INTRODUCTION TO ORACLE 10G

INTRODUCTION TO ORACLE 10G

James Perry

University of San Diego

Gerald Post

University of the Pacific

UPPER SADDLE RIVER, NEW JERSEY 07458

Library of Congress Cataloging-in-Publication Data

Perry, James T.
   Introduction to Oracle 10g / James Perry, Gerald Post.-- 1st ed.
    p. cm.
 1. Oracle (Computer file) 2. Database management. 3. Relational databases. I. Post, Gerald V. II. Title.
   QA76.9.D3P4844 2005
   005.75'85--dc22
                                                      2005028079

Acquisitions Editor: Bob Horan
Editorial Director: Jeff Shelstad
Managing Editor (Editorial): Jeannine Ciliotta
Editorial Assistant: Ana Cordero
Media Project Manager: Nancy Welcher
Marketing Manager: Debbie Clare
Marketing Assistant: Joanna Sabella
Senior Managing Editor (Production): Cindy Regan
Senior Production Editor: Anne Graydon
Permissions Supervisor: Charles Morris
Manufacturing Buyer: Michelle Klein
Design and Formatting Manager: Christy Mahon
Cover Design: Jayne Conte
Cover Illustration/Photo: Getty Images
Multimedia Artist: Richard Bretan
Composition/Full-Service Project Management: Interactive Composition Corporation/Jennifer Crotteau
Printer/Binder: Bindright
Typeface: 10/12 Times Ten Roman

Certain portions of copyrighted Oracle screen displays of software programs have been reproduced herein with the permission of Oracle.

Microsoft® and Windows® are registered trademarks of the Microsoft Corporation in the U.S.A. and other countries. Screen shots and icons reprinted with permission from the Microsoft Corporation. This book is not sponsored or endorsed by or affiliated with the Microsoft Corporation.

Copyright © 2007 by Pearson Education, Inc., Upper Saddle River, New Jersey, 07458.
Pearson Prentice Hall. All rights reserved. Printed in the United States of America. This publication is protected by Copyright and permission should be obtained from the publisher prior to any prohibited reproduction, storage in a retrieval system, or transmission in any form or by any means, electronic, mechanical, photocopying, recording, or likewise. For information regarding permission(s), write to: Rights and Permissions Department.

Pearson Prentice Hall™ is a trademark of Pearson Education, Inc.
Pearson® is a registered trademark of Pearson plc
Prentice Hall® is a registered trademark of Pearson Education, Inc.

Pearson Education LTD.   Pearson Education Australia PTY, Limited
Pearson Education Singapore, Pte. Ltd   Pearson Education North Asia Ltd
Pearson Education, Canada, Ltd   Pearson Educación de Mexico, S.A. de C.V.
Pearson Education–Japan   Pearson Education Malaysia, Pte. Ltd

10 9 8 7 6 5 4 3 2 1
ISBN 0-13-195740-6

DEDICATION

This textbook is dedicated to the following people:

Kelly Carling and Tobias Carling
Jim's daughter and son-in-law

and

Sarah Post
Jerry's wife

BRIEF CONTENTS

CHAPTER 1	Introduction to Relational Database Systems and Oracle 10g	1
CHAPTER 2	Overview of SQL and SQL*Plus	48
CHAPTER 3	Creating, Modifying, Renaming, and Deleting Database Tables	91
CHAPTER 4	Modifying Data and Auditing Table Operations	142
CHAPTER 5	Querying a Database	199
CHAPTER 6	Creating Multitable Queries and Views	264
CHAPTER 7	Using PL/SQL to Your Advantage	319
CHAPTER 8	Understanding and Using Forms Builder	372
CHAPTER 9	Customizing Forms	413
CHAPTER 10	Creating and Modifying Reports	469
CHAPTER 11	Building an Integrated Application	521
CHAPTER 12	Maintaining Database Security	556
CHAPTER 13	Database Administration	590

CONTENTS

Preface   xix

CHAPTER 1   Introduction to Relational Database Systems and Oracle 10g   1

Database Management Systems   1
Personal Systems   2
Server-based Systems   2

Describing Systems as Entities and Relationships   4

Understanding the Relational Database Model   6
Primary Keys   7
Normal Forms   8
Relationships and Foreign Keys   13
Object Relational Model   14

Installing Oracle Tools   16
Installing the Oracle Database Management System   17
Removing the Oracle Database Management System   19
Installing Developer Suite Tools   21
Enterprise Forms and Reports Services   24

Exploring the Oracle Environment   26
SQL*Plus and iSQL*Plus   26
Developer Suite Tools   28
Oracle Enterprise Manager   30

Introduction to the Book's Databases   33
Redwood Realty   33
Coffee Merchant   35
Rowing Ventures   38
Broadcloth Clothing   41

CHAPTER 2   Overview of SQL and SQL*Plus   48

Introduction   48
Types of SQL Commands   49
Anatomy of a SQL Statement   50
Obtaining Online Help   51

Interfacing with the Database   52

Using the DOS Command-Line SQL*Plus   53
Logging into Oracle   53
Entering and Running SQL Commands   54
Editing SQL Commands   55

Using SQL*Plus for Windows   55
Logging into Oracle   56
Entering and Running SQL Commands   56
Editing SQL Commands   57
Exiting SQL*Plus   59

Using iSQL*Plus 59
   Logging into Oracle 60
   Entering and Running SQL Commands 60
   Editing SQL Commands 61
   *Exiting iSQL*Plus* 62

Understanding SQL Statements 62
   Running SQL Queries 63
   Examining Data Definition Language Statements 64
   Exploring Data Manipulation Language Statements 66
   Discovering Transaction Control Statements 71
   Reviewing Data Control Language Statements 72

Using SQL*Plus Command Extensions 74
   Describing a Table's Structure 75
   Capturing Files for Printing 76
   Formatting Commands 76
   *Customizing Your SQL*Plus Environment* 78
   Executing Script Files 80
   Using Variables 81
   *Discovering Other SQL*Plus Commands* 82
   Building and Running a Script 83

CHAPTER 3 Creating, Modifying, Renaming, and Deleting Database Tables 91

Designing a Relational Database 91
   Talking to the Database User 91
   Identifying User Requirements 92
   Recognizing Business Objects 92
   Normalizing the Design 93

Understanding Oracle User Accounts 95

Further Instructions for Personal Oracle Users 95
   Creating a User 95
   Logging in with Another Username and Password 96
   Changing a User's System Privileges 96
   Changing Other Users' Passwords 97
   Changing Your Own Password 98
   Removing a User 99

Creating Tables 99
   Oracle Data Types 100
   *Creating a Table Using SQL*Plus* 106
   Adding Table and Column Comments 107

Defining and Using Constraints 110
   Understanding Constraints 110
   Naming Constraints 110
   Defining Constraints 111
   Creating Column and Table Constraints 115
   Assigning Default Values to Columns 118

Altering a Table and Its Constraints 119
   Adding, Enabling, or Disabling Constraints 119
   Dropping or Renaming Constraints 120
   Changing a Column's Default Value or Data Type 121
   Adding, Dropping, and Renaming Columns 122
   Marking Columns as Unused and Dropping Unused Columns 124

Displaying Tables' Names, Structures, and Comments 124
   Listing your Database Tables 126
   Reviewing Information on Columns 128
   Reviewing Table and Column Constraints 129
   Reviewing Table and Column Comments 132

Dropping, Reinstating, and Renaming Tables 133
   Dropping a Table 133
   Reincarnating a Dropped Table 135
   Purging the Recycle Bin 135
   Renaming a Table 136

Creating Tables Based on Other Tables 136

CHAPTER 4 Modifying Data and Auditing Table Operations 142

Inserting Rows into Tables 142
   Specifying a Column List 145
   Dealing with Integrity Constraints 146
   Omitting the Column List 147
   Inserting Dates and Times 149
   Inserting Data from Other Database Tables 152
   Creating and Using Sequences 153

Updating Data 157
   Update Statement 157
   Introducing the CASE Structure 161
   Updating Data Using the CASE Structure 162
   Substitution Variables 163

Deleting Rows and Truncating Tables 168
   Deleting Selected Rows 168
   Deleting All Rows 169

Merging Rows 171

Database Transactions 174
   Commit 174
   Rollback 175
   Savepoints 176

Creating and Using Database Triggers 178
   Introducing Triggers 179
   Creating and Using a BEFORE Trigger 181
   Creating an AFTER Trigger to Audit Table Operations 183
   Creating and Using a Statement-Level Trigger 186
   Displaying, Altering, and Dropping Triggers 190

CHAPTER 5 Querying a Database 199

Displaying Data from a Single Database Table 199
   Writing a SELECT Statement 200
   Selecting All Columns 203
   Using DISTINCT to Display Unique Rows 204
   Breaking a Runaway Query 204
   Using Search Conditions to Filter the Results 205
   Sorting 211
   Including Computations in Queries 216

Introducing SQL Functions   221
   Using Single Row Functions in Queries   222
   Using Aggregate Functions   239
   Grouping Results   246
   Filtering Groups with the HAVING Clause   247
   *Formatting SQL*Plus Output and Creating*
      Simple Reports   249

CHAPTER 6 Creating Multitable Queries and Views   264

Creating and Using Multitable Queries   264
   Joining Tables Having Matching Column Values   265
   Understanding Other Join Types and
      Join Conditions   273
   Exploring Set Operators   282
   Using Subqueries   286

Creating and Using Views   299
   What Views Provide   300
   Defining and Querying One-Table Views   300
   Modifying Data Using One-Table Views   304
   Producing Complex Views   305
   Creating Synonyms to Simplify Table References   309
   Listing View Definitions   310
   Dropping Views   311

CHAPTER 7 Using PL/SQL to Your Advantage   319

Introduction to PL/SQL   319
   Benefits of PL/SQL   319
   PL/SQL Block Types   320

Understanding Anonymous Blocks   321
   Exploring the Declarative Section   321
   Exploring the Executable Section   323
   Exploring the Exception Handling Section   324

Creating Anonymous Blocks   325
   Initializing the Redwood Realty Database   325
   Writing an Anonymous Block   325
   *Setting up the SQL*Plus Environment   328*
   Running an Anonymous PL/SQL Block   328
   Modifying an Anonymous Block to Display
      Multiple Rows   329
   Handling Exceptions   330

Understanding Explicit Cursors   333
   Introducing PL/SQL Iteration Constructs   333
   Using Explicit Cursors and Loops to
      Process Rows   335
   Using FOR Loops to Process Explicit Cursors   339
   Introducing the IF Statement   341

Introducing Named Blocks   347

Creating, Using, Listing, and Dropping Functions   347
   Creating and Storing a Function   348
   Invoking a Function   350
   Modifying a Function   352
   Listing and Dropping a Function   353

Creating, Using, Listing, and Dropping Procedures 356
  Advantages of Procedures 356
  Creating and Storing a Procedure 357
  Invoking a Stored Procedure 360
  Modifying a Procedure and Recompiling and Saving It 361
  Listing and Dropping Procedures 362

CHAPTER 8 Understanding and Using Forms Builder 372

Introduction to Forms 372
  Three Main Form Types 373
  Forms Services Architecture 374
  The Basic Structure of Oracle Forms 376

Creating a Simple Main Form with the
  Forms Builder 377
  Forms Builder Wizards 378
  Testing a Form with the Run Form Button 382
  Displaying Data with Form Queries 384

Modifying Forms 385
  The Layout Editor 385
  The Object Navigator 387
  Basic Properties 388
  Adding Images 390
  Adding Lookup Columns 394
  Creating a List of Values 395
  Automating the Execute Query Step 398
  Radio Buttons and Check Boxes 398

Creating Tabular Forms and Sub Forms 402
  Creating Tabular Forms 402
  Creating Main and Sub Forms 402
  Adding Display Columns to the Grid 406
  Setting Format Masks 407

CHAPTER 9 Customizing Forms 413

Setting the Form Structure 413
  Creating a Canvas and Simple Data Block 415
  Creating a Data Block for a Query 417
  Making the Search Work 420

Designing Form Triggers 421
  Defining Form Events 422
  Creating and Editing Triggers 424
  Debugging Triggers 428
  Handling Errors 431
  *Understanding Scope and Lifetime in
    Forms Programs 434*

Creating Useful Forms Tools 435
  Creating Sequences 435
  Validating Form Input 438
  Computing Subtotals for Grid Data 441

Using Multiple Canvases 443
  Adding a Canvas 443
  Stacked Canvas 444
  Tab Canvas 447
  Evaluating Form Styles 450

Creating Web Forms with JDeveloper   451
   Modify the Listings Table and Set up your
      Server Files   *452*
   Create a Data Connection and Workspace   *453*
   Create the Business Components Data Model   *454*
   Create a Java Server Page to Display Data   *456*
   Adding a Search Form   *457*

CHAPTER 10   Creating and Modifying Reports   469

Introducing Reports Developer   469
   Web Publishing and Paper Reports   *469*
   Types of Reports   *470*
   Oracle Reports Services   *472*

Building and Modifying Reports   473
   The Report Structure   *473*
   The Reports Builder   *475*
   The Paper Design and Layout Windows   *478*
   The Object Navigator Window   *481*

Enhancing a Report   483
   Aligning and Justifying Columns   *485*
   Setting Format Masks and Properties   *486*
   Adding Shading and Borders   *486*
   Inserting Page Numbers and Dates   *487*
   Adding Text Boxes   *488*

Customizing Reports   489
   The Data Model   *489*
   Adding Fields   *492*
   Data Group Structure and Frames   *493*
   Creating a Report Manually   *495*
   Displaying Images from the Database   *499*

Controlling Data in a Report   500
   Creating User Parameters   *500*
   Using Filters to Limit Reports   *503*
   Creating Report Triggers   *504*

Creating Custom Templates   504
   Designing Custom Templates   *505*
   Applying Templates   *507*
   Registering Templates   *507*

Customizing a Web Report   509
   The Dynamic Report Environment   *510*
   Modifying a Web Report   *510*
   Adding a Chart to a Web Report   *514*

CHAPTER 11   Building an Integrated Application   521

Designing an Integrated Database Application   521
   Organizing Redwood Realty   *522*
   A Consistent Look   *523*
   Creating Template Forms   *524*
   Creating and Applying Property Classes and Visual Attributes   *525*
   Applying Template Forms and Properties   *527*

Connecting Forms and Reports into an Application   530
   Startup Form   *530*
   Opening Connected Forms   *532*

*Displaying Reports   534
Deploying Forms and Reports in OracleAS   538*

Creating Menus   540
*The Role of Menus   540
Building Menus   542
Creating Menu Actions   543
Deploying and Using Menus   546*

Creating Help Files   547
*The Oracle Web Help System   548
Creating HTML Help Files   548
Deploying and Using Help Files   551*

CHAPTER 12 Maintaining Database Security   556

Creating and Editing User Accounts   556
*User Authentication   557
User Roles   559
System and Object Privileges   560*

Controlling User Access to Objects   563
*Creating Roles   564
Granting and Revoking Permissions   565*

Enforcing Privileges through Views and Procedures   568
*Restricting Access to Selected Rows and Columns   569
Restricting Updates through Procedures   570
Virtual Private Database and Label Security   573
Limiting Access within an Application   573*

Protecting Data with Encryption   575
*Securing Internet Transmissions   576
Encrypting Selected Data in the Database   576
Protecting Source Code with Wrap   579*

Auditing the Database   579
*Enabling Auditing   581
Viewing Audit Trails   582
Creating Triggers for Auditing   583
Fine-Grained Auditing   585*

CHAPTER 13 Database Administration   590

Overview of a DBA's Duties   590

Using the Enterprise Manager   591

Understanding Oracle Storage Files   594
*Protecting Control Files   596
Creating Tablespaces and Datafiles   596
Configuring Undo and Redo Operations   600*

Configuring Space for Schema Objects   602
*Setting Table Storage Parameters   602
Defining Clusters   604
Creating Partitions   605*

Exporting and Importing Data   606
*Using SQL Scripts   607
Using the Data Pump   607
Using SQL*Loader and External Tables   608*

Maintaining the DBMS 610
   Patches and Updates   *610*
   Starting and Shutting Down the Database   *612*

Backing up the Database 614
   Complications in Backing up Databases   *614*
   Shutdown and System Backups (Cold)   *616*
   Continuous Backups and Archives (Hot)   *617*

Monitoring and Improving Database Performance 618
   Monitoring Tools   *618*
   Optimizing Queries   *623*

Obtaining Useful Information from System Views 631

Glossary 636

Index 645

ABOUT THE AUTHORS

James T. Perry is a Professor of Information Systems in the School of Business at the University of San Diego. He has a Ph.D. in computer science from the Pennsylvania State University and a Bachelor of Science in mathematics from Purdue University. He is the coauthor of over eighty textbooks and trade books covering topics such as database management systems, the Internet, accounting information systems, Microsoft Office, and electronic commerce. Some of his most popular books have been translated into Chinese, Dutch, French, and Korean. Jim's prior teaching appointments, spanning over 30 years, include the Information Systems Department at San Diego State University and the Computer Science Department at the University of Nebraska. He has worked as a computer security consultant to various private and governmental organizations, including the Jet Propulsion Laboratory. He was a consultant on the Strategic Defense Initiative (Star Wars) project and served as a member of the computer security oversight committee. When he is not writing or teaching, Jim can be found refereeing rowing regattas throughout California.

Gerald V. Post is a Professor of Management Information Systems at the University of the Pacific. He has a Ph.D. in economics and statistics from Iowa State University and a Bachelor's degree in mathematics and economics from the University of Wisconsin-Eau Claire. The author of textbooks on database management and management information systems, he has published dozens of professional papers in journals including *Communications of the ACM, Management Information Systems Quarterly,* and *Decision Sciences*. Jerry has taught MIS and database classes for over twenty years. He has developed several database applications for commercial businesses. When he is not writing, you can find him riding his bike or chasing his dogs through the hills.

PREFACE

TO THE STUDENT

This text describes how to use the Oracle 10g database management system.

Chapter 1 opens the book by describing database terminology, differentiating between personal database management systems (DBMS) and client server systems such as Oracle, entities and relationships, and database normalization and primary keys. Next, you learn about installing Oracle on your own system. Then you get an overview of the Oracle environment by exploring SQL*Plus, the Developer Suite tools, and the Oracle Enterprise Manager. Finally, we introduce you to the structure and contents of the book's four databases: Redwood Realty, Coffee Merchant, Rowing Ventures, and Broadcloth Clothing.

Chapter 2 introduces the SQL database language and Oracle's database interfaces, including the operating system prompt, SQL*Plus for Windows, and *i*SQL*Plus. With step-by-step instructions, you learn how to launch a script file to build the Redwood Realty database and then write and execute SQL statements in the SQL*Plus and *i*SQL*Plus environments. Using Oracle's SQL*Plus statements, which are extensions to the SQL*Plus language, you review how to describe a table's structure, capture results for later printing, and customize your SQL*Plus environment.

Chapter 3 describes how to build database tables to hold your data. It includes a comprehensive discussion of Oracle data types including character, numeric, date, and image data. You learn how to specify constraints, or conditions, on table columns including primary and foreign key constraints, unique constraints, and check constraints specifying ranges of allowed values for the columns to which they are attached. In this chapter, you learn how to list names of tables, how to list their columns and any constraints placed on them, and how to drop and rename tables. Chapter 3 concludes with an example illustrating how to create a table from an existing one.

Chapter 4 discusses SQL data manipulation language (DML) statements, database transactions, and database triggers. Using both description and step-by-step practice, you learn how to insert new rows into existing tables and how you can create and use Oracle sequences to generate any required primary key column values automatically. You learn to modify data with the SQL UPDATE statement and practice deleting rows with the DELETE statement. A complete description of database transactions and their associated COMMIT and ROLLBACK statements appears in Chapter 4. Using transactions, you learn how to undo errant data manipulation statements. Finally, this chapter introduces database triggers. You discover how triggers can intercept column values that are about to be changed and log the changes to a file to maintain an audit trail for selected tables and their columns.

Chapter 5 introduces the SELECT statement, that all-important SQL statement, which retrieves information from database tables and describes how to retrieve information from a single database table. You learn about the SELECT statement clauses including FROM, WHERE, and ORDER BY in addition to the SQL operators. Computing elapsed dates, using mathematical operators to perform numeric calculations, and using column aliases all are important concepts that appear in Chapter 5. Many of the most commonly used Oracle functions are described in this chapter. The function categories described in Chapter 5 include character functions, numeric and date functions, conversion functions, special functions to convert NULL values to some other value, and the aggregate functions. The chapter concludes with a comprehensive discussion about using SQL*Plus output formatting and report creation commands.

Chapter 6 expands the discussion of the SELECT statement to show you how to interrogate multiple tables in a single query. You learn about join types and join conditions including equijoins, left-, right-, and self-joins, and Cartesian products. Set operators UNION, MINUS, and INTERSECT provide you with additional tools to retrieve information, and their description appears in this chapter. You study database views and learn how to create views and use them to your advantage. A thorough discussion of potential problems associated with inserting, updating, and deleting data through views is presented. You learn about some of Oracle's important data dictionary views, which provide information about your tables and other resources you own.

Chapter 7 introduces programming to the mix. You learn how to write anonymous PL/SQL code blocks, implicit cursors, explicit cursors to process multiple row results, and named PL/SQL code blocks. Using well-planned steps, you walk through creating, using, and listing both PL/SQL functions and PL/SQL procedures. Naturally, you learn the advantages of using functions and procedures over using anonymous blocks.

Chapter 8 introduces the concept of database forms. Forms are commonly used in building applications. Users interact with your database through the forms. New data entered into the forms are transferred to the database tables. This chapter explores the capabilities of Oracle's Forms Builder. You will use the automated tools to create the three basic form types: main form, tabular form, and sub forms.

Chapter 9 shows you how to go beyond the automated features provided by the Forms Builder. By learning to create forms from scratch, you gain more control over the appearance of the form. You also learn to add useful features such as form triggers to respond to events and how to compute subtotals and other calculations on a form. You learn to use multiple canvases, such as the popular tab canvas, to use a form to display data from multiple tables without overwhelming the user.

Chapter 10 covers the other important aspect of applications: building reports. Reports are designed to display summary data. You learn to use the report wizard to create reports. From there, you can modify and customize the overall report structure and add more features. You learn to control the overall layout, the various subtotals, and formatting. You will see that it is relatively easy to add graphs to reports and provide interactive filters so that users can select the data they want to see. You will also see how to create and deploy reports that can be viewed by managers across the Internet using only a Web browser.

Chapter 11 puts the pieces together and shows you how to build an integrated application. Users should never see tables or SQL. In fact, they might never know that a database lies beneath the application. Instead, they see your forms and reports. A key step in building an application is to standardize the forms and reports using templates. You then use trigger code to connect the forms and reports and hide details from the users. You can create custom menus and even write your own help files. When you are done, you can deploy your application on an Oracle Application Server (if you have access to one).

Chapter 12 explores some of the basic concepts you need to maintain security. Securing a database application requires that developers and administrators think about security right from the start. You learn how to create user accounts and assign security permissions through roles. You can also limit access to data using views and application controls. You learn how to encrypt database records in case someone steals the entire database. The chapter also explains how to establish and monitor security audits so you will know if someone tries to attack your database.

Chapter 13 provides an introduction to the role and tools of the database administrator. The chapter begins by explaining the various features of the Enterprise Manager. This tool is an interactive introduction to the many DBA tasks. However, because most DBAs use SQL commands, the chapter also shows how to handle basic configuration tasks using commands. If you want to run your own copy of Oracle, you eventually need to be able to perform these tasks. Even if you do not have your own copy, you can read the chapter to see the tasks that need to be performed so you can decide if you want to become an Oracle DBA. You will see how to configure storage files, and maintain and update the database software. You will also learn how to export and import data and back up the database and recover from crashes. The chapter also introduces tools to monitor and improve the performance of the database operations.

Our hope is that you will be an active reader and participant as you read the text. Perhaps the most important tool to learning and remembering what you read is to work through the step-by-step examples. By following these detailed instructions, you will learn by doing and by making the occasional mistake. No matter what you do to the database in a particular chapter, it will have no negative effect on learning material in any other chapter. The database safeguard in place is that you reload the entire database or at least the parts of it you will touch at the beginning of each chapter. That way, you start with a fresh, new, and correct database.

Each chapter has a set of review questions at the end to reinforce your learning. The terminology review questions include true/false questions, fill-in questions, and multiple-choice questions. Following these questions are four hands-on exercises that ask you to use Oracle to solve a problem. The same four cases appear in each chapter. The first hands-on exercise is an extension of the chapter that asks you to do additional work with the Redwood Realty database. It contains explicit instructions for every step you need to execute. Hands-on exercise Number Two is the case of Coffee Merchant, a retail and wholesale distributor of fine coffee. Like the Redwood Realty case, it contains detailed instructions that lead you to a solution to the problem. Case Three involves a rowing regatta. It consists of several tables and other database objects needed to hold information about the race, its participants, and their affiliations. Called Rowing Ventures, it has a brief discussion of the database tables and the deliverables required to finish the problem, but you design all the steps needed to produce the requested deliverables or results yourself. The fourth case is Broadcloth Clothing, which is an international problem involving clothing manufacture and distribution, with distribution and manufacturing plants around the world. This problem is particularly interesting because it emphasizes foreign currencies, factory production timetables, and several other issues that appear when one deals with a global company. Here too, you are expected to provide your own steps, using Oracle, to solve the problem. However, the problem is frequently less difficult to solve than the other three hands-on exercises.

By studying the text, working the step-by-step exercises faithfully, and using the end-of-chapter materials to reinforce what you have read, you will learn how to use the Oracle database system software to create and maintain a reasonably large number and volume of tables. Once you complete this book and the course that uses it, you will be well on your way to becoming very knowledgeable about database systems in general and Oracle in particular.

TO THE INSTRUCTOR

APPROACH AND FEATURES OF THE BOOK

This book presents a mix of both database theory and application steps that illustrate the theory. Students learn the reason particular database statements are required for the activities they are about to perform. This is followed by short, step-by-step sequences directing them to perform the database activities needed to complete a task. For example, Chapter 4 contains a complete presentation about database triggers, including why and when they should be used. Following the description of triggers are steps that the student is asked to execute to create a trigger (before update) on a particular table. Text following the trigger creation steps describes circumstances in which one might want to report a database table update and log it into an audit table. Then, the student follows another set of steps to update the table upon which a trigger is defined, to see the effects of the update operation. Finally, the student follows a few short steps to display the audit table rows containing information collected and logged by the trigger that the student created.

Important terms appear in a special typeface in the sentence where each is defined. Because basic terminology is an important component in learning about database management systems, the end-of-chapter material reinforces their importance with a key term summary and an extensive review. The review, which follows the chapter summary, includes true/false, fill-in, and multiple-choice questions to help students understand and remember the key terms.

Four databases accompany the text. One database, called Redwood Realty, is used in each chapter and in all the steps within each chapter to illustrate various concepts. The first hands-on exercise in the end-of-chapter materials is always an extension of the Redwood Realty case. It asks the student to follow the steps included in the problem to further strengthen understanding of the concepts introduced in each chapter. This hands-on example provides students with an example database that is already familiar to them and that requires little further explanation to get them up to speed.

The three other databases appear in each chapter as the database for the same hands-on example in each chapter. The Coffee Merchant, a coffee wholesale and retail business, consists of seven tables. Several of the Coffee Merchant tables contain several thousand rows so that students can experience dealing with nontrivial database tables. The Consumers table, for example, contains 1,587 rows chock-full of customer contact information. Inventory contains a comprehensive list of the coffees and teas available worldwide, ranging from Guatemalan Huehuetenango coffee to Russian Caravan tea. The description column of the Inventory table contains a lengthy description of the characteristics of each tea and coffee, some exceeding 100 words.

Rowing Ventures represents a typical sporting event with teams, team affiliations, different race events with individual starting times, and various boat configurations. Containing six tables with a small number of rows, this problem affords the student a chance to work, step-by-step, with a smaller database and yet use the same tools and methods as for any other comprehensive database. Students are expected to solve the problem by carefully reading the problem, but it contains no step-by-step instructions.

The fourth and final database is used in the fourth and last hands-on exercise. Called Broadcloth Clothing, it is an international problem, containing many of the challenges of dealing with a large international organization. It involves factories whose employees speak languages other than English, and several different world currencies. Broadcloth contains seventeen tables, including Customer, which contains customer information; Factory, which lists the factories manufacturing clothing around the world; and Compliance, which lists the safety compliance record of factories. Like the Rowing

Ventures case, this hands-on problem provides a problem statement and a description of the deliverables the student is to produce without step-by-step instructions.

INSTRUCTIONAL SUPPORT: www.prenhall.com/perrypost

The textbook is equally well suited for database courses in four-year institutions and in other settings, including community college courses offering product-specific instruction in Oracle leading to a database certification.

No matter what type of institution you teach in, we want to make your job easier by providing a rich variety of instructional support materials for the book. It is likely that not everyone will want to use all the supplied support materials, but we believe there are subsets of the tools and supporting material that each person will like. Student and instructor materials can be found on the Web site, www.prenhall.com/perrypost. Instructor materials can also be accessed through the catalog page, www.prenhall.com

INSTRUCTOR RESOURCES

- An **Instructor's Resource Manual** provides materials describing the chapter, hints, tips, and traps. Solutions to end-of-chapter exercises will be found in the additional files described below.

- **PowerPoint slide presentations** contain figures from the text plus selected script file text showing important SQL statements to help you organize lectures and activities.

- A **Test Item File** and **TestGen** contain a full complement of over 1,500 test questions in multiple-choice, true-false, and short-answer format. The Test Item File is available in Microsoft Word and as the computerized Prentice Hall TestGen software, a comprehensive set of tools for testing and assessment. TestGen allows instructors to create and distribute tests for their courses, either by printing and distributing through traditional methods, or by online delivery via a Local Area Network server. The software features Screen Wizards for assistance, and is backed with full technical support.

- The **Image Library** is a collection of the text illustrative material organized by chapter. It includes all of the figures, tables, and screenshots from the book. Images can be used to enhance lectures and slide presentations.

- **Solutions** and **Data Files** contain all the databases, database script files to load them, other data files required to complete each step within the text, and data for the hands-on exercises. They also contain solutions or script files that generate the solutions, example output results that match those the student will generate, plus all problem solutions. All of these files are available to the instructor at the book's Web site, www.prenhall.com/perrypost, and are protected by usernames and passwords that are available to instructors. The script files available for students run with minimal feedback so that no one is confused, for example, by messages generated when the script file drops tables. Some progress messages appear on the screen to reassure students (and instructors) that database loading is occurring as expected. When complete, the database initialization script displays, for selected databases, table names and row counts. Students can take a screen shot of the database loading summary messages, if needed, as reassurance that the tables loaded as expected.

We suggest that students run the database-initializing script file at the beginning of each chapter (steps appear in the text requesting the student to do so) to ensure that each chapter's database manipulations do not affect any work in any other chapters. That way, there are no surprises or side effects caused by the previous chapter's script files; each chapter starts the Redwood Realty database back at its initial, pristine state.

Most end-of-chapter hands-on exercises require students to generate two or three reports of various types. You can choose to simply print the reports we have created and saved in Notepad format, or you can generate your own reports by solving the problems yourself. If you choose to execute the steps to solve a problem, then either you can run the script files we supply to the instructor, or you can work the problem from scratch just to experience any potential problem areas that students might encounter. Please direct students to download data files from the book's Web site shown below.

STUDENT RESOURCES

The Companion Web site, at www.prenhall.com/perrypost, contains additional materials for students:

- A **PowerPoint** slide presentation that highlights key text terms and concepts.
- A full **Glossary** of key terms, in alphabetical order.
- **Student Data Files** that contain all the databases, database script files to load them, any other data files required to complete each step within the text, and data for the hands-on exercises. Note that the Web site is the single source for all data files for the book.

PATHS THROUGH THE BOOK

There are as many ways to teach database management systems and Oracle as there are instructors. We designed this book to be flexible enough to satisfy several teaching approaches and styles. The book contains thirteen chapters, which is just right for a full semester, three-credit course introducing databases in general or Oracle in particular. However, the book will serve equally well in a variety of situations. For example, if you have limited time or a course that is one or two credit hours, you can present just the SQL portion of Oracle by assigning readings in Chapters 1 through 7. If you are teaching an overview of Oracle, then you will prefer to use all the chapters. Although we have arranged the topics in a particular order, you might prefer to assign chapter readings in a slightly different way. Chapter 1, which introduces relational database management systems, contains foundation material that no student should miss. You will want to assign that chapter first. Chapter 2, which introduces SQL and SQL*Plus, is a handy overview of what will appear in chapters that follow it. A complete discussion of SQL queries appears in Chapters 5 and 6. However, you might wish to present SQL queries before you present chapters describing SQL data definition language statements and data manipulation language statements. In that case, assign Chapter 5 following Chapter 2. We suggest that you not assign Chapter 6 before students read Chapters 3 and 4, however. Chapter 6 is advanced querying and views. It involves multiple tables and the several ways to join them (left outer join, equijoin, and so on). Chapter 6 also describes views in great detail and it probably should not be the third chapter assigned. Chapter 7 is programming using PL/SQL. It is definitely a nontrivial topic. You can choose to omit this chapter if you do not want to discuss programming, and use defined subprocedures and functions. It is an advanced topic that could be assigned near the end of the course following Chapter 13.

Chapters 8 through 11 discuss forms and reports, and they build on the student's knowledge of earlier SQL chapters. Chapter 12 describes database security and requires, in some cases, that the student have DBA privileges. If you do not want to allow that level of access, we suggest that they can still gain a lot by reading the chapter even if they do not have the privileges needed to execute every step-by-step exercise. Many of the developer-security exercises can be performed without DBA permissions. The capstone chapter, database administration, presents an overview of database administration. It provides an introduction to the topic and a nice segue to the database administration standalone course that many educational institutions offer following the introductory database course.

A NOTE ABOUT USING ORACLE

You can install the Oracle 10g software that comes with the book on your own computer, or you can use Oracle supplied by your school. Except for a select few optional exercises found in the later chapters, none of the steps or exercises you are requested to perform require special privileges. You merely need a valid username and password and minimal privileges (create objects such as tables and session privilege) to perform any of the steps or end-of-chapter exercises in this book. Of course, if you install Oracle on your own machine, you can grant yourself DBA privileges and thereby create other users and perform DBA-level tasks. This book doesn't require you to be able to do that, however.

ACKNOWLEDGMENTS

Creating a textbook is a collaborative effort between the publisher and the authors. Like most meaningful endeavors, creating the best textbook in a topic area involves teamwork and coordination among the team members. We want to thank the reviewers who provided suggestions and insights to help us craft the book most likely to help students succeed and instructors to teach and mentor their students. In particular, we thank

> Vladan Jovanovic, Georgia Southern University
> Jennifer Kreie, New Mexico State University
> Karen Nantz, Eastern Illinois University
> Jeremy Smith, Carnegie Mellon University
> Thomas P. Sturm, University of St. Thomas, Minnesota
> William H. Thomas, Juniata College, Pennsylvania

The authors acknowledge the work of the dedicated professionals at Pearson Prentice Hall. We especially thank Bob Horan, Jeannine Ciliotta, Ana Cordero, and Anne Graydon for the care and attention they provided us every step of the way. They are true professionals!

Finally, we want to thank our spouses, Nancy and Sarah, for their patience as we worked long hours to complete this book on an extremely tight schedule. We couldn't do it without you.

If you would like to contact us about the book, we would be happy to hear from you and respond to your comments, suggestions, and even praise! You can e-mail your messages to us at **perrypost@prenhall.com**. For the latest information, data files, updates, and support materials for *Introduction to Oracle 10g,* please visit the book's Web site at www.prenhall.com/perrypost.

—James Perry

—Gerald Post

READ THIS BEFORE YOU BEGIN

The CDs packaged with the book contain the Oracle 10g Personal Edition and Developer Suite software, which you can install on your own computer. At the beginning of each chapter are steps that you should follow to initialize the Redwood Realty database before executing any other steps in the chapter. The data files, script files, and any other data for the chapters is exclusively on the book's Web site (www.prenhall.com/perrypost). Look for data files there. By initializing the database at the beginning of *each* chapter, you are assured that any changes you make to the database in other chapters will not adversely affect the database for the current chapter. In other words, each chapter reinitializes the database to its initial state. A few of the early chapters do not install the full Redwood Realty database because you need only a few tables and other objects to complete them. Chapters beyond the first four install a full Redwood Realty database when you run the requested steps. Feel free to examine all the script files before you run them. They are all compatible with Notepad, so you can use Windows Explorer to locate a script file, open it, and examine or print it.

CHAPTER 1

INTRODUCTION TO RELATIONAL DATABASE SYSTEMS AND ORACLE 10G

Learning Objectives

In this chapter, you will learn:

- The basic purpose and uses of database systems.
- The basic steps of designing a database.
- How to install the Oracle tools needed for this book.
- Some background information on the databases used in the book.

DATABASE MANAGEMENT SYSTEMS

A ***database management system (DBMS)*** is one of the most important computer tools in organizations today. Most companies use a DBMS to record business transactions and handle financial accounting records. Many companies use a DBMS to provide easy access to research data. Most commercial Web sites use a DBMS in the background to hold inventory and transaction data. The purpose of a DBMS is to provide reliable storage and easy access to data. The DBMS is software that works with the computer's operating system to store and retrieve the data. The data is stored in a carefully designed ***database.*** To be more precise, the database consists of the data, the DBMS—or simply database system—is the software that controls the database.

Database systems have gone through several changes over the years. One of the most important changes was the development of the relational database model. Most existing database systems, including Oracle, are based on this model. You will learn more about the relational approach throughout the book, but the fundamental concept is that all data is stored in tables consisting of simple rows and columns.

A DBMS has several components—to store and retrieve the data, identify users, and create applications. Users interact with the database through a query language, data-entry forms, and reports. SQL is the standard query language used by most major systems, including Oracle. Several elements of SQL are defined by standards, which makes it easier to apply your knowledge to different systems. Oracle is heavily based on SQL—to do almost anything in Oracle, you first need to learn the SQL language. Ultimately, you also need to know how to create forms and reports, for those are the primary ways that people will use your database. The Oracle Developer Suite contains tools to help you build data-entry forms and create several types of reports with minimal programming.

Applications consist of the database, plus the forms and reports needed by users to perform specific tasks. *Developers* are people who design the databases, write queries, and build the forms and reports. *Database administrators (DBAs)* are people who are responsible for managing the DBMS, including installing and updating software, monitoring for problems, and handling backup and recovery in case anything goes wrong.

PERSONAL SYSTEMS

In small organizations, you might run a DBMS on a single personal machine. As a developer, you would probably install everything on a single machine and perform your initial application tests that way. However, the true strength of a DBMS lies in its ability to handle multiple users making changes simultaneously. A personal database system can be useful if only one or two people are going to need it. You might choose this approach because of the ease of creating applications with the forms and reports builders. However, you would be surprised how many people will want to use the system once you get it built. In other words, applications might start small, but they have a tendency to grow. Using a DBMS makes sense in these situations, because it is flexible enough to support change and growth. The tables, queries, forms, and reports you build for a small application can all be extended and used when several people want to use the same application.

SERVER-BASED SYSTEMS

Most production database systems use an approach in which the database is held on a primary server and the users connect to it through separate machines—sometimes called client computers. The server is a central repository for the data, so all users see the same information and changes are immediately visible to everyone. Of course, this approach requires that all of the machines be connected by some type of network. Because of its flexibility and availability, the most common approach today is to use Internet protocols to connect the machines. This approach also makes it easier for clients to access the database when they travel. In fact, the client computers today usually connect through an Internet browser. One advantage of this approach is that all the software needed to access the database and run forms and reports can be downloaded across the Internet. Consequently, it is relatively easy to set up a client computer so that it can be used with the database application. Another advantage is that the end user can use a small, inexpensive client machine to interact with Oracle—expensive client machines are not required.

As shown in Figure 1.1, most Oracle applications run on a three-tier system. One tier, the back-end database server, handles the database itself. This computer, or server, is responsible for storing and retrieving data. It handles backup operations and transaction passing to the database. Often, it consists of a cluster of computers to provide continuous, robust service in case one of the database servers fails. The middle tier is Oracle's Application Server, which handles user logins and processes forms and reports. It retrieves data from the DBMS by sending queries across the network. When

CHAPTER 1 Introduction to Relational Database Systems and Oracle 10g

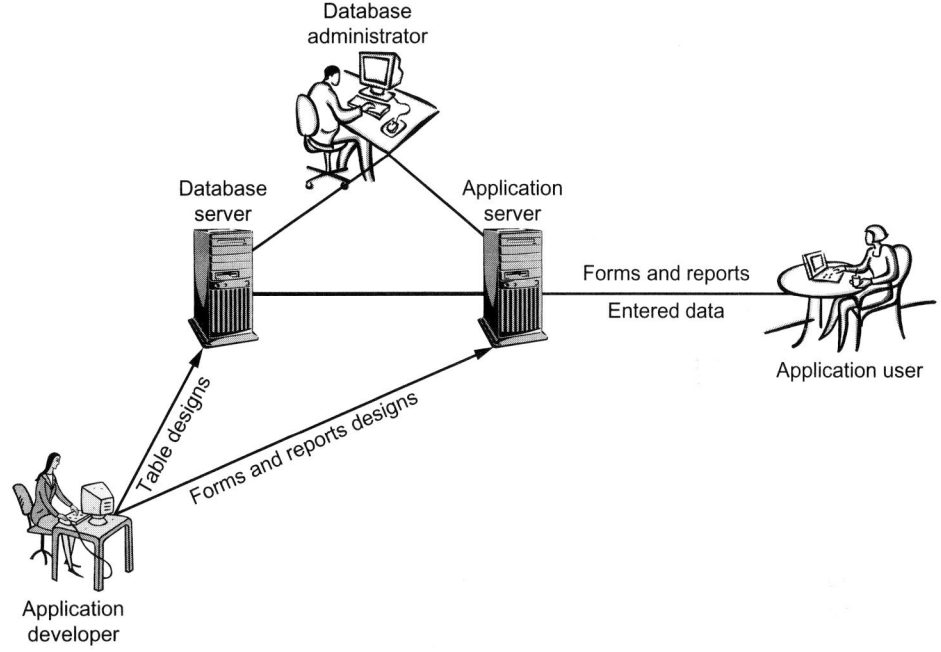

FIGURE 1.1 Three-tier DBMS approach.

it receives data rows in response, it processes them and integrates them into the forms and reports that it sends to the users. The middle tier can also be a cluster of computers to handle heavier loads and compensate for hardware failures. The front-end tier is the client side—running on almost any computer that supports an Internet browser. One requirement Oracle places on the front-end tier is that the browser has the Java engine installed. Commonly, client tasks are relatively easy and are limited to the basic display and collection of simple data items, for example. Because users often insist that their information-gathering be portable, they often use different computers. Therefore, it is helpful to keep the client side hardware and software requirements as simple as possible to reduce support costs. If something goes wrong with a client machine, users simply switch to another computer and reconnect to the application server.

As you might surmise, a primary goal in a multiple user, multi-tier system is to keep the database and the applications running continuously. In mission-critical applications, the system should be able to keep working, even if some of the components fail. The only sure way to solve this problem is to build in redundancy at each level. Of course, it costs more money to build a system this way—particularly because your organization has to pay more license fees to Oracle for each processor that runs their software. But, if your system and data are truly important, the added cost is minor compared to the lost business and expense of recovering from a hardware failure.

Running a database on multiple tiers has several advantages, but it also has a drawback—particularly when the client side runs in a Web browser. Because of potentially slow network connections, data is downloaded to the client's computer. Changes made to that data are not stored on the server database until the user clicks a button to save the data. Think about what happens if several people are working on the same project. By delaying the updates, the probability increases that someone else will alter the data before you save your changes. The DBMS can recognize this situation, but the delays make it a little more difficult to determine which of the changed values are correct.

Because Oracle relies on Java, be sure that the Java engine (or add-in) is installed with your Web browser. The basic engine is commonly installed by default, but some organizations disable it for security reasons. Locate it at the Java Web site (http://www.java.com) and download and install the most current version available.

DESCRIBING SYSTEMS AS ENTITIES AND RELATIONSHIPS

The point of a database is to collect all of the information needed and store it efficiently so that it can be updated and retrieved quickly. One of the challenges is to identify exactly what data is needed by the organization. Developers begin the process by talking to users and managers to identify the problems that need to be solved. The catch is that users do not know much about databases. Instead, you need to ask them about the business operations and the data that is collected and used in making decisions. You need to organize this information so it can be stored efficiently in the database. At the same time, it helps if you can draw a diagram that you can show to users so they can verify that you understand the organization.

The entity-relationship or class approach is a useful way to model a database system. Note that some people still use the older *entity-relationship diagram (ERD)* terminology and drawings. More recently, people have adopted the *unified modeling language (UML)* terminology and drawings. The two approaches have similar goals and the differences mostly are related to drawing diagrams. The UML approach is easier to read and it is standardized so it is simpler to present. But, you can use whatever terms and diagrams you want.

The fundamental step of the modeling approach is to identify the entities or classes of objects for which you need to collect data. Each *entity* or *class* has *attributes* that define the type of data being collected. For example, a Customer is a common entity in many databases. The Customer entity has attributes such as CustomerID, Last Name, First Name, Phone, Address, and City. The attributes represent the data to collect for each class. For example, a particular instance of Customer data might be:

```
151, 'Jones', 'Mary', '111-2222', '123 Main', 'Eureka'
```

Ultimately, you also have to record the type of data held by each attribute. In the preceding example, most of the attributes hold text data—data that includes characters, numbers, and punctuation. Table 1.1 shows the various generic *data types* that you are likely to encounter. As you identify the attributes that you will store, you need to record the type of data each one will hold. Some attributes are relatively clear, such as using Text to store customer addresses. For others, you will have to examine existing

TABLE 1.1 Generic data types.

Data Type	Description	Examples
Text	Any type of characters, numbers, or most punctuation.	123 Main Street
Number	Numbers are stored so they can be aggregated or manipulated arithmetically. You can usually specify the number of decimal places, such as zero to get integers. Also used by Oracle to hold monetary values.	1.2345 15.32 153
Date	Used to hold dates and time values. It is important to use this type instead of text when possible, because the system can compute the difference between dates.	13-JUL-2006
Binary	Used to hold data for non-traditional objects such as pictures, spreadsheet files, or other large items.	Picture.jpg

data and question users. Number and Date data types are available for data that participate in calculations. For example, you would store employees' birth data, instead of their ages, in a database field. With a birth date column, you can later determine each employee's age by computing the difference between today's date (from the computer's clock) and an employee's birth date. Similarly, an invoice number could be a character string because you would not perform mathematical calculations on the InvoiceID. An invoice's unit price field should be a numeric field so that a database calculation can sum it, or compute the product of quantity and unit price, to determine the total cost of an item. If you made everything a text data type, then you would be able to store and retrieve the data, but you could not calculate totals or compute the difference between two dates.

A database will almost always have more than one entity, sometimes hundreds of them. Generally, the entities are related to each other. These *associations* or *relationships* are eventually made by storing related data in similar columns. For example, a Customer Order is another common business entity. It represents orders placed by customers (another entity). The Customer Order contains attributes such as OrderID and OrderDate. It also contains a CustomerID attribute. This attribute provides a link back to the Customer table. For example, a specific Customer Order might contain data: 1201, '06-JUN-2006', 151. The 151 is the CustomerID, and you can use it to look up the rest of the data by finding CustomerID 151 in the Customer entity.

Figure 1.2 shows how you can draw the relationship between the Customer and CustomerOrder entities. Each entity is represented by a box. The attributes appear within the box, and the entity name appears at the top. A connecting line defines the relationship between the two entities. Usually it is drawn to show that the values for CustomerID in the CustomerOrder class will connect to the values of CustomerID in the Customer table. A notation near each end of a line indicates the type of relationship. In this case, it is a *one-to-many* relationship, because a "1" appears on the left end of the line and "*" (an asterisk) appears on the right end of the line. The asterisk indicates the many side of the one-to-many relationship. Reading left to right in this example, any customer can place many orders as indicated by the asterisk (*) on the CustomerOrder side of the link. Going the other way, a given order can only come from one customer as indicated by "1" on the Customer side of the link. That is, if you are looking at an order form, there is space only for one customer. Two customers cannot share an order. How do you know that? It represents an organizational rule, so either you have to know it is the standard approach in business or you have to ask the users.

In a project, your basic job at this point is to talk to the users and identify all of the entity classes and corresponding attributes. You should begin drawing a diagram to show the classes and relationships between them. You might struggle with some of the associations initially, but the next section will provide some rules to guide your design.

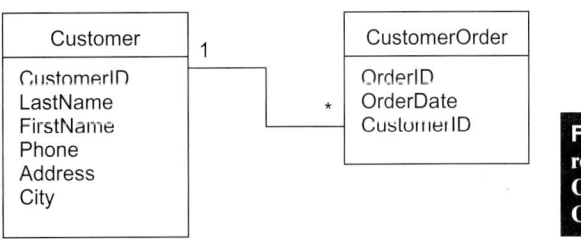

FIGURE 1.2 One-to-many relationship between Customer and CustomerOrder.

UNDERSTANDING THE RELATIONAL DATABASE MODEL

Database researchers have demonstrated, to date, that relational databases are the most efficient way to store and retrieve most data. To achieve this efficiency, you need to design the database carefully. The fundamental component of a relational database is a table. E. F. Codd, the acknowledged father of relational databases, who developed the approach, used the term *relation* instead of *table*. That explains how the databases designed according to Dr. Codd's founding principles became known as *relational database systems*.

A *table* consists of rows and columns and holds data that represents a single entity in the business model. Its columns are known as attributes. A row of data represents a single instance of data. It is easiest to understand the terminology by looking at an example, so Figure 1.3 shows two sample tables that might exist in a relational database. These tables represent, more concretely, the relationship diagram shown in Figure 1.2. Notice that each row is simple in the sense that it represents exactly one thing. Each piece of data is simple because it contains data values that describe only one thing. For instance, you cannot store two phone numbers for one person. If you need to store multiple phone numbers for a customer, you either have to add new columns to the table (CellPhone, HomePhone, and so on), or put them into a separate table. Also, notice that the tables connect to each other through the data in the CustomerID column. If you look at the first row in the CustomerOrders table, you see that it was placed by the customer with ID equal to 151. You can take that CustomerID value and use it to look up the data about that customer by finding the matching row in the Customers table. This joining of tables is not an accident. You have to build it into the database design. It is matching column values in two related tables that allow the database system to couple, or join, separate, related rows from two tables. In other words, matching column values in two distinct tables is the glue that allows Oracle or another database system to synthesize information from separate tables of facts.

FIGURE 1.3 Sample tables in a relational database.

CustomerOrders

OrderID	OrderDate	CustomerID
1201	06-JUN-2006	151
1202	06-JUN-2006	155
1203	07-JUN-2006	151

Customers

CustomerID	LastName	FirstName	Phone	Address	City
151	Jones	Mary	111-2222	123 Main	Eureka
152	Smith	Susan	222-5555	738 Elm	Eureka
153	Brown	David	111-2355	235 East	Eureka
154	Sanchez	Maria	999-3332	351 Ocean	Arcata
155	Steuben	Saul	555-2351	111 Main	Orick
156	Hayworth	Michele	231-3252	761 West	Loleta

PRIMARY KEYS

There are a few basic rules for designing tables that will work efficiently and correctly in a relational database system. But to understand the rules, you need to learn a few definitions first. A ***relational database*** is a collection of related tables. A table is a collection of rows and columns (attributes) that describe an entity. An attribute is a characteristic of an entity. A ***row*** holds data for a single instance of an object.

Each table must have a primary key. A ***primary key*** is a value that uniquely identifies each row and resides in a particular column or collection of columns. For many objects, you will create your own primary key column and allow the relational database management system to automatically populate the column with unique values. In this small example, the CustomerID is likely to be a generated key. If the system automatically generates the primary key, then it will be unique. However, if people create it manually, then it is difficult to guarantee that a key value will always be unique. People can make mistakes and assign the same value to two customers—particularly with a large system, or a system in which multiple users interact with a database and may be simultaneously entering primary keys independent of one another. Fortunately, Oracle has tools to generate primary key values that are guaranteed to be unique. Furthermore, you can ask Oracle to automate the process of key generation. In the example shown in Figure 1.3, the OrderID key might also be generated by the database, but it could also be created by the sales department—perhaps taken from a preprinted form.

For each table that is stored and maintained by the database, you will have to talk with the users to determine how you will pick primary key values. Some keys are better choices than others. For example, in the case of the Customer table, you would not want to use a customer's phone number as the customer row's primary key. What happens if two people from the same family want to place orders? Do you need to tell them apart? Or worse, what happens when they change their phone number and it gets assigned to someone else?

Be careful with primary keys. You will not generate new keys for every table. In fact, you will often encounter tables where the primary key consists of multiple columns. These situations have a special meaning that is critical to understanding relational database design. When two (or more) columns are part of a primary key, it means there is a ***many-to-many*** relationship between the entities they represent.

Figure 1.4 provides an example of a many-to-many relationship that you have probably encountered. The Student entity is straightforward and holds common data about students, especially the names and phone numbers. The Organization entity represents clubs, sports teams, and other organizations on campus. The Participants entity stands in the middle and tracks which students participate in each organization. In the Participants entity, both the OrganizationID and StudentID form the primary key. Both columns are required to be part of the key to uniquely identify a row. Figure 1.5 shows sample data for the entity tables.

FIGURE 1.4 One-to-many and many-to-many relationships.

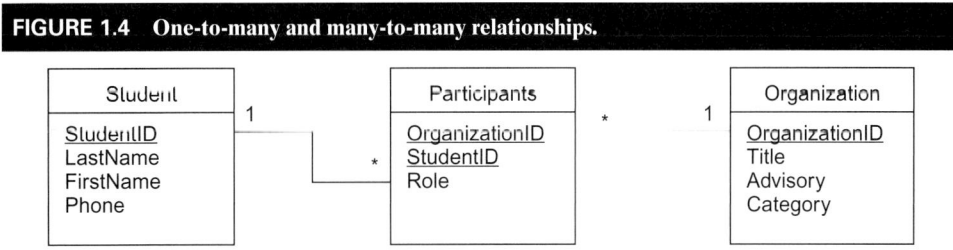

Organization

OrganizationID	Title	Advisor	Category
101	Lacrosse	Amerit	Sports
115	Phi-Beta	Smith	Fraternity
125	Student Council	Antonio	Governance

Student

StudentID	LastName	FirstName	Phone
12013	Fellini	Federico	111-4444
12315	Bergman	Ingmar	222-3331
12551	Truffaut	Francois	888-2221
23664	Kurosawa	Akiro	999-4491

Participant

OrganizationID	StudentID	Role
101	12013	Captain
101	12551	Member
115	12013	Member
115	23664	President
125	12551	Treasurer
125	12315	Member

FIGURE 1.5 Sample data showing the need for two columns to be part of the key.

OrganizationID has to be keyed because each student might belong to many organizations. StudentID has to be keyed because each organization might have many student participants. If only OrganizationID is part of the key, it does not uniquely identify a row because most ID values are entered more than once—in fact, they are entered once for each student. If only StudentID is part of the key there would be duplicate values again, because a student could belong to more than one organization. By building the *composite primary key* from both the OrganizationID and StudentID, a row is uniquely identified because a student is only listed once for each organization in which he or she is a member.

NORMAL FORMS

Identifying columns for primary keys is an important step in designing tables for a relational database. But tables require additional thought. Each table in a relational database must meet certain conditions. If these conditions are not met, the database will exhibit many problems including the loss of important data. Generally, you start with a form or description of data. From there, you create entities. You convert these entities into tables using a *normalization* process. The steps of the procedure guide you to creating tables that have nice features. The easiest way to understand the process is to follow a demonstration.

Figure 1.6 shows a relatively common business form for a customer order or sale. Look at the form and see if you can identify the main entities. The Customer entity is relatively obvious—particularly since it is marked in a separate box. If you think about it for a minute, the overall CustomerOrder itself should be an entity. That leaves the rest of the data items on the form. Because they are also displayed in a separate box, it is tempting to say that the items being ordered represent the third and final entity. That answer is a good start, but it needs improvement.

Customer Order

OrderID　　　　　　　　　　　　　　　　Date

CustomerID
First Name   Last Name
Phone
Address
City, State Zipcode

ItemID	Price	Description	Quantity	Value
1526	32.95	Basketball	1	32.95
3921	79.92	Running shoes	1	79.92
4797	1.59	Racquetballs	3	4.77

FIGURE 1.6 Form data to be normalized.

To understand the reasons why applying normalization to your database design is important, you could try building a database table without doing any design. What happens if you take the data from Customer Order form and put all of it into a single table? Figure 1.7 shows some sample data. First, notice that you do not have to store the Value column because it can be computed from the existing data. Most of the time, anything that can be computed does not need to be stored. The database has tools to handle the computations for you, and there is no need to waste the space.

If you try to enter data into this proposed table you will quickly see some of the problems—mainly the huge amount of repetition. For each of the three items being ordered, you would have to re-enter all of the order data. Plus, you would have to enter all of the customer data each time. Repeating the same data over and over is a waste of space. But there are other problems. What happens if Customer 155 cancels his order and you delete the two rows in the table? You would lose all information about the customer! Similarly, what can you tell me about product 1577? It has not been ordered yet, so there is no place to store its data, so you do not know anything. You can find similar problems throughout the proposed table. How do you fix the design to avoid these problems? The answer is to ensure that all tables conform to three normalization rules or forms. Normalization rules are applied in sequence, beginning with the first normal form.

First Normal Form

To be in *first normal form,* a proposed table must have only atomic elements. *Atomic* means that values cannot be broken down any further. In other words, each cell in the table holds simple data values. They cannot be repeating or have nested values. Technically, every cell in Figure 1.7 is atomic. But, we cheated a little to make it that way. In reality, the ItemID repeats for each OrderID, which is clear by looking at the original order form in Figure 1.6.

If you wanted to reduce some of the obvious repetition within the order, you might consider organizing the table as shown in Figure 1.8. In many ways, this approach is even worse, because now the relational database does not know how many items might be ordered on each form, so it is hard to allocate the space and to search the database for the items. The proposed table in Figure 1.8 is not in first normal form. You might consider fixing it by repeating the data and forcing it to look like Figure 1.7, but that

FIGURE 1.7 Placing all data into one table is a bad design.

OrderID	OrderDate	CustID	FName	LName	Phone	Address	City	State	ZIP	ItemID	Price	Description	Qty
1201	06-JUN-06	151	Mary	Jones	111-2222	123 Main	Eureka	CA	95001	1526	32.95	Basketball	1
1201	06-JUN-06	151	Mary	Jones	111-2222	123 Main	Eureka	CA	95001	3921	79.92	Running Shoes	1
1201	06-JUN-06	151	Mary	Jones	111-2222	123 Main	Eureka	CA	95001	4797	1.59	Racquetballs	3
1202	06-JUN-06	155	Saul	Steuben	555-2351	111 Main	Orick	CA	95022	1526	32.95	Basketball	1
1202	06-JUN-06	155	Saul	Steuben	555-2351	111 Main	Orick	CA	95022	3144	15.72	Baseball	1

FIGURE 1.8 Reducing repetition by using non-atomic columns is still bad.

OrderID	OrderDate	CustID	FName	LName	Phone	Address	City	State	ZIP	ItemID	Price	Description	Qty
1201	06-JUN-06	151	Mary	Jones	111-2222	123 Main	Eureka	CA	95001	1526	32.95	Basketball	1
										3921	79.92	Running Shoes	1
										4797	1.59	Racquetballs	3
1202	06-JUN-06	155	Saul	Steuben	555-2351	111 Main	Orick	CA	95022	1526	32.95	Basketball	1
										3144	15.72	Baseball	1

OrderID	OrderDate	CustID	FName	LName	Phone	Address	City	State	ZIP
1201	06-JUN-06	151	Mary	Jones	111-2222	123 Main	Eureka	CA	95001
1202	06-JUN-06	155	Saul	Steuben	555-2351	111 Main	Orick	CA	95022

OrderID	ItemID	Price	Description	Quantity
1201	1526	32.95	Basketball	1
1201	3921	79.92	Running Shoes	1
1201	4797	1.59	Racquetballs	3
1202	1526	32.95	Basketball	1
1202	3144	15.72	Baseball	1

FIGURE 1.9 Split out the repeating data section.

does not seem to be an improvement. Instead, the answer is to split the proposed table into two new tables. You would also split the version in Figure 1.7 into the same two new possible tables, but for a slightly different reason. Essentially, you pull out the data that was on the repeating section in the original form and place it into a new possible table. However, you have to include the OrderID column from the original set because that is how the tables will be linked back together.

Figure 1.9 shows the resulting changes. Notice that the first proposed table will use OrderID as the primary key because you no longer have to repeat the order and customer data for each item being purchased. The second proposed table will use both OrderID and ItemID as the primary key because of the many-to-many relationship. Each order can have many items on it, and each item can be ordered many times. Both of these proposed tables hold atomic data and are now in first normal form.

SECOND NORMAL FORM

If you look closely at the second proposed table in Figure 1.9 you will see that it still has some problems. In Figure 1.9, each time you enter ItemID 1526, you have to enter the description and price. Besides wasting space and data-entry time, embedding the information about items in this order table means that you still do not have any way of finding data on products that have not yet been ordered. The problem arises because the item description and price depend only on the ItemID. If someone asks you about ItemID 1526, it will have the same description and price today as it did yesterday. These values do not depend on the OrderID.

A table is in *second normal form* if all of the non-key columns depend on the entire key. It also has to be in first normal form. This example is not in second normal form, because the description and price depend only on the ItemID, not on the OrderID. On the other hand, the quantity ordered does depend on both the OrderID and ItemID because it tells us how many units of each item to ship for a specific order.

If you can handle a little confusion for a minute, think again about the price column. Is there always one price for an item, or can prices depend on a specific order? There is no single answer, because any business could have different rules. These dependency issues might be different for any organization. Some have traditional answers that work in most cases, but you still need to talk to users and understand how they approach the problem. If you are building this order form for a real company, you would most likely use two prices: (1) a list price that depends only on the ItemID, and (2) a sale price that depends on both the OrderID and the ItemID. That way the order-customer

OrderID	OrderDate	CustID	FName	LName	Phone	Address	City	State	ZIP
1201	06-Jun-06	151	Mary	Jones	111-2222	123 Main	Eureka	CA	95001
1202	06-Jun-06	155	Saul	Steuben	555-2351	111 Main	Orick	CA	95022

OrderItems

OrderID	ItemID	Quantity
1201	1526	1
1201	3921	1
1201	4797	3
1202	1526	1
1202	3144	1

Items

ItemID	Price	Description
1526	32.95	Basketball
3144	15.72	Baseball
3921	79.92	Running Shoes
4797	1.59	Racquetballs

FIGURE 1.10 Split out the columns that depend only on the ItemID.

company can offer a discount based on any characteristics it chooses. But, for the rest of this discussion, we will stick with the easier case of using one price that does not change.

To fix a proposed table that is not in second normal form, you once again split it. Take the columns that depend on just the partial key and put them in their own table. Figure 1.10 shows the results. The OrderItems and Items tables are now in second normal form. Actually, the proposed order-customer table is also in second normal form—because it has only one column in the primary key.

THIRD NORMAL FORM

The proposed order-customer table in Figure 1.10 still has problems. If you look back at the originally proposed table in Figure 1.7, the problems are even more obvious. The table still repeats the same customer information for each order. In the original, it repeats the customer information for each item ordered. The problem is that the customer data (name, address, and so on) depends only on the CustomerID and does not depend on the OrderID at all. Once you know a CustomerID, you should know everything about that customer, and you do not need to be told their OrderID.

A table is in *third normal form* when each non-key column depends on nothing but the key. It also has to be in second normal form. In this example, the customer data columns depend on the CustomerID which is not part of the primary key, so it is not in third normal form. Again, the answer is to split the table. Take out the columns that depend only on the CustomerID and put them into their own table.

Figure 1.11 shows the resulting tables. You can go through each table and verify that it is in third normal form. Use the simple rule: A table is in third normal form if, and only if, each cell contains atomic data and every non-key column depends on the whole key, and nothing but the key.

In the Orders table, the OrderID is the primary key, and it identifies both the OrderDate and the CustomerID placing the order. The Customers table is keyed by the CustomerID and each of the non-key columns represents simple attributes for customers. Similarly, the Items table is keyed by ItemID, and it identifies the price and description of each item. The OrderItems table arose because of the repeating section on the order form. Both OrderID and ItemID have to be keyed because of the

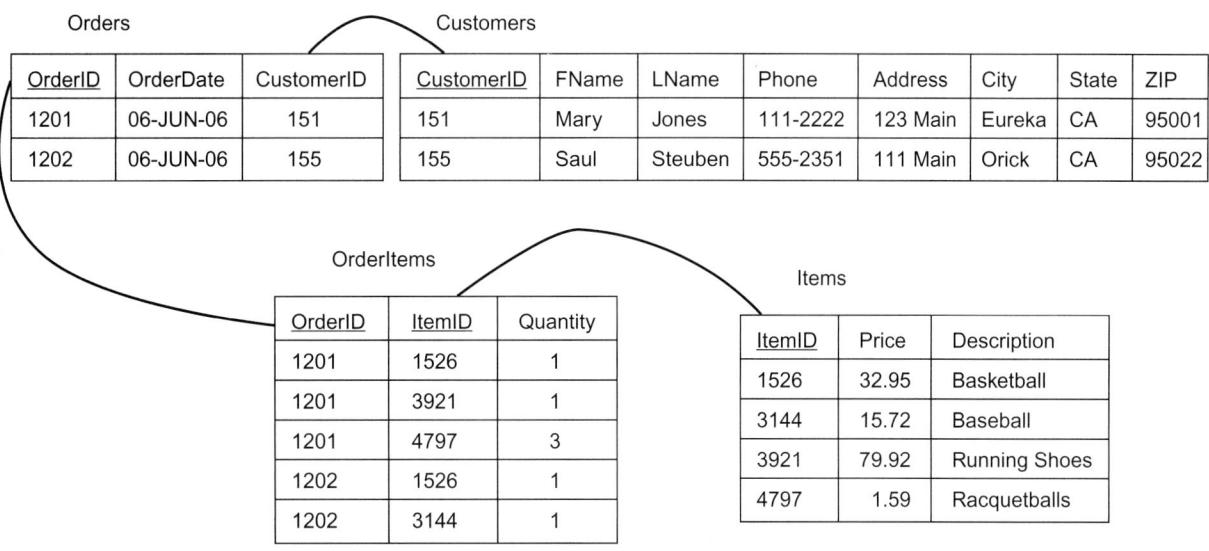

FIGURE 1.11 Split out the columns that depend only on the CustomerID.

many-to-many relationship. The quantity column depends on both the order and the item, so this table is also in third normal form.

Tables in third normal form are relatively well behaved. Each table represents a single concept and there is minimal duplication of data. You can add rows to a table or even delete rows without losing critical data in the other tables. For example, if you delete an order, you still retain the customer contact data.

Third normal form is not the final stop in normalization, but the other situations are relatively rare and are beyond the scope of this book. You can read more about them in any good database design textbook. However, you always have to at least get your tables into third normal form before trying to create them in a relational database.

RELATIONSHIPS AND FOREIGN KEYS

Figure 1.11 also shows how the tables are connected so that the data can reconstruct the original form. These relationships are not accidental. You must also be careful when splitting the tables to ensure that they can be recombined through their relationships. Usually, these connections are made through key columns, because the keys provide an efficient reference to the underlying data. For example, the Orders table holds the CustomerID value which can be used to find the related data in the Customers table.

Look at the Orders table more closely for a minute. The OrderID column is the primary key because it is the only column needed to ensure that each row is unique. In particular, notice that the CustomerID column is not part of the primary key in the Orders table. If you did make it a key, you would be saying that there is a many-to-many relationship between orders and customers—specifically, that a given order could have many customers. That statement is false in most business transactions. Companies almost always sell an order to a single customer. Hence, you do not key the CustomerID column in the Orders table.

However, since the CustomerID column is the primary key in the Customers table, it is called a ***foreign key*** when placed in the Orders table. The name is similar to having a king (or diplomat) visit another country. While in the other country, the king or key is "foreign." You will see later that this terminology is important in Oracle, because you define relationships by specifying the foreign keys. Notice that the OrderItems table has two foreign keys: OrderID and ItemID, because both are primary keys in their home tables.

Notice that the Customers and Items tables have no foreign keys. Sometimes they are referred to as **base tables** because the data in them does not depend on any other table. The advantage of base tables is that you can create and load data into them without concern for related tables. Conversely, if foreign key and primary key relationships are known to the database system, then you cannot load data into the Orders table until after you have created a few customers. For example, if you attempted to load data into the OrderItems table (see Figure 1.11) *before* loading data into the Items table upon which the OrderItems table rows depend, Oracle would issue an error message. More specifically, if you try to create an order and enter a CustomerID value of 190, you must already have a matching row in the Customers table with that key value. This property is called *referential integrity,* and means that you cannot insert data into one side of a relationship unless the matching value already exists in the other table.

OBJECT RELATIONAL MODEL

In the 1990s, programmers began using a new approach called object-oriented programming (OOP). It is particularly effective for programming in a graphical environment, because many common tasks can be performed by predefined objects. By using existing objects, the programmer saves considerable time by not having to rewrite the same code. Eventually, programmers needed to store some of their object data on disk drives. Developers also tried to extend the ideas of classes and objects into the business world. It was hoped that classes could be defined and reused across an entire organization. For instance, a company could have a Customers class that would be available to all application developers. In OOP terms, a class is a description of an entity. It consists of a title, a set of attributes, and methods or functions that it can perform. Notice that this definition is similar to the entity definition used to create tables for the database, except that databases probably do not need to hold the internal function procedures for the classes. Several companies attempted to create object-oriented databases. A few decided to try to combine the benefits of the object model with the relational model. So far, neither the pure object-oriented nor the object-relational database features have seen much commercial success. However, Oracle supports several object-type features that you can use to define tables. Whether you gain enough value in using them depends on the type of problem you face.

The object-oriented approach introduces two primary features to the relational database model: (1) you can store more complex data types, and (2) you can create sub-tables when you have a hierarchy of classes. The first feature is the easiest to understand. Recall that relational databases require that data be atomic. But, you are constrained to storing data in the common types that are defined by the DBMS (text, number, date, and binary). What if you need a new type of data? For instance, you might want to store the geographical location of stores or warehouses. Location is defined by latitude and longitude coordinates, but you might also include altitude if users needed it. To humans, the concept of location is represented by those three values. Any function to compute distance requires that you pass in all of the values. But a relational database would require you to store those as three separate columns. While it is not a major disaster, it means the database does not truly represent the way we view the data. With the object-oriented approach, you can simply define a new own data type called Location and specify that it consists of three values: Longitude, latitude, and altitude. Those three values are then treated as a single item when copying

CHAPTER 1   Introduction to Relational Database Systems and Oracle 10g   **15**

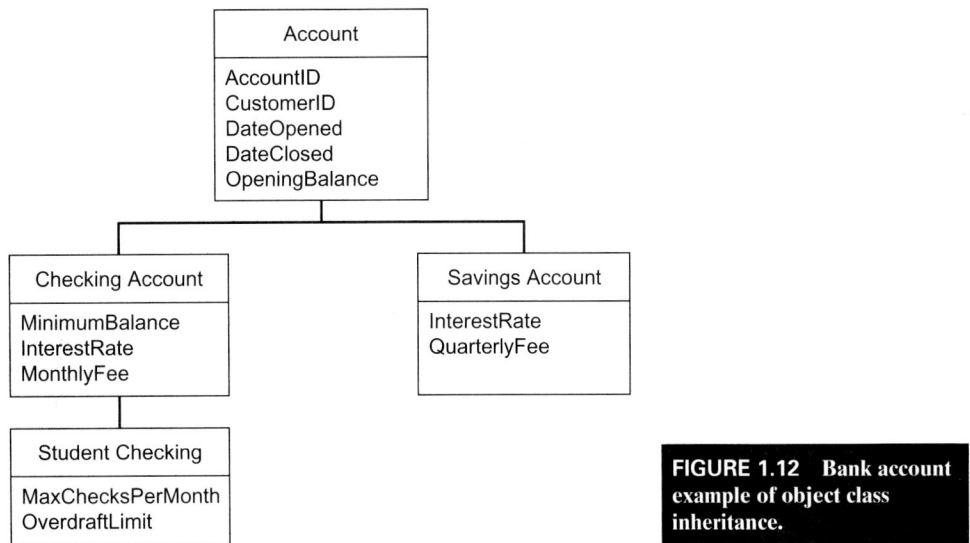

FIGURE 1.12 Bank account example of object class inheritance.

the data or passing it to a function. Oracle provides the CREATE TYPE command to define a new type of composite data. It is a flexible way to customize your database. However, be cautious. Creating a composite data type in Oracle could make it more difficult to transfer your data to other systems in the future.

Inheritance is a key feature of object-oriented programming. *Inheritance* means permitting objects to be defined and created that are specialized types of existing objects, which allows sharing of the object's behavior without having to implement that behavior anew. Programmers first define a generic class, and then derive more detailed object classes from this generic super class. Figure 1.12 shows a simple example for a bank computer system. The generic Account class holds data that is needed for every type of account. In programming, it also contains methods to create and close accounts, but the methods would not be stored in the database, so they are not shown here. Developers can then define sub-classes such as the Checking Account and Savings Account classes. As the drawing indicates, both of these are derived from the generic Account class. That means they inherit all of the properties and methods of the super class. (It is called a *super class* because it is above the derived classes.) Inheritance makes it easy to define new types of accounts, such as a Student Checking Account. Programmers have to define only the new properties—all of the other properties and methods are handled by the super class.

Oracle uses a combination of data types with sub-types and nested tables to handle inheritance. Basically, you can define different data types for each type of account and store them as nested table columns within the Account table. The details are beyond the scope of this book.

The interesting aspect to the object inheritance model is that it is hierarchical. Part of the motivation for developing the relational model was the need to overcome the shortcomings of the hierarchical approach. In some ways, the object-oriented (OO) approach represents an attempt to add more structure to a relational database. In fact, you do not need to use the OO features. You can always find a way to implement what you want within the relational framework. In the bank account example, you simply define all four of the classes as separate tables. Then, you would store the data for an individual account across whatever tables you needed. The one requirement is that you would define the AccountID as the primary key in all of the tables. With a true OO

16 Introduction to Oracle

approach, the DBMS automatically handles the connections across the tables. Of the possible OO features, the one you are most likely to use is the CREATE TYPE command to define your own data types.

INSTALLING ORACLE TOOLS

The Oracle database management system is a complex software package. It consists of dozens of applications, each of which has dozens or hundreds of components. The system integrates closely with the operating system. However, Oracle strives to maintain platform independence, so that applications you build within the Oracle system will run on any platform that has the Oracle system installed. Figure 1.13 illustrates the basic elements of the system. A Database Administrator (DBA) is usually responsible for installing and managing the database system, including backups and recovery. An application developer designs the database tables, forms, reports, queries, and code to handle some process required by the user. The DBMS itself integrates with the operating system, with a primary focus on storing and retrieving data on the disk drives. It has a *data engine* that handles most of the actual exchanges with the computer system. Internally, all data is stored in tables, and the DBMS maintains a *data dictionary* to identify all of the tables and columns stored in the database. The DBMS also has a *security subsystem* that identifies users and applies access rights to control the actions of all users. All the components of the engine, dictionary, and security systems are installed automatically. The DBMS has a *query processor* that uses the PL/SQL language to determine how to store and retrieve data in response to user and application requests. It is a powerful system that optimizes the way data is retrieved. The system also has *administration tools* to help the DBA configure and monitor the DBMS status and performance. In Oracle, these consist of several queries and packages, in addition to the Enterprise Manager. The *Enterprise Manager* is a separate graphical-based tool that

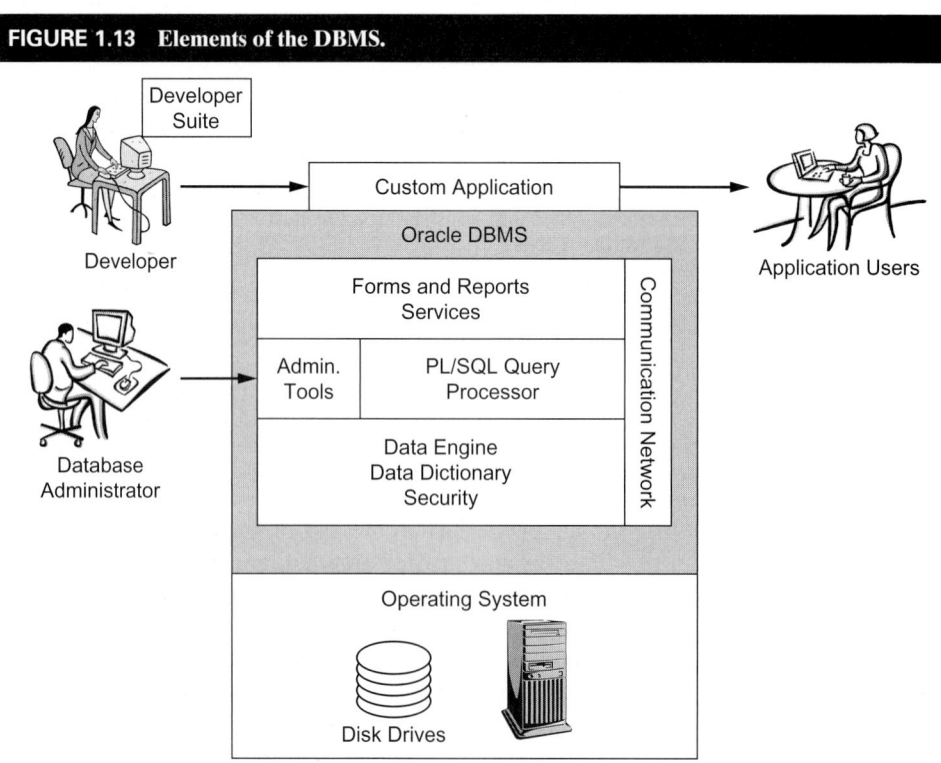

FIGURE 1.13 Elements of the DBMS.

provides DBAs with easy access to several important Oracle administration tools in one location. The entire system relies on a ***communications network*** to connect to users and other computers. When you install a database, you have to configure the system so that it has a unique identity on the Oracle network.

Forms and reports services are a separate component of the DBMS. If you install the DBMS on a server for a production environment, you will have to install the forms and reports services separately. They are part of the Oracle Enterprise system. In fact, most organizations install the forms and reports services on a separate computer. However, Oracle does provide a separate forms and reports services component that can be installed on the same server as the DBMS.

Once the components are installed, the application developer installs the ***Developer Suite*** tools. In most cases, these are installed on separate machines. However, it is possible to install both the Oracle DBMS and the Developer Suite on the same computer. Note that you should not attempt to install the Developer Suite on the same machine that runs the enterprise forms and reports services.

INSTALLING THE ORACLE DATABASE MANAGEMENT SYSTEM

It is important to understand that the Oracle tools are installed in multiple pieces. It is also critical to understand that the system integrates tightly with your operating system. As vendors tighten security on the operating systems (Linux, Windows XP, UNIX, and so on), you may experience more challenges installing the Oracle software. In some cases, you might have to disable various security features. For example, firewalls can interfere with most of Oracle's tools.

Oracle 10g is heavily based on Internet protocols. That means that most of the tools run within Web browsers. It also means that most communications are based on Internet standard protocols. This approach is generally good because most systems understand how to support standard Internet protocols. The one drawback is that base Internet security is minimal, so vendors, companies, and educational institutions have been adding more security tools. In their default configurations, many of these tools will block the Oracle connections. For example, Oracle forms and reports, and the Enterprise Manager, connect through specific TCP/IP ports that are normally blocked. If you install the DBMS software on multiple machines, someone will have to configure the firewalls to allow the specified connections. If you install the DBMS and the Developer Suite on your own machine, you should have fewer problems. However, you might still have to open some ports or disable an internal firewall.

Always try the standard installation first, write down all connections and ports used by the system, and test the result. If a component fails, try opening the specified ports on your firewall. If that still fails, try turning off the firewall software.

Next, you will install the Oracle database system on your own computer. If you are using an existing Oracle system, then you need not execute these steps. However, it is helpful if you read the steps to understand what is involved in installing the database system.

To install the Oracle database management system:

1. Find the main database installation disk or folder. If you have a high-speed Internet connection, you can download current copies from the Oracle Technology Network (http://otn.oracle.com). Either way, you will have to register your copy and agree to Oracle's terms.
2. Make sure you have at least a couple of gigabytes of space on the target machine and start the installation of the main database by opening the folder. If necessary, run the **setup.exe** file. When the installer starts, click the **Install/Deinstall Products** button.

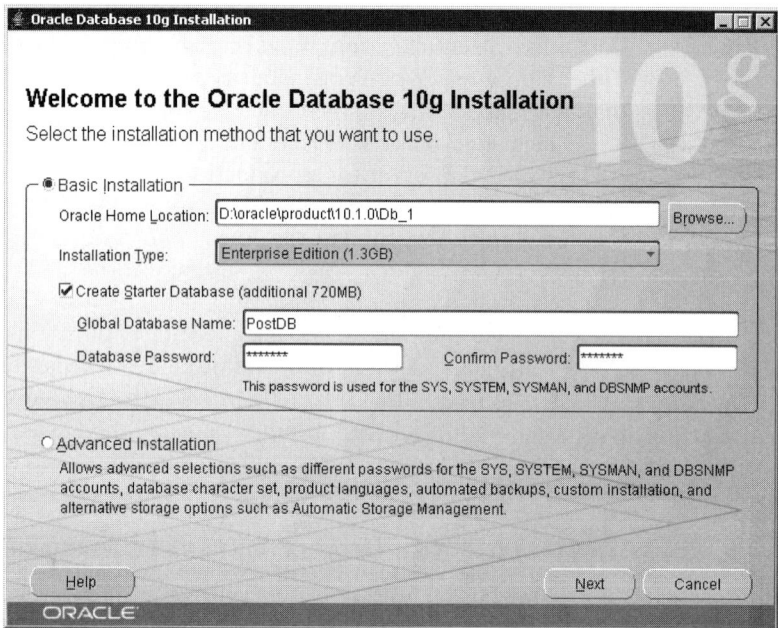

FIGURE 1.14 Oracle basic installation choices.

3. You have to fill out all of the options on the main installation screen, but you can accept the default values if they make sense for your computer. First, enter a **password** and enter it again in the confirmation box. Write down the password so you do not forget—it is the system password that you will need later. Remember it and keep it safe!

4. As shown in Figure 1.14, check the **Oracle Home** location and make sure it is on a disk with at least 2 gigabytes of free space. Choose the installation type—you might only have the choice of Personal Oracle. If you want, you can change the Global Database Name to something more personal than ORCL.

5. This step is critical: Write down everything on this screen, you will need most of it later.

6. Click the **Next** button and you will be shown a list of the components to be installed. Click the **Install** button and take a break for several minutes. After the DBMS software is installed and the initial database created, you will be given the option to change passwords. You can skip that option for now because the accounts are all disabled. Click the **OK** button.

7. You should see a screen similar to Figure 1.15 that shows the installation was successful. More important, it also lists the addresses and TCP/IP ports needed for several tools. Copy this list and write down the data. If you are installing on a production network, you will have to give the data to your security or network engineers so they can open ports to those utilities. Click the **Exit** button when you are ready.

8. The system will start the Enterprise Manager. If it does not start correctly, you will have to shut down the computer and restart it. Start your browser and use the address you copied in Step 7. (*Hint*: http://<server name>:5500/em). When it runs, you should put a shortcut to the site on your desktop because you will need it later.

9. You should log into the Enterprise Manager with the **system** username and the password you entered in Step 3.

CHAPTER 1   Introduction to Relational Database Systems and Oracle 10g   **19**

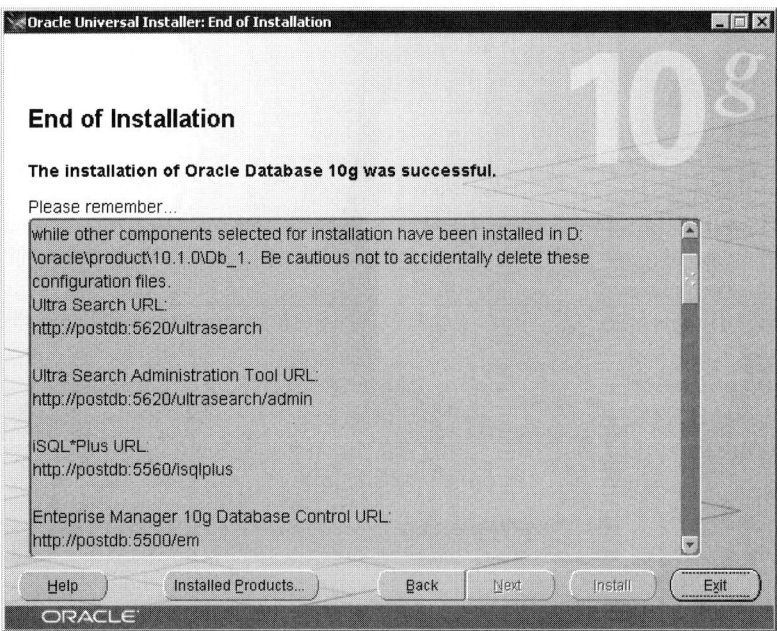

FIGURE 1.15   Installation successful, but be sure to copy the URLs.

10. Create a new account for yourself, because you want to avoid using the system account. Click the **Administration** link, then click **Users** under the Security heading. Click the **Create** button. Enter a username and a password and click the **OK** button to create the new user. Write these down in your list.

At this point, you have the main database engine and query system running on your system. You also have an account that you can use to create your own tables and queries. You still need to install the Developer Suite that gives you the tools to create forms and reports.

REMOVING THE ORACLE DATABASE MANAGEMENT SYSTEM

If major errors occur during the installation, or if you find that you need to specify different options, you will have to reinstall the software. Removing the software requires some patience and time.

To remove the Oracle database system from your computer:

1. Begin by using the Windows service manager to stop all of the Oracle services. On the main Windows menu choose **Start/All Programs/Administrative Tools/Computer Management,** then open the **Services** node under **Services and Applications.** As shown in Figure 1.16, scroll down until you find all of the running Oracle services. For each one, click the **Stop** button. Right-click the entry, choose the **Properties** option and change its default mode from **Automatic** to **Manual.** Restart the computer.

2. When the computer restarts, Oracle will not be running. On the main Windows menu, choose **Start/All Programs/Oracle . . . home/Oracle Installation Products/Universal Installer.** Click the button to **Deinstall Products.** Select the checkbox for all of the items displayed. Figure 1.17 shows a system with both the Oracle database and forms services installed. Click the **Remove** button to start the process. If prompted, click the **Yes** button to verify and continue.

20 Introduction to Oracle

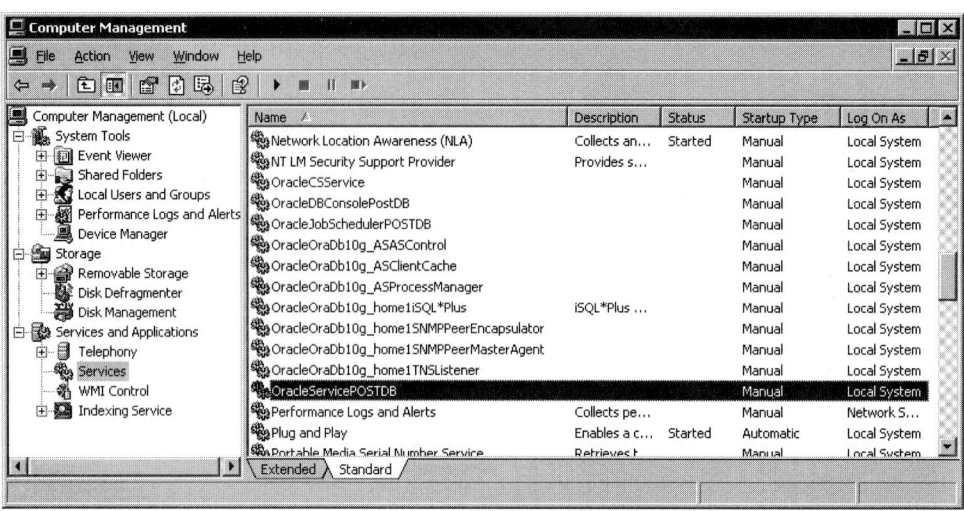

FIGURE 1.16 Oracle services to be stopped.

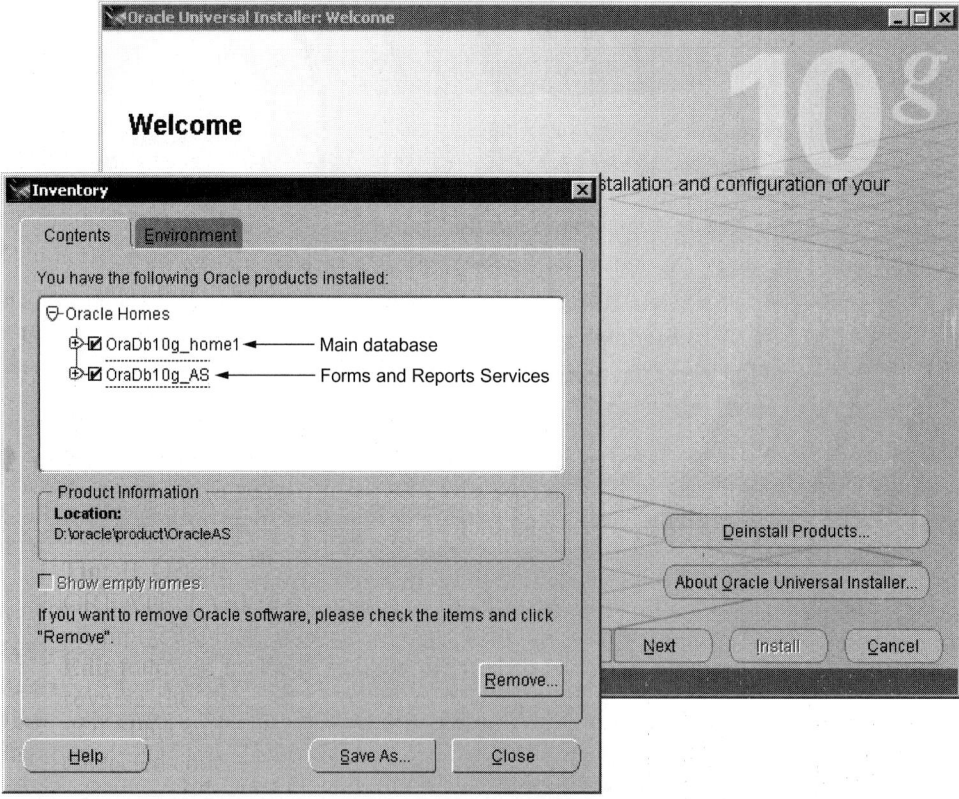

FIGURE 1.17 Oracle products to be removed.

3. When the process finishes, close and exit the installer. You now have to manually delete the files from your computer. Use Windows Explorer to browse to the Oracle Home folder and delete everything. You also might want to delete everything in the C:\Program Files\Oracle folder.

4. To get a clean uninstall, you have to remove some Oracle entries from your computer's registry. Be very careful and double-check before you delete anything. It

CHAPTER 1 Introduction to Relational Database Systems and Oracle 10g

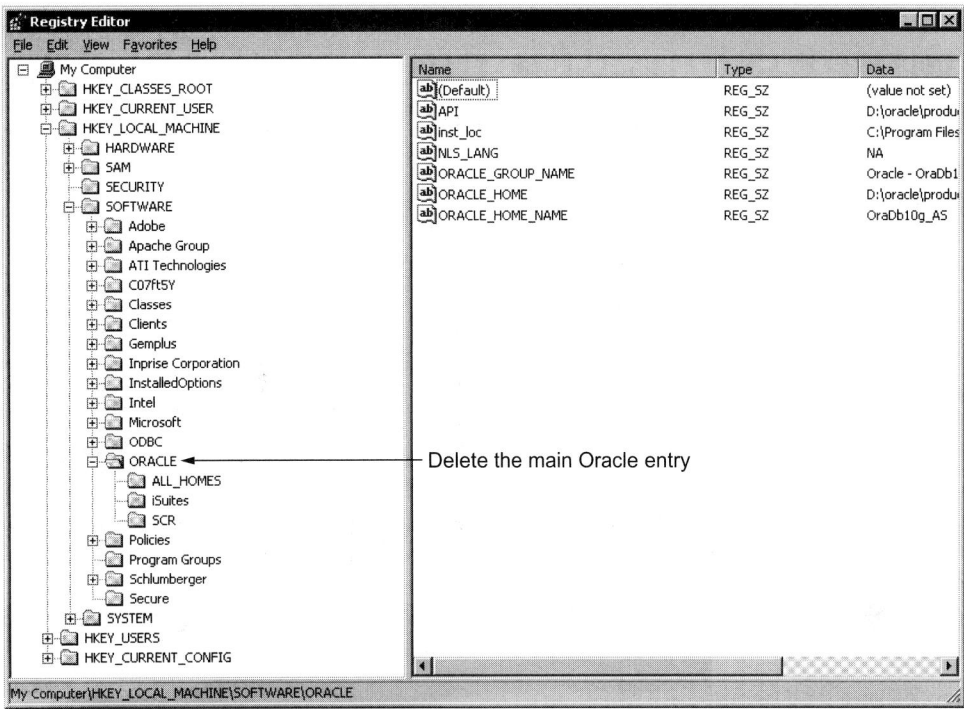

FIGURE 1.18 Oracle registry entries to be deleted.

cannot be restored. Using the main Windows menu, choose **Start/Run,** then enter **regedit** and hit the Enter key. As shown in Figure 1.18, expand the node for **HKEY_LOCAL_MACHINE,** followed by the **SOFTWARE** node. Highlight the **ORACLE** entry and hit the Delete key.

5. You should also find the entries for the services and delete them. They are under the node: **HKEY_LOCAL_MACHINE\SYSTEM\ControlSet001\Services,** and **HKEY_LOCAL_MACHINE\SYSTEM\ControlSet002\Services.** You want to delete any service with Oracle in the name: OracleOraDb10g_home1TNS Listener, Oracle.<dbname>, OracleDBConsole<dbname>, OracleOraDB10g_home1iSQL* Plus, OracleCSService, OracleDBConsole<dbname>, and OracleService <dbname>. Once you find the first one, use the Edit/Find facility in the registry editor to search for Oracle to find the others. When you have deleted them, close the editor.

6. You will also want to remove the existing entries from your Start menu. Open the Windows Start menu, locate the Oracle entries, **right-click** them and choose the **Delete** option. Additionally, you might want to remove the Oracle directory from the environment path variable. You can do that in the registry (**HKEY_LOCAL_ MACHINE\SYSTEM\ControlSet002\Control\Session Manager\ Environment**) or by right-clicking the My Computer icon and selecting the Advanced tab.

At this point, you have removed most of the Oracle fragments. To be safe, you should reboot the computer. Once the machine restarts, you can insert the Oracle database disk and re-install whatever you need.

INSTALLING DEVELOPER SUITE TOOLS

The Developer Suite tools need to be installed on the developer's computers. They should never be installed on a machine that is running the Oracle Application Server forms and reports services. It is fine to install them on a machine that is already

22 Introduction to Oracle

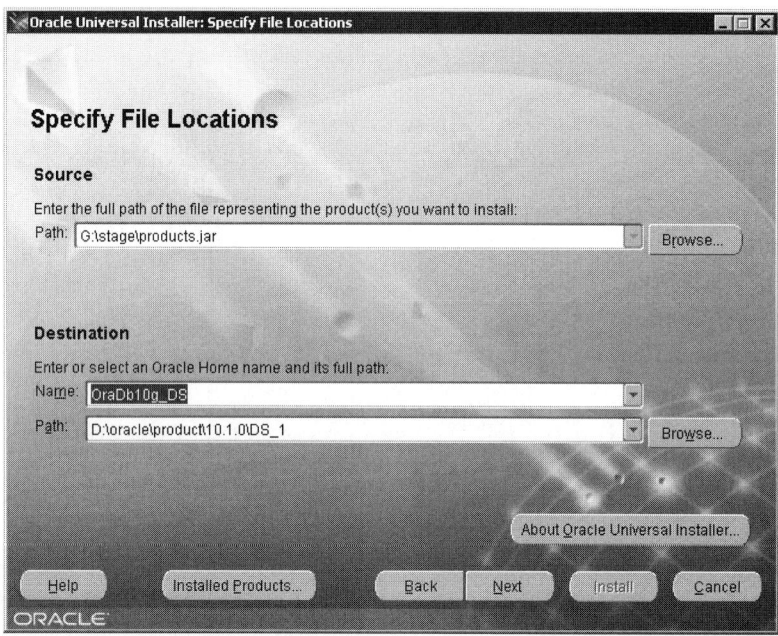

FIGURE 1.19 Specify a unique home name and path.

running personal Oracle—you just have to be sure to put the Developer Suite in a different home directory.

To install developer suite tools:

1. Find and start the first Developer Suite disk. When the setup program runs, click the **Install** button to begin. After the installer checks your machine you will see a Welcome screen. Click the **Next** button.

2. As shown in Figure 1.19, you need to set the destination for the Oracle Home folder. If you have already installed the database on this machine, you must enter a new folder **path** and a new **Name** for the Developer Suite home. Be sure you have at least one gigabyte of free space at the destination location. Click the **Next** button when you are ready.

3. You can select different levels of the development tools if you have a limited amount of space. However, you need at least the **Rapid Application Development** suite, so you might as well pick the **Complete** option, because it uses the same amount of space. Click the **Next** button to continue.

4. If you want to test the option to e-mail reports, you have to provide the name of the outgoing SMTP mail server. This option might require some cooperation from your network and security administrators. You can leave it blank for now and add a value later if you need it, so click the **Next** button.

5. You can scroll through the Summary list of items to be installed; just click the **Install** button when you are ready. You can take a break for a few minutes but you might need someone available to insert the second disk around the 70 percent mark. When the installer finishes, you can exit and close it.

You now have the ability to create forms and reports. If you look at the Windows start menu, you will see several entries for Oracle, including a long list of items under the Oracle Developer Suite.

Oracle components can be installed in many different configurations, and it is difficult to cover all the possibilities. However, one variation needs a bit more

CHAPTER 1 Introduction to Relational Database Systems and Oracle 10g

explanation. It is relatively common to install the primary database on a separate server—even in a development shop. Then you install the Developer Suite on individual computers. This approach is useful because if someone crashes a development computer, it does not affect anyone else, and everyone shares the same database. But, when you install the Developer Suite on each machine, you have to perform one more set of steps. You need to configure the Oracle network on the developer machines so the tools know how to locate the database server. If it is a large organization that has installed Oracle Internet Directory or an Oracle Names Server, you can usually skip these steps. Also, if you installed the main database software on the same machine as the developer software, you can skip these steps.

To configure the Oracle network on a developer machine:

1. From the Windows start menu, choose the options: **Oracle Developer Suite/Configuration and Migration Tools/Net Manager.** Expand the **Service Naming** node to see if any names have been entered. As shown in Figure 1.20, you will usually see only the extproc entry. Leave this one alone, but you have to add one that points to the server.
2. Click the **Service Naming** node and click the **Create** + button. Enter a Service Name for the server. It can be almost anything, but pick something you will associate with the server, such as **LabDB** and click the **Next** button.
3. On the Protocol screen, stick with the default TCP/IP connection and click the **Next** button.
4. On the third setup screen you have to enter the name of the server that is hosting the database. You might need to get the name from your work administrator, but usually it is just the machine network name assigned in Windows. You should accept the default port number of 1521, so click the **Next** button.

FIGURE 1.20 Oracle network configuration.

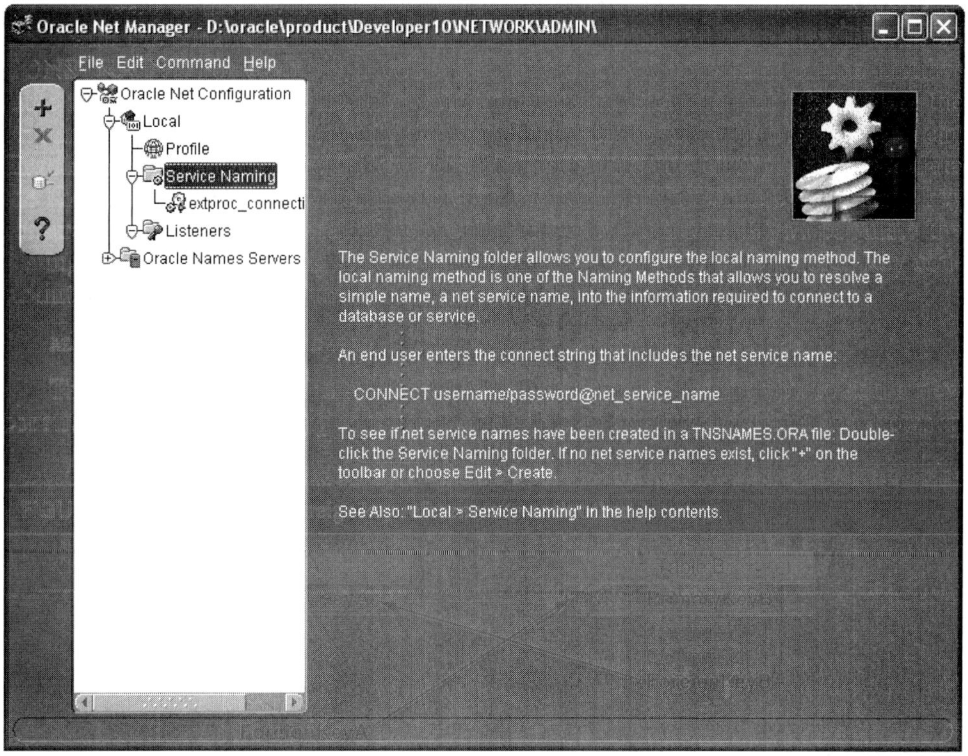

24 Introduction to Oracle

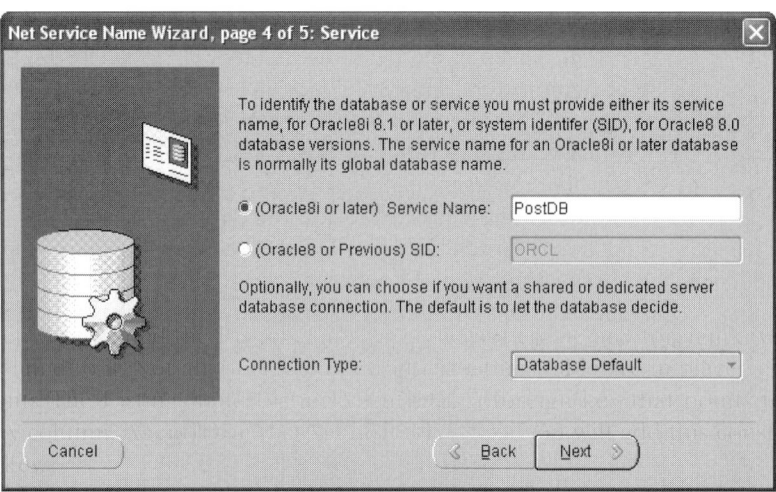

FIGURE 1.21 Entering the global database name.

5. You now have to enter the global database name that was assigned in Step 4 of the database installation procedure. The default value is ORCL, but you might have changed it to something more meaningful. As shown in Figure 1.21, enter the value and click the **Next** button.

6. This step is critical. You will be given the option to test your values. Click the **Test** button. The test first tries to use the default database login, but that account (scott) is normally locked so the first test will fail. Click the **Change Login** button and enter your own username and password. Then click the **Test** button again.

7. When the test process successfully connects to the database, close the test form and click the **Finish** button. Back on the main Net Manager screen use the **File/Save Network Configuration** menu option to save the new connection. Then close the Net Manager.

8. If the test does not connect successfully to the database, you can retry your account or try the system account. If you continue to experience problems, it is most likely because the name of the database server was entered incorrectly. Or, perhaps a firewall or network problem is blocking access to the server. You will need the help of your network administrator.

At this point, your machine should be able to run the Oracle development tools and connect to the database server.

ENTERPRISE FORMS AND REPORTS SERVICES

The Application Server and Forms and Reports Services software is not included with the software on the student disk. You will not need it to do any work, steps, or assignments in this book. However, the Application Server and Forms and Reports Services can be useful to practice real-world deployment. If you want to experiment with them, you can download them from OTN. However, you need a minimum of two computers, and probably three. If you want to run the full Application Server, you need to install the enterprise database on one server, the Application server on a second, and put the Developer Suite on a workstation. If you have only one server and a workstation and want to experiment with the application server, you can install the Developer Suite on your workstation. Then install the database on the server, followed by the forms and

CHAPTER 1   Introduction to Relational Database Systems and Oracle 10g   **25**

reports services. This section describes the basic steps to install the forms and reports services in this situation.

To install forms and reports services:

1. Download the separate Forms and Reports services from OTN. It is not the full Application Server, just a portion of it, so look through the site carefully. Unzip the files into a temporary folder and run the setup.exe program. Click the **Next** button on the Welcome screen.

2. You must install the forms and reports services into a new Oracle home, so change the destination path and enter a new name for the home. Pick a path with at least one gigabyte of spare space, and enter a name like **OraDB10g_AS** so you remember it is the partial application server. Click the **Next** button to start the installation.

3. You have the option to add other languages to the forms and reports server. You can add some if you want to experiment with applications that use multiple languages, or just stick with the default language. Click the **Next** button.

4. You have to name the database instance, enter **Ora10gAS.** You also have to enter another administrator password. Write down the username (ias_admin) and the password you choose. Click the **Next** button.

5. If you want the server to e-mail reports to users, you have to enter the name of the outgoing SMTP server. You can get this name from your network administrator, and you will probably need the network and security administrators to configure the network so you can use the server. For now, leave it blank. You can always enter a value later. Click the **Next** button to continue. Then click the **Install** button and take a break for a few minutes.

6. As shown in Figure 1.22, when the installation is complete, the screen will show you two URLs. Write them down or remember them. Port 80 is the standard Web port. You can test it simply by pointing your browser to the server. It should show

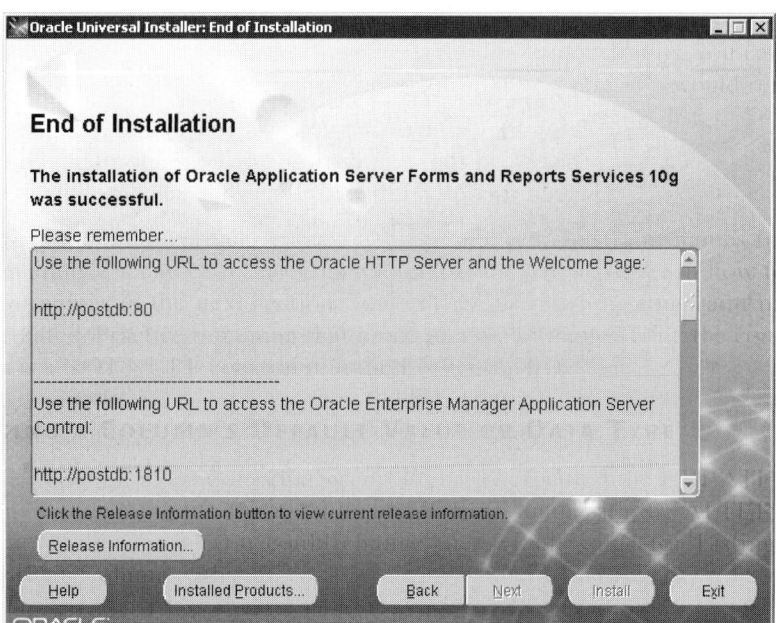

FIGURE 1.22   Copy and save the Forms and Reports Services configuration.

you a basic information page. The other URL uses TCP/IP port 1810 to access the application server enterprise manager. You use this address to configure options for the forms and reports services. You use the ias_admin login with the password you created in Step 4.

The Application Services run somewhat independently and have their own management and monitoring systems. Configuration is a little complicated, but ultimately, the services are required if you want to use the forms and reports in a production setting.

EXPLORING THE ORACLE ENVIRONMENT

Now that you have installed the Oracle systems, you probably want to play with them to see what they can do. However, as you have seen, database systems require you to define and create tables carefully before you can do almost anything. But you really should start to get familiar with the tools and capabilities of Oracle. So this section will focus on relatively simple tasks using a single small table. It does not really show you the power of the database system, but it will help you learn the overall organization of some of the tools.

SQL*PLUS AND *i*SQL*PLUS

The best way to become familiar with the two Oracle interfaces, SQL*Plus and *i*SQL*Plus, is to use them. First, you will create a table, then you will load some sample data into the table. Because we do not want this to become a typing exercise, you will perform this step by running a SQL script file that does all the work for you. (In chapters to follow, as you learn about creating tables and populating them, you will type the SQL statements yourself.) You will use the popular Oracle database interface tool called SQL*Plus to run the script. Prepare by locating the student data file for this exercise called Ch01Explore.sql. It is located in the folder Ch01Data among the data files that came with your book. Note the full path to the data file.

1. Start SQL*Plus from the main Windows Start menu. Your menu choices should be similar to those in Figure 1.23 but will not be exactly the same. Look for the main **Oracle home** options, expand **Application Development,** and select the **SQL Plus** choice.
2. Log into the database. Figure 1.24 shows the standard login screen. If you are running the database on your own machine, you need to look up the username and password that you created for yourself after you installed the DBMS. You also need to look up the name of your machine, which you enter into the Host String space. If someone else installed Oracle for you, you will be given the three values that you need. Enter them now and then click the **OK** button.

FIGURE 1.23 Starting SQL*Plus.

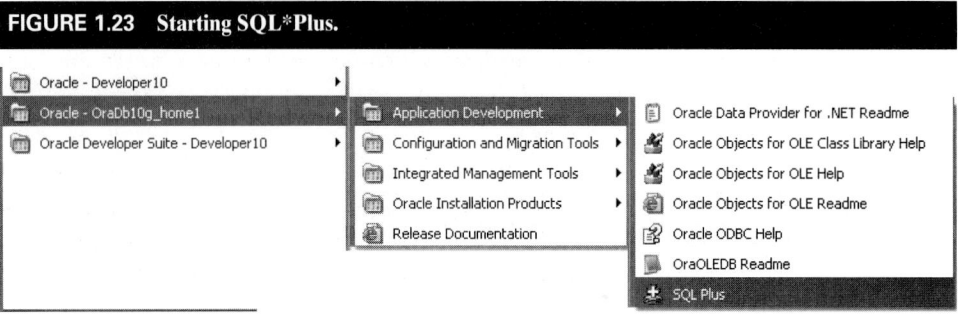

CHAPTER 1 Introduction to Relational Database Systems and Oracle 10g **27**

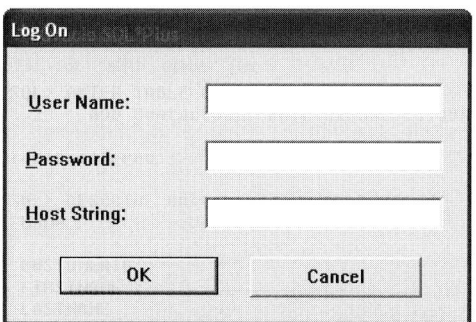

FIGURE 1.24 Standard login screen.

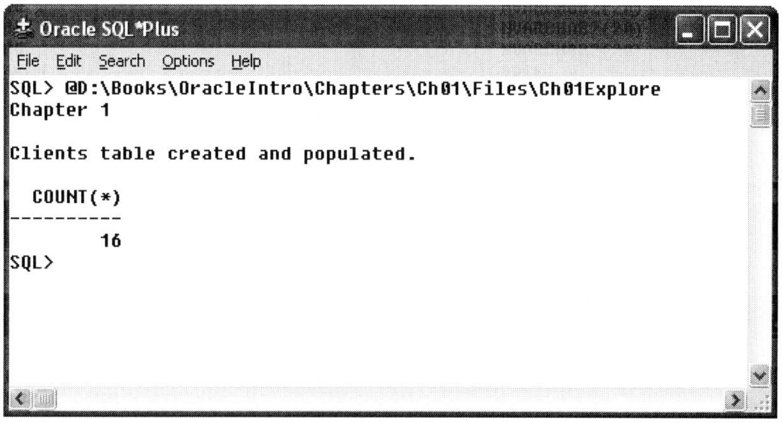

FIGURE 1.25 Running the setup script.

3. SQL*Plus starts as a mostly empty page. You need to run the SQL script for this chapter. Use Windows Explorer to find the exact location on the student data disk. In SQL*Plus, type

   `@<path>\Ch01Explore`

   but substitute your path for "<path>" above. Figure 1.25 shows the sample command and the result.

   The script creates a Clients table for you and loads it with 16 names. The table consists of five columns: ClientID, FirstName, LastName, Category, and Balance. The Category simply represents the job of the client (Builder, Banker, and so on). The Balance is the amount the client currently owes you for services you performed earlier.

4. To see the data, type the command: **SELECT * FROM Clients;** and press **Enter** to execute it. Be sure to include the semicolon at the end of the statement. You will see rows of data, but they are probably messy because SQL*Plus wraps the rows to a new line.

5. Log off of Oracle and exit SQL*Plus by typing **Exit** and then pressing **Enter.**

Oracle also includes a more graphical-oriented query tool called *i*SQL*Plus. It has the additional feature that it runs across the Internet using a simple Internet browser. This tool is not on the standard menu. Instead, start your Internet browser and then connect to the server.

Introduction to Oracle

To launch *i*SQL*Plus and access your Oracle database:

1. Start your Internet browser. In the address line, enter the URL of the *i*SQL server that appeared when you installed the database. If you left the default values unchanged, then the address will be the following (substitute your machine name for "<server name>" below):

   `http://<server name>:5560/isqlplus`

   > **Tip:** If you cannot determine your machine name, then you can use the following URL. It almost always works if you have installed the database on your own machine.
   > `http://127.0.0.1:5560/isqplplus`
   > (It *does not* work if you are accessing a remote server. In that case, ask your instructor for the proper URL to access *i*SQL*Plus.)

2. Type your Oracle username in the Username text box, and type your password in the Password text box. You do not need to enter or change the Connect Identifier. Click the **Login** button. The Workspace window appears.
3. Click the Workspace text box and type the following. You do not need to press Enter at the end of the line, unlike in SQL*Plus.

   `SELECT * FROM Clients;`

4. Click the **Execute** button to execute the command. Oracle retrieves the 16 rows from the Clients table and displays them (see Figure 1.26).

Figure 1.26 shows the command and the results. Notice that the browser formats the table to make it easy to see the rows and columns of the results. For the most part, you can use either SQL*Plus or *i*SQL*Plus for just about every exercise in this book. We tend to use SQL*Plus in almost all the examples because it is the most common tool available, and it works on a wide variety of platforms—not just Windows. In any case, both tools support standard queries. The main drawbacks to SQL*Plus are that you need it installed on your machine, and the results often need to be formatted to be readable. On the other hand, although *i*SQL*Plus is easy to run, it does not support all of the configuration options available in SQL*Plus. Most people still use SQL*Plus because it has been around the longest and they have learned how to use it.

To remove the table created earlier with a SQL statement:

1. Clear the Workspace window by clicking the **Clear** button on the right side of the screen, just below the dividing line. The Workspace text box clears and *i*SQL*Plus removes the query results.
2. Click the **Workspace** text box and type the following. Then press the **Execute** button to execute the query.

   `DROP TABLE Clients PURGE;`

3. Because you are done with *i*SQL*Plus for the time being, click the **Logout** link to log out of Oracle.
4. Close your browser.

DEVELOPER SUITE TOOLS

The two main tools in the Developer Suite are the Forms Builder and the Reports Builder. They both have many options and take some time to learn. Nevertheless, it helps to see at least a simple form and report so that you understand their purposes. The one catch is that it takes several steps to run the two builders, and complications

CHAPTER 1 Introduction to Relational Database Systems and Oracle 10g

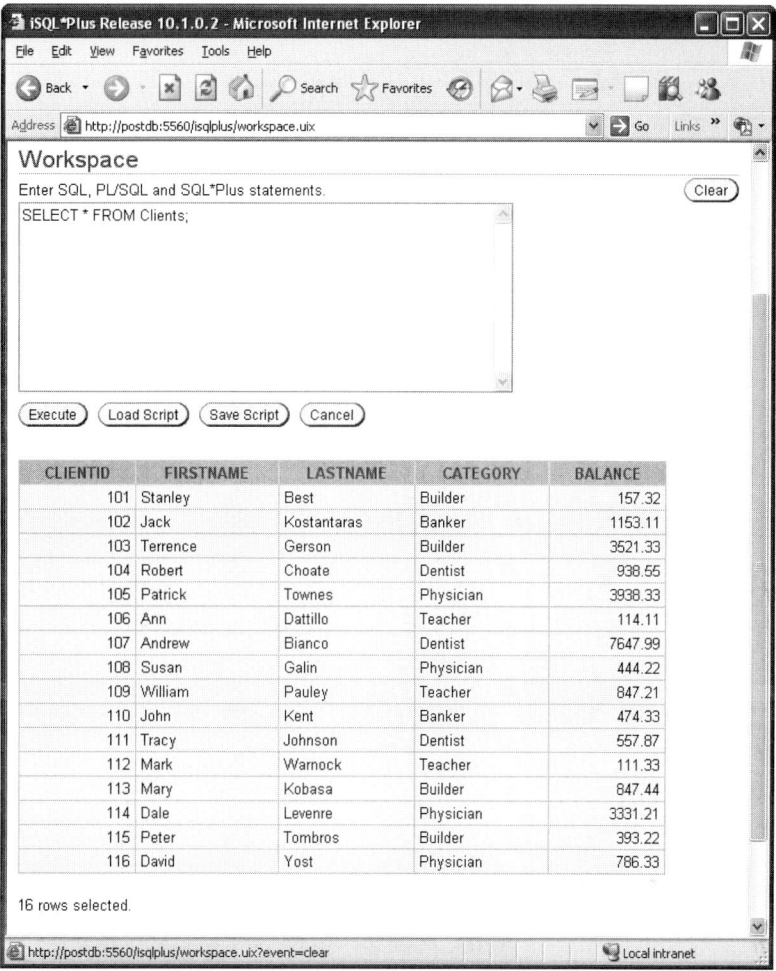

FIGURE 1.26 Running a simple query with *i*SQL*Plus.

can arise that take too long to solve right now. So, you will have to be content with the pictures for now.

Figure 1.27 shows a simple form that can be used to view and enter data into the Clients table. Since it is a single table, the form is relatively simple. You can scroll through the rows of data by clicking the Next Record ▶ and Previous Record ◀ buttons on the toolbar. If you make changes to the data, you click the Save button to write the changes to the database. You can even use the form as a query tool. You can click the Enter Query button; enter values onto the form, such as Banker in the Category box; and click the Execute Query button. The form will then show you only records that match the values you entered. More complex forms compute totals and use lookup lists to make it easier for users to enter data.

Figure 1.28 shows a sample report based on the data in the Clients table. It is a grouped report because it computes totals for each of the entries in the Category column (Banker, Builder, and so on). The detail section shows the balance of each client within the specified category. The Report Wizard did most of the work to create this report. You can print the form or view it through a Web browser. For printed reports, Oracle can generate Adobe Acrobat Portable Document Format (PDF) reports that you can e-mail to users so they can view or print them.

■ **30** Introduction to Oracle

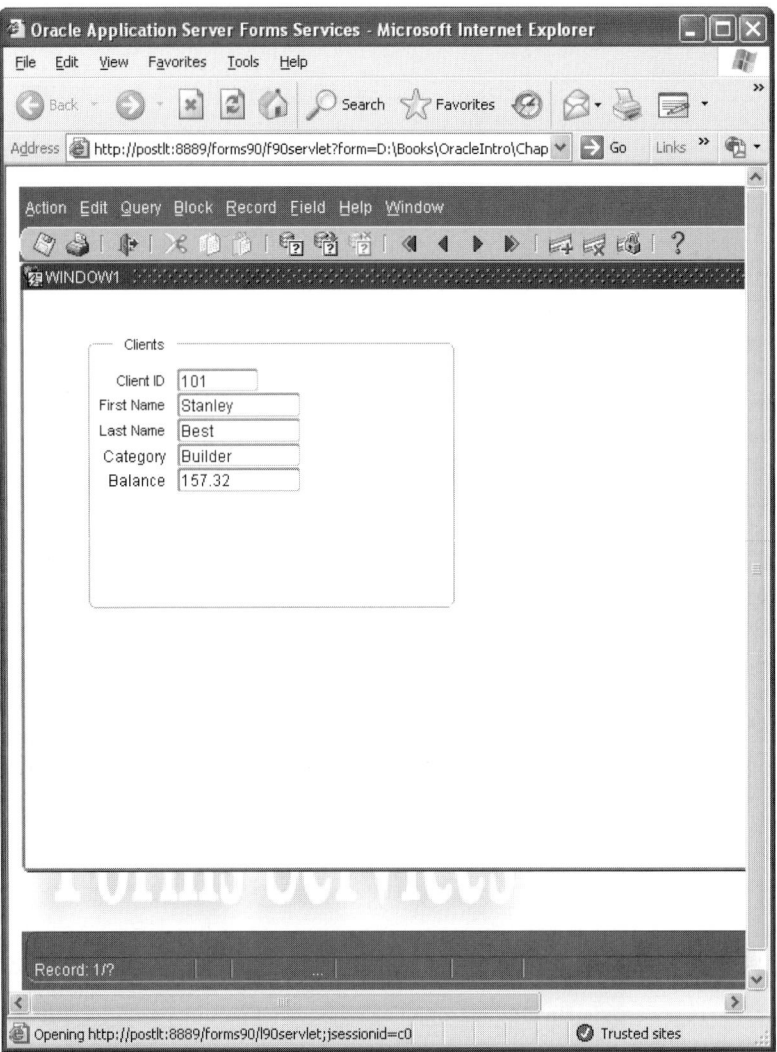

FIGURE 1.27 A simple form for the Clients table.

This book will show you how to use the wizards to quickly create useful forms and reports. You will also learn how to edit the forms and reports and customize them to provide even more features. If you are curious, both the sample form (Clients.fmb) and the sample report (ClientBalances.jsp) are included on the student data disk in the files folder for this chapter. You can click on either file to open it in the respective Oracle editor. You should be able to view the report if you want to see it run. However, it takes a little more effort to run forms, and you do not need to take the time to go through that process now. The detailed steps are covered in Chapter 8, where you will have many opportunities to work with reports.

ORACLE ENTERPRISE MANAGER

The Oracle Forms and Reports Builders are used primarily by application developers. The results of those efforts are utilized by end users. Developers also use the SQL*Plus or *i*SQL*Plus query tools. Only rarely will you allow users direct access to the query tools. Even if you restrict them to doing simple read-only queries, it takes time to

Client Balances

Category	Client ID	First Name	Last Name	Balance
Banker	110	John	Kent	$474.33
	102	Jack	Kostantaras	$1,153.11
	Total:			$1,627.44
Builder	101	Stanley	Best	$157.32
	103	Terrence	Gerson	$3,521.33
	113	Mary	Kobasa	$847.44
	115	Peter	Tombros	$393.22
	Total:			$4,919.31
Dentist	107	Andrew	Bianco	$7,647.99
	104	Robert	Choate	$938.55
	111	Tracy	Johnson	$557.87
	Total:			$9,144.41
Physician	108	Susan	Galin	$444.22
	114	Dale	Levenre	$3,331.21
	105	Patrick	Townes	$3,938.33
	116	David	Yost	$786.33
	Total:			$8,500.09
Teacher	106	Ann	Dattillo	$114.11
	109	William	Pauley	$847.21
	112	Mark	Warnock	$111.33
	Total:			$1,072.65
Total:				$25,263.90

FIGURE 1.28 Sample report for Clients.

explain the details of SQL syntax to them, and there is a risk that they will misunderstand the query results. However, some advanced users might request access to those tools. The query tools are also heavily used by database administrators. Almost any task the DBA needs to perform can be handled with special queries or packages. However, it takes time to learn the names and functions of all of these tools. And, DBAs generally have to memorize the commands, because the query systems do not provide any prompting.

The Enterprise Manager is a tool created to help DBAs monitor the database and perform basic tasks. It is a graphical interface that runs in a browser over the Internet. Consequently, it is relatively easy to use, even for beginning DBAs, and makes the database controls accessible from more locations. The main drawback is that only a DBA may use the Enterprise Manager. If you have installed a copy of the Oracle DBMS on your own machine, you can use the System account which has the DBA role. If you are limited to accessing a shared computer in a lab setting, the DBA will not want to give the DBA role to students; so you probably will not be able to run the exercises in this book that use the Enterprise Manager.

If you do have DBA privileges, running the Enterprise Manager is straightforward. Just be careful and do not try to change anything until you know what you are doing. If you crash some parameters, you might have to remove and reinstall the database system.

To start the Enterprise Manager:

1. Look up the TCP/IP port that was configured when the system was installed. Start your Web browser and enter the URL into the address line. The default location is (Enter the name of your server without the angle brackets.):

   `http://<server name>:5500/em`

32 Introduction to Oracle

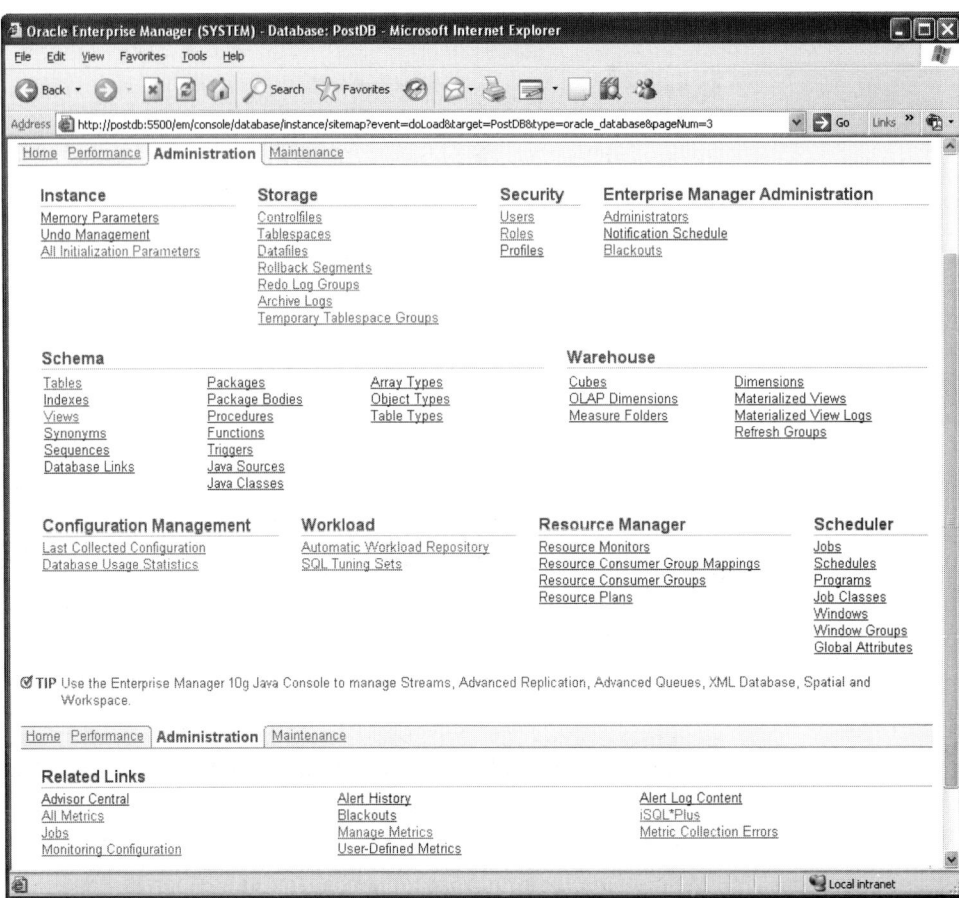

FIGURE 1.29 Administration tasks in the Enterprise Manager.

2. When asked, enter your username and password to log in. You will then see the Home page of the Enterprise Manager. It contains basic status information about the database.

3. Notice the main tabs near the top of the browser (Home, Performance, Administration, and Maintenance). These give you access to most of the features of the tool. Figure 1.29 shows the main options on the **Administration** page.

   The options are grouped by primary task, such as Storage and Security.

4. For example, click the **Users** link under the **Security** option to add users to the database or modify the access rights of existing users. If you installed Oracle on your own machine, you may use this option to create a new account for yourself so that you do not have to use the System account.

   The other tabs provide even more controls and links, which demonstrate the large number of tasks a DBA performs. Again, avoid making any changes at this point. A DBA account has considerable privileges on the database, because DBAs need wide access to configure the database and help users. However, these privileges also give the account the power to cause serious damage.

5. Click the **Logout** link at the top of the page and close the browser before you scare everyone.

INTRODUCTION TO THE BOOK'S DATABASES

The best way to learn about database systems is to build sample databases and experiment with them. The case for each chapter in this book is based on a fictitious real estate company called Redwood Realty. This small office of 29 real estate professionals and support staff is in Arcata, California, and it serves all of Humboldt County, near the northern border of California. The chapters show you, using step-by-step examples, how to build elements of the application for this real estate company. At the end of each chapter, you will find four hands-on exercises. The first exercise in every chapter refers to the chapter case, Redwood Realty, and requests you to extend the work you did in the chapter body to add features, or simply do more of what you learned. You use Redwood Realty as the backdrop application. The other three end-of-chapter exercises also ask you to use what you learned in the chapter to create or extend database objects for the three distinct examples.

A major objective of the book is to show you how to create specific features that you probably will need to understand in other database work you will encounter. As you work on cases in the future, the examples in this book will provide guidance to create the foundation for almost any DBMS case. This section provides a brief description of each of the four end-of-chapter cases. All four of the cases have SQL scripts that you may use to create and load the data into the tables to initialize everything for the databases. These scripts are on the student data disk and are organized by chapters. Each chapter might have additional files, such as sample forms and reports. Generally, you will be asked to copy these files onto a folder on your hard drive, so you should set up a special folder for this book and create subfolders for each chapter.

REDWOOD REALTY

The Redwood Realty case appears in every chapter in this book as the backbone case used to teach the database concepts in general, and Oracle concepts in particular. The body of each chapter explains Oracle using the Redwood Realty database throughout. As you are probably aware, a real estate firm helps people buy and sell houses and charges a commission for that service. By convention, real estate professionals charge the real estate sellers a commission, not the real estate buyers. There are several advantages to using real estate professionals when purchasing or selling real estate. Principal among these advantages is that real estate professionals are familiar with all the rules and regulations surrounding real estate and can help their clients navigate the mountain of paperwork involved in both selling an purchasing a home. Agents are employees who have earned a state license by passing a state exam. This license allows them to sell real estate in the state in which they hold the license (California, in this example). Real estate professionals contact possible sellers, and investigate recent sales to establish a listing price for a house or property. Houses are listed for sale and entered into the regional multiple listing service (MLS) database. The agent working with the seller is called the selling or listing agent. Potential buyers can contact the original listing agent, or they might work with a second agent—possibly from a different company. When any of the agents working for Redwood Realty list a house, they need to enter the description into the company's database. They also need to track the customer information.

Figure 1.30 shows a concise diagram outlining the relationship among the eight tables that make up the Redwood Realty database. Each box represents a table, and the table's name appears at the top of each box in the shaded area. A table's primary key or keys are located below the table's name and are underlined. Primary key columns contain the notation "PK" to their left. The notation "FK" appears to the left

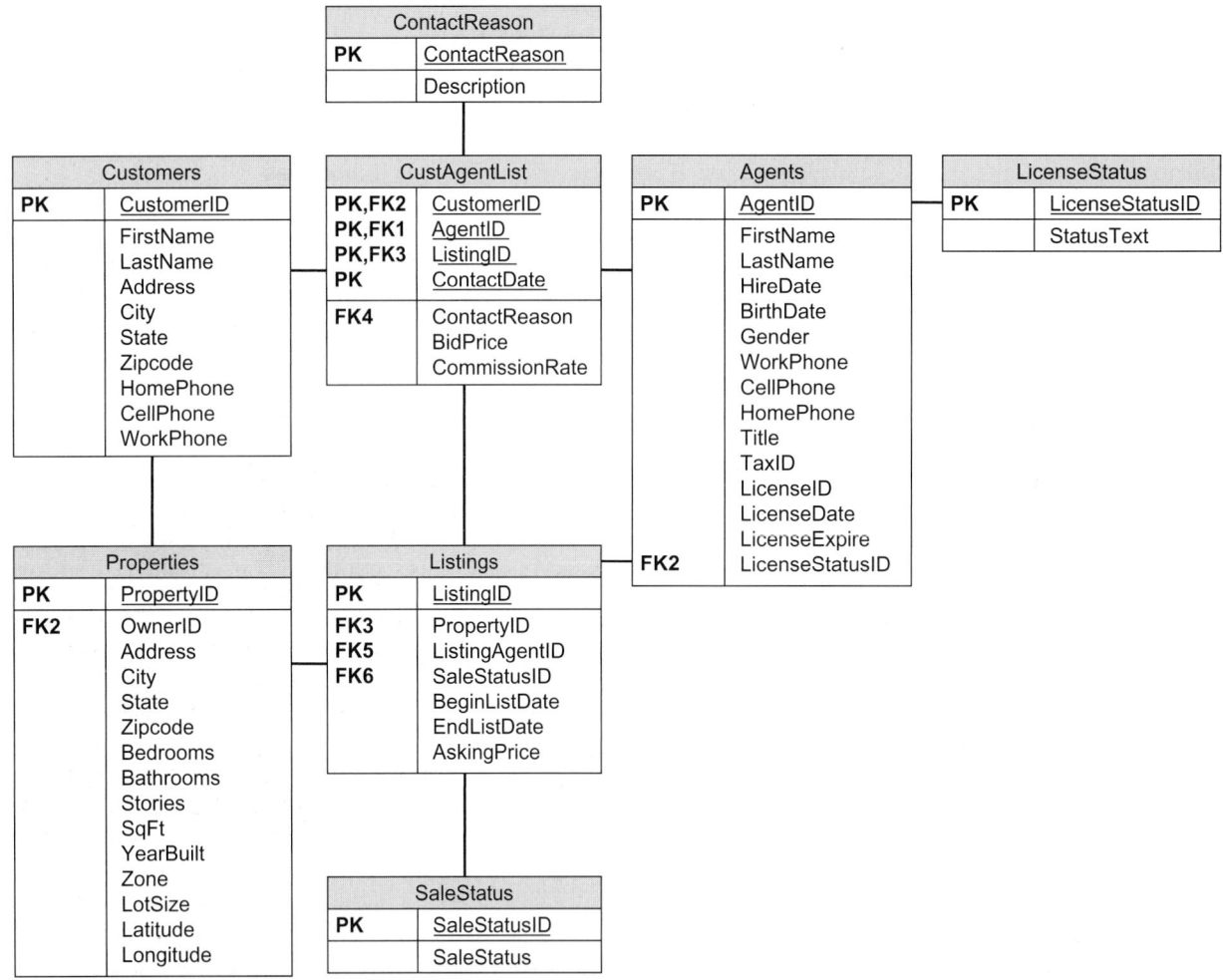

FIGURE 1.30 Diagram of the Redwood Realty database.

of any table column that is a foreign key. Some primary key columns are also foreign key columns (see the CustAgentList table in Figure 1.30, for example). In that case, both *PK* and *FK* appear to the left of the column. (There is no significance to any digit that appears next to the FK notation. It is just Visio's way of tracking distinct foreign keys.) You will probably refer to Figure 1.30 a lot. So, we suggest you use a sticky flag to mark its place in your book.

Briefly, the meaning of the tables are as follows. The *ContactReason* table contains three rows with reasons that people contacted Redwood Realty: Buy, Sell, or Casual are the three values, with longer explanations attached. The *Customers* table lists the 2,500 buyers and sellers who have contacted Redwood Realty recently. Data includes all the requisite contact information. *Agents* is a 29-row table listing information about the real estate agents working for Redwood Realty. *Listings* contains a row for each property for sale. Its 502 rows reference the listing agent and the property description, found in other tables, along with begin and end listing dates. In this table is the owner's desired selling price, called AskingPrice, for each property. *Properties* contains all the details about 2,000 properties referenced in the Listings table and in the Customers tables. Not all homes listed in Properties are for sale—only 502 of them. The others (1,492 of them) are simply properties in Humboldt County. Besides the typical information about the properties, each record contains data available in the public record of the county assessor, such as square footage living space, the year the structure was built, the zoning, lot size, bedrooms, bathrooms, and the longitude and latitude! The *SaleStatus* table is a tiny table containing three rows: For Sale, Pending, and Sold. Mostly useful as a table referenced by forms drop-down lists, the SaleStatus table provides a consistent spelling for the status of properties in the Listings table that references it. The *LicenseStatus* table contains the 16 rows that describe the various conditions associated with a real estate license in California. Status indicators range from "Licensed" to "Surrendered." Their exact meaning, except for obvious categories, is unimportant. But they are real conditions that indicate whether an agent can practice in the state. Finally, the CustAgentList table is the glue that binds together each of three tables whose abbreviations make up the table's name. CustAgentList contains foreign key references to the Customers, Listings, Agents, and ContactReason tables. It contains 1,018 rows. In this table is the only place you will find the price that prospective buyers have bid on a property. Therefore, only those properties for which the ContactReason is "Buy" contain a non-null BidPrice, if any.

When the real estate market heats up, agents get busy and can be working with several buyers and sellers at the same time. Sales are particularly difficult because buyers and sellers often go through several rounds of negotiations before deciding on a final price. The agents need to keep track of all offers. In fact, the contact list is one of the most important pieces of data to an agent. People who look at one house might not make an offer on it, but they are likely to be interested in other houses. A good agent has a detailed knowledge of the inventory of houses available and can direct potential buyers to one that fits their needs. Agents earn their money through commissions on the sale or purchase of a house. Typically, the listing and purchasing agent split the overall commission, and a portion of the commission is paid to the agent's real estate company. Traditionally, agencies write sales contracts with a 6 percent commission, but sometimes that number is negotiable. Figure 1.31 shows the contact form that agents want to use for tracking offers and listings by agents. Of course, the company collects additional data about employees and customers, but there is not space to display all of it on this form. The main body of this form will become the CustomerAgentList table. Other forms are used to enter that data.

Figure 1.32 shows part of the listings report for agents. The report shows some of the pertinent data about the properties that are listed by each agent. Again, considerably more detail is collected about properties, including the number of bathrooms, number of stories, the size of the house measured in square feet, and the year it was built. Agents also store contact data on property owners.

COFFEE MERCHANT

The Coffee Merchant is a small store that ships coffee and tea around the world to its many customers. It is primarily a Web-based company. Its computer needs are relatively simple: Record orders and track customers. The Coffee Merchant's inventory of coffee and teas is extensive. It offers coffee beans ranging from Kona Extra Fancy, grown in the United States, to varieties from Sumatra, Ethiopia, Yemen, Colombia, Costa Rica, and Papua New Guinea—to name a few.

There are seven Oracle tables representing the Coffee Merchant's business model, so far. As the expertise develops, the managers plan to include shipping in the database. The tables are: States, Consumers, Employees, OrderLines, Orders, Inventory, and Countries. *States* contains information about the 50 U.S. states and the District of Columbia. Columns include the state abbreviation, full state name, sales tax rate, population, state size in square miles, and a URL that takes you to the official state Web

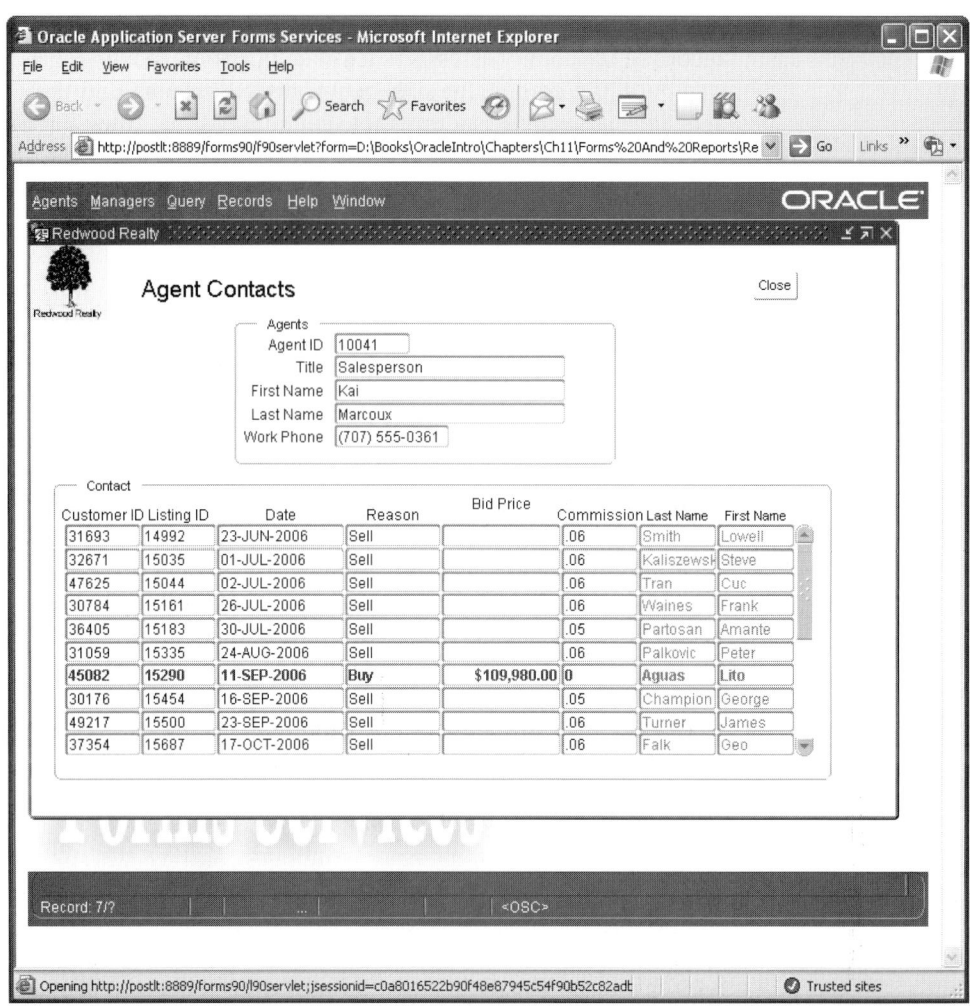

FIGURE 1.31 Contact form for agents and customers.

site (in case you become curious about the state flower of Mississippi, for example!). The *Consumers* table holds name and address information about past and present customers. The table holds over 1,500 customer rows. *Employees* stores data for the 22 employees such as hire date, commission rate, birth date, gender, and name. Orders placed with the Coffee Merchant are placed in the Orders and OrderLines tables. The 500 rows in the *Orders* table contain pointers to consumers and employees involved, the order dates, and the customer purchase orders, if any. *OrderLines* holds 2,192 rows of individual lines for every order, and each entry points back to the parent order with appropriate foreign/primary key pairs. The *Inventory* table lists all the teas and coffees that the Coffee Merchant is able to supply customers. The 128 unique products in the Inventory table range from the most exotic Oolong teas to the commonplace Colombian coffees. Though not used extensively in this textbook, Inventory's Description field contains a lengthy description of the coffee or tea including origin, characteristics of the taste, and facts about how the product is processed. *Countries* is a 256-row table describing countries in the world, fixed at a particular point in time. The Inventory table points to the Countries table to indicate the country of origin of

Agent Listings

Redwood Realty

Last Name Allee　　　　**First Name** Lora　　　　**Agent ID** 15293
Work Phone (707) 555-9990

Listing ID	List Date	Asking Price	City	Bedrooms
15099	12-JUL-06	$230,000	Eureka	4
15863	11-NOV-06	$208,000	Arcata	4
15461	17-SEP-06	$200,000	Eureka	3
15537	26-SEP-06	$178,035	Arcata	3
16120	18-DEC-06	$163,360	Eureka	3
15982	29-NOV-06	$155,010	Eureka	3
15480	18-SEP-06	$149,228	Arcata	3
15232	06-AUG-06	$145,000	Loleta	3
15623	04-OCT-06	$145,000	Arcata	5
15699	20-OCT-06	$130,950	Eureka	3
16135	19-DEC-06	$129,800	Arcata	3
15705	20-OCT-06	$129,740	Eureka	3
15045	03-JUL-06	$125,000	Arcata	3
15384	05-SEP-06	$119,000	Eureka	3
15715	22-OCT-06	$105,000	Arcata	3
15663	10-OCT-06	$101,000	Arcata	3
15268	10-AUG-06	$100,000	McKinleyville	3
Total: 17		**$2,514,123**		

FIGURE 1.32 Simple sales listing report.

the inventory item. Some details about the company and how employees process orders is described next.

To fulfill the orders received on the Web site and over the phone, the Coffee Merchant employs 22 people. To monitor who is doing the best job of selling, management tracks which employee is responsible for each order. Only the employee who takes the order is associated with it, and Web orders are assigned to an employee on a rotating basis.

The company does not separate out shipping details. Based on a long-standing tradition, the company prefers to use the Oracle order forms rather than the Web forms available to online shoppers. Besides, the Oracle forms are designed for use by employees and not potential customers.

Figure 1.33 shows the basic order form used by the Coffee Merchant. The customer information is entered on a separate form, and a lookup list is used on this form to select the appropriate customer. Likewise, the company maintains a separate list of items in inventory. They are identified by number on this order form, but a lookup list is used to provide more details about each item. Note that the Value column is calculated on the form and is not actually saved in the database. The company does introduce two items that were not handled in the simpler order form of the chapter. First, it supports both a list price and a sale price of the item. The sale price is assigned at the time of the sale—based on data not stored in the database. Second, employees can offer additional discounts to customers. This percentage discount is deducted from the sale price.

Figure 1.34 shows a typical management report for the Coffee Merchant. It computes total sales by quarter for each state and for each inventory category. At the moment, the store has only two inventory categories, coffee and tea, but they might add other items in the future. The company uses a calendar year, so the value of the quarter is easy to compute from the order date. The company does use separate tables of states and countries to reduce data entry errors.

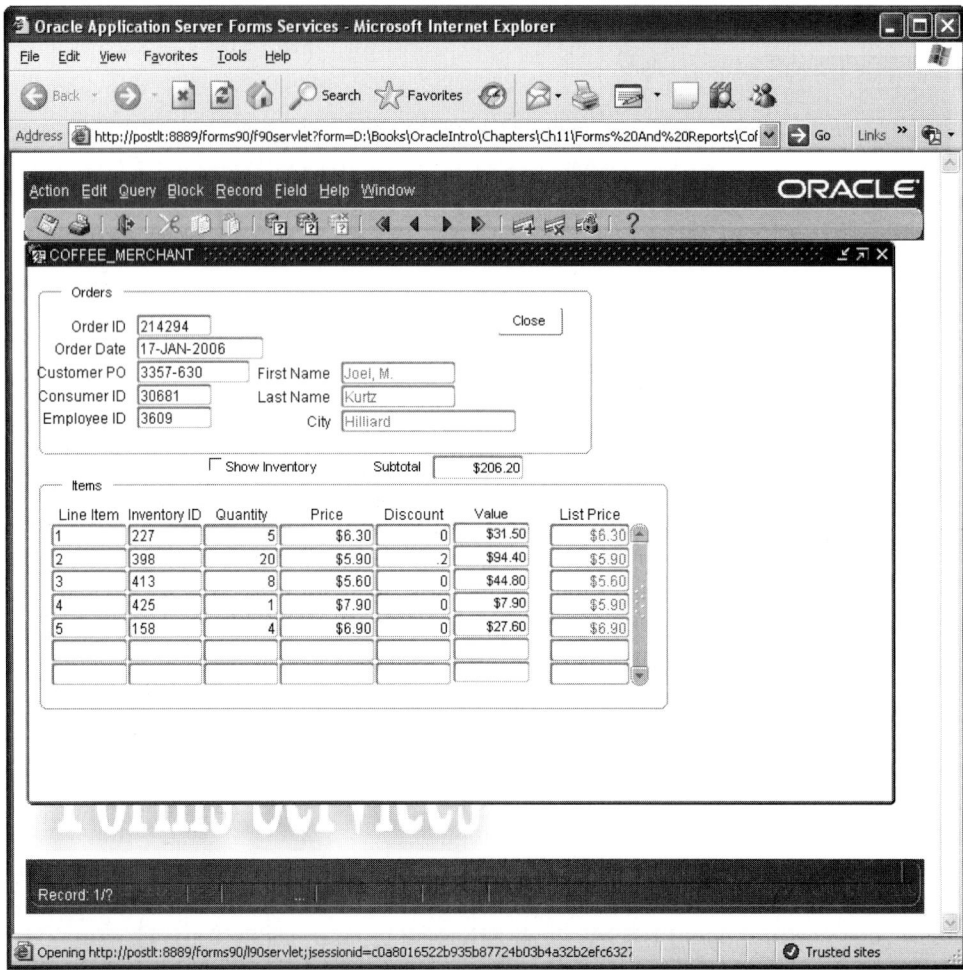

FIGURE 1.33 Basic order form for the Coffee Merchant.

ROWING VENTURES

Rowing Ventures is responsible for coordinating rowing regattas at more than a dozen venues around the United States and abroad. Besides overseeing the venue and providing vendor display and merchandising space at the rowing events, Rowing Ventures (RV) stores a myriad of details about the races at each regatta, the participants, their sponsors, the boats in each race, boat bow numbers, and crews in each boat.

Six tables make up this relatively small database. The *Boat* table lists the boat category, assigned lane number (called the *bow* number), and the club or organization with which the crew is affiliated. The *Organization* table holds details about the club or college participating in one or more races. Data in this table include phone, address, nation, the organization's name, and a major news outlet affiliated with the group or region where the group is based. *RaceTimes* holds finish time, finish order, and pointers to the race and boat. *Race* holds the names of all groups of races that have finished the race. Only two types of races are in this table, so far: Club Eights Men and Club Fours Men. Joining Race, RaceTimes, and Boat together provides a roster of the races run so far, team names, finish times, and order of finish. *BoatCrew* lists the people who are actually racing in each boat. The *Person* table lists the name, gender, weight, and birth

Quarterly Sales By State

Item Type C

Year/Quarter	2005-4	2006-1	2006-2	
State	Value	Value	Value	Total
AL	$487	$288	$158	$933
AZ	$216	$1,049		$1,264
CA	$3,676	$2,934	$354	$6,964
CO	$492	$321		$813
CT	$1,504	$1,366	$311	$3,180
DC	$315			$315
DE	$138	$636		$775
FL	$1,281	$1,144	$105	$2,530
GA	$931	$561		$1,492
IA	$561	$67		$628
IL	$1,675	$1,590	$602	$3,868
IN	$298	$361		$658
KS		$392	$226	$618
KY	$198	$434	$202	$834
LA	$314	$615		$929
MA	$1,556	$933	$707	$3,196
MD	$81	$424		$504
ME	$89			$89
MI	$749	$836	$154	$1,740
MN	$1,120	$1,159	$494	$2,773
MO	$1,304	$1,077	$455	$2,835
MS	$809	$644		$1,453
NC	$450	$866	$86	$1,401
NE	$44			$44
NH	$251	$226		$478
NJ	$2,413	$1,080	$220	$3,714
NM		$345	$200	$546
NV	$529	$424		$952
NY	$4,733	$4,245	$85	$9,063
OH	$2,406	$1,688	$385	$4,479
OK	$195	$368		$563
OR	$299	$210		$508
PA	$1,797	$2,966	$414	$5,177
RI		$600		$600
SC	$9	$256		$265
TN	$556	$1,011	$144	$1,711
TX	$4,657	$2,752	$333	$7,742
UT	$643	$269		$912
VA	$889	$458	$444	$1,791
VT	$76			$76
WA	$342	$796		$1,138
WI	$1,738	$1,151	$38	$2,927
WV		$73		$73
	$39,820	$36,612	$6,118	$82,551

FIGURE 1.34 Quarterly sales organized by inventory type and state.

date of each participant. Information in the Person table determines which races a person can legitimately participate in, and any age handicaps applied (in the case of master rowers). Joining Race, RaceTimes, Boat, BoatCrew, and Person gives a complete list of who raced in which race, and the result.

Key elements of the database are the ability to register participants. Most boats are crewed, which means they have multiple people rowing. The boats are expensive, so they are owned and raced by organizations. Many of the organizations are university rowing clubs, but a few private teams compete. When registering a boat for a race, Rowing Ventures has to track data about all crew members, and about the organization itself. Races have many categories that are based on the type of boat, number of rowers, and often the gender and age of the crew. All boats in a given race are provided bow numbers that correspond to the lane in which they race, so they can be easily identified on the water and at the finish line.

The sport has a unique terminology. If you read Web sites, or go to a race, you should know the details. For instance, sweep rowing involves one oar per person. Sculling is two oars. A person rowing a single is always sculling. An eight-person boat (shell) always has a coxswain whose position is noted as "0" in the Position column in the BoatCrew table. Called an "eight," the shell contains eight rowers who have one oar per person. Their positions are numbered from the bow to the stern in descending order beginning with position 8. Rowing alternates from the left, or port side, to the right, or starboard side as you work from the bow to the stern. High school rowers, known as juniors, and college rowers typically row either bow or starboard. Masters rowers, 27 years old or older, often commit to being port or starboard rowers. Fours—a four-seat boat—can contain a coxswain ("cox") or not. This type of boat is either a "four" or a "quad." A four is four people with four oars. A quad is four people and eight oars. (No, this is *not* on the quiz!)

Figure 1.35 shows a version of the form used to record results of a race. Places are assigned based on the finish order, and the times of each boat are recorded. All of the

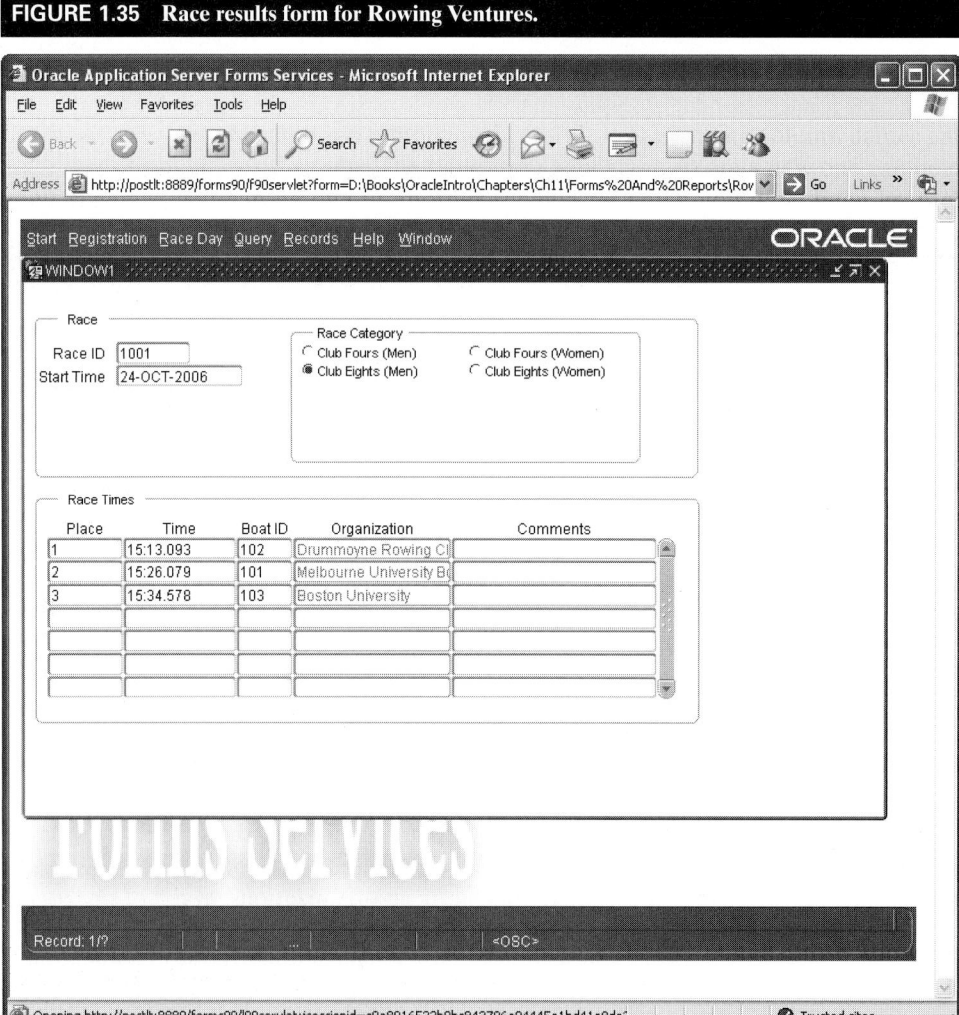

FIGURE 1.35 Race results form for Rowing Ventures.

CHAPTER 1 Introduction to Relational Database Systems and Oracle 10g 41

Race Results
Rowing Ventures

Race ID	Start Time	Category	Place	Time	Boat ID	Position	Last Name	First Name
1001	24-OCT-06	Club Eights (Men)	1	15:13.093	102	0	Rogers	June
				Drummoyne Rowing Club		1	Pangburn	Richard
						2	Berry	Glenn
						3	Farrar	Donald
						4	Wood	Larry
						5	Wheeler	Michael
						6	Miller	Ralph
						7	Moore	Paul
						8	Sutter	Robert
			2	15:26.079	101	0	Wolfe	Carole
				Melbourne University Boat Club		1	Rappaport	Scott
						2	Eklund	Gene
						3	Cory	Lou
						4	Simpson	Ted
						5	Briggs	Dan
						6	Lewis	Donald
						7	Witte	Charles
						8	Johnson	Douglas
			3	15:34.578	103	0	Rose	Barbara
				Boston University		1	White	Dwight
						2	Kern	Ray
						3	Morrow	Ray
						4	Brown	Mark
						5	King	Michael
						6	Wisefield	Joey
						7	Wolfod	Harry
						8	Jones	Bruce

FIGURE 1.36 Race results with crew names.

supporting data was recorded before the race—predominantly when the boats and crews were registered. After a race, the clerk simply picks the appropriate race, enters the place numbers and times, and picks the boats from a list.

Results from the race are printed and posted for teams and fans to see (see Figure 1.36). Eventually, the results are sent to various news outlets. Crew members are happy to see their names in the newspaper—even if it is just the student paper. The PDF version of some of the results are also posted on the Web site so fans and participants can check later and compare results for all events.

BROADCLOTH CLOTHING

Broadcloth Clothing is a relatively complicated case. In terms of data collected, it is much larger than the other examples. It represents a company that manufactures clothing that is sold largely through department and chain stores. The complication is that the company really focuses on design and coordination. Most of the clothing is made in various factories around the world that are independently owned. Broadcloth develops new clothing lines, gets orders from the stores (who are the customers), and then contracts with various factories to make a certain number of items. Each design is really a model or style of clothing, such as a new skirt, blouse, or pants. Each model can be made in multiple sizes and colors. For example, a style of blouse from a predetermined type of fabric is one model of clothing. That model in blue at size 6 is a specific item of clothing.

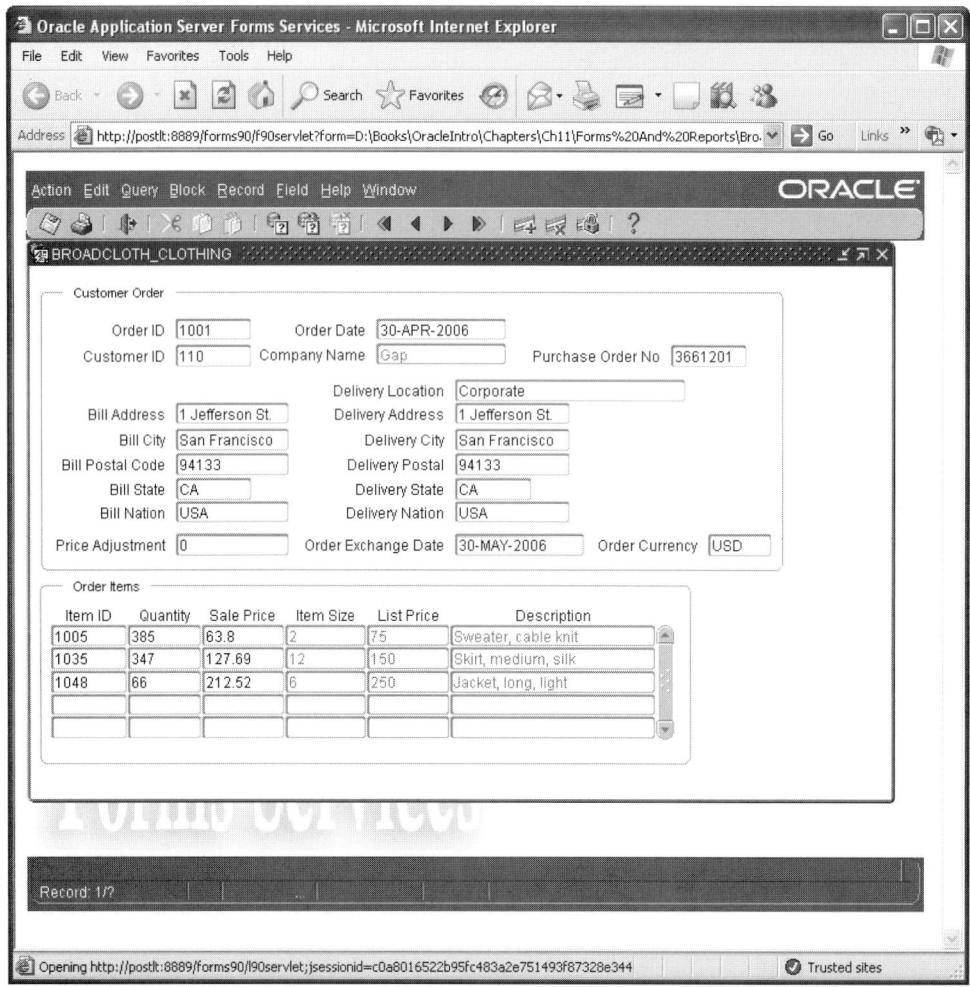

FIGURE 1.37 Order form for Broadcloth Clothing.

As shown in Figure 1.37, customers order multiple quantities of individual items. Generally, they order a selection of sizes and colors based on the model. But the company has to track the individual items. Later, reports can produce aggregate totals by model style if desired.

The international nature of the production makes it somewhat more complicated to deal with shipping. Many nations impose customs taxes on clothing. All of them require that the shipments go through customs for evaluation. A factory tries to mass-produce items to hold down costs, but it needs to batch the shipments together for a company to reduce shipping costs. For example, on Monday, a factory might make thousands of blouses and make pants on Tuesday. These items are sorted on Wednesday and boxed so that some of the blouses and pants go to one customer, and the rest are shipped to other customers. When a large enough shipment is created, the clothes are sent to the shipper along with the invoice shown in Figure 1.38. Each shipment is assigned an ID number to go through customs. Occasionally, an explanation is provided to the customs agents.

One of the more difficult jobs of managers at Broadcloth Clothing is to schedule production. They have to collect the orders from the customers and determine how

CHAPTER 1   Introduction to Relational Database Systems and Oracle 10g

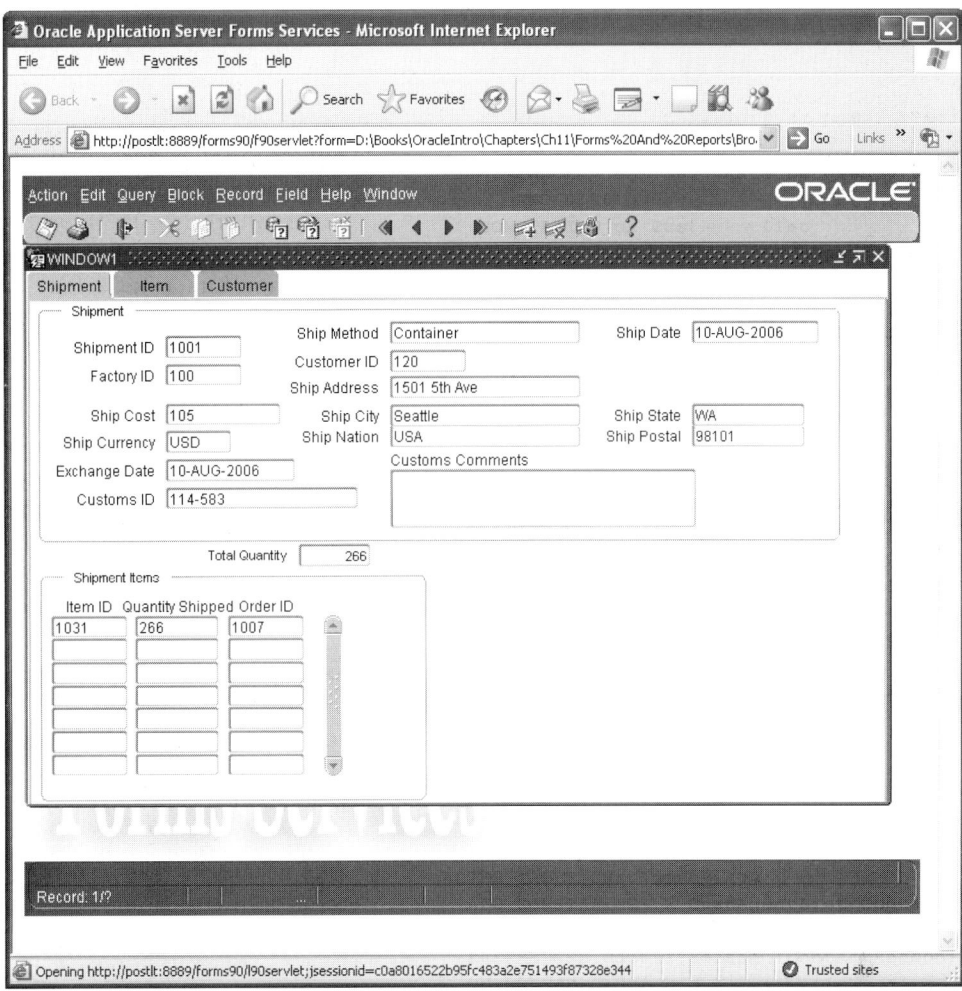

FIGURE 1.38   Shipping from factory to customer.

many items of each product need to be produced. Then they have to determine which factory should be given each order. Since the factories also produce goods for other companies, the managers need to juggle orders across several factories. Broadcloth also tracks quality measures from each production batch, to identify the best suppliers. Lately, the company has also performed spot checks on working conditions. It sends inspectors to factories to evaluate various conditions and ensure that all workers are old enough to work, are healthy, and are being paid a reasonable wage for the area. Figure 1.39 shows one version of a factory report. This one simply computes total production of various clothing styles at the different factories. By printing the report for different time periods, the company can determine which factories to use for similar products in the future.

Once they are set up correctly, production systems are impressive. However, daily operations are always more complex than many people expect. When everything runs correctly, the right clothes are produced on time and are shipped to the correct customers. The challenge is that many things can go wrong. Managers need to check the orders, production, and shipping data constantly, so they can recognize problems as they arise. They also need data to be able to create workarounds. For

BC Broadcloth Clothing

Production Analysis

Model ID	Description	Factory ID 100 City Bangkok Total Produced	101 Quezon City Total Produced	102 Zhongshan City Total Produced
1001	Sweater, scoop neck		283	
1002	Sweater, cable knit			
1004	Blouse, long collar			
1005	Blouse, frills		387	
1006	Sweater, button			
1007	Pants, plain front, narrow leg			
1009	Skirt, pleated, single color			
1010	Skirt, pleated, plaid			73
1011	Skirt, long, wool	266		
1012	Skirt, medium, silk			347
1013	Jacket, fitted, short			
1014	Jacket, loose, long			
1016	Jacket, long, light		42	
1017	Scarf, wool			
1018	Stockings, stripes			
1019	Hat, floppy			
1020	Tie, silk		341	
		266	1053	420

FIGURE 1.39 Factory production report.

example, if a customer is shipped the wrong items, a manager might have to find the correct items, or schedule a new production run at an available factory. With the right data in the database, managers can quickly search for alternatives. They will still have to call the customers and factories to verify data, but the database provides an easier starting point.

Summary

Database management systems are powerful software tools that make it easy to share data safely and create applications. However, you have to design databases carefully to take advantage of the features of the relational database approach. You can begin the design process by identifying the major entities involved. Then use the three main normalization rules to create well-behaved tables. The basic rule for third normal form is that every column must contain single-valued data, and each non-key column depends on the whole key and nothing but the key. Along the way, you must be sure each table is identified by a primary key. You also have to ensure that the relationships between tables reflect the way the company operates.

Installing Oracle software is normally handled by a database administrator, but you will often have to install a copy on your own machine. To work on the exercises in this book, you must install at least the main database, plus the Developer Suite tools. If you install the two products in different homes (folder locations); you can install both products on a single computer. Removing the Oracle software is more challenging because it requires editing the Windows registry file.

You will learn to use several Oracle tools in this book that provide the foundation for application development and database administration. Because almost all tasks in Oracle can be handled with SQL, you will spend considerable time using SQL*Plus. The Web-based *i*SQL*Plus is useful when you need to connect to the server with an Internet connection. The Developer Suite tools provide the ability to build forms and reports quickly, and with minimal programming. The tools support customization and you can use programming elements to create powerful applications. The Enterprise Manager is Oracle's graphical tool to handle basic database administration tasks. It is slightly easier for novices to use the Enterprise Manager instead of memorizing administrative queries. However, you need the DBA role to use the tool, and ultimately, you need to learn many of the routine DBA queries.

Key Terms

- administration tools
- applications
- associations
- atomic
- attributes
- base tables
- class
- communications network
- composite primary key
- data dictionary
- data engine
- data types
- database
- database administrators (DBAs)
- database management system (DBMS)
- developer suite
- developers
- enterprise manager
- entity
- entity-relationship diagram (ERD)
- first normal form
- foreign key
- forms and reports services
- inheritance
- many-to-many
- normalization
- one-to-many
- primary key
- query processor
- referential integrity
- relational database
- relationships
- row
- second normal form
- security subsystem
- super class
- table
- third normal form
- unified modeling language (UML)

Review

TRUE/FALSE

1. In a production situation, the application server should be installed on a server separate from the database server.
2. It is possible for a table to be in third normal form, but still violate the conditions of first normal form.
3. A column that is a foreign key must always be part of the primary key in the same table.
4. If Developer Suite is installed on the same computer as the main database, it must be installed in a separate home (path).
5. You need the DBA role to use the Enterprise Manager.

FILL IN

1. When you create a table and define two columns as part of the primary key, you are indicating there is a(n) _____ relationship between these two columns.
2. For a table to be in first normal form, all columns in the table must hold _____ data.
3. One of the main object-relational features that Oracle provides is the _____ command to enable users to define their own objects.
4. A primary key that consists of multiple columns is called a(n) _____ key.
5. To ensure accurate data, the principle of _____ ensures that a user can only enter values for CustomerID into the Order table if data for that customer already exists in the Customer table.

Multiple Choice

1. Which tool would you use if you wanted to look up the phone number for an employee?
   a. SQL*Plus
   b. Enterprise Manager
   c. Forms Builder
   d. Reports Builder
   e. Application Server

2. You have a proposed table:

   `ListingProperty(ListingID, StartDate, AgentID, PropertyID, Bedrooms, Bathrooms, Size)`

   where the bedrooms, bathrooms, and size depend on the PropertyID. This proposed table violates the conditions of
   a. First normal form.
   b. Second normal form.
   c. Third normal form.
   d. Both second and third normal form.
   e. Entity-relationship design.

3. The _____ is responsible for creating the forms and reports in an application system.
   a. User
   b. Database administrator
   c. Query builder
   d. Application developer
   e. CEO

4. The first step to removing the Oracle database is
   a. Run the Windows Add/Remove programs tool.
   b. Run the Oracle installer and pick the deinstall option.
   c. Remove the Oracle entries from the Windows registry.
   d. Stop the Oracle services.
   e. Cancel your payments to Oracle.

5. In a relational database table, data that describes a single instance of an entity is stored
   a. In a column of a table.
   b. In a row of a table.
   c. As a complete table.
   d. As a primary key in a table.
   e. In the data dictionary.

Hands-on Exercises

1. Extending the Chapter Case

Ultimately, you need to create a list of normalized tables to be able to build a database for an organization. At this stage, it would be helpful to start with a diagram of the main entities and their relationships.

1. Reread the basic case description and write down the main entities. Your list should at least include Properties, Agents, Listings, Customers, and CustomerAgentList, since all of these have been mentioned in the case description.

2. You should think about additional lookup tables, such as a ContactReason table that might have three or four rows of data. Its purpose is to provide data for a drop-down list so users can pick a reason from the list instead of typing it by hand. Besides making it easier for the user to enter data, lookup lists reduce errors due to abbreviations and typographical errors.

3. Look at the form and report displayed in the text and identify the entities needed to create them. Draw an entity diagram for this case. Identify the columns that belong to each normalized table. Draw lines to show the relationships and add markings to indicate one-to-many relationships. Hint: Unless you create several additional lookup tables, your solution should have about eight tables. Sketch your diagram and turn it in.

2. Coffee Merchant

Ultimately, you need to create a list of normalized tables to be able to build a database for an organization. At this stage, it would be helpful to start with a diagram of the main entities and their relationships.

1. Reread the basic case description and write down the main entities. The case is similar to the basic order problem discussed in the chapter, so you should include at least the four tables created for that normalization: Orders, OrderLines, Inventory, and Consumers.

2. The company uses a States table so that employees can pick the appropriate state from a list instead of typing it. This approach provides consistent values for the report. Similarly, the company lists the country of origin for each

inventory item, and so it maintains a separate country table.

3. Draw an entity diagram for this case. Identify the columns that belong to each normalized table. Draw lines to show the relationships and add markings to indicate one-to-many relationships. Hint: Unless you create several additional lookup tables, your solution should have about seven tables. Sketch your diagram and turn it in.

3. ROWING VENTURES

Using the form and report displayed in the text for this case, identify the major entities and relationships needed to create this database. Look up at least one Web site regarding races and create a list of racing classes. Draw the relationship diagram and turn in it in. You should have at least six tables in the diagram, but there can be more if you add lookup tables.

4. BROADCLOTH CLOTHING

Using the form and report displayed in the text for this case, identify the major entities and relationships needed to create this database. This case is relatively large, so build it one section at a time. Start with the basic order form and then add shipping information. Factory production can be complex by the time you collect production and quality data for shifts. The working conditions element adds several more tables. The base diagram without lookup tables should be around thirteen tables.

CHAPTER 2

OVERVIEW OF SQL AND SQL*PLUS

Learning Objectives

In this chapter, you will learn how to:

- Classify and recognize types of SQL statements
- Edit and save SQL statements
- Use three different SQL interface tools available in Oracle
- Write SQL statements to create tables and insert data into tables
- Write SQL statements to delete rows, add columns, and remove tables
- Use SQL*Plus extensions to capture output and format results

INTRODUCTION

Structured Query Language, or SQL (pronounced either as the word "sequel" or as the letters "S-Q-L"), is the industry standard language for interacting with relational databases. SQL owes its origin to the seminal work by Dr. E.F. Codd, who developed IBM's System R and SQL in the 1970s. All of Oracle's access tools are based on this standard. Two committees establish the industry standards for SQL. They are the American National Standards Institute, or ANSI, and the International Standards Organization, or ISO. The American National Standards Institute standardized SQL in 1986. Then, in 1989, ANSI/ISO published the SQL89 (or SQL1) standard. ANSI later revised this first standard and dubbed it SQL92 ("SQL2"). The latest ANSI standard, SQL99 ("SQL3"), provides guidance for object-oriented relational database concepts. SQL is very portable—you can use SQL to access a large number of database systems including Oracle, DB2 (IBM), SQL Server (Microsoft), or MySQL.

SQL is not a programming language. Instead, it provides statements to enter, retrieve, modify, remove, and display data stored in database tables. With SQL, you can pose ad hoc questions, create various objects, and perform database maintenance operations. Several versions of the standard have evolved over the years. The latest one, called SQL99, is fully recognized by the Oracle database management system. An advantage of a standard is that any SQL statements and skills you learn using Oracle are directly transferable to other relational database management systems. There may be some small variations among database vendors' implementations of SQL, but they are often no more significant than using square brackets to surround names instead of double quotation marks. In other words, when you learn SQL here, you have learned the interface of almost all other database management "systems."

Even though Oracle implements ANSI SQL, it also provides a rich set of extensions to SQL. These extensions are called SQL*Plus commands. Although SQL*Plus extensions cannot be used with all SQL-based database systems, they are quite useful for those using Oracle. SQL*Plus extensions provide a variety of developmental aids including, but not limited to, formatting the data returned from a query, or question, posed in standard SQL. Throughout this book and in other documentation provided by Oracle, these helpful extensions are called SQL*Plus commands.

Types of SQL Commands

There are five types of SQL statements. They are: Query statements, Data Definition Language (DDL) statements, Data Manipulation Language (DML) statements, Transaction Control (TC) statements, and Data Control Language (DCL) statements.

Query Statements

Query statements allow you to retrieve rows from one or more tables. The single query statement is SELECT (we follow the convention that SQL reserved words—words that define SQL language elements and that should not be used as identifiers—are in all capital letters).

Data Definition Language Statements

SQL statements in this group allow you to define structures, such as tables and views, that make up a database. We will use five of them in this text: CREATE, ALTER, DROP, RENAME, and TRUNCATE. They allow you to create and define tables or users, modify a database structure, eliminate a database structure such as a table, change the name of a structure, and delete all entries in a table, respectively.

Data Manipulation Language Statements

As the name implies, data manipulation statements permit you to modify the contents of tables by inserting new data, changing existing data, or removing entire rows of data from tables. DML statements include INSERT, UPDATE, and DELETE. You will learn how to use all of these statements in chapters that follow.

Transaction Control Statements

Transaction control statements provide the tools to make permanent any changes made to table rows, or to revoke those changes. The COMMIT statement makes permanent any changes made to table rows. The ROLLBACK statement does the opposite—it repeals any changes that have occurred to table rows since the last time they were made permanent. A related statement in this group, called SAVEPOINT, allows you to bookmark a point back to which you may want to undo changes.

Data Control Language Statements

Data control language statements control who has access to what tables, who can log into the Oracle system, and what accesses and privileges each user has for various database tables. You use the GRANT statement to provide a wide variety of access rights and privileges to users, whereas you issue the REVOKE statement to rescind selected accesses and privileges. For example, you can specify which user can retrieve data from another user's data, or you can prevent a user from creating a table.

ANATOMY OF A SQL STATEMENT

You can write a SQL statement to accomplish a database task. Following the command word or phrase (for example, CREATE) you include a phrase to further qualify the basic action you want to perform. SQL statements entered through the SQL*Plus interface can occupy one or more lines. SQL statements are continued to other lines by pressing the Enter key. This moves the insertion point to the beginning of a new line and does *not* require the use of a continued-line indicator. However, you must not split a word between lines. If you are using a line-by-line style interface such as SQL*Plus provides, then it numbers each successive line. There is no requirement to type a complete SQL statement on one line. Frequently, SQL statements in this text appear on multiple lines, each line containing a separate SQL phrase. Figure 2.1 shows an example of a SQL SELECT statement entered through the SQL*Plus interface.

You cannot abbreviate words in a SQL statement (though you can abbreviate selected SQL*Plus words, which we describe later). Separate individual words by at least one white space character (Spacebar, Tab, or Enter). You can type SQL words in upper- or lowercase. SQL keywords—those that are specially defined in the SQL language to mean something specific to SQL—appear in all uppercase in this textbook so they are easy to identify. Common SQL punctuation appearing in SQL commands includes comma (used to separate a list of names such as column names) and parentheses to set off discrete elements. Use a period to delimit two names from one another, such as Inventory.Price, to fully qualify the name of an object. Single quotation marks, or apostrophes, enclose literal character strings, including dates. Double quotation marks enclose other strings that serve, for example, as alternative names for columns. A semicolon indicates the end of a SQL statement. Typing a semicolon and

FIGURE 2.1 Example of a SQL command entered with SQL*Plus for Windows.

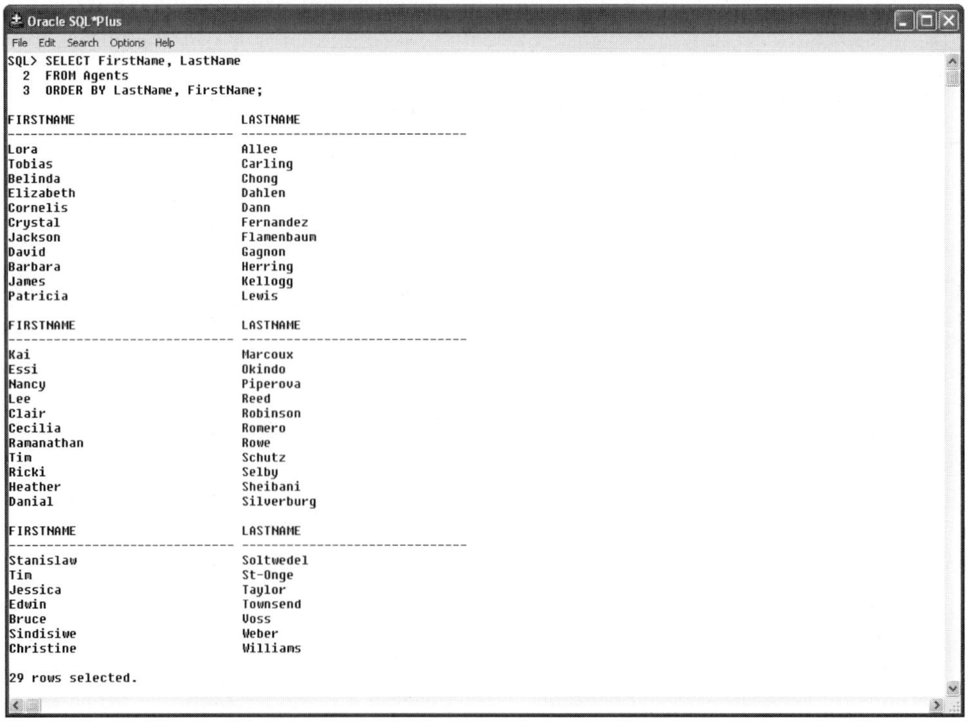

```
Oracle SQL*Plus
File  Edit  Search  Options  Help
SQL> SELECT FirstName, LastName
  2    FROM Agents
  3    ORDER BY LastName, FirstName;

FIRSTNAME                     LASTNAME
----------------------------- -----------------------------
Lora                          Allee
Tobias                        Carling
Belinda                       Chong
Elizabeth                     Dahlen
Cornelis                      Dann
Crystal                       Fernandez
Jackson                       Flamenbaum
David                         Gagnon
Barbara                       Herring
James                         Kellogg
Patricia                      Lewis

FIRSTNAME                     LASTNAME
----------------------------- -----------------------------
Kai                           Marcoux
Essi                          Okindo
Nancy                         Piperova
Lee                           Reed
Clair                         Robinson
Cecilia                       Romero
Ramanathan                    Rowe
Tim                           Schutz
Ricki                         Selby
Heather                       Sheibani
Danial                        Silverburg

FIRSTNAME                     LASTNAME
----------------------------- -----------------------------
Stanislaw                     Soltwedel
Tim                           St-Onge
Jessica                       Taylor
Edwin                         Townsend
Bruce                         Voss
Sindisiwe                     Weber
Christine                     Williams

29 rows selected.
```

```
± Oracle SQL*Plus                                    _ □ X
File  Edit  Search  Options  Help
SQL> CREATE TABLE ContactReason
  2       (ContactReasonID NVARCHAR2(10)
  3        Description NVARCHAR2(30)
  4       );
   (ContactReasonID NVARCHAR2(10)
   *
ERROR at line 2:
ORA-00922: missing or invalid option

SQL>
```

FIGURE 2.2 SQL command error message and associated error code.

pressing Enter in SQL*Plus causes the SQL command to execute. There are additional punctuation marks. Discussion of them appears when their use arises later in the text.

OBTAINING ONLINE HELP

One of the most useful skills when first learning Oracle is how to obtain help. For example, if you type a SQL command that contains an error, the SQL*Plus interpreter displays an error message and an associated error number. It indicates the line number containing the error and marks the error's position within the line. Figure 2.2 shows an example of an error generated by a CREATE TABLE statement. In attempting to create a new table called ContactReason, we typed the command describing the table's structure incorrectly. Some errors may be self-evident, but others are difficult to spot. The Windows-based SQL*Plus interpreter indicates that the error is on line 2, displays the error number ORA-00922, and the message "missing or invalid option." Most Oracle error messages are typically terse. If you cannot readily identify the problem, it is reassuring to know there is additional information online to help you interpret and then fix the mistake. The Oracle error prefix of "ORA" indicates that the database system generated the error (sometimes called an exception). The five-digit number following ORA, assigned by the Oracle Corporation, indicates the exact nature of the error—in this case, that we omitted a comma in the second line. An asterisk in the error message often pinpoints the exact location of the mistake in the offending statement. In the error shown in Figure 2.2, however, the asterisk simply marks the beginning of the statement or phrase in which the mistake is detected. In particular, the asterisk indicates that the mistake occurs at the opening parenthesis, which precedes the definition of the first column in the ContactReason table. The message "missing or invalid option" is not specific enough to be helpful.

Oracle error message help is available on the Oracle Technology Network (OTN) Web site and on other Web sites. If you go to the Web site http://ora-code.com, you will find a complete list of ORA error codes in numeric order. It may take a couple of clicks to find the exact error number among the several Web pages of listings, but it will yield good results.

To display more information about an ORA style error message:

1. Start your Web browser, type **http://ora-code.com** in the address bar, and press **Enter.** The Oracle Database Error Code Web page appears.
2. Click **3** in the page hyperlinks at the bottom of the page to go to the third page of error listings.

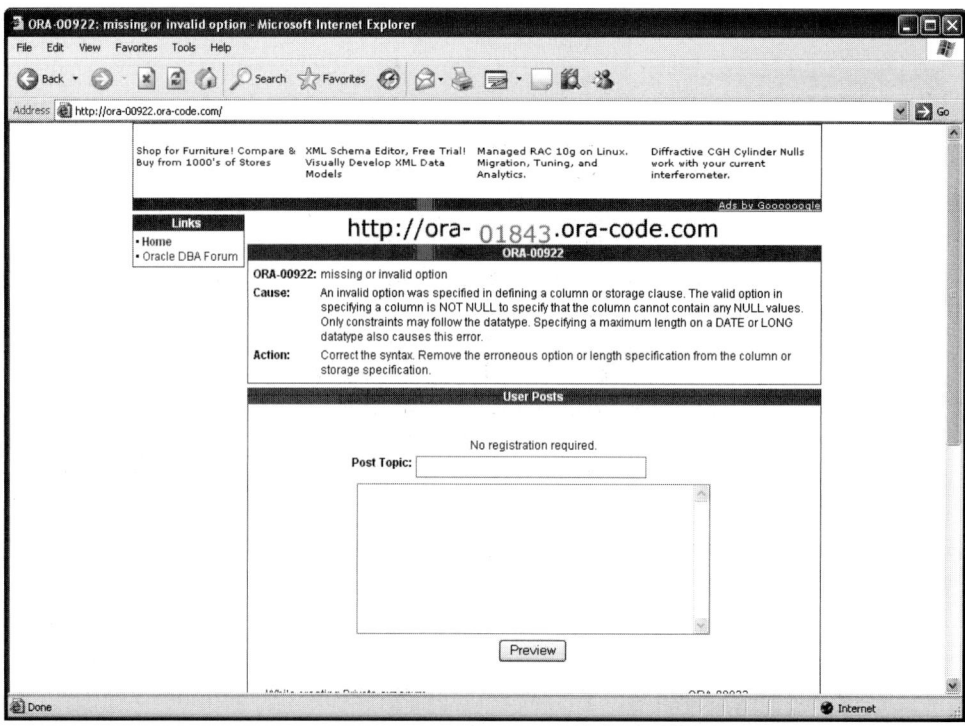

FIGURE 2.3 Displaying additional information about an Oracle error code.

3. Click the **ORA-00922** hyperlink (the values increase left to right, row by row).
4. A complete description of the error appears. Apparently Oracle thinks we have added an invalid clause. If you inspect the SQL line carefully, you will find that a comma is missing from the end of line 2. We don't need to fix the error at this time.
5. Close your Web browser.

INTERFACING WITH THE DATABASE

Besides defining the SQL language, the SQL99 standard provides directives on how SQL statements are to be executed. In particular, these directives, which are known as *binding styles,* dictate the minimal set of SQL statements that must be supported for a particular binding style. There are four distinct methods of execution: Direct execution, module binding, embedded SQL, and call-level interface (CLI).

Direct execution allows you to communicate with the database management system directly through a client application such as command line SQL, SQL*Plus, or *i*SQL*Plus. The SQL*Plus interpreter checks the command line to ensure that it contains no syntax errors. If it is correct, then it submits it to the database for execution. SQL commands are case-insensitive. Even though we show SQL reserved words in all capital letters, the SQL*Plus interpreter and the Oracle database that executes the commands are case-*insensitive*—commands and any words they contain can be in uppercase, lowercase, or any combination. Furthermore, the SQL*Plus ignores spaces and line breaks wherever they occur in the statement. We use white space and line breaks to make commands more readable, and you should, too.

The SQL interpreter communicates with the database server on the same computer or on another computer on the network. With direct execution, you type a SQL statement directly into the client and press a key to send the statement to the database server. Shortly, the server returns results back to the client interface. In the case of a SQL data retrieval statement, result rows are sent back to the client interface.

The module binding method permits you to create blocks of SQL statements. Once created, the module can be combined into a complete application with a program called a linker. The result is a complete procedure that contains all that is needed to perform a series of database manipulations.

Embedded SQL statements are placed directly into some host programming language (C++ or COBOL, for instance). An Oracle preprocessor examines the SQL statements for correctness and separates them from the other compiled programming language code. The SQL code is converted into a form that the database system can understand. Embedding SQL statements directly into a host programming language provides the program with access to database tables through the SQL statements that retrieve the actual data rows.

A call-level interface provides a way to invoke SQL statements through a specific code "door" by passing the SQL statements directly to subroutines that process them. The statements are not compiled or otherwise transformed before being received by the database server. Instead, they are executed directly by the relational database management system.

Next, you learn about three different ways you can interrogate and modify Oracle databases: The command-line interface through your operating system, SQL*Plus command-line client product from Oracle, and the Web-based environment from Oracle called iSQL*Plus.

Sometimes the distinctions between SQL and SQL*Plus are not clear at first glance. They are different, and you should be aware of their differences. SQL is a nonprocedural language to communicate with relational database management systems. SQL*Plus, on the other hand, is an environment developed by Oracle in which you can execute SQL statements. Later in this chapter, you will read about a second use of the term SQL*Plus— SQL*Plus commands. **SQL*Plus commands** are Oracle's own extension to SQL. They provide a wide variety of tools to format results, display table definitions, and edit and save files. You will learn about these in the section entitled Using SQL*Plus Extensions.

Next, you will use three different methods to log into the Oracle database system using SQL*Plus on a Windows machine. First, you will invoke SQL*Plus from the DOS (Disk Operating System) prompt. Next, you will use the more user-friendly SQL*Plus for Windows, which is the Windows-based version. Finally, you will invoke iSQL*Plus, which is a Web-based interface to Oracle's database. Each of these has its advantages and disadvantages. Once you have finished this textbook, you can opt to use whichever interface suits you best.

USING THE DOS COMMAND-LINE SQL*PLUS

If you are running Oracle on your own Windows-based PC or are using a Windows PC to interact with Oracle on a server, then you can use a DOS (Disk Operating System) window to interact with the database or use the SQL*Plus environment. We'll describe the DOS version briefly, but we encourage you to use SQL*Plus instead, as you have many familiar Windows tools, such as copy and paste, available to you.

LOGGING INTO ORACLE

You can invoke SQL*Plus from the DOS prompt. Once you have the DOS prompt, you can invoke SQL*Plus, log onto Oracle, and issue SQL commands. The steps that follow show you how to invoke SQL*Plus.

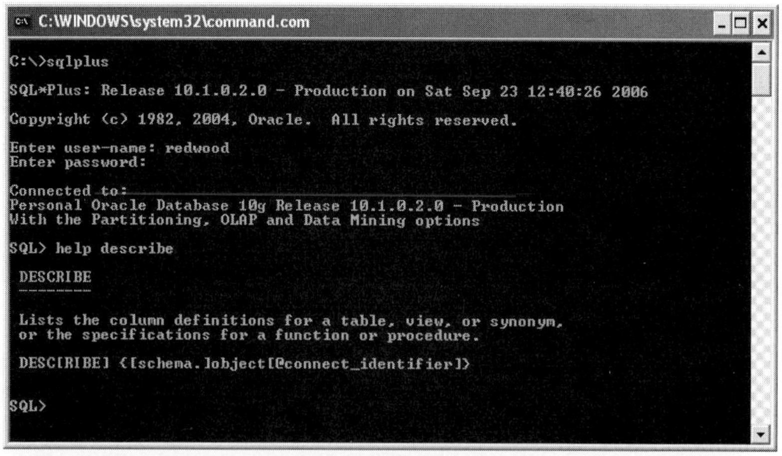

54 Introduction to Oracle

```
C:\>sqlplus

SQL*Plus: Release 10.1.0.2.0 - Production on Sat Sep 23 12:40:26 2006

Copyright (c) 1982, 2004, Oracle.  All rights reserved.

Enter user-name: redwood
Enter password:
Connected to:
Personal Oracle Database 10g Release 10.1.0.2.0 - Production
With the Partitioning, OLAP and Data Mining options

SQL> help describe
 DESCRIBE
 --------
 Lists the column definitions for a table, view, or synonym,
 or the specifications for a function or procedure.

 DESC[RIBE] {[schema.]object[@connect_identifier]}

SQL>
```

FIGURE 2.4 Using SQL*Plus in a DOS window.

To open a DOS window and invoke SQL*Plus in the Windows operating system:

1. Click the **Start** button on the task bar, click **Run** on the Start menu, type **command** in the Open text box, and click **OK.** The DOS window opens.
2. Type **sqlplus** and press **Enter.** Oracle prompts you for a username.
3. Type your username (ask your instructor, if necessary) and press **Enter.** The *Enter password* prompt appears.
4. Type your password (it will *not* echo on the screen) and press **Enter.** If you have entered a correct username and password combination, the SQL> prompt appears.
5. Type **help describe** and press **Enter** to display help about the SQL*Plus help command (see Figure 2.4).
6. To log out of Oracle, type **exit** and press **Enter.** Oracle logs you out and returns the DOS C> prompt.
7. To close the DOS window, type **exit** again and press **Enter.** The DOS window closes.

ENTERING AND RUNNING SQL COMMANDS

In the previous series of steps, you ran a SQL*Plus command—one defined by Oracle to extend the standard SQL command set. That command described the structure of the omnipresent Dual table that Oracle installs automatically. Before executing the steps that follow, locate the file Ch02SaleStatus.sql, and copy it to your computer. Note the full path where you save the file. Avoid saving it in the Windows folder My Documents, because that is a "deep" path. Instead, save it in a location such as the root of drive C (C:\) or in the Temp folder of C (C:\Temp\).

To run a SQL command in SQL*Plus open a DOS window:

1. Open a DOS window: Click the **Start** button on the task bar, click **Run** on the Start menu, type **command** in the Open text box, and click **OK.** The DOS window opens.
2. Launch SQL*Plus: Type **sqlplus** <username>**/**<password>, and press **Enter,** where you substitute your username for <username> and your password for <password>, separated by a slash. (Be aware that the password *is not* hidden when you use this technique!)
3. Type the SQL*Plus command **CLEAR SCREEN** (either uppercase or lowercase) and press **Enter** to clear the screen.

4. At the SQL> prompt, type **START,** press the **Spacebar,** type the complete path to the Ch02SaleStatus.sql file, followed by a backslash, followed by **Ch02SaleStatus.sql** (capitalization is unimportant). Then, press **Enter.** For example, if you saved the file (called a script) in the root directory of C, then you would type the following and press **Enter:**

```
SQL> START C:\Ch02SaleStatus.sql
```

Oracle responds by displaying the confirming message "Table created."

5. Leave the DOS window open for the next steps that follow.

EDITING SQL COMMANDS

When you want to make changes to a SQL command you just entered—perhaps there is a mistake you need to correct—invoke the editor by typing **edit** at the SQL> prompt. Windows opens Notepad, allowing you to make changes and then save them.

To run a SQL command in SQL*Plus, make active the DOS window you opened previously. Then, do the following:

1. Type **edit** and press **Enter.** Windows opens Notepad, the editor of choice for the DOS window. The CREATE TABLE script that is stored in the file Ch02SaleStatus.sql file appears in the Notepad window. Its contents are written to a temporary file called afiedt.buf, an Oracle-defined file name.
2. If necessary, click the mouse just to the left of the first line—immediately to the left of the word *CREATE.*
3. Type**--Create a new table** and press **Enter.** Any line beginning with two consecutive hyphens (minus signs) is a comment and is ignored by Oracle.
4. Click **File** on the menu bar, click **Exit,** and click the **Yes** button when asked if you want to save changes.
5. The newly changed SQL statement, including the comment you inserted, appears below the message *Wrote file afiedt.buf,* ready to be executed.
6. To execute the modified SQL statement, type **/** (slash) and press **Enter.** Oracle generates an error message (ORA-00955) because the table already exists, and the SQL statement is attempting to re-create it.
7. Type **exit** and press **Enter** to exit SQL*Plus. Type **exit** and press **Enter** again to close the DOS window.

USING SQL*PLUS FOR WINDOWS

A much easier to use SQL*Plus environment is SQL*Plus for Windows. It provides a Windows dialog box and a cleaner interface. Specifying the location of files is also much simpler in the Windows based version of SQL*Plus. If you have a choice between an operating system interface such as DOS and a Windows version of that same interface, you will probably prefer the latter.

When you log into Oracle with SQL*Plus for Windows, SQL*Plus displays the SQL> prompt and provides you with an environment that:

- Accepts SQL statements that you type and passes them to the Oracle server.
- Interprets editor, formatting, and file commands.
- Formats the results returned from SQL query statements and displays reports on screen.

- Remembers environment controls you set, such as the number of lines between headings and the width of the display line.
- Provides a simple line editor that supports entry and modification of statements you type.
- Accepts SQL statements that are stored in files.

LOGGING INTO ORACLE

To log into Oracle with SQL*Plus for Windows:

1. Click **Start,** point to **All Programs** (Windows XP), point to **Oracle-OraDb10g_home1,** point to **Application Development,** and click **SQL Plus.** The Log On dialog box appears.

   > **Tip:** You may want to create a shortcut to SQL*Plus by right-clicking SQL Plus, pointing to **Send To**, and clicking **Desktop (create shortcut).**

2. Type your username in the User Name text box and press **Tab.** Type your password in the Password text box. If necessary, press **Tab** and type the host string in the Host String text box—ask your instructor if a host string is required.

   > **Tip:** If you inadvertently press Enter after typing your username, Oracle will close the Log On dialog box and prompt you for a password. Simply type your password and press **Enter.**

3. Click **OK** to log into the Oracle database. You may want to maximize the SQL*Plus window.

If you have entered everything correctly, SQL*Plus will log you into the Oracle database, display the SQL*Plus release number, the date and time, and a copyright notice. In addition, it displays the Oracle database (e.g., Personal Oracle) to which you are connected. The last line displayed is the SQL> prompt, indicating SQL*Plus is ready to receive commands. (Leave the SQL*Plus window open for additional steps to follow.)

If you receive an error message such as *ORA-01017: invalid username/password; logon denied* that means you have entered an incorrect username or password. Ask your instructor or your database administrator to determine what your correct username and password are. If you see an error message with the number ORA-12154 such as *ORA-12154: TNS: could not resolve the connect identifier specified,* then contact your instructor.

Once you log in successfully and the SQL> prompt appears, you have started a new Oracle session. You can enter only one SQL*Plus command at the prompt. For very long commands, simply press Enter between words in the command to continue the line. There is no limit on the number of continued lines in a single SQL*Plus command. Try it next.

ENTERING AND RUNNING SQL COMMANDS

Once logged into Oracle through the Windows SQL*Plus interface, you can execute SQL and SQL*Plus commands.

To display the structure of the SaleStatus table and add data rows to it:

1. With the SQL prompt displayed, type the SQL*Plus command **describe salestatus,** which lists the table column names and their data types, and press **Enter.** Oracle retrieves and displays information about the salestatus table. Notice that the column names appear capitalized. Table column names are stored in uppercase.

2. Enter some data into the table using the INSERT command. Type the following line at the SQL> prompt, pressing **Enter** after *SaleStatus*. Type the semicolon but *do not* press Enter at the end of the second line.

```
INSERT INTO SaleStatus
VALUES (101, 'For Sale');
```

3. Press **Enter** to send the complete SQL statement to SQL*Plus and on to Oracle for execution. Oracle executes a command when a semicolon is the last character preceding the Enter key press—for single or multi-line commands alike. The message "1 row created." appears to indicate that you successfully added a data row to the table.

4. Type the following two SQL statements, pressing **Enter** at the end of each line following the semicolon. (Uppercase is immaterial *except* for the data within single quotes. Capitalize those values exactly as shown.)

```
INSERT INTO SaleStatus VALUES (102, 'Pending');
INSERT INTO SaleStatus VALUES (103, 'Sold');
```

SQL*Plus displays the Oracle generated message after each statement, if correctly entered, "1 row created." (See Figure 2.5.)

5. Type **CLEAR SCREEN** and press **Enter** to clear the SQL*Plus screen, and leave the SQL*Plus window open for steps that follow.

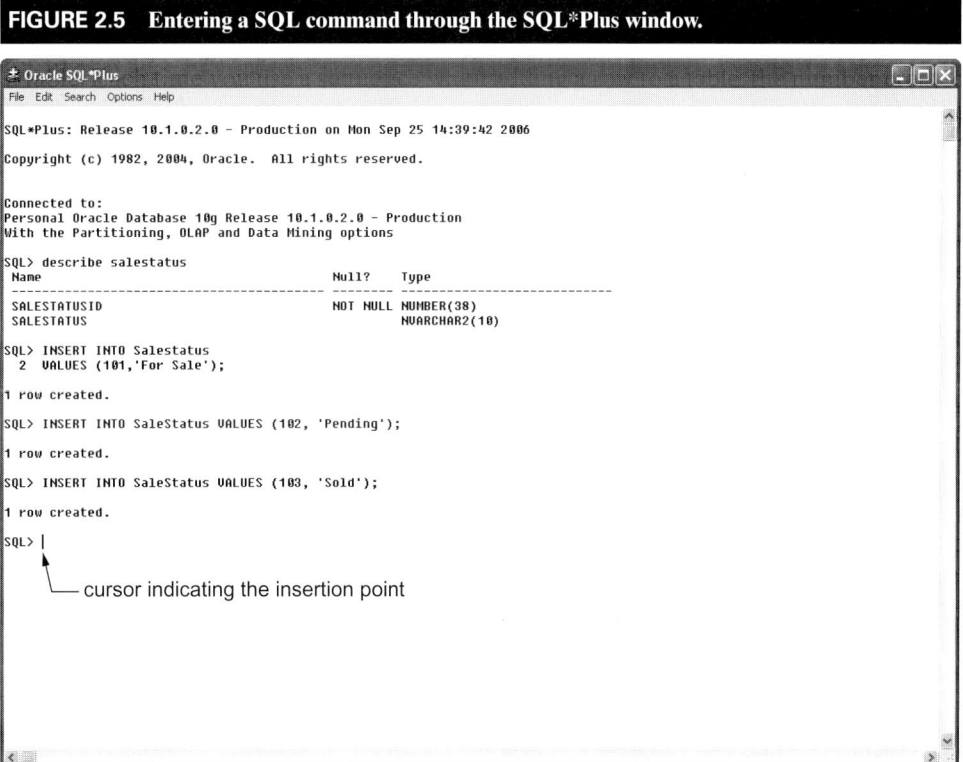

FIGURE 2.5 Entering a SQL command through the SQL*Plus window.

EDITING SQL COMMANDS

You can change what you wrote in SQL*Plus by typing *edit* at the SQL> prompt, and the procedures are identical to those presented for editing SQL commands in the DOS window. However, we think you should use a different technique throughout the textbook so you can preserve everything you type and edit it easily. Often, SQL commands are long, and retyping them completely to correct mistakes is daunting. We think an excellent alternative is to create SQL and SQL*Plus commands using a text editor such as Notepad (not a word processor such as Word, however).

Once you have typed your SQL command, you can copy it to the Windows Clipboard (Ctrl+A to select all text, and then click **Copy**), activate the SQL*Plus window, and paste in the command and run it. If an error occurs, simply ignore the SQL*Plus window, return to Notepad, correct the error, and copy and paste it back into SQL*Plus. The advantage of this is that you can save the Notepad file and replay or reload it into SQL*Plus later if needed. Using Edit at the SQL*Plus prompt is a bit more cumbersome. Any SQL commands you save—or groups of individual commands in one file each terminated with a semicolon—is called a *script.* It is handy to keep a copy of many, if not all, of the lines of SQL you create as a record of the table structures and the data they contain. With scripts safely stored on disk, you can run them on another computer with Oracle by opening SQL*Plus and typing **start,** followed by the fully qualified path and filename of the script file. Practice this technique next.

To edit a SQL command in Notepad and then execute it in SQL*Plus:

1. With SQL*Plus open, type the following command exactly as shown. Press **Enter** after typing the table name, SaleStatus, and again following the semicolon on the second line.

   INSERT INTO SaleStatus
   VALUES (101, 'Unknown');

   Oracle returns an error message indicating that it has detected a *unique constraint* violation.

2. Click the mouse just to the left of the first line and drag it down and through the semicolon on the second line. Do not select the SQL prompt, the line numbers, the echoed command, or the error message (see Figure 2.6).

3. Click **Edit** on the menu bar and click **Copy.**

   Tip: Press **Ctrl+C** to copy the selected text to the Clipboard to save time.

4. Start Notepad (Click **Start,** point to **All Programs,** point to **Accessories,** and click **Notepad**), or launch another text editor of your choice.

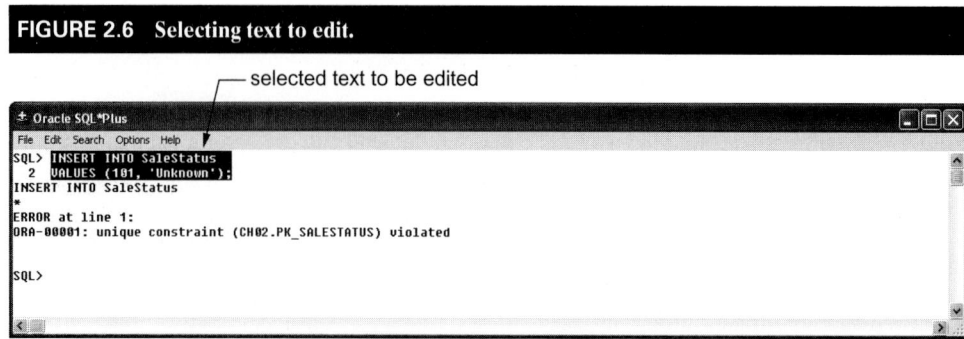

FIGURE 2.6 Selecting text to edit.

5. In Notepad, click **Edit** and then click **Paste** (or, press **Ctrl+V** for a shortcut equivalent). The SQL command appears in Notepad. Now you can correct it and save the command as a file.

6. Correct the command: Change the value 101 to **104,** a new row identification number.

7. Copy the corrected command back into SQL*Plus: Press **Ctrl+A** to select all text, press **Ctrl+C** to copy the text to the Clipboard, switch to the SQL*Plus window, press **Ctrl+V** to paste the new code into the SQL*Plus window, and press **Enter** to run the command. This time, it executes correctly and Oracle returns the confirming message "1 row created."

8. Switch back to the Notepad window, Click **File,** and then click **Save.** Using the *Save in* list box, navigate to the folder where you wish to store your Chapter 2 script files, type **Ch2<yourname>SaleStatus.sql** in the *File name* list box (type your last name in place of "<yourname>"), open the **Save as type** list box, click **All Files,** and then click **Save.**

9. Close Notepad. While actively running SQL*Plus commands, you will want to keep Notepad open.

EXITING SQL*PLUS

There are three ways to exit SQL*Plus:

- Click File on the menu bar and then click Exit.
- Type Exit at the SQL> prompt.
- Click the title bar Close button (an X).

When you exit SQL*Plus, Oracle logs you off and automatically closes your database connection. Complete the previous steps by logging off of Oracle.
To exit SQL*Plus:

1. Make SQL*Plus the active window.
2. Type **exit** at the SQL prompt, and press **Enter.** Oracle disconnects you and the SQL*Plus window closes.

USING *i*SQL*PLUS

Yet another way to access Oracle is through *i*SQL*Plus, which is a Web-based SQL*Plus environment. You access *i*SQL*Plus by entering a URL of the form http://machinename.domainname:port/isqlplus/

In the preceding example, *machinename* is the machine name, and the port is 5560. If you have installed Oracle on your own computer, you may be able to access *i*SQL*Plus with this URL:

http://127.0.0.1:5560/isqlplus/

If you are unsuccessful with either of the preceding URLs, then check with your instructor to obtain the exact URL for your location or institution. Figure 2.7 shows the login screen for *i*SQL*Plus using the machine name PURDUE. There is no domain name because *i*SQL*Plus is located on the same machine as the Oracle database, and that machine has been named PURDUE. Just as when you use SQL*Plus, you enter your username, password, and (perhaps) a connect identifier, and press the login button to log into the Oracle database. If you are unsure about the connect identifier, consult your instructor.

60 Introduction to Oracle

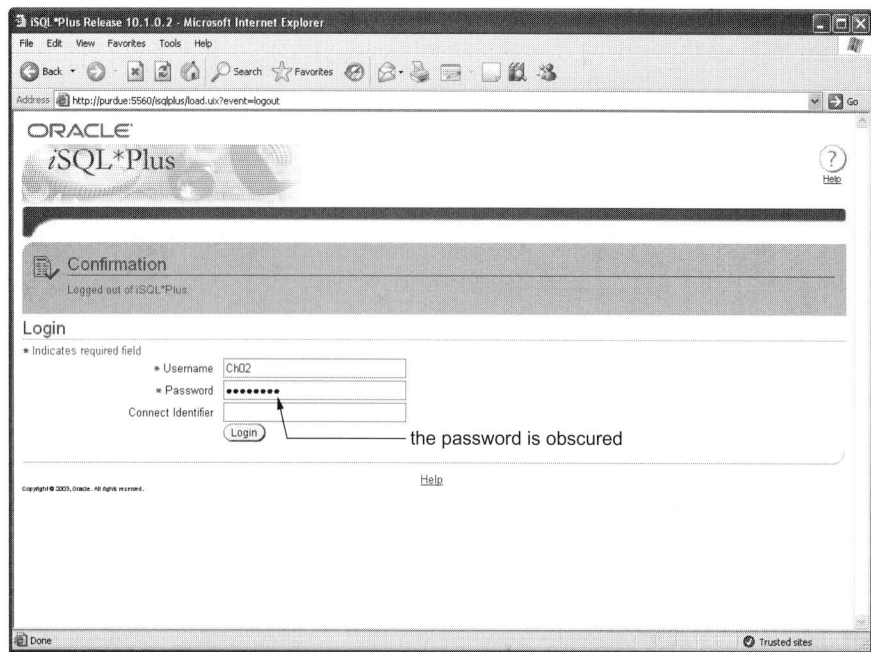

FIGURE 2.7 Logging into Oracle using *i*SQL*Plus.

LOGGING INTO ORACLE

Let's try logging into Oracle through an *i*SQL*Plus Web-based version of SQL*Plus. To log into Oracle with *i*SQL*Plus and enter a SQL command:

1. Launch a Web browser and enter the URL for your Oracle database. Be sure to check with your instructor if you are unsure about the URL. The *i*SQL*Plus Web page appears.
2. Click the **Username** text box, type your username, press **Tab,** and type your password.
3. If you require a Connect Identifier, press **Tab** and type the connect identifier (check with your instructor). Figure 2.7 shows the *i*SQL*Plus Web page with our chosen username, *Ch02,* and the undisclosed password in place.
4. Click the **Login** button to log into the Oracle database. If you entered your correct username and password, *i*SQL*Plus displays the Workspace Web page.
5. Click in the Workspace window labeled *Enter SQL, PL/SQL and SQL*Plus statements* to place the insertion point inside the window.

ENTERING AND RUNNING SQL COMMANDS

Entering SQL and SQL*Plus commands is very straightforward. You may prefer this method because you can easily move anywhere within the command, make changes at will, and then submit the command for processing by clicking the **Execute** button.

To enter a SQL command and execute it:

1. Type the following SQL statement exactly as written:

```
SELECT *
FROM SaleStatus;
```

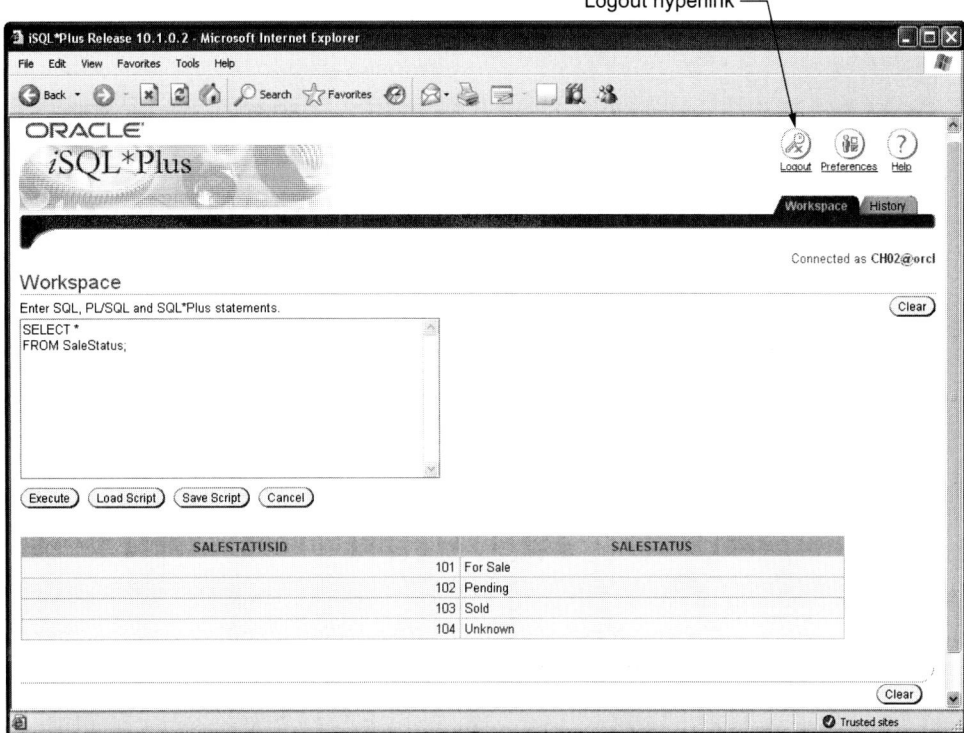

FIGURE 2.8 SQL command and retrieved rows in a browser.

2. Click the **Execute** button located just below the box in which you entered the SQL statement. The results appear near the bottom of the window. The rows stored in the SaleStatus table that you created and populated appear (see Figure 2.8).

As you observe, you type a command in the work screen and the output appears in the bottom. If the result is larger than fits on one screen, then *i*SQL*Plus displays a Next Page button at the bottom of the screen, allowing you to view subsequent output screens. The *i*SQL*Plus environment also lets you execute commands you have typed, load SQL script files, save the script appearing on screen, and check the history of commands you have typed (the *History* hyperlink), in addition to having other features. Clicking the Help button at the top of the screen delivers online help.

EDITING SQL COMMANDS

Edit a SQL or SQL*Plus command the same way you would alter a word-processed document: Move to the position you want to change, make any change, and click the **Execute** button to execute the altered command. Save the altered command by pressing the **Save Script** button and follow the familiar prompts to save the file in any folder you want.

To edit a SQL command in the *i*SQL*Plus browser window:

1. Click the mouse between the word *SaleStatus* and its terminating semicolon.
2. Press **Enter** to move to a new line, and then type
   ORDER BY SaleStatus DESC
3. Click the **Execute** button to display the new results. Oracle sorts the returned rows in descending order on the SaleStatus field.

4. Save the new script as a file: Click the **Save Script** button: if you see a warning dialog box indicating risks of files from the Internet, then click the **Save** button.
5. Use the *Save in* list box to navigate to the folder in which you save your Chapter 2 scripts, type the name **Ch2<yourname>ReverseSaleStatus.sql**, click the **Save as type** list box, click **All Files,** and click **Save**. *i*SQL*Plus saves your script file. You can load it at another time by clicking the **Load Script** button, clicking the **Browse** button, and locating the file you want to load (you will practice this later).
6. Click the **Clear** button. The Workspace window is cleared.

EXITING *i*SQL*PLUS

To exit *i*SQL*Plus:

1. Click the **Logout** link (located both at the top and bottom of the window) to log out of Oracle. Oracle displays a confirming screen indicating you logged out correctly.
2. Close the Web browser.

UNDERSTANDING SQL STATEMENTS

The SQL commands for querying a database, creating and deleting various database objects including tables, and inserting, updating, and deleting database table rows are the fundamental operations performed through the SQL*Plus interface. Next, you will examine the structure of each of the five types of SQL statements, see specific examples of each one used with the Redwood Realty database, and periodically issue SQL commands to observe the results with your database. To try out various SQL statements, you will first run a SQL script to define two more tables and insert data into them. With some of the Redwood Realty tables in place, you can try out some of the SQL commands described here.

To use a script file to create two tables and insert data:

1. Locate the Chapter 2 script file named Ch02Agents.sql, and write down the full path to the file (for example, C:\Temp\ or C:\My Documents\SQL\).
2. Launch SQL*Plus, if necessary, and type your username and password to log in.
3. At the SQL> prompt, type **START <path>\Ch02Agents.sql,** where "<path>" is the full path to the script file.
4. Press **Enter** to run the series of SQL commands located in the script file. Oracle returns two error messages (see Figure 2.9) below each of the DROP TABLE SQL commands. Ignore those, since they are merely there to ensure that you start with a clean copy of the two tables.

FIGURE 2.9 Error messages generated from DROP TABLE commands.

```
Oracle SQL*Plus
File Edit Search Options Help
DROP TABLE Agents        CASCADE CONSTRAINTS PURGE
           *
ERROR at line 1:
ORA-00942: table or view does not exist


DROP TABLE LicenseStatus CASCADE CONSTRAINTS PURGE
           *
ERROR at line 1:
ORA-00942: table or view does not exist

SQL>
```

5. Type the SQL*Plus statement **CLEAR SCREEN** (lowercase is fine too) and press **Enter** to clear the SQL*Plus screen of all messages.
6. Type **exit** and press **Enter** to close SQL*Plus and log out of Oracle.

The script file creates two tables, called *Agents* and *LicenseStatus,* and places data into the tables. The Agents table contains 29 rows listing Redwood Realty real estate agents. The LicenseStatus table contains 16 rows, which contain information about the nature of the agents' real estate licenses (Licensed, Expired, Revoked, and so on).

RUNNING SQL QUERIES

Perhaps the main purpose of the SQL language is the ability to ask questions of the database and receive answers from it—an activity called *querying* the database. The SELECT command is the SQL data retrieval command. The SELECT command retrieves information from one or more tables. The command specifies which table fields, including calculations on those fields, to retrieve, which tables to query to locate requested fields, which rows of a table to include in the returned set, and the order in which returned rows are to appear.

The SELECT command has the following syntax. A statement's syntax means the rules regarding the spelling and grammar of a language—SQL in this case. Syntactical rules are inflexible and respond only if you type the statement correctly—as the rules of syntax indicate. In this and all examples in this textbook, brackets ([and]) enclose *optional* portions of a statement, braces ({ and }) enclose a list from which you must choose one entry, and a vertical bar indicates alternative choices.

```
SELECT [DISTINCT|ALL] {* | [column_expression [AS new_name]] [,…]}
FROM table_name
[JOIN table_name [alias] ON (table_column <operator>table_column)]…
WHERE search_condition]
[GROUP BY column_list] [HAVING search_condition]
[ORDER BY column_list]
```

At first glance, the syntax for the SELECT command looks a bit daunting. Don't be concerned. You will use SELECT in enough different forms to become comfortable with it in no time. For example, you could list the contents of the Agents table—all rows and all columns—with this SELECT statement:

```
SELECT * FROM Agents;
```

The asterisk indicates that all existing columns in the table are to be listed, and the FROM clause indicates that Oracle is to return rows from the Agents table. The returned rows consist of 15 columns and 29 rows. You can request a subset of that information with a SELECT query such as:

```
SELECT firstname, lastname, gender
FROM agents
WHERE gender = 'F'
ORDER BY lastname, firstname;
```

The column names following "SELECT" indicate that only an agent's first name, last name, and gender are to be returned from the Agents table. Furthermore, the WHERE clause restricts the results to rows to female agents (*gender* = 'F'). Prior to displaying results, the ORDER BY clause sorts the rows into order by last name and then by first name within matching last name groups. Let's try a SQL SELECT statement using the *i*SQL*Plus interpreter. First, close the SQL*Plus client program if it is still running by typing **exit** at the SQL> prompt.

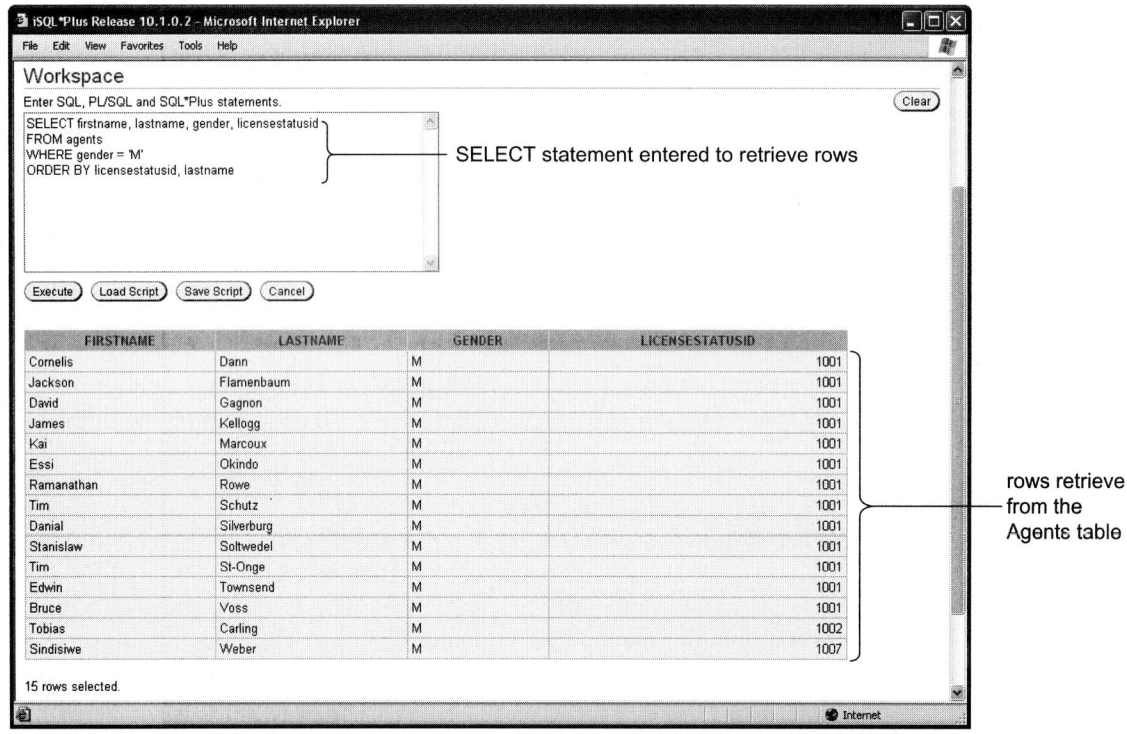

FIGURE 2.10 Rows returned by a SELECT statement.

To display selected rows from the Agents table with a SELECT statement:

1. Launch your Web browser, then launch *i*SQL*Plus. (Type in your username and password, and then click the **Login** button.)
2. Click the Workspace window and type the following on four lines. All capitalization is optional except for the letter *M* inside single quotation marks on the third line. It *must* be capitalized. Notice that we have omitted the statement-terminating semicolon, because *i*SQL*Plus does not require it.

```
SELECT firstname, lastname, gender, licensestatusid
FROM agents
WHERE gender = 'M'
ORDER BY licensestatusid, lastname
```

3. Click the **Execute** button to pass the statement to Oracle. Oracle returns 15 rows (see Figure 2.10).
4. Click the **Logout** button. (There is a logout button at the top and bottom of the screen.)
5. Close your browser.

There are other ways to write a SELECT statement, and you will explore these further in Chapter 3.

EXAMINING DATA DEFINITION LANGUAGE STATEMENTS

SQL statements in the data definition language (DDL) group you will use frequently include CREATE TABLE, ALTER TABLE, and DROP TABLE. There are DDL statements you will use in later chapters, but these are representative of this group.

Creating a Table

One of the fundamental data definition language (DDL) statements is CREATE TABLE. SQL supports three types of tables: Base tables, derived tables, and viewed tables. Most of the time you will be dealing with base tables. **Base tables** are schema objects that hold data—just like the Agents table that you created when you ran the Ch02Agents.sql script file. *Derived tables* are the results returned by the database system when you query (SELECT) the database. *Viewed tables,* which you will study in detail in Chapter 6, are named, derived tables. Viewed tables are usually more complex SELECT statements that are named so they can be run simply by referring to them as you would a simple base table within a query. Here, you will study the structure and use of the CREATE TABLE statement to construct a base table.

A simplified syntax of the CREATE TABLE syntax to create a base table is as follows. (For full details of the CREATE TABLE syntax, see the SQL Reference manual from Oracle Corporation.)

```
CREATE TABLE table_name
(column_name type [NOT NULL]
[CONSTRAINT constraint_definition DEFAULT expression]
[,column_name type [NOT NULL]
[CONSTRAINT constraint_definition DEFAULT expression]…]
)
[PRIMARY KEY (column_name [,column_name …])
[FOREIGN KEY (column_name [,column_name …])
REFERENCES foreign_table (column_name [,column_name …])]
```

The CREATE TABLE statement that follows creates a Redwood Realty table called ContactReason, which contains two columns indicating the reason a customer contacted the agency. To date, there are three contact reasons: *Buy, Casual, Sell.* A *Buy* contact means an associated client (customer) is interested in purchasing a home. A *Casual* contact indicator means that someone was "just looking" at a home—perhaps at an open house—but is not actively in the market to purchase a home. *Sell* indicates that the associated client contacted Redwood Realty wanting to sell a property. Here is the CREATE TABLE statement to create the ContactReason table and identify the ContactReason as the primary key field. A primary key field, as you recall, uniquely identifies each row of a table.

```
CREATE TABLE ContactReason
    (ContactReason NVARCHAR2(15) NOT NULL,
     Description NVARCHAR2(50),
     CONSTRAINT pk_ContactReason PRIMARY KEY (ContactReason)
    );
```

The first line names the table. Then a list of column names and their data types appear enclosed in a pair of parentheses. The third line contains a constraint definition for one of the columns. A **constraint** is a restriction on the value a column can have. The constraint indicates that the first column, ContactReason, is a primary key. As such, each value in this column must be unique within the table (*Buy, Casual,* and *Sell* are unique—each appears in only one row of the table).

Each column name is followed by a data type and size. The ContactReason column has the data type NVARCHAR2, a national character set character string of variable size up to a maximum of 15 characters. (The **national character set** permits storage of information from languages whose individual characters cannot be represented by an eight-bit coding scheme.) The optional NOT NULL clause indicates that the value in this column cannot be omitted. The second column, named Description, permits national characters of varying lengths up to a maximum of 50 characters.

Adding and Dropping Columns

A handy feature of relational databases is the ability to add, change, and remove columns whenever needed. Suppose an employee table contains a few hundred rows with typical information about employees including name, address, phone, hire date, and birth date columns. Over the last year or so, every employee in the sales division is given a mobile phone to use when traveling. Originally, the table did not have a mobile phone column. Can you simply add a column to hold the new information? Yes. Simply use the SQL ALTER TABLE statement. The following shows how you might add a column called MobilePhone to an Employee table:

```
ALTER TABLE Employee
    ADD MobilePhone VARCHAR2(14);
```

Oracle adds the MobilePhone column as the last column of the table and assigns the NULL value to each entry. Later, someone can insert mobile phone numbers into selected rows of the table. Similarly, you can modify or remove existing table columns. Execute the ALTER TABLE statement with the MODIFY or DROP COLUMN phrase to modify a column or remove it, respectively. For instance, the SQL statement:

```
ALTER TABLE Employee
    DROP COLUMN YearStarted;
```

removes the YearStarted column from the table. Similarly, the statement:

```
ALTER TABLE Employee
    Modify YearStarted DATE DEFAULT SYSDATE;
```

changes the data type of the column to DATE type. In addition, the DEFAULT statement ensures that any unfilled YearStarted field is automatically filled in with today's date—the value returned by the SYSDATE function.

Periodically, you may want to remove unwanted tables entirely. Suppose you no longer need the CheapWebHost table, which contains the names and URLs of Web hosts. You've settled on a Web host, so that table has become useless. You could delete all the table's rows, but the table's structure persists. To purge a table's definition along with any rows it may contain, use the DROP TABLE statement. The DROP TABLE syntax is simple.

```
DROP TABLE table_name [CASCADE CONSTRAINTS] [PURGE]
```

When a table is deleted with the CASCADE CONSTRAINTS option, the table and its data are deleted (moved to the recycle bin) along with any other objects that reference the table or depend upon the table including views, routines, and triggers (discussed later). The optional PURGE clause is deleted, but it is not moved to the recycle bin. Instead, it is irrevocably dropped from the system. For example, the following statement deletes the CheapWebHost table and empties the recycle bin.

```
DROP TABLE CheapWebHost CASCADE CONSTRAINTS PURGE;
```

Exploring Data Manipulation Language Statements

One of the fundamental functions of any database is to allow the manipulation of the data it contains. Data manipulation language (DML) statements include the SQL statements to add, modify, and remove data in a database table. Being able to insert new data rows, alter errant or changed information in tables, and delete obsolete records is required to maintain a database's currency and accuracy. INSERT, UPDATE, and DELETE are the SQL statements that provide these capabilities.

INSERTING DATA

Use the INSERT statement to insert a value for each column, or field, in a table, or to insert values into selected columns. The syntax for a basic INSERT statement is straightforward:

```
INSERT INTO table_name [(column_name [, column_name ...])]
VALUES (value [, value...])
```

If you are inserting values into every column in the table, then you can use the form:

```
INSERT INTO table_name
VALUES (value, value, value, ...)
```

Notice that in the preceding form you omit the list of table columns, specifying only values they receive. When you choose to insert values for *every* column in the INSERT statement, the VALUES clause must contain a value for each column—none can be omitted. If you do not know the value to insert for a column, insert the word NULL in its place. *NULL* is a reserved word meaning that a value is unknown. The following INSERT statement illustrates how you would add a new row to the LicenseStatus table knowing all the values and the order in which the table fields occur in the table.

```
INSERT INTO LicenseStatus
VALUES (1017, 'Reactivated');
```

If you use this form, then the list of values must conform to the following:

- If column names are not specified in the INSERT statement, there must be one value for each column, and the values must be in the same order as they are defined in the table.
- Unknown values must be represented by the NULL value.

If you choose to insert only a few of the values, then you can list the column names receiving values, in any order, followed by the VALUES list corresponding to those values. For example, suppose you want to add a new real estate agent to the Agents table and you only have the new agent's broker-assigned AgentID and the agent's first and last names. In this situation, it is simpler to issue an INSERT statement with the list of three columns followed by the three values in the VALUE clause. Let's try it with SQL*Plus.

To add a new agent to the Agents table knowing only three columns' values:

1. Open SQL*Plus and log into Oracle with your username and password.
2. At the SQL> prompt, type the following:

```
INSERT INTO Agents (AgentID, FirstName, LastName)
VALUES (10001, 'Melinda', 'Whitmore');
```

3. Press **Enter** to execute the command. SQL*Plus checks the command and passes it to the Oracle database. Oracle responds with the message *1 row created*, indicating Oracle added the row (see Figure 2.11).
4. Verify the insertion by displaying the agent information. Type this statement at the SQL> prompt:

```
SELECT AgentID, FirstName, LastName
FROM Agents
WHERE AgentID < 10200;
```

5. Press **Enter** to execute the statement. Oracle displays the two rows that match the criteria, one of which is the row you inserted. Leave SQL*Plus open for more steps that follow later.

```
SQL*Plus: Release 10.1.0.2.0 - Production on Sat Sep 30 09:42:54 2006

Copyright (c) 1982, 2004, Oracle.  All rights reserved.

Connected to:
Personal Oracle Database 10g Release 10.1.0.2.0 - Production
With the Partitioning, OLAP and Data Mining options

SQL> INSERT INTO Agents (AgentID, FirstName, LastName)
  2  VALUES (10001, 'Melinda', 'Whitmore');

1 row created.

SQL>
```

FIGURE 2.11 Inserting a new row and verifying its values.

A third form of the INSERT statement uses a SELECT clause to copy rows from another table. In this form, the SELECT clause replaces the VALUES clause:

```
INSERT INTO table_name (column_name1, column_name2, …)
    SELECT column1, column2, …
    FROM table_name [WHERE search_condition]
```

You list the columns you into which you want to insert values followed by a SELECT statement that retrieves a like number and type of columns for the insertion. An optional WHERE clause filters rows. For example, you could add rows to the Agents table with this statement, which copies values from another table whose columns are the same data type as those of the Agents table:

```
INSERT INTO Agents (AgentID, LastName, FirstName)
    SELECT NewAgentNumber, AgentLastName, AgentFirstName
    FROM NewlyLicensedAgents;
```

Remember that the data type for the Agent table columns must be identical to those of the NewAgentNumber table, and each row added to the table must have a NewAgentNumber that is unique and that doesn't match any already in the Agents table. You can see that using this method is a handy way to copy possibly large amounts of data from one table to another.

Updating Rows

It should not be surprising to you that periodically, information in tables must be corrected due to data input errors, or updated because the information has changed. Customers' addresses change regularly, employees get merit increases, and product inventories are continually changing. The UPDATE statement allows you to modify one or more fields in one or more rows of your Oracle tables. The syntax for the UPDATE statement is:

```
UPDATE table_name
    SET column_name = expression [, column_name = expression, …]
    [WHERE search_condition]
```

The UPDATE syntax indicates the SET clause is required, but the WHERE clause is optional. You specify the name of the table to be updated along with pairs of column names and update values. If you specify a WHERE clause, then only rows that satisfy the search condition are updated.

Suppose you wanted to add Melinda Whitmore's cell phone number and license status identification number—information you did not have when you first inserted her record. You could use the UPDATE statement to locate her record and then add those values.

CHAPTER 2 Overview of SQL and SQL*Plus **69**

To update three values for a particular real estate agent:

1. With SQL*Plus still active, type **CLEAR SCREEN** to clear the screen of any previous information.
2. Open Notepad and type the following on multiple lines (press Enter to move to a new line for the first three lines, but *do not* press Enter at the end of the fourth line). Be very careful to insert single quotation marks around the cell phone number and around the first and last name values. Spell and capitalize the first and last names exactly as shown. (You will learn about the COMMIT statement in paragraphs to follow.)

```
UPDATE Agents
SET CellPhone = '(707) 555-8099', LicenseStatusID = 1001
WHERE FirstName = 'Melinda' AND LastName = 'Whitmore';
COMMIT;
```

3. In Notepad, press **Ctrl+A** to select all the text and press **Ctrl+C** to copy it to the Clipboard.
4. Switch to SQL*Plus, press **Ctrl+V** to paste the text into SQL*Plus, and press **Enter** to execute the COMMIT statement. If SQL*Plus indicates any syntax errors, then switch to Notepad, make any corrections, and repeat steps 3 and 4. Oracle displays the message *1 row updated* (see Figure 2.12) and *Commit complete.* Both the CellPhone and LicenseStatusID fields for Melinda Whitmore's record are updated with their new values. (You can issue a SELECT statement to verify the change if you want.)
5. Switch to Notepad, save your SQL statement if you want, and close Notepad. However, leave SQL*Plus running.

DELETING TABLE ROWS

Use the SQL DELETE statement to remove rows from a database table. You can remove one, two, several, or all rows from a table. When you want to remove *all* rows from a table, issue the TRUNCATE statement. The difference between issuing a DELETE statement to remove all table rows and a TRUNCATE statement is that under certain circumstances, rows removed by a DELETE statement can be reinstated with a ROLLBACK statement, which is described in the next section. However, a table's rows cannot be reinstated if they are removed by using a TRUNCATE statement. TRUNCATE also does additional housekeeping chores such as releasing extra table space no longer needed. The syntax for a DELETE statement is:

```
DELETE FROM table_name
[WHERE search_condition]
```

FIGURE 2.12 Updating a row in the Agents table.

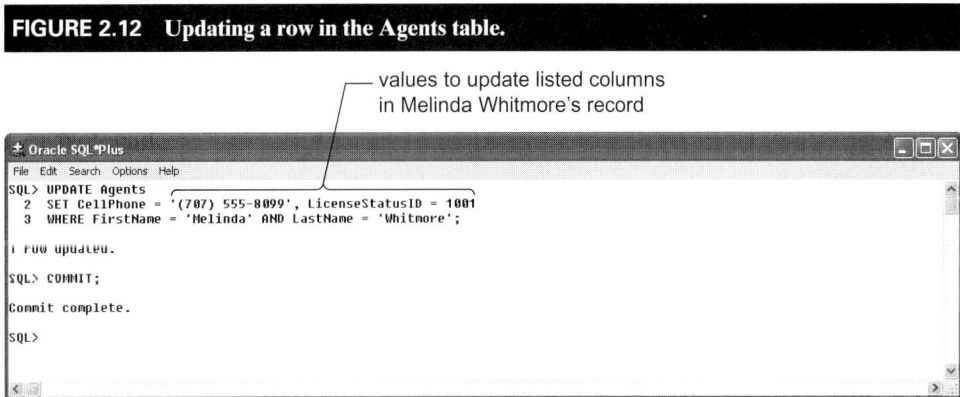

The DELETE FROM clause requires you to name the table from which you are deleting rows. The optional WHERE clause serves the same purpose as it does in a SELECT or UPDATE statement: it carries a search condition specifying the conditions that a row must satisfy to be deleted. If you omit the WHERE clause, a common mistake for those new to SQL, then Oracle will delete all rows in the table. Both the DELETE and the TRUNCATE statements delete rows from a table, but they do not delete the table definition itself. To remove a table and its rows, issue the DROP TABLE command (described earlier in this chapter).

To delete a row from the Agents table:

1. If you closed SQL*Plus, open it and log into the database with your username and password. Type **CLEAR SCREEN** and press **Enter** to start with a SQL prompt and a clean screen.

2. Type the following command following SQL> to delete the newly added agent, Melinda Whitmore, from the Agents table. Press **Enter** at the end of both lines.

   DELETE FROM Agents
   WHERE AgentID = 10001;

   Oracle displays the confirming message "1 row deleted."

3. Verify that Melinda Whitmore's record is no longer in the table by displaying all the agents' first and last names. At the SQL> prompt type:

   SELECT FirstName, LastName
   FROM Agents
   ORDER BY LastName DESC;

   and press **Enter** to execute the command (see Figure 2.13).

FIGURE 2.13 Deleting a row and verifying its removal.

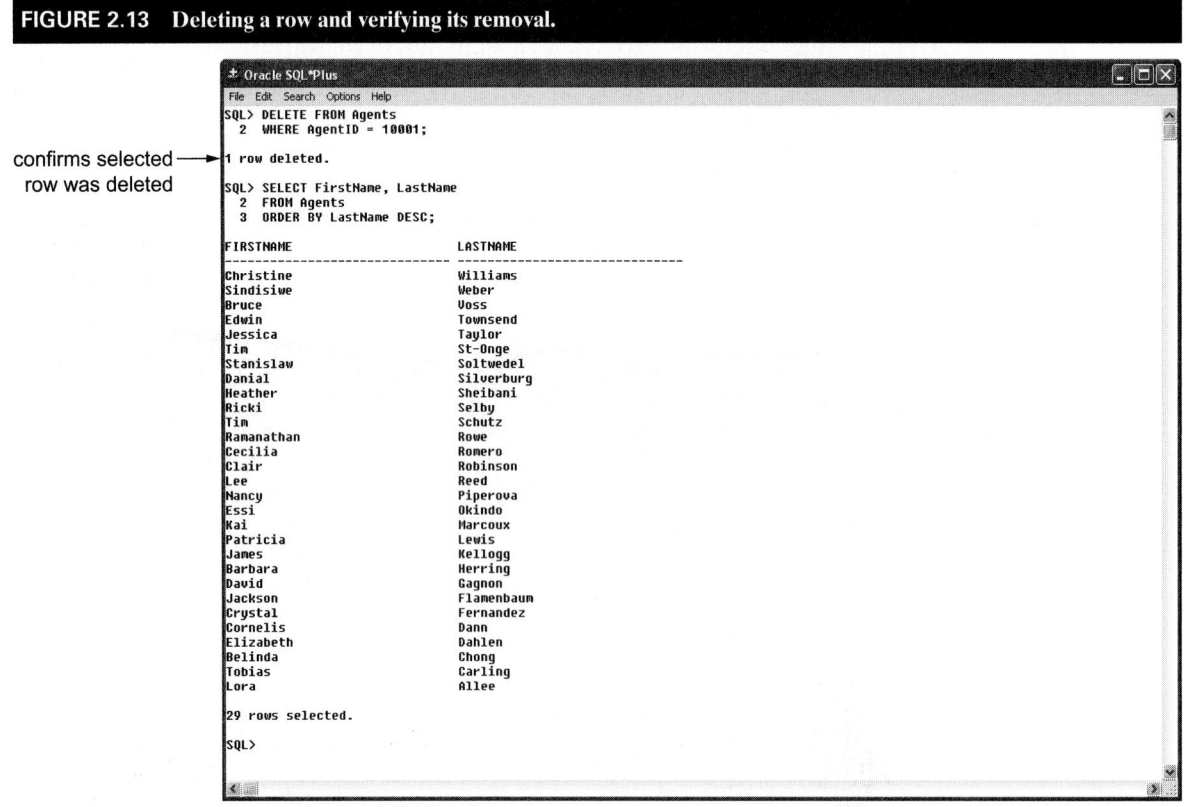

4. Notice that the Melinda's record is no longer in the list of agents. (Your display might have more column headings interspersed in the listing, depending on a SQL*Plus environment setting called LINESIZE. We discuss LINESIZE in the next section.) Leave SQL*Plus open. If you close SQL*Plus and then reopen it in the next section, some of the steps will not work properly.

DISCOVERING TRANSACTION CONTROL STATEMENTS

SQL commands in the transaction control (TC) statements category govern database transactions. A database *transaction* is a group of SQL statements that are a logical unit of work. Statements in a transaction are a cohesive, inseparable group whose individual statements must succeed. Otherwise, the entire collection of SQL statements must be backed out so that the database is returned to its original state *before* the transaction is executed. A common example is transferring money from your savings account to your checking account. One UPDATE statement would reduce your savings account by the amount of the transfer, while a subsequent UPDATE statement would increase your checking account by a like amount. If either of these individual UPDATE statements failed for any reason, there would be funds floating in cyberspace and the bank's books would not balance. Transaction control statements prevent this possibility by binding these two statements together in a single transaction, requiring that both UPDATE statements be permanently recorded in the database; or reversing their effect to restore the database to its original state prior to executing the transaction.

MAKING CHANGES ENDURE OR REPEALING THEM

When you execute a DDL statement such as CREATE TABLE to add a new table to your database, Oracle changes the database immediately so that it is visible to any user allowed to access the table. However, this is not true for DML statements (INSERT, UPDATE, and DELETE), unless you set a special SQL*Plus variable, called AUTOCOMMIT, to on. When AUTOCOMMIT is set to on (SET AUTOCOMMIT ON), every change caused by a DML statement is written to the database as soon as it is executed.

To permanently record the results of one or more SQL statements which constitute a series of statements in a transaction, you *commit* a transaction by executing the transaction control statement COMMIT. To reverse the result of one or more SQL statements which make up a transaction, you *roll back* the instructions with a ROLLBACK statement. Any database changes performed before executing a ROLLBACK statement—back to the last COMMIT statement—are discarded. When you disconnect from the database, Oracle automatically commits all database changes made by that user. Figure 2.14 shows a single transaction, which is bracketed between COMMIT statements.

FIGURE 2.14 Example transaction structure.

Recall that in previous steps, you inserted a new agent, Melinda Whitmore, updated her cell phone number, and issued a COMMIT statement to make permanent the added and updated agent record. Following that, you deleted Whitmore's record from the Agents table. If you did not log off Oracle since you executed the DELETE statement, then you will be able to restore Whitmore's record. If you happened to log off after deleting her record, then you will not be able to restore her record because Oracle executed a "silent" commit statement for you. Execute the following steps to reverse the DELETE statement, restoring Melinda Whitmore's record in the Agents table.

To reverse all operations since the last COMMIT:

1. Type **ROLLBACK**, type **;** (semicolon), and press **Enter**. Oracle responds "Rollback complete."
2. At the SQL> prompt type:

```
SELECT LastName, CellPhone
FROM Agents
ORDER BY LastName DESC;
```

and press **Enter** to verify that Melinda Whitmore's record is restored. Notice that her name reappears in the list of agents, second from the top, along with her updated cell phone number. You reversed the DELETE statement—the last transaction since a previous COMMIT statement.

Because you do not want Whitmore's record in the Agents table, execute the following steps to permanently delete her record from the database.

To delete a record and make the deletion permanent:

1. With SQL*Plus still running, at the SQL> prompt type the following:

```
DELETE FROM Agents
WHERE AgentID = 10001;
```

and press **Enter** to execute the command.
2. Make the deletion permanent. Type

```
COMMIT;
```

and press **Enter**. Oracle responds *Commit complete.*
3. Type **Exit** and press **Enter** to log out of Oracle and close SQL*Plus.

ESTABLISHING ROLLBACK SIGNPOSTS

You can also set a savepoint at any point within a transaction. A savepoint allows you to roll back any changes to that savepoint. Savepoints are commonly used in very long transactions to minimize the number of statements you have to roll back if some transactions fail. The syntax of a SAVEPOINT statement is:

```
SAVEPOINT savepoint_name
```

where savepoint_name is any meaningful name. For example, you can declare a savepoint by typing:

```
SAVEPOINT AfterFinancialUpdates;
```

If you execute DML statements before and after the SAVEPOINT statement, you can restore the database to its state at the AfterFinancialUpdates point by executing the statement:

```
ROLLBACK TO SAVEPOINT AfterFinancialUpdates;
```

REVIEWING DATA CONTROL LANGUAGE STATEMENTS

Users' access must be controlled in a multiuser Oracle database. Any user's access to the database itself can be restricted, and a user may be allowed or denied access to various database objects such as tables, views, and reports. Data control language (DCL) statements provide database security with SQL statements that allow and deny access to the system and objects which it contains. When you create tables and other objects in your schema (username), other users cannot access those objects unless you explicitly give them that privilege. Also, newly installed users cannot do very much except log into Oracle unless a database administrator (DBA), who is the most trusted system user, grants system and object privileges to users. The GRANT statement provides privileges. The REVOKE statement takes away privileges. While you do not have much control over the privileges *you* have, yourself, you can grant privileges to objects you control to others. Likewise, you control revoking any privileges on objects you have created.

There are two types of privileges: system privilege and object privilege. A ***system privilege*** allows a user to perform selected actions in Oracle (creating tables, creating views, etc.). An object privilege allows a user to take particular actions on database objects (insert data into another user's table, for example).

GRANTING PRIVILEGES

You grant system and object privileges with the GRANT command. Its syntax is:

```
GRANT privilege [, privilege [, privilege] …] | ALL PRIVILEGES
ON object
TO user [IDENTIFIED BY password] [, user2 [, user3]…] | PUBLIC
[WITH GRANT OPTION]
```

where you substitute appropriate names for all italicized words. For example, suppose your username is Pine and you own a table named Agents. You want to allow username Elm the ability to list the entries in your Agents table. However, you *do not* want Elm to have the ability to alter or delete any records in the Agents table. Pine grants Elm those rights by logging into the database and entering the SQL command:

```
GRANT SELECT ON Pine.Agents TO Elm;
```

REVOKING PRIVILEGES

Anyone owning an object can disallow access by other users to database objects owned (created) by that user. The syntax for the REVOKE statement is:

```
REVOKE privilege [, privilege [, privilege] …] | ALL PRIVILEGES
ON object
FROM user [, user2 [, user3]…] | PUBLIC
```

To revoke user Elm's ability to display rows in the Agents table owned by Pine, user Pine would execute the SQL statement:

```
REVOKE SELECT ON Pine.Agents FROM Elm
```

There are several object privileges that you can grant to others. They include SELECT, INSERT, UPDATE, DELETE, and EXECUTE.

Database administrators (DBAs) have sufficient privileges to grant other users a variety of system privileges. These include CREATE SESSION, CREATE TABLE, CREATE USER, CREATE VIEW, and CREATE SYNONYM, to name a few. You can check what system privileges you have by executing a simple SELECT statement. Log into Oracle using SQL*Plus and execute the steps that follow to see what system privileges you possess.

To check what system privileges you have:

1. Launch SQL*Plus, if necessary, and log into the database with your username and password.
2. Type the following (spell the table name very carefully, including the two underscores):

SELECT *
FROM user_sys_privs;

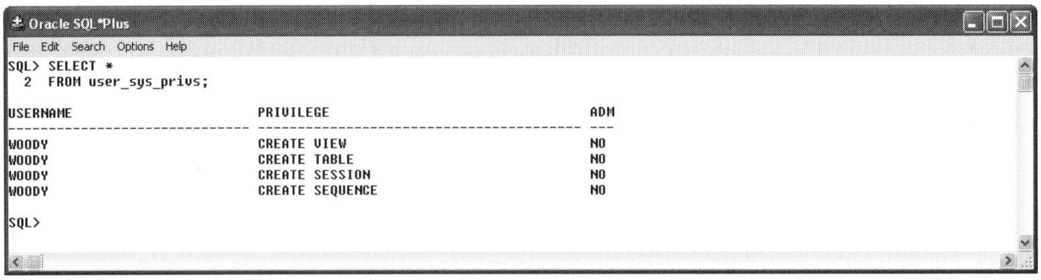

FIGURE 2.15 Displaying a list of system privileges.

3. Press **Enter** to pass the command to Oracle. Oracle lists your username and any privileges you have—the create table privilege, for example.
4. Type **exit** and press **Enter** to log out of the Oracle database and close SQL*Plus.

The rows returned indicate your username in the first column and all privileges, one per row. In addition, it indicates whether or not you can grant the privilege to other users. Figure 2.15 shows a list of system privileges granted to user Woody. Your list will be different, of course.

You will find details and examples of granting and revoking object and system privileges in Chapter 12, *Maintaining Database Security*. We defer any more discussion about privileges until that chapter.

USING SQL*PLUS COMMAND EXTENSIONS

The SQL*Plus client provided by Oracle provides several commands, called SQL*Plus commands. Different from standard SQL commands, SQL*Plus commands allow you to format retrieved columns, capture returned results in a buffer, run external script files, display a table's structure and data type definitions, change your password, and connect to the database system—among almost 80 individual commands. You have used some of these special commands in this chapter (CLEAR SCREEN, for example). They are defined only in the SQL*Plus environment (but not necessarily in the *i*SQL*Plus environment), and only for Oracle. An example of a SQL*Plus command that saves time is START. You used it earlier in this chapter to launch a script file containing SQL commands.

There's no need to introduce all of the SQL*Plus commands here, but we will discuss several of them by category or function that they perform. You will notice in examples herein that SQL*Plus commands do not end with a semicolon. It is okay to abbreviate many of the SQL*Plus commands (DESCRIBE or DESC), but you cannot abbreviate any of the SQL commands. Finally, some SQL*Plus commands are not supported in *i*SQL*Plus. Therefore, all examples in the discussions that end this chapter appear in the context of the SQL*Plus client program.

> **Note:** By now you know that in SQL*Plus, you must press Enter at the end of each line to move to a new line or execute a SQL statement terminated with a semicolon. Beginning here, we will frequently omit that detail, trusting you to remember it. Instead, we instruct you to *type* a command or *execute* a command, omitting the instruction to "press Enter."

CHAPTER 2   Overview of SQL and SQL*Plus   **75**

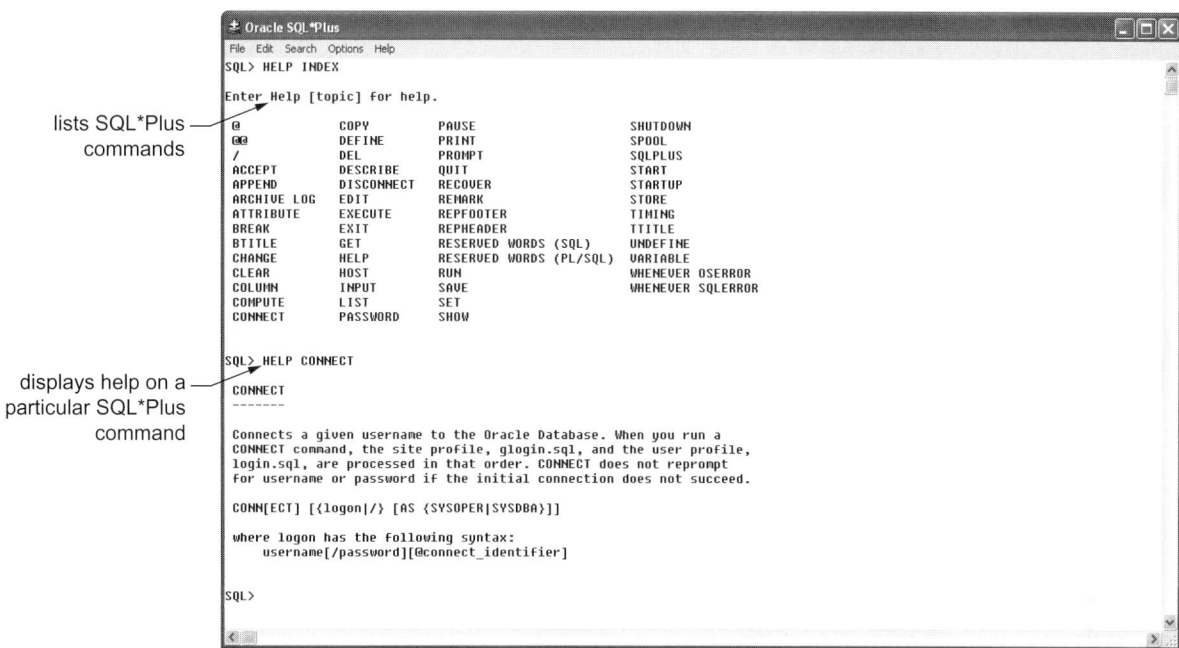

FIGURE 2.16 Listing SQL*Plus commands and help on the CONNECT command.

It is simple to display a list of all the SQL*Plus commands. Execute SQL*Plus, and request help.

To display a comprehensive list of the Oracle SQL*Plus commands:

1. Launch SQL*Plus, if necessary, logging in with your username and password.
2. Type **CLEAR SCREEN** to clear the display.
3. Execute **HELP INDEX** (lowercase is fine), omitting a semicolon, to display a list of over 50 SQL*Plus commands.
4. Type **HELP CONNECT** (see Figure 2.16).

When you type HELP CONNECT, SQL*Plus displays information about the SQL*Plus command's use and its syntax. If you request help about a SQL command, such as CREATE TABLE, SQL*Plus returns an error message indicating it could not find help on the topic. Remember, use the Oracle Technical Network for SQL questions. Use the SQL*Plus HELP command for SQL*Plus questions.

DESCRIBING A TABLE'S STRUCTURE

The SQL*Plus DESCRIBE command displays the column definitions for a table, view, or synonym. It also lists the specifications for a function or procedure (described in later chapters). When you cannot remember the names of some of the columns of a table you created, simply list them.

To list the column names and data types in a table:

1. At the SQL*Plus prompt execute:

   DESCRIBE Agents

   Oracle displays the column names and data types for the 15 columns in the Agents table.

2. Type **DESCRIBE SaleStatus**
3. Type **DESCRIBE LicenseStatus** (see Figure 2.17). Leave SQL*Plus running.

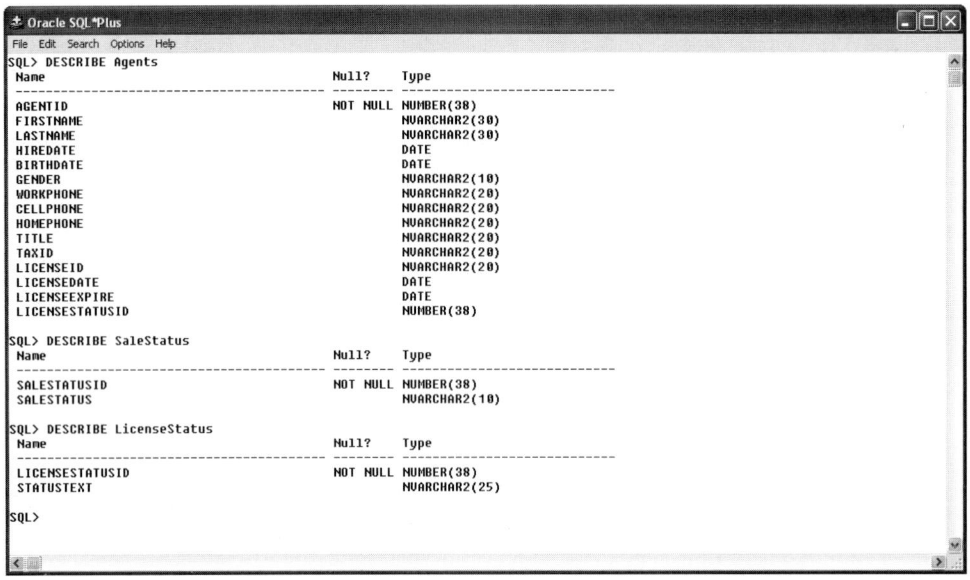

FIGURE 2.17 Displaying tables' column definitions.

CAPTURING FILES FOR PRINTING

You may be required, as part of an assignment, to save the results of your SQL*Plus sessions—both the SQL and SQL*Plus statements and the results they return. By saving the statements Oracle executes, and any confirming messages and query results, you can print the file to turn in to your instructor for credit. Although you can use Windows tricks such as pressing the PrtScrn key to capture one screen's worth of SQL*Plus output, this breaks down when Oracle produces more than a page of output. The SQL*Plus SPOOL command allows you to capture any text that appears on the SQL*Plus screen—either commands that you enter or results returned from the database—into a named file. The SPOOL SQL*Plus command is not available in *i*SQL*Plus. (If you try to execute SPOOL in *i*SQL*Plus, it returns an error message indicating it is not available.) SPOOL is a toggle, meaning you can capture the screen on a continuing basis, or you can turn it off. You can type HELP SPOOL to see the syntax. It is:

```
SPOOL [file_name[.ext] [CREATE | REPLACE| APPEND | OFF | OUT]
```

Each of the capitalized words above can be abbreviated to their first three letters, except OFF and OUT (for example, *SPO* instead of *SPOOL*). You turn on the spooling facility by typing the SPOOL command followed by a fully qualified file name, including the path. Once you designate a file, *everything* you type or that displays is captured to the file until you either log off SQL*Plus or you type SPOOL OFF. You can practice in the next section, where you learn to use formatting commands.

FORMATTING COMMANDS

The COLUMN SQL*Plus command formats the display of column headings and column data. The full COLUMN syntax is long, but the abbreviated version is this:

```
COLUMN [{column_name | expression}[option...]]
```

Some of the most important options include CLEAR, FORMAT, HEADING, JUSTIFY, and WRAP. The COLUMN command specifies the display attributes for a column, including the column heading text, the column alignment, format for numeric data, and whether or not the column data wraps within the column if needed. For example, the SQL*Plus command:

```
COLUMN AgentID FORMAT 99999 HEADING 'Agent ID'
```

sets the display characteristics, for the rest of this SQL*Plus session, for the AgentID column. In particular, only five digits appear for AgentID values, and the heading is changed from the default (the table column name) to the case-sensitive heading "Agent ID." You can specify as many column names and settings as you want on multiple SQL*Plus lines. To remove any column formatting that you set up during this SQL*Plus session, execute CLEAR COLUMNS. Doing so erases all column formatting. The COLUMN command is particularly handy inside a script file, which you can run repeatedly. Let's try out the SPOOL and COLUMN SQL*Plus commands.

To copy output to a spool file and format SQL*Plus columns:

1. With SQL*Plus running, open Notepad.
2. In Notepad, type the following SQL*Plus statements. Do *not* press Enter at the end of the last line, "FROM Agents;".

```
CLEAR SCREEN
CLEAR COLUMNS
COLUMN AgentID FORMAT 99999 HEADING 'Agent ID'
COLUMN FirstName FORMAT A15 HEADING 'First Name'
COLUMN LastName FORMAT A15 HEADING 'Last Name'
SELECT AgentID, FirstName, LastName
FROM Agents;
```

3. Save the preceding in a Notepad file named **Ch2<yourname>FormatColumns.sql** in a folder and disk of your own choosing.
4. Copy all the Notepad text into SQL*Plus. SQL*Plus immediately interprets the COLUMN instructions, but it does not run the SQL SELECT statement (if you did not press Enter following the semicolon in the Notepad version).
5. Press **Enter** to submit the SELECT statement for execution, and format the columns as specified (see Figure 2.18).

The *format model* A15 following the FORMAT modifier indicates the column is alphanumeric and limits what is displayed to 15 columns. Anything longer is truncated on the right. The format mask 99999 indicates the column is numeric and that SQL*Plus is to display a maximum of five digits. If you change the format mask to 999, for example, then #### appears in the column, indicating that the column values are wider than the numeric format mask allows. Simply increase the number of digits indicators. If you specify:

```
COLUMN AgentID FORMAT 99,999 HEADING 'Agent ID'
```

Then the agent identifications appear with a comma between the third and fourth most significant digits (e.g., 10,041).

Notice that the column headings are different from their usual format. Each heading contains two words, and they are not uppercase text, as is the default. You probably see that only 11 agent rows appear under their headings. Add the two lines for the heading and a blank line preceding each heading, and the total is 14 lines. This is the SQL*Plus default value for the PAGESIZE environment variable. The PAGESIZE variable determines the number of lines displayed between the top of the title and the end of the page. You can change it temporarily by adding the SQL*Plus statement SET PAGESIZE <value>, where "<value>" is the number of lines in a page. The maximum value of PAGESIZE is 50,000.

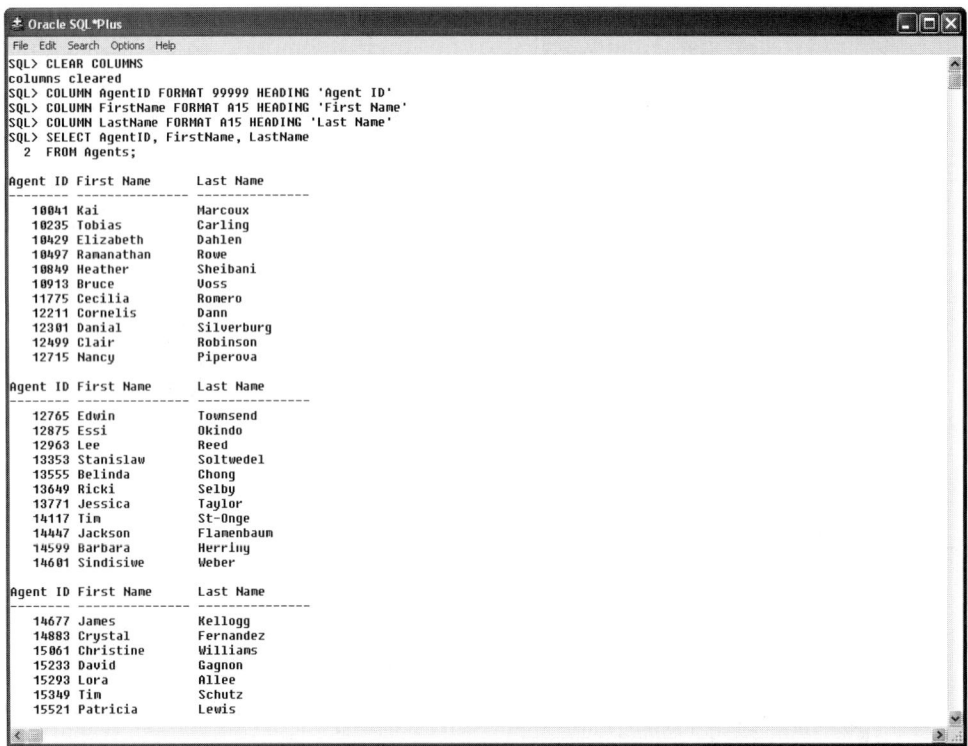

FIGURE 2.18 Altering column headings.

To modify a SQL script file:

1. Open your FormatColumns script file in Notepad, click to the left of the CLEAR COLUMNS statement, and press **Enter** to open up a blank line. On the blank line between CLEAR SCREEN and CLEAR COLUMNS, type the statement:

   `SET PAGESIZE 45`

2. Click **File** and click **Save** to save the modified SQL*Plus file.
3. Copy and paste all the lines in Notepad into the SQL*Plus window.
4. In the SQL*Plus window, press **Enter** to execute the SELECT statement (see Figure 2.19).
5. In SQL*Plus, type:

   `SET PAGESIZE 14`
   `CLEAR SCREEN`

   to restore the original default value for the PAGESIZE environment variable and clear the screen.
6. Close the Notepad window, but leave SQL*Plus running.

There are other SQL*Plus formatting commands that you will encounter throughout this textbook. We will discuss their use when we introduce them.

CUSTOMIZING YOUR SQL*PLUS ENVIRONMENT

You can permanently set some of the SQL*Plus environment variables such as PAGESIZE so that you do not have to reestablish them every time you log into Oracle through SQL*Plus. For example, you might like to always have PAGESIZE set to 50, and the

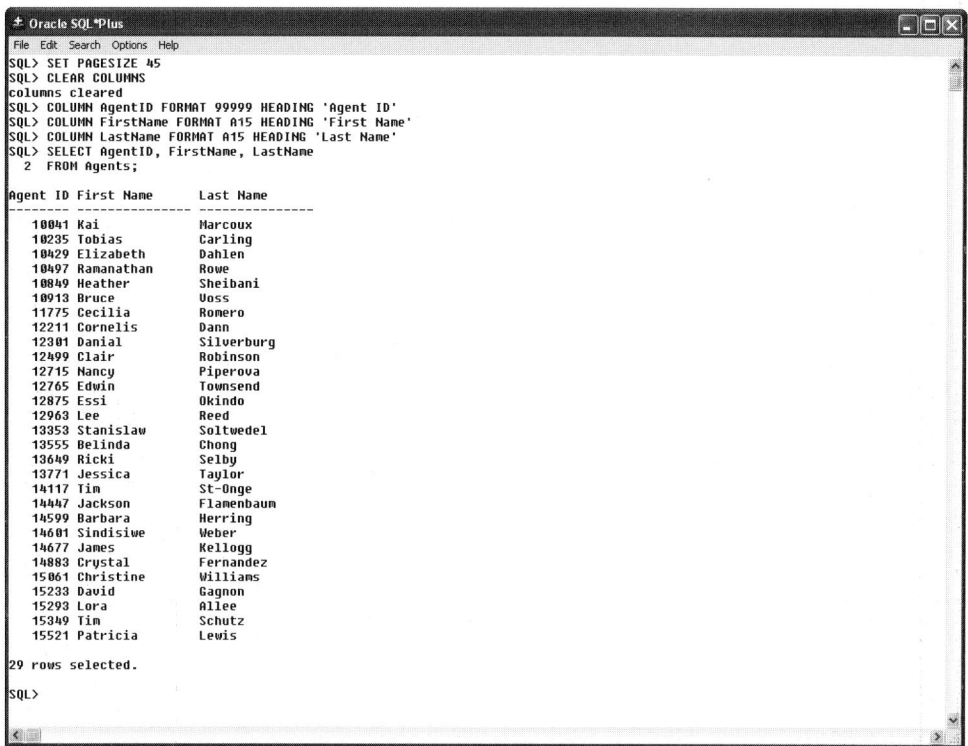

FIGURE 2.19 Altering the PAGESIZE environment variable.

number of characters per line, called LINESIZE, set to 75. Customize your SQL*Plus environment using SQL*Plus commands located in the menu bar. Change any of the SQL*Plus environment variables by opening SQL*Plus, clicking **Options** on the menu bar, and then clicking **Environment.** If you are using SQL*Plus in a public location, the SQL*Plus menus may not be available. Institutions often do that so that SQL*Plus appears the same across all laboratory computers. It's still important to know how.

To modify selected SQL*Plus environment variables:

1. With SQL*Plus open (not *i*SQL*Plus), click **Options** on the menu bar and click **Environment.** SQL*Plus opens the Environment dialog box.
2. Drag the Set Options scroll box down until you see *pagesize* in the list. Click **pagesize** to highlight it, and click the **Custom** radio button in the Value panel. Notice that 14 appears in the text box, indicating pagesize's current value (you reset it to 14 in preceding steps).
3. Double-click **14** to select the entire string and type **45** (see Figure 2.20).
4. Drag the scroll box down until you see sqlprompt in the list. Click **sqlprompt.** Click the **Custom** option button. Notice that the default prompt, SQL>, appears in the box in the Value group. There is no need to change its setting.
5. Click **OK** to confirm the linesize change you made. The Environment dialog box closes.
6. With the SQL*Plus prompt displayed, type **SHOW PAGESIZE** and press **Enter** to display the current value of the PAGESIZE variable.
7. What is the value of the LINESIZE variable? Type **SHOW LINESIZE** and press **Enter** to find out.

80 Introduction to Oracle

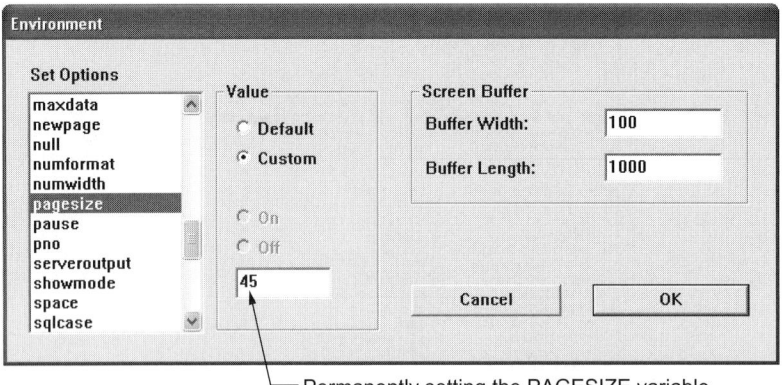

Permanently setting the PAGESIZE variable

FIGURE 2.20 Customizing the SQL*Plus environment.

You can customize any of the SQL*Plus variables whose names are displayed in the Set Options list of the Environment dialog box. By the way, if you want the long list of *all* the environment variable values, type **SHOW ALL**.

EXECUTING SCRIPT FILES

You will find that you write some SQL and SQL*Plus statements that you run frequently. Rather than rewrite the dozens of lines, it is more convenient to save your SQL*Plus statements in a file so that you can rerun the entire set, much as you have been doing when you copy the lines from Notepad into SQL*Plus and then run the lines. A collection of SQL and SQL*Plus statements in a file is called a script or script file. Once saved, you can invoke the entire file, without involving Notepad and without going to the bother of copying and pasting, by using two SQL*Plus commands that serve an identical purpose: To locate, load, and run script files. These commands are START and @. Both accomplish the same result. They load up a script file and execute all the lines it contains.

To execute a stored script file:

1. Locate the folder containing the script file you saved earlier called Ch2<yourname>FormatColumns.sql and remember the path to it.
2. At the SQL*Plus prompt, type:

   `START <path>\Ch2<yourname>FormatColumns`

   where "<path>" is the full path to the disk and folder where you stored your script file, and "<yourname>" is the name you substituted previously. For example:

   `START C:\My Documents\Ch2ElmFormatColumns`

3. Press **Enter** to execute the START command. SQL*Plus loads the script file and executes the instructions it contains. Your SQL*Plus screen should show three columns and 29 rows of real estate IDs and names—all with only one page heading at the top (see Figure 2.21).

   > Note: We removed the first line, CLEAR SCREEN, so you could see the START instruction that launched the script file. Your screen *will not* display that line.

If you prefer, you can substitute the at sign (@) in place of the word START and accomplish exactly the same thing.

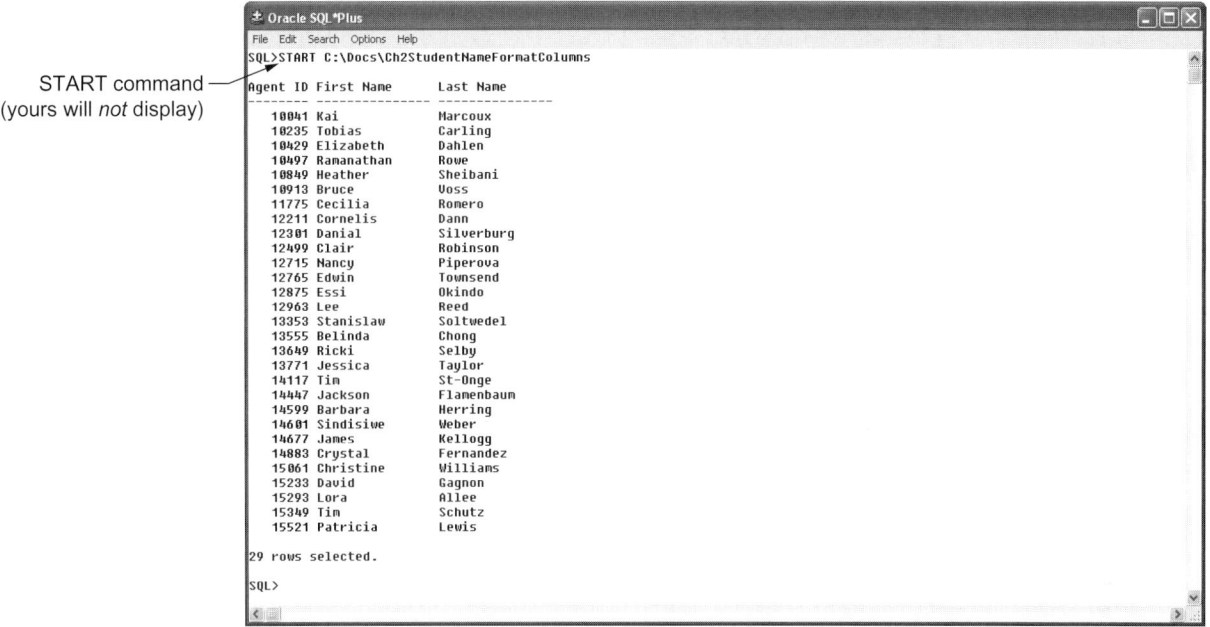

FIGURE 2.21 Launching a script file in SQL*Plus.

USING VARIABLES

SQL*Plus allows you to define variables that you can use in place of actual values in SQL statements. The variables known as ***substitution variables*** are substitutes for values in SQL statements. They are particularly useful inside SQL script files. Variables are identified easily because they are ordinary text strings that look like they might be table column names. However, they are variables because they begin with an ampersand (&). So, when SQL*Plus runs the following SELECT statement:

```
SELECT AgentID, FirstName, LastName
FROM Agents
WHERE LastName = '&lastnameplease';
```

It requests that the user supply "lastnameplease" before submitting the query to Oracle for processing. Using variables provides a way of generalizing script files. In the preceding example, several people could list an agent's information by supplying the agent's last name at "run time." An actual example helps you see how this works.

To use a substitution variable in a script file:

1. Switch to SQL*Plus and type **CLEAR SCREEN** (press **Enter**) to clear off the work surface.

2. Open Notepad, type the following SQL script, and then save the Notepad file as **Ch2<yourname>SubVar.sql**

   ```
   SELECT AgentID, FirstName, LastName, BirthDate
   FROM Agents
   WHERE LastName = '&lastnameplease';
   ```

3. Switch back to SQL*Plus, and type:

   ```
   @<path>\Ch2<yourname>SubVar
   ```

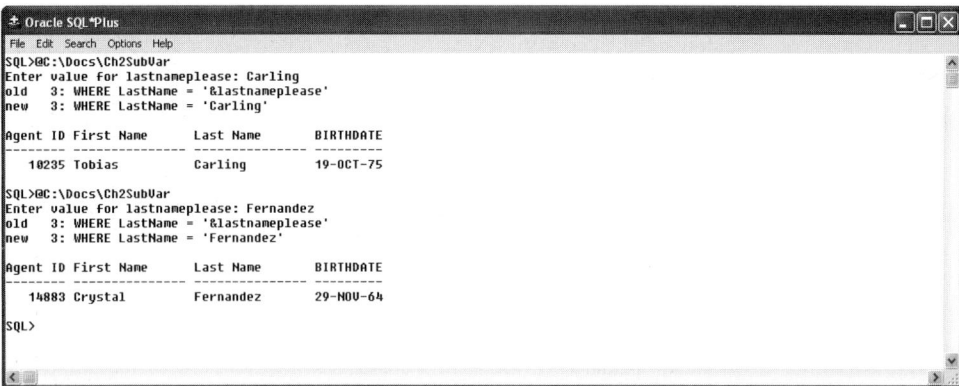

FIGURE 2.22 Using a substitution variable in a script file.

where "<path>" is the full path to the disk and folder where you stored your script file, and "<yourname>" is the name you substituted previously.

4. Press **Enter** to launch the script file. After you press enter, SQL*Plus first prompts you for the last name.
5. Type **Carling** and press **Enter.** Be sure to spell the last name exactly as shown, including capitalization. Oracle displays the selected columns for the Agent whose last name is Carling.
6. Repeat Steps 3 and 4.
7. When prompted with "Enter value for lastnameplease," type **Fernandez** and press **Enter.** SQL*Plus substitutes the string you typed into the variable and passes the completed query to Oracle for execution. Oracle returns another row (see Figure 2.22).
8. Exit SQL*Plus by typing **Exit** and pressing **Enter**.
9. Close Notepad.

DISCOVERING OTHER SQL*PLUS COMMANDS

There are several SQL*Plus commands that you will use in this textbook that you may want to learn more about online. Remember that SQL*Plus command descriptions and syntax are available in SQL*Plus by typing HELP followed by the command. Remember that you can list all the SQL*Plus commands by typing HELP INDEX. Here, we mention more of these commands without as much detail as for other commands. While these commands are useful, they are easy to understand and use.

The HOST command, not available in *i*SQL*Plus, executes host operating system commands without leaving SQL*Plus. You can type $ at the SQL> prompt, also. Both commands invoke the operating system. In the case of Windows, a DOS box opens and the OS prompt, indicating the current path, appears. You can return back to SQL*Plus by typing **Exit** and pressing **Enter**. For example, if you want to list the SQL script files on the current directory, you can type HOST and then type DIR *.SQL at the DOS prompt. Further, if you want to automate a DOS command, you can list the command following "HOST." For example, if you execute the command:

```
HOST DEL C:\Docs\myfile.sql
```

in SQL*Plus, then SQL*Plus will invoke the host operating system and ask it to delete (DEL) the file myfile.sql found on the path *C:\Docs* and then close the DOS window, returning to SQL*Plus almost before you realize it happened. You'll use this in the script file that you will build shortly. Of course, you can execute a variety of commands, including changing the current directory, at the host OS prompt.

The TERMOUT and PAGESIZE environment variables are very useful inside a script file when you want to perform a series of SQL and SQL*Plus commands. TERMOUT is handy when you do not want a SQL*Plus script file to display informative messages such as "1 row created." Issuing SET TERMOUT OFF (or SET TERM OFF) suppresses the output to the screen from within a script file (only). Issuing SET TERM ON toggles screen display back on. Once a script containing the TERMOUT statement is completed, TERMOUT is automatically turned on. FEEDBACK is another SQL*Plus environment variable that determines whether *informative* messages appear on the screen—messages such as "1 row created" or "table dropped." Execute the command SET FEEDBACK OFF to suppress informative messages, and execute SET FEEDBACK ON to reinstate them. FEEDBACK remains OFF for the remainder of the SQL*Plus session until you turn it back on, regardless of whether or it was set inside a script file. Executing SET PAGESIZE 0 suppresses printing of column headings. This is handy when you want to spool the results of a query to a file without its column headings.

You can document script files by including comments. Begin a single-line comment with two hyphens (--). Multiline comments begin with a slash followed by an asterisk (/*) and end with an asterisk followed by a slash (*/). You can also use the REM command to start a single-line comment. We recommend you avoid the /* and */ form of comments, since it is easy to forget to terminate a comment. Omitting the terminating */ means the rest of the script file is treated as comments.

The PROMPT command sends a message or a blank line to the screen. The PROMPT command is especially handy inside a script file when you want to display a progress message indicating the status of the running script file. For example, the statement:

```
PROMPT Successfully ran script to delete files.
```

displays on the screen everything that follows the PROMPT command.

BUILDING AND RUNNING A SCRIPT

A script file, as you learned earlier, is a collection of SQL and SQL*Plus statements that accomplishes some task. Recall that a script file is invoked by typing START followed by the path and script file name. SQL*Plus loads the script file and executes every line, in turn. To wrap up this chapter, it is helpful to put together some of the statements you learned in this chapter into a script file that you can run to review its results. In addition, you will draw upon some system tables maintained by the database that contain the names of all the objects owned by the schema (user). Oracle keeps a list of objects owned by the current user in a view called user_tables. The table is a "table of tables" because it holds more than 45 columns describing characteristics of the tables you own, including the number of rows in each table, the percentage of free space, and all table names. (Type *DESCRIBE user_tables* to display a list of columns in this system table.) You will build a script to display the names of all tables you own, the number of rows they contain, and a description of the columns in each of these tables—all from a single script file that you can run as often as you need as your database changes.

Next, you will write a script file that describes the names of files that belong to you (your schema). The script file will call upon a system table to list the names of tables in your account. You will use this list of table names to dynamically build another script file containing a series of DESCRIBE commands, one for each table that is found in your account. Finally, your script file will execute the dynamically built script file and

84 Introduction to Oracle

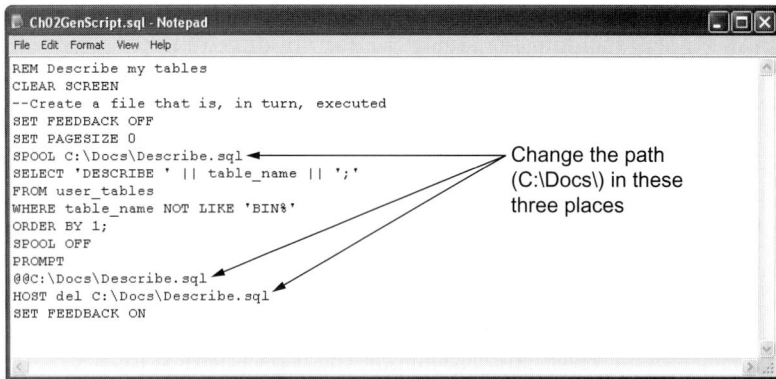

FIGURE 2.23 Script file.

then delete when it is done executing. The end result is a SQL*Plus display of table names and a list of the columns each contains along with the data type assigned to each column. Don't be concerned if you do not understand every line of the script file. The main lesson is that you can create script files that you subsequently ask SQL*Plus to execute.

To create a script file and save it:

1. First, determine a location on disk where you can save your script file. For example, you might be able to save a script file in C:\Temp or in the root directory, C:\.

2. Open Notepad, and type the code shown below. Remember to substitute, in place of "C:\Docs\," the exact path where you will save your script file. There are three places you must change the path. (Figure 2.23 also shows the code in Notepad.)

```
REM Describe my tables
CLEAR SCREEN
--Create a file that is, in turn, executed
SET FEEDBACK OFF
SET PAGESIZE 0
SPOOL C:\Docs\Describe.sql
SELECT 'DESCRIBE' || table_name || ';'
FROM user_tables
WHERE table_name NOT LIKE 'BIN%'
ORDER BY 1;
SPOOL OFF
PROMPT
@@C:\Docs\Describe.sql
HOST del C:\Docs\Describe.sql
SET PAGESIZE 14
SET FEEDBACK ON
```

3. Click **File,** click **Save,** click the **Save as type** list box, select **All Files,** navigate to the disk and folder where you want to save your script file, type **Ch2<yourname>GenScript.sql** (substitute your last name for "<yourname>") in the File name list box, (remember to select **All Files** in the *Save as type* list box) and click the **Save** button to save your script. Leave Notepad open in case you encounter errors in SQL*Plus.

4. Open SQL*Plus and log in with your username and password. At the SQL prompt, type:

START <path>Ch2<yourname>GenScript

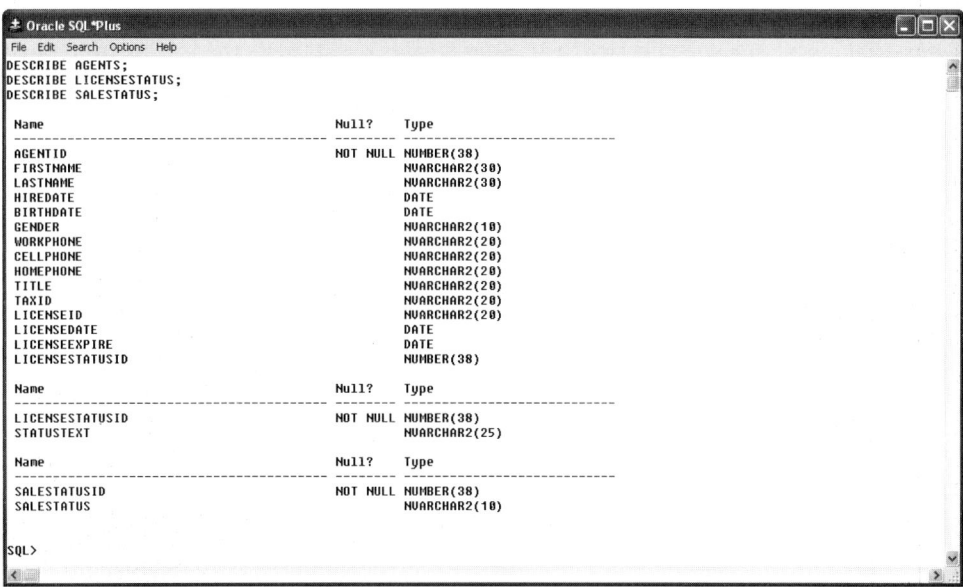

FIGURE 2.24 Output from the script file.

Substitute the path to your script file for "<path>" and your last name for "<yourname>."

5. Press **Enter** to launch your script file. Your output should match Figure 2.24.
6. If you encounter errors, switch to Notepad, correct the mistakes, resave the file, and execute Step 4 again. Seek your instructor's help if you cannot locate the error or don't know how to correct it.
7. Close Notepad and exit SQL*Plus.

Summary

There are five categories of Structured Query Language (SQL) statements: Query, data definition, data manipulation, transaction control, and data control language. SQL queries retrieve information from a database. DML statements INSERT, UPDATE, and DELETE modify data. Data definition language statements define structures in the database such as tables. Transaction control statements repeal or make permanent any changes made by the most recent uncommitted DML statements. Data control language statements provide security by allowing (or not) users access to selected database objects. Access to the Oracle client/server model database is available from the host operating system, from a Windows client called SQL*Plus, and from a Web-based interface called iSQL*Plus. Each method has its own distinct advantages, but the most common access is using the SQL*Plus client program.

Oracle extensions to standard SQL are called SQL*Plus statements. These proprietary statements allow you to format output, capture retrieved results, run script files, display a table's structure, and customize the SQL*Plus client interface's environment. You can review these helpful extensions to the SQL by typing **HELP INDEX** at the SQL prompt. Typing **HELP** and a command name displays additional help on the SQL*Plus command in question. Collections of SQL and SQL*Plus statements constitute a SQL script file. By collecting related statements into a file, you can repeatedly invoke the statements by running the script file whenever needed. Script files can contain variables whose values a user specifies when the script files are run. Variables allow the names of objects and actions taken to be deferred until execution time, providing a dynamic and customizable script that satisfies the information needs of a wide audience of database users.

Key Terms

- Base table
- Commit
- Constraint
- Derived table
- Format model
- National character set
- NULL
- Query
- Rollback
- Script
- SQL*Plus commands
- Substitution variable
- System privilege
- Transaction
- Viewed table

Review

True/False

1. Structured Query Language is a programming language.
2. Data manipulation language (DML) SQL statements allow you to create objects such as tables and views.
3. Interfacing with Oracle directly through a host operating system is a lot easier than using SQL*Plus.
4. Execute the DELETE FROM statement to remove records from a database table.
5. If you delete a record from a table, you can restore the original record if you issue a ROLLBACK statement before logging off the system or making the deletion permanent.

Fill In

1. Execute the _____ SQL statement to add records to a table.
2. The DESCRIBE statement is a _____ statement, not a SQL statement.
3. To remove a table from a schema, issue the _____ command.
4. When you want database changes resulting from INSERT, DELETE, and UPDATE statements to be permanent, issue the _____ SQL statement.
5. The _____ SQL*Plus statement, with the appropriate modifiers, allows you to control the format of returned columns of data in SQL*Plus.

Multiple Choice

1. Which of the following allows you to capture everything that appears on the SQL*Plus screen to a file?
   a. PRINT ON
   b. SPOOL <filename>
   c. SPOOL OFF
   d. CAPTURE <filename>
2. Which of these clears any column formatting you may have set during a SQL*Plus session?
   a. FORMAT COLUMN OFF
   b. COLUMN FORMAT CLEAR
   c. CLEAR COLUMNS
   d. None of the preceding is correct

3. Which of the following is the correct statement to add a row to the LicenseStatus table, assuming the proposed data values are the correct data type for each table column?
   a. INSERT INTO LicenseStatus VALUES (876, 'Out of commission');
   b. INSERT LicenseStatus VALUES (876, 'Out of commission');
   c. INSERT FROM LicenseStatus VALUES (876, 'Out of commission');
   d. CREATE FROM LicenseStatus VALUES (876, 'Out of commission');
4. Which of the following deletes Danial Silverburg from Redwood Realty's Agents table?
   a. DELETE FROM Agents LastName = 'Silverburg' AND FirstName = 'Danial';
   b. DROP FROM Agents WHERE LastName = 'Silverburg' AND FirstName = 'Danial';
   c. DELETE FROM Agents WHERE LastName = 'Silverburg' AND FirstName = 'Danial';
   d. DELETE Agents WHERE LastName = 'Silverburg' AND FirstName = 'Danial';
   e. Both c and d are correct
5. You can suppress further display of informative messages such as "3 rows deleted" by issuing what statement?
   a. SET TERMOUT ON
   b. SET PAGESIZE 0
   c. SET SPOOL OFF
   d. SET INFORM OFF
   e. SET FEEDBACK OFF

Hands-on Exercises

1. Extending the Chapter Case

The Redwood Realty database administrator wants you to create a table called ContactReason in the Redwood Realty database. It contains the three reasons people contact the company: To buy a home, to sell a home, or to make contact with a broker on a casual basis. The three categories are to be stored in the table along with a longer description. Table 2.1 shows the three rows you are to insert into the ContactReason table.

1. Log into Oracle using SQL*Plus. Open Notepad and immediately save the file as **Ch2<yourname>RedwoodEOC.sql.** Remember to click **Save as type** and then select **All Files.**
2. In Notepad, type the following and press Enter at the end of the first two lines. *Do not* press Enter following the semicolon.

   ```
   CREATE TABLE ContactReason
   (ContactReason NVARCHAR2(15) PRIMARY KEY,
    Description NVARCHAR2(50)
   );
   ```

TABLE 2.1 Data to be entered into the ContactReason table.

ContactReason	Description
Buy	Offer to buy a property
Casual	General customer probably looking for properties
Sell	Listing to sell a property

3. Copy and paste all four Notepad lines into SQL*Plus. Press **Enter** to execute the CREATE TABLE statement. Oracle should display "Table created."
4. If an error occurs in the preceding step, occurs, then identify and fix it in Notepad. Repeat Step 3.
5. Switch back to Notepad, press **Enter** to move to a new line, and type the following INSERT statements. Press **Enter** on the last line too.

   ```
   INSERT INTO ContactReason VALUES ('Buy',
   'Offer to buy a property');
   INSERT INTO ContactReason VALUES ('Casual',
       'General customer probably looking for
       properties');
   INSERT INTO ContactReason VALUES ('Sell',
   'Listing to sell a property');
   ```

6. In Notepad, carefully click and drag across the three Insert Statements, dragging through the third semicolon on the third INSERT statement and the empty line below it. Paste the text into SQL*Plus. The three commands execute immediately.
7. Switch to Notepad, save the file, exit Notepad, and switch back to SQL*Plus.
8. Type **COMMIT;** (remember the semicolon at the end) and press **Enter** to make permanent the insertion of these three rows.

9. In SQL*Plus, type and execute the following INSERT statement (be sure to type two consecutive single quotation marks between *n* and *t* in the word *Don't.*):

   ```
   INSERT INTO ContactReason VALUES
   ('Don''t know', 'Unknown reason');
   ```

10. In SQL*Plus, type the following statement and press **Enter** to execute it:

    ```
    SELECT *
    FROM ContactReason;
    ```

11. Type **ROLLBACK;** (remember the terminating semicolon) and press **Enter** to revoke the last action.

12. To create a text file you can print and turn in, execute the following instructions in SQL*Plus. Substitute a full path (for example, C:\Main\) for the string "<path>" in the statement below.

    ```
    SPOOL <path>Ch2ContactReasonList.txt
    DESCRIBE ContactReason
    SELECT * FROM ContactReason;
    SPOOL OFF
    ```

13. Locate the file Ch2ContactReasonList.txt you just created, open it in Notepad, insert a new line at the top, type your name, save the file, print it, and then close Notepad.

14. Switch back to SQL*Plus and erase the spool text file by executing (substitute a real path to your file in place of "<path>") the instruction:

    ```
    HOST del <path>\Ch2ContactReasonList.txt
    ```

15. Type the following instruction to remove the table and its contents:

    ```
    DROP TABLE ContactReason;
    ```

16. Exit SQL*Plus.

2. COFFEE MERCHANT

The Coffee Merchant DBA wants you to create some tables and make some modifications to the data. You are to use both SQL*Plus and *i*SQL*Plus in this exercise. If, for any reason, you cannot use *i*SQL*Plus, the browser-based database interface, then simply use SQL*Plus instead to accomplish the tasks. The DBA wants you to create and populate the States table, which will contain 50 states and the District of Columbia when you are done. Fields in that table include the two-character state abbreviation, the full state name, the state sales tax rate, the estimated population, the size of the state in square miles, and the state's official Web site URL, if available.

1. Launch SQL*Plus and log into Oracle. Open Notepad and immediately save the file as **Ch2<yourname>CoffeeEOC.sql.** Remember to click **Save as type** and then select **All Files.**

2. Type the following in Notepad, pressing **Enter** at the end of each line. (Remember to type the final right parenthesis followed by a semicolon.)

   ```
   CREATE TABLE States
       (StateID NCHAR(2) PRIMARY KEY,
        StateName NVARCHAR2(20) NOT NULL,
        TaxRate NUMBER(7,4),
        Population INTEGER,
        LandArea INTEGER,
        WebURL NVARCHAR2(50)
   );
   ```

3. Save the Notepad file, copy to the Clipboard all text through and including the terminating semicolon, but not the blank line following it. Close Notepad.

4. In SQL*Plus, press **Ctrl+V** to paste the text, and press **Enter** to execute the script command. Oracle responds with the message "Table created."

5. In SQL*Plus, type and execute the following SQL statements:

   ```
   INSERT INTO STATES
     VALUES ('AK', 'Alaska', 0, 643786,
   571951, 'www.state.ak.us');
   CLEAR SCREEN
   COLUMN StateID FORMAT A7
   COLUMN StateName FORMAT A15
   COLUMN TaxRate FORMAT 0.9999
   COLUMN Population FORMAT 99,999,999
   COLUMN LandArea FORMAT 99,999,999
   COLUMN WebURL FORMAT A15
   SELECT * FROM STATES;
   COMMIT;
   DELETE FROM STATES;
   SELECT * FROM STATES;
   ROLLBACK;
   SELECT * FROM STATES;
   ```

6. Locate the file Ch02PopulateStates.sql and note its full path on your computer. Then type the following in SQL*Plus, pressing **Enter** to run the script file. (Substitute the path to the script file for "<path>" statement shown.

   ```
   START <path>\Ch02PopulateStates.sql
   ```

   The last message displayed after a series of *1 row created* messages is *Commit complete.*

7. Type **Exit** to log off Oracle and close SQL*Plus.

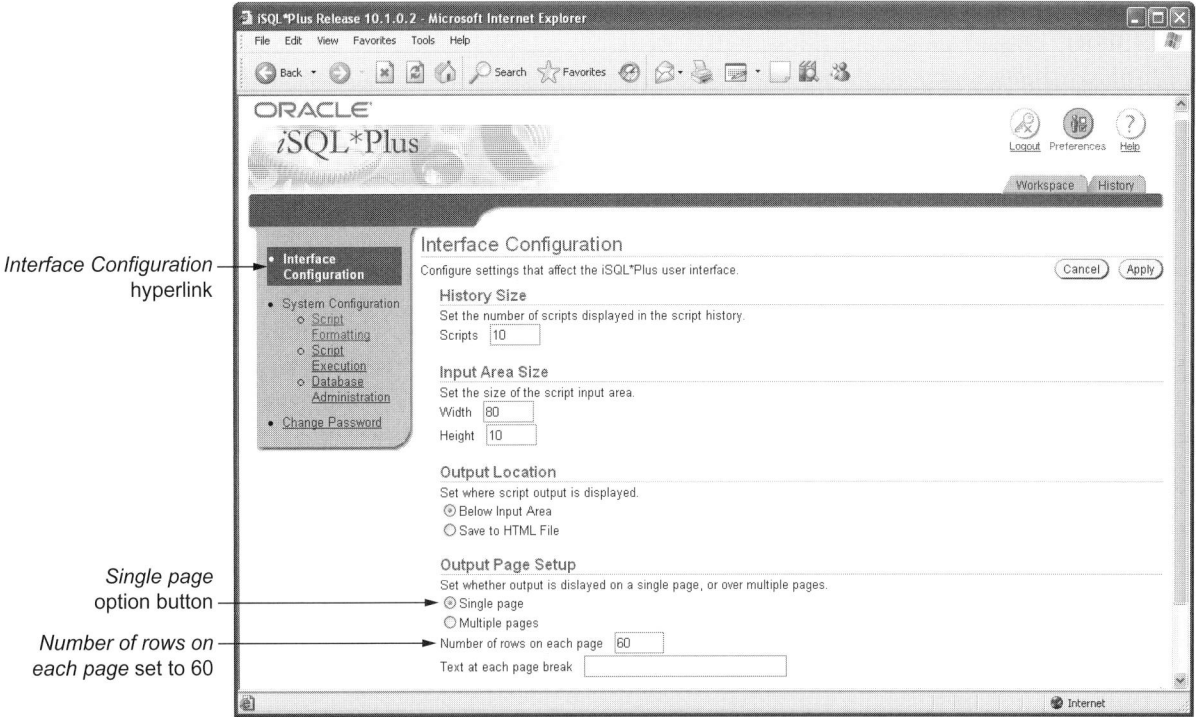

FIGURE 2.25 Changing an *i*SQL*Plus environment variable.

8. Open your Web browser, open *i*SQL*Plus, and log into Oracle with your username and password.

9. Click the **Preferences** link near the top right side of the screen, and click the **Interface Configuration** link on the left side, if necessary. Next, click the **Single page** option button under the Output Page Setup heading, double-click the **Number of rows on each page** text box, and type **60** (see Figure 2.25). Click the **Apply** button and then click the **Workspace** tab located at the top right side of the page.

10. Click the **Workspace** text box and type the following, pressing **Enter** at the end of each line:

    ```
    COLUMN Density FORMAT 9,999
    SELECT StateID, StateName,
    Population/LandArea AS Density
    FROM States
    ORDER BY Density DESC;
    ```

11. Click the **Execute** button to view the results: The list of states (and the District of Columbia) appears. The most densely populated state appears at the top of the list and the least densely populated appears at the bottom (what is it?).

12. Click **File** on your browser's menu bar, click **Print** on the menu, and click **Print** in the Print dialog box to print the *i*SQL*Plus query and results pages. Write your name on each output page and be prepared to turn in the results to your instructor.

13. Click the **Logout** hyperlink to log out of the database. When the logout confirmation Web page appears, close the browser.

3. ROWING VENTURES

Rowing Ventures is responsible for coordinating rowing regattas in more than a dozen venues around the U.S. and abroad. Besides overseeing the venue and providing vendor display and merchandising space at the rowing events, Rowing Ventures stores a myriad of details about the races at a regatta, the participants, their sponsors, the boats in each race, boat bow numbers, and crews in each boat.

Launch SQL*Plus and log into Oracle. Next, open your data disk containing files accompanying this textbook and locate and run the script file called Ch02RowingVentures.sql. It creates tables called Boat and Organization. Open a spool file to save the next steps to disk, and execute the statements **DESCRIBE Organization** and **DESCRIBE Boat** to display column names in those tables. Print the spool file for reference, but keep it open. Next, use a SELECT statement to display the following Organization table fields for all records: OrganizationID, Phone, and the address fields. Close the spool file and print it. Clear the screen, then display the BoatID and BoatCategory columns of all the records in the Boat table. Delete the first two records listed by referring to their BoatID values in the DELETE statement. Create another spool file (for example. SPOOL C:\Docs\Myfile.txt), and display the BoatID and BoatCategory columns of all rows in the Boat table. Execute a statement to undo your previous record deletions. Print the spool file. Close SQL*Plus. Be sure to write your name on all printouts so that you can turn them in to your instructor, if requested.

4. BROADCLOTH CLOTHING

Broadcloth Clothing, a manufacturer of fine women's clothing, wants you to list the contents of several of its database tables, redirecting those listings to a file which you can print. First, locate the script file Ch02Broadcloth.sql among the data files for this chapter and note its path. Next, launch SQL*Plus, log into Oracle with your username and password. Start a spool file by executing:

```
SPOOL
<path>\<yourname>Ch02BroadclothSpool.txt
```

where you substitute a real path for "<path>" and substitute your last name for "<yourname>" so that the file's name is unique in the directory you choose. Next, using the path you noted earlier, run the script file Ch02Broadcloth.sql to create and populate two tables that you will need to complete this exercise. The tables the script file creates are *Factory* and *WorkingConditions*. Using the DESCRIBE statement, list the field names and their data types for both tables. Next, list the values in the columns ComplianceID and ConditionCategory for all rows in the WorkingConditions table. Delete all rows in the WorkingConditions table whose ComplianceID is equal to 2003. Display the same two columns again for all rows with a SELECT statement. Rescind the deletions. Stop the spool file. Edit the spool file in Notepad and add your name as a new first line in the spool file. Save the spool file and print it. Close Notepad and type Exit in SQL*Plus to leave SQL*Plus and log off Oracle.

Launch *i*SQL*Plus, log into the database, display the structure of the Factory table (names and data types), and print the Web page showing these results. Click the **Clear** button to clear the Workspace and results. Next, write a SELECT statement to display all the columns of the Factory table. Print the query and results displayed in the Web page. Click the **Clear** button to erase the query and the results. Then, type and execute a DELETE statement to remove any rows in the Factory table in which the Greenwich Mean Time difference (GMTDifference) is exactly positive eight hours. Display all rows in the Factory table again, and print this Web page. Click the **Logout** button to exit Oracle. Close your browser.

CHAPTER 3

CREATING, MODIFYING, RENAMING, AND DELETING DATABASE TABLES

Learning Objectives

In this chapter, you will learn:

- How to create normalized tables.
- How to create a user account and assign a password to it.
- How to grant object and system privileges to a user account.
- Oracle commands to create tables.
- Data types that are available in Oracle.
- Techniques to add integrity constraints and domain constraints to tables.
- How to add and delete table columns.
- Which system tables hold table descriptions, column names, and table names.
- How to rename or remove tables.

DESIGNING A RELATIONAL DATABASE

After reading Chapter 2, you have an understanding of how to create tables, and you have written code to create tables. In this chapter, you will get a detailed description of table creation, the data types that Oracle supports, how to ensure that your table data remains consistent, and how to constrain the values that table columns can hold. First, you will examine the larger issue of database design by considering how to determine what tables you need for an application and what columns individual tables should contain.

TALKING TO THE DATABASE USER

Perhaps the most important task in crafting a database is to design tables that store the organization's data and support its business rules. Because Oracle provides several options for accessing data from a database, you can design database tables that store related information in separate tables and still display the disparate data in one report. For any database project, you must understand the data elements constituting the data that is to be stored in the database. A successfully designed database must reflect business rules that you gather from various sources. One of the first steps in designing the database is to determine exactly what data is required. You do this by talking to people—the users—who deal with the data regularly and must make sense of it. People generally have only a vague notion of what they want from a database system. You must be persistent in preliminary data gathering. In particular, you must: (1) identify exactly what data to collect, (2) determine how the different data are related, and (3) establish how long the data is kept in the database system.

Having identified the data elements, you need to organize them into groups or objects. Part of this process involves, again, determining business rules that govern the groups. For example, consider the business rules surrounding the customers object. Can a customer's record reflect more than one order or sale involving multiple items during the lifetime of that customer's data? On the other hand, can a customer's data be recorded in a database if there are no unfilled orders and the previous order was placed more than a year ago? Answers to questions like these affect the database design. Therefore, a correctly designed database reflects all the identified business rules. Identifying business rules and weaving them into the database design always has problems and usually involves some database redesign as those problems are identified and resolved. Several problems have common themes and are presented herein.

IDENTIFYING USER REQUIREMENTS

One way to identify user requirements is to observe a company's operations. Identify the data needs of various groups in the organization, being careful to collect the data and organize it. Collecting documents, from the Web or paper documents, is one method to obtain information about the basic data and information needs of the firm. Collect these critical pieces of information before forming the initial database design: (1) the data that must be collected, (2) the type of data (numeric, characters, etc.), and (3) the volume of data required.

RECOGNIZING BUSINESS OBJECTS

By identifying all the data that a business needs to store in a database and forming the fundamental storage units, database tables, you can design required business reports and forms with the data in mind later. Capturing the fundamental data, organizing it into tables, and establishing the relationships between them are fundamental to a successful database design. Companies deal with business objects, or entities, without calling them by those names. From a database designer's view, an ***entity*** or ***object*** is a person, place, or thing (a noun) that the business wants to record and track. Familiar examples of entities include customers, employees, and airline passengers. Each entity is described by its attributes or properties. An entity along with its properties is called a ***class.*** Every row in the customer entity has attributes or characteristics that describe (adjectives) its members. Attributes include name, address, phone number, and so on. As a database designer, it is your job to define these entities and the attributes that describe them. As you collect information and forms from users, you can group related data together into their respective entities. On an employment form, for example, much of an applicant's contact information would likely be part of an entity that might be called *applicant.* Some information on the application would not be in that entity—information such as job skills and previous employers and their addresses. Those would likely be stored in separate entities, but linked to the application entity.

Relational databases store entities in tables. Tables contain columns corresponding to each of the attributes identified for the entity, one column per attribute. Each row of a table represents an instance, or example, of that entity and contains the data that uniquely describes one member of that class. As you identify data classes, or tables, you will also identify linkages, or relationships, between those tables. Tables always have relationships to other tables in the database. In the Redwood Realty database, for example, the Customers table has a relationship with the Properties table, which contains homes owned by those customers. The table that contains information about Redwood Realty real estate agents is related to a table containing real estate license information. The Agents table is also related, indirectly, to Customers, because each customer in the Customers table is there because they contacted a real estate agent, who is listed in the Agents table. Thus, a relational database is a collection of related and carefully designed tables. A *table* is a collection of columns, or attributes, that describe an entity.

It is important to identify associations or relationships among entities. These relationships represent the company's business rules, and therefore it is important to represent them correctly. The relationship between two tables is classified in one of three ways: (1) One-to-one, (2) one-to-many, or (3) many-to-many. A one-to-one relationship means that any given row in table A is related to exactly one row in table B, and vice versa. This does not occur very often, because both tables could be combined into one. A one-to-many relationship is the most common one. In this relationship, one row of a table is related to possibly many rows of another table. The second table is related to only one row of the first table. An example is the relationship between a customer and the orders that customer places. A customer can place none, one, or many orders with a particular company. However, any given order can be placed by only one customer. The third relationship, many-to-many, exists when a row in table X is related to many rows in table Y and a row in table Y is related to many rows in table X. An example is the relationship between students and instructors: A student can have several instructors (he or she *can* take more than one class), and any instructor almost always has more than one student. This type of relationship does not work well in a relational database system, so it must be replaced with two one-to-many relationships involving the original two tables and a third table containing key columns from the original two tables (described later).

Normalizing the Design

Once you have collected data and grouped it into tables, you can examine the tables to further refine their structure. The process of data normalization requires you to split your data into several tables that are connected to one another based on the data each holds. A handy, compact method of representing the contents of each of your database tables is to use a notation like the one shown in Figure 3.1 depicting tables called Customers, Listings, and SaleStatus—all part of the Redwood Realty database. The notation lists the table name and a parenthesized list of column names in the table. A column whose name is underlined indicates a primary key, and primary key fields are usually listed first. A ***primary key*** uniquely identifies a row within a table, much as a

FIGURE 3.1 Representing tables by listing their names and their column names.

Customers(CustomerID, FirstName, LastName, Address, City, State, Zipcode, HomePhone, CellPhone, WorkPhone)
Listings(ListingID, PropertyID, ListingAgentID, SaleStatusID, BeginListDate, EndListDate, AskingPrice)
SaleStatus(SaleStatusID, StatusText)

student ID identifies one student at an educational institution. When more than one column is underlined—meaning the primary key consists of several fields of a table—the fields are called a **composite primary key.** A table's primary key is not enough to connect it to other, related tables. A foreign key is required to complete the connection. A foreign key is a field that uniquely identifies a row in another table. In other words, a foreign key in one table matches the value of a primary key in another related table. In Figure 3.1, the foreign key *SaleStatusID* in the Listings table identifies the like-named primary key in the SaleStatus table. Although both keys' names are the same in this example, they don't have to be. (A foreign key and a primary key are identified as such when you create the tables containing them, and you will get practice doing this later.)

The advantage of this notation is that you do not need special graphics software to create it. You can write it by hand or use a word processor. The main disadvantage is that it is more difficult to show the relationships between tables. In any case, this table notation is a good starting point to begin the normalization process, which usually involves reducing the number of columns in a table and shifting some columns into another table or into a new table.

Chapter 1 described the meaning of first, second, and third normal form. You can examine the design of your initial table layout by first ensuring that they all conform to first normal form. While a detailed discussion of normalization is beyond the scope of this textbook, it is instructive to look at a few examples before moving on. Consider the Redwood Realty database tables. Suppose after your discussions with real estate professionals at Redwood about their data needs, you decide that a Customers table should contain the usual customer contact information. In addition, for those customers who want to sell a property, the Customers table contains details about the property for sale including the address, square feet, number of bedrooms, and so on.

Figure 3.2 shows a simplified form of such a design. It can spell trouble, however. What, for example, do you do if a seller decides not to sell a property? Redwood Realty could delete the record containing the property description, because it is no longer on the market. But in so doing, they also delete the seller's information—a contact they might wish to maintain for future mailings or casual contact. That design violates rules of second normal form. As it stands, the Customer table stores two facts: facts about customers and facts about properties. While those two topics are *related* to one another, they should not be coresident. The solution is to break the table into two tables—one to store customer information and the other to store property information. The obvious question arises: How do you maintain a connection between these two facts when they are stored in two different tables? The answer is to add a foreign key to the property table which contains the value of one of the customers' primary key values. The connection is made by posing a query—a SELECT statement—in which Oracle matches the foreign key in the property table with a primary key in the customer table. This is called a join operation, and it is explained fully in Chapter 5.

The complete process of normalizing a database, while extremely important, is outside the scope of this textbook. Here, you want to learn how to use Oracle to create tables, query tables, and use other Oracle tools. If you want to learn all about

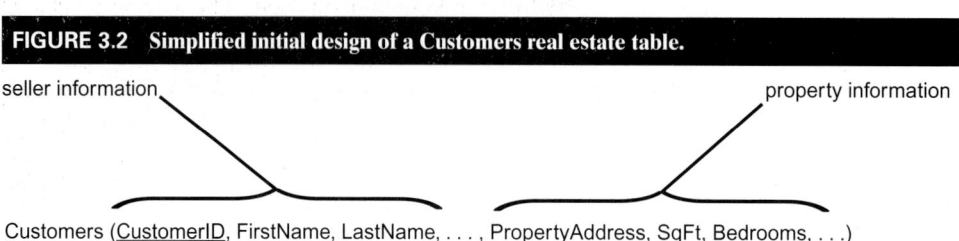

FIGURE 3.2 Simplified initial design of a Customers real estate table.

normalization, we urge you to consult textbooks devoted to database design and normalization. In addition, there are an almost limitless supply of Web sites which contain a wealth of information about databases in general and Oracle in particular. Search by using Google (www.google.com).

UNDERSTANDING ORACLE USER ACCOUNTS

When you work with a personal database such as Microsoft Access, you start the database system and either create a new database or open an existing one. In either case, you are probably the only person using the database, and Access does not require you to possess a username or password to use its database. The Oracle database allows a large number of concurrent users to share the same database system, which is usually stored on a separate server. Database files stored and maintained by Oracle provide security by keeping a user's database tables and other objects in a separate, protected area. This area is called a *user schema. Schema objects* or *database objects* are the names given to all the objects stored in the user schema. A client/server, industrial-strength database such as Oracle requires that each user who wants to access the database possess credentials—a username and password. This username and password is usually assigned, upon request, by the database administrator (DBA) or by your instructor. If you installed and are using Personal Edition of the Oracle database on your own computer, then you had the opportunity to change the password for several system (DBA) accounts including SYSTEM and SYSDBA. If you have already established your own username and password, then you may want to read the next section anyway. Besides showing how to create a new user account and password, the next section gives step-by-step instructions for Personal Oracle users on establishing certain critical object and system privileges. The privileges are needed for you to create tables, build views, and access your schema. If you are not using Personal Oracle, then you can skip the next section, *Further Instructions for Personal Oracle Users,* and proceed directly to the section titled *Creating Tables.*

FURTHER INSTRUCTIONS FOR PERSONAL ORACLE USERS

If you have installed Personal Oracle, then you likely assigned a new password to the special account SYSTEM. You should use the SYSTEM account very sparingly and should not use it on a regular basis to create tables or any of the activities in this book. Instead, use a "normal" account whose privileges are restricted so that you can limit damage caused by any errant commands. However, you need to log in with the SYSTEM username to create a new username and password and establish privileges for the new account. Here's how.

CREATING A USER

To create a user in the database, you must log on as a privileged user and then issue a CREATE USER statement. As a privileged user, you can assign object privileges and system privileges. Then log off the privileged account, log into the newly created "ordinary" user account, and go about your business of creating tables and performing other duties in your schema. The simplified syntax of the CREATE USER command is as follows:

```
CREATE USER <username> IDENTIFIED BY <password>
  [DEFAULT TABLESPACE <tablespace_name>]
  [TEMPORARY TABLESPACE <tempspace_name>]
```

96 Introduction to Oracle

The "<username>" stands for the username you assign, and "<password>" stands for the password you assign. In the steps that follow, you will need to connect to the database as a privileged user. Here, we log in using the SYSTEM user in the example, which has a default password of MANAGER. Log in with the same account and whatever password you assigned to the SYSTEM account.

To create a new user account in Oracle:

1. Using SQL*Plus, log onto Oracle with the SYSTEM account and the password you assigned during the install process.
2. Issue this statement to create a new user. You select your own username and password. Remember both! We select *Chapter3* for the username and *ChangeMe* for the password in this example. Press **Enter** to execute the command.

   `CREATE USER Chapter3 IDENTIFIED BY ChangeMe;`

3. Oracle responds with the message "User created." Leave SQL*Plus running.

Next, you will temporarily log out of the SYSTEM account and log into the new account to ensure that you have it correct. We continue using the username and password shown above, but you use whatever username and password you assigned.

LOGGING IN WITH ANOTHER USERNAME AND PASSWORD

Next, you will log out of the system account to try out the newly created username/password pair.

To log into Oracle under a different username and account while already connected to Oracle:

1. Type this statement at the SQL prompt, pressing **Enter** to execute it. Substitute the username and password you created above. The username precedes the slash, and the password follows it.

   > **Tip:** Usernames and passwords are case insensitive in Oracle. Most people prefer to type them in lowercase, because it doesn't require using the Shift key.

   `CONNECT chapter3/changeme;`

2. Oracle issues the error message
   ERROR:
   ORA-01045: user CHAPTER3 lacks CREATE SESSION privilege; logon denied
3. Oracle logs off the system account, leaving SQL*Plus running without a user logged in (see Figure 3.3)

CHANGING A USER'S SYSTEM PRIVILEGES

The error indicated in the preceding steps, ". . . lacks CREATE SESSION privilege . . . ," indicates that the newly created username and password exist, but they cannot log into the system. As a system manager, all you did in the previous steps was reserve the username *Chapter3* for a user, but you disallowed its use. A system manager must grant the user the ability to connect to the database, which requires that the user be able to create a session. The ability to do that is called the CREATE SESSION system privilege. Only a database administrator (DBA) or other super user can grant that privilege. You will do that next, because you can morph into a DBA by logging in via a privileged account, SYSTEM.

CHAPTER 3 Creating, Modifying, Renaming, and Deleting Database Tables

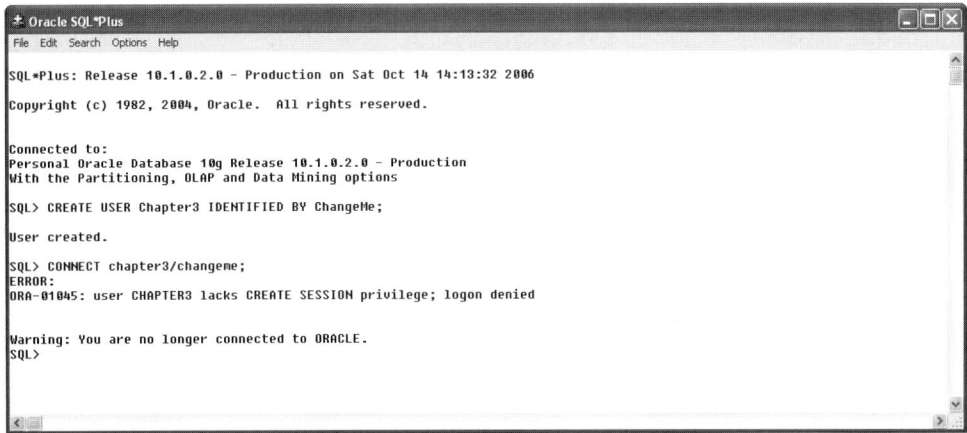

FIGURE 3.3 Attempting to log in with a new user account having no privileges.

To grant additional privileges to a user name:

1. Connect to Oracle through the DBA account, system. At the SQL prompt execute the statement. (We log in with username *system* and password *manager*. You use any suitable DBA-privilege account, as in the previous steps.):

   `CONNECT system/manager;`

2. Oracle issues the message "Connected." to indicate that you are logged in again.

3. Grant the CREATE SESSION and CREATE TABLE privileges, substituting the username you created previously for *chapter3*, by executing:

   `GRANT CREATE SESSION, CREATE TABLE TO chapter3;`

   Oracle responds "Grant succeeded."

4. Test the new user by logging on again. Type the username and password you created previously, such as:

   `CONNECT chapter3/changeme;`

   Oracle responds "Connected." Leave SQL*Plus running and remain logged in under your user account.

Changing Other Users' Passwords

If you can log on to Oracle using one of the database administrator (DBA) accounts such as SYSTEM, then you can change the password of any other user who has an account on your system. The same holds true for a database manager overseeing a client/server Oracle enterprise-class system. If users forget their passwords, or if you forget your password, the DBA can assign a new one. Because passwords are enciphered using a one-way encryption algorithm, even a DBA cannot reconstruct a forgotten password. However, a DBA can assign a new one to a user and cause the user to change it to a new password upon its first use. The optional PASSWORD EXPIRE phrase of the ALTER USER statement provides this capability. The simplified syntax for the ALTER USER statement to modify the password and require the user to change it upon first use is as follows:

`ALTER USER <username> IDENTIFIED BY <newpassword> PASSWORD EXPIRE`

The next steps change the chapter3 user's password to *Columbus* and force the user to change it when first logging into Oracle.

To change another user's password:

1. With SQL*Plus still open, switch back to the SYSTEM account by executing the following at the SQL prompt. (This assumes that the SYSTEM user still has the password *MANAGER*.):

   CONNECT SYSTEM/MANAGER;

2. Issue the following command to change the password for username Chapter3 to *Columbus*

   ALTER USER Chapter3 IDENTIFIED BY Columbus PASSWORD EXPIRE;

   Oracle responds with the affirming message "User altered."

3. Remember the password you type following the phrase "IDENTIFIED BY" because only you know it until you tell it to your user, Chapter3.

4. Type **CONNECT Chapter3/Columbus;** and press **Enter** to log into Oracle using the newly assigned password. Oracle indicates the password has expired and requests that the user change the password.

   > **Tip:** Passwords *are* case sensitive when you perform step 5, below. Be sure to capitalize the password the same way both times in step 5. Once changed, the password is no longer case sensitive.

5. Following the "New password:" prompt, type the new password, **Sherlock,** press **Enter,** type the password again (very carefully), and press **Enter.** If both spellings match and the case of each letter matches, Oracle responds with "Password changed" followed by "Connected." (See Figure 3.4.) Leave SQL*Plus running.

If you do not have the ability to log in to Oracle with DBA level privileges, you must ask the DBA to assign you a new password. On the other hand, it is a good idea to change your Oracle password periodically for security reasons.

CHANGING YOUR OWN PASSWORD

Any users can change their own passwords, and they can do so without asking the DBA. Once you are logged onto Oracle via SQL*Plus or *i*SQL*Plus, simply issue the PASSWORD command. After you enter PASSWORD, SQL*Plus prompts you to enter the old password and then asks you to enter the new password twice. Be sure to carefully spell the new password correctly both times and use matching case for every letter both times.

FIGURE 3.4 Changing another user's password.

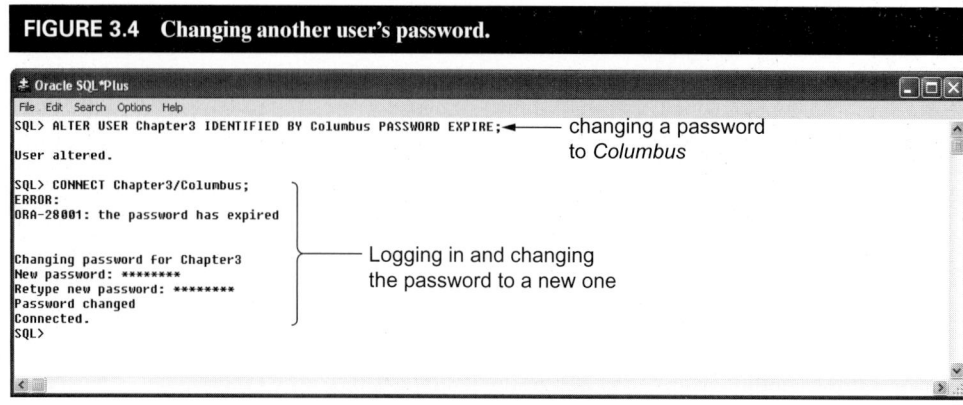

CHAPTER 3   Creating, Modifying, Renaming, and Deleting Database Tables   **99**

```
Oracle SQL*Plus
File  Edit  Search  Options  Help
SQL> DROP USER Chapter3 CASCADE;

User dropped.

SQL>
```

FIGURE 3.5   **Removing a user.**

To change your password:

1. Type **PASSWORD** and press **Enter**
2. Type the old password, **Sherlock** and press **Enter**
3. Type the new password, **Timecrunch** (or make up another one of your choosing) and press **Enter,** and repeat this once more.
4. The response "Password changed" appears, confirming that you changed the password. Leave SQL*Plus running.

REMOVING A USER

To make this session a round trip, you will remove the username *Chapter3* from the system. To remove a user, you must be logged in with the privileges that the SYSTEM account has. An "ordinary" user cannot delete a user from the system (thankfully). You delete a user with the DROP USER statement. Its syntax is pretty simple:

```
DROP USER <username> [CASCADE]
```

To delete a user:

1. Connect as a system user:

   CONNECT SYSTEM/MANAGER;

2. Drop the user Chapter3; type **DROP USER Chapter3 CASCADE;** and press **Enter.** Have patience. It takes a couple of seconds to remove the user and search for and remove any objects in the user's schema. Soon, Oracle responds "User dropped." (see Figure 3.5).
3. Type **Exit** and press **Enter** to log off Oracle and close SQL*Plus.

CREATING TABLES

Database tables are the structure in which all data is stored, and they are fundamental to a database. You create a new database table by specifying its name, the name of each data column, the type of data stored in that column, and the size of the data field. Optionally, you may specify column ***constraints,*** or restrictions, on the values that a field can hold. For instance, you might want the Gender field of an employee table to accept only M or F (uppercase only), or you might want the Title column in the Agents table or the Redwood Realty database to contain only the values "Broker" or "Salesperson." Another type of constraint prevents an empty value, called NULL, in a field because the user forgot to enter its value. (The next section discusses Constraints in detail.)

Oracle table names must adhere to the following rules. Table names:

- are from 1 to 30 characters long,
- begin with a character,
- can contains letters, numbers, and the special symbols $, _ (underscore), and #,
- must not contain blanks,
- must not duplicate the name of another object owned by the user (in the schema),
- must not be an Oracle reserved word,
- must not be the word DUAL, which is the name of a dummy table.

Table names are case insensitive. Therefore, the name *Customer, customer,* and *CuStOmEr* are identical in any SQL statement.

Delimited names are less restrictive than regular names described above. **Delimited names** refer to object names—tables, columns, etc.—that are enclosed in a set of double quotation marks such as the "CreditLimit" identifier. Although the quotation marks are not stored in the database, all the other characters are stored exactly as they appear in the SQL statement. Delimited names are case sensitive, so the names "CreditLimit" and CREDITLIMIT are different names, even though they are spelled the same. However, "CREDITLIMIT" and CreditLimit *are* the same name, because Oracle converts to uppercase all names that are not delimited. Spaces are allowed in delimited names, and SQL reserved words are permitted in delimited names. However, we recommend against using either SQL reserved words or spaces in delimited names. Whether you decide to user delimited names or not, the more important issue is to decide on one or the other and use it consistently.

As you may recall from Chapter 2, you use the CREATE TABLE statement to create a table. As a reminder, the simplified version of the state is as follows:

```
CREATE TABLE [schema.]table_name
(column_name type [NOT NULL]
[CONSTRAINT constraint_definition DEFAULT expression]
[,column_name type [NOT NULL]
[CONSTRAINT constraint_definition DEFAULT expression]…]
)
[PRIMARY KEY (column_name [,column_name …])
[FOREIGN KEY (column_name [,column_name …])
REFERENCES foreign_table (column_name [,column_name …])]
```

Table_name is the name you assign to the table, *column_name* is the name you assign to a column, and that is followed by one of the acceptable data types, such as numbers, dates, or characters. (The next section describes Oracle data types in detail.) The value following *DEFAULT* prevents NULL values from entering columns by inserting the default value specified. *Constraint_definition* specifies the definition of a constraint, or limitation, on the column. (Another section in this chapter describes constraints and gives several examples.) The full CREATE TABLE syntax is far richer than that shown above, and its details can be found in the SQL Reference manual from Oracle Corporation.

ORACLE DATA TYPES

Notice in the syntax of the CREATE TABLE statement that each column has its own data type, which follows the column name. The **data type** specifies, or limits, the type of data that the field holds. Oracle is particular about the data that each column stores for two reasons. First, knowing the type of data allows Oracle to allocate table space more

TABLE 3.1 Oracle character data types.

Type	Oracle Designation	Description
Fixed	CHAR(size)	Fixed-length character data of *size* characters padded with spaces. Maximum `size` is 2000 bytes.
Fixed National	NCHAR(size)	Same as CHAR except stores National characters of maximum length 2000 bytes.
Variable	VARCHAR2(size)	Variable-length character data of *size* characters. Maximum `size` is 4000 bytes.
Variable National	NVARCHAR2(size)	Variable-length character data of *size* National characters. Maximum `size` is 4000 bytes.
Memo	LONG	Character data of variable length up to 2 gigabytes. (Not recommended. Use CLOB data type instead.)

efficiently. Second, it allows Oracle to check for errors. If you attempt to store a character string in a salary field meant to hold numeric values, Oracle issues an error message and disallows the operation—before it can cause any harm. Oracle data types fall into four groups: character, numeric, date/time, and image. Of these, you will use character, numeric, and date/time most often.

CHARACTER DATA

Character data fields store alphanumeric values containing both text and numbers that are *not* used in calculations. Examples are student identification numbers, inventory parts numbers, and postal codes such as the U.S. ZIP code. Table 3.1 summarizes the Oracle character data types.

CHAR and NCHAR hold fixed-length character data and National character data. ***Fixed-length character*** data means character data in which the fields for different records are identical in length. You would use a CHAR field to store a student ID number of a ZIP code. They are always the same length. The syntax for a fixed-length character data type is:

```
<fieldname> CHAR(<length>)
```

For example, you could declare a ZIP code field in a Customer table this way:

```
Zipcode CHAR(5)
```

VARCHAR2 is a very popular and versatile data type. It holds a maximum of 4,000 characters. ***Variable-length character*** data is data whose length can vary from one record to another. For example, one employee's last name might be 20 characters long, whereas another person's last name in another record might be only 5 characters long. Variable length records conserve storage because they are not padded on the end to fill out the rest of the field to its maximum allowed length. NVARCHAR2 is similar to VARCHAR2, but it can hold National characters, which accommodate languages with a larger, more complex alphabets. You declare a VARCHAR2 field with this syntax:

```
<fieldname> VARCHAR2(maximum_size)
```

Most character fields in the Redwood Realty database are declared as variable-length National character fields to accommodate the widest types of character data. The LastName field in the Redwood Realty Agents table is declared this way:

```
LastName NVARCHAR2(30)
```

TABLE 3.2 Oracle numeric data types.

Type	Oracle Designation	Description
INT, INTEGER, SMALLINT	NUMBER(38)	An integer with up to 38 digits of precision.
Fixed precision	NUMBER(p,s)	A variable length number. Precision is the maximum number of digits, scale is the maximum number of digits to the right of the decimal point.
FLOAT, DOUBLE PRECISION	NUMBER	A floating-point number with up to 38 digits of precision.

This declaration supports variable length names up to 30 characters long. Memo fields, which are declared as LONG, are not often used. In its place, Oracle encourages you to use the CLOB data type (see below).

Numeric Data

Oracle uses the NUMBER data type for all numeric data. Numeric data stores signed, fixed-, and floating-point numbers with 38 digits of precision. (Any of those 38 digits may be in front of or behind the decimal point.) Always use the NUMBER field for any table columns upon which you want to perform arithmetic calculations. Table 3.2 lists the numeric data types along with a brief description of them. Oracle allows you to use INTEGER, INT, SMALLINT, DOUBLE PRECISION, FLOAT, REAL, DEC, DECIMAL and NUMERIC declarations. However, all such declarations are converted to the NUMBER data declaration. You declare all numeric fields with this syntax:

```
<fieldname> NUMBER [([precision,] [scale])]
```

Precision refers to the total number of digits that are stored in a number, and ***scale*** specifies the number of digits to the right of the decimal space. Because precision includes all the digits in the number, precision is always greater than or equal to scale. For example, the declaration

```
AmountDue NUMBER(7,2)
```

can store numbers as large as 99,999.99—seven total digits, two of which are to the right of the decimal point. NUMBER(4,4) specifies a number with four places to the right of the decimal point and none to the left.

An ***Integer*** is a whole number with no fractional part—you omit the scale part of the declaration. For instance,

```
AnnualSalary NUMBER(6)
```

specifies an integer field whose maximum value is the whole number 999,999 and whose minimum value is −999,999. If you attempt to store a number larger than the specified precision, Oracle generates an error. If you enter a value such as 23986.59 into the preceding AnnualSalary field, Oracle rounds the value to the nearest whole number—23,987 in this case.

A ***fixed-precision number*** contains a specific number of decimal places. Fixed-precision numbers appear with both the precision and scale specified. Both the latitude and the longitude of homes listed in the Redwood Realty Properties contain numbers with a precision of 8 and a scale of 5. Latitude and longitude values such as 183.5456 are represented in the database, pinpointing where the properties are in the world. The latitude column is declared this way:

```
Latitude NUMBER(8,5)
```

CHAPTER 3   Creating, Modifying, Renaming, and Deleting Database Tables   **103**

and can represent both positive and negative values corresponding to locations north and south of the Equator, respectively.

A *floating-point number* contains a variable number of decimal places. Digits can appear on either side of the decimal point, including numbers with no decimal places to the left of the decimal point and numbers with no decimal places to the right of the decimal point. Declare floating point numbers by specifying simply NUMBER, omitting the parentheses and numbers between them. Floating-point numbers are widely used in the scientific community, for example, to represent numbers very close to zero, and extremely large numbers. An example from the Redwood Realty database is the field holding the realtors' commission rates, which can be a percentage such as 4.125 percent (4 1/8 percent).

DATE AND TIME DATA

Oracle stores date and time values using three available data types: DATE, INTERVAL, and TIMESTAMP. DATE stores date and time information (*date/time* information), with the time portion rounded to the nearest full second. Oracle supports dates in the range January 1, 4712 B.C. to December 31, 4712 A.D. TIMESTAMP is a close relative of Date. It stores year, month, day, and time data. Unlike the DATE data type, TIMESTAMP also stores fractional seconds. An example is 17-OCT-06 11.02.24.00 AM. INTERVAL stores elapsed time interval between two date/time data types. Table 3.3 shows a summary of the Date and time data types available in Oracle.

The default output format of DATE columns is DD-MON-YY where DD is a two-digit date, MON is a three-character month abbreviation capitalized, and YY represents the last two digits of the year. The default time format is HH:MI:SS a.m., which displays the hour, minutes, and seconds using a 12-hour clock. If you omit the time when entering data into a DATE column, Oracle sets it to 12:00:00 A.M. If you omit setting the date when entering the time, the date portion of the column is set to the first day of the current month by default. Declare a DATE data type this way:

```
HireDate DATE
```

Several of the Redwood Realty database fields store DATE data, including the Agents table fields HireDate and BirthDate.

TIMESTAMP data stores date values with more precision in the time component—fractions of seconds. You can use timestamp data to record the exact time, based on the Oracle system clock, when a table was altered—or to track any time-sensitive changes

TABLE 3.3 Oracle date and time data types.

Type	Oracle Designation	Description
Date and time to whole seconds	DATE	Date and time with the century, all four digits of the year, month, day, hour, minute, and second.
Time interval in years	INTERVAL YEAR(p) TO MONTH	Time in years and months, where precision is the number of digits in the YEAR date/time field.
Time interval in days	INTERVAL DAY(p) TO SECOND(f)	Time in days, hours, minutes and seconds. Precision, p, is the max. number of digits in the day, and f is the number of fractional digits in the seconds field.
Date and Time to fractions of a second	TIMESTAMP(p)	Stores date and time to fractions of a second. Decimal places specified by precision in parentheses.

to database tables. It is the best way to store very precise time values. (You will learn how to use TIMESTAMP data in Chapter 4 in the auditing discussion.) You declare a TIMESTAMP column this way:

```
UpdateTableDateTime TIMESTAMP(2)
```

The value in parentheses—the precision—specifies the number of decimal places stored for fractional seconds. If you omit this value, Oracle uses the default of six decimal places.

The INTERVAL YEAR TO MONTH data type stores a time interval in years and months as a positive or negative value. If you add a positive time interval to a particular date/time value, it results in a date after the particular date. Conversely, adding a negative time interval to a given date results in a date earlier than the given date. The form of stored value is:

```
+ or - <elapsed years>-<elapsed months>
```

Where the + or – indicates a positive or negative time interval and precedes the number pair. The "<elapsed years>" represents the years part of the interval, and the "<elapsed months>" represents the months portion of the time interval. They are separated by a hyphen. For example, the elapsed interval of +06−09 represents a positive time interval of six years and nine months. You declare a time interval in this way:

```
TimeSinceLastOfficeVisit INTERVAL YEAR(2) TO MONTH
```

and indicate that the year portion of the time interval is expressed in two digits (for example, 02 for 2002). Such fields can be useful in capturing the time spent, year to date, on an annual work project.

The INTERVAL DAY TO SECOND data records elapsed time expressed in hours, minutes, and seconds. The data form is

```
+ or - <days>  <hours>:<minutes>:<seconds>
```

For example, the date +06 07:26:51.00 represents a positive elapsed time of 6 days, 7 hours, 26 minutes, and 51 seconds. Following is an example of how you might declare an INTERVAL DAY TO SECOND column:

```
TimeTrials INTERVAL DAY TO SECOND
```

You will need to understand some of these data types and the way they appear when you display them. Execute the following steps to run a script to review some number and date data types. You have the choice, as usual, of using SQL*Plus or *i*SQL*Plus. In this case, running the script file using the *i*SQL*Plus interface is better because some of the columns are very wide and do not display as well in SQL*Plus. The script file builds a table called DemoDataTypes, places one row into the table, issues a SELECT statement to display the row, and deletes the table to return the database to its original state. First, locate the data file Ch03DataTypes.sql. Make a note of its full path.

To review some data types available in Oracle:

1. Launch *i*SQL*Plus and log into Oracle with your username and password.
2. Once you are logged in, click the **Load Script** button, click the **Browse** button next to the *File* text box, use the *Look in* list box to navigate to the folder containing Ch03DataTypes.sql, click **Ch03DataTypes.sql**, and click the **Open** button.
3. Click the *i*SQL*Plus **Load** button to load the script into the Workspace text box. Scroll the box to examine the code. It begins with a CREATE TABLE statement to create three types of numeric fields followed by three types of date/time fields.

CHAPTER 3 Creating, Modifying, Renaming, and Deleting Database Tables   **105**

4. Click the **Execute** button to run the script. Two informative messages appear along with a display of the single row of the table followed by a *Table dropped* statement (see Figure 3.6).
5. Optionally, you can print the Web page to examine it in detail later.
6. Click the **Logout** hyperlink near the top of the page to exit *i*SQL*Plus, and then close your browser.

The first three values displayed are all the same number stored in three different numeric data types. Study their differences. The next two fields are date/time values. Notice the difference between DATE and TIMESTAMP in the fractions of seconds. Finally, you see an example of a time interval of almost 326 days.

IMAGE DATA

To store amorphous data such as employees' pictures, sounds, or binary files such as Word or Excel documents, turn to one of the Oracle large object (LOB) data types. Table 3.4 summarizes the LOB data types.

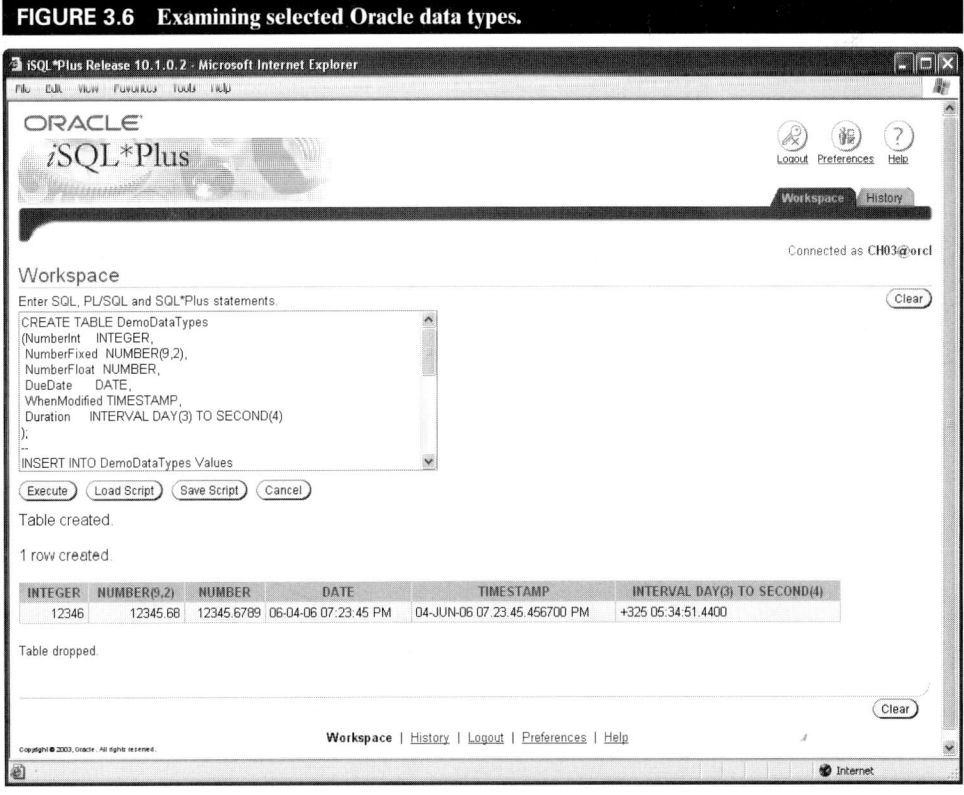

FIGURE 3.6 Examining selected Oracle data types.

TABLE 3.4   Oracle image data types.

Oracle Designation	*Description*
BLOB	Binary LOB stores binary, unstructured data up to 128 terabytes.
CLOB	Character LOB stores character data for very large objects—up to 128 terabytes.
NCLOB	Variable length Unicode national character data up to 128 terabytes.

TABLE 3.5 Customers table column names and data types.

Column Name	Data Type	Maximum Length	Special Conditions
CustomerID	Integer		primary key
FirstName	National, variable length string	30	not null
LastName	National, variable length string	30	not null
Address	National, variable length string	40	
City	National, variable length string	30	
State	National, variable length string	20	
Zipcode	National, variable length string	20	
HomePhone	National, variable length string	20	
CellPhone	National, variable length string	20	
WorkPhone	National, variable length string	20	

Declare a column to have one of the data types shown in Figure 3.4 using this:

```
<imageitemname> BLOB
```

You can substitute the appropriate LOB item for "BLOB" above for other data types in the same family. Do not specify a length, because Oracle automatically allocates enough space to hold the item. An extension to the Redwood Realty database would be to include a column containing a picture of each home for sale. A convenient place for such a column would be in the Listings table, which lists properties for sale.

CREATING A TABLE USING SQL*PLUS

A central table in the Redwood Realty database is Customers. Its rows will contain contact information about customers including first and last names, address, and phone numbers. Table 3.5 shows the Customers table column names and their data types and lengths. You will create this table next. However, before building any tables in your schema, you must clear out previously created Redwood Realty tables so that there is no conflict with the new ones you will create.

> **Tip:** We will ask you to do this as one of the first activities in each chapter so you start with a "clean" database. The script file you are about to run deletes all the Redwood Realty tables, but no others.

Before executing the steps below, note the full path to the script file we have supplied called Ch03InitializeRedwood.sql and write it down. You will need it in the exercise.

To initialize the Redwood Realty database:

1. Launch SQL*Plus: click **Start,** point to **All Programs,** point to **Oracle-OraDb10_home1,** point to **Application Development,** and click **SQL Plus.** (Consider making SQL Plus a shortcut on your desktop to simplify launching it.) The Log On dialog box appears.

2. Type your username in the User Name text box, type your password in the Password box, and click **OK.** (These instructions assume you are using Personal Oracle. You may have to use a Host String value on other installations. In this case, check with your instructor.)

3. Type the following and press **Enter** to execute the script file:

   START <path>\Ch03InitializeRedwood.sql

   No messages appear because the script file suppresses them. Your schema is initialized.

4. Leave SQL*Plus running.

CHAPTER 3   Creating, Modifying, Renaming, and Deleting Database Tables   **107**

Next, you will create the Customers table. All the character string fields are defined with the data type NVARCHAR2, which allows National characters to be used, and varying length strings. The only other data type is INTEGER, which defines a fixed-point number that is the unique identifier assigned to each customer in the table.

To create the Customers table:

1. Ensure that you are still logged into Oracle using the SQL*Plus client.
2. Type **CLEAR SCREEN** and press **Enter** to clear the screen.
3. Type the following, pressing **Enter** at the end of each line to move to the next line. Remember to type the right parenthesis and terminating semicolon on the last line:

> **Tip:** You do not have to add spaces at the beginning of each line for the column definitions. Also, you need not bother with capitalization of any words below. We did so to separate Oracle key words from user-defined names. Ignore capitalization everywhere to save time. The results are the same either way.

```
CREATE TABLE Customers
 (CustomerID INTEGER,
  FirstName NVARCHAR2(30),
  LastName NVARCHAR2(30),
  Address NVARCHAR2(40),
  City NVARCHAR2(30),
  State NVARCHAR2(20),
  Zipcode NVARCHAR2(20),
  HomePhone NVARCHAR2(20),
  CellPhone NVARCHAR2(20),
  WorkPhone NVARCHAR2(20)
 );
```

4. If needed, press **Enter** to send the CREATE TABLE statement to SQL*Plus for validation and on to Oracle for execution. If mistakes occur, type **Edit** at the SQL prompt, correct the mistakes in the Notepad editor, click **File,** click **Save,** and close Notepad. SQL*Plus becomes active with the altered statement rewritten. Press **/** (slash) and press **Enter** to execute the corrected statement.

   Oracle responds with the message "Table created."

5. Type **Describe Customers** and press **Enter** to display the way Oracle defined the table you just created (see Figure 3.7). Notice that Oracle created a NUMBER(38) CustomerID field in place of your INTEGER declaration.
6. Leave SQL*Plus running for the time being.

ADDING TABLE AND COLUMN COMMENTS

Oracle stores information about all your objects—tables, views, columns, and so forth—in a set of its own system tables. (We'll make use of Oracle's system tables near the end of this chapter.) For example, Oracle stores commentary data about tables and columns in its own system tables. The SQL command COMMENT allows you to add comments about tables or columns. The comments you add do not affect the contents or operation of the tables or columns to which they are attached. Comments provide a small amount of documentation about the purpose and use of a table or its columns. They can be particularly useful to anyone who is unfamiliar with all the tables in a database and needs to learn quickly why they exist and how they relate to other tables.

108 Introduction to Oracle

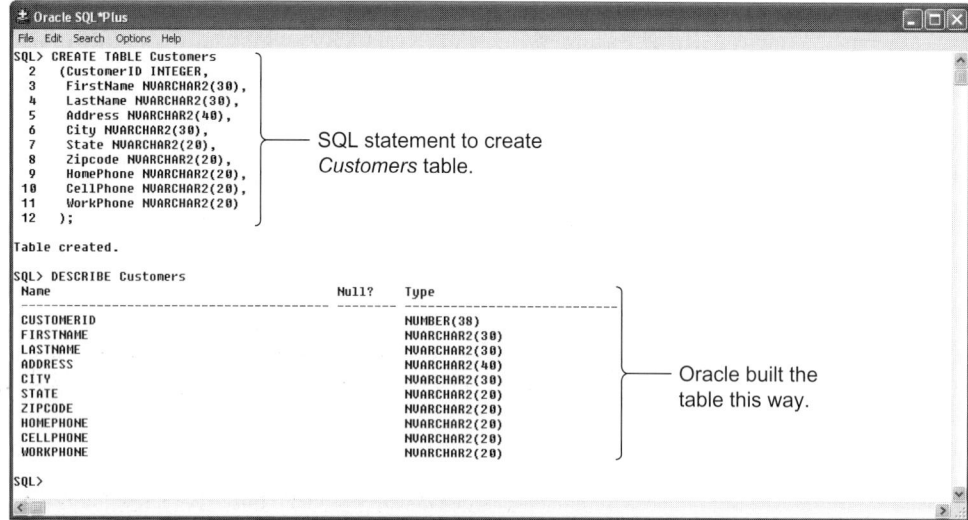

FIGURE 3.7 Creating a table using the SQL*Plus interface.

Next, you'll add comments to the Customers table you create and then display the comments you added by interrogating one of Oracle's system tables. The simplified syntax of the COMMENT command to add a table comment is:

```
COMMENT ON TABLE <tablename> IS '<text>'
```

You can remove a comment from a table by entering an empty string (leave the text out) with the COMMENT command.

To add a comment to a table:

1. With SQL*Plus running and you logged into Oracle, type **CLEAR SCREEN** to clear the display.
2. Type the following SQL command and press **Enter** to execute it.

   ```
   COMMENT ON TABLE Customers IS
   'People who want to buy or sell a property';
   ```

   Oracle responds with "Comment created."
3. Display the comment by executing these SQL*Plus and SQL statements. Be sure to type CUSTOMERS in uppercase or the statement will not work properly:

   ```
   COLUMN comments FORMAT A40 WORD_WRAPPED
   SELECT table_name, comments
   FROM user_tab_comments
   WHERE table_name = 'CUSTOMERS';
   ```

   Figure 3.8 shows the result.
4. Type **Exit** to log out of Oracle and close the SQL*Plus dialog box.

You create *column* comments in a similar way. For example, to place a comment on the State column of the Customers table, you would execute the command:

```
COMMENT ON COLUMN Customers.State IS
'The state should ALWAYS be California';
```

CHAPTER 3 Creating, Modifying, Renaming, and Deleting Database Tables 109

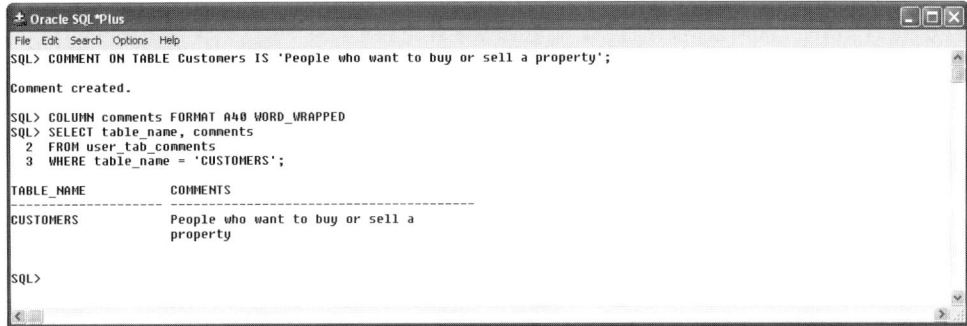

FIGURE 3.8 Creating and displaying a table comment.

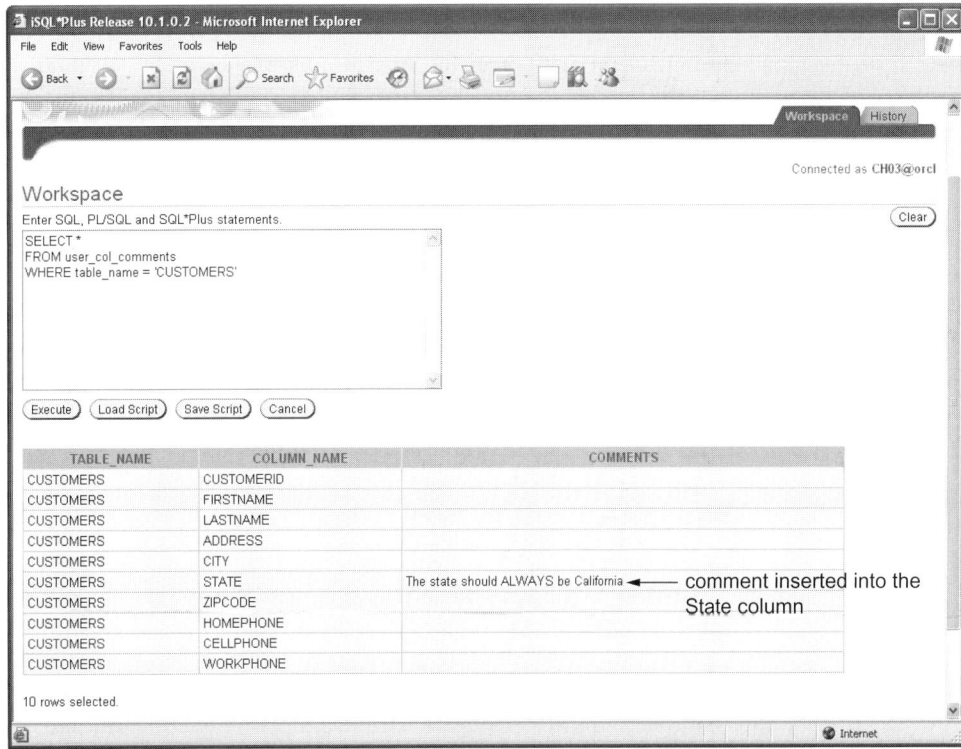

FIGURE 3.9 Column comment example.

in which you use a table name followed by a period followed by the field name, State. The table name is needed in case there is more than one table in your schema that has a State column. You can execute a statement such as this one to display column comments in the Customers table:

```
SELECT *
FROM user_col_comments
WHERE table_name = 'CUSTOMERS';
```

Figure 3.9 shows the result of the preceding query.

DEFINING AND USING CONSTRAINTS

The Customers table you created above contains column names and data types properly defined. It's not sufficient for Oracle to simply store data. Its tables must ensure that the data they contain are accurate and consistent, and that they maintain integrity with other, related tables.

UNDERSTANDING CONSTRAINTS

SQL defines a series of integrity and domain constraints that enforce rules on tables, ensuring that the data remains reasonable and accurate. *Integrity constraints* are rules that are applied to tables and table columns in which they appear that constrain the values that are inserted into the tables. Specifically, integrity constraints identify which columns are primary keys (PRIMARY KEY) and which are foreign keys (FOREIGN KEY . . . REFERENCES). Recall that a primary key is one or more columns that uniquely identify a row in a table; a foreign key, remember, is a column that matches a primary key in another table. *Domain constraints* define specific data values or value ranges that are permitted in columns in which they appear. They can specify that a column value cannot be empty (NOT NULL), that it must be unique among all the other values (UNIQUE) in that column, or that only selected ranges of values are allowed in the column (CHECK). For example, a domain constraint might state that the value of the Gender column must be either M (for male) or F (for female)—capitalized. A range constraint might indicate that the CommissionRate column values are limited to the range of 1 percent to 6 percent and cannot be empty (NOT NULL). You can apply constraints to individual columns, called column constraints, to individual tables, or to multiple tables. The latter two are called table constraints. You can list column constraints immediately following the column name and data type declaration, or you can list some or all column constraints at the end of the CREATE TABLE command, just before the terminating right parenthesis. Table constraints must appear at the end of the CREATE TABLE command.

NAMING CONSTRAINTS

SQL provides these five constraints: CHECK, FOREIGN KEY, NOT NULL, PRIMARY KEY, and UNIQUE. Every constraint in the user schema must have a unique name. Either you define the name or Oracle generates it automatically. If you choose to name all your constraints explicitly, then you should decide on a naming convention for them and stick to it. In this text, we follow this procedure to create unique and informative constraint names. Any convention established to name a constraint is called a *constraint naming convention.* The constraint naming convention we follow throughout this textbook is that integrity constraints names are of the form:

```
{pk|fk}_<primary_key_table_name>_<foreign_key_table_name>
```

For example, a primary key column in the Customer table would have the name pk_customer, where *pk* refers to primary key. Similarly, a foreign key column in the Agents table referring to a primary key column in the LicenseStatus table would be named fk_licensestatus_agents (primary key table first, foreign key table second). Of course, Oracle stores object names in uppercase unless you use quotation marks to surround the name (resist doing it, though), so capitalization doesn't matter.

We name domain constraints with this general form:

```
{nn|un|cc}_<tablename>_<columnname>
```

TABLE 3.6 Constraint prefixes and example constraint names.

Constraint Type	Constraint Type Prefix	Example Constraint Name
CHECK	ck	ck_customers_zipcode
FOREIGN KEY	fk	fk_customers_properties
NOT NULL	nn	nn_agents_lastname
PRIMARY KEY	pk	pk_agentid
UNIQUE	un	un_contactreason_description

For instance, nn_agents_lastname is the name you assign the NOT NULL domain constraint of the LastName column in the Agents table. Due to the 30-character length limitation, you may need to shorten some names. For example, ck_custagentlist_commrate is the shortened name we assign to a check constraint for the CommissionRate column of the CustAgentList table. Table 3.6 summarizes these constraint naming conventions. There are several online resources you can consult to learn about naming constraints.

DEFINING CONSTRAINTS

Before you create tables containing constraints, let's look at the individual constraints in more detail, starting with the integrity constraints.

PRIMARY KEY CONSTRAINTS

A *primary key constraint* ensures that all values in the column in which it is declared are not null and are unique. Every table should have one primary key consisting of one column or a combination of columns. When multiple columns constitute a table's primary key, the *combination* of column values must be unique, although individual column values may not be. A multicolumn primary key is also called a **compound primary key** (another synonym for *composite primary key*). You define a single-column primary key either as a column constraint or as a table constraint. You must define a compound primary key as a table constraint.

Define a primary key column constraint by including the phrase PRIMARY KEY at the end of the primary key's column definition. For example, you could declare the CustomerID column of the Customers table to be the primary key by substituting this phrase in the CREATE TABLE statement you executed earlier:

```
CustomerID INTEGER PRIMARY KEY
```

Alternatively, you can define a name for the primary key using this form:

```
CustomerID INTEGER CONSTRAINT pk_customers PRIMARY KEY
```

where <constraint-name> is a unique name identifying the constraint and follows our convention of *pk* followed by an underline followed by the table name (all in lowercase). You can define a primary key as a table constraint by placing it at the end of the CREATE TABLE statement, after all field declarations. In the CREATE TABLE statement that employs a table constraint to declare the primary key, the last three lines are:

```
...
WorkPhone NVARCHAR2(20),
CONSTRAINT pk_customers PRIMARY KEY (CustomerID)
);
```

Declare a composite primary key at the end of the CREATE TABLE statement. For example, the Redwood Realty table CustAgentList table's primary key consists of the columns CustomerID, AgentID, ListingID, and ContactDate. Its PRIMARY KEY phrase is:

```
…
CommissionRate NUMERIC(4,4),
CONSTRAINT pk_CustAgentList PRIMARY KEY (CustomerID, AgentID, ListingID,
ContactDate)
);
```

Notice that a primary key column constraint, unlike a table constraint form, does not name the primary key column. That is because the phrase is part of the column declaration. However, column names do appear in the table constraint version of the primary key declaration.

FOREIGN KEY CONSTRAINTS

Foreign key constraints are related to primary key constraints. While primary key constraints ensure the integrity of the data in a table and uniquely identify each row, a *foreign key constraint* specifies that a field must exist as a primary key in another, referenced table. This is known as a *referential constraint.* Using the metaphor that foreign key tables are the children of a primary key row, a foreign key ensures that the child has a parent. A common example is the relationship between a table containing orders and a table containing line items comprising those orders. Maintaining a database table's integrity means preserving the primary key-to-foreign key relationships. With a referential constraint in place, you cannot delete a primary key field containing rows unless you first delete all the rows that refer to it via their foreign keys.

As with primary key constraints, you can declare a foreign key along with the column declaration (column constraint) or independently of it at the end of the CREATE TABLE statement (table constraint). The simplified syntax of the column constraint foreign key is:

```
<column-name> <datatype> [CONSTRAINT <constraint-name>]
REFERENCES <tablename> [(column-name)] [ON DELETE {CASCADE | SET NULL}]
```

The optional clause ON DELETE specifies what to do if parent rows are deleted. CASCADE indicates that all child rows are deleted when a related parent table row is deleted. If you omit the CASCADE option, Oracle prevents deletions of referenced parent table rows if there are dependent rows in the child table.

Here are some examples of column constraint foreign keys in which the foreign key, OwnerID, references the primary key CustomerID in the Customers table:

```
OwnerID INTEGER CONSTRAINT fk_customers_properties              (1)
    REFERENCES Customers (CustomerID)
OwnerID INTEGER REFERENCES Customers (CustomerID)               (2)
OwnerID INTEGER REFERENCES Customers                            (3)
```

In Example 1, we name the constraint, the table, and column it references. Example 2 doesn't name the constraint. Example 3 is the shortest way to specify a foreign key for OwnerID. It does not mention the CustomerID column. When you omit the name of the primary key following the name of the referenced table, Oracle automatically assigns the referenced table's primary key field. The name of the foreign key and primary key do not have to be identical, but the data type and length of the two fields must agree. Foreign keys usually reference primary keys, but occasionally they can reference unique fields in another table. The UNIQUE constraint is covered later in this section.

Adding a foreign key *table constraint* is similar, except that the statement appears at the end of the CREATE TABLE statement and contains the phrase "FOREIGN

KEY." The simplified form of the foreign key table constraint is:

```
[CONSTRAINT <constraint-name>] FOREIGN KEY (<column-name>)
REFERENCES <primary-key-tablename> [(primary-key-column-name)]
[ON DELETE {CASCADE | SET NULL}]
```

In the preceding syntax, "<column-name>" identifies the column that is the foreign key, "<primary-key-tablename>" identifies the name of the table containing the referenced primary key, and "<primary-key-column-name>" identifies the column containing the referenced primary key. You have the option of writing a table constraint to identify a foreign key. For example, the following foreign key table constraint links the foreign key LicenseStatusID to the like-named column in the LicenseStatus table.

```
CREATE TABLE Agents
(AgentID INTEGER PRIMARY KEY,
...
CONSTRAINT fk_licensestatus_agents FOREIGN KEY (LicenseStatusID)
    REFERENCES LicenseStatus(LicenseStatusID)
);
```

> **Tip:** Before you can create a foreign key referencing another table, the referenced table must already exist and must contain a PRIMARY KEY constraint.

NOT NULL CONSTRAINTS

The ***NOT NULL*** constraint prevents a column's values from being empty, or NULL. In other words, you must specify a value for any column containing the NOT NULL statement or arrange for a default value to be supplied if you don't supply one explicitly. The NOT NULL constraint is a column constraint only. Use NOT NULL constraints sparingly, because the value of noncritical columns is not always known when someone inserts a new record into a table. Primary key columns automatically have the NOT NULL constraint because a primary key, by definition, cannot be null. Though not required, most foreign key columns are implicitly NOT NULL because they almost always point to an existing primary key column in another table. You can supply an optional constraint name for NOT NULL declarations. We have chosen to not name them throughout this book.

The first few columns of the Redwood Realty Properties table contain two columns whose values cannot be omitted—Address and City. To request Oracle to enforce that rule, simply include the NOT NULL option in the column declaration for each column you want to always contain a value:

```
CREATE TABLE Properties
(PropertyID INTEGER PRIMARY KEY,
...
Address NVARCHAR2(30) NOT NULL,
City NVARCHAR2(30) NOT NULL,
State NVARCHAR2(20),
...
```

The preceding NOT NULL statements ensure that every property has an address and city. A value in the State column is not required, however. You can choose to name the NOT NULL constraints, but the columns containing NOT NULL are distinguished from others when you issue the DESCRIBE <tablename> statement. Figure 3.10 shows an example with columns of the Coffee Merchant's Orders table explicitly marked "NOT NULL." ORDERID is the primary key column. Thus, it is automatically assigned the NOT NULL constraint.

114 Introduction to Oracle

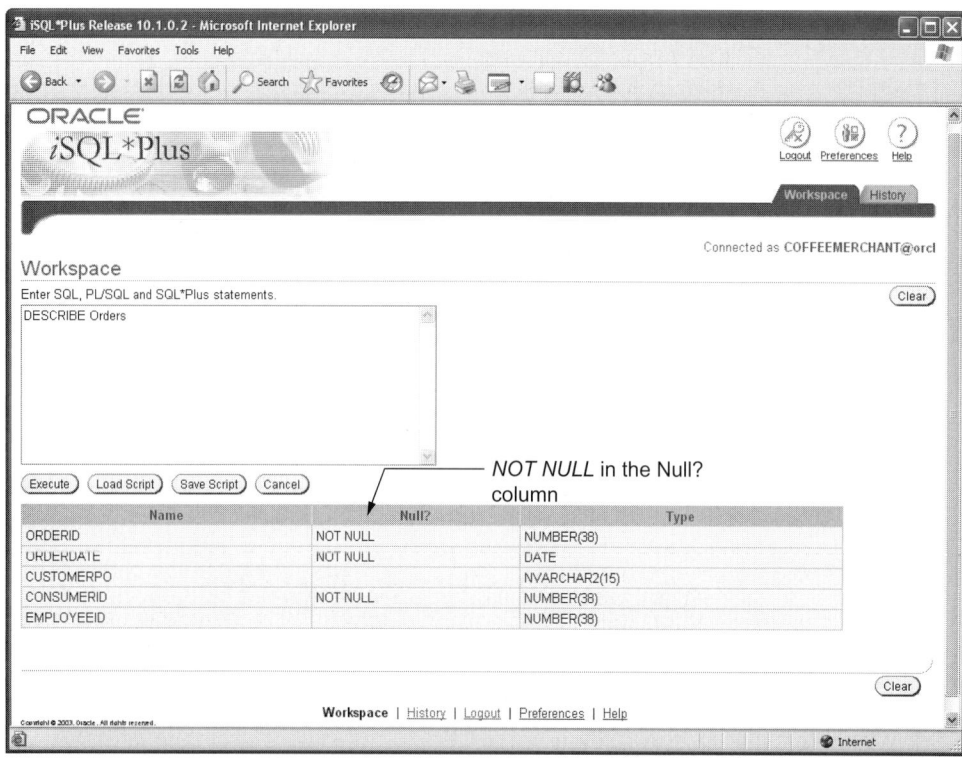

FIGURE 3.10 Displaying NOT NULL constraints using the DESCRIBE statement.

UNIQUE CONSTRAINTS

A *UNIQUE constraint* specifies that all the values in the column in which it occurs must be the only one of its kind—no value may be repeated. All primary keys have the UNIQUE constraint automatically, because primary keys must be unique. The major difference between a PRIMARY KEY constraint and a UNIQUE constraint is that a UNIQUE constraint allows null values. You can write a UNIQUE constraint as either a column constraint or a table constraint. Phone numbers or social security numbers are examples of columns that should have the UNIQUE constraint—if they are not primary keys. For example, the Redwood Realty LicenseStatus table that contains the number and descriptions for real estate license conditions holds unique text values such as "Licenses" and "Revoked" to describe a realtor's license situation. To ensure that those values are unique—without duplicates, you can include UNIQUE in the column definition for StatusText when you create the Redwood table. From that point forward, Oracle always ensures that any value anyone attempts to insert into the StatusText column is one of a kind. Here's an example using the column constraint form of the UNIQUE constraint.

```
CREATE TABLE LicenseStatus
   (LicenseStatusID INTEGER PRIMARY KEY,
    StatusText NVARCHAR2(25) UNIQUE);
```

An example of a UNIQUE table constraint is as follows:

```
CREATE TABLE MovieCollection
   (MovieID INTEGER PRIMARY KEY,
    DirectorName VARCHAR2(30) NOT NULL,
    CONSTRAINT un_directorname_moviecoll UNIQUE(DirectorName));
```

One major difference between the column and table forms of the UNIQUE constraint is that only one column in a table may have the column constraint UNIQUE stated. You can have many columns with the UNIQUE constraint if you use the table constraint form.

CHECK CONSTRAINTS

A **CHECK constraint** enforces a logical expression on a column that must evaluate to true for all values in the column. This is a terrific tool for enforcing business rules limiting the acceptable values that can appear in a column. For example, a business rule for the Redwood Realty database is that the commission rate can range from, say, 1 percent to 6 percent—no higher and no lower. Similarly, the Gender column can contain only M or F (uppercase). Be careful specifying CHECK constraints. Once you define a CHECK constraint and a table is filled, it is very difficult to alter the constraint. The CHECK condition must evaluate to true or false to be valid, and you can use relational operators, logical operations, and set operators (described later) to write the CHECK condition that Oracle tests for each new value about to be inserted into a column containing the CHECK constraint. The syntax for the CHECK column constraint is

```
CONSTRAINT <constraint-name> CHECK (<logical expression>)
```

For instance, you could include the following CHECK constraint in the CREATE TABLE statement to constrain values of the Agents table Title column values to "Broker" or "Salesperson" to ensure consistent spelling and capitalization:

```
CREATE TABLE Agents
...
HomePhone NVARCHAR2(20),
Title NVARCHAR2(20) CONSTRAINT ck_agents_title
     CHECK ((Title = 'Broker') OR (Title = 'Salesperson')),
...
```

Enforcing business rules to ensure that values fall within a range are straightforward. Use a CHECK condition such as the following, which allows values for ComRate of 1 percent to 6 percent, inclusive. The constraint is not named in this example. If you do not assign a constraint name, Oracle generates an internal, unique, and inscrutable name for you.

```
...
ComRate NUMBER(4,4) CHECK (ComRate >= 0.01 AND ComRate < 0.06),
...
```

If you subsequently attempt to insert a value such as 0.08 percent into the ComRate column, Oracle returns the error message

```
ORA-02290: check constraint(<yourschema>.SYS_<checkname>) violated
```

where "<yourschema>" is your username and "<checkname>" is the Oracle-generated constraint name assigned to the ComRate CHECK constraint.

CREATING COLUMN AND TABLE CONSTRAINTS

You learn how to create column and table constraints by using the Oracle's database interface tools, SQL*Plus and *i*SQL*Plus. If you feel more comfortable with one of these tools, please feel free to use it exclusively. We feature a mixture of both interfaces so you become comfortable using them. As you recall, you start the SQL*Plus program and then you log into Oracle. You will create several of the Redwood Realty tables and assign various constraints to selected fields. First, you will create the ContactReason table. When populated later, the ContactReason table rows will contain a text phrase indicating why someone contacted the broker (buy, sell, casual) and a primary key for each row. In the future, bear in mind that when you create tables that contain foreign

TABLE 3.7 ContactReason column names, data types, and constraint.

Column Name	Data Type	Length	Constraint
ContactReason	NVARCHAR2	15	PRIMARY KEY
Description	NVARCHAR2	50	

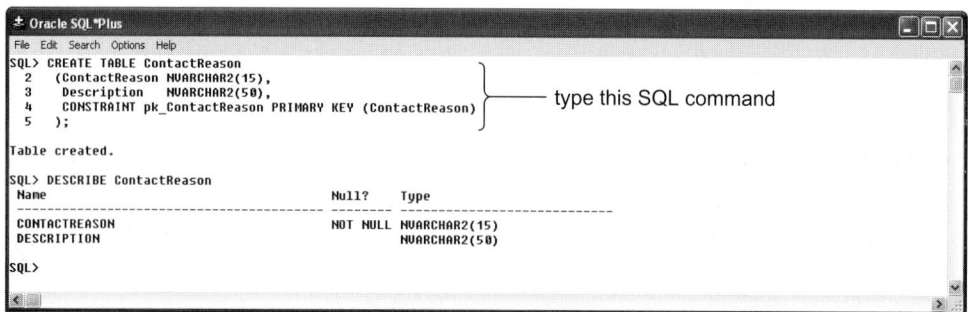

FIGURE 3.11 Defining a primary key.

key references to other tables, you should build the tables to which they refer first—tables which contain no foreign keys—if possible. Sometimes you cannot do this. In this case, you will have to either defer the foreign key constraints or alter affected tables *after* building them. Both of these topics—deferring constraints and altering tables—appear later in this chapter in detail.

Table 3.7 shows the column names, column characteristics, and constraints for the ContactReason table you are about to create.

To create the ContactReason table:

1. Launch SQL*Plus, if necessary, and log into the database.
2. In SQL*Plus, type the command on multiple lines as shown in Figure 3.11, but do not type the line numbers, because SQL*Plus adds those automatically. Remember: Press **Enter** to move to a new line.
3. Type **;** (semicolon) as the last character of the last line and then press **Enter** to execute the CREATE TABLE statement.

> **Tip:** If Oracle generates an error message, remember you can select the CREATE TABLE statement in its entirety (but not the line numbers, SQL prompt, or Oracle messages), click **Edit,** click **Copy,** open Notepad, and click **Edit** followed by **Paste** to copy the text to Notepad. Correct the mistake, then reverse the process: Copy from Notepad to the Clipboard, then switch to SQL*Plus and paste the corrected code. Press **Enter,** if needed, to execute the corrected code.

4. Type **DESCRIBE ContactReason** and press **Enter** to display the structure of the newly defined table (see Figure 3.11). Notice the ContactReason column contains the NOT NULL constraint applied automatically because the column is a primary key.

In the steps above, you defined and named a primary key as a table constraint, because it appears after both columns are defined. Table 3.8 lists the columns and constraints for the Agents table. Refer to it as you create the table in the following steps.

CHAPTER 3 Creating, Modifying, Renaming, and Deleting Database Tables

TABLE 3.8 Structure of the Agents table.

Column Name	Data Type	Length	Constraint
AgentID	INTEGER		PRIMARY KEY
FirstName	NVARCHAR2	30	NOT NULL
LastName	NVARCHAR2	30	NOT NULL
HireDate	DATE		
BirthDate	DATE		
Gender	NVARCHAR2	10	Only allowed values are 'M' and 'F'
WorkPhone	NVARCHAR2	20	
CellPhone	NVARCHAR2	20	UNIQUE
HomePhone	NVARCHAR2	20	
Title	NVARCHAR2	20	
TaxID	NVARCHAR2	20	
LicenseID	NVARCHAR2	20	
LicenseDate	DATE		
LicenseExpire	DATE		
LicenseStatusID	INTEGER		

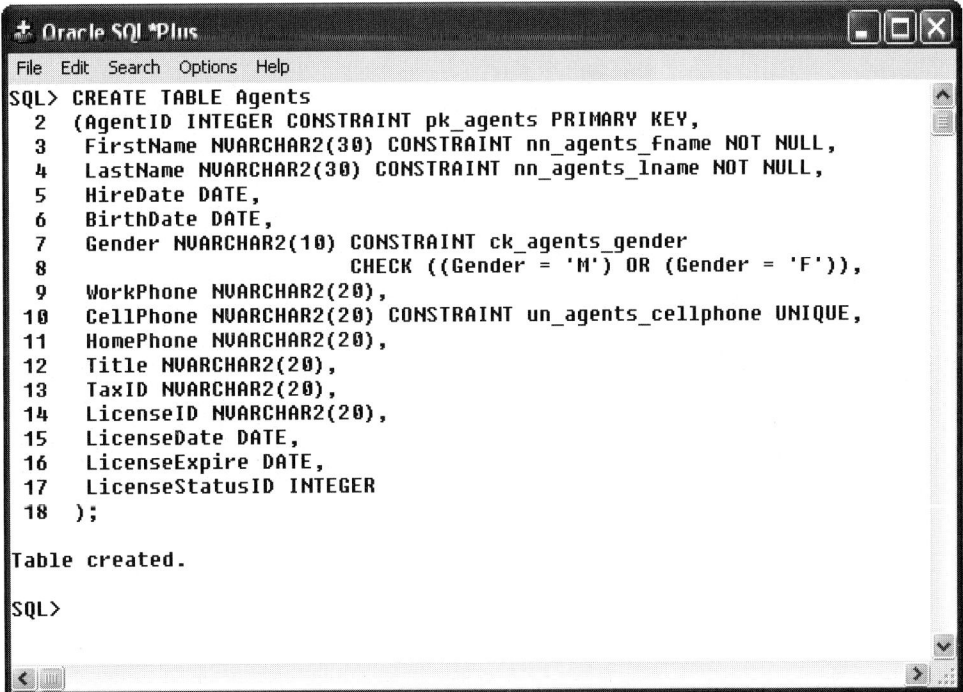

FIGURE 3.12 Creating the Agents table with constraints.

To create the Agents table:

1. Type **CLEAR SCREEN** and press **Enter** to clear the screen.
2. Type and execute the CREATE TABLE statement shown in Figure 3.12. Remember to use Notepad to make any corrections and copy the corrected statement back to SQL*Plus.
3. Type **DESCRIBE Agents** and press **Enter** to list the columns and the NOT NULL constraints.

You probably noticed that only the NOT NULL constraint appears when you execute the DESCRIBE command. How do you verify that the other constraints are in effect on your tables? Read on.

ASSIGNING DEFAULT VALUES TO COLUMNS

Specifying a default value for a column is a handy feature supported by SQL. A default value is one that is inserted into a table column whenever a user omits it while inserting other fields in the row of the table. You declare that a column has a default value followed by that value in this way in the CREATE TABLE statement:

```
<column-name> <column-type> DEFAULT <expression>
```

The default value, indicated by "<expression>" above, can be a constant, an expression involving mathematical operators, and most SQL functions (with a few exceptions), to name a few. In its simplest form, a default value is a constant.

In the steps that follow, you will create the Listings table and designate a primary key (PK) constraint, a NOT NULL constraint, and two default values. The Listings table lists all the properties for sale. The latter will automatically insert values into two optional columns if the data entry person omits them during an INSERT operation. The Oracle built-in function SYSDATE, which delivers the current date and time, automatically fills the BeginListDate field, if omitted during data entry. A date 180 days from the current date fills in the EndListDate field if it is omitted during row insertion. That guarantees that the two DATE columns have a value—either user supplied or automatically supplied.

To create the Listings table, complete with constraints and default values:

1. Type **CLEAR SCREEN** and press **Enter** to clear the display.
2. Type the CREATE TABLE statement shown in Figure 3.13. You can use Notepad to compose the SQL statement and then copy it into SQL*Plus.
3. Execute the CREATE TABLE statement by pressing **Enter** following the semicolon ending the statement. Oracle responds with "Table created." Correct any errors, and execute the corrected statement. Leave SQL*Plus running.

Notice that we omitted the constraint name for the NOT NULL constraint on the ListingAgentID column. Oracle automatically generates a unique constraint name of its own for that column constraint.

FIGURE 3.13 Designating default values for selected table columns.

```
SQL> CREATE TABLE Listings
  2   (ListingID       INTEGER   CONSTRAINT pk_listings PRIMARY KEY,
  3    PropertyID      INTEGER   CONSTRAINT nn_listings_propertyid NOT NULL,
  4    ListingAgentID  INTEGER   NOT NULL,
  5    SaleStatusID    INTEGER,
  6    BeginListDate   DATE      DEFAULT SYSDATE,
  7    EndListDate     DATE      DEFAULT SYSDATE + 180,
  8    AskingPrice     NUMERIC(9)
  9   );

Table created.

SQL>
```

ALTERING A TABLE AND ITS CONSTRAINTS

After creating a table, you sometimes have to change some attribute in the table. You issue the ALTER TABLE command, in concert with the DROP, MODIFY, ADD, and RENAME clauses to make those changes. Transformations you can make include adding or deleting columns, altering the data type or length of columns, and changing the default values for columns. In addition, you can drop, add, enable, disable, or rename tables' constraints. The ALTER TABLE statement can avoid the tricky problem of creating tables in a particular sequence so no foreign key referential integrity constraints are violated. Figure 3.14 shows an example of two tables, each of which contains a foreign key reference to the other. The conundrum is which table to create first. You cannot create table A first, because it contains a foreign key reference to table B, which has not yet been created—Nor can you create Table B first, for the same reason. ALTER TABLE solves the problem by allowing you to add foreign key clauses to the tables *after* both are created, thus avoiding the "chicken and the egg" problem altogether.

ADDING, ENABLING, OR DISABLING CONSTRAINTS

Any of the constraints you included in the CREATE TABLE statements earlier can be omitted from that statement and added to a table later with the ALTER TABLE... ADD command. When you create a constraint, it is enabled automatically. You can disable the constraint when you create it by using the ALTER TABLE ADD CONSTRAINT... DISABLE command, which creates the constraint but disables it immediately. A ***disabled constraint*** is a constraint that is named but not enforced. Alternatively, you can disable an existing constraint by issuing the ALTER TABLE... DISABLE CONSTRAINT command. Later, you can enable any constraints by issuing the ALTER TABLE... ENABLE CONSTRAINT. Naturally, if you want to either enable or disable constraint, you must know its name. When you create a constraint, you may want to disable it temporarily. To do so, you use the ALTER TABLE statement with the constraint name you want to disable. Then add the clause DISABLE CONSTRAINT. For example, if you create a foreign key constraint on the Listings table for the field PropertyID, then you cannot insert data into that table unless the primary key field to which it points exists and has data. To solve this problem, you can disable the PropertyID foreign key constraint, populate the Listings table, populate the LicenseStatus table to which the foreign key points, then reenable the foreign key constraint. This avoids generating referential integrity violations as you populate the Listings table. The following statement will disable the PropertyID foreign key constraint in the Listings table until you later reenable it:

```
ALTER TABLE Listings DISABLE CONSTRAINT fk_propertieslistings
```

The general forms of the ALTER TABLE statement allowing you to add a new constraint, enable an existing constraint, or disable an existing constraint are shown in

FIGURE 3.14 Tables with foreign key references to each other.

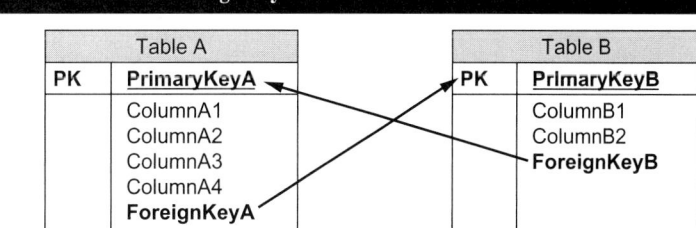

forms 1, 2, 3, and 4 below. Notice that NOT NULL requires the MODIFY CONSTRAINT clause.

```
ALTER TABLE <table-name>
   ADD CONSTRAINT <constraint-name> <constraint-type>            1
ALTER TABLE <table-name>
   MODIFY CONSTRAINT <constraint-name> NOT NULL                  2
ALTER TABLE <table-name>
   ENABLE CONSTRAINT <constraint-name>                           3
ALTER TABLE <table-name>
   DISABLE CONSTRAINT <constraint-name>                          4
```

When you created the Listings table, you did not create any foreign keys to other tables related to it. Not all tables related to the Listings table are in place yet, but one is—Agents. The Listings field ListingAgentID is a foreign key that points to the primary key column, AgentID, in the Agents table. Next, you will add this constraint as a foreign key.

To add a foreign key constraint to the Listings table:

1. Type the following, pressing **Enter** following the semicolon:

```
ALTER TABLE Listings
   ADD CONSTRAINT fk_agents_listings FOREIGN KEY (ListingAgentID)
   REFERENCES Agents (AgentID)
   ON DELETE CASCADE;
```

2. Oracle responds with the confirming message "Table altered."

When you created the Customers table, you did not designate a column as the table's primary key. You will issue the ALTER TABLE statement to designate the primary key for an existing column. In addition, you will add the NOT NULL constraint to the FirstName and LastName columns so their values can never be omitted. The MODIFY clause adds NOT NULL constraints to existing table columns.

To add a primary key constraint to the Customers table:

1. Execute the following command. Remember to press **Enter** at the end of the second line.

```
ALTER TABLE Customers
   ADD CONSTRAINT pk_customers PRIMARY KEY(CustomerID);
```

Oracle responds with the confirming message "Table altered."

2. Execute the following statement to add a NOT NULL constraint to the FirstName column:

```
ALTER TABLE Customers
   MODIFY FirstName CONSTRAINT nn_customers_fname NOT NULL;
```

3. Execute the following statement to add a NOT NULL constraint to the LastName column:

```
ALTER TABLE Customers
   MODIFY LastName CONSTRAINT nn_customers_lname NOT NULL;
```

Figure 3.15 shows the four ALTER TABLE statements and Oracle responses to them.

DROPPING OR RENAMING CONSTRAINTS

When a database constraint is no longer required, you can drop it with the ALTER TABLE statement with the DROP clause. You can drop a constraint by mentioning its

CHAPTER 3 Creating, Modifying, Renaming, and Deleting Database Tables

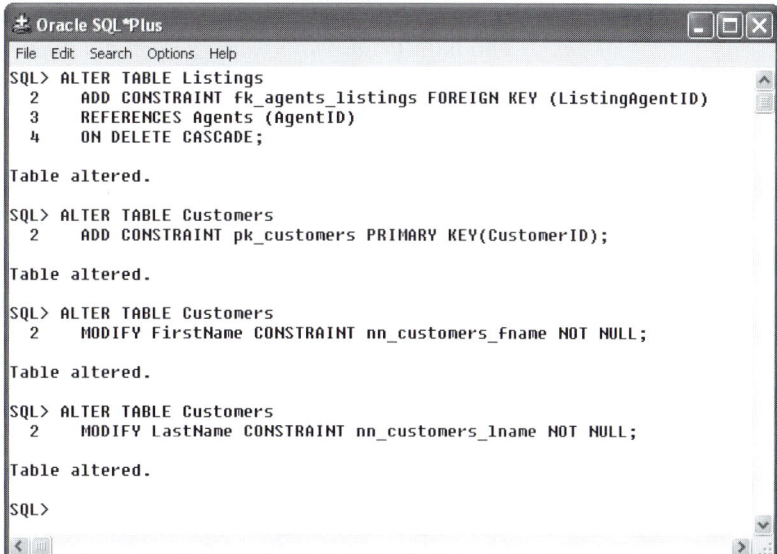

FIGURE 3.15 Adding constraints with the ALTER TABLE statement.

name explicitly, or not mentioning it at all. For example, you could drop the NOT NULL constraint on the LastName column of the Customers table with the following command:

```
ALTER TABLE Customers DROP CONSTRAINT nn_customers_lname;
```

Similarly, you could drop the Listings table's primary key by executing either of the following:

```
ALTER TABLE Listings DROP PRIMARY KEY;
```

or

```
ALTER TABLE Listings DROP CONSTRAINT pk_listings;
```

If you choose poor names for one or more of your constraints, you can use the ALTER TABLE statement to change their names. Here's how you would rename the ListingAgentID foreign key, called fk_agents_listings, to fk_agents_list:

```
ALTER TABLE Listings RENAME CONSTRAINT fk_agents_listings
  TO fk_agents_list;
```

It is a good idea to rename any system-generated constraint names from their rather meaningless names to more meaningful ones. When you learn how to display constraint names in the next section, you will see there is one constraint name that Oracle created. Practice renaming that name to a better name. (Hint: the constraint in question is a NOT NULL constraint in the Listings table.)

CHANGING A COLUMN'S DEFAULT VALUE OR DATA TYPE

Like other column alterations that occur after you executed the CREATE TABLE statement, you can modify the *default value* for a column with the ALTER TABLE statement. For instance, you could change the default value for Listings table's BeginListDate column with:

```
ALTER TABLE Listings MODIFY BeginListDate DEFAULT SYSDATE -2;
```

If you want to remove a default value from the column, then you have to set the DEFAULT to NULL this way:

```
ALTER TABLE Listings MODIFY BeginListDate DEFAULT NULL;
```

By setting the DEFAULT to NULL, you remove it. Oracle will no longer supply a default value for the BeginListDate column if its value is omitted during data entry.

You can modify just about any aspect of a column anytime after creating it with a CREATE TABLE statement. Here are some of the characteristics of a column you can change with the ALTER TABLE statement:

- Data type
- Default value
- Size of a column for a data type that has an explicit size
- Precision of a numeric column

For instance, the following example changes the precision of the AskingPrice column from its original NUMBER(9) to NUMBER(12,2) allowing one more significant digit and two places after the decimal point:

```
ALTER TABLE Listings MODIFY AskingPrice NUMBER(12,9);
```

Because the table alteration statements described in this chapter (CREATE TABLE and ALTER TABLE) are classified as data definition language (DDL) statements, they take effect immediately and are not affected by a ROLLBACK instruction. If you want to undo a table alteration statement, you will have to execute an ALTER TABLE statement, explicitly reversing the change.

ADDING, DROPPING, AND RENAMING COLUMNS

One of the terrific things about a relational database is that you can add or remove columns whenever needed without causing long and expensive delays. Renaming columns is equally easy. When you add a column to a table, Oracle adds it as the last column in the table. Let's add a column called ContactDate to the Customers table. ContactDate is a DATE data type holding the date of the first contact with the customer whose default value is today's date, supplied by the SYSDATE function.

To add a column to a table:

1. With SQL*Plus still running, type the following and press **Enter**:

   ```
   ALTER TABLE Customers
     ADD ContactDate DATE DEFAULT SYSDATE;
   ```

2. Type **DESCRIBE Customers** and press **Enter** to verify that Oracle added the column (see Figure 3.16).

Deleting a column is just as easy. Be very careful. Once you delete a column of a table that is not empty, the column cannot be rolled back. The only way to undo a column deletion operation is to add the column back in and then reconstruct all the data in that column by hand—using INSERT statements—a long and painful prospect. Because none of your Redwood Realty tables have any data yet, deleting a column is inconsequential. Try it.

To delete a table's column:

1. Type the following command to drop the HomePhone column. Be sure to press **Enter** to execute it:

   ```
   ALTER TABLE Customers
     DROP COLUMN HomePhone;
   ```

CHAPTER 3 Creating, Modifying, Renaming, and Deleting Database Tables **123**

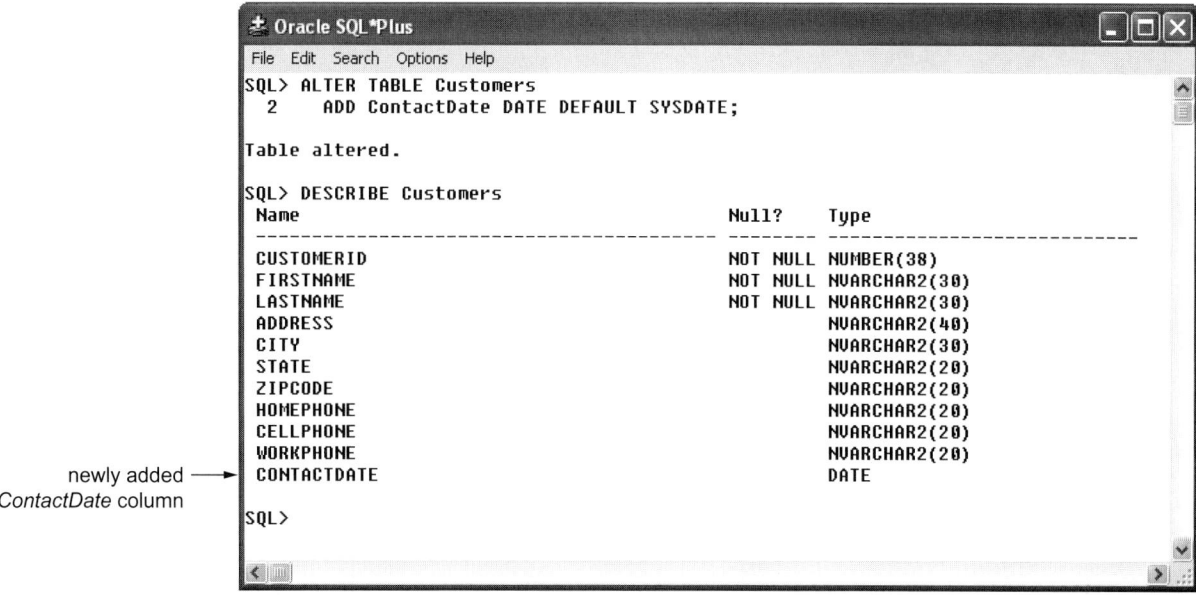

newly added ContactDate column

FIGURE 3.16 Adding a column to a table.

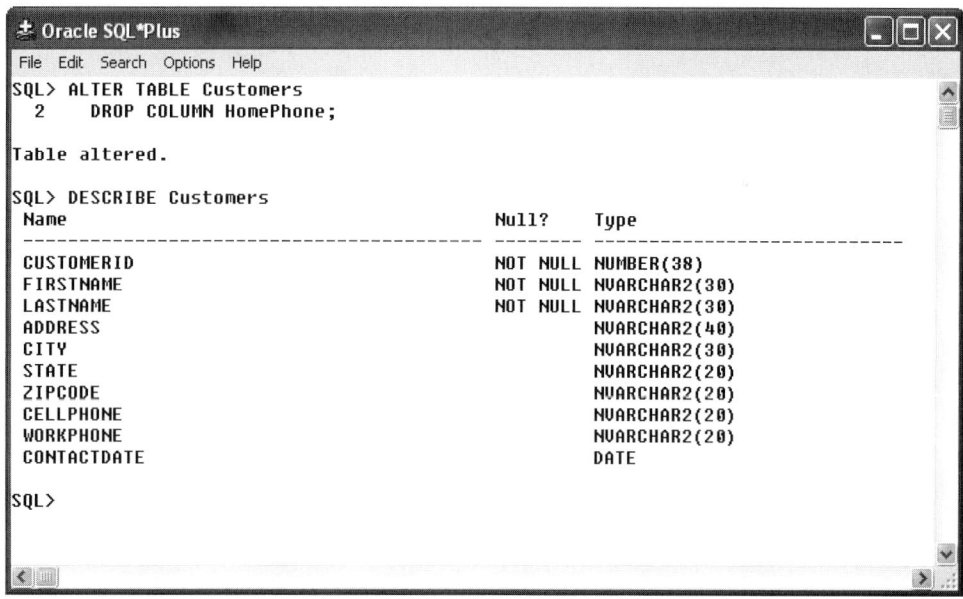

FIGURE 3.17 Dropping a column from a table.

2. Execute the statement **DESCRIBE Customers** to display the table's changed structure (see Figure 3.17).

If you want to drop multiple columns in one statement, simply omit the keyword "COLUMN" and separate the column names with commas:

```
ALTER TABLE Customers
   DROP (BirthDate, Gender, WorkPhone);
```

With the RENAME COLUMN phrase of the ALTER TABLE statement, you can change a column's name.

> **Warning:** If you rename a column, then any objects that reference that table column become invalid.

Suppose you want to rename the Agents table Title column to AgentTitle. This ALTER TABLE statement will rename the column:

```
ALTER TABLE Agents RENAME COLUMN Title TO AgentTitle;
```

MARKING COLUMNS AS UNUSED AND DROPPING UNUSED COLUMNS

Instead of dropping unwanted, unused, or unnecessary columns, you can mark them as unused. What's the difference between dropping a column and marking it as unused? An unused column (one marked as unused) is not visible to Oracle users. The DESCRIBE statement does not reveal the column exists, and no query can reference the marked column. Effectively, columns marked as unused are invisible. The alternative is to drop a column. Doing so removes the column physically and causes all the data that the column contained to be discarded. For a large table, this can be a large performance penalty because it takes a lot of time to remove the data and rewrite the row to the table. It is not a command you would want to unleash on a database during the middle of the day when lots of users are logged into Oracle. Marking a column unused takes much less time, and there is no recourse if you want to revive a dropped column—the drop operation is irreversible. The simple syntax to mark a column unused is form 1. Use form 2 to mark multiple columns in one command (the word *COLUMN* is omitted in form 2):

```
ALTER TABLE <table-name> SET UNUSED COLUMN <column-name>;                 1
ALTER TABLE <table-name> SET UNUSED (<col-name₁>, … ,<col-nameₙ>)         2
```

Later, you can execute an ALTER TABLE with the DROP COLUMN clause or an ALTER TABLE with the DROP UNUSED COLUMNS clause to physically remove the column(s) from the database. It is helpful to learn how to use this command. You will hide the columns LicenseID, LicenseDate, and LicenseExpire in the Agents table.

To mark columns as unused:

1. If necessary, launch SQL*Plus and log into Oracle.
2. Type **DESCRIBE Agents** to review the columns it contains. Near the bottom are LicenseID, LicenseDate, and LicenseExpire.
3. Type the following ALTER TABLE statement and press **Enter** to execute it.

   ```
   ALTER TABLE Agents
     SET UNUSED (LicenseID, LicenseDate, LicenseExpire);
   ```

4. Type **DESCRIBE Agents** (and press **Enter**) again to verify that the three marked columns are absent (see Figure 3.18).
5. Exit SQL*Plus by typing **Exit** and pressing **Enter**. You will use *i*SQL*Plus for the remaining examples in this chapter.

DISPLAYING TABLES' NAMES, STRUCTURES, AND COMMENTS

When adding information to a table or altering its structure, you can review the table's column names and data types, as you often have in this text, by issuing the DESCRIBE <tablename> command. The only constraint that is revealed with the DESCRIBE statement is NOT NULL. It does not reveal which columns are primary and foreign keys, except that both keys carry the NOT NULL constraint. For example, Figure 3.19 shows the result of the DESCRIBE Listings command. Notice that the first three

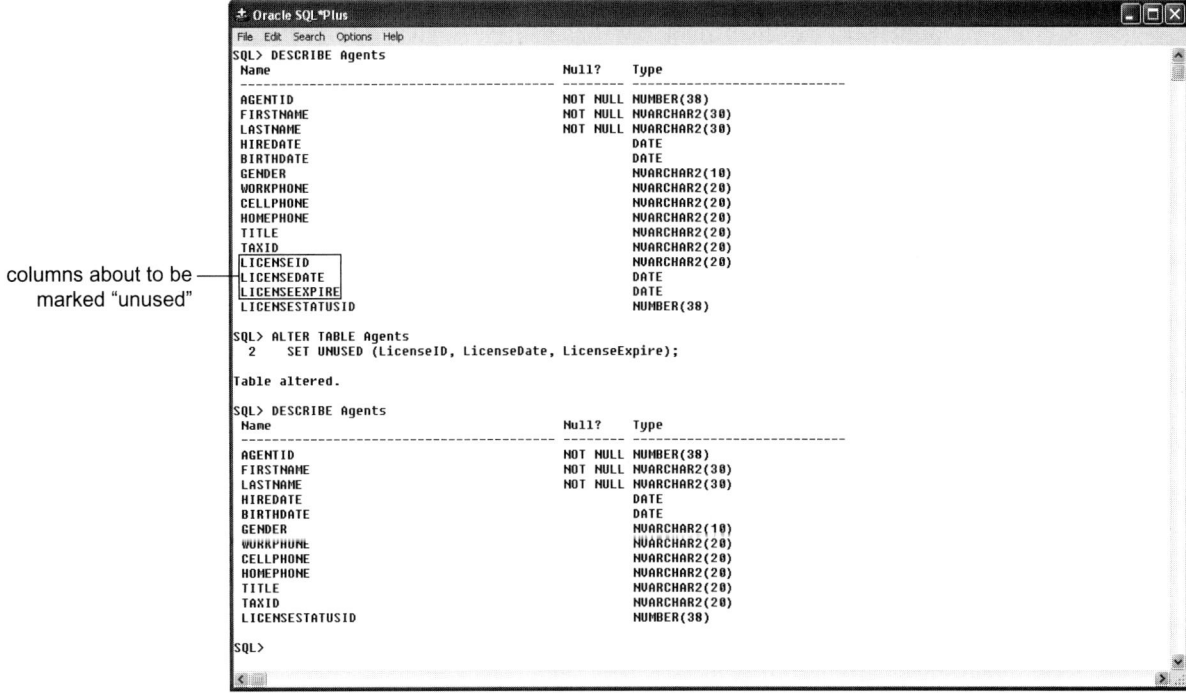

FIGURE 3.18 Marking multiple columns unused.

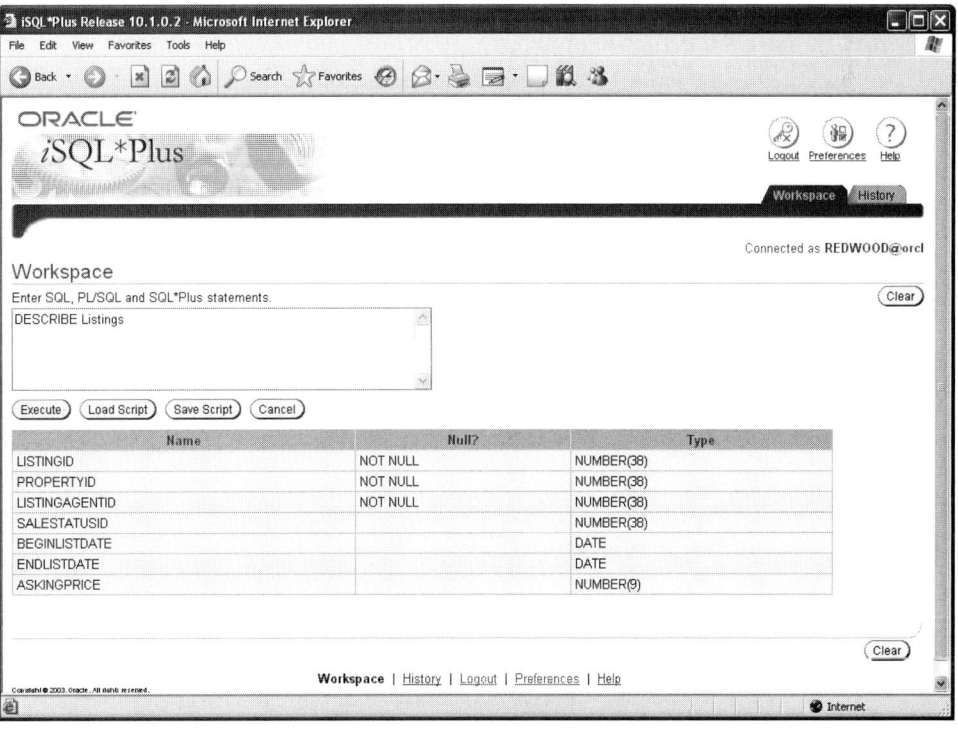

FIGURE 3.19 Describing the Listings table.

columns show "NOT NULL." There is no indication that ListingID is the primary key or that ListingAgentID is the foreign key. To view information about table constraints and the names of the tables you have created, query Oracle's data dictionary tables. The ***Oracle data dictionary*** contains of tables of information about its own tables and all objects in the database. Oracle creates the data dictionary whenever the database administrator creates a new database. Any changes to the users' tables or other objects are noted in the data dictionary. For instance, each of the columns' names for a particular user table, along with data type information, is stored in a data dictionary table. The DESCRIBE command merely interrogates these system-maintained "tables about tables" to retrieve column names and data types for the named table.

The data dictionary is owned by a privileged Oracle account, SYS. Normally, users and database administrators alike do not insert, update, or delete entries in the data dictionary. Doing so could wreck the database. Rather than interacting with tables directly, users can view information in the data dictionary through database views. A ***view*** is an object that displays a subset of the rows and columns of a base table. Although views look like ordinary (base) database tables, they are used to restrict what the view user can retrieve from the base table. You retrieve information through views the same way you do with tables—with a SELECT command. Because data dictionary views define which rows and columns appear in the view, they provide wide-ranging control over who can use them and what is revealed through them, a type of "need-to-know" protection that is not available with base tables. Data dictionary views fall into three groups: DBA, USER, and ALL. DBA views allow users with database administrator level access to view all information about all database objects. USER views display information about objects (tables, etc.) belonging to the current user—in that user's schema. The ALL views group permits any user access to objects in a schema and also to objects to which the user has been given access—usually other users' objects. (Though you will learn about the SELECT command in detail in Chapter 5 and creating your own views in Chapter 6, you will practice using the SELECT command in a limited way to review your database objects.)

LISTING YOUR DATABASE TABLES

The simplified syntax to retrieve information about objects you have created or to which you have access is:

```
SELECT view_columnname₁, …, view_columnnameₖ
FROM groupprefix_objectname;
```

where "view_columnname" are the names of the columns you want to retrieve and "groupprefix" is one of *USER, DBA,* or *ALL.* Objectname is the type of object you want to examine. It can be TABLES or CONSTRAINTS, among others. Putting these pieces together, you can retrieve the names of tables you own by issuing the command:

```
SELECT table_name
FROM user_tables;
```

"Table_name" is one of the columns that data dictionary view "user_tables" stores, and is the name of the tables you own. This particular view restricts the table names retrieved to those you created in your schema, but not other tables to which Oracle has granted you read access. For example, the following SELECT command displays *view* names for *all* views which you have created or to which you have been granted access privileges (several thousand objects):

```
SELECT view_name
FROM all_views;
```

The best way to understand this is to try it. You can use either *i*SQL*Plus or SQL*Plus, whichever you prefer.

To display names of your tables:

1. Launch SQL*Plus and log into Oracle with your username and password.
2. Type the following command, pressing **Enter** at the end of each line:

```
SELECT table_name
FROM user_tables;
```

Oracle displays the four tables you created. Additional temporary table names may also appear.

3. Launch Notepad so you can edit the statement and later save it. Switch to SQL*Plus, drag across the SELECT statement, including the semicolon, and then press **Ctrl+C** to copy it to the Clipboard.
4. Switch to Notepad and press **Ctrl+V** to paste the statement. Modify the SELECT statement to this:

```
SELECT table_name
FROM user_tables
WHERE table_name NOT LIKE '%BIN%';
```

Be sure to capitalize "BIN" and surround it with percent signs.

5. Save the file as **<yourname>Ch3GetTableNames.sql**. Copy the statement back into SQL*Plus, and close Notepad.
6. With SQL*Plus active, press **Enter** to execute the copied command. Oracle returns your table names without the temporary table names (see Figure 3.20).

What other information is in the view *user_tables*? Execute *DESCRIBE user_tables* to find out. There are 47 columns in that view, but only a few are of interest to most users. Figure 3.21 shows some of the columns in the view.

Table 3.9 displays selected database objects from which you can retrieve information. You can execute SELECT statements similar to the ones above to retrieve information. You will examine several of these objects as you read this text.

Each of the data dictionary views in Table 3.9 has different columns. If you are curious about their contents, first reveal the names of the columns in the view of interest by

FIGURE 3.20 Displaying table names using a data dictionary view.

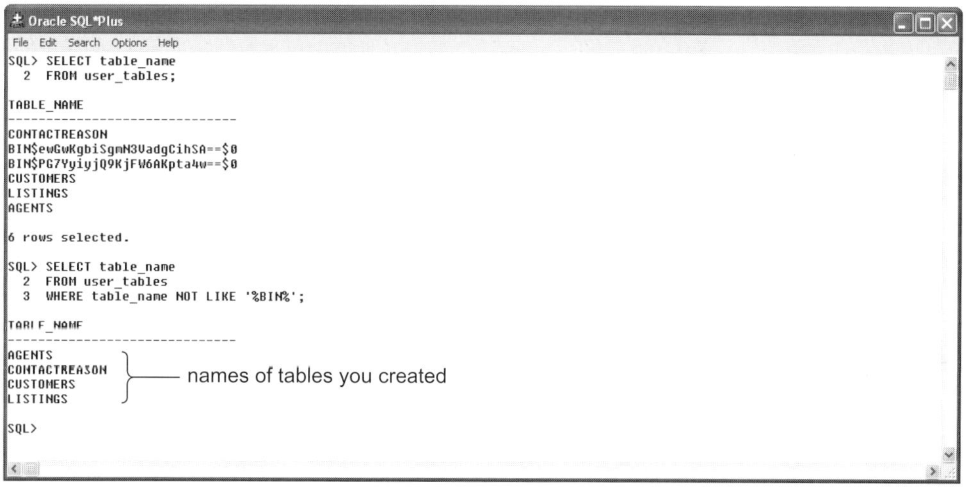

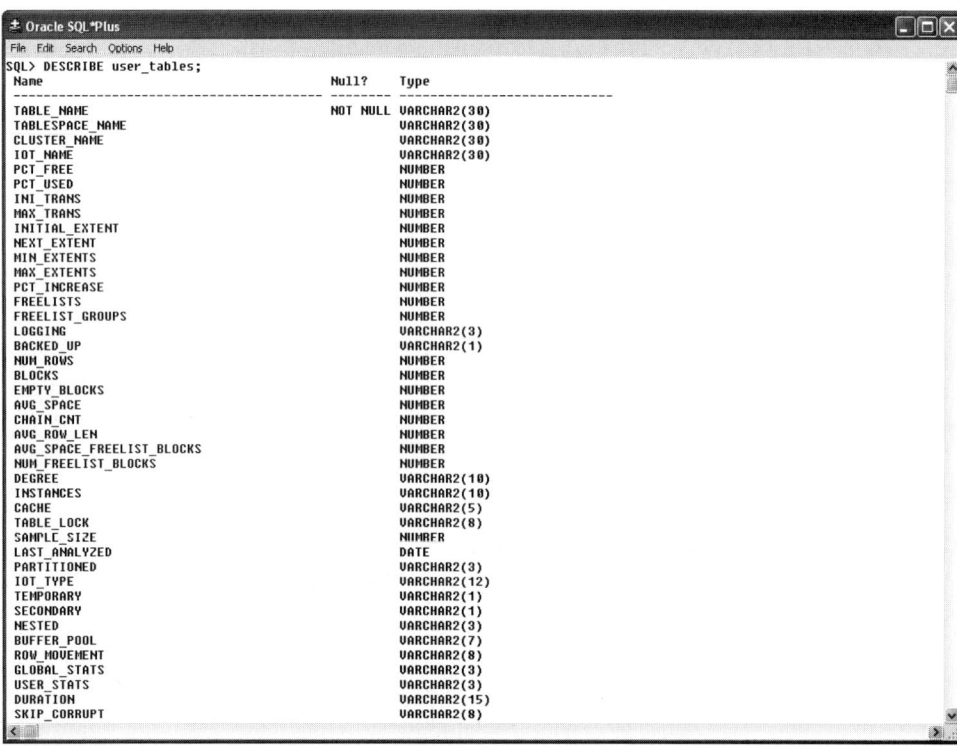

FIGURE 3.21 Some of the columns in the user_tables view.

TABLE 3.9 Selected objects available through data dictionary views.

Object	Description
CONS_COLUMNS	Table columns having constraints
CONSTRAINTS	Table constraints
INDEXES	Table indexes
OBJECTS	All database objects
SEQUENCES	Sequences generating unique keys
TAB_COLUMNS	Table columns. (USER_TAB_COLUMNS are the current user's columns)
TABLES	Database tables
USERS	Names of all database users (ALL_USERS)
VIEWS	Database views

issuing a DESCRIBE <viewname> command. Then note the columns that you want to review. Be careful! Some views contain many rows.

REVIEWING INFORMATION ON COLUMNS

More detailed information on columns of your tables is available in the view user_tab_columns. (The "user" prefix restricts the rows returned in any query to those that belong to your schema.) You issue a SELECT statement referencing the data dictionary view user_tab_columns. If needed, you can review the columns it contains by executing the statement DESCRIBE user_tab_columns. Next, you will review more details about the table Listings you created earlier. Ensure that SQL*Plus is running and you are still logged into Oracle.

CHAPTER 3 Creating, Modifying, Renaming, and Deleting Database Tables

```
Oracle SQL*Plus
File Edit Search Options Help
SQL> COLUMN column_name FORMAT A15
SQL> COLUMN data_type   FORMAT A9
SQL> COLUMN nullable    FORMAT A8
SQL> SELECT column_name, data_type, data_length,
  2         data_precision, data_scale, nullable
  3  FROM user_tab_columns
  4  WHERE table_name = 'LISTINGS';

COLUMN_NAME     DATA_TYPE DATA_LENGTH DATA_PRECISION DATA_SCALE NULLABLE
--------------- --------- ----------- -------------- ---------- --------
LISTINGID       NUMBER             22                         0 N
PROPERTYID      NUMBER             22                         0 N
LISTINGAGENTID  NUMBER             22                         0 N
SALESTATUSID    NUMBER             22                         0 Y
BEGINLISTDATE   DATE                7                           Y
ENDLISTDATE     DATE                7                           Y
ASKINGPRICE     NUMBER             22              9          0 Y

7 rows selected.

SQL>
```

FIGURE 3.22 Displaying details about a table's columns.

TABLE 3.10 Some of the user_constraints columns.

Column	Description
owner	Owner of the constraint (username).
constraint_name	Name of the constraint.
constraint_type	Type: P, R, C, U, V or O.
table_name	Table containing the constraint.
status	Either ENABLED or DISABLED.

To review additional details about a table:

1. Type the following, pressing **Enter** (as usual) at the end of each line. Be sure to capitalize the name *LISTINGS*. Figure 3.22 shows the result that should match your query result.

```
CLEAR SCREEN
COLUMN column_name FORMAT A15
COLUMN data_type FORMAT A9
COLUMN nullable FORMAT A8
SELECT column_name, data_type, data_length,
       data_precision, data_scale, nullable
FROM user_tab_columns
WHERE table_name = 'LISTINGS';
```

2. Type **CLEAR COLUMNS** and press **Enter** to clear the column formatting.

Notice that the data length is probably not what you expect. The data length for numbers allows a maximum number of digits, but the DATA_PRECISION column indicates that the user table's AskingPrice column has a nine-digit maximum length. The NULLABLE column indicates whether or not NULL values are allowed.

REVIEWING TABLE AND COLUMN CONSTRAINTS

You have added several constraints. Occasionally, it is a good idea to review those constraints. Oracle supplies several views that contain information about the objects in your schema. One of those views, called *user_constraints*, contains information about the constraints applied to your tables. Table 3.10 shows some of the columns found in *user_constraints*. Although you have not been introduced formally to queries in the

130 Introduction to Oracle

text in any significant way, you will run a query to retrieve information about the constraints on all your tables. Chapter 5 describes queries in exquisite detail. Chapter 6 describes a cousin of the query, called views.

The meaning of the constraint_type column in Table 3.10 may not be obvious. Values that can appear in that column define the type of constraint that has been assigned. P stands for primary key; R indicates foreign key; C is either check or not null; U is unique; V is check option of a view definition; and O is a read-only view. The codes P, R, C, and U are the important ones.

Next you will retrieve information about constraints you have defined on your tables by querying the user_constraints view.

To review your table constraints:

1. With SQL*Plus still running, type the following lines, pressing **Enter** at the end of each line. Be sure to capitalize *BIN* and follow it with "%" in the code below.

   ```
   CLEAR SCREEN
   SET PAGESIZE 20
   COLUMN table_name FORMAT A15
   COLUMN constraint_type FORMAT A10
   SELECT table_name, constraint_type, constraint_name, status
   FROM user_constraints
   WHERE table_name NOT LIKE 'BIN%'
   ORDER BY table_name;
   ```

   Oracle displays the thirteen constraints you established on your tables, sorted by table name (see Figure 3.23).

2. Reset the PAGESIZE SQL*Plus environmental variable and clear the column formatting by typing and executing the following SQL*Plus statements:

   ```
   SET PAGESIZE 14
   CLEAR COLUMNS
   ```

   Notice that one of the Listings constraints displays an unusual constraint name beginning with SYS. (Yours will be different from the one shown in the figure.) That is an example of a constraint *name* that Oracle automatically assigned when you omitted it for one of the constraints on the Listings table. Which constraint did you not name when you assigned it to a column? You have to consult another data dictionary view called user_cons_columns to find out. Three of the most important columns in that view are

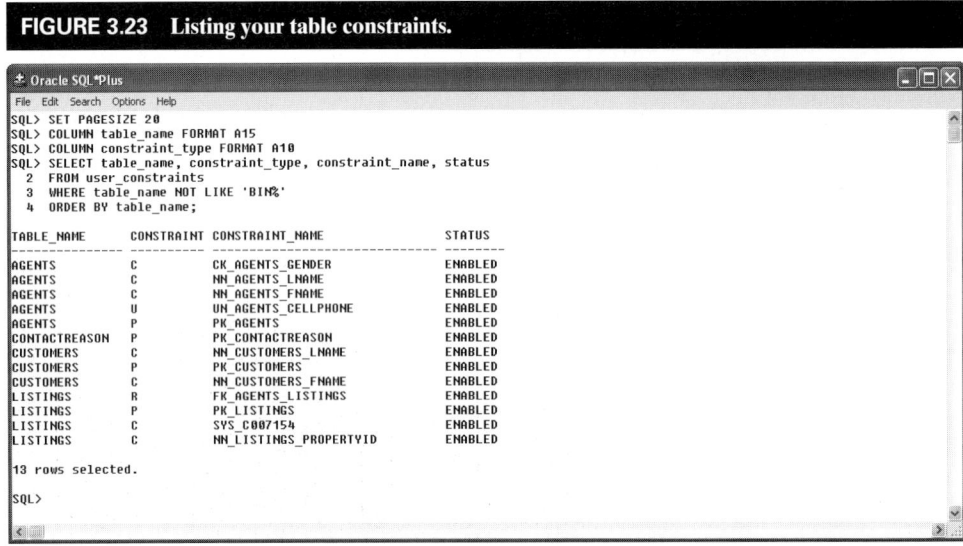

FIGURE 3.23 Listing your table constraints.

CHAPTER 3 Creating, Modifying, Renaming, and Deleting Database Tables

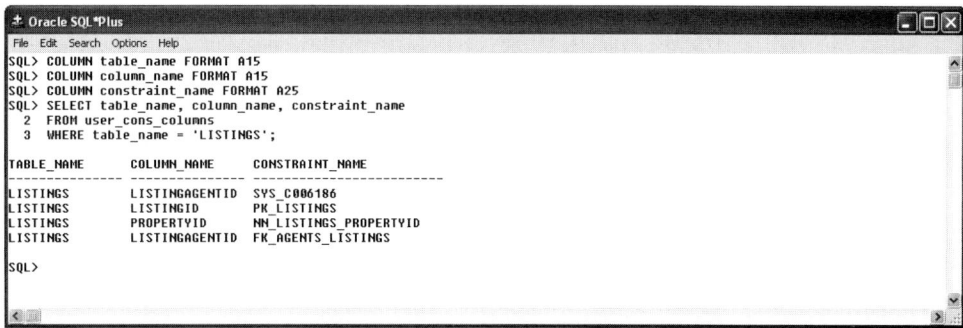

FIGURE 3.24 Reviewing column constraints for the Listings table.

table_name, column_name, and constraint_name. The view user_cons_columns displays more details about a column's constraints.

To review the constraints on a particular table:

1. Enter the following code in SQL*Plus and press **Enter** at the end of each line. Remember to type *LISTINGS* in the last row in uppercase, because Oracle stores object names in uppercase (unless you use quotation marks around the object names).

```
CLEAR SCREEN
COLUMN table_name FORMAT A15
COLUMN column_name FORMAT A15
COLUMN constraint_name FORMAT A25
SELECT table_name, column_name, constraint_name
FROM user_cons_columns
WHERE table_name = 'LISTINGS';
```

2. Exit SQL*Plus by typing **exit** and pressing **Enter**.

Figure 3.24 should match your results. Notice that the unnamed column constraint is assigned to the ListingAgentID column of the Listings table. You cannot tell from the previous result, but it is either an unnamed CHECK constraint or an unnamed NOT NULL constraint. (It is the latter.)

If you want to pull together information from both views to get a more complete picture of what constraints are assigned to which columns, that involves a more complicated query—one which we do not want you to attempt at this stage. It is available as a script file called Ch03TableConstraintsISP.sql. Reviewing columns sometimes looks better in *i*SQL*Plus, because that interface does a good job of lining up columns and ensuring that no rows wrap to new lines. For that reason, we suggest you do these next steps using *i*SQL*Plus.

To review all the constraints on your tables and columns:

1. Launch *i*SQL*Plus and log into the database.
2. Click the **Load Script** button, click the **Browse** button located next to the File text box, and navigate to the folder containing the file Ch03TableConstraintsISP.sql.
3. Click **Ch03TableConstraintsISP.sql** in the *Choose file* dialog box, click the **Open** button, and click the **Load** button to load the script file and display it in the Workspace text box.
4. Click the **Execute** button to run the query. Oracle displays a complete set of constraint information including table names, column names, constraint types, constraint names, and status (see Figure 3.25).
5. Leave *i*SQL*Plus running for the next set of steps.

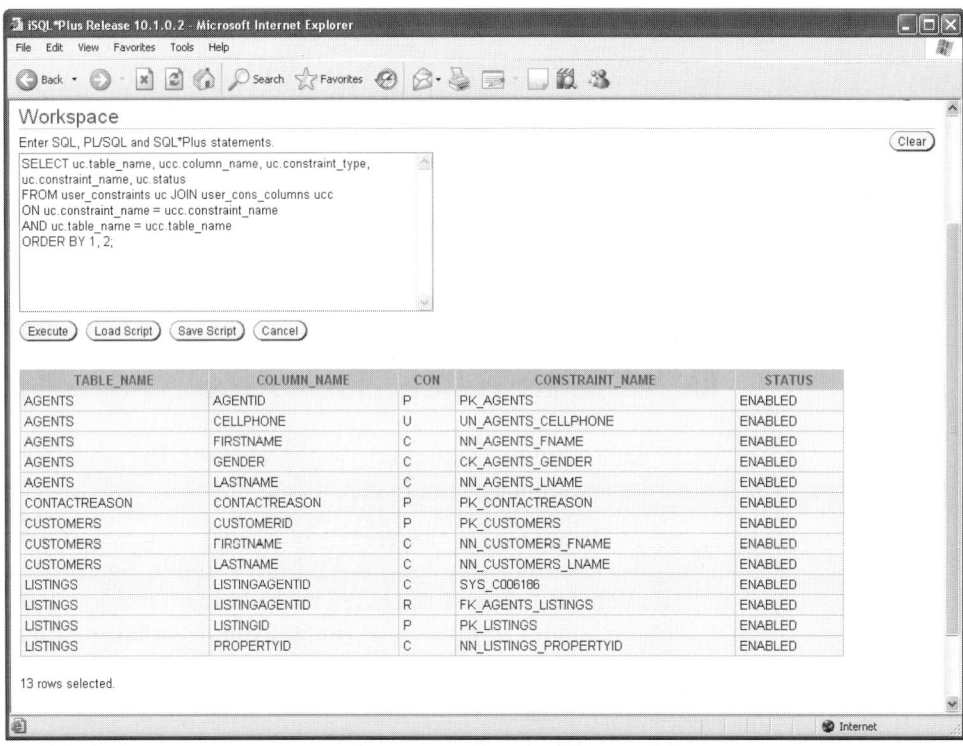

FIGURE 3.25 Displaying more complete constraint information.

If you prefer to use SQL*Plus, then the alternative script file you should run is called Ch03TableConstraints.sql. That script file contains additional code to format columns so they are more readable in the SQL*Plus environment.

REVIEWING TABLE AND COLUMN COMMENTS

Storing comments about a table or its columns can help you remember what the purpose of the table or column is. You added comments earlier in this chapter to the Customers table and to the State column of that table. You reviewed those comments at the same time by issuing a SELECT statement. The data dictionary view user_tab_comments contains your table and view names and any comments they may contain. Even your tables having no comments are noted. As you would expect, all_tab_comments contains owner names, table names, and comments for *all* database tables and views. This table has thousands of rows, so be very careful if you query it.

Recall that you can list comments on any of your tables by executing

```
SELECT *
FROM user_tab_comments
```

Similarly, you can list comments that you may have on your table columns by executing the SQL statement

```
SELECT *
FROM user_col_comments
```

By using the optional WHERE clause following either of the preceding two SELECT commands, you restrict which table's comments or column comments Oracle retrieves and lists. Carefully, you will examine some comments stored in

CHAPTER 3 Creating, Modifying, Renaming, and Deleting Database Tables **133**

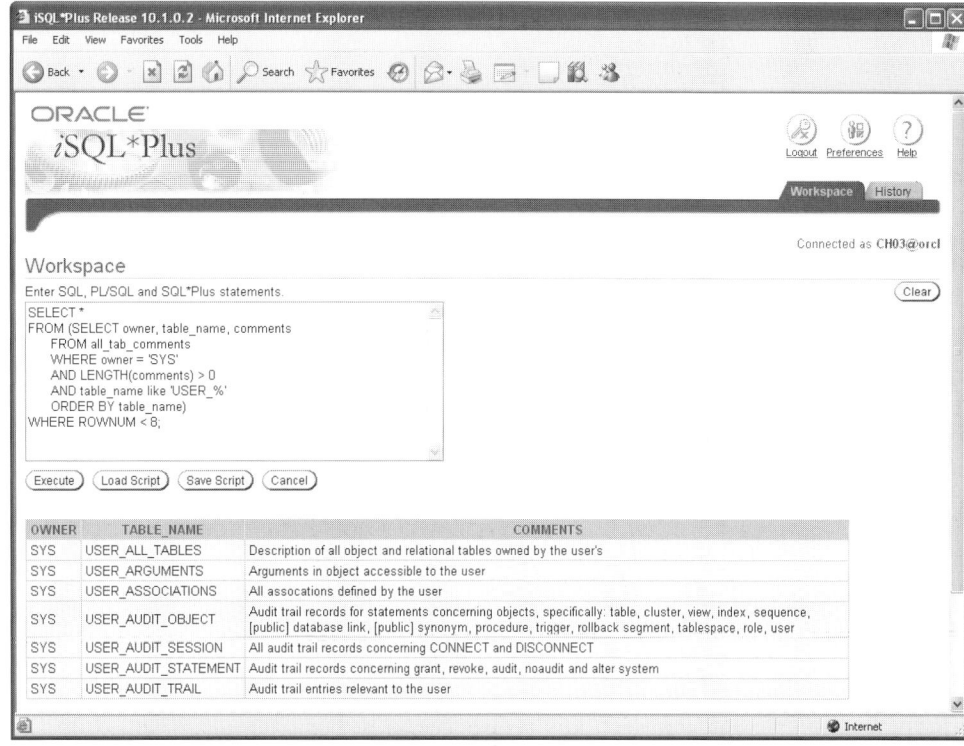

FIGURE 3.26 Seven rows showing schema SYS' table comments.

the SYS account, which has DBA privileges, and display selected table comments. Because this query you are about to type could return thousands of rows, we have created a script file you simply load and execute. The query, which is more complex than you have seen before, ensures that only seven rows are returned by Oracle. If you choose to use SQL*Plus instead of iSQL*Plus, run the alternative script Ch03TableComments.sql.

To display table comments from selected SYS account tables:

1. With *i*SQL*Plus still running, click the **Load Script** button, click **Browse**, navigate to the folder containing the file Ch03TableCommentsISP.sql, click **Open**, and click **Load**. The script contents appear in the Workspace text box.
2. Click the **Execute** button to view the results (see Figure 3.26).
3. Click the **Logout** hyperlink to log out of the database, and then close the browser window.

DROPPING, REINSTATING, AND RENAMING TABLES

SQL provides statements to DROP tables or RENAME them. Both dropping a table and renaming it can cause other objects in the schema to become invalid when they refer to dropped or renamed tables.

DROPPING A TABLE

When you no longer need a database table, you can delete it by issuing the DROP command. You should do so carefully, because other tables, views, and users may refer

```
Oracle SQL*Plus
File Edit Search Options Help
SQL> DROP TABLE Agents;
DROP TABLE Agents
           *
ERROR at line 1:
ORA-02449: unique/primary keys in table referenced by foreign keys

SQL>
```

FIGURE 3.27   DROP TABLE attempt with resulting error message.

to the table. Tables are not trivial to recreate and populate, either. When you delete a table, its data along with the table's structure are removed. When you delete a table, Oracle deletes all rows from the table, removes all information about the table from its data dictionary, and it deletes all of the table's indexes, triggers, and constraints. Versions prior to Oracle 10g permanently removed the table and reclaimed the space for other use. Beginning with Oracle 10g, a dropped table is moved to a recycle bin. This is called a *flashback drop,* because you can recover the table later. If you are sure you never want to recover the table, you can skip putting it in the recycle bin by adding the optional phrase PURGE. The DROP TABLE syntax is

```
DROP TABLE <tablename> [CASCADE CONSTRAINTS] [PURGE]
```

Remember that other tables may depend on the dropped table because they contain foreign key references to it. For example, if you drop the Agents table, Oracle issues an error message because the ListingAgentID column in the Listings table references the AgentID column in the Agents table. (See Figure 3.27.) Referential integrity rules prevent a parent table from being dropped if one or more tables reference it. There are three ways to handle this problem: (1) Disable or drop the individual foreign key constraints with ALTER TABLE statements on each of the dependent tables, (2) drop, first, all tables with foreign key references to the table you want to drop in the first place, or (3) ask Oracle to drop the foreign key constraints for you with the CASCADE CONSTRAINTS option. If you choose the third option, Oracle first drops all foreign key constraints referencing the table to be dropped. Then, Oracle drops the table. Before you drop a table to which other tables may have foreign key references, you can query the data dictionary view *all_dependencies* or *user_dependencies.*

> **Warning:** Be careful querying the all_dependencies data dictionary view. It has more than 60,000 rows!

Next, you will attempt to drop the Agents table. Following that, you will add the CASCADE CONSTRAINTS option and issue the modified command.

To drop a table:

1. If necessary, launch SQL*Plus and log into Oracle.
2. Execute the following statement:

   DROP TABLE Agents;

   Oracle issues an error message like the one shown in Figure 3.27

3. Type and execute the following, corrected statement:

   DROP TABLE Agents CASCADE CONSTRAINTS;

   Oracle drops the table and displays the confirming message "Table dropped."

CHAPTER 3 Creating, Modifying, Renaming, and Deleting Database Tables

REINCARNATING A DROPPED TABLE

If you are using 10g or a later version of Oracle, then you can restore a dropped table—as long as you do not include PURGE in the DROP TABLE command. The FLASHBACK TABLE command allows you to restore a dropped table from Oracle's recycle bin. In addition, Oracle restores any triggers, constraints, or indexes associated with the restored table. Referential integrity constraints to other tables that are in the restored table are *not* reinstated. The simplified syntax to restore the table to its state before a DROP TABLE statement is:

```
FLASHBACK TABLE <tablename> TO BEFORE DROP;
```

When you drop a table, you can inspect the recycle bin to verify it is there by querying the user_recyclebin, a data dictionary view. Or, you can issue the SHOW RECYCLEBIN statement, which displays some of the same columns of the RECYCLEBIN data dictionary view.

To peek into the recycle bin and then reinstate a dropped table:

1. Type the following command and press **Enter** to review the recycle bin's contents:

```
COLUMN type FORMAT A10
SELECT original_name, object_name, type
FROM user_recyclebin;
```

Oracle displays several rows including one with Agents as the original_name value.

2. Reinstate the Agents table by executing:

```
FLASHBACK TABLE Agents TO BEFORE DROP;
```

Oracle responds "Flashback complete." Of course, your object- and original-names will be slightly different from those in Figure 3.28.

PURGING THE RECYCLE BIN

You can purge the recycle bin—empty the trash—entirely, or you can purge an individual table, or index from it using the PURGE command. The simple syntax to purge a single table is:

```
PURGE TABLE <tablename>
```

The syntax to purge the entire recycle bin is simply:

```
PURGE RECYCLEBIN
```

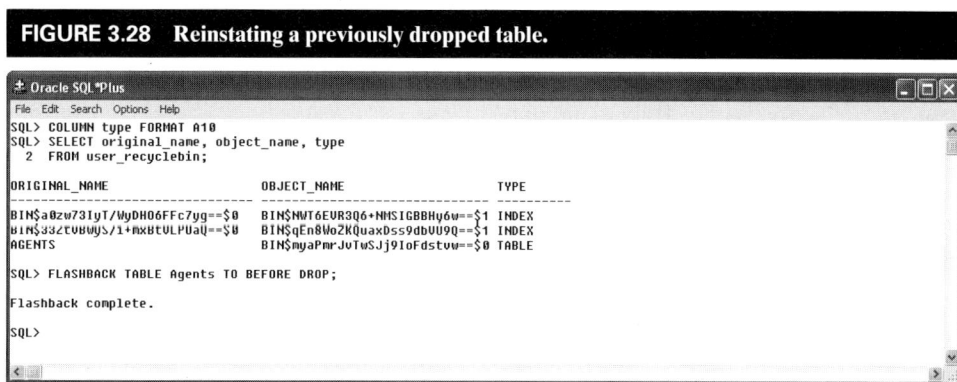

FIGURE 3.28 Reinstating a previously dropped table.

To purge the recycle bin:

1. Type the following command and press **Enter** to empty the recycle bin:

   `PURGE RECYCLEBIN;`

2. Oracle displays the confirming message "Recyclebin purged."

RENAMING A TABLE

Execute the RENAME command to rename a table and other database objects such as views and synonyms. Alternatively, you can issue the ALTER TABLE statement to rename a table. Either way, Oracle renames the table and automatically transfers to the newly named table all the integrity constraints, indexes, and other objects that referenced the old table name. However, some objects that referenced the old table such as stored procedures (Chapter 7), functions (Chapter 7), and views (Chapter 6) no longer work. Always be careful when you contemplate renaming a table, because it can cause unanticipated consequences throughout your database. Rename a table with this simple syntax:

`RENAME <old-tablename> TO <new-tablename>`

CREATING TABLES BASED ON OTHER TABLES

Another way to create a table is to borrow the definition, including column names and data types from an existing table. The table from which you create a new one can be in your schema, or it can be one in another schema to which you have been granted SELECT access. When you issue a CREATE TABLE AS statement with the optional SELECT query construct, the query creates a table whose structure is identical to the original one. Then, it copies the contents of any selected rows to the new table. The simplified CREATE TABLE AS syntax is:

```
CREATE TABLE <new-tablename> AS
SELECT *
FROM <old-tablename>
```

You could build an exact duplicate of a table in your schema. For example, suppose you wanted to create a copy of the Listings table just so you have a backup in case something happens to the original.

To create a table from an existing table:

1. With SQL*Plus running, type the following command and press **Enter** to execute it:

   ```
   CREATE TABLE NewListings AS
   SELECT *
   FROM Listings;
   ```

   Oracle responds "Table created."

2. Verify the new table's structure by executing the SQL*Plus command:

   `DESCRIBE NewListings`

   The results of executing these two statements should match those shown in Figure 3.29.

3. Type **exit** and press **Enter** to log off Oracle and close SQL*Plus.

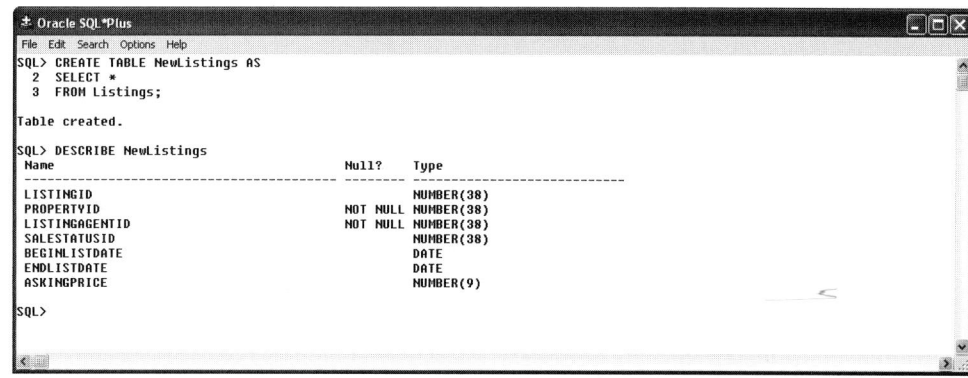

FIGURE 3.29 Creating a table from another table.

Summary

Designing a relational database to meet or exceed the needs of your customers requires discussing with them how their organizations operate and what data they store to support their business units. You can design required reports and forms to support desired business outcomes. Tables are the single storage facility for data, and a table consists of columns and rows. Each row describes a single entity in the "fact" that is represented by each table. A primary key uniquely identifies each row in a table and provides a linkage column to other tables related to it. A foreign key in one table matches the value of a primary key in the parent table. Such a relationship enforces referential integrity, which disallows deleting a parent table row without first deleting the child table rows related to it.

Any given column in a table stores only one type of data, and Oracle provides four basic data types. They are character, numeric, date and time, and image. If you forget a column, you can add one later using the ALTER TABLE command. That command allows you to modify columns including changing the scale or precision of numeric columns, assigning default values, and adding constraints. Constraints enforce rules including limiting the range of values that can be stored in a column, enforcing value uniqueness within a column, disallowing omission of a column's value, and primary and foreign key designations enforcing integrity rules.

Oracle provides a command-line interface to the database and a Web-based interface. SQL*Plus is the command-line interface, allowing you to type a command and press Enter to execute it immediately. The Web-based interface, *i*SQL*Plus, works through your browser to execute SQL and SQL*Plus commands, returning neatly organized columns to the browser.

Several Oracle data dictionary views allow you to extract a wide range of information about table names, column constraints, table constraints, and column comments. Using the DROP TABLE command, you can eliminate a table from the database and optionally recycle the space it occupies. Placed in a recycle bin, dropped tables can be restored, under certain circumstances, with the FLASHBACK command. The PURGE RECYCLEBIN command empties the Oracle recycle bin.

Key Terms

- Check constraint
- Class
- Composite primary key
- Compound primary key
- Constraint
- Constraint naming convention
- Data type
- Delimited names
- Disabled constraint
- Domain constraints
- Entity
- Fixed length character
- Fixed-precision number
- Flashback drop
- Floating-point number
- Foreign key constraint
- Integer
- Integrity constraint
- NOT NULL
- Oracle data dictionary
- Precision
- Primary key
- Primary key constraint
- Referential constraint
- Scale
- Schema object
- Table
- Unique constraint
- User schema
- Variable length character
- View

Review

TRUE/FALSE

1. Once you have been assigned a username and password, you cannot change your own password.
2. A column with a VARCHAR2(30) data type declaration is always 30 characters long. Oracle supplies additional spaces to pad the string to 30 characters if it is short.
3. Column constraints are optional, but they are one way to enforce business rules such as maximum or minimum allowable values, for example.
4. A foreign key constraint enforces referential integrity.
5. The largest number you could store in a column whose data type declaration is NUMBER(7,2) is 99.9999.

FILL IN

1. By convention prescribed by this book, a foreign key constraint name begins with _____ and is followed by an underscore.
2. A(n) _____ _____ (two words) uniquely identifies the row in which it is contained.
3. A(n) _____ constraint limits the values that a column can store.
4. The Oracle name where dropped tables are temporarily placed until purged is called the _____.
5. A database _____ is the general name of the object that displays a subset of a table's rows and columns.

MULTIPLE CHOICE

1. If you have database administrator privileges, you can create a new username and password by issuing what command?
   a. MODIFY USER <username> as identified by <password>
   b. CONNECT <username>/<password>
   c. CREATE USER <username>/<password>
   d. CREATE USER <username> IDENTIFIED BY <password>
   e. None of the preceding is correct
2. Which of the following data type declarations would you use to define the *Quantity* column containing whole numbers whose limit maximum value is 96,785?
   a. Quantity NUMBER(38)
   b. Quantity NUMBER(7,2)
   c. Quantity NUMBER(96785)
   d. Quantity NUMBER(5)
3. This constraint ensures that the values in a particular column of a given table are not duplicated.
   a. PRIMARY KEY
   b. FOREIGN KEY
   c. CHECK
   d. UNIQUE
   e. Both a and d are correct
4. The database object *user_tables* is found in Oracle's data dictionary and is called a _____.
   a. view
   b. table
   c. recycle bin table
   d. constraint
   e. none of the preceding is correct
5. When you drop a table using this option, Oracle does not place the table in the recycle bin. Instead, it is permanently removed from the database and all the space it occupied is relinquished.
   a. CASCADE CONSTRAINTS
   b. DUMP
   c. PURGE
   d. FLASHBACK
   e. NO RECYCLE

Hands-on Exercises

1. EXTENDING THE CHAPTER CASE

Robert Stirling, the office manager for Redwood Realty, wants you to drop a table in the Redwood Realty database and create a new one. The new table, called CustAgentList, will tie together the Agents, Customers, ContactReason, and Listings tables. Some of those tables exist and some do not. The fields in the CustAgentList table are: CustomerID, AgentID, ListingID, ContactDate, ContactReason, BidPrice, and CommissionRate. The table has a composite primary key consisting of the first four columns listed. The first three columns listed are also foreign keys pointing to related tables. ContactReason is the fourth foreign key. BidPrice can be empty. If a value is inserted into it, the range of allowed values is from 90,000 to 800,000. When specified, CommissionRate must range from 2 percent to 6 percent, inclusive.

1. Start SQL*Plus and log into Oracle. You can use Notepad in conjunction with SQL*Plus if you wish to save your commands as a script file—or in case you need to make corrections.

2. Type the following, pressing **Enter** at the end of each line. Note that the *extra* white space is not required. We did that to make the statements more readable. You can compress two or more spaces down to one space to save typing and time. Substitute a real path for "<path>" and your last name for "<yourname>" below in line 4.

```
REM Drop the NewListings table
DROP TABLE NewListings CASCADE CONSTRAINTS;
COLUMN type FORMAT A10
SPOOL C:\<path>\<yourname>Ch3Redwood.txt
SHOW USER
SELECT original_name, object_name, type
FROM user_recyclebin;
SPOOL OFF
REM Permanently eliminate the NewListings
PURGE RECYCLEBIN;
DROP TABLE CustAgentList CASCADE
CONSTRAINTS PURGE;
CREATE TABLE CustAgentList
   (CustomerID INTEGER NOT NULL,
    AgentID INTEGER NOT NULL,
    ListingID INTEGER NOT NULL,
    ContactDate DATE NOT NULL,
    ContactReason NVARCHAR2(15),
    BidPrice NUMERIC(9) CONSTRAINT
    cc_cuaglistBidPrice
      CHECK ((BidPrice >= 90000) AND
      (BidPrice <= 800000)),
    CommissionRate NUMERIC(4,4) CONSTRAINT
    cc_cuaglistCommRate
      CHECK (CommissionRate Between 0.02
      AND 0.06),
    CONSTRAINT pk_CustAgentList
      PRIMARY KEY (CustomerID, AgentID,
      ListingID, ContactDate));
```

3. Type the following, pressing **Enter** at the end of each line. Here you will add the constraints *after* creating the table with ALTER TABLE statements.

```
ALTER TABLE CustAgentList
  ADD CONSTRAINT fk_CustAgentList_Cust
  FOREIGN KEY (CustomerID)
  REFERENCES Customers (CustomerID) ON
  DELETE CASCADE;
ALTER TABLE CustAgentList
  ADD CONSTRAINT fk_CustAgentList_Agent
  FOREIGN KEY (AgentID)
  REFERENCES Agents (AgentID) ON DELETE
  CASCADE;
ALTER TABLE CustAgentList
  ADD CONSTRAINT fk_CustAgentList_Listing
  FOREIGN KEY (ListingID)
  REFERENCES Listings (ListingID) ON DELETE
  CASCADE;
ALTER TABLE CustAgentList
  ADD CONSTRAINT fk_CustAgentList_Contact
  FOREIGN KEY (ContactReason)
  REFERENCES ContactReason (ContactReason)
  ON DELETE CASCADE;
```

4. Type the following to display the constraints you created. You will add to the spool file result, so be sure you specify the same file name as you did above in step 2, line 4.

```
COLUMN table_name FORMAT A15
COLUMN column_name FORMAT A15
COLUMN constraint_name FORMAT A25
SPOOL C:\<path>\<yourname>Ch3Redwood.txt
APPEND
DESCRIBE CustAgentList
SELECT table_name, column_name,
constraint_name
FROM user_cons_columns
WHERE table_name = 'CUSTAGENTLIST';
SPOOL OFF
CLEAR COLUMNS
```

5. Type **exit** and press **Enter** to exit SQL*Plus.

6. Open Notepad, click **File**, click **Open**, navigate to the folder where your <yourname>Ch3Redwood.txt spool is stored, click

\<yourname\>Ch3Redwood.txt, and then click the **Open** button.

7. Move the insertion point to the leftmost position in the first line and press **Enter** to open a new line. Move up to the empty line and type your first and last names to identify the file.
8. Click **File** and then click **Print** to print the spool file. Close Notepad, and click **Yes** when asked if you want to save the changes. Be prepared to turn in this output to your instructor, if requested.

2. Coffee Merchant

The Coffee Merchant DBA wants you to create two tables and include several constraints on columns of the tables you build. You will use SQL*Plus for all your work. The DBA would like you to build the *Inventory* table, which will hold coffee and tea items for sale; the DBA has asked that you also build a *Countries* table that will hold the identification number and names of all the world's countries. When populated, the Inventory table will contain foreign keys for each coffee and tea that point to the country of origin.

As you type and execute SQL*Plus and SQL commands, mistakes may occur. You can opt to create the text in Notepad, and then copy and paste each step's instructions to SQL*Plus. Just be careful to correct any mistakes in Notepad and recopy them to SQL*Plus before continuing. Any mistakes will appear in your spool file. When you open it in Step 9 below, simply delete the mistake lines from the spool file. Begin by locating and running the script file Ch03InitializeCoffee.sql. It cleans up the Coffee Merchant database so that you start with a "clean slate."

1. Launch SQL*Plus and log into Oracle.
2. Type **SPOOL \<path\>\\\<yourname\> Ch3Coffee.txt** and press **Enter.** Be sure to substitute a suitable path (for example, C:\Temp) for "\<path\>" and type your last name in place of "\<yourname\>".
3. Type the following:

```
COLUMN type FORMAT A10
SHOW USER
DROP TABLE States;
SELECT original_name, object_name, type
FROM user_recyclebin;
PURGE RECYCLEBIN;
```

4. Next, create the Countries table by typing the following commands and pressing Enter at the end of each line:

```
CREATE TABLE Countries
 (CountryID INTEGER CONSTRAINT pk_countries
 PRIMARY KEY,
  CountryName NVARCHAR2(40) CONSTRAINT
  nn_CountriesCountryName NOT NULL);
```

5. Create the Inventory table by typing the following commands and pressing Enter at the end of each line. The last line ends with a parenthesis and a semicolon.

```
CREATE TABLE Inventory
 (InventoryID INTEGER CONSTRAINT
 pk_inventory PRIMARY KEY,
  Name NVARCHAR2(40) NOT NULL,
  Price NUMBER(6,2) CONSTRAINT cc_InvPrice
    CHECK (Price >=3 AND PRICE <= 400),
  OnHand INTEGER CONSTRAINT cc_InvOnHand
    CHECK (OnHand BETWEEN -1000 AND 25000),
  Description NVARCHAR2(500),
  ItemType NVARCHAR2(1) CONSTRAINT
  cc_InvItemType
    CHECK (ItemType = 'C' OR ItemType = 'T'),
  CountryID INTEGER CONSTRAINT
  fk_CountriesInventory
    REFERENCES Countries(CountryID) ON
    DELETE CASCADE);
```

6. Type the following to examine the constraint names you created and the names Oracle assigned for ones you did not name. As usual, press **Enter** at the end of each line.

```
DESCRIBE Inventory
DESCRIBE Countries
COLUMN table_name FORMAT A15
COLUMN column_name FORMAT A15
COLUMN constraint_name FORMAT A25
SELECT table_name, column_name,
constraint_name
FROM user_cons_columns WHERE table_name =
'INVENTORY';
SPOOL OFF
CLEAR COLUMNS
```

7. Type **exit** to exit SQL*Plus and log off of Oracle.
8. Open Notepad, click **File,** click **Open,** navigate to the folder where your \<yourname\> Ch3Coffee.txt spool is stored, click **\<yourname\> Ch3Coffee.txt,** and then click the **Open** button.
9. Click **File** and then click **Print** to print the spool file. You can turn in this output to your instructor, if requested. Close Notepad.

3. Rowing Ventures

Rowing Ventures wants your help to ensure that the data they enter into various tables that make up their regatta information is consistent, values entered into selected columns are within reasonable limits, and related tables have their foreign keys set properly. Before beginning, initialize Rowing Ventures' tables by locating and running the script file called Ch03InitializeRowing.sql. Next, open Notepad and create all the instructions to accomplish what follows in a file you save as <yourname>Ch3Rowing.sql. Next, create two tables called BoatCrew and Person. BoatCrew contains three columns: BoatID, PersonID, and Position. BoatID and PersonID are both integer numbers and are the composite primary key for BoatCrew. Neither column can be empty. Position is a single-digit integer whose values are limited to 0 through 8, where 0 indicates the coxswain and 1 through 8 indicates the position in which the crew member rows. PersonID is a foreign key referencing the PersonID column in the Person table. The third column, Position, can be empty. Because the PersonID column references a table not yet built, build the Person table and then use an ALTER TABLE statement to define the foreign key in the BoatCrew table.

The Person table contains six columns: PersonID, LastName, FirstName, Gender, Weight, and DateOfBirth. PersonID is the primary key, an integer value with no scale specified. LastName, FirstName, and Gender are all National character strings whose maximum length is 50. LastName and FirstName must not be empty, but the other fields can be empty. Gender is limited to 'M' and 'F' (uppercase, only), with a default value of 'F' when omitted during data entry. (*Hint:* enter the default *before* typing the constraint for the column.) Weight is any integer value (no scale specified) in the range of 85 to 250. Add the table comment *Position 0 indicates the coxswain* to the BoatCrew table. Create the two tables as described above. Then, open a spool file to save the following results: (1) your user name (SHOW USER), (2) the two table's descriptions, (3) the BoatCrew table's comments (*hint:* include the clause **WHERE table_name = 'BOATCREW'** to limit the results displayed), and (4) a listing of each table's constraints. (*Hint:* query the user_constraints view and add the limiting phrase **WHERE table_name IN ('BOATCREW', 'PERSON')** to reduce the rows to just the constraints on the two tables you created.) Print the completed spool file, and print the script file you saved in Notepad.

4. Broadcloth Clothing

The Broadcloth database administrator wants your help to ensure that the data they enter into the Broadcloth Customer table contains the appropriate constraints and data types. Launch *i*SQL*Plus and then locate, load, and execute the script file Ch03InitializeBroadcloth.sql. (Running the script will eliminate any Broadcloth tables lying around from previous chapters.) Ignore any error messages such as "table or view does not exist." Create the Customer table with columns and constraints shown below in Table 3.11. Assign a meaningful name to all constraints. After you create the table, print the *i*SQL*Plus Web page showing the message "Table created."

Add the column comment *Currency appropriate for home country* to the BaseCurrency column. Display the constraints for the table Customers only. *Hint:* use the user_constraints view and add the clause **WHERE table_name = 'CUSTOMER'** to restrict the constraints to those in the Customer table. Print the resulting Web page. Display the column comments for the Customer table, only (see hint above). Execute DESCRIBE Customer and print the resulting Web page.

TABLE 3.11 Customer columns and their constraints.

Column Name	Data Type	Length	Constraint
CustomerID	Integer		Primary key; default 0
CompanyName	String	Variable up to 50	NOT NULL
City	String	Variable up to 50	NOT NULL
Nation	String	Variable up to 50	(none)
ContactID	Integer		(none)
BaseCurrency	String	Variable up to 50	(none)

CHAPTER 4

MODIFYING DATA AND AUDITING TABLE OPERATIONS

Learning Objectives

In this chapter, you will learn how to:

- Insert rows into tables.
- Insert data into tables containing domain and integrity rules.
- Insert data from other database tables.
- Update data in one or more columns.
- Use substitution variables in a SQL script file.
- Delete one, several, or all rows from a table.
- Truncate a table.
- Start and end database transactions.
- Audit insert, update, and delete operations with triggers.

INSERTING ROWS INTO TABLES

In Chapter 3 you learned how to use several of Oracle's DDL statements to create tables, name constraints, and drop tables. When you executed the CREATE TABLE statement, Oracle created the database object immediately. As you remember, DDL statements take effect immediately without the need to COMMIT them. In this chapter, you will learn how to use Oracle's DML, or data manipulation language, statements to insert, update, and delete database table records. Whenever you execute DML statements, you can choose to make any database changes permanent periodically by issuing the database transaction control statement COMMIT. Occasionally, you will use the SELECT query statement to review some of the changes you make to data. Chapters 5 and 6 present the SELECT statement in detail. *Query* statements allow users to view database data, and they often answer questions such as "how many customers live in California?" The DML commands that you issue to insert, update, and delete data in database tables are sometimes called *action queries* because they cause changes to data in tables.

Action queries make changes to tables, and those changes could lead to irreparable damage and cause great data loss if formulated incorrectly. You will learn how to monitor action queries by noting who ran them, and data values before and after the queries were run using a handy tool called triggers. A ***trigger*** is a program that Oracle automatically executes—*fires* in database lingo—whenever an INSERT, UPDATE, or DELETE statement is run against a specified database table.

To initialize database tables used in this chapter, you will run a script file we have supplied. Recall that a script file is a text file containing SQL and SQL*Plus statements. Using SQL*Plus, you run a script file by issuing the START command followed by a space and the path and name of the script file. The path is any legitimate Windows path, but it cannot contain blanks. Recall that you can substitute @ for the word *start*. Initialize the Redwood Realty database by executing the following steps.

To initialize the Redwood Realty database for use in Chapter 4:

1. Launch SQL*Plus, log into the database with your username and password, type **CLEAR SCREEN** and press **Enter** to clear the screen.
2. Locate the script file Ch04InitializeRedwood.sql, and note the Windows path to that file. (The script file creates two tables and establishes constraints on selected table columns.)
3. Next, type

    `@C:\<path>Ch04InitializeRedwood.sql`

    and press **Enter** to run the script. (Substitute your actual path for "<path>" shown above). You can also type `START C:\<path>Ch04InitializeRedwood` in which you omit the extension ".sql" and substitute START for @.
4. To verify that two Redwood Realty tables have been created, type and execute the following statements to display the tables' structures:

    `DESCRIBE LicenseStatus`
    `DESCRIBE Agents`

The script you ran in the preceding steps dropped all Redwood Realty tables and created the LicenseStatus and Agents tables. Neither table has any data rows, because you will add rows to those tables during the course of this chapter. The Agents table contains information about the brokers and realtors in the Redwood Realty office including their names, contact information, birthday, hire date, and real estate license status. One of the Agents table columns, LicenseStatusID, is a foreign key that is related to a corresponding primary key column in the LicenseStatus table. Besides the primary key LicenseStatusID, the LicenseStatus table contains a full description of type of license that each realtor or broker holds. For each primary key code there is a corresponding full text description. Figure 4.1 shows the table column names and the primary key and foreign key relationship between them. Table 4.1 shows the constraints that the Agents table enforces. (The only constraint on the LicenseStatus table is the primary key column, LicenseStatusID). The constraints are part of the two CREATE TABLE statements that you ran in the steps above. You can open the script file Ch04InitializeRedwood.sql in Notepad and print it if you want to examine the DDL and SQL*Plus statements it contains.

In this chapter, you will add, delete, and modify rows in both tables to understand how INSERT, UPDATE, and DELETE SQL statements operate. As you execute SQL statements to become familiar with them, you will see a few error messages generated by Oracle which illustrate how Oracle provides domain and referential integrity.

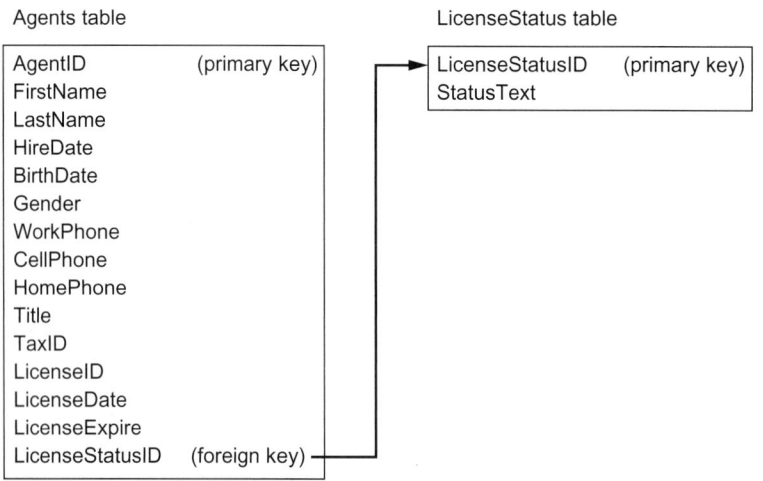

FIGURE 4.1 Structure of two related Redwood Realty tables.

TABLE 4.1 Constraints and structure of the Agents table.

Column	Description	Data type	Constraint(s)
AgentID	Unique number assigned to each agent	INTEGER	Primary key
Gender	Agent's sex	NVARCHAR2(10)	Check: only 'M', 'm', 'F' or 'f'
Title	Internal title assigned to each employee	NVARCHAR2(20)	Check: only 'salesperson' or 'broker' (any combination of upper- and lowercase letters allowed)
LicenseStatusID	Code representing an agent's real estate license status	INTEGER	Foreign key; value must be found in the LicenseStatus table's primary key column, LicenseStatusID

You issue INSERT statements to add new rows to a database table. With the INSERT statement you can specify:

- the table into which the row is to be inserted,
- a list of columns for which you want to insert values,
- a list of values inserted into specific columns.

The general syntax of the INSERT command is:

```
INSERT INTO <table-name> [(column, column,…)]
   VALUES (expression, expression, …);
```

where "<table-name>" is the table into which you are inserting values. You can omit specifying the table column names if you supply a value for *every* column in the table. If you wish to omit values for some columns, then you must specify the column names and the values to be inserted. In any case, you need to supply a value for the primary key column and any other columns that have a NOT NULL constraint—including a foreign key column. You do not have to specify values for columns with default values specified in the table definition.

If you choose to insert values for each column in the table, then you do not need to list the column names in the INSERT statement. However, you must specify values for each column in the table, and they must be in the same order as they are listed in the CREATE TABLE statement that created the table. For any columns whose values are unknown, place the word *NULL*. For instance, to insert three rows into the LicenseStatus table, you could issue the commands

```
INSERT INTO LicenseStatus VALUES (1001, 'Licensed');
INSERT INTO LicenseStatus VALUES (1004, 'Deceased');
INSERT INTO LicenseStatus VALUES (1003, NULL);
```

Because you did not specify the column names, Oracle places the first value in the LicenseStatusID column and places the second value, a string, in the StatusText column. The third line shows an example in which you don't know the description for code 1003. Oracle inserts NULL into that column, indicating that value for the StatusText column corresponding to LicenseStatusID 1003 is unknown at this time. Because the data type for the StatusText column is NVARCHAR2, a character string, you must enclose any text in single quotation marks. Any text within single quotation marks is case sensitive. If you want to insert a character string that contains a single quotation mark, you must type two single quotation marks. For example, you type the value *'Realtor's license suspended'* to include a single quotation mark to make the word *Realtor* possessive. Always use two single quotation marks, not a double quotation mark, when you want to include a single quotation mark in a stored text string.

Whenever you want to insert values into only selected table fields—not all fields—use the INSERT INTO form:

```
INSERT INTO <table-name> (column, column,…)
  VALUES (expression, expression,…);
```

When you use this form of the INSERT command, you must specify the column names into which you want to insert values along with a corresponding set of values (expressions) in the VALUES clause. The *order* of the column names in your INSERT statement does not have to match the order of the column names in the CREATE TABLE statement. However, the data values in the VALUES clause must be in the same order as their corresponding column names in the column list of the INSERT INTO statement. For instance, the following are examples of inserting data into the Agents table. The only required column in the Agents tables is AgentID, the primary key.

```
INSERT INTO AGENTS(AgentID, LastName, FirstName)
  VALUES (12345, 'Frockmeister', 'Robert');
INSERT INTO AGENTS(LastName, TaxID, LicenseStatusID, AgentID)
  VALUES ('Kellog', '1234-rtu', NULL, 40335);
INSERT INTO AGENTS(AgentID, Gender, LastName, BirthDate)
  VALUES(21334, 'f', 'Pennypacker', To_Date('04-JUN-1979'));
```

In the three preceding statements, all the columns are in a slightly different order from the order of the columns in the table. However, the values are inserted into the corresponding columns according to the column names. Practice inserting data by executing the steps that follow.

SPECIFYING A COLUMN LIST

Steps that follow illustrate what happens when you attempt to insert a row containing a foreign key reference to a table that is empty or not fully populated yet.

To insert a row into the Agents table:

1. If you logged out of SQL*Plus and Oracle, then launch SQL*Plus and log into Oracle.
2. Open Notepad so you can easily modify the SQL statements you are about to type. First, save the file as Ch4<yourname>Insert41.sql, and then type the

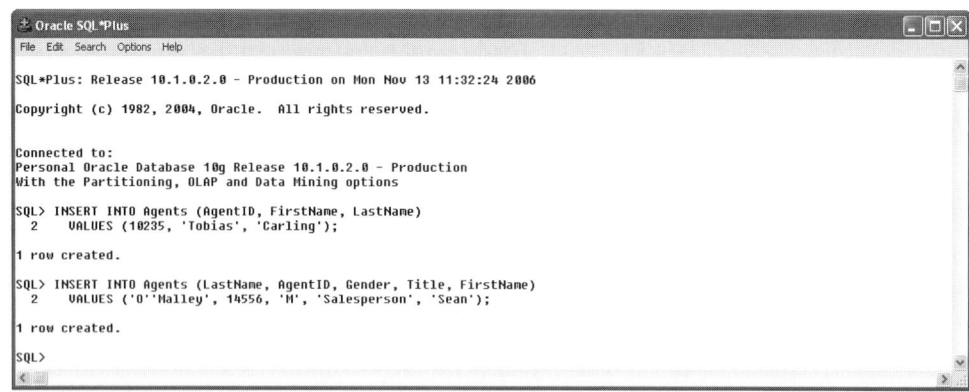

FIGURE 4.2 Inserting rows into the Agents table.

following in Notepad:

```
INSERT INTO Agents (AgentID, FirstName, LastName)
  VALUES (10235, 'Tobias', 'Carling');
```

3. Copy and paste the preceding into SQL*Plus, and press **Enter** to execute it. Oracle adds a new row (see Figure 4.2).
4. Switch back to Notepad and type the following INSERT statement, copy and paste it into SQL*Plus, and execute it:

```
INSERT INTO Agents (LastName, AgentID, Gender, Title, FirstName)
  VALUES ('O''Malley', 14556, 'M', 'Salesperson', 'Sean');
```

> **Tip:** Type two single quotation marks following the O in O'Malley. Remember: for every two consecutive single quotation marks you type within a quoted string, Oracle stores one quotation mark.

DEALING WITH INTEGRITY CONSTRAINTS

Before you can add rows containing a foreign key value referencing another table's primary key, the referenced table's values must already be in place. For example, you cannot add an Agent table row with the value 1006 in the LicenseStatusID column unless the LicenseStatus table already has a row containing 1006 in its primary key column. You have at least two choices to solve this primary key/foreign key relationship conundrum. One choice is to first populate the table containing the primary key column referenced by other tables as a foreign key. The second choice is to specify *NULL* for the foreign key field and defer populating the primary key column of the referenced table until later. The second approach means you will have to later update the foreign key column of all rows once you have inserted all the rows in the referenced table. A popular solution is to first populate all tables containing primary keys referenced by other tables through a foreign key reference. Then, populate all the other tables. Let's try to insert an Agent table row that violates a referential integrity constraint—its foreign key points to an empty LicenseStatus table.

To try to insert a row with a foreign key integrity constraint violation:

1. Save the present contents of Notepad. Next, click **File** and then click **New** to create a new file. Save it as Ch4<yourname>IntegrityTest42.sql. (Substitute your last name for "<yourname>.")

2. Type the following SQL command into Notepad, copy and paste it into the SQL*Plus dialog box, and then execute it.

```
INSERT INTO Agents (AgentID, LastName, LicenseStatusID, Gender)
  VALUES (14883, 'Fernandez', 1001, 'F');
```

Oracle generates an error message because there is no value of 1001 in the LicenseStatus table. Because there is no "parent" primary key to match Fernandez' foreign key, Oracle traps the error.

3. Switch to notepad and type **NULL**, replacing *1001* as the third item in the VALUES clause. Copy and paste it into SQL*Plus, and execute the modified INSERT statement. Oracle inserts the corrected row (see Figure 4.3).

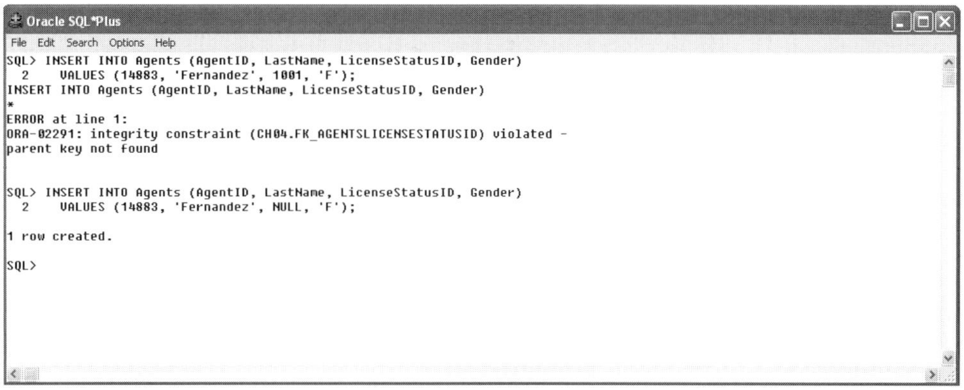

FIGURE 4.3 Correcting an integrity constraint violation.

The modified INSERT statement executed correctly because you inserted NULL in a field that is a foreign key. Because its value is NULL, Oracle does not bother to check to see if a corresponding primary key value exists in the LicenseStatus table. The problem is not completely solved, because eventually, you will want to link the two tables together. At that time, you will have to populate the LicenseStatus table. Then, you can modify any NULL LicenseStatusID values, replacing them with valid LicenseStatusID values matching values in the primary key of the LicenseStatus table.

OMITTING THE COLUMN LIST

You can omit the parenthesized list of table column names in the INSERT INTO statement as long as: (1) you supply values for *every* table column, and (2) the values you supply are in the same order as the column definitions in the CREATE TABLE statement. Inserting rows into a table without specifying the column names can save a great deal of typing. In fact, most of the script files we supply that you run which populate tables use this method. Because the Agents table LicenseStatusID column depends on (references) values in the like-named column in the LicenseStatus table, filling the LicenseStatus table is first priority.

To insert values without using a column list:

1. Ensure that you are logged into SQL*Plus and then type the following statements. Use Notepad as you have in the past to copy and paste statements into SQL*Plus. At the end of this sequence of steps, save the Notepad file under a unique name on your disk.

```
INSERT INTO LicenseStatus VALUES (1001, 'Licensed');
INSERT INTO LicenseStatus VALUES (1002, 'Licensed NBA');
INSERT INTO LicenseStatus VALUES (1003, 'Canceled Officer');
```

148 Introduction to Oracle

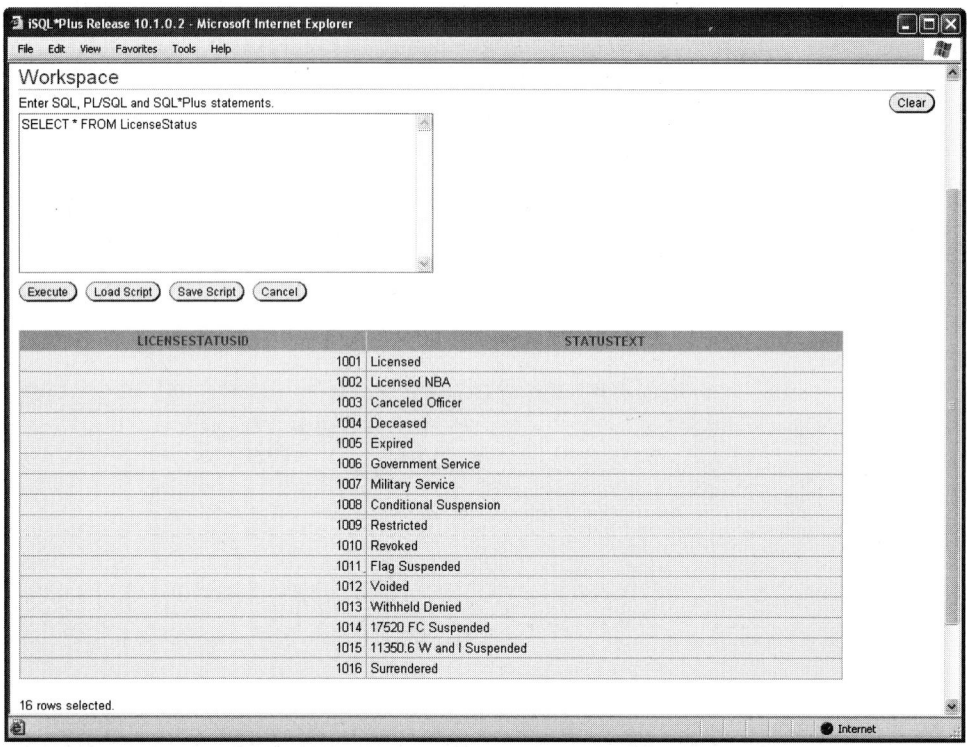

FIGURE 4.4 Displaying the contents of the LicenseStatus table.

Oracle indicates three rows have been inserted.

2. Locate the file Ch04InsertLS.sql, open it in Notepad, copy and paste the entire contents into SQL*Plus, and execute its INSERT statements. (You can also run it as a script file using the START command as you have done before.) Oracle adds 13 rows to the LicenseStatus table.

3. In SQL*Plus type **Exit** and press **Enter** to logout of Oracle and close SQL*Plus.

4. Open your Web browser and then launch *i*SQL*Plus. Log into *i*SQL*Plus with your username and password. (If you prefer, you can do this activity from SQL*Plus. We find *i*SQL*Plus is better when you *display* table columns, because it squeezes in all the columns so that each row appears on one line and it aligns values below the column names.)

5. Type `SELECT * FROM LicenseStatus` in the Workspace text box, and click the **Execute** button to view the LicenseStatus table's contents (see Figure 4.4).

6. After reviewing your results, click the **Logout** hyperlink and close your browser.

Next, you will add in the remaining agent rows to the Agents table. Instead of running a series of INSERT INTO statements, you can run a script file that will populate the remaining rows for you.

To populate the remaining Agents rows:

1. Launch SQL*Plus, log in with your username and password.

2. Locate the script file Ch04InsertAgents.sql, note its path, and type and execute the following START statement to add more rows to the Agents table. Be sure to use your own path to the script file. Your results should match those shown in Figure 4.5.

CHAPTER 4 Modifying Data and Auditing Table Operations

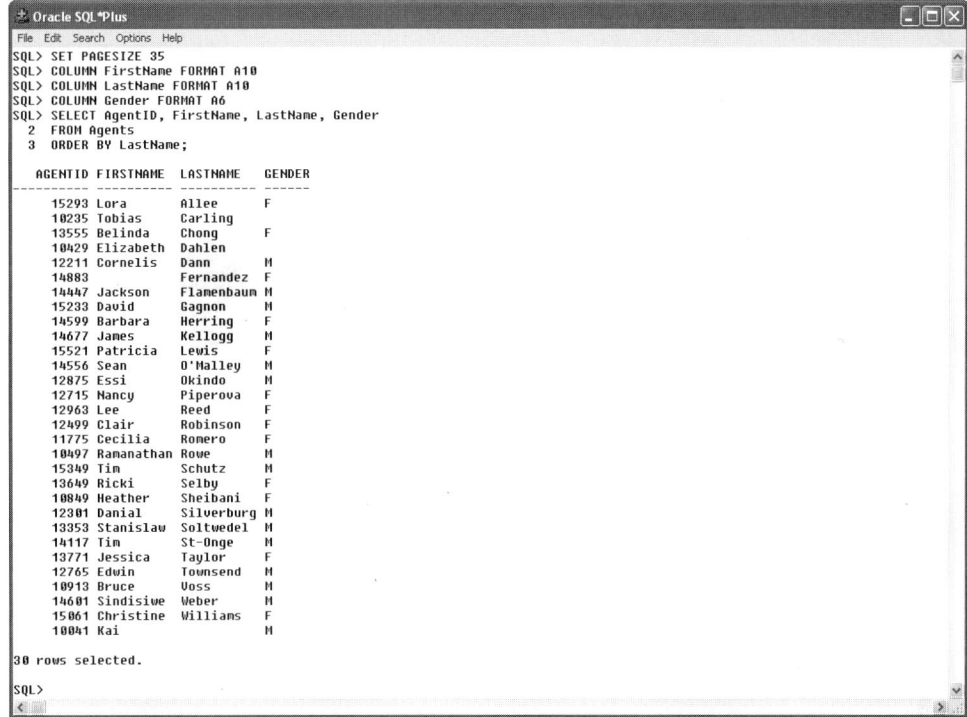

FIGURE 4.5 Displaying selected columns from the Agents table.

> **Tip:** You can omit the suffix .sql for script files when using the START or @ commands. Oracle knows that .sql files are script files.

```
START C:\Ch04InsertAgents
```

Oracle displays a series of "1 row created." messages indicating that it inserted the rows. You can open the script file in Notepad to review its contents.

3. Display selected columns of the Agents table by executing the following SQL*Plus and SQL statements:

```
CLEAR SCREEN
SET PAGESIZE 35
COLUMN FirstName FORMAT A10
COLUMN LastName FORMAT A10
COLUMN Gender FORMAT A6
SELECT AgentID, FirstName, LastName, Gender
FROM Agents
ORDER BY LastName;
```

Your results should match those shown in Figure 4.5.

INSERTING DATES AND TIMES

When you enter numeric data into a table, do not enclose it in single quotation marks. As you recall, you must enclose both character and date type values in single quotes. Regardless of the data type you enter with an INSERT statement, Oracle stores all values in an internal binary format. SQL statements that retrieve data from a table also convert data to a printable form.

The default Oracle formats to enter a date are DD-MON-YY and DD-MON-YYYY, which are both format models. For example, you could issue the following INSERT statements to add two agents' AgentID and BirthDate fields using both of the preceding two default date formats:

```
INSERT INTO Agents (AgentID, BirthDate) VALUES (99887, '12-OCT-1970')
INSERT INTO Agents (AgentID, BirthDate) VALUES (55678, '08-JUN-82')
```

Observe that in both cases, the date fields are enclosed in single quotation marks.

If a two-digit year has a value between 0 and 49, then it is assumed to be a date in the 21st century. Two-digit year values greater than 50 are stored as 20th century dates. For example, the date value '20-OCT-35' represents October 20, 2035. Similarly, the date value '04-JUL-51' represents July 4, 1951. It is best to always use four-digit years when inputting dates to avoid any confusion.

When retrieving or inserting data or time information, you can use a format model to specify a different input or output format. A *format model* is an alphanumeric string that specifies the way a value appears on output or the interpretation of a value for input into a database. Format models do not affect the way data is stored, however. Format models are especially important when you are inputting or displaying date or time values. To insert a date into a DATE field not using either of the default date formats, specify the date as a character string and use the Oracle TO_DATE function to convert the date character string into an internal date form acceptable to Oracle. The general form of the TO_DATE function is

```
TO_DATE('date string', 'date format model')
```

where *date string* represents the date value enclosed in single quotation marks and *date format model* is the format representing the date string's format. For example, the following INSERT statements add an agent's HireDate and AgentID using a date format other than the default:

```
INSERT INTO Agents (HireDate, AgentID)
    VALUES (TO_DATE('July 14, 2005', 'Month DD, YYYY'), 77777);

INSERT INTO Agents (AgentID, HireDate)
    VALUES (88888, TO_DATE('10/17/1946', 'DD/MM/YYYY');
```

Both the spelling and capitalization of date format model elements indicate to Oracle the format of a date value being input. Date models can contain forward slashes (/), hyphens (-), and colons (:) between date elements in the formatting model when they also appear in the date string. As a convenient reminder, Table 4.2 shows examples of date format model symbols.

TABLE 4.2 Common date format model symbols.

Format Model Symbol	Displayed or Input Value
MONTH	FEBRUARY
Month	February
MM	02
DD	15
DDD	251
DAY	WEDNESDAY
Day	Wednesday
DY	WED
YYYY	2006
YY	06

Let's practice adding agent information to the Agents table, specifying date information constants and their corresponding date format models.

To add rows to the Agents table:

1. If necessary, launch SQL*Plus, log in with your username and password. Open Notepad as you have in the past.

2. Type the following SQL command into Notepad, copy and paste it into the SQL*Plus dialog box, and then execute it. Make any needed corrections in Notepad, then recopy to SQL*Plus to execute the corrected statement:

```
INSERT INTO Agents(AgentID, HireDate, BirthDate)
VALUES(23456,TO_DATE('January 12, 2004', 'Month DD, YYYY'),
'10-JUN-1981');
INSERT INTO Agents(HireDate, AgentID)
VALUES(TO_DATE('2004/02/03', 'YYYY/MM/DD'),56789);
```

3. Press **Enter**, if needed, to execute the second SQL statement. Oracle responds with two separate messages "1 row created."

4. Display the rows added by executing this simple SELECT statement. (Chapter 5 presents the SELECT statement in detail.)

```
SELECT AgentID, BirthDate, HireDate
FROM Agents WHERE AgentID > 16000;
```

Figure 4.6 shows the results of executing these three SQL statements. Your results should match those. Remain logged into SQL*Plus, because you will execute additional steps in the next section.

Inserting times is similar to inserting dates. Use the time-specific format model elements HH, MI, SS, AM, and PM to indicate hours, minutes, seconds, and the meridian indicator (AM or PM can be written with or without periods). For instance, to insert a time such as a boat race's beginning time, you might issue the following INSERT statement:

```
INSERT INTO BoatRace(RaceID, BeginTime)
     VALUES(1237, TO_DATE('08:20:25 AM', 'HH:MI:SS AM');
```

Storing times is vital in an application such as the Rowing Ventures exercise, in which the whole point of the race is to record the start and finish times to calculate which boat finished with the shortest elapsed time.

FIGURE 4.6 Inserting date values into a table.

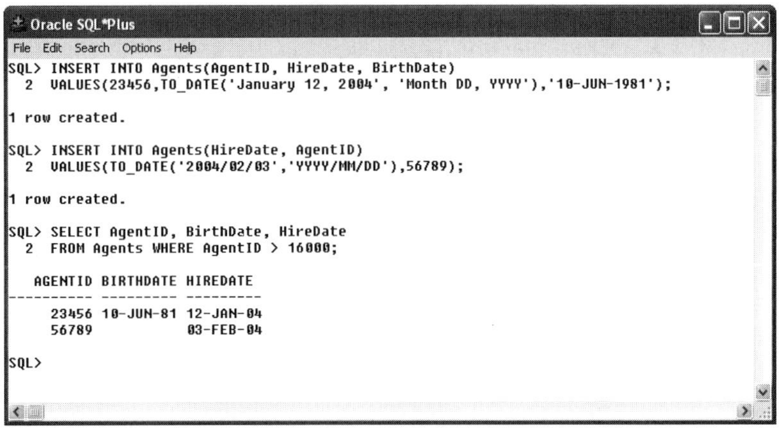

INSERTING DATA FROM OTHER DATABASE TABLES

You can use the INSERT statement with an optional clause—the SELECT subquery—to select data from the other table. The subquery may return zero, one, or several rows from another table, inserting them into the target table. The number of columns and the types of each column in the source and target tables must match. However, the corresponding columns in the source and target tables need not match. For example, you could insert selected rows from a table called NevadaRealtors into the Agents table. Assuming that each primary key field from the source table NevadaRealtors does not clash with those of existing agents' AgentID columns in the Agents table, you could issue the following INSERT statement with the SELECT subquery to copy rows from the NevadaRealtors table for realtors whose home city is Winnemucca.

```
INSERT INTO Agents(AgentID, FirstName, LastName, BirthDate, LicenseID)
   SELECT RealtorID, Fname, Lname, DOB, LicNumb
   FROM NevadaRealtors
   WHERE LOWER(HomeCity) = 'winnemucca';
```

Oracle searches the NevadaRealtors table extracting the listed columns for which the source table's HomeCity value (converted to lower case letters) matches *winnemucca*. Source table columns are extracted and inserted into corresponding target table (Agents) columns, one row at a time. If fourteen rows in the NevadaRealtors table are retrieved, Oracle inserts those fourteen rows into the Agents table. Drop the WHERE clause if you want to insert *all* rows from a source table. Experimenting with this form of the INSERT statement will give you a firm grasp of how it works.

To add rows to the Agents table from another table:

1. Locate the script file Ch04NevadaRealtors.sql, note its path, and type and execute the following statement. Be sure to use your own path to the script file.

   START C:\Ch04NevadaRealtors

2. Type the following in SQL*Plus. Of course, you can first launch Notepad, type the statement in Notepad, and the copy and paste to SQL*Plus. Press Enter to execute the statement.

   ```
   INSERT INTO Agents(AgentID, FirstName, LastName, BirthDate, LicenseID)
      SELECT RealtorID, Fname, Lname, DOB, LicNumb
      FROM NevadaRealtors
      WHERE LOWER(HomeCity) = 'winnemucca';
   ```

   If your statement is successful, Oracle displays the message "5 rows created."

3. To display the newly inserted rows, type and execute the following SQL SELECT statement:

   ```
   SELECT AgentID, FirstName, LastName
   FROM Agents WHERE AgentID > 515432;
   ```

   Figure 4.7 shows the results of steps 2 and 3.

4. To complete this series of steps, drop the NevadaRealtors table by issuing the following SQL command:

   DROP TABLE NevadaRealtors CASCADE CONSTRAINTS PURGE;

   Oracle removes the table, frees up any space it occupies, and issues the confirming message "Table dropped."

5. Type **Exit** and press **Enter** to log out of Oracle and close the SQL*Plus interface.

```
Oracle SQL*Plus
File Edit Search Options Help
SQL> START C:\Ch04NevadaRealtors
SQL> INSERT INTO Agents(AgentID, FirstName, LastName, BirthDate, LicenseID)
  2     SELECT RealtorID, Fname, Lname, DOB, LicNumb
  3     FROM NevadaRealtors
  4     WHERE LOWER(HomeCity) = 'winnemucca';

5 rows created.

SQL> SELECT AgentID, FirstName, LastName
  2  FROM Agents WHERE AgentID >515432;

   AGENTID FIRSTNAME                      LASTNAME
---------- ------------------------------ ------------------------------
    515602 Doc                            Bishop
    518444 Bill                           Jeffords
    516344 Jim                            Case
    516476 John L.                        Peterson
    515894 Craig                          Cardoza

SQL>
```

FIGURE 4.7 Inserting rows from another table.

CREATING AND USING SEQUENCES

A *sequence* is a database object that generates a series of unique integers. Unique integers are commonly used to generate a unique primary key for each new record added to a table. Each time you use a sequence when adding a row to a table, the number created by the sequence is guaranteed to be new, ensuring that no two rows in a table have the same number. Sequences free the data input personnel from attempting to assign unique numbers themselves. The value of automatic generation of unique integer values becomes even more evident when you consider what could happen when dozens or hundreds of people are simultaneously entering information—sales orders for example—into a database. For each new order they enter, data entry people must ensure that the primary key they enter is different from all the other numbers being assigned by members of the same order entry team. A sequence accomplishes this task, as long as all data entry people reference the same sequence, by name, as they issue an INSERT statement. The named sequence hands out integer numbers in rapid fire to anyone requesting them. Because the maximum value of an integer number generated through a sequence is 10^{27}, there is no chance that you will run out of unique numbers.

Creating a Sequence

You issue the SQL statement CREATE SEQUENCE to create a sequence, and you can have as many uniquely named sequences as you desire in a particular database. The syntax of the CREATE SEQUENCE statement is:

```
CREATE SEQUENCE <sequence name>
[START WITH <value>]
[INCREMENT BY <value>]
[{MAXVALUE <value> | NOMAXVALUE}]
[{MINVALUE <value> | NOMINVALUE}]
[{CYCLE | NOCYCLE}]
[{ORDER | NOORDER}]
[{CACHE <value> | NOCACHE}];
```

Each of the phrases in square brackets is optional, and phrases in curly braces indicate that you must choose one of the options in the list.

Like other objects in a database, every sequence in your user schema must have a unique sequence name. Use the suffix _seq for sequences to easily identify the object type. The START WITH clause allows you to specify a starting value for the sequence. Unless you specify a value, Oracle will begin the sequence with *one*. The INCREMENT BY clause indicates a positive or negative integer that Oracle adds to the latest sequence value to create the next one. Sequences can be ascending order (positive increment value) or descending order (negative increment value), and sequence values can be negative. The values you specify for MINVALUE and MAXVALUE set the minimum and maximum values, respectively, for the sequence. A MINVALUE is meaningless for positive INCREMENT BY values, and a MAXVALUE is meaningless for negative INCREMENT BY values. CYCLE determines whether Oracle should issue values from the sequence when the maximum or minimum are reached. CYCLE specifies to start the sequence over again. NOCYCLE, the default, indicates that Oracle should not generate any numbers once it reaches the maximum or minimum value. ORDER specifies that integers should be released to requesters in the same time order as they are requested—the first request gets the next number first, the second requester gets the second number next, and so on. NOCYCLE is the default. CACHE or its opposite and default NOCACHE specifies whether or not Oracle can generate a series of unique numbers ahead of time, before they are requested, and store them in a memory location for quick distribution to requesters. The default, NOCACHE, means that numbers are not generated in batches ahead of time. Perhaps the most important concept surrounding sequences is that once a sequence value has been generated and assigned, that same value cannot be regenerated until the sequence repeats—a very remote possibility.

You will create a sequence that you can use to create a unique primary key whenever you insert a new real estate agent into the Agents table. By using the sequence in conjunction with the INSERT statement, you ensure that a unique primary key is assigned the first time and every time. First, you must create and name the sequence. You will start the new sequence of numbers at 654321 because you want all new agents to be assigned a six-digit ID greater than any entered so far.

To create and name a sequence:

1. Launch SQL*Plus, log in with your username and password. Open Notepad as you have in the past, and use Notepad as your editor. As in the past, copy and paste what you create in Notepad into SQL*Plus and press **Enter** to execute the statement in SQL*Plus. If needed, correct any mistakes and repeat.
2. In SQL*Plus, type **CLEAR SCREEN** and press **Enter**.
3. Type the following statement in SQL*Plus:

   ```
   CREATE SEQUENCE AgentID_seq
   START WITH 654321
   INCREMENT BY 2 NOCACHE NOCYCLE;
   ```

4. Press **Enter** to execute the preceding statement in SQL*Plus. Oracle responds with the confirming message "Sequence created."

You can list any sequences you have created in your schema by displaying columns from the USER_SEQUENCES data dictionary view.

To display names of sequences and details about an individual sequence:

1. Type and execute the following to display information about the USER_SEQUENCES columns:

   ```
   DESCRIBE user_sequences
   ```

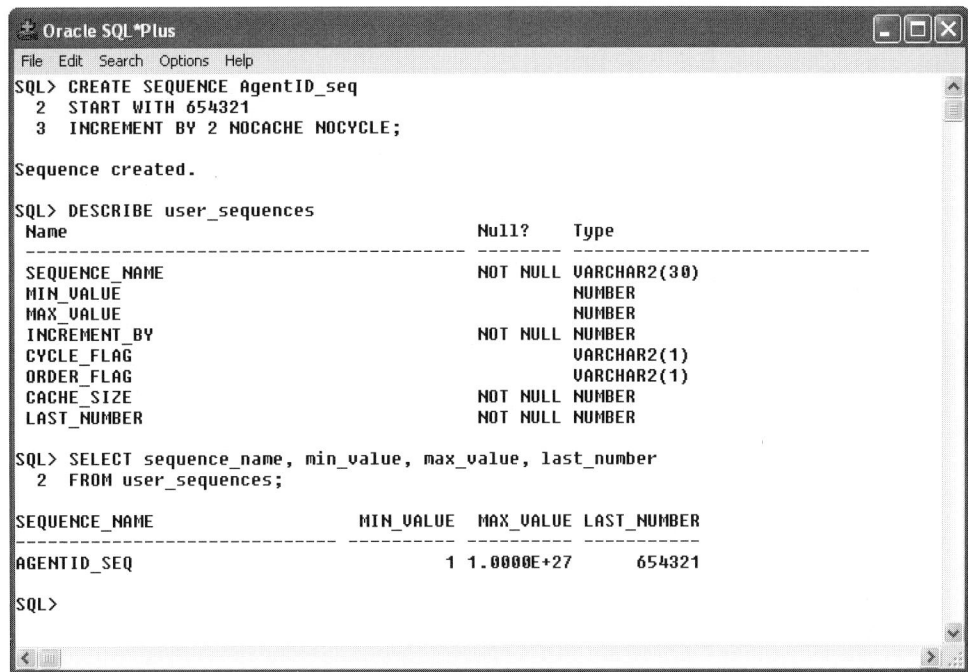

FIGURE 4.8 Creating a sequence and displaying its characteristics.

2. Type and execute the following statement:

```
SELECT sequence_name, min_value, max_value, last_number
FROM user_sequences;
```

Examine the result from the last step. Notice that the MAXVALUE for the sequence AGENTID_SEQ (Oracle stores object names in uppercase) is 10^{27}, an extraordinarily large number of values! (See Figure 4.8.)

Using Sequence Values for Primary Keys

With the AgentID_seq sequence defined, you can invoke it to create unique integer numbers for any purpose. Here, you will use the AgentID_seq sequence to create primary keys for each new agent's information you add to the Agents table. You access sequence values by referring to two pseudocolumns, NEXTVAL and CURRVAL. An Oracle *pseudocolumn* appears to be a field from a database table, but it is a command that returns a value. NEXTVAL (NEXT VALue) is a pseudocolumn that actually generates the sequence value. Once that value is generated, it is stored in the pseudocolumn CURRVAL (CURRent VALue). CURRVAL is handy, because you can reference it to see what value Oracle generated and, for example, populate a related table's foreign key field with the value just generated. To generate a new, unique integer from a sequence, use the following in an INSERT statement:

```
<sequencename>.NEXTVAL
```

To refer to the latest value that has been generated, use the following syntax within a SQL statement:

```
<sequencename>.CURRVAL
```

Next, you will insert three new rows into the Agents table, each row representing information about three newly hired real estate agents. In these examples, you will fill in only a few of the data columns for each agent to save time.

To insert a new row using the AgentID_seq sequence:

1. Type and execute the following INSERT statements:

```
INSERT INTO Agents (AgentID,FirstName,LastName)
  VALUES (AgentID_seq.NEXTVAL,'Angelica','Francis');
INSERT INTO Agents (AgentID,FirstName,LastName)
  VALUES (AgentID_seq.NEXTVAL,'Hershel','Wickstrom');
INSERT INTO Agents (AgentID,FirstName,LastName)
  VALUES (AgentID_seq.NEXTVAL,'Bryan','Wilson');
```

2. Type the following to display the newly entered rows. Observe the values for the primary key column of each of these last three rows listed. Do their primary keys coincide with the sequence you created above?

```
SELECT AgentID, FirstName, LastName
FROM Agents
WHERE AgentID > 123456
ORDER BY AgentID;
```

3. Type the following to display the value of the pseudocolumn CURRVAL for the sequence AgentID_seq:

```
SELECT AgentID_seq.CURRVAL
FROM DUAL;
```

Dual is a table that Oracle has defined which contains one row and one column. It is used when you want to display a value—a calculation or a date for example—that is not a column of any particular table. You will see the Dual table used more in Chapter 5.

Figure 4.9 shows the results of executing the two SELECT statements in steps 2 and 3. As you can see, the primary keys generated for the AgentID by the AgentID_seq sequence are 654321, 654323, and 654325—just as you would expect. As you probably agree, sequences are very convenient for creating primary key values.

ALTERING OR DROPPING SEQUENCES

Settings for any sequence can be changed by issuing the ALTER SEQUENCE statement. Any changes you make to a sequence are applied to values generated *after* the sequence modifications occur. Restrictions to the ALTER SEQUENCE statement are: The START WITH clause cannot be changed, and any changes to the sequence cannot invalidate the existing sequence values. For example, you cannot alter a sequence by lowering MAXVALUE lower than a sequence value that has already been generated. A simplified form of the statement is:

```
ALTER SEQUENCE <sequencename>
[INCREMENT BY <value>]
[{MAXVALUE <value> | NOMAXVALUE}]
[{MINVALUE <value> | NOMINVALUE}]
[{CYCLE | NOCYCLE}]
[{ORDER | NOORDER}]
[{CACHE <value> | NOCACHE}];
```

When you no longer need a sequence, you can delete it by issuing the DROP SEQUENCE statement. Its form is simply

```
DROP SEQUENCE <sequencename>>;
```

Let's drop the sequence AgentID_seq you created in this section.

CHAPTER 4 Modifying Data and Auditing Table Operations

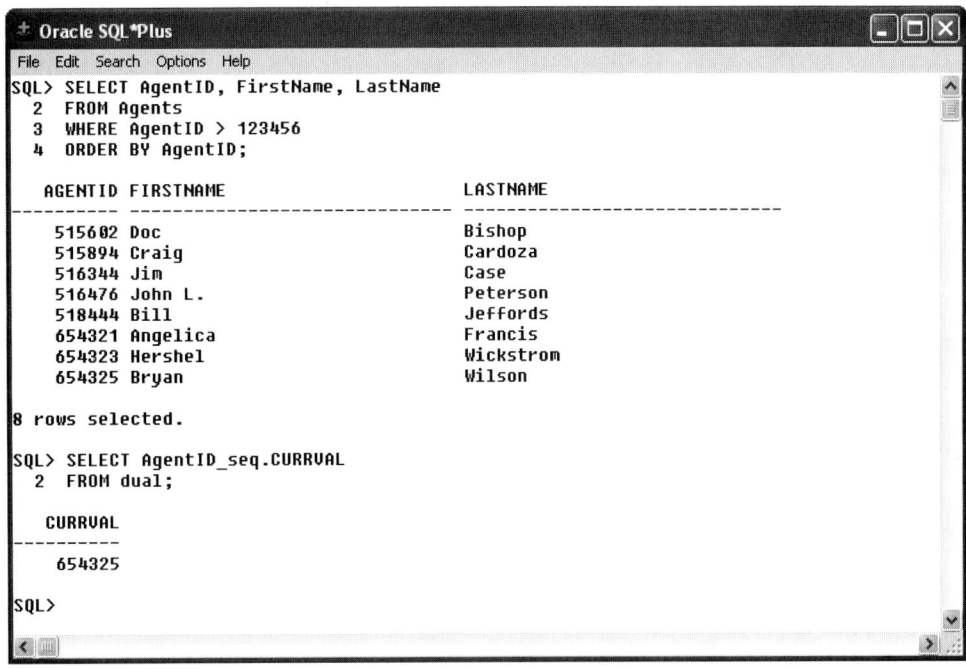

FIGURE 4.9 Reviewing sequence values and CURRVAL.

To drop a sequence:

1. Type and execute the following SQL statement:

   DROP SEQUENCE AgentID_seq;

   Oracle drops the sequence and issues the confirming message "Sequence dropped."

2. Leave SQL*Plus running for steps that follow.

UPDATING DATA

Buyers, sellers, and properties for sale in the Redwood Realty database tables change frequently, and properties move from "for sale" status to "sold" on a regular basis. Redwood Realty realtors renew their real estate licenses, which requires that their LicenseExpire column values be updated from time to time. Most tables in any business require updates on a continuing basis. Inventories of items sold in a store must be reduced to reflect the moment's, hour's, or day's sales of any number of products. Information about people, products, and events require modification as conditions change. The SQL UPDATE statement provides the capability to alter values stored in table columns.

UPDATE STATEMENT

SQL provides the UPDATE statement to make modifications to data. You can update only one table at a time with a single UPDATE statement, but you can modify more than one table column at a time. The general syntax of the UPDATE statement, sometimes called an action query, is this:

```
UPDATE <tablename>
SET <columnname1> = <expression1> [, <columnname2> = <expression2>, …]
[WHERE <condition>];
```

where "<tablename>" specifies the table whose values you want to update, "<columnname>" is the name of a table column, and "<expression>" is a value or an expression that evaluates to a value of the same data type as the column definition. The WHERE clause, which is optional, specifies the search condition and restricts the rows whose columns are affected. If you omit it, then columns in all rows are updated. The "<condition>" consists of column names, relational operators, values, and logical operators. A WHERE clause condition must evaluate to true or false. Oracle's relational operators, like other database systems and programming languages, consist of those shown in Table 4.3.

Oracle's logical operators are shown in Table 4.4. They are the same as logical operators in other database systems.

The record for real estate agent Tobias Carling contains a lot of NULL values because you did not know what values to enter for Title, LicenseDate, and so on at the time you inserted his other information. (See Figure 4.2.) To supply the missing columns for that single record, write an UPDATE statement, supplying the FirstName and LastName, to select the single row to be changed, and supply values for any or all columns you want to fill in or modify. In the steps that follow, you will fill in values for HireDate, BirthDate, Gender, and Title. Then, you can display the row corresponding to Tobias Carling to verify the modifications visually.

TABLE 4.3 Oracle's relational operators.

Relational Operator	Meaning
=	Equal to
<> or !=	Not equal to
>	Greater than
<	Less than
<=	Less than or equal to
>=	Greater than or equal to

TABLE 4.4 Oracle's logical operators.

Logical Operator	Meaning	WHERE Clause Example
AND	True only if both conditions are true; false otherwise	WHERE State = 'MN' AND Gender = 'M'
OR	True if either condition is true; false otherwise	WHERE LicenseStatusID = 1001 OR LicenseStatusID = 1002
NOT	Negate expression	WHERE NOT State = 'NE'
IN	True if among set of discrete values listed	WHERE City IN('Arcata', 'Fortuna', 'Orick')
LIKE	Wildcard expression allowing "don't care" conditions	WHERE LastName LIKE 'Mc%'
BETWEEN … AND …	True if within the value range, inclusive	WHERE SqFt BETWEEN 1500 AND 2000

CHAPTER 4   Modifying Data and Auditing Table Operations   **159**

To update a single row with the UPDATE statement:

1. With SQL*Plus running, type the following statements which format some of the columns and display part of the row corresponding to Carling. Save this set of statements so you can execute them again at the end of these steps. You may want to use Notepad to create and save all the statements you type; then, copy them to SQL*Plus to execute them.

```
CLEAR SCREEN
COLUMN FirstName FORMAT A10
COLUMN LastName FORMAT A10
COLUMN Gender FORMAT A6
SELECT FirstName, LastName, HireDate, BirthDate, Gender, Title
FROM Agents
WHERE FirstName = 'Tobias' AND LastName = 'Carling';
```

> **Tip:** Be careful to capitalize the values for first and last names exactly the way you see them above—with initial uppercase letters. Otherwise, Oracle will not find and display the corresponding row.

2. To uniquely identify the row to be changed, specify the values for first and last names in the WHERE clause in the UPDATE statement also. In a small table, there's very little chance that more than one record will match those column values. Type and execute the following statement:

```
UPDATE Agents
SET HireDate = TO_DATE('12/19/2000', 'MM/DD/YYYY'),
    BirthDate = TO_DATE('10/19/1975', 'MM/DD/YYYY'),
    Gender = 'M',
    Title = 'SALESPERSON'
WHERE FirstName = 'Tobias' AND LastName = 'Carling';
```

Oracle responds with "1 row updated."

3. Verify the changes by issuing this SELECT statement to display Carling's row. Rerun the code you saved from step 1 or retype and run the following:

```
SELECT FirstName, LastName, HireDate, BirthDate, Gender, Title
FROM Agents
WHERE FirstName = 'Tobias' AND LastName = 'Carling';
```

Observe that Oracle updated the four fields you modified in step 2 above (See Figure 4.10).

4. Leave SQL*Plus running.

UPDATE statements can affect more than one row. If you omit the WHERE clause, Oracle applies all the changes to every record in the table. Always be careful when using the UPDATE statement without a WHERE clause. Mistakes using the UDPATE statement can cause great damage. If you do make a mistake and want to undo your previous statements, you can issue a ROLLBACK statement. Details about the effects of ROLLBACK and how to use it and its opposite, COMMIT, appear in the section *Database Transactions*, which appears later in this chapter.

Lora Allee, one of the Redwood Realty brokers, noticed that the values for the Title field of recent additions to the Agents table are empty. In particular, she points out that salespeople with AgentID values of 515602 and greater should be modified so the Title column contains "Salesperson." Lora asks you to modify just that field for those agents. How do you modify one column for several rows? If possible, you locate some characteristic—a value for one or more columns—that uniquely identifies those

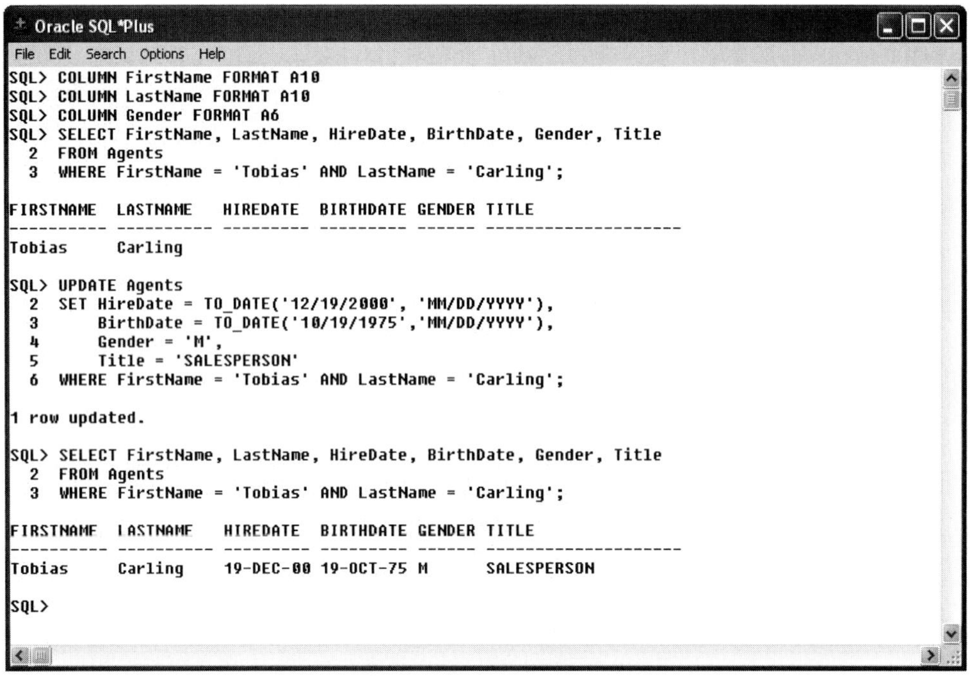

```
SQL> COLUMN FirstName FORMAT A10
SQL> COLUMN LastName FORMAT A10
SQL> COLUMN Gender FORMAT A6
SQL> SELECT FirstName, LastName, HireDate, BirthDate, Gender, Title
  2  FROM Agents
  3  WHERE FirstName = 'Tobias' AND LastName = 'Carling';

FIRSTNAME  LASTNAME   HIREDATE  BIRTHDATE GENDER TITLE
---------- ---------- --------- --------- ------ --------------------
Tobias     Carling

SQL> UPDATE Agents
  2  SET HireDate = TO_DATE('12/19/2000', 'MM/DD/YYYY'),
  3      BirthDate = TO_DATE('10/19/1975','MM/DD/YYYY'),
  4      Gender = 'M',
  5      Title = 'SALESPERSON'
  6  WHERE FirstName = 'Tobias' AND LastName = 'Carling';

1 row updated.

SQL> SELECT FirstName, LastName, HireDate, BirthDate, Gender, Title
  2  FROM Agents
  3  WHERE FirstName = 'Tobias' AND LastName = 'Carling';

FIRSTNAME  LASTNAME   HIREDATE  BIRTHDATE GENDER TITLE
---------- ---------- --------- --------- ------ --------------------
Tobias     Carling    19-DEC-00 19-OCT-75 M      SALESPERSON

SQL>
```

FIGURE 4.10 Updating multiple columns in a single row.

rows and only those rows. In this case, that qualifying value is the AgentID value. You will specify it in the WHERE clause of the UPDATE statement.

To update the value of one column in multiple, qualifying rows:

1. With SQL*Plus running, type and execute the following:

```
UPDATE Agents
SET Title = 'Salesperson'
WHERE AgentID >= 515602;
```

Oracle responds with the message "8 rows updated."

Currently, all values in the Title column are in mixed case—Salesperson and Broker, for example. You decide it is better if the values are all uppercase letters. An UPDATE statement can take the current value of a column and modify it based on its current value. In this case, you will use the Oracle built in function UPPER to convert Title values to upper case. By writing an UPDATE statement without a WHERE clause, all rows are modified.

To modify a column in all rows:

1. Type **CLEAR SCREEN** and press **Enter** to clear the screen.
2. Type and execute this statement:

```
UPDATE Agents
SET Title = UPPER(Title);
```

Oracle responds with the message "40 rows updated."

3. Execute the following to display selected columns of all rows to review the changes.

```
SELECT FirstName, LastName, Title
FROM Agents;
```

Notice that all values in the Title column are uppercase (see Figure 4.11).

CHAPTER 4   Modifying Data and Auditing Table Operations

FIGURE 4.11 Updating multiple rows with a single expression.

INTRODUCING THE CASE STRUCTURE

There are more than a few instances in which the column update value depends on a column in the table. For instance, you might want to modify a realtor's commission rate based on the number of years that realtor has been with the company. As another example, you might want to insert or alter a real estate brokerage fee based on the suggested sales price of a property. The CASE structure performs this type of if-then-else logic in which the value you want to update a column with is not a constant. You can use a CASE structure anywhere Oracle allows expressions in SQL statements. The general syntax of CASE is:

```
CASE
   WHEN <condition1> THEN <result1>
   WHEN <condition2> THEN <result2>
   ...
   [ELSE <default result>]
END
```

Oracle checks each WHEN condition, beginning with the first one. It proceeds, in turn, to the next WHEN condition until it finds a condition that evaluates true. If Oracle locates a condition that is true, it returns the result value that follows the THEN clause and skips the remaining WHEN/THEN clauses. If none of the conditions evaluate to true, then Oracle returns the value that follows the ELSE as the result. However, if there is no ELSE clause and none of the preceding WHEN conditions is true, then the CASE statement returns NULL.

For example, the following SQL statement updates a hypothetical column called CommissionRate. The value by which the column is updated is based on a salesperson's Paygrade column value, and the SET clause uses a CASE structure to supply one of four possible values for the updated CommissionRate. The value by which the CommissionRate is updated depends on the row's Paygrade column value:

```
UPDATE AgentPayGrade
  SET CommissionRate =
   CASE
      WHEN Paygrade = 1 THEN 0.06
      WHEN Paygrade = 2 THEN 0.075
      WHEN Paygrade = 3 THEN 0.08
      ELSE 0.09
   END
WHERE PositionType = 'SALESPERSON';
```

If a row has a Paygrade value of 1, then the CommissionRate is updated to 0.06, if the Paygrade is 2, then CommissionRate is updated to 0.075, and so on.

UPDATING DATA USING THE CASE STRUCTURE

Although a CASE structure is not limited to use with the UPDATE statement, it is particularly handy when altering columns' values based on conditions specified by other columns in the row. For example, suppose the Redwood Realty office manager discovered that the expiration dates for real estate licenses are incorrect. For licenses obtained on or after January 1, 2002, the expiration date should be five years after the LicenseDate value. Licenses issued (LicenseDate) from January 1, 2000 and December 31, 2001 have expiration dates that are four years after the LicenseDate value. All older licenses are unchanged. You can issue a single UPDATE statement, using a CASE structure, to handle the three cases. In the steps that follow, we will use the Oracle built-in function ADD_MONTHS. Its form is

```
ADD_MONTHS(<date column>,<months>)
```

The argument "<date column>" is the column containing a date value and the second argument, "<months>", is the integer number of months to add to the date column. To add five years to the date column value, specify the value 60 (5 years times 12 months per year) as the second argument.

To update a column using a CASE structure:

1. Launch SQL*Plus, if necessary, log in with your username and password, and locate the script file Ch04ListAgents.sql. In SQL*Plus, type **START C:\ Ch04ListAgents** and press **Enter** to execute the script. Remember to substitute your path in place of "C:\" in the preceding statement. The script file displays rows from the Agents table in ascending order by LicenseDate (see Figure 4.12).

2. Launch Notepad, type the following SQL statement, copy it to SQL*Plus, and execute it.

```
UPDATE Agents
  SET LicenseExpire = CASE
      WHEN LicenseDate >='01-JAN-02' THEN ADD_MONTHS(LicenseDate,60)
      WHEN LicenseDate >='01-JAN-00' THEN ADD_MONTHS(LicenseDate,48)
      ELSE LicenseExpire
   END;
```

If there are errors, correct them in Notepad and repeat the copy/paste/execute process until you get successful completion. Oracle issues a message indicating "40 rows updated" to indicate successful completion.

```
FIRSTNAME       LASTNAME        LICENSEDATE LICENSEEXPIRE
--------------- --------------- ----------- -------------
Bruce           Voss            27-AUG-95   01-SEP-98
Lora            Allee           22-NOV-95   01-DEC-98
Essi            Okindo          26-APR-96   01-MAY-99
Belinda         Chong           22-JAN-97   01-FEB-00
Kai                             30-JAN-97   01-FEB-00
Stanislaw       Soltwedel       04-MAY-97   01-JUN-00
Christine       Williams        03-AUG-97   01-SEP-00
Tim             St-Onge         25-JUN-98   01-JUL-01
Danial          Silverburg      24-OCT-98   01-NOV-01
Jackson         Flamenbaum      16-FEB-99   01-MAR-02
Ramanathan      Rowe            06-APR-99   01-MAY-02
Cecilia         Romero          02-MAY-99   01-JUN-02
Jessica         Taylor          23-OCT-99   01-NOV-02
Lee             Reed            20-FEB-00   01-MAR-03
David           Gagnon          14-MAR-00   01-APR-03
Cornelis        Dann            10-SEP-00   01-OCT-03
James           Kellogg         06-JUN-01   01-JUL-04
Ricki           Selby           23-DEC-01   01-JAN-05
Nancy           Piperova        27-MAY-02   01-JUN-05
Barbara         Herring         10-SEP-02   01-OCT-05
Heather         Sheibani        27-NOV-02   01-DEC-05
Tim             Schutz          17-MAR-03   01-APR-06
Elizabeth       Dahlen          22-DEC-04   01-JAN-08
Edwin           Townsend        26-MAR-06   01-APR-09
Clair           Robinson        29-MAR-06   01-APR-09
Sindisiwe       Weber           21-FEB-07   01-MAR-10
Patricia        Lewis           29-JUN-07   01-JUL-10

27 rows selected.

SQL>
```

FIGURE 4.12 Selected Agents rows before being updated.

3. Re-execute the statement below, substituting your path to the script file. Remember to press **Enter** at the end of the line.

   START C:\Ch04ListAgents

   The script displays the same list as in Figure 4.12, except that the LicenseExpire column values are updated for selected rows (see Figure 4.13). Verify that the update worked correctly by examining your results and comparing those in Figures 4.12 and 4.13. Notice that the LicenseExpire date for David Gagnon is "14-MAR-04," which is exactly four years following his LicenseDate value.

4. Type **Exit** and press **Enter** to log off Oracle and close the SQL*Plus client.

SUBSTITUTION VARIABLES

When you need to update several table rows, it can be tedious and time-consuming to retype an UPDATE statement ten or twenty times. Oracle provides relief from the drudgery with substitution variables. Another reason substitution variables are handy is you can use them in SQL script files and vary any part of a SQL statement at execution time. In other words, substitution variables allow you to create a more general SQL statement which defers statement details until execution time, when you fill in the missing pieces.

Substitution variables are so named because they are used in SQL statements as substitutes for values at the time the SQL statement is executed. When you run a SQL statement containing substitution variables, Oracle prompts you for values that you

```
FIRSTNAME      LASTNAME       LICENSEDATE  LICENSEEXPIRE
-------------- -------------- ------------ -------------
Bruce          Voss           27-AUG-95    01-SEP-98
Lora           Allee          22-NOV-95    01-DEC-98
Essi           Okindo         26-APR-96    01-MAY-99
Belinda        Chong          22-JAN-97    01-FEB-00
Kai                           30-JAN-97    01-FEB-00
Stanislaw      Soltwedel      04-MAY-97    01-JUN-00
Christine      Williams       03-AUG-97    01-SEP-00
Tim            St-Onge        25-JUN-98    01-JUL-01
Danial         Silverburg     24-OCT-98    01-NOV-01
Jackson        Flamenbaum     16-FEB-99    01-MAR-02
Ramanathan     Rowe           06-APR-99    01-MAY-02
Cecilia        Romero         02-MAY-99    01-JUN-02
Jessica        Taylor         23-OCT-99    01-NOV-02
Lee            Reed           20-FEB-00    20-FEB-04
David          Gagnon         14-MAR-00    14-MAR-04
Cornelis       Dann           10-SEP-00    10-SEP-04
James          Kellogg        06-JUN-01    06-JUN-05
Ricki          Selby          23-DEC-01    23-DEC-05
Nancy          Piperova       27-MAY-02    27-MAY-07
Barbara        Herring        10-SEP-02    10-SEP-07
Heather        Sheibani       27-NOV-02    27-NOV-07
Tim            Schutz         17-MAR-03    17-MAR-08
Elizabeth      Dahlen         22-DEC-04    22-DEC-09
Edwin          Townsend       26-MAR-06    26-MAR-11
Clair          Robinson       29-MAR-06    29-MAR-11
Sindisiwe      Weber          21-FEB-07    21-FEB-12
Patricia       Lewis          29-JUN-07    29-JUN-12

27 rows selected.

SQL>
```

FIGURE 4.13 Selected Agents rows after updating them.

enter to replace the substitution variables. The following UPDATE scenario illustrates why substitution variables can save you work.

Suppose you are asked to add a column called AnnualBonus to the Agents table and then update the column value with each employee's annual bonus amount. The bonus amount varies depending on how long the employee has been with Redwood Realty. Therefore, several UPDATE statements are required to replace empty AnnualBonus column values with actual bonus amounts. In addition to being time-consuming, running a few dozen individual UPDATE statements is also error-prone. Using substitution variables reduces this drudgery considerably. The following example shows an UPDATE statement using substitution variables to modify the AnnualBonus column.

```
UPDATE Agents
SET AnnualBonus = &BonusAmount
WHERE HireDate > &MinHireDate;
```

Two of the substitution variables in the preceding statement, &BonusAmount and &MinHireDate, cause SQL*Plus to prompt you for those values when you run the statement in SQL*Plus. You respond by typing, first, the value for &BonusAmount and press **Enter**. Next, SQL*Plus prompts you for the value for &MinHireDate, you type a value, and press **Enter**. SQL*Plus places the two values you entered into the SQL statement and sends the modified statement to SQL, and Oracle executes it. If you want to update other rows in the Agents table, simply type slash (/) and press **Enter**. SQL*Plus repeats the steps of requesting you to enter values for the two substitution variables and then sends the statement to Oracle for execution. Let's try it, but with a slightly more complex business rule.

Robert Stirling wants you to modify the Agents table by adding the AnnualBonus column. Then, he wants you to update the annual bonus values with variable amounts,

CHAPTER 4 Modifying Data and Auditing Table Operations

TABLE 4.5 Annual bonus schedule based on employment longevity.

Length of service (months)	Annual bonus amount
12 or less	$0
13 to 24	$500
25 to 48	$700
49 to 72	$1,000
73 or greater	$1,500

depending on agents' length of service with Redwood. Table 4.5 shows the annual bonus schedule.

To calculate how long each agent has worked for Redwood Realty, you can use two Oracle date functions: SYSDATE and MONTHS_BETWEEN. The SYSDATE function returns the current date from your computer. MONTHS_BETWEEN returns the number of months between two dates. Its general form is

```
MONTHS_BETWEEN(<date1>, <date2>)
```

The function calculates the number of months between the two dates and returns a real number including any fractional part of a month. If the first date is more recent then the second date, it returns a positive number. Otherwise, it returns a negative number. To calculate the length of time employees have worked for Redwood, you could use the function as follows:

```
MONTHS_BETWEEN(SYSDATE, HireDate)
```

This calculates the elapsed months since today's date. However, to obtain a consistent result, you will use an artificial date in the steps that follow. That way, everyone will get the same result no matter what the actual date is.

To add a column and update its contents with substitution variables:

1. Launch SQL*Plus, log into Oracle, type **CLEAR SCREEN**, and press **Enter**.
2. Launch Notepad and then immediately save the empty as Ch04<yourname>SubVars.sql to preserve it for possible later use. (Substitute your name for "<yourname>".)
3. Type the following in Notepad:

```
ALTER TABLE Agents
  ADD(AnnualBonus NUMBER(5) DEFAULT 0);
```

4. Copy the statement into SQL*Plus and press **Enter** to execute it. Oracle responds "Table altered."
5. Switch back to Notepad, and type the following UPDATE statement on lines below the Alter Table statement. When you are done, save the Notepad file, copy the UPDATE statement (only) to SQL*Plus, and press **Enter** to execute it. Close Notepad.

```
UPDATE Agents
  SET AnnualBonus = &BonusAmount
WHERE MONTHS_BETWEEN('01-JAN-2006', HireDate)
  BETWEEN &LowMonths AND &HighMonths;
```

SQL*Plus responds by requesting a value for BonusAmount.

6. Type **500** and press **Enter**. Oracle displays the old and new values.
7. Type **13**, press **Enter**, type **24**, and press **Enter**. Oracle responds with "3 rows updated" (see Figure 4.14).

```
Oracle SQL*Plus
File Edit Search Options Help
SQL> ALTER TABLE Agents
  2    ADD (AnnualBonus NUMBER(5) DEFAULT 0);

Table altered.

SQL> UPDATE Agents
  2    SET AnnualBonus = &BonusAmount
  3    WHERE MONTHS_BETWEEN('01-JAN-2006', HireDate)
  4      BETWEEN &LowMonths AND &HighMonths;
Enter value for bonusamount: 500
old   2:    SET AnnualBonus = &BonusAmount
new   2:    SET AnnualBonus = 500
Enter value for lowmonths: 13
Enter value for highmonths: 24
old   4:      BETWEEN &LowMonths AND &HighMonths
new   4:      BETWEEN 13 AND 24

3 rows updated.

SQL>
```

FIGURE 4.14 Running a SQL statement containing substitution variables.

As you can see, SQL*Plus substituted 500, 13, and 24 for the three substitution variables and passed the statement to Oracle. Oracle updated three rows based on the modified update statement:

```
UPDATE Agents
   SET AnnualBonus = 500
 WHERE MONTHS_BETWEEN('01-JAN-2006', HireDate)
   BETWEEN 13 and 24;
```

SQL*Plus displays both the old and new SQL*Plus lines in the output along with the line number where it substituted the values. Because you are going to execute this line at three more times, you can suppress the display of the old and new lines' verifications by executing the SQL*Plus command SET VERIFY OFF. Because the SQL statement is still in its internal buffer, you can re-execute it simply by typing the forward slash key (/) and pressing **Enter**.

To execute a SQL statement in the buffer with different substitution values:

1. With SQL*Plus still running, type **SET VERIFY OFF** and press **Enter**.
2. Type **/** and press **Enter** to re-execute the SQL statement in the buffer.
3. Type **700**, press **Enter**, type **25**, press Enter, type **48** and press **Enter**.
4. Type **/** and press **Enter**; type **1000**, press **Enter**, type **49**, press **Enter**, type **72** and press **Enter**.
5. Type **/** and press **Enter**; type **1500**, press **Enter**, type **73**, press **Enter**, type **678** and press **Enter** (see Figure 4.15). (The value 678 you just typed is an arbitrarily high value to mean a *very* long time.)
6. Type **SET VERIFY ON** to reset it.
7. View the modifications to the Agents table by typing and executing the following in SQL*Plus:

   CLEAR SCREEN
   SELECT LastName, HireDate, AnnualBonus
   FROM Agents
   WHERE HireDate IS NOT NULL
   ORDER BY HireDate;

   Notice that the AnnualBonus amount varies by length of service. Sorting by HireDate makes this obvious (see Figure 4.16).
8. Type **Exit** and press **Enter** to log off Oracle and close SQL*Plus.

CHAPTER 4 Modifying Data and Auditing Table Operations **167**

```
SQL> UPDATE Agents
  2    SET AnnualBonus = &BonusAmount
  3  WHERE MONTHS_BETWEEN('01-JAN-2006', HireDate)
  4    BETWEEN &LowMonths AND &HighMonths;
Enter value for bonusamount: 500
Enter value for lowmonths: 13
Enter value for highmonths: 24

3 rows updated.

SQL> SET VERIFY OFF
SQL> /
Enter value for bonusamount: 700
Enter value for lowmonths: 25
Enter value for highmonths: 48

4 rows updated.

SQL> /
Enter value for bonusamount: 1000
Enter value for lowmonths: 49
Enter value for highmonths: 72

4 rows updated.

SQL> /
Enter value for bonusamount: 1500
Enter value for lowmonths: 73
Enter value for highmonths: 678

13 rows updated.

SQL>
```

FIGURE 4.15 Processing substitution variables.

```
SQL> SELECT LastName, HireDate, AnnualBonus
  2  FROM Agents
  3  WHERE HireDate IS NOT NULL
  4  ORDER BY HireDate;

LASTNAME              HIREDATE   ANNUALBONUS
--------------------- ---------- -----------
Chong                 30-AUG-95         1500
Okindo                20-DEC-95         1500
Williams              08-JAN-96         1500
Soltwedel             04-MAY-96         1500
Voss                  05-JUN-96         1500
Allee                 14-JUL-96         1500
                      03-OCT-96         1500
St-Onge               13-JUL-97         1500
Rowe                  05-SEP-97         1500
Silverburg            21-SEP-97         1500
Taylor                29-JUN-98         1500

LASTNAME              HIREDATE   ANNUALBONUS
--------------------- ---------- -----------
Gagnon                17-JAN-99         1500
Romero                01-NOV-99         1500
Flamenbaum            08-FEB-00         1000
Reed                  18-SEP-00         1000
Carling               19-DEC-00         1000
Dann                  02-SEP-01         1000
Selby                 05-JAN-02          700
Kellogg               05-FEB-02          700
Piperova              24-DEC-02          700
Sheibani              18-JUL-03          700
Herring               07-DEC-03            0

LASTNAME              HIREDATE   ANNUALBONUS
--------------------- ---------- -----------
                      12-JAN-04          500
                      03-FEB-04          500
Schutz                21-JUN-04          500
Dahlen                23-MAY-05            0
Lewis                 30-MAY-06            0
Weber                 25-AUG-06            0
Townsend              12-SEP-06            0
Robinson              16-OCT-06            0

30 rows selected.

SQL>
```

FIGURE 4.16 Displaying updated table.

Notice that Robinson's AnnualBonus amount (at the bottom) is zero. Her AnnualBonus was not updated because she has been with the company less than 13 months based on the arbitrary date of '01-JAN-2006' we used earlier. The value is zero because that is the default set when you altered the table.

An alternative way to define substitution variables is with the SQL*Plus ACCEPT command. The ACCEPT command contains an optional PROMPT phrase that displays a prompt and waits for the user to type a value. ACCEPT is similar to substitution variables you used in the preceding steps, but it allows you to control the order in which the prompts appear. Because the ACCEPT statements often are used with stored procedures and PL/SQL (Chapter 7), we defer discussion until that chapter.

DELETING ROWS AND TRUNCATING TABLES

When you need to remove one, several, or all rows from a table, use the DELETE statement (also called a *DELETE action query*). Deleting rows from a table does not remove the table from the database—the DROP TABLE statement does that. DELETE is probably the simplest SQL command you can write. The simplified DELETE command syntax is:

```
DELETE [FROM] [schema.]{<tablename> | <view>}
[WHERE <condition>];
```

Notice that the DELETE command does not reference any column names because it deletes entire rows, not individual columns. Although *FROM* is optional, the statement reads better if you include it. *Schema* is the name of the table or view owner. (Views are presented in Chapter 6.) The optional WHERE clause identifies rows to be deleted—rows which match the condition specified by "<condition>". Be careful. Not only is the DELETE command simple to write, it can be dangerous to execute. That is because it is easy to accidentally omit the WHERE clause in a DELETE statement. If you omit it, then Oracle deletes *all* rows in the specified table. Imagine the consequences if someone accidentally deleted all the customer names and addresses from the Redwood Realty database, for example! Fortunately, you can reinstate rows accidentally deleted by executing the SQL command ROLLBACK, which is described in the Database Transactions section of this chapter. Normally, if you attempt to remove rows that are referenced by other tables via a primary key and foreign key relationship, Oracle will not remove the rows, and instead will generate an error message. That is the nature of referential integrity—it protects rows from becoming orphans. You can specify an optional clause, ON DELETE CASCADE, on the foreign key column when you create the table. Doing so causes the delete to "ripple" from the row being deleted and containing the primary key to include any dependent rows in other tables to be deleted. This is the case with the relationship between the LicenseStatus table and the Agents table. The Agents table contains the LicenseStatusID foreign key column referencing a row in the LicenseStatus table—linked to its primary key. If you were to delete the row in LicenseStatus containing the primary key value 1001, Oracle would automatically ripple the delete to all rows in the Agents table whose foreign key was 1001. Omit the ON DELETE CASCADE clause on a foreign key field if you want to avoid that possibility.

DELETING SELECTED ROWS

Several times within this chapter you have executed steps that add rows to the Agents table. Now it is time to remove several of those rows.

CHAPTER 4   Modifying Data and Auditing Table Operations   **169**

To delete rows from a table:

1. Start SQL*Plus and log into Oracle (if needed), type **CLEAR SCREEN**, and press **Enter**.
2. Execute the following DELETE statement

   ```
   DELETE FROM Agents
   WHERE FirstName IS NULL AND LastName IS NULL;
   ```

   Oracle responds with the affirming message "2 rows deleted." There were two rows in which *both* the first and last names were empty (null). Those rows are gone now.

3. Type and execute the following

   ```
   DELETE FROM Agents
   WHERE AgentID = 515602;
   ```

   Again, Oracle indicates it deleted the single row.

4. Type and execute the following:

   ```
   DELETE FROM Agents
   WHERE Title = 'Salesperson';
   ```

   In the last step above, Oracle indicates "0 rows deleted." That usually means that the DELETE statement is syntactically correct, but that no rows met the column conditions specified. That, in turn, indicates a misspelled literal value or a relational operator that is not correct. Recall that earlier you updated the Title column to all uppercase data.

   Robert Stirling has been forced to temporarily reduce the number of agents on staff. He is furloughing the agents who have been with Redwood Realty the shortest time—everyone hired in 2006. Write a DELETE action query to remove rows meeting that criterion.

   To remove selected rows based on HireDate:

1. Type and execute the following:

   ```
   DELETE FROM Agents
   WHERE HireDate >= TO_DATE('2006/01/01', 'YYYY/MM/DD');
   ```

   Oracle removes four rows.

2. Remove rows in which the HireDate is unknown—has the value NULL. Type and execute the following:

   ```
   DELETE FROM Agents
   WHERE HireDate IS NULL;
   ```

   This time, Oracle deletes nine rows (see Figure 4.17). That is, there are nine rows whose HireDate column contains NULL.

3. Leave SQL*Plus running.

DELETING ALL ROWS

You can remove all rows from a table, leaving the table structure in place, in two different ways. If you omit the WHERE clause from the DELETE statement, all table rows are removed. For example, the statement

```
DELETE FROM Agents;
```

removes all the Agents table rows, leaving it empty. Removing rows from a large table with thousands of rows is "expensive" because Oracle keeps a copy of all the delete

```
SQL> DELETE FROM Agents
  2  WHERE FirstName IS NULL AND LastName IS NULL;

2 rows deleted.

SQL> DELETE FROM Agents
  2  WHERE AgentID = 515602;

1 row deleted.

SQL> DELETE FROM Agents
  2  WHERE Title = 'Salesperson';

0 rows deleted.

SQL> DELETE FROM Agents
  2  WHERE HireDate >= TO_DATE('2006/01/01', 'YYYY/MM/DD');

4 rows deleted.

SQL> DELETE FROM Agents
  2  WHERE HireDate IS NULL;

9 rows deleted.

SQL>
```

FIGURE 4.17 Deleting selected rows from a table.

transactions in case you need to reverse this action. For a large table, this can take a long time and can occupy a significant amount of space—until you finalize the delete operation with the COMMIT transaction control statement described later in this chapter.

There are times when you need to delete all the records in a table that you are certain you will never need to reinstate. For example, you may have created a new table with the records from another table whose records are outdated. Or, perhaps you have moved data from a table into several other tables to normalize the database but still need the table for data input. In these cases, you can use the TRUNCATE TABLE statement instead of the DELETE statement. When Oracle *truncates* a table, it removes all the table data without saving any rollback (undo) information. When SQL Server truncates a table, the records are permanently removed, but the table's structure remains intact. The general form of the TRUNCATE TABLE is simply:

```
TRUNCATE TABLE <tablename>;
```

If a table has foreign key constraints (without the ON DELETE CASCADE option), you cannot truncate the table. You must first disable the constraint using the ALTER TABLE statement. For example, you could remove the Agents table foreign key constraint by executing:

```
ALTER TABLE Agents
DISABLE CONSTRAINT fk_AgentsLicenseStatusID;
```

Let's remove all rows from the Agents table with the TRUNCATE TABLE statement.

To alter a referential integrity constraint and then remove all rows from a table:

1. With SQL*Plus running, execute the following:

   ALTER TABLE Agents
   DISABLE CONSTRAINT fk_AgentsLicenseStatusID;

2. Truncate the table by executing the following:

   TRUNCATE TABLE Agents;

   Oracle responds "Table truncated." (See Figure 4.18.)

CHAPTER 4 Modifying Data and Auditing Table Operations **171**

```
Oracle SQL*Plus
File Edit Search Options Help
SQL> ALTER TABLE Agents
  2  DISABLE CONSTRAINT fk_AgentsLicenseStatusID;

Table altered.

SQL> TRUNCATE TABLE Agents;

Table truncated.

SQL>
```

FIGURE 4.18   **Truncating the Agents table.**

MERGING ROWS

The SQL statement MERGE allows you to merge row from a source table to a target table, combining the features of INSERT, UPDATE, and DELETE into one statement. The syntax of MERGE is as follows:

```
MERGE INTO <target-tablename>
USING <source-tablename or query>
ON (<condition>)
[WHEN MATCHED THEN UPDATE <set-clause>
  [DELETE <condition>]]
[WHEN NOT MATCHED THEN INSERT <insert-clause>];
```

A typical example where MERGE is handy is refreshing a master inventory table with new item prices and quantities held in a transaction table. New inventory items in the transaction table are inserted into the master inventory table, while transaction inventory table items that match the master inventory update the master inventory table quantity and item price columns. The INSERT, UPDATE, and DELETE data manipulation commands provide all the functionality needed to add, modify, or remove rows. However, the MERGE statement accomplished in a single command execution what would require multiple DML statements to accomplish using INSERT, UPDATE, and DELETE. Because it combines UPDATE and INSERT statements into one statement, MERGE is informally called "upsert." An example will illustrate how this works.

The MERGE INTO clause specifies the name of the table into which Oracle merges rows. The USING ON clause identifies the two tables involved—the source table and the target table—and the two columns that are to be compared for matching values—the two primary key fields. The WHEN MATCHED clause specifies what to do when a USING ON clause is satisfied for a row—when the primary keys match. The WHEN NOT MATCHED clause specifies what action Oracle takes when a source table row does not match a corresponding row in the target table. In most cases, the unmatched row, a new one, is inserted into the target table.

The LicenseStatus table contains two columns and sixteen rows shown in Figure 4.19 (see "LicenseStatus target table"). The table UpdateLicenseStatus (see "UpdateLicenseStatus source table" in Figure 4.19) contains new rows to add to the LicenseStatus table along with existing rows (identified by matching LicenseStatusID values) which will update the LicenseStatus table (see "LicenseStatus table following MERGE" in Figure 4.19). The following MERGE statement uses the source table UpdateLicenseStatus to modify the target table, LicenseStatus:

```
MERGE INTO LicenseStatus LS
USING UpdateLicenseStatus ULS
  ON (LS.LicenseStatusID = ULS.LicenseStatusID)
```

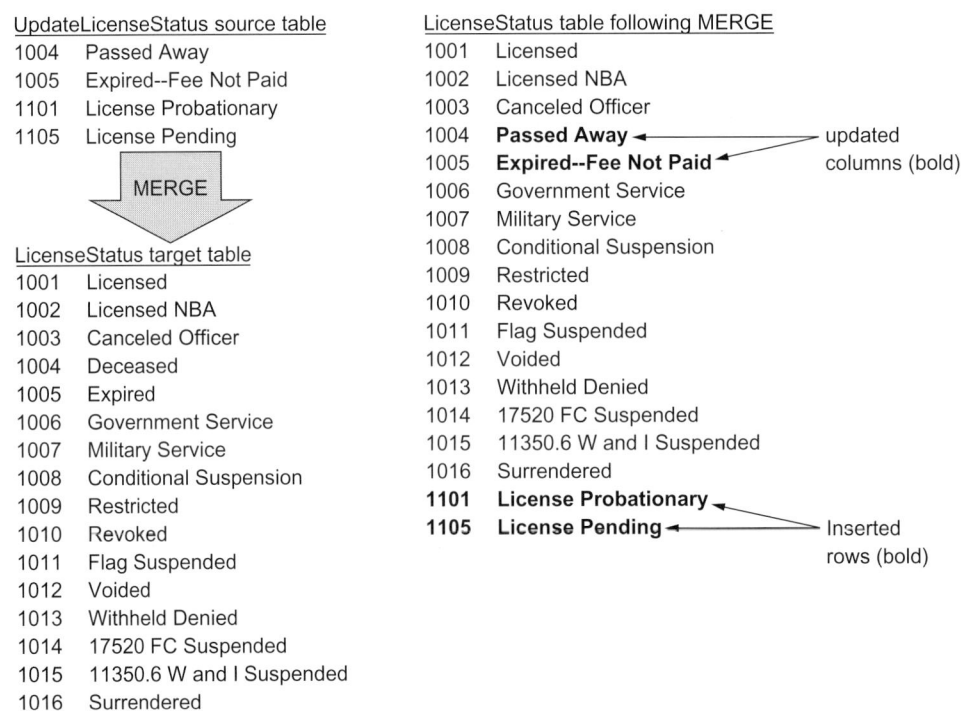

FIGURE 4.19 MERGE example.

```
WHEN MATCHED THEN
    UPDATE SET LS.StatusText = ULS.StatusText
WHEN NOT MATCHED THEN
    INSERT (LS.LicenseStatusID, LS.StatusText)
    VALUES (ULS.LicenseStatusID, ULS.StatusText);
```

LS and ULS are aliases. In database parlance, an *alias* is an alternative name for a table or column. It is often defined and used to shorten the table or column name for subsequent references. In the preceding example, the alias LS is shorter than the name *LicenseStatus* that is used in four other places, and ULS is much shorter than *UpdateLicenseStatus.*, which is also used in four other places in the same statement.

The MERGE statement tells Oracle to update the selected fields when the primary key in the source table matches the primary key in the target table. The WHEN NOT clause tells Oracle to insert the source table row whenever its primary key is not found in the target, because that indicates a new row to be inserted. If you wanted to delete rows from the target table, then you include the DELETE statement as part of the WHEN MATCHED clause.

Stirling Leonard wants you to update two rows and insert two other rows into the LicenseStatus table. The two rows to update have the primary key values 1004 and 1005, respectively, and the LicenseText values *Passed Away* and *Expired—Fee Not Paid*. The two rows to be inserted are the second and third rows under the heading "UpdateLicenseStatus source table" in Figure 4.19. Their primary key values, 1101 and 1105, do not occur in the LicenseStatus table, so Oracle adds those two rows to the LicenseStatus table.

To create the MERGE source table:

1. With SQL*Plus running, clear the screen (type **CLEAR SCREEN** and press **Enter**). Type and execute the following statement to create the source table

CHAPTER 4 Modifying Data and Auditing Table Operations   **173**

containing rows that update the LicenseStatus table. Feel free to use Notepad to create the statements, then copy/paste them into SQL*Plus as you have in the past.

```
CREATE TABLE UpdateLicenseStatus
  (LicenseStatusID INTEGER PRIMARY KEY,
   StatusText NVARCHAR2(25));
```

Oracle indicates success with "Table created."

2. Populate the UpdateLicenseStatus table by typing and executing the following INSERT statements. Press **Enter** at the end of each line.

```
INSERT INTO UpdateLicenseStatus VALUES (1004, 'Passed Away');
INSERT INTO UpdateLicenseStatus VALUES (1005, 'Expired--Fee Not Paid');
INSERT INTO UpdateLicenseStatus VALUES (1101, 'License Probationary');
INSERT INTO UpdateLicenseStatus VALUES (1105, 'License Pending');
```

Oracle responds after each INSERT statement with "1 row created."

With the source table containing the rows to be modified and rows to be inserted in the UpdateLicenseStatus table, you can execute the MERGE statement.

To execute a MERGE statement to update and add rows to a target table:

1. Carefully type the following statement in Notepad, copy it to SQL*Plus, and execute it. Make corrections in Notepad, if needed, and re-execute the statement.

```
MERGE INTO LicenseStatus LS
USING UpdateLicenseStatus ULS
   ON (LS.LicenseStatusID = ULS.LicenseStatusID)
WHEN MATCHED THEN
   UPDATE SET LS.StatusText = ULS.StatusText
WHEN NOT MATCHED THEN
   INSERT (LS.LicenseStatusID, LS.StatusText)
   VALUES (ULS.LicenseStatusID, ULS.StatusText);
```

Oracle responds with the affirming message "4 rows merged." (See Figure 4.20.)

FIGURE 4.20 Issuing MERGE to modify a table.

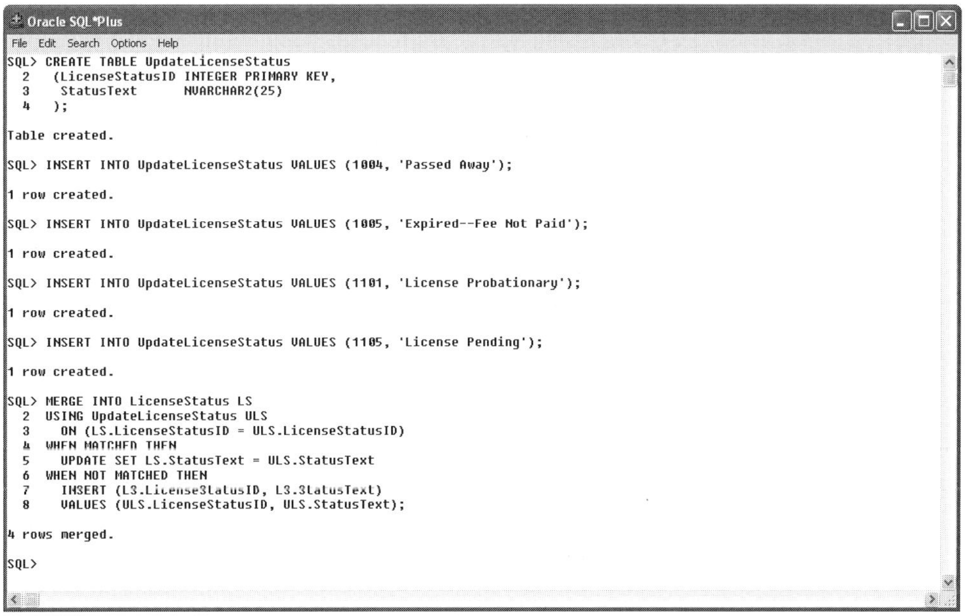

2. Display rows of the newly updated LicenseStatus table by executing the following:

   ```
   SELECT *
   FROM LicenseStatus
   ORDER BY LicenseStatusID;
   ```

   Compare your list to Figure 4.19. The last two rows are new and should contain 1101 and 1105 as primary keys. Rows identified by 1004 and 1005 should contain modified values.

3. Remove the now superfluous table UpdateLicenseStatus by typing an executing

   ```
   DROP TABLE UpdateLicenseStatus;
   ```

4. Log off Oracle and exit SQL*Plus plus by typing **Exit** and pressing **Enter**.

DATABASE TRANSACTIONS

An important concept to consider whenever you use data manipulation language (DML) statements is a database transaction. A database *transaction* is a group of statements that are a logical work unit. It is one or more inseparable set of SQL statements that should all execute successfully and be made permanent or undone as a whole. Common examples include the events that should occur when you pay a bill by check to someone with an account at your bank. As the bank processes a check, it subtracts (debits) the amount of the check from your checking account, reducing its balance. Simultaneously, the bank adds (credits) the check amount to the account of whomever is depositing the check. Both the subtraction and addition operations must occur successfully, or both transactions must be voided. Otherwise, money will be lost in the system—floating around in space.

The preceding situation is an example of two UPDATE statements that must be grouped into a single transaction to ensure that both update operations succeed, or that both are revoked. Often, transactions consist of any number of INSERT, DELETE, and UPDATE operations. Transactions are defined by the COMMIT, ROLLBACK, and SAVEPOINT statements.

When you issue DML statements such as INSERT or DELETE during your session, you can see the changes in the database tables. However, Oracle prevents another *session* (an individual connection to the Oracle database server) from seeing the changes or accessing the affected rows while the changes are uncommitted. Among other advantages, locking rows prevents another user from changing a table row while another user is simultaneously modifying it. If such a scenario were allowed, then one user's modifications to a table would be nullified by another's. You do not explicitly start a transaction. Instead, a transaction begins automatically when you log into Oracle via SQL*Plus or *i*SQL*Plus and ends when you commit the current transaction. When one transaction ends, another one begins automatically.

COMMIT

The COMMIT command makes permanent any database changes. For the duration of a transaction, Oracle locks any affected rows. Issuing a COMMIT statement unlocks affected rows and allows other users to examine or modify them. Data definition language (DDL) statements, such as CREATE TABLE, CREATE SEQUENCE, and DROP TABLE, and data control language statements (DCL) such as GRANT cause Oracle to implicitly issue a COMMIT statement. When you create a table, for example, it is made permanent immediately after executing the command

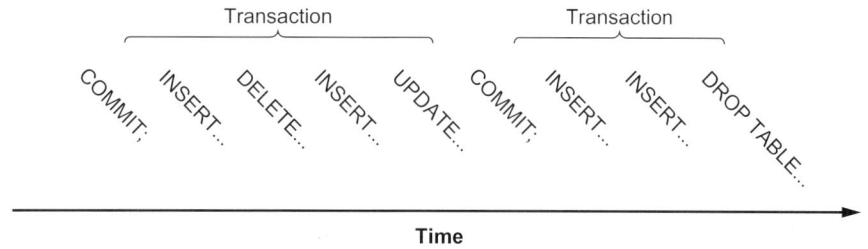

FIGURE 4.21 Illustration of transactions.

and does not require a COMMIT statement. In addition, Oracle issues an implicit COMMIT statement when you log off Oracle. For example, if you insert 25 rows and update 12 others following a COMMIT statement, those changes since the last COMMIT statement are made permanent—and the transaction ends—the moment you log off Oracle.

After executing one or more DML statements, you can commit all of the changes made in the transaction. When you *commit* changes, they are made permanent. All previously uncommitted changes are committed, and they cannot be reversed. The syntax of the COMMIT statement is as simple as it gets:

```
COMMIT;
```

A transaction is measured from the last time a COMMIT was issued by the current session to the present one. Figure 4.21 shows a timeline representing DML statements comprising a transaction.

Rollback

When you *rollback* a database, you undo any pending changes to a database. If you start a transaction that does not finish correctly or with incorrect results, then you can rollback the database to restore the original data. The SQL command ROLLBACK does that: It reverses any DML commands during the current transaction—back to the beginning of the transaction or to a savepoint. ROLLBACK unlocks any pending changes caused during the transaction and unlocks affected records. In addition, it ends the transaction and erases all savepoints. While ROLLBACK is an "undo" for DML statements, it cannot undo DDL statements. Any DDL statements (CREATE TABLE, and so on) can be reversed only by issuing the appropriate DROP statements. The ROLLBACK syntax is quite simple:

```
ROLLBACK [WORK] [TO [SAVEPOINT] <savepoint-name>];
```

"<Savepoint-name>" is the name previously defined in the current transaction. (See *Savepoints* in the next section.) For example, you could issue the statement ROLLBACK TO SAVEPOINT Alpha23, where Alpha23 is a savepoint defined in the transaction. Doing so causes the following to happen:

- Changes made to the database since the specified savepoint was marked are reversed.
- All savepoints marked after the specified savepoint are erased.
- All row and table locks acquired since the specified savepoint are released.

The scope of SQL statements affected by either a ROLLBACK or a COMMIT is the current transaction. Recall, a transaction begins when one of the following events occurs:

- You connect to Oracle and perform a DML statement.
- You end a previous transaction and then execute another DML statement.

A transaction ends when one of the following events occurs:

- You perform a DML statement that does not complete successfully. Oracle issues a ROLLBACK command for the failed instruction only.
- You execute a COMMIT or ROLLBACK statement.
- You disconnect from Oracle normally.
- You issue a data control language statement such as GRANT.
- You execute a DDL statement such as CREATE TABLE.

SAVEPOINTS

Savepoints are named points within a transaction, and they allow you to rollback changes to any savepoint within the transaction. Savepoints are useful if you have a long transaction and want the option of reversing a small portion of the transaction, instead of the entire transaction, when you make a mistake. This allows you to avoid reverting way back to the beginning of the long transaction and reissuing a large number of DML statements. The syntax of the SAVEPOINT statements is:

```
SAVEPOINT <savepointname>;
```

If you execute a ROLLBACK statement without specifying a savepoint, then all the DML statements are reversed back to the beginning of the transaction and all savepoint names are erased. Figure 4.22 shows an example of a transaction containing DML statements, SAVEPOINT statements, and a ROLLBACK statement.

In Figure 4.22 the transaction begins at the top of the screen—directly after logging in. The first savepoint, called SaveFirst, is set after inserting the Carling data. We add the Voss row and then create the savepoint SaveSecond. Next, the Voss' title is changed to Salesperson. When the ROLLBACK executes, changes from SaveSecond are revoked—Voss' title change to Salesperson is revoked. The SELECT clause shows the two records added since the start of the transaction, except for the UPDATE change. Finally, the COMMIT statement closes the transaction, begins a new one, and makes permanent the two INSERT actions.

Recall from your previous Oracle sessions that you deleted all rows from the Agents table by executing TRUNCATE TABLE Agents. In the steps below, you will issue data manipulation, ROLLBACK, and COMMIT statements to understand how transactions control statements (TCL) work. As usual, we suggest you carefully type each statement in Notepad, copy it to SQL*Plus, and then execute it. Make any needed corrections in Notepad, and then follow the copy/paste/execute regimen in SQL*Plus.

To execute DML statements, create savepoints, and rollback transactions:

1. Start SQL*Plus, log into Oracle, and type the following SQL*Plus commands to format the display. Press **Enter** at the end of each line.

```
CLEAR SCREEN
COLUMN AgentID FORMAT 999999
COLUMN FirstName FORMAT A12
COLUMN LastName FORMAT A12
COLUMN Gender FORMAT A6
```

CHAPTER 4 Modifying Data and Auditing Table Operations

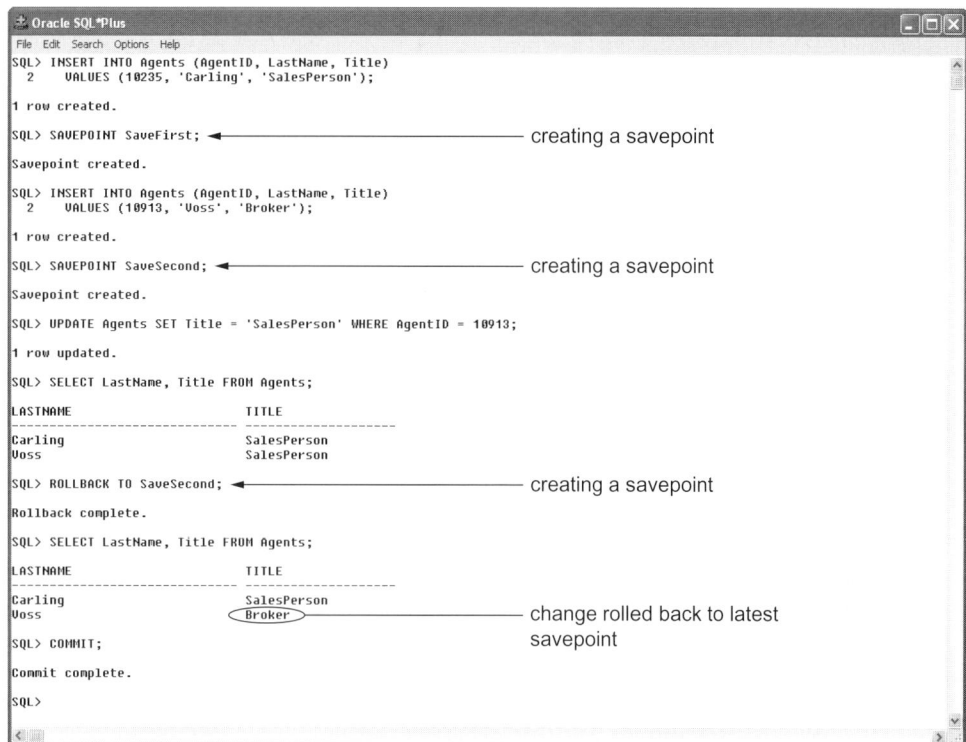

FIGURE 4.22 Using savepoints in a transaction.

2. Next, type and execute the following statements:

   ```
   INSERT INTO Agents (AgentID, FirstName, LastName, Gender)
     VALUES (10429, 'Elizabeth', 'Dahlen', NULL);
   SAVEPOINT InsertOne;
   INSERT INTO Agents (AgentID, FirstName, LastName, Gender)
     VALUES (10497, 'Ramanathan', 'Rowe', 'M');
   INSERT INTO Agents (AgentID, FirstName, LastName, Gender)
     VALUES (10849, 'Heather', 'Sheibani', NULL);
   UPDATE Agents SET Gender = 'M' WHERE LastName = 'Dahlen';
   SAVEPOINT InsertTwo;
   ```

   If you entered the preceding correctly, Oracle will respond with "1 row created" and "Savepoint created" following each INSERT and SAVEPOINT command, respectively.

3. Display the rows in Agents by typing and executing this statement:

   ```
   SELECT AgentID, FirstName, LastName, Gender FROM Agents;
   ```

   Notice that NULL is recorded for Sheibani's Gender column (see Figure 4.23).

4. Type and execute the following statements. Notice the changes. You've rolled back the database to the InsertOne savepoint—a point before the latest two INSERT statements and the UPDATE statement.

   ```
   CLEAR SCREEN
   ROLLBACK TO InsertOne;
   SELECT AgentID, FirstName, LastName, Gender FROM Agents;
   ```

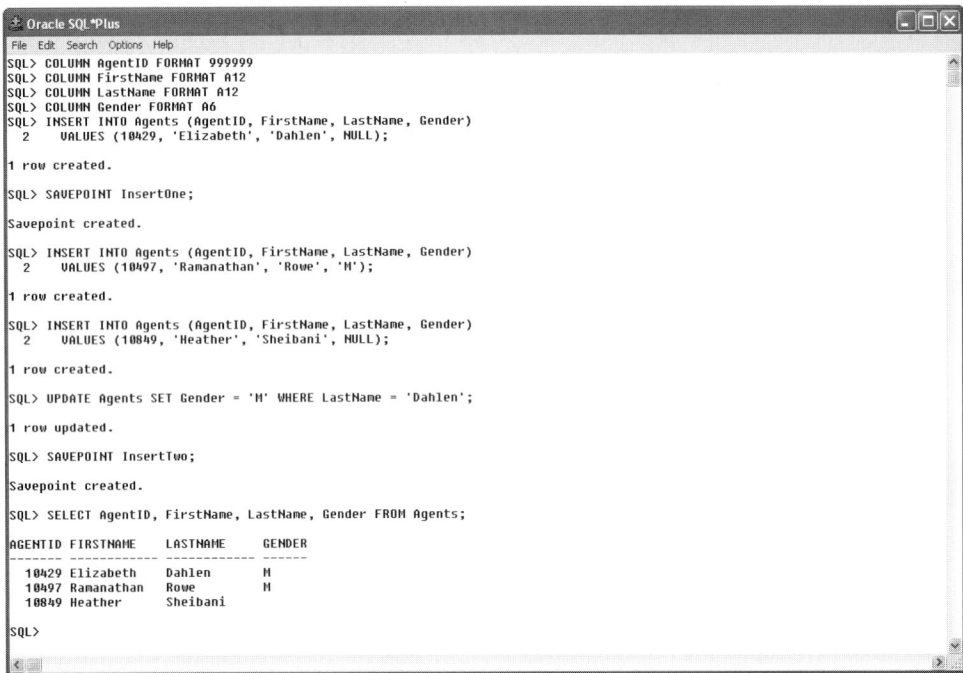

FIGURE 4.23 Modifying the Agents table.

5. Finally, commit your changes and attempt to roll them back by executing the following statements in SQL*Plus:

```
COMMIT;
SELECT AgentID, FirstName, LastName, Gender FROM Agents;
ROLLBACK;
SELECT AgentID, FirstName, LastName, Gender FROM Agents;
```

Figure 4.24 shows the result of executing the preceding statements: Once you have executed a COMMIT statement, Oracle makes the changes permanent and there's "no going back."

6. Finally, remove all records from Agents and type **Exit** and press **Enter** to log off Oracle. Oracle executes an implicit COMMIT for you when you end your session.

```
DELETE FROM Agents;
exit
```

CREATING AND USING DATABASE TRIGGERS

A database trigger is associated with a table, view (see Chapter 6), a schema, or the database. It automatically executes (or *fires*) whenever certain events occur to that table, view, schema, or database event. In this chapter, you learn about triggers associated with database tables. In the case of table triggers, the events the triggers monitor are the execution of the DML statements INSERT, UPDATE, or DELETE. Triggers are frequently used to monitor changes occurring to particular columns of specified tables. You write Oracle triggers in Oracle's programming language, PL/SQL. When you create a trigger, Oracle compiles the code and stores it in the data dictionary.

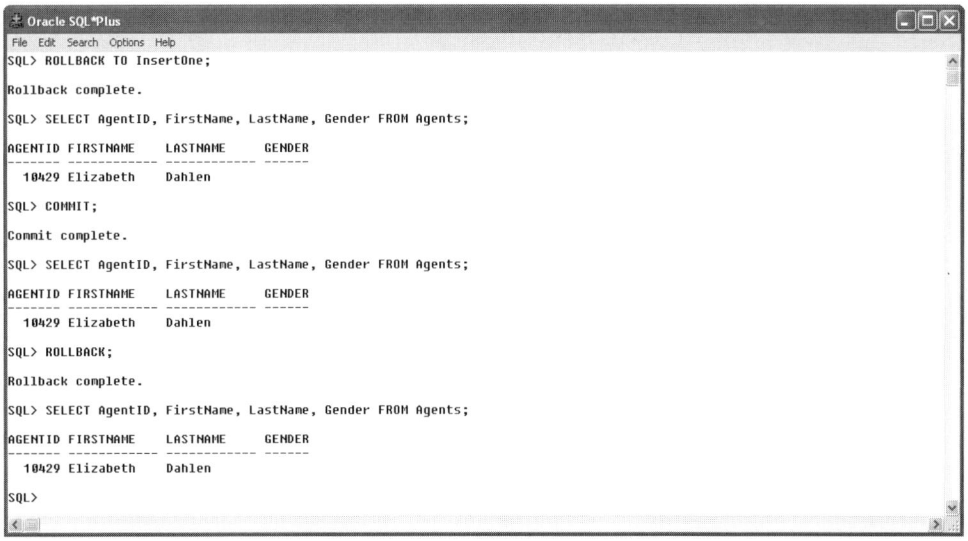

```
Oracle SQL*Plus
File Edit Search Options Help
SQL> ROLLBACK TO InsertOne;

Rollback complete.

SQL> SELECT AgentID, FirstName, LastName, Gender FROM Agents;

AGENTID FIRSTNAME     LASTNAME     GENDER
------- ------------- ------------ ------
  10429 Elizabeth     Dahlen

SQL> COMMIT;

Commit complete.

SQL> SELECT AgentID, FirstName, LastName, Gender FROM Agents;

AGENTID FIRSTNAME     LASTNAME     GENDER
------- ------------- ------------ ------
  10429 Elizabeth     Dahlen

SQL> ROLLBACK;

Rollback complete.

SQL> SELECT AgentID, FirstName, LastName, Gender FROM Agents;

AGENTID FIRSTNAME     LASTNAME     GENDER
------- ------------- ------------ ------
  10429 Elizabeth     Dahlen

SQL>
```

FIGURE 4.24 Ending a transaction with COMMIT.

INTRODUCING TRIGGERS

You can use triggers to enforce referential integrity constraints instead of using foreign key constraints, but it is preferable to use Oracle's built-in foreign key integrity constraints. Triggers are particularly handy when you want to prevent invalid table entries, perform validity checks on column values, or enforce access security. For example, if your business rules state that a Redwood Realty agent's LicenseDate must be earlier than today's date, you can create a table trigger to enforce that rule. Similarly, a table trigger can ensure that an agent's license expiration date is greater than the LicenseDate column value before inserting a new agent's row into the Agents table.

Another popular use of table triggers is tracking modifications to database tables. By defining triggers on particular tables, Oracle can log data about any modifications to tables. When an Oracle user executes an INSERT, UPDATE, or DELETE statement on a table, triggers specified on that table can be set up to record information in an audit table. Information stored in the audit table might include the Oracle username of the user modifying the table, the table name, type of table modification, column values both before and after the operation, and the modification date and time stamps. This is very handy in maintaining accounting audit trails and in collecting information about anyone attempting to hack into a table and change it without authorization.

Triggers can fire before, after, or instead of a DML operation. A trigger that fires *before* the event can collect data about the row before any modifications, and a trigger that fires *after* the event can collect the new, modified row value(s). A trigger that fires *instead of* the DML event is handy when you want to disallow selected types of modifications to a table.

The code that defines a trigger can be run once for every affected row, or it can run just once per statement execution—regardless of the number of rows affected. A trigger that fires for each row is called a ***row-level trigger,*** whereas a trigger that fires once per DML event for any number of affected rows is called a ***statement-level trigger.*** For instance, if you deleted twelve rows of a table and had a row-level trigger defined for a delete operation, the trigger would fire twelve times. On the other hand, a statement-level trigger of the same type would fire exactly once.

To define a trigger, use the CREATE TRIGGER statement. Its general syntax is

```
CREATE [OR REPLACE] TRIGGER <trigger-name>
{BEFORE | AFTER | INSTEAD OF} <trigger-event> ON <table_name>
  [FOR EACH ROW [WHEN <condition>]]
[DECLARE
    <declaration statements>]
BEGIN
  <trigger-body>
END;
```

where CREATE indicates the trigger is new, and REPLACE indicates that an existing trigger is being replaced with this one. REPLACE is an optional phrase, but you should use it only to modify a trigger. When you use REPLACE, Oracle replaces an existing trigger by the same name. However, if you create a trigger and later replace it with a trigger defined on another table, Oracle generates an error. "<Trigger name>" is the trigger's name. BEFORE or AFTER specifies that the trigger fires before or after the event occurs. INSTEAD OF specifies that the trigger fires in place of the DML event, but its use is restricted to database *views*. Database views are described in Chapter 6.

> **Tip:** We suggest you name triggers this way: <table-name>_{bi|bu|bd|ai|au|ad}_trg, where "bi" stands for before insert, "bu" for before update, "ai" for after insert, and so on. An AFTER UPDATE trigger on the Agents table would be named "Agents_au_trg" for example. Trigger names must be unique among the trigger names of a single schema, but they do not have to be unique with respect to other objects. That is, two triggers cannot have the same name, but a trigger and a table can have the same name, though that is not recommended.

"<Trigger event>" specifies the event that causes the trigger to fire and can be INSERT, UPDATE, DELETE, or any combination of those words separated by "OR." The "<table-name>" names the table upon which the trigger is defined. The option FOR EACH ROW indicates that the trigger is a row-level trigger, causing it to fire on *every* affected row. The trigger is a statement-level trigger if you omit "FOR EACH ROW" from the statement. The "WHEN <condition>" optional phrase holds a Boolean expression that restricts when the code in the trigger body actually executes. The "<trigger-body>" consists of PL/SQL code that carries out the trigger's chores.

There are some restrictions you must consider when creating triggers. Among them are these: A procedure or function called by a trigger cannot execute transaction control statements (COMMIT, ROLLBACK, and SAVEPOINT). Any statements performed by the trigger are part of the transaction. Trigger actions are committed or rolled back along with the events that cause the trigger to fire.

Within the trigger body, you can refer to the values of any column in the current record both before and after the trigger executes. Two **correlation names** exist for every column of the table being modified and contain the old and new column values of the current row affected by the triggering event. They are available only for row-level triggers, not statement-level triggers. The correlation name :OLD (a colon precedes "OLD") holds the column value before executing the SQL statement that causes the trigger to fire. Similarly, :NEW (colon followed by "NEW") holds the value for the column in the SQL statement that causes the trigger to fire. For example, suppose you have defined a BEFORE UPDATE trigger on the Agents table. If you execute an UPDATE statement on the Agents table, its BEFORE UPDATE trigger fires. Within the trigger body, the correlation values :NEW and :OLD are available for each column being updated. If you are updating the LicenseExpire column, you can refer to the before-update value with :OLD.LicenseExpire and the proposed, updated value with

TABLE 4.6 Values supplied in trigger body by correlation names NEW and OLD.

SQL Statement	Correlation Name	Value
INSERT	NEW	Value supplied for the column in the statement that originated the transaction.
	OLD	NULL
UPDATE	NEW	Value supplied for the column in the statement that originated the transaction.
	OLD	Value of the column that was last committed into the table prior to the transaction.
DELETE	NEW	NULL
	OLD	Value of the column that was last committed into the table before the transaction.

:NEW.LicenseExpire. Table 4.6 shows values for the OLD and NEW correlation names for the INSERT, UPDATE, and DELETE statements.

CREATING AND USING A BEFORE TRIGGER

Earlier in this chapter (see *Creating and Using Sequences*) you created a sequence called Agent_ID to supply primary key values for the Agents table. While sequences are a terrifically handy device to supply primary key values when inserting rows, you must remember to request a new sequence number each time as part of the INSERT statement. That is, sequences are not automatically associated with any particular table's primary key column. This slightly annoying problem is easily solved with a trigger.

CREATING A BEFORE TRIGGER

Once you create this trigger, you can insert new real estate agents into the Agents table without entering a value for AgentID. A sequence value will be provided by a BEFORE INSERT trigger you will write. First, you will recreate the sequence that you dropped earlier in this chapter.

To drop a sequence and recreate it anew:

1. Launch SQL*Plus, log into Oracle, type and execute the following lines:

```
CLEAR SCREEN
DROP SEQUENCE AgentID_seq;
CREATE SEQUENCE AgentID_seq
  START WITH 12345
  INCREMENT BY 2;
```

Oracle probably generated an error message after the DROP statement above because you already dropped the sequence. It won't hurt anything, and it guarantees that you start from scratch defining the sequence. Oracle should respond "Sequence created."

2. Very carefully type the following lines, pressing **Enter** at the end of each line. Notice the terminal forward slash (**/**). Press **Enter** after that line too. The forward slash tells Oracle to compile and store the procedure.

```
CREATE OR REPLACE TRIGGER Agents_bi_trg
BEFORE INSERT ON Agents FOR EACH ROW
BEGIN
  SELECT AgentID_seq.NEXTVAL INTO :NEW.AgentID FROM DUAL;
END;
/
```

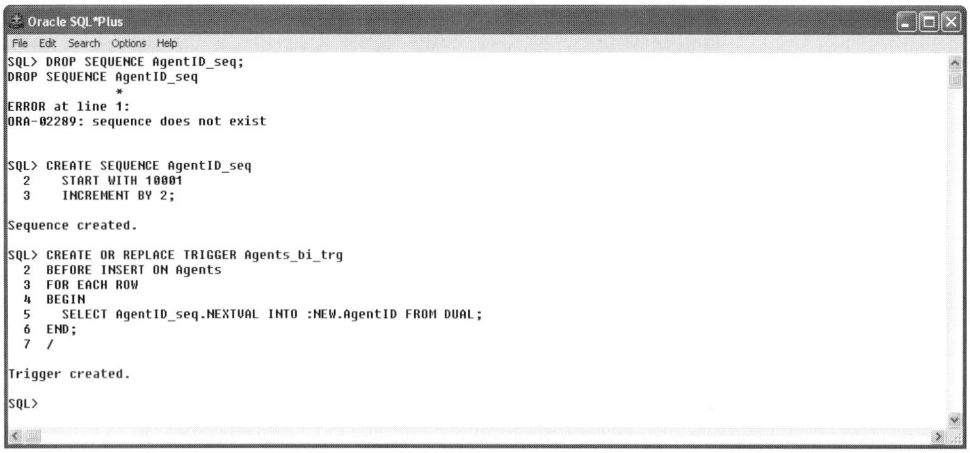

182 Introduction to Oracle

```
Oracle SQL*Plus
File Edit Search Options Help
SQL> DROP SEQUENCE AgentID_seq;
DROP SEQUENCE AgentID_seq
              *
ERROR at line 1:
ORA-02289: sequence does not exist

SQL> CREATE SEQUENCE AgentID_seq
  2    START WITH 10001
  3    INCREMENT BY 2;

Sequence created.

SQL> CREATE OR REPLACE TRIGGER Agents_bi_trg
  2  BEFORE INSERT ON Agents
  3  FOR EACH ROW
  4  BEGIN
  5    SELECT AgentID_seq.NEXTVAL INTO :NEW.AgentID FROM DUAL;
  6  END;
  7  /

Trigger created.

SQL>
```

FIGURE 4.25 Creating a Sequence and a BEFORE INSERT trigger.

Oracle signals success with the message "Trigger created." (See Figure 4.25.)

> **Tip:** If Oracle displays the error message "*Warning: Trigger created with compilation errors,*" then you probably mistyped the SELECT line. Simply correct the mistake and resubmit the entire collection of lines in step 2.
>
> **Tip:** You can display trigger compile errors by typing
>
> ```
> SHOW ERRORS TRIGGER <trigger-name>
> ```
>
> **Tip:** Substitute your trigger name for "<trigger-name>".

3. Leave SQL*Plus running.

Here's an explanation of the trigger you created in step 2 above. The trigger is named *Agents_bi_trg*. It is a BEFORE INSERT trigger, which means it fires when anyone executes an INSERT INTO Agents statement—just before the statement actually adds a row to the Agents table. The trigger code is sandwiched between the BEGIN and END words. It simply selects the next value in the sequence (AgentID_seq.NEXTVAL) and places it into the AgentID column of the correlation name :NEW. Oracle supplies NEW and OLD correlation names inside a trigger body whenever an INSERT or UPDATE statement executes that causes a trigger to fire. The Oracle ubiquitous table DUAL is referenced in the SELECT clause because you cannot extract a value from thin air—you must reference a table. With the newly acquired, unique primary key value stored in the NEW row, Oracle takes the values the user supplies in the INSERT statement plus any NEW correlation column values and inserts them into the Agents table.

TESTING A BEFORE TRIGGER

Let's test the trigger by inserting three new rows into the currently empty Agents table. Execute the following steps.

To insert rows into a table and invoke the newly defined trigger:

1. Using SQL*Plus, type and execute the following INSERT statements:

```
INSERT INTO Agents(LastName, FirstName)
  VALUES('Marcoux', 'Kai');
```

```
INSERT INTO Agents(LastName, FirstName)
  VALUES('Silverburg', 'Danial');
INSERT INTO Agents(LastName, FirstName)
  VALUES('Taylor', 'Jessica');
```

Oracle responds after each INSERT statement with "1 row created."

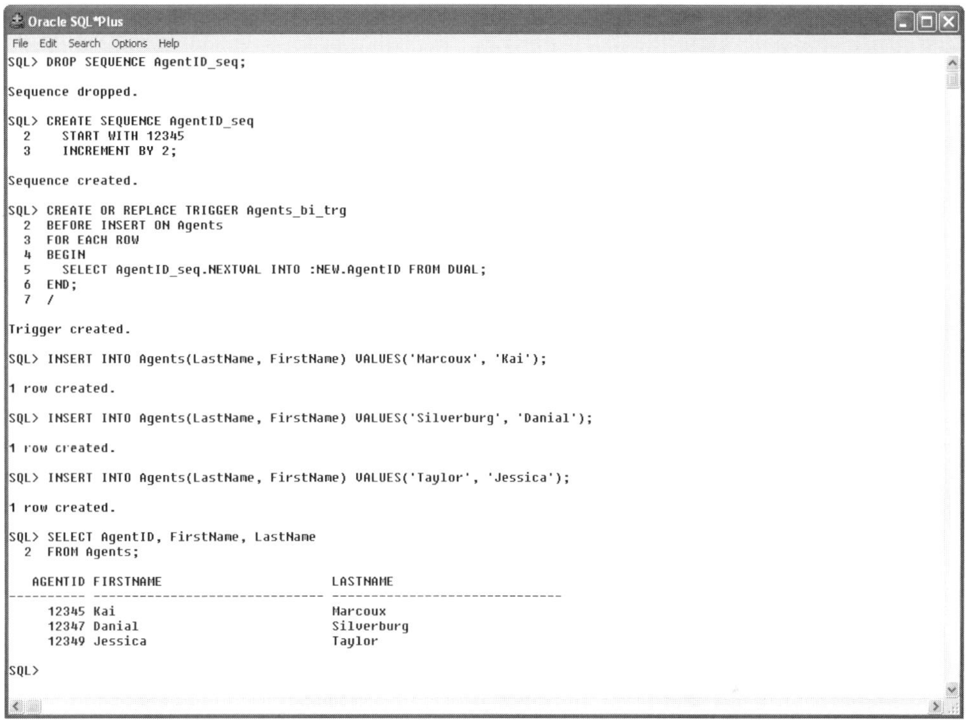

FIGURE 4.26 Displaying Agents rows with trigger-supplied primary key values.

2. Type and execute the following SELECT statement to display the three newly inserted rows. Primary keys are supplied by the trigger you defined in earlier steps.

```
SELECT AgentID, FirstName, Lastname
FROM Agents;
```

Figure 4.26 shows the results of the SELECT statement. Notice that the primary key values that are automatically inserted by the trigger are 12345, 12347, and 12349.

3. Type **exit** and press **Enter** to log off Oracle and close the SQL*Plus window. Doing so automatically commits all database changes you have made since you logged into Oracle.

CREATING AN AFTER TRIGGER TO AUDIT TABLE OPERATIONS

Although Oracle provides rich auditing tools, you can define your own customized auditing tools. By defining UPDATE, INSERT, or DELETE triggers on selected tables, you can log any modifications to those tables. Known as an audit trail, the table modification data is stored in one or more audit tables whose structure you define. Typical audit trail data you can capture includes the date and time the modification occurred, the nature of the modification (update, delete, or insert statement), the username of the logged user making the modification, and the old and new values, as appropriate.

Robert Stirling wants to monitor, but not prevent, all UPDATES to the Agents table. Whenever anyone with access rights to the Agents table issues an UPDATE command for the Agents table, Robert would like Oracle to quietly log information to an audit table. Information he wants you to record there includes the event that occurred (INSERT in this example), the username of the person making the change, and the date and time the change occurred. In addition, you are to insert into the audit table the values in seven of the Agents columns: AgentID, FirstName, LastName, HireDate, BirthDate, Gender, and Title. Although a full audit table normally includes all columns from the table you are monitoring, recording these seven columns is fine for now. Later, Robert may ask you to add more columns to the audit table, and he will probably want you to write triggers to fire for INSERT and DELETE statements too.

CREATING AN AUDIT TABLE TO LOG TABLE MODIFICATIONS

Fulfilling Robert's request requires you to first create a new audit table to hold the recorded data about the changes to the Agents table. Second, you need to create a trigger that fires whenever an UPDATE statement on the Agents table executes. Begin by creating the audit table, AuditAgents.

To create an audit table to hold selected information about changes to the Agents table:

1. Launch SQL*Plus, log into Oracle, and type and execute **CLEAR SCREEN**.
2. Launch Notepad and then use the method of creating SQL statements in Notepad and then copy/paste them into SQL*Plus. Execute the SQL*Plus script. If needed, make corrections in SQL*Plus, then repeat.
3. Type the following in Notepad, copy it to SQL*Plus, and execute it to create the AuditAgents table:

```
CREATE TABLE AuditAgents
   (AuditEvent     NVARCHAR2(6),
    BeforeAfter    NVARCHAR2(6),
    AuditUsername  NVARCHAR2(30),
    AuditDate      DATE,
    AgentID        INTEGER,
    FirstName      NVARCHAR2(30),
    LastName       NVARCHAR2(30),
    HireDate       DATE,
    BirthDate      DATE,
    Gender         NVARCHAR2(1),
    Title          NVARCHAR2(11));
```

4. Save your Notepad file with a name unique to you such as <yourname> CreateAudit.sql. Remember to change the *Save as type* list box to *All Files*.

CREATING AN AFTER TRIGGER

Next, you will create a trigger that fires when an UPDATE is issued for the Agents table. It can fire after the update operation occurs and must occur for every row updated. Therefore, it will be a row-level AFTER UPDATE trigger.

To create an AFTER UPDATE trigger on the Agents table:

1. Type the following in Notepad, then copy and paste it into SQL*Plus.

```
CREATE OR REPLACE TRIGGER Agents_au_trg
AFTER UPDATE ON Agents
```

```
      FOR EACH ROW
      BEGIN
        INSERT INTO AuditAgents
          VALUES ('Update', 'Before', user, sysdate,
             :OLD.AgentID, :OLD.FirstName, :OLD.LastName,
             :OLD.HireDate, :OLD.BirthDate, :OLD.Gender, :OLD.Title);
        INSERT INTO AuditAgents
          VALUES ('Update', 'After', NULL, NULL,
             :NEW.AgentID, :NEW.FirstName, :NEW.LastName,
             :NEW.HireDate, :NEW.BirthDate, :NEW.Gender, :NEW.Title);
      END;
```

FIGURE 4.27 Creating an audit table and an AFTER UPDATE trigger.

2. In SQL*Plus, press **Enter** to move to a new line below "END", type a slash (/), and press **Enter** to compile the code. Oracle responds "Trigger created." (See Figure 4.27.) If an error occurs, check your code carefully against what appears in this step. Then, make any necessary corrections, and repeat this step.
3. Switch to Notepad and save your file again.

The update trigger is in place. It fires whenever you update an Agents table row. When it fires, it records four special audit values and seven of the Agents columns. The trigger inserts two rows: one with values *before* the update operation and one with values *after* it.

TESTING AN AFTER TRIGGER

To test your new AFTER UPDATE trigger, you will execute three UPDATE statements on the Agents table. The statements will modify one of the seven Agents columns that are logged into the audit table, though you can update any column. Then, you will display the contents of the AuditAgents table to examine the data it has collected when the AFTER UPDATE trigger executed. For every row you update in the Agents table, there should be two rows in the AuditAgents table. Let's test the trigger.

To modify Agents table rows and activate the AFTER UPDATE trigger:

1. Type and execute the following UPDATE statements. Use Notepad, if you want, to type the code, copy the code to SQL*Plus, and execute it. Save your Notepad file when you are done.

```
UPDATE Agents SET Gender = 'M' WHERE AgentID = 12345;
UPDATE Agents SET Title = 'Salesperson' WHERE LastName = 'Silverburg';
UPDATE Agents SET HireDate = '29-JUN-98' WHERE AgentID = 12349;
```

Oracle responds with three messages, in turn, indicating "1 row updated."

2. Type and execute one additional update for a row already updated in Step 1:

```
UPDATE Agents SET LastName = 'Wahlberg' WHERE AgentID = 12345;
```

3. You'll switch to *i*SQL*Plus, for a change, to display the audit table's columns, so type **exit** and press **Enter** to log off Oracle and exit SQL*Plus. (If you prefer, you *can* continue the next steps in SQL*Plus.)

4. In Notepad, if necessary, click **File** and then click **Exit** to close it.

You have inserted four rows into the Agents table. Nothing else seems to have happened. However, your AFTER UPDATE trigger has been recording the four sets of changes you made and has stored that information in the audit table, AuditAgents. Next, you temporarily take on the role of the database auditor and examine who has been modifying the Agents table and when they did it.

To display the audit table's AuditAgents:

1. Launch your browser, launch *i*SQL*Plus, click the **Username** text box, type your username, press **Tab,** type your password in the Password text box, and click the **Login** button.

2. Click in the **Workspace** text box and type the following:

```
SELECT * FROM AuditAgents;
```

3. Click the **Execute** button. Oracle returns the eight rows from the AuditAgents table. Your results should match those in Figure 4.28.

4. Click the **Logout** button to log out of *i*SQL*Plus. Close your browser.

Look at Figure 4.28 carefully. Notice the *Before* and *After* rows for each modification. In the first two lines, you see the gender (column "G" in the figure) has changed. In the third and fourth rows, you see that the Title value appears after the update. The last two rows show the change to the LastName column. If you wanted to display the time and the date of the change, you could simply specify that the AuditDate column display a date and a time by using the TO_CHAR and an appropriate format model. For example, the following displays date and time details:

```
SELECT TO_CHAR(AuditDate, 'MM/DD/YY HH:MM:SS');
```

> **Tip:** The results would be the same if you created a BEFORE UPDATE trigger rather than the AFTER UPDATE as above. It makes no difference for this application.

CREATING AND USING A STATEMENT-LEVEL TRIGGER

The triggers you have learned about and used in this chapter are all row-level triggers. That is, they fire for every affected row when the triggering event occurs. Recall that statement-level triggers trigger only once per event, regardless of the number of table

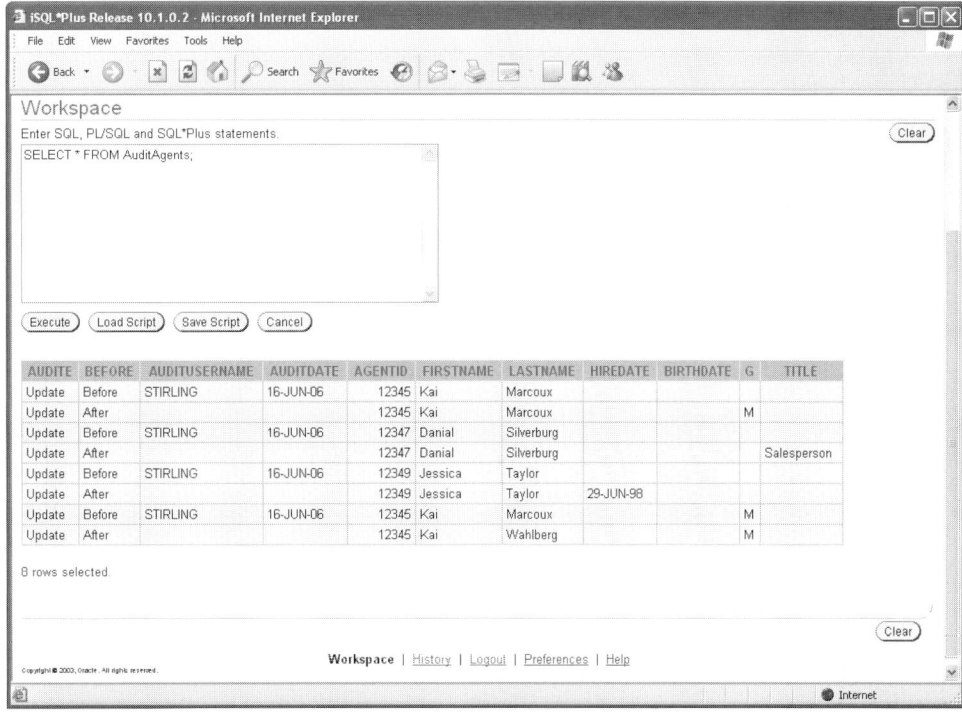

FIGURE 4.28 Displaying the audit table.

rows involved. In this section, you will see an example in which a seemingly correct row-level trigger generates an Oracle error. When replaced with a statement-level equivalent trigger, it works correctly. The trigger's purpose is simple. Every time someone executes an INSERT or DELETE statement on the Agents table, you want Oracle to display a message indicating the number of rows remaining in the table. You will create an AFTER trigger specifying both INSERT and DELETE so you catch both events. Recall that there already is a BEFORE INSERT trigger for Agents, which you created earlier, and there is also an AFTER UPDATE trigger on Agents. There is no problem having multiple triggers on a table for a particular event (INSERT, etc.), but Oracle does not guarantee the firing order of multiple triggers declared at the same level for the same type of DML statement. That is okay because your triggers do not depend on any timing sequence to operate correctly.

Let's experiment with a row-level trigger that simply displays the number of rows in the Agents table whenever anyone executes an INSERT or DELETE statement on the Agents table. It will fire after the modification occurs. You will test the trigger using SQL*Plus, and produce output on the screen (console) using the DBMS_OUTPUT package. The DBMS_OUTPUT package enables you to send messages from triggers to the screen. Specifically, the package's PUT and PUT_LINE procedures allow you to place information on the screen. For example, the following trigger body line displays the updated value of LastName of the Agents table:

```
BEGIN
   DBMS_OUTPUT.PUT_LINE('New LastName value: ' || :NEW.LastName);
END;
```

To see output from a trigger, you have to run the SQL*Plus command:

```
SET SERVEROUTPUT ON
```

A new feature you will use in the trigger you are about to write is a variable. The internal variable is a temporary memory location that exists only as long as the trigger is executing. The variable is needed to hold the integer number that is the count of the rows in the Agents table. It is declared in the optional trigger header, which begins with the word DECLARE and ends with the word BEGIN. BEGIN also marks the beginning of the trigger code body.

To create a trigger to display a row count on an INSERT or UPDATE event:

1. Launch SQL*Plus. Then type and execute the following statements. They clear the screen and set up the output. Press **Enter** at the end of each line. You should use Notepad as your editor, and then copy/paste to SQL*Plus.

   ```
   CLEAR SCREEN
   SET SERVEROUTPUT ON
   ```

2. Type the following code, copy it to SQL*Plus, and press **Enter** following the line containing END;

   ```
   CREATE OR REPLACE TRIGGER Agents_adai_trg
   AFTER INSERT OR DELETE ON Agents
   FOR EACH ROW
   DECLARE
     V_RowCount NUMBER;
   BEGIN
     SELECT COUNT(*) INTO V_RowCount FROM Agents;
     DBMS_OUTPUT.PUT_LINE(V_RowCount ||' rows in Agents');
   END;
   ```

3. In SQL*Plus, type slash (/) and press **Enter** to compile the trigger (see Figure 4.29). Oracle responds with the affirming message "Trigger created."

Keep Notepad open with your trigger code available, because you will need to modify it shortly. Next, test the trigger to see what happens.

To test the trigger:

1. In SQL*Plus, type and execute the following DELETE statement to invoke the trigger:

   ```
   DELETE FROM Agents WHERE Lastname = 'Silverburg';
   ```

   Oracle displays an error message.

2. Undo the deletion by typing and executing:

   ```
   ROLLBACK;
   ```

3. Switch to Notepad in preparation for changes to your trigger.

FIGURE 4.29 Trigger execution error.

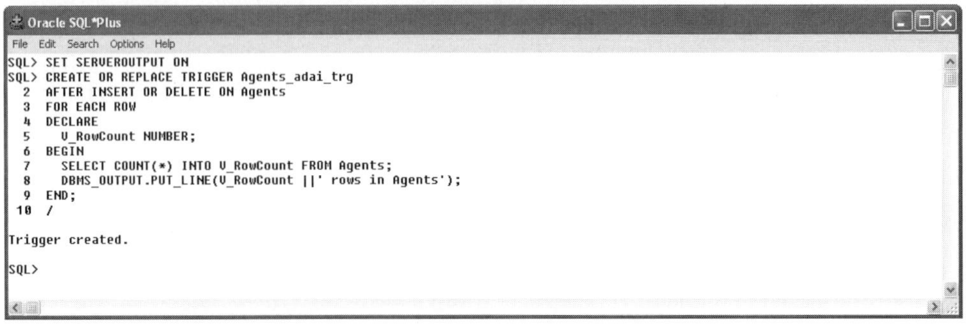

CHAPTER 4 Modifying Data and Auditing Table Operations

There is something wrong with the trigger. The message "... AGENTS is mutating, trigger/function may not see it" appears. A ***mutating table*** is a table that is being modified by a DML statement that has triggered the event. SQL statements in a trigger body (for example, the SELECT in the preceding trigger) are not allowed to read from or modify any table of the triggering statement. This includes the triggering table itself. The trigger is trying to change or examine something that's already being changed. This confuses Oracle. When a row-level trigger is about to fire for the second row in a multirow delete, what is Oracle to do? Does the application intend that Oracle see the table in its pre-delete state? Or does it intend to see it after the deletion occurs? It seems as if we have a Catch-22. The problem goes away if we simply change the trigger from a row-level trigger to a statement-level trigger.

To modify and recompile the trigger:

1. In Notepad, delete the code line "FOR EACH ROW" from the trigger body, save the code under a name of your own choosing (select a .sql suffix), and copy/paste the trigger definition into SQL*Plus.
2. Type slash (/) and press **Enter** to recompile the trigger.
3. Test the trigger again by typing and executing the following in SQL*Plus:

   `DELETE FROM Agents WHERE Lastname = 'Silverburg';`

   This time, the trigger works correctly. Notice the message "2 rows in Agents" appears directly below the DELETE statement. The statement-level trigger message indicates that there are two rows remaining ("2 rows in Agents" appears on the console) after the delete operation. Oracle follows this with a message indicating "1 row deleted." See Figure 4.30.

FIGURE 4.30 Correctly executing statement-level trigger.

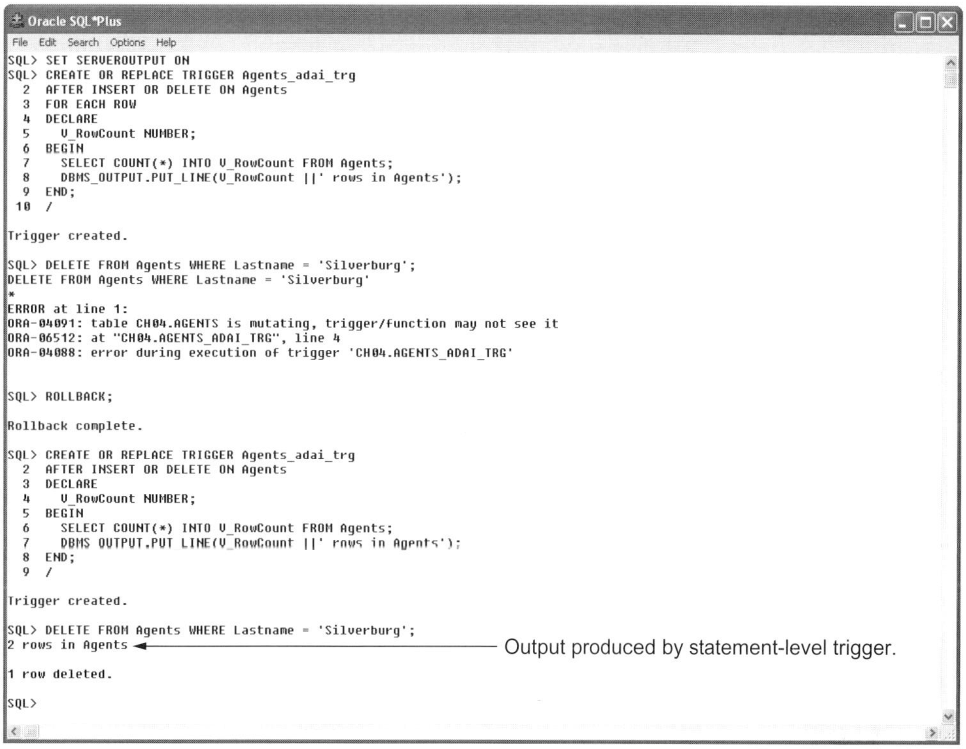

TABLE 4.7 Columns available in the user_triggers data dictionary view.

Column name	Data type	Meaning
Trigger_Name	VARCHAR2(30)	Name of trigger
Trigger_Type	VARCHAR2(16)	Type of trigger
Triggering_Event	VARCHAR2(227)	Event that causes trigger to fire
Table_Owner	VARCHAR2(30)	User who owns the table that the trigger references
Base_Object_Type	VARCHAR2(16)	Type of object referenced by the trigger
Table_Name	VARCHAR2(30)	Table referenced by the trigger
Column_Name	VARCHAR2(4000)	Column referenced by the trigger
Referencing_Names	VARCHAR2(128)	Name of the OLD and NEW aliases.
When_Clause	VARCHAR2(4000)	Trigger condition WHEN clause
Status	VARCHAR2(8)	Whether the trigger is enabled or disabled
Description	VARCHAR2(4000)	Description of trigger
Action_Type	VARCHAR2(11)	Action type of the trigger
Trigger_Body	LONG	Code contained in trigger body

4. Type **COMMT;** and press **Enter** to make permanent the changes so far.

5. Type **Exit** and press **Enter** to log off SQL*Plus, because you will use *i*SQL*Plus in the next section.

DISPLAYING, ALTERING, AND DROPPING TRIGGERS

Like any other Oracle object, information about triggers is saved in the data dictionary. You can get information on triggers from the data dictionary view user_triggers. A more comprehensive list of all triggers is in the view all_triggers, though it is a longer list and the information spans thousands of characters. (The column_name column, for example, is 4000 characters long). Table 4.7 shows the columns available in the user_triggers view.

DISPLAYING TRIGGER INFORMATION

Several of the columns are of little interest to us. However, important ones are trigger_name, trigger_type, triggering_event, table_name, and status. Examine those columns for your triggers by following these steps:

To display selected trigger information:

1. Launch *i*SQL*Plus (you can use SQL*Plus, if you prefer), log into Oracle with your username and password, and click the **Workspace** text box.

2. Type the following in the Workspace text box:

   ```
   SELECT Trigger_Name, Triggering_Event, Trigger_Type, Table_Name, Status
   FROM user_triggers;
   ```

   Figure 4.31 shows the selected information for the three triggers you own.

3. If you are using *i*SQL*Plus, then click the **Logout** hyperlink to log out of Oracle and close your browser. If you are using SQL*Plus, *do not* close it. You will use it again in a moment.

DISABLING AND ENABLING TRIGGERS

When you create and compile a trigger, it is automatically enabled. If you need to turn off a trigger temporarily, you can issue an ALTER TRIGGER statement to disable or enable it. When a trigger is disabled, it is still defined but inactive and will not fire. The ALTER TRIGGER syntax is:

```
ALTER TRIGGER [schema.]<trigger-name> {ENABLE | DISABLE};
```

CHAPTER 4 Modifying Data and Auditing Table Operations

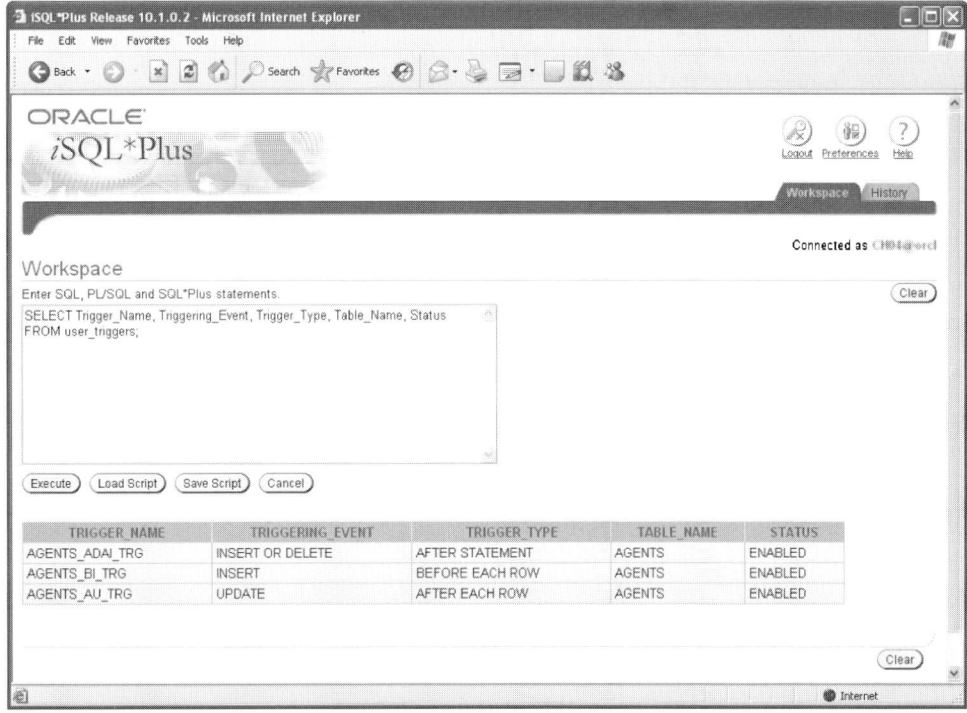

FIGURE 4.31 Displaying trigger information.

Schema is the optional schema name. For any triggers you have created (own), you can omit your schema (login) name. If you have delete rights to a trigger owned by another schema, then you must use the qualifying schema name. You could disable the Agents_au_trg trigger that you created and thus own it so that it no longer fires. To do so, execute the SQL command:

```
ALTER TRIGGER Agents_au_trg DISABLE;
```

Later, if you decide to reinstate the trigger, you can enable it by executing:

```
ALTER TRIGGER Agents_au_trg ENABLE;
```

DROPPING TRIGGERS

If you know that you no longer need one or more triggers, you can remove them and their definitions entirely. Like other database objects, triggers are removed by issuing a DROP statement. The syntax is:

```
DROP TRIGGER [schema.]<trigger-name>
```

Because we no longer need any of the triggers created in this chapter, you will delete all of them. If you forget their names, simply run the SELECT statement (query) you ran previously. It displays the triggers' names.

To drop triggers you have created:

1. Launch SQL*Plus, if needed, and then type and execute the following statements:

```
DROP TRIGGER Agents_au_trg;
DROP TRIGGER Agents_bi_trg;
DROP TRIGGER Agents_adai_trg;
```

After each individual statement, Oracle displays "Trigger dropped."

2. Just to satisfy yourself that all of your triggers are gone, type and execute the following:

   `SELECT Trigger_Name from user_triggers;`

   Oracle responds "no rows selected," which confirms you have removed all your triggers.

3. Type **exit** and press **Enter** to log out of Oracle and close SQL*Plus.

Summary

Oracle's data manipulation language (DML) statements include INSERT, UPDATE, and DELETE. The INSERT SQL statement allows you to add new rows to a table. Using it, you specify an optional list of column names and a corresponding list of values. There must be as many values, including NULL, as there are column names and the values must correspond, left to right, with the list of column names. However, the list of column names need not be in the same order as they are in the table. Oracle assigns any column omitted from the INSERT statement its default value, if designated, or NULL. If you execute an INSERT statement for a table containing a foreign key constraint referencing another table's primary key, you must be careful. Normally, the referenced table must be populated first. Alternatives include disabling, temporarily, the constraint or inserting NULL in the foreign key column. Enter date values in the standard form enclosed in apostrophes, DD-MON-YY, or use the TO_DATE function with a format model that matches the format of the date value you are inserting.

A sequence is a database object that generates a series of unique numbers suitable for primary keys. You create a named sequence, specify optional starting and increment integers, and then reference its pseudocolumn NEXTVAL to supply the next unique integer. The pseudocolumn CURRVAL provides the last value generated. The Oracle table Dual provides a one-row, one-column table to which you can refer when you need to display the value of a pseudocolumn or a calculation.

The UPDATE statement makes modifications to data. You can update one or several columns of a single table with UPDATE, which is called an action query. The optional WHERE clause contains a logical expression consisting of relational operators, logical operators, constants, and column references. The logical expression limits the scope of the rows affected, whereas omitting the WHERE clause causes modifications to all rows of the table. Using the CASE structure is a convenient way to provide many alternative update values for a column. Oracle's substitution variables provide substitutes for values in SQL statements when run. Oracle prompts you for the actual values to replace the substitution variables when you execute a script containing them, or when you run a single-line SQL statement with them.

The DELETE action query deletes rows from a table. The optional WHERE clause determines which rows are deleted. Omitting the WHERE clause causes all rows to be removed, but the table remains. The TRUNCATE TABLE statement deletes all rows from a table permanently—without the possibility of reversing that action. A TRUNCATE statement does not affect a table's structure. It remains intact.

The MERGE statement combines the INSERT, UPDATE, and DELETE actions into one statement and merges rows from a source table into a target table. Oracle inserts rows present in the source table but not in the target table. MERGE updates rows with the source table values when both the source and target tables have rows with matching primary key fields. MERGE deletes rows from the target table not found in the source table. Its actions are specified by the WHEN MATCHED and WHEN NOT MATCHED clauses.

Database transaction statements include COMMIT, ROLLBACK, and SAVEPOINT. COMMIT makes permanent any DML actions. ROLLBACK reverses some or all of the DML statement actions since the beginning of the transaction. Transactions begin when you log into Oracle, when you issue a DDL statement (CREATE TABLE, for instance) or you issue a COMMIT statement closing out a previous transaction. Savepoints allow you to establish markers so that you can rollback the database to any marker within the current transaction.

CHAPTER 4 Modifying Data and Auditing Table Operations **193**

Triggers are blocks of code that are associated with a table and that execute, or fire, before or after a particular DML statement on a table executes. Triggers are a handy way to enforce business rules such as checking the value of proposed changes to rows or the acceptable range of values for salary. Triggers can be defined for non-DML statements, but normally are defined for INSERT, UPDATE, and DELETE events—or any combination of them—on a table. Triggers can occur before or after a DML statement executes. Tracking information about changes to a particular table, called auditing a table, is a common use for triggers. You can disable, enable, or drop triggers at any time.

Key Terms

- Action query
- Alias
- Commit
- Correlation names
- Dual
- Fire
- Format model
- Mutating table
- Pseudocolumn
- Query
- Rollback
- Row-level trigger
- Sequence
- Session
- Statement-level trigger
- Substitution variable
- Transaction
- Trigger
- Truncate

Review

TRUE/FALSE

1. An UPDATE statement always makes changes to values in a table, and those changes cannot be reversed.
2. When you insert a row into a table, you do not need to supply a column-name/value pair for every column in the table.
3. Truncating a table is slightly different from deleting all rows in that table. Deleted rows are reversible, but a truncated table's rows cannot be rolled back.
4. COMMIT makes permanent any changes to a database.
5. Within the body of a BEFORE INSERT (FOR EACH ROW) trigger, your code has access to non-NULL values stored in the OLD and NEW correlation values for every column in the row being inserted.

FILL IN

1. In an INSERT statement containing a column and values list, you place a(n) _____ when the value is unknown.
2. Use the Oracle function _____ to insert a date, including its format model.
3. The _____ parameter of the CREATE SEQUENCE statement sets the smallest value to be generated.
4. After executing the SQL _____ command, none of the changes to the database can be rescinded.
5. You specify _____ _____ _____ in a trigger definition so it fires before modifying the LicenseDate column in the Agents table. If you want the trigger to fire only once, regardless of the number of rows affected, then you *omit* the three words _____ _____ _____ in the trigger creation statement.

Multiple Choice

1. Which of the following INSERT statements is correct, knowing what you do about the Agents table?
   a. INSERT INTO Agents(AgentID, LastName) (96743, 'Gilbert');
   b. INSERT INTO Agents VALUES (96743, 'Gilbert');
   c. INSERT INTO Agents(AgentID, LastName) VALUES ('96743', 'Gilbert');
   d. INSERT INTO Agents(AgentID, LastName) VALUES (96743, 'Gilbert');

2. Which of the following is an incorrectly formed DELETE statement?
   a. DELETE FROM Agents;
   b. DELETE FROM Agents WHEN AgentID = 12345;
   c. DELETE Agents WHERE LastName = 'Ellison';
   d. DELETE FROM Agents WHERE FirstName = 'Leonard' AND LastName = 'Smythe';

3. When issuing the MERGE INTO command, what phrase precedes an INSERT statement when you want to add rows missing from the target table?
   a. WHEN MATCHED THEN UPDATE.
   b. WHEN NOT MATCHED THEN UPDATE.
   c. WHEN MATCHED THEN INSERT.
   d. WHEN NOT MATCHED THEN INSERT.

4. An individual connection to an Oracle database server is called what?
   a. A transaction.
   b. A mutating table.
   c. A schema.
   d. A session.

5. Oracle allows BEFORE and AFTER triggers for INSERT, UPDATE, and DELETE statements. What is the name of the trigger type that is allowed for views but not tables?
   a. AUDIT.
   b. INSTEAD OF.
   c. IN VIEW OF.
   d. IN REVERSE OF.

Hands-on Exercises

1. Extending the Chapter Case

Robert Stirling wants you to add a table to the Redwood Realty database called Customers. It will contain contact information about customers interested in buying and selling real estate. Robert has prepared a script file that creates the table and inserts an initial ten customer rows into it. After you run that script file, you will drop the existing sequence, AgentID_seq, create a new one to supply primary keys for the Customers table when new customers are inserted, establish some savepoints, insert new customers, rollback the database, delete selected customers, and create a trigger that fires automatically when you insert a new customer into Customers. Finally, you will drop the trigger and drop the sequence you created. Demonstrate the work you accomplish in this problem by turning on a spool file that captures your keystrokes and Oracle's responses. Launch SQL*Plus and log into Oracle.

When you have completed this exercise, print the spool file and turn it in to your instructor. Use Notepad as your text editor, then copy and paste pieces of it to SQL*Plus. First, locate the script file Ch04Problem1.sql and note its path. Substitute its path on your computer for "<path>" in Step 1, and substitute any suitable path for "<mypath>" below and your last name for "<yourname>."

Important note: You should complete this exercise in one session. If you do some of the steps, log out of Oracle, and then return, then Oracle will commit the changes and some of the ROLLBACK statements will not work the same way.

1. Type and execute the following:

```
START C:\<path>\Ch04Problem1.sql
COLUMN CustomerID FORMAT 99999
COLUMN LastName FORMAT A10
COLUMN City FORMAT A10
COLUMN State FORMAT A10
```

```
COLUMN Zipcode FORMAT A7
CLEAR SCREEN
SPOOL C:\<mypath>\<yourname>Ch04Redwood.txt
SHOW USER
CREATE SEQUENCE CustomerID_seq
   START WITH 34567
   INCREMENT BY 2;
```

2. Update Customer rows and set a savepoint:

```
UPDATE Customers
SET City = 'Aracta', State = 'California'
WHERE Zipcode = '95570';
SAVEPOINT SaveAfterUpdate;
```

3. Insert a new customer and set another savepoint:

```
INSERT INTO Customers (CustomerID,
FirstName, LastName)
   VALUES (25599, 'Lora', 'Dietrich');
SAVEPOINT SaveAfterInsert;
```

4. Delete all customers, display them to prove they are deleted, change your mind (oops) and restore them, and display them again to show they are reinstated. Delete selected customers, display the remaining ones, reinstate everything all the way back to the first savepoint, and display selected columns:

```
DELETE FROM Customers;
SELECT CustomerID, LastName, City, State,
Zipcode FROM Customers;
ROLLBACK TO SAVEPOINT SaveAfterInsert;
SELECT CustomerID, LastName, City, State,
Zipcode FROM Customers;
DELETE FROM Customers WHERE WorkPhone IS
NULL;
SELECT CustomerID, LastName, City, State,
Zipcode FROM Customers;
ROLLBACK TO SAVEPOINT SaveAfterUpdate;
SELECT CustomerID, LastName, City, State,
Zipcode FROM Customers;
```

5. Create a trigger to automatically insert primary key values into Customers when they are inserted. Insert several customers. Display the newly inserted customers.

```
CREATE OR REPLACE TRIGGER Customers_bi_trg
BEFORE INSERT ON Customers
FOR EACH ROW
BEGIN
   SELECT CustomerID_seq.NEXTVAL INTO
   :NEW.CustomerID FROM DUAL;
END;
/
INSERT INTO Customers (LastName, FirstName,
City, State, Zipcode)
   VALUES ('Chang', 'Y.F.', 'Arcata', 'CA',
   '95518');
INSERT INTO Customers (LastName, FirstName,
City, State, Zipcode)
   VALUES ('Newman', 'Richard', 'Blue Lake',
   'CA', '95525');
INSERT INTO Customers (LastName, FirstName,
City, State, Zipcode)
   VALUES ('Nasser', 'Jehad', 'Eureka',
   'CA', '95503');
COMMIT;
SELECT CustomerID, LastName, City, State,
Zipcode
FROM Customers ORDER BY CustomerID;
```

6. Turn off the spool file, drop the trigger, drop the sequence(s), drop all tables, and close the spool file.

```
SPOOL OFF
DROP TRIGGER Customers_bi_trg;
DROP SEQUENCE CustomerID_seq;
DROP SEQUENCE AgentID_seq;
DROP TABLE Agents CASCADE CONSTRAINTS
PURGE;
DROP TABLE AuditAgents CASCADE CONSTRAINTS
PURGE;
DROP TABLE LicenseStatus CASCADE
CONSTRAINTS PURGE;
DROP TABLE Customers CASCADE CONSTRAINTS
PURGE;
```

7. Type **exit** and press **Enter** to exit SQL*Plus.

8. Open Notepad, click **File,** click **Open,** navigate to the folder where your <yourname>Ch04Redwood.txt spool is stored, click **<yourname>Ch04Redwood.txt,** and then click the **Open** button.

9. Press **Enter** at the top of the spool file to open a line, type your first and last names in the first line of the spool file. Click **File** and then click **Print** to print the spool file. You can turn in this output to your instructor, if requested. Close Notepad.

2. COFFEE MERCHANT

The Coffee Merchant database administrator wants you to create and populate the Employees table, which holds information about current Coffee Merchant employees. Then, he wants you to create a special table called AuditEmployees which holds information about every insert, update, or delete operation that takes place on the Employees table. A trigger you will write stores into the table before and after images of the affected Employees rows. In the audit table the trigger will store the word *Before* or *After,* the Oracle user making the modification, the date and time when the change occurred, the primary key field EmployeeID, and the LastName and CommissionRate fields. You will create savepoints and insert, update, and delete Employees rows to test the trigger. After making modifications to the Employees table, you will print the AuditEmployees rows to reveal what information the table holds, spooling the results to a file so you can print it and turn it in to your instructor.

We ask that you use Notepad or another suitable text editor to hold *everything* you submit to SQL*Plus for execution. When you have completed the assignment, save the Notepad file containing the SQL*Plus and SQL commands and print it. In addition, print the spool file. Be sure to place your name and other information your instructor requests at the top of both printouts. If you make mistakes midway through the problem, you can start from the top. If you start over, do so from the beginning and rerun the initialization file, Ch04Problem2.sql. It will remove any objects you have created and reset the Coffee Merchant Tables. Type each of the steps below in Notepad, copy/paste them to SQL*Plus, and execute them.

1. Launch SQL*Plus, log into Oracle, and type and execute the following to initialize the Coffee Merchant tables and create an Audit Employees table. Locate the path to the file Ch04Problem2.sql and replace "<path>" (below) with it.

```
CLEAR SCREEN
START C:\<path>\Ch04Problem2.sql
CREATE TABLE AuditEmployees
  (BeforeAfter    NVARCHAR2(6),
   AuditUsername  NVARCHAR2(30),
   AuditDate      DATE,
   EmployeeID     INTEGER,
   LastName       NVARCHAR2(30),
   Commission     Number(4,4)
  );
```

2. Create a trigger which fires after an INSERT, UPDATE, or DELETE on the Employees table. (The table Employees was created and populated in Step 1 within the Ch04Problem2.sql script.) Remember to type a slash (/) and press **Enter** to compile and store the trigger.

```
CREATE OR REPLACE TRIGGER
Employees_aiauad_trg
AFTER INSERT OR UPDATE OR DELETE ON
Employees
FOR EACH ROW
BEGIN
 INSERT INTO AuditEmployees VALUES
 ('Before', user, sysdate,
    :OLD.EmployeeID, :OLD.LastName,
    :OLD.CommissionRate);
 INSERT INTO AuditEmployees VALUES
 ('After', NULL, NULL,
    :NEW.EmployeeID, :NEW.LastName,
    :NEW.CommissionRate);
END;
/
```

3. Create a savepoint and insert three employee rows.

```
SAVEPOINT BeforeInsert;
INSERT INTO Employees (EmployeeID,
FirstName, LastName, Gender)
  VALUES (1528, 'Luca', 'Pacioli', 'M');
INSERT INTO Employees (EmployeeID,
FirstName, LastName, Gender)
  VALUES (3432, 'Melinda', 'English', 'F');
INSERT INTO Employees (EmployeeID,
FirstName, LastName, Gender)
  VALUES (3692, 'Steve', 'Ballmer', 'M');
```

4. Create another savepoint and update several employee rows using a CASE structure.

```
SAVEPOINT BeforeUpdate;
UPDATE Employees
  SET CommissionRate =
    CASE
        WHEN CommissionRate IS NULL THEN
        0.025
        WHEN CommissionRate < 0.07 THEN
        CommissionRate * 1.15
        WHEN CommissionRate BETWEEN 0.07 and
        0.09 THEN CommissionRate * 1.1
        ELSE CommissionRate * 1.05
    END;
```

5. Create another savepoint, delete several employees, display a count of the remaining rows, reverse the DELETE, COMMIT the changes, and display the Employees row count again to demonstrate the one-SQL statement ROLLBACK worked.

```
SAVEPOINT BeforeDelete;
DELETE FROM Employees WHERE Gender = 'M';
SELECT COUNT(*) FROM Employees;
ROLLBACK TO SAVEPOINT BeforeDelete;
COMMIT;
SELECT COUNT(*) FROM Employees;
```

6. Begin spooling SQL*Plus to a spool file, display the Oracle username, display the audit table rows, disable the trigger, delete selected Employees rows, show the row count,

rollback all changes, and show the changed row count.

```
SPOOL C:\Ch04Problem2-spoolfile.txt
SHOW USER
SELECT * FROM AuditEmployees;
ALTER TRIGGER Employees_aiauad_trg DISABLE;
DELETE FROM Employees Where Gender = 'F';
SELECT COUNT(*) FROM Employees;
ROLLBACK;
SELECT COUNT(*) FROM Employees;
```

7. Display information about the trigger including its name, the type, and the table with which it is associated. Drop the trigger, drop all tables created in this problem, and turn off the spool file.

```
SELECT Trigger_Name, Trigger_Type,
Table_Name FROM User_Triggers;
DROP TRIGGER Employees_aiauad_trg;
DROP TABLE AuditEmployees CASCADE
CONSTRAINTS PURGE;
DROP TABLE Employees CASCADE CONSTRAINTS
PURGE;
SPOOL OFF
```

8. Type **exit** and press **Enter** to log off Oracle and close SQL*Plus.
9. Finally, save your Notepad file containing all the preceding SQL*Plus and SQL statements. Open the spool file, press **Enter** to open up a row at the top, type your first and last names, and save and print the spool file. Do the same thing for the SQL*Plus/SQL script file—enter your name on the top line preceding all script file lines, and print the file.

3. Rowing Ventures

There are some fears that someone will inadvertently alter the Rowing Ventures' *Person* table, which holds the name, gender, weight, and birth date information. According to most regatta rules, any coxswain whose weight is less than a particular value must carry a bag containing extra weight to compensate. Because the weight of the coxswain, in particular, and rowers, in general, is so critically important, the race officials want to monitor any changes to the Person table. If anyone were to alter the coxswain's weight by increasing it, that boat would have a definite advantage. You are to create and execute a series of SQL statements that do the following.

First, launch Notepad and launch SQL*Plus. Locate the script file Ch04Problem3.sql, which initializes the database for this problem. Run the script file by issuing the START statement. Include the path and script file name following START. Next, create a table called AuditPerson containing columns that record the username, current date/time, and Person table columns PersonID, Weight, and DateOfBirth. Create an AFTER trigger, named *Person_aiauad_trg,* that fires whenever anyone executes an INSERT, UPDATE, or DELETE statement on the Person table. The trigger records both the before and after values for the Person table in corresponding AuditPerson columns. Insert two rows with values for PersonID (greater than 1100), LastName, FirstName, Gender, Weight, and DateOfBirth. Make their birthdates *after* 1972. Update the Weight column for males (Gender = 'M') by 6 percent. Commit all changes so far to the database. Set a savepoint called *BeforeDeleteFemale.* Delete rows from the Person table in which the rower's birth date (DateOfBirth) is anytime between 1971 and 1972, inclusive. Undo this last change, rolling back to the savepoint you created. Start a spool file, and then display the contents of the AuditPerson file by executing:

```
SELECT * FROM AuditPerson;
```

Display trigger information including the trigger's name, type, the table it monitors, and its status. Drop the trigger, and drop the two tables Audit Person and Person. Turn off the spool file. Print the entire SQL*Plus session, including all statements you executed. Print the spool file. Be sure to identify both outputs with your name at the top of the page. Log out of SQL*Plus and close SQL*Plus.

4. Broadcloth Clothing

The Broadcloth database comprises seventeen tables. None is more important to the company's DBA than the Contact table. It contains customer contact information including each customer's assigned ContactID, name, phone (land and mobile), address, e-mail address, and so on. If this table were to be corrupted or modified by unauthorized people, restoring the original values could be very expensive. Naturally, the company has maintained backups, but the DBA wants you to implement some fundamental monitoring that records all INSERT, UPDATE, and DELETE accesses to the Contact table. First, launch SQL*Plus, locate the file Ch04Problem4.sql, and run it in SQL*Plus to initialize selected Broadcloth tables. Then, create an audit table called AuditContact. Its columns are described in the following table.

Column Name	Data Type	Contents
OperationType	VARCHAR2(6)	Operation performed on the table: INSERT, UPDATE, or DELETE.
BeforeAfter	VARCHAR(6)	Indicates selected values before ('BEFORE') or after ('AFTER') changes are made.
Username	VARCHAR(30)	Oracle username of user making the change.
ModDate	Date	Date and time when row was altered.
RecordPK	INTEGER	Copy of the ContactID table column to identify changed row.
RecordLastName	NVARCHAR(20)	LastName of changed or inserted record.

Next, create three separate triggers to log changes to Contact. Be sure to save the code for each of these triggers so you can print them and turn them in to your instructor. *Contact_bu_trg* is the before update, row-level trigger that stores two rows in the audit table—one with the before value of the columns listed above (store "UPDATE" in OperationType and store "BEFORE" in BeforeAfter) and one with the values after the update (store "UPDATE" in OperationType and store "AFTER" in BeforeAfter). *Contact_bi_trg* is the before insert, row-level trigger that inserts only one row into AuditContact. The trigger places "INSERT" into OperationType, "(new)" into BeforeAfter, and fills out the remaining AuditContact columns with Oracle user name, current date/time, the new record's primary key, and the new record's LastName value. (Hint: use :NEW correlation names.) Finally, the *Contact_bd_trg* is the before delete row-level trigger that inserts only one row into AuditContact. The trigger places "DELETE" into OperationType, "(old)" into BeforeAfter, and fills out the remaining AuditContact columns with Oracle user name, current date/time, the old record's primary key and LastName values. (Hint: use :OLD correlation names.) Insert two records (use primary keys whose value is greater than 1234 and supply only FirstName and LastName values.) Remember to use DESCRIBE to review Contact's structure. Delete any rows in contact in which the Nation column equals either Pakistan or Malaysia (initial capital letter). Update the GMTDifference value to its current value plus two for rows in which the PrimaryLanguage is "Chinese" (spelled and capitalized as shown). Make all changes permanent. Turn on a spool file named appropriately and easy to locate when you are done, and then type and execute the statement: SELECT * FROM AuditContact; Then, turn off the spool file, locate and edit it by placing your name in the top line. Save and then print the spool file for your instructor, and print the script files showing how you created the triggers. Finally, execute DROP statements to drop all triggers, drop the Contact table, and drop the AuditContact table.

CHAPTER 5

QUERYING A DATABASE

Learning Objectives

In this chapter, you will learn how to:

- Write a SELECT statement to retrieve data from a single table.
- Write a SELECT statement to filter rows and display unique values.
- Sort returned rows into ascending and descending order on returned column values.
- Write expressions to form computations and create column aliases.
- Write SQL character, numeric, conversion, and special functions in SELECT statements.
- Use SQL aggregate functions avg, count, max, min, and sum.
- Group results by common elements.
- Filter groups with the HAVING clause.
- Use SQL*Plus report formatting statements.

DISPLAYING DATA FROM A SINGLE DATABASE TABLE

In previous chapters, you created tables, populated tables with data, established constraints, and modified and deleted data from tables. In this chapter you learn to extract information from the database tables. Relational databases ensure that you can access data elements from one or more database tables and display then in a two-dimensional, table format. Using the structure query language and the SQL*Plus client, you can write English-like structured data access statements that are the industry standard for querying databases. With SQL, you specify where to locate the data, how to connect multiple tables, which columns of information you want, the filtering criteria to apply to candidate rows, and the order in which rows are to be returned in the resulting table. The SELECT statement is the SQL command that extracts information from relational database tables. Unlike DML commands, SELECT does not alter information in any table.

In this chapter, and the one that follows, you will learn how to get exactly the information you want. For example, you might want to know which Redwood Realty agent sold the highest total dollar volume of real estate this month. Or, you might want a list of properties for a potential buyer that are located within a certain ZIP code and whose asking price is within a particular range. These questions and more are just a few examples of queries you pose by writing SELECT statements.

WRITING A SELECT STATEMENT

The simplest form of the SELECT statement has the syntax

```
SELECT * FROM <table-name>;
```

where "<table-name>" is the name of a table whose rows you want to retrieve and the *asterisk* (*) in the select list indicates that Oracle is to retrieve *all* of the table's columns. They appear in the result in the same column order as they are defined in the table. Writing the asterisk wild card column selector saves you from having to type each column name individually. On the other hand, you do not have any options about the order in which columns are listed in the returned rows when you use the asterisk. The SELECT statement can be complex and, frankly, a bit daunting. The following is a slightly simplified, general form of the SELECT statement syntax with its major clauses represented.

```
SELECT [DISTINCT] <select-list>
FROM {<table-list>}
[WHERE <conditions>]
[GROUP BY <group-by-list>]
[HAVING <group-conditions>]
[ORDER BY <order-list> [ASC | DESC]]
[FOR UPDATE <for-update-options>];
```

The optional word DISTINCT suppresses display of duplicate rows—rows having matching values across *every* column in the select list. The *select list* is a comma-separated list of table column names and expressions. When you reference columns from a table owned by another schema, you refer to a column with the form *schema.column-name*. The **table list** following the reserved word *FROM* contains a list of one or more tables from which the result data is retrieved. The optional **WHERE clause** defines the filter or search conditions that each row in the table(s) must meet to be returned. Oracle includes only rows meeting the conditions in the result set of rows. The optional **GROUP BY clause** partitions the result set into groups. Each distinct group is identified by matching results in all of the columns listed in the group by list. **HAVING,** another optional clause, provides an additional filter on the grouped result rows. (The WHERE clause applies to individual rows.) The optional **ORDER BY clause** sorts the resulting rows into order on individually listed column names. When ASC or DESC appears following any given column name, the rows are sorted in ascending or descending order on the column. Sorting is applied from left to right, and you can sort on as many columns as you wish. You can sort by columns regardless of whether they appear in the returned set of columns. If you omit the ORDER BY clause, Oracle returns rows in unpredictable order.

A popular use of the FOR UPDATE optional phrase is to lock selected rows. The clauses SELECT, FROM, WHERE, HAVING, and ORDER BY must appear in this order; however, you may write a SELECT statement on as many or as few lines as you want. In other words, Oracle does not care if there are hard returns or extra white space *between* words and phrases. Traditionally, database users write each phrase at the beginning of a new line, however.

Here is a simple example requesting Oracle to retrieve selected columns from the Customers table. The filter *City = 'Arcata'* limits rows to customers living in Arcata, and the ORDER BY clause sorts the rows by LastName and then by FirstName for matches on LastName. Although you can specify Oracle keywords, table name, and column names in lowercase, uppercase, or a mixture of both, it is best to adopt one style. Throughout this textbook, we use uppercase for SQL reserved words and a combination of uppercase and lowercase for column names. Of course, any criteria you specify inside single quotation marks *must* match the capitalization in the database. (*Arcata,* in the following example, has an initial capital letter followed by lowercase letters—just like all data values in the City column of the Properties table.)

```
SELECT FirstName, LastName, Address, City, State, Zipcode
FROM Customers
WHERE City = 'Arcata'
ORDER BY LastName, FirstName;
```

Before going further, let's set up the entire Redwood Realty database. The script file to create Redwood Realty tables, populate them, and set up the primary key and foreign key references is in the data files supplied with this book. Before launching SQL*Plus, locate the script file called BuildRedwood.sql among the data files for Chapter 5. Note the path to that file. Besides the preceding script file, there are ten additional script files that BuildRedwood.sql invokes. Keep all the script files in the same folder. Follow these steps to build the Redwood Realty database from scratch. The script file takes a few moments to run—perhaps a minute or so, depending on the capabilities of your computer. The script file provides mileposts as it creates the eight tables constituting the database. When complete, the script also produces a row count of each of the tables.

To build the Redwood Realty database:

1. Launch SQL*Plus and log into the Oracle database. (Note, *do not* use *i*SQL*Plus for this task.)
2. Locate the path and folder to the Redwood Realty database script files found in the RedwoodRealty folder. Substitute that path for "<path>" below and press **Enter** at the end of the line:

   START <path>\BuildRedwood

   Oracle takes several moments and then produces affirming messages as it creates and populates each table. See Figure 5.1.

With the Redwood Realty database built, run a SELECT statement to display information from one of the tables.

To display information from a table:

1. Type these commands and press **Enter** after each line. These SQL*Plus commands clear the screen and format columns so they fit more compactly on your screen:

   **CLEAR SCREEN
   COLUMN FirstName FORMAT A12
   COLUMN LastName FORMAT A12
   COLUMN Gender FORMAT A6
   COLUMN Title FORMAT A11**

2. Type the following statement to display all rows in the Agents table. (Press **Enter** at the end of the last line to compile and execute the SELECT statement.)

   **SELECT FirstName, LastName, Gender, Title
   FROM Agents;**

   Figure 5.2 shows the results. Selected columns of all Agents rows appear. Rows are in no particular order.

3. Type **exit** and press **Enter** to log out of Oracle and close SQL*Plus. You will be using both SQL*Plus and *i*SQL*Plus in this chapter.

202 Introduction to Oracle

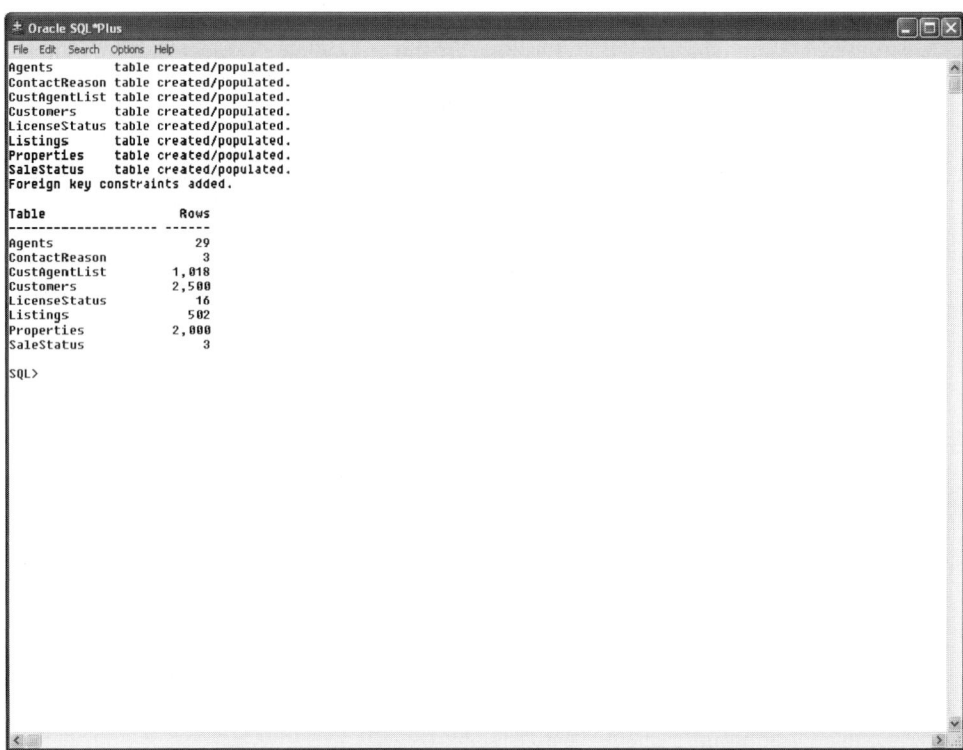

FIGURE 5.1 Messages produced by the BuildRedwood script file.

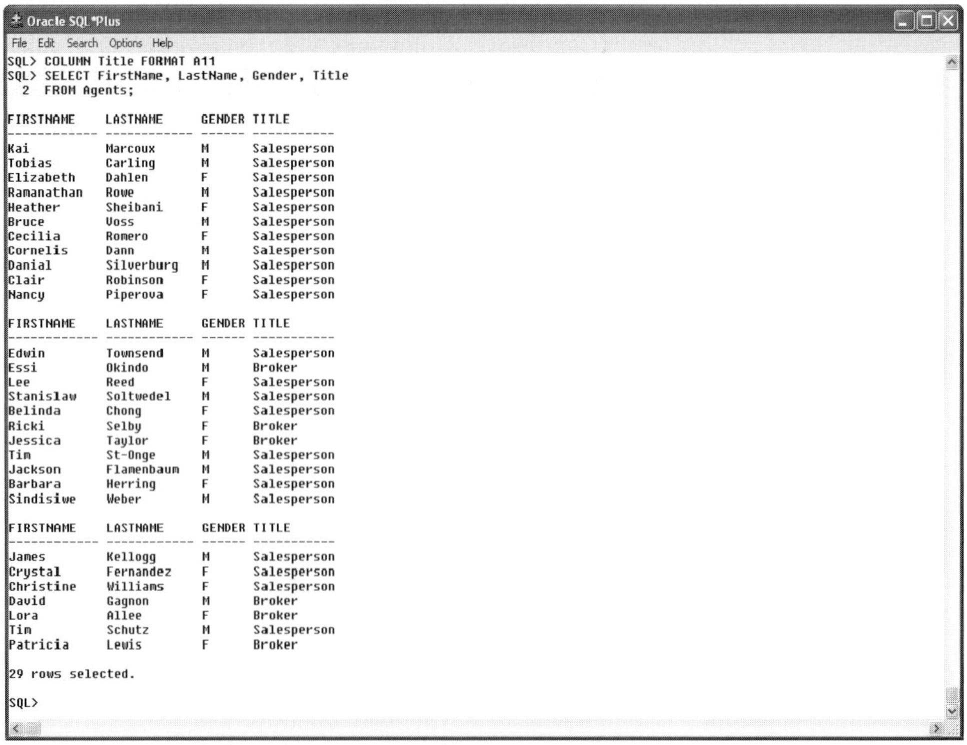

FIGURE 5.2 SELECT statement returning real estate agent information.

SELECTING ALL COLUMNS

If you want to return all columns from a table, you have two ways to write the select list. You can list each of the columns, separated by commas, following the word SELECT. For long lists of columns, this may be undesirable. The second, shorter way is to type an asterisk character (*) in the select list. The main drawback to typing an asterisk in the column list is that columns are listed in the same order, left to right, as they are in the table definition. Therefore, you lose control of the column order. If that doesn't matter, it's a lot shorter way to write the query. Let's try it in *i*SQL*Plus, because *i*SQL*Plus displays a table with lots of columns much better than SQL*Plus does.

To display all columns and all rows of a table:

1. Launch your browser and then launch *i*SQL*Plus. Log into Oracle with your username and password.
2. Click the **Workspace** text box and type the following. (In *i*SQL*Plus, the statement-terminating semicolon is not needed. We type it anyway for consistency.)

```
SELECT *
FROM Agents;
```

3. Click the **Execute** button to execute the statement. If needed, correct any errors in the Workspace text box and repeat this step. Oracle displays several rows and all columns of the Agents table (see Figure 5.3). Use the horizontal and vertical scroll bars to review the retrieved information.
4. Click the **Logout** button to log out of Oracle and then close your browser.

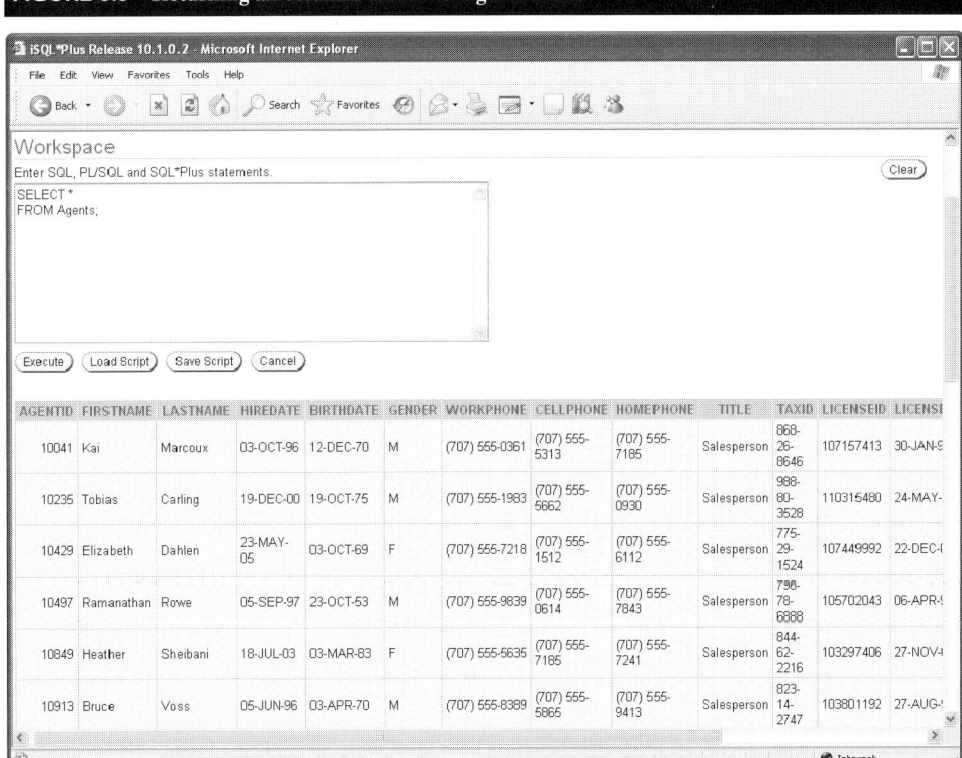

FIGURE 5.3 Returning all columns from the Agents table.

Using DISTINCT to Display Unique Rows

Including the optional phrase DISTINCT preceding the select list in the SELECT statement eliminates duplicate rows. A duplicate row occurs when *all* of the column values returned by a SELECT statement match those of at least one other row. Duplicate rows are relatively unlikely if you return many columns from a table—especially if one of the columns is the rows' primary keys. But, if you display just a few columns, then DISTINCT shows its worth. For example, suppose you want to know the range of commission rates that the buyers have negotiated with the agency. That column is found in the CustAgentList table. You can get that information by running the following query:

```
SELECT CommissionRate
FROM CustAgentList;
```

Then, you can scan the long list (1,018 rows) to find the different values for commission rates. Clearly, that is not easy. By including the DISTINCT phrase to suppress duplicate rows, only the unique row values appear. The revised query is

```
SELECT DISTINCT CommissionRate
FROM CustAgentList;
```

Running the preceding query yields just five rows. Figure 5.4 shows a DESCRIBE statement displaying CustAgentList column names followed by the SELECT statement shown above. Reviewing the list, it is obvious that there are four distinct percentages: 3 percent, 4 percent, 5 percent, and 6 percent. (Zero percent indicates a buyer in this scheme.)

Breaking a Runaway Query

More than a few times while learning Oracle, you might run a SELECT statement in SQL*Plus that runs on endlessly. It could return hundreds or even thousands of rows.

FIGURE 5.4 Retrieving unique rows using DISTINCT.

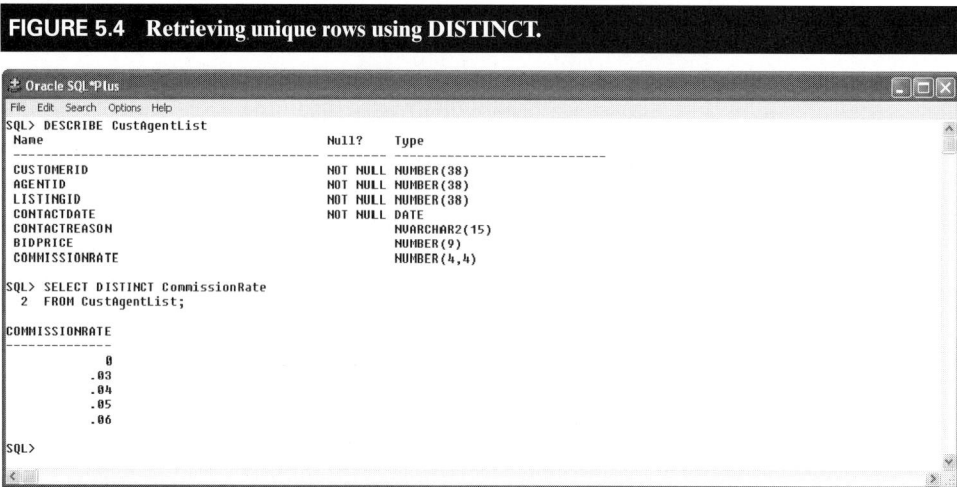

You can get SQL*Plus' attention and break the long processing loop very simply: Press **Ctrl+C** to interrupt the current instruction. Let's try it.

To interrupt a long-running SQL statement in SQL*Plus:

1. Launch SQL*Plus, log into Oracle, and type the following statement. Press **Enter** on the last line to submit the instruction to Oracle. The SELECT statement will return 1018 rows!

   ```
   SELECT *
   FROM CustAgentList
   ```

2. After watching for a few seconds, you can interrupt SQL*Plus and halt the values returned. Press **Ctrl+C.** That is, hold down the Ctrl key, press C and release both. SQL*Plus will stop displaying results, will display the number of rows shown so far, and then redisplay the SQL> prompt (see Figure 5.5).

USING SEARCH CONDITIONS TO FILTER THE RESULTS

Use the optional WHERE clause in a SELECT statement to filter rows that Oracle returns from the database. You used a WHERE clause in Chapter 4 in the UPDATE and DELETE statements. WHERE serves the exact same function in the SELECT statement. The *search condition,* which follows the WHERE clause, identifies specific rows in a table or tables that Oracle is to retrieve by specifying expressions and values that must match or be true for the rows to be retrieved. To review, the form of the WHERE clause is:

```
WHERE <column-name> <comparison-operator> <search-expression>
```

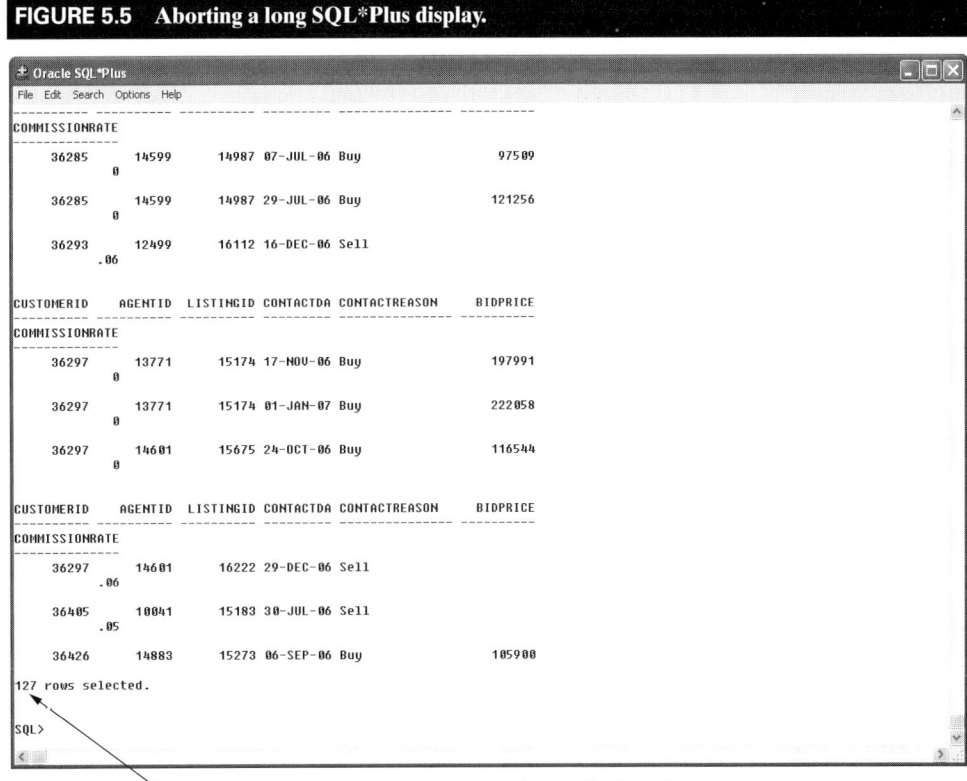

FIGURE 5.5 Aborting a long SQL*Plus display.

indicates the number of rows displayed prior to the interrupt

Column-name specifies the table column whose value Oracle checks. *Comparison-operator* is one of the comparison operators. It compares the value in the table column to the search-expression for each row in the table. Table 4.3 on page 158 lists the comparison operators. The *search-expression* often is a value such as a character string or a number. Several of the preceding column-name/comparison-operator/search-expression pairs can occur together when connected by logical operators. (Logical operators appear in Chapter 4, Table 4.4 on page 158.)

USING COMPARISON OPERATORS

Comparison operators allow you to compare two items and determine whether one is less than, equal to, greater than, or not equal to the other—and combinations. Examples of WHERE clauses that retrieve selected rows from the Customers table are these:

```
...WHERE City = 'Blue Lake'
...WHERE CustomerID = 25343
...WHERE FirstName <> 'Randy'
```

To better understand the WHERE clause, let's try a few queries in SQL*Plus against various Redwood Realty tables. Even though the SELECT statements reference tables that contain 1,000 and 2,000 rows, Oracle returns only a relatively few rows because the WHERE clause establishes search conditions that only a handful of rows satisfy.

To experiment with the WHERE clause:

1. Launch SQL*Plus, type **CLEAR SCREEN** and press **Enter,** and execute the following SELECT statement:

```
SELECT CustomerID, FirstName, LastName
FROM Customers
WHERE LastName = 'Nguyen';
```

Oracle returns eight rows, each with a different CustomerID value.

2. Type and execute the following:

```
SELECT OwnerID, Bedrooms, Bathrooms, Stories, SqFt
FROM Properties
WHERE SqFt = 2100;
```

Oracle returns five rows—one for each property whose home's SqFt value exactly matches 2100.

3. Type and execute the following:

```
SELECT AgentID, LastName, FirstName
FROM Agents
WHERE Title <> 'Salesperson';
```

Oracle returns six rows. These represent agents whose title *is not* 'Salesperson.'

4. Type and execute the following. (Setting the SQL*Plus linesize value to 90 allows each row to appear on one line.)

```
SET Linesize 90
SELECT *
FROM CustAgentList
WHERE BidPrice > 350000;
```

5. Type and execute the following to display selected rows from the Listings table:

```
SELECT ListingID, BeginListDate, EndListDate, AskingPrice
FROM Listings
WHERE BeginListDate <= '26-JUN-2006';
```

```
SQL> SET Linesize 90
SQL> SELECT *
  2  FROM CustAgentList
  3  WHERE BidPrice > 350000;

CUSTOMERID   AGENTID  LISTINGID CONTACTDA CONTACTREASON    BIDPRICE COMMISSIONRATE
----------   -------  --------- --------- -------------    -------- --------------
     35979     15293      15685 29-JAN-07 Buy                369836              0
     40341     12301      14998 06-AUG-06 Buy                485196              0
     41040     12875      15685 15-FEB-07 Buy                399745              0
     25571     10849      15685 22-JAN-07 Buy                355326              0
     26075     14677      16021 13-JAN-07 Buy                402402              0
     31588     10497      15375 08-OCT-06 Buy                563091              0
     31588     10497      15375 04-NOV-06 Buy                608638              0
     32809     10429      15028 13-SEP-06 Buy                377155              0
     32809     10429      15028 29-OCT-06 Buy                417423              0
     48207     15233      15390 24-SEP-06 Buy                361185              0
     48207     15233      15390 25-SEP-06 Buy                382746              0

11 rows selected.

SQL> --
SQL> SELECT ListingID, BeginListDate, EndListDate, AskingPrice
  2  FROM Listings
  3  WHERE BeginListDate <= '26-JUN-2006';

 LISTINGID BEGINLIST ENDLISTDA ASKINGPRICE
 --------- --------- --------- -----------
     14979 23-JUN-06 23-NOV-06      126000
     14981 23-JUN-06 23-DEC-06      127000
     14987 23-JUN-06 23-AUG-06      124950
     14992 23-JUN-06 23-JUL-06      154685
     14994 23-JUN-06 23-OCT-06      282500
     14997 23-JUN-06 23-SEP-06      145000
     14998 24-JUN-06 24-OCT-06      495000
     15001 25-JUN-06 25-JUL-06      114950
     15005 26-JUN-06 26-SEP-06      122000
     15007 26-JUN-06 26-NOV-06      107000
     15010 26-JUN-06 26-NOV-06      129950

11 rows selected.

SQL>
```

FIGURE 5.6 Using the WHERE clause to filter table rows.

Oracle returns rows in which the listing was obtained earlier than June 27, 2006. Figure 5.6 shows the results of Steps 4 and 5.

RULES FOR CHARACTERS AND DATES

When using characters in the search condition of a WHERE clause, remember that uppercase letters are *not* equivalent to lowercase letters. For example, the WHERE search condition in the SELECT statement

```
SELECT LastName
FROM Agents
WHERE Title = 'salesperson'
```

returns no rows from the Agents table. That is because all titles in the Agents table are stored in mixed case. Any given title in the table begins with an uppercase letter followed by lowercase letters. That means that a character string such as "salesperson" does not match the character string "SALESPERSON" (nor any combination of uppercase and lowercase letters). (Later, you will learn ways around this conundrum using a few simple Oracle functions.) Remember, too, that you must enclose a character string in single quotation marks when it is part of a literal constant in a WHERE clause. By contrast, numbers in a search condition are *not* enclosed in single quotation marks.

You will probably need to create WHERE clauses that use dates in the search condition. Recall that dates appear in the default Oracle format of DD-MON-YY, where DD is the day, MON is the three-letter abbreviation for the month, and YY is the two-digit year. You learned previously that YY values greater than 50 indicate the previous century, whereas YY values less than or equal to 50 indicate the current century.

Search conditions using dates and relational operators are perfectly valid, as you saw with a previous example of a date in a WHERE clause. Suppose you want to list all real estate agents whose real estate license expires on or after June 1, 2005. The following SELECT clause selects rows in which the LicenseExpire dates are greater than or equal to '01-JUN-05.'

```
SELECT FirstName, LastName
FROM Agents
WHERE LicenseExpire >= '01-JUN-05';
```

Similarly, you could list all agents whose licenses have expired by selecting those whose LicenseExpire value is less than (before) today's date (supplied by the pseudo-column SYSDATE) with the following SELECT statement:

```
SELECT FirstName, LastName
FROM Agents
WHERE LicenseExpire < SYSDATE;
```

USING SQL OPERATORS

SQL Operators, sometimes lumped in with the comparison operators, allow you to filter or restrict rows returned based on string-pattern matching, lists of allowed values, NULL values, or ranges of allowed values. Selected SQL operators appear in Table 5.1.

Between The *between operator,* BETWEEN . . . AND, is a convenient way to search for rows whose column values fall within a particular range of values. Figure 5.7 shows that there are 12 rows retrieved in which the AskingPrice ranges from $212,000 to

TABLE 5.1 Selected SQL relational Operators.

Operator	Meaning
BETWEEN . . . AND	Matches a range of values.
IN	Matches a finite list of acceptable values.
IS NULL	Matches the null value. It is the *only* way to use NULL in a search condition.
LIKE	Matches patterns in character strings.

FIGURE 5.7 Using the BETWEEN . . . AND operator.

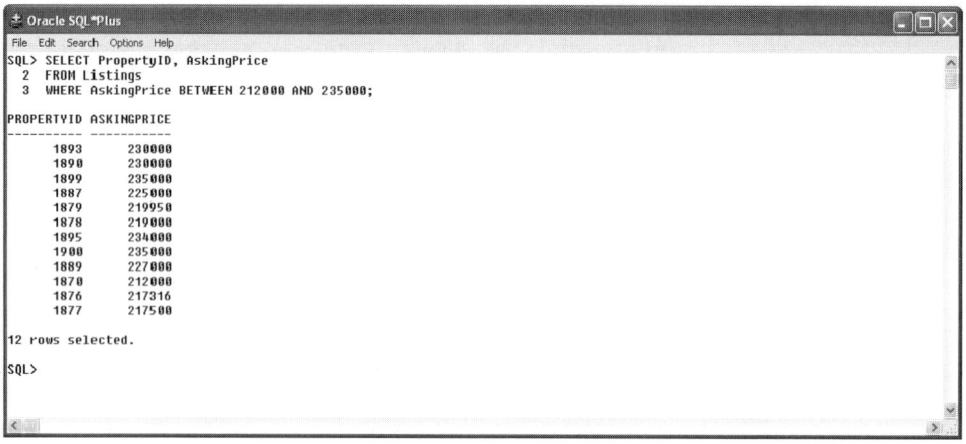

```
SQL> SELECT PropertyID, AskingPrice
  2  FROM Listings
  3  WHERE AskingPrice BETWEEN 212000 AND 235000;

PROPERTYID ASKINGPRICE
---------- -----------
      1893      230000
      1890      230000
      1899      235000
      1887      225000
      1879      219950
      1878      219000
      1895      234000
      1900      235000
      1889      227000
      1870      212000
      1876      217316
      1877      217500

12 rows selected.

SQL>
```

$235,000, inclusive. Notice that one property exactly equals the low price in the range and two properties are equal to the high price in the range.

IN   The *IN operator* returns rows in which values match one of the values in a list of acceptable values. Table column values must exactly match one of the listed values to be returned in the answer set. The IN operator is particularly convenient when you want to match a small number of distinct values. For example, you might want to display information about any customers who live in Ohio, Indiana, Michigan, or Illinois. The easiest WHERE clause to write is

```
WHERE State IN ('Ohio','Indiana','Michigan','Illinois')
```

Contrast this to the equivalent but much longer version using comparison operators and logical operators (presented next):

```
WHERE State = 'Ohio' OR State = 'Indiana'
   OR State = 'Michigan' OR State = 'Illinois'
```

LIKE   The *LIKE operator* uses wildcard characters to search for patterns of characters in a character string. *Wildcard characters* are special symbols that stand for one or more characters in a search string. Use wildcard characters in conjunction with the LIKE operator in a WHERE clause to determine if any of the character strings in a table column match the character pattern you specify. Construct character search patterns with normal characters and the two Oracle wildcard characters, % and _ (underscore). The underscore character (_) matches exactly one character in the specified position. The percent character (%) matches any number of characters (including none) in the specified position. For instance, you could list all Customers whose last name begins with *H* with the following:

```
SELECT FirstName, LastName, Address, City, State
FROM Customers
WHERE LastName LIKE 'H%';
```

If you wanted to locate customers whose ZIP code begins with 955 and ends with a 1, regardless of the fourth digit, then you would specify the following WHERE clause using the underline wildcard character in the fourth digit position:

```
…WHERE ZipCode LIKE '955_1';
```

If you need to search for either a percent or underscore in a column, use the ESCAPE option. The ESCAPE option specifies a character that precedes any wildcard characters used with the LIKE operator. For example, you can search for the occurrence of percent (for example, "… almost 35% of all people … ") in a column with the following WHERE clause and optional ESCAPE option specifying the backslash as the escape character. The backslash inside the quoted string at its beginning marks the percent that follows as a wildcard character, not a literal character.

```
…WHERE StatusText LIKE '\%almost 35% of all people' ESCAPE '\'
```

> **Tip:** Beginning with Oracle 10g, an even more powerful set of string match tools have become available called *regular expressions*. Although this topic is beyond the scope of this book, you may want to read about regular expressions. Use a Web search engine and the phrase *regular expressions* to locate articles describing them.

IS NULL   Occasionally, you will want to write a query that displays rows containing the NULL value in a particular column—meaning the value is not known. For example, you might want to list real estate properties in which the YearBuilt is NULL.

Or, you might want to list rows of the Agents table in which the LicenseExpire date is NULL. Because NULL is the absence of information, you cannot use a comparison operator to determine if the column value is empty. Instead, you use IS NULL in the WHERE clause to search for null values. Of course, you can use IS NOT NULL to search for all values *except* for NULL in a column. The following lists selected columns from the Agents table in which the LicenseExpire field is unknown.

```
SELECT FirstName, LastName
FROM Agents
WHERE LicenseExpire IS NULL;
```

Using Logical Operators

Recall from Chapter 3 that the three logical operators are AND, OR, and NOT. They are part of an expression appearing in the WHERE clause that limit the rows returned based on whether both conditions are true simultaneously (AND) or separately (OR). They are used to combine parts of search conditions. NOT negates the logical expression that follows it. For example, suppose you want to purchase a house in Arcata built after 1999 and whose size (SqFt) is at least 2,000 square feet. Furthermore, it must have three or more bedrooms and between two and four bathrooms. Whereas comparison operators enforce each of the preceding individual considerations (SqFt > 2000, for example), the logical operator AND connects together two or more of the individual conditions to ensure that *all* conditions are met.

It is important to understand operator precedence when writing conditional expressions. **Operator precedence** refers to the order in which Oracle evaluates subexpressions. In a WHERE conditional expressions such as

```
WHERE City = 'Arcata' AND YearBuilt < 2004 OR Bedrooms = 3;
```

Oracle does not evaluate the expression from left to right. An operator's precedence indicates in what order it is evaluated. Each of the comparison operators has higher precedence than any of the logical operators. Parentheses are at the top of the precedence list. So any subexpression inside parentheses is evaluated first. Then, subexpressions with <, =, >, and other combinations of relational operators are evaluated next. Finally, all subexpressions with logical operators are evaluated. In the preceding WHERE clause, *City = 'Arcata'* is evaluated first and determined to be true or false based on the current table row. Next, the subexpression *YearBuilt < 2004* is evaluated, and so on. Finally, Oracle evaluates the three true/false results connected by the two logical operators. Among the logical operators, NOT has the highest precedence, so it is evaluated first. AND is second highest, and OR is last. In a subexpression in which precedence is equal among them, the subexpressions are evaluated left to right.

Try out some of the search conditions you have just learned about using SQL*Plus. As usual, we suggest you use Notepad to create the individual statements, copy the statements, paste them into SQL*Plus, and press Enter to execute them. That way, you will have a Notepad file that is a permanent record of every statement you executed in SQL*Plus.

To create SELECT statements using various search conditions:

1. Launch SQL*Plus, if necessary, and log into Oracle.
2. Type **CLEAR SCREEN**, and press **Enter.**
3. Execute the following to display the addresses and other data about homes in Arcata that were built after 1991 and have at least 2,000 square feet of living space:

```
SELECT Address, YearBuilt, SqFt, Bedrooms, Bathrooms
FROM Properties
WHERE City = 'Arcata' AND YearBuilt > 1991 AND SqFt >= 2000;
```

4. Execute the following to display properties in either Blue Lake or Trinidad whose street name ends with "Ln". Because you do not know if it has been capitalized in the table, there are at least four possible combinations. (You'll learn a much easier method using functions later.) The OR expression takes care of these possibilities.

```
SELECT Address, City
FROM Properties
WHERE City IN ('Blue Lake', 'Trinidad') AND
  (Address LIKE '%Ln' OR Address LIKE '%lN'
  OR Address LIKE '%LN' OR Address LIKE '%ln');
```

5. Execute the following to list the SaleStatusID, BeginListDate, and SellingPrice of properties for sale (SaleStatusID equals 101) whose listings were first established (BeginListDate) in June, 2006.

```
SELECT SaleStatusID, BeginListDate, AskingPrice
FROM Listings
WHERE SaleStatusID = 101
  AND BeginListDate BETWEEN '01-JUN-2006' AND '30-JUN-2006';
```

6. Modify the preceding query, adding the restriction to include properties whose AskingPrice value is greater than 130,000.

```
SELECT SaleStatusID, BeginListDate, AskingPrice
FROM Listings
WHERE SaleStatusID = 101
  AND BeginListDate BETWEEN '01-JUN-2006' AND '30-JUN-2006'
  AND AskingPrice > 130000;
```

Figure 5.8 shows the last query and its resulting rows. Your results should match.

SORTING

So far, all SELECT statement examples shown here or that you have created return rows in random order. To control the order in which rows are displayed, you must use the optional ORDER BY clause of the SELECT statement. Its syntax is

```
ORDER BY {<column-name>|<result-column-number>} [ASC|DESC]
    [NULLS FIRST|NULLS LAST]
    [,{<column-name>|<result-column-number>} [ASC|DESC]
    [NULLS FIRST|NULLS LAST]]...
```

FIGURE 5.8 Example query with logical and comparison operators.

```
SQL> SELECT SaleStatusID, BeginListDate, AskingPrice
  2  FROM Listings
  3  WHERE SaleStatusID = 101
  4    AND BeginListDate BETWEEN '01-JUN-2006' AND '30-JUN-2006'
  5    AND AskingPrice > 130000;

SALESTATUSID BEGINLIST ASKINGPRICE
------------ --------- -----------
         101 23-JUN-06      154685
         101 22-JUN-06      145000
         101 24-JUN-06      495000
         101 27-JUN-06      178128
         101 28-JUN-06      183000
         101 29-JUN-06      138950

6 rows selected.

SQL>
```

Column-name is any column name in the table—even a column that is not returned in the result. *Result-column-number* refers to the position that a returned result occupies in the list of columns. The number ranges from 1 to the number of columns (or values) returned. *ASC* stands for *ascending,* and *DESC* stands for *descending.* *NULLS FIRST/LAST* specifies whether NULL values in a column sort to the top or the bottom (LAST is the default). You can specify the optional sort order keywords for each column or result column number specified. Multiple sort columns are separated by commas, and sort columns after the first break tie in all preceding sort orders. If you specify more than one column, the sorting is done from left to right. Oracle arranges returned rows based on the first sort column specified. Given equal values within a column, Oracle sorts on the second column within the group, and so on.

Character columns or values are evaluated from left to right to return them in ascending or descending order. Numeric values are sorted from low to high (ascending) or high to low (descending). For dates, ascending order means from the oldest date to the most recent; descending dates, from most recent to oldest. The default sort order is ascending when none is specified, and the sort orders of multiple columns are independent of one another—you can specify ASC for one column and DESC for another—in any combination. The ORDER BY clause is the last one in a SELECT statement, and Oracle sorts the rows before returning them to the client machine.

> **Caution:** If you use the keyword DISTINCT to qualify columns in a SELECT statement, the column(s) to which the keyword pertains must also be listed in the ORDER BY clause.

Sorting by one or more columns makes locating rows far easier. For example, if you are continuously referring to a customer list by customers' last names, then the SELECT clause producing such a list should order the list by LastName and then FirstName (a *telephone book* sort). On the other hand, if you want to refer to real estate by city and then neighborhood within a city, it makes sense to sort by those columns. Here is a SELECT statement that sorts properties by city (ascending), then by number of bedrooms (ascending), and finally by year built (descending).

```
SELECT YearBuilt, City, Bedrooms, SqFt
FROM Properties
WHERE YearBuilt > 1989
  AND City IN ('Fortuna', 'McKinleyville', 'Loleta')
  AND SqFt >= 2000
ORDER BY City, 3, YearBuilt DESC;
```

Oracle selects rows based on the WHERE clause criteria, extracts four columns from the selected rows, sorts the answer by the three ORDER BY clause columns, and returns the 26 rows. Notice the value 3 in the ORDER BY clause. That stands for the third column in the column-list (Bedrooms) and is the second sort key, just behind City. Using numbers is particularly handy when you use a long expression in the SELECT list, because referring to a column by its position is much easier than repeating a long column expression in the ORDER BY clause.

NULL VALUES AND THE ORDER BY CLAUSE

When the ORDER BY specifies a column that contains NULL values, those values always sort to the end of the list, by default, for both ascending and descending orders. If you want NULL values in a sorted column to appear at the beginning of the list, specify the optional phrase NULLS FIRST following the column it is to affect. For example, the following query sorts NULL values to the top of the list, regardless of either a DESC or ASC modifier:

```
SELECT BidPrice FROM CustAgentList
ORDER BY BidPrice DESC NULLS FIRST;
```

TOP-N QUERIES

So called top-N queries are queries that sort rows and select the first N largest (or smallest) values. For example, you could sort a sales table in descending order by SalesAmount and then display just the first ten rows. This would produce the top ten sales amounts for the selected period. Similarly, if you sorted a SalesAmount column in ascending order (the default), the top-N query might select the first five values. They might be the bottom, or worst five sales amounts. You use a top-N query to find the latest realtors hired, the youngest salespersons, or the best five products. SQL does not provide an optional phrase that selects the top-N or bottom-N values. Instead, you have to use a simple trick.

To produce a top-N list, the first requirement is that the list be sorted in ascending order for the smallest (numbers) or oldest (dates) values, or in descending order for the largest (numbers) or most recent (dates) values. Second, you use an Oracle pseudocolumn called ROWNUM to clip off as many rows from the top of the returned set of rows as you need. The sorted rows are numbered by the ROWNUM pseudocolumn, beginning at 1. Select as many of the top rows as you want by using the comparison (relational) operators < or <=. You *cannot* use the > or >= comparison operators with a ROWNUM pseudocolumn. For example, suppose you want to list the top five AskingPrice values from the Listings table, which holds the current listings of homes for sale. The following statement produces the desired result—the top five most expensive homes currently listed. Notice that you need not actually display ROWNUM to use it in a WHERE clause.

```
SELECT AskingPrice
FROM (SELECT AskingPrice
      FROM Listings
      ORDER BY AskingPrice DESC)
WHERE ROWNUM <= 5;
```

Here's how it works. The subquery following the FROM statement is a query within a query, and the innermost query is called an ***inline view.*** It is executed first and returns *all* the rows from the Listings table in descending order by AskingPrice—all 502 of them. The results produce a temporary table (the inline view) that is queried by the outer query. Among the columns returned by the inline query is the pseudocolumn ROWNUM—in order from 1 through 502. Because the inline view produces rows in descending order by selling price, the top five represent the highest five asking prices. The outer query's WHERE clause extracts only the first five rows based on the ROWNUM value.

A slight complication arises with NULL values in the returned set. You will see that in the SELECT clause results you generate next. Let's experiment with the ORDER BY clause.

To sort rows using the ORDER BY clause:

1. If necessary, launch SQL*Plus and log into Oracle. Type **CLEAR SCREEN** and press **Enter** to clear the screen.
2. Determine the *highest seven* BidPrice values placed by possible property purchasers by typing and executing the following:

```
CLEAR SCREEN
SELECT BidPrice
FROM (SELECT BidPrice FROM CustAgentList
      ORDER BY BidPrice DESC)
WHERE ROWNUM <= 7;
```

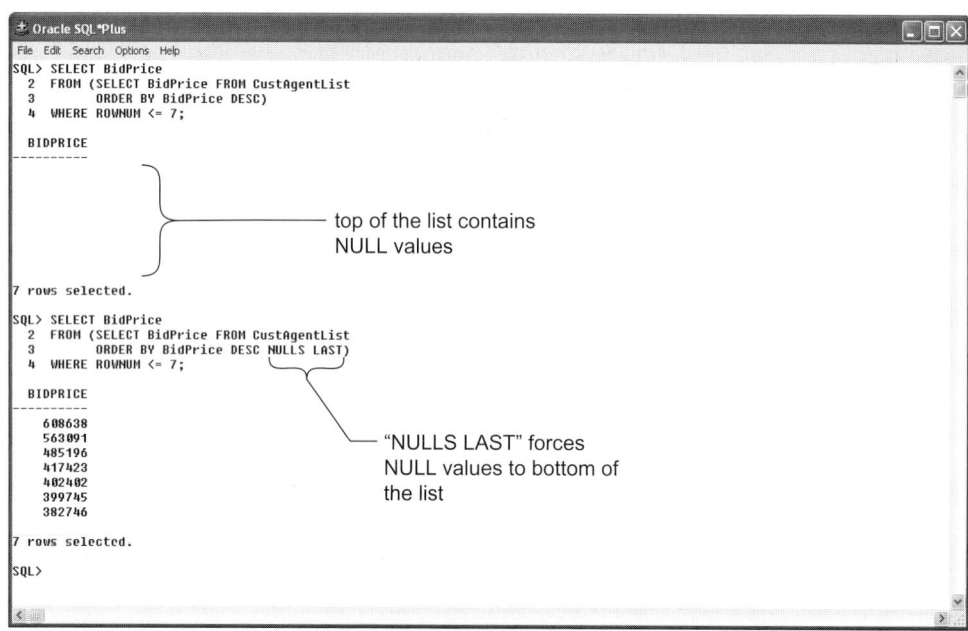

FIGURE 5.9 Top-N analysis results for two queries.

Oops! Oracle returned a lot of nothing! Because BidPrice is NULL for properties in which there is no active interest, the NULL values populate the top of the list when a DESC sort occurs.

3. Force the NULL values to the bottom of the list so you can pick "real" values from the top of the list. Edit the query to add the phrase NULLS LAST immediately after the word DESC and inside the right parenthesis. Execute the modified query.

```
SELECT BidPrice
FROM (SELECT BidPrice FROM CustAgentList
      ORDER BY BidPrice DESC NULLS LAST)
WHERE ROWNUM <= 7;
```

Oracle returns the top seven BidPrice values. See Figure 5.9.

4. List the real estate agents' last names, first names, and dates of birth. Sort from the youngest to oldest, up to and including the birthdays occurring in July 1969. Type and execute the following SQL*Plus and SQL statements:

```
CLEAR SCREEN
COLUMN LastName FORMAT A15
COLUMN FirstName FORMAT A15
SELECT LastName, FirstName, BirthDate
FROM Agents
WHERE BirthDate >= '01-JUL-69'
ORDER BY BirthDate DESC;
```

Compare your results to Figure 5.10.

5. Type the following SQL*Plus and SQL statements to return rows using three columns to organize the results: City, Bedrooms, and Bathrooms. Notice that two of the sort columns are in descending order, whereas the third (Bathrooms) defaults to ascending.

```
CLEAR SCREEN
COLUMN Address FORMAT A20
```

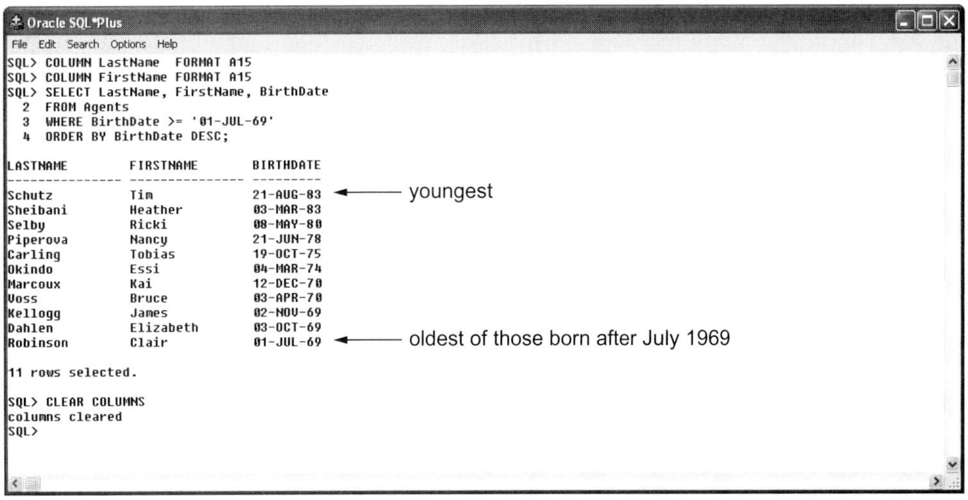

FIGURE 5.10 Sorting agent rows by descending birth date.

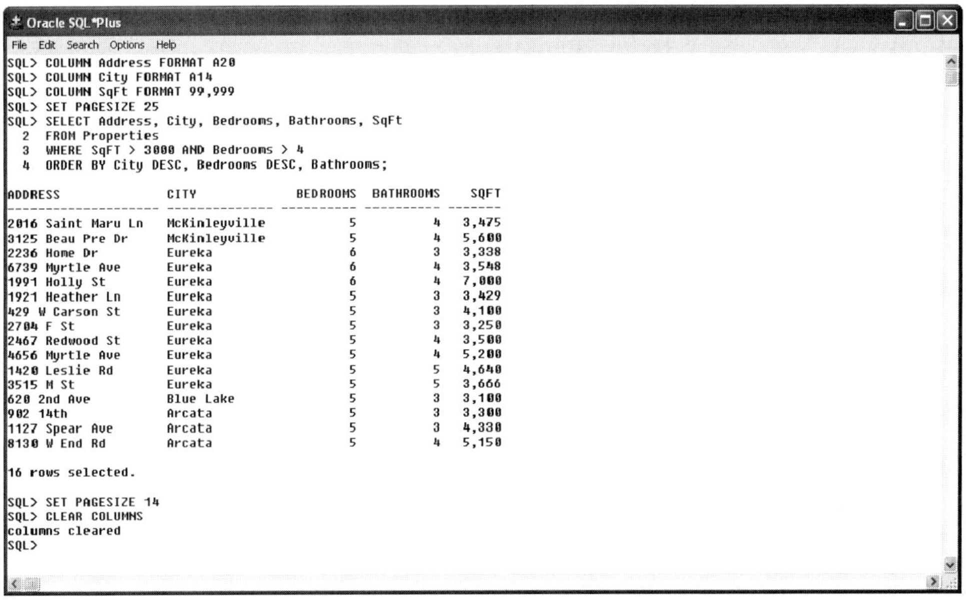

FIGURE 5.11 Using multiple sort columns to break ties.

```
COLUMN City FORMAT A14
COLUMN SqFt FORMAT 99,999
SET PAGESIZE 25
SELECT Address, City, Bedrooms, Bathrooms, SqFt
FROM Properties
WHERE SqFT > 3000 AND Bedrooms > 4
ORDER BY City DESC, Bedrooms DESC, Bathrooms;
SET PAGESIZE 14
CLEAR COLUMNS
```

Compare your results to Figure 5.11.

6. You can leave SQL*Plus running for later steps, or you can type **exit** and press **Enter** if you want to take a break.

INCLUDING COMPUTATIONS IN QUERIES

Most database applications display information both directly from tables, such as names and addresses, in addition to information *derived* from other table columns in the same or other tables. In fact, table normalization rules disallow storing information in a table that can be derived from the table. For example, it would be unwise to store an invoice's line item subtotal, the product of the quantity purchased and the unit cost, in an invoice line item table. If you stored, say, a quantity sold of 12, a unit price of $5.00, and a total of $60.00 in an invoice line item table row, there exists a non-primary key dependency in a row—a violation of normalization rules. Furthermore, a change in an erroneous unit price does not automatically update the product, so errors can propagate.

Fortunately, SQL allows calculations along with column names in the SELECT column list. Placing calculations such as extended cost (quantity X unit price) ensures that the product is always current, regardless of any prior changes to either unit price or quantity sold. In a similar way, you can specify a simple expression to calculate an employee's age based on the date of birth column stored in a table. (Of course it would not make sense to store age in such a table, because it is an ever-changing value.) You can create SQL queries containing calculations in addition to table columns ranging from simple expressions up to arbitrarily complex calculations involving arithmetic operators and built-in functions.

USING MATHEMATICAL OPERATORS TO PERFORM NUMERIC CALCULATIONS

Oracle performs arithmetic on expressions in SQL statements containing the operators addition, subtraction, multiplication, and division. The mathematical operators are the standard +, −, *, and /. The precedence among operators in an expression, recall, is that addition and subtraction are equal and lowest; multiplication and division are equal and are evaluated before addition and subtraction. Expressions inside parentheses are always evaluated first.

You can form expressions with mathematical operators on columns whose data type is NUMBER, DATE, or INTERVAL. Some mathematical operations do not make sense with DATE or INTERVAL data types, as you will see in sections that follow.

You can write arithmetic expressions involving column names, constants, and SQL functions in the list following a SELECT statement. It is separated from subsequent columns or expressions by a comma. When you want to try out a simple calculation involving only constants or the time of day (stored on the server), you can query the DUAL table mentioned previously. Recall that DUAL is a single row, single column table that exists so that you can write and test expressions. Because you cannot simply write an expression without a FROM <table> clause, DUAL serves that purpose. For example, suppose you want to calculate the sales tax (6 percent) on an item costing $37.85 and the total amount due, you can issue a simple SQL query such as:

```
SELECT 0.06 * 37.85, 1.06 * 37.85
FROM DUAL;
```

(Your cell phone probably can perform this calculation too, but this is simply an illustration.) The sales tax and the total amount appear as two columns in the result, and the DUAL table serves as the dummy table on which you can "hang" the two calculations.

You can perform calculations on columns with NUMERIC data types by specifying the columns involved and using the appropriate mathematical operators between them. For example, you can write a SELECT statement that determines the total real estate sales commission that is split between buying realtor, selling realtor, and the broker(s). One of the columns stored in the Listings table needed to perform this calculation is AskingPrice, which is the price the seller would like to receive for a property. You want to display the commission that would accrue at the 6 percent commission rate.

In addition, you want to know the net sale amount, which is (here) the asking price minus the commission. The following displays the AskingPrice column and the two computed values. Note that the parentheses are not needed in this example (multiplication is computed first). We used them to clarify the calculations.

```
SELECT AskingPrice, AskingPrice*0.06, AskingPrice-(AskingPrice*0.06)
FROM Listings;
```

Let's try a few calculations. In preparation for the steps that follow, launch either SQL*Plus or *i*SQL*Plus and log into Oracle.

To perform calculations in a SQL query:

1. List the asking price, commission, and net amount received for selected properties by typing the statements below. You will restrict the rows returned to more expensive properties to make the result manageable.

```
CLEAR SCREEN
SELECT AskingPrice, AskingPrice*0.05, AskingPrice*0.06,
  AskingPrice-(AskingPrice*0.05), AskingPrice-(AskingPrice*0.06)
FROM Listings
WHERE AskingPrice > 350000
ORDER BY AskingPrice DESC;
```

Oracle returns eight rows showing calculated values for commission and net price in the second and third columns, respectively.

2. The Properties table contains a column, called YearBuilt, that holds the numeric, four-digit year the home was built. Calculate and display the age of the home for the top ten oldest homes in the Properties table, assuming the current year is 2006.

```
COLUMN Address FORMAT A20
COLUMN City FORMAT A7
SELECT Address, City, YearBuilt, 2006-YearBuilt
FROM (SELECT Address, City, YearBuilt, 2006-YearBuilt
      FROM Properties ORDER BY 4 DESC)
WHERE ROWNUM < 11;
```

3. You can leave SQL*Plus (or *i*SQL*Plus) running for steps that follow. If you are using *i*SQL*Plus, it may log you off after a prescribed period of inactivity. If so, simply launch *i*SQL*Plus again and log back into Oracle.

Your results from these two steps should match Figure 5.12. The column formatting makes the SQL*Plus output a bit more attractive by limiting the column widths of the Address and City columns.

CALCULATING WITH DATES

Performing calculations using date columns is common in database applications. An accounting manager might want a list of all accounts that are 30, 60, and 90 days past due. A realtor needs a list of the names and agents whose real estate license is within a month of expiring. Both of the preceding examples implicitly use today's date in the calculation. Recall that the SYSDATE pseudocolumn returns the current date and time. You can display today's date simply by executing

```
SELECT SYSDATE FROM DUAL;
```

If you retrieve the current date along with other columns, you can replace the DUAL table name with the table you query. For example, suppose you want to display the LicenseExpire column and the number of days until each real estate agent's license expires sorted from longest to shortest number of days. The following SELECT provides the answer.

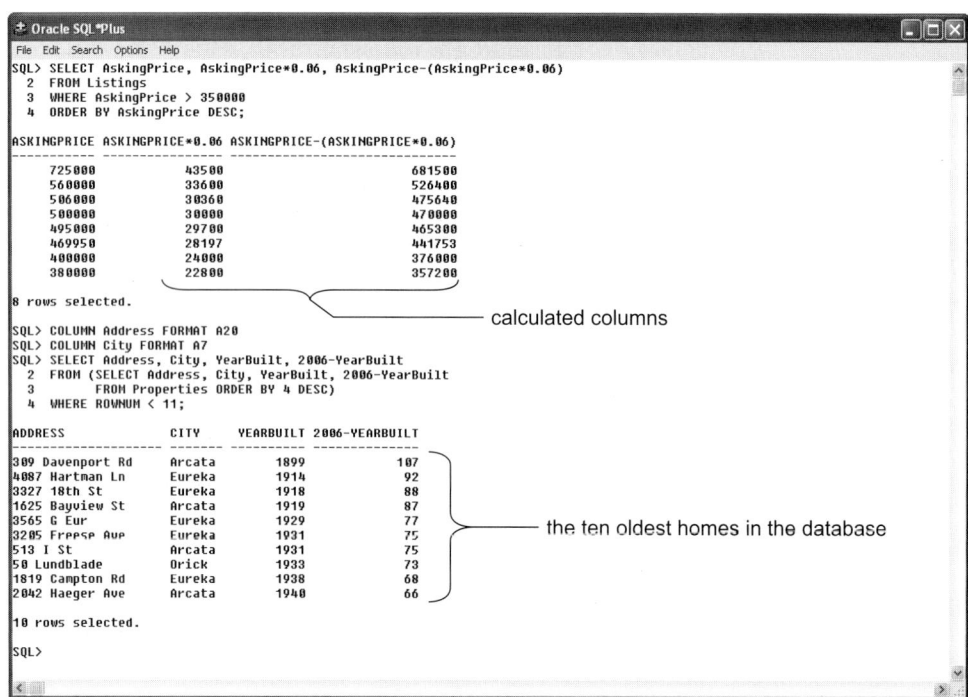

FIGURE 5.12 Writing expressions in SELECT statements.

```
SELECT LicenseExpire, LicenseExpire-SYSDATE
FROM Agents
ORDER BY LicenseExpire-SYSDATE DESC;
```

Alternatively, you can calculate the number of months or years until the license expires by dividing the expression by 30 or 365, respectively. For instance, the following displays the approximate number of years until the license expiration date.

```
SELECT LicenseExpire-SYSDATE
FROM Agents
ORDER BY 1 DESC;
```

The "1" preceding *DESC* above tells Oracle to sort by the first item in the select list. The calculation is *approximate,* because there are slightly more than 365 days, on the average, in each year. A more accurate number of average days per year is 365.24, because every fourth year is a leap year and every year evenly divisible by 400 is a leap century. You can add and subtract small numbers to date values to give a number of days in the past or in the future, respectively. Of course, you can subtract two date values to get elapsed days. You should not add two date values, nor should you divide or multiply date values. Such calculations are nonsense. (What is the meaning of today's date, in days, divided by 2?) There are a bevy of date functions available, and you will learn about them later in this chapter. The following are all legitimate mathematical operations on dates, assuming HireDate and BirthDate are both date values. The last example in the following list calculates age from a birth date column and today's date. The age is expressed in days.

```
SYSDATE + 27
SYSDATE – HireDate
HireDate – BirthDate
InvoiceDate – 60
SYSDATE – BirthDate
```

INTRODUCING COLUMN ALIASES

As you can see from Figure 5.12 and from numerous other SELECT statement results shown so far, Oracle uses the uppercase version of the column name or the entire expression for the column heading in displayed results. In Figure 5.12, for example, you specified "Address" in the SELECT list. Oracle heads that column with the uppercase version, "ADDRESS." When you use an expression in the SELECT list, Oracle removes any spaces and uses the entire expression as the column's header. In Figure 5.12, notice that the column label "2006-YEARBUILT" heads the column displaying the age of houses. You do not need to use the Oracle-generated column headers. You can specify your own column heading using a *column alias.* Using a column alias has several advantages: A column alias (or simply, alias) provides a more meaningful column heading for an otherwise complex expression; an alias simplifies any reference to a column in ORDER BY clauses; and an alias provides you control over the use of uppercase and lowercase letters in headings.

You write a column alias following the column it renames. An alias consists of a sequence of letters, numbers, and underscores (but no spaces). Its maximum size is 30 characters, and the alias follows the optional keyword AS. (The ANSI standard *requires* the AS keyword.) If you want to preserve the case or use spaces in an alias, then you must enclose it in double quotation marks. The following is an example showing column aliases.

```
SELECT AskingPrice-0.06*AskingPrice AS NET_PRICE,
       AskingPrice*0.06 "Commission Rate"
FROM Listings;
```

Notice that the keyword "AS" is omitted in the second column. Though we prefer that you use the ANSI standard calling for AS, you can omit it. We think AS makes it more apparent to anyone reading the SELECT statement that a column alias has been assigned.

CONCATENATING COLUMNS

Periodically you will want to merge together the output of two columns into one. *Concatenation* is the term that describes combining together, end-to-end, a consecutive series of symbols. Concatenation provides a way to display a sometimes more meaningful result. In a database, concatenation joins a character string to a column, joins two columns together, or joins two character strings. The two vertical bars (||), or pipe symbols, are the concatenation operator, which indicates that the column or string to the right of the operator is to be added to the end of the string or column value to its left. (The pipe symbol appears above the backslash character on the right side of your keyboard.) For example, the Agents table has first name and last name columns. It is handy to be able to combine both columns into one character string for envelope labels, inside addresses in letters, and so on. The following concatenates both columns by using concatenation, or "string addition."

```
SELECT FirstName||LastName
FROM Agents;
```

You'll see a small problem with the preceding statement if you try it: the first and last names appear together but without a space between the names (for example "AlecBaldwin"). You can include literal characters in a concatenated sequence of literals and column names to form the string expression. Concatenated strings are another example where column aliases are handy. To correct the output, simply sandwich a blank character between the two columns, forming a three-part concatenated string.

220 Introduction to Oracle

The ORDER BY clause sorts by last name and then first name, even though neither column appears by itself in the result:

```
SELECT FirstName||' '||LastName AS "Name"
FROM Agents
ORDER BY LastName, FirstName;
```

> **Tip:** Don't confuse the use of the apostrophe (') and the double quotation mark (") in SQL statements. The apostrophe encloses literal strings, whereas the double quotation mark encloses column aliases. They are not interchangeable.

It's time to experiment with date calculations, aliases, and column concatenations. Launch SQL*Plus or *i*SQL*Plus and log into Oracle, if needed.

To experiment with SELECT statement date calculations, aliases, and concatenation:

1. Type and then execute the following to list agents in descending age order:

```
CLEAR SCREEN
COLUMN "Name" FORMAT A20
COLUMN "Age when hired" FORMAT 99
SELECT FirstName||' '||LastName AS "Name",
    (HireDate-BirthDate)/365.24 AS "Age when hired"
FROM Agents
ORDER BY "Age when hired" DESC, LastName, FirstName;
```

Agents' names appear in descending order by age (see Figure 5.13). The age is rounded to the nearest year due to the column formatting specification, "99."

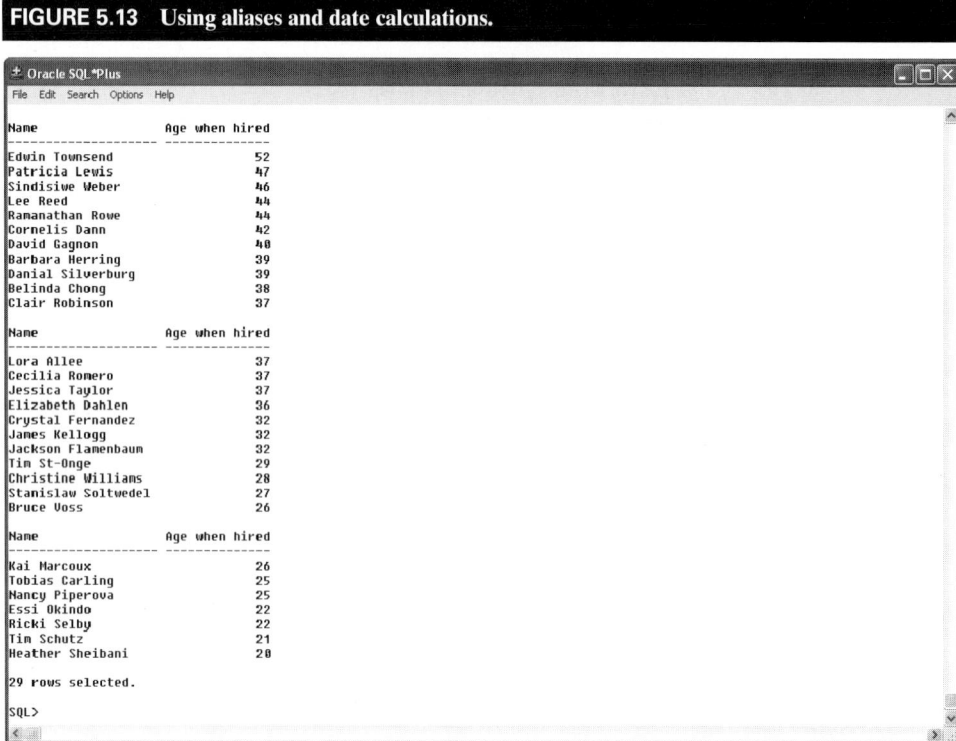

FIGURE 5.13 Using aliases and date calculations.

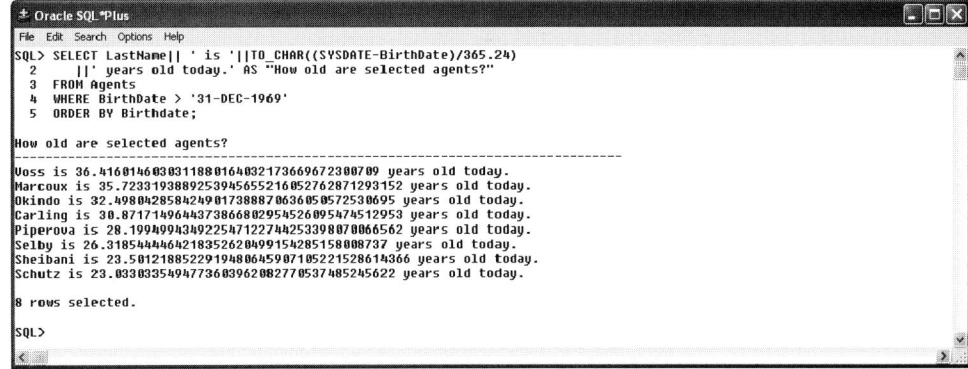

FIGURE 5.14 Producing a single, long line with concatenation.

2. Calculate each agent's approximate age today. Naturally, your results depend on the actual date when you run these statements.

   ```
   COLUMN FirstName FORMAT A15
   COLUMN LastName FORMAT A15
   SELECT FirstName, LastName, (SYSDATE-BirthDate)/365.24 AS Age
   FROM Agents
   ORDER BY LastName, FirstName;
   ```

   Notice the Age alias displays in uppercase because it does not appear within quotation marks. Therefore, its case is not preserved.

3. Try changing the *Age* alias in the preceding SELECT statement to *Age Today* (without double quotation marks. What happens? Oracle generates an error message.

4. Type and execute the following:

   ```
   SELECT LastName|| ' is '||TO_CHAR((SYSDATE-BirthDate)/365.24)
       ||' years old today.' AS "How old are selected agents?"
   FROM Agents
   WHERE BirthDate > '31-DEC-1969'
   ORDER BY Birthdate;
   ```

   Oracle produces a long value for age (see Figure 5.14). The reason is that the TO_CHAR function converts both the date and time to a character string, and the time includes a lot of digits.

5. Exit from SQL*Plus or *i*SQL*Plus, whichever you are running.

INTRODUCING SQL FUNCTIONS

Oracle provides a rich variety of built-in functions. A *function* accepts zero or more input values, or parameters, and returns an output parameter. Oracle's functions fall into one of two groups: Single row functions and aggregate functions. A *single row function* operates on one table row at a time and returns one row for each input row. An *aggregate function* operates on multiple table rows simultaneously and returns one row of output. An example of a single row function is the UPPER function that takes in a character string and returns its value as all uppercase characters—one for each row retrieved by a SELECT statement. Aggregate functions are used to compute summary information. You can use the AVG function to compute the average sale by ZIP code, or you could use the SUM function to tally sales by realtor. We begin with the single row functions.

USING SINGLE ROW FUNCTIONS IN QUERIES

Single row functions return wherever they are used for each row retrieved by the SELECT statement. Single row functions are not limited to appearing in select lists. They can occur in WHERE clauses and ORDER BY clauses as well. Oracle has a number of single row functions, and they are subdivided into these categories:

- *Character functions.* They allow you to manipulate character strings and result in character string output.
- *Numeric functions.* They allow you to perform calculations and result in numeric output.
- *Conversion functions.* They allow you to convert a value from one data type to another.
- *Date functions.* They allow you to manipulate dates and times.
- *Regular expression functions.* They allow you to use regular expressions to search data.

USING CHARACTER FUNCTIONS

A character function accepts character input, processes the character, and returns the result. An example of a character function is LOWER( ), which converts all the characters in the string to lowercase, returning the converted string as a result. Another character function, INITCAP( ), converts the initial letter of each word to uppercase. Character functions anywhere in a SELECT statement do not affect the columns to which they refer. Instead, they retrieve the column (or expression based on a column) and produce a result. For example, if you wanted to display the agents' names and ensure that they appeared with proper initial uppercase letters for each name, then you would issue the following:

```
SELECT INITCAP(FirstName), INITCAP(LastName)
FROM Agents;
```

That way, no matter how the data was entered into a table, it would appear in proper form on output. Table 5.2 summarizes commonly used SQL single-row character functions.

To use a single-row character function, write the function name, a left parenthesis, the argument (a column name, usually), and a closing parenthesis in the SELECT list, WHERE clause, or ORDER BY clause. You can experiment with the single-row character functions by executing the following steps in SQL*Plus:

To use selected single-row character functions:

1. Launch SQL*Plus, log into Oracle, clear the screen **(CLEAR SCREEN),** and type the following to review some of the character functions:

   ```
   SELECT UPPER('oracle') "Upper", LOWER('DATABASE') AS "Lower",
     INITCAP('for whom the bell tools') AS "Initcap",
     LENGTH('for whom the bell tools') AS "Length"
   FROM DUAL;
   ```

2. Type and execute the following to list customers having the longest street addresses. Use an inline view to collect the addresses and their lengths and to sort them by descending address length. Then ask Oracle to extract just the top ten rows:

   ```
   SELECT Address, LENGTH(Address) AS "Addr. Size"
   FROM (SELECT Address, LENGTH(Address)
         FROM Customers
         ORDER BY 2 DESC)
   WHERE ROWNUM < 11;
   ```

TABLE 5.2 Selected single-row character functions.

Function	Description
INSTR(<str1>,<str2>)	Searches <str1> and returns the position at which <str2> occurs.
LENGTH(<str>)	Returns the number of characters in <str>.
LOWER(<str>)	Returns the lowercase version of <str>.
UPPER(<str>)	Returns the uppercase version of <str>.
INITCAP(<str>)	Converts the initial letter of each word of <str> to uppercase.
NVL(<str>, <value>)	Returns <value> if <str> is NULL; else, <str> is returned.
NVL2(<str>, <value1>, <value2>)	Returns <value1> if <str> is *not* NULL; else, returns <value2> if <str> is NULL.
REPLACE(<str1>,<str2>, <str3>)	Searches <str1> for occurrence of <str2>. If found, it replaces <str2> with <str3>.
LPAD(<str>, <width>, [,<pad string>])	Pads string <str> with spaces to the left to right align the <str> for a total width of <width>. You can supply an optional pad character.
RPAD(<str>, <width>, [,<pad string>])	Pads string <str> with spaces to the right to bring total length to <width> characters. You can supply an optional pad character.
SUBSTR(<str>, <start> [, <length>])	Returns the substring of <str> that begins at position <start>. <Length> is an optional length to return.
TRIM(<str>)	Trims spaces from the left and the right of <str>.
LTRIM(<str>)	Trims spaces from left side of <str>.
RTRIM(<str>)	Trims spaces from right side of <str>.

3. Type and execute the following to display customers' names in proper case for customers whose last names end with "ling." Display just the first initial, a period, and full last name:

```
SELECT SUBSTR(FirstName,1,1) || '. '||LastName AS "Name"
FROM Customers
WHERE UPPER(LastName) LIKE '%LING';
```

Figure 5.15 shows the results Oracle returns for these three queries.

4. Type and execute the following to display agents' names with trailing dots and work phone numbers right-aligned. Issue the SQL*Plus PAGESIZE command to set the page longer. (Reset the PAGESIZE following the SELECT clause.):

```
SET PAGESIZE 40
SELECT
   RPAD(FirstName||' '||LastName,40,'.') AS "Agent",
   LPAD(WorkPhone,18) AS "Work Number"
FROM Agents
ORDER BY LastName, FirstName;
SET PAGESIZE 14
```

Figure 5.16 shows the use the use of UPPER, LPAD (left pad), and RPAD (right pad) single-row character functions.

USING NUMERIC FUNCTIONS

Several single-row numeric functions are available. They provide capabilities far beyond those of the mathematical operators. They allow you to round values to various

224 Introduction to Oracle

```
SQL> SELECT UPPER('oracle') "Upper", LOWER('DATABASE') AS "Lower",
  2     INITCAP('for whom the bell tools') AS "Initcap",
  3     LENGTH('for whom the bell tools') AS "Length"
  4  FROM DUAL;

Upper  Lower     Initcap                    Length
------ --------- -------------------------- ------
ORACLE database For Whom The Bell Tools        23

SQL> SELECT Address, LENGTH(Address) AS "Addr. Size"
  2  FROM (SELECT Address, LENGTH(Address)
  3        FROM Customers
  4        ORDER BY 2 DESC)
  5  WHERE ROWNUM < 11;

ADDRESS                                  Addr. Size
---------------------------------------- ----------
Washington Dulles International                  31
5794 West Las Positas Boulevard                  31
3001 John F. Kennedy Boulevard                   30
2525 East El Segundo Boulevard                   30
460 Point San Bruno Boulevard                    29
1450 Fashion Island Boulevard                    29
1100 North Washington Street                     28
2600 West Magnolia Boulevard                     28
691 South Milpitas Boulevard                     28
11812 San Vicente Boulevard                      27

10 rows selected.

SQL> SELECT SUBSTR(FirstName,1,1) || '. '||LastName AS "Name"
  2  FROM Customers
  3  WHERE UPPER(LastName) LIKE '%LING';

Name
---------------------------------
A. Gibeling
M. Pilling
R. Colling
H. Hotaling

SQL>
```

FIGURE 5.15   Using several single-row character functions.

```
SQL> SET PAGESIZE 40
SQL> SELECT
  2     RPAD(UPPER(LastName)||', '||FirstName,50,'.') AS "Agent",
  3     LPAD(WorkPhone,17) AS "Work Number"
  4  FROM Agents
  5  ORDER BY LastName, FirstName;

Agent                                              Work Number
-------------------------------------------------- -----------------
ALLEE, Lora.......................................   (707) 555-9990
CARLING, Tobias...................................   (707) 555-1983
CHONG, Belinda....................................   (707) 555-0962
DAHLEN, Elizabeth.................................   (707) 555-7218
DANN, Cornelis....................................   (707) 555-9652
FERNANDEZ, Crystal................................   (707) 555-1652
FLAMENBAUM, Jackson...............................   (707) 555-5551
GAGNON, David.....................................   (707) 555-8668
HERRING, Barbara..................................   (707) 555-3355
KELLOGG, James....................................   (707) 555-2075
LEWIS, Patricia...................................   (707) 555-8690
MARCOUX, Kai......................................   (707) 555-0361
OKINDO, Essi......................................   (707) 555-0719
PIPEROVA, Nancy...................................   (707) 555-0492
REED, Lee.........................................   (707) 555-7213
ROBINSON, Clair...................................   (707) 555-1950
ROMERO, Cecilia...................................   (707) 555-2430
ROWE, Ramanathan..................................   (707) 555-9839
SCHUTZ, Tim.......................................   (707) 555-6005
SELBY, Ricki......................................   (707) 555-3933
SHEIBANI, Heather.................................   (707) 555-5635
SILVERBURG, Danial................................   (707) 555-5865
SOLTWEDEL, Stanislaw..............................   (707) 555-0089
ST-ONGE, Tim......................................   (707) 555-4697
TAYLOR, Jessica...................................   (707) 555-4529
TOWNSEND, Edwin...................................   (707) 555-9485
VOSS, Bruce.......................................   (707) 555-8389
WEBER, Sindisiwe..................................   (707) 555-0616
WILLIAMS, Christine...............................   (707) 555-5525

29 rows selected.

SQL> SET PAGESIZE 14
SQL>
```

FIGURE 5.16   Using the LPAD and RPAD character functions.

CHAPTER 5   Querying a Database   **225**

TABLE 5.3   Selected single-row numeric functions.

Function	Description	Examples
ABS(\<n\>)	Returns the absolute value of \<n\>.	ABS(5) = 5 ABS(−58) = 58
CEIL(\<n\>)	Returns smallest integer greater than or equal to \<n\>.	CEIL(6.8) = 7 CEIL(−34.5) = −34
FLOOR(\<n\>)	Returns largest integer less than or equal to \<n\>.	FLOOR(78.9) = 78 FLOOR(−3.1) = −4
MOD(\<n\>,\<m\>)	Returns the remainder of \<n\> divided by \<m\>.	MOD(7,3) = 1 MOD(29,6) = 5
POWER(\<n\>,\<k\>)	Returns \<n\> raised to the \<k\> power.	POWER(2,3) = 8 POWER(5,2) = 25
ROUND(\<n\> [,\<m\>])	Returns \<n\> rounded to \<m\> decimal places. If \<m\> is omitted, then rounds to nearest integer.	ROUND(7.467,2) = 7.47 ROUND(96.87,−1) = 100
SIGN(\<n\>)	Returns −1 if \<n\> is negative, 0 if \<n\> is zero, and +1 if \<n\> is positive.	SIGN(−23) = −1 SIGN(456) = 1
SQRT(\<n\>)	Returns the square root of \<n\>.	SQRT(81) = 9 SQRT(7) = 2.645751
TRUNC(\<n\> [,\<k\>])	Returns the truncated value of \<n\> to \<k\> decimal places. Second argument is optional.	TRUNC(56.999) = 56 TRUNC(789.559,1) = 789.5

decimal places, calculate the remainder, truncate a number to its closest whole value, and raise a number to a power. Table 5.3 lists several of the more commonly used numeric functions. Consult Oracle documentation for a complete list of all built-in functions, including single-row numeric functions.

You use single-row numeric functions to perform calculations. This class of functions accepts as arguments an input number from a table or an expression that evaluates to a number. The function performs its built-in mathematical manipulation on the input expression and produces a numeric result. Not all numeric functions perform calculations on their inputs. Instead, they return some characteristic about the input number. The SIGN( ) function, for instance, returns −1 if the input number is negative; it returns 1 if it is positive, and it returns 0 if the input number is zero. Next, launch SQL*Plus and log into Oracle, if needed. Then, type **CLEAR SCREEN** and press **Enter** to clear the screen in preparation for the next steps.

To use selected single-row numeric functions:

1. Type and execute the following:

    ```
    SELECT ABS(-234), CEIL(23.112), MOD(21,6),
      ROUND(567.93537,2), SQRT(5280)
    FROM DUAL;
    ```

2. Type and execute the following statements to review the differences between the TRUNC and ROUND functions. Figure 5.17 shows the results. Of course, the age values Oracle returns will depend on today's date:

    ```
    COLUMN LastName FORMAT A15
    SELECT LastName,
      TRUNC((SYSDATE-BirthDate)/365.25)    AS "Age",
      ROUND((SYSDATE-BirthDate)/365.25,2) AS "Rounded-2",
    ```

```
    ROUND((SYSDATE-BirthDate)/365.25,3) AS "Rounded-3",
    (SYSDATE-BirthDate)/365.25 AS "Full"
FROM Agents
WHERE BirthDate < '01-JAN-61'
ORDER BY 5;
```

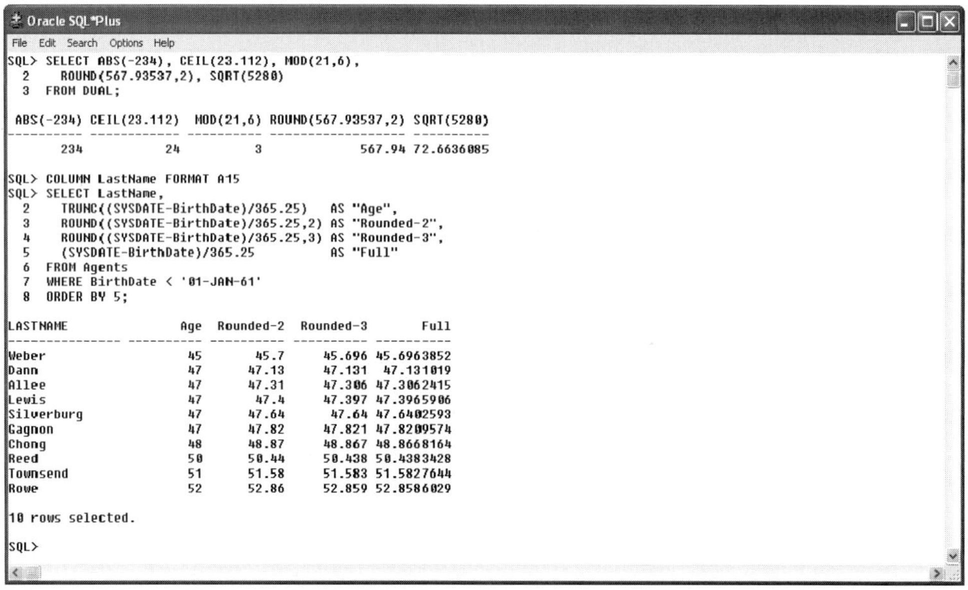

FIGURE 5.17 Experimenting with selected numeric functions.

3. You can keep SQL*Plus running for exercises that follow.

   USING DATE FUNCTIONS

   Oracle provides several built-in single-row date functions that operate on date data types. Several date functions appear in Table 5.4. The table also contains two conversion functions because they convert to date types from strings and back. The latter are TO_CHAR and TO_DATE.

   The best way to become acquainted with the date functions and related conversion functions is to use them.

   To execute queries containing date and date-conversion functions:

1. Using SQL*Plus, type and execute **CLEAR SCREEN**.
2. Type and execute the following:

   ```
   SELECT
       EXTRACT(YEAR FROM HireDate) AS "Hire Year",
       EXTRACT(MONTH FROM HireDate) AS "Hire Month",
       EXTRACT(DAY FROM HireDate) AS "Hire Day",
       HireDate,
       ADD_MONTHS(HireDate,5) AS "+5 Months"
   FROM Agents
   WHERE HireDate > '14-JUN-02'
   ORDER BY 1;
   ```

3. Using a conversion function, display the current time by typing and executing the following SQL*Plus and SQL statements. (Naturally, this will be different for everyone based on the date and time when they executed the query.)

TABLE 5.4 Date functions and date-related conversion functions.

Function	Description	Example
ADD_MONTHS(<date>, <no. of months>)	Adds specified <no. of months> to date value. (Subtracts if <no. of months> is negative.)	ADD_MONTHS('10-OCT-06',3) returns 10-JAN-07.
EXTRACT(<ymd> FROM <date>)	Extracts an integer value that is the year, month, or day of the date.	EXTRACT(YEAR FROM '10-OCT-85') returns 1985.
LAST_DAY(<date>)	Returns the last day of the month that contains the date.	LAST_DAY(SYSDATE) returns the last day of this month.
MONTHS_BETWEEN (<date1>,<date2>)	Returns the months between two dates. If <date1> is more recent than <date2>, then the result is positive.	MONTHS_BETWEEN (SYSDATE, HireDate) returns the number of elapsed months between today and the HireDate field for each row.
NEW_TIME(<date>, <cur-time-zone>, <new-time-zone>)	Returns the date and time in another time zone.	NEW_TIME(SYSDATE, 'PST','EST')
NEXT_DAY(<date>, <string>)	Returns the date of the first day of the specified name (<string>) that is later than the date, <date>, specified.	NEXT_DAY('14-JUN-2006', 'Tuesday') returns the date '20-JUN-06.'
SYSDATE	Returns the current date and time. (SYSDATE has no arguments.)	'07-OCT-06' if that is the current date.
TO_CHAR(<date>, <format>)	Convert date/time to a string whose format is specified by <format>.	TO_CHAR(SYSDATE, 'MM/DD/YYYY HH24:MM;SS')
TO_DATE(<str>,<format>)	Convert <str> to a date using <format> to interpret the string.	TO_DATE('10/30/2006' 'MM/DD/YYYY')

```
COLUMN "Quarter" FORMAT A7
COLUMN "1 hour later" FORMAT A12
COLUMN "1 Day later" FORMAT A11
SELECT
   TO_CHAR(SYSDATE, 'MM/DD/YYYY HH:MM:SS AM') AS "Year and time",
   TO_CHAR(SYSDATE, 'YYYY') AS "Year",
   TO_CHAR(SYSDATE, 'Q') AS "Quarter",
   TO_CHAR(SYSDATE+1/24, 'HH24:MM:SS') AS "1 hour later",
   TO_CHAR(SYSDATE+1, 'MM/DD/YYYY') AS "1 Day later"
FROM DUAL;
```

Figure 5.18 shows typical results, though your exact results will vary because your current time and date are different.

4. Determine how many years each employee has worked for Redwood Realty. First type **CLEAR SCREEN** and press **Enter** to maximize available screen. Then type and execute the following:

```
SET PAGESIZE 40
COLUMN "Unrounded Hire Age" FORMAT A20
SELECT TO_CHAR(BirthDate,'MM/DD/YYYY') AS "Birth date",
   TO_CHAR(HireDate,'MM/DD/YYYY') AS "Hire date",
   TRUNC(MONTHS_BETWEEN(HireDate, BirthDate)/12,0) AS "Hire Age",
```

```
        TO_CHAR(MONTHS_BETWEEN(HireDate, BirthDate)/12, '99.99')
          AS "Unrounded Hire Age"
        FROM Agents ORDER BY 3 DESC;
```

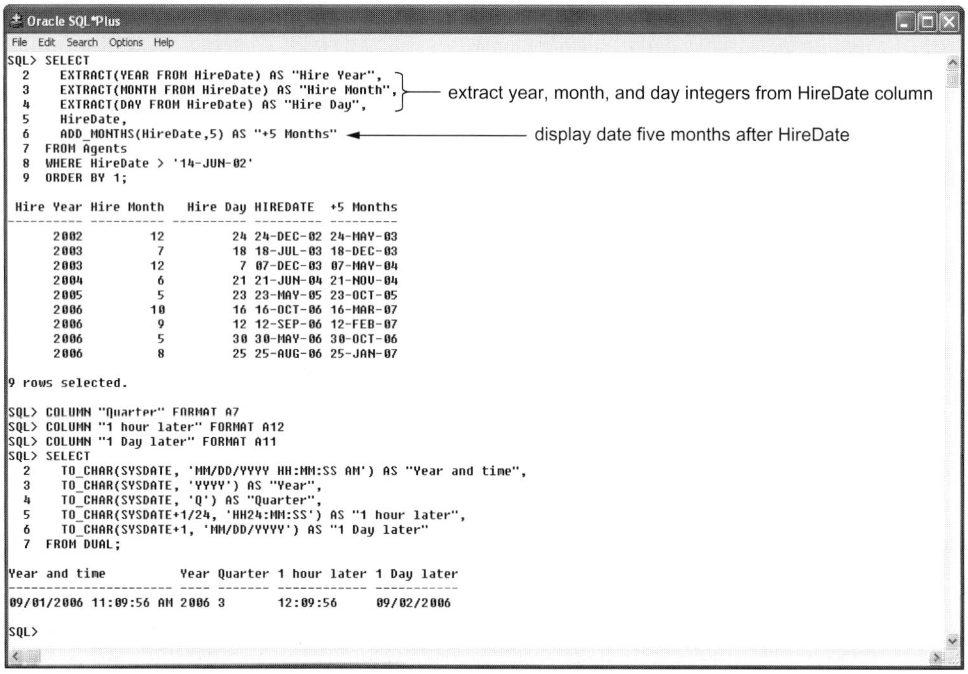

FIGURE 5.18 Using date and conversion functions.

Figure 5.19 shows the full-page results in descending order by employees' ages when they were hired by Redwood Realty.

5. Type and execute the following to compute the amount of time each listing is active. Express the end date minus the begin date in days, whole weeks, and whole months:

```
CLEAR SCREEN
SELECT DISTINCT
  (EndListDate-BeginListDate) AS "Market Time: Days",
  TRUNC((EndListDate-BeginListDate)/7) AS "Weeks",
  FLOOR(MONTHS_BETWEEN(EndListDate,BeginListDate)) AS "Months"
FROM LISTINGS
ORDER BY 1 DESC;
```

Oracle computes and displays the several unique, elapsed times between listings' begin and end dates.

6. Type the following to display the first day of the LicenseExpire month, the LicenseExpire date, and the last day of the month when the license expires. Do this only for Agents that are brokers whose license expires before the year 2002:

```
SELECT ADD_MONTHS(LAST_DAY(LicenseExpire),-1)+1 AS "Beginning",
  LicenseExpire AS "Actual",
  LAST_DAY(LicenseExpire) AS "Ending"
FROM Agents
WHERE UPPER(TITLE) = 'BROKER' AND EXTRACT(YEAR FROM LicenseExpire) < 2002;
```

Figure 5.20 shows the results following Steps 5 and 6.

CHAPTER 5 Querying a Database **229**

```
SQL> SET PAGESIZE 40
SQL> COLUMN "Unrounded Hire Age" FORMAT A20
SQL> SELECT TO_CHAR(BirthDate,'MM/DD/YYYY') AS "Birth date",
  2    TO_CHAR(HireDate,'MM/DD/YYYY')  AS "Hire date",
  3    TRUNC(MONTHS_BETWEEN(HireDate, BirthDate)/12,0) AS "Hire Age",
  4    TO_CHAR(MONTHS_BETWEEN(HireDate, BirthDate)/12, '99.99') AS "Unrounded Hire Age"
  5  FROM Agents ORDER BY 3 DESC;

Birth date Hire date   Hire Age Unrounded Hire Age
---------- ----------  -------- --------------------
02/01/1955 09/12/2006        51  51.61
04/10/1959 05/30/2006        47  47.14
12/21/1960 08/25/2006        45  45.68
03/25/1956 09/18/2000        44  44.48
10/23/1953 09/05/1997        43  43.87
07/16/1959 09/02/2001        42  42.13
11/06/1958 01/17/1999        40  40.20
01/11/1959 09/21/1997        38  38.69
02/04/1965 12/07/2003        38  38.84
10/21/1962 11/01/1999        37  37.03
10/20/1957 08/30/1995        37  37.86
05/13/1959 07/14/1996        37  37.17
07/01/1969 10/16/2006        37  37.29
09/26/1961 06/29/1998        36  36.76
10/03/1969 05/23/2005        35  35.64
11/02/1969 02/05/2002        32  32.26
11/29/1964 05/30/1997        32  32.50
05/03/1968 02/08/2000        31  31.76
05/19/1968 07/13/1997        29  29.15
08/16/1967 01/08/1996        28  28.40
04/04/1969 05/04/1996        27  27.08
04/03/1970 06/05/1996        26  26.17
12/12/1970 10/03/1996        25  25.81
10/19/1975 12/19/2000        25  25.17
06/21/1978 12/24/2002        24  24.51
03/04/1974 12/20/1995        21  21.79
05/08/1980 01/05/2002        21  21.66
03/03/1983 07/18/2003        20  20.37
08/21/1983 06/21/2004        20  20.83

29 rows selected.

SQL>
```

FIGURE 5.19 Computing age using the TRUNC and MONTHS_BETWEEN functions.

```
SQL> SELECT DISTINCT
  2    (EndListDate-BeginListDate) AS "Market Time: Days",
  3    TRUNC((EndListDate-BeginListDate)/7) AS "Weeks",
  4    FLOOR(MONTHS_BETWEEN(EndListDate,BeginListDate)) AS "Months"
  5  FROM LISTINGS
  6  ORDER BY 1 DESC;

Market Time: Days      Weeks     Months
-----------------  ---------  ---------
              184         26          6
              183         26          6
              182         26          6
              181         25          6
              153         21          5
              151         21          5
              123         17          4
              122         17          4
              121         17          4
              120         17          4
               92         13          3
               91         13          3
               90         12          3
               62          8          2
               61          8          2
               31          4          1
               30          4          1

17 rows selected.

SQL> SELECT ADD_MONTHS(LAST_DAY(LicenseExpire),-1)+1 AS "Beginning",
  2    LicenseExpire AS "Actual",
  3    LAST_DAY(LicenseExpire) AS "Ending"
  4  FROM Agents
  5  WHERE UPPER(Title) = 'BROKER' AND  EXTRACT(YEAR FROM LicenseExpire) < 2002;

Beginning Actual    Ending
--------- --------- ---------
01-MAY-99 01-MAY-99 31-MAY-99
01-DEC-98 01-DEC-98 31-DEC-98

SQL>
```

FIGURE 5.20 Calculating unique elapsed times and start/end dates.

> **Tip:** Your screen resolution might not match the screen shown in the figures, but the results should be the same. Just scroll the SQL*Plus window up and down to review the results, if needed.

7. Type **exit** and press **Enter** to exit SQL*Plus.

Review your results and the preceding figures. Notice, for instance, that an integer number of days is the result when you subtract two dates. Furthermore, the amount of detail that a date-valued result displays depends on the formatting you use in the TO_CHAR function. You can display just the date, or the time, or both.

USING CONVERSION FUNCTIONS

Oracle provides over 30 single-row conversion functions that allow you to convert a value from one data type to another. An example of one of the most popular conversion functions is TO_CHAR, which converts a date or time value to a character string. Other conversion functions include TO_DATE, and TO_NUMBER. Additional conversion functions include conversions from binary to floating-point, from multi-byte characters to single-byte characters, and from numeric or character to character large object (CLOB). Here, you will learn about the three popular conversion functions TO_CHAR, TO_DATE, and TO_NUMBER by using them. If you are interested in learning details about other conversion functions, consult Oracle documentation or any of many available online sources.

The TO_CHAR Function Use the single-row conversion function TO_CHAR to convert a date or time value to a character string. Its general syntax is:

    TO_CHAR(<date-number> [,<format-string>])

The parameter "<date-number>" is a date/time value or a numeric value, column, or expression followed by an optional "<format-string>". The "<format-string>", formally called the *format model,* specifies the exact format of the output character string. For example, you could convert the HireDate column in the Agents table to an output string in another format by using the TO_CHAR function in a SELECT list such as the following:

    SELECT FirstName, LastName, (HireDate, 'Month, DD, YYYY')
    FROM Agents;

The result is the first and last names followed by dates such as each agent's hire date, such as "October 03, 1996" or "August 30, 1995." Alternatively, you can omit the format string, in which case the output format is Oracle's default DD-MON-YY format (for example, 03-OCT-96).

The TO_CHAR function is frequently used to format numeric results into more pleasing forms. For example, you can convert and display the BidPrice values formatted with leading currency symbol, commas, and two decimal places with the following TO_CHAR function:

    SELECT TO_CHAR(BidPrice, '$99,999,999.99')
    FROM CustAgentList;

The format model, '$99,999,999.99' indicates that a dollar sign should appear, and the mask character 9 indicates the position of digits. Period marks the position of an inserted decimal place, and the "99" appearing after the decimal point indicates that two decimal places (even 00, if needed) are required. There are several format model characters you can employ to produce formatted dates or numbers. Table 5.5 shows

CHAPTER 5   Querying a Database   **231**

TABLE 5.5   Selected number format elements.

Element	Example	Description
9	9999	Returns a value with the specified number of digits and leading space, if positive or hyphen if negative. The 9s dictate the maximum number of digits to display.
, (comma)	9,999	Returns a comma in the specified location. Comma cannot occur as the first element or after a decimal character.
. (period)	99.99	Returns a period and marks the location of the beginning of any decimal places.
0	0999	Returns leading zeroes.
	9990	Returns trailing zeroes.
$	$999,999	Returns a leading dollar sign.
B	B999	Returns blanks for the integer part of a fixed number when the integer part is zero.
MI	9999MI	When the value is negative, it returns a trailing minus sign ($-$). Positive values return a trailing blank.
RN	RN	Returns a value as Roman numerals in uppercase.
	rn	Returns a value as Roman numerals in lowercase.
S	S9999 or	Returns a *leading* minus sign (S999) for negative values or a positive sign ($+$) for a positive value.
	9999S	Returns a *trailing* minus sign (999S) for negative values or a positive sign ($+$) for a positive value.
EEEE	9.99EEEE	Returns a value in scientific notation (e.g., 1.78E+03).

several of the most important number format characters. These can be used in the format string in limited combination with one another to produce the desired, formatted character output.

Issuing several SELECT statements with several different format model elements will help you understand exactly how they work.

To use the TO_CHAR function to format date and number columns and expressions:

1. Launch SQL*Plus, log into Oracle, type **CLEAR SCREEN,** and press **Enter.**
2. Type and execute the following to display a formatted BidPrice value for a select few higher-priced homes:

```
SET PAGESIZE 20
SELECT TO_CHAR(BidPrice, '$99,999,999.00') AS "Bid Price"
FROM CustAgentList
WHERE BidPrice > 360000;
```

3. Type and execute the following to review how numbers are signed and the use of Roman numerals. Be sure to enter the WHERE clause accurately. Otherwise Oracle will return many (or no) rows. In particular, there are no blanks within the quoted string following the word *LIKE*.

```
SELECT TO_CHAR(Longitude, 'S9999.99') AS "S9999.99",
   TO_CHAR(Longitude, '000999.99MI') AS "000999.99MI",
   TO_CHAR(Latitude, 'S9999.9') AS "S9999.9",
   TO_CHAR(Latitude, 'RN') AS "Roman Latitude"
FROM Properties
WHERE UPPER(Address) LIKE '%RIVER%';
```

Your results for Steps 2 and 3 should match Figure 5.21.

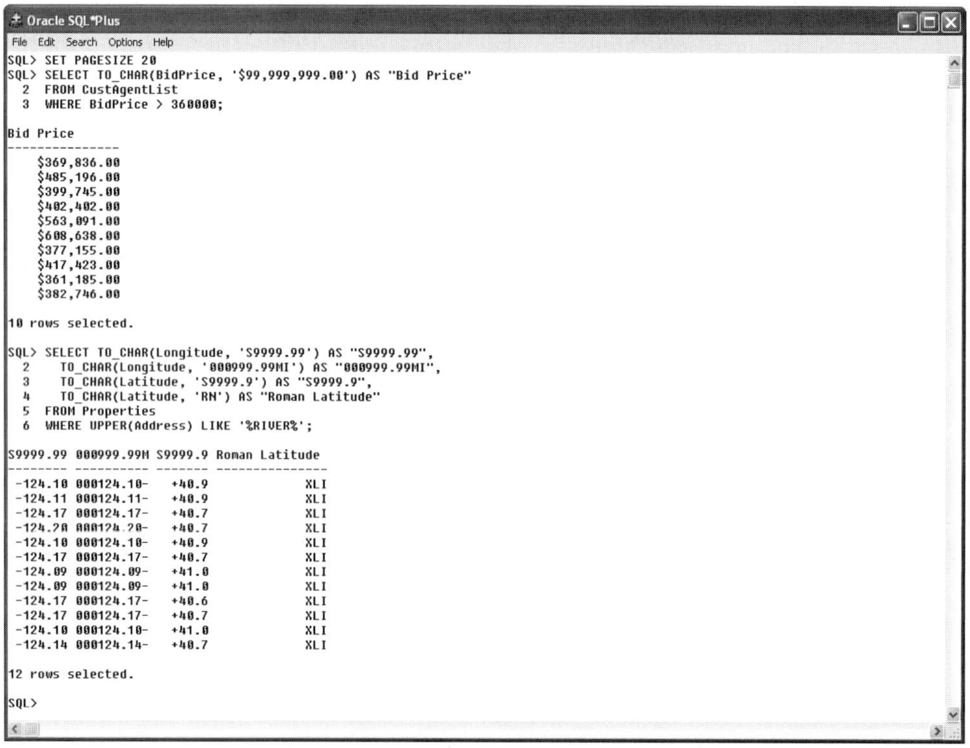

```
SQL> SET PAGESIZE 20
SQL> SELECT TO_CHAR(BidPrice, '$99,999,999.00') AS "Bid Price"
  2  FROM CustAgentList
  3  WHERE BidPrice > 360000;

Bid Price
---------------
    $369,836.00
    $485,196.00
    $399,745.00
    $402,402.00
    $563,091.00
    $608,638.00
    $377,155.00
    $417,423.00
    $361,185.00
    $382,746.00

10 rows selected.

SQL> SELECT TO_CHAR(Longitude, 'S9999.99') AS "S9999.99",
  2  TO_CHAR(Longitude, '000999.99MI') AS "000999.99MI",
  3  TO_CHAR(Latitude, 'S9999.9') AS "S9999.9",
  4  TO_CHAR(Latitude, 'RN') AS "Roman Latitude"
  5  FROM Properties
  6  WHERE UPPER(Address) LIKE '%RIVER%';

S9999.99 000999.99M S9999.9 Roman Latitude
-------- ---------- ------- --------------
 -124.10 000124.10-   +40.9            XLI
 -124.11 000124.11-   +40.9            XLI
 -124.17 000124.17-   +40.7            XLI
 -124.20 000124.20-   +40.7            XLI
 -124.10 000124.10-   +40.9            XLI
 -124.17 000124.17-   +40.7            XLI
 -124.09 000124.09-   +41.0            XLI
 -124.09 000124.09-   +41.0            XLI
 -124.17 000124.17-   +40.6            XLI
 -124.17 000124.17-   +40.7            XLI
 -124.10 000124.10-   +41.0            XLI
 -124.14 000124.14-   +40.7            XLI

12 rows selected.

SQL>
```

FIGURE 5.21 Using numeric format characters.

4. Type and execute the following constants and format models to see how other format elements work:

```
CLEAR SCREEN
SELECT TO_CHAR(345.678,'S99,999.99') AS "S99,999.99",
  TO_CHAR(0.00678,'9.999EEEE') AS "9.999EEEE",
  TO_CHAR(5280, '09.99') AS "09.99",
  TO_CHAR(1256, 'RN') AS "RN: 1,256",
  TO_CHAR(1234.5678, '$999,999.00') AS "$999,999.00"
FROM DUAL;
```

Notice that the third column contains a series of pound signs (#). That indicates the format string is too short to accommodate the value. Edit the third line to

```
TO_CHAR(5280, '09999.99') AS "09999.99",
```

And then execute the corrected query. Your results should match those shown in Figure 5.22.

5. Type **exit** and press **Enter** to log out of Oracle and close SQL*Plus.

The TO_DATE Function The TO_DATE function converts a string to a date and a time. It is a handy function when you want to insert a data value into a column. You specify the date as a string and an optional format string. The function converts the string into an internal date/time format according to the supplied format string. If you omit the format string, the date string must be in the default format of either DD-MON-YY or DD-MON-YYYY (enclosed in apostrophes). The function's syntax

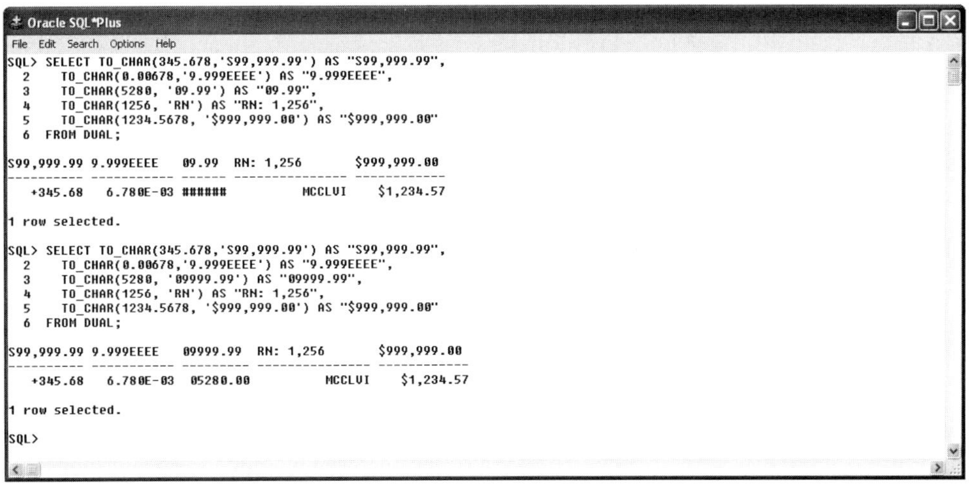

FIGURE 5.22 Additional numeric format characters.

is similar to that of the TO_CHAR function:

```
TO_DATE(<date-string> [,<format-string>])
```

where "<date-string>" is the string that is to be converted to a date and "<format-string>" is an optional format model string that guides Oracle in interpreting the date string. Examples of the TO_DATE function are:

```
TO_DATE('January 10, 2006', 'Month DD, YYYY')
TO_DATE('10/17/2004 10:27:48', 'MM/DD/YYYY HH24:MI:SS')
TO_DATE('7.14.03', 'MM.DD.YY')
TO_DATE('2006/9/23','YYYY/MM/DD')
TO_DATE('10-OCT-2006')
```

In the first line above, the format model indicates the role that each part of the date string plays. It indicates that the date begins with a full month name followed by a two-digit day of the month (DD). That is followed by a comma, and a four-digit year (YYYY). Other format strings reflect the exact *form* of the date string to its left, with the exception of the fifth example. The last date string above is in default form, so Oracle will interpret it correctly without the aid of a format string. Table 5.6 lists several important date format model elements and their meanings. Table 5.7 lists several important time format model elements along with their meanings and examples.

It is likely you will use only some of the elements at first. Later, as you encounter increasingly sophisticated database applications, you might want to revisit these tables to refresh your memory. Next, you will become familiar with several of these format model elements by using them in the following exercise.

To experiment with the TO_DATE function and several format model elements:

1. Launch SQL*Plus, log into Oracle, and clear the screen.
2. Type and execute the following:

```
SELECT TO_DATE('January 10, 2006','MONTH DD, YYYY') AS "Date-1",
   TO_DATE('10/17/1999 14:23:39', 'MM/DD/YYYY HH24:MI:SS') AS "Date-2"
FROM DUAL;
```

Notice that the result displays in Oracle default format: DD-MON-YY. Even though that shows the values have been entered correctly, time details are absent.

TABLE 5.6 Date-related format model elements.

Perspective	Parameter	Description	Example
Century	CC	Two digit century.	20, 21
Quarter	Q	One-digit quarter of the year.	1, 2, 3, or 4
Year	YYYY, YYY, YY, Y, RR	Year represented by four, three, two, or one digit. RR is rounded to nearest year.	2006, 006, 06, 6
Month	MONTH, Month, MON, Mon	Month represented as full name or abbreviated. Capitalization matches result.	JANUARY, January, JAN, or Jan, respectively
	MM	Two-digit month of the year.	01, 02, ..., 12
Week	WW, W	Two-digit week of the year or one-digit week of the month.	01-52; 1-5
Day	DDD, DD, D	Three-digit day of the year; two-digit day of the month; one-digit day of the week.	
	DAY, Day, DY, Dy	Day of the week: complete, abbreviated, and capitalized or not.	SUNDAY, Sunday, SUN, Sun

TABLE 5.7 Time-related format model elements.

Perspective	Parameter	Description	Example
Hour	HH24, HH	Two-digit hour in 24- or 12-hour format.	23, 11
Minute	MI	Two-digit minute.	Range: 0–59
Second	SS	Two-digit second.	Range 0–59
Separators	- / ; , : . (hyphen, slash, semicolon, comma, colon, period)	Characters that you can use to separate date and time values.	DD-MON-YYYY; HH:MM:SS; YYYY/MM/DD
Time suffixes	AM, A.M., PM, P.M.	AM, A.M., PM, or P.M. as appropriate (specify one or the other).	12:45 P.M.
	AD, BC, A.D., B.C.	AD, BC, A.D., or B.C. as needed. Specify only AD or BC (with or without periods).	1452 B.C.
	TH	Supplies suffix for numbers as needed.	1ST, 2ND, 3RD, or 15TH
	SP	Number is spelled out.	DDSP produces FIFTEEN for a day value of 15
	TZR	Time zone region.	PST, EST

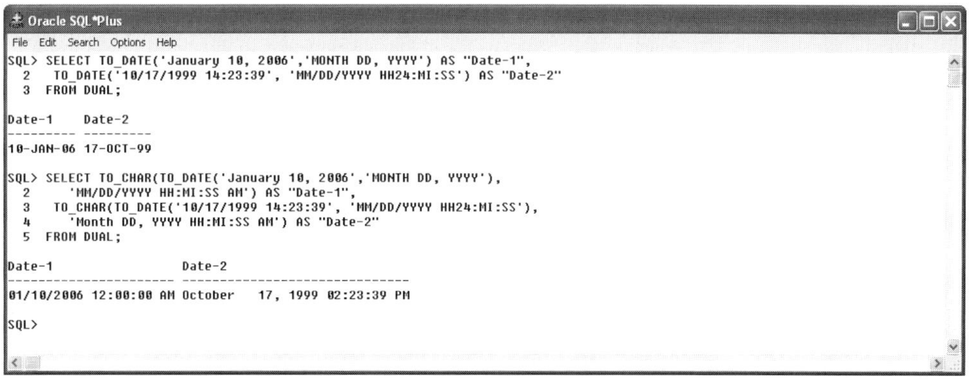

```
SQL> SELECT TO_DATE('January 10, 2006','MONTH DD, YYYY') AS "Date-1",
  2    TO_DATE('10/17/1999 14:23:39', 'MM/DD/YYYY HH24:MI:SS') AS "Date-2"
  3  FROM DUAL;

Date-1    Date-2
--------- ---------
10-JAN-06 17-OCT-99

SQL> SELECT TO_CHAR(TO_DATE('January 10, 2006','MONTH DD, YYYY'),
  2     'MM/DD/YYYY HH:MI:SS AM') AS "Date-1",
  3     TO_CHAR(TO_DATE('10/17/1999 14:23:39', 'MM/DD/YYYY HH24:MI:SS'),
  4     'Month DD, YYYY HH:MI:SS AM') AS "Date-2"
  5  FROM DUAL;

Date-1                        Date-2
----------------------------  ----------------------------
01/10/2006 12:00:00 AM        October   17, 1999 02:23:39 PM

SQL>
```

FIGURE 5.23 Examples of the TO_DATE function.

> **Tip:** As is customary, use the DUAL table whenever you want to display expressions that do not depend on any table columns—expressions consisting of functions, mathematical operators, character strings, and other literals.

3. Modify the SELECT statement in Step 2 by enclosing each TO_DATE function in a TO_CHAR function as the first argument. Then, add a format model statement that shows more details of the time portion of the date/time value. The modified statement is as follows:

```
SELECT TO_CHAR(TO_DATE('January 10, 2006','MONTH DD, YYYY'),
   'MM/DD/YYYY HH:MI:SS AM') AS "Date-1",
   TO_CHAR(TO_DATE('10/17/1999 14:23:39', 'MM/DD/YYYY HH24:MI:SS'),
   'Month DD, YYYY HH:MI:SS AM') AS "Date-2"
FROM DUAL;
```

Figure 5.23 shows the results of these two steps.

4. Type and execute the following to display dates from the Redwood Realty database in a format that you control:

```
CLEAR SCREEN
SELECT TO_DATE('01/01/'||YearBuilt, 'MM/DD/YYYY') AS "Computed",
   YearBuilt AS "Data Col."
FROM Properties
WHERE YearBuilt > 1994 AND UPPER(City) = 'MCKINLEYVILLE';
```

Figure 5.24 shows the result of the preceding. Notice that the integer, four-digit year is concatenated to the string "01/01" to form a date.

5. Type **exit** and press **Enter** to log off Oracle and exit SQL*Plus.

The TO_DATE and TO_CHAR functions are not limited to *displaying* values. They are used just as often to insert date and character data into database tables. Their form in an INSERT statement is identical to the examples above, except that the TO_CHAR function and its arguments are part of the VALUES list.

The TO_NUMBER Function   The TO_NUMBER function has the syntax

```
TO_NUMBER(<str> [,<format-string>])
```

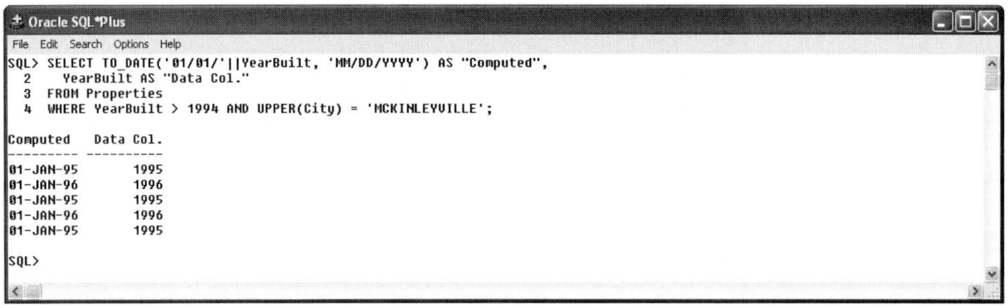

FIGURE 5.24 Creating date values from constants and a column containing numbers.

where "<str>" is the input argument (an expression, a table column name, and so on) that is converted to a number. Like the TO_CHAR and TO_DATE functions, it has an optional format model that you can supply to indicate how to interpret the first argument. The format model string can contain the same elements listed in Table 5.5. The following converts the column StreetNumber, row by row, to a number, adds 400 to it, and displays the result.

```
SELECT TO_NUMBER(StreetNumber) + 400
FROM DUAL;
```

USING SPECIAL FUNCTIONS

Several functions perform highly specialized transformations on data and are collectively called special functions. Popular special functions presented here include DECODE, NVL, NVL2, TRANSLATE, and CASE. A comprehensive discussion of the CASE expression appears in Chapter 4 under the heading *Introducing the CASE Structure*, so it is not presented again here.

The DECODE Function One of the most interesting Oracle built-in functions is DECODE. DECODE substitutes values using a condition and allows you to use if-then-else logic in SQL without resorting to PL/SQL. DECODE's syntax is:

```
DECODE(<value>, <search-value1>, <result1>,
    [<search-value2>, <result2>,…] <default-result>)
```

The "<value>" is compared to "<search-value1>". If "<value>" and "<search-value1>" are equal, then Oracle returns "<result1>" as the answer. If the value is not equal to the first "<search-value1>" and other, optional "<search-value>"/"<result>" pairs exist, then the "<value>" is compared to the next "<search-value>". This continues until a match is found or no equality is found with all "<search-values>". If the comparison is completed without finding a match, then the "<default-result>" is returned if it is present. If not, then NULL is returned. Here are some examples of the DECODE function.

```
SELECT DECODE(YearInSchool,1,'Freshman',2,'Sophomore',3,'Junior',4,'Senior')
FROM SchoolData;

SELECT InventoryID, ItemName,
 DECODE(InventoryStatus,
        0,'Backordered',
        1,'Available',
        2,'Near reorder point',
          'Unknown')
FROM Inventory;
```

The first decode displays Freshman, Sophomore, Junior, or Senior based on the value of the column YearInSchool being 1, 2, 3, or 4, respectively. It provides a more meaningful output than a number would without modifying the underlying column values. In the second example, meaningful words appear in place of numeric codes indicating the status of the inventory item. If the InventoryStatus column is NULL or a value other than 0, 1, or 2, the DECODE function returns the default value, *Unknown.*

The NVL and NVL2 Functions The NVL function converts a NULL value to a non-null value. The NVL2 value is similar to NVL except that it has the option to convert a NULL value to a non-null value or another value if the argument is not null. The syntax of NVL is as follows:

```
NVL(<input>,<value>)
```

where the "<input>" parameter is, typically, a table column name and "*<value>*" is the value to substitute if that instance of the column value is NULL. Note that the data type of "<value>" must agree with the data type of the input parameter. If this is a problem, simply convert the "<input>" value to another data type using a conversion function compatible with the "<value>". For instance, the following generates the Oracle error message "ORA-01722: invalid number" when executed:

```
SELECT NVL(BidPrice,'Null BidPrice') FROM CustAgentList;
```

Instead, use the TO_CHAR function to convert BidPrice to a character string so it is compatible with the character datatype of the NVL substitution value, *Null BidPrice* as follows:

```
SELECT NVL(TO_CHAR(BidPrice),'Null BidPrice')FROM CustAgentList;
```

Another handy use of NVL is to supply a value in a numeric calculation when a column value can be NULL. When you add a value to a column containing NULL, the result is NULL. Therefore, NVL solves the problem of adding a salesperson's base pay plus any incentive amounts, whether or not the incentive column is NULL. A hypothetical SELECT such as this will display NULL regardless of the base pay if the Incentive column is NULL:

```
SELECT BasePay+Incentive FROM Employees;
```

The solution is to use the NVL function to substitute a zero whenever a NULL value appears for an employee's row. Doing so allows the two values to be summed without returning a NULL result. This SELECT solves the problem:

```
SELECT BasePay+NVL(Incentive,0) AS Compensation FROM Employees;
```

With the NVL2 function, Oracle displays one of two values that appears in the function—not the table column. Its form is:

```
NVL2(<input>,<value-if-not-null>,<value-if-null>)
```

where the second argument is returned if "<value>" is not NULL, or the third argument is returned if "<input>" is NULL. Unlike the NVL function, the data types of the second and third arguments *do not* need to agree with the "<input>" value.

The TRANSLATE Function The TRANSLATE function converts the occurrences of characters in one string with corresponding characters from another string. However, it replaces a single character at a time. The TRANSLATE function syntax is:

```
TRANSLATE (<string1>, <string-chars-to-replace>, <replacement-chars>)
```

where "<string1>" is the string whose characters Oracle examines and performs the replacement operation. Oracle uses the second argument to determine which individual source characters are to be replaced. Replacement characters are found in the third argument. The number of characters in each should be identical. A simple use of TRANSLATE is to encode a message using a (very insecure) character-for-character substitution reminiscent of a decoder ring used by kids to encrypt messages. Another handy use of TRANSLATE is in a WHERE clause to check the *format* of a column's values, but not its *content*. The following ensures that all employees' TaxID values, which correspond to their Social Security numbers, are in the proper form. The proper form is XXX-XX-XXXX, regardless of their actual values. The following TRANSLATE function highlights any TaxID numbers that don't correspond to the accepted format:

```
SELECT FirstName, LastName, TaxID AS "Bad Format"
FROM Agents
WHERE TRANSLATE(TaxID,'0123456789','XXXXXXXXXX') <> 'XXX-XX-XXXX';
```

In the preceding WHERE clause, Oracle examines the TaxID field and substitutes the letter *X* for each occurrence of a digit (there are ten digits and a matching list of ten Xs in the second argument string). That converts the output TaxID numbers (but not the database values) to a common form that you can compare to a reference string, "XXX-XX-XXXX." Any differences appear in the output of the SELECT. If all TaxID fields conform to the format, then the query returns no rows.

Try out these special functions for yourself. Prepare by launching SQL*Plus, logging into Oracle, and clearing the screen. Then, execute the steps below to test the special functions.

To experiment with various special functions:

1. Type and execute the following to display the unique values for SaleStatusID values in the Listings table. The DECODE translates the codes into meaningful terms:

```
SELECT DISTINCT DECODE(SaleStatusID,
  101,'For Sale',
  102,'Pending',
  103,'Sold',
  'UNKNOWN') AS "Status"
FROM Listings;
```

2. Type and execute this SQL statement to return either *Licensed* or *Something Else* for all possible LicenseStatusID values:

```
SELECT DISTINCT DECODE(LicenseStatusID,
   1001,'Licensed', 'Something Else') AS "License Status"
FROM Agents;
```

Oracle returns two rows, which indicates only that there are codes corresponding to Licensed and to any other code. Be sure to use DISTINCT to reduce the number of rows Oracle returns.

3. Type and execute this SQL statement to list a sample of the cell, work, and home phone numbers of customers. The WHERE clause artificially limits the number of returned rows.

```
SELECT
   NVL(HomePhone,'unknown') AS "Home Phone",
   NVL(CellPhone,'unknown') AS "Cell Phone",
   NVL(WorkPhone,'unknown') AS "Work Phone"
FROM Customers WHERE CustomerID < 25030;
```

Figure 5.25 shows the results of running these steps. Your output should match the figure.

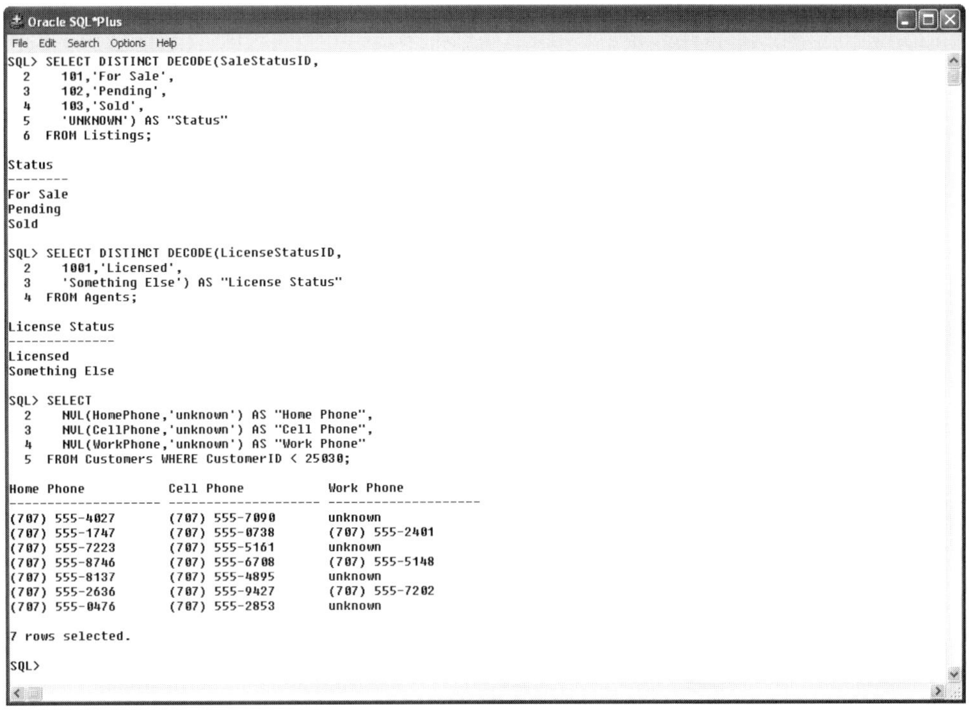

FIGURE 5.25 Using special functions.

4. Next, you will update a column in the Agents table so it "shows up" in the SELECT statement as being of the wrong form. Type and execute these statements:

   ```
   CLEAR SCREEN
   COMMIT;
   UPDATE Agents
   SET WorkPhone = TO_CHAR(SYSDATE, 'HH:MI:SS')
   WHERE Gender = 'F';
   ```

5. Now, use the TRANSLATE statement to highlight any WorkPhone numbers whose form does not follow the traditional form "(ddd) ddd-dddd" (where "d" stands for a digit). Execute the following:

   ```
   SELECT LastName, WorkPhone FROM Agents
   WHERE TRANSLATE(WorkPhone,'9876543210','aaaaaaaaaa') <> '(aaa) aaa-aaaa';
   ```

   Figure 5.26 shows the phone numbers that do not conform to the standard layout.

6. Finally, rescind the updates you made to help illustrate how TRANSLATE works by typing and executing:

   ```
   ROLLBACK;
   ```

7. Type **exit** and press **Enter** to log off Oracle and close SQL*Plus.

USING AGGREGATE FUNCTIONS

All the functions you have studied up to this point are single row functions. They return one row for each row processed. In this section you will learn about aggregate functions. *Aggregate functions* operate on a group of related rows and return a single row for each

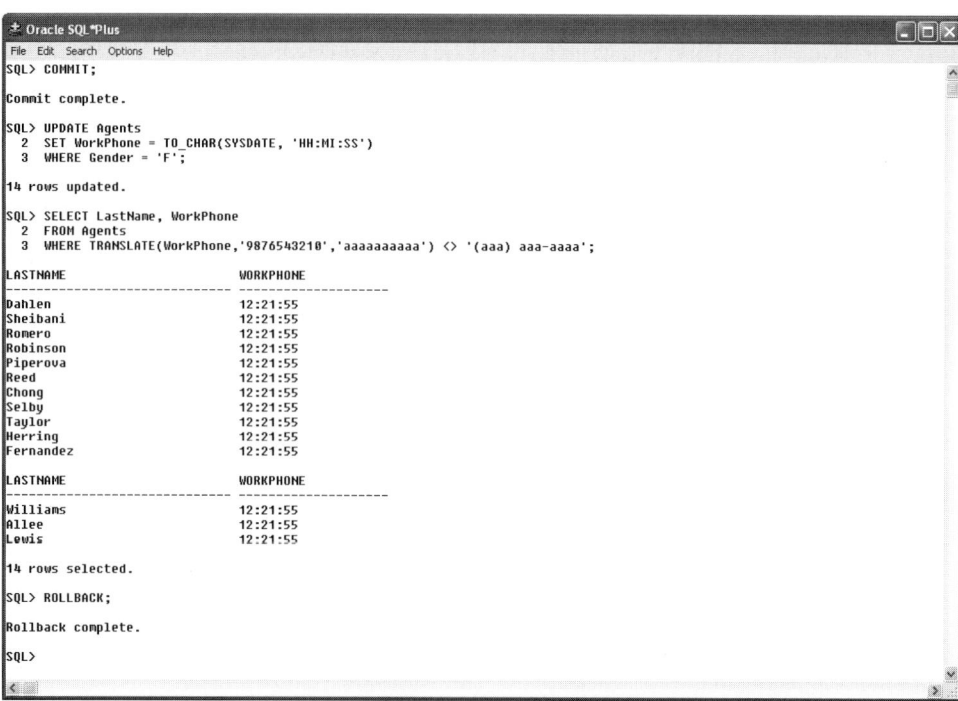

FIGURE 5.26 TRANSLATE locates nonconforming data formats.

group of rows. The functions are called "aggregate" because the word means to form by a collection of related units. Because they operate on groups, the aggregate functions are also called *group functions.* Examples of aggregate function usage abound. You might want to total home sales in a particular neighborhood or ZIP code. Or, you might want to compute the average commission received by male realtors versus female. Other uses include displaying the maximum and minimum sales prices for homes listed in Arcata.

The aggregate functions mostly return numeric results, and you usually include them to compute a statistic of some type. The group functions presented here are AVG, COUNT, MAX, MIN, and SUM. Related to the aggregate function is the GROUP BY clause of the SELECT statement that groups rows by one or more common characteristics. Additionally, the optional clause HAVING filters which groups are returned. Both GROUP BY and HAVING are presented in this chapter. Table 5.8 lists selected multiple row, or aggregate, functions.

The general syntax of an aggregate function is:

```
Aggregate-function-name([DISTINCT|ALL] expression)
```

The optional ALL need not appear because that is the default behavior of aggregate functions, and it instructs Oracle to include all values (except NULL). The DISTINCT clause uses only distinct, non-null values when Oracle evaluates the function.

There are a few special considerations you should know about the data that these aggregate functions analyze.

- Aggregate functions ignore NULL values because NULL, which is an absence of a value, is not applicable when computing any sort of meaningful statistic.

TABLE 5.8 Selected multiple-row functions.

Function	Description
AVG(<n>)	Returns the average of <n>.
COUNT(*)	Returns the number of rows retrieved by the query.
MAX(<n>)	Returns the maximum value of <n>.
MIN(<n>)	Returns the minimum value of <n>.
SUM(<n>)	Returns the sum of <n>.

- You can use the COUNT, MAX, and MIN functions with strings and date and time values, in addition to numbers.
- The DISTINCT keyword excludes duplicate values from the aggregate value calculation.

EXPLORING THE AVG, MAX, AND MIN FUNCTIONS

The AVG function calculates the average of the numeric values in the specified column. If you want to know a few simple statistics about the minimum asking prices, average asking prices, and maximum asking prices of all properties listed, execute the following query:

```
SELECT MIN(AskingPrice), AVG(AskingPrice), MAX(AskingPrice)
FROM Listings;
```

You can deliver a bit finer detail by adding a WHERE clause to limit the rows that are returned and subsequently evaluated. For example, you might want to know the same statistics as indicated above—but just for sales in which the end listing date is in the first quarter of 2007. The following selects a subset of the listings and performs the aggregate calculations of the subset:

```
SELECT MIN(AskingPrice), AVG(AskingPrice), MAX(AskingPrice)
FROM Listings
WHERE EndListDate BETWEEN '01-JAN-07' AND '31-MAR-07';
```

Expressions are allowed as arguments of aggregate functions. To compute the average profit from a hypothetical table called Products, issue a SELECT statement that averages the difference between each row's Price and Cost columns, and format it nicely with the containing TO_CHAR function:

```
SELECT TO_CHAR(AVG(Price-Cost),'$999.99) AS "Average Profit"
FROM Products;
```

By placing the AVG function inside the TO_CHAR function, Oracle computes the average over all rows in the Products column whose Price and Cost columns are not NULL, and then formats the result using the TO_CHAR's format model.

As you can guess, MIN computes the smallest value in a specified column or of the computed expression for all the involved rows. Similarly, MAX displays the maximum value of its column or expression for all involved rows. MIN and MAX functions can also have non-numeric data. You can compute the smallest or greatest date, time, or character string. The most recent date is considered the highest value, and the least, the lowest. For character strings, the letter *A* is lower than the letter *B* or *C*. Applying the MAX function to a character string will display the alphabetically highest title. For example, the following produces the highest street address of all the homes in the Properties table:

```
SELECT MAX(Address) FROM Properties;
```

and produces 991 Bayside Rd as the answer, because numbers are even higher than all alphabetic characters. Similarly, the following yields the customer last name with the lowest name—*Aaron:*

```
SELECT MIN(LastName) FROM Customers;
```

If you attempt to find the average of a character string, Oracle generates the error message "ORA-01722: invalid number."

The optional phrase DISTINCT ensures that only unique values are gathered and participate in the aggregate function calculation. For instance, suppose you want to know the average square feet in homes that are in the Properties table. You can compute it in two different ways:

```
SELECT AVG(SqFt) FROM Properties;                                    (1)
```

or

```
SELECT AVG(DISTINCT SqFt) FROM Properties;                           (2)
```

The result of query (1) above is 1784.57 (rounded), whereas the result of query (2) above is 1874.41—slightly higher. In the second case, homes with matching SqFt values were reduced to one for all matches. Then the average was computed. To understand this further, suppose the following list of values were in the Bedroom column: 2, 3, 2, 5, 3, 3. The AVG of those values yields (2+3+2+5+3+3)/6, or 3.00 The AVG (DISTINCT) version yields (2+3+5)/3.0, or 1.67.

INTRODUCING THE SUM AND COUNT FUNCTIONS

The SUM function totals the values stored in a column or an expression based on a column. Summations of date, time, or character fields don't make sense, so Oracle throws an error when you attempt to SUM anything except a number column or expression. The option DISTINCT instructs Oracle to eliminate duplicate numeric values before totaling them. The default ALL, which you can omit, tells Oracle to total all non-null numeric values in the column. Like any query, you can include a WHERE clause to control which rows are selected for the summation. You could total the potential commissions that the realtors might generate if they all each got 3 percent commission based on the BidPrice. The following specifies the time period of November 2006 as the target to be summed.

```
SELECT SUM(BidPrice * 0.03)
FROM CustAgentList
WHERE ContactDate BETWEEN '01-NOV-06' AND '30-NOV-06';
```

The query gathers BidPrice values between the specified dates, multiplies each, in turn, by 0.03, and sums the products. If you were to run the preceding query against the Redwood Realty database, the result would be 322069.77 (unformatted). Executing the same query *without* the WHERE clause yields a much larger total: 2119914.81 (unformatted).

The COUNT function is slightly different from the other aggregate functions. It can refer to any data type including numeric, character, or date/time. The function has three variations.

- **COUNT(*)** counts all the rows in the referenced table, including those with null values in various places.
- **COUNT(<expression>)** calculates the number of rows with non-null values in a specific column or expression.
- **COUNT(DISTINCT <expression>)** computes the number of distinct, non-null values in a column or expression.

The syntax of the COUNT function is

```
COUNT(* | [|DISTINCT|ALL] <expression>)
```

If you want to know how many records there are in a table, then

```
COUNT (*)
```

will do the trick. If you want to count the number of unique values in a column, then the COUNT function

```
COUNT(DISTINCT <column-name>)
```

is just what you need. Finally, if you simply want to count all non-null occurrences of a value in a column, including duplicate values, then

```
COUNT(<column-name>)
```

works just fine.

When you want to count the number of rows for a particular subset of rows, then include the WHERE clause to restrict the rows that Oracle retrieves before counting rows, values, or unique values. For instance, suppose you wanted to know how many rows there are in Redwood Realty's Properties table. You would write this simple statement that returns one row displaying the count:

```
SELECT COUNT(*) FROM Properties;
```

Alternatively, you can count the rows returned by using a constant in place of "*"—a constant such as 1 or 7 or 'wow' inside the parentheses:

```
SELECT COUNT(7) FROM Properties;
```

In any case, the result is the same: 2000. Oracle counts "*" or the number of 1s or the number of 7s for each row returned. That is, there are 2,000 homes in the Properties table. On the other hand, your broker might want to know how many Customers live in Orick. (She wants to send out a mailing to them, but she wants to consider the approximate postage cost first.) The following tallies the number of Orick residents in the Customers table:

```
SELECT COUNT(*)
FROM Properties
WHERE City = 'Orick';
```

Be careful when you use the keyword DISTINCT with the COUNT function. If you place DISTINCT immediately after the SELECT, such a query returns the count of rows in the table. On the other hand, placing DISTINCT following COUNT and inside the parentheses tells Oracle to count the unique column values—a vastly different result. What does that mean? Let's issue two queries and discuss the difference. Start SQL*Plus, log into Oracle, and clear the screen.

To use the COUNT function:

1. Type and execute the following.

   ```
   SELECT DISTINCT COUNT(City) AS "Unique Cities"
   FROM Customers;
   ```

   What answer did you get? The number, 2500, is the number of rows in the Customers table, *not* the number of distinct cities contained in it.

2. Modify the preceding query to the following and execute it.

   ```
   SELECT COUNT(DISTINCT City) AS "Unique Cities"
   FROM Customers;
   ```

What is the answer now? (If you are concerned about variations in capitalization in the database, then substitute *DISTINCT UPPER(City)* for *DISTINCT City* above.) Oracle returns the answer 9. There are nine distinct city names in the City column of the Customers table.

3. For how many customers in the Customers table is the WorkPhone column empty? Type and execute the following to answer that question:

```
SELECT COUNT(*)
FROM Customers
WHERE WorkPhone IS NULL;
```

Oracle returns the answer 1991. Of the 2,500 customers listed, 1,991 do not have work phone numbers listed—that value is missing.

4. How many properties exist in the Properties table from Arcata, CA? Type and execute the following to find out:

```
SELECT COUNT(*) FROM Properties WHERE LOWER(City) = 'arcata';
```

5. How many properties for McKinleyville, CA are there in the Properties table? Type and execute the following to generate the answer. (Because you might be concerned with the exact spelling of names, remember that you can use wild cards. Be careful to not use too short an abbreviation, else other cities may match the criteria and contribute to the count.)

```
SELECT COUNT(*) FROM Properties
WHERE LOWER(City) LIKE 'mck%';
```

Figure 5.27 displays the results of these five steps.

6. Leave SQL*Plus running for another exercise illustrating the COUNT function in a different role.

FIGURE 5.27 COUNT function examples.

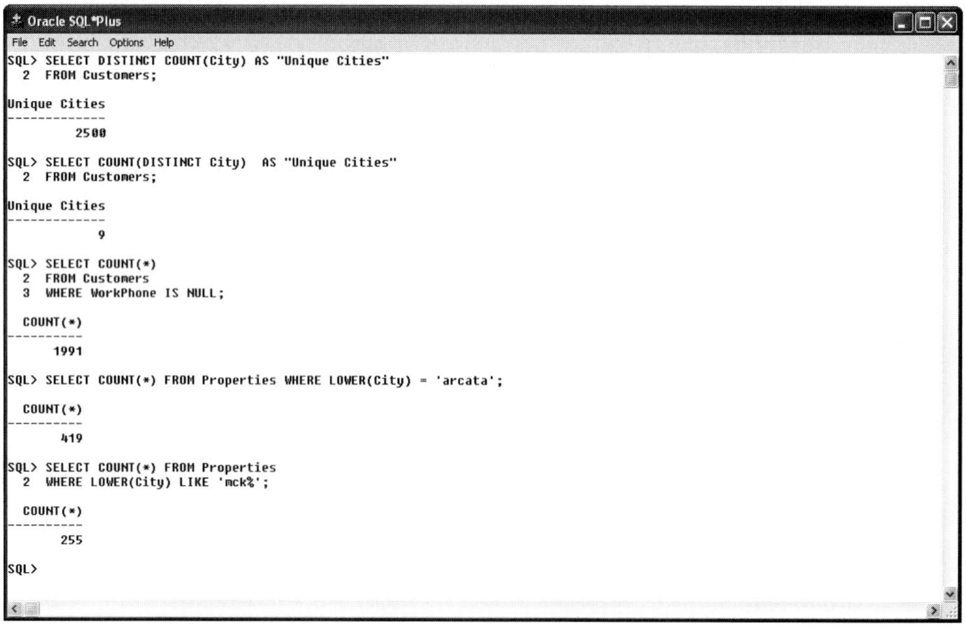

```
SQL> SELECT DISTINCT COUNT(City) AS "Unique Cities"
  2  FROM Customers;

Unique Cities
-------------
         2500

SQL> SELECT COUNT(DISTINCT City) AS "Unique Cities"
  2  FROM Customers;

Unique Cities
-------------
            9

SQL> SELECT COUNT(*)
  2  FROM Customers
  3  WHERE WorkPhone IS NULL;

  COUNT(*)
----------
      1991

SQL> SELECT COUNT(*) FROM Properties WHERE LOWER(City) = 'arcata';

  COUNT(*)
----------
       419

SQL> SELECT COUNT(*) FROM Properties
  2  WHERE LOWER(City) LIKE 'mck%';

  COUNT(*)
----------
       255

SQL>
```

Remember that we introduced the CASE structure in Chapter 4. Here, you will use CASE to count the number of properties for sale in various price ranges. You will produce a price range frequency analysis using the COUNT function and the CASE statement. Suppose you wanted to know the number of homes in various price ranges. You could issue a series of statements such as this one:

```
SELECT COUNT(1)
FROM Listings
WHERE AskingPrice BETWEEN 100001 and 200000;
```

Oracle returns 455, because there are that many homes in the price range $100,001 and $200,000, inclusive. However to get the whole picture, you would have to issue a series of SELECT statements, each with a different price range. Of course, you could use a substitution variable for the two ends of the price range, but that still involves running several queries. Is there a way to run a single query that delivers the frequency distribution you want? Yes. You can use the CASE statement in conjunction with the COUNT statement to partition the home AskingPrice column values and then tally each group. The GROUP BY phrase that you learn about in the next section will not help you, because the groups are very fine-grained—prices are different from one another by just a few dollars. The groups you want might be every $100,000 increment.

Here's the solution, which you will try out next: You can construct a CASE/WHEN/ELSE inside each COUNT function. The CASE produces a 1 when an AskingPrice is in the range, otherwise it produces a NULL value. When the statement executes, each COUNT tallies its selected range of values and produces the frequency distribution. The best way to understand it is to write and execute the query.

Redwood Realty wants a frequency distribution of AskingPrice values in $100,000 increments up to $600,000. The last "bucket" is every price above $600,000 and catches all the remaining, high-end prices.

To create a frequency distribution query using COUNT and the CASE statement:

1. With SQL*Plus running, type **CLEAR SCREEN,** press **Enter,** and then type and execute the following statement:

```
SELECT
 COUNT(CASE WHEN AskingPrice BETWEEN 0 AND 100000
      THEN 1 ELSE NULL END) "<= 100000"
FROM Listings;
```

Oracle displays the value 6 under the heading "<= 100000".

2. Modify the SELECT statement in Step 1 to this more complete version. Check it carefully, making sure none of the price ranges overlap, and then execute it. (You should use Notepad to create the SELECT statement and then copy it to SQL*Plus. Editing any mistakes is easier that way.) Your results should match Figure 5.28.

```
SELECT
 COUNT(CASE WHEN AskingPrice BETWEEN 0 AND 100000
      THEN 1 ELSE NULL END) "<= 100000",
 COUNT(CASE WHEN AskingPrice BETWEEN 100001 AND 200000
      THEN 1 ELSE NULL END) "<= 200000",
 COUNT(CASE WHEN AskingPrice BETWEEN 200001 AND 300000
      THEN 1 ELSE NULL END) "<= 300000",
 COUNT(CASE WHEN AskingPrice BETWEEN 300001 AND 400000
      THEN 1 ELSE NULL END) "<= 400000",
 COUNT(CASE WHEN AskingPrice BETWEEN 400001 AND 500000
      THEN 1 ELSE NULL END) "<= 500000",
```

```
       COUNT(CASE WHEN AskingPrice BETWEEN 500001 AND 600000
             THEN 1 ELSE NULL END) "<= 600000",
       COUNT(CASE WHEN AskingPrice > 600000
             THEN 1 ELSE NULL END) "> 700000"
FROM Listings;
```

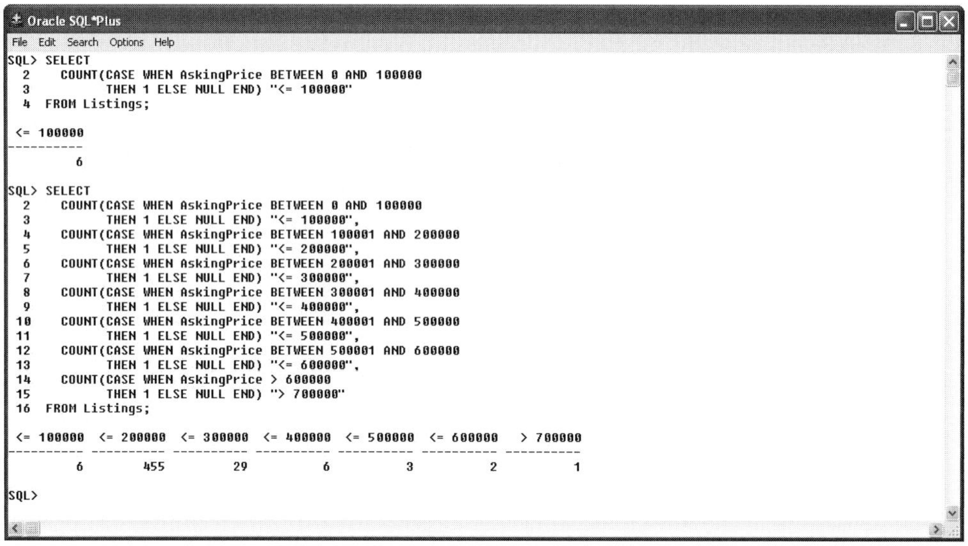

FIGURE 5.28 Creating a frequency distribution.

3. In SQL*Plus, type **exit** and press **Enter** to log out of Oracle and close the SQL*Plus client program.

GROUPING RESULTS

Using the GROUP BY optional phrase of the SELECT statement, you can generate summary statistics using aggregate functions based on row groupings. In the previous section, you created aggregate results based on *all* selected rows. Using the GROUP BY phrase lets you identify groups sharing a common characteristic and then generating statistics for each group. Oracle returns as many rows as there are identified groups.

To understand how handy the GROUP BY phrase is, consider how you might collect statistics about properties. Suppose you wanted to know the average square footage of properties in each city in the Properties table and the number of them. First, run a query that returns all the unique names of cities:

```
SELECT DISTINCT City FROM Properties ORDER BY City;
```

Oracle returns an ordered list of nine cities beginning with Arcata. Next, you might run nine queries similar to the following to determine two statistics you want—one time for each unique city:

```
SELECT COUNT(*), AVG(SqFt), 'Arcata' AS "City"
FROM Properties WHERE City = 'Arcata';
```

What a time-consuming process it is to run nine queries! Furthermore, even if you save all nine queries as a script file and run it again in the future, there is always the possibility that a row with a new city name will appear in the Properties table. There has to be a better way. There is, with the addition of the GROUP BY phrase to the SELECT statement.

To form multiple row outputs that display aggregate values for various groups, add one or more column names to the SELECT list. The column(s) you add identify the groups and tell Oracle to group aggregate results by first sorting the rows into groups by the group columns and then producing aggregate results for each group. The following shows the single SELECT statement that produces the statistics you sought with the nine SELECT statements above.

```
SELECT City, COUNT(*), AVG(SqFt)
FROM Properties
GROUP BY City;
```

The City column in the SELECT list is the grouping column. Oracle groups together rows by City and then produces the count and average values for each of the nine city groups and produces a nine-row output.

When you include a GROUP BY phrase, the SELECT statement has some new restrictions. You must specify only a column or combination of columns that are the basis for the groupings, a constant, or an aggregate function in the SELECT list. Furthermore, the grouping column(s) that you specify in the SELECT list must be included in the GROUP BY list. If there is more than one column, separate them with commas. For example, in the following SELECT statement,

```
SELECT City, Bedrooms, COUNT(*), AVG(SqFt)
FROM Properties
GROUP BY City, Bedrooms;
```

the groups are formed around combinations of City *and* Bedrooms values—every combination—because those two SELECT list elements are *not* aggregate functions. Therefore, the GROUP BY clause must contain both column names. The order in which you list each column in the GROUP BY clause determines the sort order of the groups: The first GROUP BY column is the primary sort order and subsequent groups are tiebreakers within alike groups. Of course, you can use the GROUP BY clause without mentioning any aggregate functions in the SELECT list. For example, the following lists all unique combinations of bedroom and bathroom values in the Properties table:

```
SELECT Bedrooms, Bathrooms FROM Properties
GROUP BY Bedrooms, Bathrooms;
```

If you run the preceding query, Oracle will produce 18 rows beginning with 2 bedrooms/1 bathroom through 6 bedrooms/4 bathrooms.

Filtering Groups with the HAVING Clause

The SELECT statement's optional HAVING clause restricts (filters) the groups of rows returned by the query. The HAVING clause appears after the GROUP BY clause and can appear only if there is a GROUP BY clause. While both the WHERE clause and the HAVING clause filter rows, the WHERE clause operates at the individual row level—*before* Oracle forms the groups and *before* groups are filtered by the HAVING clause. If you code a WHERE clause, then you eliminate selected rows from being considered for any grouping operation. In contrast, the HAVING clause only works after groups are formed, and only then does it determine which groups will appear in the output. You can think of HAVING as a WHERE clause for groups. The syntax of the HAVING clause and its relative position in a SELECT clause is:

```
SELECT ...
FROM ...
WHERE ...
```

```
GROUP BY ...
HAVING ...
ORDER BY ...;
```

The HAVING clause need not include any aggregate function from the SELECT list. For example, you could form groups around city names and count the number of entries in each group; but the HAVING clause could filter groups by another aggregate value. The next SELECT illustrates this:

```
SELECT City, COUNT(*)
FROM Properties
GROUP BY City
HAVING AVG(SqFt) > 1800;
```

The results display three city names and the count of their rows, but only for cities whose average square feet is greater than 1800—a statistic Oracle calculates invisibly and then uses to filter the groups. It's time to try out both the GROUP BY and HAVING clauses. Launch SQL*Plus, if needed, in preparation for steps that follow.

To group and filter aggregate information:

1. Clear the SQL*Plus screen and then type and execute the following to get a count of the Properties by city and sorted in descending order by count:

```
SELECT City, COUNT(*)
FROM Properties
GROUP BY City
ORDER BY 2 DESC;
```

2. Modify the preceding by adding a WHERE clause that eliminates properties with fewer than 5 bedrooms:

```
SELECT City, COUNT(*)
FROM Properties
WHERE Bedrooms >= 5
GROUP BY City
ORDER BY 2 DESC;
```

(See Figure 5.29.)

3. Modify the preceding query by removing the WHERE clause and adding a HAVING clause to display only cities with more than 300 customer rows. Delete the ORDER BY clause. Type and execute the following statements:

```
CLEAR SCREEN
SELECT City, COUNT(*)
FROM Properties
GROUP BY City
HAVING COUNT(*) > 300;
```

4. Finally, compute several aggregate values from the Properties table and group them by City. Using selected column formatting cleans up the display:

```
COLUMN AVG(SqFt)       FORMAT 9999
COLUMN AVG(YearBuilt) FORMAT 9999
SELECT City, MIN(SqFT), AVG(SqFt), MAX(SqFT), AVG(YearBuilt)
FROM Properties
GROUP BY CITY
ORDER BY City DESC;
```

Figure 5.30 shows the results of Steps 3 and 4. Your results should be comparable.

5. Type **CLEAR COLUMNS** and press **Enter** to clear residual column formatting.

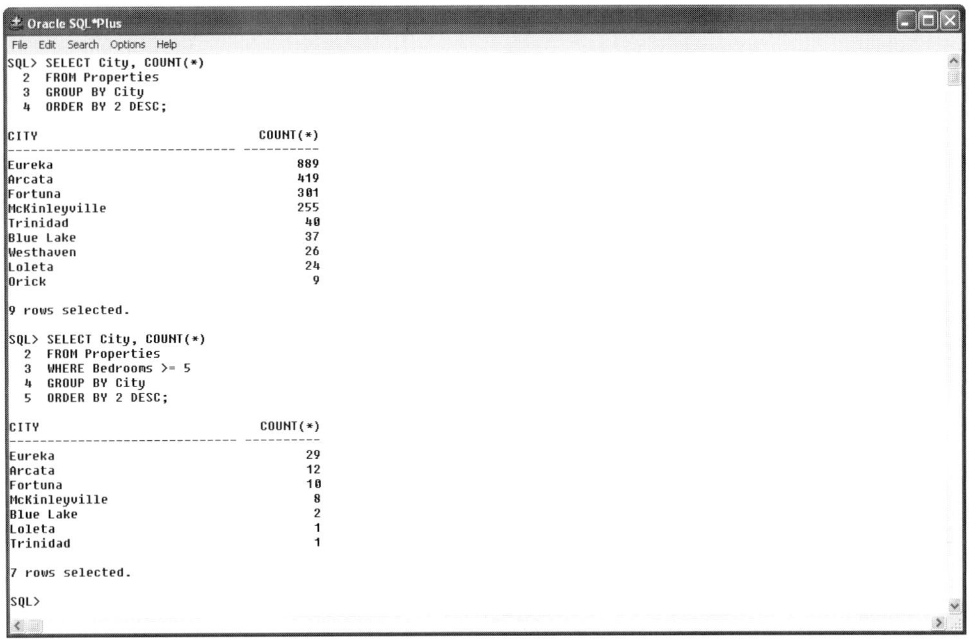

CHAPTER 5   Querying a Database   **249**

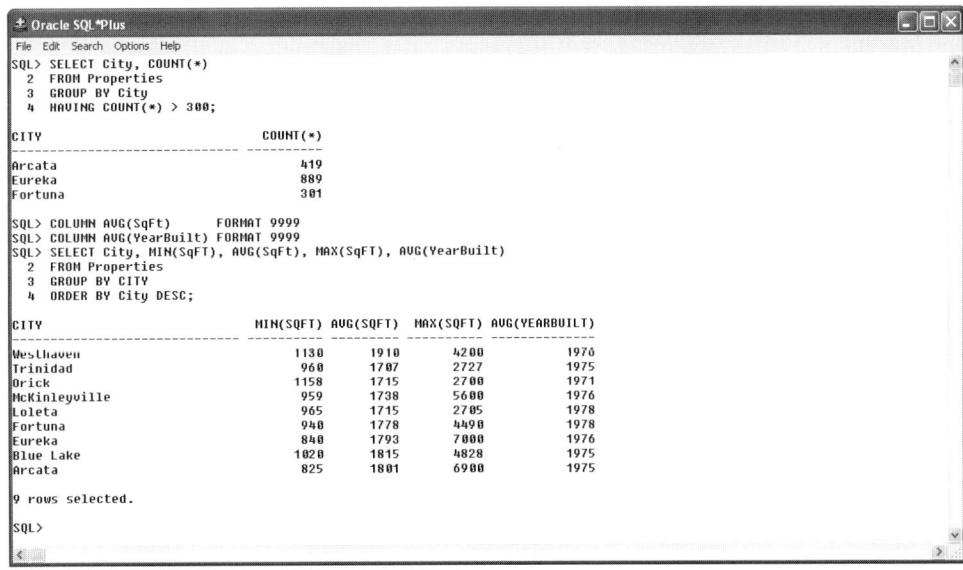

FIGURE 5.29   GROUP BY with a WHERE clause.

FIGURE 5.30   GROUP BY with a HAVING clause and another query.

6. If you want to take a break, now is a good time to exit SQL*Plus: Type **exit** and press **Enter.**

FORMATTING SQL*PLUS OUTPUT AND CREATING SIMPLE REPORTS

Throughout Chapter 5, you have used *i*SQL*Plus (a little) and SQL*Plus (a lot) to issue queries to display selected information from a table. You have used column

TABLE 5.9	Selected SQL*Plus commands.
@ pathname	Run a SQL Script (see START).
ACCEPT	Reads a line of input and stores it in a given substitution variable.
BREAK	Specifies where and how formatting will change.
BTITLE	Places and formats a title at the bottom of each page.
CLEAR	Clears the SQL*Plus screen, buffer, headings, etc.
COLUMN	Changes display characteristics of a column.
COMPUTE	Calculates and displays totals.
EXIT [n]	Commits logoff and exit (n = error code).
LINESIZE	Sets the maximum number of characters in a single output line.
PAGESIZE	Establishes the maximum number of lines on an output page. It includes the heading line, underline, and blank line at the end.
PROMPT	Sends the specified message or a blank line to the screen.
SET	Displays or changes SQL*Plus settings.
SHOW	Lists the value of a system variable.
SPOOL file	Stores query results in *file*.
SPOOL OFF	Turns off spooling.
SPOOL OUT	Sends results to printer.
TTITLE	Defines a page title.
UNDERLINE	Specifies the character used for the underline character. The default is hyphen (-).

aliases several times, issued CLEAR COLUMN, and even executed a few COLUMN commands. You have not used most of the SQL*Plus commands (as opposed to SQL commands or statements) to produce a nicely formatted report. In fact, SQL*Plus contains a large number of commands to create report headings and footings, suppress the display of duplicate information, format columns of character strings and numbers, and perform calculations. Collectively, these features are often called **report formatting** features. Although there are a large number of report formatting statements, we will present the most important ones here, in Table 5.9. Even though SQL*Plus provides a number of commands that help you create simple reports, nothing rivals Oracle Reports when you have more complex reporting needs (see Chapter 10).

Although you will learn how to use several of the SQL*Plus commands listed in Table 5.9 interactively, by issuing individual commands at the SQL*Plus prompt, reports look best when you create a complete script file and run the script file to a spool file. That way, the individual SQL*Plus prompts do not appear in the report—only the results. After experimenting with various SQL*Plus formatting commands, you will build a report by entering all the page, line, and column formatting commands first. Those code lines are followed by the query that delivers the payload—the rows from one or more tables. First, let's look at setting up several crucial SQL*Plus environment variables.

Setting SQL*Plus Environment Variables

SQL*Plus has several environment variables that you can set to various values. An **environment variable,** also known as a SQL*Plus system variable, is an internal value that SQL*Plus uses to determine how various elements appear when they are displayed. One of the environment variables, for example, is the SQL*Plus prompt. By setting the SQLPROMPT environmental variable to a different character string, you can change its default from "SQL>" to something else. For example, you can change the prompt to "Oracle" by issuing the statement:

```
SET SQLPROMPT Oracle>
```

Other more important environment variables include UNDERLINE, which indicates the character that appears below column headings (usually a hyphen) in output displays. Others shown in Table 5.9 include LINESIZE and PAGESIZE. Of course, you can write any SQL*Plus environment variable in uppercase, lowercase, or any mixture, but we choose to show them in uppercase to distinguish them from database object names. You can list all the SQL*Plus environment variables by launching SQL*Plus and typing:

```
SHOW ALL
```

SHOW ALL displays an alphabetical list of variable names and their current settings. For example, the default setting of the LINESIZE variable is 80 (80 characters per output line maximum); the usual setting for PAGESIZE is 14.

When you create reports, they are usually created by spooling the output to a spool file. Therefore, the value of the SPOOL environment variable is changed to ON. You usually change the value of the environment variable FEEDBACK to OFF so that a response such as "29 rows selected." does not appear in (and clutter) the report you produce. You will learn about setting and using the other environment variables in this section, including BTITLE, COLUMN, TTITLE, and so on. Perhaps the most important point to remember about environment variables is that they maintain their default values or the values you explicitly set for the life of your SQL*Plus session. Not until you log off the session does SQL*Plus revert to its default SQL*Plus environment variables, which are stored in a special file. Therefore, when you run several reports in a row, remember that each report should establish anew the environment variables it needs independently of other script files. That is, each report script file should begin with a series of SQL*Plus statements setting the variables upon which it depends.

FORMATTING COLUMNS

The SQL*Plus COLUMN command establishes the column heading and the format of the data appearing under it. If you forget the syntax and settings available, simply type HELP COLUMN at the SQL*Plus prompt to display a list of keywords that COLUMN allows. The general syntax is:

```
COLUMN [column-name|column-alias] [options]
```

Column-name or column-alias identifies the column or alias from the SELECT query to which this particular COLUMN setting applies. If a SELECT statement provides an alias for a column or expression in the SELECT list, then you must use the alias rather than the column name. The *options* include CLEAR, which erases the setting for the named column, FORMAT, which provides explicit character or number formatting, and ON or OFF, which turn on or suppress any column settings. Other options include WRAPPED, WORD WRAPPED, JUSTIFY, and NULL. The following COLUMN command specifies formatting for the FirstName column of the Agents table:

```
COLUMN LastName FORMAT A15 HEADING "Last Name"
```

Whenever a SELECT statement displays the LastName column value, it appears in a column that is 15 characters wide and has the column heading *Last Name*. The following specifies a format for the AskingPrice column of the Listings table:

```
COLUMN AskingPrice FORMAT $9,999,999 HEADING "Asking|Price"
```

In this COLUMN command, the AskingPrice column values appear with leading dollar signs, internal commas where needed, and a two-row heading *Asking* followed by *Price* on the next line. If you want to temporarily turn off formatting for the AskingPrice column, then issue:

```
COLUMN AskingPrice OFF
```

Reinstate it by issuing:

```
COLUMN AskingPrice ON
```

If you want a display of a column's formatting, then issue:

```
COLUMN <column-name>
```

Permanently delete a column's formatting by issuing:

```
COLUMN <column-name> CLEAR
```

Let's try out the column formatting commands next. First, launch SQL*Plus and log into Oracle.

To establish column formats:

1. Open Notepad, save the new file as <yourname>Ch05Report1.sql, and then type the following SQL*Plus lines. Copy and paste the lines to SQL*Plus and press **Enter** on the last line to execute it:

```
CLEAR SCREEN
SET FEEDBACK OFF
CLEAR COLUMNS
SET LINESIZE 60
SET PAGESIZE 40
SET UNDERLINE =
COLUMN Address       FORMAT A25       HEADING "Address" TRUNCATED
COLUMN City          FORMAT A10       HEADING "City"
COLUMN SqFt          FORMAT 9,999     HEADING "Square|Feet"
COLUMN YearBuilt     FORMAT 9999      HEADING "Year|Built"
```

The first six lines set SQL*Plus environment variable to clear the screen, clear any residual column formats sitting around, set line sizes, page lengths, and the new underline character, and suppress display of the number of rows selected by any subsequent SELECT statements.

2. Next, display selected columns from the Properties table—columns whose formats have been set in Step 1. Type the following in your Notepad file, copy and paste this piece to SQL*Plus, and execute it:

```
SELECT Address, City, Sqft, YearBuilt
FROM Properties
WHERE City = 'Loleta'
ORDER BY 2,4 DESC;
```

You may have to scroll your display to see the rows returned, but your results should match those in Figure 5.31.

3. Display the column settings for the Address column by executing:

```
COLUMN Address
```

SQL*Plus displays four lines of the Address column's formatting characteristics.

4. Reset all the environment variables to their defaults, just for practice, and clear the column formats by typing the following in Notepad and then copying them to SQL*Plus and executing them.

```
CLEAR COLUMNS
SET LINESIZE 80
SET PAGESIZE 14
SET UNDERLINE '-'
SET FEEDBACK ON
```

```
Oracle SQL*Plus
File Edit Search Options Help
SQL>SET FEEDBACK OFF
SQL>CLEAR COLUMNS
columns cleared
SQL>SET LINESIZE 60
SQL>SET PAGESIZE 40
SQL>SET UNDERLINE =
SQL>COLUMN Address   FORMAT A25    HEADING "Address" TRUNCATED
SQL>COLUMN City      FORMAT A10    HEADING "City"
SQL>COLUMN SqFt      FORMAT 9,999  HEADING "Square|Feet"
SQL>COLUMN YearBuilt FORMAT 9999   HEADING "Year|Built"
SQL>SELECT Address, City, Sqft, YearBuilt
  2  FROM Properties
  3  WHERE City = 'Loleta'
  4  ORDER BY 2,4 DESC;

                                   Square  Year
Address                   City       Feet Built
========================= ========== ===== =====
676 Scenic Dr             Loleta     1,349  1991
552 Pershing              Loleta     2,060  1991
632 Pershing              Loleta     2,552  1989
794 Eel River Rd          Loleta     1,900  1987
229 Church                Loleta     1,764  1987
3840 Tompkins Hill Rd     Loleta     1,912  1985
508 Echo Ln               Loleta     2,705  1985
460 Singley Hill Rd       Loleta       965  1983
281 Table Bluff Rd        Loleta     1,857  1982
51 Loleta Dr              Loleta     1,328  1981
6121 Tompkins Hill Rd     Loleta     1,877  1981
166 Hay Rake Ln           Loleta     1,695  1981
51 Clough Rd              Loleta     1,440  1978
48 Table Bluff Rd         Loleta     1,831  1978
356 Loleta Dr             Loleta     1,714  1977
4363 Tompkins Hill Rd     Loleta     1,695  1977
296 Spring                Loleta     1,640  1976
12 Table Bluff Rd         Loleta     1,640  1975
1107 Singley Hill Rd      Loleta     1,420  1975
321 Hookton Cemetary Rd   Loleta     1,450  1971
3146 Copenhagen Rd        Loleta     1,918  1968
700 Singley Hill Rd       Loleta     1,360  1966
119 Bay View Dr           Loleta     1,941  1957
849 Perrott Ave           Loleta     1,138  1955
SQL>
```

FIGURE 5.31 Formatting columns.

> **Tip:** Notice the apostrophes around the hyphen in the fourth line (prev. page). The hyphen is also a continuation character in SQL*Plus, so you must enclose it in single quotation marks so SQL*Plus does not misinterpret its meaning.

5. Type **exit** and press **Enter** to close your SQL*Plus session and log out of Oracle.
6. Switch back to Notepad, click **File,** and click **Save** to save the latest modifications. Close Notepad.

Because you exited SQL*Plus, SQL*Plus will reset all the environment variables to their default values the next time you launch SQL*Plus. Executing the statements in Step 4 simply reminds you that it is a good idea to reset any variables you changed. That way, subsequent SQL statements on other tables with like-named columns won't be formatted unless you specifically want them to be.

SETTING PAGE AND REPORT HEADERS, FOOTERS, AND DIMENSIONS

Having defined the columns of your new report, Ch05Report1.sql, you can move on to providing headers and footers for it. The TTITLE and BTITLE SQL*Plus commands establish the lines that appear at the top and the bottom of the display, respectively. These heading/footing statements have the following form:

    TTITLE | BTITLE [options [text|variable]…] | [ON|OFF]

Similar to the COLUMN command, issuing:

    TTITLE OFF

temporarily suspends any TTITLE (or BTITLE) options set. Specifying ON makes those options active. Options include LEFT, CENTER, or RIGHT, which align text information in the way indicated. FORMAT applies a format model to data displayed. Its format model elements are the same as the COLUMN statement. The SKIP *n* option specifies the number of lines to skip following the title before displaying data. The text of the BTITLE or TTITLE command can be literal text or a SQL*Plus variable. You can incorporate the SQL*Plus variables SQL.LNO, SQL.PNO, and SQL.USER in either title. SQL.LNO holds the current line number of a report. SQL.PNO holds the current report page number, and SQL.USER holds the name of the logged user running the report. An example of the TTITLE statement with several options and text is:

```
TTITLE LEFT SQL.USER CENTER 'Properties Available' -
RIGHT 'Confidential' SKIP 3
```

The hyphen at the right end of the first line is a SQL*Plus continuation character (space followed by a hyphen). It is needed because the long TTITLE line continues to the second line. Without it, SQL*Plus interprets the second line as another command. The user's name appears left-aligned followed by a centered literal title. The string Confidential appears right-aligned on the same line. Finally, the statement SKIP 3 is similar to pressing **Enter** three times. The first SKIP causes printing to continue on the next line. Then SQL*Plus inserts two empty lines inserted below the title. You can suppress TTITLE (or BTITLE) by executing:

```
TTITLE OFF
```

You can reset either top or bottom title by specifying an empty string ('') following BTITLE or TTITLE:

```
TTITLE ''
```

The following BTITLE statement places the current page number, centered, on the bottom of each page (defined by the PAGESIZE environment variable):

```
BTITLE CENTER 'Page ' FORMAT 999 SQL.PNO
```

When enough lines appear to reach the value of PAGESIZE, SQL*Plus spills out the BTITLE according to the specifications (and then a new TTITLE, if required). In the preceding example, BTITLE indicates that the word "Page", followed by a blank and a three-digit page number, appear centered on the bottom of each page. SQL*Plus determines the center of a line by the value of the LINESIZE variable. If LINESIZE is 60, then the page number is centered at about column 30.

Let's modify your Ch05Report1.sql file to incorporate these new elements. Launch SQL*Plus, log into Oracle, and open the Notepad file <yourname>Ch05Report1.sql. Then, make modifications as follows:

To modify the report script file:

1. In Notepad, add the following three statements below the statement SET FEEDBACK OFF, in the third through fifth lines:

```
TTITLE LEFT 'Properties' CENTER 'Redwood Realty' -
  RIGHT 'Confidential' SKIP 2
BTITLE CENTER 'Page ' FORMAT 99 SQL.PNO
BREAK ON City SKIP PAGE
```

> **Tip:** The BREAK command above tells SQL*Plus to jump to a new page (spilling out a footer and header) whenever the City column changes. Of course, you want the query to produce output sorted on the BREAK column for this to work correctly.

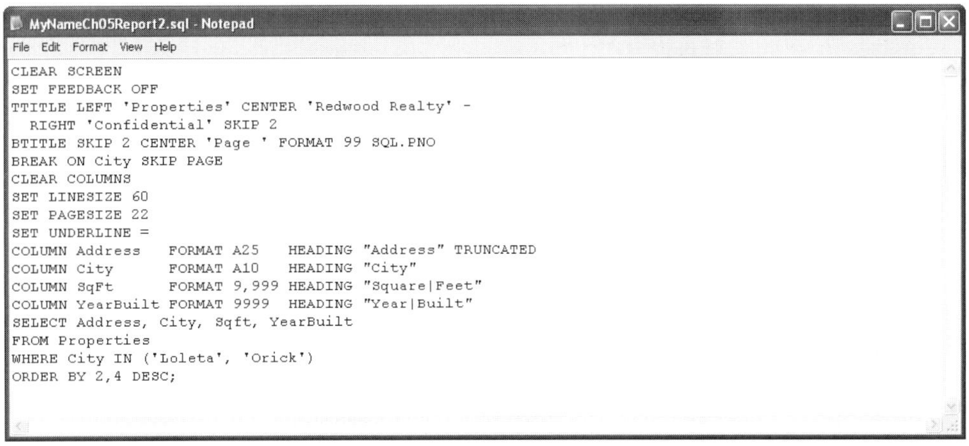

```
MyNameCh05Report2.sql - Notepad
File Edit Format View Help
CLEAR SCREEN
SET FEEDBACK OFF
TTITLE LEFT 'Properties' CENTER 'Redwood Realty' -
   RIGHT 'Confidential' SKIP 2
BTITLE SKIP 2 CENTER 'Page ' FORMAT 99 SQL.PNO
BREAK ON City SKIP PAGE
CLEAR COLUMNS
SET LINESIZE 60
SET PAGESIZE 22
SET UNDERLINE =
COLUMN Address    FORMAT A25   HEADING "Address" TRUNCATED
COLUMN City       FORMAT A10   HEADING "City"
COLUMN SqFt       FORMAT 9,999 HEADING "Square|Feet"
COLUMN YearBuilt  FORMAT 9999  HEADING "Year|Built"
SELECT Address, City, Sqft, YearBuilt
FROM Properties
WHERE City IN ('Loleta', 'Orick')
ORDER BY 2,4 DESC;
```

FIGURE 5.32 Modified report script file.

2. Edit the line containing PAGESIZE to this:

   `PAGESIZE 22`

3. Modify the SELECT query WHERE clause to include the city of Orick. The modified WHERE clause is:

   `WHERE City IN ('Loleta', 'Orick')`

4. Remove all the lines that follow the SELECT query—lines beginning with "Column Address" through "SET FEEDBACK ON.":

   Your modified script file should match Figure 5.32.

5. Save the modified script file under the new name <yourname>Ch05Report2.sql.

6. Copy and paste the entire, modified script file to SQL*Plus, press **Enter** to execute the last line, if necessary, and review the results. Figure 5.33 shows the last two pages of the report. Notice that no city name repeats, and a new page appears for Orick.

7. Type **exit** and press **Enter** to log off Oracle and close SQL*Plus. This also resets, to their original values, the environment variables you set in recent exercises.

CREATING HTML REPORTS WITH SQL*PLUS

SQL*Plus allows you to share your reports on the Web by providing a special command that produces HTML-formatted results that you can post on the Web. You produce a Web-formatted report by spooling it to a file, and then immediately display it in your Web browser or upload it to a Web site. It is best to produce HTML reports by executing a script file. If you produce a report interactively, SQL*Plus produces the SELECT statement on output and the report results. The SQL*Plus command that does the HTML formatting is:

`SET MARKUP HTML ON SPOOL ON`

which you embed in the script file or execute interactively. The MARKUP command merely specifies that SQL*Plus output be HTML-encoded. The SPOOL ON portion of the command causes SQL*Plus to write <html>, <head>, and <body> HTML tags, before writing data produced by the query, to the spool file. The MARKUP command

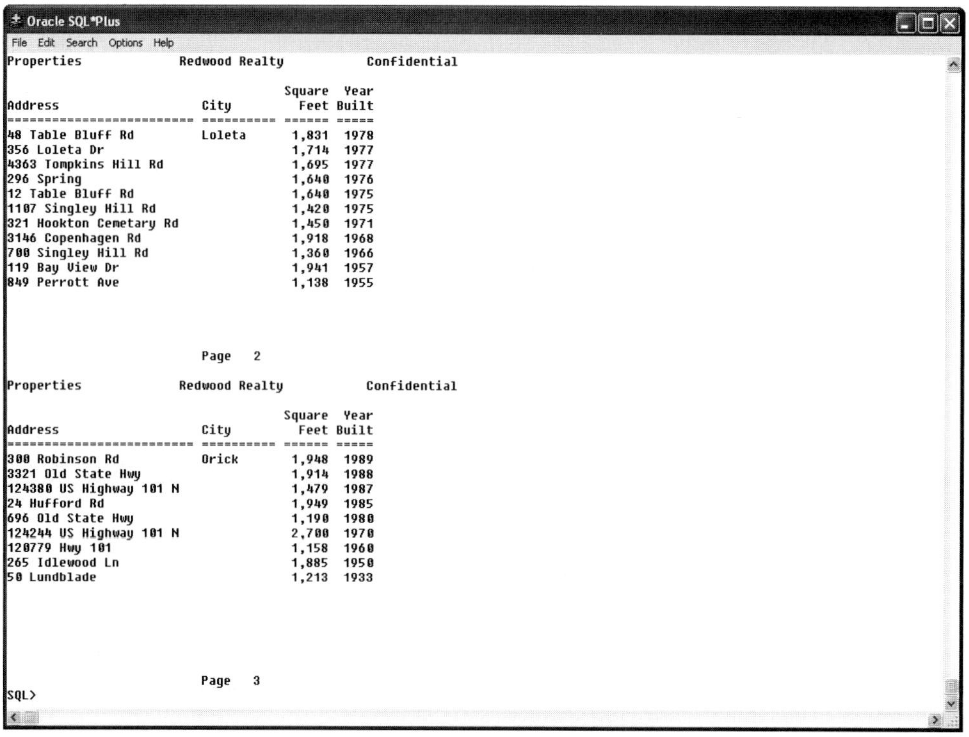

FIGURE 5.33 Modified report results.

does not actually write HTML to a spool file—only the SPOOL <filename> causes that to happen.

After closing the spool file with the SQL*Plus SPOOL OFF command, you tell SQL*Plus to cease producing HTML code by executing:

```
SET MARKUP HTML OFF
```

If you forget to turn off HTML code production, you will see a series of HTML table commands (<td>, <tr>, and so on) on the screen instead of the usual SQL*Plus output. You can inject your own HTML code to make the Web reports even more interesting, but you need not. SQL*Plus' MARKUP command produces attractive Web results.

Before producing results yourself, be aware of a couple of things. First, Web pages are infinitely long displays, so you will want to set the SQL*Plus PAGESIZE variable to a value that is longer than the likely number of output rows. Headings in the middle of a Web page aren't attractive. Second, you should set the FEEDBACK variable to OFF, because you don't want a message such as "354 rows selected" to appear on the Web report along with the returned rows. Finally, remember to reset any SQL*Plus variables back to their original values. That way there will be no surprises when you continue using SQL*Plus interactively.

Next, you will write a short SQL*Plus script file, save it, and then execute it to produce a Web page. The script file will list the Customers from any city that the user selects. Several columns from the Customers table will populate a Web-formatted file you produce called *CustomerReport.html*. Finally, you will launch your Web browser to view the Web page that you generated.

To create and save a script file to produce an HTML report:

1. Open Notepad and immediately save the empty files as <yourname>Ch05WebReport.sql in any folder of your choice, substituting your last name for "<yourname>".

2. In Notepad, type the following to display available city names, set a few environment variables, and prompt the user for the name of the city to use as selection criteria in the Web report. (Be sure to insert a space following the colon in the ACCEPT line.)

```
SET FEEDBACK OFF
CLEAR SCREEN
SELECT DISTINCT City "City Names" FROM Customers ORDER BY City;
PROMPT
ACCEPT cityname PROMPT 'List Customer rows for city: '
```

3. Add the following lines below what you have typed so far:

```
SET TERMOUT OFFSET VERIFY OFF
SET PAGESIZE 50000
SET MARKUP HTML ON SPOOL ON
SPOOL C:\CustomerReport.html
```

4. Immediately after the last line above, write the SELECT statement that will retrieve the requested rows, filtering then with a substitution variable, "&cityname":

```
SELECT FirstName, LastName, Address, City,
  HomePhone, CellPhone, WorkPhone
FROM Customers
WHERE UPPER(City) = UPPER('&cityname')
ORDER BY 2,1;
```

5. Immediately below the last line above, type the following lines to turn off spooling, and reset SQL*Plus environment variables to their default values:

```
SPOOL OFF
REM Reset SQL*Plus variables
SET MARKUP HTML OFF
SET PAGESIZE 14
SET VERIFY ON
SET FEEDBACK ON
SET TERMOUT ON
```

6. Save the completed script file by clicking **File** on the menu bar and pressing **Save.**
7. Click **File,** and then click **Exit** to exit Notepad.

Next, run the script file and then load the Web page to review the results.

To run the script file in SQL*Plus and then review the results in a Web browser:

1. Launch SQL*Plus, log into Oracle, and then execute the script file you produced above by typing and executing the statement below. Be sure to substitute the full path to your script file for "<path>" and your last name for "<yourname>":

```
START <path><yourname>Ch05WebReport
```

2. Type **orick** and press **Enter** to respond to the prompt.
   Figure 5.34 shows the displayed cities, the prompt, and the city name entered.
3. Type **exit** and press **Enter** to exit SQL*Plus.

FIGURE 5.34 City names and prompt displayed by the script file.

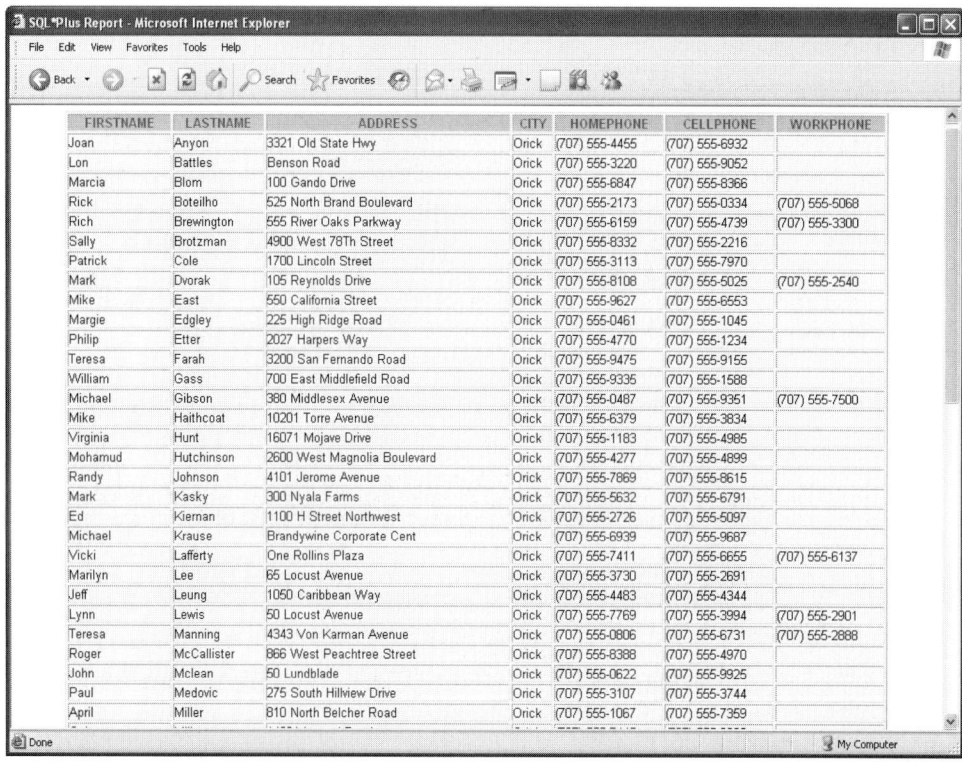

FIGURE 5.35 Web page produced by the script file.

4. Using your favorite Web browser, locate the Web page *CustomerReport.html* and open it to review the Web-formatted list of customers living in Orick. Figure 5.35 shows the top portion of the page.
5. Close your Web browser when you are finished examining the report. You can delete the file *CustomerReport.html* if you want.

Summary

The SQL SELECT statement queries tables and returns rows. Specify the table(s) from which the rows are retrieved and optional clauses. The search criteria in the optional clause WHERE determines which rows appear in the result. GROUP BY forms groups from retrieved rows; the HAVING clause filters groups, and the ORDER BY clause sorts the rows before returning them to the user. Use the DISTINCT keyword preceding the select list to produce unique rows.

WHERE conditions consist of comparison operators, column names, expressions, and literals whose combination is a logical expression. When the logical expression is true, the table row is returned in the result set; otherwise, it is not. SQL provides several SQL operators including BETWEEN . . . AND, IN, IS NULL, and LIKE that allow you to search value ranges and discrete lists of values, determine if a value is null, or use wildcard characters, respectively.

The optional ORDER BY clause, which is the last phrase of a SELECT statement, sorts rows on one or more values or expressions separated by commas—in ascending or descending order for each value or expression. ORDER BY can reference columns or expressions that are not in the select list. When used in conjunction with an inline view, the ORDER BY clause provides a convenient way to produce top-N analysis—the top or bottom N rows in an ordered set.

SQL supports a full complement of mathematical operators to perform calculations in the select list or support expressions in the WHERE clause. They include addition, subtraction, multiplication, and division. SQL functions provide many built-in programs to perform calculations on characters, numeric values, and dates. SQL conversion functions convert data from one data type to another. Special functions such as NVL provide support for determining when columns contain NULL values, and return other values when they do.

Aggregate functions allow you to calculate summary information on groups of rows including summation and counting values from grouped rows, and calculation of average, minimum, and maximum values.

Finally, SQL*Plus supports production of HTML output suitable for review by a Web browser. Issuing the MARKUP HTML ON SPOOL ON command initiates production of HTML output. Setting several SQL*Plus environment variables appropriately and using the SPOOL command produces attractively formatted HTML code that browsers can display. The result of a query is a formatted table with evenly spaced columns and a standard color background and text.

Key Terms

- Aggregate function
- ASC/DESC
- Asterisk (*)
- BETWEEN operator
- Character function
- Column alias
- Concatenation
- Conversion function
- Date function
- Environment variable
- Format model
- Function
- GROUP BY clause
- Group function
- HAVING clause
- IN operator
- Inline view
- LIKE operator
- Numeric function
- Operator precedence
- ORDER BY clause
- Regular expression functions
- Report formatting command
- Search condition
- Select list
- Single row function
- Table list
- WHERE clause
- Wildcard character

Review

TRUE/FALSE

1. A SELECT statement must contain a FROM clause. All other SELECT statement clauses are optional.
2. If you wanted to return Agent rows in which the birthdays were any date within a specified year, you would probably use the IN operator in the WHERE clause to restrict the retrieved rows.
3. You must use a column alias when you want to sort rows based on an expression. In other words, you cannot use expressions in an ORDER BY clause.
4. Aggregate functions such as AVG ignore null values in their calculations. For example, an average of five values, one of which is NULL, would equal the sum of the four non-null numbers divided by four.
5. At least one of the select list members must be a table column name or nonaggregate function, because you cannot write a SELECT statement whose select list is exclusively aggregate functions.

Fill in

1. The _____ clause provides row filtering for SELECT statements before groups are formed.
2. The character % in an expression such as **LIKE '%month'** is called a(n) _____ character.
3. Determining the order to evaluate subexpressions in an expression is based on operator _____.
4. You write a(n) _____ _____ (two words) following *FROM* to help generate a list of the top ten home prices.
5. To compute someone's age given a column containing birth date, you would compute elapsed days with the help of the _____ function and do some additional math.

Multiple Choice

1. If a select list is *City, MAX(BidPrice)*, then the SELECT statement must also contain what phrase?
   a. ORDER BY
   b. DISTINCT
   c. GROUP BY
   d. HAVING
2. You add what keyword to display unique city names in the SELECT statement *SELECT City FROM Properties;*?
   a. GROUP BY
   b. UNIQUE
   c. NVL
   d. DISTINCT
3. Combining two character strings together in a select list such as *SELECT FirstName|| LastName FROM Agents;* is called what?
   a. aggregation
   b. concatenation
   c. conversion
   d. formatting
4. In the TO_DATE function, you use a _____ _____ to indicate the exact layout of the date?
   a. syntax string
   b. format model
   c. date constant
   d. system variable
5. What SQL*Plus environment variable can you set to suppress messages such as *15 rows selected*, which appears following execution of a SELECT statement?
   a. SQLPROMPT
   b. PAGESIZE
   c. LINESIZE
   d. FEEDBACK

Hands-on Exercises

1. Extending the Chapter Case

Robert Stirling has asked you to query several Redwood Realty database tables and produce some ad hoc reports. He is excited about the possibility of being able to run the reports whenever he needs information about Redwood Realty's business. For that reason, he asks you to create SQL script files so that Robert can simply issue the command *START <scriptfilename>* to run any given query. Some of the queries will produce data files, others will simply produce on-screen results only, and yet another one will result in an HTML formatted file that Stirling can open in his browser. You have talked to Robert and he has discussed his information and reporting needs.

1. Begin by launching SQL*Plus and logging in with your username and password. Next, launch Notepad (or other suitable text processor) so you can capture and save any code you generate as files.
2. First, compute minimum, average, maximum AskingPrice values found the Listings table, and count the number of listings. Group the results by AgentID. Type the following into Notepad,

and save the Notepad file as <yourname>Ch05Prob1Script1.sql. Then copy and paste the Notepad text into SQL*Plus and execute it. Type your full name in place of "<Your full name here>."

```
REM <Your full name here>
CLEAR COLUMNS
SET PAGESIZE 35
SET FEEDBACK OFF
CLEAR SCREEN
COLUMN Stat1 FORMAT $9,999,999 HEADING
  'Minimum'
COLUMN Stat2 FORMAT $9,999,999 HEADING
  'Average'
COLUMN Stat3 FORMAT $9,999,999 HEADING
  'Maximum'
COLUMN Stat4 FORMAT 999 HEADING 'Count'
SELECT ListingAgentID "Agent ID",
   MIN(AskingPrice) AS "Stat1",
   AVG(AskingPrice) AS "Stat2",
   MAX(AskingPrice) AS "Stat3",
   COUNT(AskingPrice) AS "Stat4"
FROM Listings
GROUP BY ListingAgentID
HAVING COUNT(AskingPrice) > 18
ORDER BY "Stat4" DESC;
SET FEEDBACK ON
```

3. Switch back to Notepad, type the following, copy/paste just this new code into SQL*Plus and execute it. Be sure to substitute a path to the spool file for "<path>" in the sixth line, and substitute your last name in the same line for "<yourname>."

```
CLEAR COLUMNS
SET PAGESIZE 35
CLEAR SCREEN
COLUMN "Name" FORMAT A25 HEADING
   'Agent"s Name'
COLUMN "Age" FORMAT A10 HEADING
   'Age at|Hire Date'
SPOOL C:\<path>\<yourname>Ch05Prob1Part1.txt
SHOW USER
SELECT LastName||', '||FirstName AS "Name",
   LPAD(TO_CHAR((HireDate-BirthDate)/365.25,
   '99'),7) AS "Age"
FROM Agents
WHERE (HireDate-BirthDate)/365.25 > 30.00
ORDER BY 2 DESC;
SPOOL OFF
SET PAGESIZE 14
```

4. Locate the spool file <yourname>Ch05Prob1Part1.txt and print it.

5. Save the current Notepad file one last time. Open a new, empty Notepad file. Type the following code. Substitute a suitable path for "<path>" in the eighth line. That path defines the folder in which to store your HTML file. Save the entire file as <yourname>Ch05Prob1Part2.sql, substituting your last name for "<yourname>." Leave Notepad open.

```
SET TERMOUT OFF
SET FEEDBACK OFF
SET VERIFY OFF
SET ECHO OFF
TTITLE OFF
CLEAR COLUMNS
SET PAGESIZE 50000
SET MARKUP HTML ON SPOOL ON
SPOOL C:\<path>\Ch05Customers.html
SELECT FirstName, LastName, Address, City
FROM Customers
WHERE UPPER(City) = 'BLUE LAKE'
ORDER BY 2,1;
SPOOL OFF
SET MARKUP HTML OFF
SET PAGESIZE 14
SET ECHO ON
SET VERIFY ON
SET FEEDBACK ON
SET TERMOUT ON
```

6. Switch to SQL*Plus and type the following, substituting the path to your SQL script file for "<path>" and substituting your last name for "<yourname>," and press **Enter** to execute the script file.

    START
    C:\<path>\<yourname>Ch05Prob1Part2.sql

7. Exit SQL*Plus (type **exit** and press **Enter**), open the Web page (Ch05Customers.html) that you created in Step 5, print your Web page, and close your browser. Be sure to write your first and last names on the printed Web page so you can turn it in to your instructor, if asked.

8. Save the Notepad file, print the Notepad file, and close Notepad.

2. COFFEE MERCHANT

The DBA wants you to produce two reports from the Coffee Merchant tables. To get warmed up, you decide to produce a practice report that calculates the population density of each state in the United States from the States table. For the DBA, you will produce a report that lists the coffees in the inventory and the total value of each inventory item on hand, including teas. Finally, you'll write a script file that the DBA can run to display the inventory in a Web page. Before beginning, locate the file BuildCoffee.sql in the *CoffeeMerchant* folder of your data files. The script file builds the Coffee

Merchant database from scratch. Note the path to that file.

1. Launch SQL*Plus, log into Oracle, an type the following at the SQL prompt, substituting the actual path for "<path>" in the following line:

   ```
   START <path>\BuildCoffee
   ```

2. Open Notepad and type the following statements. Copy and paste them into SQL*Plus. Execute the statements in SQL*Plus. Save the Notepad file, in a folder of your choosing, as <yourname>Ch05Problem2Part1.sql. Substitute your last name for "<yourname>" and in the code below. Substitute a full path, including drive name, for "<path>" in the third line below.

   ```
   REM Calculate the population density of
   REM each state
   CLEAR SCREEN
   SPOOL
   <path>\<yourname>Ch05Problem2Report1.txt
   SHOW USER
   SET PAGESIZE 55
   CLEAR COLUMNS
   COLUMN StateID FORMAT A03
       HEADING 'ID'
   COLUMN StateName FORMAT A14
       HEADING 'State'
   COLUMN Population FORMAT 99,999,999
       HEADING 'Population'
   COLUMN LandArea FORMAT 999,999
       HEADING 'Land Area'
   COLUMN Density FORMAT 99,999
       HEADING 'Density'
   SELECT StateID, StateName, Population,
     LandArea, Population/LandArea AS Density
   FROM States
   WHERE UPPER(StateID) <> 'DC'
   ORDER BY Density DESC;
   SPOOL OFF
   ```

3. Type the following in Notepad, below the last line above. Copy and paste this new code to SQL*Plus and execute it. Observe that the column formatting persists, as you would like it to. The code displays the 15 states with the longest names. Make appropriate changes to the third line for "<path>" and "<yourname>".

   ```
   REM Display states with the 15 longest
   REM names
   CLEAR SCREEN
   SPOOL
   <path>\<yourname>Ch05Problem2Report2.txt
   SHOW USER
   SELECT StateName, "Length"
   FROM (SELECT StateName, LENGTH(StateName)
   AS "Length"
   FROM STATES
     WHERE UPPER(StateID) <> 'DC'
     ORDER BY "Length" DESC)
   WHERE ROWNUM < 16;
   SPOOL OFF
   CLEAR COLUMNS
   SET PAGESIZE 14
   ```

4. Save your Notepad file to preserve your work. Next, type the following in Notepad and then copy it to SQL*Plus. The code in this step displays all inventory products in order by coffee first and then tea. Column statements format the columns attractively. Again, make necessary changes to the third line to personalize the location and name of the spool file.

   ```
   REM List coffees in inventory and their
   total values
   CLEAR SCREEN
   SPOOL
   <path>\<yourname>Ch05Problem2Report3.txt
   SHOW USER
   COLUMN Name FORMAT A33
       HEADING 'Coffee Name'
   COLUMN OnHand FORMAT 99,999
       HEADING 'In Stock'
   COLUMN Price FORMAT $999.99
       HEADING 'Price'
   COLUMN TotValue FORMAT $999,999
       HEADING 'Total|Value'
   SELECT Name, OnHand, Price, Price*OnHand AS
   TotValue
   FROM Inventory
   WHERE UPPER(ItemType)='C' AND OnHand > 0
   ORDER BY 4 DESC;
   SPOOL OFF
   ```

5. Save the Notepad file once again, and then open a new one. Name it <yourname>Ch05Problem2Part2.sql. Type the following into the Notepad file. In the seventh line, change the "<path>" and "<yourname>" as needed to personalize them. When you are done typing the following, save the Notepad file and close Notepad.

   ```
   SET TERMOUT OFF
   SET FEEDBACK OFF
   SET ECHO OFF
   CLEAR COLUMNS
   SET PAGESIZE 234
   SET MARKUP HTML ON SPOOL ON
   SPOOL
   <path>\<yourname>Ch05Problem2Part2WebPage.html
   SELECT Name, Price, OnHand, Description,
       CASE WHEN ItemType='C' THEN 'Coffee'
       ELSE 'Tea' END AS "Type"
   FROM Inventory
   ORDER BY "Type", Name;
   ```

```
SPOOL OFF
SET MARKUP HTML OFF
SET PAGESIZE 14
SET ECHO ON
SET FEEDBACK ON
SET TERMOUT ON
```

6. Switch to SQL*Plus and execute the script file you created above. Type the following, substituting the path for "<path>" and your name for "<yourname>."

   ```
   START
   <path>\<yourname>Ch05Problem2Part2.sql
   ```

7. Load the Web page you created in Step 6 into your browser and print it.

8. Print the other spool files you created and close any open programs including SQL*Plus.

3. ROWING VENTURES

Produce reports from the Rowing Ventures database which contains information about crew races involving both eight-person shells and four-person shells. First, you must populate the database by locating the data file BuildRowing.sql found in the *RowingVentures* folder of your Chapter 5 data files. Make a note of the names of the Rowing Ventures tables displayed in SQL*Plus as the script file runs. When necessary, execute the DESCRIBE statement to reveal the columns defined for each table. Produce the following reports that you spool to an output file. Print your script file. Edit each spool file to contain your name at its top. Then, print the spool files.

- Create a report called <yourname>Ch05Problem3Report1.txt that lists the Nation, OrganizationName, Address, City, and State columns (in that order) from the Organization table. Use the BREAK command to eliminate duplicate values in the Nation column, and sort the results by nation, then state within nation. Format all columns using the COLUMN command to ensure that the column headings are initial uppercase (for example, "Organization ID" or "Address") and that no column is longer than 15 characters. Allow a maximum of 25 lines in a SQL*Plus page. Suppress messages such as "10 rows selected." Issue the TTITLE statement to include a page title that displays your name in the left, "Organizations by Nation" in the center, and the page number on the right. Reset all environment variables to their original values following the SPOOL OFF command.

- Create a report called <yourname>Ch05Problem3Report2.txt that lists the contents of the Person table. Concatenate FirstName and LastName into one column. Display nicely formatted columns with column headings that are in title case (initial capital letters for each word). Make column widths as small as possible without truncating any values or column labels. (Find the actual largest size of values in each column with the expression MAX(LENGTH(<columnname>)) to determine column width.) Set up a title (TTITLE) with your name (left) and the name of the table (centered). Sort the output in ascending order by birth date. Display only rows for people born after 1963.

4. BROADCLOTH CLOTHING

First, you must populate the database by locating the data file BuildClothing.sql found in the *Broadcloth* folder of your Chapter 5 data files. Make a note of the names of the Broadcloth tables displayed in SQL*Plus as the script file runs. When necessary, execute the DESCRIBE statement to reveal the columns defined for tables you are asked to query. Produce a Web page from the Contact table. Print the script file that creates the Web page and print the first two pages of the Web page, itself. Second, run an ad hoc query to compute some statistics. Print the script file and the spool file it produces. Be sure to identify all files with your name. Here are details about the queries and their reports:

- Display all columns from the ProductionBatch table, but select only rows in which the StartDateTime value is any day in August, 2006. Sort the returned rows in descending production cost.

- Write an ad hoc query that displays the minimum, average, and maximum shipping cost and the count grouped by factory identification number and sorted in ascending order by maximum shipping cost. Display only groups whose average shipping cost is less than 200. All the required information is in the Shipment table. (Execute **DESCRIBE Shipment,** if needed.) Spool the results to a file so you can print it.

CHAPTER 6

CREATING MULTITABLE QUERIES AND VIEWS

Learning Objectives

In this chapter, you will learn how to:

- Create queries that join two or more tables.
- Use table aliases in multitable queries.
- Construct natural join, inner join, self join, and outer join queries.
- Use set operators UNION, MINUS, and INTERSECT.
- Create scalar, multiple row, and multicolumn subqueries.
- Write correlated subqueries.
- Create both single-table views and complex views.
- Update, insert, and delete data through views.
- List view definitions and drop views.

CREATING AND USING MULTITABLE QUERIES

One of the strengths of SQL is its ability to relate data that is stored in separate tables. This allows you to store information about real estate agents in one table, homes for sale in another, and names and addresses of owners in a third table. Using a properly constructed query, you can combine information when necessary. The queries you studied and created in Chapter 5 involved one table only. In this chapter, you learn how to write queries that reference several tables by joining them. A *join* is a temporary relationship you create between two tables. Often this relationship is formed by associating rows from one table with rows from another table based on columns in each that have the same value. Usually, the database system joins tables by matching the foreign key of one table with the primary key of another, though other join conditions are allowed—including inequalities. The condition that Oracle evaluates to determine if the two values meet the criteria for joining is called a *join condition*. The join condition is part of the FROM clause or (in older systems) is in the WHERE clause. Checking to see if rows from two tables satisfy the join condition occurs for each pair of rows and produces none, one, or several matching pairs. The most common type of join condition looks for matching values in two tables. This

Employees		
ID	Name	Div
1001	Bob	Mkt
1002	Dawn	Sales
1003	Betty	Sales
1006	Nancy	Mkt
1009	Fred	Sales

Sales		
PK2	Emp#	Amount
21	1002	$2,000
22	1002	$2,200
23	1003	$1,800
24	1003	$200
25	1009	$600
26	1009	$750
27	1009	$425

Result of joining the Employees and Sales tables:

```
         from Employees        from Sales
        ┌──────────────┐    ┌──────────────────┐
        1002  Dawn  Sales  21  1002  $2,000
        1002  Dawn  Sales  22  1002  $2,200
        1003  Betty Sales  23  1003  $1,800
        1003  Betty Sales  24  1003    $200
        1009  Fred  Sales  25  1009    $600
        1009  Fred  Sales  26  1009    $750
        1009  Fred  Sales  27  1009    $425
```

FIGURE 6.1 Joining two tables.

particular join condition is called an *equijoin,* because the database system is attempting to locate *equal* values in specified columns of both tables.

There are other ways to join tables in which the values do not have to match. These non-equijoin techniques also are described in detail in this chapter. Figure 6.1 shows a hypothetical example with primary key and foreign key values from two tables. The columns that Oracle scans for matches are the ID column in Employees and Emp# in Sales. Note that the Sales table is sorted by Emp# to make showing join lines convenient. Normally, the Emp# column, which is the foreign key pointing to the Employees, is *not* in any particular order.

Joining two or more tables is necessary because databases and the tables they hold have been normalized to some degree. That means that distinct but related information is housed in separate tables. For example, the Redwood Realty database contains eight tables of facts. One of those tables contains information about real estate agents. Another contains information about properties that are for sale. By joining those two tables on a common column, the real estate agent's identification number, you can determine which real estate agent has listed which properties. That information is not available in either table. But, by joining these tables of separate facts you can ascertain more information. Similarly, you can write a query that joins the Customers table to the CustAgentList table and the join the CustAgentList to the Listings table. By joining pairs of these three tables, you can extract information about customers who have properties for sale and the date when they listed them for sale. Heretofore, this information was not available with the single-table queries you created in Chapter 5. Assembling information from disparate but related tables is the way you generate useful information from relational databases.

JOINING TABLES HAVING MATCHING COLUMN VALUES

The FROM clause of the SELECT statement joining two or more tables specifies a join condition. An *inner join,* sometimes called a simple join, is a join of two or more tables that returns only rows that satisfy the join condition. One of the most popular join conditions, and one defined above, is equijoin. Recall that it is an inner join in which the values in a column of one table must *equal* the values in the column of another table. There is no requirement that the column names from each table be the same, though it is often convenient and provides a hint as to how tables are joined. A ***natural join*** is a special case of an equijoin. It occurs when the column *names* match in both tables. A natural join requires that all values in identically named columns match for the join to occur. Frequently, identically named columns are the primary key and foreign key that are defined for the two tables, but they need not be.

USING AN INNER JOIN

Using the American National Standards Institute (ANSI) SQL99 compliant form of the join, you specify in the FROM clause the table names and the column names whose values satisfy the join condition. (Versions of Oracle prior to 8 allowed conditions to appear only in the WHERE clause, along with non-join filtering criteria.) The ANSI join has several advantages over the older, traditional method of joining tables:

- Accidentally forming a Cartesian product (every row of one table joined to every row of another) is less likely because you must explicitly state the join criteria.
- ANSI SQL99 join syntax is easier to understand.
- Using the standard assures that other ANSI-compliant databases will execute the queries properly.
- Join criteria appear separately from row filtering criteria.
- The optional USING clause, when applicable, requires less typing.

The inner join syntax is as follows. The word *INNER* is optional. If omitted, it is assumed to be an inner join. (Only the FROM clause is shown, though the SELECT statements can also have other optional clauses such as WHERE, ORDER BY, and so on.)

```
SELECT <column-list>
FROM <table1> [<alias1>] [INNER] JOIN <table2> [<alias2>]
  ON {<table1>|<alias1>}.<join-column1> =
     {<table2>|<alias2>}.<join-column2>;
```

The FROM statement specifies a pair of tables with optional table aliases (introduced later) along with the ON phrase which specifies the names of the column from each table. The equal operator between each column name in the ON phrase indicates that the two columns' values must match in order to join the two rows and display any columns mentioned in the select list. If the values do not match, they are not joined and thus do not appear in the column list. For example, suppose you want to display the first and last names of customers and the street and city of any properties that they own. The query retrieves information from two database tables: the Customers table containing customer information and the Properties table that contains the street and city data for properties owned by customers. The way that Oracle associates related rows from both tables is through the OwnerID column in the Properties table and the corresponding CustomerID column in the Customers table. Each property's OwnerID value appears in the CustomerID column of the Customers table. To match property owners (Customers) to their properties, Oracle must simply find matching CustomerID/OwnerID value pairs. Here's the SELECT statement that will join the two tables:

```
SELECT FirstName, LastName, Properties.Address, Properties.City
FROM Customers INNER JOIN Properties
  ON Customers.CustomerID=Properties.OwnerID;
```

Notice that the third and fourth items in the select list have the table name and a dot preceding the column name. Called a ***qualified name,*** it designates both the table name and the column name it contains. You must use a qualified name for those two columns because the columns Address and City appear in both tables. If you omit the table name qualifier, then Oracle indicates the column references are ambiguous—it does not know which City column you mean. Let's experiment with equijoin by issuing SELECT statements containing table join conditions.

The preceding SELECT example conforms to the ANSI/ISO SQL99 join syntax. (Versions of Oracle prior to 9i did not allow this form.) We strongly suggest you use it. However, you may encounter SELECT statements that use the older method of joining tables. The older method—one which we will not use in this book after this example—places the join condition in the WHERE clause. The problem with join conditions mixed in with filtering criteria in the WHERE clause is just that—it is difficult to distinguish join conditions from row filtering criteria. Here is the one and only example of this older syntax:

```
SELECT FirstName, LastName, Properties.Address, Properties.City
FROM Customers, Properties
WHERE Customers.CustomerID=Properties.OwnerID;
```

Before you can proceed with hands-on database activities, you must initialize the Redwood Realty database. Even if you have done this activity in Chapter 5, it is important that you run the initialization script for this chapter. The script introduces new tables not available in earlier chapters, and it safely drops older versions of them from previous chapters. No tables you create are affected, other than those for Redwood Realty.

To initialize the Redwood Realty for Chapter 6 usage:

1. Locate the folder called RedwoodRealty. Within the RedwoodRealty folder, locate the script file called BuildRedwood.sql. That is the file you will run to initialize the database (the same script file you ran at the beginning of Chapter 5). Note the path to that file, as you will need it in the next step. Part of the path should be <path>\RedwoodRealty\
2. Launch SQL*Plus and log into Oracle.
3. Substitute the path you noted in step 1 for "<path>" below, and then type and execute the following:

    START <path>\BuildRedwood

    Oracle displays the table names as they are populated. Table names and their row counts appear also.

The SELECT statement you are about to write contains ***display columns,*** which are the columns that appear following SELECT and preceding FROM, and ***search columns,*** which appear in the WHERE clause. The primary and foreign key columns which Oracle uses to join two tables together are called ***join columns.***

To join two tables and retrieve columns from both of them:

1. With SQL*Plus running, launch Notepad so you can save and edit your SQL statements easily.
2. Type the following statements to clear the screen and establish column formatting. As usual, copy and paste the statements from Notepad to SQL*Plus, and then execute them.

    ```
    CLEAR SCREEN
    COLUMN FirstName FORMAT A12
    COLUMN LastName  FORMAT A12
    COLUMN City      FORMAT A15
    COLUMN Address   FORMAT A25
    ```

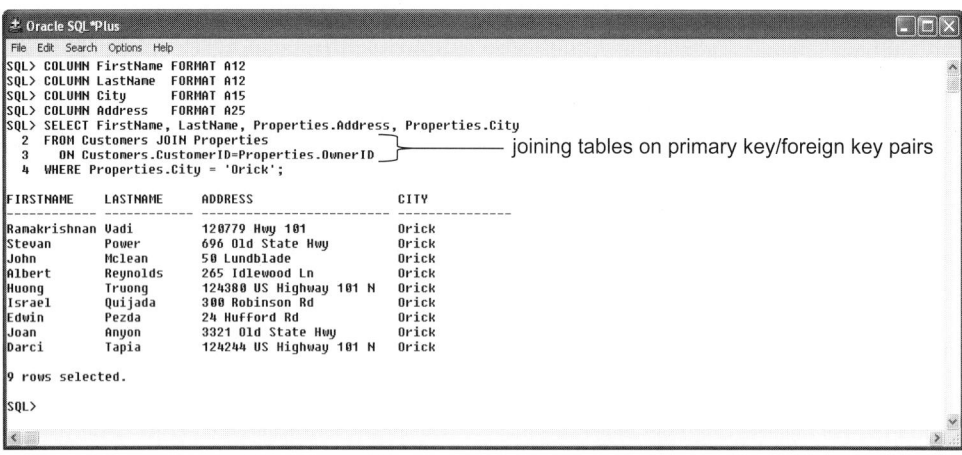

FIGURE 6.2 Joining the Customers and Properties tables.

3. Type the following in Notepad, copy and paste it to SQL*Plus, and execute it to join two related tables and display selected columns for properties that are located in Orick:

```
SELECT FirstName, LastName, Properties.Address, Properties.City
FROM Customers JOIN Properties
   ON Customers.CustomerID=Properties.OwnerID
WHERE Properties.City = 'Orick';
```

Oracle joins the two tables on matching CustomerID/OwnerID column values (see Figure 6.2).

4. Switch back to Notepad and save the entire script as <yourname>Ch06Query01.sql, substituting your last name for "<yourname>."

5. Modify the SELECT statement by removing the "Properties" qualifier and period following it from the two instances in the select list (but not anywhere else). Execute the modified query, which should match the following. What happens?

```
SELECT FirstName, LastName, Address, City
FROM Customers JOIN Properties
   ON Customers.CustomerID=Properties.OwnerID
WHERE Properties.City = 'Orick';
```

6. Leave SQL*Plus running.

In Step 5 above, Oracle reports that the reference is ambiguous by issuing the error message "ORA-00918: column ambiguously defined."

An alternative and slightly simpler way to join tables is available whenever the two tables' join columns have the same name. This alternative FROM-clause syntax is:

```
SELECT <column-list>
FROM <table1> [<alias1>] [INNER] JOIN <table2> [<alias2>]
   USING (<join-column>);
```

Be sure you enclose the join column name in parentheses, otherwise Oracle will generate a syntax error.

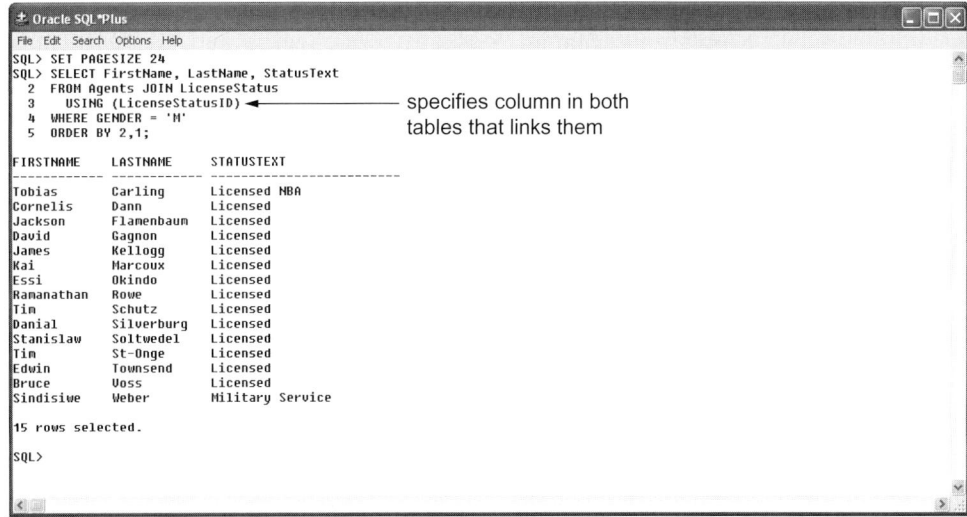

FIGURE 6.3 Joining tables on like-named columns.

To join two tables whose foreign and primary key columns have the same name:

1. Switch back to Notepad and type the following lines below the text you have typed so far.

```
CLEAR SCREEN
SET PAGESIZE 24
SELECT FirstName, LastName, StatusText
FROM Agents JOIN LicenseStatus
   USING (LicenseStatusID)
WHERE GENDER = 'M'
ORDER BY 2,1;
```

2. Copy the preceding code—just the lines in Step 1—into SQL*Plus and execute it. Notice that the COLUMN formatting still applies for FirstName and LastName as long as you did not close SQL*Plus. Your results should match Figure 6.3.
3. Leave SQL*Plus running.

Using a Natural Join

A natural join is a close relative of an inner join. The difference between them is that a natural join requires that the values of the join columns be the same and that the column *names* must match too. Natural joins look for value matches in columns in both tables that have the same names. Therefore, if table A has two columns whose names match columns in table B, then the values in both column pairs must match for their corresponding rows to be joined. Using a natural join means you must be careful that you intend for Oracle to match *all* value pairs in columns with the same name. (An inner join looks for matches of column values, just like a natural join, but the join columns can be different names.) Both natural joins and inner joins require that join columns are the same data type. A natural join has a slightly simpler structure because it does not require an ON clause. The syntax of a natural join between two tables is:

```
SELECT <column-list>
FROM <table1> [<alias1>] NATURAL JOIN <table2> [<alias2>];
```

Several of the Redwood Realty tables have primary keys and foreign keys whose names match. For example, the CustAgentList table and the Customers table both have a column called CustomerID. This indicates that the two tables are related by a common column. Similarly, the Agents and LicenseStatus tables both have a LicenseStatusID column. Likewise, the Properties and Listings tables both have a column named PropertyID. Try a natural join by running the steps that follow. In these steps, you will link the Properties and Listings tables to display related columns from both. You will list the address, city, bedrooms, bathrooms, and sqft columns from the Properties table along with the AskingPrice from the Listings table. Rows from these two tables are joined on matching PropertyID column values, and only that column is identically named in both tables. Therefore a natural join is, well, a natural choice.

To join two tables with a natural join:

1. Open Notepad and type the following. Then copy it to SQL*Plus and execute it. (Be sure to press **Enter** following the last line so that it executes.) The formatting renders the resulting rows easier to read.

```
CLEAR SCREEN
SET PAGESIZE 20
COLUMN Address      FORMAT A25       HEADING 'Address'
COLUMN City         FORMAT A15       HEADING 'City'
COLUMN Bedrooms     FORMAT 99        HEADING 'Br'
COLUMN Bathrooms    FORMAT 99        HEADING 'Ba'
COLUMN SqFt         FORMAT 9,999     HEADING 'Square|Feet'
COLUMN AskingPrice  FORMAT $9,999,999 HEADING 'Asking|Price'
BREAK ON CITY SKIP 1
```

2. Type the following SELECT statement to join two tables and return common rows. You greatly restrict the number of returned rows with the WHERE criteria. You could loosen or remove the criteria to return hundreds of rows if you want.

```
SELECT Address, City, Bedrooms, Bathrooms, SqFt, AskingPrice
FROM Properties NATURAL JOIN Listings
WHERE SqFt >= 2000 AND Bathrooms > 3 AND Bedrooms > 3
ORDER BY City, AskingPrice;
```

Oracle returns nine row pairs from the joined tables (see Figure 6.4).

3. Leave SQL*Plus running.

JOINING THREE OR MORE TABLES

You are not limited to joining just two tables. Oracle permits you to join an unlimited number of tables. To join three or more tables, Oracle first joins two of the tables using the join conditions specified for the two tables. Then, it joins the result to another table based on join conditions containing columns of the joined tables and the new table about to be joined. This process continues until all tables are joined into the result. (Oracle's query optimizer determines the order in which to join tables based on the join conditions, indexes on tables, and available statistics on the table. Optimization is described in Chapter 13.)

For example, to join the Agents, Listing, and Properties tables, specify the table names and the join conditions for each table pair, in turn, in the FROM clause. The following SELECT statement joins the three tables based on matching column values in two pairs of columns:

```
SELECT FirstName, LastName, Address, City,
  Bedrooms, Bathrooms, AskingPrice
FROM Agents INNER JOIN Listings
  ON AgentID = ListingAgentID
        INNER JOIN Properties
  ON Listings.PropertyID = Properties.PropertyID;
```

```
SQL> SET PAGESIZE 20
SQL> COLUMN Address       FORMAT A25       HEADING 'Address'
SQL> COLUMN City          FORMAT A15       HEADING 'City'
SQL> COLUMN Bedrooms      FORMAT 99        HEADING 'Br'
SQL> COLUMN Bathrooms     FORMAT 99        HEADING 'Ba'
SQL> COLUMN SqFt          FORMAT 9,999     HEADING 'Square|Feet'
SQL> COLUMN AskingPrice   FORMAT $9,999,999 HEADING 'Asking|Price'
SQL> BREAK ON CITY SKIP 1
SQL> SELECT Address, City, Bedrooms, Bathrooms, SqFt, AskingPrice
  2  FROM Properties NATURAL JOIN Listings
  3  WHERE SqFt >= 2000 AND Bathrooms > 3 AND Bedrooms > 3
  4  ORDER BY City, AskingPrice;

                                           Square     Asking
Address                   City       Br Ba  Feet       Price
------------------------- ---------- -- --  ------ ----------
8130 W End Rd             Arcata      5  4  5,150    $560,000

5990 Stover Rd            Blue Lake   4  4  4,828    $725,000

2312 Myrtle Ave           Eureka      5  4  2,845    $180,000
6739 Myrtle Ave                       6  4  3,548    $219,000
3209 W St                             4  4  3,200    $325,000
1845 Quaker St                        4  4  3,249    $335,000

1591 Kings Row            Fortuna     4  4  4,490    $495,000

3340 Dows Prairie Rd      McKinleyville  4  4  2,500  $235,000
1138 Perini Rd                        4  4  3,000    $380,000

9 rows selected.

SQL>
```

FIGURE 6.4 Using a natural join.

To join two tables, simply list the table names, pair-wise, and their join columns. The phrase

```
FROM Agents JOIN Listings
   ON AgentID = ListingAgentID
```

tells Oracle to join the Agents and Listings columns by matching values in their respective columns, AgentID and ListingAgentID. The third and fourth FROM lines (spacing or location of the ON statement on a separate line is optional):

```
        JOIN Properties
   ON Listings.PropertyID = Properties.PropertyID;
```

join the Listings table to the Properties table on matching column values. In the preceding code segment, the join columns are qualified by their respective table names. For example, Listings.PropertyID designates column PropertyID in the Listings table. Similarly, Properties.PropertyID designates column PropertyID in the Properties table. To avoid ambiguity, you must use qualified names in select list items when identical column names appear in joined tables. Additionally, you can save keystrokes by assigning a short name, called a *table alias*, to a table. Then, you can and should use the table alias to qualify *all* column names everywhere in a select list.

An alternative way of writing a FROM statement joining two tables is to place all ON statements together in the following way. You can adopt either convention, because the outcome is the same. Be sure to nest the ON statements in reverse order of join order by table name (see below).

```
SELECT FirstName, LastName, Address, City,
   Bedrooms, Bathrooms, AskingPrice
FROM Agents JOIN Listings JOIN Properties
   ON Listings.PropertyID = Properties.PropertyID
   ON AgentID = ListingAgentID;
```

Because LastName and FirstName only occur in the Agents table in this particular three-table join, you can use unqualified names in the select list. The three-table join in the exercise below illustrates the use of table aliases.

To join three tables using table aliases:

1. With SQL*Plus still running, type the following in Notepad, copy it to SQL*Plus, and press **Enter** to clear the display, clear breaks, and apply additional column formatting. (Be sure to type two single quotation marks between the word *Agent* and the letter *s* in the COLUMN statement so a single quotation mark appears in the column heading.)

   ```
   CLEAR SCREEN
   CLEAR BREAKS
   COLUMN Agent FORMAT A25 HEADING 'Agent''s|Name'
   ```

2. Next, type the following, copy it to SQL*Plus, and execute it. Oracle links the three tables and displays four columns selected from among the three tables. Your results should match Figure 6.5.

   ```
   SELECT ag.FirstName||' '||ag.LastName AS Agent,
          pr.Address, pr.City, li.AskingPrice
   FROM Agents ag INNER JOIN Listings li
     ON ag.AgentID = li.ListingAgentID
              INNER JOIN Properties pr
     ON li.PropertyID = pr.PropertyID
   WHERE UPPER(pr.City) IN ('ORICK','BLUE LAKE','LOLETA')
   ORDER BY pr.City, li.AskingPrice;
   ```

3. Type **CLEAR COLUMNS** and press **Enter** to clear out all column definitions.
4. Switch back to Notepad and save the file to preserve your work.
5. Close Notepad and close SQL*Plus. (Closing SQL*Plus ensures that any lingering environmental settings—pagesize, headings, and so on—that you set previously are reset to their default values.)

FIGURE 6.5 Joining three tables and filtering rows.

```
SQL> CLEAR BREAKS
breaks cleared
SQL> COLUMN Agent FORMAT A25 HEADING 'Agent''s|Name'
SQL> SELECT ag.FirstName||' '||ag.LastName AS Agent,
  2          pr.Address, pr.City, li.AskingPrice
  3  FROM Agents ag INNER JOIN Listings li
  4    ON ag.AgentID = li.ListingAgentID
  5              INNER JOIN Properties pr
  6    ON li.PropertyID = pr.PropertyID
  7  WHERE UPPER(pr.City) IN ('ORICK','BLUE LAKE','LOLETA')
  8  ORDER BY pr.City, li.AskingPrice;

Agent's                                                      Asking
Name                      Address              City           Price
------------------------- -------------------- ---------- ----------
James Kellogg             540 Broad            Blue Lake    $112,000
Lee Reed                  2115 Chezum Rd       Blue Lake    $139,500
Tobias Carling            830 Railroad Ave     Blue Lake    $145,000
Stanislaw Soltwedel       833 Blue Lake Bl     Blue Lake    $159,446
Lee Reed                  741 2nd Ave          Blue Lake    $190,463
Ramanathan Rowe           5990 Stover Rd       Blue Lake    $725,000
Bruce Voss                3146 Copenhagen Rd   Loleta       $104,000
Heather Sheibani          356 Loleta Dr        Loleta       $111,950
Barbara Herring           296 Spring           Loleta       $114,000
Lora Allee                229 Church           Loleta       $145,000
Sindisiwe Weber           552 Pershing         Loleta       $154,000
Edwin Townsend            119 Bay View Dr      Loleta       $162,500
Lora Allee                632 Pershing         Loleta       $282,500
David Gagnon              124380 US Highway 101 N  Orick    $129,950
Cecilia Romero            120779 Hwy 101       Orick        $170,266
Lee Reed                  124244 US Highway 101 N  Orick    $184,950

16 rows selected.

SQL>
```

Understanding Other Join Types and Join Conditions

All of the join conditions you have seen so far in this chapter are equijoins or their equivalent, natural joins. In all cases, the comparison that Oracle performed was for equality (=) between two columns forming the join condition. The other join condition is non-equijoin, in which an operator other than equality appears between column names in the join condition. These types of operators include BETWEEN, >, <, and so on. Examples of these are presented later in this chapter. In addition, there are three join types, one of which you have already seen. They are inner joins, outer joins, and self joins. You have already seen several examples of inner joins at work. An ***outer join*** returns a row when join conditions are met and even when one of the join column conditions contains a null value. It is a type of extended inner join—an inner join plus all other rows from another table. A ***self join*** returns rows from the same table, joining a table to itself and then evaluating the join condition. Next, you will study outer join queries.

Using Outer Join Queries

Recall that an inner join query retrieves rows from two tables only when values exist in all tables being joined (and are equal, in the case of equijoin). If a join column in a table is null, the row is not returned. Imagine, for example, a join query involving a Salesperson table, containing salesperson's names, and a Sales table, containing a record of each sale made and the ID of the salesperson making the sale. If you joined the Salesperson table to the Sales table, the returned rows would display the salespersons' names and the sales they made. What would not be evident is whether there are salespersons who have made no sales at all. An outer join query would uncover hidden information such as that by returning all the inner join rows, as usual, and additional rows with salesperson names and NULL for sales values when they are absent in the sales row. Likewise, an inner join query would not reveal which inventory items did not sell at all in a given month—only the items that *did* sell that month. An outer query would provide that information. Figure 6.6 shows a simple example of sales people and their sales. When you use an outer join query, the result reveals that three salespersons

FIGURE 6.6 Outer join illustration.

Salespersons

ID	Name	Div
1001	Bob	Mkt
1002	Dawn	Sales
1003	Betty	Sales
1006	Nancy	Mkt
1009	Fred	Sales

Sales

PK2	Emp#	Amount
21	1002	$2,000
22	1002	$2,200
23	1003	$1,800
24	1003	$200

Result of joining the Salespersons and Sales tables:

```
    from Salespersons    from Sales
    ┌─────────────────┐ ┌──────────────────┐
    1002 Dawn   Sales   21 1002  $2,000
    1002 Dawn   Sales   22 1002  $2,200
    1003 Betty  Sales   23 1003  $1,800
    1003 Betty  Sales   24 1003    $200
    1001 Bob    Mkt     null null   null
    1009 Nancy  Mkt     null null   null
    1009 Fred   Sales   null null   null
```

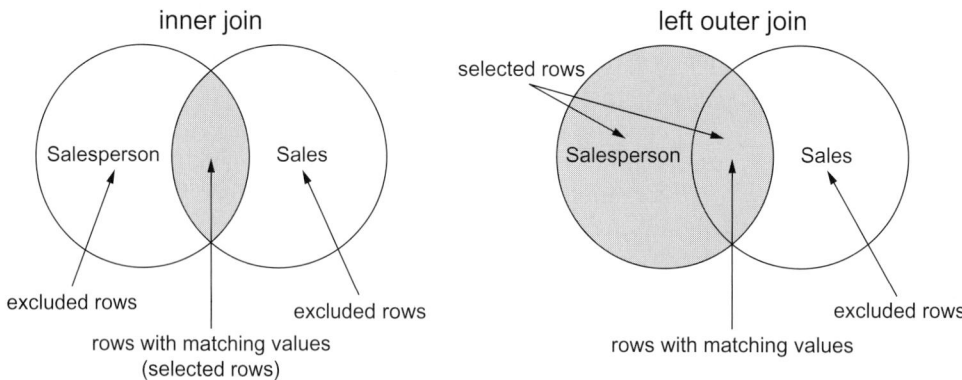

FIGURE 6.7 Venn diagrams showing inner join and left outer join.

had no sales at all — a fact that an inner join cannot unearth. Figure 6.7 illustrates this concept with Venn diagrams.

There are three types of outer join queries you can pose: Left outer join, right outer join, and full outer join. The syntax is similar to an inner join:

```
SELECT <column-list>
FROM <table1> [<alias1>]
     {LEFT|RIGHT|FULL} [OUTER] JOIN <table2> [<alias2>]
  ON {<table1>|<alias1>}.<join-column1> =
     {<table2>|<alias2>}.<join-column2>;
```

The word OUTER is optional, though it helps document that the query is an outer join. A ***left outer join*** refers to the table listed on the left side in the FROM clause. It further means that if there are unmatched rows in the left table, then it should be matched with a NULL record and returned in the results. Similarly, a ***right outer join*** refers to the table listed on the right side of *RIGHT OUTER JOIN* in the FROM clause. If there are unmatched rows in the right table, then it should be matched with a NULL record and returned in the results. A ***full outer join*** instructs Oracle to return rows from either table that do not have matching rows in the other table along with those that do have matches in both.

> **Tip:** Of course, a left outer join query will return the same results as its equivalent right outer join if you reverse the table names in FROM clause.

It would be interesting to know what Redwood Realty agents do not have any listings in the Listings table. Any underproductive agents, especially those who have no active listings, should consider another line of work! An outer query would reveal any agents who have no listings. Currently all twenty-nine Redwood Realty agents are hardworking, and have listings in the Listings table. Therefore, you will add three new agents to the Agents table. Because they are new, no entries in the Listings table will appear with a ListingAgentID foreign key matching any of the three new agents' AgentID primary keys. In the next exercise, you will add new agents to the Agents table, execute a standard inner join with Agents and Listings, and then execute an outer join with those same two tables.

To experiment with a left or right outer join query:

1. Launch SQL*Plus, log into Oracle, and start Notepad. Then type (in Notepad followed by a copy/paste operation) and execute the following insert new rows into the Agents table. Be very careful typing the three INSERT statements (on the next page).

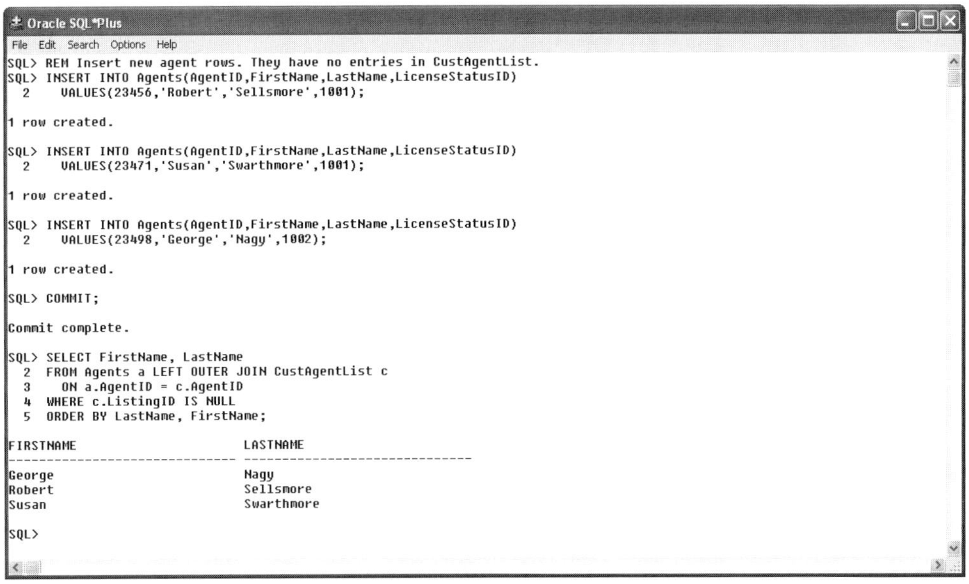

CHAPTER 6 Creating Multitable Queries and Views

FIGURE 6.8 Using a left outer join.

```
CLEAR SCREEN
REM Insert new agent rows. They have no entries in CustAgentList.
INSERT INTO Agents(AgentID,FirstName,LastName,LicenseStatusID)
   VALUES(23456,'Robert','Sellsmore',1001);
INSERT INTO Agents(AgentID,FirstName,LastName,LicenseStatusID)
   VALUES(23471,'Susan','Swarthmore',1001);
INSERT INTO Agents(AgentID,FirstName,LastName,LicenseStatusID)
   VALUES(23498,'George','Nagy',1002);
```

2. Type **COMMIT;** and press **Enter** to make the insertions permanent.
3. Type the following in Notepad, and then copy it to SQL*Plus and execute it.

```
SELECT FirstName, LastName
FROM Agents a LEFT OUTER JOIN CustAgentList c
   ON a.AgentID = c.AgentID
WHERE c.ListingID IS NULL
ORDER BY LastName, FirstName;
```

Oracle lists three agents who have no matching rows in the Listings table. Your screen should match Figure 6.8.

4. Construct a left outer join to see the "missing rows" another way. Type and execute the following SQL*Plus statements and modified SELECT statement shown below.

```
SET PAGESIZE 50
CLEAR SCREEN
SELECT FirstName, LastName, COUNT(ListingID)
FROM Agents a LEFT OUTER JOIN CustAgentList c
   ON a.AgentID = c.AgentID
GROUP BY FirstName, LastName
ORDER BY LastName, FirstName;
```

Your results show that for three of the agents, the count function returns zero. That means their rows did not match any rows in the Listings table. See Figure 6.9.

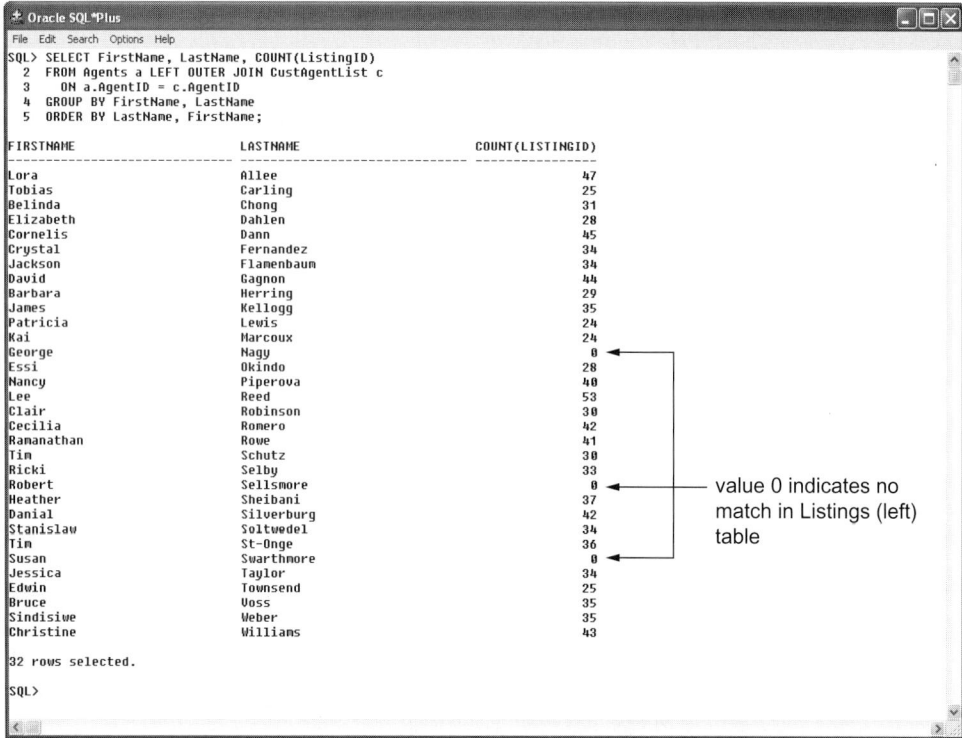

FIGURE 6.9 Showing non-matching rows with a COUNT function.

5. Type and execute the following to reset the PAGESIZE environment variable:

   SET PAGESIZE 14

6. Leave SQL*Plus running.

USING SELF JOIN QUERIES

Recall that a self join is an inner or outer join between two columns that are collocated in the same table. A frequently cited example is an employee table that contains employees and their supervisors. A column such as ManagerID might contain the identification of the employee's supervisor. A column such as EmployeeID, which typically is a primary key, is each employee's unique identifier. You join a table to itself by listing it twice in the FROM clause of a SELECT statement. You must use a table alias in this case to distinguish between the manager's ID and the matching employee's ID. For instance, the following hypothetical self join lists employees and their managers, where both managers and employees are in the same table called Employees.

```
SELECT w.FirstName, w.LastName, s.FirstName, s.LastName
FROM Employees w INNER JOIN Employees s
  ON w.ManagerID = s.EmployeeID;
```

The equijoin condition matches each employee's ManagerID column (w.ManagerID) with an employee who has the EmployeeID (s.EmployeeID). The left FirstName and LastName form the employee's name, whereas the right FirstName/LastName pair in any returned row is the manager's name. The Redwood Realty tables do not have any such hierarchical arrangement, but you can see how a self join works by creating and populating a stand-alone table that is *not* part of the Redwood Realty database. You will do that next.

CHAPTER 6 Creating Multitable Queries and Views 277

To create an Employee table and populate it:

1. Launch SQL*Plus and log into Oracle, if necessary.
2. Using Windows Explorer or another suitable file/folder display program, locate the file Ch06EmpSelfJoin.sql, which is one of the Chapter 6 data files. Note the path to that file.
3. Type and execute the following, substituting the actual path to the script file for "<path>" below, including the drive name.

    START <path>\Ch06EmpSelfJoin

    The script file displays *EmpSelfJoin created and populated* to indicate that it was successful.

Now you can experiment with a self join query. Begin by displaying the columns' contents.

To display the contents of the columns and to perform a self join:

1. Type and execute the following statement in SQL*Plus:

    CLEAR SCREEN
    SELECT * FROM EmpSelfJoin;

2. Type and execute:

    DESCRIBE EmpSelfJoin

Figure 6.10 shows the 21 rows of EmpSelfJoin, its column names, and column data types.

Consider Figure 6.10. The EmployeeID column contains each employee's unique identification number. The rightmost column, called BossID, contains the identification number of that employee's boss. For example, examine the row for

FIGURE 6.10 Displaying the EmpSelfJoin table.

```
Oracle SQL*Plus
File Edit Search Options Help
SQL> SELECT * FROM EmpSelfJoin;
EMPLOYEEID FIRSTNAME        LASTNAME         HIREDATE  BIRTHDATE G     BOSSID
---------- ---------------- ---------------- --------- --------- - ----------
     10497 John             Warner           05-SEP-97 23-OCT-53 M
     12765 Kent             Conrad           12-SEP-06 01-FEB-55 M      10497
     12963 Bobby            Durbin           18-SEP-00 25-MAR-56 F      10497
     13555 Susan            McCain           30-AUG-95 20-OCT-57 F      10497
     15233 Mike             DeWine           17-JAN-99 06-NOV-58 M      10497
     12301 Thomas           Daschle          21-SEP-97 11-JAN-59 M      12963
     15521 Celia            Pryor            30-MAY-06 10-APR-59 F      12963
     14601 Mitch            McConnell        25-AUG-06 21-DEC-60 M      12963
     13771 Felicity         Dorgan           29-JUN-98 26-SEP-61 F      12963
     11775 Patty            Murray           01-NOV-99 21-OCT-62 F      12963
     14883 Connie           Burns            30-MAY-97 29-NOV-64 F      13555

EMPLOYEEID FIRSTNAME        LASTNAME         HIREDATE  BIRTHDATE G     BOSSID
---------- ---------------- ---------------- --------- --------- - ----------
     14599 Clair            Baucus           07-DEC-03 04-FEB-65 F      13555
     14117 Christopher      Dodd             13-JUL-97 19-MAY-68 M      13555
     13353 John             Sununu           04-MAY-96 04-APR-69 M      13555
     12499 Barbara          Fitzgerald       16-OCT-06 01-JUL-69 F      15233
     10429 Jessica          Chafee           23-MAY-05 03-OCT-69 F      15233
     10913 Ted              Stevens          05-JUN-96 03-APR-70 M      15233
     10041 Bob              Graham           03-OCT-96 12-DEC-70 M      15233
     12875 John             Edwards          20-DEC-95 04-MAR-74 M      12765
     10849 Lora             Gregg            18-JUL-03 03-MAR-83 F      12765
     15349 Bill             Frist            21-JUN-04 21-AUG-83 M      12765

21 rows selected.

SQL> DESCRIBE EmpSelfJoin
 Name                                      Null?    Type
 ----------------------------------------- -------- ----------------------------
 EMPLOYEEID                                NOT NULL NUMBER(38)
 FIRSTNAME                                          NVARCHAR2(15)
 LASTNAME                                           NVARCHAR2(15)
 HIREDATE                                           DATE
 BIRTHDATE                                          DATE
 GENDER                                             NVARCHAR2(1)
 BOSSID                                             NUMBER(38)

SQL>
```

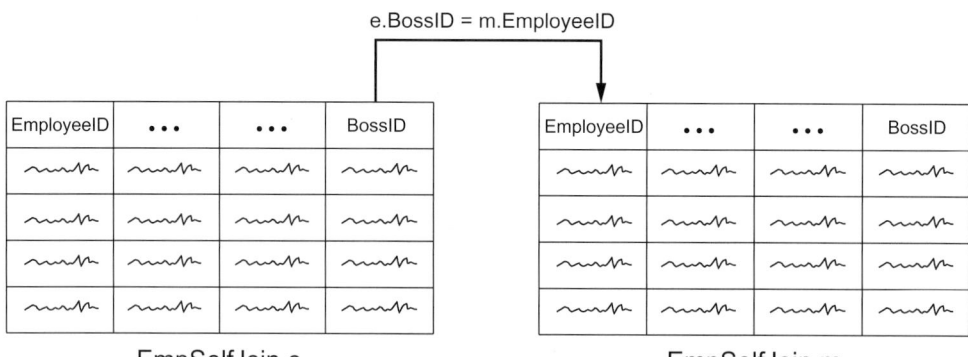

FIGURE 6.11 Illustration of a table joined to itself by using aliases.

Kent Conrad—EmployeeID value 12765. The value of his BossID column is 10497, which is a foreign key pointing back into the same table. In particular, that value is the EmployeeID for John Warner. Therefore, John Warner is Kent Conrad's boss. Consider Bill Frist's row at the bottom. His BossID value is 12765. The employee row having that EmployeeID value is Kent Conrad's row. Kent Conrad is Bill Frist's boss.

How can we display this relationship—a table containing a column that references another column in the same table—in a meaningful display? You can do this by writing a self join query, which can be an inner join query or an outer join query. In particular, you write the table name *twice* in the query and use two table aliases to differentiate between them. Think of a single table as two tables, side-by-side. You relate them to each other just as you would two distinct tables—by telling Oracle which column in one table is associated with which table in another table. Figure 6.11 shows the EmpSelfJoin table as two tables, each with an alias assigned. The alias "e" implies EmpSelfJoin from an employee's standpoint, and the alias "m" is the same EmpSelfJoin table from a manager's viewpoint.

The keys to joining a table to itself are: (1) using aliases, and (2) using an equijoin with the correct alias-qualified columns for each table. You will create the SQL statement to join the EmpSelfJoin table to itself on matching EmployeeID/BossID pairs by executing the steps that follow.

To join a table to itself:

1. Clear the screen by typing and executing:

    `CLEAR SCREEN`

2. Type the following in Notepad to make editing easy. Then copy it to SQL*Plus and execute it. Make any corrections in Notepad and recopy, if needed.

    ```
    SELECT m.FirstName||' '||m.LastName AS Manager,
           e.FirstName||' '||e.LastName AS Employee
    FROM EmpSelfJoin e INNER JOIN EmpSelfJoin m
      ON e.BossID = m.EmployeeID
    ORDER BY m.LastName, e.LastName;
    ```

Oracle displays twenty rows with the manager in the first column and the employee reporting to that manager in the second column (see Figure 6.12). But wait! There are twenty-one employees in the list (Figure 6.10). Where is the 21st employee? Examine the employee rows in Figure 6.10 and you will see that John Warner's BossID is null because he is the CEO. He reports to no other employee. Because inner joins do

```
SQL> SELECT m.FirstName||' '||m.LastName AS Manager,
  2         e.FirstName||' '||e.LastName AS Employee
  3  FROM EmpSelfJoin e INNER JOIN EmpSelfJoin m
  4  ON e.BossID = m.EmployeeID
  5  ORDER BY m.LastName, e.LastName;

MANAGER                         EMPLOYEE
------------------------------  ------------------------------
Kent Conrad                     John Edwards
Kent Conrad                     Bill Frist
Kent Conrad                     Lora Gregg
Mike DeWine                     Jessica Chafee
Mike DeWine                     Barbara Fitzgerald
Mike DeWine                     Bob Graham
Mike DeWine                     Ted Stevens
Bobby Durbin                    Thomas Daschle
Bobby Durbin                    Felicity Dorgan
Bobby Durbin                    Mitch McConnell
Bobby Durbin                    Patty Murray

MANAGER                         EMPLOYEE
------------------------------  ------------------------------
Bobby Durbin                    Celia Pryor
Susan McCain                    Clair Baucus
Susan McCain                    Connie Burns
Susan McCain                    Christopher Dodd
Susan McCain                    John Sununu
John Warner                     Kent Conrad
John Warner                     Mike DeWine
John Warner                     Bobby Durbin
John Warner                     Susan McCain

20 rows selected.

SQL>
```

FIGURE 6.12 Listing managers and their employees with a self join query.

not join rows in which one or both of the join columns is null, John Warner does not appear in the employee column—only as a manager. To include him along with his other employees, consider him accountable to the board of directors. Using the NVL function and replacing the inner join with an outer join will correct the misstep.

To use an outer join to display all employees and their managers:

1. Execute **CLEAR SCREEN** to clear the screen.
2. Modify the previous SELECT to the following and re-execute the query:

```
SELECT
  NVL2(m.LastName, m.FirstName||' '||m.LastName, 'Board of Directors')
    AS Manager,
  e.FirstName||' '||e.LastName AS Employee
FROM EmpSelfJoin e LEFT OUTER JOIN EmpSelfJoin m
  ON e.BossID = m.EmployeeID
ORDER BY m.LastName, e.LastName;
```

3. You can delete the EmpSelfJoin table, because you no longer need it. Type and execute the following:

```
DROP TABLE EmpSelfJoin CASCADE CONSTRAINTS PURGE;
```

Oracle responds with the message "Table dropped."

Figure 6.13 shows the query's result: A full list of twenty-one managers and their employees including the CEO, John Warner. Notice John Warner's manager is "Board of Directors," because the NVL2 function returns that string if the manager's last name is null (it is null for a row that cannot be joined because the BossID is null). Otherwise, NVL2 returns the manager's first and last names, concatenated.

USING FULL JOIN QUERIES

The SQL standard provides for a FULL OUTER JOIN in which unmatched join attributes from either table are joined with null values on the unmatched side. There is little need for this in most well-designed databases.

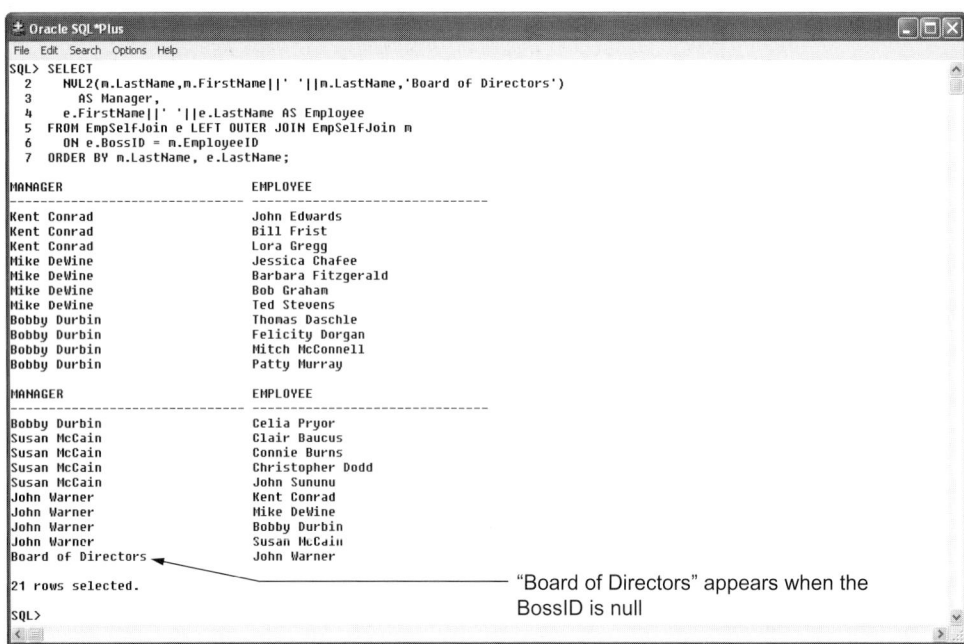

FIGURE 6.13 Managers and their employees produced using an outer join query.

Using Non-Equijoin Queries

When you use an equality join, the values in the two referenced columns must match. There are several cases where a non-exact match is useful. A ***non-equality join,*** or non-equijoin, is a query that uses a join condition with something other than the equality operator. Operators in a non-equality join include BETWEEN, <, <=, >, >=, <>, and =. Specifically, a non-equijoin is useful when you join two tables in which the join attribute from one table falls within a specified range of values that are found in the second table. An example is the following query, which locates the employees who were hired between two dates whose date values ranges are found in another table:

```
SELECT e.LastName e.HireDate
FROM Employees e JOIN CompanyHistory h
  ON e.HireDate BETWEEN h.BeginDate AND h.EndDate;
```

In the preceding example, you want to list the employees' last names and hire dates for employee hire dates that fall within values stored in another table, not some constant value you hardwired into the query. Another common example is using a non-equality join to look up a shipping charge in a table based on the weight of an object in another table. The non-equality join allows a "match" on any value within the range of values specified.

The Redwood Realty manager wants to tally the number of properties in categories by their AskingPrice. This type of tally, called a ***distribution,*** shows the count of homes in each price category. You have written a query to do something similar using the CASE structure and the COUNT function. In this example, the manager wants to change the categories from time to time. The categories are simply a table that contains a primary key and a column each for the low price and high price. This three-column table is altered whenever the manager wants different low/high price ranges or finer/coarser-grained price differences. You can use a non-equality join to compare the AskingPrice value in the Listings table to the low/high values in a table. Tallying the

TABLE 6.1 Asking price distribution table.

CategoryID	LowLimit	HighLimit
1000	$0	$50,000
1010	$50,000	$100,000
1020	$100,000	$150,000
1030	$150,000	$200,000
1040	$200,000	$250,000
1050	$250,000	$300,000
1060	$300,000	$350,000
1070	$350,000	$400,000
1080	$400,000	$2,000,000

results simply means using the COUNT function for each value pair to sum the count. The first thing that you must do is build a table to hold the low and high asking price value. Table 6.1 suggests the contents of the table used to tally the frequency distribution. It contains primary keys so that the manager can add, delete, or update the table as statistics granularity needs change.

Begin by constructing the PriceCat table, which holds the database equivalent of Table 6.1. Once that table is in place, you can write a query that employs a non-equality join to generate the price distribution.

To create the price category distribution table and display its contents:

1. Locate the script file Ch06PriceRange.sql among your Chapter 6 data files. Note the path on your disk to that file.

2. Launch SQL*Plus, if needed. Type **CLEAR SCREEN** and press **Enter** to clear the SQL*Plus work surface. Then, type and execute the following, substituting the actual path to the script file for "<path>" below, including the drive name.

   `START <path>\Ch06PriceRange`

   Oracle quietly creates the PriceCat table and populates it. The message "PriceCat table created and populated" appears.

3. Display the table's contents by typing and executing the following:

   `SELECT * FROM PriceCat ORDER BY LowLimit;`

4. Open Notepad and type the following. Then copy it to SQL*Plus. That way, it is easy to modify the statement in Notepad and copy it to SQL*Plus for execution:

   ```
   SELECT c.LowLimit, c.HighLimit, COUNT(AskingPrice) AS "Frequency"
   FROM Listings s JOIN PriceCat c
     ON s.AskingPrice >= c.LowLimit AND
        s.AskingPrice <  c.HighLimit
   GROUP BY c.LowLimit, c.HighLimit
   ORDER BY c.LowLimit;
   ```

   Oracle displays a frequency distribution of the prices (see Figure 6.14). The non-equality appears in the ON phrase (the >= and < comparison operators).

5. You can clean things up a bit by including the other categories for which there were *no* properties. Recall that a null in a join condition (non-equijoin or equijoin) omits the row. Revise the SELECT statement by changing the (inner) JOIN to a RIGHT OUTER JOIN. Execute the modified SELECT statement shown below:

   ```
   SELECT c.LowLimit, c.HighLimit, COUNT(AskingPrice) AS "Frequency"
   FROM Listings s RIGHT OUTER JOIN PriceCat c
   ```

```
           ON s.AskingPrice >= c.LowLimit AND
              s.AskingPrice <  c.HighLimit
    GROUP BY c.LowLimit, c.HighLimit
    ORDER BY c.LowLimit;
```

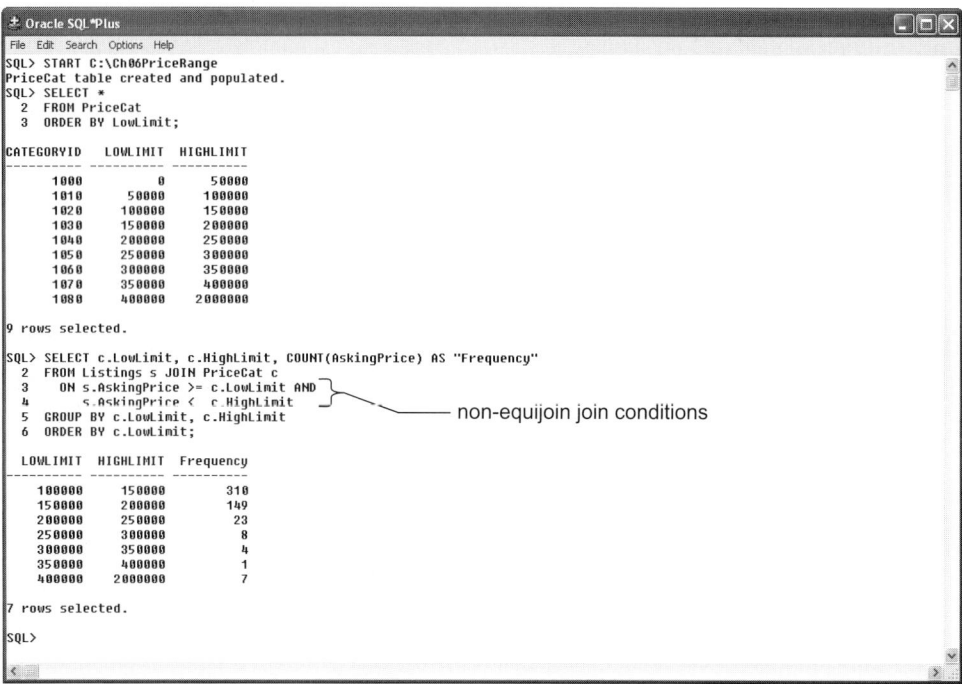

FIGURE 6.14 Creating the PriceCat table and running a non-equijoin query.

Figure 6.15 shows the difference between the script files and the results. Notice that the two categories containing no homes now appear and their frequencies are both zero.

6. You do not need the PriceCat table any more. Type and execute the following to remove it:

   `DROP TABLE PriceCat CASCADE CONSTRAINTS PURGE;`

7. Type **exit** and press **Enter** to exit SQL*Plus. Save any Notepad script files and close Notepad.

EXPLORING SET OPERATORS

There are times when you need to combine the results from multiple SELECT statements into one outcome. SQL provides this capability through *set operators.* The result of each SELECT statement is considered a set, and you can combine these sets using the set operators UNION, UNION ALL, MINUS, and INTERSECT. Table 6.2 summarizes these operators.

SQL statements that contain set operators are called *compound queries,* and each query in the compound query is called a *component query.* There are some rules and restrictions regarding compound queries:

- The data type of each column in the second query must be identical to the data type of the corresponding column in the first query.
- The number of columns returned by both component queries must be the same.

CHAPTER 6 Creating Multitable Queries and Views

- The first SELECT determines the column names for the result set.
- If you want to use ORDER BY in a compound query, you must place the ORDER BY clause at the end of the entire statement.

Sometimes, compound queries are called ***vertical joins*** because the retrieved rows are formed based on columns instead of rows. The syntax of a set operation is as follows:

```
<component query>
{UNION | UNION ALL | INTERSECT | MINUS}
<component query>
```

In the preceding syntax, you select one of the choices UNION, UNION ALL, INTERSECT, or MINUS as the set operator. Compound queries consisting of three SELECT statements contain two set operators; four SELECTS have three set operators; and so on.

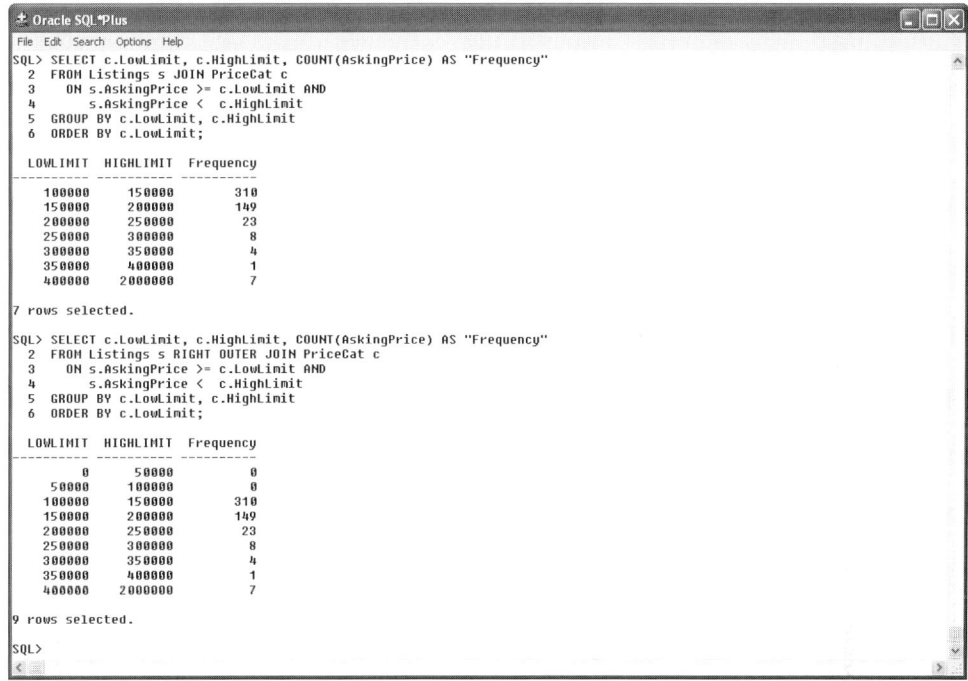

FIGURE 6.15 Comparing a non-equijoin and a right outer non-equijoin.

TABLE 6.2 SQL set operators.

Set Operator	Description
UNION	Returns all unique rows retrieved by the queries.
UNION ALL	Returns all the rows retrieved by the queries, including any duplicate rows.
INTERSECT	Returns rows that are retrieved by both queries.
MINUS	Returns the rows that remain when the rows retrieved by a second query are removed (subtracted) from the rows retrieved by the first query.

USING UNION AND UNION ALL

You may recall that Chapter 3 contains an explanation of how to list information about the tables you own. Likewise, Chapter 4 contains a section explaining how to list the triggers you have created in your schema. It is handy to be able to list *all* of the objects in your schema that you own. A UNION set operator is just right for this type of integration—combining rows from distinct SELECT statements and organizing them. The following compound query returns information about your tables, your triggers, and your sequences.

```
SELECT Table_Name AS "Object", 'Table' AS "Type"
FROM User_Tables
    UNION
SELECT Sequence_Name "Object", 'Sequence' AS "Type"
FROM User_Sequences
ORDER BY 2,1;
```

The first component query retrieves table names and the constant "Table" to identify them as tables in the output. The second component query retrieves sequence names and the constant string "Sequence" for identification of those rows. Oracle sorts the resulting union of the rows returned by the two component queries. Try it in a moment. First, though, you need to create a sequence and a trigger so that they show up in the result.

To create triggers and sequences in your schema:

1. Launch SQL*Plus, log into Oracle, and type **CLEAR SCREEN** to erase the display.
2. Locate the script Ch06CreateObjects.sql, and execute the script by typing the following. Substitute the actual path to the script file, including the drive, for "<path>" in the statement below:

    START <path>\Ch06CreateObjects

    Oracle invisibly creates two sequences and two triggers.

Now you are ready to create a compound query using the UNION set operator to list all your object types. Follow these steps. You will probably want to save the code you create as a script file, so be sure to use Notepad and save the lines when you are done.

To use the UNION set operator to combine results from multiple queries:

1. Type the following in Notepad, copy it to SQL*Plus, and execute it.

```
CLEAR SCREEN
SELECT Table_Name AS "Object", 'Table' AS "Type"
FROM User_Tables
WHERE Table_Name NOT LIKE 'BIN%'
    UNION
SELECT Sequence_Name "Object", 'Sequence' AS "Type"
FROM User_Sequences
    UNION
SELECT Trigger_Name "Object", 'Trigger' AS "Type"
FROM User_Triggers
ORDER BY 2,1;
```

Oracle returns three types of rows: sequences, tables, and triggers (see Figure 6.15). The aliases keep all columns like-named from the three component queries. The WHERE clause filters out Oracle table names that begin with "BIN."

```
± Oracle SQL*Plus
File Edit Search Options Help
SQL> SELECT Table_Name AS "Object", 'Table' AS "Type"
  2  FROM User_Tables
  3  WHERE Table_Name NOT LIKE 'BIN%'
  4     UNION
  5  SELECT Sequence_Name "Object", 'Sequence' AS "Type"
  6  FROM User_Sequences
  7     UNION
  8  SELECT Trigger_Name "Object", 'Trigger' AS "Type"
  9  FROM User_Triggers
 10  ORDER BY 2,1;

Object                          Type
------------------------------  --------
AGENTID_SEQ                     Sequence
CUSTOMER_SEQ                    Sequence
AGENTS                          Table
CONTACTREASON                   Table
CUSTAGENTLIST                   Table
CUSTOMERS                       Table
LICENSESTATUS                   Table
LISTINGS                        Table
PROPERTIES                      Table
SALESTATUS                      Table
AGENTS_BI_TRG                   Trigger

Object                          Type
------------------------------  --------
CUSTOMERS_BI_TRG                Trigger

12 rows selected.

SQL>
```

FIGURE 6.16 Using UNION in a compound query.

> **Tip:** Of course, the tables, triggers, and sequences you see in your list may be different because you may have additional objects besides the 12 just created and shown in the figure.

2. Type the following to delete the sequences and triggers that Oracle created in Step 1:

```
DROP SEQUENCE AgentID_seq;
DROP SEQUENCE Customer_seq;
DROP TRIGGER Agents_bi_trg;
DROP TRIGGER Customers_bi_trg;
```

Oracle drops the sequences and triggers.

The UNION ALL operator is similar to UNION, except that any duplicate rows are not eliminated. It can be useful for listing *all* the rows from two or more SELECT statement but not eliminating duplicates.

USING THE MINUS OPERATOR

The MINUS operator returns the rows that remain when the rows retrieved by the second query are subtracted from rows retrieved by the first query. To understand this concept, consider a very simple pair of one-column tables. Suppose Table1 contains the values A, C, D, F, G, H, and Z. Suppose Table2 contains values A, B, C, H, and W. The SQL statement

```
SELECT *
FROM Table1
MINUS
SELECT *
FROM Table2;
```

would return the values D, F, G, and Z—the values in Table1 that *are not* in Table2. The second table removes A, C, and H because the two tables have those rows in common.

How is the MINUS operator useful in the Redwood Realty database? You can issue the MINUS set operator to "subtract" the Orick properties for sale from the Customers who live in Orick. The result is a list of Orick residents who do not have their properties for sale. In effect, the query is "Customers in Orick" minus "Properties in Orick for sale." The query to reveal this list of addresses, which you can try on your own, is as follows:

```
SELECT Address, City
FROM Customers
WHERE City = 'Orick'
MINUS
SELECT Address, City
FROM Properties
WHERE City = 'Orick';
```

If you execute the preceding query, Oracle lists 53 rows. Since there are 62 people from Orick in the Customers database and there are nine Orick properties for sale, the result makes sense (62 − 9 = 53). However, the numbers need not "add up," because some owners who list their properties for sale may live in other cities or states.

> **Tip:** A handy trick you can use to ensure that two tables are identical is to use the MINUS and UNION ALL set operators. Assume GoodTable and TestTable are the two tables you want to ensure have the same contents (GoodTable is the gold standard). The following query returns *no rows* if the two tables have identical contents. Otherwise, discrepancy rows appear in the result.
>
> (SELECT * FROM GoodTable MINUS SELECT * FROM TestTable)
> UNION ALL
> (SELECT * FROM TestTable MINUS SELECT * FROM GoodTable);
>
> (The parentheses are important because they force evaluation of the two component queries prior to executing the UNION ALL set operation.)

USING THE INTERSECT OPERATOR

The INTERSECT operator returns rows that are retrieved by both queries—rows that are in both tables, but not rows that are in one table but not the other. Suppose you would like to compare the Customers table, containing name and address information about anyone who has contacted Redwood Realty, and the Properties table, which contains the addresses of properties for sale. In particular, you want to know which customers in the Customers table live in the homes that they are listing for sale (in the Properties table). To restrict the results to a manageable size, you will examine only those customers who live in Orick. An INTERSECT query is one way to find the answer. The query shown below will return address and city values for homes that appear in *both* the Customers and Properties tables—at the intersection of those two tables. If you choose to run the query in SQL*Plus, you will see nine entries that satisfy the query.

```
SELECT Address, City
FROM Customers
WHERE City = 'Orick'
INTERSECT
SELECT Address, City
FROM Properties
WHERE City = 'Orick';
```

USING SUBQUERIES

A *subquery* is a query that is contained within another SQL statement—often a query, itself. It is a complete SELECT statement nested within another SQL statement. Here's an example. Suppose you want a list of Agents who were hired by Redwood

Realty after Tobias Carling was hired. If you had not completed this chapter, you would solve this problem in two steps: (1) Issue a query to return Tobias Carling's HireDate from the Agents table, and then (2) execute a query to list all real estate agents whose HireDate value is greater than Tobias Carling's HireDate. You can use a subquery in a SQL data manipulation (DML) statement. Imagine that you are asked to delete (retire) all agents whose hire date is before Tobias Carling's hire date. Use a subquery in a DELETE statement to deliver Carling's hire date, which is plugged into the DELETE statement WHERE clause to remove the record—all in one statement.

This chapter describes how to retrieve the results in one step using a subquery. Subqueries are of two basic types: Single row Subqueries and multiple row subqueries. A *single row subquery* returns zero or one row to the outer SQL statement. A *multiple row subquery* returns two or more rows to the outer SQL statement. Of these two basic types, there is a further subdivision of subqueries: A *multiple column subquery* returns more than one column to the outer SQL statement. A *correlated subquery* references one or more columns in the outer SELECT statement.

UNDERSTANDING AND WRITING SINGLE ROW SUBQUERIES

The simplest subquery is a single-row and single-column subquery. A single row/single column query has the special name *scalar subquery* because it returns one value. You can place a scalar subquery anywhere in a SQL statement that you can write a string: as one of the SELECT clause list items, in the FROM clause, in the WHERE clause, or in the HAVING clause, for instance. The following scalar subquery, for example, lists agents whose age is greater that the average age of all agents.

```
SELECT FirstName, LastName
FROM Agents
WHERE MONTHS_BETWEEN(SYSDATE,BirthDate) >
   (SELECT AVG(MONTHS_BETWEEN(SYSDATE,BirthDate))
    FROM Agents);
```

The subquery, the SELECT clause in parentheses following the greater than (>) comparison operator, executes first. It returns the average age (in months) of all agents. That number replaces the subquery and the remainder of the outer query executes. The WHERE clause selects rows in which the agent's age exceeds the average of all agents' ages. Computing an average means that about half of the rows should always be returned in the answer in a query like this one.

To write and execute a scalar subquery:

1. Start SQL*Plus and log into Oracle, if necessary. Start Notepad to use it as your text editor. Type the following in Notepad, then copy it to SQL*Plus and execute it to list properties that are at least 18 years younger than the average for all Arcata properties:

```
CLEAR SCREEN
SELECT Address, YearBuilt
FROM Properties
WHERE City = 'Arcata' AND
      YearBuilt > (SELECT AVG(YearBuilt)
                   FROM Properties
                   WHERE City = 'Arcata')+18
ORDER BY Address;
```

2. Type the following to list the real estate agents who have the same title as Jessica Taylor. (The UPPER function used throughout eliminates concern over how words are capitalized.) (The code continues on the next page.)

```
COLUMN FirstName FORMAT A10
COLUMN LastName FORMAT A10
```

```
COLUMN TITLE FORMAT A11
SELECT FirstName, LastName, Title
FROM Agents
WHERE UPPER(Title) =
   (SELECT UPPER(Title)
    FROM Agents
    WHERE LOWER(FirstName) = 'jessica'
      AND LOWER(LastName) = 'taylor');
```

Figure 6.17 shows the results of these two steps.

UNDERSTANDING AND WRITING MULTIPLE ROW SUBQUERIES

Multiple row queries are queries within queries that *can* return more than one row to the containing query. Usually, multiple row queries appear in WHERE and HAVING clauses. To properly handle a multiple row subquery, the outer, or parent query uses the multiple row operators IN, ANY, or ALL. Recall that the IN operator attempts to match a column with a list of values enclosed in parentheses. The ANY operator compares one value with *any* value in a list of values; the ALL operator compares one value with *all* values in a list. Bear in mind that you must use a multiple row operator with a subquery that *might* return multiple rows. The comparison operators you have used so far, including >, >=, <, <=, =, and <> will cause an error if the subquery returns more than one row. For example, the following will probably generate an error message because the subquery may return more than one birthday value.

```
SELECT LastName
FROM Agents
WHERE Birthdate > (SELECT Birthdate FROM Agents
                   WHERE Gender = 'M');
```

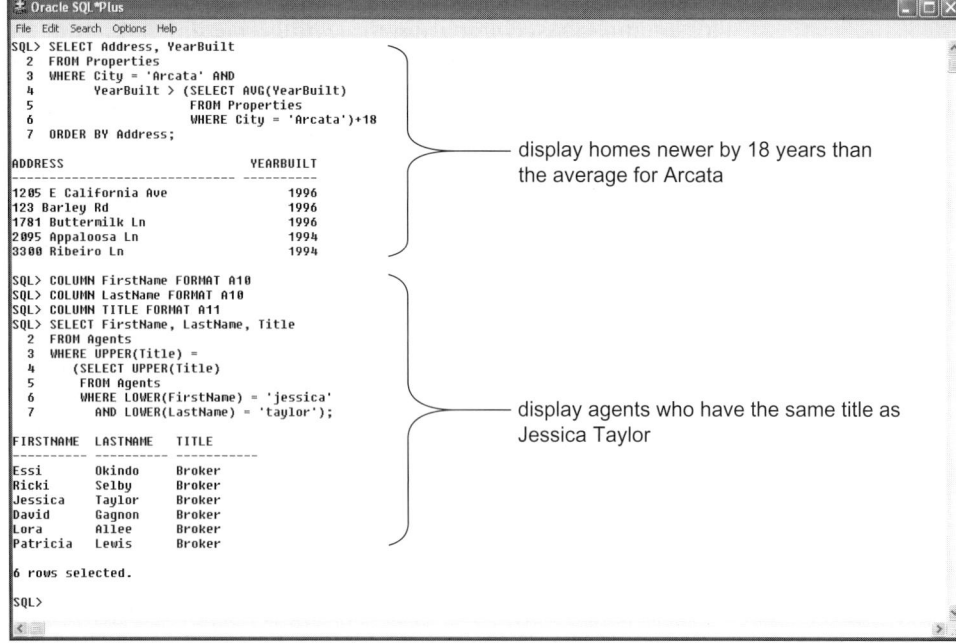

FIGURE 6.17 Using subqueries in WHERE clauses.

The error message is *ORA-01427: single-row subquery returns more than one row* and it indicates that the greater than (>) operator can only compare one value to one other value—not a list of possible values.

Using the IN Operator with a Multiple Row Subquery The IN operator is handy for checking if a value is in a list of values in another table. The list of values is generated by a subquery. You can also use NOT IN to find a value that is not in a list of values. For example, the following query containing two subqueries determines which parts of a fictitious supplier are manufactured in Encino:

```
SELECT * FROM Parts
WHERE PartNumber IN (SELECT PartNumber FROM Shipments
                WHERE SupplierNumber IN
                    (SELECT SupplierNumber FROM Suppliers
                     WHERE UPPER(City) = 'ENCINO'));
```

The most deeply nested query returns the SupplierNumber located in Encino. Those value(s) are compared against SupplierNumber and are used to select a PartNumber from the Shipments table. The PartNumber from the Parts table is compared against the list of PartNumber values from the Shipments table. All the columns from the Parts table are displayed for rows in which the PartNumber is in a shipment from a supplier whose plant is in Encino.

To list agents who have no listings;

1. Open Notepad so you can save all the lines of the script you type in these steps.
2. Type the script in Notepad, copy it to SQL*Plus, and execute it. The SELECT statement determines which agents *do not* have customers buying or selling homes.

```
CLEAR SCREEN
SELECT DISTINCT FirstName, LastName
FROM Agents
WHERE AgentID NOT IN (SELECT AgentID FROM CustAgentList);
```

The subquery returns a list of agent IDs from the CustAgentList corresponding to agents that have a customer. That AgentID from the Agents table is compared against the list. Names of agents not found in the list appear in the result.

3. List the Agents' first and last names for agents with customers in Orick. This is, essentially, an alternative to joining three tables:

```
SELECT DISTINCT FirstName, LastName
FROM Agents
WHERE AgentID IN (SELECT AgentID FROM CustAgentList
                WHERE CustomerID IN (SELECT CustomerID
                                    FROM Customers
                                    WHERE City = 'Orick'));
```

4. Type and execute a different version of the preceding query to display seller's agents—agents who represent sellers. (Remember: type the script in Notepad if you want to save it later. Then copy the new portion to SQL*Plus for subsequent execution.)

```
SELECT DISTINCT a.FirstName, a.LastName
FROM Agents a JOIN CustAgentList c USING (AgentID)
WHERE c.ContactReason = 'Sell'
  AND c.CustomerID IN (SELECT CustomerID FROM CUSTOMERS
                    WHERE UPPER(City) = 'ORICK');
```

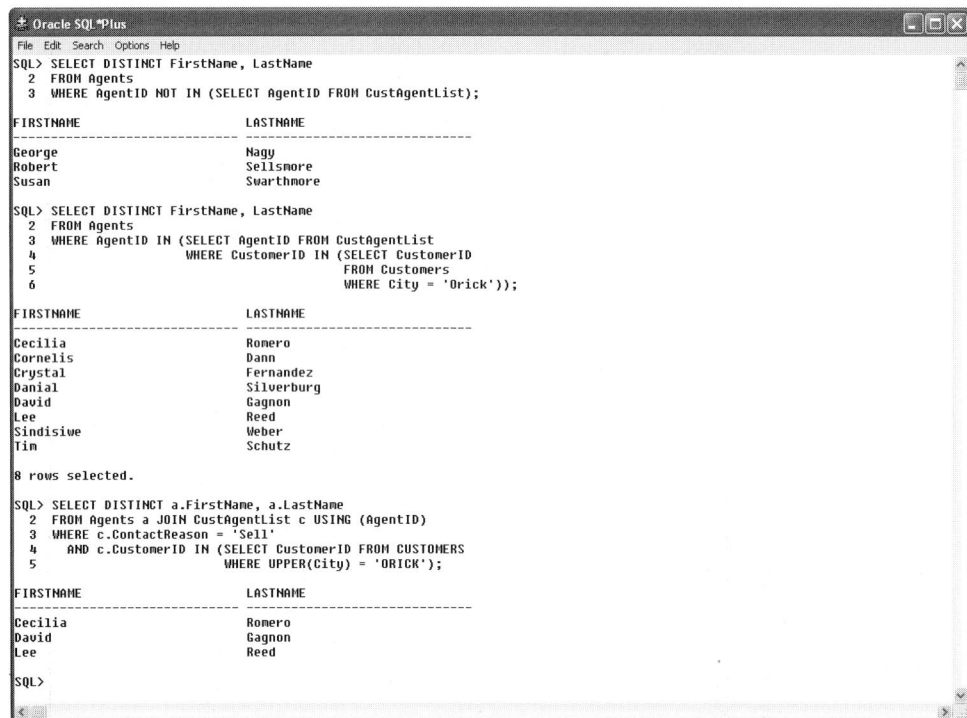

FIGURE 6.18 Examples of the IN operator and subqueries.

Figure 6.18 shows the results of these steps. Notice that only two real estate agents have clients in Orick who want to sell their homes. They may have many listings, however.

Using the ANY and ALL Operators You use the ANY and the ALL operators to compare a value with the values in a list. You combine the ANY or ALL operators with any of any of the comparison operators (>, >=, <, <=, =, or <>). The results of the subquery are a set of values, rather than individual values. One of the comparison operators must precede ANY or ALL in your query. Table 6.3 summarizes the meaning of ANY and ALL when used with several of the comparison operators.

Before investigating the ANY and ALL operators, install a new Redwood Realty table called AgentsHR. It contains more sensitive information about the agents including the number of dependents, base salary, marital status, social security number, ethnicity, vacation weeks, and the sales team within Redwood Realty to which they

TABLE 6.3 ANY and ALL operator descriptions.

Operator	Meaning
=ANY	Equal to any value the subquery returns. It is the same as the IN operator.
<ANY	Smaller than the largest value the subquery returns.
>ANY	Larger than the smallest value the subquery returns.
>ALL	Larger than the largest value the subquery returns.
<ALL	Smaller than the smallest value the subquery returns.

CHAPTER 6   Creating Multitable Queries and Views   291

belong. There are five sales teams organized around neighborhoods about which they are most familiar. First, use your file browser to locate the script file called Ch06AgentsHR.sql. Note the path to that file, or copy it to a convenient location and remember its new path.

To add a new table to the Redwood Realty database:

1. In SQL*Plus, type the following, substituting the actual path for "<path>" to the file Ch06AgentsHR.sql.

```
START <path>\Ch06AgentsHR
```

Oracle creates a table and populates it with additional agent information.

2. Type the following to display the new table's structure and list its contents:

```
CLEAR SCREEN
DESCRIBE AgentsHR
SELECT * FROM AgentsHR;
```

Your results should closely resemble Figure 6.19

The new table provides a bit more numeric information in a smaller table. It is handy for demonstrating the ANY and ALL operators to perform comparative analysis with salaries and team group averages. First you will write a query containing a subquery to determine which real estate agents who make more in base salary than the highest paid member of team 10. Naturally, this excludes members from team 10 by definition—because you want those who make more than the "highest paid member . . . ," the appropriate operator is ALL.

FIGURE 6.19   Description and contents of the AgentsHR table.

```
SQL> DESCRIBE AgentsHR
 Name                                      Null?    Type
 ----------------------------------------- -------- ----------------------------
 AGENTID                                   NOT NULL NUMBER(38)
 DEPENDENTS                                         NUMBER(38)
 BASESALARY                                         NUMBER(38)
 MARITAL                                            NVARCHAR2(1)
 SSN                                                NVARCHAR2(11)
 ETHNICITY                                          NUMBER(38)
 VACATION                                           NUMBER(38)
 TEAM                                               NUMBER(38)

SQL> SELECT * FROM AgentsHR;

  AGENTID DEPENDENTS BASESALARY M SSN         ETHNICITY   VACATION       TEAM
--------- ---------- ---------- - ----------- ---------   --------   --------
    10041          5       3051 M 193-82-2099         3          4         14
    10235          1       2642 S 299-39-6678         1          2         11
    10429          4       2985 S 113-60-1549         1          4         13
    10497          1       4377 M 306-16-5360         4          2         14
    10849          4       2585 D 313-36-4309         2          4         14
    10913          2       3493 D 486-11-3733         4          4         13
    11775          4       2216 M 817-28-2690         1          4         14
    12211          2       3520 D 327-25-8620         1          2         14
    12301          2       3637 D 152-64-9996         1          2         14
    12499          1       3413 W 675-31-4312         2          3         13
    12715          1       2066 M 709-98-2311         1          3         11

  AGENTID DEPENDENTS BASESALARY M SSN         ETHNICITY   VACATION       TEAM
--------- ---------- ---------- - ----------- ---------   --------   --------
    12765          2       2360 W 667-78-9822         2          2         11
    12875          2       2343 M 861-49-4737         1          3         14
    12963          2       4433 S 944-32-6394         4          3         14
    13353          4       4064 S 687-13-4756         2          3         14
    13555          2       3420 M 928-51-8656         1          4         10
    13649          1       4171 D 679-68-1774         3          2         14
    13771          5       3838 M 312-74-1536         1          2         10
    14117          1       2567 M 934-97-5021         2          3         14
    14447          3       3723 W 393-17-5206         5          3         12
    14599          4       4260 M 251 32 2456         5          2         11
    14601          3       2135 W 487-39-2872         1          2         12

  AGENTID DEPENDENTS BASESALARY M SSN         ETHNICITY   VACATION       TEAM
--------- ---------- ---------- - ----------- ---------   --------   --------
```

(additional rows are out of sight)

To use the ANY and ALL operators in a subquery:

1. Using Notepad as your text editor, type the following statements, and then copy it to SQL*Plus and execute it:

```
CLEAR SCREEN
COLUMN BaseSalary FORMAT $9,999
SELECT AgentID, BaseSalary, Team
FROM AgentsHR
WHERE BaseSalary >ALL (SELECT BaseSalary
                      FROM AgentsHR
                      WHERE Team = 10);
```

Oracle returns five rows indicating that only five of the thirty-two agents make more than *every* agent in team 10.

2. Modify the query slightly to list agents (their IDs, at least) for any agent *not in team 10* who makes more in base salary than *any* agent in team 10. Edit the previous SELECT statement by replacing >ALL with >ANY, adding the additional WHERE clause condition AND Team <> 10, and rerunning the query. The modified SELECT statement is:

```
SELECT AgentID, BaseSalary, Team
FROM AgentsHR
WHERE BaseSalary >ANY (SELECT BaseSalary      modified line
                      FROM AgentsHR
                      WHERE Team = 10)
   AND Team <> 10;                             modified line
```

Oracle displays eleven rows indicating that eleven agents not in team 10 make more than the lowest-paid member of team 10 (see Figure 6.20).

3. Leave SQL*Plus and Notepad running.

FIGURE 6.20 Using ALL and ANY operators in a query.

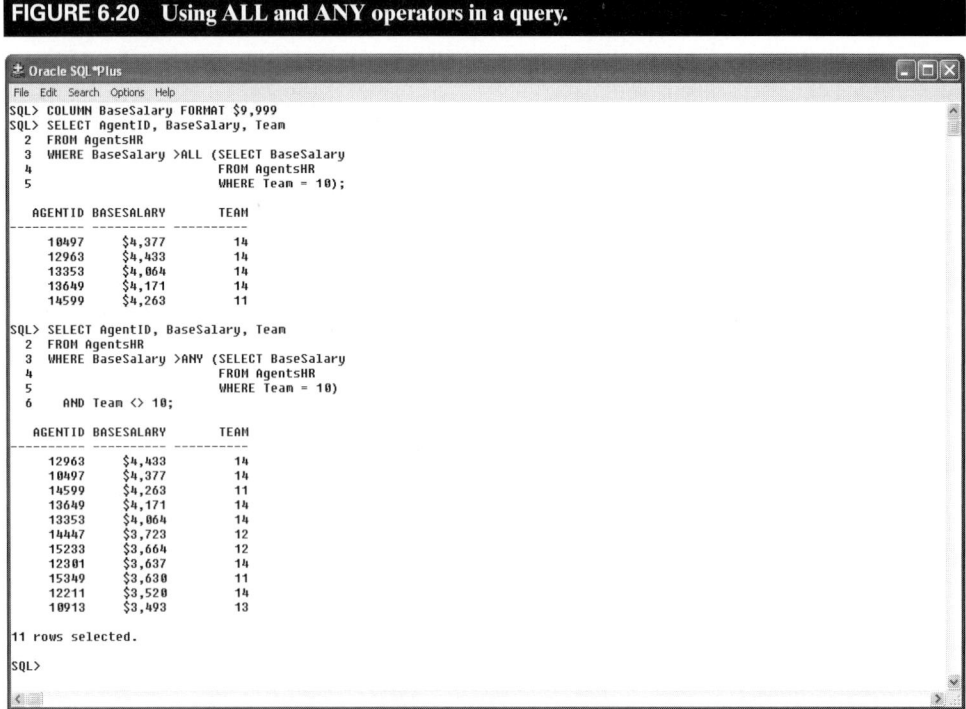

CHAPTER 6 Creating Multitable Queries and Views

It would be interesting to see the maximum base salary of team 10 so it is easy to validate the results from queries such as the ones you just ran. Let's join the Agents table to the AgentsHR table to display names, instead of ID numbers. In addition, use a SELECT subquery in an outer query's select list to compute and display the maximum salary of team 10. Finally, display the base salary of anyone whose base salary is larger than the greatest salary of a team 10 member. This query is similar to step 1 above, except that the agents' names and a maximum salary appear.

To display the names of anyone making more than the highest-paid team 10 member:

1. Type the following to clear the screen and format columns you are about to display in a SELECT statement:

   ```
   CLEAR SCREEN
   COLUMN Agent       FORMAT A22    HEADING 'Agent''s Name'
   COLUMN BaseSalary  FORMAT $9,999 HEADING 'Base|Salary'
   COLUMN TeamMax     FORMAT $9,999 HEADING 'Team 10|Max. Salary'
   ```

2. Type the following query and its *two* subqueries. Be sure to use Notepad so you can easily edit the query, if needed. Type it very carefully, then copy it to SQL*Plus and execute it.

   ```
   SELECT FirstName || ' '|| LastName AS Agent, BaseSalary,
         (SELECT MAX(BaseSalary)
          FROM AgentsHR
          WHERE Team = 10) AS TeamMax, Team
   FROM Agents INNER JOIN AgentsHR USING (AgentID)
   WHERE BaseSalary >ALL (SELECT BaseSalary
                          FROM AgentsHR
                          WHERE Team = 10);
   ```

   Oracle returns the same rows as Step 1 in the preceding exercise, except that more information is available when two tables are joined and another subquery returns the actual maximum salary for verification. Your results should match Figure 6.21.

3. Type **CLEAR COLUMNS** to remove all column formatting
4. Type **exit** and press **Enter** to log off Oracle and exit SQL*Plus.
5. Save everything you have typed in Notepad and close Notepad.

FIGURE 6.21 Using two subqueries and the ALL operator.

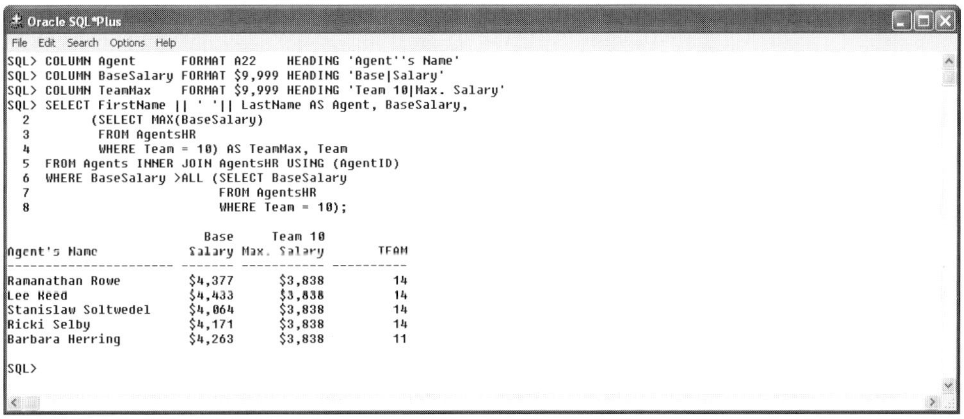

Understanding and Writing Correlated Subqueries

Correlated subqueries are quite different from subqueries you have studied in this chapter so far. Because a correlated subquery references one or more columns in the outer or containing query, Oracle executes the inner query once for each row in the outer query. A correlated subquery is handy when you want to answer a question that depends on the value of a column in the outer query for every row in the outer query. While correlated subqueries are an extremely powerful tool, they can be expensive, too. Consider the following subquery which lists agent IDs corresponding to agents who have a higher than average number of vacation days than others in their same team:

```
SELECT *
FROM AgentsHr outer
WHERE outer.Vacation >
   (SELECT AVG(Vacation)
    FROM AgentsHR inner
    WHERE outer.Team = inner.team)
ORDER BY Team;
```

First, Oracle selects a row from the outer query (SELECT *...). Then it determines the values of the correlated columns (outer.Team and inner.Team). Then, Oracle executes the inner query for each row of the outer query, passes the results of the inner query to the outer query, and executes the outer query. Then, Oracle picks the next row from the outer query and repeats the preceding procedure. When you consider the query, it becomes clear that tables with a large number of rows that are the subject of a correlated query can be extremely expensive. Consider the cost in terms of the number of rows retrieved and examined. If a table contains 1,000 rows, the inner query is executed against 1,000 rows for *each* row in the outer query. Because the table in the outer query also contains 1,000 rows, the total cost is 1,000 times 1,000, or 1,000,000 rows! This will take even the fastest database a fair amount of time. The need for a correlated subquery is clear, but use them judiciously.

Using Comparison Operators For your first experiment with correlated subqueries, you will answer the interesting question: "Which properties that are for sale have an asking price that is above the average for their city." You will use a correlated subquery to answer this question, hoping to pinpoint some properties that might be overpriced for their area. Any real estate professional will tell you this is a coarse-grained question that really depends on many factors. Nevertheless, it is a valuable tool in your database arsenal. Launch SQL*Plus and open Notepad in preparation for the next interactive steps. The query you are about to write joins the Listings and Properties tables so that both the AskingPrice and City columns are available simultaneously. The subquery also joins the two tables so that the average asking price can be determined for each city. Because a large number of rows could be returned, the outer query restricts the analysis to three small cities: Loleta, Orick, and Trinidad. The query works perfectly well if you remove that restrictive clause, but Oracle returns 194 rows.

To write a correlated subquery:

1. Type the following in Notepad and then copy and execute the lines in SQL*Plus. Begin with column formatting lines:

```
CLEAR SCREEN
COLUMN Address FORMAT A30
COLUMN City       FORMAT A16
COLUMN AskingPrice FORMAT $9,999,999
```

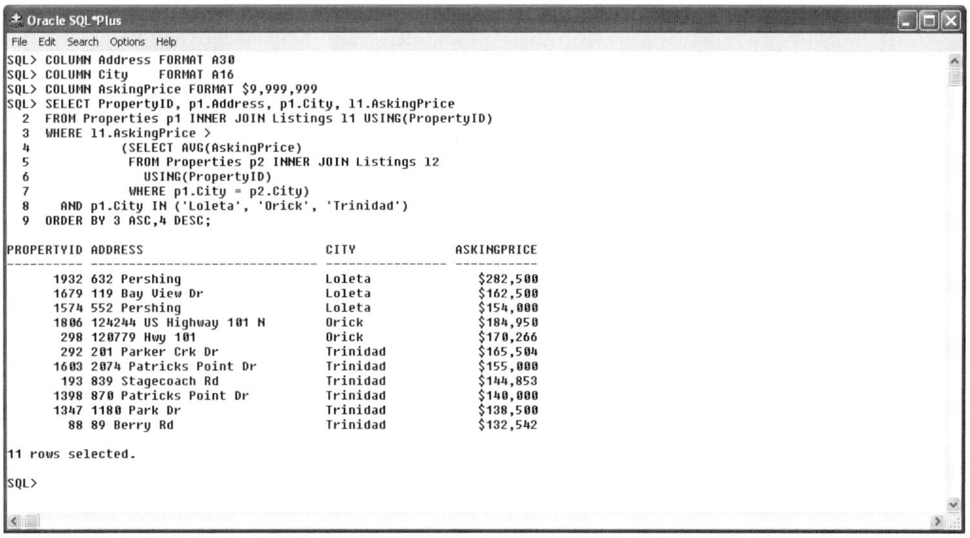

CHAPTER 6 Creating Multitable Queries and Views 295

FIGURE 6.22 A correlated subquery to locate above-average asking prices.

2. Next, type the following and execute it in SQL*Plus to display properties with above average asking prices when compared to others in their respective cities:

```
SELECT PropertyID, p1.Address, p1.City, l1.AskingPrice
FROM Properties p1 INNER JOIN Listings l1 USING(PropertyID)
WHERE l1.AskingPrice >
         (SELECT AVG(AskingPrice)
           FROM Properties p2 INNER JOIN Listings l2
             USING(PropertyID)
           WHERE p1.City = p2.City)
   AND p1.City IN ('Loleta', 'Orick', 'Trinidad')
ORDER BY 3 ASC,4 DESC;
```

Figure 6.22 shows the eleven properties in one of three selected cities whose average price is greater than the average price for their cities.

3. To clean things up, type and execute the following:

```
CLEAR COLUMNS
```

The correlation columns are found in the WHERE clause near the bottom of the SELECT statement:

```
WHERE p1.City = p2.City
```

It compares the city name from the outer query to the city name currently available from the subquery. If they do not match, that AskingPrice of the inner query is not considered in the current average price calculation. The inner query continues retrieving every row in the joined Properties and Listings tables until no more exist. Then the next row of the outer query is fetched and the inner query begins anew from the top.

You can modify an earlier query you ran to yield more specific base salary information and list each agent who has an above average salary when compared to others on the team. It is different from the earlier query because the salary is compared to the team's average, not the overall average. A correlated subquery suits our needs here, and the cost is low because there are only twenty-nine agents.

To use a correlated subquery to determine who earns more than their group average:

1. In Notepad, type the following and copy to SQL*Plus and execute:

```
CLEAR SCREEN
SET PAGESIZE 30
COLUMN BaseSalary FORMAT $9,999 HEADING 'Base|Salary'
BREAK ON Team SKIP 1
```

2. Type and execute the following:

```
SELECT Poss.Team, Poss.AgentID, Poss.BaseSalary
FROM   AgentsHR Poss
WHERE  BaseSalary >
  (SELECT   AVG(BaseSalary)
   FROM     AgentsHR Aver
   WHERE    Poss.Team = Aver.Team)
ORDER BY 1,2;
```

Oracle displays the sixteen rows for team members with salaries over their respective team's average. Your result should match Figure 6.23.

3. Type and execute the following to reset columns, breaks, and page size values:

```
CLEAR BREAKS
CLEAR COLUMNS
SET PAGESIZE 14
```

4. Save your Notepad file, if you want to preserve these last steps. You can exit SQL*Plus if you want to take a break, or leave it running for steps that follow.

Using EXISTS The ***EXISTS operator*** is used when you want to determine whether a condition is true in a subquery. The EXISTS operator returns true if the condition

FIGURE 6.23 A correlated subquery to display above-average salaries.

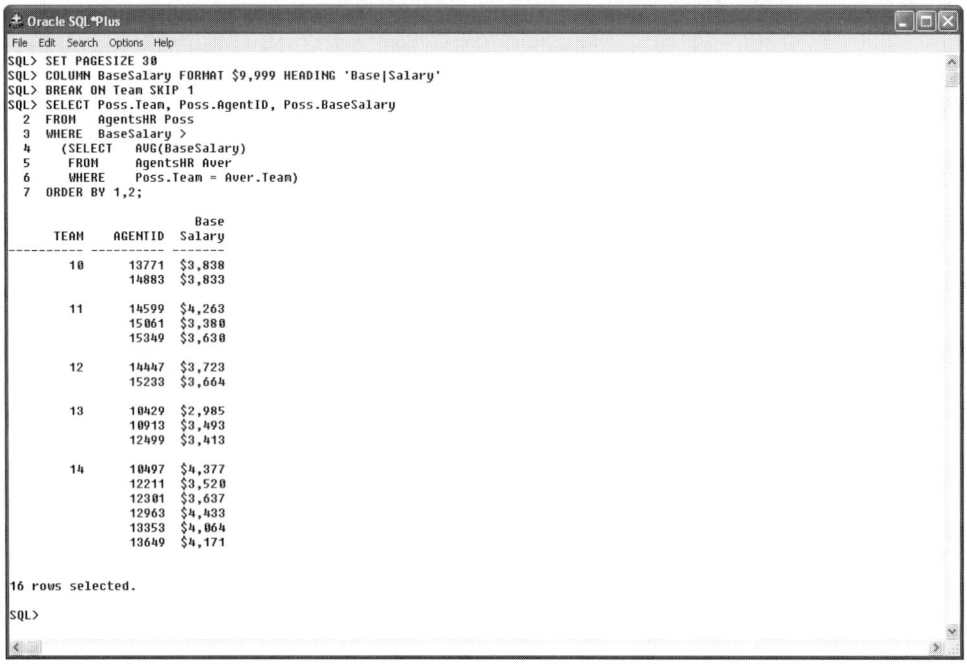

```
Oracle SQL*Plus
File Edit Search Options Help
SQL> SET PAGESIZE 30
SQL> COLUMN BaseSalary FORMAT $9,999 HEADING 'Base|Salary'
SQL> BREAK ON Team SKIP 1
SQL> SELECT Poss.Team, Poss.AgentID, Poss.BaseSalary
  2  FROM   AgentsHR Poss
  3  WHERE  BaseSalary >
  4    (SELECT   AVG(BaseSalary)
  5     FROM     AgentsHR Aver
  6     WHERE    Poss.Team = Aver.Team)
  7  ORDER BY 1,2;

                          Base
      TEAM    AGENTID   Salary
---------- ---------- -------
        10      13771  $3,838
                14883  $3,833

        11      14599  $4,263
                15061  $3,380
                15349  $3,630

        12      14447  $3,723
                15233  $3,664

        13      10429  $2,985
                10913  $3,493
                12499  $3,413

        14      10497  $4,377
                12211  $3,520
                12301  $3,637
                12963  $4,433
                13353  $4,064
                13649  $4,171


16 rows selected.

SQL>
```

exists or false if it does not. Although you can use EXISTS with non-correlated subqueries, careful consideration of them will soon convince you that their only practical use is with correlated subqueries. In other words, an EXISTS operator is very interesting when the subquery result depends on the outer query—in other words, a correlated subquery. NOT EXISTS is the logical opposite of EXISTS. You use it if you want to know when a subquery does not find the corresponding row. Because EXISTS tests only if a row exists or not, the subquery select list columns are irrelevant. It is common to use '1' or 'X' and even the keyword NULL in the subquery select list, for instance. The following is the syntax for a typical EXISTS query and its accompanying subquery.

```
SELECT <outer select list>
FROM <outer table>
WHERE EXISTS
   (SELECT 'X'
    FROM <inner table> inner
    WHERE <outer table.columnname> = <inner table.column name>);
```

You can use a correlated subqueries with the EXISTS condition to determine if anyone with outstanding orders has ordered a particular item by correlating user orders with inventory stock. Similarly, the EXISTS operator in conjunction with a correlated subquery will efficiently determine if a customer has a real estate agent or a real estate agent has any properties in the Listings table. You can determine the latter with the following correlated subqueries involving the two Redwood Realty tables Agents and Listings—but not joined as you might think:

```
SELECT LastName, FirstName, 'No Listings' AS "Situation"
FROM Agents
WHERE NOT EXISTS (SELECT 'X'
                  FROM Listings
                  WHERE AgentID = ListingAgentID);
```

Observe that the subquery select list contains a constant, because *what* is returned by the subquery in an EXISTS (or NOT EXISTS) subquery is irrelevant. You only want to know is there a row that satisfies the subquery criterion. The NOT EXISTS here poses the question "Are there any real estate agents whose AgentID is not found in the Listings table?" and returns the answer yes. There are three. Test it for yourself.

To pose a correlated subqueries using the EXISTS operator:

1. Launch SQL*Plus and log into Oracle, if needed. Type and execute **CLEAR SCREEN** to clear SQL*Plus' display.
2. Type the following SELECT statement and execute it. It counts the unique customers who do not have a real estate agent assigned.

```
SELECT COUNT(*) AS "Customers w/o agents"
FROM Customers outer
WHERE NOT EXISTS
  (SELECT 'X'
   FROM CustAgentList inner
   WHERE outer.CustomerID = inner.CustomerID);
```

The query returns the value 1745, meaning that 1,745 customers in the Customers table do not have ID numbers that match the agents' ID numbers in the Agents table.

3. Write another query to count the number of customers who do not have properties listed in the Properties table. Type and execute the following.

(Though you could list the customer names, it is a long list and would scroll for a while.)

```
SELECT COUNT(LastName) AS "Customers w/o properties"
FROM Customers
WHERE NOT EXISTS
  (SELECT 123
   FROM Properties
   WHERE CustomerID = OwnerID);
```

Don't be concerned that the subquery select list has 123. We did that to drive home the point that the subquery select list is immaterial when used with an EXISTS condition.

4. Finally, list the agents whose license status is not "Licensed." Do so without joining the tables—by using a correlated subquery and EXISTS. Type and execute the following:

```
SELECT FirstName, LastName, AgentID
FROM Agents a
WHERE EXISTS (SELECT 'X'
              FROM LicenseStatus b
              WHERE a.LicenseStatusID = b.LicenseStatusID
                AND UPPER(StatusText) <> 'LICENSED')
ORDER BY LastName, FirstName;
```

Your results should match those shown in Figure 6.24.

5. If you have been using Notepad as your editor, then save the code you created in this session and close Notepad.
6. Type **Exit** and press **Enter** to log off Oracle and close SQL*Plus.

FIGURE 6.24 Using the EXISTS operator in several correlated subqueries.

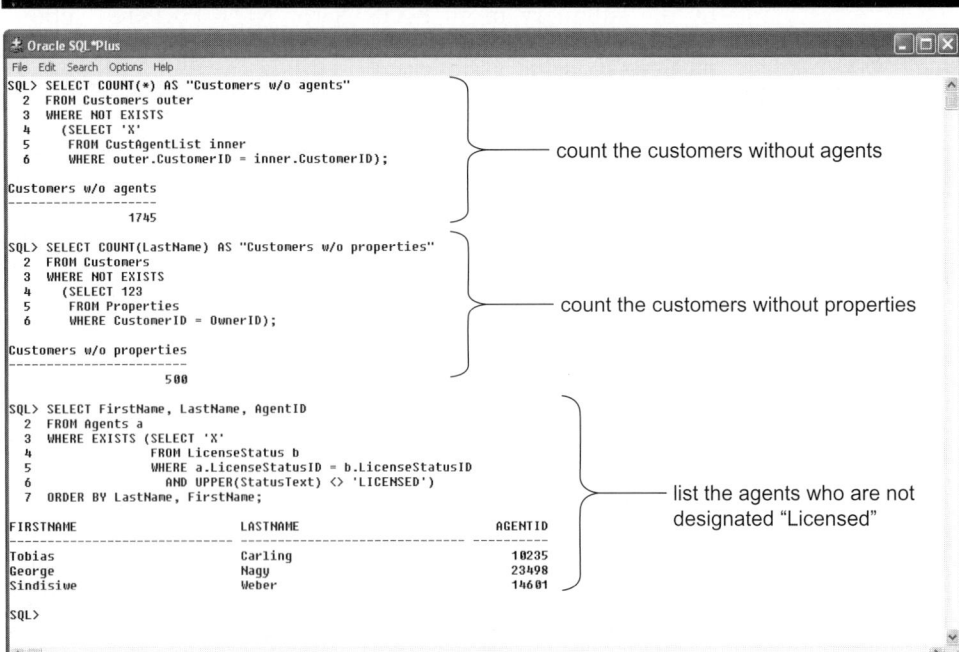

USING SUBQUERIES IN DML STATEMENTS

Subqueries are not restricted to use with SELECT statements. You can use subqueries in DML statements including INSERT, DELETE, and UPDATE statements. For example, the following DELETE statement deletes agents from the Agents tables if they have no listings in the listings table. (Don't do this, because three agents that have no listings are new!)

```
DELETE
FROM Agents
WHERE NOT EXISTS
   (SELECT 'X' FROM Listings
    WHERE AgentID = ListingAgentID);
```

Here, the subquery merely determines if the AgentID, supplied by the outer query, is found in any of the Listings' ListingAgentID column values. If not, then that agent has no listings. If you were to run this, it would identify and delete three agents (Susan Swarthmore, George Nagy, and Robert Sellsmore) from the Agents table. In an application where you are selling items, you might want to insert an inventory item into a table of items that should be ordered when they are in short supply.

You can use a correlated subquery to update a table. For instance, the following ALTER TABLE and SELECT statements add a column to the AgentsHR table and then populate it with corresponding values from the Agents' birthdays, which are found in the BirthDate column of the Agents table. Notice that a correlated subquery is required to tie each agent to the correct birth date in the outer query.

```
REM Add a column to the AgentsHR table to hold BirthDate:
ALTER TABLE AgentsHR
   ADD (BirthDate DATE);
REM Place each agent's birthdate into the correct row:
UPDATE AgentsHR hr
SET BirthDate = (SELECT BirthDate
                 FROM Agents ag
                 WHERE hr.AgentID = ag.AgentID);
```

CREATING AND USING VIEWS

A *view* is a predefined query on one or more tables called *base tables*. It can consist of a subset of a base table, or it can be a combination of an arbitrary number of tables joined in the same way that you join base tables. A view is not stored as a physical table. Instead, Oracle stores the information you use to create a view, its *definition,* in its system tables. When you use a view, Oracle activates its definition and performs SELECT or DML statements based on the view's definition. For example, you retrieve information from a view, or virtual table, in the same way you do from any other table in the database. You specify a view name in the FROM clause of the SELECT statement, just as you would a base table's name. From the user's viewpoint, views and tables are indistinguishable. Although you can always use a view to retrieve information from the underlying base tables, you cannot always perform arbitrary DML statements such as INSERT, UPDATE, or DELETE. (An explanation appears later in this chapter.) You have used views in previous chapters—data dictionary views. For example, when you display information about tables, you can query the data dictionary view user_tables. Similarly, the data dictionary view user_sequences contains information about sequences users create, and the data dictionary view user_triggers holds the definition of all users' triggers.

In the remainder of this chapter, you will learn how to define and query views. In addition, you will use DML statements with views and learn how views can help protect important tables from unwanted modifications or even from unwanted examination. You will learn how views can provide need-to-know security for selected tables, and how they provide query simplification.

WHAT VIEWS PROVIDE

You create views by specifying a SELECT statement that prescribes what rows, columns, and tables are accessed to create the view. Like other objects, you can grant access to other users to your views. Some of the benefits of a view are:

- Security: Views can restrict a user's access to base table rows and columns, hiding the information the user should not see.
- Query simplification: Views provide query simplification. When a complex, multi-table SELECT statement is required to deliver information, you can capture the query as a view, allowing users to access information through the simpler view.
- Privacy: Views can hide the names of the base tables that constitute the view from users.
- Data independence: If a commonly accessed table is restructured into multiple tables, a view joining the multiple tables together masks the structure change.

Views allow you to define exactly what information is delivered from underlying base tables upon which the views are defined. By restricting different classes of database users to particular views of a table or collection of related tables, you provide a type of security known as discretionary access control. ***Discretionary access control*** means that different users can see different rows and columns from the same base tables. A personnel director might need to access employees' sensitive information such as ethnicity, date of birth, number of dependents, health insurance coverage, and so on. From the same table or collection of tables, a manager might need to display employees' identification numbers, address information, and job skills. With carefully honed views, you can tailor the information to which distinct groups have access, rather than granting blanket access to the base tables containing all employee information.

Views act like filters, allowing certain information to pass through the filter to users but preventing other information from passing. A ***column subset view,*** for example, hides selected columns from some users but makes them accessible to others. This is possible by eliminating columns from the view definition. A ***row subset view*** makes rows meeting stated criteria inaccessible to selected user groups. This is accomplished by using a WHERE clause in the SELECT statement of the view definition to filter rows that should be hidden.

There are two fundamental types of views—complex views and simple views. A ***complex view*** contains a subquery that retrieves data from multiple tables, or groups rows using a GROUP BY or DISTINCT clause, or contains a function call. A ***simple view*** retrieves rows from *one* base table. Simple views are described next.

DEFINING AND QUERYING ONE-TABLE VIEWS

To create (define) a view, issue the CREATE VIEW statement. Its simplified syntax is as follows (and is continued on the next page):

```
CREATE [OR REPLACE] [FORCE | NOFORCE] VIEW <view-name>
  [(<column-name>,…,<column-name>)]
```

```
AS <subquery>
[WITH CHECK OPTION [CONSTRAINT <constraint-name>]]
[WITH READ ONLY];
```

where the optional phrase OR REPLACE indicates that Oracle should replace an existing view by the same name in the user's schema, if it exists. There is no way to modify a view, so you have to recreate the entire view, replacing any older identically named one. The FORCE option allows you to create a view on a base table that does not yet exist. NOFORCE, the default if omitted, means that the view cannot be created unless the table it refers to exists already. "<View-name>" is the name of the view being created, and "<column-name>" is the name of the view's column corresponding to an expression or column in the subquery. Subquery is the subquery that retrieves the data from the base table(s). The WITH CHECK OPTION specifies that only rows that satisfy the subquery WHERE clause criteria can be inserted, updated, or deleted. If you omit the WITH CHECK OPTION, Oracle processes the rows without determining if they would be available through the view. READ ONLY specifies that rows may only be read with the view, not updated, deleted, or inserted. "<Constraint-name>" specifies the name of the WITH CHECK OPTION constraint.

A simple view is based on *one* base table. The following example creates a row subset view of the Agents table which will display only rows with male real estate employees. Furthermore, the WITH READ ONLY clause prevents anyone from accidentally changing any of the Agents table column values.

```
CREATE OR REPLACE VIEW MaleEmployees
AS SELECT *
    FROM Agents
    WHERE Gender = 'M'
WITH READ ONLY;
```

The view is called MaleEmployees. It returns the same columns that the underlying table, Agents, contains. As with a base table, you can issue the SQL*Plus statement DESCRIBE to display a view's column names and data types.

Views restrict which columns are available by omitting them from the subquery defining the view. For example, the following CREATE VIEW statement omits most of the Agents table columns:

```
CREATE OR REPLACE VIEW Employees
AS SELECT AgentID, FirstName, LastName, Title
    FROM Agents;
```

Only the AgentID, FirstName, LastName, and Title columns are available through the preceding view.

Once you have created a one-table view, querying it is a snap. You simply use the view name where you would otherwise write a table name. A SELECT statement querying a view can have a select list to return a subset of a view's columns, and it can have the other optional SELECT statement clauses including WHERE, GROUP BY, HAVING, and ORDER BY. The following SELECT statement queries the view Employees whose definition appears above.

```
SELECT LastName||', '||FirstName, Title
FROM Employees
WHERE Title = 'Broker'
ORDER BY 1;
```

The preceding query uses the view called Employees to retrieve the name fields concatenated and the title for each row in which the title is "Broker." Oracle sorts the rows returned through the view before displaying them.

It is time to define a view or two and then query them. In preparation, launch SQL*Plus and log into Oracle. You might want to launch a text editor to serve as your editor and allow you to save the SQL statements when you are done.

To create and query a one-table view:

1. Type **CLEAR SCREEN** and press **Enter** to clear the screen.
2. Type the following, copy it to SQL*Plus, and execute to create a view named Brokers. It is a row subset view displaying all columns for agents whose title is "Broker":

```
CREATE OR REPLACE VIEW Brokers
AS SELECT *
   FROM Agents
   WHERE UPPER(Title) = 'BROKER'
WITH CHECK OPTION;
```

Oracle signals that the view has been created with the message "View created."

3. Create a column subset view for agents who have titles other than *Broker*. Type and execute the following statement to create the view called NonBrokers:

```
CREATE OR REPLACE VIEW NonBrokers
AS SELECT AgentID, LastName, FirstName, BirthDate
          Gender, HireDate, Title, TaxID
   FROM Agents
   WHERE UPPER(Title) <> 'BROKER'
WITH CHECK OPTION;
```

Oracle signals the view has been created with the message "View created."

4. Type the following to display information about the NonBrokers view:

```
DESCRIBE NonBrokers
```

Oracle displays column names and data types for the NonBrokers view. Your display, to this point, should be similar to Figure 6.25

FIGURE 6.25 Creating and describing views.

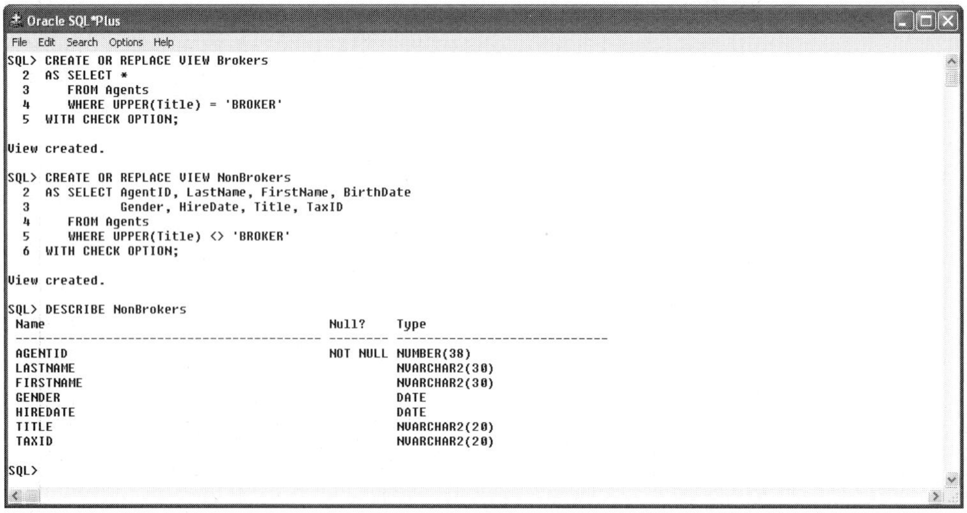

CHAPTER 6 Creating Multitable Queries and Views   303

```
Oracle SQL*Plus
File Edit Search Options Help
SQL> COLUMN FirstName FORMAT A15
SQL> COLUMN LastName  FORMAT A15
SQL> COLUMN Title     FORMAT A12
SQL> SELECT FirstName, LastName, Title
  2  FROM NonBrokers
  3  ORDER BY LastName, FirstName;

FIRSTNAME        LASTNAME        TITLE
---------------  --------------- ------------
Tobias           Carling         Salesperson
Belinda          Chong           Salesperson
Elizabeth        Dahlen          Salesperson
Cornelis         Dann            Salesperson
Crystal          Fernandez       Salesperson
Jackson          Flamenbaum      Salesperson
Barbara          Herring         Salesperson
James            Kellogg         Salesperson
Kai              Marcoux         Salesperson
Nancy            Piperova        Salesperson
Lee              Reed            Salesperson

FIRSTNAME        LASTNAME        TITLE
---------------  --------------- ------------
Clair            Robinson        Salesperson
Cecilia          Romero          Salesperson
Ramanathan       Rowe            Salesperson
Tim              Schutz          Salesperson
Heather          Sheibani        Salesperson
Danial           Silverburg      Salesperson
Stanislaw        Soltwedel       Salesperson
Tim              St-Onge         Salesperson
Edwin            Townsend        Salesperson
Bruce            Voss            Salesperson
Sindisiwe        Weber           Salesperson

FIRSTNAME        LASTNAME        TITLE
---------------  --------------- ------------
Christine        Williams        Salesperson

23 rows selected.

SQL>
```

FIGURE 6.26 Displaying rows through the NonBrokers view.

5. Type and execute the following to clear the screen, format some columns, and query the views you created:

```
CLEAR SCREEN
COLUMN FirstName FORMAT A15
COLUMN LastName  FORMAT A15
COLUMN Title     FORMAT A12
SELECT FirstName, LastName, Title
FROM NonBrokers
ORDER BY LastName, FirstName;
```

Your display should be similar to Figure 6.26. In the last step above, Oracle displays the twenty-three rows of the NonBrokers table from the Agents base table. No row contains "Broker" in the Title column because the view filters out those rows. If you have set the PAGESIZE value to a value other than 14, the number of headings on your display will vary.

You can modify the names of the columns defined in a view by specifying column names between the word *VIEW* and the view name. Create one more view to try out this view-creation option.

To create a view that defines alternative column names:

1. Type the following statements in SQL*Plus (or Notepad then copy to SQL*Plus):

```
CLEAR SCREEN
CREATE OR REPLACE VIEW
   Cust (CustNo, LName, FName, Addr, City, St, Zip)
AS SELECT CustomerID, LastName, FirstName,
          Address, City, State, Zipcode
   FROM Customers;
```

```
SQL> CREATE OR REPLACE VIEW
  2      Cust (CustNo, LName, FName, Addr, City, St, Zip)
  3    AS SELECT CustomerID, LastName, FirstName,
  4              Address, City, State, Zipcode
  5       FROM Customers;

View created.

SQL> DESCRIBE Cust
 Name                                      Null?    Type
 ----------------------------------------- -------- ----------------------------
 CUSTNO                                    NOT NULL NUMBER(38)
 LNAME                                     NOT NULL NVARCHAR2(30)
 FNAME                                     NOT NULL NVARCHAR2(30)
 ADDR                                               NVARCHAR2(40)
 CITY                                               NVARCHAR2(30)
 ST                                                 NVARCHAR2(20)
 ZIP                                                NVARCHAR2(20)

SQL>
```

FIGURE 6.27 Defining a view with alternative column names.

2. Type the following and press **Enter** to display information about the view:

   `DESCRIBE Cust`

   Figure 6.27 shows the results. They should match what you see.

3. Type **exit** and press **Enter** to exit SQL*Plus and log off Oracle.

MODIFYING DATA USING ONE-TABLE VIEWS

You can perform DML statements on views to update, insert, or delete data in the base tables on which they are defined. There are some restrictions, however. If you have defined a view with the WITH READ ONLY option, Oracle will not allow any DML operation using the view. If you prefer using the view for DML operations, you must re-create the view without the phrase WITH READ OPTION. Similarly, update operations or insert statements issued on a view defined with the WITH CHECK OPTION will fail if the attempted modification would otherwise make the modified record unavailable through the view. For example, if you attempted to insert a new row using the Brokers view and the title were "Salesperson," the insert would fail. Oracle issues the error message *ORA-01402: view WITH CHECK OPTION where-clause violation*. If you create simple views without the check option, you can update, insert, and delete rows that are not otherwise retrieved by the view.

Several rules about using DML statements apply to simple views and complex ones. If the view does not include the WITH READ ONLY option, DML statements you issue will execute correctly on a simple view subject to a condition—the modification must not violate the base table's domain or referential integrity rules. In particular, all modifications must abide by the table's constraints including: (1) PRIMARY KEY, (2) NOT NULL, (3) UNIQUE, (4) FOREIGN KEY, and (5) WITH CHECK OPTION constraints. Let's try some DML operations on views you have created above.

To insert, update, and delete rows using a simple view:

1. Launch SQL*Plus, log into Oracle, and launch Notepad if you want to use it as your editor. Type **CLEAR SCREEN** to clear the SQL*Plus screen.
2. Type and execute the following to insert a row into the Brokers view:

   ```
   INSERT INTO Brokers (AgentID, LastName, FirstName, Title)
       VALUES (87654, 'Foxworthy', 'Robert', 'Salesperson');
   ```

   Oracle rejects the attempted INSERT because the Brokers view only allows insertions for Titles equal to *Broker*.

3. Type and execute the following to insert a new customer using the Cust view:

   ```
   INSERT INTO Cust (CustNo, FName, LName, Addr, City)
       VALUES (76543,'Allison', 'Honeycutt', '123 Main','Loleta');
   ```

4. You forgot to include the ZIP code in the preceding INSERT. Update it by typing and executing the following. (Be sure to write the WHERE clause as shown, or else many rows may be affected.)

   ```
   UPDATE Cust
   SET St = 'CA', Zip = '95551'
   WHERE CustNo = 76543;
   ```

5. Make the insert and update permanent by typing and executing the following:

   ```
   COMMIT;
   ```

6. Display the row you just inserted by typing and executing the following:

   ```
   SELECT CustNo, FName, LName, City, St, Zip
   FROM Cust
   WHERE CustNo = 76543;
   ```

7. Delete the newly committed row by typing and executing the following:

   ```
   DELETE FROM Cust
   WHERE CustNo = 76543;
   ```

   Figure 6.28 shows the results of the preceding steps.

Producing Complex Views

You create a complex view with the same CREATE VIEW you use for a simple one-table view. Recall that a complex view contains a subquery that retrieves rows from multiple base tables, groups rows using a GROUP BY or a DISTINCT clause, or

FIGURE 6.28 Executing DML statements on a view.

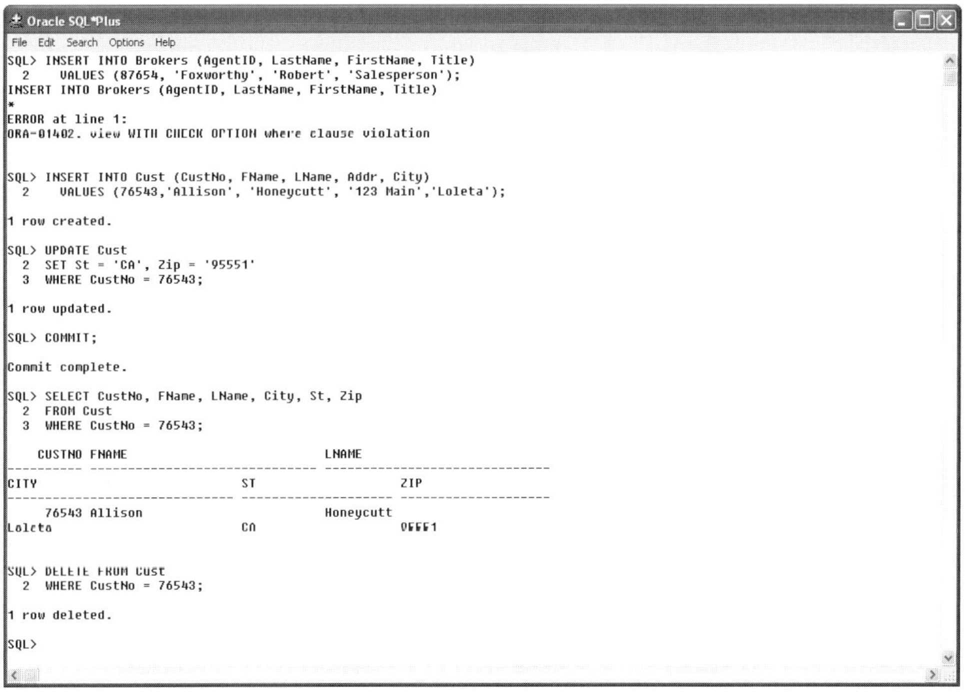

contains one or more functions or expressions. Any of the preceding renders the view a complex view. Complex views are different from simple views mainly because DML operations are not allowed on some complex views.

EXAMINING A ONE-TABLE COMPLEX VIEW

The best way to tackle complex views is to begin with a one-table view and discover why it is a complex view and what problems you encounter when trying to use it for DML operations. You will create a view based on the Agents table and then execute a couple of DML statements on the view. As usual, use SQL*Plus to execute the statements in the steps.

To create a complex one-table view and run DML statements on it:

1. Type and execute the following in SQL*Plus to create a new view. It retrieves and displays four of the Agents columns and creates a new column for each agent's age.

```
CREATE OR REPLACE VIEW AgentView AS
  SELECT AgentID, FirstName, LastName,
         BirthDate, (SYSDATE-BirthDate)/365.25 AS Age
  FROM Agents;
```

2. Modify an agent's birth date through the newly created view by typing and executing the following:

```
UPDATE AgentView
SET BirthDate = TO_DATE('10/17/1962', 'MM/DD/YYYY')
WHERE Agentid = 10041;
```

Oracle updates the row with the new birth date.

3. Modify an agent's age through the view by typing and executing the following:

```
UPDATE AgentView
SET AGE = 50
WHERE Agentid = 10041;
```

Oracle rejects the update attempt and issues the error message

ORA-01733: virtual column not allowed here

4. Rescind all updates by executing:

```
ROLLBACK;
```

Figure 6.29 shows these steps and their results. Your screen should match the figure.

FIGURE 6.29 Disallowing an update on a one-table complex view.

```
Oracle SQL*Plus
File Edit Search Options Help
SQL> CREATE OR REPLACE VIEW AgentView AS
  2    SELECT AgentID, FirstName, LastName,
  3           BirthDate, (SYSDATE-BirthDate)/365.25 AS Age
  4    FROM Agents;

View created.

SQL> UPDATE AgentView
  2  SET BirthDate = TO_DATE('10/17/1962', 'MM/DD/YYYY')
  3  WHERE Agentid = 10041;

1 row updated.

SQL> UPDATE AgentView
  2  SET AGE = 50
  3  WHERE Agentid = 10041;
SET AGE = 50
    *
ERROR at line 2:
ORA-01733: virtual column not allowed here


SQL> ROLLBACK;

Rollback complete.

SQL>
```

Executing the ROLLBACK rescinds the update in step 2 above. However, it does not affect the view, because CREATE VIEW is a DDL statement. Clearly, Oracle rejects any attempts to change a virtual column—one that is calculated—through a view. So, some one-table views are, in fact, complex views. Therefore, single table complex views that contain expressions are not 100 percent updatable. That is neither good nor bad. You must simply be aware of that situation.

EXAMINING MULTIPLE TABLE COMPLEX VIEWS

More frequently, you will encounter views that consist of multiple tables. Often, people create multiple table views to simplify otherwise difficult, multiple table join statements. Another reason to create views is to protect the underlying table from unauthorized viewing of sensitive columns or unauthorized modifications. The best way to experience this is to create a few multiple table views. Once created, you will probably agree that the views created here simplify querying the database. They do pose some data modification problems.

First, let's create a very useful view that displays many of the objects that you have created in this chapter and displays their names. Recall that Oracle stores information about your objects—tables, sequences, views, and so on—in its data dictionary views (user_tables, user_sequences, user_views, etc.). Armed with that knowledge, you will create a view called *MyOwnObjects* that displays many of these objects.

To create a multiple table view:

1. Using SQL*Plus, type **CLEAR SCREEN** and press **Enter,**
2. Type and execute the following to create the MyOwnObjects view:

```
CREATE OR REPLACE VIEW MyOwnObjects (ObjType, ObjName) AS
  SELECT 'Table', Table_Name FROM User_Tables
  WHERE Table_Name NOT LIKE 'BIN%'
    UNION
  SELECT 'View', View_Name FROM User_Views
    UNION
  SELECT 'Sequence', Sequence_Name FROM User_Sequences
    UNION
  SELECT 'Trigger', Trigger_Name FROM User_Triggers;
```

Oracle creates the view, which will display several of your object types when you query it.

3. Query your objects by typing and executing the following:

```
SELECT ObjType, ObjName
FROM MyOwnObjects
ORDER BY 1,2;
```

Oracle displays your nine tables and five views, including the one that produced the listing, *MyOwnView* (see Figure 6.30).

Sometimes multiple table views are handy when a select query is difficult to form, complicated, or otherwise cumbersome to write. Views can save time when users issue multiple table views frequently. Here is an example of a multiple table view that simplifies an otherwise complicated SELECT statement. You will create a view called ForSale. It joins five tables together to list information about sellers, the homes for sale, and the sellers' agents. The five tables you will join are, in no particular order, Agents, CustAgentList, Listings, Properties, and Customers. This is a long CREATE VIEW statement, so type it very carefully. As usual, white space is up to you, but we indent with white space to make the statement simpler to read. You will want to use a text editor for this example so it is easy to make small changes and tweak the script. We suggest Notepad. Also, launch SQL*Plus and log into Oracle, if needed.

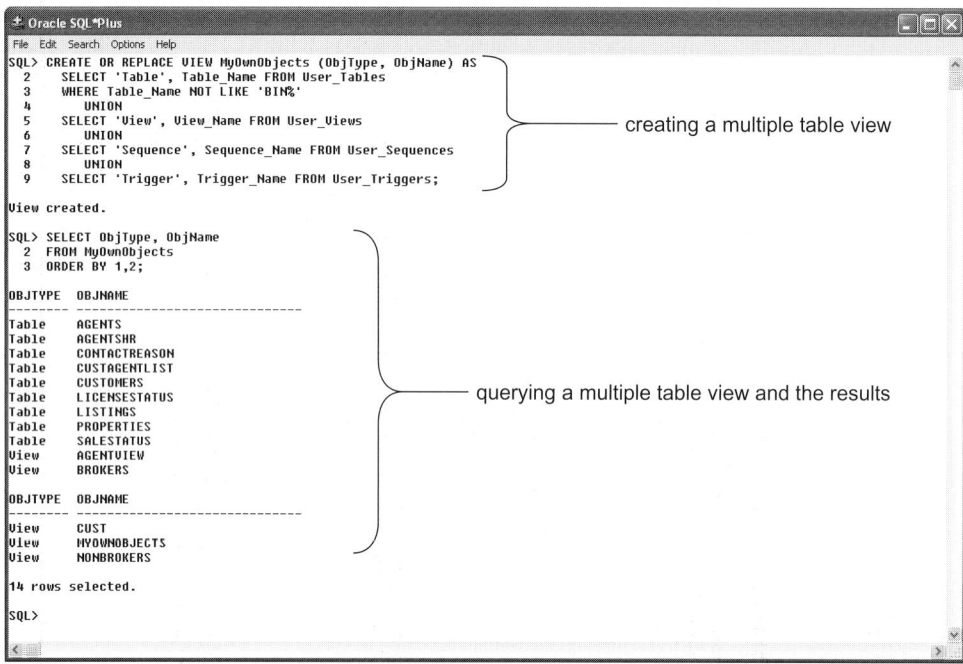

FIGURE 6.30 Creating a multiple table view and querying it.

To create a multiple table view to simplify a complex join query:

1. Type **CLEAR SCREEN** and press **Enter** to clear the SQL*Plus screen.
2. Type and execute the following to create the five-table view:

```
CREATE OR REPLACE VIEW
   ForSale(AgID, AgentFirst, AgentLast, Bid, Ask,
           Addr, City, Br, Ba, Ft,
           SellerFirst, SellerLast) AS
   SELECT
      a.AgentID, a.FirstName, a.LastName, b.BidPrice, c.AskingPrice,
      d.Address, d.City, d.Bedrooms, d.Bathrooms, d.SqFt,
      e.FirstName, e.LastName
   FROM Agents a
      INNER JOIN CustAgentList b ON a.AgentID = b.AgentID
      INNER JOIN Listings c ON b.ListingID = c.ListingID
      INNER JOIN Properties d ON c.PropertyID = d.PropertyID
      INNER JOIN Customers e  ON d.OwnerID = e.CustomerID
   WHERE b.ContactReason = 'Sell';
```

Oracle indicates it created the view. If you get syntax errors, then check, line by line, your script against the one here. Make any corrections and resubmit.

3. Now that the view called ForSale, joining five tables, exists, you can query it using the column names defined by the view (*AgID, AgentFirst, Br* and so on). Type and execute the following SQL*Plus statements to format columns so they are easy to read:

```
COLUMN Asking      FORMAT $9,999,999
COLUMN Addr        FORMAT A25
COLUMN City        FORMAT A10
COLUMN SellerLast  FORMAT A14
COLUMN Br          FORMAT 99
COLUMN Ba          FORMAT 99
COLUMN Ft          FORMAT 9,999
```

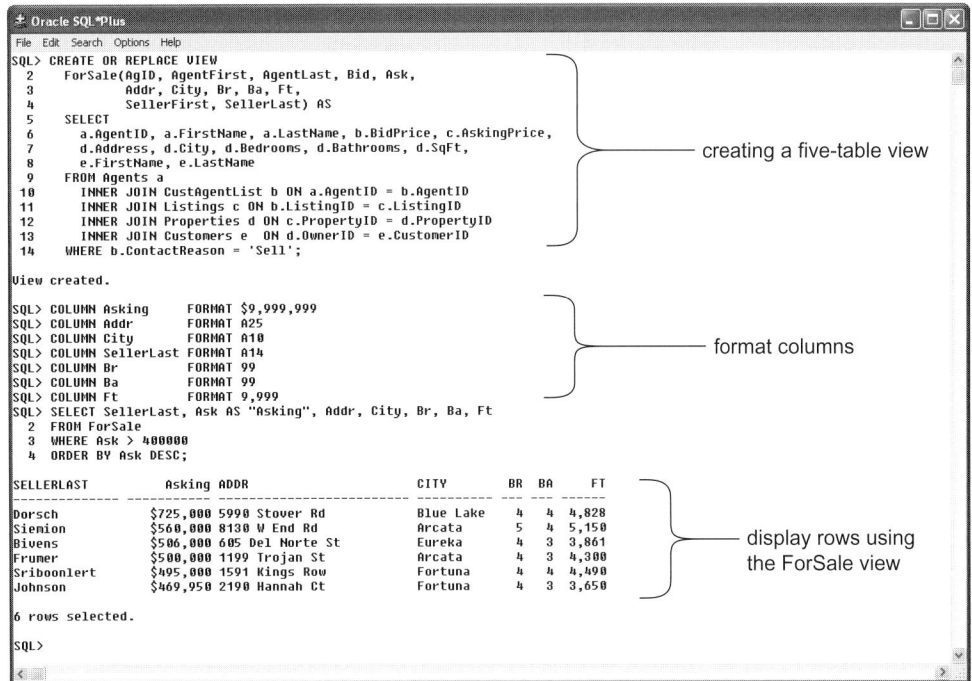

FIGURE 6.31 Creating a multiple table view joining five tables.

4. Finally, write a query to select particular columns from the ForSale view by typing and executing the following in SQL*Plus:

```
SELECT SellerLast, Ask AS "Asking", Addr, City, Br, Ba, Ft
FROM ForSale
WHERE Ask > 400000
ORDER BY Ask DESC;
```

Oracle returns six rows that match the criteria. Your results should match Figure 6.31.

5. In SQL*Plus, type **exit** and press **Enter** to log off Oracle and close SQL*Plus. Save your Notepad script file and close Notepad.

CREATING SYNONYMS TO SIMPLIFY TABLE REFERENCES

If you have been granted access to another user's tables or other objects, you can access those tables and other objects in ways limited by the owner granting the access. For instance, if user CoffeeMerchant grants you SELECT access to the table Merchandise, you can issue a SELECT statement to retrieve rows from that table if you qualify the table name with the schema name CoffeeMerchant. For example, the following would retrieve all rows and columns from the table from a different schema having access to it:

```
SELECT *
FROM CoffeeMerchant.Merchandise;
```

When you have access to multiple tables in another's schema, then writing the qualifying schema name for each table name can be time-consuming and error-prone. A very handy feature that reduces keystrokes is to assign a synonym to each qualified table name to which you have access. Then, you can use the synonym in place of the qualified table name wherever it is needed. You can assign a private synonym (if you have the CREATE SYNONYM privilege) by executing the CREATE SYNONYM statement. Its simplified syntax is:

```
CREATE SYNONYM <synonym-name> FOR <qualified-name>;
```

For example, suppose you have the CREATE SYNONYM privilege and you also have SELECT access to the table mentioned above. Then you could create a synonym called MyCoffee to simplify references to the actual table by executing the following:

```
CREATE SYNONYM MyCoffee FOR CoffeeMerchant.Merchandise;
```

Once you have created the synonym, you can issue a select statement using the synonym. For example,

```
SELECT * FROM MyCoffee;
```

retrieves rows from the Merchandise table owned by the CoffeeMerchant schema. You will learn more about granting access to others' tables in Chapter 12.

LISTING VIEW DEFINITIONS

Oracle maintains information on views you create in data dictionary views. The data dictionary view *user_views* (as you can probably guess by now) contains information about the views you create. The view *all_views* contains views to which you have access—views that you do not necessarily own but to which their owners have granted you access. Of course, you can execute the DESCRIBE statement followed by the view name to review a display of a views column names and data types. However, user_views has much more information. Table 6.4 lists some of the columns available in user_views.

It is instructive to look at your view definitions next.
To review the definition of one or more views you own:

1. Launch SQL*Plus, log into Oracle, and clear the screen.
2. Next, type and execute the set column and page formatting to display view information in an attractive way:

```
SET PAGESIZE 50
COLUMN view_name FORMAT A15
COLUMN text_length FORMAT 99,999
COLUMN text FORMAT A40 WRAPPED
```

3. Type and execute the following to display information about the views you own:

```
SELECT view_name, text_length, text
FROM user_views
ORDER BY view_name;
```

Oracle displays six rows with view information (see Figure 6.32).

TABLE 6.4 Description of some of the user_views columns.

Column Name	Data Type	Description
view_name	VARCHAR2(30)	Name of the view.
text_length	NUMBER	Number of characters in the view's subquery.
text	LONG	Text of the view's subquery that created the view.

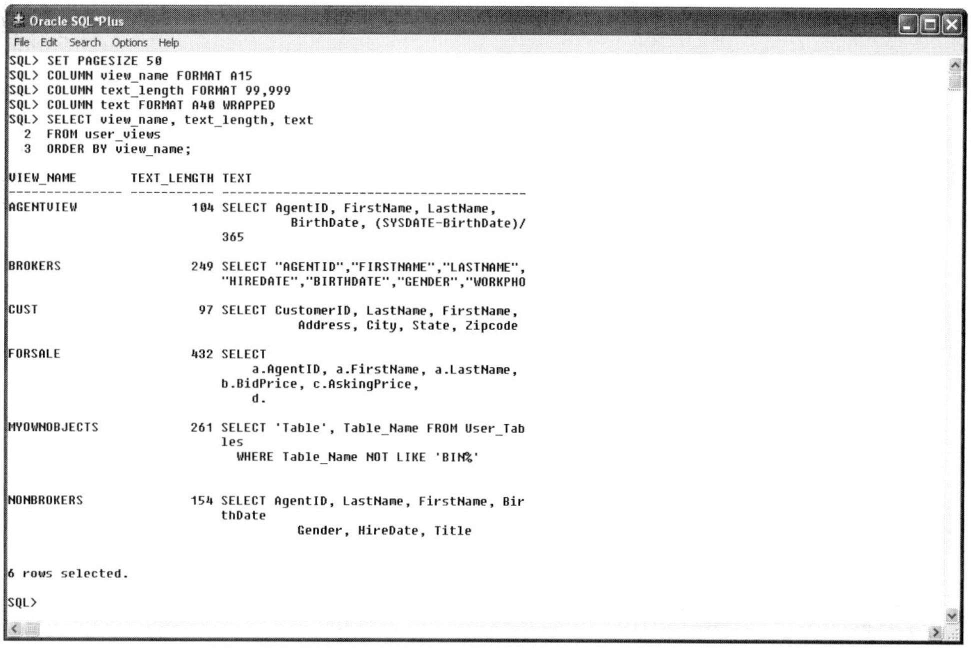

```
± Oracle SQL*Plus
File Edit Search Options Help
SQL> SET PAGESIZE 50
SQL> COLUMN view_name FORMAT A15
SQL> COLUMN text_length FORMAT 99,999
SQL> COLUMN text FORMAT A40 WRAPPED
SQL> SELECT view_name, text_length, text
  2  FROM user_views
  3  ORDER BY view_name;

VIEW_NAME       TEXT_LENGTH TEXT
--------------- ----------- ----------------------------------------
AGENTVIEW              104 SELECT AgentID, FirstName, LastName,
                                  BirthDate, (SYSDATE-BirthDate)/
                            365

BROKERS                249 SELECT "AGENTID","FIRSTNAME","LASTNAME",
                                  "HIREDATE","BIRTHDATE","GENDER","WORKPHO

CUST                    97 SELECT CustomerID, LastName, FirstName,
                                  Address, City, State, Zipcode

FORSALE                432 SELECT
                                  a.AgentID, a.FirstName, a.LastName,
                               b.BidPrice, c.AskingPrice,
                                     d.

MYOWNOBJECTS           261 SELECT 'Table', Table_Name FROM User_Tab
                            les
                                WHERE Table_Name NOT LIKE 'BIN%'

NONBROKERS             154 SELECT AgentID, LastName, FirstName, Bir
                            thDate
                                  Gender, HireDate, Title

6 rows selected.

SQL>
```

FIGURE 6.32 Displaying view information.

4. Type and execute the following to reset columns and page sizes:

```
CLEAR COLUMNS
SET PAGESIZE 14
```

If you want to list *all* the views to which you have access, then you can change the query in step 3 to the following. Warning: running the query below produces hundreds of views because Oracle allows each user access to a lot of views—not just the views you create in your own schema.

```
SELECT view_name, text_length, text
FROM all_views
ORDER BY view_name;
```

By our count, there over 1,500 views available to any user. So, avoid displaying all_views unless you restrict the results with a finely tuned WHERE clause.

DROPPING VIEWS

You drop a view by issuing

```
DROP VIEW <view-name>
```

similar to the way you drop other objects such as sequences or tables. Finish this chapter by cleaning house and dropping all the views you created so far. Remember that you can query MyOwnObjects *prior* to dropping all views to see what views you own. Display views only by executing the query:

```
SELECT *
FROM MyOwnObjects
WHERE LOWER(ObjType) = 'view';
```

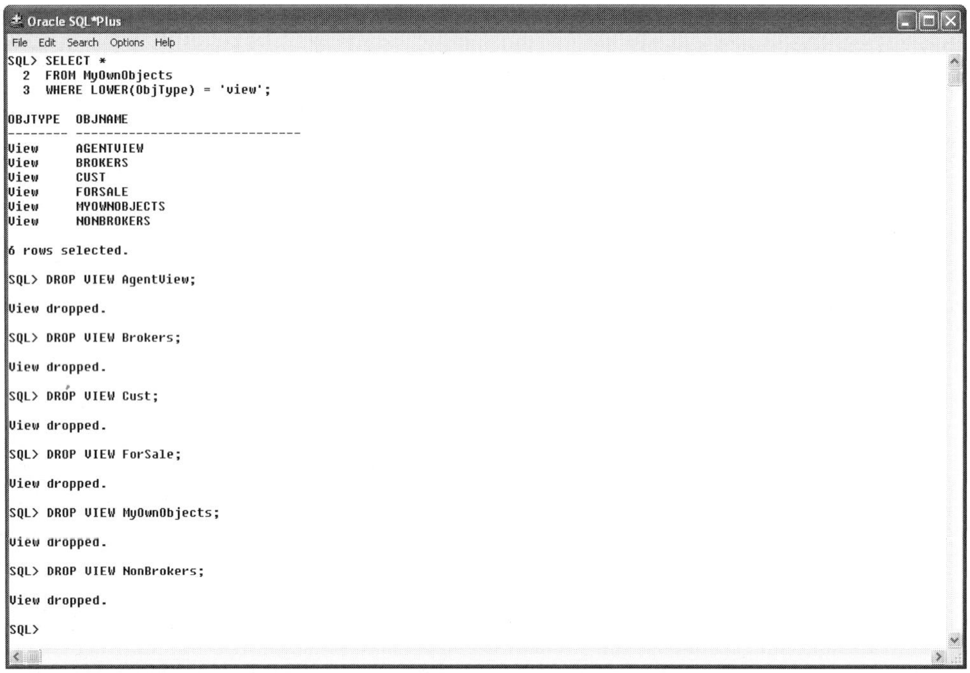

```
SQL> SELECT *
  2  FROM MyOwnObjects
  3  WHERE LOWER(ObjType) = 'view';

OBJTYPE   OBJNAME
--------  ------------------------------
View      AGENTVIEW
View      BROKERS
View      CUST
View      FORSALE
View      MYOWNOBJECTS
View      NONBROKERS

6 rows selected.

SQL> DROP VIEW AgentView;

View dropped.

SQL> DROP VIEW Brokers;

View dropped.

SQL> DROP VIEW Cust;

View dropped.

SQL> DROP VIEW ForSale;

View dropped.

SQL> DROP VIEW MyOwnObjects;

View dropped.

SQL> DROP VIEW NonBrokers;

View dropped.

SQL>
```

FIGURE 6.33 Listing and then dropping views you created.

Run the following steps to display your views and then drop them all. To drop all views you created in this chapter:

1. In SQL*Plus type and execute the following:

```
CLEAR SCREEN
SELECT *
FROM MyOwnObjects
WHERE LOWER(ObjType) = 'view';
```

Oracle displays the six views you created in this chapter.

2. Delete the views by typing and executing the following:

```
DROP VIEW AgentView;
DROP VIEW Brokers;
DROP VIEW Cust;
DROP VIEW ForSale;
DROP VIEW MyOwnObjects;
DROP VIEW NonBrokers;
```

Oracle drops all views you created. (See Figure 6.33.)

3. Type **exit** and press **Enter** to log off Oracle and close SQL*Plus.

Summary

SELECT statements allow you to join an unlimited number of tables together, pair-wise, on common columns. When joining tables, you list them in the FROM clause and use the ON phrase to indicate the column(s) in each table that are used to join the two tables. Use an equijoin when columns of two tables are to match (=). Table aliases simplify table references in multiple table join statements. Assign a table alias by listing it following the table name in the FROM clause. Inner join operations return rows from table pairs in which columns match. Outer joins include the left, right, and full outer join. Outer joins allow tables returning null values for a potential match to be included in the result. Using a left or right outer join reveals which rows in one table have no corresponding related rows in another—a fact that is hidden in an inner join.

Set operators UNION, UNION ALL, MINUS, and INTERSECT to combine the results of multiple SELECT statements in various ways. UNION and UNION ALL combine all returned rows. UNION ALL allows duplicate rows, but UNION does not. MINUS extracts rows returned by one SELECT statement that match rows returned by another. INTERSECT excludes returned rows from two SELECT statements that they do not have in common.

Subqueries are queries within queries. They can return one row and one column, multiple rows and one column, or multiple rows and multiple columns. A subquery executes before its outer query executes, except in the case of a correlated subquery.

Using a correlated subquery, the outer query executes for one row, then the subquery executes for all rows using the information from the outer query. Subqueries can appear in a query's select list, in a query's FROM statement (an inline view), in a SELECT statement's WHERE clause (the most common), or in selected DML statements such as CREATE TABLE. The operators ANY and ALL provide additional WHERE clause options, when combined with relational operators, to determine if a value is larger or smaller than some or all values returned by a subquery.

Views are uniquely named and predefined SELECT statements that reference base tables and retrieve subsets of information. Their definitions are stored and activated whenever the view name is used in place of a table. They provide data integrity and need-to-know security, and simplify otherwise complex queries. You can create private synonyms to simplify references to other schema's tables to which you have been granted access. Synonyms provide aliases for existing objects.

Key Terms

- Column subset view
- Complex view
- Component query
- Compound query
- Correlated subquery
- Discretionary access control
- Display columns
- Distribution
- Equijoin
- Exists
- Full outer join
- Inner join

- Join
- Join column
- Join condition
- Left outer join
- Multiple column subquery
- Multiple row subquery
- Natural join
- Non-equality join
- Outer join
- Qualified name
- Right outer join
- Row subset view

- Scalar subquery
- Search columns
- Self join
- Set operator
- Simple view
- Single row subquery
- Subquery
- Table alias
- Vertical join
- View

Review

TRUE/FALSE

1. When you join two tables, each table's join field must match the other table's join field.
2. Using table aliases provides additional security and simplifies table references.
3. You can use a subquery in a SELECT statement FROM clause and in selected DDL statements.
4. The result of an EXISTS operator and the subquery to which it applies are only the values TRUE or FALSE.
5. A view acts just like a table, but it can be defined to return a subset of a base table's rows, columns, or both.

Fill In

1. A(n) _____ join returns rows which satisfy the join condition.
2. When you return all the rows of one table and only columns that satisfy the join condition from another table, that is called a(n) _____ join.
3. A(n) _____ subquery returns one row and one column.
4. A(n) _____ subquery depends on a value from the outer query to execute the inner query.
5. You can create a(n) _____ to simplify references to qualified table names.

Multiple Choice

1. Which of the following FROM clauses correctly joins tables People and Sales on matching values of PeopleID columns, which both tables have?
   a. FROM People JOIN Sales BY People.PeopleID IN Sales.PeopleID
   b. FROM Sales JOIN People USING PeopleID = PeopleID
   c. FROM People p JOIN Sales s ON PeopleID = PeopleID
   d. FROM Sales JOIN People USING (PeopleID)
2. Which of the following WHERE clauses would you write to return all Employee rows and selected Sales rows in which the join columns (EmpID for Employee and EmployeeID for Sales) match?
   a. FROM Employee RIGHT OUTER JOIN Sales ON EmpID = EmployeeID
   b. FROM Employee LEFT OUTER JOIN Sales ON EmpID = EmployeeID
   c. FROM Employee FULL OUTER JOIN Sales ON EmpID = EmployeeID
   d. FROM Employee INNER JOIN Sales ON EmpID = EmployeeID
3. Which of these WHERE clauses displays rows in which an agent's BaseSalary is less than or equal to the highest BaseSalary of all the agents?
   a. WHERE BaseSalary >= ALL (SELECT BaseSalary FROM AgentsHR)
   b. WHERE BaseSalary >=ANY (SELECT BaseSalary FROM AgentsHR)
   c. WHERE BaseSalary <=ALL (SELECT BaseSalary FROM AgentsHR)
   d. WHERE BaseSalary <=ANY (SELECT BaseSalary FROM AgentsHR)
   e. None of the preceding is correct.
4. Which of the following is *incorrect* as shown?
   a. CREATE OR REPLACE VIEW Someone AS SELECT * FROM Agents;
   b. CREATE VIEW Someone AS SELECT * FROM Agents WHERE AgentID > 13000;
   c. CREATE VIEW Someone (F1,F2) AS SELECT HireDate FROM Agents;
   d. CREATE VIEW Someone (AgID) AS (SELECT AgentID FROM Agents);
   e. All of the preceding are correct.
5. Which of the following lists views (by name) that only you have created?
   a. SELECT view_name FROM user_views;
   b. SELECT view_name FROM all_views;
   c. SELECT view_name FROM views;
   d. SELECT viewname FROM userviews;
   e. None of the preceding is correct.

Hands-on Exercises

1. Extending the Chapter Case

You are to create a new table and run several queries. The table contains bonus amounts for salespersons who have particular numbers of properties in the Listings table. Those with between 16 and 20 receive a $300 bonus; those with between 21 and 30 receive a $600 bonus; and those with more than 30 listings receive a $1,000 bonus. The table has low and high limits that you will use to bracket the bonus amount based on the number of listings using an INNER JOIN, an inline view, and an inequality (use > or < instead of =) join condition.

Open a Notepad text file and save everything you type and execute in SQL*Plus in the Notepad file. When you have completed the assignment, print the Notepad file and be prepared to turn it in to your instructor, if requested.

Execute the following steps for part 1 of this exercise. Launch Notepad and save the empty file as <yourname>Ch06Prob1Part1.sql. Then, type the following in Notepad, copy it into SQL*Plus, and execute it. Locate the file Ch06BuildBonus.sql among the data files supplied with your book or available online. Note the path on your computer to that file.

1. Type the following to initialize the database for this problem, substituting the actual path to the data file for "<path>" below. Type your name in place of "<your name here>."

```
REM <your name here>
CLEAR SCREEN
START <path>\Ch06BuildBonus.sql
```

2. Next, type and execute the following to display the newly complete table, BonusSchedule:

```
SELECT * FROM BonusSchedule;
```

3. Type and execute the following to set up columns and then display bonus amounts:

```
SET PAGESIZE 35
COLUMN Bonus FORMAT $9,999
SELECT a.LastName, a.ListCount, b.Bonus
FROM (SELECT AgentID, LastName, COUNT(*) as ListCount
      FROM Agents INNER JOIN Listings
      ON AgentID = ListingAgentID
      GROUP BY AgentID, LastName) a
        INNER JOIN BonusSchedule b
        ON a.ListCount BETWEEN b.LowLimit
        AND b.HighLimit
ORDER BY b.Bonus DESC, a.LastName ASC;
```

4. Type and execute the following to repeat the preceding query and spool it to a text file. Substitute your name for "<yourname>" in the following script, and substitute an appropriate path for "<path>" below:

```
SPOOL
<path>\<yourname>Ch06Prob1P1-spool.txt
SHOW USER
/
SPOOL OFF
```

5. Restore default environment variables and delete the newly created table by executing the following:

```
CLEAR COLUMNS
SET PAGESIZE 14
DROP TABLE BonusSchedule CASCADE CONSTRAINTS
PURGE;
```

6. Save everything you have typed in Notepad one final time. Print the Notepad file and print the spool file you created in Step 4 above.

Next, you are to write execute statements to list all properties in the Redwood Realty database whose status is "Sold." Open a new Notepad file, save it as <yourname>Ch06Prob1Part2.sql, and launch SQL*Plus if necessary. Then follow the steps below.

7. Type and execute the following, substituting your name for "<your name here>."

```
REM <your name here>
CLEAR SCREEN
CLEAR COLUMNS
COLUMN LastName FORMAT A15
COLUMN City     FORMAT A15
COLUMN Address  FORMAT A20
COLUMN Owner    FORMAT A15
```

8. Next, type and execute the following to join multiple tables and list only those that have sold:

```
SELECT p.City, p.Address, p.PropertyID,
c.LastName AS "Owner"
FROM Properties p INNER JOIN Customers c
  ON p.OwnerID = c.CustomerID
WHERE PropertyID IN
    (SELECT PropertyID
     FROM Listings
     WHERE SaleStatusID = (SELECT
                            SaleStatusID
                            FROM SaleStatus
                            WHERE SaleStatus
                            = 'Sold')
    )
ORDER BY 1,2;
```

9. Save the Notepad file once again, and print the Notepad script file. Close Notepad.

Next, you are to write execute statements to create a view called MyListings and then test the view. Open up a new Notepad file, save it as <yourname>Ch06Prob1Part3.sql, and launch SQL*Plus if necessary. Then follow the steps below. Substitute a path in the first line. Substitute your name for "<yourname>" above and in first and second lines of the script below.

```
SPOOL <path><yourname>Ch06Prob1
Part3-spoolfile.txt
REM <yourname>
CLEAR SCREEN
CREATE OR REPLACE VIEW MyListings (Agent,
Addr, City, Price) AS
  SELECT LastName, Address, City, AskingPrice
```

```
    FROM Agents INNER JOIN Listings ON
    AgentID = ListingAgentID
            INNER JOIN Properties USING
            (PropertyID)
    ORDER BY LastName, City;
REM Describe the new view:
DESCRIBE MyListings
REM Display information about Carling using
REM view
SELECT Agent, City, Price
FROM MyListings
WHERE UPPER(Agent) = 'CARLING'
ORDER BY City, Price DESC;
```

10. Clean up by typing the following to drop the view and close the spool file:

```
DROP VIEW MyListings;
SPOOL OFF
```

11. Save the Notepad file once again, print the Notepad script file, and print the spool file(s). Close Notepad.

12. In SQL*Plus, type **exit** and press **Enter** to log off Oracle and exit SQL*Plus.

2. COFFEE MERCHANT

The Coffee Merchant manager has asked that you produce several reports.

1. Launch SQL*Plus, log into Oracle, and launch Notepad. Save your Notepad file as <yourname>Ch06Problem2Part1.sql, where you substitute your last name for "<yourname>." For this problem, type all statements in Notepad, then copy them to SQL*Plus to execute them. This way, you will have a complete script file when you are finished.

2. Initialize the Coffee Merchant database by typing and executing the following. It will ensure that all your Coffee Merchant files are in their original, mint condition no matter what you did to them in previous chapters. First, determine the full path to BuildCoffee.sql. (It is in the CoffeeMerchant folder of the data files supplied with the textbook.) Then, issue the following START command with the full path (for "<path>"to BuildCoffee.sql.

```
START <path>\CoffeeMerchant\BuildCoffee
```

Oracle builds the seven Coffee Merchant tables and sets all foreign keys.

3. Start a spool file by executing the following (make the path to an appropriate folder and plug in your name for "<yourname>").

```
SPOOL C:\<yourname>Ch06Prob2Part1.txt
```

4. Type and execute the following query to list the names of people who have ordered coffee that is grown in Yemen. The government is restricting imports from Yemen, and you want to know which customers to contact. Substitute your name for "<yourname>" in the second line.

```
CLEAR SCREEN
REM <yourname>
COLUMN CNAME    FORMAT A20 HEADING 'NAME'
COLUMN Street   FORMAT A30
COLUMN City     FORMAT A15
COLUMN State    FORMAT A5
COLUMN Zipcode FORMAT A5   HEADING 'ZIP'
SET PAGESIZE 40
SELECT a.FirstName||' '||a.LastName AS
CNAME, a.Street,
       a.City, a.State, a.Zipcode
FROM Consumers a
     JOIN Orders     b USING (ConsumerID)
     JOIN OrderLines c USING (OrderID)
     JOIN Inventory  d USING
     (InventoryID)
     JOIN Countries  e USING (CountryID)
WHERE UPPER(e.CountryName) LIKE 'YEM%'
  AND UPPER(d.ItemType) = 'C'
ORDER BY a.Zipcode;
```

5. Type the following in SQL*Plus to turn off the spool file and reset columns and PAGESIZE:

```
SPOOL OFF
CLEAR COLUMNS
SET PAGESIZE 14
```

6. Save all that you have typed in the Notepad file, and press **Ctrl+N** to open a new Notepad file in preparation for part 2 to follow.

   For part 2 of this exercise, you will list customer names and order numbers for anyone who placed an order during October 2005. This query will join three tables to extract the required information. Because you want to print the results, you will open a spool file.

7. Start a spool file by executing the following (make the path to an appropriate folder and plug in your name for "<yourname>").

```
SPOOL C:\<yourname>Ch06Prob2Part2.txt
```

8. Type the following in a Notepad file to set up columns and formatting, replacing "<yourname>" with your first and last names to identify the script file. Then, save the file as <yourname>Ch06Problem2Part2.sql, and copy it to SQL*Plus for execution.

```
REM <yourname>
REM List Customers and their order totals
REM for October 2005
```

```
CLEAR SCREEN
COLUMN OrderID  FORMAT 999999
COLUMN CNAME    FORMAT A30
COLUMN Total    FORMAT $99,999.99
SET PAGESIZE 80
```

9. Next, type the following query and SQL*Plus statements in Notepad, copy them to SQL*Plus, and execute them.

```
SELECT OrderID, a.FirstName|| ' ' ||
a.LastName AS "CNAME",
       SUM(c.Quantity*c.Price*(1-
       c.Discount)) AS "Total"
FROM Consumers a JOIN Orders b USING
                 (ConsumerID)
                 JOIN OrderLines c USING
                 (OrderID)
WHERE b.OrderDate BETWEEN '01-OCT-05' AND
'31-OCT-05'
GROUP BY OrderID, a.FirstName, a.LastName
ORDER BY "Total" DESC;
SPOOL OFF
CLEAR COLUMNS
```

10. Save your Notepad file and print it. Press **Ctrl+N** to open an new Notepad file.

11. The next query will determine which consumers placed orders with an employee named Hillary Flintsteel. Type the following in a Notepad file to set up columns and formatting, replacing "<yourname>" with your first and last names to identify the script file. Then, save the file as <yourname>Ch06Problem2Part3.sql, and copy it to SQL*Plus for execution.

```
SPOOL C:\<yourname>Ch06Prob2Part3.txt
REM <yourname>
REM What consumers have orders placed by
Flintsteel?
CLEAR SCREEN
COLUMN FirstName   FORMAT A12
COLUMN LastName    FORMAT A12
COLUMN Street      FORMAT A27 WORD_WRAP
COLUMN City        FORMAT A15 WORD_WRAP
COLUMN State       FORMAT A02
COLUMN Zipcode     FORMAT A05 HEADING 'ZIP'
SET PAGESIZE 55
```

12. Type the following SQL and SQL*Plus code in Notepad, and save the completed Notepad file. Copy the code segment to SQL*Plus and execute it.

```
SELECT DISTINCT c.FirstName, c.LastName,
c.Street,
    c.City, c.State, c.Zipcode
FROM Consumers c JOIN Orders USING
                 (ConsumerID)
                 JOIN Employees USING
                 (EmployeeID)
WHERE EmployeeID = (SELECT EmployeeID
                    FROM Employees
                    WHERE LOWER(LastName)
                    LIKE 'flint%')
ORDER BY c.Zipcode;
SPOOL OFF
CLEAR COLUMNS
SET PAGESIZE 14
```

13. Close SQL*Plus, and close Notepad.

14. Print all three script files, and print all three spool files you created.

3. ROWING VENTURES

Create the following SQL script files and accompanying reports. Be sure to print all script files and all spool files. Be sure to place your name in the header of all script files and spool files when you print them.

Launch SQL*Plus, log into Oracle, and execute the script file BuildRowing.sql, which is found in the RowingVentures folder of the data files. Produce a spool report file following these guidelines: Create a query that joins the Rowing Ventures tables Boat, BoatCrew, and Person. In the query, list the following columns, in the order listed: BoatCategory, BowNumber, Position, and LastName, Firstname (concatenated and separated by a comma). Sort the rows into ascending order on BoatCategory, BowNumber, and Position. Use COLUMN formatting commands to limit the rowers' concatenated names to 30 characters, the position to three characters, the boat category to seven characters and the bow number to three characters. Instead of listing the Position column directly, display "Cox" in place of the position value zero (0). Otherwise, display the character string equivalent of the position (1-8). Set breaks on (first) BoatCategory (SKIP PAGE) and then BowNumber (SKIP 1 DUP, which allows bow numbers to list). At end of the script file, clear all breaks and columns.

Report 2: Write a query to list the names of everyone who is in the same boat as Ted Simpson. (*Hint*: Join tables BoatCrew and Person to determine which boat Simpson is in. Then list names of everyone with those same BoatIDs.) Be aware that Ted Simpson *could* be in multiple boats and races. Print the query and print the spool file. Format the report in an attractive way.

Report 3: Write and run a script file that creates (or replaces) a view named RowerOrganizations. The view displays the rowers names and the organizations (OrganizationName) to which they belong.

The view joins four tables: Person, BoatCrew, Boat, and Organization. List only the OrganizationName, FirstName, and LastName (in that order). Print the query that creates the view, and run a query using the view to display the three columns. Precede the query with column formatting and page sizing SQL*Plus statements. Set the PAGESIZE to 60, format the OrganizationName column to 40 characters (maximum) and format each name column to 15 characters maximum width. Sort the results by OrganizationName, then by LastName, and then by FirstName. After running the query, clear all columns, reset the page size to 14, and drop the view.

4. BROADCLOTH CLOTHING

Launch SQL*Plus, log into Oracle, and execute the script file BuildClothing.sql, which is found in the Broadcloth folder of your Chapter 6 data files. Create a read only view called ContactInfo that displays rows and columns from the Contact table. The view displays only the following columns, in the order given: FirstName, LastName, Address, City, State, Nation, and PrimaryLanguage. Display only rows for which the nation is China, India, Malaysia, or Thailand. After creating the view, open a spool file, and run SQL*Plus commands to limit the width of the Nation, City, and LastName columns to 25 characters. Run a query using the view to display LastName, City, and Nation (in that order) sorted by Nation, then City, then LastName. Identify the spool file and the script file by placing your name in the header before printing each. Then, print the script and spool files.

Write a query with a subquery that lists the FactoryID, City, Nation, and MaxWorkers values for all factories which employ more than the average number of MaxWorkers. Spool the output to a file. *Hint*: Only the Factory table is involved. Use COLUMN commands to format the City and Nation columns to a maximum width of 15 characters, and format the MaxWorkers to show up to four digits with a comma separator for thousands. Sort the result on the Nation and then City (ascending for both). Print the script file and print the spool file. Remember to type your name in the header of both files to identify them.

CHAPTER 7

USING PL/SQL TO YOUR ADVANTAGE

Learning Objectives

In this chapter, you will learn how to:
- Write PL/SQL anonymous blocks.
- Use and declare PL/SQL variables.
- Write PL/SQL code.
- Create, open, execute, and close cursors to process multiple database table rows.
- Write functions and procedures using PL/SQL.
- Use PL/SQL LOOP and IF statements to iterate and make selections.
- Handle exceptions when they occur.

INTRODUCTION TO PL/SQL

PL/SQL stands for *Programming Language/Structured Query Language*. It is unique to Oracle and is the procedural language extension of SQL. It combines the SQL database language with a procedural programming language. The programming language is built on a basic building unit called a block, and a ***block*** contains SQL and PL/SQL statements. Once you create a block of PL/SQL, Oracle can compile it and store it in the database. When Oracle ***compiles*** a PL/SQL block, it converts the higher level PL/SQL instructions into a lower-level format, which a computer can execute more quickly. Alternatively, you can save the PL/SQL code as a script file and execute it whenever you need to. PL/SQL provides all the familiar third generation programming language constructs including looping, selection, variable declaration, and error handling. PL/SQL is considered a member of the object-oriented class of programming languages. Figure 7.1 illustrates how Oracle processes SQL and PL/SQL blocks.

BENEFITS OF PL/SQL

Even though the established relational database access language SQL provides all the requisite statements needed to interact with databases, SQL has few programming

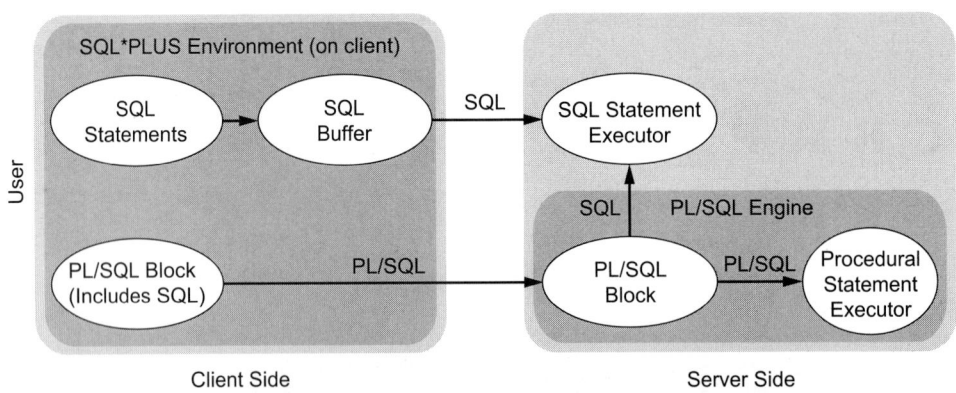

FIGURE 7.1 PL/SQL processing.

constructs that help in selecting and analyzing retrieved data. For example, SQL does not provide any of the following very useful capabilities:

- Intercepting exceptions that may occur while processing data.
- Allowing iteration through returned rows, examining each one, in turn, for selected values or characteristics.
- Securing code through encryption.
- Storing code in the database rather than on the client's machine.
- Permitting decision making and alternative branching while processing returned database table rows.

Though SQL is a very powerful and at once straightforward data access language, PL/SQL adds powerful procedural language constructs and adds features not found in SQL alone. Tightly integrated with the Oracle database, PL/SQL is improved continually to provide both closer integration to the database and increased efficiency, through improvements such as native compilation of PL/SQL code. That means that PL/SQL is compiled to the C language, the same language in which Oracle is written, to yield very fast execution times for compiled code. In addition to supporting the SELECT statement, PL/SQL allows SQL data manipulation statements including INSERT, UPDATE, and DELETE. However, PL/SQL does not allow SQL data definition (DDL) statements such as CREATE.

PL/SQL reduces overhead, increases productivity, and improves performance. Without PL/SQL, Oracle processes SQL one statement at a time. Processing each SQL statement means another call to the server. On the other hand, PL/SQL can send an entire SQL statement block to the server, cutting down on the interaction between the client and the server. PL/SQL is trim, because you can create a simple PL/SQL block simply by enclosing a SELECT statement into a PL/SQL block by preceding it with BEGIN and following it with END.

PL/SQL is tightly integrated with the Oracle server. Most PL/SQL data types are also available in Oracle. PL/SQL provides a special attribute that you use by typing %TYPE to assign an internal PL/SQL variable the same data type as defined for a table column.

PL/SQL BLOCK TYPES

There are three types of blocks available in PL/SQL. They are anonymous blocks, procedures, and functions. An ***anonymous block,*** also called an unnamed block, is a collection of PL/SQL statements that are compiled and executed. Anonymous blocks do not have a name and they cannot be stored in the database. A *subprogram* is a computer program contained within another program that operates semi-independently of the enclosing program and that can be invoked from the enclosing program. PL/SQL provides two types of subprograms called procedures and functions which aid you in creating more robust database access and integrated, complete database solutions. A *procedure* is a named PL/SQL block that is stored on the Oracle server and that performs some action or series of actions. A *function* is a named PL/SQL block that is stored on the Oracle server and returns a value. You will learn more about procedures and functions later in this chapter.

UNDERSTANDING ANONYMOUS BLOCKS

Anonymous blocks of PL/SQL code are not stored on the Oracle server. Instead, they are typically saved as SQL script files with the file name extension .sql. You can execute the code block as often as you want to by launching SQL*Plus and executing the script file by issuing:

```
START <PL/SQL code block file name>
```

Anyone with access to the computer, disk, and file on which you stored the code block can also run the script file when needed. Anonymous blocks are very useful for performing activities involving activities you don't need to repeat often. An anonymous PL/SQL block can contain three sections called declarative, executable, and exception handling. Only the executable section is required in every PL/SQL program; the others are optional. The fundamental syntax of an anonymous block is as follows:

```
[DECLARE}
BEGIN
[EXCEPTION]
END;
```

The optional *declarative section* begins with DECLARE and defines any variables or constants required in the program block. Any variables needed *must* be declared there, and the declaration includes the variable name, its data type, and an optional initial value. A PL/SQL *variable,* like other programming language variables, is used to reserve temporary storage to hold values contained wholly within the PL/SQL block. Variables are unavailable outside the block, so they are known as *private variables.* A *constant* occupies storage space, exists as long as the PL/SQL block is available, and holds a value that does not change during the PL/SQL code's execution. The *executable section* is enclosed with BEGIN and END statements. It contains the PL/SQL code and SQL statements to be executed. SQL statements access database tables, whereas PL/SQL statements manipulate data within the PL/SQL block without accessing database tables. The optional *exception handling section* of the PL/SQL block begins with the keyword EXCEPTION and gets program control whenever any of a number of errors occurs. Typically, the exception section displays error messages and indicates the origin of the error. Control automatically jumps to the exception handling code near the end of the PL/SQL block. Whether or not the PL/SQL block contains an exception handling section, the last statement in a PL/SQL block is END, which is followed by a semicolon. The keyword *END* closes the PL/SQL block. Semicolons also end each statement within the PL/SQL block, including statements in the declaration and exception handling sections. Figure 7.2 shows an example of a PL/SQL block.

EXPLORING THE DECLARATIVE SECTION

Examine Figure 7.2 for a moment and consider its sections. The declarative section contains a comment at the top. Comments provide a hint about what succeeding lines

```
DECLARE
  /* Declare variables */
  c_date CONSTANT DATE := '10-OCT-2006';
  v_first Agents.FirstName%TYPE;
  v_last Agents.FirstName%TYPE;
  v_yearsonjob NUMBER(4,2);
BEGIN
  /* Retrieve values into internal variables */
  SELECT FirstName, LastName, (c_date-HireDate)/365.25
  INTO v_first, v_last, v_yearsonjob
  FROM Agents
  WHERE LastName = '&AgentLastName';

  /* Display the result on the screen */
  DBMS_OUTPUT.PUT_LINE
    ('Agent '||v_first||' '||v_last||
    ' has worked here '||v_yearsonjob||' years.');
  /* Handle exceptions such as row not found */
EXCEPTION
  WHEN OTHERS THEN
    DBMS_OUTPUT.PUT_LINE ('Did not find an agent by that name');
END;
```

FIGURE 7.2 Example PL/SQL block.

are doing. You can insert comments by enclosing them in /*...*/ pairs that span any number of physical lines. Alternatively, you can begin a single-line comment with two hyphens. Four variables are declared in the declarations section. They include one constant (c_ is the customary prefix for constants) and three variables (v_ is the usual prefix for variables). The variables are assigned the same data type as their corresponding table columns. The syntax for assigning column data types to PL/SQL variables is:

```
<table_name>.<column_name>%TYPE
```

Table_name is the table's name, and column_name is the corresponding name of the column. In Figure 7.2, you see that v_first is assigned the same data type as the LastName column of the Agents table (Agents.LastName). The general syntax for declaring a variable is:

```
<variable_name> [CONSTANT] <datatype> [NOT NULL]
    [:= | DEFAULT <value or expression>];
```

For example, the following declares v_taxrate a numeric variable with an initial value of 18.75 percent. Always remember to terminate statements with a semicolon.

```
v_taxrate NUMBER (4,4) := .1875;
```

Variable names can be up to 30 characters long, begin with a character, and contain numbers, letters, or special symbols. A variable name must not be the same as a column name referenced in the PL/SQL block. If you violate that rule, Oracle assumes that the name refers to the table column and *not* the variable. Most professionals follow the convention of prefixing the variables in a PL/SQL block with c_, v_, or g_ for a constant, a variable, or a global variable. A ***global variable*** is one that can be referenced by the host environment from outside the PL/SQL block.

A constant looks like a variable but, in fact, cannot change during the program execution. Programmers follow the practice of naming most constants used in code, so it is easy to change the value, if needed, simply by changing the value in the declaration. The alternative is to use a constant (e.g., 0.1875) repeatedly. However, changing the constant becomes onerous because you must locate *every* instance of the constant and change it. It is always better to use a constant construct—even for a single-use constant. It's good documentation.

There are four categories of PL/SQL variables: scalar, composite, reference, and large object (LOB). A scalar data type, similar to a scalar subquery defined in Chapter 6, holds a single value. Scalar data types are the same ones used to declare table columns. Additionally, a Boolean data type is available in PL/SQL. A Boolean data element can have the value of TRUE, FALSE, or NULL.

The NOT NULL optional phrase in a variable declaration indicates that the variable *cannot* contain null. That implies that the variable must be initialized or Oracle will throw an exception. (Programmers often say *throw an exception* to mean that an exception is generated.) If you write the optional ":=" following the variable name and other optional phrases, the variable is assigned that initial value before the execution section begins. Otherwise, its initial value is NULL.

EXPLORING THE EXECUTABLE SECTION

The key word BEGIN marks the beginning of the executable section, and it is the only *required* section in a PL/SQL block, as mentioned previously. You can include a SELECT statement to retrieve information from database tables. However, you use a modified form of SELECT—it must contain an INTO clause to assign retrieved column values to variables. Otherwise, you cannot display whatever the SELECT statement retrieves. Recall that this form of the SELECT statement has the simplified syntax as follows:

```
SELECT <column_name1> [, <column_name2>, ...]
INTO <variable_name1> [, <variable_name2>,...]
FROM <table_Name> | <view_name>
WHERE <condition>;
```

When a SELECT statement is encountered in a PL/SQL block, Oracle allocates memory to hold the retrieved table or view rows. This area is called a ***cursor.*** There are two types. Oracle creates an ***implicit cursor*** for a SELECT statement or a DML statement that returns one row. It occurs without your intervention. If a SELECT statement returns more than one row, you must manually create and manage an ***explicit cursor.*** You will learn about explicit cursors later in this chapter. For now, you will use SELECT statements that return none or only one row. Therefore, you need not be concerned with cursors yet.

In the PL/SQL block shown in Figure 7.2, for example, only one row is returned. The substitution variable &AgentLastName causes a prompt to appear requesting you to

```
Enter value for agentlastname:
```

You type a response (for example, *Carling*) and press **Enter.** That value replaces the substitution variable (e.g., 'Carling') in the SELECT statement WHERE clause. The SELECT statement can then retrieve the contents of two columns and the value of a calculated virtual column for the selected agent name. Those values are placed into the variables identified in the declarations section by placing the variable names following the keyword INTO. The select-list expression

```
(C_date-HireDate)/365.25
```

computes the number of years the selected agent has worked for Redwood Realty. Once Oracle places the values of the retrieved columns and the calculated value into the variables, they are displayed using the PUT_LINE function of the DBMS_OUTPUT package. Think of it as a way to display lines on the screen from within PL/SQL code.

SELECT statements in PL/SQL blocks do not display on the screen like they do when issued directly from SQL*Plus. Instead, you rely on the DBMS_OUTPUT package that contains a bundle of various functions that you invoke to display any values you wish.

> **Tip:** If you type and execute the PL/SQL block shown in Figure 7.2 and no output appears, the reason is that you must first set the SQL*Plus environmental variable SERVEROUTPUT to the value ON. Simply type SET SERVEROUTPUT ON and press **Enter** at the SQL prompt.

The argument of the PUT_LINE function (see Figure 7.2) is the string you want to display. In this case, it is formed by concatenating variables and string constants.

EXPLORING THE EXCEPTION HANDLING SECTION

The optional exception handling section of a PL/SQL block specifies what to do if an exception occurs during the execution of the PL/SQL block. **Exceptions** are error conditions or unexpected results that occur when executing a PL/SQL block. When an exception occurs, it is *raised* and the code in the exception handler takes over. For example, if you code the statement

```
SELECT 12/0
INTO v_numbervar
FROM DUAL;
```

the attempted division by zero throws an exception. If the PL/SQL block contains an EXCEPTION section, control transfers to it, and Oracle executes any statements it contains and exits the PL/SQL block. A different type of exception is raised or thrown when a SELECT statement returns no rows.

There are two types of exceptions: user-defined and predefined. A ***user-defined exception*** is an error that the user defines. A user-defined exception is not necessarily an Oracle error. Instead, it may be a convenient way to throw control of the program to another section of the PL/SQL block. You declare user-defined exceptions in the declarative section of the block. The syntax is simple. It is:

```
<exception_name> EXCEPTION;
```

You can cause a user-defined exception to occur—called raising the exception—by executing the RAISE statement. Its syntax is:

```
RAISE <exception_name>;
```

You write code to handle user-defined exceptions in the exceptions section. You will see examples of these later in this chapter.

Oracle's predefined exceptions correspond to commonly occurring Oracle errors. They include unique constraint violation, division by zero, and an attempt to assign values to a NULL object. Some of these and their error codes are listed in Table 7.1.

The exception handler called OTHERS, which appears in the exceptions section of Figure 7.2, handles *all* exceptions that are not listed in any other WHEN clauses of the EXCEPTION statement. In other words, it is a catchall exception handler. Use it when you don't need to worry about the exact nature of the exception that occurred in the PL/SQL block.

TABLE 7.1 Selected Predefined Oracle Exceptions.

Oracle Error Code	Meaning
ORA-0001	Unique constraint violated.
ORA-1001	Illegal cursor operation.
ORA-1403	No data found.
ORA-1422	A SELECT INTO statement returns more than one row.
ORA-1476	Division by zero has occurred.
ORA-1722	Conversion to a number failed; (Attempt to convert a character string, for instance).
ORA-6502	Truncation, conversion error, or arithmetic error.
ORA-6511	Attempt to open a cursor that is already open.

CREATING ANONYMOUS BLOCKS

Creating anonymous blocks is about the same as writing SQL and SQL*Plus statements. The main difference is that PL/SQL follows the structure conventions mentioned above—named sections in a particular order and each statement ends with a semicolon. Before beginning, you should restore the Redwood Realty database to its original form.

INITIALIZING THE REDWOOD REALTY DATABASE

Before you start writing PL/SQL blocks, we want you to initialize the database. Doing so minimizes the possibility that your results will be different from those shown here. All the activity in this chapter uses SQL*Plus as the platform of choice. Every step in this chapter assumes you have launched SQL*Plus and logged into Oracle, unless otherwise indicated. Launch SQL*Plus and log into Oracle.

To initialize the database:

1. Locate the path to the BuildRedwood.sql script file in the Redwood Realty folder among the data files associated with this textbook. Substitute that path for "<path1>" below and then type and execute the following:

   `START <path1>\RedwoodRealty\BuildRedwood`

2. Note the path and folder to the script file *Ch07AgentsHR* in your Chapter 7 data files. Substitute that path for "<path2>" below, and then type and execute the following:

   `START <path2>Ch07AgentsHR`

   Your screen should match the results shown in Figure 7.3.

3. Leave SQL*Plus running.

WRITING AN ANONYMOUS BLOCK

To write an anonymous PL/SQL block, simply launch your favorite text editor (Notepad in the case of Windows) and write the code. When completed, you can copy the code to SQL*Plus and then execute it, or you can save it as a script file (with the file extension *.sql*) and then execute it by referencing it in a START command such as:

   `START C:\AnonymousBlockExample.sql`

or

   `@C:\AnonymousBlockExample.sql`

FIGURE 7.3 Initializing the Redwood Realty database.

You will create an anonymous block and save it on your disk. Because the block is anonymous, it is *not* saved in the database. Thus, anyone who might benefit from running the PL/SQL block must: (1) have access to the host machine on which it is stored, (2) know the path to the file, and (3) know the PL/SQL anonymous block file name.

The PL/SQL block you are about to write will query the Agents table to count the number of agents. Then, it will query the AgentsHR table to compute the average base salary and the average vacation time. Finally, the code will execute an Oracle formatting function to convert a number to a formatted dollar amount, and the code will display the results in three lines on the screen. In preparation, launch Notepad or another suitable text editor. You may launch SQL*Plus now, but you don't need to yet.

To create an anonymous PL/SQL block:

1. Open Notepad. In Notepad, start by typing the declarations section. Remember to type a semicolon to end the lines as indicated (except DECLARE):

```
DECLARE
   v_AvgSal AgentsHR.BaseSalary%TYPE;
   v_AvgVac AgentsHR.Vacation%TYPE;
   v_Count INTEGER NOT NULL := 0;
   v_AvgSalChar VARCHAR2(15);
```

2. Continue by typing the execution section in Notepad. The empty lines, or white space, aid readability by separating distinct code sections. (The indent following BEGIN is two spaces for each line, though you can change that to more or fewer spaces.)

```
BEGIN
   /* Count the number of agents in the table */
   SELECT COUNT(AgentID) INTO v_Count FROM Agents;

   /* Compute averages */
   SELECT AVG(BaseSalary), AVG(Vacation)
   INTO v_AvgSal, v_AvgVac
   FROM AgentsHR;

   /* Convert to a formatted character string */
   v_AvgSalChar := TO_CHAR(v_AvgSal, '$99,999.99');

   /* Display results */
   DBMS_OUTPUT.PUT_LINE('Average Salary: '||v_AvgSalChar);
   DBMS_OUTPUT.PUT_LINE('Average Vacation: '|| v_AvgVac|| ' weeks');
   DBMS_OUTPUT.PUT_LINE('Based on: '|| v_Count|| ' agents');
```

3. Finally, type the following code to complete the PL/SQL anonymous block. Remember to type a semicolon after END. Note that the last line contains the slash (/), which tells Oracle to compile the code when the block is loaded into SQL*Plus.

```
EXCEPTION
  WHEN OTHERS THEN
    DBMS_OUTPUT.PUT_LINE(SQLERRM);
END;
/
```

4. In Notepad, click **File,** click **Save As,** click the **File name** text box, and navigate to the folder on your computer where you want to save the code. (Remember it!) Type **<yourname>AnonBlockOne.sql,** substituting your own name for "<yourname>," click the **Save as type** list box, and click **All Files.** Click the **Save** button to save the file. Figure 7.4 shows the completed PL/SQL block in Notepad.

5. Click **File,** and then click **Exit** to close Notepad.

Let's examine and discuss each line of the code before attempting to execute it. The declarations section defines three local variables. (A *local variable* is a variable that is available and can be referenced only within the PL/SQL block in which it is defined.) The local variable v_AvgSal will hold the average salary, and its data type is the same as the BaseSalary of the AgentsHR table. Similarly, v_AvgVac will hold the average vacation time calculated from the Vacation column in the AgentsHR table. V_Count will hold an integer that is the number of agent rows found in Agents. Finally, the local variable v_AvgSalChar will hold the formatted character string version of the average salary.

The execution section has several comment lines enclosed by /* and */. The first SELECT statement computes the number of agent rows in the Agents table and puts

FIGURE 7.4 An anonymous PL/SQL block.

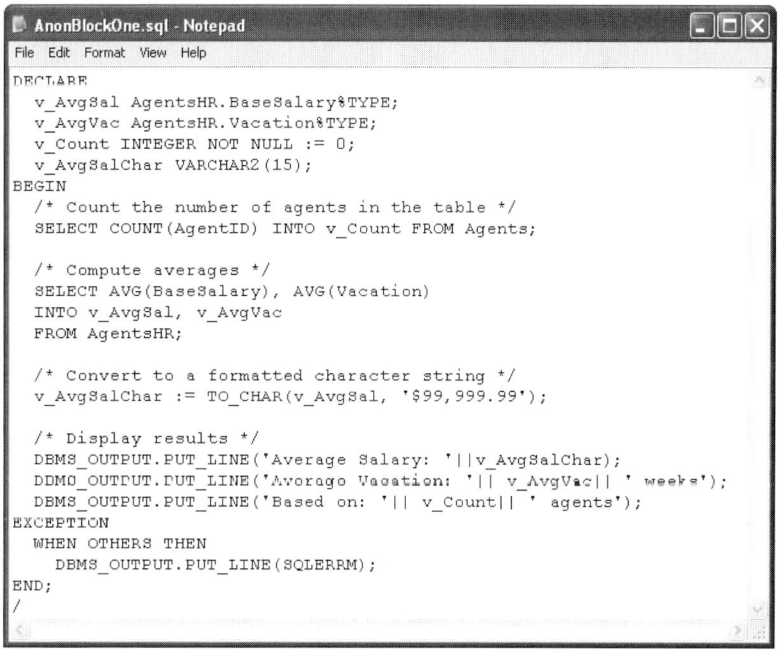

```
DECLARE
  v_AvgSal AgentsHR.BaseSalary%TYPE;
  v_AvgVac AgentsHR.Vacation%TYPE;
  v_Count INTEGER NOT NULL := 0;
  v_AvgSalChar VARCHAR2(15);
BEGIN
  /* Count the number of agents in the table */
  SELECT COUNT(AgentID) INTO v_Count FROM Agents;

  /* Compute averages */
  SELECT AVG(BaseSalary), AVG(Vacation)
  INTO v_AvgSal, v_AvgVac
  FROM AgentsHR;

  /* Convert to a formatted character string */
  v_AvgSalChar := TO_CHAR(v_AvgSal, '$99,999.99');

  /* Display results */
  DBMS_OUTPUT.PUT_LINE('Average Salary: '||v_AvgSalChar);
  DBMS_OUTPUT.PUT_LINE('Average Vacation: '|| v_AvgVac|| ' weeks');
  DBMS_OUTPUT.PUT_LINE('Based on: '|| v_Count|| ' agents');
EXCEPTION
  WHEN OTHERS THEN
    DBMS_OUTPUT.PUT_LINE(SQLERRM);
END;
/
```

the returned value into the local variable v_Count. The second SELECT statement computes the average BaseSalary and the average value for Vacation and stores the answers in two local variables for later use. Finally, an assignment statement converts the average salary to a formatted string by executing:

```
V_AvgSalChar := TO_CHAR(v_AvgSal, '$99,999.99');
```

The last three lines of the execution section display the results using concatenated string literals and local variables.

The exception handling section displays an error message (SQLERRM) with the catchall condition OTHERS. If an error occurs in the execution section, control transfers here and the message appears on the screen. Although we could remove the exception handling section with no ill effects, any error condition that might arise due to a database table changing would be masked from you because there would be no provision for even noting the error. It is always a good habit to include an exception handling block in any PL/SQL code blocks—anonymous or otherwise.

The word *END* followed by a semicolon marks the end of the PL/SQL anonymous code block. The slash tells Oracle to run the PL/SQL block. You could omit the slash and type it manually after loading the PL/SQL block in SQL*Plus, but it is more convenient to store the slash in the file containing the PL/SQL code. It is one less thing to remember to type.

SETTING UP THE SQL*PLUS ENVIRONMENT

If you were to run the PL/SQL block you just created in SQL*Plus, nothing would appear to happen. The only visible result would be the line Oracle displays to indicate that the code completed:

```
PL/SQL procedure successfully completed.
```

For the PUT_LINE output from the DBMS_OUTPUT package to appear on the screen (console), you must turn on the SQL*Plus environment variable SERVEROUTPUT. Do so by executing

```
SET SERVEROUTPUT ON
```

You might prefer to place that statement within the anonymous code block so you don't have to remember to type it.

RUNNING AN ANONYMOUS PL/SQL BLOCK

With the anonymous PL/SQL block safely saved, you can run the block to see the results. There's no need to have Notepad open, but you can launch SQL*Plus and log into Oracle.

To run an anonymous PL/SQL block:

1. Type and execute the following to run the PL/SQL block you saved previously. Substitute the actual path to the file for "<path>" and your name for "<yourname>" below.

    START <path>\<yourname>AnonBlockOne

    The only message displayed is the one mentioned previously indicating that "... procedure successfully completed."

2. The SERVEROUTPUT SQL*Plus environmental variable is OFF. Type and execute the following to turn it on:

    SET SERVEROUTPUT ON

CHAPTER 7   Using PL/SQL to Your Advantage   **329**

FIGURE 7.5 Executing an anonymous PL/SQL block.

3. Because the anonymous PL/SQL block is still in the SQL*Plus buffer, type slash
   (/) and press **Enter** to execute it.

   Three result lines produced by the anonymous PL/SQL block appear, along with
   the Oracle successful completion line. See Figure 7.5.

4. Type **exit** and press **Enter** to log off Oracle and close SQL*Plus.

The preceding code used an *implicit cursor* because the SELECT statement
retrieves exactly one row from the table—the average base salary and average vacation days for all agents. Next, you will modify the anonymous block to return the average salary and vacation of each agent *team,* grouped by team number. All the requisite columns are found in the AgentsHR table, so that doesn't change. What does change is that the SELECT statement will return five rows, one row for each of the five numbered teams.

MODIFYING AN ANONYMOUS BLOCK TO DISPLAY MULTIPLE ROWS

Modifying an anonymous block is the same process as modifying any other SQL script file: Open the anonymous block in a text editor, make any desired changes, and save the anonymous PL/SQL block under its existing name or a new one. After you have modified the anonymous block, you can run it from SQL*Plus using the START command to test the results of your changes. Let's modify the anonymous PL/SQL block you created above to change its behavior. To preserve the anonymous block you created earlier, you will open it and immediately save it under a new name.

The purpose of the modified anonymous PL/SQL block you are about to change is to produce statistics about the five Redwood Realty agent teams. In particular, instead of an average based on all realtors, the anonymous block will display averages for each team. There are five teams numbered 10 through 14. Before you modify the anonymous block, launch Notepad (or another suitable text editor).

To modify an anonymous PL/SQL block and save it under a new name:

1. Click **File,** click **Open,** click the **Look in** list box to navigate to the folder where you previously stored the file AnonBlockOne.sql (prefixed by your name, of course), click the **Files of type** list box, and select **All Files,** and double-click **AnonblockOne.sql** in the list of files to open it.

2. Insert an empty line between the v_AvgVac and v_Count variable declarations in the declarations section and in that open line type:

   `v_Team AgentsHR.Team%TYPE;`

3. Modify the SELECT statement to the following form by adding *Team* in select list, adding *v_Team* as the first variable in the INTO list of the SELECT statement, by

typing GROUP BY Team at the end of the SELECT statement, and by adding a PUT_LINE line. Your modified code should match the following code (added/changed lines are marked):

```
DECLARE
   v_AvgSal AgentsHR.BaseSalary%TYPE;
   v_AvgVac AgentsHR.Vacation%TYPE;
   v_Team AgentsHR.Team%TYPE;                              (added line)
   v_Count INTEGER NOT NULL := 0;
   v_AvgSalChar VARCHAR2(15);
BEGIN
   /* Count the number of agents in the table */
   SELECT COUNT(AgentID) INTO v_Count FROM Agents;

   /* Compute averages */
   SELECT Team, AVG(BaseSalary), AVG(Vacation)            (changed line)
   INTO v_Team, v_AvgSal, v_AvgVac                        (changed line)
   FROM AgentsHR                                          (changed line)
   GROUP BY Team;                                         (added line)

   /* Convert to a formatted character string */
   v_AvgSalChar := TO_CHAR(v_AvgSal, '$99,999.99');

   /* Display results */
   DBMS_OUTPUT.PUT_LINE('Team: '||v_Team);                (added line)
   DBMS_OUTPUT.PUT_LINE('Average Salary: '||v_AvgSalChar);
   DBMS_OUTPUT.PUT_LINE('Average Vacation: '|| v_AvgVac|| ' weeks');
   DBMS_OUTPUT.PUT_LINE('Based on: '|| v_Count|| ' agents');
EXCEPTION
   WHEN OTHERS THEN
      DBMS_OUTPUT.PUT_LINE(SQLERRM);
END;
/
```

4. Save the changed file under a new name: Click **File,** click **Save As,** click the **Save as type** list box, click **All Files,** click the **File name** list box, type **<yourname> AnonBlockTwo.sql** (substitute your last name for "<yourname>"), and click the **Save** button. Notepad saves your changed file.

5. Launch SQL*Plus (if necessary), log into Oracle, and type and execute the following to clear the screen and allow output from the PL/SQL block:

```
CLEAR SCREEN
SET SERVEROUTPUT ON
```

6. To make it easier to talk about the selected lines of the PL/SQL block, switch back to Notepad and copy all the code from Notepad to SQL*Plus. Doing so produces SQL line numbers to which you can refer as we discuss the outcome.

7. In SQL*Plus, press **Enter** at the end of the last line containing the slash (/) to run the code block. Oracle issues an error message which the exception section displays (see Figure 7.6).

What caused the error message indicating "... more than the requested number of rows ..." were fetched in the previous exercise? The error occurred because the SELECT statement (lines 12 through 15 in Figure 7.6) in the modified PL/SQL block returns more than one row from the database—five rows, in fact—one of the exceptions described in the next section.

HANDLING EXCEPTIONS

In the preceding code, your code contains an exception section that handles any exception thrown during execution of the anonymous PL/SQL block because you coded the

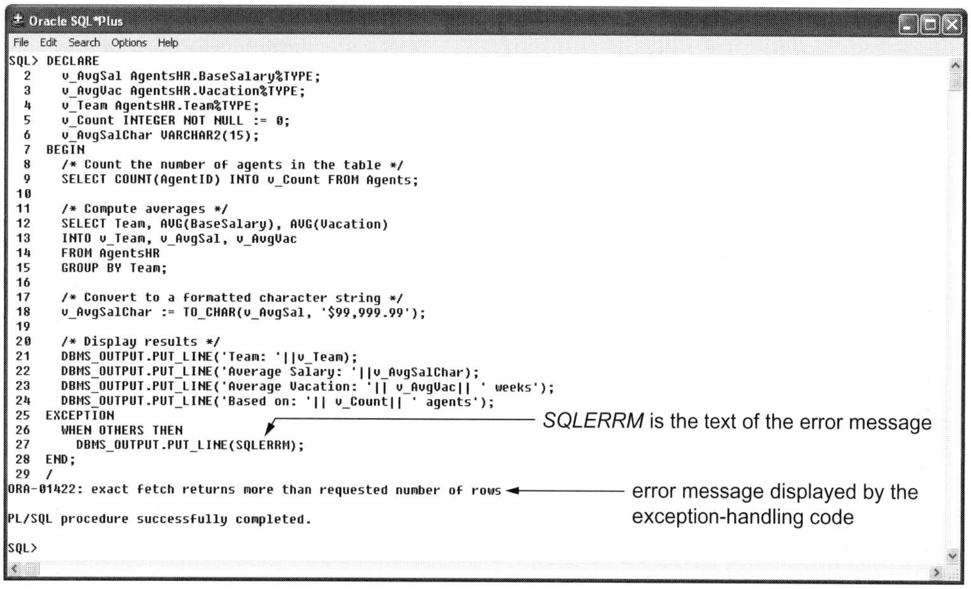

CHAPTER 7 Using PL/SQL to Your Advantage **331**

```
SQL> DECLARE
  2    v_AvgSal AgentsHR.BaseSalary%TYPE;
  3    v_AvgVac AgentsHR.Vacation%TYPE;
  4    v_Team AgentsHR.Team%TYPE;
  5    v_Count INTEGER NOT NULL := 0;
  6    v_AvgSalChar VARCHAR2(15);
  7  BEGIN
  8    /* Count the number of agents in the table */
  9    SELECT COUNT(AgentID) INTO v_Count FROM Agents;
 10
 11    /* Compute averages */
 12    SELECT Team, AVG(BaseSalary), AVG(Vacation)
 13    INTO v_Team, v_AvgSal, v_AvgVac
 14    FROM AgentsHR
 15    GROUP BY Team;
 16
 17    /* Convert to a formatted character string */
 18    v_AvgSalChar := TO_CHAR(v_AvgSal, '$99,999.99');
 19
 20    /* Display results */
 21    DBMS_OUTPUT.PUT_LINE('Team: '||v_Team);
 22    DBMS_OUTPUT.PUT_LINE('Average Salary: '||v_AvgSalChar);
 23    DBMS_OUTPUT.PUT_LINE('Average Vacation: '|| v_AvgVac|| ' weeks');
 24    DBMS_OUTPUT.PUT_LINE('Based on: '|| v_Count|| ' agents');
 25  EXCEPTION
 26    WHEN OTHERS THEN                        ──── SQLERRM is the text of the error message
 27      DBMS_OUTPUT.PUT_LINE(SQLERRM);
 28  END;
 29  /
ORA-01422: exact fetch returns more than requested number of rows ◄──── error message displayed by the
                                                                        exception-handling code
PL/SQL procedure successfully completed.

SQL>
```

FIGURE 7.6 A run-time error using an implicit cursor.

TABLE 7.2 Some named exceptions and their meanings.

Exception name to test	Meaning
ACCESS_INTO_NULL	Attempted to assign a value to an attribute of an uninitialized object.
CASE_NOT_FOUND	None of the WHEN clauses of a CASE structure were selected and there was no ELSE default clause.
CURSOR_ALREADY_OPEN	Program tried to open a cursor that is already open.
INVALID_CURSOR	Program tried to perform an illegal cursor activity such as closing an open cursor.
NO_DATA_FOUND	A SELECT INTO statement returns zero rows.
ROWTYPE_MISMATCH	A cursor variable and a PL/SQL variable have incompatible data types.
TOO_MANY_ROWS	A SELECT INTO statement returned more than one row.
VALUE_ERROR	A conversion, arithmetic, truncation, or size-constraint error occurred. (For example, an attempt to select a long character column into a shorter PL/SQL variable causes this exception.)
ZERO_DIVIDE	Attempted to divide a number by zero.

catchall phrase "WHEN OTHERS . . . " More fine-grained exception handling is possible when you use the names of individual exceptions in the exception handling code. The names of several exceptions and their meanings appear in Table 7.2. The exception handling code that follows shows how you might process named exceptions individually.

```
EXCEPTION
   WHEN VALUE_ERROR THEN
      DBMS_OUTPUT.PUT_LINE('Value error was generated.')
   WHEN ZERO_DIVIDE THEN
      DBMS_OUTPUT.PUT_LINE('Code performs a divide by zero.')
```

```
    WHEN TOO_MANY_ROWS THEN
      DBMS_OUTPUT.PUT_LINE('Query returned more than one row.')
    WHEN OTHERS THEN
      DBMS_OUTPUT.PUT_LINE('Error: '||SQLERRM)
END;
```

where the first three WHERE clauses test specific error conditions, and the WHERE OTHERS traps all other exceptions.

When an exception occurs in a PL/SQL block, control transfers to the exception handling section. If there is no WHEN clause to handle the particular exception, then control passes to the WHEN OTHERS exception handler. If there is no exception handler, including the generic WHEN OTHERS, then the error appears on the screen and is not processed further. Once control jumps to the exception handling section, it cannot return to the main PL/SQL code body. It is easier to understand exception handling if you write a simple PL/SQL block to illustrate two of them. Launch SQL*Plus, launch Notepad or your favorite text editor, and follow the steps below to experiment with generating exceptions and handling them.

To write a PL/SQL block to generate and handle specific, named exceptions:

1. Type the following in SQL*Plus to set up the environment.

   ```
   SET SERVEROUTPUT ON
   ```

2. Type the following in your text editor, copy it to SQL*Plus. Press **Enter** following the slash (/) in the last line to compile and execute the PL/SQL block. Keep the text editor open to make changes in subsequent steps.

   ```
   CLEAR SCREEN
   DECLARE
     v_TeamNo AgentsHR.Team%TYPE;
   BEGIN
     SELECT Team INTO v_TeamNo FROM AgentsHR;
     SELECT 123/0 INTO v_TeamNo FROM DUAL;
     SELECT Team INTO v_TeamNo FROM AgentsHR
       WHERE Vacation = 20;
   EXCEPTION
     WHEN ZERO_DIVIDE THEN
       DBMS_OUTPUT.PUT_LINE('Divide by zero');
     WHEN TOO_MANY_ROWS THEN
       DBMS_OUTPUT.PUT_LINE('Multiple rows returned');
   WHEN OTHERS THEN
       DBMS_OUTPUT.PUT_LINE('Something else went wrong');
   END;
   /
   ```

   The message "Multiple rows returned" appears, indicating that Oracle has raised the TOO_MANY_ROWS exception. Ignore the subsequent message from Oracle "PS/SQL procedure successfully completed."

3. Switch back to the text editor, and type -- (two hyphens) in the first two columns just to the left of the first SELECT statement. That turns the statement into a comment. Copy and paste the entire modified script into SQL*Plus, and press **Enter** to execute the modified block. This time, the ZERO_DIVIDE exception is raised and your message handling that case appears (see Figure 7.7).

4. Switch back to the text editor, and type -- (two hyphens) in the first two columns just to the left of the second SELECT statement to turn it into a comment also. Copy and paste the entire script into SQL*Plus, and press **Enter** to execute the modified block. This time, the OTHERS exception is raised and your message *Something else is wrong* appears.

```
SQL> DECLARE
  2    v_TeamNo AgentsHR.Team%TYPE;
  3  BEGIN
  4    -- SELECT Team INTO v_TeamNo FROM AgentsHR;         ← two hyphens turn the SELECT
  5    SELECT 123/0 INTO v_TeamNo FROM DUAL;                 statement into a comment
  6    SELECT Team INTO v_TeamNo FROM AgentsHR
  7       WHERE Vacation = 20;
  8  EXCEPTION
  9    WHEN ZERO_DIVIDE THEN
 10       DBMS_OUTPUT.PUT_LINE('Divide by zero');
 11    WHEN TOO_MANY_ROWS THEN
 12       DBMS_OUTPUT.PUT_LINE('Multiple rows returned');
 13    WHEN OTHERS THEN
 14       DBMS_OUTPUT.PUT_LINE('Something else went wrong');
 15  END;
 16  /
Divide by zero

PL/SQL procedure successfully completed.

SQL>
```

FIGURE 7.7 Exploring exception handling.

5. Type **exit** and press **Enter** to log out of Oracle and close SQL*Plus. Switch to your text editor and save your exception-testing PL/SQL block in an appropriate folder.

6. Close Notepad or other text editor.

Next, you will learn how to fix the error previously indicated when you attempted to display team numbers and average salaries and average vacation days. The solution to the TOO_MANY_ROWS exception issued earlier is to use an *explicit cursor* to retrieve the information from the Redwood Realty tables.

UNDERSTANDING EXPLICIT CURSORS

Recall that a SELECT statement in a PL/SQL block that returns one row uses an *implicit cursor*. Using an implicit cursor in a PL/SQL block means that default mechanisms allow Oracle to pass a single row, returned from a database table, to a PL/SQL block and into the variables set up to receive the returned column(s). But an implicit cursor cannot handle more than one row being returned by a SELECT statement. It is like asking a one-seat motor bike to accommodate a busload of passengers. Instead, you have to modify a PL/SQL block whose SELECT statement could return multiple rows. To accept multiple rows from a database table, the code uses an *explicit cursor*. Setting up an explicit cursor involves moving the SELECT statement to the declarations section and turning it into a cursor. Then, you have to initialize the cursor, write code to explicitly retrieve information from the database, and, at the end, shut down the cursor. Several additional code lines are required to implement an explicit cursor. And, you need a programming construct not mentioned yet—a loop.

INTRODUCING PL/SQL ITERATION CONSTRUCTS

PL/SQL supplies three types of loops that allow a program to repeatedly execute a code section until (or while) some condition is met. As you will see shortly, having a looping structure allows you to instruct Oracle to pass one retrieved row at a time to your program and then pass additional rows, one at a time, each time the loop executes. There are three types of loop structures in PL/SQL: Simple loops, WHILE loops, and FOR loops. A ***simple loop*** executes repeatedly until you explicitly end the loop. A ***WHILE loop*** runs until a specified condition occurs. A ***FOR loop*** runs a predetermined number of times.

A simple loop, like all looping structures, executes a section of PL/SQL code it encloses repeatedly. To end a loop, you must include the code statement EXIT or EXIT WHEN. The syntax for a simple loop is:

```
LOOP
   statements
END LOOP;
```

The EXIT statement ends a loop immediately. An EXIT WHEN statement ends the loop when the condition attached to it becomes true. For example, the following code section executes until the value v_Counter reaches 15.

```
v_Counter := 1;
LOOP
  v_Counter := v_Counter + 3;
  EXIT WHEN v_Counter > 15;
  DBMS_OUTPUT.PUT_LINE(v_Counter);
END LOOP;
```

If you ran the preceding in a PL/SQL block, the loop would execute five times and display the values 4, 7, 10, and 13. The loop begins with the word *LOOP* and ends with the words *END LOOP* and the semicolon that follows it. The loop body is any code between those statements. The EXIT or EXIT WHEN statement can occur anywhere in the loop body. It is the EXIT WHEN statement, shown above, that determines when to exit the loop.

A warning is appropriate here. If you *omit* the EXIT WHEN or EXIT statement from any simple loop such as the preceding one, the loop will execute without ever stopping. A loop that does not stop is called an ***infinite loop.*** They occur more often than you might think. Just be very careful to include an EXIT WHEN statement and ensure that the condition can become true. For instance, the following is an infinite loop even though it *does* contain an EXIT WHEN statement. Can you see why the loop never stops?

```
/* Do not run this! */
v_Counter := 1;
LOOP
  v_Counter := v_Counter - 1;
  EXIT WHEN v_Counter > 15;
  DBMS_OUTPUT.PUT_LINE('Infinite loop. Help!');
END LOOP;
```

WHILE loops execute until a specified condition becomes true. The syntax for the WHILE loop is:

```
WHILE <condition> LOOP
   statements
END LOOP:
```

For example, the following loop displays five values and terminates when the loop counter, v_Counter, is no longer less than or equal to 15.

```
v_Counter := 1;
WHILE v_Counter <= 15 LOOP
   DBMS_OUTPUT.PUT_LINE(v_Counter);
   v_Counter := v_Counter + 3;
END LOOP;
```

Unlike the simple loop above, the WHILE loop tests the condition (v_Counter <= 15) *before* executing the loop body—at the top of the loop. If the condition is true, then the loop body executes. Otherwise, the body is not executed and control passes to the statement following the END LOOP statement.

A FOR loop executes a predetermined number of times. Sometimes called a counting loop, it is especially handy when you know the number of times to execute a loop beforehand. The loop runs a number of iterations based on the value of a lower and upper bound of a loop variable. The FOR loop syntax is:

```
FOR <loop_variable> IN [REVERSE] <lower_bound>..<upper_bound> LOOP
   statements
END LOOP;
```

where the loop variable ("<loop_variable>" in the syntax above) specifies a variable that is initialized to the "<lower_bound>" value (or "<upper_bound>" if REVERSE is specified) and determines when the loop executes. The loop variable is incremented (decremented if REVERSE is specified) by one each time through the loop. Execution of a FOR loop halts when the loop variable exceeds the upper bound (or the loop variable is less than the lower bound if REVERSE is specified). If REVERSE is omitted, the lower bound specifies the loop variable's initial value, and the upper bound specifies the loop variable's highest value. If REVERSE is specified, then the opposite is true; the upper bound value is loop variable's initial value and the lower bound is the loop variable's lowest value. Here is an example of a FOR loop that executes 15 times. Unlike both the simple loop and the WHILE loop, it is not necessary to declare the loop variable in a FOR loop.

```
FOR v_Counter IN 1..15 LOOP
   DBMS_OUTPUT.PUT_LINE(v_Counter);
END LOOP;
```

In the preceding example, the loop variable v_Counter is initialized to 1 the first time the FOR statement is executed. Then, the DBMS_OUTPUT statement executes. Control transfers to the top of the loop, the code increases the value of v_Counter by 1, and the FOR loop compares the newly incremented value to the loop limit, 15. If the value does not exceed 15, the loop continues. This process repeats until the loop variable is 15. Then, the loop variable's value is incremented to 16, which is compared to the loop limit of 15. Because the loop variable's value is greater than 15, control transfers to the statement following END LOOP.

USING EXPLICIT CURSORS AND LOOPS TO PROCESS ROWS

You might wonder why loop constructs are introduced in the middle of discussion about explicit cursors. Explicit cursors and loop constructs go together like cookies and milk. Because explicit cursors, by definition, are a result of a SELECT statement returning more than one row, loop constructs are required to step through multiple rows and process them one at a time.

USING EXPLICIT CURSORS

Whenever a PL/SQL block contains a SELECT statement that returns more than one row from a database table, you use a cursor to process the rows within the PL/SQL block. Think of a cursor as a set of rows returned by Oracle, stored in memory, that you process one row at a time. You request Oracle to retrieve rows into the cursor using a SELECT statement. Once Oracle places the requested rows in the cursor, you can fetch each one row at a time from the cursor and process it. To use a cursor, you usually follow five steps.

1. Declare variables to store the values returned from the SELECT statement.
2. Define the cursor by specifying a SELECT statement to retrieve rows.
3. Open the cursor, which causes Oracle to retrieve rows from the database and place all of them in the cursor (memory).

4. Fetch a row from the cursor and process it in the PL/SQL block. Repeat this step until all rows are processed.
5. Close the cursor, which releases the memory space occupied by the cursor and makes retrieved rows unavailable.

The best way to understand the process is to write a PL/SQL block that uses a cursor and to write code corresponding to each of the preceding five steps. Rather than modify the already modified PL/SQL block you have been using so far, you will create a new one from scratch. It will be similar to the one you saved called AnonBlockTwo.sql, except it will return just the average base salaries for each team, grouped by team number. It requires a cursor because the SELECT statement retrieves five rows.

Declaring Variables to Hold Column Values and the Cursor

First, you declare variables to hold the column values returned by the SELECT statement. In addition, you declare a variable to define the cursor. The cursor is the SELECT statement that retrieves the rows. To get started, open Notepad (or another text editor) to create the anonymous PL/SQL block using a cursor. Then follow the sequence of steps in this section to complete the PL/SQL block.

The syntax for defining a cursor is as follows:

```
CURSOR <cursor_name> [<parameter_list>]
   [RETURN <return_type>] IS
   <query>
[FOR UPDATE [OF (<column_list>)][NOWAIT]];
```

where "<cursor_name>" is any valid Oracle identifier. "<Parameter_list>" is optional and can be any list of arguments needed for execution. The optional RETURN phrase specifies the type of the value, if any, returned. The "<query>" is any SELECT statement. It retrieves one or more columns from one or more database tables. The optional FOR UPDATE clause locks database rows when the cursor opens. The NOWAIT option causes the program to terminate immediately when the cursor opens if the SELECT statement cannot obtain exclusive access to the database table rows.

To define variables to hold column values and the cursor:

1. Open Notepad and save the empty Notepad file to establish its name by doing the following: Click **File**, click **Save As**, click the **Save as type** list box, click **All Files**, click the **File name** list box, type **<yourname>AnonCursorOne.sql** (substitute your last name for "<yourname>"), and click the **Save** button.

2. Type the following to create the local variables to store retrieved column values.

```
DECLARE
   v_AvgSal AgentsHR.BaseSalary%TYPE;
   v_TeamNo AgentsHR.Team%TYPE;
   v_AvgSalChar VARCHAR2(15);
```

3. Next, type the following to define the cursor and mark the beginning of the PL/SQL code body. Notice the prefix, cv_, for the cursor ("cursor variable"). The cursor is defined by a complete SELECT statement:

```
   CURSOR cv_TeamCursor IS
      SELECT Team, AVG(BaseSalary)
      FROM AgentsHR
      GROUP BY Team
      ORDER BY Team;
BEGIN
```

Leave Notepad open for steps to follow.

OPENING THE CURSOR

The next step is to open the cursor. You do that by executing the OPEN statement. The OPEN command prepares the cursor, launches the SELECT statement, and retrieves rows from the database. Rows are placed into memory. A cursor's *active row* is the only row available to the PL/SQL program. When OPEN executes, the first row retrieved becomes the active row.

4. Continue by typing the following line to open the cursor:

```
OPEN cv_TeamCursor;
```

5. Type the following line to display column headers on the display:

```
DBMS_OUTPUT.PUT_LINE('Team'||'   Average Salary');
```

Leave Notepad open.

LOOPING AND FETCHING ROWS FROM THE CURSOR

Once you open the cursor, rows retrieved into the cursor are available for processing inside the PL/SQL program.

FETCH retrieves rows from the cursor, or context area, into variables so that the code can process the variables obtained from the row. The FETCH command operates on only one row and proceeds through the entire record set. The syntax of the FETCH statement is as follows:

```
FETCH <cursor_name>
INTO <variable_name(s)>;
```

where "<cursor_name>" is the cursor's name, and "<variable_name(s)>" is a list of comma-separated, previously defined variables. There must be as many variables in the list as there are returned columns in the cursor. Data types of the variables must match the data types of the returned columns.

In the next steps, you will write code to retrieve each row, one row at a time, and display it. The code will be enclosed in a simple loop that exits when there are no more rows available—after the last active cursor row is processed. Because the cursor may retrieve many rows, there must be a way to determine when to end the loop. The loop should end after processing the last row available. Therefore, there must be a way to know when the cursor has no more rows. There is. The Boolean variable %NOTFOUND is true after the FETCH statement reaches the last available row and there are no more rows to be fetched. The variable is appended to the cursor name. In this case, cv_TeamCursor%NOTFOUND is the complete Boolean variable you test to determine when to exit the loop.

6. Type the following lines to fetch rows within a simple loop, format one of the values, and display a single line on the console. (There are seven spaces in the string literal between v_TeamNo and v_AvgSalChar to align values beneath their respective column headers. The number of spaces is not crucial, though.)

```
LOOP
  FETCH cv_TeamCursor
  INTO v_TeamNo, v_AvgSal;
  EXIT WHEN cv_TeamCursor%NOTFOUND;
  v_AvgSalChar := TO_CHAR(v_AvgSal, '$99,999.99');
  DBMS_OUTPUT.PUT_LINE(v_TeamNo||'       '||v_AvgSalChar);
END LOOP;
```

Leave Notepad running.

Closing the Cursor and Writing the Exception Handler

The last bit of work to do is to close the cursor. You should always close explicit cursors. Until you close the cursor, the memory area occupied by the cursor's retrieved rows is not available for any other purpose. They syntax to close a cursor is simply

```
CLOSE <cursor_name>;
```

where "<cursor_name>" is the name of the open cursor. If you attempt to close a cursor that is not open, Oracle issues the error following error message (see Table 7.2):

```
ORA-01001: invalid cursor
```

To complete the code you are creating to process rows, follow these steps.

7. Type the following to close the open cursor, cv_TeamCursor:

```
CLOSE cv_TeamCursor;
```

8. Type the following code to create the exception handler and mark the end of the PL/SQL block:

```
EXCEPTION
  WHEN OTHERS THEN
    DBMS_OUTPUT.PUT_LINE('Error: '||SQLERRM);
END;
/
```

9. The code is complete. It is time to save the anonymous PL/SQL block. In Notepad, press **Ctrl+S** to save the final form of the file. Figure 7.8 shows the completed anonymous PL/SQL block in a Notepad window. Your code should match it.
10. Close Notepad.

FIGURE 7.8 A completed PL/SQL block containing an explicit cursor.

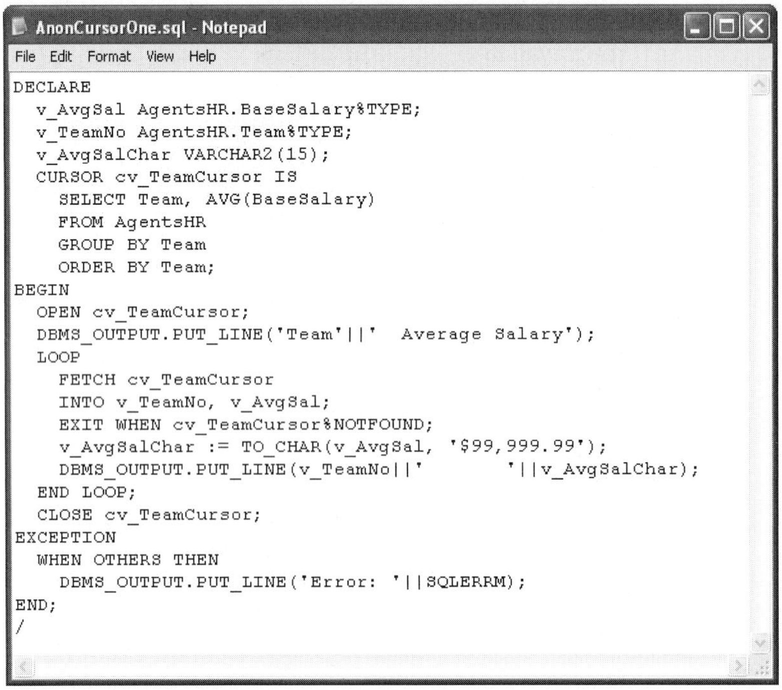
AnonCursorOne.sql - Notepad
File Edit Format View Help
DECLARE
v_AvgSal AgentsHR.BaseSalary%TYPE;
v_TeamNo AgentsHR.Team%TYPE;
v_AvgSalChar VARCHAR2(15);
CURSOR cv_TeamCursor IS
SELECT Team, AVG(BaseSalary)
FROM AgentsHR
GROUP BY Team
ORDER BY Team;
BEGIN
OPEN cv_TeamCursor;
DBMS_OUTPUT.PUT_LINE('Team'||' Average Salary');
LOOP
FETCH cv_TeamCursor
INTO v_TeamNo, v_AvgSal;
EXIT WHEN cv_TeamCursor%NOTFOUND;
v_AvgSalChar := TO_CHAR(v_AvgSal, '$99,999.99');
DBMS_OUTPUT.PUT_LINE(v_TeamNo||'   '||v_AvgSalChar);
END LOOP;
CLOSE cv_TeamCursor;
EXCEPTION
WHEN OTHERS THEN
DBMS_OUTPUT.PUT_LINE('Error: '||SQLERRM);
END;
/

FIGURE 7.9 Testing an anonymous PL/SQL block containing an explicit cursor.

It is time to test the anonymous PL/SQL block. With the block saved, launch SQL*Plus, log into Oracle, and follow these steps to test the code. If you encounter any errors, open Notepad, correct any mistakes, paste the code into SQL*Plus, and press **Enter** to rerun the corrected code. Save the perfected anonymous PL/SQL block if you make changes to it to preserve the final copy.

To test the anonymous PL/SQL block containing an explicit cursor:

1. Type the following in SQL*Plus to clear the screen and ensure that output from the PL/SQL block appears on the console:

   ```
   CLEAR SCREEN
   SET SERVEROUTPUT ON
   ```

2. Type the following to test the anonymous PL/SQL block you saved called AnonCursorOne.sql. Substitute the actual path to your code for "<path>" and your name for "<yourname>" below:

   ```
   START <path>\<yourname>AnonCursorOne
   ```

   If coded correctly, your results should match those shown in Figure 7.9. In other words, the five teams' team numbers and average salaries appear below their labels and the affirming message "PL/SQL procedure successfully completed."

3. Type **exit** and press **Enter** to log off Oracle and close SQL*Plus.

USING FOR LOOPS TO PROCESS EXPLICIT CURSORS

When you need to create a loop to process rows of an explicit cursor, there is no better choice than a special form of the FOR loop called a cursor FOR loop. When you use a *cursor FOR loop,* you do not have to open or close the cursor, and you do not have to issue a FETCH instruction. The cursor FOR loop does those three activities automatically for you. Thus, the advantage of using a cursor FOR loop with an explicit cursor is that the PL/SQL block code is simplified. The cursor FOR loop syntax is:

```
FOR <record_name> IN <cursor_name> LOOP
  <statement1>;
  <statement2>;...
END LOOP;
```

Instead of retrieving table columns and subsequently assigning them to internal PL/SQL variables, the cursor FOR loop assigns a retrieved row to a record. A *record* is a composite structure that has the same structure as the row Oracle retrieved with the explicit cursor.

To see the difference, you will create a new PL/SQL block containing a cursor FOR loop and an explicit cursor that returns multiple rows and displays them. Prepare for the exercise by launching SQL*Plus and Notepad. Type the text in Notepad, make any required changes in Notepad, and copy/paste it into SQL*Plus to execute the code. For convenience, you will place the CLEAR SCREEN and SET SERVEROUTPUT ON statements *inside* the anonymous PL/SQL block.

The procedure will retrieve the first and last names of all sellers who live in Loleta, California. Later, you will make this procedure more general to accommodate *any* city name that the user wants. Observe the FOR statement and how it interacts with the cursor.

To write a FOR loop in conjunction with an explicit cursor:

1. Type the following to clear the screen and set a SQL*Plus environmental variable:

```
CLEAR SCREEN
SET SERVEROUTPUT ON
```

2. Continue by typing the following declarations section:

> **Tip:** You do not need to match the spacing and indentation shown here, but it aids readability.

```
DECLARE
  CURSOR cv_Sellers IS
    SELECT a.FirstName, a.LastName, c.AskingPrice
    FROM Customers a
      INNER JOIN Properties b ON a.CustomerID = b.OwnerID
      INNER JOIN Listings c USING (PropertyID)
      INNER JOIN CustAgentList d USING (ListingID)
    WHERE UPPER(d.ContactReason) = 'SELL'
      AND a.City = 'Loleta'
    ORDER BY LastName, FirstName;
```

3. Continue by typing the following to implement the cursor FOR loop to process retrieved rows, and the exception handler to process two of the many possible exceptions:

```
BEGIN
  DBMS_OUTPUT.PUT_LINE(RPAD('Seller''s Name',24,' ')||'Asking Price');

  FOR v_Counter IN cv_Sellers LOOP
    DBMS_OUTPUT.PUT_LINE(
      RPAD(v_Counter.FirstName||' '||v_Counter.LastName,30,' ')||
      v_Counter.AskingPrice
    );
  END LOOP;

EXCEPTION
  WHEN NO_DATA_FOUND THEN
    DBMS_OUTPUT.PUT_LINE('No sellers in that city');
  WHEN OTHERS THEN
    DBMS_OUTPUT.PUT_LINE('Error of unknown type occurred');
END;
/
```

> **Tip:** The RPAD function is not strictly necessary, but it ensures that the displayed columns line up nicely. You probably recall that RPAD adds space on the right side of the first argument to extend it to a stated length.

4. Now you can test the cursor FOR loop. Copy the all the code you have typed in steps 1 through 3 above into SQL*Plus and press **Enter** to execute it. If errors occur,

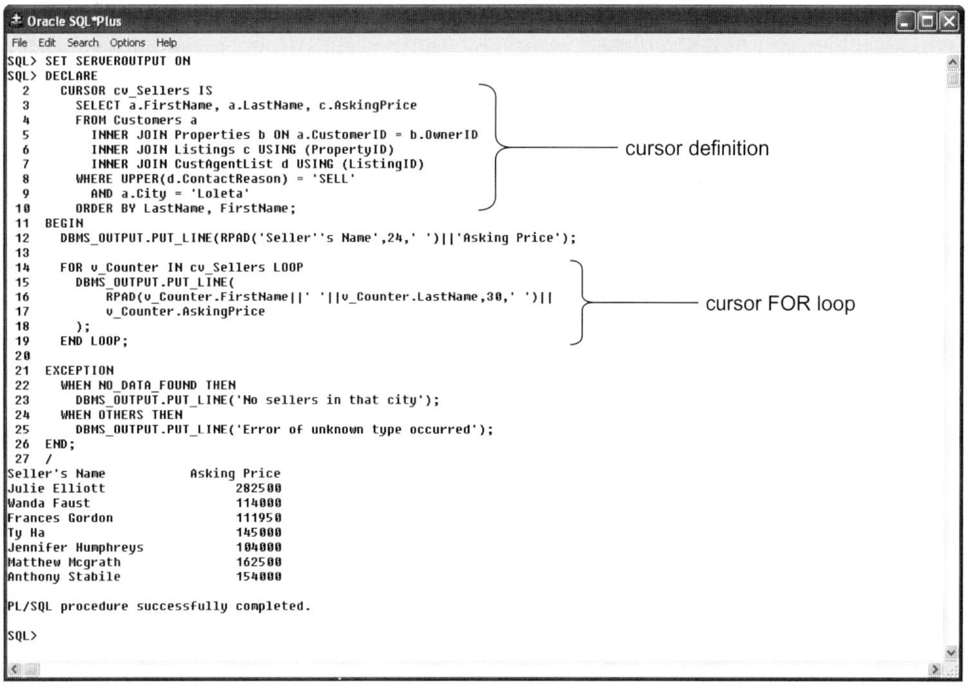

```
SQL> SET SERVEROUTPUT ON
SQL> DECLARE
  2     CURSOR cv_Sellers IS
  3       SELECT a.FirstName, a.LastName, c.AskingPrice
  4       FROM Customers a
  5         INNER JOIN Properties b ON a.CustomerID = b.OwnerID
  6         INNER JOIN Listings c USING (PropertyID)
  7         INNER JOIN CustAgentList d USING (ListingID)
  8       WHERE UPPER(d.ContactReason) = 'SELL'
  9         AND a.City = 'Loleta'
 10       ORDER BY LastName, FirstName;
 11  BEGIN
 12     DBMS_OUTPUT.PUT_LINE(RPAD('Seller''s Name',24,' ')||'Asking Price');
 13
 14     FOR v_Counter IN cv_Sellers LOOP
 15        DBMS_OUTPUT.PUT_LINE(
 16           RPAD(v_Counter.FirstName||' '||v_Counter.LastName,30,' ')||
 17           v_Counter.AskingPrice
 18        );
 19     END LOOP;
 20
 21  EXCEPTION
 22     WHEN NO_DATA_FOUND THEN
 23        DBMS_OUTPUT.PUT_LINE('No sellers in that city');
 24     WHEN OTHERS THEN
 25        DBMS_OUTPUT.PUT_LINE('Error of unknown type occurred');
 26  END;
 27  /
Seller's Name            Asking Price
Julie Elliott                  282500
Wanda Faust                    114000
Frances Gordon                 111950
Ty Ha                          145000
Jennifer Humphreys             104000
Matthew Mcgrath                162500
Anthony Stabile                154000

PL/SQL procedure successfully completed.

SQL>
```

(lines 2–10 are labeled "cursor definition"; lines 14–19 are labeled "cursor FOR loop")

FIGURE 7.10 Using a cursor FOR loop with an explicit cursor.

they are simply typos. Correct them in Notepad, and then recopy the entire PL/SQL block to SQL*Plus and re-execute it. Your result should match Figure 7.10.

5. Save the Notepad code under an appropriate name and in a folder of your own choosing. Close Notepad.
6. Type **exit** and press **Enter** to log off Oracle and close SQL*Plus.

INTRODUCING THE IF STATEMENT

Statements in a PL/SQL block are executed in sequence—one after another—by default. If you use a looping structure, then statements within a loop are executed repeatedly until (or while) some condition exists. Only one other programming structure completes the toolkit of statement types needed to write any PL/SQL program: the IF statement. Sometimes called a *selection construct,* the IF statement allows alternative statement choices to be executed based on whether a condition is true or false. You have seen one of these constructs called CASE in Chapter 4. Like the IF statement, the CASE statement allows alternative execution choices based on the value of one or more conditions. The IF statement syntax is:

```
IF <condition> THEN
   <statements>;
[ELSIF <condition> THEN
   <statements>;]
[ELSE
   <statements>;]
END IF;
```

where "<condition>" is an expression that evaluates to either true or false. In its simplest form, the IF statement has only a THEN phrase. If the condition evaluates to FALSE or NULL, the rest of the IF statement is skipped and nothing is done. When an IF statement condition is FALSE, Oracle evaluates the first ELSIF (notice the spelling omits a second *E*) condition, if any. The optional ELSIF clause contains statements that are the alternative to the statements following THEN. Subsequently, if the condition following ELSIF is true, the statements following the next THEN keyword are executed. Otherwise, statements in the ELSIF or the ELSE, whichever occurs next, are executed. Every IF statement ends with an END IF (two words) and a terminating semicolon. Semicolons also end all statements following the THEN, ELSIF, and ELSE keywords.

MAKING ALTERNATIVE CHOICES USING THE IF STATEMENT

The following examples illustrate how alternative statements execute depending on a condition. In particular, the PL/SQL block determines if there is an agent named *Franklin* in the Agents table. If there is not, the agent is added to the table. Otherwise, nothing more happens. DML statements such as UPDATE, INSERT, and so on are frequently implemented via PL/SQL blocks, both anonymous and named.

```
DECLARE
  v_Tally INTEGER := 0;
BEGIN
  SELECT COUNT(*) INTO v_Tally FROM Agents
    WHERE LastName = 'Franklin';
  IF v_Tally = 0 THEN
    INSERT INTO Agents (AgentID, FirstName, LastName, LicenseStatusID)
          VALUES (23456, 'Ben', 'Franklin',1001);
  ELSE
    DBMS_OUTPUT.PUT_LINE('Agent already in table: not added');
  END IF;
END;
```

Here, the SELECT statement computes the number of times an agent with the last name Franklin occurs in the Agents table. That resulting count is stored in v_Tally. The IF condition tests the result, determining if the value retrieved is zero or not. If it is zero, the expression is true. Otherwise, the expression is false (for values greater than zero). If the expression is TRUE, Oracle executes the INSERT INTO statement. If the expression is FALSE, the statement in the ELSE side of the statement executes and displays an informative message.

If it were unnecessary to inform the user when the name is found in the table, you can omit the ELSE statement. The alternative IF statement that inserts a row when one does not already exist is this simpler IF/THEN statement:

```
IF v_Tally = 0 THEN
  INSERT INTO Agents (AgentID, FirstName, LastName, LicenseStatusID)
        VALUES (23456, 'Ben', 'Franklin',1001);
  END IF;
```

The statements following THEN statements and those following ELSE are mutually exclusive. That is, only one or the other group of statements can be executed. Both sets can never be executed. Figure 7.11 shows a graphic representation of the IF statement with the optional ELSE phrase.

EXECUTING DML STATEMENTS IN PL/SQL BLOCKS

In addition to executing SELECT statements, PL/SQL blocks can execute data manipulation statements (but not DDL statements). Carefully constructed PL/SQL blocks can provide enhanced support for inserting, modifying, or deleting records. Rather than simply execute an INSERT, UPDATE, or DELETE statement, you can code a PL/SQL block that provides background information that helps you to determine if or how rows should be modified. For example, the human resources (HR) director for Redwood Realty has noticed that the base salaries of some of the Redwood

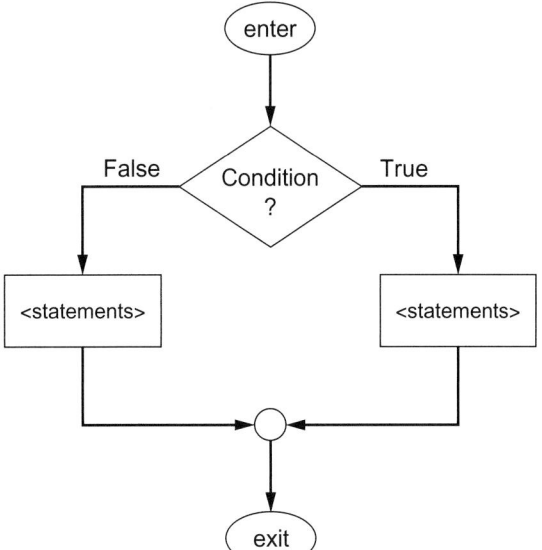

FIGURE 7.11 IF statement logic.

TABLE 7.3 Proposed salary increase rules.

Base Salary to Dependent Ratio	Base Salary Increase
$0 – $1,000	10%
$1,001 – $1,500	8%
$1,501 – $2,000	6%
$2,001 – $3,000	3%
Above $3,000	No increase

Realty agents—a perk meant to sustain agents during periods when home sales are low—are inequitable and require some minor modifications. She would like to increase the base salary of agents based on the ratio of each agent's base salary divided by their number of dependents. An example of that ratio is an agent's $3,000 base salary divided by the agent's five dependents, which yields the value of $600 per dependent. The ratio is, in the HR director's opinion, a fair way to ensure that agents have coverage based on the number of dependents in their households. The HR director proposes the graduated scale for increasing agents' base salary values shown in Table 7.3.

The type of graduated scale with different salary increase percentages is a typical situation where the IF statement is exactly what is needed. The IF statement provides the multiple condition evaluations required to determine which of an alternative set of actions should occur. In this case, the alternative actions are a choice among five alternatives, four of which are UPDATE statements affecting the AgentsHR table. This is a good example for you to code to understand how the IF statement works. Figure 7.12 shows the logic diagram to aid in implementing a PL/SQL block containing an IF statement and UPDATE statements.

Beginning directly below the ENTER oval, the logic determines if each agent's salary ratio is less than or equal to 1,000. If that condition is TRUE, then the code increments the BaseSalary value by 10 percent and exits the code block. If not, then the next test determines if the salary ratio is less than or equal to 1,500. If it is, then the agent's

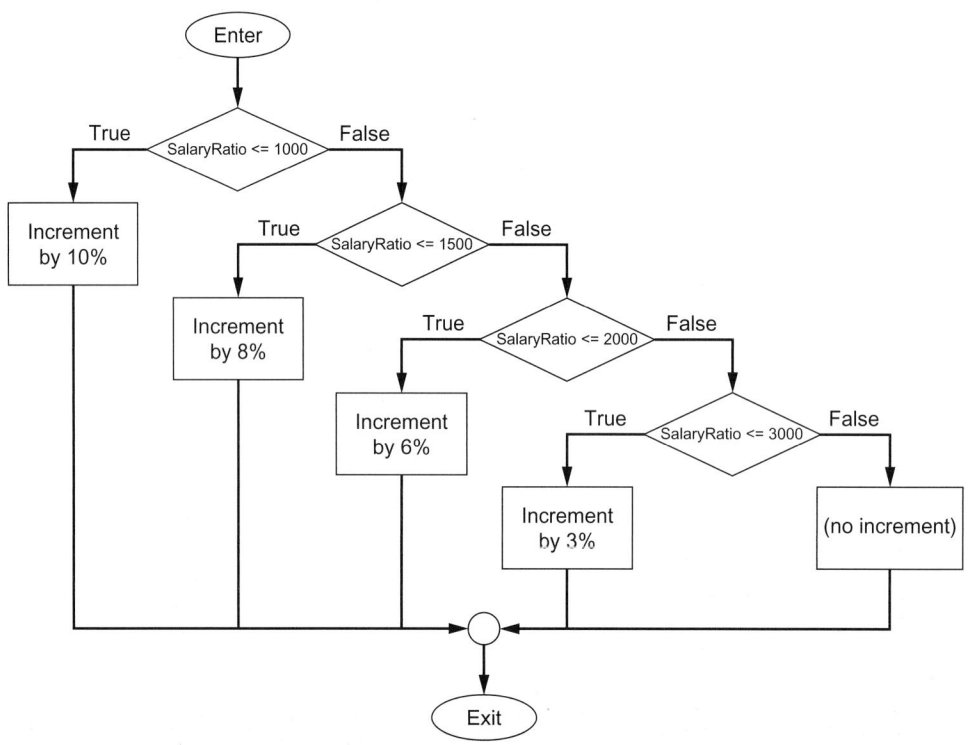

FIGURE 7.12 Business rule logic diagram.

BaseSalary value is augmented by 8 percent and execution exits the block. Testing conditions continues. If none of the first four conditions are TRUE, then the FALSE side of the catchall ELSE executes, indicating that no increment occurs.

Notice the way the testing logic is arranged. The less than or equal conditions are arranged in increasing order by values against which they are tested. The alternative is to test for "greater than" in descending order by values tested. Either way works, but do not randomly test values in willy-nilly order by increasing and then decreasing values. That logic arrangement will not work correctly.

Next, you will implement an UPDATE statement within an anonymous PL/SQL block with the aid of the IF statement. Prepare by launching SQL*Plus, logging into Oracle, and then launching Notepad or another text editor. Save the empty text file under a convenient name in a folder of your choice.

To write a PL/SQL block to conditionally update a table's column values:

1. After opening a new Notepad file and saving it under a name of your choice, type the following in your Notepad file.

```
CLEAR SCREEN
SET SERVEROUTPUT ON
```

2. Continue by typing the following declarations section lines in your Notepad file:

```
DECLARE
  v_Amount NUMBER(2,2);
  CURSOR cv_Agent IS
    SELECT AgentID, BaseSalary/Dependents AS SalaryRatio
    FROM AgentsHR;
```

3. Type the following execution section in Notepad or another text editor:

```
BEGIN
  FOR v_Counter IN cv_Agent LOOP
    IF v_Counter.SalaryRatio <= 1000 THEN
      v_Amount := 0.10;
    ELSIF v_Counter.SalaryRatio <= 1500 THEN
      v_Amount := 0.08;
    ELSIF v_Counter.SalaryRatio <= 2000 THEN
      v_Amount := 0.06;
    ELSIF v_Counter.SalaryRatio <= 3000 THEN
      v_Amount := 0.03;
    ELSE
      v_Amount := 0;
    END IF;
    DBMS_OUTPUT.PUT_LINE
      (v_Counter.AgentID|| ' updated by '||
       TO_CHAR(v_Amount*100,'99')||'%'
      );
    UPDATE AgentsHR
      SET BaseSalary = BaseSalary * (1+v_Amount)
      WHERE AgentID = v_Counter.AgentID;
  END LOOP;
  COMMIT;
```

4. Continue in Notepad by typing the following exception handling section, including the slash, which will cause the code to be compiled and executed when you copy the entire block to SQL*Plus and press **Enter** following the slash.

```
EXCEPTION
  WHEN OTHERS THEN
    DBMS_OUTPUT.PUT_LINE('Error; transactions rolled back');
    ROLLBACK;
END;
/
```

5. Save the Notepad file once again to preserve the code you have typed, then copy all the code to SQL*Plus. Then, close Notepad. Figure 7.13 shows the code in SQL*Plus prior to execution.

6. Press **Enter** in SQL*Plus to execute the PL/SQL block. Figure 7.14 shows part of the completed code and the messages indicating the AgentID and the salary increment percentage, indicating successful completion.

7. Close SQL*Plus if you want to take a break. Otherwise, keep it running for steps you will execute later in this section.

In a business application, you would normally omit the DBMS_OUTPUT line inside the FOR loop. It is there just to reassure you that Oracle took the correct actions.

Using the cursor FOR loop and the conditional logic, Oracle updates each agent's BaseSalary column by the appropriate percentage. For each agent's row, the IF statement records the percentage increase in the internal variable v_Amount. Outside the IF statement but within the FOR loop, the UPDATE statement applies the stored v_Amount for the selected agents to update their salaries. The COMMIT statement outside the FOR loop makes all the changes permanent. However, if an error should occur while the FOR loop executes, control transfers to the exception handling section, and the ROLLBACK statement it contains rolls back all uncommitted updates.

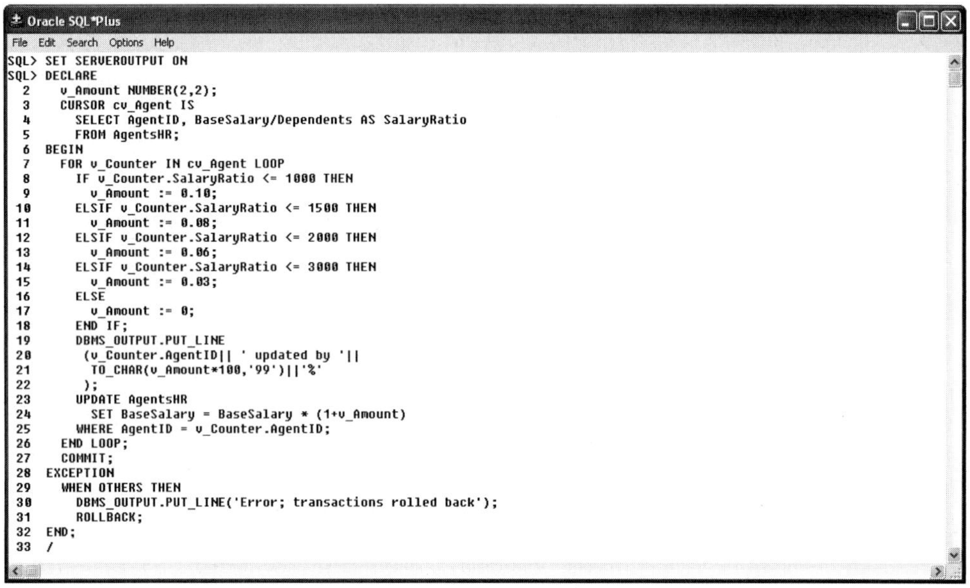

```
SQL> SET SERVEROUTPUT ON
SQL> DECLARE
  2     v_Amount NUMBER(2,2);
  3     CURSOR cv_Agent IS
  4       SELECT AgentID, BaseSalary/Dependents AS SalaryRatio
  5       FROM AgentsHR;
  6  BEGIN
  7     FOR v_Counter IN cv_Agent LOOP
  8       IF v_Counter.SalaryRatio <= 1000 THEN
  9         v_Amount := 0.10;
 10       ELSIF v_Counter.SalaryRatio <= 1500 THEN
 11         v_Amount := 0.08;
 12       ELSIF v_Counter.SalaryRatio <= 2000 THEN
 13         v_Amount := 0.06;
 14       ELSIF v_Counter.SalaryRatio <= 3000 THEN
 15         v_Amount := 0.03;
 16       ELSE
 17         v_Amount := 0;
 18       END IF;
 19       DBMS_OUTPUT.PUT_LINE
 20         (v_Counter.AgentID|| ' updated by '||
 21          TO_CHAR(v_Amount*100,'99')||'%'
 22         );
 23       UPDATE AgentsHR
 24         SET BaseSalary = BaseSalary * (1+v_Amount)
 25         WHERE AgentID = v_Counter.AgentID;
 26     END LOOP;
 27     COMMIT;
 28  EXCEPTION
 29     WHEN OTHERS THEN
 30       DBMS_OUTPUT.PUT_LINE('Error; transactions rolled back');
 31       ROLLBACK;
 32  END;
 33  /
```

FIGURE 7.13 Implementing a DML statement in a PL/SQL code block.

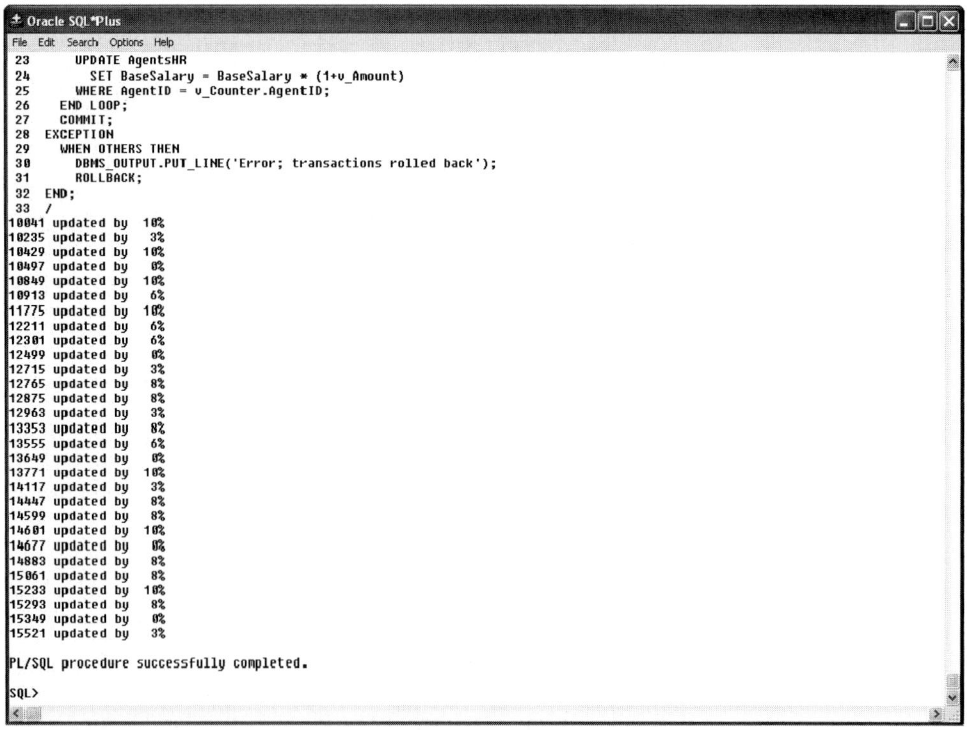

```
 23       UPDATE AgentsHR
 24         SET BaseSalary = BaseSalary * (1+v_Amount)
 25         WHERE AgentID = v_Counter.AgentID;
 26     END LOOP;
 27     COMMIT;
 28  EXCEPTION
 29     WHEN OTHERS THEN
 30       DBMS_OUTPUT.PUT_LINE('Error; transactions rolled back');
 31       ROLLBACK;
 32  END;
 33  /
10041 updated by  10%
10235 updated by   3%
10429 updated by  10%
10497 updated by   0%
10849 updated by  10%
10913 updated by   6%
11775 updated by  10%
12211 updated by   6%
12301 updated by   6%
12499 updated by   0%
12715 updated by   3%
12765 updated by   8%
12875 updated by   8%
12963 updated by   3%
13353 updated by   8%
13555 updated by   6%
13649 updated by   0%
13771 updated by  10%
14117 updated by   3%
14447 updated by   8%
14599 updated by   8%
14601 updated by  10%
14677 updated by   0%
14883 updated by   8%
15061 updated by   8%
15233 updated by  10%
15293 updated by   8%
15349 updated by   0%
15521 updated by   3%

PL/SQL procedure successfully completed.

SQL>
```

FIGURE 7.14 Messages indicate the salary increment amount for each agent.

INTRODUCING NAMED BLOCKS

Named blocks are PL/SQL blocks with a name. In addition, named blocks have a slightly different structure from anonymous blocks. Named blocks contain a fourth section called the header section. A named block's **header section** tells Oracle the name of the block and whether the block is a function or a procedure—the two types of named blocks available. As you may recall from the introduction, a function is a named PL/SQL block that is stored on the Oracle server and returns one value. A procedure is a named PL/SQL block that is stored on the Oracle server and performs some action. You can execute a function or procedure directly from SQL*Plus or from within another function or procedure. The action of executing a function or procedure is termed *calling* the function or procedure. In other words, you *call* a function or procedure by using its name in a SQL*Plus statement or other PL/SQL block. You can call a function by placing its name and any arguments in a SQL statement. However, you call a procedure from a PL/SQL block or by running the EXECUTE command in SQL*Plus. A procedure cannot be used in a SQL statement.

Both functions and procedures can, and usually do, accept parameters. *Parameters* are the list of values, separated by commas and enclosed in parentheses that follow the function or procedure name and through which information passes to or from the function or procedure. Parameters are designated as input (IN), output (OUT) or both (IN OUT). The **IN** parameter designator means that a value passed into the function or procedure cannot be changed within the function or procedure during its execution. The designation **OUT** on a parameter means that a value is computed within the function or procedure and passed back to the statement through the parameter and back to the code that called it. The **IN OUT** parameter designation means that a value passed into a function or procedure may be changed and passed back out to the calling statement. If omitted, an argument is implicitly designated IN. That is a nice, safe default, meaning that any attempted changes to an argument passed into a function or procedure are protected from being changed when control returns to the statement that called the function or procedure.

You can create, modify, or drop functions and procedures. Naturally, you must create a function or procedure before you can use it. Once created, the function or procedure definition is stored in the database. Unlike a script file whose location (path) you must remember in order to execute it (e.g., START C:\Ch07AgentsHR.sql), functions and procedures are always available to their owner. In addition, any user (schema) can execute a function or procedure if they have permission granted to them by their owner. First, you learn how to create, modify, call, and drop functions.

CREATING, USING, LISTING, AND DROPPING FUNCTIONS

A function returns a value to the statement from which it is called. Examples of functions that a database administrator or programmer might create include a function to calculate an agent's age from the BirthDate field, a function that computes an agent's tenure at Redwood Realty, or the total value of an agent's real estate listings. Although none of the preceding examples are onerous to create with SQL statements, it is very handy to have commonly used ones encapsulated in a function. That way, whenever you need a value such as the value of a selected agent's listings or the value of all properties for sale in a particular city, you can invoke it by simply writing the function name in a SELECT statement. In other words, functions allow you to write a definition of the procedure needed to calculate a particular value. Once created, you can execute the function to calculate the requisite value whenever it is needed.

CREATING AND STORING A FUNCTION

Before you can use a function, you have to create it. When you create a function, Oracle stores it in the database and automatically makes it available to the schema that created it. The syntax to create a function is:

```
CREATE [OR REPLACE] FUNCTION <function_name>
[(<parameter_name [IN|OUT|IN OUT] <datatype>[,…])]
RETURN <datatype> {IS|AS}
BEGIN
  <function_body>
[EXCEPTION
  <exception_handling_statements>;
END [<function_name>];
```

Notice that the OR REPLACE phrase is optional. Including it allows you to either create a new function or replace a like-named one without error. The "<function_name>" is the function's name. Following that is an optional list of parameters, including IN, OUT, or IN OUT designators. Each parameter is separated from the next one by a comma. The function returns a value, so RETURN contains the data type of the returned result. The SQL and PL/SQL statements making up the function appear between the BEGIN and END keywords. The optional exception-handling section begins with the keyword EXCEPTION and ends with the END keyword, which marks the end of the entire function. As usual, you type a slash (/) and press **Enter** to compile and store the definition. If compile errors occur, then the definition is not stored in the database. In that case, you must correct any errors and recompile the corrected code to store the definition.

Next, you will create a simple function that computes the age of an agent. The function's only argument is an IN variable containing the agent's identification number. The function returns the agent's age, an integer number. Prepare to write the function by launching SQL*Plus, logging into Oracle, and by launching Notepad. It is especially important to use a text editor for the upcoming exercise because you will write the function with a small error. Then, you will investigate the error, and finally, you will correct it. When the code compiles without error, Oracle will store it in the database.

To create, compile, and store a function:

1. In SQL*Plus, type **CLEAR SCREEN** and press **Enter** to start with an empty screen.
2. Open a new Notepad file, and type this line to turn on server output:

   `SET SERVEROUTPUT ON`

3. Continue by typing the function header and declaring its variables. You will notice that we have omitted, on purpose, the semicolon on the last of these lines. You do the same.

   ```
   CREATE OR REPLACE FUNCTION Age(InputAgentID IN NUMBER)
     RETURN INTEGER AS
     v_BirthDate Agents.Birthdate%TYPE;
     v_TodaysDate DATE;
     v_Age INTEGER                         (omit semicolon on this line)
   ```

4. Type the remainder of the function including its body and exception handling sections. Remember to type the slash (/) in the last line but *do not* press Enter following the slash:

```
BEGIN
   SELECT BirthDate, SYSDATE
   INTO v_BirthDate, v_TodaysDate
   FROM Agents
   WHERE AgentID = InputAgentID;
   v_Age := TRUNC((v_TodaysDate-v_BirthDate)/365.25);
RETURN v_Age;
EXCEPTION
   WHEN OTHERS THEN
      DBMS_OUTPUT.PUT_LINE(SQLERRM);
END Age;
/
```

5. Save the Notepad file as <yourname>Ch07AgeFunction.sql in a folder of your choice. As usual, substitute your last name for "<yourname>" in the script file. (The reason you save a function that also will be stored in the database is in case you want to change its definition.)

6. In Notepad, copy the code and paste it into SQL*Plus. Press **Enter** to compile the code.

   Oracle generates an error message indicating that there are compilation errors. How do you peek inside the compilation to see what is wrong? The answer is, with the SHOW ERRORS command. SHOW ERRORS shows the problems that were found by the compiler along with indicators of the line and column numbers that are possible errors.

7. Continue by typing the following in SQL*Plus. Press **Enter** at the end of the command to execute it:

   SHOW ERRORS

   Oracle displays information that helps you pinpoint the problem (see Figure 7.15)

8. Keep SQL*Plus and Notepad running.

It is apparent that Oracle did not expect to see the BEGIN keyword yet. Examining the error message, you see that Oracle expected some sort of punctuation. That usually means that a statement preceding the one Oracle did not expect to run into is at fault. Indeed, the line

```
V_Age INTEGER
```

in the declarations section is missing its statement-terminating semicolon. Whenever you compile a function or procedure and the generic error message

Warning: Function created with compilation errors.

appears, execute SHOW ERRORS to get more detailed information on the problem. Edit the function by inserting the missing semicolon:

To edit a function:

1. Locate and open in Notepad the function you stored as a script file.
2. Move to the end of the v_Age variable declaration and type a semicolon.
3. Save the modified Notepad script file to preserve your changes.
4. Copy and paste the modified script to SQL*Plus.
5. Close Notepad.

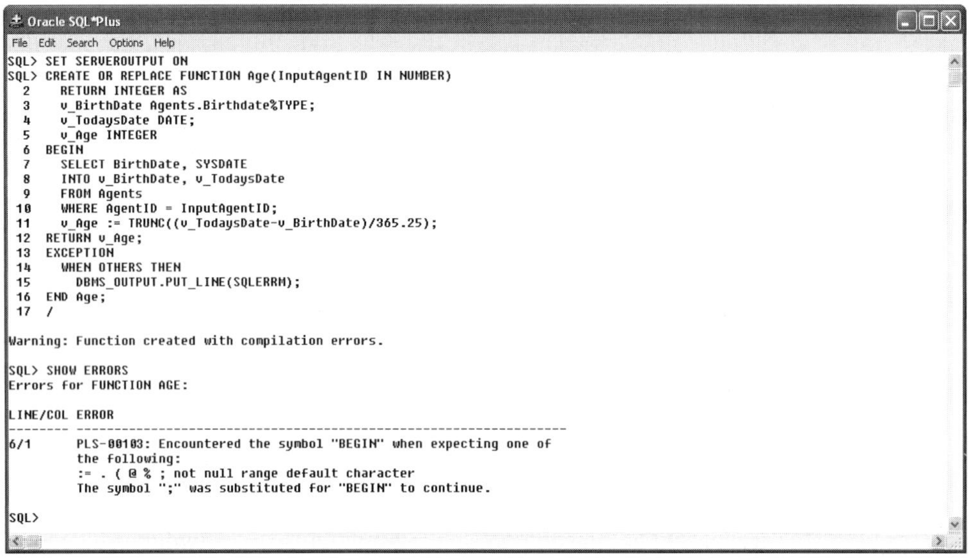

```
Oracle SQL*Plus
File Edit Search Options Help
SQL> SET SERVEROUTPUT ON
SQL> CREATE OR REPLACE FUNCTION Age(InputAgentID IN NUMBER)
  2      RETURN INTEGER AS
  3      v_BirthDate Agents.Birthdate%TYPE;
  4      v_TodaysDate DATE;
  5      v_Age INTEGER
  6  BEGIN
  7      SELECT BirthDate, SYSDATE
  8      INTO v_BirthDate, v_TodaysDate
  9      FROM Agents
 10      WHERE AgentID = InputAgentID;
 11      v_Age := TRUNC((v_TodaysDate-v_BirthDate)/365.25);
 12  RETURN v_Age;
 13  EXCEPTION
 14      WHEN OTHERS THEN
 15      DBMS_OUTPUT.PUT_LINE(SQLERRM);
 16  END Age;
 17  /

Warning: Function created with compilation errors.

SQL> SHOW ERRORS
Errors for FUNCTION AGE:

LINE/COL ERROR
-------- -----------------------------------------------------------------
6/1      PLS-00103: Encountered the symbol "BEGIN" when expecting one of
         the following:
         := . ( @ % ; not null range default character
         The symbol ";" was substituted for "BEGIN" to continue.

SQL>
```

FIGURE 7.15 Displaying compile-time error information.

6. In SQL*Plus, press **Enter** at the end of the line containing slash (/) to move to a new line in SQL*Plus and tell Oracle to compile the function.

7. Leave SQL*Plus running.

The message *Function created* appears, indicating that the function compiled without errors this time. When the compilation is error-free, Oracle stores the function in the database in the schema of the user who created it. Now, you can call the function to compute agents' ages.

INVOKING A FUNCTION

You call (invoke) your new function the same way you would any Oracle built-in database function. Recall that you call a built-in database function by using a SELECT statement followed by the function name and any arguments it requires. If you are not retrieving any other database fields, use the DUAL table in the FROM clause. Give your new function a test run. You will use two different ways to call it.

To call a function:

1. Switch to SQL*Plus, type the following to increase the pagesize environmental variable and clear the screen. Press **Enter** after each line:

```
SET PAGESIZE 50
CLEAR SCREEN
```

2. In SQL*Plus, type the following to test your Age function. Of course, the results you see depend on the current date stored in your computer.

```
SELECT Age(10041)
FROM DUAL;
```

Oracle returns a value that depends on your system clock (and the current date that it holds). It should be approximately 35.

CHAPTER 7 Using PL/SQL to Your Advantage **351**

```
Oracle SQL*Plus
File  Edit  Search  Options  Help
SQL> SELECT Age(10041)
  2  FROM DUAL;

AGE(10041)
----------
        35

SQL> SELECT AgentID, LastName, Age(AgentID) AS "Agent's Age"
  2  FROM Agents;

  AGENTID LASTNAME                      Agent's Age
---------- ------------------------------ -----------
    10041 Marcoux                                35
    10235 Carling                                30
    10429 Dahlen                                 36
    10497 Rowe                                   52
    10849 Sheibani                               23
    10913 Voss                                   35
    11775 Romero                                 43
    12211 Dann                                   46
    12301 Silverburg                             47
    12499 Robinson                               36
    12715 Piperova                               27
    12765 Townsend                               51
    12875 Okindo                                 32
    12963 Reed                                   49
    13353 Soltwedel                              36
    13555 Chong                                  48
    13649 Selby                                  25
    13771 Taylor                                 44
    14117 St-Onge                                37
    14447 Flamenbaum                             37
    14599 Herring                                41
    14601 Weber                                  45
    14677 Kellogg                                36
    14883 Fernandez                              41
    15061 Williams                               38
    15233 Gagnon                                 47
    15293 Allee                                  46
    15349 Schutz                                 22
    15521 Lewis                                  46

29 rows selected.

SQL>
```

FIGURE 7.16 Calling a user-defined function.

3. Type the following to call your function in conjunction with other information in the Agents table:

   ```
   SELECT AgentID, LastName, Age(AgentID) AS "Agent's Age"
   FROM Agents;
   ```

   Oracle displays the 29 agents' ID numbers, last names, and ages (see Figure 7.16). Of course, their calculated ages depend on your system clock. In this example, each agent's ID is an input parameter to the Age function.

4. Type the following to test the robustness of the Age function:

   ```
   CLEAR SCREEN
   SELECT Age(12345)
   FROM DUAL:
   ```

   Oracle displays an error message and the exception handler displays its own, separate error message: *ORA-01403: no data found* (see Figure 7.17)

5. Leave SQL*Plus running.

Why did the error occur? The AgentID value 12345, an argument, is passed to the Age function. The value is plugged into the WHERE clause of the function's SELECT statement (see line 10 in Figure 7.15). Because there is no agent with that AgentID value, Oracle returns no rows. That is the source of the problem. Is there a way to prevent an error message from being generated and to display, instead, a more user-friendly error message? Yes there is. You can modify and enhance the Age function. One way to improve it is to make it more robust in the face of possible user errors.

```
± Oracle SQL*Plus
File Edit Search Options Help
SQL> SELECT Age(12345)
  2  FROM DUAL;
SELECT Age(12345)
       *
ERROR at line 1:
ORA-06503: PL/SQL: Function returned without value
ORA-06512: at "CH07.AGE", line 16


ORA-01403: no data found
SQL>
```

FIGURE 7.17 Error messages indicating an invalid AgentID value.

MODIFYING A FUNCTION

To improve the Age function, you can add a test to determine if the AgentID value entered by the user exists in the table before executing the statement that calculates the age. If the AgentID value passed to the function does not exist, the function can display a simple message indicating the AgentID is incorrect, and then exit the function. If the AgentID does exist, the function can compute an age and return normally. That way, the user never sees the messy, three-line error message after entering an invalid AgentID. You will make modifications to the Age function next.

To add conditional logic to test for an invalid AgentID:

1. Launch Notepad and then open the Age function script file <yourname>Ch07AgeFunction.sql you saved earlier.

2. In Notepad, edit the file as follows: At the top of the declarations section, add the line:

   `v_Count INTEGER;`

3. Immediately after the BEGIN keyword, and before the SELECT statement, add the following code. (Type the digit 1, not the letter l (ell) in the parentheses following the word *COUNT* on the second line.):

   ```
   /* Test AgentID to see if it exists */
   SELECT COUNT(1)
   INTO v_Count
   FROM Agents WHERE AgentID= InputAgentID;
   IF v_Count = 0 THEN
     v_Age := -1;
   ELSE
   ```

4. Indent each of the existing SELECT statement lines two more spaces (*SELECT Birthdate, SYSDATE, INTO...*).

5. Indent the assignment statement v_Age := TRUNC... two spaces also.

6. Immediately following the v_Age assignment statement, press **Enter** to add a new line, and type (indented two spaces)

   `END IF;`

7. Save the modified script file to preserve your changes. Figure 7.18 shows the modified script file. Arrows indicate the new lines you inserted so you can see them easily. Check your code against Figure 7.18.

8. Leave Notepad running.

The modified code is ready for testing. You will copy and paste the newly modified Age function into SQL*Plus and press **Enter** to recompile it. Because the function

CHAPTER 7 Using PL/SQL to Your Advantage **353**

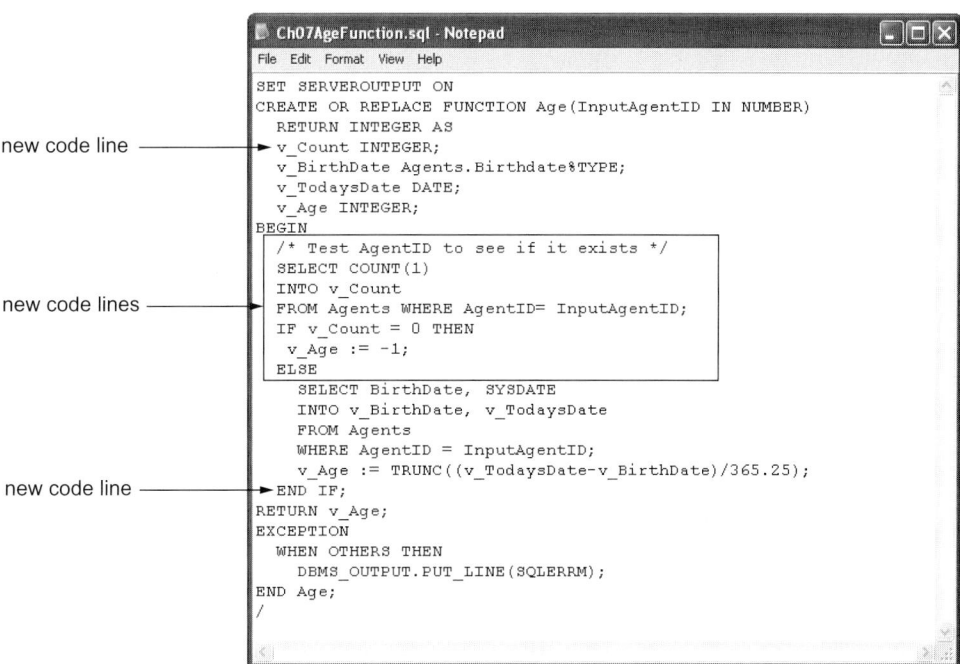

FIGURE 7.18 Modified Age function.

header has "CREATE OR REPLACE FUNCTION," the new, error-free version replaces the older one in the database.

To recompile the modified Age function:

1. In SQL*Plus, type **CLEAR SCREEN** and press **Enter.**
2. Switch to the open Notepad file and copy and paste all the newly modified Age code to SQL*Plus. Press **Enter** to compile and replace the previous version in the database.

   Oracle responds "Function created." If you have syntax errors, switch to Notepad, make any changes, and repeat this step until the code is error-free.
3. Close Notepad. (Save the file if you made changes since the last save operation.)
4. Type the following, pressing **Enter** to test the new code:

   ```
   SELECT Age(10497) AS "Agent that exists" FROM DUAL;
   ```

   Oracle displays a value.
5. Type the following, pressing **Enter** to test the new code for a non-existing agent:

   ```
   SELECT Age(12345) AS "Agent that does not exist" FROM DUAL;
   ```

   The function returns the answer -1, indicating there is an error. However, the multiple error messages do not appear. That's an improvement. See Figure 7.19.
6. Keep SQL*Plus running, though you can exit if you want to take a break.

LISTING AND DROPPING A FUNCTION

When you request PL/SQL compiler to compile a function or procedure, it generates p-code, short for *pseudocode*. ***P-code*** is a portable form of code for a function or procedure that executes on any computer platform by the PL/SQL engine. If you want

354 Introduction to Oracle

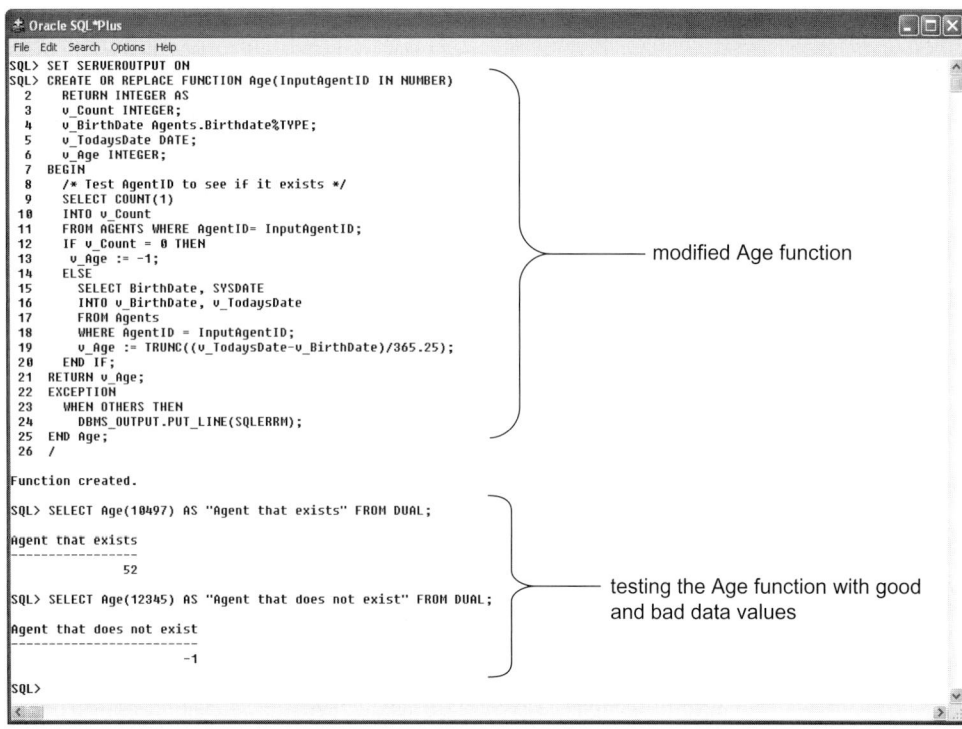

FIGURE 7.19 Testing the modified Age function.

more efficient code, you can request that PL/SQL produce native code when it compiles your function or procedure. *Native code* is machine code that executes on a particular computer directly without separate, line-by-line interpretation. However, native code requires that your computer have the C compiler installed.

LISTING A FUNCTION'S DEFINITION

When you create a function or a procedure with CREATE OR REPLACE, Oracle stores it in the data dictionary. Oracle stores both the source text of a function or procedure and its compiled (p-code) form in the database. When the function or program is called, Oracle reads the p-code from disk and stores it in memory for execution. You can access and display information about your functions and programs from several data dictionary views. The view USER_OBJECTS contains high-level information about the objects you own. You have seen this view before. Another data dictionary view called USER_SOURCE contains the original source code of the function or procedure. USER_ERRORS, another data dictionary view, contains information about compile errors.

To list information about functions you have created:

1. In SQL*Plus, type **CLEAR SCREEN** and press **Enter.**
2. Type the following to list the names of any of your own functions and procedures stored in the database:

```
COLUMN Object_Name FORMAT A20
COLUMN Object_Type FORMAT A12
SELECT Object_Name, Object_Type
FROM USER_OBJECTS
WHERE Object_Type IN ('FUNCTION', 'PROCEDURE');
```

CHAPTER 7 Using PL/SQL to Your Advantage

Oracle displays the name and type of Age, the only function (or procedure) you have created so far. (Other function or procedure names might appear if you have created other ones.)

3. Type the following two SQL*Plus statements. (Press **Enter** at the end of the statement two execute each):

```
SET PAGESIZE 40
CLEAR SCREEN
```

4. Display the User_Source column names and data types by typing and executing this:

```
DESCRIBE User_Source
```

5. Type the following, pressing **Enter** after each line, to display detailed information about your Age function's source code:

```
SELECT Text
FROM User_Source
WHERE Name = 'AGE'
ORDER BY Line;
```

After a brief pause, Oracle displays the Age function source code (see Figure 7.20).

6. Leave SQL*Plus running.

DROPPING A FUNCTION

Like all objects that you own, you remove them from the database by dropping them. Dropping functions, you use the following syntax:

```
DROP FUNCTION <function_name>;
```

FIGURE 7.20 Displaying User_Source's structure and information about a stored function.

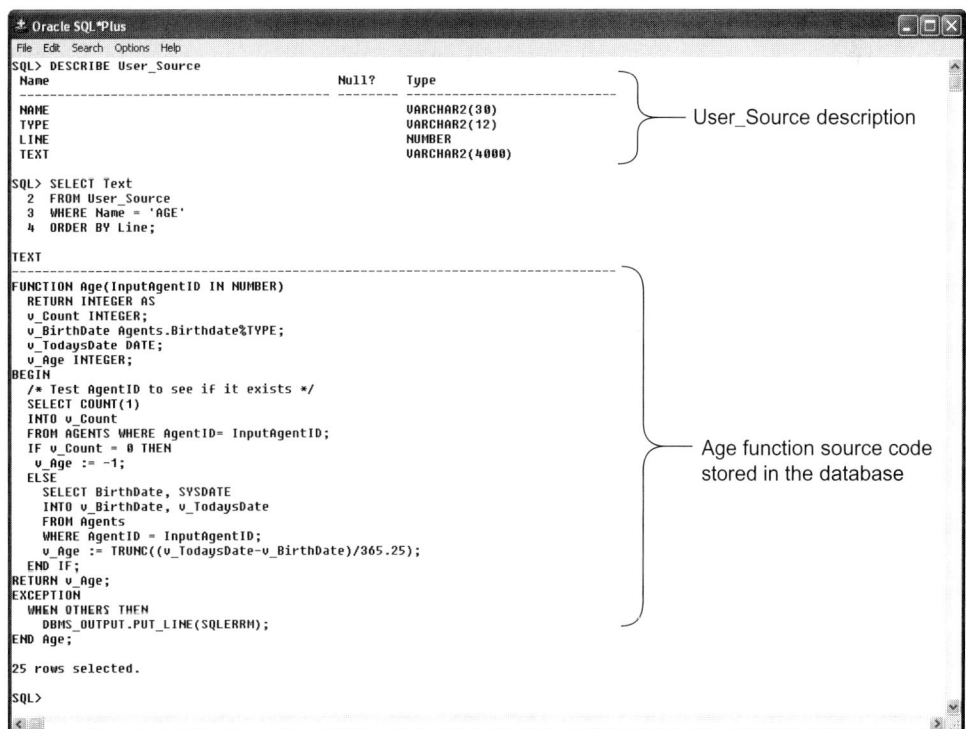

Clean things up by dropping the function you created in this section. To drop a function you own:

1. In SQL*Plus, type the following (and press **Enter**) to drop the Age function:

   `DROP FUNCTION Age;`

   Oracle responds with the message "Function dropped."

2. Just to see that it is gone, type the code you typed earlier to list any functions and procedures and execute it in SQL*Plus:

   ```
   SELECT Object_Name, Object_Type
   FROM USER_OBJECTS
   WHERE Object_Type IN ('FUNCTION', 'PROCEDURE');
   ```

   Oracle responds "no rows selected" (assuming you have no other functions or procedures in your schema) indicating you currently have no functions or procedures stored in the database.

3. Type **exit** and press **Enter** to log off Oracle and exit SQL*Plus.

CREATING, USING, LISTING, AND DROPPING PROCEDURES

Recall that a procedure contains SQL and PL/SQL statements that accomplish some task, and has parameters that represent values passed into the procedure, out of the procedure, or both. Unlike a function, a procedure does not return a value. However, a procedure can return one or more values back to the calling program through one or more of its parameters. Viewed as one- or two-way streets, any parameters you define appear in the procedure's header and are declared with data types there. Following the procedure header is the optional declarations section in which you declare local variables and cursors. Unlike anonymous PL/SQL code blocks, the declarations section does not begin with the keyword DECLARE. You omit it. Following the declarations section is the execution section and an optional exception-handling section.

Before you can use a procedure, you must create it. Once it is created, or stored in the database, you can invoke it from SQL*Plus or another procedure with a CALL statement. To rewrite or redefine a subprogram, you modify it in a text editor and then re-create it. Finally, you can list the contents of a procedure's source code, and remove the procedure by dropping it.

ADVANTAGES OF PROCEDURES

Stored procedures have several advantages over accomplishing the same task in SQL*Plus or using an anonymous PL/SQL block. A stored procedure is compiled once and the executable code is invoked when the procedure is called. Execution is quick and efficient using compiled code—either p-code or native code. Grouping SQL statements in a single procedure cuts down on traffic over the network between the SQL client machine and the Oracle server because procedures present the server with all the SQL code at once. Building and maintaining collections of useful procedures reduces the proliferation of same-purpose code by multiple users. Stored procedures that are tested and trusted instill confidence and promote their use in multiple applications, reducing the development time for new database applications. Procedures promote database security by allowing access to sensitive information only through stored procedures. Instead of granting access to views, synonyms, or tables directly, users are disallowed access to those objects and provided access to them indirectly through stored procedures that manipulate the tables, synonyms, or views on the user's behalf.

Procedures can restrict update operations on sensitive or valuable tables by requiring all updates to the table(s) be made with selected stored procedures. Stored procedures can capture and document a company's business rules in an easy-to-understand form. Stored procedures are particularly helpful when used in conjunction with data entry. In that context, stored procedures can provide front-end data validation to ensure that values for customer records, for example, fall within acceptable ranges. Using a stored procedure is the only general, reliable way to ensure that additional database activities occur when a row in a separate but related table is updated, inserted, or deleted. For example, a stored procedure can implement an INSERT operation to create a new customer order. Within the same procedure, additional code ensures that all the related customer items being ordered are stored in a separate order entry table, and that the two tables are linked together on a common primary key/foreign key value.

CREATING AND STORING A PROCEDURE

Before you can use a stored (named) procedure, you must create it. The syntax for creating (or replacing) a named procedure is as follows:

```
CREATE [OR REPLACE] PROCEDURE <procedure_name>
  [(<parameter_name> [IN|OUT|IN OUT] <data_type> [, …])]
  {IS|AS}
  [<local_variable_declarations>]
BEGIN
  <procedure_body>
[EXCEPTION
  <exception_handling_code>]
END [<procedure_name>];
```

Notice that the OR REPLACE phrase is optional. Including it allows you to either create a new function or replace a like-named one without error. The "<procedure_name>" is the procedure's name. Following that is an optional list of parameters, including IN, OUT, or IN OUT designators. Each parameter is separated from the next one by a comma. Following the procedure header are optional local variable declarations, including cursors and scalar variables. Their form is identical to those found in the declarations section of an anonymous PL/SQL block.

Unlike in an anonymous block, you omit the keyword DECLARE in a stored procedure. The SQL and PL/SQL statements composing the body of the procedure are not optional. They appear between the BEGIN and END keywords. The optional exception-handling section begins with the keyword EXCEPTION and ends with the END keyword, which marks the end of the entire procedure. As usual, you type a slash (/) and press Enter to compile and store the definition. Thus, it is convenient to store the slash with the script file to create the procedure so you don't have to remember to type it to compile the code—just copy it to SQL*Plus and press Enter to compile the code. If compile errors occur, the proposed new definition is not stored in the database. In that case, you must correct any errors and recompile the corrected code to store the definition.

Next, you will create a stored procedure called *ForSale* that retrieves and displays properties for sale in a particular city. The city name (called *CityIn* in the procedure) is an input parameter (IN) to the procedure. It determines which city to search in for properties offered for sale. The procedure is particularly helpful because the SQL statement is slightly complex. Requiring agents to construct a three-table join along with a filtering WHERE clause is unreasonable. Therefore, you will capture that logic in a procedure that the agents can invoke to return the properties they want.

Launch SQL*Plus and then launch Notepad so you can save the script file that you are writing when it is complete. Log into Oracle and then follow these steps to create the stored procedure *ForSale*.

To create a stored procedure to return homes for sale in a particular city:

1. In Notepad, type the following to set the stage by clearing the screen and ensuring the SERVEROUTPUT environment variable is set ON:

```
CLEAR SCREEN
SET SERVEROUTPUT ON
```

2. Continue by typing, in Notepad, the procedure header and the declarations section, which contains only a declaration for the cursor that retrieves the properties. The cursor joins three Redwood Realty tables to gather information needed from all three, ensuring that only properties for sale are retrieved:

```
CREATE OR REPLACE PROCEDURE ForSale(CityIn IN VARCHAR2) AS
   CURSOR cv_Properties IS
      SELECT PropertyID,AskingPrice,Address,City
      FROM Properties JOIN Listings USING(PropertyID)
         JOIN CustAgentList USING(ListingID)
      WHERE UPPER(City) = UPPER(CityIn)
        AND UPPER(ContactReason) = 'SELL';
```

3. Continue by typing the procedure body. It consists of a cursor FOR loop and a couple of DBMS_OUTPUT lines that display a heading and format retrieved rows. The spacing is not critical. However, spacing is critical within single quotation marks. There are four spaces following *Prop ID* and three spaces following *Asking* in the first DBMS_OUTPUT statement. Also, the format model in the TO_CHAR statement for the PropertyID contains zeroes, not the letter o ("oh"), repeated five times.

```
BEGIN
   DBMS_OUTPUT.PUT_LINE('Prop ID    '||'Asking   '||'Address');
   FOR a IN cv_Properties LOOP
      DBMS_OUTPUT.PUT_LINE(
         TO_CHAR(a.PropertyID,'00000')||
         ' '||TO_CHAR(a.AskingPrice,'$9,999,999')||
         '   '||a.Address||',  '||INITCAP(CityIn)
      );
   END LOOP;
```

4. Finally, type the exception-handling section, the terminating keyword and procedure name, and the slash:

```
EXCEPTION
   WHEN OTHERS THEN
      DBMS_OUTPUT.PUT_LINE(SQLERRM);
END;
/
```

Your completed ForSale script file should match the code in Figure 7.21.

5. With the code completed, save the script file in case you need to modify it later or print the source code. Save the script file as <yourname>Ch07ForSale.sql. Substitute your last name for "<yourname>".

6. Leave Notepad running in case you need to correct syntax errors. Copy all the code from Notepad (or other text editor), including the final slash, to SQL*Plus.

7. After you copy the entire script file to SQL*Plus, press **Enter** to compile it and store it in the database. If there are any errors, switch back to your text editor,

FIGURE 7.21 Completed ForSale source code (shown in Notepad).

FIGURE 7.22 Message indicating the procedure is syntax-error free.

modify it, save the text editor file again, and repeat Steps 6 and 7. Oracle signals that it successfully compiled the code with the message "Procedure created." (See Figure 7.22.)

8. Close Notepad or other text editor but leave SQL*Plus running.

When the *Procedure created* message appears, that indicates that Oracle compiled the procedure without syntax errors. There may be run-time errors, but that is yet to be determined. Simultaneously, Oracle stores the source code and the object code in the database so it is available to the owning schema and any other schemas to which the owner has granted access.

The procedure executes as follows. When users call the procedure, they type in a city name (e.g., 'Loleta') as the only input parameter. The DBMS_OUTPUT line following BEGIN produces column headers. Inside the cursor FOR loop, the cursor retrieves related information from three tables in which the ContactReason column contains the value *sell* (both converted to uppercase to ensure no capitalization errors thwart retrieval). The user-input city name formal parameter (CityIn) is substituted in the WHERE clause of the cursor shown in the declarations section. Therefore, the cursor FOR loop retrieves rows corresponding to properties that are for sale in the city whose name is sent to the procedure through the formal parameter, CityIn. The input city name also appears in the DBMS_OUTPUT line appearing just before the END LOOP keyword. The city is converted by INITCAP to appear in a properly capitalized form on output. The TO_CHAR functions in the DBMS_OUTPUT lines merely format the data into a more attractive form. The exception handler contains the catchall WHERE OTHERS THEN phrase to display an error message. Later, you can upgrade that to detect particular errors to make the message more finely grained if you wish.

INVOKING A STORED PROCEDURE

You call a procedure using the CALL statement. Alternatively, you can use EXECUTE, or its shortcut form EXEC, to run a names subprogram. In this text, we use CALL exclusively. Test the procedure you created by selecting SQL*Plus and invoking the procedure.

To call a named procedure from SQL*Plus:

1. In SQL*Plus, type the following to initialize SQL*Plus—just in case you logged off and are reactivating it:

```
SET SERVEROUTPUT ON
CLEAR SCREEN
```

2. Next, call the ForSale procedure to display information about properties for sale in Loleta, California. Type the following and press **Enter** to execute it.

```
CALL ForSale('loleta');
```

The ForSale procedure returns information about seven homes for sale.

3. Next, call the ForSale procedure to display information about properties for sale in Orick, California. Type the following and press **Enter** to execute it. (Type the city in all uppercase to ensure that the procedure works no matter how you capitalize the input city name.):

```
CALL ForSale('ORICK');
```

Three properties appear in the list, along with the confirming message *Call completed*.

4. Call the ForSale procedure a third time, requesting information about properties for sale in Blue Haven:

```
CALL ForSale('Blue Haven');
```

This time, only the column header appears. No properties appear to be for sale.

5. Oops! The city in step 4 should be Blue Lake. Try it again. Type the following and press **Enter:**

```
CALL ForSale('BLUE lake');
```

Okay. That was the problem. There are six properties for sale in Blue Lake.

CHAPTER 7 Using PL/SQL to Your Advantage **361**

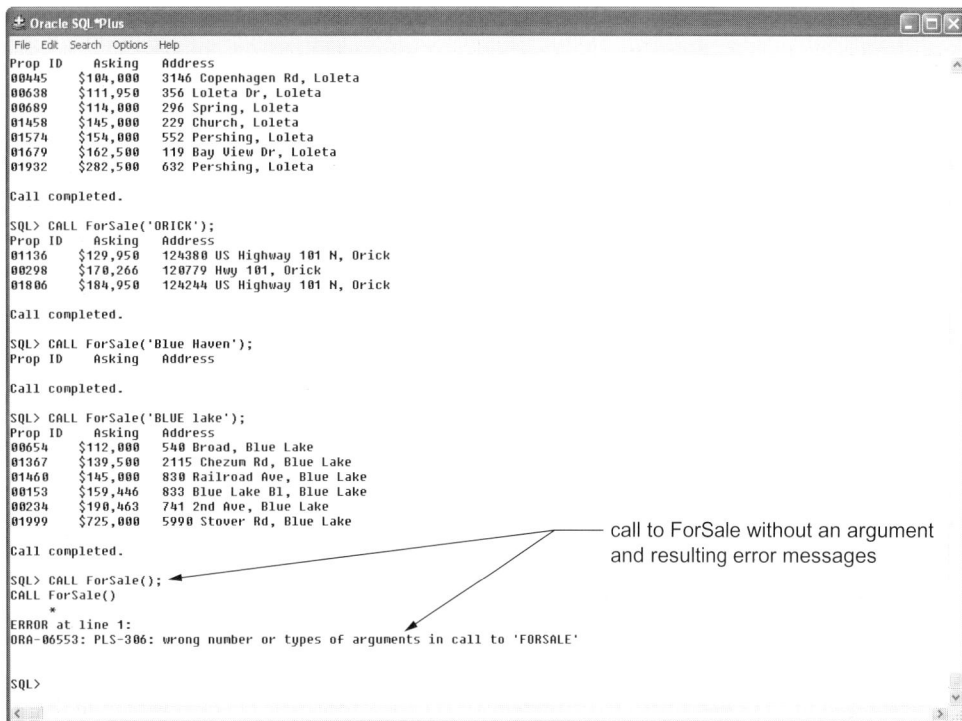

FIGURE 7.23 Testing the ForSale procedure.

6. Try one more test. Call the ForSale procedure without any argument. Type the following and press **Enter:**

`CALL ForSale();`

Oracle responds with an error message. The exception handler displays the error number and the full text of the error message (see Figure 7.23).

One enhancement to the procedure to make it slightly more robust is to determine if no rows are returned, and display a user-friendly message indicating that no homes are for sale in the given city.

MODIFYING A PROCEDURE AND RECOMPILING AND SAVING IT

You can modify a procedure by opening the original source code in a text editor, making changes to it, and then recompiling it in SQL*Plus—as long as the procedure header contains the phrase CREATE OR REPLACE. If you simply recompile the procedure and the header omits "OR REPLACE," Oracle will generate an error message and indicate that a like-named procedure already exists.

Because you had the foresight to save the procedure source code as the script file named Ch07ForSale.sql, you can easily retrieve it and make changes. It is best to preserve the original so you always have it as a benchmark. Prepare for the next steps by opening Notepad or another text editor and then opening the script file you saved earlier called <yourname>Ch07ForSale.sql.

To modify a procedure script file and recompile it:

1. Immediately save the script file under a new name to preserve the original. Click **File,** click **Save As,** and type the new file name **<yourname>Ch07ForSale2.sql,**

where you substitute your last name for "<yourname>" in the preceding file name.

2. Insert a new line below the procedure header and above the cursor definition, and type the following in the empty line (indented two spaces):

```
v_PropCount INTEGER NOT NULL := 0;
```

The v_PropCount local variable will hold the number of rows returned. If none are retrieved, then its value remains zero.

3. Insert the following line immediately *after* the loop heading, "FOR a IN cv_Properties LOOP"

```
v_PropCount := v_PropCount + 1;
```

4. Insert the following three lines immediately after the END LOOP: statement—above the keyword EXCEPTION:

```
IF v_PropCount = 0 THEN
  DBMS_OUTPUT.PUT_LINE('******No homes for sale in '||INITCAP(CityIn));
END IF;
```

5. Save the script file again, now that the changes are complete.
6. In SQL*Plus, type **CLEAR SCREEN** and press **Enter** to start with an empty screen. Then, copy the entire procedure from Notepad to SQL*Plus, and press **Enter** to recompile and save the newly modified version. Oracle should respond: *Procedure created.* If not, type **SHOW ERRORS** and press **Enter** to discover the errors.
7. Correct any errors in your text editor and repeat Step 5, if needed.
8. Test the modified code by typing the following two lines (press **Enter** after the second line to execute the call):

```
CALL ForSale('Loleta');
CALL ForSale('Mitchell');
```

The procedure works, as usual, for Loleta. However, the new message appears for the city Mitchell because it contains no properties for sale. See Figure 7.24.

9. Close Notepad or whatever text editor you are using.
10. Leave SQL*Plus running for the last steps that follow.

LISTING AND DROPPING PROCEDURES

You can list a procedure's definition just as you did earlier for a function. In addition, you can drop procedures you no longer need.

LISTING A FUNCTION'S DEFINITION

As mentioned earlier, when you create a function or a procedure with CREATE OR REPLACE, Oracle stores it in the data dictionary. Oracle stores both the source text of a function or procedure and its compiled (p-code) form in the database. You can access and display information about your procedures from several data dictionary views. The view USER_OBJECTS contains high-level information about the objects you own. You have examined this view before. Another data dictionary view called USER_SOURCE contains the original source code of the function or procedure. In preparation, launch SQL*Plus. You need not save the code you are about to type. If you want to save the code, be sure to launch a text editor and save the lines at the end of this series of steps.

```
SQL> CREATE OR REPLACE PROCEDURE ForSale(CityIn IN VARCHAR2) AS
  2    v_PropCount INTEGER NOT NULL := 0;            ← new line
  3    CURSOR cv_Properties IS
  4      SELECT PropertyID,AskingPrice,Address,City
  5      FROM Properties JOIN Listings USING(PropertyID)
  6        JOIN CustAgentList USING(ListingID)
  7      WHERE UPPER(City) = UPPER(CityIn)
  8        AND UPPER(ContactReason) = 'SELL';
  9  BEGIN
 10    DBMS_OUTPUT.PUT_LINE('Prop ID    '||'Asking    '||'Address');
 11    FOR a IN cv_Properties LOOP
 12      v_PropCount := v_PropCount + 1;             ← new line
 13      DBMS_OUTPUT.PUT_LINE(
 14        TO_CHAR(a.PropertyID,'00000')||
 15        '  '||TO_CHAR(a.AskingPrice,'$9,999,999')||
 16        '  '||a.Address||', '||INITCAP(CityIn)
 17      );
 18    END LOOP;
 19    IF v_PropCount = 0 THEN                       ← three new lines
 20      DBMS_OUTPUT.PUT_LINE('******No homes for sale in '||INITCAP(CityIn));
 21    END IF;                                       ←
 22  EXCEPTION
 23    WHEN OTHERS THEN
 24      DBMS_OUTPUT.PUT_LINE(SQLERRM);
 25  END;
 26  /

Procedure created.

SQL> CALL ForSale('Loleta');
Prop ID   Asking    Address
00445     $104,000   3146 Copenhagen Rd, Loleta
00638     $111,950   356 Loleta Dr, Loleta
00689     $114,000   296 Spring, Loleta
01458     $145,000   229 Church, Loleta
01574     $154,000   552 Pershing, Loleta
01679     $162,500   119 Bay View Dr, Loleta
01932     $282,500   632 Pershing, Loleta

Call completed.

SQL> CALL ForSale('Mitchell');
Prop ID   Asking    Address
******No homes for sale in Mitchell

Call completed.
```

FIGURE 7.24 Testing the newly modified ForSale procedure.

To list information about any procedures you own:

1. In SQL*Plus, type **CLEAR SCREEN** and press **Enter.**
2. Type and execute the following to list the names of any functions or procedures you own that are stored in the database:

```
COLUMN Object_Name FORMAT A20
COLUMN Object_Type FORMAT A12
SELECT Object_Name, Object_Type
FROM USER_OBJECTS
WHERE Object_Type IN ('FUNCTION', 'PROCEDURE');
```

Oracle displays the name and type of the procedure, ForSale. It is the only procedure you have created and not dropped. (You dropped the Age function earlier. Otherwise, its name and type would appear also.)

3. Type the following two SQL*Plus statements. (Press **Enter** at the end of the statement to execute each):

```
SET PAGESIZE 40
CLEAR SCREEN
```

4. Type the following, pressing **Enter** after each line, to display detailed information about the ForSale procedure's source code. Be sure to type *FORSALE* in the third line in all uppercase letters:

```
SELECT Text
FROM User_Source
WHERE Name = 'FORSALE'
ORDER BY Line;
```

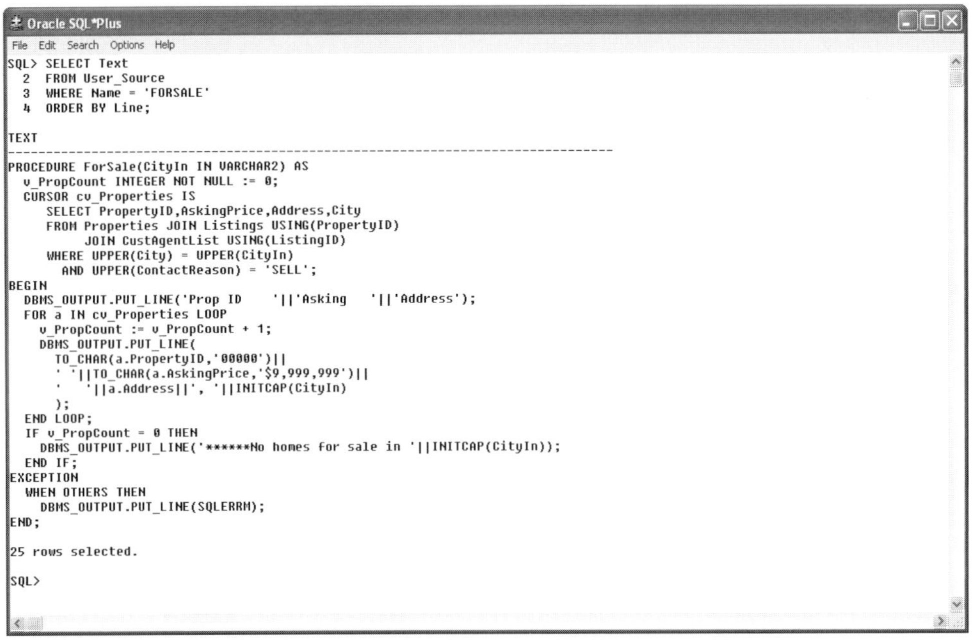

```
SQL> SELECT Text
  2  FROM User_Source
  3  WHERE Name = 'FORSALE'
  4  ORDER BY Line;

TEXT
--------------------------------------------------------------------------------
PROCEDURE ForSale(CityIn IN VARCHAR2) AS
  v_PropCount INTEGER NOT NULL := 0;
  CURSOR cv_Properties IS
    SELECT PropertyID,AskingPrice,Address,City
    FROM Properties JOIN Listings USING(PropertyID)
      JOIN CustAgentList USING(ListingID)
    WHERE UPPER(City) = UPPER(CityIn)
      AND UPPER(ContactReason) = 'SELL';
BEGIN
  DBMS_OUTPUT.PUT_LINE('Prop ID    '||'Asking    '||'Address');
  FOR a IN cv_Properties LOOP
    v_PropCount := v_PropCount + 1;
    DBMS_OUTPUT.PUT_LINE(
      TO_CHAR(a.PropertyID,'00000')||
      ' '||TO_CHAR(a.AskingPrice,'$9,999,999')||
      '  '||a.Address||', '||INITCAP(CityIn)
    );
  END LOOP;
  IF v_PropCount = 0 THEN
    DBMS_OUTPUT.PUT_LINE('******No homes for sale in '||INITCAP(CityIn));
  END IF;
EXCEPTION
  WHEN OTHERS THEN
    DBMS_OUTPUT.PUT_LINE(SQLERRM);
END;

25 rows selected.

SQL>
```

FIGURE 7.25 Displaying a procedure's source code.

After a brief pause, Oracle displays the 25 lines of the ForSale procedure (see Figure 7.25).

5. Leave SQL*Plus running.

DROPPING A FUNCTION

In the same way as you did previously, you can remove any object you own from the database by dropping it. To drop a procedure, use the now-familiar syntax:

```
DROP PROCEDURE <procedure_name>;
```

Clean things up by dropping the procedure you created in this section.

To drop a procedure you own:

1. In SQL*Plus, type the following (and press **Enter**) to drop the Age function:

    DROP PROCEDURE ForSale;

    Oracle responds with the message "Procedure dropped."

2. To verify that Oracle removed the procedure, type the code you typed earlier to list any functions and procedures and execute it in SQL*Plus:

    ```
    SELECT Object_Name, Object_Type
    FROM USER_OBJECTS
    WHERE Object_Type IN ('FUNCTION', 'PROCEDURE');
    ```

    Oracle responds "no rows selected" indicating that you currently have no functions or procedures stored in the database.

3. Type **exit** and press **Enter** to log off Oracle and exit SQL*Plus.

4. If you launched Notepad to capture everything you typed, save the file under a name and in a folder of your own choosing. Close Notepad or other text editor.

Summary

PL/SQL is Oracle's procedural language extension to SQL. PL/SQL blocks can be anonymous or named. Anonymous blocks are not named and are not stored in the database, but named blocks are. Anonymous PL/SQL blocks can contain up to three distinct sections: an optional declarations section in which local variables are declared, a required execution section beginning with BEGIN, and an optional exception-handling section. The execution section contains the code that runs when the block is executed. The exception-handling section executes whenever selected run-time conditions occur. When they do, control transfers immediately to the code in the exception-handling section designated to respond to the particular condition. The PUT_LINE procedure in the DBMS_OUTPUT package produces output to the screen, but you must set to ON the SQL*Plus environmental variable SERVEROUTPUT to see any output from the PUT_LINE procedure.

Unlike SQL, PL/SQL has an iteration construct that permits code it encloses to execute repeatedly until (or while) a condition holds. A simple loop consists of statements book-ended by LOOP and END LOOP keywords. To end a simple loop, you use an EXIT or EXIT WHEN statement, which jumps out of the loop upon execution (EXIT) or when the condition becomes true (EXIT WHEN). The WHILE loop iteration construct executes until a specified condition becomes true. When you need to count the number of iterations a loop executes, the FOR loop is the answer. It iterates until a loop variable's value exceeds (positive counting) or becomes less than (down counting) an upper bound value. A cursor FOR loop is a special version that executes until no more records, fetched by the cursor, are found in the database.

Oracle creates an implicit cursor when you write PL/SQL code to retrieve a single row from a database table. Oracle automatically opens, processes, and closes an explicit cursor. To retrieve more than one row from one or more database tables, you must use an explicit cursor. Code must explicitly open a cursor before you can retrieve database information. Inside a looping construct, FETCH retrieves records, one at a time, from the cursor. The SELECT statement to fetch columns must use the INTO optional phrase and list local PL/SQL variables into which Oracle places columns from the row fetched from the database. Terminate processing of a cursor by closing it. A cursor FOR loop automatically opens a cursor, fetches a row from the cursor, and closes a cursor on completion of the task.

There are two types of PL/SQL named blocks: functions and procedures. Functions contain a function header and an optional list of comma-separated arguments. The arguments pass information into and out from the function. Named PL/SQL blocks are compiled and saved in the database so that anyone with the appropriate privileges may call them. A function returns a single value, in addition to returning information through the argument list elements. Procedures are similar in structure and purpose to functions, with one major difference: procedures do not return a single value. The procedure that references a function or other procedure does so by calling it. Because both the source code and the compiled (p-code) are stored in the database, you can list the source of any function or procedure you own, in addition to their names and types, through the data dictionary view USER_OBJECTS.

Remove unwanted named PL/SQL functions or procedures by dropping them. Once dropped, the function or procedure is no longer available and its name and definition are erased from the data dictionary.

Key Terms

- Active row
- Anonymous block
- Block
- Calling
- Compile
- Constant
- Cursor
- Cursor FOR loop
- Declaration section
- END
- Exception
- Exception-handling section
- Executable section
- Explicit cursor
- FOR loop
- Function
- Global variable
- Header section
- Implicit cursor
- IN
- IN OUT
- Infinite loop
- Local variable
- Named block

- Native code
- OUT
- Parameter
- P-code
- Private variable
- Procedure
- Record
- Simple loop
- Subprogram
- User-defined exception
- Variable
- WHILE loop

Review

TRUE/FALSE

1. An anonymous block must contain a declarations section.
2. In a PL/SQL block, it is not necessary to declare a loop variable used by a FOR loop.
3. Executing code in a PL/SQL block is more efficient than running the same code as a series of statements in SQL*Plus because the code in a PL/SQL code block is passed to the server as one unit.
4. You can change the value of any argument that is passed into a procedure or subprogram inside the procedure.
5. A PL/SQL cursor that can return multiple rows must use an implicit cursor to pass the rows, one-by-one, to the PL/SQL code.

FILL IN

1. The _____ loop iteration structure executes until a specified condition occurs.
2. A(n) _____ returns a single value to the calling program.
3. A(n) _____ is a memory area that holds rows retrieved by a SELECT statement in a PL/SQL block.
4. PL/SQL blocks are either anonymous blocks or _____ blocks.
5. Code that executes on a particular computer directly without line-by-line interpretation is called _____ code.

MULTIPLE CHOICE

1. When Oracle _____ a PL/SQL block, it converts the higher level PL/SQL instructions into a more efficient form that a computer can more quickly execute.
   a. identifies
   b. extracts
   c. executes
   d. compiles
2. PL/SQL blocks may *not* contain what?
   a. SELECT statements with subqueries.
   b. Data definition language statements such as CREATE TABLE.
   c. Data manipulation language statements such as UPDATE.
   d. Arithmetic statements such as
      `v_Variable := 24;`
3. Anonymous PL/SQL blocks cannot contain what?
   a. A declarations section.
   b. An execution section.
   c. A header section.
   d. An exception-handling section.
4. If you are processing multiple rows retrieved from database tables, the easiest looping structure to use to process each row in turn is a(n) _____ loop.
   a. FOR
   b. cursor FOR
   c. WHILE
   d. simple
5. You invoke a stored procedure with the _____ statement.
   a. RUN
   b. EXECUTIVE
   c. INVOKE
   d. CALL

Hands-on Exercises

1. EXTENDING THE CHAPTER CASE

Robert Stirling wants his agents to be able to run a procedure to list all the properties for which they are the listing agent. (The listing agent is the one who originally placed the property on the for sale list by request from the seller.) Any agent can execute the MyListings using the following syntax in either SQL*Plus or *i*SQL*Plus:

```
CALL MyListings('<ListAgentLastName>'|
'all');
```

where "<ListAgentLastName>" is the listing agent's last name and limits the output to the agent named. The other possible input value is *all*, which indicates that the caller wants a list of all listing agents and their properties. To keep things simple, you will produce only the following columns from the procedure: ListingID, buyer's agent, listing agent, BidPrice, and AskingPrice. Later, you can expand the procedure to include the property's address if you wish.

Launch SQL*Plus and log in to Oracle. Then follow these steps to: (1) create the MyListings procedure and then (2) test the procedure. The deliverables are a listing of the procedure and a spool file showing the results of running the procedure with three test cases. Be sure to place your name in the first line of both outputs using a text editor of your choice.

1. Type the following heading and declarations sections in Notepad and save it as <yourname>Ch07Prob1Part1.sql, substituting your last name for "<yourname>":

```
CREATE OR REPLACE PROCEDURE
MyListings(AgentNameIn IN VARCHAR2) AS
  v_Count INTEGER;
  CURSOR cv_AllAgents IS
    SELECT ListingID, d.LastName AS
    LISTAGENT,
        a.LastName AS BUYAGENT,
        BidPrice, AskingPrice
    FROM Agents a JOIN CustAgentList b ON
    a.AgentID = b.AgentID
        JOIN Listings c ON b.ListingID =
        c.ListingID
        JOIN Agents d ON
        c.ListingAgentID = d.AgentID
    WHERE UPPER(ContactReason) = 'BUY'
    ORDER BY d.LastName, a.LastName;
  CURSOR cv_OneAgent IS
    SELECT ListingID, d.LastName AS
    LISTAGENT,
        a.LastName AS BUYAGENT,
        BidPrice, AskingPrice
    FROM Agents a JOIN CustAgentList b ON
    a.AgentID = b.AgentID
        JOIN Listings c ON b.ListingID =
        c.ListingID
        JOIN Agents d ON
        c.ListingAgentID = d.AgentID
    WHERE UPPER(ContactReason) = 'BUY'
      AND UPPER(d.LastName) =
      UPPER(AgentNameIn)
    ORDER BY a.LastName;
```

2. Next, type the following body just below the preceding lines in your text editor:

```
BEGIN
  /* See if agent name in Agents table */
  SELECT COUNT(*)
  INTO v_Count FROM Agents
  WHERE UPPER(LastName) =
  UPPER(AgentNameIn);
--Three possibilities: ALL, a particular
--  agent, invalid name
  IF UPPER(AgentNameIn) = 'ALL' THEN
    FOR X IN cv_AllAgents LOOP
      DBMS_OUTPUT.PUT_LINE(
        ' '||X.ListingID||
        ' '||RPAD(X.LISTAGENT,15)||
        ' '||RPAD(X.BUYAGENT,15)||
        ' '||TO_CHAR(X.BidPrice,
        '$99,999,99')||
        ' '||TO_CHAR(X.AskingPrice,
        '$99,999,99')
      );
    END LOOP;
  ELSIF v_Count > 0 THEN
    FOR X IN cv_OneAgent LOOP
      DBMS_OUTPUT.PUT_LINE(
        ' '||X.ListingID||
        ' '||RPAD(X.LISTAGENT,15)||
        ' '||RPAD(X.BUYAGENT,15)||
        ' '||TO_CHAR(X.BidPrice,
        '$99,999,99')||
        ' '||TO_CHAR(X.AskingPrice,
        '$99,999,99')
      );
    END LOOP;
  ELSE
    DBMS_OUTPUT.PUT_LINE('Invalid Agent
    Name');
  END IF;
```

3. Type these last few lines of the procedure definition in Notepad or another text editor. The last line is a slash (/). Do not press Enter after that line.

```
EXCEPTION
  WHEN OTHERS THEN
    DBMS_OUTPUT.PUT_LINE(SQLERRM);
END MyListings;
/
```

4. Save the script file again, then copy and paste the entire contents into SQL*Plus.
5. Press **Enter** in SQL*Plus to compile the code. If compilation errors occur, remember to execute SHOW ERRORS in SQL*Plus plus to identify erroneous lines. Make any corrections in Notepad and repeat Steps 4 and 5.
6. Test your newly minted *MyListings* file by typing and executing the following in SQL*Plus (substitute your last name and a suitable path as usual). Note that you must increase the size of the buffer with the SIZE parameter in line 3 below.

```
SPOOL <path>\<yourname>Ch07Prob1Part2.txt
SET SERVEROUTPUT ON SIZE 123456
CALL MyListings('Carling');
CALL MyListings('Quinn');
CALL MyListings('all');
SPOOL OFF
```

7. Delete the MyListings procedure by executing the following in SQL*Plus:

```
DROP PROCEDURE MyListings;
```

8. Locate both the *MyListings* script file and the spool file you created in Step 6. Open Notepad or another text editor and add your name to a new line at the top of each text file. Print both files.
9. Close SQL*Plus, and close your text editor.

2. Coffee Merchant

Create the following function and procedure described below. Execute the steps following the compilation of each to test the function and the procedure. Save the function-creation script file and save the procedure-creation script file. Print all script files and spool files so you can turn them in to your instructor. Be sure to place you name and other identifying information at the top of each document, if not already there, before printing it.

Launch SQL*Plus, log into Oracle, and execute the script file BuildCoffee.sql, which is found in the CoffeeMerchant folder of your data files. Running the script file ensures that all tables are in their initial states before you begin this assignment.

Part 1: First, you will create a function called SalesTax that returns the sales tax rate from the state name that is the input argument. Having the SalesTax function simplifies displaying a state's sales tax or using it in a tax computation. An example of how you might invoke the function is:

```
SELECT SalesTax('CA')*Price*Quantity FROM OrderLines;
```

where the input parameter in this example is California and the returned value is the sales tax rate that is used to compute sales tax.

1. Type the following function in Notepad and then copy and paste it to SQL*Plus. Remember: *Do not* press Enter following the slash (/) on the last line of this script file. Type your first and last names in place of "<your name here>" in the first line, but leave the two hyphens in place.

```
-- <your name here>
CREATE OR REPLACE FUNCTION
SalesTax(StateInParm IN VARCHAR2)
  RETURN NUMBER AS
  v_Count NUMBER;
  v_TaxRate NUMBER(4,4) := -0.05;
BEGIN
  /* Test to see if state exists */
  SELECT COUNT(*)
  INTO v_Count
  FROM States WHERE UPPER(StateID) =
  UPPER(StateInParm)
          OR UPPER(StateName) =
             UPPER(StateInParm);
  IF v_Count > 0 THEN
    SELECT TaxRate
    INTO v_TaxRate
    FROM States
    WHERE UPPER(StateID) =
    UPPER(StateInParm)
       OR UPPER(StateName) =
          UPPER(StateInParm);
  END IF;
RETURN v_TaxRate;
EXCEPTION
  WHEN OTHERS THEN
    DBMS_OUTPUT.PUT_LINE(SQLERRM);
END SalesTax;
/
```

2. Press **Enter** to compile the function. Make any needed corrections if syntax errors occur, and remember to execute SHOW ERRORS to list any errors in SQL*Plus. Save any Notepad text file changes. Then copy and paste the corrected text to SQL*Plus and recompile it, if necessary.

Part 2: Test your function. Type and execute the following in SQL*Plus. Substitute an appropriate path and your own name for "<path>" and "<yourname>" (twice), respectively, in the code below.

3. Type the following and execute it in SQL*Plus to test your SalesTax function:

```
SPOOL <path>\<yourname>Ch07Prob2Part2.txt
-- <yourname>
SET SERVEROUTPUT ON
SELECT StateName AS "State",
       TO_CHAR(SalesTax(StateID)
       *100,'90.99')||'%' AS "Tax (%)"
FROM States
WHERE Population/LandArea < 20
ORDER BY 2;
SELECT SalesTax('CaLiFoRnIa')*10*24.95 FROM
DUAL;
SELECT SalesTax('NoSuchState') FROM DUAL;
SPOOL OFF
```

4. Print the spool file produced by Step 3.

   Part 3: You are to create a procedure named CustomerOrder that has two parameters: a consumer's first and last names. It retrieves all orders placed by that customer in the database and joins four tables. As usual, type carefully and use a text editor to capture the entire set of lines. Then copy them to SQL*Plus to execute them. Once you create the procedure, you will test it by locating Jerry Peterson's order(s).

5. Type the following in Notepad, save it from Notepad, and then copy it to SQL*Plus:

```
CREATE OR REPLACE PROCEDURE CustomerOrder(
    Fname IN VARCHAR2,
    Lname IN VARCHAR2) AS
  v_Count INTEGER;
  CURSOR cv_GetOrd IS
    SELECT OrderID,OrderDate,Name,
    Quantity,Price,Discount,
           TO_CHAR(Price*Quantity*(1-
           Discount),'$9,999.99') AS
           ExtPrice,
           TO_CHAR(Price*Quantity*(1-
           Discount)*SalesTax(State),
           '99.99') AS Tax
    FROM Consumers a
      INNER JOIN Orders     b USING
      (ConsumerID)
      INNER JOIN OrderLines c USING
      (OrderID)
      INNER JOIN Inventory  d USING
      (InventoryID)
    WHERE LOWER(FirstName) = LOWER(Fname)
    AND LOWER(LastName) = LOWER(Lname)
    ORDER BY OrderID, LineItem;
BEGIN
  /* See if customer exists */
  SELECT COUNT(*) INTO v_Count FROM
  Consumers
  WHERE LOWER(FirstName) = LOWER(Fname) AND
  LOWER(LastName) = LOWER(Lname);
  CASE
    WHEN v_Count > 0 THEN
      FOR X IN cv_GetOrd LOOP
        DBMS_OUTPUT.PUT_LINE(
        ' '||X.OrderID||' '||X.OrderDate||
        ' '||RPAD(X.Name,20)||
        ' '||TO_CHAR(X.Quantity,'999')||
        ' '||TO_CHAR(X.Price,'$9999.99')||
        ' '||X.ExtPrice||' '||X.Tax
        );
      END LOOP;
    ELSE
      DBMS_OUTPUT.PUT_LINE('No orders for
      that customer');
  END CASE;
EXCEPTION
  WHEN OTHERS THEN
    DBMS_OUTPUT.PUT_LINE(SQLERRM);
END CustomerOrder;
/
```

6. Press **Enter** to compile the code. Modify the code if compile errors show up. Resubmit to the compiler until you get a clean compile.

   Part 4: Test the CustomerOrder procedure. Create a spool file, and print it after you run the following code.

7. Once the code is compiled successfully, test it by executing the following in SQL*Plus. Substitute, as usual, your name for "<yourname>" (twice) and a path of your own choosing for "<path>" in the code for this step.

```
SPOOL <path>\<yourname>Ch07Prob2Part4.txt
-- <yourname>
SET SERVEROUTPUT ON
CALL CustomerOrder('Jerry','Peterson');
CALL CustomerOrder('Abe','Lincoln');
SPOOL OFF
```

8. Finish by dropping the function and the procedure you created. Type the following:

```
DROP FUNCTION SalesTax;
DROP PROCEDURE CustomerOrder;
```

9. Close Notepad and close SQL*Plus.

3. Rowing Ventures

Create the following procedure and execute the steps following that to test the procedure and display information about it. Save every one as a script file, and print each out to turn in to your instructor. Be sure to place your name and other identifying information in each document header before printing it.

Launch SQL*Plus, log into Oracle, and execute the script file BuildRowing.sql, which is found in the RowingVentures folder of your data files. Running the script file ensures that all tables are in their initial states before you begin this assignment.

Part 1: Create a named procedure called RaceInfo which has two input-only arguments: BoatCat and BowNo, both having data type VARCHAR2. The procedure joins the Rowing Ventures tables Boat, BoatCrew, and Person, and retrieves the following columns from their respective tables: BoatCategory, BowNumber, Position, LastName, and FirstName. The rows retrieved correspond to the particular boat category (BoatCat) and bow number (BowNo) you input as arguments. Only that particular boat's category and bow number appears in the result. If you enter the value 'all' for the BoatCat parameter and any string for the BowNo, all the rows retrieved by the cursor appear in the output.

Sort the rows into ascending order by BoatCategory, BowNumber, and Position. Convert the Position value of zero (0) to "Cox" whenever it appears. (Do that in the cursor, not in the FOR loop.) Leave all other Positions values as right-padded, three-character strings of numbers. (*Hint*: Use TO_CHAR for numbers with the appropriate format model to right-align them.)

Use a cursor FOR loop to process the rows, and an IF/THEN/ELSIF structure within the loop to determine if all rows display, or only ones determined by the two input parameters. Display any rows using the DBMS_OUTPUT package procedure PUT_LINE. Compile the procedure.

Part 2: Test the RaceInfo procedure by executing the following in SQL*Plus after you have successfully compiled the procedure. Substitute an appropriate value for "<path>" and your last name for "<yourname>" in two places in the code below. Then, print the spool file.

```
CLEAR SCREEN
SPOOL <path>\<yourname>Ch07Problem3
Part1.txt
PROMPT <yourname>
SET PAGESIZE 100
SET SERVEROUTPUT ON
CALL RaceInfo('ALL','X');
CALL RaceInfo('Crew-8','3');
SPOOL OFF
```

Part 3: Spool the following to a file so you can print the results when you have finished.

- List the source code of the RaceInfo procedure using a database view.
- List the object_name and object_type from another database view you have used before.
- Drop the procedure RaceInfo.

Use the COLUMN command to size the columns to 20 and 12 characters, respectively. Add your name to the top line of the spool file using a text editor and then print the amended file.

4. BROADCLOTH CLOTHING

Create the function described below. First, launch SQL*Plus, log into Oracle, and execute the script file BuildClothing.sql, which is found in the Broadcloth folder of your Chapter 7 data files. Running the script file ensures that all tables are in their initial states before you begin this assignment.

Create a function called ItemTC that has two arguments. The first argument is a character whose value can be either *C* or *S* (either lowercase or uppercase). The second argument is a four-digit number. The ItemTC function uses an implicit query based on the OrderItem table of the Broadcloth database to either count or sum the value of all items in the OrderItem table for the corresponding ItemID. The function answers the questions: (1) "How many total orders contain ItemID number so and so?" and (2) "What is the total value (OrderQuantity times SalePrice) of orders for the item whose ItemID is so and so?" Here is the syntax of the ItemTC function:

```
ItemTC(<character>,<itemID_number>)
```

where "<character>" is 'C' if you want a count of the item whose ItemID matches the second argument, "<itemID_number>" or "<character>" is 'S' if you want a sum of the product of OrderQuantity and SalePrice for the ItemID you input to the function. ItemID, OrderQuantity, and SalePrice are all columns in the OrderItem table.

Part 1: Create a function ItemTC that returns a number using an implicit query and that displays an error message, if any, in the exception-handling section. When completed and working correctly, insert your name as a comment in a new first line of the script file containing the function definition. Print the file containing the function creation code.

Part 2: Test your function by turning on a spool file named <yourname>Ch07Prob4Part2.txt and then running the statements referencing your function shown below. Substitute your name for "<yourname>" in the spool file name above and the script below. The second SELECT statement will generate the error messages. The first one is likely

ORA-06503: PL/SQL: Function returned without value

because there are no items by that number. That message is okay for this exercise, but the first and third SELECT tests will return answers.

```
--<yourname>
SET SERVEROUTPUT ON
SELECT ItemTC('S',1017), ItemTC('C',1017)
FROM DUAL;
SELECT ItemTC('C',12345)
FROM DUAL;
SELECT ItemTC('c',1005), ItemTC('s',1005)
FROM DUAL;
```

Close the spool file and then print it. As a guideline, the answers that your function should return for the third SELECT statement are 2 and 40530.5.

Part 3: Improve your function so that an invalid ItemID number displays the message

```
Order item with ItemID xxxxxx was not
found.
```

in addition to the Oracle-issued error message shown above when the input ItemID does not match any ItemID in the Order Item table. (Insert the errant ItemID value where "xxxxxx" appears in the message above). (*Hint*: test so see if there are *any* items in the OrderItem table that have the input ItemID number that is the second argument of the function. Then, execute RETURN -1 and exit the function.) Print the improved function definition.

Part 4: Test your improved ItemTC function by starting another spool file named <yourname>Ch07Prob4Part4.txt and then running the following statements in SQL*Plus. Print the spool file.

```
--<yourname>
SET SERVEROUTPUT ON
SELECT ItemTC('C',12345) FROM DUAL;
DROP FUNCTION ItemTC;
```

Save all text editor files, and then close SQL*Plus.

CHAPTER 8

UNDERSTANDING AND USING FORMS BUILDER

Learning Objectives

In this chapter, you will learn:
- The three basic types of forms.
- The structure of Oracle forms.
- How to create main forms with the Forms Builder.
- How to use a form to filter data with simple queries.
- How to modify and improve forms.
- How to create grid and sub forms.

INTRODUCTION TO FORMS

Relational databases are designed to store data efficiently. You create tables and establish links across the tables using the data in the key columns. Storing data this way is efficient, but it is difficult for users to understand. For example, in the case of Redwood Realty, think about the confusion agents would face if you asked them to enter data directly into the CustAgentList table. Take a look at that table again and you will see that it contains row after row of key values for CustomerID, AgentID, and ListingID. You cannot expect users to memorize those key values. It also would be difficult to ask users to write queries to retrieve and format the data they want to see. The answer is to create forms.

Database *forms* are interactive applications that are used to enter and edit related data stored in tables. Sometimes they are used simply to retrieve and display data in response to a few choices by the user. Forms run in an environment that allows you to create complex applications that can respond to user input, perform calculations, and alter multiple tables in the database. Originally, forms ran as applications on the local computers of the users. Today, Oracle forms run as Web applications. Users open and run your forms using a Java-enabled Web browser.

THREE MAIN FORM TYPES

Many common database applications can be built using three basic types of forms: (1) a main form that displays data for a single row at a time, (2) a tabular form that displays multiple rows on one page, and (3) a combination of the two that shows one row of primary data with a sub form to display multiple rows of data in a grid. Once you know how to build and modify these three types of forms, you will be able to create most applications. When building forms, it is critical to remember that the purpose of forms is to make it easier for users to accurately enter and review data. You select the type of form that best matches the needs of the user.

One of the simplest types of forms is the main form that shows one row of data on the screen. Figure 8.1 shows a sample Agent form for Redwood Realty. All of the data for one agent is displayed on the screen. When the owner or agent makes changes and clicks the Save button, the changes are written to the underlying Agent table in the database. Although this form is somewhat plain, you have the ability to change the layout completely. You can rearrange the labels and input text boxes and put them anywhere on the page. Of course, you should pick a layout that makes sense to the user. You can add colors or images to improve the readability. Later, you can add programming code that responds to various events on the page. For example, you might want to automatically generate new ID values when an agent is added to the list.

Tabular forms are even simpler. Figure 8.2 shows the License Status form that makes it easy to edit the listing of all possible license conditions. The strength of the grid listing is that users can see several entries at one time. When users need to compare items, or enter short lists, the tabular form is a good choice. Its main drawback is that you have only limited control over the layout. You can control the width of the columns or the number of rows to be displayed, or make minor changes to the font. But, the grid is designed for users to enter basic lists, so it is only useful for tables with a limited number of columns.

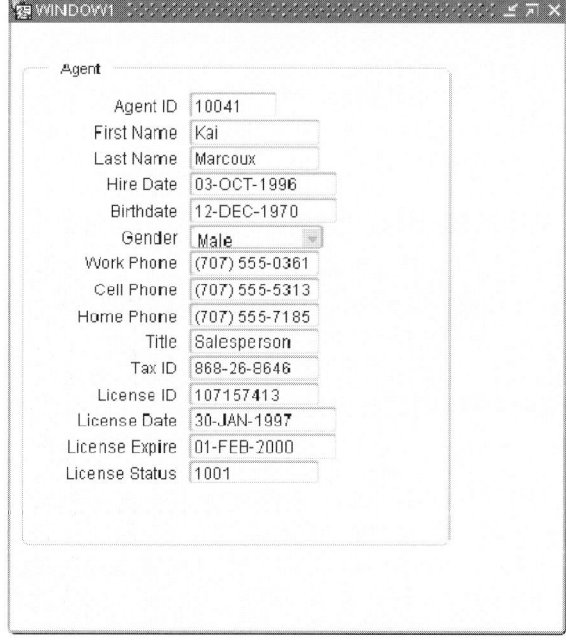

FIGURE 8.1 The Agent form for Redwood Realty shows one agent at a time.

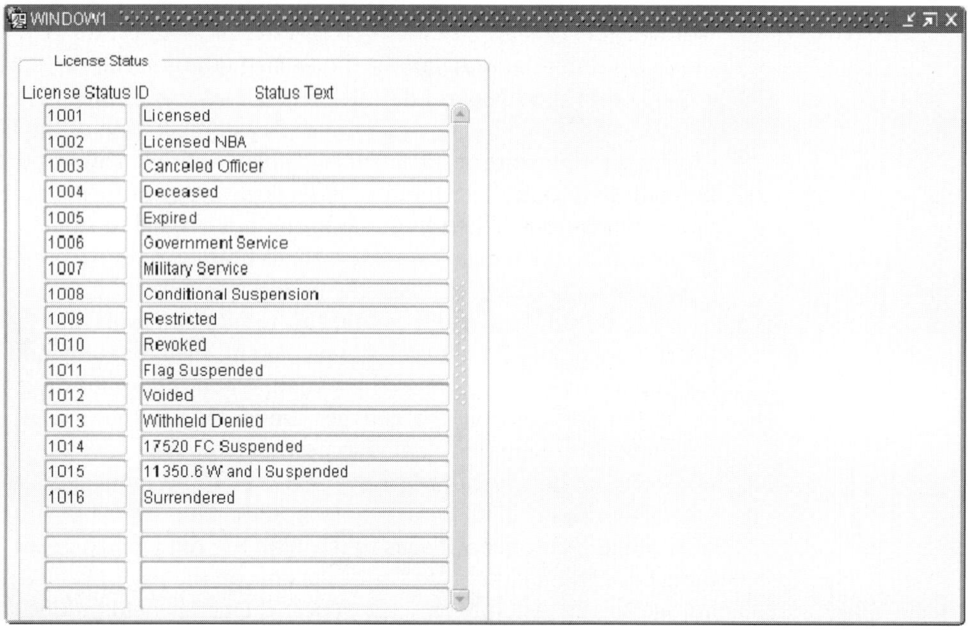

FIGURE 8.2 The License Status form uses a grid layout to display multiple rows.

Many business forms are more complex than the two basic types. For example, common order forms contain at least two major sections: the top part listing the date and the customer information; and the bottom section that holds a repeating list of items being ordered. Figure 8.3 provides an example that displays one agent at a time and shows a repeating list of contacts made by that agent. The one-to-many relationship between agent and contacts is handled by using the grid sub form to display multiple contacts for each agent.

The main/sub form approach allows you complete flexibility at the main (agent) level. You can rearrange the columns in any order or layout. You can add lines or compute subtotals. Notice that the grid sub form is linked to the data displayed in the main form. When the user selects a new agent, the grid contacts list is updated so that it displays only contacts made by the agent being displayed in the main form.

FORMS SERVICES ARCHITECTURE

It is important to understand the environment that hosts your database form. Older versions of Oracle forms used a client-server approach, where forms ran on the client machines of users and queried data on the server. Since version 9i, Oracle forms are designed to run as Java-based Web applications. This approach requires that developers understand the potential strengths and weaknesses of the Internet when creating applications.

One of the strengths of a Web-based approach is that the user's client hardware and software become less critical. Users need only a computer that can run a Java-enabled Web browser. Web browsers are installed on almost all machines. However, they might not have a Java engine installed and enabled. Fortunately, you can download the complete Java system from Sun if needed (www.java.com). Since the Java system is relatively standard, versions exist for most computer platforms. It is relatively easy to set up client computers for use within a company. On the other hand, you

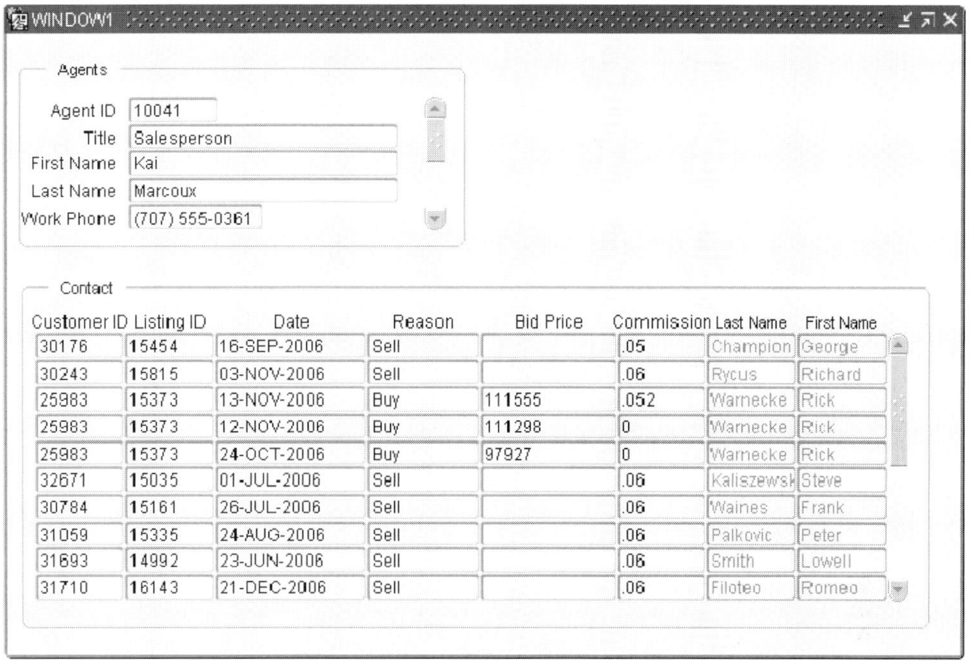

CHAPTER 8 Understanding and Using Forms Builder

[Screenshot of WINDOW1 form showing Agents section with Agent ID 10041, Title Salesperson, First Name Kai, Last Name Marcoux, Work Phone (707) 555-0361, and a Contact tabular section with columns Customer ID, Listing ID, Date, Reason, Bid Price, Commission, Last Name, First Name containing multiple rows of data.]

FIGURE 8.3 The Agent Contacts form combines a main form with a tabular form.

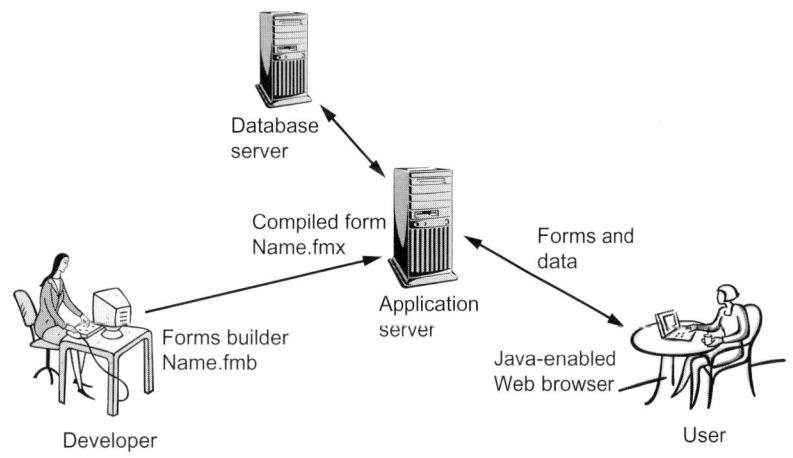

FIGURE 8.4 Web services architecture.

cannot expect random customers to install the system, so these forms are not a good way to conduct electronic commerce with the general public.

Tip: Forms Builder is easier to use if you create a Windows environment variable. Right-click **My Computer** to set its Properties. Choose the Advanced tab and click the **Environment Variables** button. Click the New button to add: name= FORMS90_HIDE_OBR_PARAMS, value=False.

As shown in Figure 8.4, forms in Oracle are created by developers using the Forms Builder tool which is part of the Developer Suite. You have to install these tools on your developer computer, but not on the database server. Each form that you create is stored as a separate file, so create a folder for your project that will hold all of the related forms. Eventually, you will compile the forms and copy the compiled versions to an application server which delivers and processes the forms using a Web interface. The forms connect to the database. In a large environment, the database will be running on a different computer. In smaller businesses, a single server can handle both the applications and the database. User machines need to install the *JInitiator* Java application provided by Oracle. The first time users (or developers) try to open an Oracle form, they will be prompted to download and install the JInitiator application. The process is relatively painless, but it does take a few minutes. Be sure that the client browser security systems (including yours) are set to allow applications to be downloaded and installed.

The overall process for creating forms is:

1. Install the Developer Suite on your computer. If you will be working with a database installed on a different machine, be sure you can connect to that computer. Use the Net Manager application if necessary to add a local connection.
2. Use Forms Builder to create and modify forms. Store them in a folder accessible to developers. Keep backups.
3. Test the forms on your computer by running the *OC4J* (Oracle Containers for Java) application on your computer. You activate it from the Windows Start menu: **Oracle Developer/Forms Developer/Start OC4J Instance.**
4. Start your Web browser and verify that your computer is added to the list of trusted sites by selecting **Tools/Internet Options/Security** from the browser's main menu. Open or run the form and test it. Install the JInitiator when asked.
5. Transfer the compiled forms to an Oracle application server, configure user browsers, and test the forms from the Web browser.

THE BASIC STRUCTURE OF ORACLE FORMS

Oracle uses specific terms to identify the various elements of forms. It is much easier to use the developer tools when you understand the terms and the overall structure of the forms. Figure 8.5 shows the design view of a simple form.

The main display area of the form is the *canvas.* You place *items* on the canvas such as labels and text boxes to display and edit data from the underlying tables. If you look through the list of *tools,* you will see that you can also draw lines or place images on the canvas. You can control the appearance of the canvas and the items by setting their properties. The *property palette* is normally hidden, but you can display it by right-clicking the canvas or individual items. Use the palette to assign properties such as colors and fonts. Some of these properties can also be assigned with the menu or toolbars at the top of the form.

The *object navigator* provides a hierarchical listing of all of the elements on the form. It can also show information for multiple forms. It is an easy way to quickly find all of the form elements. A *data block* is used to represent the transfer of data from the database to the form. Ultimately, you create a data block for each underlying table. Only the Agents table is used in this example, so there is only one data block. The individual items on the form are mapped to specific columns in the table. For most elements, you can set properties either by selecting the item on the form or by selecting it in the object navigator. A few things can be found only by using the object navigator list. You can select multiple items at the same time in either the object navigator or on the canvas by using the mouse to select them, or using **Ctrl+click** to individually pick items. When multiple items are selected, you can set display properties for all of them at the same time.

CHAPTER 8 Understanding and Using Forms Builder

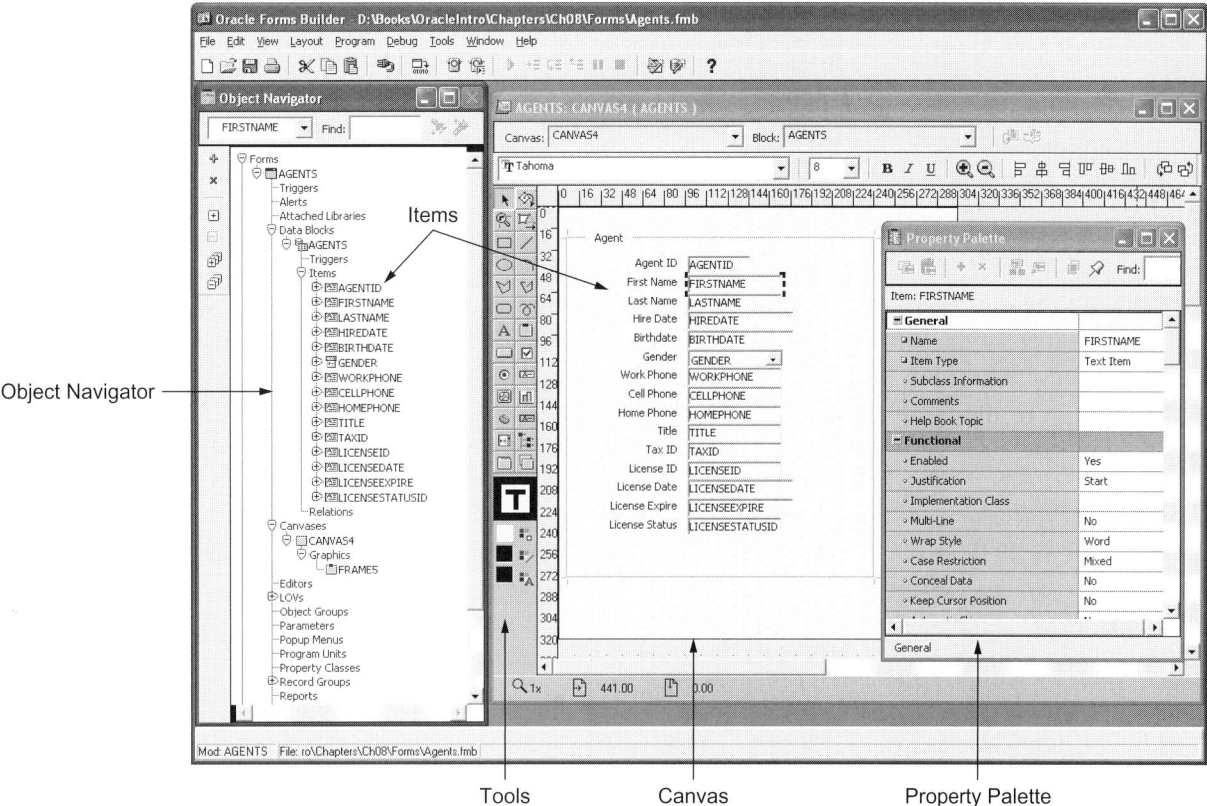

FIGURE 8.5 Design view of the structure of an Oracle form.

A *trigger* is code that is executed when some event arises on the form. Many events exist, and you can write PL/SQL code to solve specific problems or assist the user. For example, whenever you place a button on a form, you will have to include at least a line or two that executes when the button is pressed. Triggers are easy to find in the object navigator. Look under the specific object to expand the trigger listing. As you will see in some of the examples, the quickest way to create a trigger is to right-click one of the objects and select the smart trigger list. The *smart trigger* list shows the most commonly used trigger events for the chosen object. You can also choose the "Other" option to see a complete list of the trigger events available for any object. You will find that the event model provides the ability to write sophisticated applications by handling multiple events including mouse rollovers and key presses.

CREATING A SIMPLE MAIN FORM WITH THE FORMS BUILDER

The first step you need to do is to delete and rebuild the database.

1. Start SQL*Plus and run the BuildRedwood.sql file to delete and rebuild the database.

Now that you have seen the forms and the basic concepts of the builder, it is time to build the first form. You could start with a blank form and add all of the canvases, data blocks, and items from scratch. However, it is much easier and more efficient to use the Oracle wizards to generate the initial form for you. Once it is created, you can go back to design mode and make style changes or add new elements.

FORMS BUILDER WIZARDS

Before starting forms builder, make sure that your computer connects successfully to an Oracle database. The database can be running on your local machine, or it can be on a connected server. If you have any doubts, check it with SQL*Plus first. Second, before building any form, you should know what you want the form to look like. Begin by classifying it as: (1) a single row form, (2) a tabular form, or (3) a main/sub form. Identify the data elements that you will want on the form. Be sure you understand the purpose of the form—most forms should be aimed at updating data in only one table (plus one for each sub form). You might want to sketch the general outline of the form and identify the tables to use.

Oracle has two main wizards for building forms: (1) the ***data block wizard*** and (2) the ***layout wizard.*** You begin by starting the data block wizard. When it finishes, it can automatically open the layout wizard. The basic steps are:

1. Start the forms builder from the main menu. This gives you the blank forms designer.
2. Run the data block wizard.
3. Choose the tables and data items.
4. Accept the default options to run the Layout wizard.
5. Choose the items and set the captions and sizes. At this point you will have an initial form.
6. Clean up the layout by setting properties and rearranging items.
7. Add any other features such as drop down lists.
8. Test the form and improve its usability.

Of course, each step has multiple options and issues. With a little practice, the steps handled by the wizard become easy. The time-consuming aspect of forms is cleaning up the design and adding features.

When you run the data block wizard, you have to click through a few default initial screens:

1. Start the data block wizard: **Tools/Data Block Wizard.**
2. Ignore the startup screen.
3. Keep the default option to select data from a **Table or View.**
4. Click the **Browse** button to connect to the database and choose your tables.
5. Pick the **Customers** table for this example.
6. Click the double arrow (>>) to select all columns for the form.

Figure 8.6 shows the table browser list. Picking the Customers table will generate a list of all of the columns in that table in the left-hand column. You want all of the columns to appear on the new Customer form, so select all of them by moving them to the right-hand column. Figure 8.7 shows the outcome.

To finish the Data Block Wizard, you will be asked to name the data block. Generally, you want to give it the same name as the table to help you remember.

7. Click the **Next** button. Enter **Customers** for the name of the data block. Finally, keep the default option to start the layout wizard by clicking the **Finish** button. You can also start the layout wizard manually later using the menu option Tools/Layout Wizard.

CHAPTER 8 Understanding and Using Forms Builder

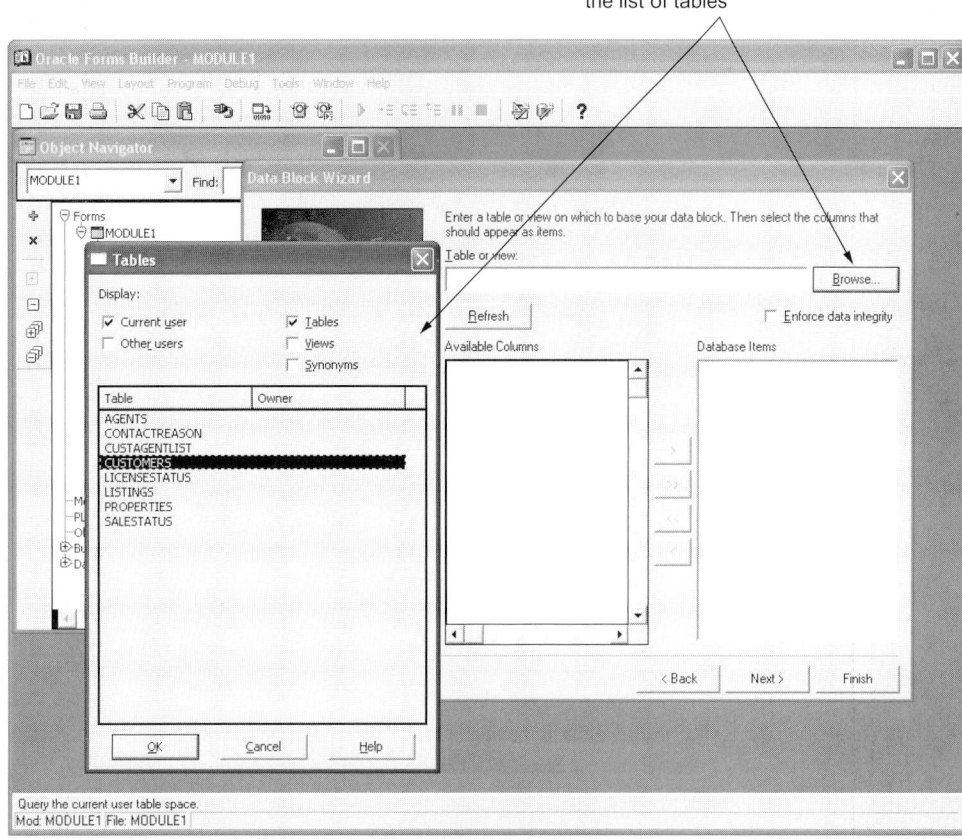

FIGURE 8.6 Choosing tables with the data block wizard.

Generally, the layout wizard displays a startup page. You can skip this page, and if you uncheck the box on the form, you can prevent it from appearing in the future. The main steps in the layout wizard are:

1. Keep the default New Canvas option and click the **Next** button.
2. Click the >> button to select all of the columns to place on the canvas. Click the **Next** button.
3. Adjust the prompts and column widths. Set most widths to **72,** which is about one inch. Longer items such as Address might use 144. Click the **Next** button.
4. Choose the **Form** type (Form or Tabular) and click the **Next** button.
5. Set the number of records to be displayed. With the standard form type, accept the default values, but enter **Customers** as the name for the frame, then click the **Next** button Click the **Finish** button on the last screen.
6. Adjust the layout and appearance of the items using the layout editor.

When creating a new form, you will always want to create a new canvas. Remember that a canvas is the drawing area on the form. In most cases, you will want to select all of the columns from the data block and place them on the canvas so they can be displayed and edited. Just as in the data block wizard, click the double arrow (>>) to move all of the columns to the right-side box.

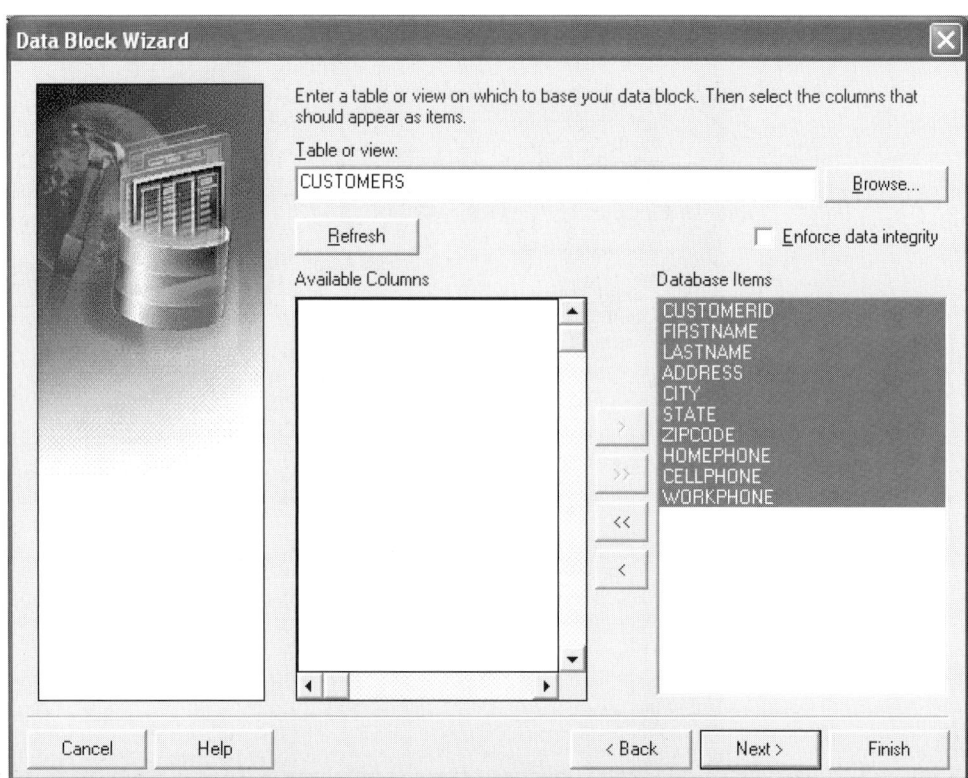

FIGURE 8.7 Choosing columns with the data block wizard.

One of the more time-consuming steps is adjusting the prompts and the widths of the columns. Figure 8.8 shows the values that you should use for the form. The prompts are the labels displayed on the form, so you clean them up by adding spaces and improving the capitalization. The widths are more challenging. You have to guess on an appropriate width for each text box. The good news is that you can always change the widths later. The reason for setting them at this point is that the initial values are usually way too large and they throw off the initial design of the form. You can save some effort later by providing better estimates now. The dimensions of most items are given in points. A *point* is a measure from typography, with 72 points in one inch. Of course, an inch on a paper form is not the same as an inch on a display screen. To estimate the number of characters that can be displayed in a text box, note that 12 digits can be displayed in one inch using a 12-point font. Keep in mind that alphabetic characters take up less space because of the variable widths of the characters.

The layout wizard asks you to select a layout of either "Form" or "Tabular." The difference is that a main form is generally used to display only one row of data at a time, rearranged in any layout on the form. The tabular layout displays data in a table or grid with multiple rows and columns. For the Customer form, you should accept the default "Form" value. The next wizard screen, shown in Figure 8.9, reveals that even if you select the tabular form layout, you will still have to enter the desired number of rows to display on the form. In the case of the Customer form, you should stick with the default value of one row.

Two other items on this form are also important: the frame title and the scroll bar. Be sure to enter a recognizable name for the frame title. It can be changed later, but because

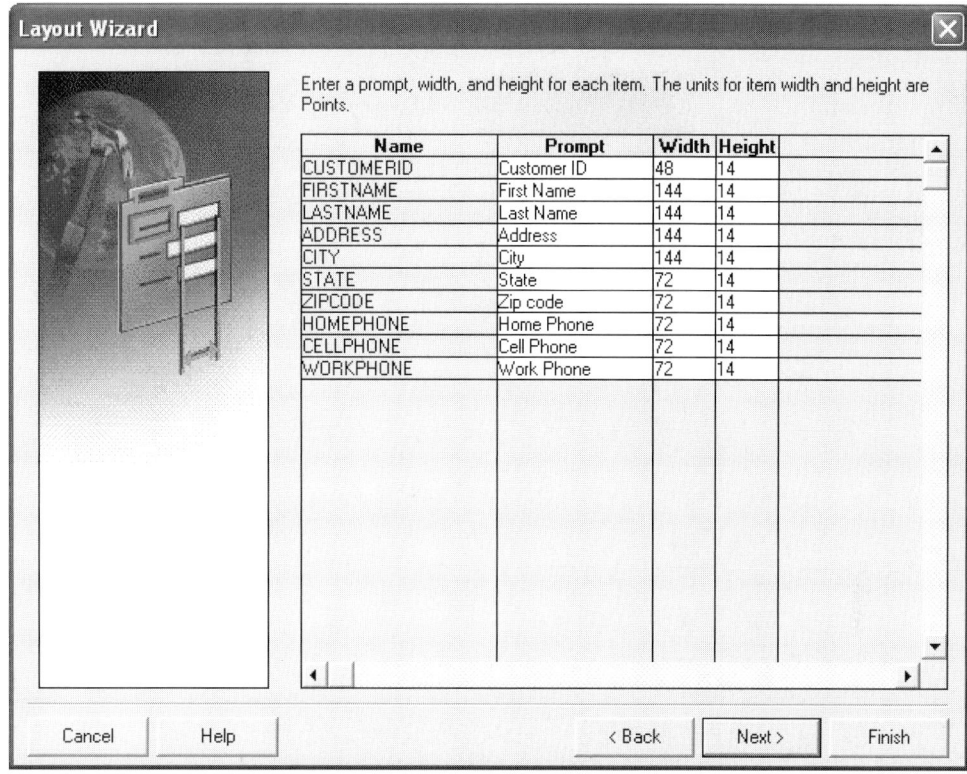

FIGURE 8.8 Setting prompts and column widths in the layout wizard.

it is displayed on the final form, you should pick a descriptive name. Use Customers in this example. The scroll bar is a more difficult choice. The scroll bar makes it relatively easy for users to move forward and back to display rows of data. It is particularly important for tabular forms because it fits with the common windows usability standards. It is less important for single-row forms, but you still might want to include it. The trick is that it is easy to add now and easy to delete later, but harder to add later. So, if you think you might want it, check the box to add it now. You can always delete it later with a couple of clicks. To test its value, include it on the Customer form. The final layout wizard screen indicates that you are done, and it builds the desired form when you click the Finish button.

Figure 8.10 shows the initial design of the Customer form as created by the two wizards. You could use the form the way it stands, but most of the time you will want to either arrange all of the items in a single column, or eliminate the columns and reorder the items anyplace on the canvas. Moving all of the items into a single column is easy. Click on the frame around the items to highlight it. Then drag the lower right-hand corner to the left and down. All of the items within the frame will be automatically rearranged to fit the new frame size. Sometimes this automatic rearrangement is useful. Sometimes it is not. The frame has an Update Layout property that is set to "Automatically" by default. At this setting, you cannot move the individual items separately. Their location is controlled by the frame. Once you get the layout close to where you want, change this property to "Manually," and you will be able to adjust and move all of the items within the frame and they will stay where you put them. For now, just create a single column for all of the items. Save the form often so that if you do not like an arrangement, you can throw it away and return to the saved version.

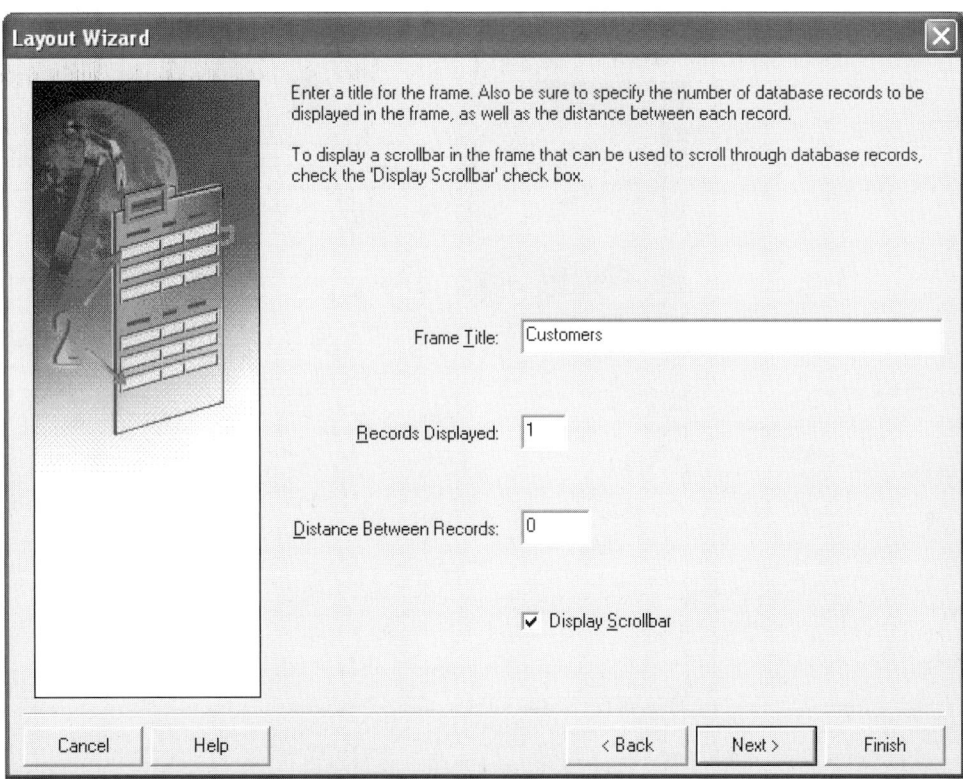

FIGURE 8.9 Choosing the number of records in the layout wizard.

TESTING A FORM WITH THE RUN FORM BUTTON

Now that you have the form designed, you can test it by running it. However, remember that the forms are designed to be run on an application server. Instead of compiling and copying the forms constantly, Oracle has provided a program to let you test the forms on your own development computer.

1. From the main Windows start menu, run the **Start OC4J Instance** program. It will take a few seconds to load. Also, your computer's security system might ask you for permission to run the program. You have to click the options to agree to let it run.
2. From the forms designer, click the traffic light icon to run the form. You can also use the menu item: **Program/Run Form.**
3. Install the JInitiator software when asked. If your computer is running a browser with high security settings (especially Windows XP with SP2), you will have to click several boxes, including the ability to allow pop-ups before the software is installed.
4. Once the form is running, you can see the actual data by clicking the Execute Query button or with the menu: **Query/Execute.**

> **Tip:** If you forget to run the OC4J before running the form, you will receive an immediate error message. Simply start OC4J and run the form again.

CHAPTER 8   Understanding and Using Forms Builder   **383**

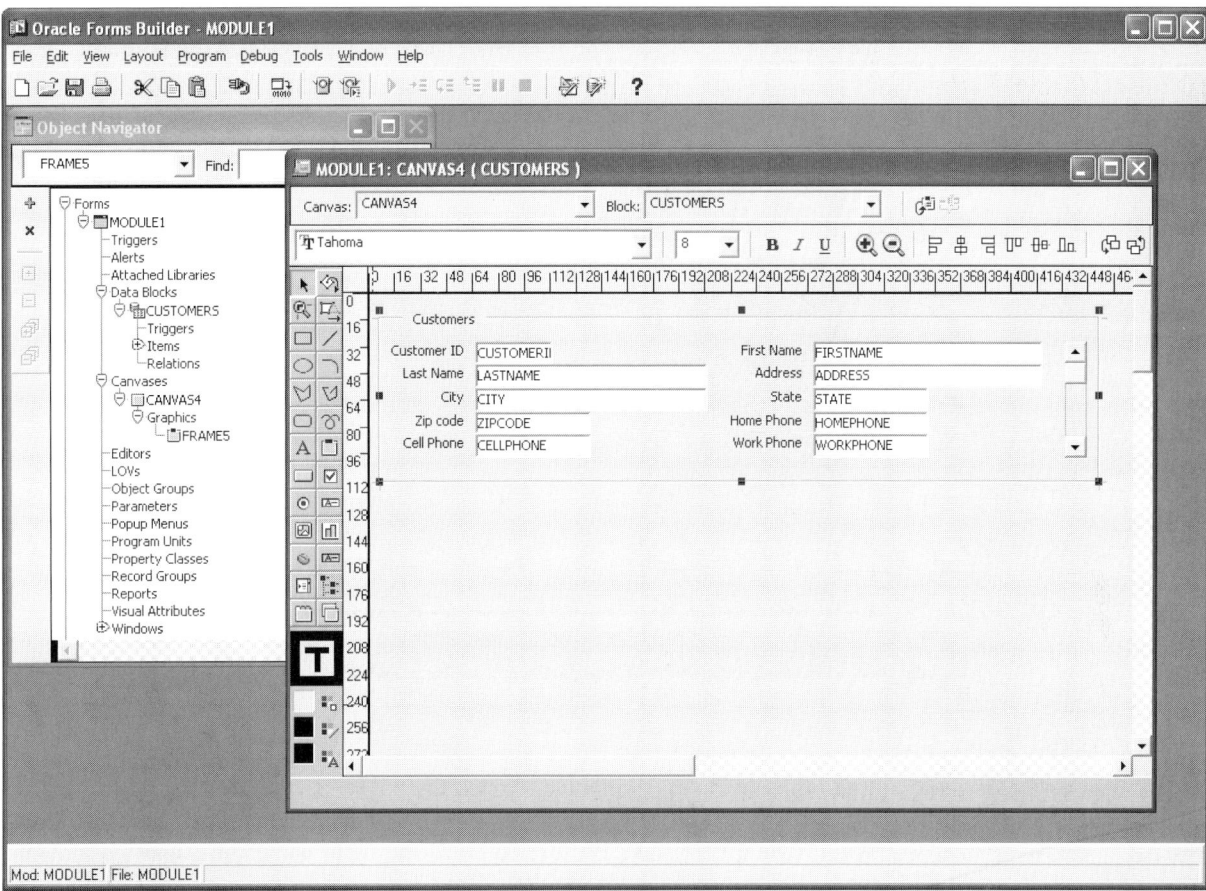

FIGURE 8.10   Design of the initial Customer form.

> **Tip:** To stop the OC4J service, use the windows Start menu option: Shutdown OC4J Instance. Do not just close the OC4J window, because that will leave the service running.

Running Oracle forms the first time requires several steps to get JInitiator installed. Higher security settings on your Internet browser add more steps. Figure 8.11 shows the startup screen that you should eventually see (but your version number is likely to be different). Follow the prompts to install the JInitiator software. Your system should then open the form you are running, but you will most likely see several more security messages. You should choose the options to enable or unblock the application as requested. If a major error arises, you might have to exit and restart the forms builder, and try again to run the form.

Figure 8.12 shows the run-time form that you should eventually see. Notice the many control buttons on the toolbar. Use these buttons to find data (Execute Query), move to another record, add or delete records, and to save the changes. You can also use menu selections, but the toolbar buttons are usually easier to find once you get used to them. Test the form now by clicking the Execute Query button. Scroll through a few records with the **Next Record** ▶ and **Previous Record** ◀ buttons and with the scroll bar. Try making a few minor changes to the data or adding a new record. Note

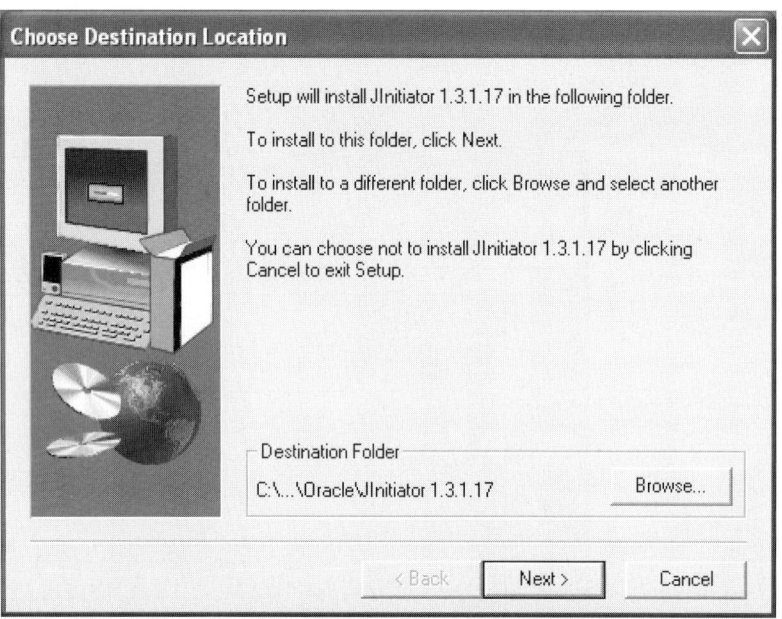

FIGURE 8.11 First step of JInitiator setup.

that you (and the final users) will have to click the **Save** button to send the changes to the database. If you close the form without saving the changes, they will be discarded. When you are finished, be sure to close the form using the **Close** button. Avoid closing the entire browser window. The Close button does some cleanup tasks and warns you about saving changes. You can leave the OC4J program running until you are finished working with forms.

DISPLAYING DATA WITH FORM QUERIES

By default, when you first run a form, it is entered into query mode. The user can enter conditions into the boxes on the form and then click the button to execute the query. The database creates a query using the conditions entered into the text boxes and returns only rows that match those conditions. To test the query system:

1. Restart the Customer form, but do not click the Execute Query button. If you are already in edit mode, you can click the **Enter Query** button to return to query mode. Figure 8.13 shows a simple query that is also relatively useful.
2. Enter **B%** into the text box for the last name. The query processor recognizes the percent sign and knows to use the pattern matching command. In SQL terms, it generates the condition: WHERE Lastname LIKE 'B%'.
3. Click the **Execute Query** button. Figure 8.14 shows the initial results you should see.

The condition acts as a filter. Scroll through the rows using the **Next Record** button. You will see that all of the customers displayed have last names that begin with the letter B. You can add more conditions, but all entries are connected with AND conditions. Rows will be matched and returned only if they meet all of the conditions. Also, remember that conditions are case sensitive. You will have to train users to enter uppercase letters for name searches. For numeric data, you can use a greater

CHAPTER 8   Understanding and Using Forms Builder

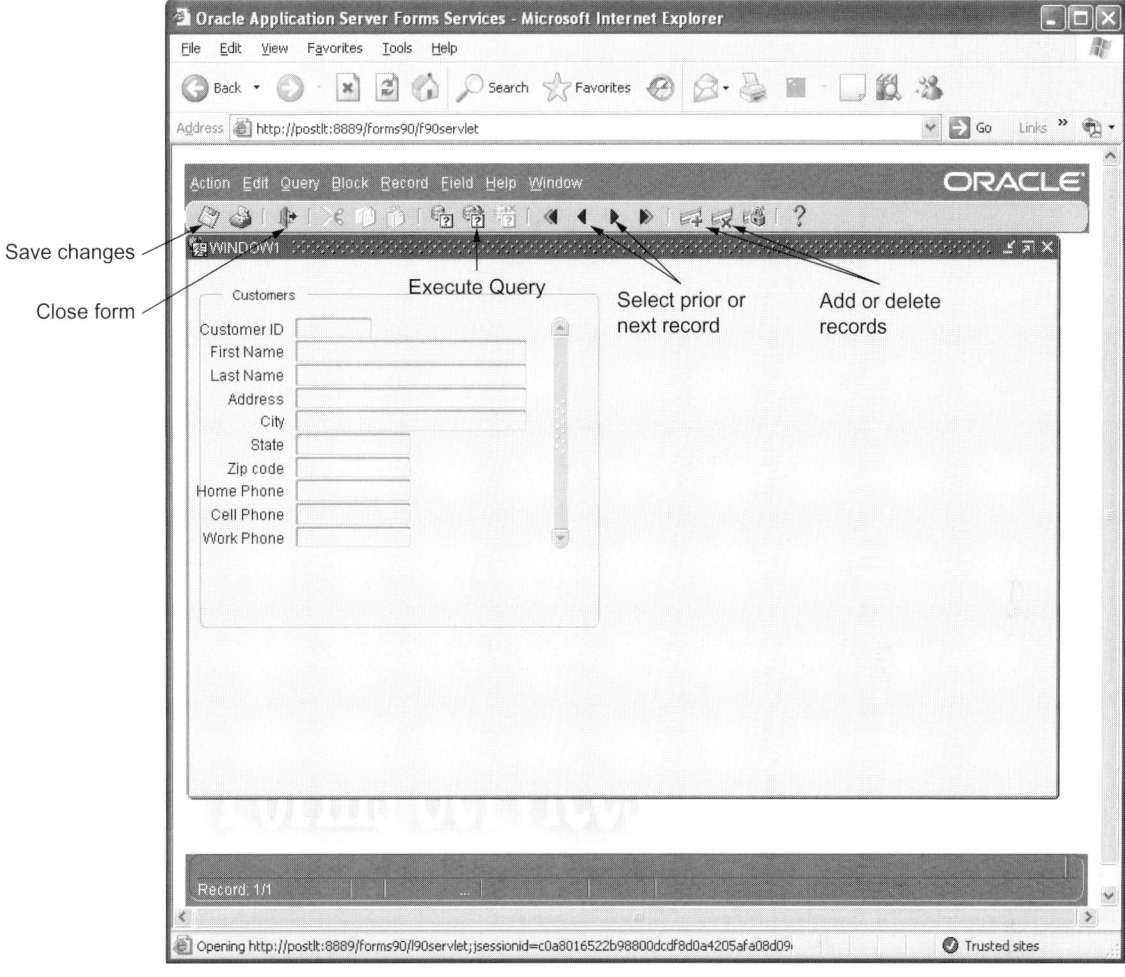

FIGURE 8.12   Initial Customer form and form controls.

than or a less than sign. Once you have retrieved the data, you can edit it or delete it as needed. The query filter provides a useful method to quickly find specific rows in a large table.

MODIFYING FORMS

The wizards do a decent job of creating the overall structure and initial layout for a form. However, you will generally want to customize the form to make it easier to use or improve the design. In fact, with practice, you can create an entire form without using the wizards.

THE LAYOUT EDITOR

The layout editor is the tool you will use the most. When you exit the form builder and re-enter to edit a form, the layout editor is not started by default. Once you open a form, you can click the F2 key or use the menu option Tools/Layout Editor to open the form for editing.

386 Introduction to Oracle

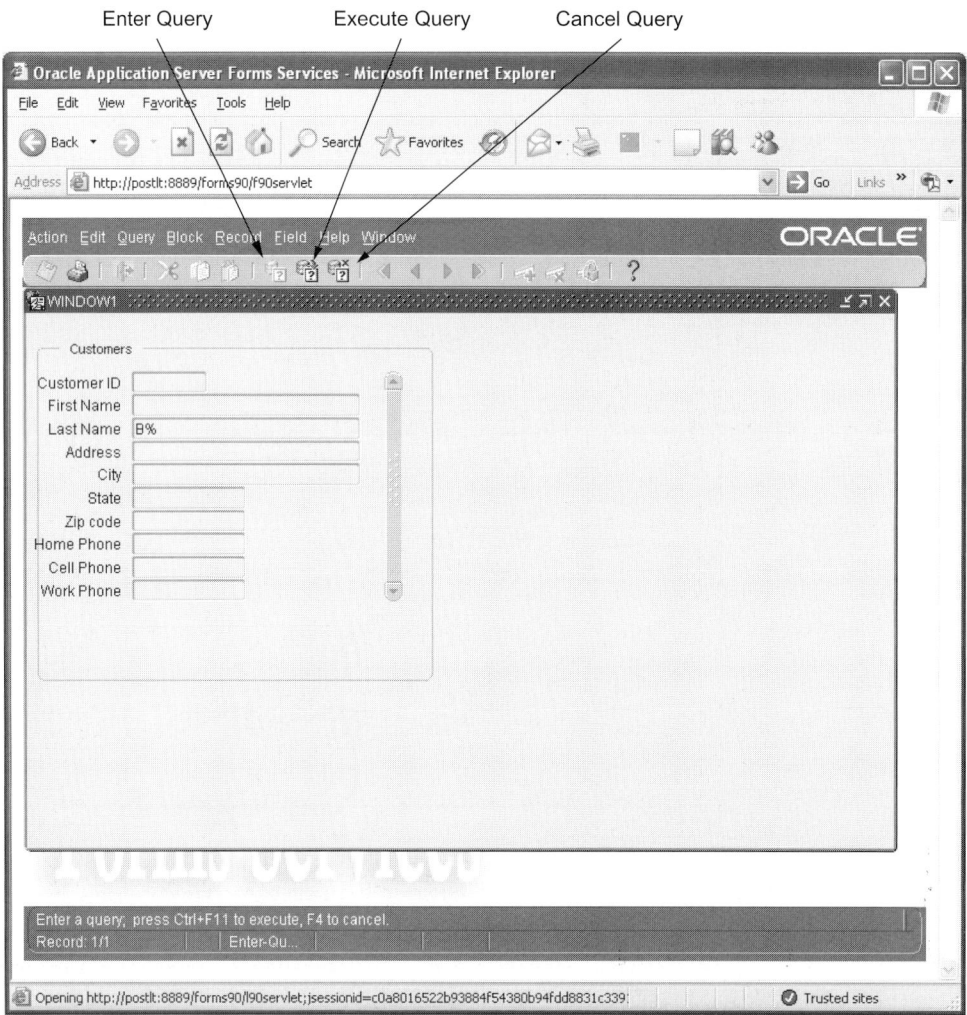

FIGURE 8.13 Simple form query to find all customers with a last name beginning with the letter B.

1. Open the **Customers** form so that you can modify its layout.
2. You need to change the frame update style to "Manually" instead of "Automatically." Right-click the frame, open the **Property Palette,** and change the **Update Layout** property to **Manually.**

Now you can move items within the frame and they will stay where you place them. To make the form easier to read, add a little more vertical space between the items. The steps are:

3. Move the **WorkPhone** text box down a dozen points.
4. Use **Ctrl+click** to select all of the text boxes and choose **Layout/Align Components.**
5. Under the column labeled **Vertically,** choose the **Distribute** option.
6. Click the **Align Left** button to set the left edges of the text boxes.

When you select the text boxes, be sure to select only the boxes and not the attached prompts. Use the mouse to draw a rectangle around only the text boxes.

CHAPTER 8   Understanding and Using Forms Builder   **387**

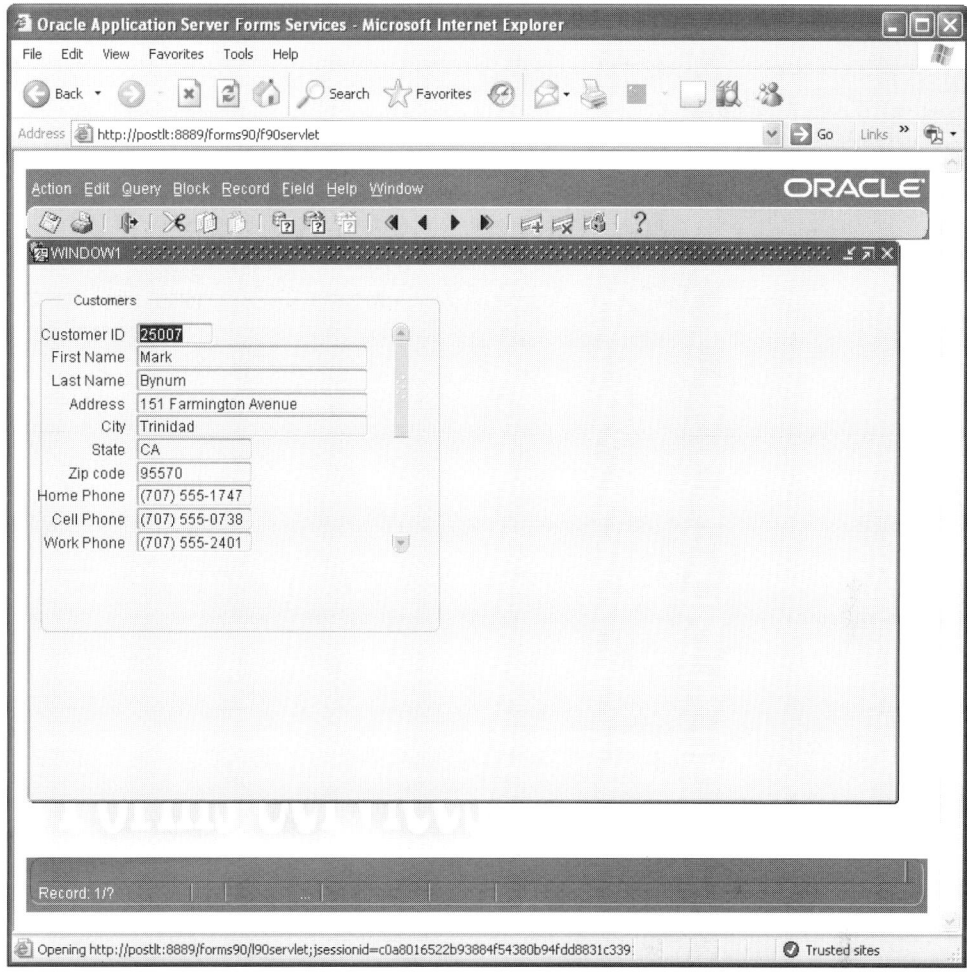

FIGURE 8.14   Rows filtered by the query.

Otherwise, use **Ctrl+click** to individually select each box. Figure 8.15 shows the many alignment options available once the boxes are selected. A few alignment buttons can be found on the main toolbar, but the distribute options are only accessible from the menu. They are useful for changing the spacing between items.

THE OBJECT NAVIGATOR

As shown in Figure 8.16, the object navigator is a hierarchical view of all of the objects in a form. Its primary purpose is to make it easy to find and select the items. Some items can be found only in the navigator. Tab order on the form is one of the trickier functions. Tab order represents the sequence of boxes on the form as the user fills in data or presses the Tab key. It is controlled by the order of the items listed in the data block in the object navigator. For example, on the Customers form, the order will move from CustomerID to FirstName to LastName, all the way down to WorkPhone. To change the order, drag an item to a different location in the list. It will not affect its position on the form, but only change the tab order.

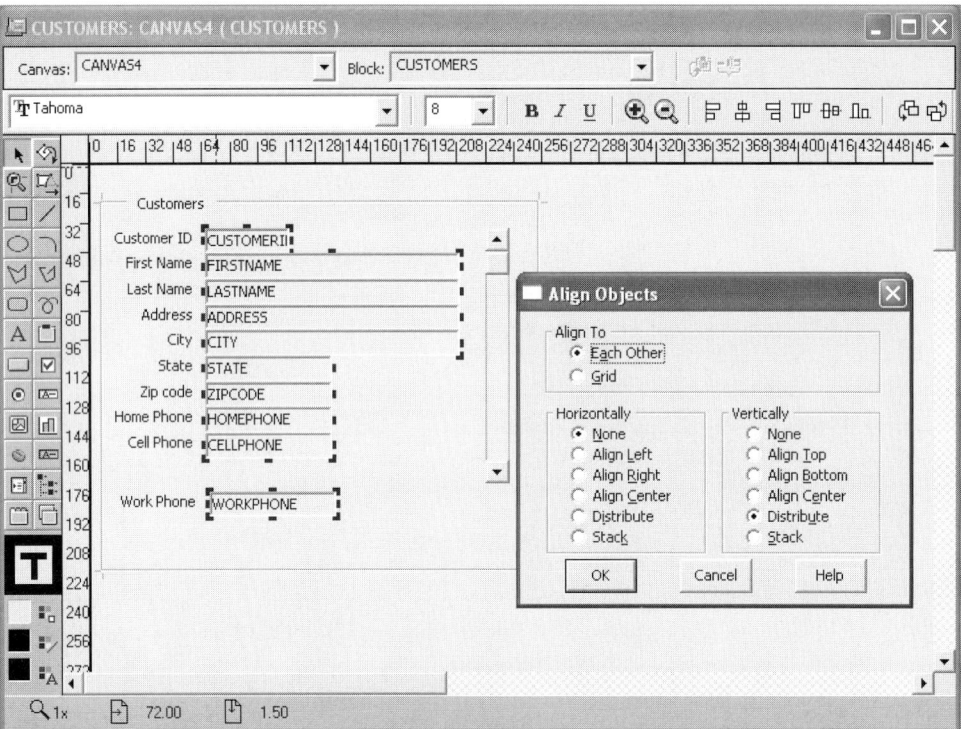

FIGURE 8.15 Object alignment options.

Another task performed in the object navigator is to provide a better name for the main window.

1. In the Object Navigator, expand the **Windows** section and find WINDOW1, which is the only window.
2. Click it twice and rename it **REDWOOD_REALTY.**

You might not think it matters, but the name is prominently displayed near the top of the browser when the form runs. You can also right-click an item to open the property palette and change various elements. Sometimes it is easier to select items on the navigator than on the layout editor. Later, you will also use the navigator to create and examine triggers or program code tied to the form events.

BASIC PROPERTIES

You use the Property Palette to set various properties. You should right-click to open the Property Palette and familiarize yourself with the many properties available for each type of item. Although you do not have to memorize the list, you do need to understand the various properties and how they affect the design and functionality of the form. For example, the properties in the Database section map an item on the form to a column in the data block. In the section on physical properties, the Height and Width are useful because they make it easy to set exact values for multiple elements. Similarly, you could use the X and Y Position entries to specify the exact location of various elements. However, the alignment buttons in the top toolbar make it easy to arrange groups of items. First, select each item to be aligned using the mouse or by using **Ctrl+click** on the item names in the object navigator. Then click the desired alignment button.

CHAPTER 8   Understanding and Using Forms Builder   **389**

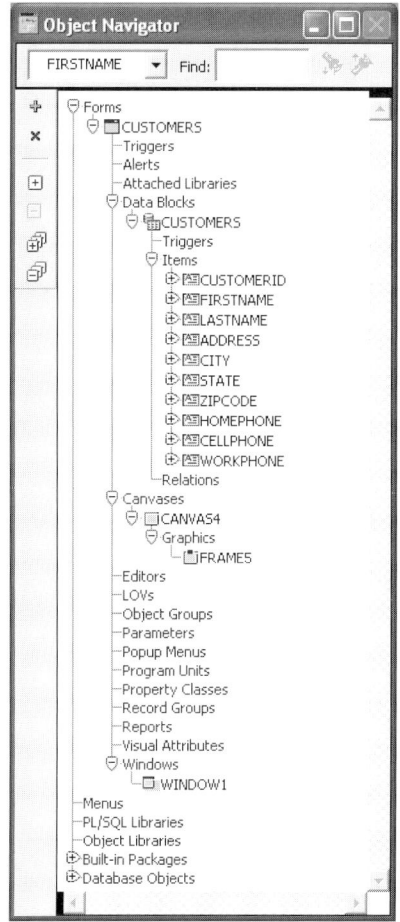

FIGURE 8.16   The object navigator.

Figure 8.17 shows some common modifications that you might want to make to forms. Many of the steps are optional, and you will have to establish your own design standards for each project. Try to be consistent across the various forms. The main steps here are:

1. Remove the scroll bar. Right-click on the scroll bar and select the **Property Palette** to edit the options for the Customers data block.

   This is a good time to learn an interesting trick with the property palette. If you know the name of the property you want, click in the **Find** box at the top right of the palette. Begin typing the name of the property, and the palette will scroll to that entry.

2. Enter **scr** into the **Find** box. Scroll the Property Palette window if necessary and set the **Show Scroll Bar** property to **No**.

3. Right-click on the frame to change the title font properties. Set the **Title Font** size to 10 points.

   You can use the font toolbar at the top of the form, or find the title properties in the property palette under the Title Font heading.

4. The last step is to change the name of the main window to Redwood_Realty.

   This name does not appear in the layout editor, but it is prominently displayed when the form runs. To change the name, open the Windows sub tree in the object navigator. Test the form and check it for alignment and balance.

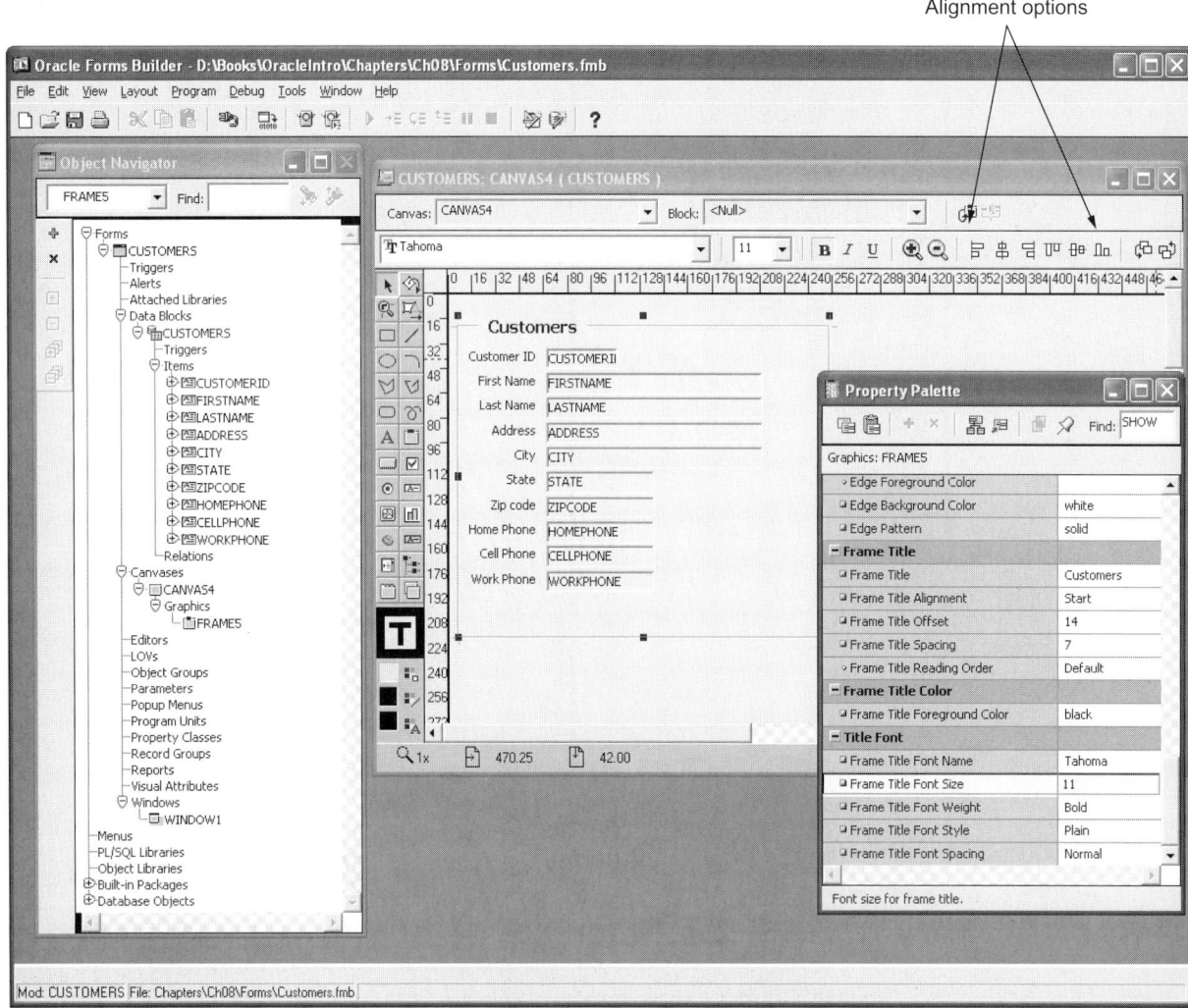

FIGURE 8.17 Common form modifications.

ADDING IMAGES

To add a logo, be sure it is stored as an image file on your computer in a standard format (such as JPEG, GIF, or TIFF). A sample file is included with the download files, or you can find or make your own logo. There is no tool to add the logo to the page.

1. Click onto the layout editor then use the menu **Edit/Import** to locate and import the file.
2. Resize it and move it as desired. When you resize a static image with the mouse, you should hold down the **Shift** key.

The shift key maintains the original aspect ratio so your image is not distorted. You can place static images anywhere on the page. If you adjust the brightness and contrast properly, you could place an image behind all of the other form items as a watermark. Be cautious with this approach because it might make the form difficult to read. Figure 8.18 shows the form with the image added to the bottom corner.

CHAPTER 8   Understanding and Using Forms Builder   **391**

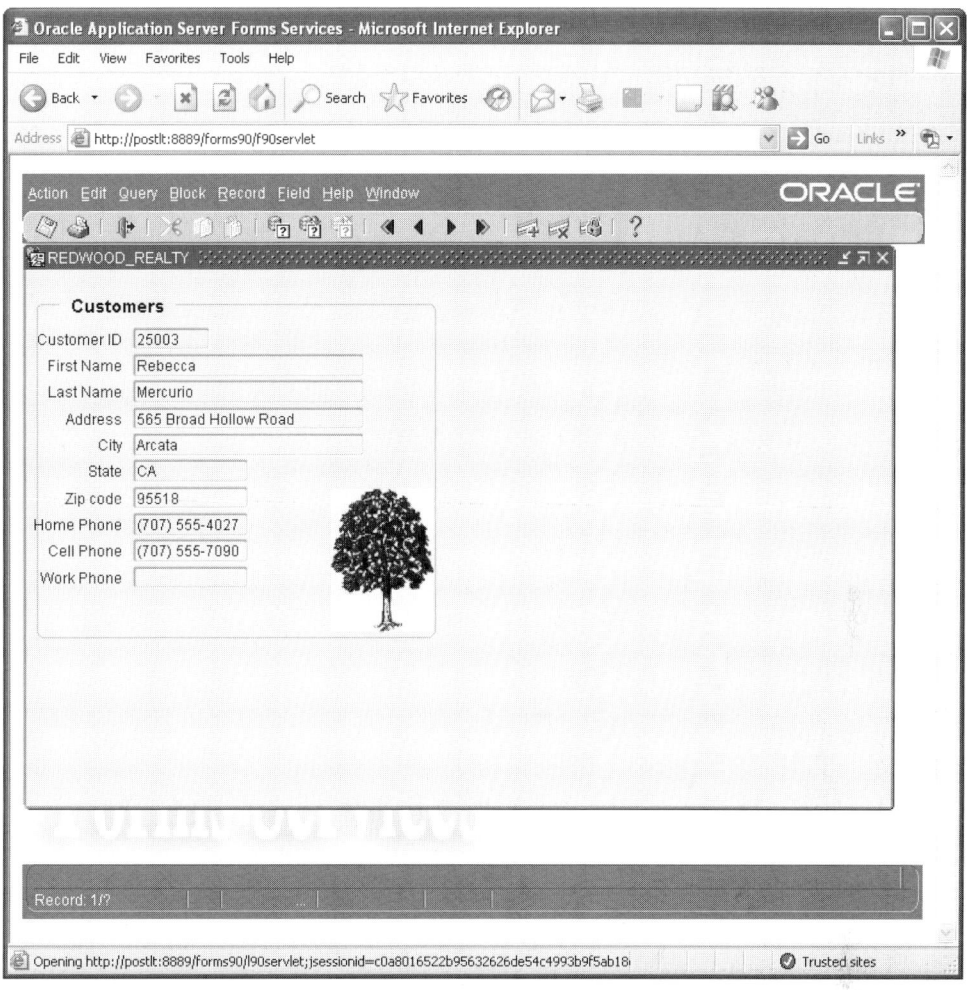

FIGURE 8.18   Adding a static image.

It is also possible to add images directly to the database. In this situation, the images are part of the data, not simply items displayed on the background of the form. For example, you might want to store pictures of employees in the database. Redwood Realty has a more important use: photographs of houses for sale. You can store a photograph or any other binary object directly in the database. You begin by creating a column in the table to hold the data. One of the strengths of a well-designed relational database is that it is easy to add a new column at any time. Adding the column does not affect existing forms and reports, so you can concentrate on using the new data without worrying about altering existing reports and forms.

1. To add the HousePhoto column to the Listings table, start SQL*Plus, connect to the database, and enter the following command

```
ALTER TABLE Listings
ADD HousePhoto LONG RAW;
```

Each row of the listing table will now be able to hold one photograph. Initially, the value will be null for each row. Assuming that agents have digital cameras and take the

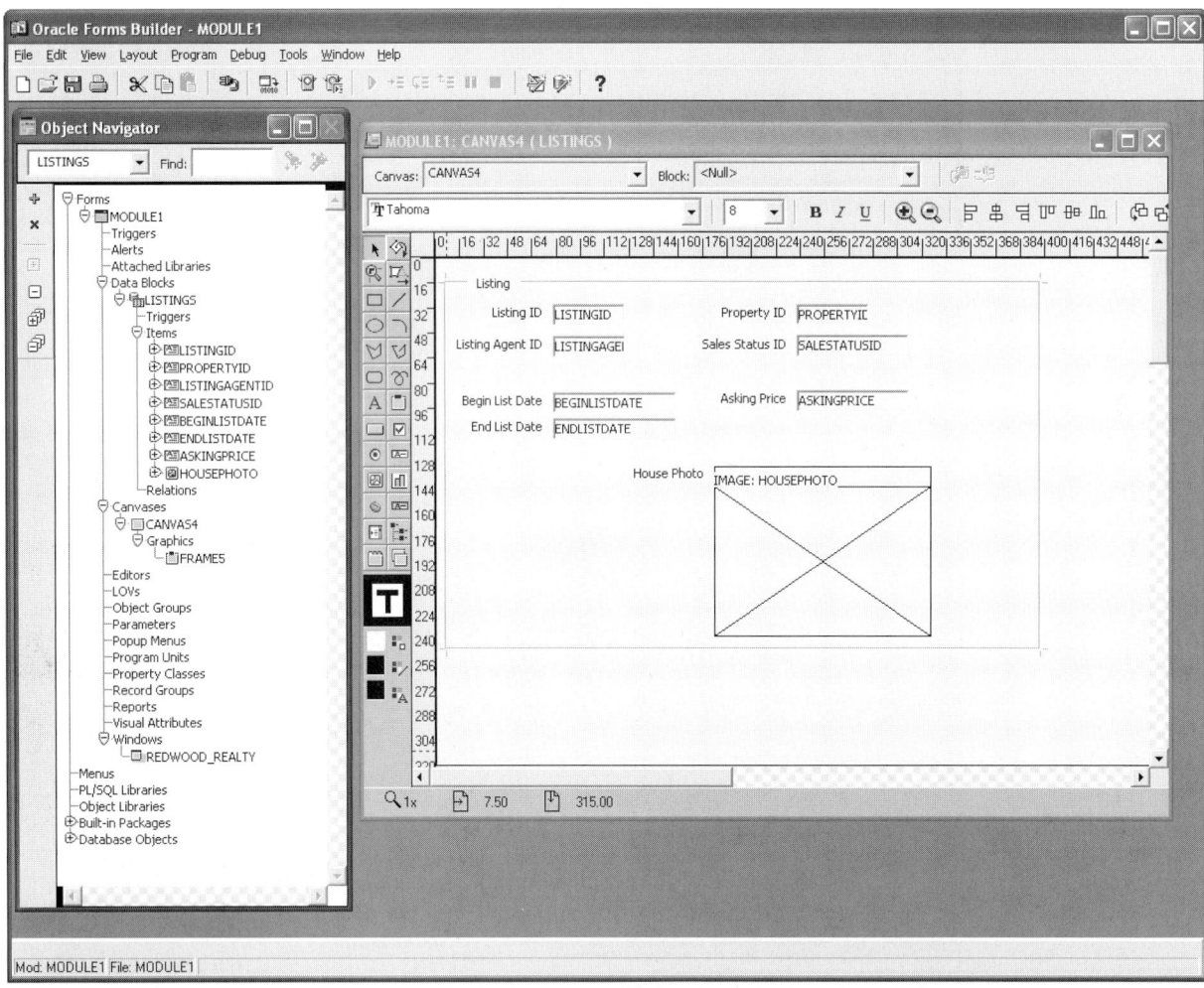

FIGURE 8.19 Design for the Listings form.

photographs, how will they load these photos into the database? The answer is that you have to create a form to display and load the photographs.

   2. Use the Data Block and Layout wizards to create a **Listings** form that is based on a single row of the Listings table. Follow the same steps used to develop the Customer form.

   Figure 8.19 shows the layout for the new form. You probably want to set the widths of the ID columns to 48. Remember to set the frame's Update Layout property to "Manually." Leave some space on the form because we need to add several items. Use the alignment commands to obtain a clean layout of the existing columns.

   Uploading a photo, or any binary object, to an Oracle database requires that the image be loaded from a file. The file has to be stored on the same computer that is processing the forms. For testing purposes, the file can be stored on your development computer. When you implement the database on a production application server, the photographs will first have to be uploaded to that server. A sample house image is included with the student files. Copy that file to a location on your development computer and remember exactly which folder you placed it in. To upload a file, you need to add an independent text box to the Listings form where the user can enter the full pathname of the file to be loaded. You also have to add a command button that will initiate the upload.

3. Use the tools to add a simple Text Item box to the form. Name it **ImageFileName**. Be sure to set the **Prompt** to **File to Load.**
4. Use the tools to add a command Button to the form. Name it **CmdLoadImage**, and be sure to set the **Label** to **Load Image.**
5. Right-click the new button, select **Triggers,** then the trigger for **WHEN-BUTTON-PRESSED.**
6. Enter one line of code into the PL/SQL Editor window:

    `READ_IMAGE_FILE(:IMAGEFILENAME,'ALL', 'HOUSEPHOTO');`

7. Click the button to **Compile PL/SQL code.** Close the code window.
8. Save the form and test it. Choose one of the listings, enter the full pathname of the image file, and click the new **Load Image** button. Be sure to click the form's **Save** button to update the database.

Figure 8.20 shows the form with the image file loaded to the database. You can delete or move the original photograph from the temporary folder. If you close the form

FIGURE 8.20 Loading an image to the database.

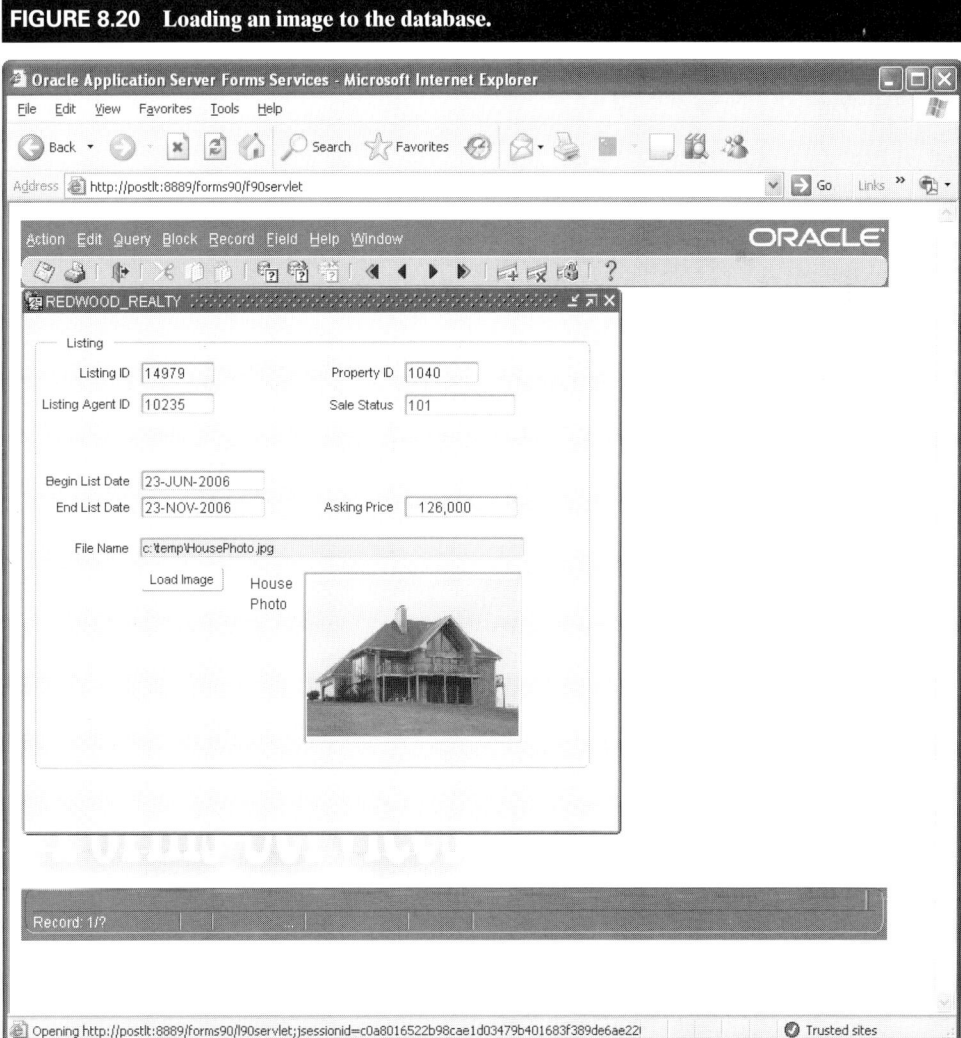

and return later, the picture will still be displayed because it is now stored within the database.

ADDING LOOKUP COLUMNS

Notice that the Listings form has only an ID value for the listing agent. If a broker is scrolling through the listings, it would be helpful to see the actual name of the listing agent. The catch is that the name is stored in the Agents table. This design was intentional because it does not make sense to repeatedly store an agent's name for every listing; and the tables are linked through the ListingAgentID. But, how can you display a value from the Agents table on the Listings form? The answer is to create a query for the underlying data block. You have to be careful when you base a form on a query. The form can write data into only one table within a data block. You can use a query to bring in additional columns for display, but they will be read-only. The values cannot be altered. And you must never add in primary key columns from a second table.

To create a query for the data block:

1. Select the data block **Listings** in the object navigator. Right-click and open the Property Palette. Find the **Query Data Source Name.** Initially, it will just be the name of the table (Listings).

2. Replace the table name with a SELECT query. However, be sure to enclose the query in parentheses:

   ```
   (SELECT ListingID, PropertyID, ListingAgentID, SaleStatusID,
   BeginListDate, EndListDate, AskingPrice, HousePhoto, FirstName, LastName
   FROM Listings INNER JOIN Agents ON
   Listings.ListingAgentID=Agents.AgentID)
   ```

   You should build and test the query in SQL*Plus before trying to paste it into the data block property. It is easier to find errors and correct them in SQL*Plus instead of waiting until you try to run the form. In this example, notice the addition of the FirstName and LastName from the Agents table. Since the form actually executes the query as a subquery, this entire listing must be in parentheses. Leaving off the parentheses is the most common mistake you will make. Check them several times.

3. Open the Query Data Source Columns property by clicking the **More...** button. Add **FIRSTNAME** and **LASTNAME** as new rows in the **Column Names** list.

   After you set the new query, open the properties for the Query Data Source Columns. You will see a list of columns currently used. Scroll to the bottom of the list and add FIRSTNAME and LASTNAME on new rows within the list. Close the property window. The two entries should now appear on the object navigator item list. You are now ready to display the values on the form.

4. Add two Text Item boxes to the form. Name them **FirstName** and **LastName** and set matching values for the prompts.

5. You now have to set several properties for both boxes. Table 8.1 shows the items that need to be set for the FIRSTNAME text box. Note that the Primary Key value is probably set to No initially, but double-check to make sure. Repeat the process and set similar values for the LASTNAME text box.

6. In the properties for the new text items, set the Database properties: **Database Item = Yes** and **Column Name = FIRSTNAME.** Do the same for LASTNAME.

Save the form and test it. Scroll through a few listings and make sure the agent name changes. Try to edit some of the entries and add a new record to make sure the basic form still works. You can use this query trick on almost any form. However, be

TABLE 8.1 Property changes for query lookup values.

Property	New Value
Name	FIRSTNAME
Prompt	First Name
Prompt Attachment Offset	7
Database Item	Yes
Column Name	FIRSTNAME
Primary Key	No
Query Only	Yes

cautious and ensure that the form works correctly before adding the query items. If something fails, return to your original copy of the form and try again.

CREATING A LIST OF VALUES

Being able to see the agent names on the listings form makes the form more useful. Brokers are unlikely to memorize agent numbers. But, what happens when you need to add a new listing? You still have to enter the appropriate value for the Agent ID. Does that mean users have to memorize ID values for every agent? Even if you require agents to enter their own listings, it would require them to memorize their own ID values. Instead, it would be nice to create a lookup list to use for selecting the agent from a list. The most powerful solution to this problem is to create a *list of values (LOV)*. A list of values is a list of all possible entries that could be selected for a specific text box. The list can be filtered and searched by the user. When a selection is made, the associated ID value is taken from the selection list and placed into the underlying table. Notice that two tables are involved in the process: (1) the listing of all agents taken from the Agents table, and (2) the Listings table that will hold the chosen value.

The easiest way to begin is to use the List of Values wizard under the Tools menu item. The wizard begins by creating a new *record group*, which holds the SQL SELECT statement to retrieve the data you displayed. The basic steps of the LOV wizard are:

1. Start the wizard with **Tools/List of Values Wizard.**
2. Accept the option to create a new record group.
3. Build a SQL query using the query designer, or enter it by hand if you have already created and tested the query in SQL*Plus.
4. The Query Builder enables you to choose tables and columns with a visual editor. It then writes the SQL SELECT statement. In this example, you want to choose the **AgentID, LastName,** and **FirstName.** Click the Sort button and choose **LastName, FirstName** as the sort condition.
5. Close the Query Builder and you will see the SQL command. Click the button to **Check Syntax.**
6. Include all of the columns in the LOV display by moving them all to the right-side window.
7. Reduce the widths of the display columns, using **48** for ID values and **72** for names. Alternatively, you can click the box to "Automatically size columns."
8. Place the cursor in the **Return Item** column for the **AgentID** row, and click the button to **Look up return item.** Choose the **ListingAgentID.** This column is where the selected entry will be placed.

Figure 8.21 shows the results of Step 8 where you have to select the return item value. Make sure that the Listings.ListingAgentID entry is placed in the return item

■ 396 Introduction to Oracle

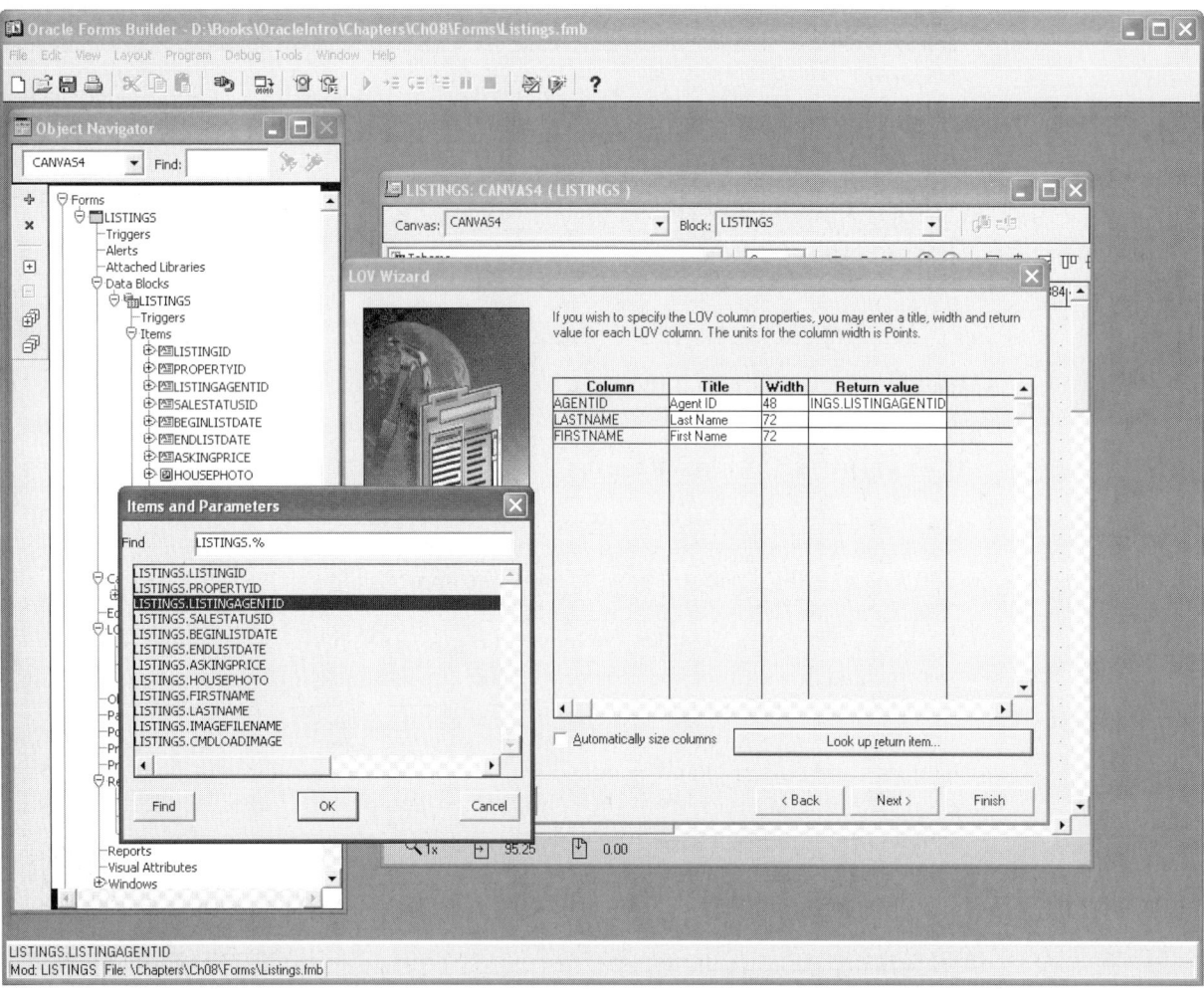

FIGURE 8.21 Choosing the return item with the List of Values Wizard.

column for the AgentID. This step ensures that the proper value (AgentID) is retrieved from the display list and placed into the desired column on the main form (Listing.ListingAgentID). Note that if you find a mistake after you close the wizard, you can select the LOV in the object navigator and then restart the wizard using the Tools/List of Values Wizard option. You can also enter changes directly into the LOV or record group properties. Note that the LOV is tied to the form by entering the name into the LOV property of the desired text item box (ListingAgentID) on the form.

9. Enter **List of Agents** as the title and set the default height to 235. Accept the default option to retrieve **20** rows at a time.
10. The last step is similar to step 8. You have to select the return item (Listings.ListingAgentID) and move it to the right side window.
11. When the wizard has finished, open the LOVs section of the object navigator and rename the LOV to **LOV_AGENTS**. Also, rename the new record group to **RG_LOV_AGENTS**.

CHAPTER 8 Understanding and Using Forms Builder

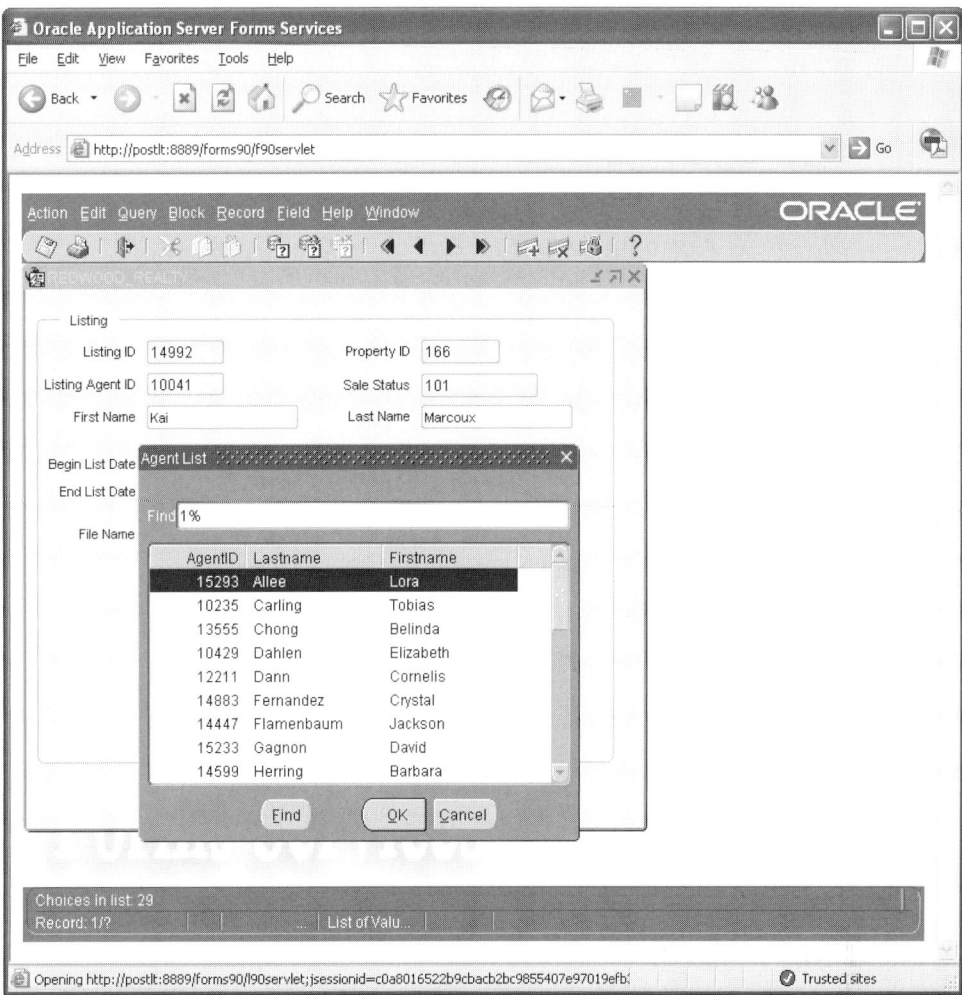

FIGURE 8.22 List of values for selecting the listing agent.

12. Run the form and it will initially appear the same as it did before. Move to the text box for the Listing Agent ID. If you look at the status bar at the bottom of the form window, you will see that "List of Values" is partially displayed. This indicator tells the user that the selected box has a supporting list of values. Click **Ctrl+L** to open the list of values.

Figure 8.22 shows the initial list. The user can scroll through the list to find the desired entry. The Find box at the top of the LOV window is a powerful feature. The user can enter search conditions to filter the rows. The one catch is that the find filter looks at each row as it is displayed. In this case, the row shows the AgentID, Lastname, and Firstname. To find an entry by last name, such as Marcoux, you would enter **%Mar%.** The leading percent sign matches any ID, the trailing percent sign matches the end of the last name and any first name.

The list of values approach is important because it enables the user to deal with names or descriptions instead of numbers. It is efficient because the LOV window never retrieves the entire list at one time. Instead, it caches a specified number of rows at one time—based on the filter. In some cases, you might want to make the LOV easier to use by placing a small button next to each text box that has an LOV. That way users know immediately when an LOV exists and can click the button to open the list. If you want to use this approach, your button needs two lines of code:

```
Go_Item('LISTINGAGENTID');
List_Values;
```

AUTOMATING THE EXECUTE QUERY STEP

To make the forms easier to use, you should consider another step. Remember that when the form first opens, it is blank. The user has to click the Execute Query button to retrieve the initial data for the form. If workers commonly use the form to scroll through records, you should consider automating that step so they immediately see the first record when the form opens. This step is straightforward and requires one line of code. The key is to place that line in the appropriate trigger event.

1. Near the top of the object navigator, find the **LISTINGS** section under the **Forms** tree. Right-click the **Triggers** entry and select the smart triggers sub menu. Choose the **WHEN-NEW-FORM-INSTANCE** entry and the PL/SQL Editor will open. Enter the code:

   ```
   EXECUTE_QUERY;
   ```

2. Compile the code and close the editor window. Test the form by running it.

This time, the form should open and display the first data row. Users can now scroll through the list without having to click the query button. If desired, they can still return to the query window and enter conditions to filter the list. Ultimately, you have to talk with users and make a design decision to determine if all of your forms should open with data displayed, or if the user should first enter filter conditions.

RADIO BUTTONS AND CHECK BOXES

Most database columns can be handled with the standard text box. You can use the properties of the text box to control and test the data being entered. You can also use a list of values to simplify data entry for key values—enabling the user to choose an item from a list instead of memorizing a number. But, sometimes, you need additional data-entry choices. In particular, you might want to use a *radio button* or *check box.* A radio button is sometimes called an option button. In principle, the only difference between a radio button and a check box is that radio buttons are drawn as circles that are filled in when an item is selected. A check box is a square box that displays a check mark when it is selected. However, most application developers have adopted the convention that multiple radio buttons are used for mutually exclusive choices. For instance, you can choose a traditional crust for your pizza or a whole wheat crust, but not both. Check boxes are used to indicate that multiple items can be chosen, such as selecting various toppings for your pizza. This convention is useful and you should follow it, because then you application will work the way users expect it to work. Just keep in mind that the forms processor does not require you to work that way, so you have to be careful when setting up groups of radio buttons.

To illustrate the use of the radio button, you are going to build a single-row form for the Properties table. The basic steps will be similar to those used for the other forms:

1. Start Forms Builder to create a new form and make sure OC4J is running. Run the Data Block wizard and choose all items from the **Properties** table.
2. In the Layout wizard, select all columns by moving them to the right-side window, but do not press the Next button yet.

CHAPTER 8 Understanding and Using Forms Builder

3. Select the **Zone** column by clicking on it. Find the **Item_type** box and change the entry from **Text Item** to **Radio Group.**

Since you want a relatively standard single-row form, begin by running the data block wizard to select the Properties table and all of its columns. The only difference is that when you get to the layout wizard, be careful. After you have moved all of the columns to the right-side window, select the Zone item and change its item type from Text Item to Radio Group. Figure 8.23 shows the location of the drop-down list for this change. After making this change, finish the wizard as usual, remembering to reset the initial lengths of the various text boxes.

4. Finish the Layout wizard, rearrange the items vertically, and set the frame to update manually.
5. Use the tools to add a Radio Button to the form. Set its properties as follows: **Name=RAD_R1, Label=Residential R1, Radio Button Value=R1.** Add similar buttons for R2, R3, and C1 (Commercial) by copying and pasting.

In the layout wizard, you created a grouping for the Zone entry. You now have to manually create the individual radio buttons. The Zone data represents the zoning of

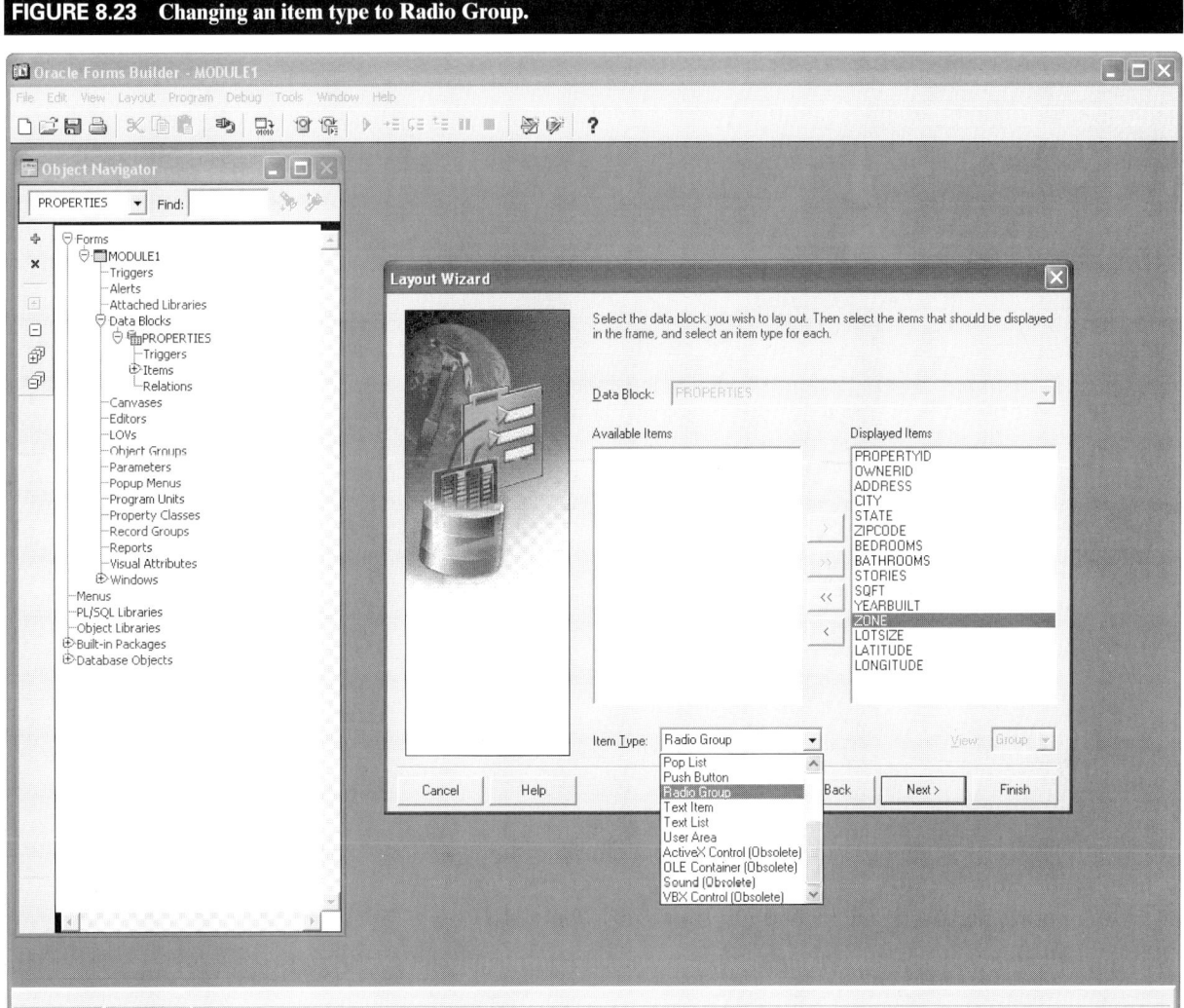

FIGURE 8.23 Changing an item type to Radio Group.

the property. Most cities use common zone terms: R1 for single-family residential, R2 and R3 for multi-family residential, and C1 for simple commercial (retail) properties. Several other designations are available, but for simplicity, assume that Redwood Realty only deals with these four types of properties.

Add the first radio button by selecting the radio button tool and placing one on the form. You will be asked to choose the group for the radio button. Since you only have the Zone group, choose that one and continue. To make the button work, you need to assign several properties. Figure 8.24 shows the values of the three main properties you need to set. Give the button a recognizable name (RAD_R1) in case you need to refer to it later in code. Assign the label (Residential R1) which is what the user will see. Finally, assign the value (R1) associated with this button. This value must match the data in the table. When a user selects a particular button, this value will be stored in the Zone column of the Properties table.

When you have finished setting the properties for the first button, copy and paste a new button onto the form. Move it below the first one and set its properties to

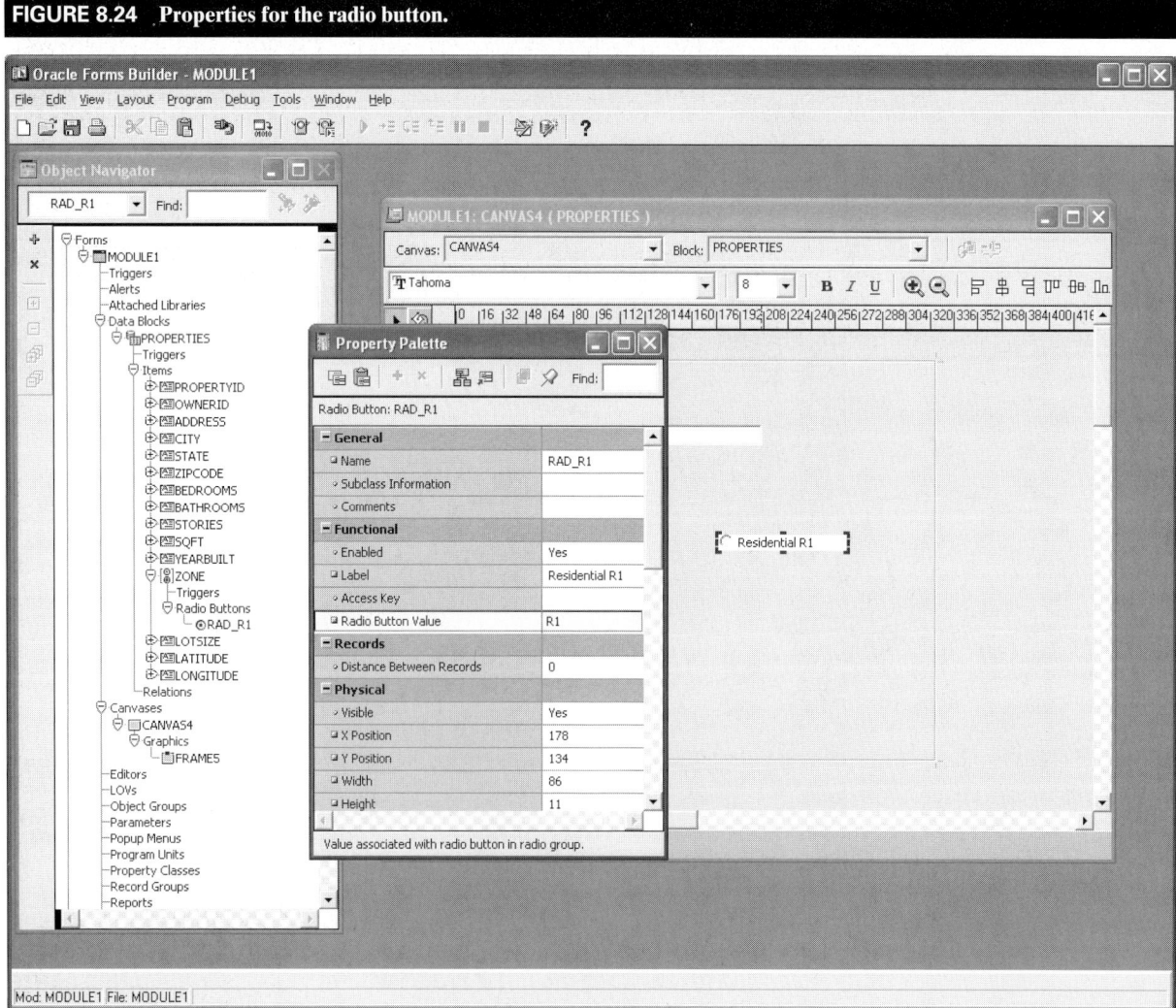

FIGURE 8.24 Properties for the radio button.

Residential R2. Do the same for Residential R3 and Commercial C1. Use the Layout/Align Components menu item to space the buttons evenly and left-align them.

Find the Zone item in the object navigator. Open its property palette and find the Initial Value property. It is currently blank, so set it to R1. This value will be the default entry, because most of the properties will be single-family housing. For visual effect, you can draw a frame around the buttons and place the Zone label in the frame.

6. Using the Object Navigator, set the **Initial Value** property for the **Zone** item to **R1**.
7. Adjust the alignment of the radio buttons. If desired, add a frame or a rectangle around the items.

Save the form and run it. Note that all of the existing properties in the database have the R1 designation, so as you scroll through the records, the selected option button will not change. Choose one of the records and change it to R2. Remember to save the change, then scroll forward and back to ensure that the display is updated properly. Figure 8.25 shows the basic form.

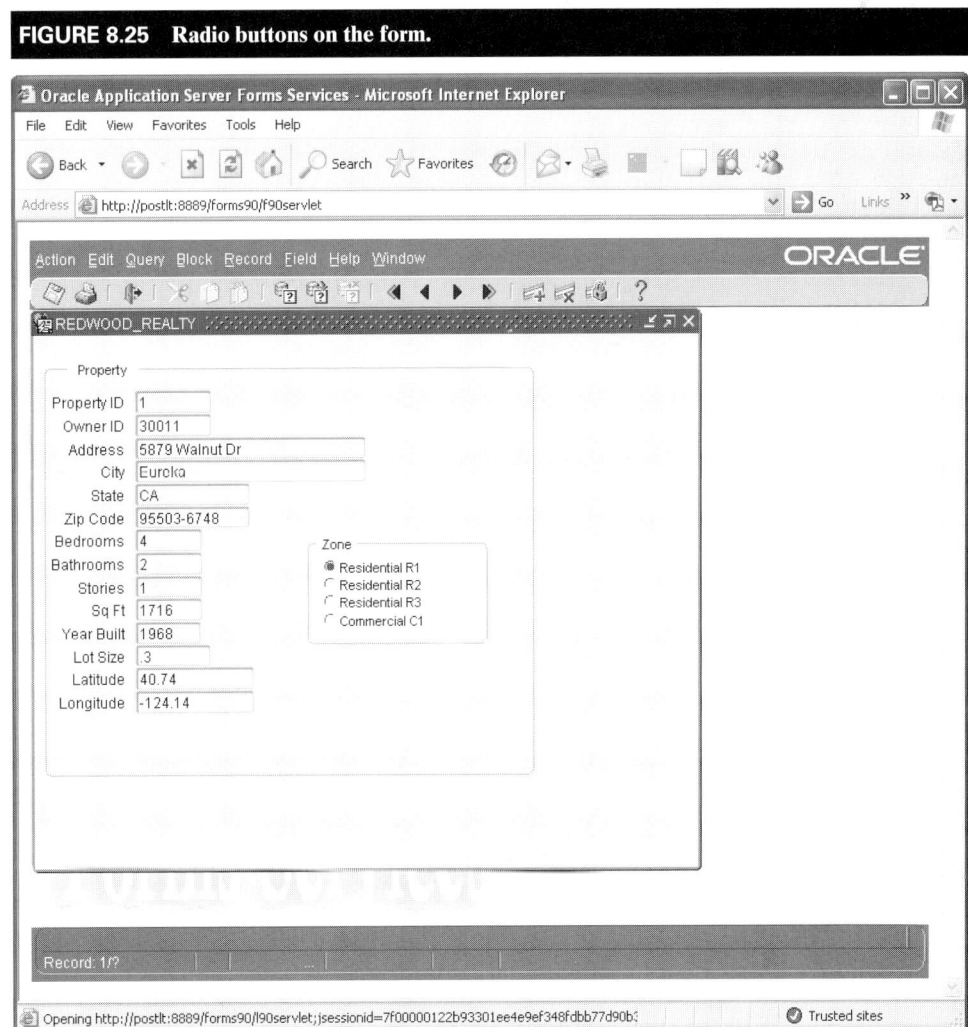

FIGURE 8.25 Radio buttons on the form.

CREATING TABULAR FORMS AND SUB FORMS

Single-row forms are useful and they give you complete control over the layout of the items on the form. However, sometimes users want to see more than one row of data at a time. For very simple tables, you might want to create a tabular form that simply displays each column of data and multiple rows. For more complicated situations, such as the common sale form, you will want to include a list of items as a sub form placed on the main form.

CREATING TABULAR FORMS

Tabular or *grid* forms are relatively simple to use and to create. To the user, the tabular form looks like a simple table editor, where data is displayed in rows and columns. The forms are really only useful when there are a limited number of columns. If you use too many columns, the user would have to scroll horizontally to see some of the data. Horizontal scrolling makes it hard to keep track of exactly which row is being edited, so you should try to use tabular forms only when all of the columns can be displayed on one screen. In general, tabular forms are used for basic administrative tasks, such as entering new values into a lookup list. The License Status form is a good application for a tabular layout. It contains only a couple of columns, and it is helpful to see multiple rows at one time. The form will be used only rarely, so it needs to be straightforward and easy to use.

The main steps in creating a tabular form are almost identical to those for a single-row form (remember to click the **Next** button when you finish a step):

1. Start the Data Block wizard and choose the **LicenseStatus** table and all of its columns.
2. Start the Layout editor and choose all of the columns.
3. Set the default column widths to **48** for the ID and **176** for the text.
4. Choose the **Tabular** layout instead of the Form layout.
5. Specify the number of rows (**20**) and include the scroll bar.

Figure 8.26 shows one of the more important setup screens, where you specify the number of rows and select the scroll bar. You should almost always include the scroll bar on tabular forms because most people expect it to be there. The number of records displayed at one time determines the size of the form, so you might want to change this value later by setting the corresponding property in the data block properties.

Figure 8.27 shows the final design for the License Status form. When you run the form and click the Execute Query button, you will see that the running version of the form looks almost the same. Users can change the data for multiple columns or rows, or even add rows, simply by typing the new values into the desired location. Remember that you have to click the Save button to commit the changes to the database. If a table contains more than the number of rows that can be displayed on the form (20 in this case), the scroll bar can be used to choose the rows displayed. You can test this function by reducing the number of displayed records and rerunning the form.

CREATING MAIN AND SUB FORMS

By themselves, tabular forms are unexciting, and are used only for simple forms. However, their real strength lies in creating more complex forms. As an application developer, you generally want to create forms that match the tasks of the users. That means that often you have to combine several elements together on one form. For example, a common sale form would contain information about the date of the sale

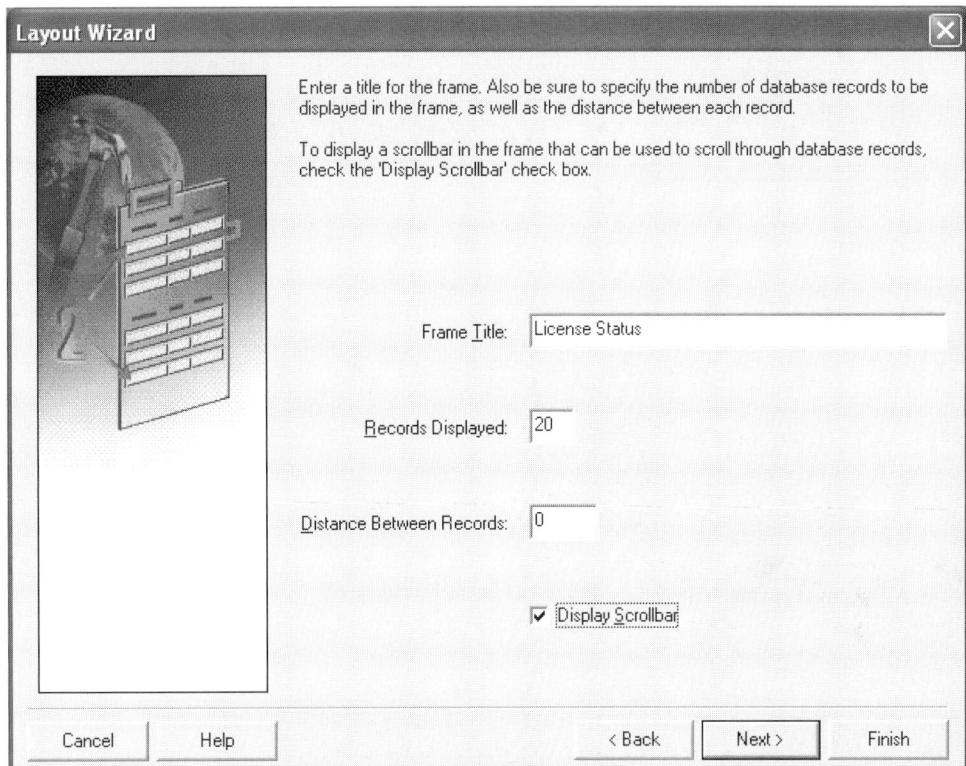

FIGURE 8.26 Setting the initial properties for a tabular form.

and possibly the customer. At the same time, it would contain a sub form to choose and display the items being sold. This sub form is commonly displayed as a grid. The data in the sub form is linked to the main form. In the sale example, the Sale Item table is linked to the Sale table by SaleID.

Redwood Realty can use a main form/sub form so that agents and managers can record and see the contacts made by each agent. Check the list of tables for the case and you will find two related tables: Agents and CustAgentList. These two are directly related through the AgentID. The goal of the CustAgentList table is to record professional contacts made with a specific agent. For example, when an agent lists a house for a customer, an entry is made in the CustAgentList table that includes the AgentID, the CustomerID, and the ListingID. The ContactReason specifies the purpose of the contact; in this case it would be to sell the customer's house. Similarly, when offers are made on a listing by another customer, the agent records the CustomerID, the ListingID, and the offer price in the table. Since most of the entries are made by individual agents, the objective is to create a main form that lists the agent information, followed by a sub form that lists all of the contacts in a grid.

Once again, the Data Block and Layout wizards do most of the initial work. The key is to create the main form first, then go back to the Data Block wizard again and add the sub form grid. Create the initial form by starting the data block wizard and choosing a few columns from the Agents table. At a minimum, include the AgentID and name columns. Complete the layout wizard and use the frame to rearrange the selected columns. Be sure there is blank space on the canvas below the Agents frame. You will put the sub form into this space with 10 rows of data, so you need at least a couple of inches.

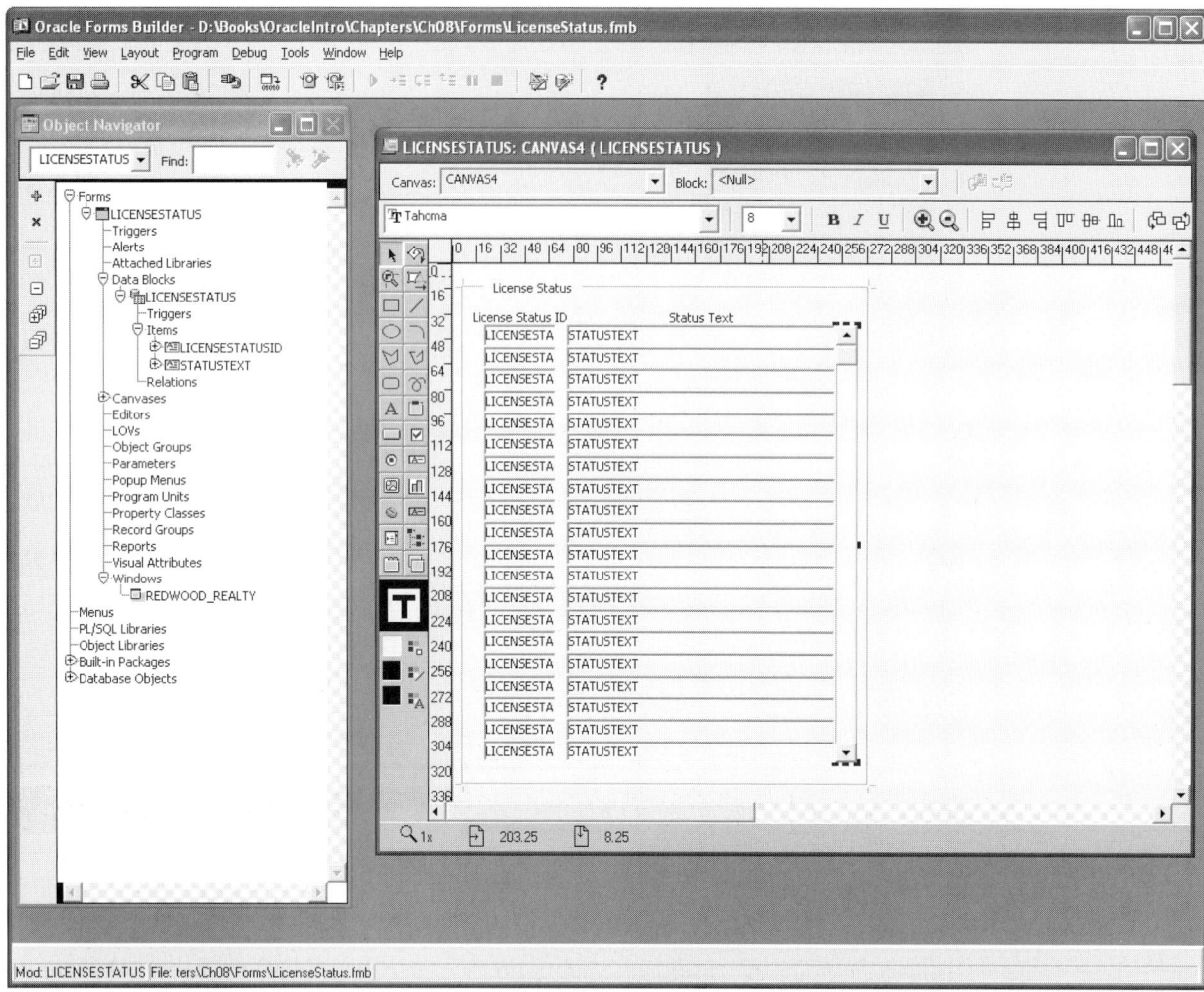

FIGURE 8.27 Tabular design for license status values.

> **Tip:** Click on the canvas before starting the data block wizard or the wizard will simply edit the original data block. If that happens, cancel the wizard and try again.

1. Create a single-row main form for the **Agents** table. Include columns for **AgentID, Title, FirstName, LastName,** and **WorkPhone.**
2. If necessary, expand the size of the canvas. Start the Data Block wizard to choose new data. Choose the **CustAgentList** table and all of its columns.
3. In the relationships screen, click **Create Relationship** to join CustAgentList to Agents through the AgentID columns.

Click on the canvas and then start the Data Block wizard again. This time, choose the **CustAgentList** table and pick all of the columns. At this point, you will be asked to create a relationship between the new data block and the existing Agents data block. These tables are connected by the AgentID column. Figure 8.28 shows the final relationship. However, you have to follow certain steps to achieve this outcome. If you

CHAPTER 8 Understanding and Using Forms Builder 405

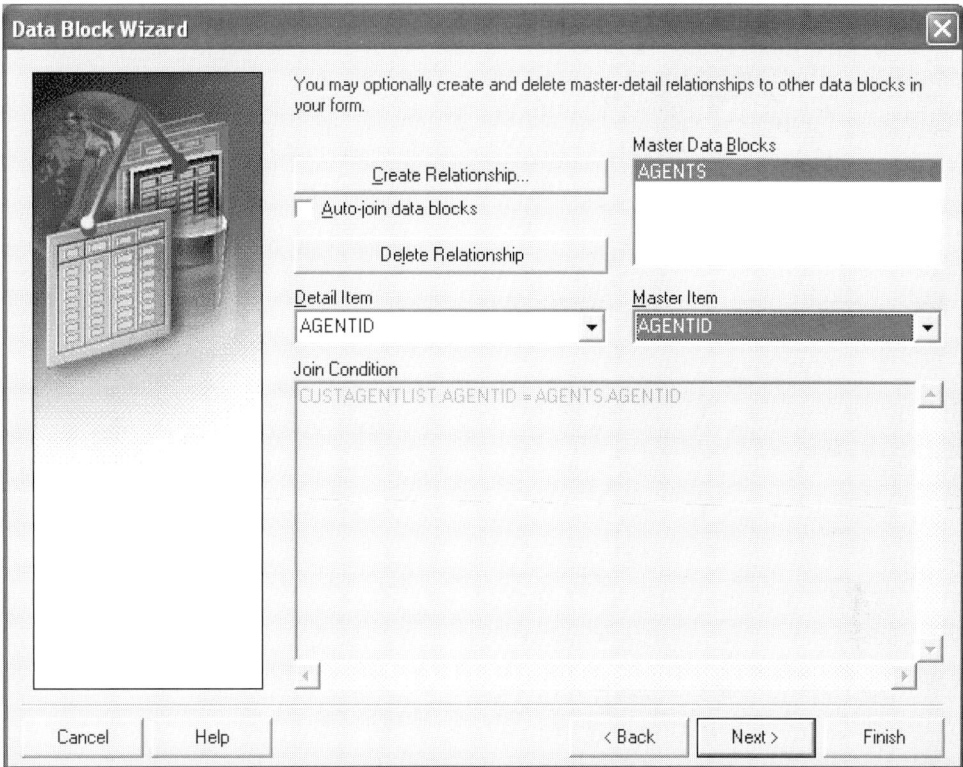

FIGURE 8.28 Creating a relationship for a main/sub form.

make a mistake, click the button to delete the relationship and try again. Your goal is to set the Join Condition so that it says CUSTAGENTLIST.AGENTID = AGENTS.AGENTID. With only two tables, you might be able to reach this outcome using the Auto-join option. Try clicking the **Create Relationship** button. If the Join Condition is created correctly, you can move to the next screen. If the condition is not correct, delete it and try the following manual steps:

1. Uncheck the **Auto-join** data blocks option.
2. Click the **Create Relationships** button.
3. In the pop-up menu, choose the default option to base it on a join.
4. In the pop-up list, choose the **Agents** table.
5. In the Detail Item drop-down list, choose the **AgentID** key column.
6. In the Master Item drop-down list, choose the **AgentID** column.

In the layout wizard, you want to display all columns from the CustAgentList table. Set the initial widths of the ID columns to 48 points. Be sure to choose the tabular option. Then set the number of records to **10** and check the box to display the scroll bar.

7. Once the relationship is correct, be sure to include all of the columns from the CustAgentList table. Later, you can hide the AgentID column by setting its width to zero. Set the number of records to **10** and include the scroll bar.

Figure 8.29 shows the initial design view of the new form. Note that you might want to simplify some of the column headings to make them fit on the display. Save the form

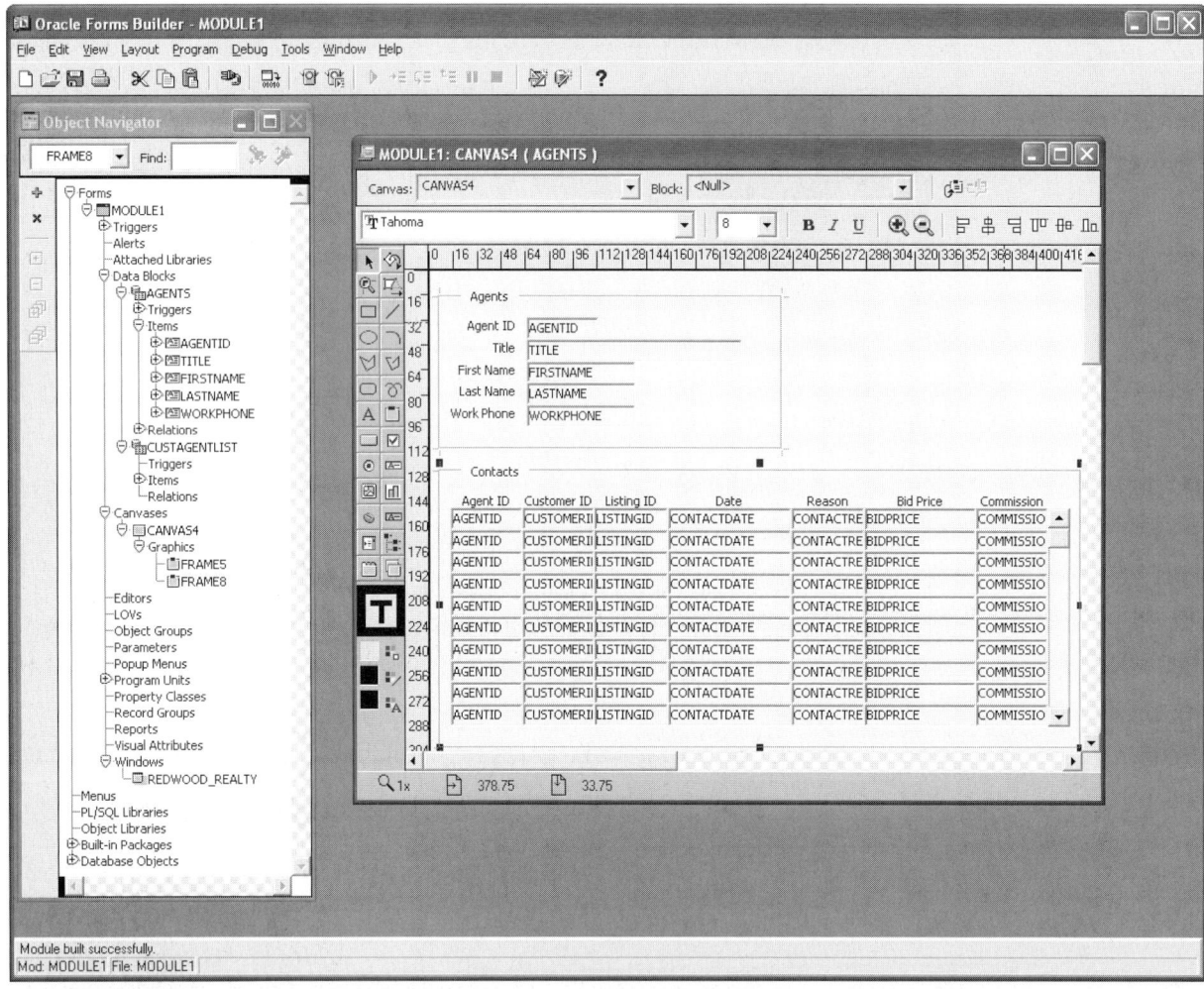

FIGURE 8.29 Initial main form and sub form design.

and run it to test it. Notice that as you select new records for the main form (Agents), the sub form display automatically updates and shows contacts only for that agent. This link works because of the relationship you created between the two data blocks.

ADDING DISPLAY COLUMNS TO THE GRID

Although the form works, it needs some additional changes to make it usable. For example, look closely at the detail section and you will notice that the AgentID value is repeated for every row. Since the AgentID is already on the main form, users do not need to see it on the detail section.

1. Use the properties to change the width of the **AgentID** box to zero and remove the prompt.

Ultimately, you will want to add LOV lookups for the CustomerID and ListingID boxes, but you can do that as an exercise. For now, it would be nice to display the customer name on the grid so agents can see the name of the person involved in the contact instead of just the ID number.

As you did with the single-row form, the key to adding the customer name is to change the data source to a query instead of just the CustAgentTable.

2. Open the Property Palette for the **CustAgentList** data block and change the **Data Source** property to:

(SELECT CUSTAGENTLIST.CUSTOMERID, AGENTID, LISTINGID, CONTACTDATE, CONTACTREASON, BIDPRICE, COMMISSIONRATE, LASTNAME, FIRSTNAME FROM CUSTAGENTLIST INNER JOIN CUSTOMERS ON CUSTAGENTLIST.CUSTOMERID= CUSTOMERS.CUSTOMERID)

Be sure to place the entire SELECT statement in parentheses as shown.

3. Since the query adds the customer last name and first name, you also need to add those two entries to the data block's **Query Data Source Columns** list.

Once the columns are in the data block, you can add them to the form. The easiest approach is to copy an existing column and paste it onto the end of the grid columns. It is best to copy the ContactReason column, because it is a text column instead of numeric, so you will have fewer properties to adjust.

4. Select the **ContactReason** column and use **Ctrl+C** to copy it. Use **Ctrl+V** to paste a copy of the column. This new column will be the **FirstName** column, so you need to set the properties as shown in Table 8.2.
5. Repeat Step 4 to create the LastName column by copying the new FirstName column.
6. You should set the Enable property for the name columns to "No," so users do not attempt to alter those entries.

Run the form and test it. Be sure you can still add rows and edit the existing data.

SETTING FORMAT MASKS

The form generally displays data using the default formats, which are similar to those you get from a query listing. In some cases, you might want to alter the way data is displayed. For example, in the contact listing, you should format the bid price as currency. The process is straightforward; you basically set two properties:

1. For the **BidPrice** item, set the property **Justification** to **End.**
2. Set the **Format Mask** property to **FML99G999G999.**

Setting the property is relatively easy. The challenge is learning the *format mask* options. The easiest approach is to press the **F1** key while the cursor is in the property box. Oracle help will provide you with an explanation of the basic choices. At first glance, the mask for the currency example seems a little odd. First, what does the "L" mean, and why not use a dollar sign instead? The "L" inserts the local currency symbol

TABLE 8.2 Properties to change to add a display column from a query.

Property	Value
Name	FIRSTNAME
Enabled	No
Column Name	FIRSTNAME
Query Only	Yes
Prompt	First Name

TABLE 8.3 Common entries for format masks.

Formatting Character	Display Effect
X	Any character or digit.
A	Only alphabetic characters.
9	Only numbers.
0	Only numbers, and displays leading zeros.
YYYY	Four-digit year.
MM	Two-digit year number.
DD	Day of month.

(such as a dollar sign), choosing the value based on the local computer settings. Similarly, you could use a comma as a thousands separator, but the "G" notation automatically picks up the national currency format and picks the appropriate delimiter. If you want a decimal separator, it is better to use the letter "D" instead of a decimal point. On machines set to U.S. standards, numbers will be displayed as 123,456.78; but on European systems, they would follow national preferences and be displayed as 123.456,78. The FM prefix indicates that numbers can be entered in fill mode, which means that users can enter numbers shorter than the length specified. Most of your format masks should include the FM notation, unless you want to force users to enter an exact number of digits.

As you can see from Table 8.3, you can create format masks for almost any type of data, including numbers, characters, and dates. Using formats for display is useful, but be cautious in how you use them for restricting data entry. For instance, you might be tempted to specify a 5-digit numeric code for ZIP codes (00000). But what would happen if users wanted to enter 9-digit ZIP codes, or postal codes from Canada or Europe that include alphabetic characters and spaces? Similar problems arise with phone numbers.

Summary

You cannot ask users to enter data directly into tables. Relational databases connect tables through data in primary keys, and it is difficult for humans to memorize primary keys and enter them correctly. Instead, you build forms that match the way users work. Users enter data into the forms just as they would in paper-based forms. The forms store the data into the underlying tables. You add features such as a list of values to help users find items by description. The LOV enters the matching primary key value into the desired table, so users do not have to memorize them. You also use check boxes and radio button groups to make it easy for users to enter data easily on the forms. Oracle forms can also be used in query mode to find specific entries or look at filtered rows of data.

To design and build forms, you need to recognize the three primary types of forms: (1) single-row main forms, (2) tabular or grid forms, and (3) main/sub forms that combine elements of the first two types. You can build more complex forms by combining elements of these types. For example, you might build a main form that has two or three separate sub forms to show detailed listings.

Creating forms is relatively easy when you use the data block and layout wizards. The LOV wizard enables you to create a list of values by selecting a few items from the database. Once the basic form has been generated, you can improve the layout and format by setting a few properties of the various items. The layout alignment controls provide several tools to help you organize objects on the form. Just remember to switch the frame's update layout method to manual instead of automatic; otherwise your changes will be discarded.

Remember that each data block on a form can write and edit data in only one table. If you base a data block on a general query, the form is likely to become read-only, where no data can be changed. However, because of the use of primary keys in relational databases, many times you will want to display lookup data from a related table. For example, you often want to show the name of a customer that matches the Customer ID value. Although you have to be careful, you can replace the data block's data source with a query that is enclosed in parentheses. The additional columns, such as customer name, can be displayed on the form; but they cannot be part of the second table's primary key, and they will be read-only columns.

The wizards make it easy to create basic forms, but it takes practice to design and build useful forms. When you begin work on a project, allocate enough time to clean up all of the details so the forms are understandable and easy to use.

Key Terms

- canvas
- check box
- data block
- data block wizard
- format mask
- forms
- grid form
- items (on a form)
- JInitiator
- layout wizard
- list of values (LOV)
- object navigator
- OC4J
- point (font measure)
- property palette
- radio button
- record group
- smart trigger
- tabular form
- tools (for forms)
- trigger

Review

TRUE/FALSE

1. You should always run the layout wizard before the data block wizard.
2. Foreign key columns on forms should have an associated list of values.
3. Tabular forms are commonly used to enter data into tables with many columns.
4. Check boxes are used to select choices that are mutually exclusive.
5. Users can view Oracle forms with any browser and its standard software.

FILL IN

1. Use a frame's _____ property to stop the frame from automatically rearranging the items within the frame.
2. When you create a list of values, the SELECT query for the list is stored in the _____ hierarchy in the object navigator.
3. When you create a radio group using the layout wizard, you have to change the _____ setting for the item that holds the selected value from Text Item to Radio Group.
4. To display a date in common U.S. (1/31/2006), you would use the format mask _____.
5. You create a main form/sub form when two tables have a _____ relationship.

MULTIPLE CHOICE

1. Items on an Oracle form are connected to the database through which object?
   a. Record group
   b. Canvas
   c. Data block
   d. JInitiator
   e. Frame
2. The best type of form to edit a base table with several columns like the Customer table is:
   a. Single row main form
   b. Tabular form
   c. Main form/sub form
   d. LOV form
   e. None of the above

3. The basic sequence of steps for creating a main form with the wizards is:
   a. Layout wizard, edit the form layout, data block wizard
   b. Edit the form canvas, data block wizard, layout wizard
   c. Layout wizard, data block wizard, edit the form layout
   d. Data block wizard, layout wizard, edit the form layout
   e. Edit the form canvas, layout wizard, data block wizard

4. The basic sequence of steps for creating a main/sub form is:
   a. Create a single-row form, add the sub form with a new data block wizard, create a relationship to link them
   b. Create the data block for the main form, create the layout for the main form, create a relationship to link them
   c. Create the layout for the main form, create the layout for the sub form, create the data blocks for both forms, link the data blocks with a relationship
   d. Create the layout for the main form, create the data block for the sub form, link the data block to the main form with a relationship
   e. Create the layout for the main form, create the layout for the sub form, create a list of values to link them

5. You can add lookup columns to a form that retrieves data from a second table by:
   a. Running the list of values wizard
   b. Changing the Query Data Source Name to a carefully built SELECT query
   c. Adding a new canvas
   d. Basing the data block on a query that includes all columns from both tables
   e. Adding a sub form with a many-to-many relationship

Hands-on Exercises

1. Extending the Chapter Case

Several agents at Redwood have asked for a form that shows them the activity on a given listing. They want to search for individual listings and see the basic listing information such as the asking price and listing dates. They also want to see some of the basic data about the property, including the number of bedrooms, bathrooms, and size in square feet. They also want to see the activity on the listing in the form of a list of offers. This form is primarily based on the Listings table, but also needs to display some columns from the Properties table. Additionally, you will need to add a sub form to show the activity, which comes from the CustAgentList table. Basic searching can be handled by the form query system. For instance, agents will be able to enter a maximum price and search for houses that have not yet sold.

1. Start the forms builder and run the data block wizard to create the initial form based on all of the columns in the Listings table.
2. Improve the layout. For example, place the beginning and ending list dates next to each other.
3. Start the data block wizard again and add all of the columns from the CustAgentList table. Make sure you set the relationship based on the ListingID column. Also, make sure you select a Tabular form with seven records and scroll bar. Edit the properties for the data block and set the ORDER BY property to **CONTACTDATE**. Save the form as **ListingActivity**.
4. For the Listings data block, modify the Query Record Source Name so that you can include some of the property data. Test your query in SQL*Plus before you change the property.

   (SELECT ListingID, Listings.PropertyID, ListingAgentID, SaleStatusID, BeginListDate, EndListDate, AskingPrice, HousePhoto, Bedrooms, Bathrooms, Stories, SQFT, YearBuilt FROM Listings INNER JOIN Properties ON Listings.PropertyID=Properties.PropertyID)

5. In the Query Data Source Columns, add **BEDROOMS, BATHROOMS, STORIES, SQFT,** and **YEARBUILT.** Set them as Number data types.
6. Create new text boxes for the five new items. Set the following properties: Name, Enabled (**No**), Database Item (**Yes**), Column Name, Query Only (**Yes**), Prompt.
7. Add an LOV for the Property ID in the main Listings form. Start the LOV wizard. Pick

PropertyID, Address, City, Bedrooms, Bathrooms, and YearBuilt from the Properties table. Resize the columns when asked. Be sure you set the Return value for the PropertyID column to **Listings.PropertyID.** Rename the LOV and Record Group. Save and test the form.

8. Create LOVs for the AgentID box in the Listings form. Then create an LOV for the CustomerID box in the sub form. Be sure to rename the LOVs and record groups. For the AgentID box in the subform, set its List of Values property to the LOV_AGENT you have already created.

9. Run the form. Enter a sample query, such as **>1990** for Year Built. Choose Action/Print to print the form to hand in. Your instructor might also ask you to hand in the file ListingActivity.fmb or to place it in a shared folder for testing.

2. COFFEE MERCHANT

Since you do not want users to enter data directly into tables, you need to create forms for the Coffee Merchant. Your first step is to determine the type of form that best matches each table. Looking at the tables, you see that two of them (States and Countries) are simple lookup tables that rarely change. You can set these up as tabular forms and one person could be responsible for minor changes once a year or so. The Employee data might change more often. More important, it has several columns and managers will rarely need to edit multiple records at one time. So you should design the Employee form as a single-row form. The same argument applies to the Consumers and Inventory tables. That essentially leaves you with the Orders and OrderLines tables. These two tables are common in business applications and have a one-to-many relationship as linked through the OrderID column. You will need a main form and sub form to handle this relationship.

1. Delete and reset the database by running the BuildCoffe.sql file on the student disk.

2. Begin with the easier forms first. Start the forms builder and use the data block and layout wizard to create tabular forms for the States and Countries tables. You will want to use at least twenty rows on each form, and you might consider using a few more rows, but check the size of your display screen and the browser to be sure the number of rows will fit.

3. The single-row main forms are also relatively easy to create. Use the data block wizard to create forms for the Employees and Consumers tables. You should use a radio button group to select the employee gender. Verify the format of the data in that column before you try to create the radio buttons.

4. The Inventory table might be small enough to build as a tabular form, but you could also create it as a single-row form. In an actual company, you would build both and ask the users which method they prefer. In fact, you might leave both forms operational and let the users pick depending on the circumstances. So, build the Inventory form twice: once as a tabular form and once as a single-row form. Be sure to create an LOV to help users pick the CountryID.

5. To build the Orders/OrderLines form, begin by creating a single-row form based on all of the columns in the Orders table. Add LOVs for ConsumerID and EmployeeID.

6. Start the data block wizard again to add the tabular sub form for the OrderLines. Save the entire form as **Orders.**

7. For the Orders data block, create a query for the Query Record Source Name that retrieves all of the columns from the Orders table in addition to the first name, last name, and city of the consumer. Display those three new values on the Orders form as read-only boxes.

8. For the OrderLines data block, create a query for the Query Record Source Name that retrieves all of the columns from the OrderLines table in addition to the Name and Price from the Inventory table. Add those two columns to the sub form display. Format the price columns.

9. Print the Orders form to hand in. Your instructor might also want copies of all of the forms.

3. ROWING VENTURES

You need to create forms to make it easier to enter data into the tables for the Rowing Ventures database. Most database activity takes place at two times: when participants register and after the race. For registration, you will need single-row forms for the Person and Organization tables. Look at the table definitions and you will see a one-to-many relationship between Boat and BoatCrew, so you need to create a main form and sub form for those two tables. Be sure to use an LOV to pick each person serving as crew for the boat. Also, you should display the person's name in the crew listing along with the PersonID. On the main form for the race, use a radio group for the RaceCategory. Write a query to check the actual data before you try to create the radio buttons.

The race results are easiest to enter when they are organized by each race. Someone will set up the race ahead of time and select the boats. That way, the person doing data entry at the event can quickly see each boat and enter only the final times and places. You need to build a main form and sub form using the Race and RaceTimes tables. Be sure to use an LOV for the BoatID in the sub form. Also, display the BowNumber and Organization for each boat. You should create an LOV to select the boats. If you want to include the organization name in the LOV, you need to create a view from the Boat and Organization tables and base the LOV on that view.

4. Broadcloth Clothing

The Broadcloth Clothing case has several tables. It will take time to create all of the forms needed for this case. For now, focus on building just some of the forms by starting with the customer side. Create forms for Customer, CustomerOrder, OrderItem, Item, and Model. You should also create tabular forms for the lookup tables PrimaryLanguage and ColorList. Before you create the Item and Model tables, make sure you understand the relationship between them. Remember that a model refers to a type of clothing, whereas an item is a specific version of that model. For instance, a woman's blouse might be a model, which leads to several item variations based on different colors and sizes. Also, be sure to create LOVs and radio groups or check boxes where appropriate.

CHAPTER 9

CUSTOMIZING FORMS

Learning Objectives

In this chapter, you will learn:
- How to build and modify forms without the wizards.
- How to create and use form triggers.
- How to compute subtotals on forms.
- How to use sequences in forms.
- How to create and use multiple canvases on forms.

SETTING THE FORM STRUCTURE

The Oracle forms wizards are nice. They help you build forms quickly to retrieve and edit data in tables. But sometimes you need a more customized form. The form still might interact with the database; for example, pulling data to fill LOV boxes or displaying selected rows from a query. You could use the wizards to build an initial form and then modify the form to get what you want. But, for some forms, it is easier to start from scratch and build the elements you want. Either way, you should understand the overall structure of an Oracle form so you know what parts to modify, and know how to add the new elements you need.

Redwood Realty wants a simplified search page, so that realtors can look for listings on the basis of common features, such as the number of bedrooms or bathrooms and price. Yes, you might consider training the realtors to write queries to find the desired listings. But, realtors are often busy and it makes more sense to build an easy-to-use form that gives them exactly what they want without requiring extensive training. Before leaping to the forms builder, you should sketch out the basic elements of the form. It is also a good idea to show the sketch to potential users to get their ideas and feedback. It is much easier to add items and make corrections at the start of the design. You might change the page layout later to make things fit better on the screen, but moving items around is easy. Rewriting queries and changing the form's logic is time-consuming. Figure 9.1 shows the basic ideas for the form.

To create custom forms you need to understand the structure of Oracle forms. You can use the wizards to create the overall structure for you, but to modify a form, you still must understand the various pieces. Figure 9.2 highlights the main components of the

414 Introduction to Oracle

Bedrooms	2 3 4 5 or more
Bathrooms	1 1.5 2 2.5 3 4 or more
Sq Feet	1000 2000 3000 4000 or more
Age/Built	1900 1970 1980 1990 2000 or later
Price	Min: Max:
Sale Status	For sale Pending Sold

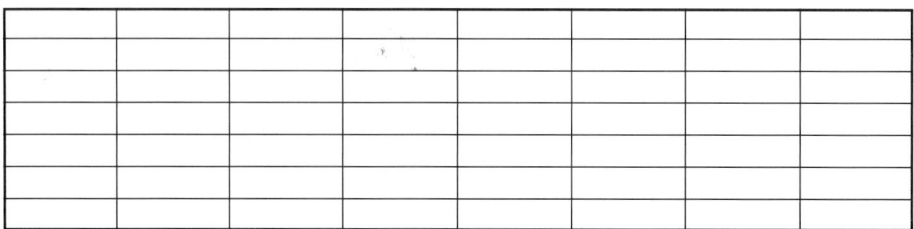

Matches

FIGURE 9.1 The initial sketch of the search form.

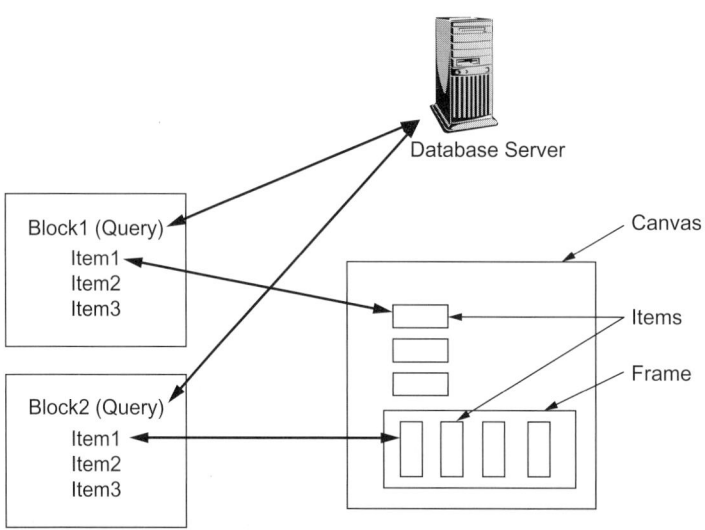

FIGURE 9.2 The structure of Oracle forms.

forms process: (1) the canvas, (2) data blocks, and (3) items. We introduced these concepts in Chapter 8, using forms wizards, but now we will examine them in more detail.

The role of the canvas is to hold items that are displayed to the users. Items can include simple boilerplate text such as titles and even images. More important, forms include a variety of items that can be linked to the database to show and edit content stored in the tables. A text box is the simplest database item type because it shows the data directly. You can also include checkboxes, radio buttons, and list boxes. Every form has at least one canvas, and you add items to the canvas by selecting them in the toolbar and positioning them on the canvas. You use the property palette to set the appearance of the canvas (e.g., background color) and control the items.

Frames are used to group items together. This grouping can be purely for aesthetic reasons and is not related to the underlying data tables. For example, automatic layout in a frame makes it easy to align groups of related textboxes quickly simply by resizing the frame. Frames are often used to group related radio box items visually. They are also used to separate data into sections. For example, they are useful to highlight sub form grids.

The canvas and frames are just basic tools to control the layout. You also must connect the form to the database to retrieve and store data, using data blocks. A data block contains a link to the database. The link can be directly into a table, or it can be to a stored view or even a stored procedure. That depends on whether you want the form to update the data in the database. If so, you should connect directly to a table whenever possible. Views and queries are useful when you want to use the form to display related data from multiple tables and do not need to alter that data.

The issue of retrieving or altering data from multiple tables drives many of your form designs in Oracle. The simple rule of thumb is that anytime you want to write data to the database, there must be a data block tied to that specific table. Just remember that each data block can update data in only one table. So, if you want to update data in multiple tables, you will need one data block for each table. If you only want to retrieve and display data, you can save a view or write a query within the data block to get any data you want—you just cannot update it.

One of the tricky parts to Oracle forms is that each data item you place on the form is connected to a single data block. You can specify or change the data block assignment by setting the data block property for the item. However, there is an easier method. Before you place a new item on a form, set the currently active data block by choosing it from the drop-down list at the top-right corner of the design form. This approach makes it easy to add multiple items to a data block quickly.

CREATING A CANVAS AND SIMPLE DATA BLOCK

The initial steps to creating the Redwood Realty search firm are straightforward:

1. Start Forms Builder and create a new form. Rename the module to **Search**.
2. Expand the Windows section and rename Window1 to **Search**, open the property palette, and set the title to **Redwood Realty**.
3. Add a new canvas to the form by highlighting the Canvases entry in the object navigator and clicking the Add (+) button. Rename it as **Search_Canvas**. You might want to set its background color, since the default values are a little dark. Try white.
4. Add a new data block to hold the basic search choice items. Select the Data Blocks entry in the Object Navigator and click the **Add** button. Be sure to choose the option to "Build a new data block manually," instead of trying to use the wizard. This data block will not connect to the database, so change properties to set its Name to **Search_Block**, and Database Data Block to **No**.

You now have a simple form with an empty canvas and data block where you can add the main search selection items. This first data block is not connected to the database because users will simply choose from the predefined list of items. Once the choices have been made, you will use a query to retrieve the matching values. But, these items will be displayed in a new data block that you will create in a few minutes. For now, concentrate on building the relatively easy search item choices.

Most of the items for the top part of the search form are relatively easy because they are not tied to the database. To control the user selections, each main item will be built as a group of radio buttons. That way the user can select only one entry for each category. First, create a title by adding a simple text label at the top of the form.

The procedure for creating the radio button groupings is similar for each of the four main categories (bedrooms, bathrooms, square feet, and year built). The easiest way to start is to add a frame to display the choices. The hard part is naming everything consistently as you create the items.

1. Create a frame. Name it **FRM_BEDROOMS** in case you need to find it later. Set its label property to **Minimum Bedrooms**.
2. Add a radio button inside the new frame. As the first button in a new category, make sure it is assigned to a new radio group. Use the object navigator to rename the radio group to **RADIO_BEDROOMS**.
3. Set the properties for the new radio button: Name=**RAD_BED_2**, Label=**2**, Radio Button Value=**2**, and Width=**20**.
4. Copy and paste the radio button to create a copy. Move it and set its properties as value 3. Do the same thing so you have buttons for 2, 3, 4, and 5 bedrooms. Double-check the labels and values. Make sure all of the buttons fit within the frame.
5. Select each of the radio buttons, and use Layout/Align Components to space them equally horizontally and align their bottom edges.
6. Use the object navigator to open the properties for the radio group. Set the Initial Value=**3**.

Once you have created the radio group for bedrooms, repeat the process for bathrooms, square feet, and year built. Be sure to choose the option to create a new radio group for the first entry in each category, then assign the subsequent values to that group. Also, be sure to set an appropriate initial value for the radio group. After the first couple of categories, you will find the process is tedious, but it will help you remember how to create them in the future.

The next step is to add the minimum and maximum price as text boxes. You might consider continuing with radio groups or even a list box. However, price is flexible and subjective, so it will be difficult to create categories that work well. Better to just leave them as input boxes. However, to make them easier to use, be sure to set the initial value and maximum and minimum properties.

1. Add a text box and name it **TXT_MinPrice**.
2. Set its properties: Data Type=**Number**, Initial Value=**0**, Lowest Allowed Value=**0**, Highest Allowed Value=**10000000**, Prompt=**Minimum Price**, Prompt Attachment Offset=**7**.
3. Create a similar box for **TXT_MaxPrice**.

The Sale Status issue is slightly different. The data tables contain a SaleStatus table that holds a list of the possible entries. Each of the three possible items is keyed by a number. For example, 101 means the property is for sale. You could use another radio group to handle this situation. However, the agents will rarely want to change the value, so a radio group would take up precious screen space. So, create a list box instead and set the initial value to the 101/For Sale option. Also, as you will see in a later section, you can load the options using a database query, so the form values can be updated automatically simply by adding or changing values in the table. Creating the list box is straightforward:

1. Add a list box to the canvas and name it **LIST_SaleStatus**.
2. Use the property palette to set the Elements in List to the three entries. Be sure to enter the matching List Item Value for each entry: **For Sale** is **101**, **Pending** is **102**, **Sold** is **103**. Set the Initial Value to **101**.

CHAPTER 9   Customizing Forms   **417**

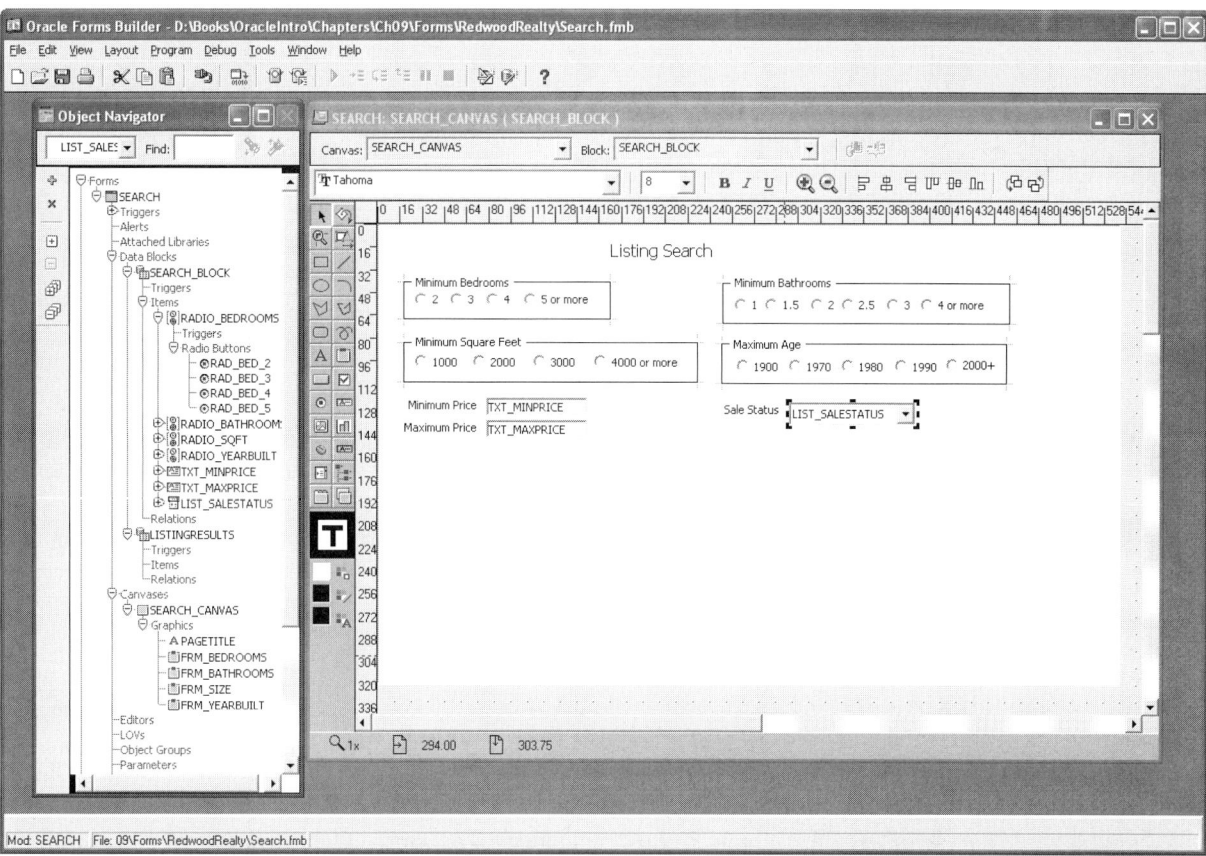

FIGURE 9.3   Initial canvas, data block, and items for search form.

3. Set Prompt=**Sale Status**, Prompt Attachment Offset=**7**, and you will probably have to reset the background color to match the color of your canvas (white).

As you are building the form, be sure to save it often. You should create a folder to hold forms for this chapter and save this form (Search.fmb) in that folder. Figure 9.3 shows a version of the initial layout. Your layout might be different, but be sure to leave enough space at the bottom of the form to display the matching records.

CREATING A DATA BLOCK FOR A QUERY

You should test the current version of the search form to make sure the radio buttons work correctly. However, at the moment, the form does not actually do anything. The next step is to create a query that retrieves matching data and displays it in a grid on the form. Since the query must connect to the database, you will have to create a new data block. However, to simplify some of the work with the data block, you should first create a view that retrieves the columns of data you want to display. You need to create a view in SQL:

```
CREATE VIEW ListingResults as
SELECT Listings.ListingID, Listings.PropertyID, Listings.SaleStatusID,
Listings.AskingPrice, Listings.EndListDate, Properties.Address,
Properties.City, Properties.State, Properties.Zipcode,
Properties.Bedrooms, Properties.Bathrooms, Properties.SqFt,
Properties.YearBuilt, Agents.LastName, SaleStatus.SaleStatus
```

```
FROM Listings INNER JOIN Properties ON
Listings.PropertyID=Properties.PropertyID
INNER JOIN Agents ON Agents.AgentID=Listings.ListingAgentID
INNER JOIN SaleStatus ON SaleStatus.SaleStatusID=Listings.SaleStatusID;
```

At a minimum, include the columns you will use to set the selection criteria in the WHERE clause, so you will need at least the Listings and Properties tables. You can add more columns if users want to see them. However, it is hard to fit more than 10 columns onto a typical display screen. Notice that there is no WHERE clause or ORDER BY clause on the query. These will be handled later through the data block. Test the view to make sure it works. For example: SELECT * FROM ListingResults WHERE rownum<5.

Now that you have a query in the database to retrieve the data, add a data block to the form that will hold the query and serve as the conduit for the data:

1. Add a new data block to the form manually. Name it **ListingResults**, and make sure that it falls below the SEARCH_BLOCK data block in the object navigator. The order in the navigator controls the tab order on the final form, and you want the SEARCH_BLOCK to be first. You can drag blocks and items around in the object navigator to change the order.

2. In the property palette, make sure the Database Data Block=**Yes**, Query Allowed=**Yes**, and Query Data Source Type=**Table**.

3. Enter the Query Data Source Name as a query that pulls the data from the view you created. The entire statement must be in parentheses: **(SELECT ListingID, PropertyID, SaleStatusID, SaleStatus, AskingPrice, EndListDate, Address, City, State, Zipcode, Bedrooms, Bathrooms, SqFt, YearBuilt, LastName FROM ListingResults)**

4. Open the columns box in the Query Data Source Columns property. Enter all fifteen of the column names into the list. Be sure to set the correct data type and length for each column.

5. Turn off the edit options in the data block properties. Insert Allowed=**No**, Update Allowed=**No**, Delete Allowed=**No**. Set the Number of Records Displayed=**7**, and Show Scrollbar=**Yes**.

Step 4 is tedious, but take your time to ensure you do not make any mistakes. Figure 9.4 shows the data entry form you will use. If you make a mistake typing a column name, it might be hard to find later. Once the data block has the query and columns defined, you can add the items to canvas. Be sure to create a frame first, and set the default data block to the new ListingResults data block.

FIGURE 9.4 Query Data Source Columns data entry.

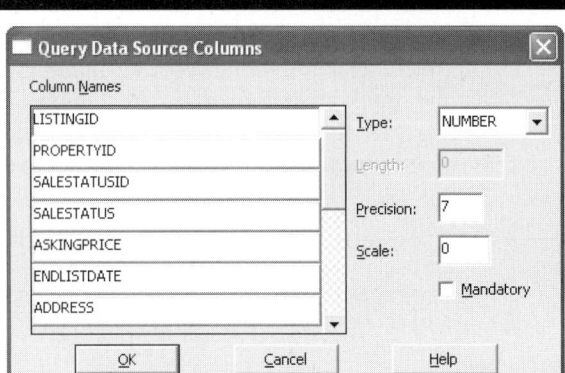

1. Set the default data block to ListingsResults in the layout designer.
2. Add a large frame to the bottom of the form. Set its properties. Name=**FRM_ListingResults**, Layout Data Block=**ListingResults**, Layout Style=**Tabular**, Number of Records Displayed=**7**, Show Scroll Bar=**Yes**, Frame Title=**Listing Results**, Background Color=**white**.

Now you can add text items inside the new frame to display the various columns. If you are careful with the widths, you can fit 10 columns of data into a standard window. Sometimes it is easiest to add a couple of items and then copy and paste them to get the others.

1. Add a text item box inside the new frame. It should automatically expand to seven rows.
2. Set its properties to match the first column (ListingID). Name=**ListingID**, Data Type=**Number**, Maximum Length=**5**, Database Item=**Yes**, Column Name=**LISTINGID**, Width=**48**, Background Color=**white**, Prompt=**Listing ID**, Prompt Attachment Edge=**Top**.
3. Repeat the steps to add display items for: **ListingID, PropertyID, SaleStatus, AskingPrice, Bedrooms, Bathrooms, SQFT, YearBuilt, City,** and agent **Lastname**.

Figure 9.5 shows the design of the form at this point. Notice the truncation of the prompts and the small widths used on the text items to ensure that everything fits across the screen. You might consider leaving out the PropertyID and ListingID

FIGURE 9.5 The intermediate search form.

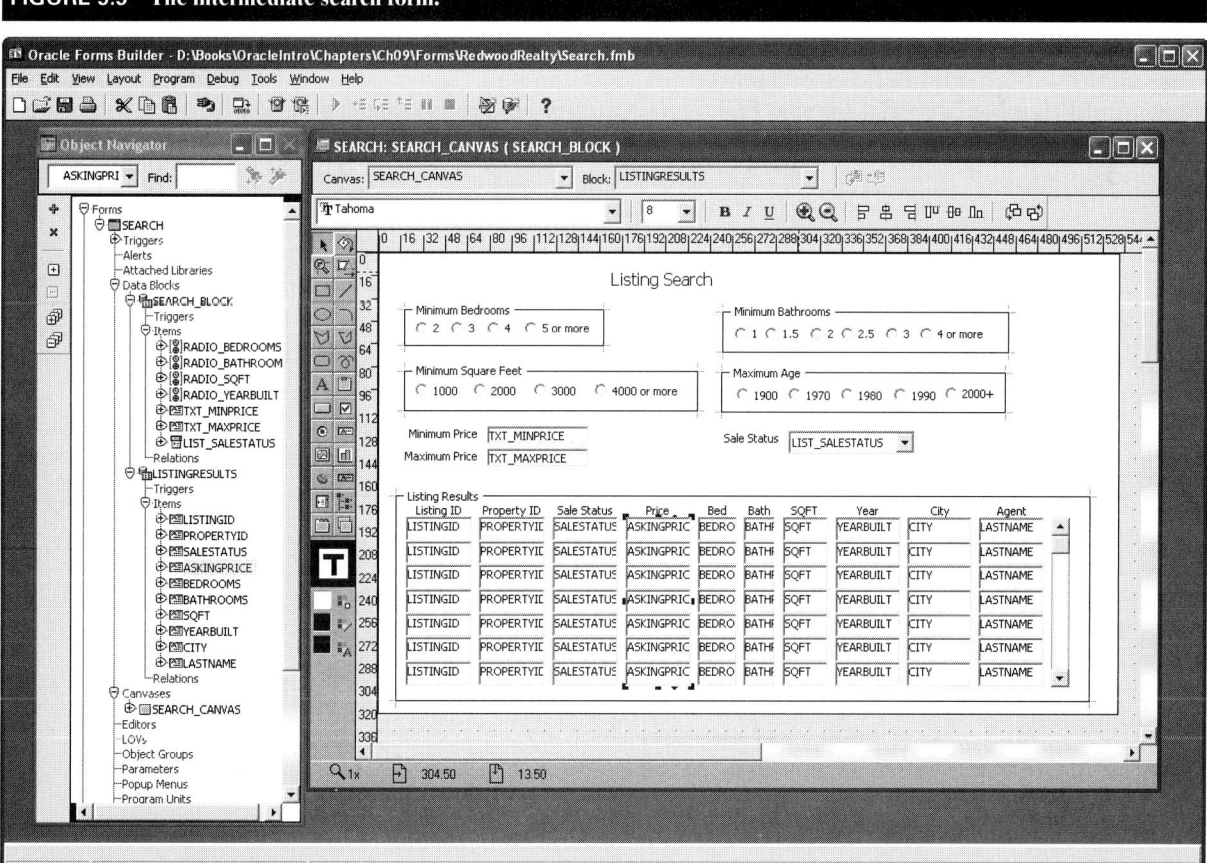

columns. However, they can be useful if the agent wants to open those forms and find the detailed information about those specific items. Ultimately, it would be better to include some type of link directly from this form that opens the other forms and displays the full detail simply by clicking a button or link.

MAKING THE SEARCH WORK

At this point, the form is almost complete. You could run it and test it, but you need a way to actually run the search. Note that the form itself will be running on the user's computer. Performing the search requires sending a query to the server, retrieving the results, and displaying them in the new grid. Most of this work is handled by the data block. However, you face an important user interface question: When should the form retrieve the data and refresh the grid? In some forms, this question is difficult to answer, and you might have to experiment with several event options to find the best one for the users. On the search form, the answer is relatively easy. Right now, you have no way of knowing when the user is finished making choices. So, you have to add a button that the user will click to indicate the choices have been made. Add a command button, and make sure it is on the Search_Block data block. Label it **Search** so the users know what it is supposed to do.

Before looking at code that the button requires to perform, there is one more important step. The data block query currently retrieves all data from the ListingResults view. You must modify that query so that it retrieves data that meets the conditions specified on the form. Open the property palette for the ListingResults data block. In the Database section, find the ***WHERE clause*** property. You want to add a relatively long statement that compares the query columns to the items on the form:

```
(ASKINGPRICE BETWEEN :SEARCH_BLOCK.TXT_MINPRICE AND
:SEARCH_BLOCK.TXT_MAXPRICE)
AND (BEDROOMS >= :SEARCH_BLOCK.RADIO_BEDROOMS)
AND (BATHROOMS >= :SEARCH_BLOCK.RADIO_BATHROOMS)
AND (SQFT >= :SEARCH_BLOCK.RADIO_SQFT)
AND (YEARBUILT >= :SEARCH_BLOCK.RADIO_YEARBUILT)
AND (SALESTATUSID = :SEARCH_BLOCK.LIST_SALESTATUS)
```

The clause is long because of the number of columns to be tested. All of them follow a similar format. You might want to enter just one condition to begin with, so you get a feel for the process and can test it. If you make a mistake typing a WHERE clause, the form will display a short error message, and you will have to go back and proofread the statement carefully. For now, look at the price statement: (AskingPrice BETWEEN :Search_Block.TXT_MinPrice AND :Search_Block.TXT_MaxPrice). First, note that the clause is enclosed in parentheses because more statements will be added later. The parentheses ensure that this statement is treated as a single statement and not mixed with the others. Second, pay careful attention to the syntax. Notice that you have to specify the name of the data block (Search_Block) when referring to the text item, because the text items are in a different data block. Also, note the use of the colon (:) to signify that the system pick up the values of the external variables and not simply look for column names. Once you understand this syntax, you can see that the WHERE clause is just like any other SQL statement. When the query is executed, the forms processor will pick up the values on the form and insert them into the WHERE clause variables, then retrieve the matching rows of data.

While you are looking at the properties of the data block, you should also specify the ORDER BY Clause. For now, just enter **AskingPrice**, since most people will want to see the results sorted by price. Later, you can think about ways to let users choose how they want the data sorted. One of the nice things about the WHERE and

ORDER BY properties is that you can write programming code that changes these values in response to user actions.

The final step to getting the form working is to write the trigger code for the Search button. Notice that because so much of the work is handled by the WHERE clause, the code for the button is simple. You assign the code to a form trigger. The most common trigger for a button is the When-Button-Pressed event. Right-click the button and select the smart trigger options and choose this event. You will then be able to enter code into a trigger window:

```
GO_BLOCK('LISTINGRESULTS');
EXECUTE_QUERY;
```

The first line (GO_BLOCK) tells the forms processor to use the ListingResults data block. Remember that the Search button is located on the Search_Block, but you want the results displayed in the ListingResults block, so you have to tell the system to switch the active block. The second line (EXECUTE_QUERY) tells the system to run the query stored in the ListingResults data block. First, the forms processor will pick up the current values on the form and insert them into the WHERE clause. Then it will retrieve the matching rows and place them in the item boxes on the form.

Test the form to ensure that it works. Change some of the search options and verify that only matching values are returned. Note that if you choose some extreme options (for example, $20,000 houses with 5 bedrooms), you might not find any matching properties. Figure 9.6 shows the results of one query, but your results can be different.

Think about what you have accomplished in this section. You created a form from scratch, without using the wizards. This form contains several items that make it easy for the user to choose properties. A data query then retrieves property listings that match the desired conditions and displays the results in a short listing. To create this connection, you added a data block based on the query. You built a WHERE clause that inserts the values on the form into the conditions. The search button contains two lines of code that execute the query. The data block handles all of the details of connecting to the database, transferring the query, and returning the matching rows.

DESIGNING FORM TRIGGERS

As you have seen from several examples, form triggers are useful tools. They enable you to control the actions that take place. So far, you have been able to use one or two lines of code to tie form sections together and execute queries. The code is capable of far more powerful actions, but do you really need to use form triggers? You can understand the use of the code if you remember that triggers are to make life easier for the user. For example, does Redwood Realty truly need the search form? Agents could write SQL queries and retrieve any data they want. Well, you have worked with queries and you have seen the search form. For a real estate agent with less database training, which method is easier to use? One of the greatest problems with SQL queries is that they often return rows of data, but you must be careful to ensure that the rows truly answer the questions you want to ask. With the form and the programming code, as the developer you write the query and double-check its results. The details are hidden from the user. So, your goal is to make life easier for the users and reduce the potential errors. Whenever possible, you will use queries and built-in form capabilities to accomplish this task. However, sometimes you need to use a few lines of code.

There are two keys to understanding form triggers: (1) they are tied to events that take place on the form, such as a user clicking a button, or a key press; and (2) you can write almost any PL/SQL code you want in response to an event. This second issue

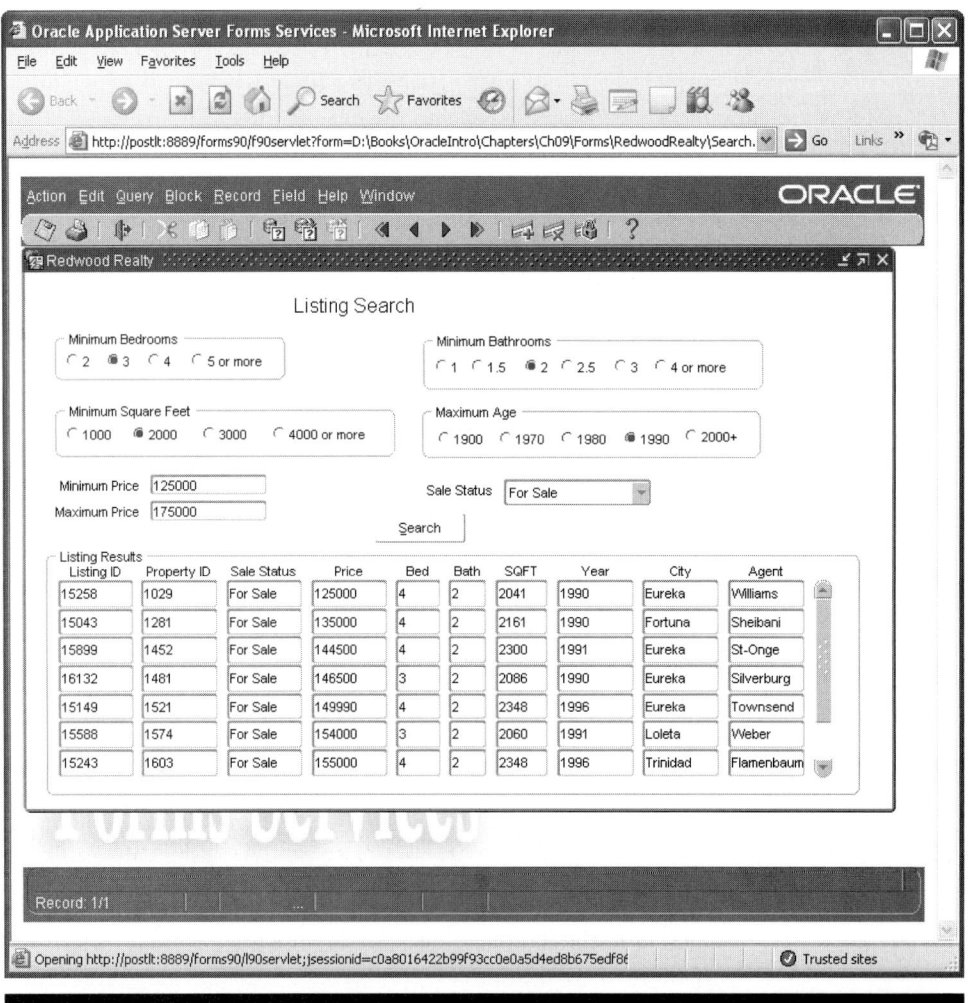

FIGURE 9.6 Search form results.

means that you have to know the basic ideas about writing code, and should learn some of the functions and options that Oracle provides. The first issue means that you have to be familiar with the various possible events on a form. Sometimes, the most difficult question you have to answer is deciding which form event to use.

DEFINING FORM EVENTS

In a visual form environment, it makes sense to attach code to various events. When some event happens, you want your code to perform some task that might analyze the input data, execute a query, start a new form, or send a message to someone. With some experience, you can find hundreds of other possibilities. One of the key strengths of a forms development environment is the number of event triggers that it supports. Oracle forms support dozens of events at the form, block, and item levels. The good news is that you will never use all of the triggers on one form. There should be multiple triggers at each level, because that is how you control when your code is executed. If you use a trigger at too low of a level (for instance tied to a key press on an item), your code will run too often. Running your code too often not only

Form	Block	Item
1. Pre-Logon		
2. On-Logon		
3. Post-Logon		
4. Pre-Form		
	5. When-Create-Record	
	6. Pre-Block	
	7. Pre-Record	
		8. Pre-Text-Item
9. When-New-Form-Instance		
	10. When-New-Block-Instance	
	11. When-New-Record-Instance	
		12. When-New-Item-Instance
		1. Post-Text-Item
	2. Post-Record	
	3. Post-Block	
4. Post-Form		
5. On-Rollback		
6. Pre-Logout		
7. On-Logout		
8. Post-Logout		

Enter: rows 1–12. Exit: rows 1–8.

FIGURE 9.7 Sequence of primary trigger events.

degrades performance, but it can result in wrong answers and bad data. If you place your code too high up in the hierarchy, it might never run at all, or might run only once when the form loads. So, more options give you a better ability to fine-tune exactly when your code executes.

Of course, the problem is that with dozens of events, it takes you longer to figure out exactly where to place your code. To help you understand the choices, Figure 9.7 shows the *sequence of primary events* that are triggered when a user enters and exits a form. The form builder will show you the complete listing of events, but the list is sorted alphabetically. You can identify the sequence of some of the triggers based on their names. Triggers labeled "PRE" occur before some major event occurs, and those labeled "POST" arise after the event. Hence, PRE-FORM indicates when the form is being opened; and POST-FORM shows when the form has been closed. Check Figure 9.10 to see when block and item events occur relative to form events.

To see an event in action, it helps to look at another tool in Oracle forms: the *Alert* message. An alert is a small form that pops up on the screen with a short message and a couple of buttons. Some people use them in applications to display messages to users. However, those alert boxes are annoying to users, so you should avoid them. They require the user to deal with the message before continuing. Instead, you would normally just display simple messages in a label or text item on the form and let users deal with issues when they want. But, once in a while a major error arises, and you have no choice but to display an alert. Or, as in this case, they are useful for debugging, so you can pop up a temporary message to see which trigger is being executed.

To demonstrate part of the event sequence, create a new form for the Agents and add three new alert forms:

1. Use the data block and layout wizards to create a simple form for the Agents table.
2. Click the Alerts entry in the object navigator and click the Add (+) button.
3. Set the properties to display a simple message. Name=**ALERT_TRIGGERS**, Title=**Trigger Fired**, Message=**test**, Alert Style=**Note**.
4. Create three triggers with almost the same code, changing the name of the message for each event:

```
DECLARE
    btn NUMBER;
BEGIN
    SET_ALERT_PROPERTY('ALERT_TRIGGER',ALERT_MESSAGE_TEXT,
        'Pre-Form trigger event');
    btn := SHOW_ALERT('ALERT_TRIGGER');
END;
```

5. Start the form and execute a query. Record the order of the events based on the alerts.

Technically, the Show_Alert function returns the value of the button clicked by the user. In this small example, you do not need to know which button was selected, so the value is not used. However, since it is a function, the syntax requires that you retrieve the value. Figure 9.8 shows the alert you receive when you execute a query on the form to display data. One of the interesting things you should see in this process is that the Post-Item event will fire again when you close the form. In fact, you will receive a Post-Item alert every time you change to a new row of data or move the cursor out of the Agent ID text item box. You might ask yourself why you would need an event to trigger every time a user moves out of a text box. You might consider using it to write code to test any changes made by the user. However, the Post-Text-Item trigger has one drawback for that purpose: it fires any time the user exits the text box—even if no changes were made. On the other hand, Oracle text items include the When-Validate-Item trigger that fires only when the user makes changes to the item and leaves the text box. If you are unsure about which event to use to handle a specific situation, you can use this trick of building alerts for each event. Then test your form as a user and see which event consistently fires when you need it. If no single event is perfect, you might have to write code for two or more events. But the situation is a little trickier when you want to share data between them.

CREATING AND EDITING TRIGGERS

Once you understand the sequence of events and know which event you want to use, you have to write the actual code for the trigger. Creating or editing a new trigger is relatively painless. To create a new trigger, find the Triggers listing in the object navigator, right-click the entry, select the Smart Triggers entry from the pop-up menu, and choose the desired event. Enter your code in the editing window. To edit an existing trigger, you can follow the same steps, or you can double-click the trigger's icon in the object navigator.

The more interesting question about creating triggers is what you can write for code within the window and how it is structured. The nice thing about Oracle form triggers is that the syntax and structure are similar to the code used in data triggers.

CHAPTER 9 Customizing Forms **425**

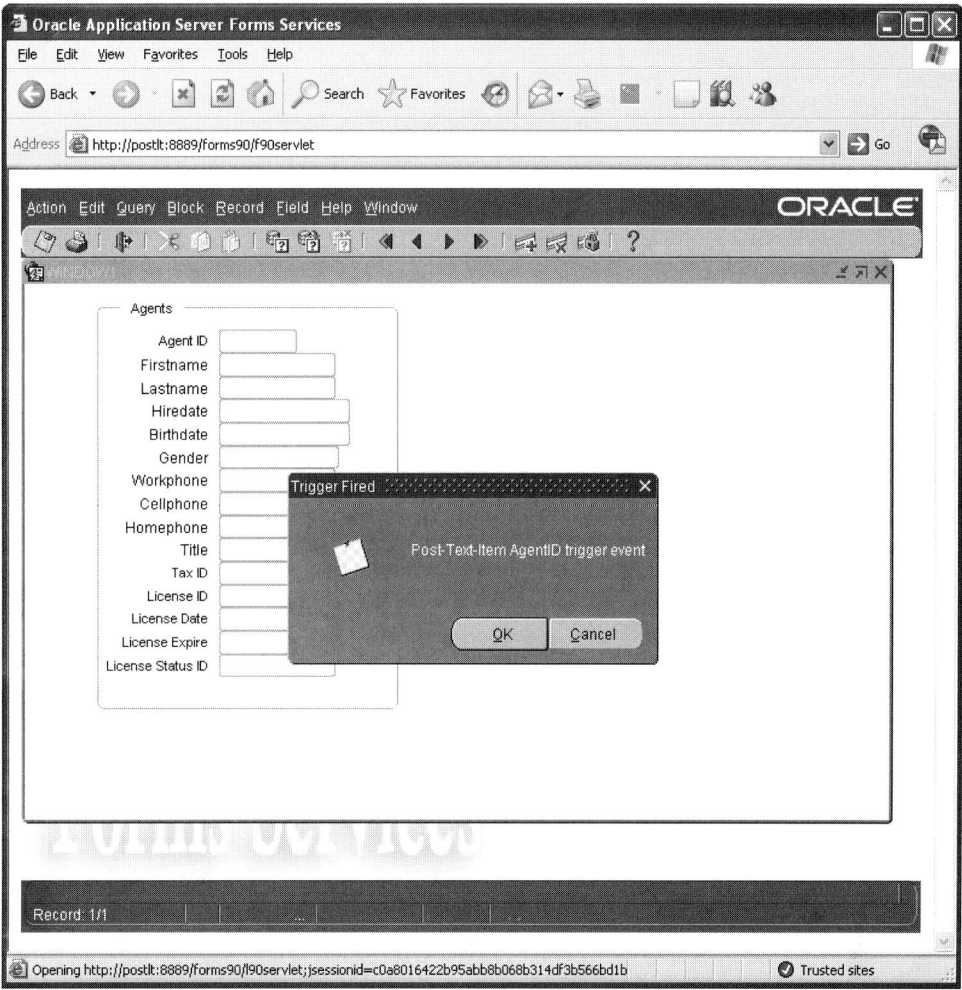

FIGURE 9.8 First firing of the Post-Item trigger.

Remember that a data trigger is created and stored in the database for events (Update, Insert, and Delete) that happen to data. The primary structure of a forms trigger is:

```
DECLARE
      --definitions of variables
BEGIN
      --PL/SQL code
      --usually with standard functions
EXCEPTION
      --statements executed if an error occurs
END;
```

Following good coding practices, all of your variables should be defined within the declaration section. The earlier examples show that the syntax is straightforward. Just list the variable name followed by its data type. Remember to end each statement with a semicolon (;).

PL/SQL code follows a fairly typical structure and syntax. Consult the PL/SQL User's Guide and Reference document available from Oracle for a complete listing of

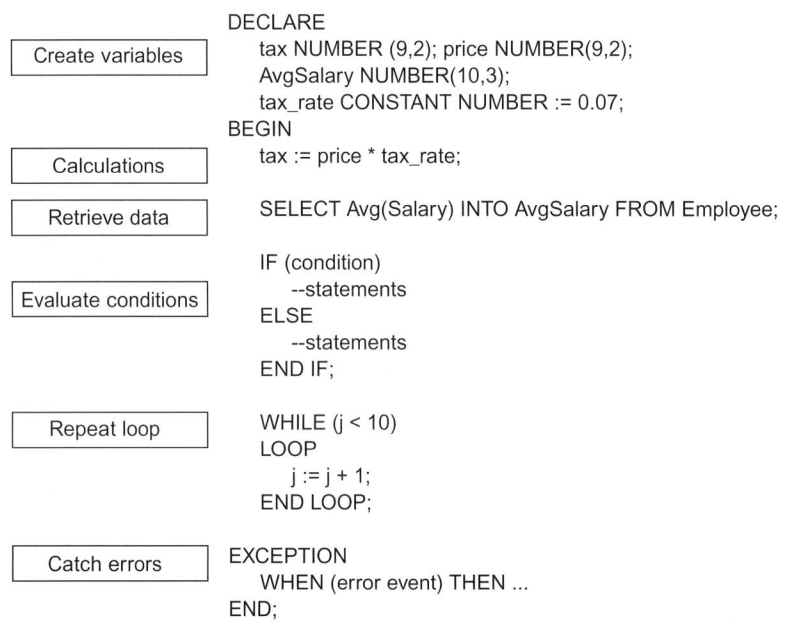

FIGURE 9.9 Common PL/SQL commands.

the syntax and structure of PL/SQL code and an alphabetical listing of commands. Essentially, you can use IF/ELSE/END statements and common looping statements such as WHILE ... LOOP and FOR ... LOOP. The common programming tasks to perform are: (1) create variables and perform calculations, (2) retrieve data from the database, (3) evaluate conditional statements, (4) perform loops, and (5) catch errors. Figure 9.9 shows the PL/SQL syntax for these actions.

Note that you require the colon-equals (:=) statement to assign values to a variable. Also notice that you can use SELECT ... INTO to retrieve single-valued items from a database query directly into a program variable. You can use basic DML commands (Insert, Update, and Delete) to transfer data from the form directly to the database. Also remember to use a leading colon when referring to items on the form, such as :Search_block.Txt_MinPrice.

Basic DML commands and SELECT INTO work particularly well to alter or retrieve a single piece of data from the database. To retrieve or edit multiple rows of data, create a cursor and step through the resulting query line by line. The Redwood Realty search form can use this capability for a specific problem. Retrieve the form in the editor and look again at the list item for SaleStatus. Remember that you entered the three choices (For Sale, Pending, and Sold) by hand. Currently, these items are *hard coded* into the form, which means that to change or add values, someone has to edit the form. That process might not seem too difficult now, but think about two years down the road when there are dozens of forms and this data might be used in several different places. Someone will have to find each usage, change the form, recompile the form, and redistribute the application. What is the probability that a new person can make all of these changes without creating additional errors or problems?

Because the descriptions and ID values already exist in a database table (SaleStatusID), your form should retrieve those values. Then, if someone decides to change them or add new ones later, they can just edit the values in the table—with a simple administration form. When this search form runs, it will pick up the current values and descriptions and display them in the form. So, how do you get the values from the table and insert them into the list box?

Begin by asking yourself **when** the list box values need to be loaded. The easiest answer is when the form opens, which means you must write your code in the Pre-Form trigger. The code to read data from a query is somewhat unique. It requires the use of a database cursor that enables the code to step through the query results one row at a time. The overall logic of this small program is: (1) set up the query to retrieve data from the SaleStatus table, (2) loop through the query results, and (3) add the description and ID value to the list box. Setting up a query and a cursor is defined in the PL/SQL documentation and is straightforward. The real trick to this code is finding a built-in function that makes it easy to assign the values to the list item. The ADD_LIST_ELEMENT command is one solution using cursors:

```
DECLARE
    CURSOR cStatus IS
        SELECT SaleStatusID, SaleStatus
        FROM SaleStatus
        ORDER BY SaleStatusID;
BEGIN
    CLEAR_LIST('LIST_SALESTATUS');
    FOR stats IN cStatus
    LOOP
        IF (stats.SaleStatusID <> 101) THEN
            ADD_LIST_ELEMENT('LIST_SALESTATUS',99,
                stats.SaleStatus, TO_CHAR(stats.SaleStatusID));
        END IF;
    END LOOP;
END;
```

The cursor is defined in the DECLARE section and it simply specifies the SELECT query. Note that you will usually want to specify an ORDER BY clause to get the data in the proper order. The body of the code uses an internal function to clear data that might already be in the list. The main section of the code is a loop that looks at each row in the cursor query. The ADD_LIST_ELEMENT function is an internal function that makes it easy to add data to the list. The parameters are: (1) the name of the list item, (2) the sequence order for the new entry, where 99 is used to add to the end of the list, (3) the descriptive entry to be displayed to the user, and (4) the ID value returned when the user picks the specified row, converted to a character value with the TO_CHAR function.

To test the new function, open the properties for the list item and remove all of the entries except the 101/For Sale default entry. To set the default value, you must have the default item in the list. When you look closely at the code in Figure 9.14, you will see that the default value causes one other difficulty. The Clear_List command does not remove a default entry. Consequently, the code to load the list box uses an IF statement to ensure that this entry is not listed twice. If you are concerned that the default description might change over time, you could write more sophisticated code to remove the initial value setting with the SET_ITEM_PROPERTY function. If you look through the Oracle functions, you will see that you could simplify the list element code by using the function POPULATE_GROUP_WITH_QUERY to retrieve the data from the database, and POPULATE_LIST to transfer the retrieved group data to the list in one statement. But, you first have to create a record group to hold the data, and writing the code with a cursor makes it easier to filter out the default value to prevent duplicates.

Your trigger code can be as complex as you need to solve a particular problem. Some code might run to hundreds of lines. However, it is usually best to keep the code as simple as possible. If you do find that the code is becoming complex, you should

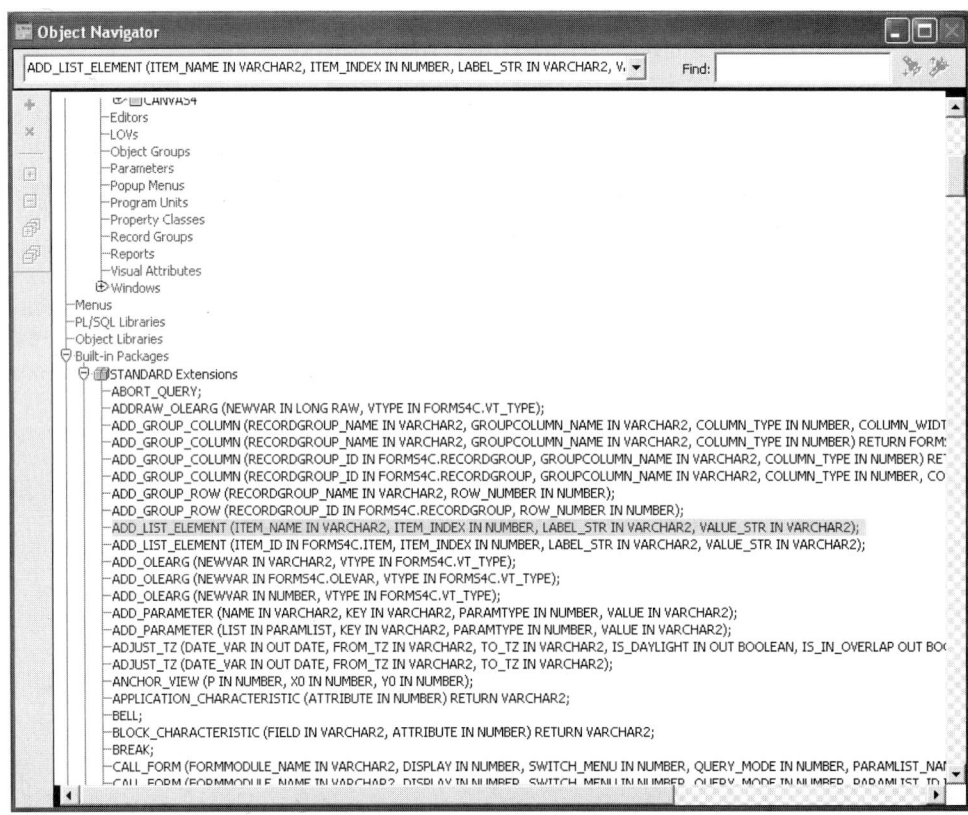

FIGURE 9.10 Some of the standard functions for Oracle forms.

rethink your overall approach to the problem. If there is no better solution, at least consider moving some of the code to the database so that it is easier to find.

You should have realized by now that most of the sample code that has been created has used built-in functions. These functions perform basic tasks such as moving to another block, altering properties of items on the form, or displaying a different record. How do you know what functions are available? As shown in Figure 9.10, you can find a listing in the object navigator. Expand the section at the bottom for Built-in Packages, then expand the section for **STANDARD Extensions**. You can scroll through the alphabetical listing to see the structure of each function. To learn more about what each function does.

Figure 9.11 shows that you can get detailed information about each function using the online Help system. You can start Help with the menu or by using Ctrl-H. Select the search tab and enter the name of the function in the search line. Select the desired topic and click the Open button to see the detailed Help. The Help description usually contains a description of all of the parameters, and sample code that shows you how to use the function. Take some time to read through the functions and their descriptions, to become familiar with the tools and their capabilities.

DEBUGGING TRIGGERS

Very rarely do you manage to write perfect code on the first attempt. Even if the code runs, you might want to check on the values of certain variables at different points in its operation. There are three basic methods for finding errors in code in Oracle

CHAPTER 9   Customizing Forms   **429**

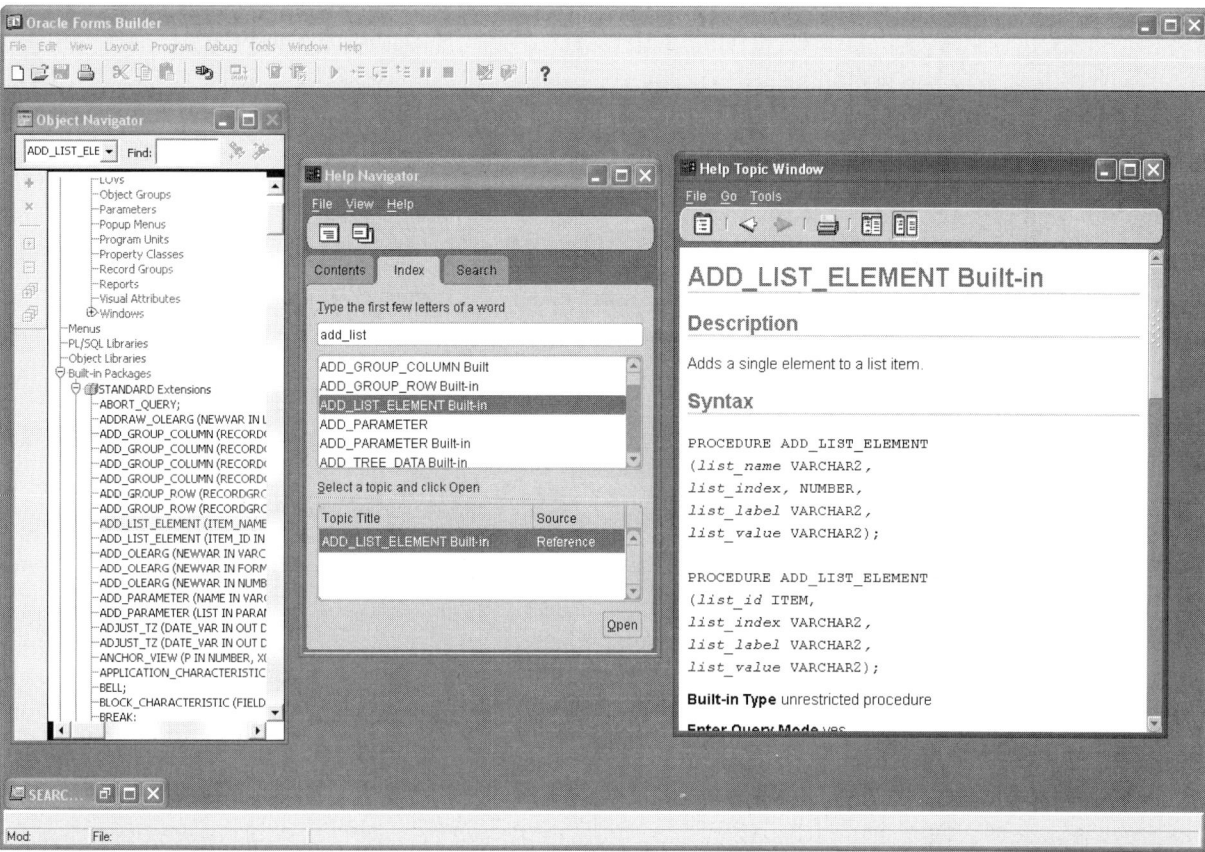

FIGURE 9.11   Help descriptions for standard functions.

forms: (1) compile the trigger code when you write it to check for syntax errors, (2) add alerts or messages at various points in your code to check the timing of events or display one or two values, and (3) run the forms debugger to step through each line of code.

The *forms debugger* with Oracle 10g is powerful. It lets you step through the code one line at a time. You can set break points and run the code until it reaches that point, or click the pause button to stop the code in the middle of a loop. You can check the values of variables (if any) within the trigger. You can look at the values of items selected on the form. You can even set breaks that stop the code when the value of a particular variable changes.

To test the debugger:

1. Open the Search form and open the trigger code for the Pre-Form trigger.
2. Double click the gray margin immediately to the left of the Clear_List line.
3. Click the icon on the main toolbar to start the debug process, or start the debugger from the main menu.
4. The form should begin to load and the debug console window should open. You might have to click somewhere on the forms builder window to see the console.

You can also right-click a line to set or remove a break point. Whichever method you choose, the break point will be indicated by a small red icon to the left of the

430 Introduction to Oracle

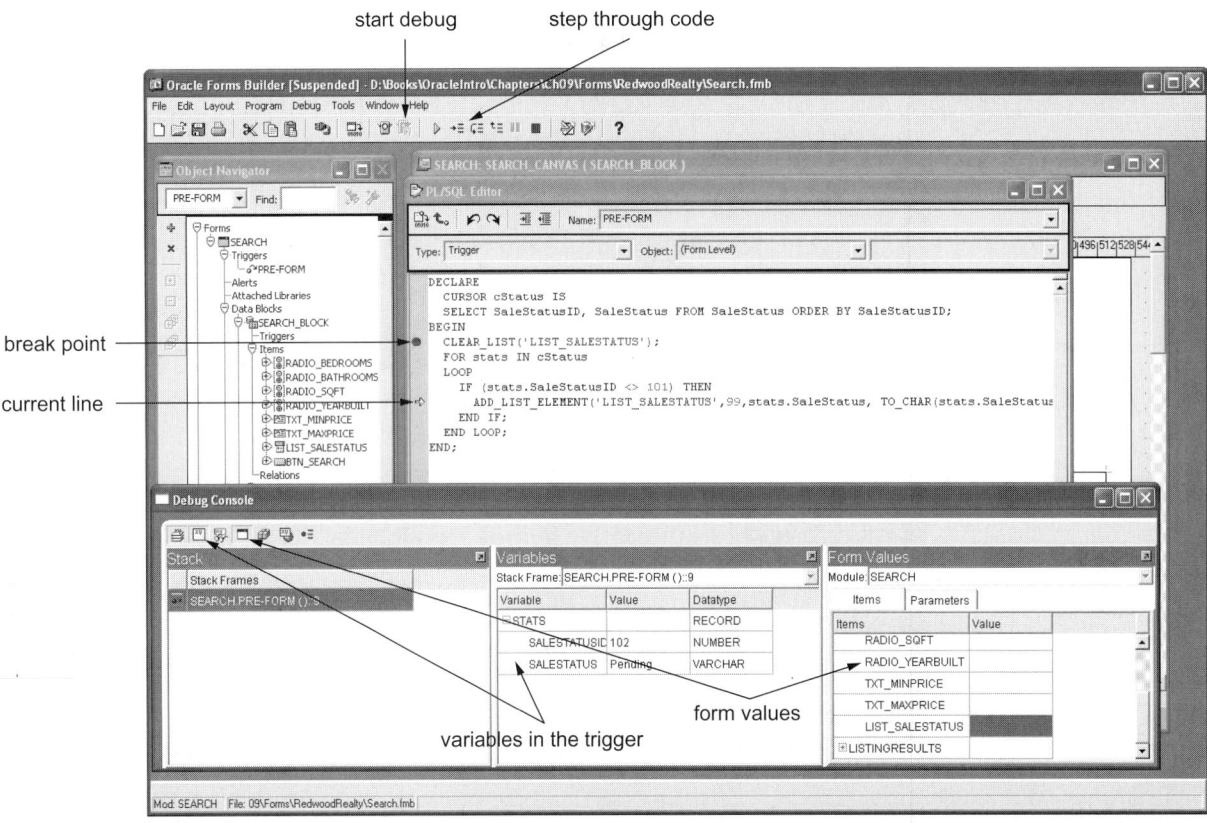

FIGURE 9.12 Some options in the forms debug console.

selected line. When the form runs, it will execute code up to, but not including, the line with the break point.

Figure 9.12 shows a few of the tools available in debug mode. Click the buttons on the top menu to display or remove the various items. The stack frames show you the current procedure and line number, and any routines that might have been executed before reaching this point. The variables window shows you the variables and their values that are declared in the current procedure. Likewise, you can see the values of items on the form.

The debug buttons in the main toolbar of the forms builder enable you to step through the code one line at a time, or to run an entire sub-procedure in one step. The current line is pointed out by a small arrow in the code editor window. Click the single-step button a few times and you will see the system execute the lines within the loop. You can check the current values being retrieved from the database by looking at the local variables. For complex problems, you can open the Watch window and set break points on the individual variables. When the variable changes, the debugger will stop and show you the code that is making the changes. This option tends to slow down the system, so use it sparingly.

> **Tip:** If you are running Windows XP and the debug console does not open, close the forms builder, use the Windows Control Panel to turn off the firewall, then follow the steps to attach the debug session to a remote computer.

The forms debugger even has the ability to attach to forms running on a server. But remember: you need to know the name of the server and the port that the forms processor is using. There is a forms command to give you that information. To test it, open the Search form and modify the When-Button-Pressed code for the Search button. Add the line: Attach.Debug; and be sure to include the semicolon at the end of the line. Add a break point to the next line (Go_Block). Run the form normally, without starting in debug mode. Click the Search button and a box will pop up showing the name of the machine and the port being used. In the forms builder, use the Debug/Attach menu option and enter the server name and port as asked. You should then be able to connect to the form and debug it remotely, using the same process as if the form were running on your machine. The debug system is relatively easy to use, but if you want more options, you can find a video tutorial on Oracle's OTN Web site.

Handling Errors

You test the syntax on all of your code by compiling it, and you can use the debugger to help track down logic errors or other problems. However, despite everyone's best efforts, unanticipated things can go wrong in a form. A ***runtime error*** is something that fails while the form is running. It might happen because a variable is assigned a bad value, such as division by zero, or perhaps you did not anticipate that a user would enter a null value. If you do not take steps to handle these errors, your form or program might crash, leaving the user facing a strange message.

To illustrate this problem and to learn how to handle these errors, create a new button on the Search form. This button (BTN_TEST) and the code will be temporary. Just add code that you know will crash:

```
DECLARE
    i NUMBER;
    j NUMBER;
BEGIN
    i := 0;
    j := 10/i;
END;
```

Compile the code to ensure that there are no syntax errors.

Figure 9.13 shows the message that is generated when you click the test button to run the code. The message is displayed in the standard message line, but it is not very informative. The most likely outcome is that users will ignore the message. If that is what you want users to do, maybe you can let it be. However, in many cases, you will want more control over what happens when an error occurs. In most cases, you would want to add exception handling to your code:

```
DECLARE
    i NUMBER;
    j NUMBER;
BEGIN
    i := 0;
    j := 10/i;
EXCEPTION
    WHEN OTHERS THEN Message(sqlerrm);
END;
```

Simply add the ***EXCEPTION statement*** above the last END command. If a runtime error arises, the forms processor will jump to the exception section and look for a matching error category. If you anticipate that certain errors might arise, you can write

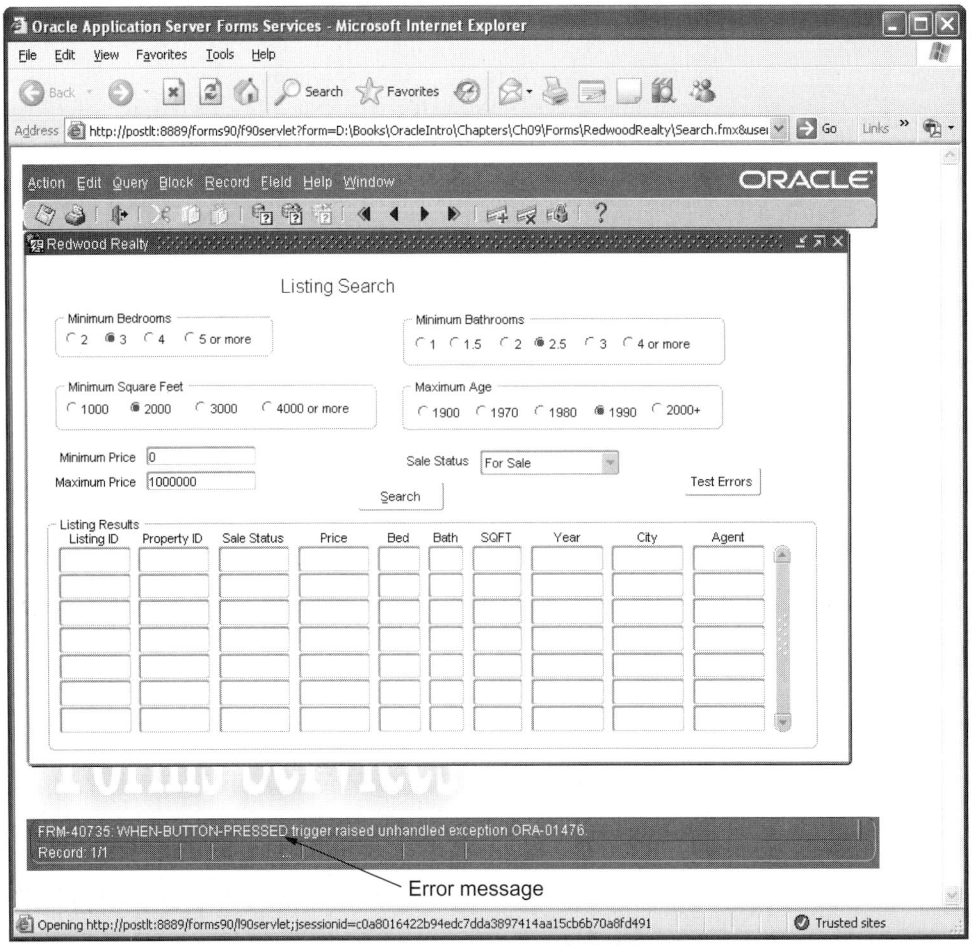

FIGURE 9.13 Message generated by the division error.

a section handler just for that particular error. In the example, you might write the error handler as:

```
EXCEPTION
    WHEN ZERO_DIVIDE THEN j:=0;
    WHEN OTHERS THEN Message(sqlerrm);
```

The PL/SQL documentation has a list of the named exceptions that you can trap individually. In many cases, it is simpler to go with the WHEN OTHERS statement, which catches all errors. Note that your code should always include the WHEN OTHERS statement someplace to ensure that all errors do get handled. Note that once an exception has been caught, you cannot return to the original block of code. The PL/SQL documentation contains several examples of how to handle various problems where you want to repeat a line after catching an error. The basic trick is to add more BEGIN/EXCEPTION/END blocks so that you trap errors immediately after a suspect line. You can also place the entire block inside a loop or a conditional statement.

CHAPTER 9 Customizing Forms **433**

You can delete the Test button and its code at this point. However, you should go back to the Pre-Form trigger and add the EXCEPTION code to trap errors that might arise.

The EXCEPTION structure will help you handle errors that arise within your code. What happens if something goes wrong within the form itself? Perhaps a user accidentally deletes a primary key and tries to save the changes. In these cases, the form processor will catch the error and return a message to the user. These errors are handled with the ON_ERROR trigger for the form. Close the Search form and open the simple Agents form.

1. Create an On-Error trigger for the form.
2. Add simple code to show the error number: **Message('Error Code is: ' || ERROR_CODE || ' DBMS Error Code is: ' || DBMS_ERROR_CODE);**
3. Run the form and execute the query to load the data.
4. Add the letter "**A**" to the end of the Agent ID and try to save the record.

Figure 9.14 shows the message generated by the new error trapping routine. In particular, you will want to record the error code number. Then you can return to the

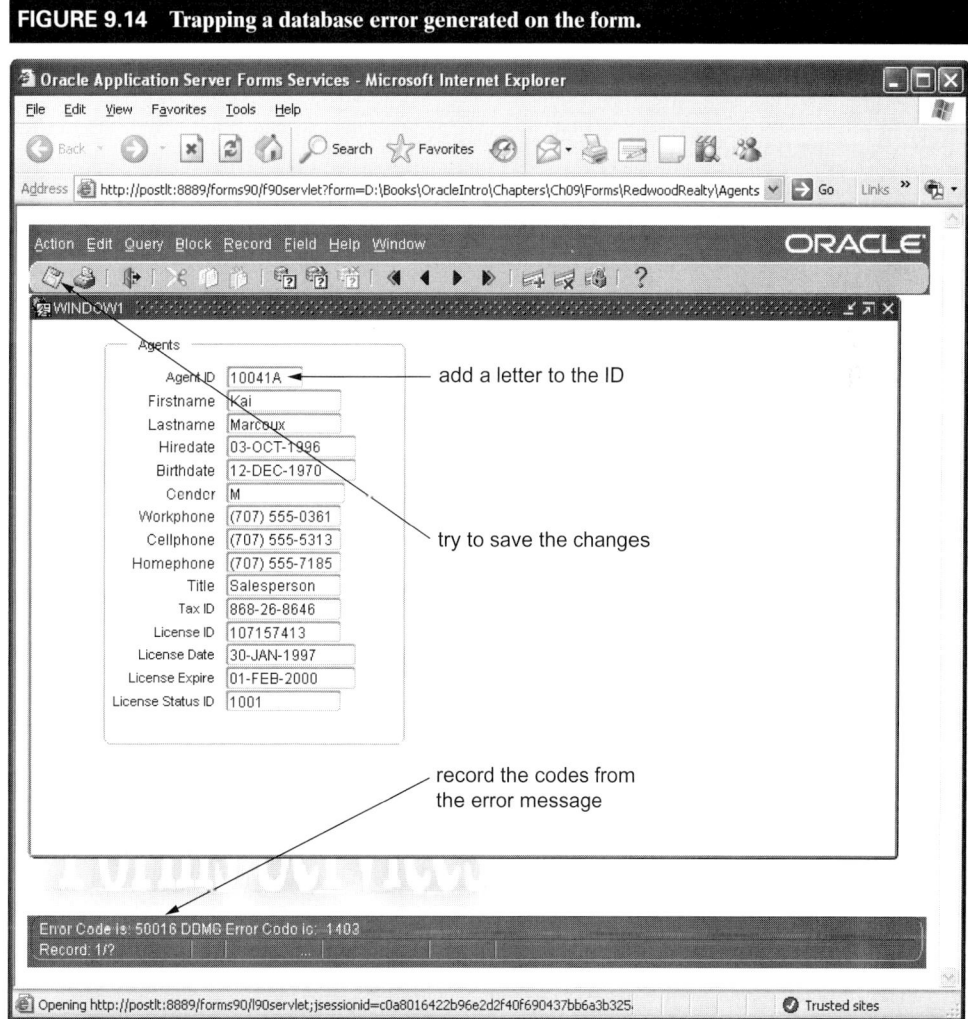

FIGURE 9.14 Trapping a database error generated on the form.

error handling code and add a condition that will enable you to write a more descriptive message. For example:

```
IF (ERROR_CODE = 50016) THEN
    Message('You must enter numbers only, not letters.');
ELSE
    Message('Error Code is: ' || ERROR_CODE
        || ' DBMS Error Code is: ' || DBMS_ERROR_CODE);
END IF;
```

You can use a similar process to determine additional error code values that you want to handle separately. You can also write more complex code to fix the error, display a more helpful message, or return the user to a different form. Note that the DBMS_ERROR_CODE returns more detailed error messages for some operations. You can find some of the codes listed in the online Oracle Help file. For instance, DBMS_ERROR_CODE = -1400 means that the user failed to enter a value for a required column.

Writing good error-handling code requires considerable practice. You need to think like the user and identify which types of problems are most likely to arise. Then you have to determine the best way to handle those errors. As always, you want to make life as easy as possible for the users. Do not simply annoy them with error messages. Whenever possible, search for a way to correct the problem automatically. In many applications, you will want to sit down with a few users and watch as they work through the form. That way you can spot potential errors and ask the users how certain problems are commonly handled.

UNDERSTANDING SCOPE AND LIFETIME IN FORMS PROGRAMS

It is important to understand the scope and lifetime of variables on forms. *Scope* refers to when the variable's value is accessible. *Lifetime* represents the time between when the variable is created and when it is destroyed. The basic rule is that a variable is created and is accessible only within the routine or section where it is defined. On a form, the most common definition is within a trigger. Consider the following code segment within a trigger:

```
DECLARE
    i1 NUMBER;
BEGIN
    i1 := 5;
    IF (i1 > 3) THEN
        DECLARE
            i2 NUMBER;
        BEGIN
            i2 := i1 + 10;
        END;
    END IF;
END;
```

You can create a new button on the form and add this code to the trigger. Put a break point in the code and step through it with the debugger to see the scope of the two variables (i1 and i2). Notice that i1 is declared at the start of the trigger, so it will be created when the trigger is fired. Its value is accessible only to code within this trigger. In addition, when the trigger code is finished (the last End statement), the variable will be destroyed. If you click the button to run the code again, all variables will start from the beginning with no values. The second variable (i2) is declared in a block within an IF statement. Its value is accessible only within that block. In fact, if you tried to refer to its value after the END IF statement, your code would generate a runtime error because the variable no longer exists.

The problem of lifetime becomes particularly important when you want to share data across multiple triggers on a form. For example, when you are testing a value entered by a user, you might want to know the value that was originally in the text box. In the Search form:

1. Create a new Pre-Text-Item trigger for the Txt_MinPrice item:

   ```
   :GLOBAL.MinPrice := :TXT_MINPRICE;
   ```

2. Create a new Post-Text-Item trigger for the Txt_MinPrice item:

   ```
   IF (:GLOBAL.MINPRICE <> :TXT_MINPRICE) THEN
       Message('Minimum price has been changed.');
   END IF;
   ```

3. Run the form and change the minimum price from 0 to 50000. Check the message line to be sure that the change message is displayed.

The trick to this example is that any variable created within the Pre-Text-Item trigger will disappear as soon as the code is finished. That means any local variables will be gone by the time the form processes the Post-Text-Item trigger. So, you need to store the original value (0) in a location with a lifetime longer than the trigger. The answer is to create a global variable. A global variable has a lifetime for the duration of the session—which can span multiple forms. The global scope makes the value accessible to any trigger on any form within the session. So, a global variable is perfect for sharing data from one trigger to another, or from one form to another form.

Note that a session is unique to each user, so a global variable created by one user cannot be accessed by another user—even if they are running the same form at the same time. That is a good thing, so you do not have to worry about collisions across global variables. If you really do want to share data with multiple users, write the data to a table in the database.

Global variables are a useful trick for many difficult situations on forms. Note that you do not declare them in advance. You simply create a name with the ***GLOBAL prefix*** (GLOBAL.name) and assign a value to it.

CREATING USEFUL FORMS TOOLS

As you have seen from the examples dealing with forms, you use code for several common types of triggers, such as when a button is pressed. In many cases, you need only a few lines of code to perform a basic task. It turns out that you need code for a few more common database tasks. This section will show you how to handle some basic functions that tend to appear in many database applications. Each example is presented independently in a separate subsection so you can refer back to this section when you need these tools in your projects. The examples also illustrate the event timing and other programming issues.

CREATING SEQUENCES

Recall that one of the most important aspects of a relational database is that each table must have a primary key. In many cases, it is easiest to create a new key column that serves as an identifier within the database. For example, the Agents table has an AgentID column to serve as its primary key. But, you always face the question: Where do you get new numbers that you can guarantee are unique? In a large organization, you might have a human resources department, and maybe you can set up some process so that new employees are always assigned unique numbers and that data is entered into the table when someone is hired. But someone would have to pay close attention to all of the numbers being assigned and would need a form to double-check their uniqueness against the database.

Instead of trusting a human-based process, it often makes more sense to let the database generate numbers to use as key values. Oracle uses sequences for this purpose. A *sequence* is a named set of numbers that Oracle uses to generate new values when requested. The two key aspects to sequences are that: (1) you have to set them up in advance, and (2) you need code to request the generation of a new value. The sequence numbers are not automatically created when a new row is entered. You have to write code to generate the value and store it in the appropriate column. Note that it is possible to write a database trigger on the Insert event for a table that will automatically generate a number. However, the more common approach in Oracle is to simply generate the key value when it is needed—which is usually on a form.

Generally, you will define a sequence when you define the original table. But, since there is no direct tie between the sequence and the table, you can set it up any time before you will have to create numbers. You only need to create the sequence once, so work through SQL*Plus.

1. Since data already exists in the table, find the highest value:

    SELECT Max(AgentID) FROM Agents;

2. The highest value should be 15521, so you will want to start the new entries with a value larger than that. You might be tempted to use 15522, and that would probably work, but just to be safe, start at 20000:

    **CREATE SEQUENCE seq_Agents
    INCREMENT BY 1
    START WITH 20000;**

3. You also use SQL to retrieve new values, which automatically increments the counter by the value specified in the sequence definition. Try it now to be sure you understand the command:

    SELECT seq_Agents.NEXTVAL FROM dual;

This command uses the synthetic dual table because PL/SQL always requires the use of the FROM clause. It should have returned the value 20000. If you repeat the command, it will return 20001 and so on. Notice that the sequence simply returned the number. It did not do anything with that number. It is up to you to use that number as the new primary key value. Actually, you could use the number for anything you want, but you should always use a sequence for only one purpose. You should also be careful to name the sequence so everyone understands its purpose.

Now that you have a sequence created, you need to add the code to your form that automatically generates a new value when a new agent is added. Start Forms Builder and open the Agents form. You should probably open the version of the form that you created in Chapter 8, so copy the Agents.fmb and Agents.fmx files that you created in Chapter 8 and place them in the folder for this chapter. If you no longer have those files, you can use the simple version you already created for this chapter.

As usual, the first step is to decide which trigger event to use. At first glance, it is tempting to use the On-Insert trigger, but that event is a little late in the process. Remember that when people use the form, they click the Insert Record option to create a blank page. This action fires the When-Create-Record event. The On-Insert event is not triggered until the user clicks the Save button.

1. Create a new trigger for the form's When-Create-Record event.
2. Use File/Connect on the main menu and log in to the database.
3. Add the code to generate a new sequence number for Agents:

```
SELECT seq_Agents.NEXTVAL INTO :AGENTS.AGENTID FROM dual;
```

4. Click the Compile button to make sure there are no typos or syntax errors.

> **Tip:** If you receive an error message about the dual table, it is most likely because you are not connected to the database.

5. Start the form and make sure a new ID is generated.

Figure 9.15 shows the Agents form when you open it. Notice that the When-Create-Record event is fired when the form is first opened. Consequently, every time someone runs the form, a new ID value will be generated. If the user is not planning to enter a new agent, clicking the Execute Query button will load the form for the existing agents. The ID value that was generated will be discarded. Since the database can

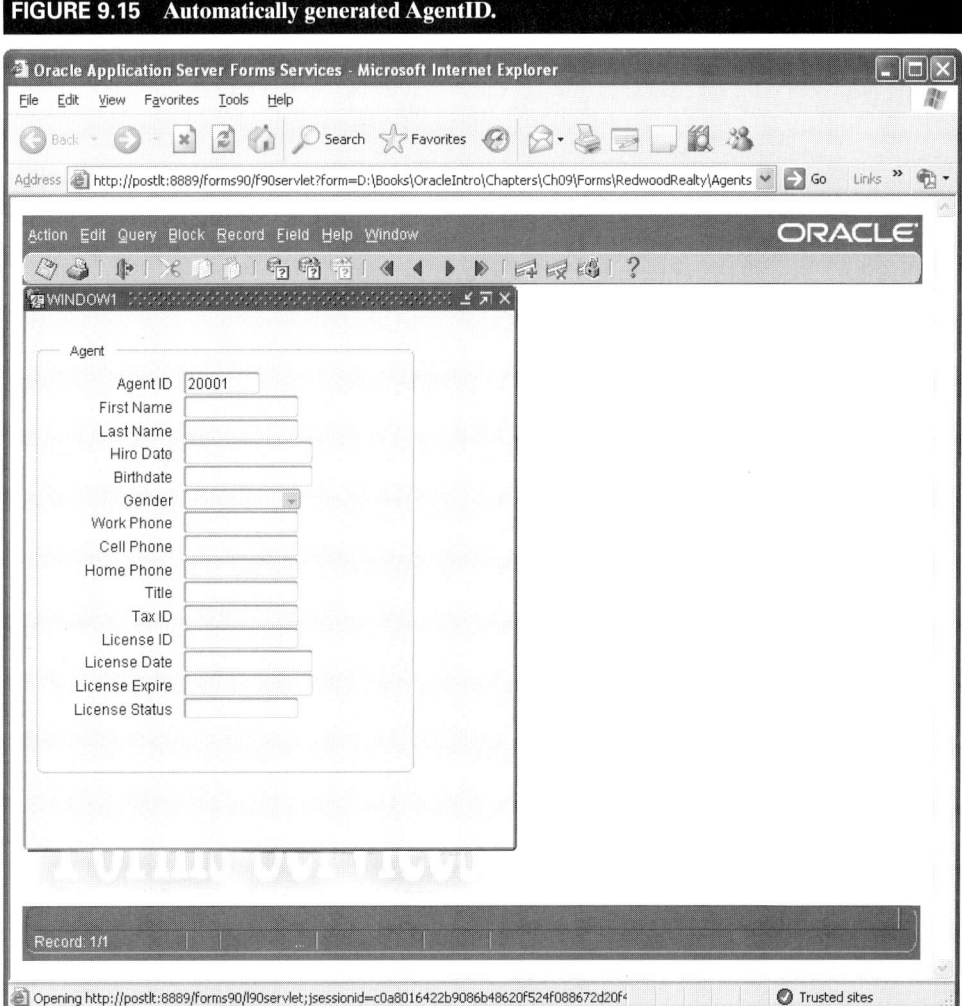

FIGURE 9.15 Automatically generated AgentID.

generate over a billion numbers, throwing a few away is not a serious problem. However, if you have a form where you expect users to rarely add new entries, you can improve the usefulness of the form. Add the Execute_Query statement to the When-New-Form-Instance trigger. This action hides the initial blank screen from the user, but the extra sequence value will still be generated.

To prevent the extra sequence value being generated, refer back to the startup events in Figure 9.7. Notice that the When-Create-Record event fires between the Pre-Form and When-New-Form-Instance events. You can use this knowledge to create a global indicator variable.

1. In the Pre-Form trigger, set **:GLOBAL.DoNotAdd := 1;**
2. In the When-New-Form-Instance trigger, reset **:GLOBAL.DoNotAdd :=0;**
3. In the When-Create-Record code, add an IF statement to decide whether to generate the ID value: **IF (:GLOBAL.DoNotAdd = 0) THEN** ...

These steps might seem annoying to you. However, they make the form easier to use, so they are important to users. These little touches make your application more professional.

VALIDATING FORM INPUT

One of the important rules in user-interface design is that errors should be caught and identified as close to the source as possible. Whenever users enter data into forms, they run the risk of making mistakes. As much as possible, your forms should identify problems immediately and inform the user, who can make corrections immediately.

Oracle forms have several ways to validate user input. Some of the simplest methods are tied to properties of the data items. Look at the Agents form again. Recall that the Gender data is entered through a pop-list box. The user must pick one of the entries in the list. Selecting from the list ensures that the data is always entered consistently. Of course, it does not prevent a user from incorrectly identifying a male as female or vice-versa, but some things like that should probably not be computerized.

Next, open the property palette for the License Status box. Scroll down to the LOV entry you created for this item. To be safe, you should set the Validate from List property to Yes. This property ensures that the user can only choose values from the list. If you look at the original database design, you will find a foreign key relationship from this column to the LicenseStatus table. This relationship also prevents the user from entering unexpected values.

Other properties give you common validation options. For example, you can set the data type, the maximum length, whether the item is required, and the minimum and maximum values for an item.

1. Open the property palette for the HireDate. Be sure that the data type is set to **Date**.
2. Set the Required property to **Yes**, set the Lowest Allowed Value to **01-Jan-1990**, and the Highest Allowed Value to **30-Dec-2050**.
3. Run the form and try to change the HireDate for an existing employee to some day in **1980**. The forms processor will disallow the change and provide an error message on the standard message line.
4. While you are at it, you should set the initial value for the HireDate to today's date: **$$DATE$$**. This way the current date will be shown as the default value when a new agent is added. The user can still change the date if necessary.

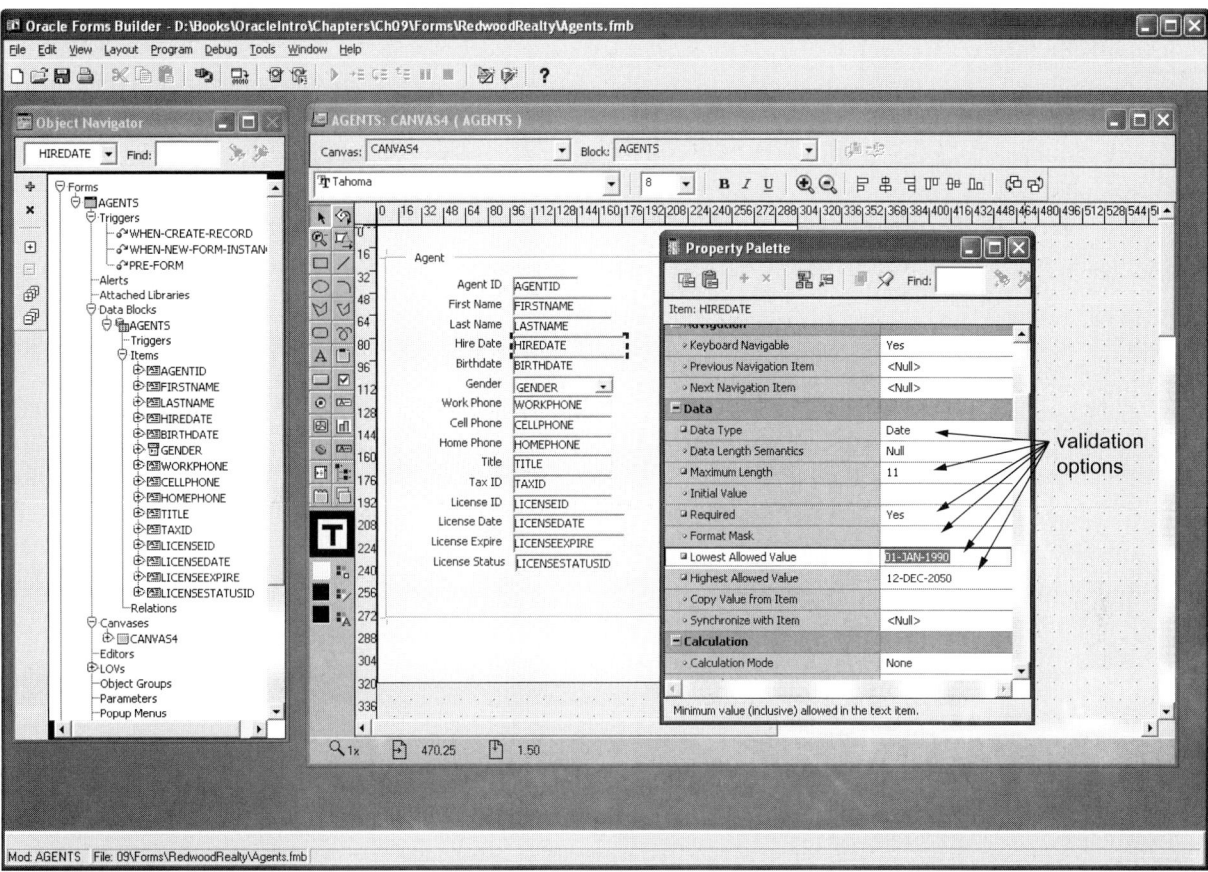

FIGURE 9.16   Basic validation properties.

Figure 9.16 shows the values for the basic validation properties. There is one more property that you can use to control user data entry in a text box. The Format Mask enables you to specify the character and numeric combinations that will be allowed. For example, you could set the Format Mask property for the work telephone to FM"("999") "999"-"9999. Notice that the delimiter characters (parentheses and dashes) are enclosed in double quotes. This format would force users to enter telephone numbers with the area code along with the other seven digits. You can also create format masks for characters and date items. But, before you go wild and set format masks for every conceivable item, think about the possible data for a few minutes. Try an easy one: ZIP codes. It might be tempting to require a five-digit numeric ZIP code, but then users will not be able to enter nine-digit codes, or worse, any codes from Canada or several other nations. You encounter similar problems with telephone numbers. Restricting phones to 10 digits blocks most international numbers and additional codes that add an extension that might be needed by a company's switchboard. It turns out that format masks are not very useful today. Occasionally, you will find some in-house numbering system that can be defined by a format mask, but it is difficult to rely on any data that is defined externally.

The third type of validation available is the ability to write PL/SQL code to perform any test that you want on the data. Oracle provides the When-Validate-Item trigger for each item on the form.

1. Right-click the birth date item to add a smart trigger for the When-Validate-Item event.
2. Add the code to ensure that the person is at least 18 years old:

```
IF (ADD_MONTHS(:BIRTHDATE, 18*12) > CURRENT_DATE) THEN
    Message('The person must be at least 18 years old.');
    RAISE FORM_TRIGGER_FAILURE;
END IF;
```

3. Run the form and test the trigger by trying to enter a recent date as a birthday.

Figure 9.17 shows what happens when you run the form and try to enter a recent date as a birthday. The validation trigger evaluates the date and notes that the person would be younger than 18 years old. It displays a message and raises an error (FORM_TRIGGER_FAILURE) which prevents the form from continuing. The power of the validation trigger is that you can write complex code to check any type of condition that you can imagine. You can use PL/SQL to issue calls to the database and compare data from multiple tables. You can write complex conditions using nested IF/THEN statements. Fortunately, most business conditions are not that complex, but it is nice to know that the capability exists if you need it. Just remember that if you

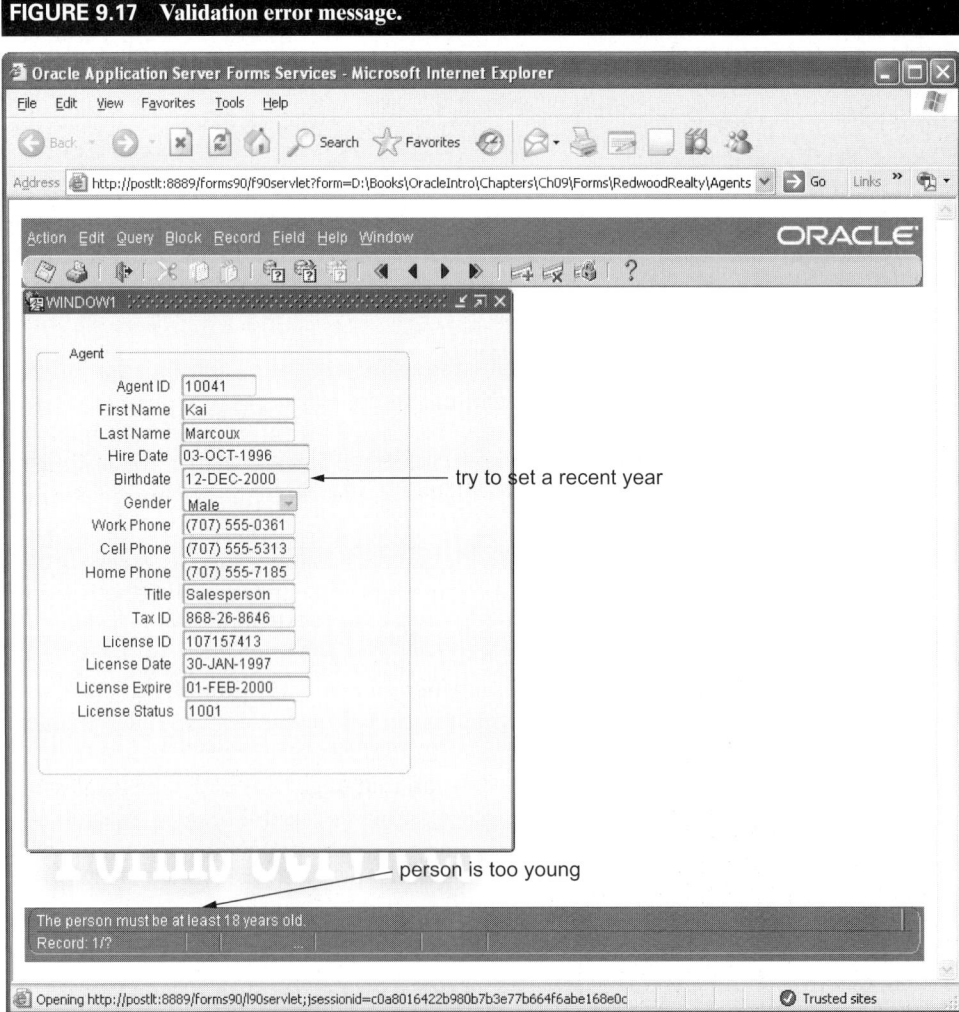

FIGURE 9.17 Validation error message.

create lengthy, complex validation code, someone else will have to read and modify that code in the future. Be sure to document it and make it easy to read.

COMPUTING SUBTOTALS FOR GRID DATA

This next tool is commonly used in sale forms. The form would display a list of items being sold along with their prices in a sub form grid. The main form would display the total value of the items being sold. The Redwood Realty case does not have a traditional sale form. However, on the Search form it would be nice to show the count of the listings that were retrieved. The count is computed almost exactly the same as a total. The only difference is in the choice of function (Count versus Sum).

The trick with subtotals is that any calculation you make must be performed in the sub form data block because that is where the numbers are. But, any data displayed in a tabular form will be repeated on each row, which could be confusing to the users. So, you want to compute the count or subtotal in the tabular data block, but you want to display the single result on the main data block.

1. Open the Search form and add a text box to the ListingResults data block. Reduce its width and place it just inside the right edge of the frame.
2. Set the properties of the text box as indicated in Table 9.1.
3. Open the property palette for the ListingResults data block. Set Query All Records to **Yes**.
4. Switch the default data block to the Search_Block and add a text box just above the frame for the tabular data.
5. Set the properties as shown in Table 9.2.
6. Save the form and run it.

Tip: If the count is not displayed in the main form text box, double-check the formula in that box and be sure you included the leading colon.

The count of the number of listings returned as matches should be displayed in the new box. The value is grayed out because the Enabled property was set to No.

TABLE 9.1 Properties for the text box in the sub form to perform the calculation.

Property	Value
Name	MatchCount
Enable	No
Keyboard Navigable	No
Data Type	Number
Calculation Mode	Summary
Summary Function	Count
Summarized Block	LISTINGRESULTS
Summarized Item	LISTINGID
Database Item	No
Visible	No
Width	5
Height	1
Prompt	Count

TABLE 9.2 Properties for the text box to display the total count.

Property	Value
Name	MatchCount
Enabled	No
Justification	Right
Data Type	Number
Format Mask	9,990
Calculation Mode	Formula
Formula	:LISTINGRESULTS.MatchCount
Database Item	No
Prompt	Number of Matches

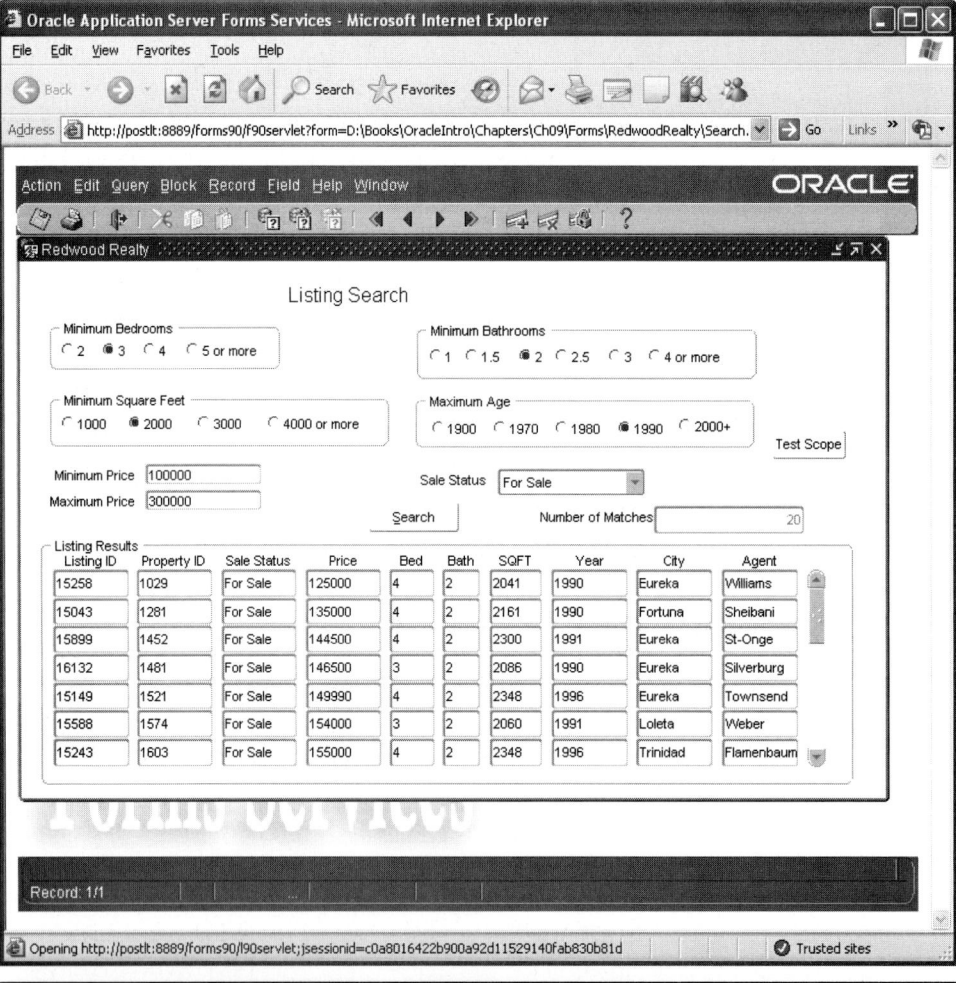

FIGURE 9.18 Sample search results with count of matches.

Figure 9.18 shows the results of a sample search. Your results will vary depending on the search conditions you choose.

It seems like a lot of work to go through to get a count of the number of matches. It might not be a critical feature of the form, but it is helpful because it displays the count in a prominent location. More important, you can use the same technique to compute subtotals, or even averages. One of the strengths of this approach is that the computations are performed on the client computer. If the tabular form is used to enter new data, the total is updated almost immediately. It does not require a new trip to the server to compute the value.

USING MULTIPLE CANVASES

All of the forms you have built to this point have been designed to show all of the data at the same time. For example, the data in sub forms is displayed at the same time as the data in the main form. Technically, all of the data was displayed on a single canvas. For many applications, this approach makes sense, since users see everything they need in one screen. Additionally, for large projects, you can split development easily by assigning one developer to each form. The forms work independently, and can be linked at the end to provide a seamless application.

However, there is a limit to the amount of data you can put on a single screen, and users might want to see several interrelated pieces of data. Although it is not possible to display all of them at the same time, Oracle forms provide another trick. You can display data on a different canvas. You or the user can then control when a canvas is displayed, so users can quickly switch between various displays of data. In fact, Oracle has three different ways to handle multiple canvases: (1) as separate displays, (2) with a stacked canvas, and (3) with a tab canvas. From a developer's perspective, all three types follow essentially the same development steps. The difference comes down to style and the way that users want to interact with the forms. Some organizations might standardize on a design structure so all applications work the same. In other cases, you might have to create a form several different ways so users can select the method that works best for the situation.

ADDING A CANVAS

To illustrate the use of multiple canvases, it is easiest to start with a form that uses two separate canvases. You already have at least one copy of the Search form. To be safe, you should work from a copy of the original Search form.

1. Use Windows to locate your forms and copy Search.fmb and Search.fmx.
2. Name them Search2.fmb and Search2.fmx.
3. Open the new Search2.fmb form and delete the Test Scope button if it still exists. Also, delete the two triggers under the Txt_MinPrice item if they exist.
4. Save the Search2 form and make two additional copies, Search3 and Search4, that you can use in the next sections.

The Search form results show the PropertyID displayed for listings that match the search condition, along with some of the basic facts about the properties. But, the users have decided that they need an easy way to see all of the information about some of the properties. You could squeeze additional columns onto the results grid, but that display is already a little crowded. Instead, you will create a new canvas to display the complete record for one property. Adding a canvas is relatively easy, and you should already be familiar with creating a data block and fine-tuning the layout.

1. Add a new canvas by clicking the Search_Properties canvas in the object navigator and clicking the Create (+) button. Name the new canvas **Properties** and make sure it falls below the Search_Canvas in the navigator list. The canvas listed first is the one displayed first when the form opens, and that should be the Search_Canvas.

2. Add a data block using the data block wizard. Select the Properties table and all of its columns. When asked, create a join using:

Properties.PropertyID= ListingResults.PropertyID.

> **Tip:** If you receive an error message trying to create the relationship, make sure the Auto Join box is unchecked.

3. In the layout wizard, the most important step is to choose the newly created Properties canvas. Actually, if you skipped step 1, you can create a new canvas at this step. As usual, set the column widths so the display is readable.
4. You now have data on a new canvas, but you need a way to display that data. Switch to the Search_Canvas and add a button on the main search form. Label it **Property**. Create a trigger for When-Button-Pressed with the code:

```
GO_ITEM('PROPERTIES.PROPERTYID');
```

You could have put the button into the results grid, but there is already limited space, so leave it at the top of the form. Also, to make life a little easier for the users, place the same code into a trigger on the PropertyID item within the display frame. Pick the trigger for When-Mouse-DoubleClick. Users will be able to see the property record either by clicking the new Property button or by double-clicking the PropertyID within the results list.

5. On the Properties canvas there should be a button so users can return to the Search page. Add a button labeled Search. Create the trigger for When-Button-Pressed as:

```
GO_ITEM('SEARCH_BLOCK.BTN_SEARCH');
```

6. Compile the code and test the form.

Figure 9.19 shows the design of the form with two canvases. When you run the form, it will appear almost identical to the original search form. Click the **Search** button and you still get a listing that matches the search criteria. However, select one of the listing items by clicking a text box on that row. Then click the new **Property** button. The canvas will switch and you will see the matching data for that property—check the PropertyID to be sure. You can click the **Search** button to return to the Search canvas and perform a new search. From the search page, you can also double-click the PropertyID box of any of the listings to bring up the details of the property on the new Property canvas. Most of the work is handled behind the scenes because you built a relationship between the Properties data block and the ListingResults data block. You can use this trick with any data tables that can be connected by relationships.

STACKED CANVAS

Using multiple canvases is a way to let users switch between related displays of data. But what if you want something more immediate? More important, what if users want to continue looking at the search criteria and the listings, and still have the ability to see the detailed property record? You have to be careful about *information overload*—trying to display too many things on one screen. However, the *stacked canvas* is designed for these tasks. Stacking a canvas means that one canvas is displayed on top of another one. The stacked canvas has a *viewport* that displays a specified portion of its screen, so it appears as if the viewport lies on top of the other canvas.

CHAPTER 9   Customizing Forms   **445**

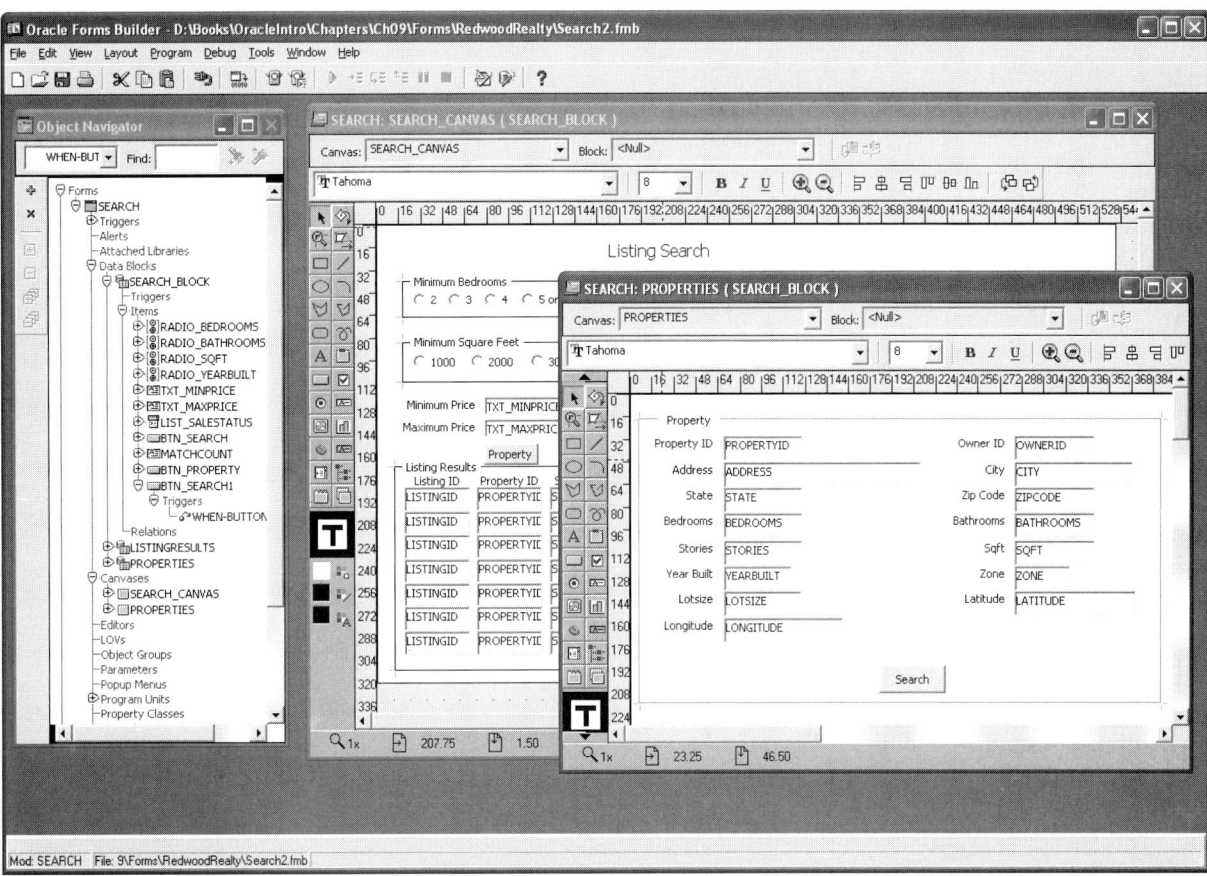

FIGURE 9.19   Form design with second canvas.

You can use code to control when the stacked canvas is visible or hidden, so users can decide when they want to see the additional data.

Creating a stacked canvas is similar to the process of creating any new canvas.

1. If necessary, close and remove all forms from the forms builder. Open a copy of the original Search form. Use Search3.fmb if you made the copy in the previous section.

2. Click the Stacked Canvas button in the tool box. Draw the viewport on top of the right side of the listings grid, but be sure users can still see at least the ListingID and PropertyID. Figure 9.20 shows the new canvas overlaying the listings. Rename the canvas as **Properties**.

3. Fire up the data block wizard and choose all of the columns in the Properties table. Be sure to create the join: Properties.PropertyID=ListingResults.PropertyID.

4. Use the layout wizard and make sure you pick the Properties canvas. When the wizard finishes, adjust the frame so that it fits within the viewport. The viewport is indicated with the darker rectangle, and only data within it will be visible. It is often helpful to center the frame's label.

5. Save everything and test the form by running it. The drawback is that the new Properties canvas permanently covers up some of the listings data. Users might want to see that data some of the time.

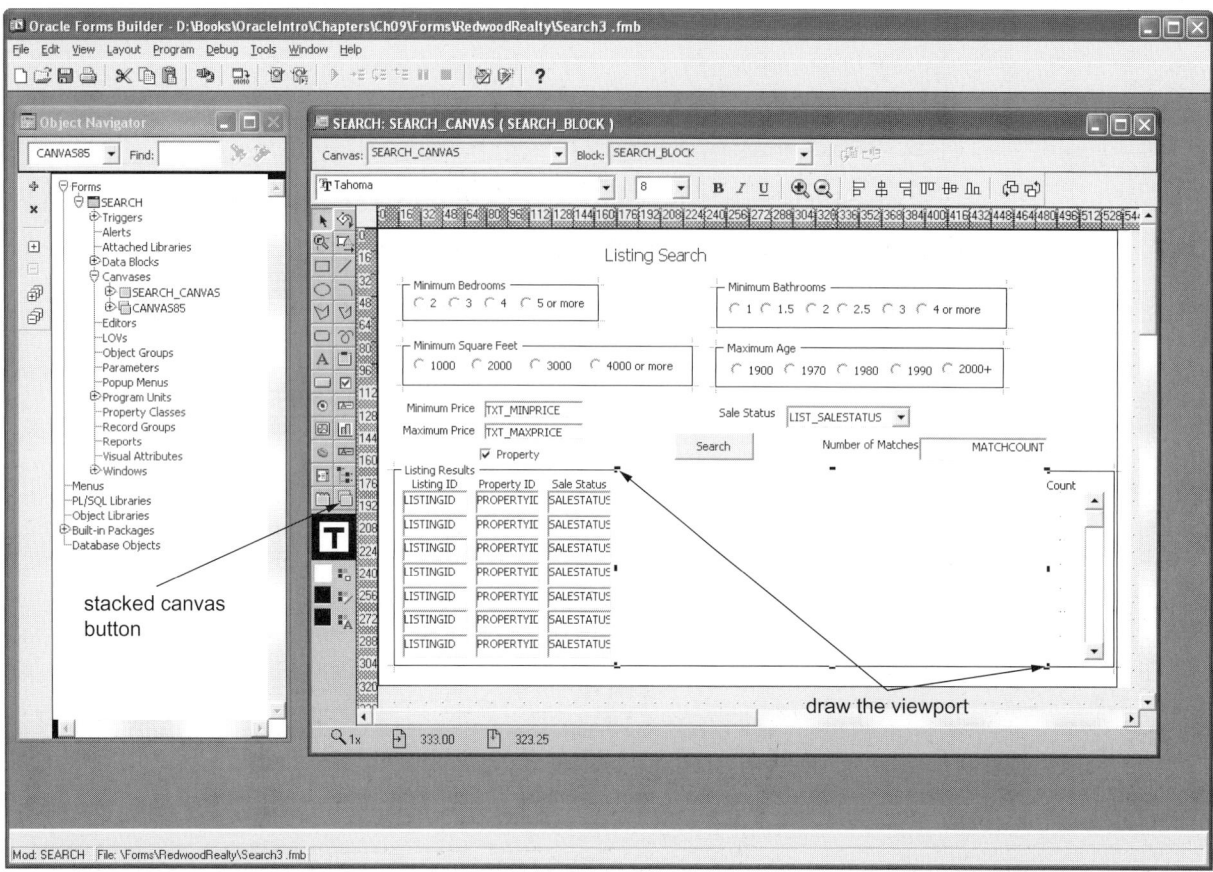

FIGURE 9.20 Adding a stacked canvas.

6. Add a check box to the Search_Block canvas, with the following properties: Name=**CHK_PROPERTY**, Label=**Property**, Value when Checked=**1**, Value when Unchecked=**0**, Data Type=**Number**, Initial Value=**0**, Database Item=**No**.

7. You want to start with the Properties canvas hidden, so edit the Pre-Form trigger and before the end of the code (above the EXCEPTION line), add:

```
HIDE_VIEW('PROPERTIES');
```

8. Create a new trigger for the checkbox When-Checkbox-Changed event:

```
IF (:CHK_PROPERTY > 0) THEN
     SHOW_VIEW('PROPERTIES');
ELSE
     HIDE_VIEW('PROPERTIES');
END IF;
```

9. Test the form and experiment with different backgrounds for the Properties canvas to improve the readability.

Figure 9.21 shows the stacked canvas in operation. Use the Property checkbox to display or hide the stacked canvas. Notice that when you leave the canvas visible, selecting a new row in the listings causes the data in the canvas to be updated. When you run this form on a local area network, the updates are instantaneous. However, if

CHAPTER 9   Customizing Forms   **447**

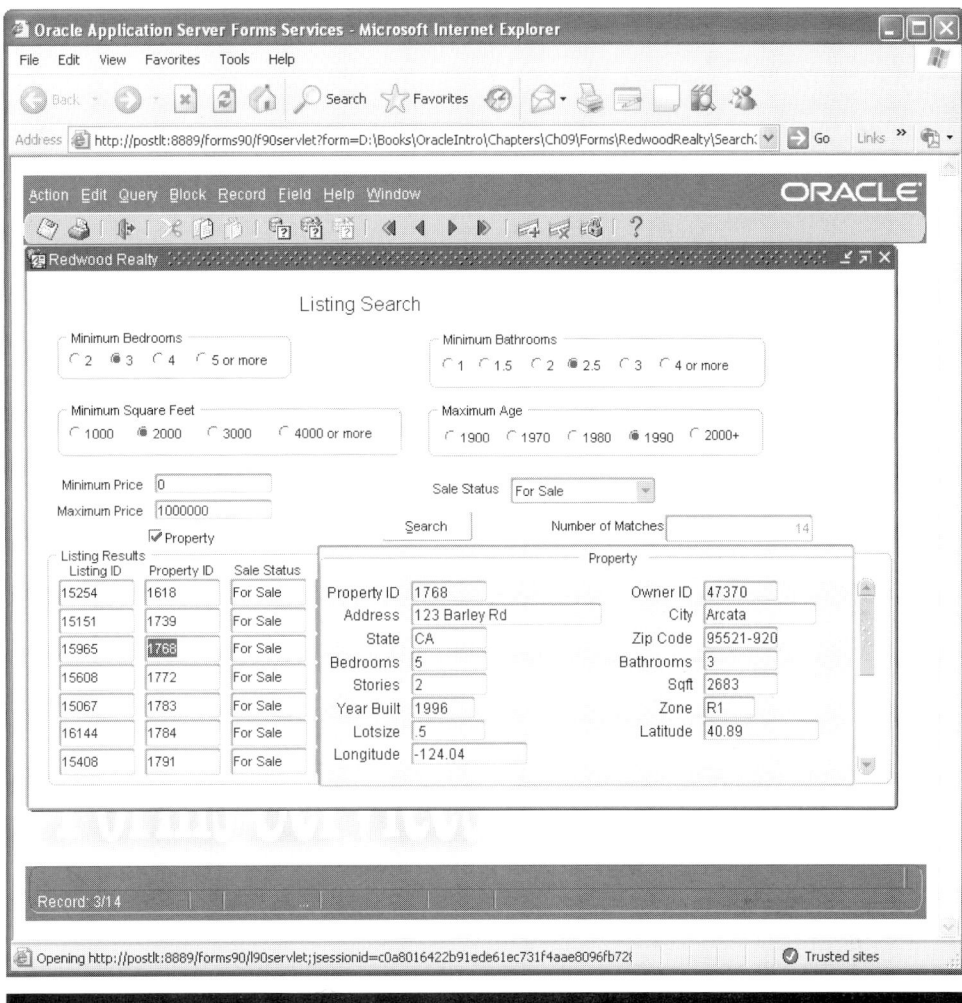

FIGURE 9.21   Displaying the stacked canvas.

users will access the forms across the Internet, you should test this feature carefully. On the other hand, if the updates are too slow, users can simply hide the Properties canvas until finding a property they want to investigate.

TAB CANVAS

In many ways, a ***tab canvas*** is just another way of displaying multiple canvases. However, it ultimately becomes an application design method. You have probably seen tab-based applications. For instance, Windows uses them to display related sets of properties. Some businesses have adopted the tab design philosophy and use it extensively. Essentially, related data sets are displayed on separate pages. A tabbed display at the top of the screen makes it easy for users to switch among the items being displayed. The concept is loosely a metaphor for a file cabinet of folders. When you click a tab, you see the contents of that folder.

Creating tab canvases for an application is a little trickier than creating a separate or stacked canvas. In fact, given a choice, you really want to start an application from the beginning knowing that it will use tabs. Because it would take too long to recreate the entire Search form, and because it is helpful to learn the process, this section will show you how to convert the Search form into tabbed canvases. The main step is to create a completely new tab canvas and transfer the original items from the original Search_Canvas.

1. Start with a clean copy of the original Search form. Use Search4.fmb if you created it in the earlier section.
2. Create a new canvas by selecting the Canvas node in the object navigator and clicking the Create button. Set some basic properties: Name=**MainTab**, Canvas Type=**Tab**, Background=**white**.
3. Initially, a tab canvas has two display pages (tabs). Use the property palette to rename each page and set its label. Use Name=**PG_SEARCH**, Label=**Search** for the first, and **PG_PROPERTY**, Label=**Property** for the second.

> **Tip:** To set properties of a page on a tab canvas, right-click on the main body of the page, not on the tab; or select the page in the object navigator.

4. You need to transfer the main graphics items from the Search_Canvas to the new MainTab canvas. The easiest method is to select them as a group beneath the navigator node Search_Canvas/Graphics and drag them to the Graphics node beneath MainTab/PG_Search/Graphics. This action will transfer the title and the frames.
5. You now have to reassign all of the data block items to the new canvas and page. You can transfer these as a group. Open the property palette, then select all of the items in the object navigator (Shift-click works well); or select all of them on the original canvas. Find the Canvas and Page properties and set Canvas to **MainTab** and set the Page to **PG_Search**. Then switch to the ListingResults data block and do the same thing for each of its items. When you have a group of items selected, be careful not to change any of the other properties because changes will be applied to every item at the same time. Figure 9.22 shows the two main properties you need to set.
6. Double-check to be sure you have transferred all of the items on the Search_Canvas. The easy method is to view the Search_Canvas and right-click any items that remain on it and change the canvas and page properties.
7. Make sure the MainTab canvas appears above the Search_Canvas in the object navigator so that it is opened by default. Run the form and test the transferred form. When it is correct, you can delete the original Search_Canvas.
8. A this point, you have simply recreated the original search form. The real power comes when you add the Properties data block. Switch to the Property page and use the data wizard to add a new data block. As before, include all columns from the Properties table and be sure to create the join:

    Properties.PropertyID= ListingResults.PropertyID.

9. Use the layout wizard and make sure you select the **MainTab** canvas and pick the **PG_Property** page at the bottom of the form.
10. You can run the form now and switch back and forth between pages simply by clicking the tabs at the top of the window. However, you can make life even easier for users by adding one line of code to let them switch to the Property page by double-clicking a PropertyID on the search page. On the search page, create a trigger for the PropertyID in the results grid for the When-Mouse-DoubleClick event:

```
GO_ITEM('PROPERTIES.PROPERTYID ');
```

Test the form, and while you are looking at the Property page, notice that it contains data for the OwnerID. It is likely that the users will also want to see more

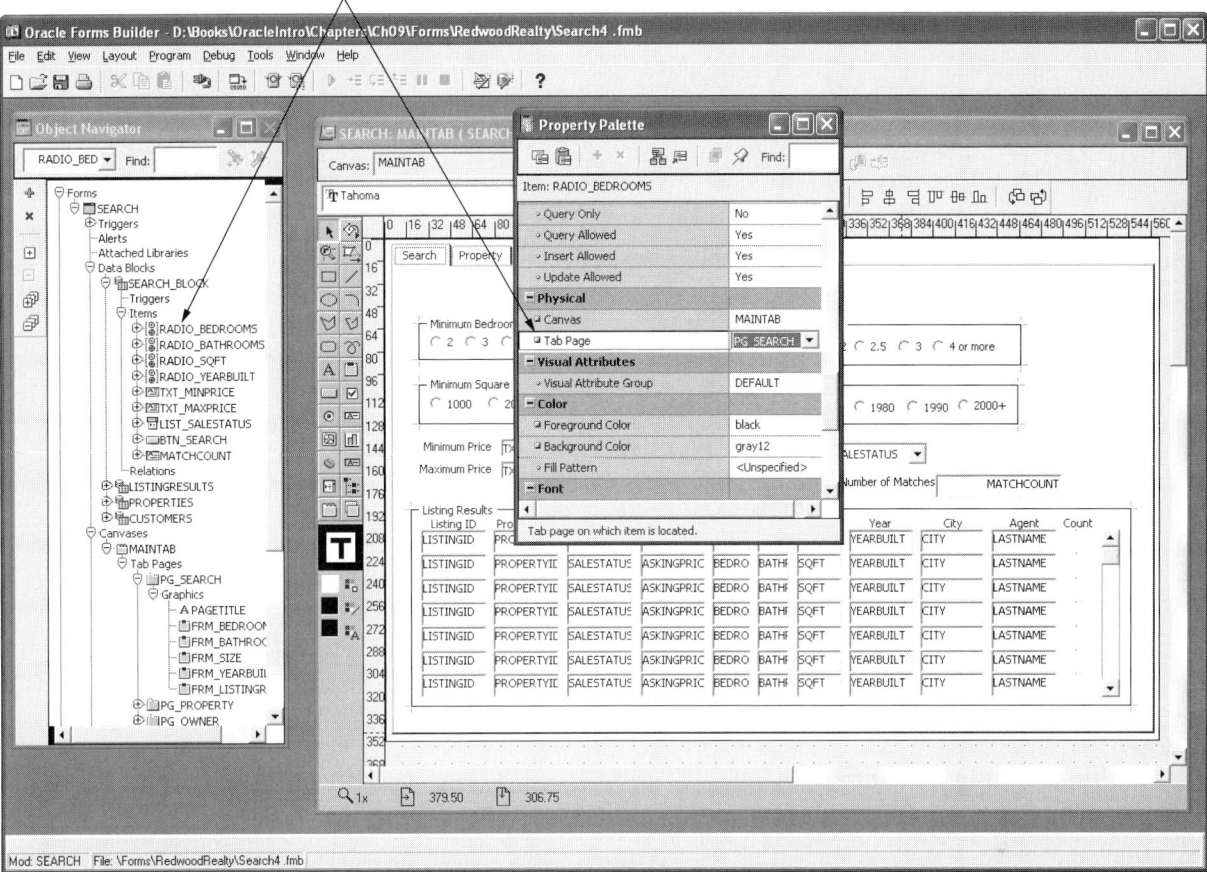

FIGURE 9.22 Specifying the canvas and page for data items.

information about the owners. With a tab canvas, it is relatively easy to add this feature without overwhelming the user. Follow the same process as you did for properties:

1. Add a new page to the MainTab canvas. Select the PG_PROPERTY in the object navigator under the MainTab/Tab Pages node. Click the Create button to add the new page. Set its properties: Name=**PG_OWNER**, label=**Owner**.
2. Use the data block wizard to add a new data block with all columns from the Customers table. Join it to the Properties data block:

Customers.CustomerID= Properties.OwnerID.

3. Use the layout wizard and make sure you pick the PG_OWNER page.
4. The form will work at this point, but you can improve it by setting the double-click trigger for the OwnerID on the Property page:

```
GO_ITEM('CUSTOMERS.CUSTOMERID');
```

Figure 9.23 shows the resulting form with three tabs. Test it by running a search and selecting a property. Double-click the PropertyID or click the Property tab to see the detailed information on the property. It is just as easy to see the detailed data on the owner. Using this form, a real estate agent can quickly search for properties with

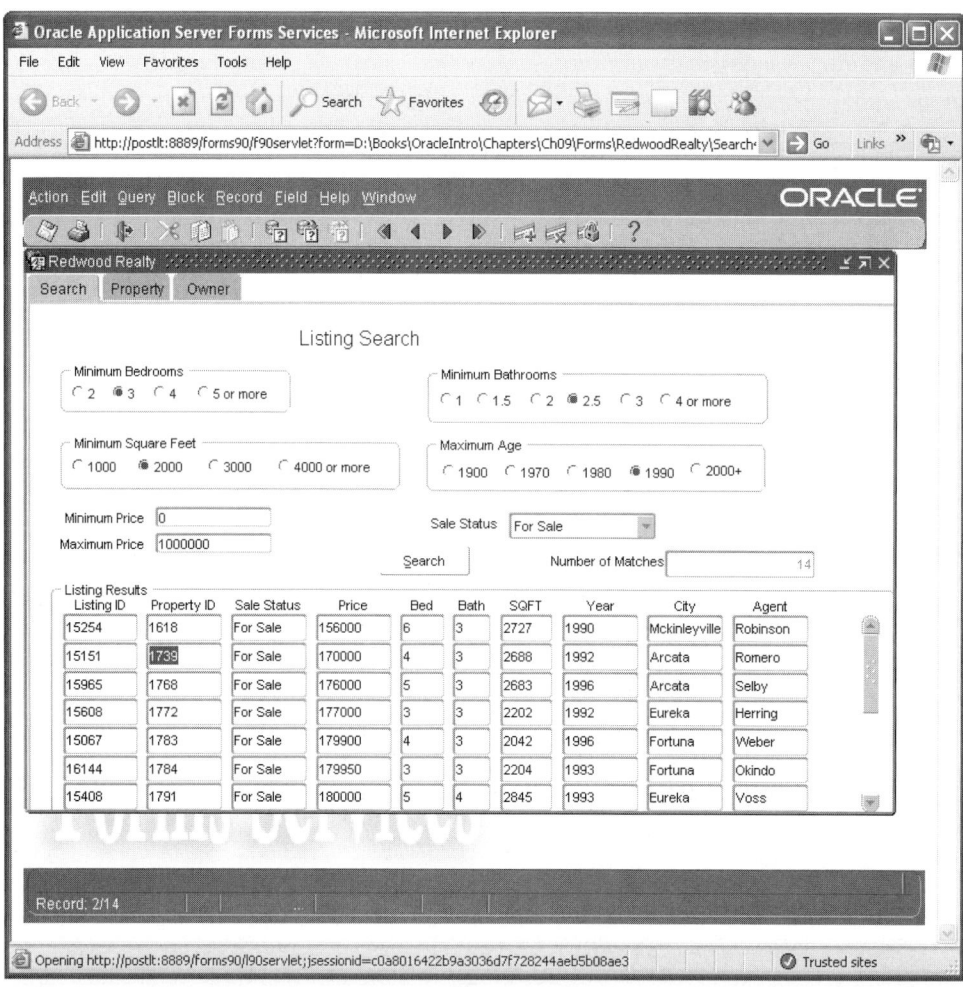

FIGURE 9.23 Tab canvas with links to Property and Owner data.

the desired attributes, get the detailed information on the property, perhaps printing the page, and quickly get the owner's name to make an appointment to show the property. Of course, you still have to work with the agents to ensure that the forms contain all of the data they need. For example, they might also want an easy method to look up the listing agent for a property.

Creating forms with a tab canvas actually requires almost no more steps than creating the forms with separate canvases. The main thing to remember is that if you want to use a tab canvas, it is best to start with one to save the step of transferring all of the data items. Whether you need to connect the pages with double-click triggers is up to you and the users. The form will work fine with just the page tabs.

EVALUATING FORM STYLES

You have now seen three ways to display related data on a form: (1) separate canvases, (2) stacked canvas, and (3) tab canvas. Actually, a fourth method exists: you can create the forms completely separately and use an OPEN_FORM command to switch to the next form. This method is slightly more difficult because it requires the use of global variables to open the form to some matching value. That is, there is no built-in join condition to match the data for you. This approach is explained in more detail in the applications chapter where it is used more heavily.

You have to choose which method to use. In some cases, performance and development teamwork play a role in the selection. However, ultimately the determining factor is user preference. The three canvas options are closely related in terms of performance and features. The biggest difference is how users want to navigate between the multiple canvases. They might prefer the tab approach that shows all of the options across the top of the window. For some forms, they might prefer to see the new data on a stacked canvas so they can compare it to data on the original form. In other cases, you might want to hide each canvas completely by using a separate canvas for each main group. This approach lets the user focus on only one step at a time. If needed, you can control the order in which the user sees each major page.

Note that in most of these new forms, the Property (and later Owner) tables are active. People could use them to change the data. You might want to restrict the ability to make changes through these forms. If so, just set the data block properties to remove UPDATE, INSERT, and DELETE.

As you build forms with multiple canvases, you will find some limitations. For example, you cannot place a stacked canvas directly on a tab canvas. Both of the specialty canvases have to be built on top of a regular content canvas. You can sometimes work around this limitation by creating a base content canvas, then drawing a tab canvas on top of it. Then you can place a stacked canvas on the main content canvas. But, you will have to work on the page layouts to create an effective user interface. In most cases, you are better off choosing one method or the other and avoid trying to mix the two.

The good news is that you now have three approaches to the same form. You can always use these as demonstration forms to show users, so they can see the differences among the three techniques. You can also use them to test for performance issues across a slower network.

CREATING WEB FORMS WITH JDEVELOPER

This section is optional because it uses a completely different form development tool. Eventually, this tool is likely to replace the Forms Designer, so you should begin to learn its capabilities. Remember that forms built with the Forms Designer require the client computer to have Java and the JInitiator installed. Consequently, these forms are not useful for deploying on the Web, particularly for customers or even suppliers. Oracle has created another technology that can be used for more traditional Web applications. At some point, it might even replace the older Forms Designer system completely. The new system is based on running Java programs on the server. This system generates relatively plain HTML pages that can be run on almost any computer. The technology is integrated with Java 2 Enterprise Edition (J2EE), and can use all of the powerful features of this system. However, J2EE is a large, complex system that takes time to learn and use. Consequently, Oracle has integrated several tools into the system to create a complete application development framework (ADF). The system relies on JDeveloper, an integrated development environment (IDE) that contains several visually oriented tools and wizards that make it easy to quickly build database-driven forms.

You need to install JDeveloper on your system. The process is relatively easy, but it does not use the standard Oracle installation tools. JDeveloper has been evolving rapidly, so you should probably download the latest release from the OTN Web site.

The package is a relatively small Zip file that you can find under the JDeveloper section on OTN.

1. Download the latest release of JDeveloper from OTN.
2. Unzip the files onto a folder on your system. Remember the location.
3. Find the main executable file (folder/jdev/bin/jdevw.exe), right-click it and use the **Send To/Desktop** option to place a shortcut on your desktop.

MODIFY THE LISTINGS TABLE AND SET UP YOUR SERVER FILES

The wizards in JDeveloper make it relatively easy to build basic forms to display data. It is even relatively easy to create master/detail forms. However, to demonstrate the power of the system, you will use it to create a simple housing search system that could be used by customers to look for houses. The first step is to build a simple main form to display basic information about a listing and the corresponding property, such as the asking price, number of bedrooms, and size of the house. However, it also would be nice to display a photo of the house if it is available. Recall that in the last chapter, you were able to store photographs of the house in the database itself. Unfortunately, this tool does not work with JDeveloper. Instead, you should follow the practice of most Web applications and store the images as files on the server. Then you can store the name of the file within the database and have the page retrieve the correct image for each house. You should set up the database and your server first.

1. Create a folder on the computer running JDeveloper to hold the images (C:\Temp).
2. Copy the sample HousePhoto.jpg file to the folder, or use one of your own pictures.
3. Use SQL*Plus to add a column to the Listings table to hold the file locations:

```
ALTER TABLE Listings
ADD PhotoFile NVARCHAR2(250);
```

4. Use SQL*Plus to assign the sample photo to one of the listings, making sure you enter the correct folder:

```
UPDATE Listings
SET PhotoFile = 'C:\Temp\HousePhoto.jpg'
WHERE ListingID=14979;
```

Now you can create a simple Web form to display the basic listing and property information. To shorten the process, you will use only a few columns for this example. You can now start JDeveloper by clicking the shortcut you created. There are three basic steps to create a Web page: (1) create a new data connection and a new Application Workspace, (2) create a data model that chooses the tables you will use, and (3) create the Web form and organize the items to be displayed.

You always have to create a data connection so that JDeveloper can find the database. But, you only have to perform this step once—you can then use the same connection for other pages and even for other projects. When you start JDeveloper, you should see a screen with several windows. The top-left window is the Application Navigator. It will contain a listing of the components that you create. Use this window to select a page or component to work on. The larger central window starts out empty, but eventually it will contain various pages of the application. The main window on the right will contain various palettes, which hold tools and items that you can place on your pages. Various secondary windows will appear at the bottom of both the left and right sides. You will need them at different times. You can rearrange the windows if you prefer, but for now it will be easier to follow the directions if you leave them in the

CHAPTER 9 Customizing Forms

default positions. If you happen to close a window, you can get it back by using the View option on the main menu at the top of the designer.

CREATE A DATA CONNECTION AND WORKSPACE

To create a data connection, you should know a few details about how the database was created. In most cases, you can use the default values, but to be safe, you should verify the database configuration with your DBA or instructor. If you installed the database, you should find your installation notes, or run the Oracle Net Manager program to look up some of the values.

1. In JDeveloper, click the **Connections** tab in the Application Navigator.
2. Right-click **Database** and choose **New Database Connection**.
3. If it appears, click **Next** on the welcome screen.
4. Figure 9.24 shows the overall screen, and that you should enter **Redwood** as the Connection Name.
5. Click **Next** and enter the username and password for the application.
6. Check the **Deploy Password** box and click **Next**.

You will generally follow the steps in the wizard, but a couple of entries in the Data Connection are a little tricky, and you probably should talk to your DBA to get accurate values. For example, if you deploy the password with the application, anyone who

FIGURE 9.24 Creating a new Data Connection in JDeveloper.

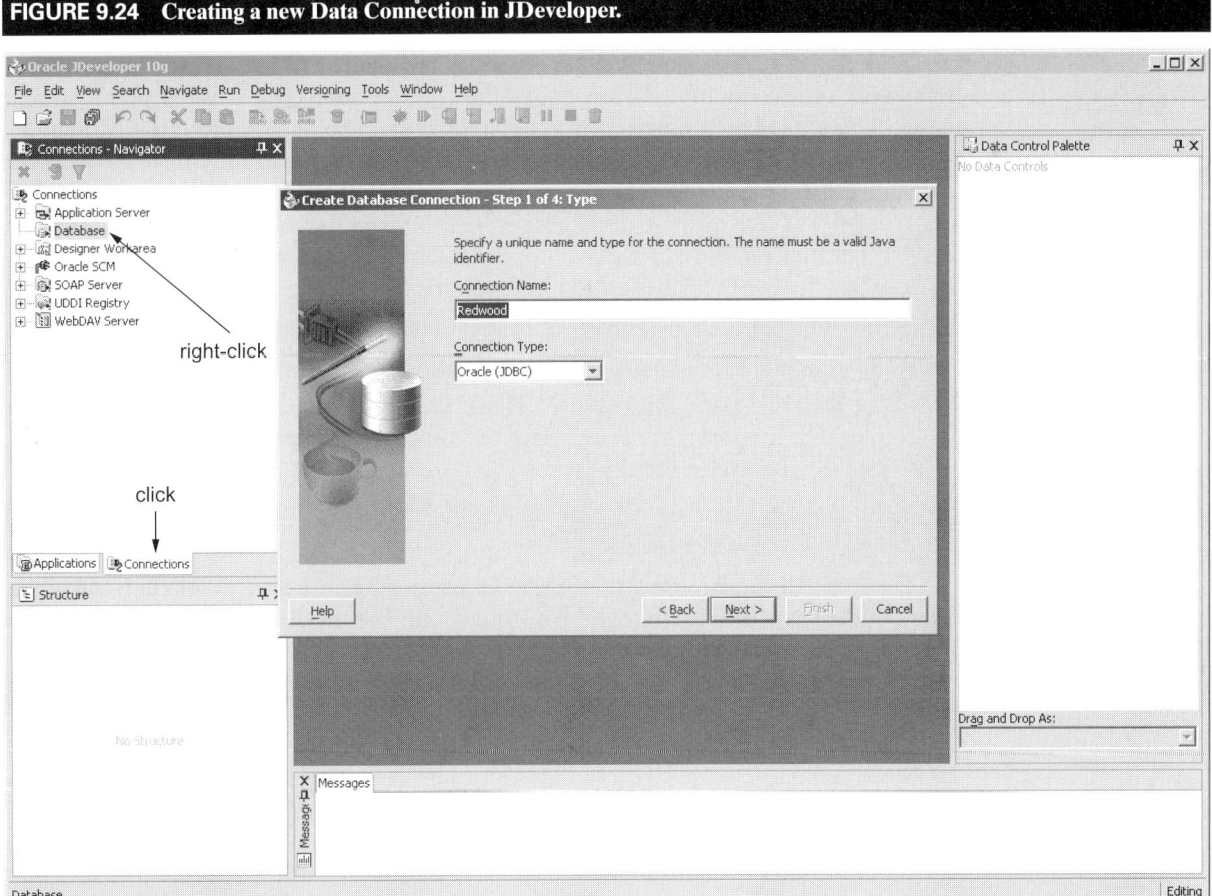

runs the form will have access to your application and the data that it provides. Since you have no way to give passwords to potential customers, you have to check this box, but your DBA might want to create a special account that has limited permissions.

7. Enter the Host Name on the database connection screen.
8. You might have to change the SID or even the port number, but try the default values first unless you know they are wrong.
9. Click **Next** and then click the button to **Test Connection**.
10. If the test is successful, click **Next** and then **Finish** to close the wizard. Otherwise, talk to your DBA to find the correct values.

Once the connection is established, you rarely will need to change it. Similarly, when you first start a new project, you have to create a workspace to hold all of your files. Ultimately, a workspace is a folder on your computer. It is usually created within the jdev\mywork subfolder in the location where you installed JDeveloper.

11. Click the **Applications** tab in the Application Navigator.
12. Right-click the Applications node and choose New Application Workspace.
13. Enter **RedwoodRealty** as the name of the workspace.
14. Select **Web Application [Default]** as the Application Template and click **OK**.

The system will add the new workspace and the Model and ViewController projects to the Application Navigator. You will use these items in the following steps.

CREATE THE BUSINESS COMPONENTS DATA MODEL

Oracle is using the Apache Jakarta framework to handle most of the server tasks. This framework relies on a model-view-controller (MVC) approach. This method is similar to the overall database approach. You begin by creating a data model. This data model has to be created within the Java server code, but since you already have defined the tables in the database, the wizard can just transfer that definition to the project. The view part means that you create pages separately from the data model. The controller is also separate from the other two components, but it is almost completely handled by the framework. For the most part, you just have to pick the data elements you need, and then build a page to display them.

1. Right-click the **Model** node in the Application Navigator and select **New**.
2. In the dialog, expand the Business Tier node and select the **Business Components** element. In the Items window, select the **Business Components from Tables** item. Click **OK** to move to the next screen.
3. Verify that the RedwoodRealty connection is chosen and click **OK**. Then, if the welcome screen appears, click **Next**.

The next three screens are similar to each other, but differ in their purpose. Figure 9.25 shows the first one. Be careful to read the top line on each screen so you understand its purpose.

4. If necessary, choose your database schema, then select the **Listings** table and click the arrow button (>) to move it to the Selected window on the right. Do the same for the Properties table and click **Next**.
5. This application will not alter any of the data, so you do not need any updateable tables. Click **Next**.
6. Again, select the **Listings** and **Properties** tables and move them to the right to use as a read-only data source. Click **Next**.

CHAPTER 9 Customizing Forms **455**

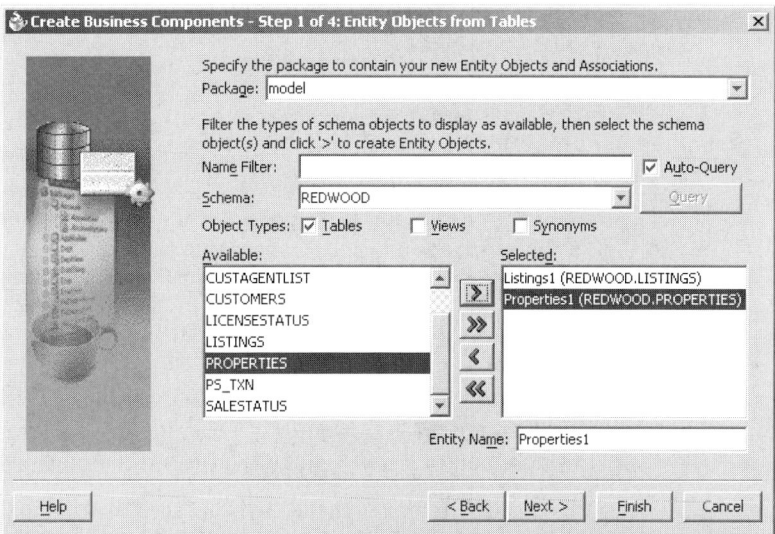

FIGURE 9.25 Choosing data tables.

7. Enter **RedwoodRealtyAM** as the name for the new Application Module and click **Next**. Click **Finish** on the last wizard screen.

The wizard will use the table definition to create the objects it needs internally. An entity object defines the fundamental data collection. If there are multiple entities, they will be connected through associations that are defined based on foreign key relationships defined in the tables. The system ultimately relies more on view objects which are similar to database views and can combine data from multiple entities. They use standard SQL statements. Both entities and views have attributes or columns. You can assign default values, set validation rules, and create calculated attributes in either an entity or a view. Simply double-click an entry in the Application Navigator and use the property editor to set the desired properties. Do not worry about those details now.

Although the system creates an association between the Listings and Properties entitics, it docs not yet allow you to select attributes from both entities to place on the form. Ultimately, you want to use Bedrooms, Bathrooms, and SQFT from the Properties table. Modify the ListingsView to accomplish this task.

1. Double-click the **ListingsView** entry in the Navigator to edit it.
2. Select the Entity Objects node in the tree, then highlight the Listings entry in the middle list. Click the arrow button (>) to move it to the Selected window. Do the same for the Properties entity.
3. Expand the Attributes node and select the Housephoto attribute. Click the Control Hints tab. Change Display Hint to **Hide**.
4. Select the Query node in the tree to see the SQL for this view. Edit the view to remove the Housephoto column.
5. Add four columns (or more) from the Properties table and add the join condition between the Listings and Properties tables. The wizard normally uses the older join syntax, but you can use INNER JOIN if you prefer.

```
SELECT Listings.LISTINGID,
       Listings.PROPERTYID,
       Listings.LISTINGAGENTID,
```

```
            Listings.SALESTATUSID,
            Listings.BEGINLISTDATE,
            Listings.ENDLISTDATE,
            Listings.ASKINGPRICE,
            Listings.PHOTOFILE,
            Properties.BEDROOMS,
            Properties.BATHROOMS,
            Properties.SQFT,
            Properties.YEARBUILT
    FROM LISTINGS Listings, PROPERTIES Properties
    WHERE Listings.PROPERTYID = Properties.PROPERTYID
```

6. Enter **LISTINGID** in the Order By line to sort the results. Click **Test** to check the syntax and fix any problems that arise.
7. Click the Attributes node. Select Bedrooms, Bathrooms, SQFT, and YearBuilt under the Properties node in the middle window and move them to the Selected window on the right. Click **OK** to close the editor.

Figure 9.26 shows the Attribute screen where you move attributes from the Properties table to make them available to the application. If you want to plan ahead, you can select all of the attributes just in case you need them later. Remember that there are three steps to combine data from multiple entities: (1) select Entity Objects and add both entities to the list, (2) select Query and write the join statement and add the new columns to the SELECT clause, and (3) select the Attributes and add the desired attributes to the selected list.

CREATE A JAVA SERVER PAGE TO DISPLAY DATA

The next step is to create a Web page to display data from the view you created. Basically, the wizard creates an HTML page and provides a mechanism for you to drag selected data items onto the page. If you are familiar with HTML, you can use tags to improve the layout and overall style. The version created here will be somewhat plain to keep it simple.

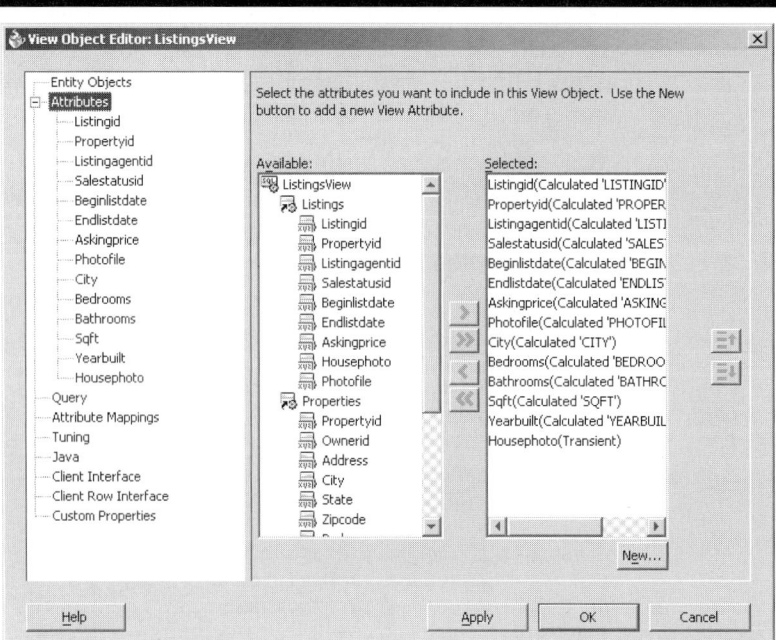

FIGURE 9.26 Selecting attributes from the Properties entity.

1. Right-click the ViewController project and select **New**.
2. In the dialog box, expand the Web Tier and select JavaServer Pages (JSP), and choose JSP Page in the Items window. Click **OK**.
3. Enter ListingProperty.jsp as the name of the new page and click **OK**.
4. Click at the top of the new page and type a title: **Property Listing**. Highlight the entry and select Heading 1 from the style box.
5. Click the Components tab at the bottom of the right-side palette. Choose CSS in the top drop-down list box. Drag the JDeveloper entry and drop it onto the form.

Notice the change in the title style when the style sheet is added. You can edit the style sheet later to change the overall look of your pages. The next step is to add a simple form and some data elements.

6. Click the form to place the cursor below the title. Click the HTML entry in the drop-down listing. Click the **Form** item.
7. Click inside the new form box and type labels for the data: Listing ID, Asking Price, Bedrooms, Bathrooms, SQFT, and Year Built. Add a blank space at the bottom of the form for buttons.
8. Click the **Data Controls** tab in the right-side palette. Expand the tree for RedwoodRealtyAMDataControl, then ListingsView1. Drag the Listingid entry to the form next to its label. Repeat the process for the other data items. Drag the Photofile item onto the form.
9. Expand the Operations node that lies inside the ListingsView1 node. Drag the Previous button onto the bottom of the form. Do the same thing to place a Next button adjacent to it.
10. Move the errors tag from the top of the form to beneath the title, but make sure it has a Paragraph style instead of Heading 1.

Figure 9.27 shows the basic form, but you can modify the layout.

11. To test the form, right-click the ViewController node and select **Run**. Click the **Next** button a couple of times to see new records.

Notice that if an image file exists, the current form simply displays the name. You really want to see the image itself. To see the image, insert an image tag that uses the file name as the source. The one catch is that if the file is blank, you will want to skip the image. You can use a JSTL "if" tag to rule out the blank entries and an HTML "img" tag to display the figure.

12. Close the browser window. Click the **Source** tab at the bottom of the display page. Find the tag that contains the Photofile name. Change that one line into the following:

```
<c:if test="${bindings.Photofile != ''}">
<img src='c:out value="${bindings.Photofile}"/>' height="100px' >
</c:if>
```

13. Save everything and run the form. Figure 9.28 shows a sample page. If you receive error messages, double-check the three new lines, noting that the Photofile reference is surrounded by curly braces, not parentheses.

Check the source on the form and you will see it is simple HTML. So any customer could use the form. You can build almost any type of form with these techniques. It is even easy to create master/detail forms.

ADDING A SEARCH FORM

To make the page more useful, you should add the ability for customers to enter search criteria, such as a price range and the number of bedrooms. There is not enough time or

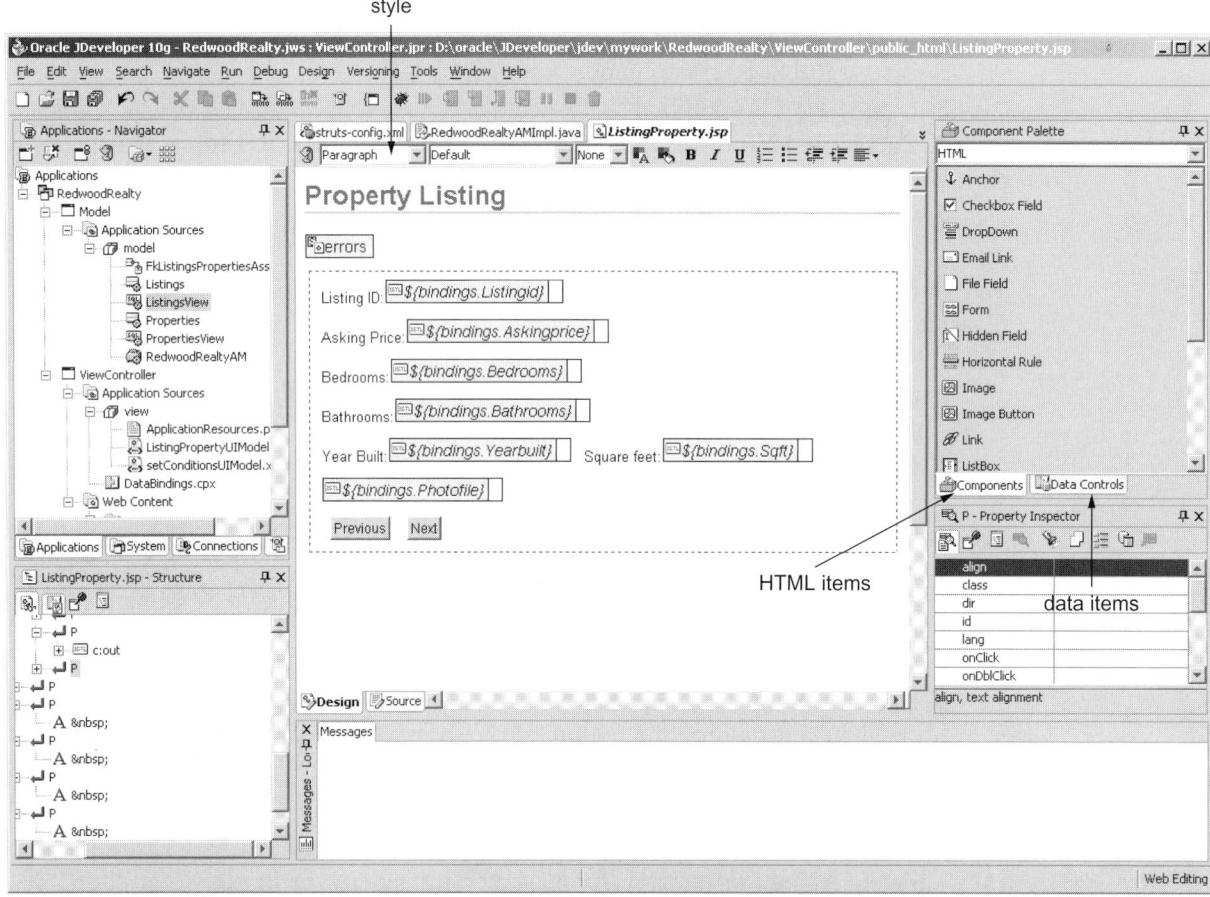

FIGURE 9.27 Design of the initial form.

space here to create a highly detailed search page, but even a simple form demonstrates the power of Oracle's system.

Four major steps are required to implement the search: (1) the most important step is to modify the query so that it applies the user values to the Where clause, (2) you create a small form to collect the user choices, (3) you create an action process between the parameter form and the results form, and (4) you link the user responses into your action process.

Altering the underlying query is the trickiest step. Oracle has several options, but the easiest is to create a separate procedure and simply append the WHERE clause to the query using string variables. However, this approach has security risks if you allow users to type text into a data field. It is called a SQL injection attack, and you should avoid letting anyone type text as a value. It is always better to use drop-down lists or radio buttons. If you do allow text, you should have a routine examine the text for special characters (especially comment characters) and limit the length of the data. But, to keep this example simple, it will use unsafe text values for the low and high price items. So, do not implement this code in a real project, but you could use it to see if you can create a SQL injection attack against your own project to understand the dangers.

1. Select the RedwoodRealtyAM node in the Application Navigator, then expand the entries in the Structure viewer and double-click the **RedwoodRealtyAMImpl.java** file so you can edit it.

CHAPTER 9   Customizing Forms   **459**

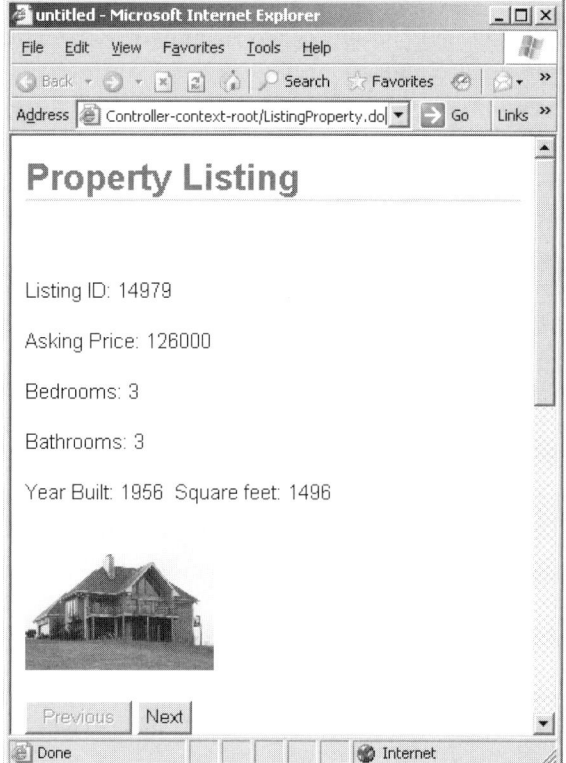

FIGURE 9.28   Initial form.

2. Scroll to the bottom of the file, and directly above the ending curly brace, add the code:

```
public void setConditions (String sLow, String sHigh,
   String nBedrooms, String nBathrooms)
{
  oracle.jbo.ViewObject LVO = findViewObject("ListingsView1");
  String sWhereClause = "SALESTATUSID=101"
    + " AND (BATHROOMS >= " + nBathrooms + ")"
    + " AND (BEDROOMS >= " + nBedrooms + ")";
  sWhereClause += " AND (ASKINGPRICE >= " + sLow + ")"
    + " AND (ASKINGPRICE < " + sHigh + ")";
  LVO.setWhereClause(sWhereClause);
  LVO.executeQuery();
}
```

3. Double-click the **RedwoodRealtyAM** node in the Navigator to open the edit dialog window. Select the Client Interface node. Select the setConditions entry and click the arrow button (>) to move it to the Selected window. Click **OK**.

Once you have created and registered the function, begin connecting it into the application. JDeveloper relies on a visual editor to help connect data pages and data actions. The Struts controller is responsible for coordinating all actions, and you can determine the page flow using the Struts Page Flow Diagram.

1. Right-click the ViewController node and select Open Struts Page Flow Diagram. Drag a Data Action from the Component palette onto the diagram page near the existing /ListingProperty page icon. Click the name or double-click the new icon and rename it as **/setConditions**.

2. Click the Data Controls tab in the palette. Expand the Redwood RealtyAMDataControlnode, then the main Operations node. Drag the setConditions entry and drop it onto the new Data Action in the diagram.
3. Click the **Components** tab to change the palette. Click the **Forward** entry. Click the **/setConditions** action icon, then click the **/ListingProperty** page icon.

Figure 9.29 shows how the /setConditions action is going to communicate with the /ListingProperty page. After the WHERE clause is applied in the new function, the query is executed and the results are passed to the ListingProperty page for display.

Of course, you still need some way to collect the user choices and pass them into the setConditions function. You could build the query form on a separate page, but it will save the user a couple of steps if you place the data entry items on the original display form.

1. On the struts diagram, double-click the **/ListingProperty** icon to open the form.
2. Click on the page to place the cursor below the existing form. Click the **Components** tab. Select Struts HTML (not just HTML) from the drop-down list.
3. Drag a form to the bottom of the JSP page, and select the setConditions.do entry as the action when the dialog box pops up. Click **OK**.
4. In the new form box, type labels for **Low Price, High Price, Bedrooms,** and **Bathrooms**.

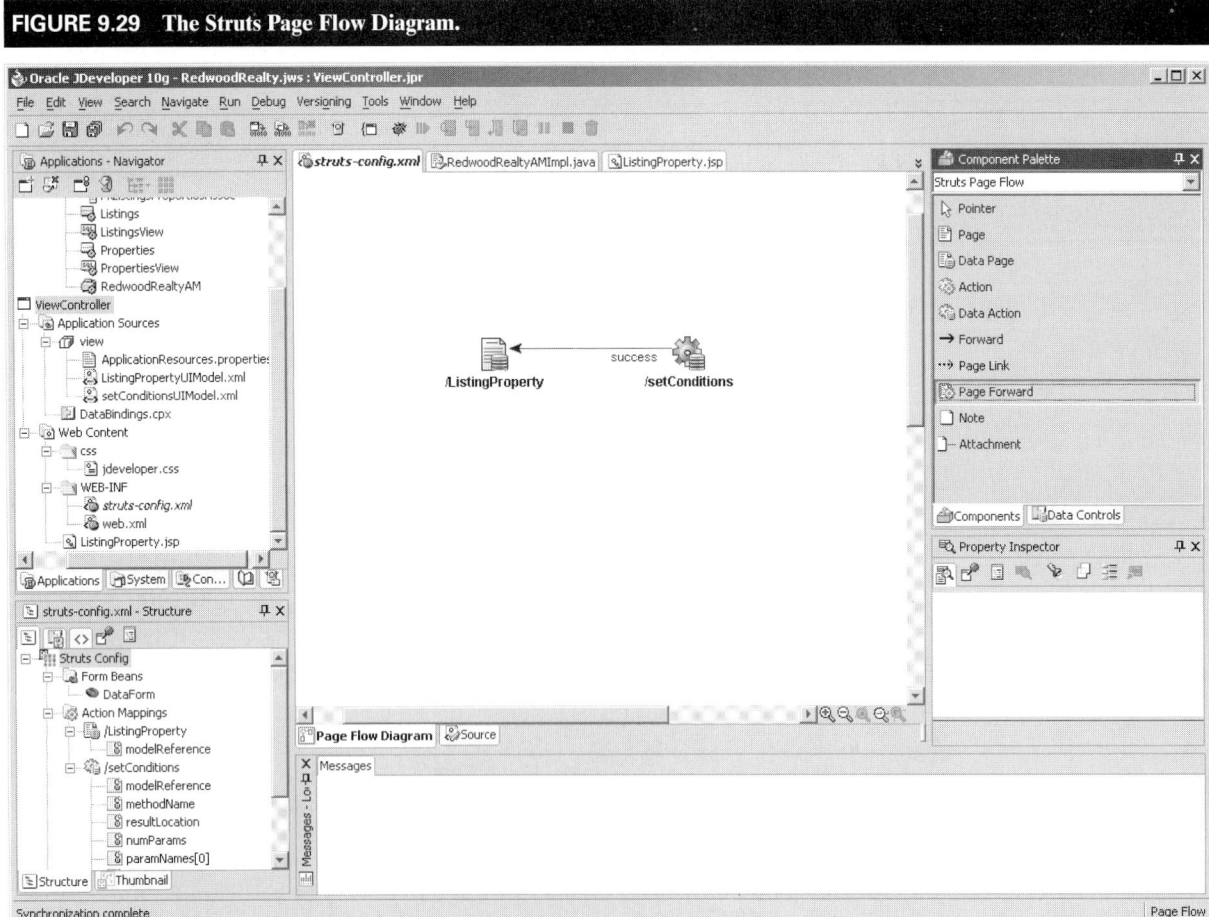

FIGURE 9.29 The Struts Page Flow Diagram.

CHAPTER 9 Customizing Forms **461**

5. Switch to plain HTML in the drop-down list. Select a Text Field and drag it onto the form adjacent to the Low Price label. Use the Property Inspector to set its name to LowPrice and set the value to **0**. Repeat the process for HighPrice with a value of **250000**.

6. Drag a Radio Button next to the Bedrooms label and type the number **1** next to it. Set its name to nBeds with a value of 1. Drag more radio buttons down so you have 1, 2, 3, 4, and 5 or more. Make sure they all have the same name to make them mutually exclusive. Set the checked property to true for the third button.

7. Repeat step 6 for bathrooms with a name of nBaths. Drag a Submit Button onto the form and change its Value to Search.

8. Switch to Source view for the page and find the first <form> entry. It needs an action element, so change the code to:

```
<form action="ListingProperty.do">
```

Figure 9.30 shows the basic structure of the new form in design view. Your layout might be different, and eventually you want to replace the text boxes with drop-down

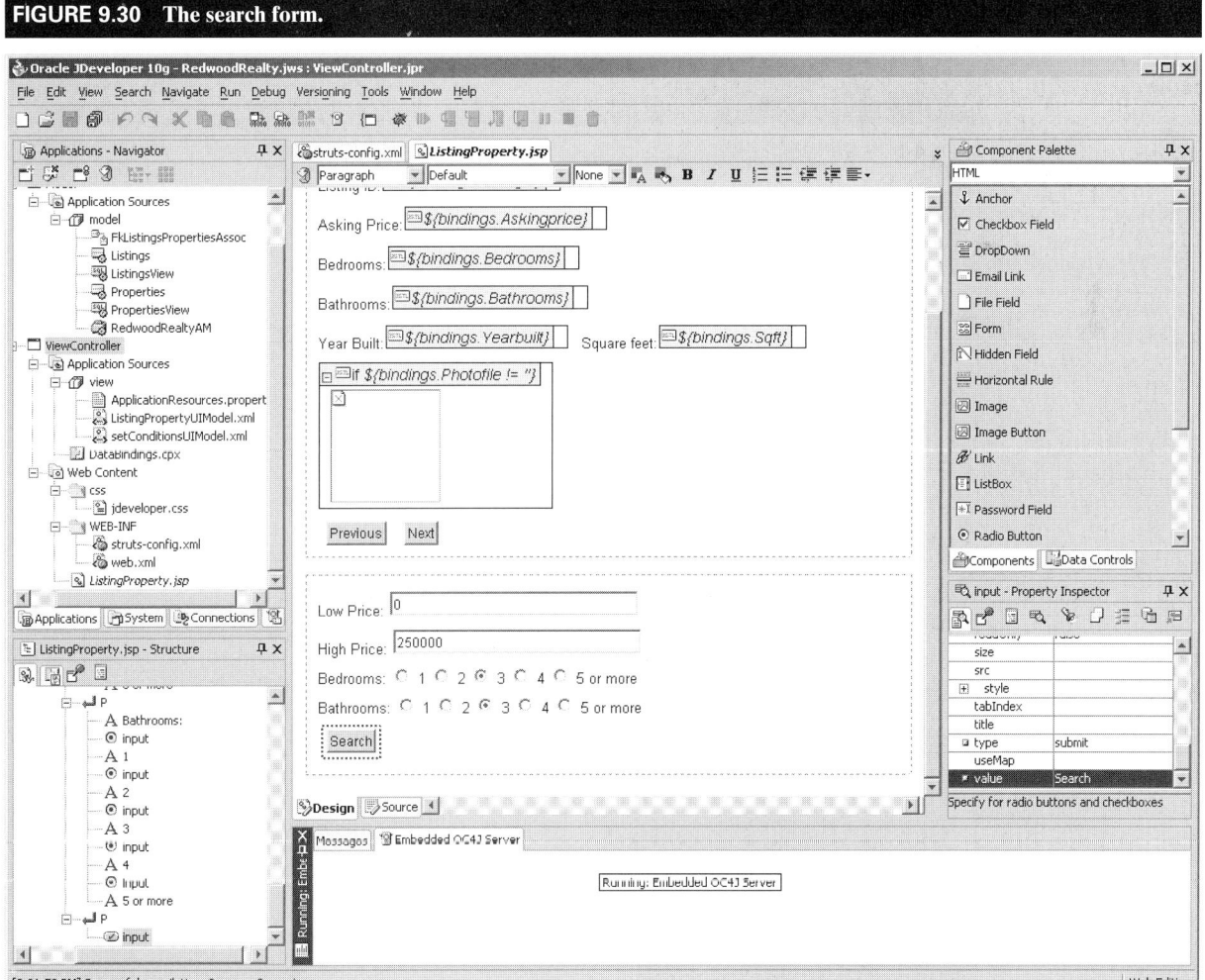

FIGURE 9.30 The search form.

lists. It is always risky to let users enter data directly into text boxes. It is highly likely that they will enter bad data. But, the text boxes will work for initial testing. It is straightforward to create drop-down lists simply by dragging them onto the form and double-clicking the box to set its values.

The next major step is to connect the query form values to the data action procedure that you wrote.

1. Click the **struts** tab in the main window to return to the page flow diagram.
2. In the Structure window at the lower left, expand Action Mappings node, then expand /setConditions. Click the entry for the first parameter: **paramNames[0]**.
3. In the Property Inspector (lower right corner), change the value entry to **${param.LowPrice}**, and remember to use curly braces and not parentheses.
4. Set the second parameter to **${param.HighPrice}**, the third to **${param.nBeds}**, and the fourth to **${param.nBaths}**.
5. Right-click an empty spot on the struts page and select Diagram/Refresh Diagram from All Pages.

As shown in Figure 9.31, your diagram should indicate that the query form on the /ListingProperty page will send data (dashed line) to the /setConditions action function. When that query is successful, the results will be transferred back to the /ListingProperty page to be displayed. Additionally, when the user clicks the Next or

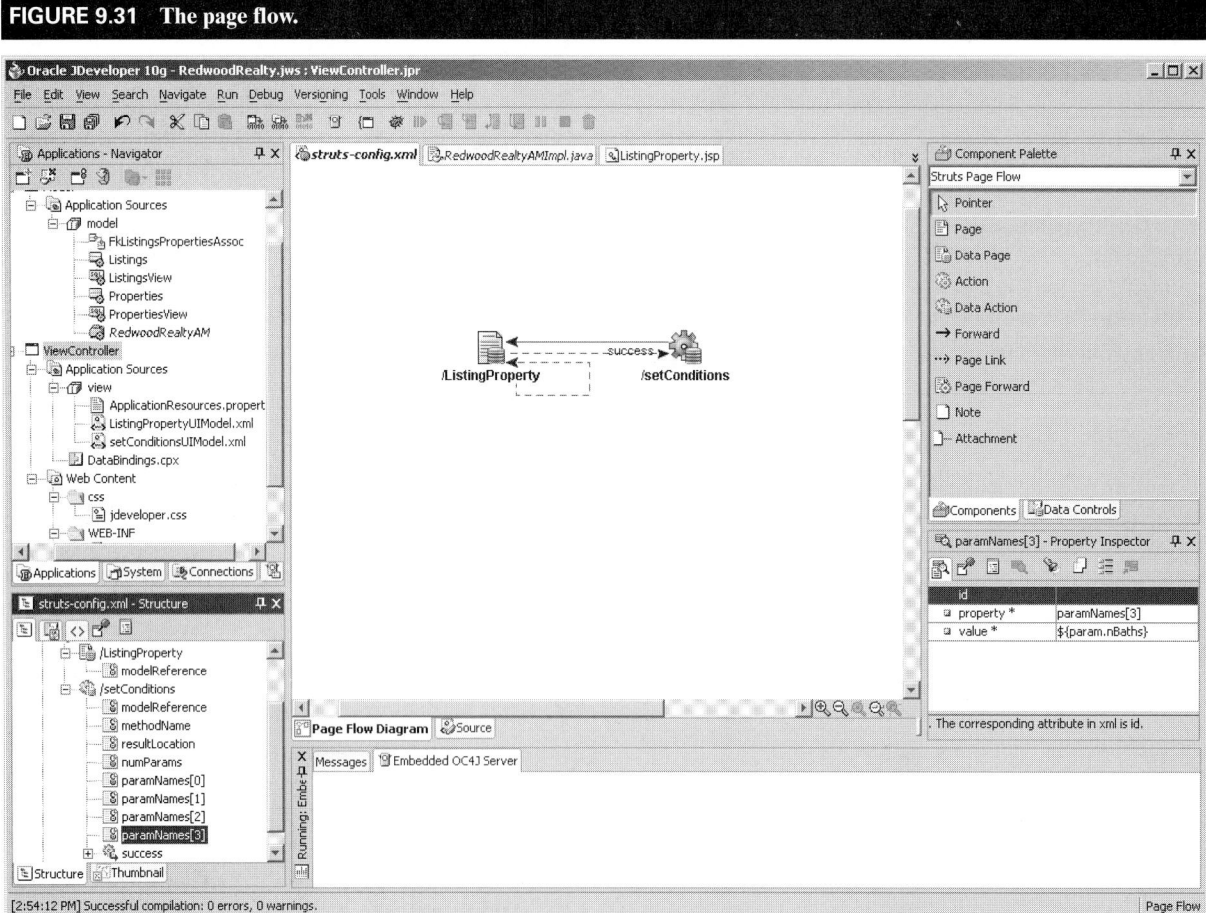

FIGURE 9.31 The page flow.

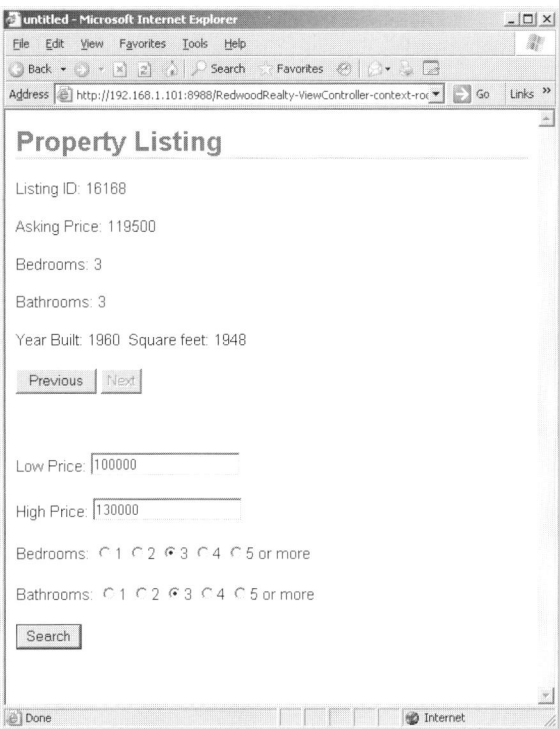

FIGURE 9.32 The final form.

Previous button, the ListingProperty page will call itself and display the next item from the query. You can now run the application and test the forms.

1. Right-click the ListingProperty icon and select **Run**.
2. Enter some values in the search form, such as **100000** and **130000** for prices and click the **Query** button.
3. Click the **Next** button to scroll through the list and ensure that all properties match your search conditions.

Figure 9.32 shows the form with some sample data. The form needs some work before you can give it to the public. Try entering prices that include commas or dollar signs and see what happens. You can see why those should be drop-down lists. You would also add more selection options based on size and city. You would also want to format the output to provide a better-looking page, and include contact information so customers know which agent to call. But all of these details are easy now that you know how to build the overall page.

Summary

The form wizards are nice tools, but eventually you have to understand the underlying structure of forms so that you can customize them. The goal of a form is to make it easy for users to perform their tasks. You can customize a form and use form triggers and multiple canvases to achieve this goal. You should understand the three primary aspects to Oracle forms: (1) a canvas holds items that are displayed to the user, (2) a data block handles the interface between the form and the database, and (3) you can write custom code to automate tasks that are triggered by events on the form.

When you want to create form elements that are not directly tied to the database, it is easier to create a canvas and data block manually. You can also manually create data blocks to retrieve and store data, but the wizards automate some of the repetitive tasks.

Oracle supports many events with form triggers. You rarely need to use all of them, but you should understand the timing of the events to choose the correct trigger for your application. The events used the most often are the Pre-Form, When-Button-Pressed, and When-Validate-Item events. However, you often need some of the others to monitor changes in data. Because of limited scope and lifetime, variables created within one trigger are not accessible to other triggers. To pass data across triggers, you will have to store it in a global variable. Be sure that you incorporate error handling in your forms. You can trap runtime errors in your code with EXCEPTION code and you can use the form's On-Error trigger to trap broader database errors. The debugger will help you find the cause of errors by enabling you to step through the code line-by-line and observe the value of the variables.

You use trigger code for several common actions, including the ability to jump to a specific item or data block on the form. Three common tasks that often require more effort are: (1) generating key values with sequences, (2) validating form input, and (3) computing and displaying subtotals. You will often use these tools in business applications. They rely on the power of form triggers, and the code is straightforward. Once you understand these basic tasks, you should be able to handle more complex issues.

Making life easier for users requires thought and access to several different options. The use of multiple canvases provides you with several choices in terms of style. A key feature of relational database systems is that data is separated into individual tables. However, users rarely think in terms of these separate tables. You use forms to display related data together. But, sometimes you cannot put every possible item onto one window. In these situations, you can place data onto multiple canvases. The types of canvases differ based on how the user switches to the different views. With simple separate canvases, you place buttons on each canvas to switch back and forth. With a stacked canvas, you can display one canvas on top of another so the user can see both sets of data at the same time. With a tab canvas, the user clicks on the display tab to see each section of data. You create each of these systems by following similar steps. The choice ultimately comes down to which method works best for the user.

Key Terms

- alert form
- EXCEPTION statement
- forms debugger
- frames
- GLOBAL prefix
- hard coded
- information overload
- lifetime of a variable
- runtime error
- scope of a variable
- sequence
- sequence of events
- stacked canvas
- standard extensions (built-in functions)
- tab canvas
- viewport
- WHERE clause

Review

True/False

1. Alert forms are good tools to use often because they interrupt the user.
2. The forms debugger is a good way to find syntax errors in your code.
3. A global variable created in a When-Button-Pressed trigger can be accessed by code in the form's Pre-Form trigger.
4. A stacked canvas is a way to let users compare data from two different tables.
5. A tab canvas cannot be combined with a stacked canvas.

Fill in

1. To create a search form that retrieves data matching the choices selected by a user, set the _____ property in the data block to connect to the items on the form.
2. The _____ built-in function can be used to display a different canvas by transferring the focus to a text box on that canvas.

3. To obtain a new key value from a sequence, you use the _____ property of the sequence.

4. With a stacked canvas, you set the _____ properties to control where data will be displayed with the new canvas.

5. To evaluate data entered by a user and to ensure that it meets certain conditions, you would write code in the _____ trigger.

MULTIPLE CHOICE

1. To catch runtime errors on a form not created by your PL/SQL code, use
   a. An EXCEPTION statement
   b. An On-Error trigger
   c. A DECLARE statement
   d. A GLOBAL prefix
   e. A Pre-Form trigger

2. To capture the value in a text box before a user changes it, you would use
   a. GLOBAL.oldValue in a Pre-Text-Item trigger
   b. GLOBAL.oldValue in a Post-Text-Item trigger
   c. Sequence.NEXTVAL in a Pre-Text-Item trigger
   d. GO_ITEM('GLOBAL') in a Pre-Text-Item trigger
   e. Local variable in a Post-Text-Item trigger

3. Which of the following is a built-in function from the standard extensions used to add entries to a list box?
   a. GO_ITEM
   b. SHOW_ALERT
   c. ADD_MONTHS
   d. ADD_LIST_ELEMENT
   e. SHOW_VIEW

4. Some of the main events when a form starts occur in the following order:
   a. Pre-Form, On-Logon, When-New-Item-Instance, Pre-Record
   b. When-New-Form-Instance, Pre-Block, When-New-Block-Instance, Post-Logon
   c. Pre-Logon, Pre-Form, Pre-Block, When-New-Block-Instance
   d. Pre-Form, Pre-Record, Pre-Text-Item, Pre-Block, Post-Form
   e. When-New-Item-Instance, When-New-Record-Instance, When-New-Block-Instance

5. For which of the following errors would the forms debugger be the most useful?
   a. Users get an error message saying they do not have permission to change the data
   b. Two sequence numbers are being generated instead of one when the form runs
   c. You consistently forget the underscores when typing names of built-in functions
   d. Users complain that the tabs on a tab canvas are not displayed correctly
   e. The form generates error messages when trying to save data

Hands-on Exercises

1. EXTENDING THE CHAPTER CASE

The manager often wants to see the total listings of sales by each agent. You need to create a form similar to the property Search form, but simpler. The manager wants to pick an agent, enter a start date and end date, pick a sale status (for sale, pending, or sold), and see the listings that match those conditions. The form should display the total value of those listings. The steps are similar to those used to create the property Search form, so refer back to those steps if you need more detailed instructions.

1. Create a new form without the wizards and add a blank canvas (**Search_Canvas**) and empty data block (**Search_Block**). Add text boxes for **Beginning Date**, **Ending Date**, and **Listing Agent**. Set the initial values for beginning and ending dates as **01-Jan-2006** and **31-Dec-2006** respectively. Add a list item box for the Sale Status with the three elements (**For Sale = 101**, **Pending = 102**, **Sold = 103**). Using the LOV wizard, create a list of values for the agents:

```
SELECT AGENTS.AGENTID, AGENTS.LASTNAME,
AGENTS.FIRSTNAME FROM AGENTS ORDER BY
AGENTS.LASTNAME, AGENTS.FIRSTNAME
```

2. For the search results, use SQL PLUS to create a new view:

```
CREATE VIEW AgentListings AS SELECT
ListingID, Listings.PropertyID,
ListingAgentID, SaleStatusID,
BeginListDate, EndListDate, AskingPrice,
City FROM Properties INNER JOIN Listings ON
Properties.PropertyID =
Listings.PropertyID;
```

3. Create a new data block (**Listings**) that pulls from the new view. Be sure to set the main properties: Query All Records=**Yes**, Query Data Name=

```
(SELECT ListingID, PropertyID,
ListingAgentID, SaleStatusID,
BeginListDate, EndListDate, City,
AskingPrice FROM AgentListings)
```

WHERE clause=

```
(BeginListDate <= :SEARCH_BLOCK.TXT_ENDDATE
AND EndListDate >= :SEARCH_BLOCK.TXT_
BEGINDATE) AND (ListingAgentID =
:SEARCH_BLOCK.TXT_AGENTID) AND
(SaleStatusID =
:SEARCH_BLOCK.LIST_SALESTATUS)
```

ORDER By=**BeginListDate**, and enter all of the columns in the Query Data Source Columns listing.

4. Add a tabular frame to the canvas to display the data from the Listings block. Add text boxes to display: **ListingID, PropertyID, BeginListDate, EndListDate,** and **AskingPrice**.

5. Add a **Search** button to the Search_Block with trigger code: **GO_BLOCK('LISTINGS'); EXECUTE_QUERY;**

6. The manager likes to use a mouse instead of a keyboard, so add a button next to the Agent text box to open the list of values. Use the trigger code: **GO_ITEM('TXT_AGENTID'); LIST_VALUES;**

7. To display and calculate the total of the asking price for the displayed items, add a text box to the LISTINGS data block and set properties similar to those in Figure 9.23, but use Prompt and Name=**Subtotal**, Summary Function=**Sum**, Summarized Block=**LISTINGS**, and Summarized Item=**ASKINGPRICE**.

8. Add a text box to the Search_Block just above the frame over the Asking Price column. Name=**Subtotal**, Justification=**Right**, Data Type=**Number**, Format Mask=**$99,999,990**, Calculation Mode=**Formula**, Formula=:**LISTINGS.Subtotal**, Database Item=**No**, Prompt=**Subtotal**.

9. Print the form to hand in. Your instructor might also want a copy of the file.

2. COFFEE MERCHANT

The Coffee Merchant needs some improvements to the Order form. The biggest problem is that workers would like an easy way to get information about the items being ordered. Recall that the form is a relatively standard main/sub form with some basic data about the order and the customer in the main form. The detail section contains a list of items being ordered. There should already be an LOV on InventoryID to help the clerks pick the correct item from the Inventory table. However, it would be nice to provide a stacked canvas so the clerks can see more of the detailed data about the inventory if necessary.

1. Begin by copying the Orders.fmb file from the work you did in Chapter 8 into a new folder for this chapter. Compile and test the form to ensure that it works. While you are editing the form, for the date, set the Initial Value=**$$DATE$$**.

2. Add a stacked canvas and draw a viewport on the right half of the sub form display. Rename the original canvas (**Main_Canvas**) and call the new one **Inventory** so you can keep them straight.

3. Use the data block wizard to add a new data block using all columns from the Inventory table. Be sure to create the relationship: **Inventory.InventoryID=OrderLines.InventoryID.** Use the layout wizard to place all of the items on the new Inventory canvas. Adjust the frame so that all of the items fit within the viewport. Use the drop-down list at the top of the form to switch to the Inventory_Canvas to help you see the viewport and frame.

4. Create a Pre-Form trigger to initially hide the new canvas, and add a check box to the main form so the user can display or hide the stacked canvas as needed:

```
IF (:CHK_INVENTORY > 0) THEN
     SHOW_VIEW('INVENTORY');
ELSE
     HIDE_VIEW('INVENTORY');
END IF;
```

5. You need to generate the OrderID automatically, so add a sequence for the Orders table (**seq_Orders** starting at 300,000) and add the trigger code to insert it in the Orders form when a new record is added. Use the example from the chapter as a guide, particularly for the global variable indicator in then Pre-Form and When-New-Form-Instance triggers.

6. You should also create a subtotal for the items being ordered. The one catch is that you need to multiply price times the quantity being purchased. To display this value on the form, you will need to delete the Name column. Create a new text box called ItemValue, set Calculation Mode=**Formula**, and the Formula= **ROUND ((:ORDERLINES.QUANTITY*:ORDERLINES.PRICE) * (1-:ORDERLINES.DISCOUNT),2)**. You also need to set the basic properties including prompt and format mask.

7. Add a new text box to the order lines grid to compute the subtotal. Follow the example in Figure 9.23, but set Name=**Subtotal**, Summary Function=**Sum**, Summarized Block= **ORDERLINES**, and Summarized Item= **ITEMVALUE**.

8. Add a text box to the Orders block just above the frame over the ItemValue column. Name=**Subtotal**, Justification=**Right**, Data Type=**Number**, Format Mask= **FML9G999D00**, Calculation Mode=**Formula**, Formula=: **ORDERLINES. Subtotal**, Database Item=**No**, Prompt=**Subtotal**. Be sure to set the Query All Records property to **Yes** for the ORDERLINES data block.

9. Print the form to hand in. Your instructor might also want a copy of the file.

3. ROWING VENTURES

The Rowing Ventures case is relatively small in terms of the number of tables. At the same time, the tables are closely related and many times users will want to reference data in multiple tables. Therefore, it makes sense to build a tab form that contains all of the related data. Users will be able to switch back and forth to see exactly the pieces they need.

So, start from scratch and build a new tab form and call it **RaceDay.** Create pages for: Race, RaceTimes, Boat + BoatCrew, Person, and Organization. Use the data block and layout wizards to create the forms for each page. For the Race and Times pages you want to use a tabular layout. Be sure to specify a sort order for the Times data block. For the Boat + BoatCrew page, you want a main and sub form similar to what you created in Chapter 8. The Person and Organization forms should display single rows. Be sure to set the correct join conditions when you create the new forms. Include LOVs where needed.

Since the race form includes all races, you should automatically load the data when the form starts. Place an **EXECUTE_QUERY;** statement in the When-New-Block-Instance trigger for the Race data block. You should also add a sequence and generate new RaceID keys automatically.

You can test the form, but note that it will not allow you to enter new values for boats, people, or organizations. Because these items are tied back to the race itself, these pages can only be used to display the people and organizations already registered. The form works reasonably well for race-day entries of the results and provides quick information about the boats and people involved. You could always use the existing forms to enter new boats or people. Or you could create additional tabs with new forms to add boats, people, and organizations. Just be careful not to build a relationship back to the race.

4. BROADCLOTH CLOTHING

To continue building forms for the Broadcloth Clothing company, you need to create the shipping forms. Because these forms contain a large amount of data, you decide to build them on a tab canvas. The primary tab will contain the Shipment and ShipmentItem tables as a main and sub form. Include a computation that shows the total number of items being shipped. The Item data should be added, as another tab canvas that can be displayed by the user when desired. The customer data should be displayed on a separate page that is linked to the shipping form. There will be no need to add new customers using this form because the customer must already exist at the time of shipping, but clerks might have to update a phone number or address. Create all necessary LOVs. Be sure to create a sequence and automatically generate values for the ShipmentID. For the Item form, create a view that includes all of the columns from the Item table along with the ModelDescription from the Model table. Similarly, for the Customer page, use a view that includes the name and phone number of the customer contact—in case the clerk needs to call the contact.

When you look at the CustomerOrder table you will see that it already includes a delivery address. It would be nice if the shipment form could automatically pick up that address and insert it as the default shipping address when a customer is chosen. You want to create the code on the validate trigger for the OrderID item in the Shipment Item sub form. The only complication is that this code will run each time an OrderID is entered—that is, it will run for each row in the tabular form. First, make sure you create an LOV for the OrderID field that displays orders only from the selected customer. Set the record group query to be:

```
SELECT ALL CUSTOMERORDER.ORDERID,
CUSTOMERORDER.CUSTOMERID,
CUSTOMERORDER.ORDERDATE
FROM CUSTOMERORDER
WHERE CUSTOMERID=:SHIPMENT.CUSTOMERID
ORDER BY CUSTOMERORDER.ORDERDATE
```

Then use the validation trigger for the OrderID field:

```
BEGIN
    SELECT DeliveryAddress,
           DeliveryCity,
           DeliveryState,
           DeliveryPostal,
           DeliveryNation
    INTO :SHIPMENT.ShipAddress,
         :SHIPMENT.ShipCity,
         :SHIPMENT.ShipState,
         :SHIPMENT.ShipPostal,
         :SHIPMENT.ShipNation
    FROM CustomerOrder WHERE
    OrderID=:SHIPMENTITEM.OrderID;
END;
```

You should look at the various text boxes and decide if you can use any validation rules. For example, since it is a shipping form, the quantity shipped would always be greater than zero. You will probably have to turn in the entire form to your instructor to be able to show the many features of this form.

CHAPTER

CREATING AND MODIFYING REPORTS

Learning Objectives

In this chapter, you will learn:

- How to create reports using the wizard.
- How to modify the structure of a form.
- How to enhance a report with detailed features and customization.
- How to filter the data for a report.
- How to create and deploy a Web report.

INTRODUCING REPORTS DEVELOPER

The original purpose of reports was to create printed listings of data to provide information to decision makers. Today, decision makers might prefer to work directly with data on a Web site and stay away from paper. In many cases, you can use forms to provide an interactive environment for decision makers to explore the data. On the other hand, reports have some powerful features that are easy to create in reports, but would require additional effort on forms. In particular, reports are really good at displaying subtotals—even at multiple levels. Even if the organization chooses to view data online, reports are useful tools to create both detailed and aggregate pictures of the data. Oracle Developer Suite includes a reports developer tool with wizards that help you build the basic report.

WEB PUBLISHING AND PAPER REPORTS

When computers were large, expensive machines, managers relied on paper reports to hold the day-to-day information they needed to make decisions. It was common for organizations to print detailed reports overnight and distribute them in the morning. With the expanding use of networks—particularly wireless networks—managers can now rely on the availability of online access. Consequently, managers often ask for interactive reports that they can open on a Web site. You can create a Web site that contains common data such as customer lists or sales reports. Managers can filter the reports for exactly the data they want, or drill down to more information by opening a more detailed report. Oracle Reports Builder can build both paper- and Web-based reports. In fact, you often use the wizard to create both layouts at the same time. Since the underlying process is the same, this chapter starts with a discussion of reports in general and focuses on the paper layout. The later sections discuss the details needed to customize Web-based reports.

TYPES OF REPORTS

You need to understand the main layouts commonly used for reports before you try to build one. The main types are: (1) *tabular report* or simple listing, (2) control break or *group report*, (3) *matrix report* or cross tab, and (4) *mailing labels*. Figure 10.1 shows an example of the tabular report. Tabular reports are simple listings of data. Sometimes there are subtotals at the bottom if the table holds numeric data. They are easy to create and easy to read. However, with decent online access, they are not particularly useful. Years ago, managers would print out huge listings of all data—primarily so they would have a copy nearby. Today, it is simpler to just issue a query and get a short list or any totals that are needed. However, you will still need to be able to produce these reports. Just remember that they should always be sorted.

Figure 10.2 is a typical example of a group report that displays sales by city and by agent. The word "by" is critical in that last sentence. Whenever you hear a manager ask for a report that includes that word, you most likely will need a group report. Essentially, the group report displays a detailed list of items, but breaks the listing into groups based

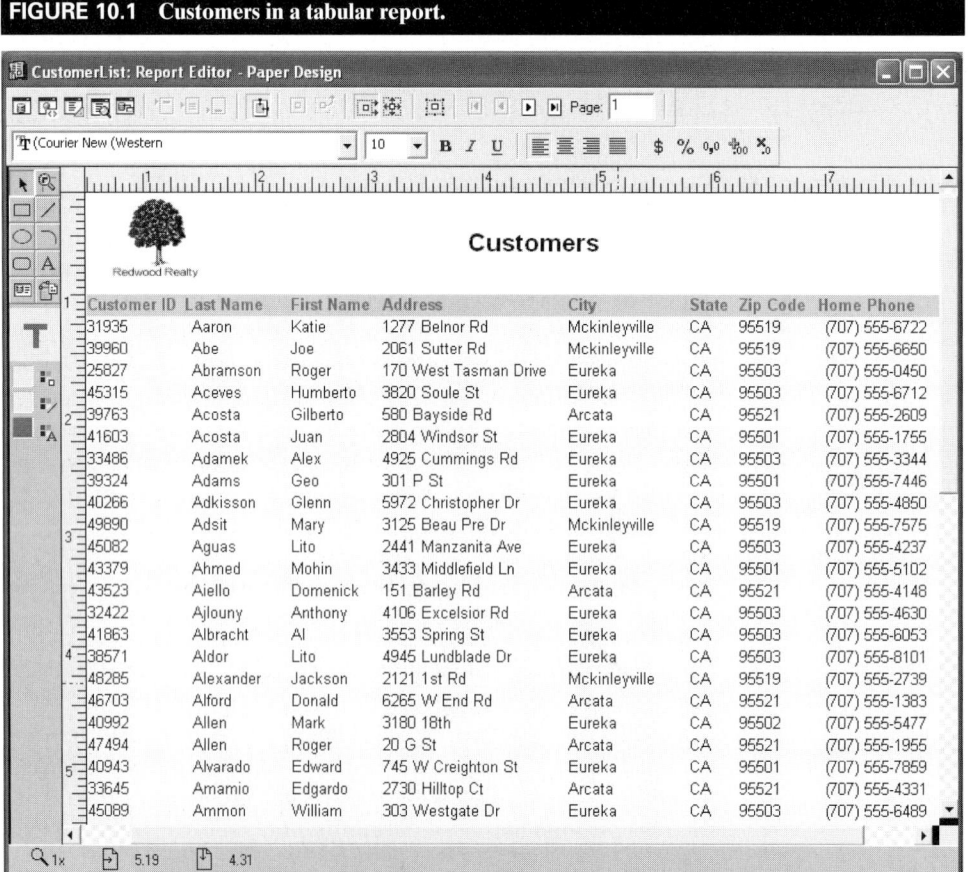

FIGURE 10.1 Customers in a tabular report.

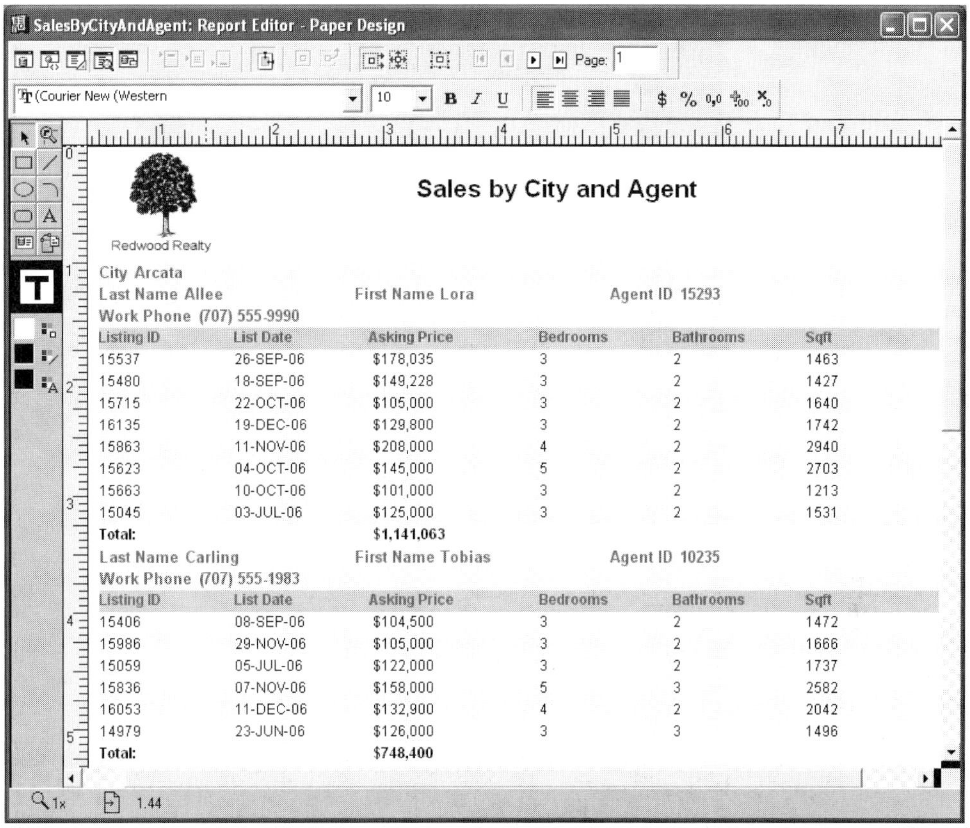

FIGURE 10.2 Grouped report shows sales by city and agent.

on some variable. In this example, it breaks it into two hierarchically related groups. That is, the manager wants to see a list of cities, and a list of agents who have sold houses in those cities. The detail section contains a list of the houses sold, including the asking price. The report computes the total of the asking price by each agent within each city, but those values do not fit on the portion of the first page displayed in the figure.

Figure 10.3 shows a matrix report that displays the total sales by agent for each month. Notice that the name of the report has two "by" clauses in it, so this report effectively contains the same data as would a grouped report. The difference is that a matrix report is a cross-tabulation that uses one of the groups as rows and the other as columns in the matrix. In this example, the month is used as a column across the top of the page. Notice that the months are displayed as numbers instead of names so they sort correctly, and that several months are missing because there were no sales in those months. More important, think about the size of this report if you built it as a typical grouped report. The matrix approach is much more compact. It is often a useful approach for time-series data. If the columns will not fit on a single page, Oracle reports will print the next set on a new page, so users could print them and tape the pages together if they want to see a large listing.

Mailing label reports are specialized—when you need them, they are the only solution; but otherwise you will not use them very often. The primary distinction of a mailing label report is that it prints multiple records across the page. Mailing label sticker paper comes precut with a certain number of labels across the page. These reports are sometimes defined in terms of the number of records on the page. For

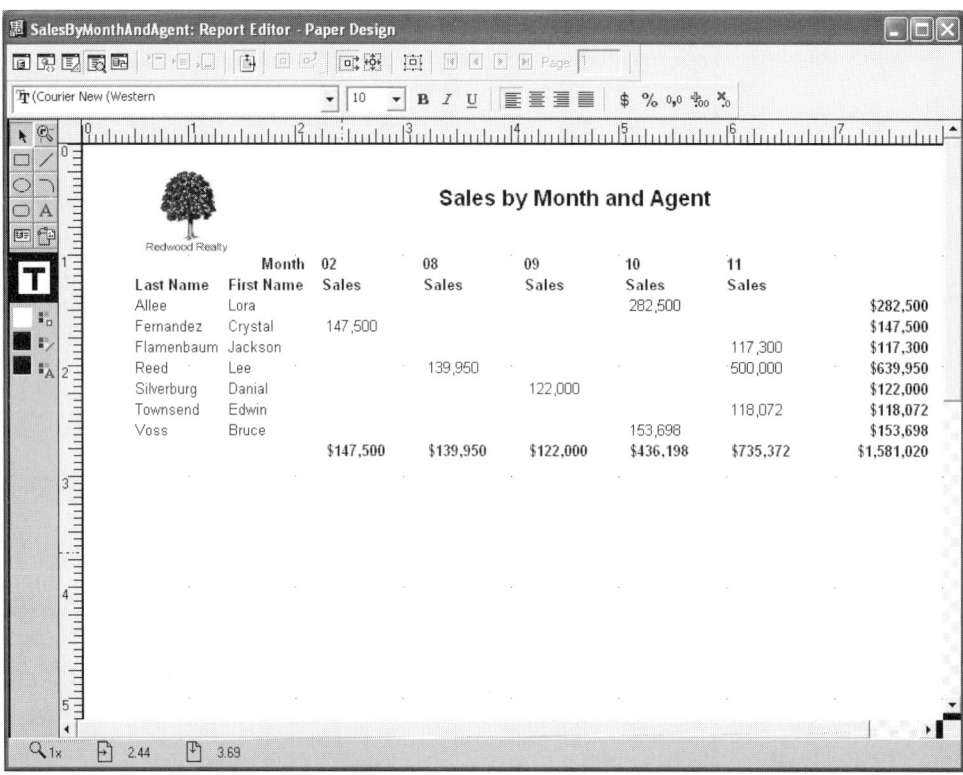

FIGURE 10.3 Matrix or cross tab report of sales by agent by month.

example, a page with three columns of records would be called a 3-up report. Most database report writers come with a set of templates predefined for commonly available mailing label sheets. You simply choose the appropriate size; pick the fields you want to display (name, address, and so on); load the paper; and print the report.

ORACLE REPORTS SERVICES

You can create and test paper-based and Web-based reports on your development computer. The paper layout is usually displayed by default, but you can use the Program/Run Paper Layout menu option (or its button on the toolbar) to view it if you close and reopen a report. Likewise, you can use the menu choice Program/Run Web Layout (or the button on the toolbar), to view a report in your browser. Unlike forms, you do not need to run the OC4J Instance to see the Web-based reports. Why not? This question is important because it helps you understand how the reports are built. The reports are built as HTML pages that incorporate Java code to handle the data processing. The Reports Builder tool handles the processing to display the data when you run the page on your development computer.

However, when you want to use Web-based reports within an organization, you need to take a few more steps. In particular, you will have to install the Oracle Forms and Reports services on a central computer. In most cases, this service is installed on a middle-tier computer running Oracle application server (AS). This product must run on a computer separate from the computer running the Oracle DBMS. That is why it is called a middle tier. The back end consists of the Oracle DBMS computer, the front end is the client computer running a Web browser, and the AS server runs in the middle.

CHAPTER 10   Creating and Modifying Reports   **473**

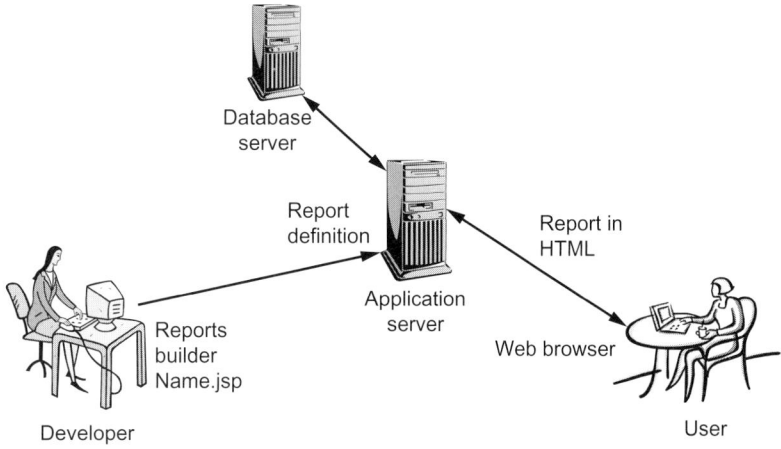

FIGURE 10.4   Oracle reports services.

Users open a Web site on the AS server that holds the reports you have defined. The reports collect data from the DBMS machine, convert everything into HTML, and send it to the client computer. As shown in Figure 10.4, you save the reports as javascript (.jsp) files. The Web server runs the Java code and creates a standard HTML file for the user.

Running all of the code on the server simplifies the environment for the user. However, it does mean that reports are less interactive than forms. Forms can process data and interact with the user relatively quickly because much of the code runs on the user's computer. Reports are designed to display data, and any interaction takes place on the server. Understanding this difference makes it easier to decide whether to build a form or a report to satisfy a user's request.

In the meantime, you will be able to build and test all of the forms in this chapter just using the Developer Suite. You do not need to install the reports services on your development computer. But, when you get to some of the more interactive tasks, such as defining user parameters, remember that the user interaction will take place on the server. In a business project, you will have to test the performance of all reports using the reports services.

BUILDING AND MODIFYING REPORTS

Oracle provides a report wizard that helps you create most common reports. Overall, it does a good job; but you will still have to modify the reports and clean them up to make them professional. One of the first challenges is to avoid putting everything on one line. The report wizard has trouble if you try to cram too many things onto the page. It first tries to reduce the font and squeeze more data onto the report. That rarely works, and you have to go back and fix it by hand. Better to hold back and let the wizard build the report with the smallest number of items that you can. If you want to add more items later, you can add them individually and see how they will fit.

THE REPORT STRUCTURE

The grouped or control break report is the most common type of report you will create. You need to understand the structure of the report and the terminology used to define this type of report. Figure 10.5 shows the overall structure of a report with a

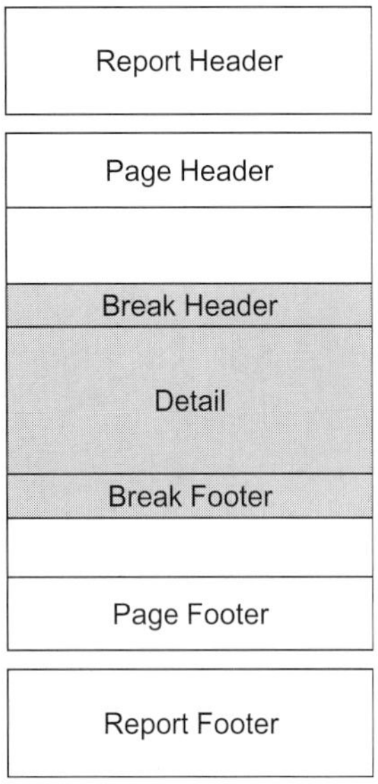

FIGURE 10.5 Overall structure of a grouped report.

[Diagram showing: Report Header, Page Header, Break Header, Detail, Break Footer, Page Footer, Report Footer]

single control break. All reports can have a ***report header*** and ***report footer***. These sections are printed only once at either the start or end of the report. They are commonly used as title pages or to display summary data across the entire report. Similarly a ***page header*** and ***page footer*** are printed at the top and bottom of each page—except that you usually do not print them on the report header and footer pages. For simple tabular listing reports, the page header often displays the column titles and a line. The page footer is generally used to display page numbers and sometimes a short message such as a copyright or security notice, or a contact number. You should ensure that the report date is displayed in one of these four primary sections. If you do not need to put the date on every page, you can put it in the report header or footer.

The main body of the report is built from the detail section. The detail section contains a list of data in columns and rows. But, unlike a simple tabular listing, the rows are grouped together based on some specified column. This variable defines a break. For each new instance, the report generator prints a set of data in the ***break header***, then prints the detail, followed by a short summary section displayed in the ***break footer***. The break header displays enough data to identify the specific individual group, and usually prints the column headings for the detail section. The break footer is almost always used to display subtotals or counts. You are not required to use both a break header and break footer. You can drop one—usually the footer—if it is not needed. Just be sure that readers can easily identify the start and end of each group. Most people use lines and shading to make it easier to see the group breaks. You can create breaks on almost any items—it just depends on the needs of the users. Common examples include breaks by customer, market location (city or state), product category, or employee. Generally, there is a one-to-many relationship between the break item and the detail fields. For example, a salesperson can participate in many sales, so you want to display each person, followed by his or her sales, followed by the total.

As shown in Figure 10.6, group break reports can become more complex because you can use multiple breaks. Multiple breaks are usually hierarchical—so that groups appear within groups. For instance, you might create a sales report that has a main grouping by customer. The second grouping would be a sale, and the detail section

FIGURE 10.6 Nested groups from customer to sale to detail.

would be the items on the sale. This report would have three levels: (1) customer, which is a group, (2) sale, which is a group, and (3) sale items, which are in the detail section. Each customer can have many sales, and each sale can have many items.

Before you start building a report, you should sketch it out and clearly identify the group breaks. Make sure you know what data will be displayed in the detail section, and which columns need totals, averages, or counts. In many ways, the most important step at the beginning is to identify the exact data needed for the detail section. Then, define the groups you need and figure out how they are hierarchically related. You can work from the top down or you can work your way from the detail section up to the top level. Just draw a picture that you can take to the users to verify the overall structure.

THE REPORTS BUILDER

Now that you understand the basic structure of a report, it is time to fire up the Reports Builder and let the wizard create a report. The goal is to create a report that shows properties sold by city and by agent. The basic design will be a group report that uses City as a group break, followed by Agent as a second group. The individual listing, along with a couple of columns from the property table, will form the detail section. Note that you need to check the SaleStatus column to determine which properties were sold. Ultimately, every report is based on a query. You could create this query ahead of time and save it as a view. A saved view is useful when the query is complex and you need to double-check the data to ensure that the query is retrieving exactly what you need. However, in this case, the query is a straightforward join of a few tables, so you can use the wizard to build the query and store it with the report.

The wizard will take you through several detailed steps, but essentially, you will perform three major tasks:

1. Create a query to retrieve the data you want on the report.
2. Choose the columns that create the group breaks.
3. Pick the report style.

Note that after the wizard finishes, you will have to clean up the layout and format the data.

Tip: You should put a shortcut to the Reports Builder on your desktop.

Of course, each of the three main steps consists of several details. These details are handled by separate forms in the wizard. For the most part, you can just run the wizard and answer the questions to create the form. It is easy to begin, but the query step takes a little more time:

1. Start the Reports Builder and choose the option to run the report wizard. Pick the next option to create both a Web and Paper Layout. Choose the **Group Above** report type because it leaves more column space than Group Left, and enter the title: **Sales by City and Agent**.
2. Choose SQL Query as the data source type, click **Next** and use the **Connect** button to connect to the database. Use the Query Builder to include the tables you need: **Agents**, **Listings**, **Properties**, and **SaleStatus**. You can select all of the columns from each table by clicking on the **select all** button at the top left corner of each table.
3. Use the sort button to sort by **City**, then **Lastname** and **Firstname**. Figure 10.7 shows the query.

You can also edit the SQL directly—either by clicking the SQL button or by returning to the wizard form. Once you know SQL, it is sometimes easier to enter the commands directly. You can also copy and paste the SQL into SQL*Plus to test and debug the query. The query in this example returns more columns than needed, but you might want some of them later, so it is easier to include them in the query now. Notice that the query builder uses the older Oracle join syntax by specifying the joins as

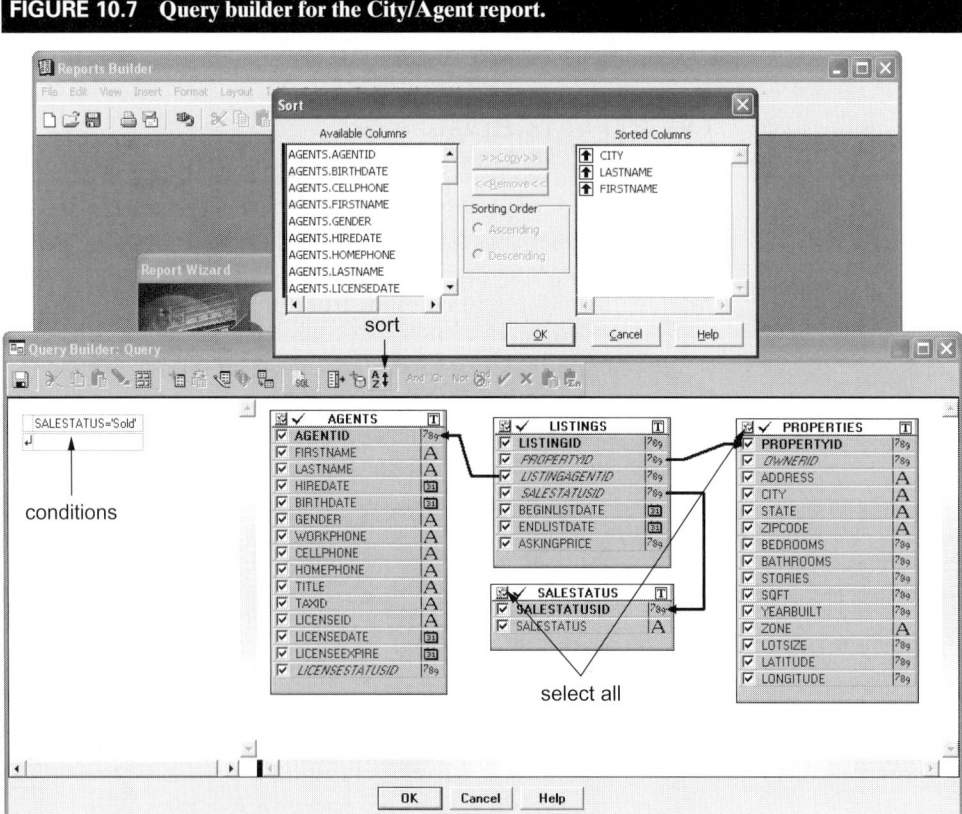

FIGURE 10.7 Query builder for the City/Agent report.

statements in the WHERE clause. You can also use the newer standard INNER JOIN syntax. The full query is:

```
SELECT ALL AGENTS.AGENTID, AGENTS.FIRSTNAME, AGENTS.LASTNAME,
AGENTS.HIREDATE,
AGENTS.BIRTHDATE, AGENTS.GENDER, AGENTS.WORKPHONE, AGENTS.CELLPHONE,
AGENTS.HOMEPHONE, AGENTS.TITLE, AGENTS.TAXID, AGENTS.LICENSEID,
AGENTS.LICENSEDATE,
AGENTS.LICENSEEXPIRE, AGENTS.LICENSESTATUSID, LISTINGS.LISTINGID,
LISTINGS.PROPERTYID, LISTINGS.LISTINGAGENTID, LISTINGS.SALESTATUSID,
LISTINGS.BEGINLISTDATE, LISTINGS.ENDLISTDATE, LISTINGS.ASKINGPRICE,
SALESTATUS.SALESTATUSID, SALESTATUS.SALESTATUS, PROPERTIES.PROPERTYID,
PROPERTIES.OWNERID, PROPERTIES.ADDRESS, PROPERTIES.CITY,
PROPERTIES.STATE, PROPERTIES.ZIPCODE, PROPERTIES.BEDROOMS,
PROPERTIES.BATHROOMS,
PROPERTIES.STORIES, PROPERTIES.SQFT, PROPERTIES.YEARBUILT,
PROPERTIES.ZONE,
PROPERTIES.LOTSIZE, PROPERTIES.LATITUDE, PROPERTIES.LONGITUDE
FROM AGENTS, LISTINGS, PROPERTIES, SALESTATUS
WHERE ((LISTINGS.LISTINGAGENTID = AGENTS.AGENTID)
  AND (LISTINGS.PROPERTYID = PROPERTIES.PROPERTYID)
  AND (LISTINGS.SALESTATUSID = SALESTATUS.SALESTATUSID))
ORDER BY PROPERTIES.CITY ASC, AGENTS.LASTNAME ASC, AGENTS.FIRSTNAME ASC
```

Close the query editor and use the **Next** button to select groupings. The second major step in the process is to set the groupings. The wizard has a form to select the columns, but the process is a little tricky. You should start with the highest level and work your way down, so the first one is easy.

1. Select the **City** in the left pane of the window and click the arrow button to move it over as the first level.
2. To add another level, you have to click on the **Level 1** entry in the right panel, just above the new City item.
3. In the left panel, select the agent **Lastname** column and click the button to move it to the right. The wizard will automatically place it under a new Level 2 section. If you do not get the Level 2 section, remove the entry and go back to Step 2.
4. Now select the other items that you want to display along with the last name: **Firstname**, **AgentID**, and **WorkPhone**. Pick one item at a time and click the arrow to move it to the right panel. Each of these columns should appear in Level 2 along with the Lastname. You do not want to create additional levels for this report.

Figure 10.8 shows the grouping levels that you need for this report. All columns listed together will be displayed on the same group header in the report. You can add other items later if necessary. Just make sure that you have both levels defined at this point.

After moving to the next wizard screen, the remaining major step is to pick the columns to display in the detail section and compute totals. Remember that you must limit the number of columns displayed in the detail section or the wizard will reduce them to an unreadable size.

1. Select the detail columns one at a time and move them to the right side panel: **ListingID**, **BeginListDate**, **AskingPrice**, **Bedrooms**, **Bathrooms**, and **Sqft**.
2. On the next wizard screen, choose the columns that will be summed (or averaged or counted). Select the AskingPrice column and click the **Sum** button to move it to the right side panel.
3. On the next screen, clean up the label text by adding spaces and capitalization.

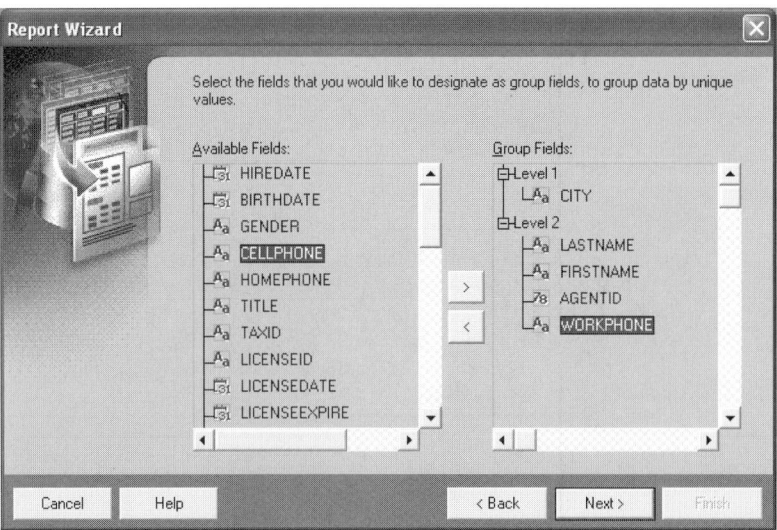

FIGURE 10.8 Choosing the groupings for the report.

4. The last wizard step is to choose a template. You can also choose to use no template, but then you will have to define all of the fonts and create shadings and lines by hand.

Tip: If the report wizard crashes at the end, it is probably because it tried to fit too many columns on the report. Rebuild the report with a smaller number of detail items.

Figure 10.9 shows the initial report created by the wizard. The object navigator window displays part of the report's structure. Notice that by choosing a template, the report uses shading to highlight the various sections.

THE PAPER DESIGN AND LAYOUT WINDOWS

The wizard and the template worked well, but you still need to clean up a couple of things. To make these changes, you can use the main Paper Design window. The Paper Design window lets you scroll through the report. However, it also lets you make minor changes to the layout and format of the data. Begin with a few simple changes.

Tip: If you save a form and come back later to open it, you need to click the **Run Paper Layout** button to see the form in the Layout window.

1. Select the report title (Sales by City . . .) and change the typeface to **Arial/Western**. Change the font size to **16** points and click the button to make it boldface as well. You will have to resize the box that holds the title. Click on the box, then click and drag the handles on the right-hand side until the full title is visible.
2. You need to format the AskingPrice column and its total. Click on the column of numbers beneath the AskingPrice heading to select it. Click the **comma** and **dollar sign** buttons on the toolbar to format the column as numeric. Do the same for the subtotal.

CHAPTER 10   Creating and Modifying Reports   **479**

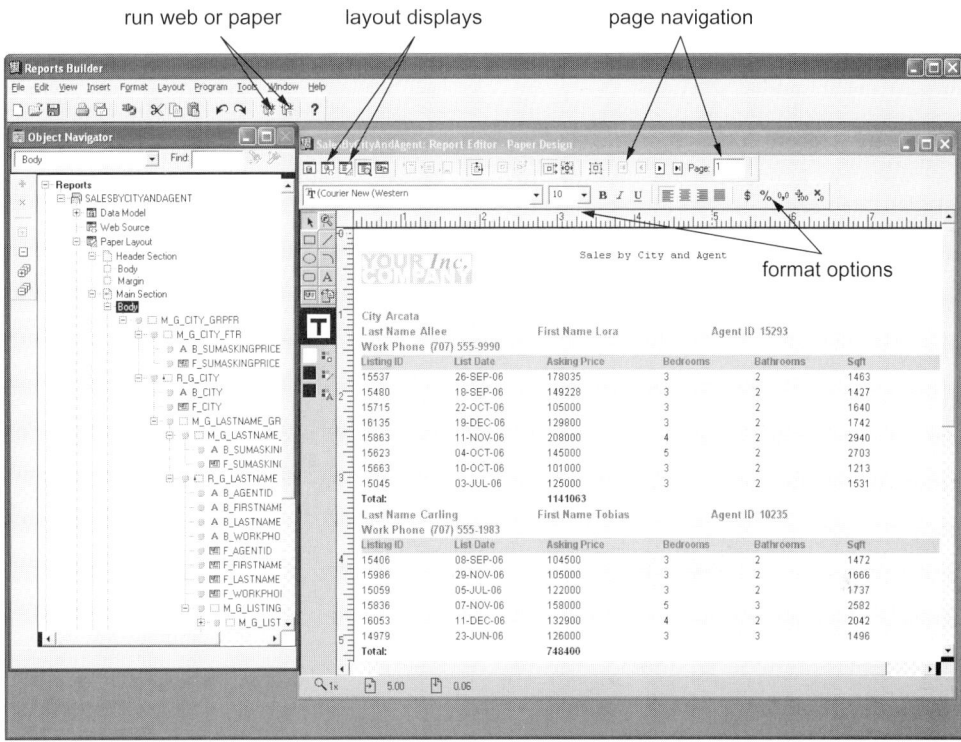

FIGURE 10.9   Initial report for sales by city and agent.

3. Last, you have to replace the logo. Click the default logo and press the **Delete** key to remove it. Use the menu option Insert/Images to browse for a better logo. You can use the simple logo that is included on the CD in the Files folder, or create your own. You will have to resize the RedwoodLogo1.jpg image to fit at the top of the report.
4. Save the report in a folder for this chapter.

Your report should be similar to the one shown in Figure 10.2 at the start of this chapter. You can also change the layout of the form if needed. In this example, only minor changes are needed. For example, in the employee group header, you might consider adding a little more space between the labels and the data. The employee names are a little close to the label. Select one of the data items (Lastname). When an item is selected, a small box with handles will appear around it. Simple drag the handles in the desired direction to change the size of the display box. You can also move the entire box; however, if you select all of the items within the group header, you will see that the boxes of the labels and data items fill most of the space, so there are almost no empty spaces. Better to just reduce the size of the display box. Of course, you could also just delete the label and let the name stand by itself.

If you look closely at your form, it is likely that you will see that an error has been introduced. Examine Figure 10.2 and you should be able to spot the problem. Somehow while adding the image and adjusting its size, the report designer altered the width of the footer that displays the totals. Compare Figure 10.2 with 10.9 and you will see that the shading does not extend to the full width. You could fix this problem in the Page Design view, but it is a good opportunity to look at the Page Layout view. If your

480 Introduction to Oracle

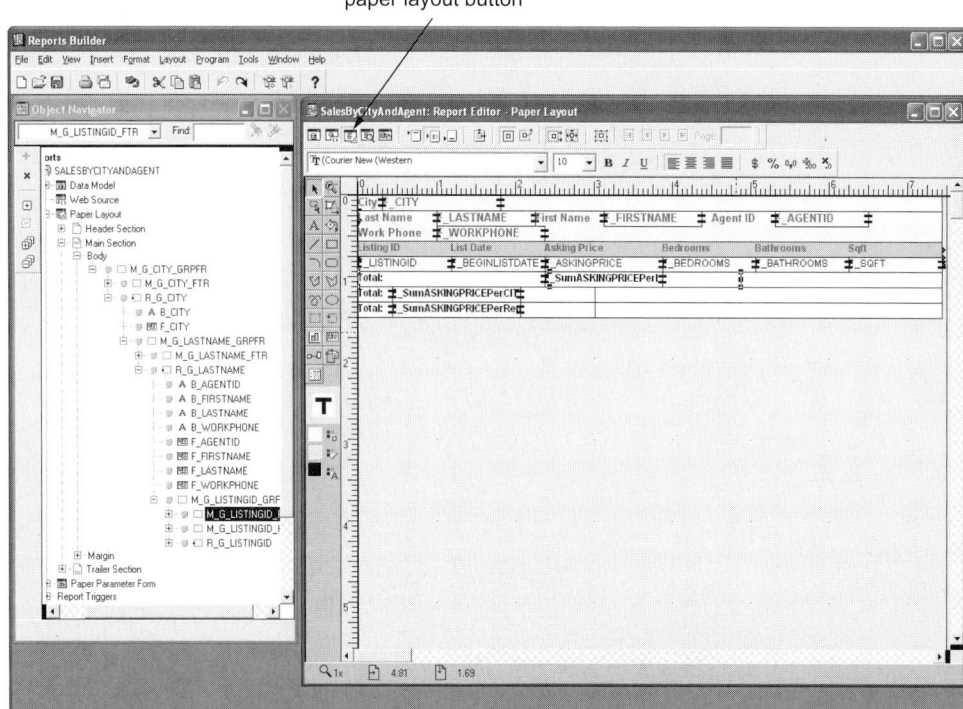

FIGURE 10.10 Page layout window.

form does not display this problem, you can use the Design view to create it. Click on the shaded area to see the frame and its handles. Then drag the right side towards the left an inch or two.

Click the **Paper Layout** button and you will see the true structure of the report. As you can see in Figure 10.10, the layout view is much simpler than the design view. It shows only the placeholders and not the actual data. It also makes the structure clearer because you can see all of the report segments on one page. The first row with the Total label is the one causing problems. It is clear that the shading does not extend all the way to the right side. Simply select the footer by clicking the shaded area. When the box and handles appear, drag the bottom-right-corner handle to the right side of the page.

> **Tip:** If you make a mistake while adjusting a report layout, use Undo **(Ctrl+Z)** and try again. If you have problems restoring a layout, throw away the changes and reload your report.

The page layout window shows the dimensions of the label and data boxes, which shows you that there is little free space on this form. However, you can use the layout view to create some additional space. First, make sure that the **Flex On** button is selected. When this button is selected, moving items within a frame causes the frame to expand. If you want to move items around but ensure that the frame size remains the same, click the **Flex Off** button. You want to add a little vertical space to the employee group header, so set flex mode to on. Select the Work Phone label and data box using **Ctrl+click.** Slowly move them down to add some space between the employee name and phone number.

> **Tip:** If you have problems moving items around on the page, click the **Flex Off** button.

Most layout adjustments can be made in Page Design or Page Layout view. Generally, it is up to you which mode you want to use. Sometimes you want to see the immediate effect of a change, so you will use Page Design view. Other times, you will find that it is easier to select multiple objects using Page Layout view. One change that can only be made in the Layout view is moving an item from one level to another. For example, perhaps you made a mistake and put an item at the detail level, but you really want it at the group header level. In Layout view, you can set **Confine Off** and the editor will allow you to drag an item from one level to another. However, back up your file first and be exceedingly cautious. It is easy to destroy the entire layout by dragging an item to the wrong location or incorrectly resizing a section. You want to make sure you can throw away the changes and reload a working copy of the report.

THE OBJECT NAVIGATOR WINDOW

Notice that regardless of your query sort, the report sorts the groups based on the first columns in that group. As long as you chose Lastname, Firstname, and then AgentID when you set up the group, the listing will be sorted alphabetically. If you first picked the AgentID column for the employee grouping, this section will be sorted by the ID number. However, you can use the query to control the order of the items in the detail section.

To sort the detail listing by BeginListDate, switch to the object navigator. Expand the node for the **Data Model**, then expand the node for **Queries** by clicking on the **plus** sign in front of the name. Open the Property Inspector for the **Q_1** query and click the button to open the **SQL Query Statement** property. At the end of the SQL statement add a clause to sort by **Listings.BeginListDate ASC**. When you switch back to the report viewer, it will refresh the query and change the sort order.

You can also use the Property Inspector to set column formats. In particular, if you want to change the format of the date column, you would need to use the Property Inspector. Right-click the item to be formatted and choose **Property Inspector**. Then set the Format Mask to the desired format. The Format Mask property uses the same formats as the one used for forms in the last two chapters.

The Object Navigator provides you with a complete list of all objects on the report. Consequently, it is often easier to find and select items in the navigator instead of trying to click a small spot in the Design or Layout windows. To demonstrate this ability, use the navigator to increase the vertical spacing between the employee groups.

1. Find the **R_G_LASTNAME** node in the Object Navigator. You have to expand Main Section, Body, M_G_CITY_GRPFR, R_G_CITY, and M_G_LASTNAME_GRPFR nodes.
2. Open the Property Inspector and set the **Vert. Space Between Frames** property to **0.5** inches.

Figure 10.11 shows the property setting and the result in the Page Design view. The vertical white space makes it easier to identify the sales and totals for each individual.

The Object Navigator lists all of the items on the form, but it takes some practice to learn how to read it. The report wizard follows a specific system in naming the elements in the hierarchy. Once you understand the basic names, it is easier to find your way around. When in doubt, you can click on an entry and it will be highlighted in the Paper Design view, so you should always double-check before making changes.

Figure 10.12 shows the expanded view of the page layout hierarchy for this report. First, notice the two main sections at the top of the list: Header Section and Main Section.

482 Introduction to Oracle

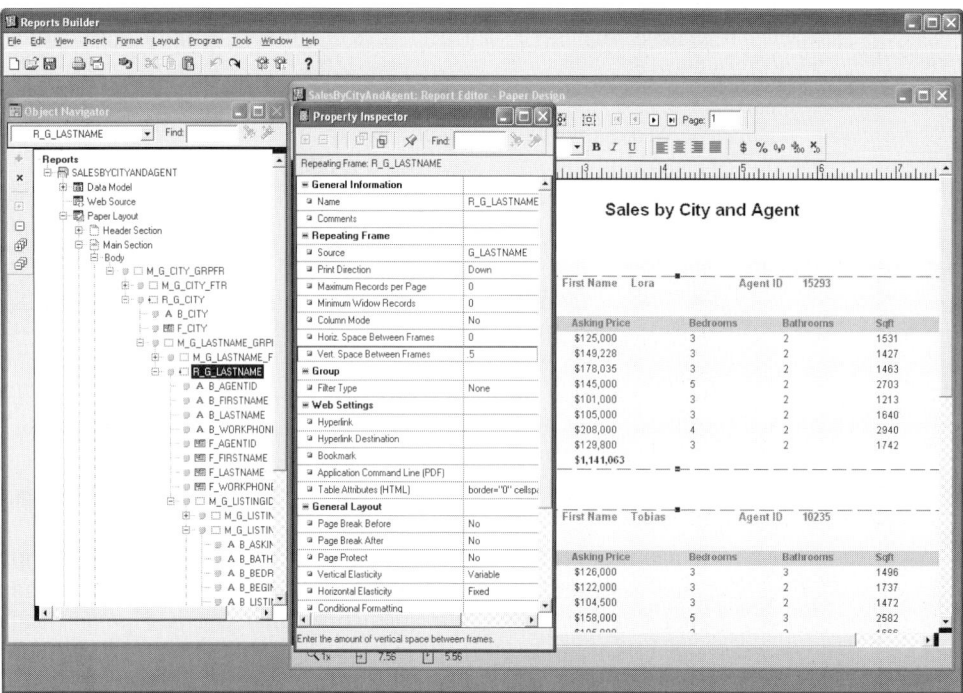

FIGURE 10.11 Using the Object Navigator to set vertical spacing.

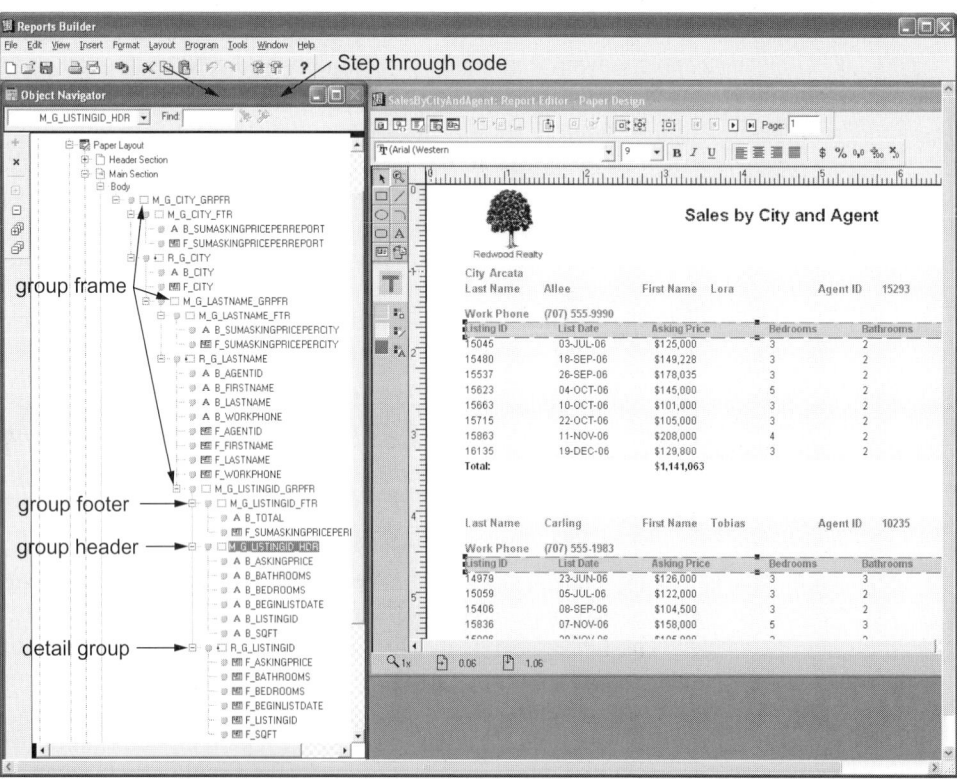

FIGURE 10.12 The Object Navigator.

The third section (Trailer) is at the bottom of the list but is not displayed here. These sections hold the data for the page header, main body, and the page footer, but the header and footer (trailer) are not used for this report, so they are empty.

The wizard groups most elements in frames. A *frame* is simply a way to group items together. By selecting the frame, you can set some properties such as the background color in one step—instead of having to assign the color to each item separately. You can also move the items as a group by moving the entire frame. You can select a frame in the Object Navigator. The primary frames are labeled with the _GRPFR suffix as an abbreviation for group frame. The other way to select frames is to select an item in the Page Design view and then click the **Select Parent Frame** button. For example, click on the total and then click the button, and the designer will highlight the immediate parent frame holding the Total item. If you continue to click the Select Parent Frame button, the designer will move to a higher-level frame.

Group headers and footers are labeled with a _HDR and _FTR suffix respectively. These entries are also frames, and the suffix is chosen to indicate their special purpose. If you look at the M_G_LISTINGID_HDR entry in the Object Navigator, you will find entries for the column headings (B_ASKINGPRICE, B_BATHROOMS, and so on). If you want to choose a different shade for this header, select the header, then pick a new color using the toolbar's **Fill Color** button.

ENHANCING A REPORT

You have already made some changes to the basic report created by the wizard in the previous section. However, some reports need more work than others. In particular, matrix reports are difficult to build on templates, so they generally need more enhancements. The main problem is that the standard templates are designed for reports with a portrait layout and can display only a limited number of columns. Matrix reports tend to have several columns and spread across multiple pages. To illustrate the process, you will use the wizard to create a matrix report that summarizes sales by month and agent. To keep the query simpler, the report will compute the total of the asking price—which is not the same as the final selling price. If you really want the final selling price, you can write a query that extracts the last BidPrice from the CustAgentList table and add that query to the report by joining on ListID. But this chapter focuses on the report writer, and the query is somewhat complex and would be distracting. Using AskingPrice simplifies the problem so that you can just start the wizard:

1. Start Reports Builder and use the wizard to create a **matrix** report entitled **Sales by Month and Agent.** Just pick the simple **Matrix** report. You do not need to add groups to this report. The matrix group creates a different matrix for each group; this report needs only one matrix.

2. Build a query from the **Agents**, **Listings**, and **SaleStatus** tables. Set the condition to include only listings that have sold (**SaleStatus.SaleStatus = 'Sold'**). Sort by agent last name and first name. Be conservative in selecting columns and pick: **LastName**, **FirstName**, and **AskingPrice**.

Now comes the tricky part. The managers want the report to show totals by month, where month is displayed across the top of the report and the agents down the left side. The Listings table includes two dates. To keep it simple, you can use the EndListDate. (If you take the time to build the query to get the actual sale price, you will also get the actual sale date, but it is not critical here.) The problem is that the date is an actual day. You need the month. The answer is to create a new column that uses the TO_CHAR(date, 'MM') function to convert the date to the appropriate month.

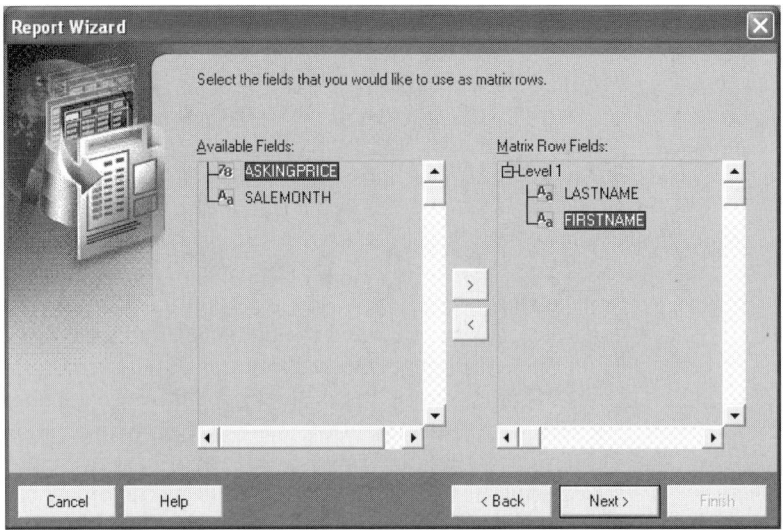

FIGURE 10.13 Choosing the fields for the matrix rows.

3. The query build has a Define Column button that you can use to add a new column. However, it might not actually save the column description, and it is usually easier to simply edit the SQL directly and add the column with the **SaleMonth** alias:

```
SELECT ALL AGENTS.LASTNAME, AGENTS.FIRSTNAME,
LISTINGS.ASKINGPRICE, TO_CHAR(LISTINGS.ENDLISTDATE, 'MM') SALEMONTH
FROM AGENTS, LISTINGS, SALESTATUS
WHERE SALESTATUS.SALESTATUS = 'Sold'
  AND ((LISTINGS.LISTINGAGENTID = AGENTS.AGENTID)
  AND (LISTINGS.SALESTATUSID = SALESTATUS.SALESTATUSID))
ORDER BY AGENTS.LASTNAME ASC, AGENTS.FIRSTNAME ASC
```

4. To define the matrix, you have to tell the wizard the fields to display in the rows, columns, and cells of the matrix. First, choose the fields for the rows. As shown in Figure 10.13 for this example, pick the **LastName** and **FirstName** fields. Because the report does not use groups, both of these fields are at Level 1.

5. In the same manner, choose the new **SaleMonth** field as the column. On the next wizard screen, select the **AskingPrice** column and click the **Sum** button, which tells the Reports Builder to compute the total of the asking price for each month for each sales agent. Similarly, on the totals screen, pick the **SumAskingPrice** and compute its **Sum** to get the row and column totals.

6. On the labels screen, clean up the labels by adding spaces and setting the capitalization. However, you need to keep the columns narrow, so set the label to **Month**, instead of Sale Month. The default widths should be fine for now. On the templates screen, you will have to choose the option to use **No template**.

Figure 10.14 shows the initial Paper Design view of the matrix report. Although it contains all of the desired data, it is somewhat plain and a little hard to read. Note that the report is sparse because there were only eight sales during the time period. If you want to see a report with more data, you can change the query condition from **Sold** to **For Sale**, but stick with the smaller report for now.

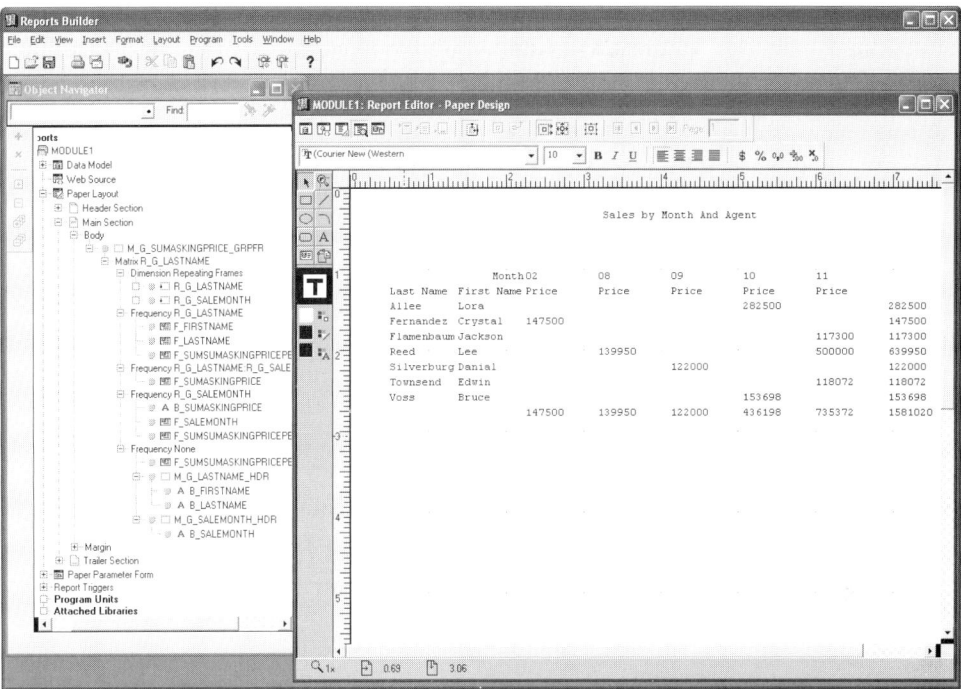

FIGURE 10.14 The initial matrix report.

To make the report look similar to the group report, you should add the logo to the top left corner. As before, use the **Insert/Image** menu option and adjust the size of the logo.

> **Tip:** You can make small layout adjustments to items by using the arrow keys on the keyboard instead of the mouse.

ALIGNING AND JUSTIFYING COLUMNS

The basic report needs some cleanup to make it more readable. To start with, all of the columns and headings are aligned, but they are left-justified. Numbers should generally be right-justified so the decimal points line up. Column headings are often centered so they are clearly displayed over the proper column.

1. In Design view, select the primary matrix of numbers by clicking one of the numbers. Use **Format/Justify/Right** to align the numbers. Do the same thing for the row and column totals. Notice that the overall total on the bottom right has to be selected separately because it is not part of the row or column groups.
2. Select the Month column headings and use **Format/Justify/Center**.
3. To add some space between first and last name, drag the First Name label to the right about a quarter of an inch. Notice that the designer automatically drags the other fields as well.
4. The simple matrix report has few display fields and generally aligns them automatically. However, you should ensure that the overall total is aligned with the row totals. Select the column of row totals and the overall total by holding down the

Shift key and clicking both items. Use **Layout/Alignment** on the menu and choose the **Align Right** option to align these two items horizontally.

SETTING FORMAT MASKS AND PROPERTIES

Since the numbers are generally in the hundreds of thousands, you need to add commas to the display to make them easier to read. You can set this format using the toolbar buttons. For more complex formatting, you can set the Format Mask property directly.

1. Click one of the numbers in the matrix display. Click the **Commas** button.
2. You can see the effect on the display, but you need to look at the properties to see how the display was changed. Right-click either one of the numbers or the **F_SumASKINGPRICE** entry in the Object Navigator, and choose the **Property Inspector** option. Notice that the Format Mask has been set to: **NNNGNNNGNNNGNN0**, which uses the global settings to insert either commas (U.S.) or dots (Europe) as separators.
3. Select all three totals (row, column, and overall) and set the comma separator. Then click the **Currency** button to add the dollar sign.

The next step is to change the typeface for the entire report. Notice that it is currently set to Courier, which is fixed-width font often used for old-style line printers. Most people find more modern typefaces easier to read.

1. Click one of the numbers in the display matrix. Press the key combination **Ctrl-A** to select all items on the page.
2. Select the **Arial/Western** typeface from the drop-down list. It should apply the new typeface to all of the items selected. If not, try again, or individually select each item and set the typeface.
3. Select just the title and set its font size to **16**. Resize its display box so that it displays the entire title.

To make the headers and totals easier to read, you should set them to boldface. Select each item and click the **standard boldface** button on the toolbar. Make sure that the row totals are sufficiently separated from the matrix columns. If not, drag the row totals (and overall total) slightly to the right.

ADDING SHADING AND BORDERS

The report is looking better, but it is still a little hard to read. It could use either shading or lines to bring out the headers and footers. Some people prefer lines to shading, but it is really just a matter of style. You can use both, but be careful to keep the data readable. Also, if the report is going to be printed on paper, you need to investigate the capabilities of the printer. Some shades will be too dark—particularly if the printer does not support colors.

1. Begin by adding a light shade to the header row. Select the labels for Last Name, First Name, and Price. In the toolbox, click the **Fill Color** button. Choose a pale yellow or beige in the color selection box. Make sure that the Last Name box runs up against the First Name box so there is no white space between them.
2. Select the column totals and the overall total and pick the same light yellow fill color as a background. Again, adjust the display boxes so they touch to ensure that there are no gaps in the background.
3. This next step is optional, but you should learn how to do it: display grid lines in the matrix to make the rows and columns easier to read. Select the matrix by

CHAPTER 10 Creating and Modifying Reports 487

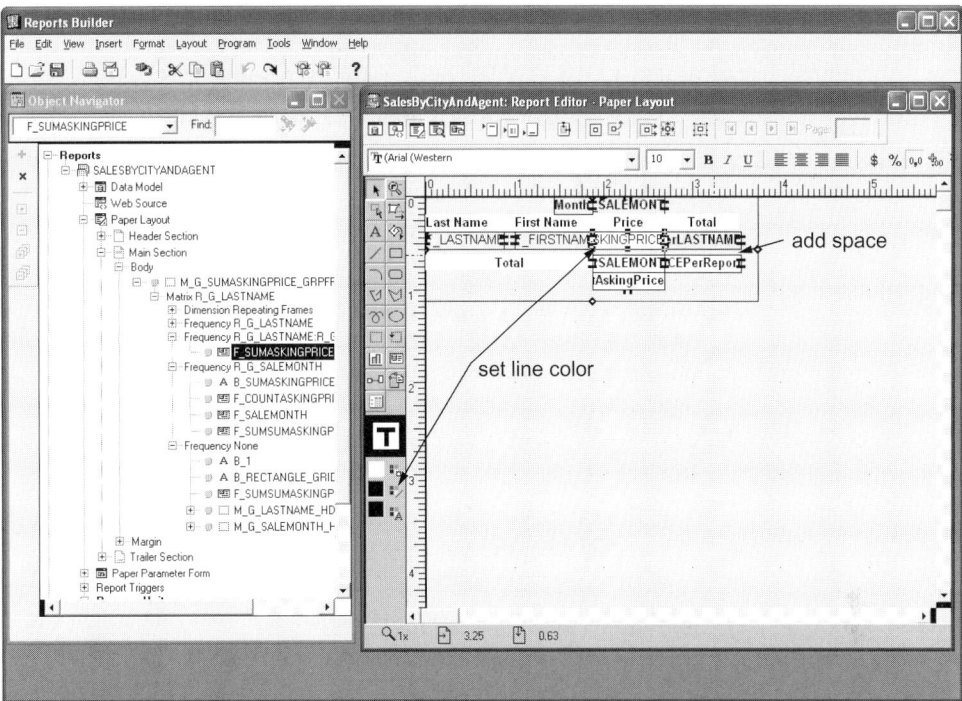

FIGURE 10.15 Adding grid lines to a matrix report.

clicking one of the numbers in the matrix. Use the Line Color option in the tool bar to pick black lines.

4. You might not be able to see the bottom line on the grid because the totals overlap it. Switch to **Layout** view. Select the items on the total row and press the **down arrow** key to open a little space. Figure 10.15 shows the new layout.

The Line Color option always affects all four lines of a rectangle. If you only want horizontal lines, or if you just want a line to separate a header, you will have to use the Line tool to draw a line on the Layout screen.

> **Tip:** To draw a horizontal or vertical line, hold down the **Shift** key while you draw the line, and it will only draw at primary angles.

INSERTING PAGE NUMBERS AND DATES

Most reports should display page numbers, and every report must have a date somewhere on the report. Users can decide if the date should appear on every page or just once in the report header or trailer page. Page numbers are generally displayed at the top or bottom of the page. In this case, you will add the date and the page number at the bottom of each report page.

1. Oracle provides a simple wizard to insert page numbers automatically. Choose **Insert/Page Number** from the main Reports Builder menu.

2. Examine the Object Navigator. In the Paper Layout/Main Section/Margin section, you will find the entry for B_PAGENUM1. If you need to format the page number, you can select it either through this entry or by selecting it on the Page Design

488 Introduction to Oracle

screen. In particular, the **Print Object On** property is useful because you can use it to control when the page number is displayed.

3. Use **Insert/Date and Time** to display the date in the bottom left margin of each page. Notice that the field is added to the same Margin section of the Object Navigator.

4. The date wizard lets you pick a data format. If you want to change the format later, use the Property Inspector to change the field's Format Mask.

ADDING TEXT BOXES

It is relatively easy to add text items to a form. In this example, it would be nice to add "Total" labels to indicate the totals computed for the row and columns. You can add labels in either the Design or Layout views, but it is a little easier to see which section you are using in the Layout view.

1. Switch to **Paper Layout** view. Select the **Text** A tool from the toolbox. Carefully draw a rectangle in the bottom-row frame to the left of the F_SumSumAskingPricePerSaleMonth field box. You must stay within the frame lines. To keep the background solid, you need the box to stretch from the left edge of the report up to the box for the total field.

2. Type **Total** into the box and click somewhere else on the screen when done. You might have to resize the box by dragging its lower-right side handle. Set the font to boldface and the background to the same pale yellow you used for the others.

3. Repeat steps 1 and 2 to add a text box above the column totals. Check the report in Design view to make sure the shading stretches across the form. Figure 10.16 shows the two new text boxes in the Layout view.

Note that text boxes hold static data that is not tied to the database. Essentially they are labels. You can control where they appear on the report or the page, but the data does not change dynamically. To display data from the database (or even page numbers), you need to place a Field onto the report. The only catch is that to add fields to a report, you first have to understand the data model.

FIGURE 10.16 Text boxes for subtotal headings.

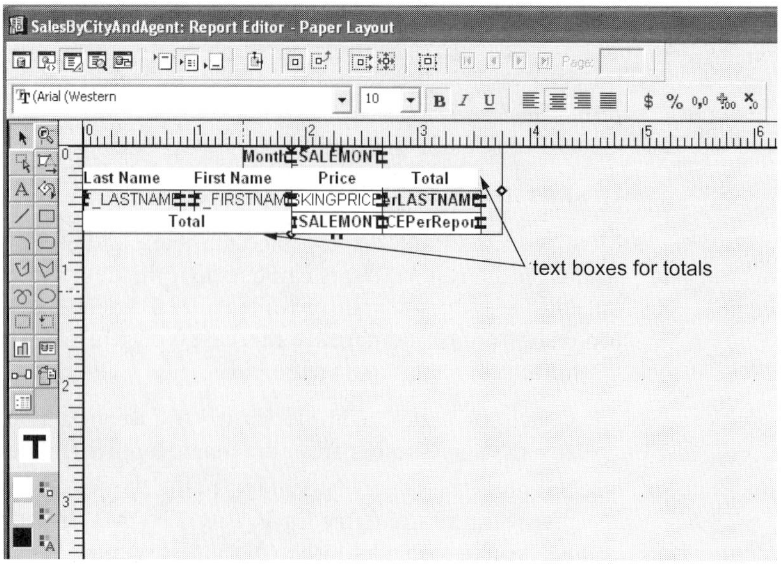

CUSTOMIZING REPORTS

The wizard makes it easy for you to choose data items, sets the basic layout of the report, and even computes subtotals. In most cases, you will use the wizard to create your report and then use the Design and Layout views to improve the appearance of the report. To add more items to the report, restart the wizard and use it to add the features you want. Use the **Tools/Report Wizard** option on the main menu. As shown in Figure 10.17, the Report Wizard provides a tab-based menu to alter all of the design selections for the report. For example, you could change the cell calculation from Sum to Average if you wanted to look at average sales prices across months. The one catch to the Report Wizard is that it will overwrite both the Web and Paper layouts. Any enhancements you made will be lost. If you need to make major changes to the report, go ahead and use the Report Wizard. If you have made major layout changes and only need to add a few things, it would be faster to make the additions by hand. But, to add anything, you need to understand and modify the data model.

THE DATA MODEL

Oracle uses a *data model* of the report to transfer data from the database into the report. The data model uses a query to specify the columns to be retrieved, the rows to be retrieved, and the primary sort order. The data model is more than just a query. It defines groups of data and relationships among the groups. The data model editor is a visual representation of the structure of the data.

1. Close the Reports Builder and start over. Open the grouped report created earlier for **Sales by City and Agent**.
2. Open the data model editor by clicking the **Data Model** button or right-click the Data Model entry and choose the **Report Editor** from the popup menu.

FIGURE 10.17 Using the Report Wizard in reentrant mode to modify a report.

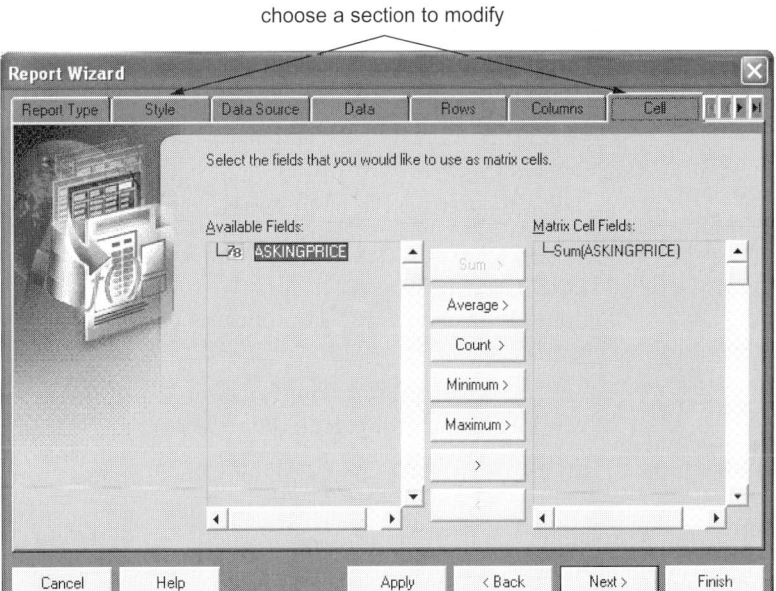

490 Introduction to Oracle

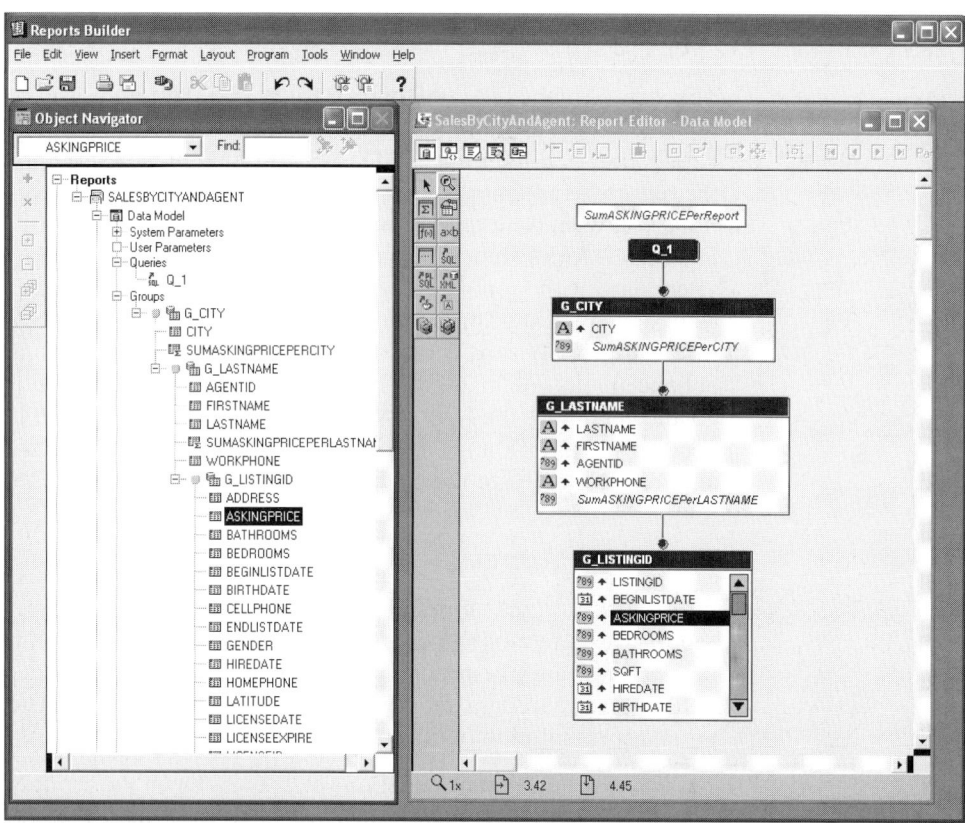

FIGURE 10.18 Data model for grouped report.

Figure 10.18 shows the data model for the grouped report. Notice that the data model clearly indicates the structure of the report. Remember that the report contains three major sections: (1) a grouping by city, (2) a grouping by agent, and (3) the detail section. Those three groups are clearly shown in the data model. More important, the data model shows the hierarchical relationship: City is the outermost level, so each city will list sales by many agents.

The data model also shows the summary fields that will be computed and displayed at each level.

3. Open the Property Inspector for the **SumAskingPricePerCity** field by double-clicking on the item in either the Data Model or the Object Navigator.

The key properties are: Column Type = Summary, Function = Sum, Source = AskingPrice, and Reset At = G_City. This last property ensures that the totals are computed for each city. Note that this particular subtotal must be located within the G_City group.

4. Drag the field **SumAskingPricePerCity** out of the **G_City** group and drop it in the **G_LastName** group. Run the report.

If you try to put a summary field in a different group, you will receive an error message that the item "references a column at a frequency below its group." The error reminds you that the location of a field within the data model is just as important as its properties. It should also warn you to be careful about moving items in the data model. Always be sure to save your work before making major changes.

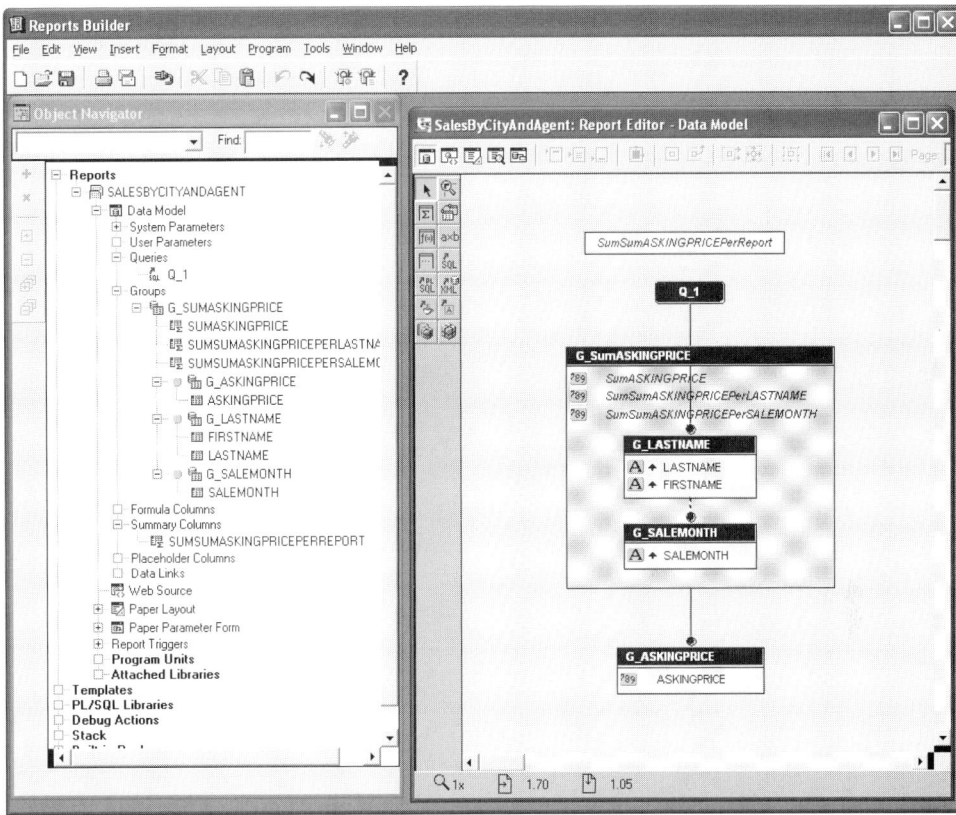

FIGURE 10.19 The initial data model for the matrix report.

5. Close the Reports Builder and **discard** the changes. Restart and this time load the matrix report **Sales by Month and Agent**. Open the data model.

Figure 10.19 shows the initial data model for the matrix report. Note that you will probably have to resize a couple of the boxes to show all of the items.

The query (Q_1) is the starting point with the data model. It defines the data being retrieved. If you follow the lines, you can see the data items that it retrieves: LastName, FirstName, SaleMonth, and AskingPrice. Each of these is displayed in a group. Remember that the agent's last name and first name are displayed together to identify the rows. Consequently, these two items form a group (G_LastName). The SaleMonth is used as the column heading, so it falls into its own group (G_SaleMonth). The asking price column forms the primary data in the cells, so again falls into a separate group.

The G_SumAskingPrice group is a critical group for this report. It is the group that defines the matrix because it holds the row and column groups. If you have enough space between the G_LastName and G_SaleMonth groups, you will see they are connected by a dashed line. This link indicates that the group was created as a Cross Product group—which is the key to creating the matrix layout. Also, note that the big group holds three summary fields: (1) SumAskingPrice, (2) SumSumAskingPricePerLastName, and (3) SumSumAskingPricePerSaleMonth. The first value is the total displayed within single cells in the matrix. The other two are the row and column totals as indicated by their names. Observe that the field for

SumSumAskingPricePerReport does not belong to a group. Because it displays the overall total and computes the sum of everything on the report, it stands alone.

The data wizard does a decent job with fairly standard reports. However, the data model has considerably more powerful capabilities. For example, instead of using one query, you can add multiple queries to a report—using each one for a separate group. More important, you can create complex group relationships. For instance, you could create a report with a primary grouping on agent. For each agent, you could have two separate repeating relationships—one to show sales by city, and a second to show sales by month. In the data model, the Agent group would be at the top and it would link to two otherwise independent groups: City and SaleMonth. Creating complex data models is beyond the scope of this book, but the process is not too difficult. Focus on the groups and remember that each group becomes a section on the report. Then think hard about how the groups and sections are related.

ADDING FIELDS

The real reason for looking at the data model for the matrix report is that the agents want you to add another field. They want to see the number of houses sold for each month along with the total value. It would have been nice if they had brought up the idea before you built the report; but they are users and you need to keep them happy. You could start from scratch and rebuild the report, but you have invested quite a bit of time in modifying the report and you would like to keep those changes. Since it is only one field, and it is similar to an existing field, it should be reasonable to add it manually.

To add any data to a report, you must start with the data model. Actually, if you need to retrieve additional columns from the database, you would first have to modify the query. To add a summary count variable, you already have the data you need.

1. Select the Summary Column button in the toolbar and click inside the G_SumAskingPrice group, to add a new summary field below the three existing ones.
2. Open the Property Inspector for the new column (CS_1) and set the following properties: Name = **CountAskingPrice**, Column Type = **Summary**, Product Order = **G_SaleMonth**, Function = **Count**, Source = **AskingPrice**, Reset At = **G_SaleMonth**.

Once you have defined the new data element, you can place it in a new field on the report. This last step is easier with grouped reports because you have more freedom to adjust the layout of the page. With the existing matrix report, you need some dexterity to move fields around to make space for the new field.

3. Switch to Paper Layout view. Find the **F_SumSumAskingPricePerSaleMonth** field that currently displays the total sales by month. Gently drag it down to open up space above it.
4. Click the **Field** button in the toolbar and draw a field above the F_SumSumAskingPricePerSaleMonth field. It is critical to keep the new field in the same group.
5. Open the Property Inspector for the new field (F_1) and set the following properties: Name = **F_CountAskingPrice**, Field Source = **CountAskingPrice**. The other properties are automatically picked up from the properties in the data model. Figure 10.20 shows the new layout.

You can switch to Paper Design view to see the report, but the new row is not very appealing. For starters, it is better to display the totals immediately below the column. Plus, you should get rid of the space between the summary value rows. Return to layout view to fix these issues.

CHAPTER 10 Creating and Modifying Reports

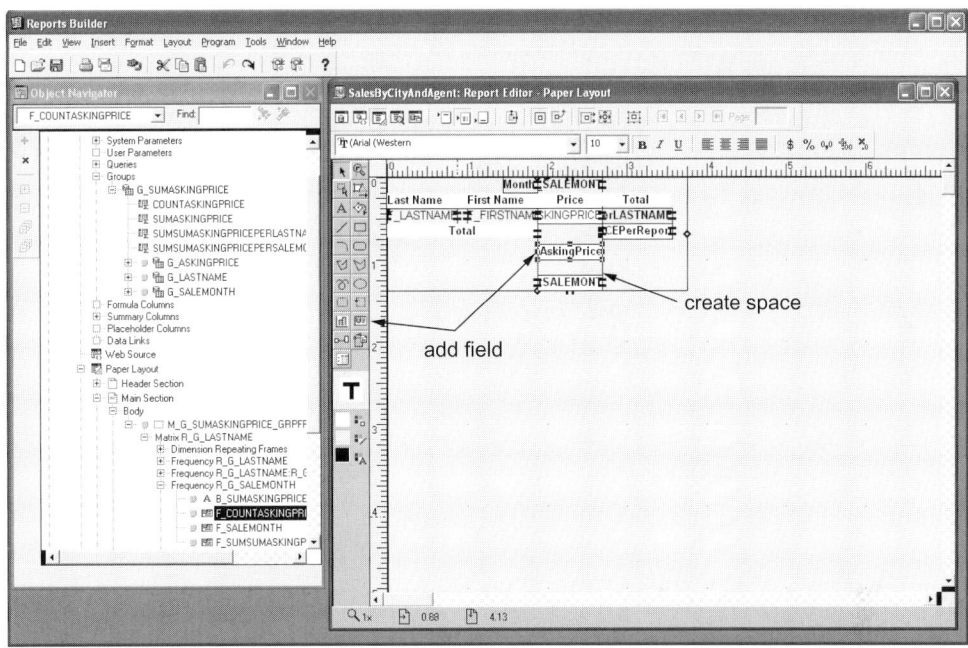

FIGURE 10.20 Adding a summary field.

6. Move the **F_SumSumAskingPricePerSaleMonth** field above the new **F_CountAskingPrice** field. Note—this step can be tricky, so be persistent and try dragging both columns around until you get what you want. Save the finished report.

It would have been nice to insert the new counting field below the sum field, but that turns out to be difficult. You have to make sure the new count field falls in the same group, and the easiest way to see the group is to drag the sum field down and open up space above it. This difficulty arises on the matrix report because space is tight. Remember, if the layout design becomes too messy, the report might not run. You can always discard your changes and try again. Figure 10.21 shows the report with the new count field. You could also add a label to describe the new row, but you can do that later.

DATA GROUP STRUCTURE AND FRAMES

In this section, you will create a report from scratch. The Data Model plays a key role in the process, so before starting, it is worth reviewing some of the tools available in the Data Model. Figure 10.22 shows the toolbox for the Data Model. The Select and Magnify tools are straightforward. You can reverse the effects of the magnifier by using the menu options under **View/Zoom**. The **Normal Size** and **Fit to Window** options are particularly useful.

Use the Summary Column, Formula Column, and Placeholder Column tools to add calculated data to the model. Summary columns are limited to internal functions such as Sum and Count. Formula columns use PL/SQL commands to perform computations. You can create user-defined functions and call them in the calculations. The functions can contain any PL/SQL code, including commands to access the database. A Placeholder column is similar to a formula, except that it can be defined selectively. That is, you can use report triggers to change the value of the placeholder depending on different events. That is the fundamental difference between a formula and placeholder

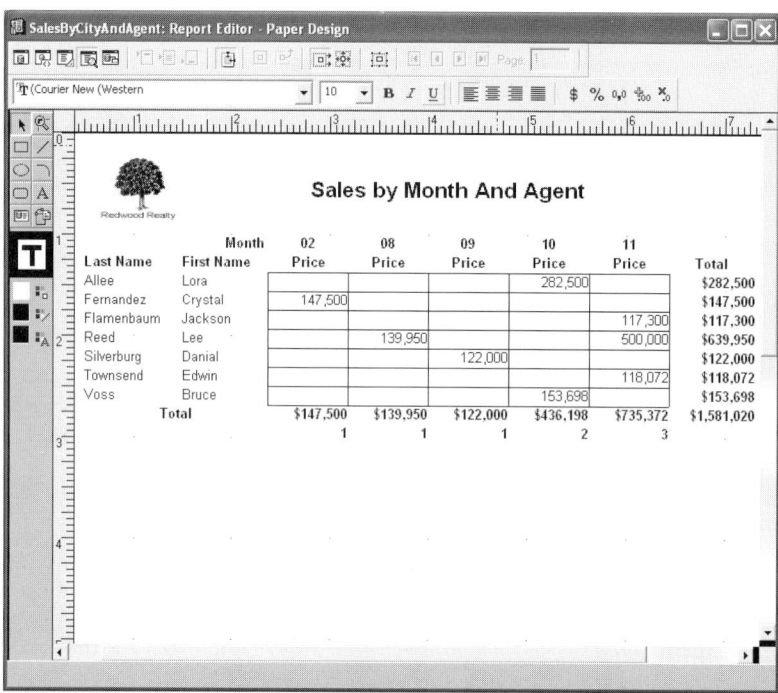

FIGURE 10.21 Count field displayed on the report.

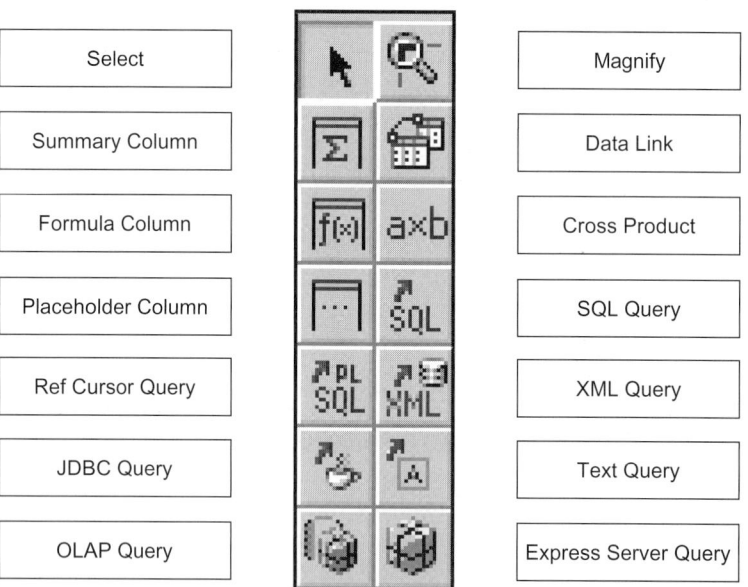

FIGURE 10.22 Data Model toolbox.

column: a formula column gets assigned values for each row on the report. You control when placeholder columns are recomputed through triggers and functions.

The Cross Product axb tool is used to create matrix reports. You use it to specify the rows, columns, and cell values of the matrix. In almost all cases, you will want to use the report wizard to help create the data model for these reports.

The Data Model needs to get data from some source, and the tool box has seven different tools to select data ranging from a basic SQL Query to an OLAP Query. Most of the time you will use the SQL Query tool to create a standard Oracle query. If a report requires complex queries and PL/SQL conditional code, you can create a PL/SQL function in the database that returns a reference cursor to each row. Then use the Ref Cursor Query to connect to the function. For some reports, you might need to connect to specialty servers using the OLAP or Express Server tools. Similarly, the XML and Text tools are designed to retrieve data from non-traditional database sources. The JDBC tool is generally used for Web-based reports. It uses the standard Java protocols to connect to a server and retrieve data.

The Data Link tool requires more explanation. It is used to create links between two queries. It establishes a master-detail (one-to-many) relationship. It is similar in effect to a grouped report, which is why it needs more explanation. Oracle makes a distinction between a report with grouped data and a master-detail report. Both are used to display data in a parent-child or one-to-many relationship. However, a grouped report uses a single query where the relationship is built into the query.

> **Tip:** If you do create a grouped report manually, the query will initially place all of the columns into one group. To create a hierarchy, drag the items for the parent group out of the existing group and a new one will be created.

A *master-detail* report uses multiple queries and you create a Data Link between them on the report. For most reports, the effect is similar and you are free to choose either method. The difference arises when you want to create a complex report—particularly one that has two master-detail relationships. For example, Redwood Realty might want a report with Agents as the master record, and two detail sections: one that shows listings by that agent, and one that shows customer contacts with that agent. Since the listings and customer contacts are not directly connected to each other, you will need to create two master-detail relationships. You cannot create this type of report with a single query and groups.

CREATING A REPORT MANUALLY

To understand the structure of a grouped (or master-detail report), it is helpful to create one from scratch. The agents need a report that shows them the properties for sale and any bids that have been made on those listings. Since there can be many bids on a property, there is a one-to-many relationship between the listing and the bids. If you really want to create a group report, you will almost always use the report wizard. If you want to create a master-detail report using multiple queries, you will have to do it manually. Even though this report could be built with groups using the wizard, the steps will follow the master-detail approach to provide you with experience.

1. If necessary, close the Reports Builder and restart it. Choose the option to **Build a new report manually**.
2. The process begins with creating a data model, so click the **SQL** button in the toolbox and click near the top left of the Data Model screen to open the Query Builder. Include the tables: **Listings**, **Properties**, and **SaleStatus**. Set the condition **SaleStatus.SaleStatus = 'For Sale'** and sort by **BeginListDate**. To save some time with the layout, keep the selected columns to a minimum.

```
SELECT ALL LISTINGS.LISTINGID, LISTINGS.PROPERTYID,
LISTINGS.BEGINLISTDATE, LISTINGS.ENDLISTDATE,
```

```
LISTINGS.ASKINGPRICE, LISTINGS.HOUSEPHOTO, PROPERTIES.CITY
FROM LISTINGS, PROPERTIES, SALESTATUS
WHERE SALESTATUS.SALESTATUS = 'For Sale'
  AND ((LISTINGS.PROPERTYID = PROPERTIES.PROPERTYID)
  AND (LISTINGS.SALESTATUSID = SALESTATUS.SALESTATUSID))
ORDER BY LISTINGS.BEGINLISTDATE ASC
```

3. Add a second query by clicking the **SQL** button again and clicking on the model screen to the right of the first query. Choose the tables for the detail section: CustAgentList and Customers. You have to include the ListingID column to make the link, and then choose five for the detail section: ContactDate, FirstName, LastName, BidPrice, and CommissionRate. Sort by ContactDate.

```
SELECT ALL CUSTAGENTLIST.LISTINGID, CUSTAGENTLIST.CONTACTDATE,
CUSTOMERS.FIRSTNAME, CUSTOMERS.LASTNAME, CUSTAGENTLIST.BIDPRICE,
CUSTAGENTLIST.COMMISSIONRATE
FROM CUSTAGENTLIST, CUSTOMERS
WHERE (CUSTAGENTLIST.CUSTOMERID = CUSTOMERS.CUSTOMERID)
ORDER BY CUSTAGENTLIST.CONTACTDATE ASC
```

4. Both queries will create groups in the data model and display them on the screen. You need to give the detail group (under query 2) a better name: **G_ContactDate**. Now you can connect the two groups with a data link. Click the **Data Link** button, then click the **ListingID** field in the first query group (**G_ListingID**) and drag the column and drop it on the **ListingID1** field in the detail group (**G_ContactDate**). Figure 10.23 shows the basic structure of the data model. Save the report as **ListingsAndOffers**.

FIGURE 10.23 The master-detail data model.

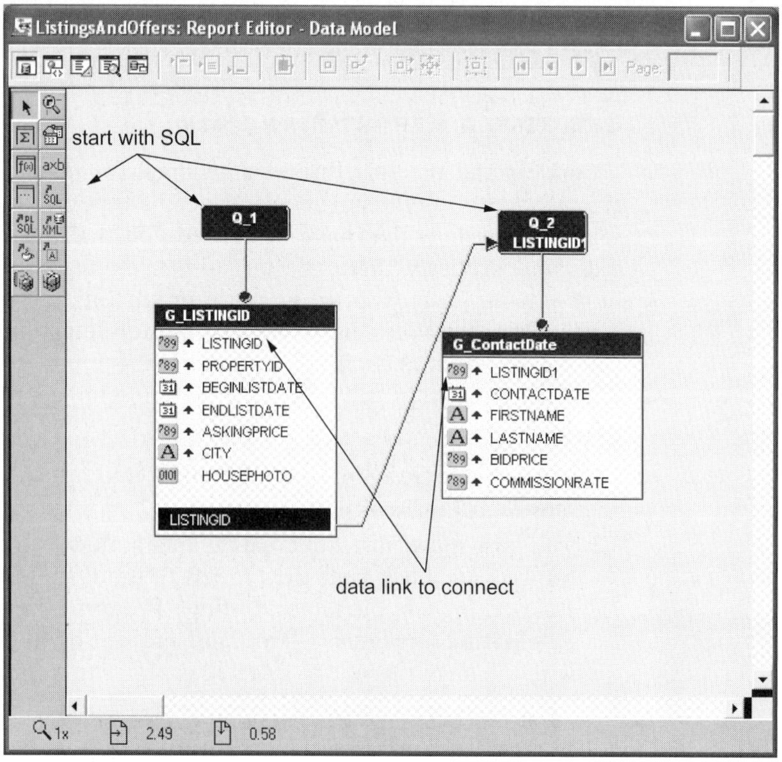

CHAPTER 10   Creating and Modifying Reports   **497**

> **Tip:** To build a master-detail data link, always drag from the master group to the detail group.

Once the data model is correct, you can create the Paper Layout for the report. The key to creating reports is to understand the role of the repeating frame. A *repeating frame* is used to collect a group of items on the report. Any piece of data that you want to display from the database must be placed within a repeating frame. In a master-detail report, you need to have at least two repeating frames: one for the master level, and a second for the detail section. The detail frame must be drawn entirely inside the master repeating frame.

To confuse the issue slightly, you can also insert simple frames, but you are not required to use them. A simple frame is used to group a logically related set of objects. It makes it easier for you to set background colors and to move all of the framed items at one time. For example, you probably want to create frames for group headers and footers.

1. Begin by placing a repeating frame on the blank layout form. This is the primary frame for each listing, so make it big enough to give yourself room to work. You can resize it later. Following the wizard's convention, name it **R_G_Listing**, and set properties Source = **G_LISTINGID**, and Vertical Elasticity = **Variable**.
2. To help define the layout, add a field near the top of the new repeating frame. Name it **F_ListingID** and set its Source to **LISTINGID**. Add a text label in front of it and type Listing ID as the label. Run the form to test it and you should get a page of Listing ID values. Follow the same process to add fields for **BeginListDate**, **AskingPrice**, and **PropertyID**. Save your work. Test it. You probably want to use the Line Color option to remove the lines from the fields.
3. Add a second repeating frame. Keep it entirely inside the original and leave some space above and below it to add column headings and a small footer. Name it **R_G_ContactDate**, set Source = **G_ContactDate**, and Vertical Elasticity = **Variable**.
4. Add the detail fields inside the new frame, near the top of the frame. Anything placed inside this inner frame will be repeated on each row. Place fields for **ContactDate**, **BidPrice**, **LastName**, and **FirstName**. You can use Layout/Alignment to vertically align the fields.
5. Draw a simple frame above the repeating frame to hold the column headings. The purpose of this frame is to make it easy to set a background. Place text labels inside this new frame as titles for the four detail columns. Test the report. Save it. Clean up the formatting by switching to an Arial typeface and setting the currency attributes for the two price fields.

> **Tip:** In the process of adding and moving items on the form, make sure everything stays within the top-level frame and make sure the top-level frame stays within the page boundaries.

The layout view in Figure 10.24 shows the basic structure of the report. Your layout should be similar in structure, but you might place the fields in slightly different locations. The two most important aspects are that: (1) the detail repeating frame lies within the master repeating frame, and (2) the fields are placed completely within their matching repeating frames.

Figure 10.25 shows the initial Design view of the report. The good news is that the report contains the data the agents want to see. The bad news is that the report still

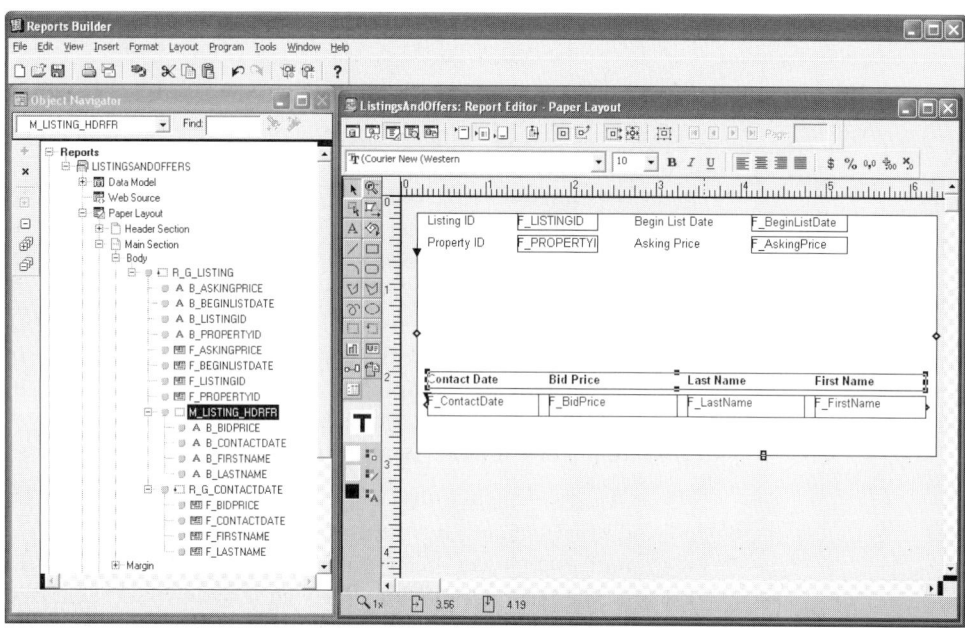

FIGURE 10.24 Paper Layout of the Listings and Offers report.

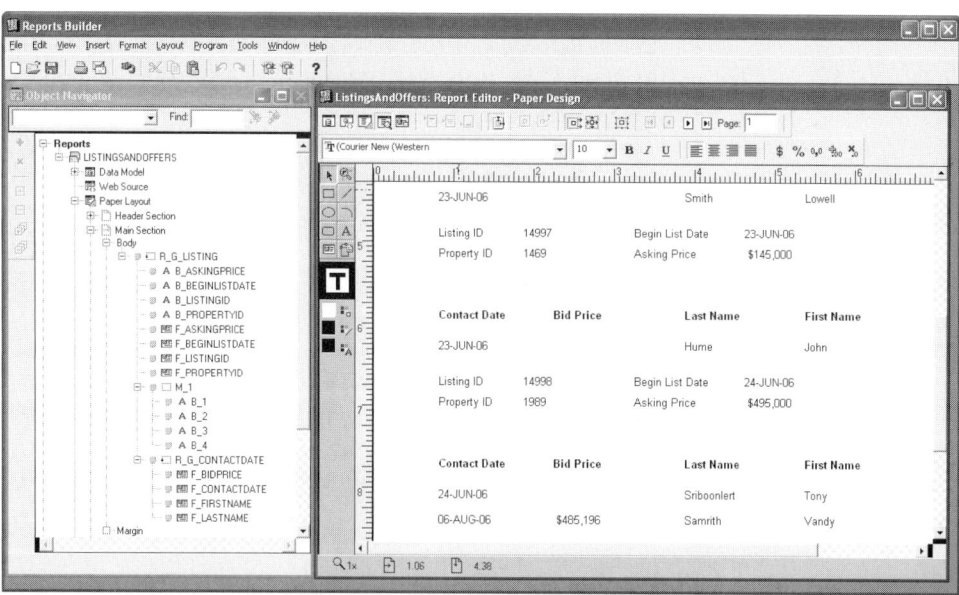

FIGURE 10.25 Design Layout of the Listings and Offers report.

needs some work to make it readable. The biggest problem is that it is difficult to identify the start and end of a listing. One thing that will help differentiate the listings is to add a footer. It might be useful to count the number of bids.

1. Switch to the Data Model. Click the **Summary Column** button and place a summary field within the **G_ListingID** group. Set its properties:

Name = **CS_CountBids**, Column Type = **Summary**, Function = **Count**, Source = **BidPrice**, Reset At = **G_ListingID**.

2. Switch to the Paper Layout view and add a simple frame as a footer group beneath the detail repeating frame. Name it **M_Listing_FTRFR** and set a light yellow shade as background. Add a text box with the label Number of Bids, followed by a field named **F_CountBids** with Source set to **CS_CountBids**.

3. You can separate the listings by displaying the lines for the main R_G_Listing frame. Another step you have to take in this case, and with many reports, is to prevent a listing from splitting on a page. In the properties for the main repeating frame, set Page Protect = **Yes**. This property prevents the report from printing the master data on one page and the details on the next page.

DISPLAYING IMAGES FROM THE DATABASE

In some situations, you might want to display images on your reports. Simple images like the logo are easy because they are static. You simply insert them when you design the report. However, recall from Chapter 8 that you can also store images in the database itself. In that chapter, you altered the Listings table to hold a photo of the house being listed. Now, the agents would like to display that same photo on the Listings and Offers report.

1. Because they are binary data, the listing photos are not included in the original database files for the Redwood case. If you have deleted and reloaded your database since Chapter 8, you need to add the photo column to the listings table, but only do this step if you skipped that section of Chapter 8 or have replaced the database. Using SQL *Plus, you can use the Describe Listings command to check. If necessary, run:

```
ALTER TABLE Listings
ADD HousePhoto LONG RAW;
```

2. If you reloaded your database, you will also have to reload the photo for at least one of the listings. You can use the Listings.fmb form to examine listings and update a sample photograph. Use the form's query facility to load the record for ListingID = **14997**, which is one of the first listings, so it will be easy to find in the report.

3. In the Reports Builder, open the ListingsAndOffers report if necessary. Switch to the data model, open the query editor and add **Listings.HousePhoto** to the SELECT statement. The Data Model will probably put the new column into the detail group (G_ContactDate). It belongs in the other group, so drag it into the G_ListingID group.

4. The next step is to add the new field to the layout. Rearrange the fields to make space in the master part of the report to show the photo. Use the **Field** button to draw the field that will display the photo. Set the following properties: Name = **F_HousePhoto**, Source = **HousePhoto**, Datatype = **Longraw**, File Format = **Image**. This last one is the main difference from a typical data field. Save the report and run it in Design view. Your report should be similar to Figure 10.26.

Ultimately, you should clean up the report a little more by adding the logo and a title. You also need to add page numbers and the report date. The steps are not listed here because you already know how to add these items.

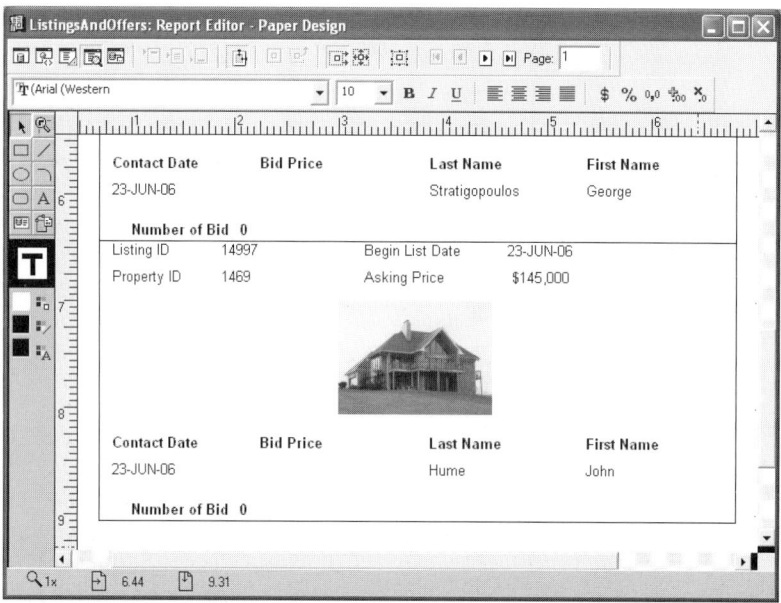

FIGURE 10.26 Design Layout with the house photo.

CONTROLLING DATA IN A REPORT

It would be nice to make reports a little more interactive. Remember the Sales by Month and Agent matrix report? Because there are few actual sales, many of the cells are blank. What if the managers want to look at listings for sale or pending instead of just those that were sold? Does that mean you have to build new reports? Remember that the Sold condition is set in the underlying query. You could copy the report and modify the query, but then you still end up with multiple copies of essentially the same report. A better solution to the problem is to create parameters.

Report parameters are used to control how a report runs. Oracle has two types of report parameters: system parameters and user parameters. ***System parameters*** control a few environmental issues. You generally set them once and rarely change them. However, they are useful if you need to move a report to run in a different region or office. The system parameters are stored with the report in the Data Model. You can find and set the values using the Object Navigator. Table 10.1 lists the parameters and their descriptions. To change the values, open the Property Inspector and change the Initial Value property.

CREATING USER PARAMETERS

As you can see from the list, the system parameters are primarily designed to control the print devices. User parameters are much more powerful. ***User parameters*** are variables that you can define and use within the report. When the report runs, the user enters values for the parameters on a form. Those values are used within your report to select data or control the report. To reduce errors and improve security, users can only pick parameter values from a list—they can never enter random data. The list can be either a static list of values that you create and store with the report, or it can be pulled

TABLE 10.1 System parameters.

Parameter Name	Description
COPIES	The number of copies to print. Default = 1.
DESFORMAT	The output format and is usually set as PDF, HTML, HTMLCSS, RTF, XLM, or DELIMITED. It can also be the printer definition. Default = dflt.
DESNAME	The name of the output device, such as a file name, printer name, or e-mail address. Default is blank.
DESTYPE	The type of output device, such as screen, file, printer, mail, sysout, cache, localfile, or preview. Default=Screen.
MODE	Whether to print the report in character or bitmap format. Default = Default.
ORIENTATION	The paper layout is portrait or landscape. Default = Default.
PRINTJOB	Controls whether the Print Job dialog box appears before the report is run. Default = Yes. However, the dialog is never called from within the Reports Builder.

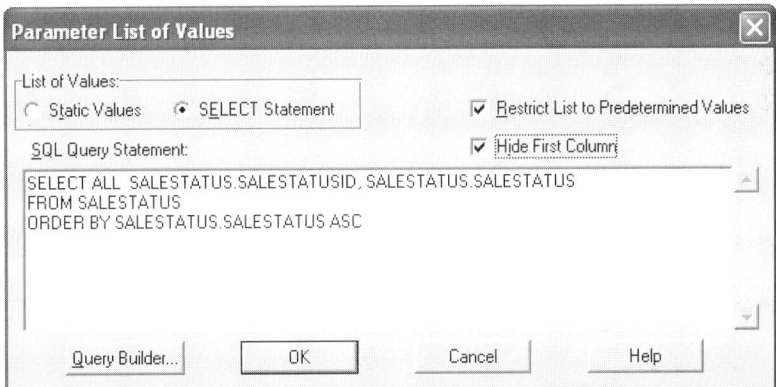

FIGURE 10.27 Parameter List of Values query.

from the database with a SELECT statement. Because SaleStatus is stored in a table, this example will use the SELECT statement.

1. Open the SalesbyMonthAndAgent report.
2. In the Object Navigator, expand the Data Model section.
3. Select the User Parameters entry and click the **Create** button to add a new user parameter.
4. Open the Property Inspector; set Name = **Sale_Status** and Datatype = **Number**.

The parameter name is eventually displayed to the users, so you need to give it a name that they will understand. Underscores are replaced with spaces, so you can use multiple words.

5. Under the List of Values property, click the **ellipses** button to open the Parameter List of Values assistant.
6. Choose the SELECT Statement option and either type in the SQL or use the Query Builder to select the SaleStatusID and SaleStatus columns from the SaleStatus table.

Figure 10.27 shows the resulting query screen. Notice the **Hide First Column** option. Ultimately, you want to use the SaleStatusID number in your report. It is risky to use the SaleStatus text value because Oracle might pad it with spaces making it more difficult to perform comparisons. Whenever possible, you should use numbers in parameters. However, you can hide those numbers from the users. By retrieving two columns, you can tell the parameter form to display the text description, but give the report the corresponding numeric value to work with.

Now that you have created a user parameter, you can use it in the report. In this case, you want to display the rows that match the condition specified by the user. Remember that this condition is specified in the main query.

7. In the Data Model, open the query and find the original condition: WHERE SaleStatus.SaleStatus = 'Sold'. Modify that line so that it reads **WHERE SalesStatus.SaleStatusID = :SALE_STATUS**

8. Save the form and run it. The *user parameter form* shown in Figure 10.28 will pop up automatically. Pick the For Sale option and click the **Run Form** button.

Figure 10.29 shows that when you run the matrix report to print houses for sale instead of only those that were sold, the report contains substantially more data. Notice that the matrix fills multiple pages. You might want to go back to Print Layout and reduce the font or shrink the column widths so the entire report fits on two pages. You might consider switching to landscape mode and going with a small enough font to fit the entire year on one page. But, the report might be too hard to read—something you always have to test with the users.

You should rerun the report and ensure that it still shows the same data when you choose only houses that were sold. While you are looking at that report, the question might occur to you: How would you display all 12 months, even though many have no data? You will not have to solve that problem here, but it is likely to come up in a business setting. The answer is that the report will display data that is retrieved by the query. So how do you get a query to return data that is Null? You use a LEFT JOIN.

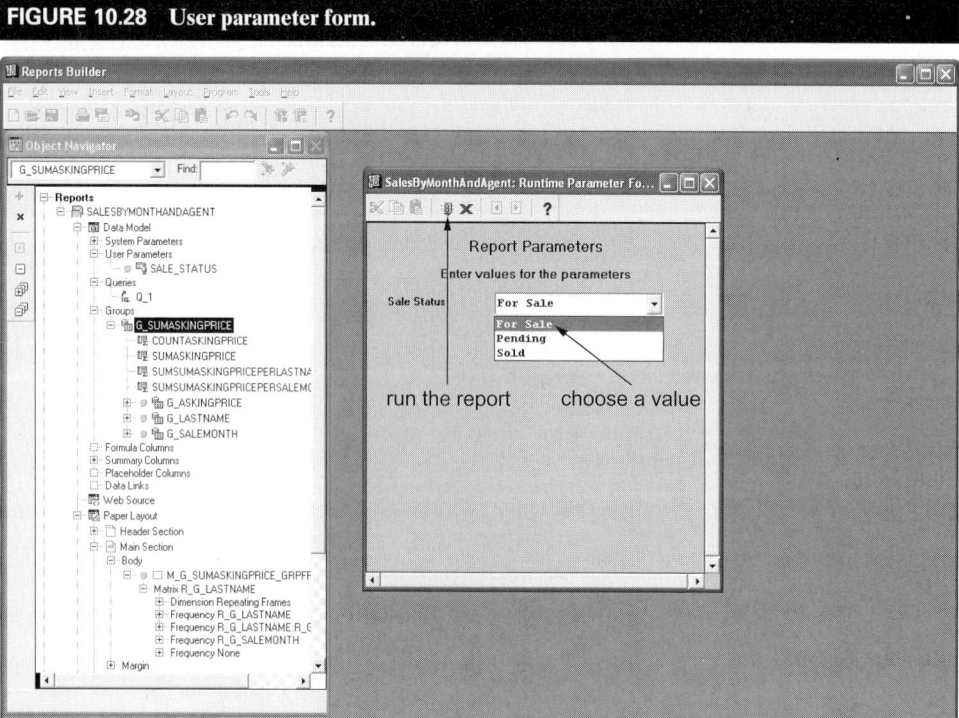

FIGURE 10.28 User parameter form.

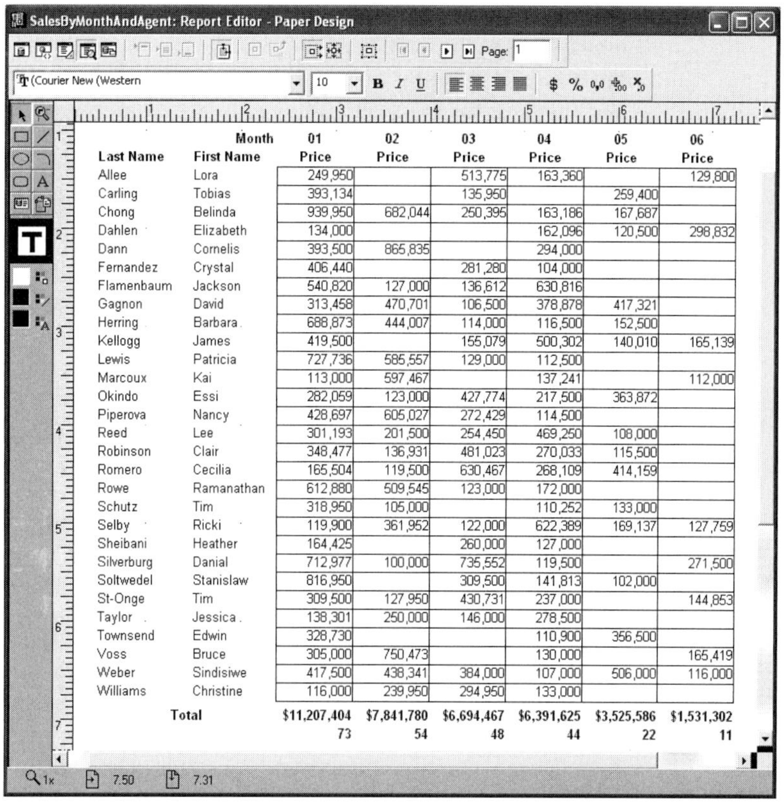

	Month	01	02	03	04	05	06
Last Name	First Name	Price	Price	Price	Price	Price	Price
Allee	Lora	249,950		513,775	163,360		129,800
Carling	Tobias	393,134		135,950		259,400	
Chong	Belinda	939,950	682,044	250,395	163,186	167,687	
Dahlen	Elizabeth	134,000			162,096	120,500	298,832
Dann	Cornelis	393,500	865,835		294,000		
Fernandez	Crystal	406,440		281,280	104,000		
Flamenbaum	Jackson	540,820	127,000	136,612	630,816		
Gagnon	David	313,458	470,701	106,500	378,878	417,321	
Herring	Barbara	688,873	444,007	114,000	116,500	152,500	
Kellogg	James	419,500		155,079	500,302	140,010	165,139
Lewis	Patricia	727,736	585,557	129,000	112,500		
Marcoux	Kai	113,000	597,467		137,241		112,000
Okindo	Essi	282,059	123,000	427,774	217,500	363,872	
Piperova	Nancy	428,697	605,027	272,429	114,500		
Reed	Lee	301,193	201,500	254,450	469,250	108,000	
Robinson	Clair	348,477	136,931	481,023	270,033	115,500	
Romero	Cecilia	165,504	119,500	630,467	268,109	414,159	
Rowe	Ramanathan	612,880	509,545	123,000	172,000		
Schutz	Tim	318,950	105,000		110,252	133,000	
Selby	Ricki	119,900	361,952	122,000	622,389	169,137	127,759
Sheibani	Heather	164,425		260,000	127,000		
Silverburg	Danial	712,977	100,000	735,552	119,500		271,500
Soltwedel	Stanislaw	816,950		309,500	141,813	102,000	
St-Onge	Tim	309,500	127,950	430,731	237,000		144,853
Taylor	Jessica	138,301	250,000	146,000	278,500		
Townsend	Edwin	328,730			110,900	356,500	
Voss	Bruce	305,000	750,473		130,000		165,419
Weber	Sindisiwe	417,500	438,341	384,000	107,000	506,000	116,000
Williams	Christine	116,000	239,950	294,950	133,000		
	Total	$11,207,404	$7,841,780	$6,694,467	$6,391,625	$3,525,586	$1,531,302
		73	54	48	44	22	11

FIGURE 10.29 The matrix report with many houses for sale.

The trick is to create a small table that includes all 12 month numbers, then LEFT JOIN that table to your data.

If you do not like the default parameter form that opens at the start of the report, you can make some simple changes to it. Use the main menu **Tools/Parameter Form Builder** option to bring up a simple editor. Basically, you can set the title and a short description. You can also choose which of the system parameters to include on the form.

Using Filters to Limit Reports

Sometimes reports get out of control. You might want to limit reports so users do not tie up a printer with giant reports. For example, the Listings and Contacts report uses space inefficiently, so it cranks out over 150 pages. It probably needs a better layout, a better decision about what users want to see, or at least a parameter form so that users can choose listings based on some parameter. However, you still might want to limit the number of listings displayed by the report. Oracle reports provide a convenient ***group filter*** property to restrict the records displayed on a report.

1. Open the **ListingsAndOffers** report and expand the Data Model in the Object Navigator.
2. Open the Property Inspector for the **G_ListingID** group. Change the **Filter Type** property to **First**. In the newly displayed **Number of Records** property, enter **50**.
3. Open the Property Inspector for the G_ContactDate group. Change the **Filter Type** property to **Last**. In the newly displayed **Number of Records** property, enter **5**.

When you run the report you will immediately see the effect of the filter on the main group—the total report now takes fewer than 20 pages. You probably will not see the effect of the filter on the detail group—only a few listings have more than five bids, and they are for houses that have already sold. Nonetheless, it is a useful trick to know. Many times you do not need to display all entries in a detail list, only the last few items.

There is one critical issue you have to be careful with. When you use a filter on a report that has subtotals (or counts), the subtotals will be applied only to the data shown on the form. In this example, if a listing had seven bids, but the report is limited to displaying no more than five, then the count would be five, not seven. If you want to display a total or count that covers the entire list of detail items—even those not shown—you have to write a separate function to perform the count and use a report trigger to compute and display the value for each group.

If you examine all of the options with the filter property, you will notice that you can write your own PL/SQL function to decide whether or not to include a record on the report. However, you should avoid this option because it is relatively slow. If you really need those features, simply embed them in your query, or use a PL/SQL function in the database to select only the rows you need.

CREATING REPORT TRIGGERS

Oracle provides several versions of report triggers to give you more detailed control over a report. For example, you can create sophisticated conditional formatting—where your PL/SQL code is executed to determine exactly how to display a data item. You might use these tools to display some values in different colors or to add additional space. The three main types of triggers you can create are: (1) *report triggers* that fire in response to basic form events unrelated to your data, (2) *validation triggers* that are used to check data returned on the user parameter form, and (3) *format triggers* that are executed every time a targeted object is displayed.

Report triggers are limited, but useful if you need them to set up a printer, open or close a network connection, or some other task when the report starts or ends. The events that support triggers are: Before Report, After Report, Between Pages, Before Parameter Form, and After Parameter Form. The Before and After report triggers are the ones you would use for setup and cleanup operations.

Validation triggers are limited to testing the value of parameters provided by the users. Since true user parameters have to come from lists, they rarely need to be tested. Validations are more useful for system parameters. However, instead of asking users to enter tricky system parameters, it is better to load values from the database. If a parameter value fails to meet your conditions, the user is returned to the parameter form.

Format triggers are the most powerful, but are still limited. A trigger attached to a single item can fire multiple times during the printing of a report. In fact, even for the same data item, the trigger can fire more than once. Consequently, you should not include calculations or DML within format triggers. In fact, your code cannot change data values. The purpose of a format trigger is to look at a data column and change the basic format properties for different values. You can change the way the data is displayed, but you cannot change the value.

CREATING CUSTOM TEMPLATES

When you use the report wizard, one of the last steps you take is to select a report template. The wizard has a default collection of templates, but they are different only in the color scheme. A powerful option with the report writer is the ability to create your own templates. With *custom templates*, all of your reports will have a similar look and feel.

Plus, you can handle some basic tasks once and have the style applied to all of your reports. For example, you can load the corporate logo onto the template so that it is always included on the reports.

The easiest way to create a custom template is to modify an existing one. The base templates are stored in the reports\templates folder beneath the directory where you installed the Developer Suite on your computer. They are given a .tdf suffix. A copy of the rwbeige.tdf file is provided on the student disk in addition.

In this section, you will modify a template and apply it to one of the reports. To be safe, the first step is to make a copy of an existing template.

1. Find an existing template, either in the Developer Suite\reports\templates folder, or the copy provided on the student disk. Use Windows to copy the file (**rwbeige.tdf**) to your working folder, and rename it **MyTemplate1.tdf**.
2. Start Reports Builder, click the **Cancel** button because you are not creating or editing a report. Select **File/Open** on the menu. Change the file types to all types (*.*), browse to your folder and open the new MyTemplate1.tdf file.
3. If necessary, expand the Object Navigator section under Templates and double-click the icon in front of the **Paper Layout** section for **MyTemplate1.**

Changes to a template are made in the Paper Layout section. However, you cannot add or delete items. Instead, you set properties for the existing items. The Paper Layout is the key to understanding templates, but there are a couple of tricky points.

The first point to understand is that there are several types of templates. The Default template is the generic version. This template defines the basic style that is applied by default to every type of form. However, each type of form (such as Group Above, Matrix, or Tabular) can have its own styles. Any styles you specify for a particular form type are called ***overrides***. A drop-down list at the top left of the Paper Layout editor lets you choose which type of form to work with. For the most part, you want to define styles to the Default layout so that they are applied to all form types.

The second point to understanding templates is that everything is grouped into four frames: (1) section or top level, (2) heading, (3) fields or detail, (4) summaries or footer. By changing properties to a section, you control the appearance of every item placed in that section when a report is built. For example, it is common to set summary frames to boldface, because it is often used to display subtotals.

The third key to understanding templates is that you need to be able to format three types of data: (1) characters or text, (2) numbers, and (3) dates. The template enables you to format each of these three types separately, and to apply different formats to the labels for each type of data. You can also assign different formats to each data type depending on which section they fall in. Keep in mind that formatting you apply to a number in the template will be applied to any number displayed in the selected section.

DESIGNING CUSTOM TEMPLATES

Figure 10.30 shows the basic elements of the template in both the Object Navigator and the Paper Layout. Three of the four frames are easy to spot in the Paper Layout. The fourth one (section) is more difficult because it covers the entire group, but you can select it by clicking on the entry in the Object Navigator or on the white rectangle in the Paper Layout. Also pay attention to the items used to define the properties for the three data types. The Object Navigator makes it easy to identify the labels and the fields. In the Paper Layout, note that the data fields are labeled with F_datatype.

Notice the Margin section in the Object Navigator. Currently, it contains one item—the image used as a placeholder for the logo. To find and position items in the

506 Introduction to Oracle

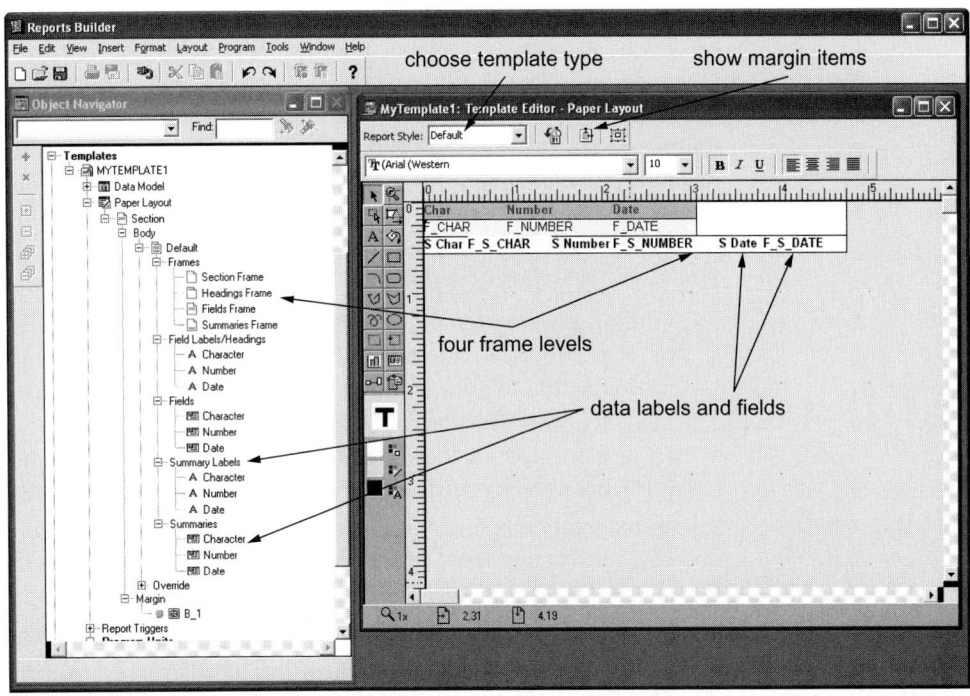

FIGURE 10.30 Initial template layout.

margins using the Paper Layout, you have to click the Margin toggle button. Since the logo is one of the biggest changes you need to make, begin with it.

1. Click the **Margin** button to display the margin items in the Paper Layout.
2. Delete the existing placeholder logo. Use **Insert/Image** to find and insert the Redwood Realty logo. Resize the logo to fit at the top of the page.
3. Click the **Insert Page Number** button to add page numbers to the margin. Choose the option to display the numbers at the bottom center of the page.
4. Click the **Insert Date and Time** button to display the standard date in the bottom-left corner of each page. Every report should display the date. Placing it on the template helps ensure that no one forgets to include it. Save your template file.

> **Tip.** If you receive a 0069 error while saving a template file, just ignore it.

The next major goal is to update the colors a little bit.

1. Click the **Margin** button again to close the margin display.
2. Expand the Paper Layout node in the Object Navigator to make it easy to find the major layout items. Select the **Headings Frame** in the Object Navigator. Click the **Fill Color** button and choose a different color—perhaps a brighter yellow.
3. Select the **Fields Frame** and use the same Fill Color button to set the property to **No Fill**, allowing the section color (white) to show through.
4. Select the three heading labels to make it easy to assign properties to all three at the same time. Use the **Text Color** button to pick a brighter blue. Verify that all three heading types pick up the new color. Save the changes.

5. Formatting the report title is a bit different. In the Object Navigator, expand nodes: **Templates/Paper Layout/Section/Body/Default**. Double-click the **properties** icon next to the Default node. Find the **Title** entry and set its Font to **Arial** at **16 points**.

Once you understand the purpose of the frames, labels, fields, and margins; it is relatively easy to modify a template. Just be careful not to get carried away and devise unreadable template styles. If in doubt, use restraint and muted colors. Better yet, consult a graphics designer for ideas on how to improve designs.

Before moving on, you should look at one of the specific report styles. Since you used the Group Above report, you might want to make some changes to its template.

1. Select the **Group Above** option in the **Report Style** drop-down list.
2. Notice that it has picked up some of the Default styles, but not all of them. In particular, you will have to reset the Text Color for the heading labels. Notice that in the Override section, there are Level 1 and Level 2 headings. Set the text color for both levels. At Level 1, be sure to set the text color for labels and for fields.
3. Save the template and close the Reports Builder.

Note that for complex templates you can also define trigger code or set default system parameter values. You will not need them for the reports in this chapter, but keep the option in mind for future reference. Sometime you might want to assign a default printer that would be used for all reports.

APPLYING TEMPLATES

Once you have a template file (and remember where you saved it), it is relatively easy to apply the new styles to a report. Do you remember the steps you followed when you created a new report? The screen that enables you to select a new template has an option to choose a template file. If you are creating a new report, you simply choose that option and find the template.

A more interesting trick is to apply the template after the report has already been created. The Oracle documentation states that when you apply a new template to an existing report, in addition to altering the frame and item display properties, the template will alter several of the basic system parameters, including page size and margin position.

1. Open the existing report **SalesByCityAndAgent**.
2. In the Object Navigator, expand the **Paper Layout** node. Select the **Main Section** entry, to make it the one where you will apply the new template.
3. Choose **Tools/Report Wizard** on the menu. Scroll the list of tabs and select the **Template** tab.
4. Choose the option to use a **Template file**. Click the **Browse** button and navigate to your new *MyTemplate1* file. Click the **Finish** button to apply the template.

Figure 10.31 shows the report with the new layout. Removing the shading from the detail section and using a darker font and stronger background for the headings has brightened up the report considerably. Whether that is a good thing depends on the users. One of the nice things about using templates is that you can show users different styles and get consensus on the best overall template. Then you can quickly apply that template to existing reports and use it for all new reports.

REGISTERING TEMPLATES

It is relatively easy to select templates from a file—as long as every reports developer knows where the templates are located and remembers to pick the option and go

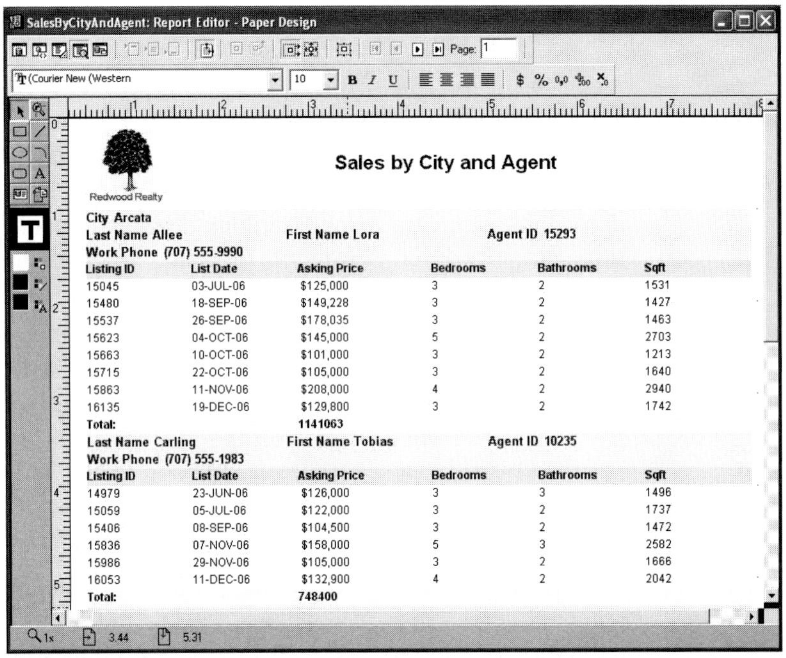

FIGURE 10.31 A brighter report with the new layout.

search for it. The other option is to modify the Oracle report configuration file so that your template shows up in the main list of templates. In fact, you could remove all of the predefined templates and replace them with your own styles. In an organization with many developers that often produces new reports it makes sense to change the main template list. However, the process is somewhat tedious and a little risky. So, if a firm only produces a few new reports, it is simpler to remind developers to browse for the template file.

If you really want to register your template, you need to modify the configuration file.

1. Use Windows explorer to find the **cauprefs.ora** file in the root Oracle Developer Suite folder. Make a backup copy of this file. This step is critical!
2. Open the **cauprefs.ora** file in WordPad or Notepad. Find the section labeled: **Reports.BreakAbove_Template_Desc**. Immediately after the Beige entry, add: **MyTemplate1**.
3. Locate the section labeled **Reports.BreakAbove_Template_File**. Immediately after the rwbeige entry, add a row with **MyTemplate1,**

```
Reports.BreakAbove_Template_Desc =
  (Beige,
  MyTemplate1,
  Blue,
  Gray,
  Green,
  Peach,
  Wine)
Reports.BreakAbove_Template_File =
  (rwbeige,
  MyTemplate1,
```

```
          rwblue,
          rwgray,
          rwgreen,
          rwpeach,
          rwwine)
```

4. Save the file.
5. Use Windows Explorer to copy your template file (MyTemplate1.tdf) into the reports\templates folder under the main Developer Suite folder.
6. You can also add a preview image of the template that is displayed when developers scroll through the list of templates. Apply the template to a report, use Print Screen to capture an image of the report. Use a graphics tool (PowerPoint will work) to edit and save the image as a bitmap (MyTemplate1.bmp) file. Copy the file to the Oracle templates folder.
7. To test your changes, close and restart Reports Builder, which forces it to reread the configuration file. Open an existing report and use Tools/Report Wizard to open the template screen. Your template should be in the list.

In the configuration file, notice that you really should add your template file to every one of the report types. However, you probably do not really want to use your sample template. So, you should clean up your Oracle configuration.

1. Move or delete MyTemplate.tdf and MyTemplate.bmp from the Oracle templates folder.
2. Restore the original backup copy of the cauprefs.ora file in the Developer Suite root folder. Close Reports Builder.

CUSTOMIZING A WEB REPORT

With improved access to the Internet, many managers are asking for reports to be delivered as Web pages instead of paper. The Reports Builder provides several ways to create Web-based reports. When you started building reports, the instructions in this chapter suggested you should choose the option to create both Web and print layouts. When you choose the Web layout, the wizard automatically builds a dynamic report using Java Server Pages (jsp). The report server reads the script in the .jsp report page, retrieves the requested data, and formats everything into a simple HTML Web page.

1. Start the Reports Builder, open the existing report **Sales by City and Agent**.
2. Click the **Run Web Layout** button and wait a few seconds. The Reports Builder has a copy of OC4J running internally, and it will process and display the report. Figure 10.32 shows the HTML version of the report still using the Beige style.

First, notice that the report contains none of the changes you made to the Paper Layout. The HTML layout is handled separately. Second, notice that HTML tends to display columns of data awkwardly. See how the phone numbers are breaking on the hyphen. These are features of HTML. If you do not like this layout, you have to create a cascading style sheet to handle the layout.

If you want an easier way to distribute reports on the Web, without having to edit HTML or style sheets, Oracle provides another option. You can save a printed report as a PDF file. However, the data in a PDF file is static. Once the report is built and distributed, the data remains fixed. On the other hand, dynamic HTML reports pick up the most recent data from the database and rebuild the HTML pages. This section will focus on the dynamic HTML approach. You can use the Reports Builder menus to create PDF files if you need them.

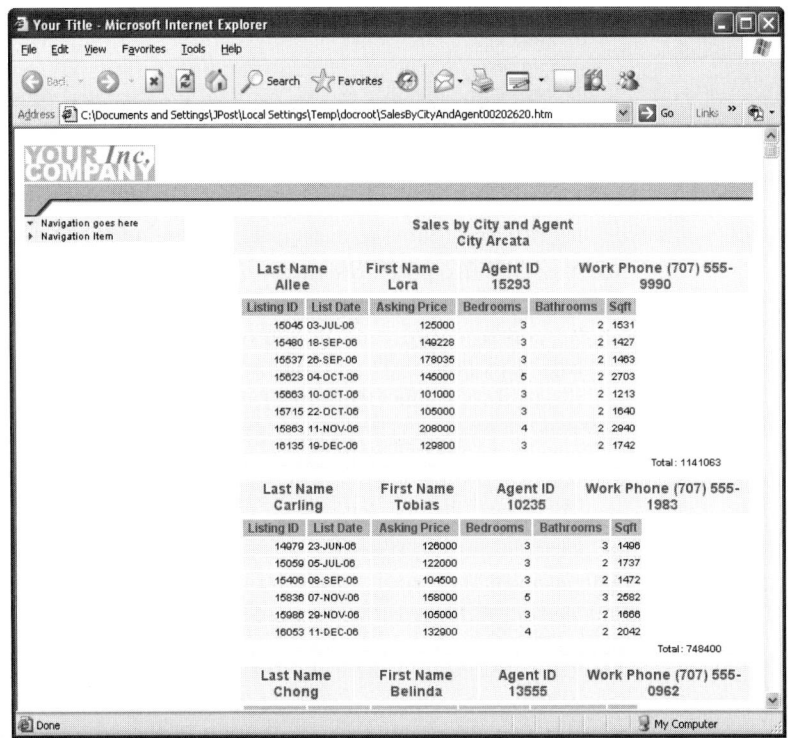

FIGURE 10.32 Initial Web view of Sales by City and Agent.

THE DYNAMIC REPORT ENVIRONMENT

To create reports dynamically, you use the Reports Builder to create a javascript text file. If you look in the folder where you have been saving reports, you will notice that all of them have been saved as javascript (.jsp) files. More specifically, the report writer has also created a Web definition file. The Oracle Web server runs a version of the Java engine that reads the report definition file, follows the Java commands to connect to the database and retrieves the data. This data is merged row by row into a new HTML page. The page layout is controlled with standard HTML TABLE tags. The basic elements of the report are tagged with style sheet classes that are defined in the accompanying cascading style sheet (CSS) file.

Figure 10.33 illustrates the overall process. You can display Web reports using the Reports Builder because it has a copy of the OC4J server built into it. To distribute the reports to users, you need to set up an Oracle Application server, then copy the report files and style sheets to that machine. For this chapter, you can simply rely on the Reports Builder to display the reports.

MODIFYING A WEB REPORT

For the most part, this section assumes that you understand the basics of Web pages and HTML. Web pages are text files, and the page display is controlled with tags that are indicated with angle brackets. Several online resources provide complete descriptions and examples of the tags, so they are not defined in this book. Note that the <TABLE> tags are important for database reports. Cascading style sheets are one aspect of Web pages that many people do not understand. A *cascading style sheet*

CHAPTER 10 Creating and Modifying Reports

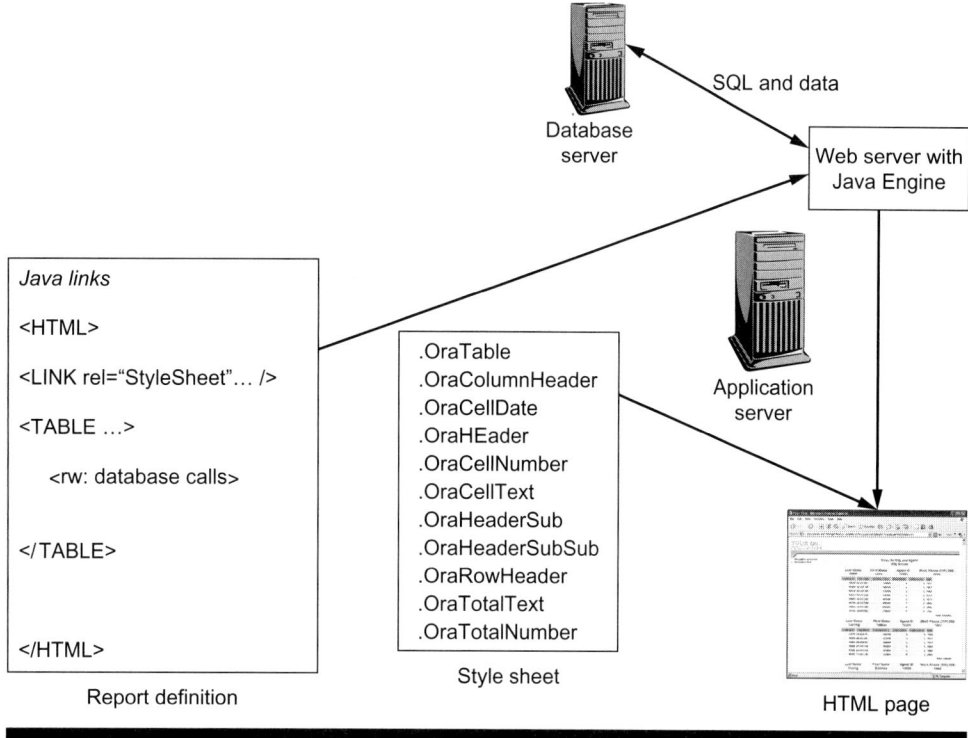

FIGURE 10.33 Dynamic HTML report components.

enables you to define properties for standard Web tags and to create your own style definitions. Style sheets are powerful and offer far more formatting options than typical HTML tags. As a result, most people do not try to memorize the style sheet options, but use a style sheet editor to help create and edit cascading style sheets.

The first step in cleaning up the Web page generated by the report writer is to examine the main Web file that it created.

1. In the Object Navigator, double-click the icon to open the **Web Source**.
2. Figure 10.34 shows the initial part of the file. Notice the style sheet and logo file references. These will have to be changed in a minute. First, scroll down a little to see the data area.

Figure 10.35 shows the start of the data retrieval section. Notice the use of three Java loops—one for each major section of the report. Technically, you can edit this section. With practice, you could even write your own Java code. However, it is risky to make changes within the data section. If you make a mistake, the report will not work at all. Always make backup copies of the original files before attempting to modify the code. You will not need to change the code for this book, but if you look through the major sections, the file will be easier to understand.

Now it is time to try making some cosmetic changes to the Web Source file. Remember, the data part works fine; you just want to change the way some things look.

1. Change the report's HTML title. Find the **<TITLE>** tag and change **Your Title** to **Sales By City and Agent**.
2. You want to replace the logo with the Redwood logo. First, copy the Redwood logo to the images folder used by the server. Use Windows Explorer to find the

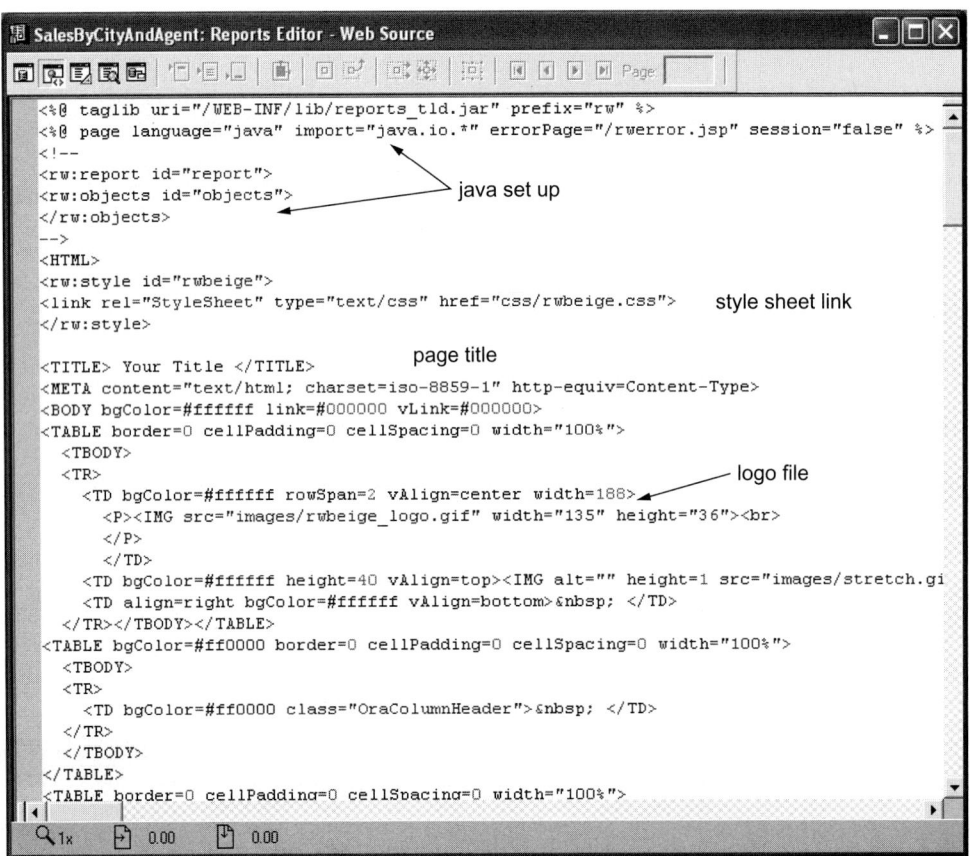

FIGURE 10.34 A portion of the Web definition file.

Developer Suite root folder. Then open the **reports\docroot\images** folder. Copy the **RedwoodLogo1.jpg** file into this folder.

> **Tip:** If you cannot find the images folder, search for the rwbeige_logo.gif file.

3. In the Web Source file, find the image link to **images/ rwbeige_logo.gif** and replace it with **images/RedwoodLogo1.jpg.** Change the width to **100** and height to **97**.

> **Tip:** Be careful with filenames. They are case sensitive.

Your Web report might not pick up the new copy of the logo file because the Web server makes a temporary copy of the Web files. If you do not see the logo, move a copy of the .jpg file into the temporary folder indicated in the address window of your Web browser. For example, C:\Documents and Settings\YourName\Local Settings\Temp\docroot\images, where YourName is your Windows username. Also, eventually you will need to create separate logo files for the Web. Image files usually have to be optimized separately for printing versus Web display.

The next thing to customize is the style sheet. These changes are made completely outside of the Reports Builder. You can make more complex changes if you have a style sheet editor available, such as the one built into Microsoft's Visual Studio. However, you will only make minor changes in this section, so you can use any text editor.

CHAPTER 10 Creating and Modifying Reports 513

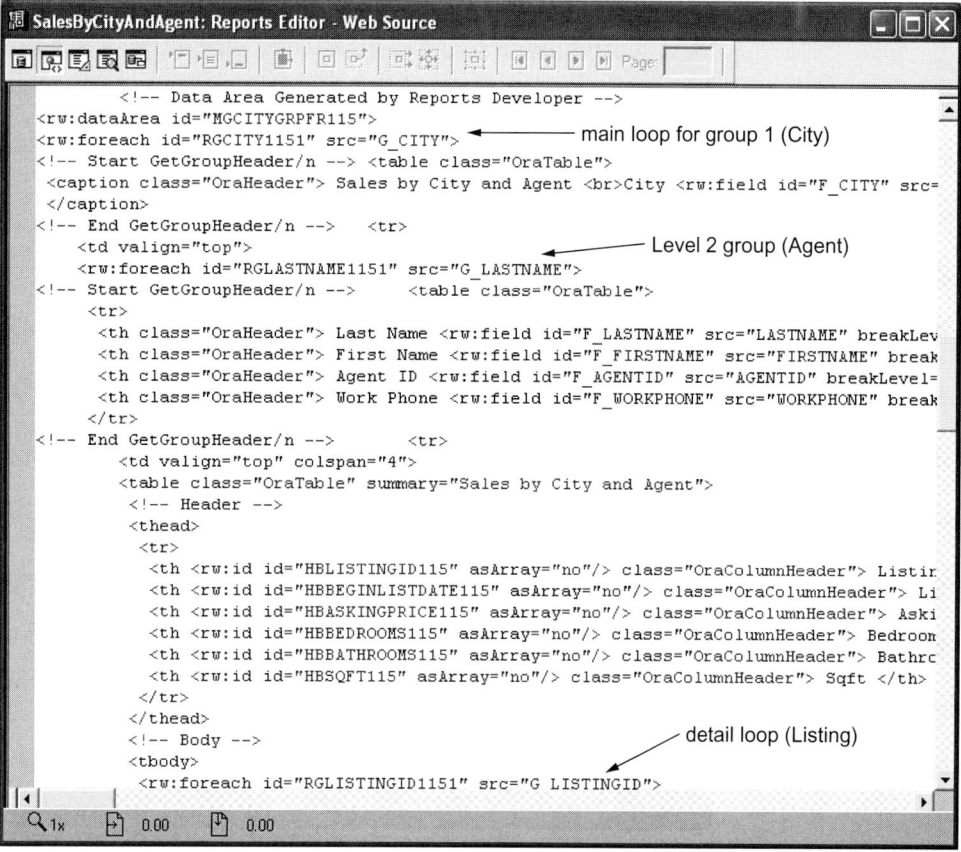

FIGURE 10.35 The data retrieval section of the Web file.

1. First, change the name of the style sheet link. In the Reports Builder Web Source, find the <link rel="StyleSheet"...> line. In the href property, change **rwbeige.css** to **CityAgent.css**. Save the file.

2. You face the same temporary directory issue with style sheets that you did with the image file. Use Windows Explorer to find the **Developer Suite root\reports\docroot\css** folder. Make a copy of the **rwbeige.css** file and rename it **CityAgent.css**.

3. Edit the new **CityAgent.css** file with WordPad or Notepad. In the row for OraColumnHeader, change the color to **0000ff**, which is the rgb code for blue. Change the background color to a yellow (**ffff66**). For the three detail data types (**OraCellDate**, **OraCellNumber**, and **OraCellText**), change the background to white (**ffffff**).

4. Save the file. Copy the file to your temporary folder (C:\Documents and Settings\YourName\Local Settings\Temp\docroot\css). Figure 10.36 shows the new file, with some space added to make it more readable.

5. In the Reports Writer, run the Web form.

Figure 10.37 shows the new report. Although you'll have to visualize the color changes, the detail section is clearer because the background is now white. For more extensive changes, you can usually figure out which styles to change based on the name. If you are uncertain about the role of the Oracle style, you can read through the Web Source to see where the style is used.

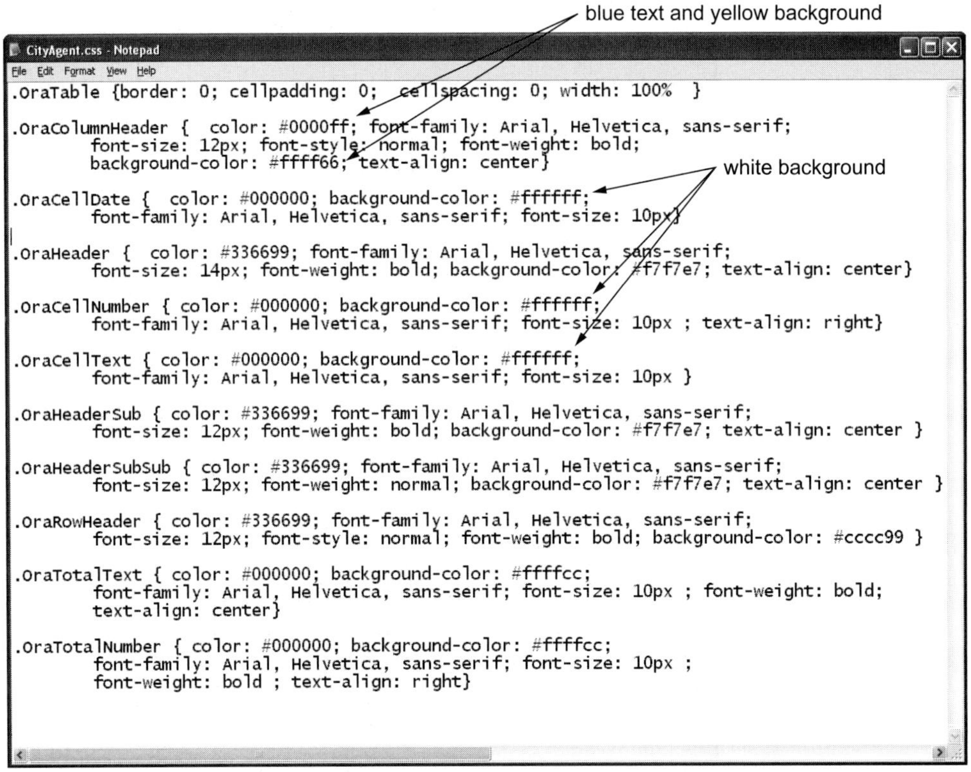


```
.OraTable {border: 0; cellpadding: 0; cellspacing: 0; width: 100% }

.OraColumnHeader {  color: #0000ff; font-family: Arial, Helvetica, sans-serif;
        font-size: 12px; font-style: normal; font-weight: bold;
        background-color: #ffff66; text-align: center}

.OraCellDate {  color: #000000; background-color: #ffffff;
        font-family: Arial, Helvetica, sans-serif; font-size: 10px}

.OraHeader {  color: #336699; font-family: Arial, Helvetica, sans-serif;
        font-size: 14px; font-weight: bold; background-color: #f7f7e7; text-align: center}

.OraCellNumber { color: #000000; background-color: #ffffff;
        font-family: Arial, Helvetica, sans-serif; font-size: 10px ; text-align: right}

.OraCellText { color: #000000; background-color: #ffffff;
        font-family: Arial, Helvetica, sans-serif; font-size: 10px }

.OraHeaderSub { color: #336699; font-family: Arial, Helvetica, sans-serif;
        font-size: 12px; font-weight: bold; background-color: #f7f7e7; text-align: center }

.OraHeaderSubSub { color: #336699; font-family: Arial, Helvetica, sans-serif;
        font-size: 12px; font-weight: normal; background-color: #f7f7e7; text-align: center }

.OraRowHeader { color: #336699; font-family: Arial, Helvetica, sans-serif;
        font-size: 12px; font-style: normal; font-weight: bold; background-color: #cccc99 }

.OraTotalText { color: #000000; background-color: #ffffcc;
        font-family: Arial, Helvetica, sans-serif; font-size: 10px ; font-weight: bold;
        text-align: center}

.OraTotalNumber { color: #000000; background-color: #ffffcc;
        font-family: Arial, Helvetica, sans-serif; font-size: 10px ;
        font-weight: bold ; text-align: right}
```

FIGURE 10.36 Style sheet changes.

Style sheets are an easy way to change the visual display of Web pages. In fact, you can modify the style sheet without changing the underlying Web page. So, if you want to change the look of your Web reports, you can simply modify the style sheet. On the other hand, you cannot use a style sheet to format numbers. In this report, you cannot set commas and dollar signs in the prices and totals. And, you cannot set numeric formats in HTML tags.

There are two ways to format numbers (or dates) on a Web page report: (1) write the format into the original SQL statement, or (2) write a Java function to format the data when it is displayed. Both methods are challenging. Setting the formatting in SQL is easy with the TO_CHAR function, but then you will have problems computing totals because they are now text values instead of numbers. Even if you know Java and J2EE, the second approach requires some configuration effort to make it work with the Reports Builder. If you are interested in pursuing the Java approach, note that Oracle has a utility library for jsp with a displayCurrency function.

Adding a Chart to a Web Report

Many managers find it easier to evaluate data by examining charts. You can include charts in a report at several levels. You could place a summary chart at the end (or beginning) of a report to show total data. You could place a chart within groups or even on the detail level so that a new chart is redrawn for each data row at that level. In this case, the chart changes based on the data at that particular level. The steps for creating a chart are the same no matter where you place the chart.

CHAPTER 10   Creating and Modifying Reports   **515**

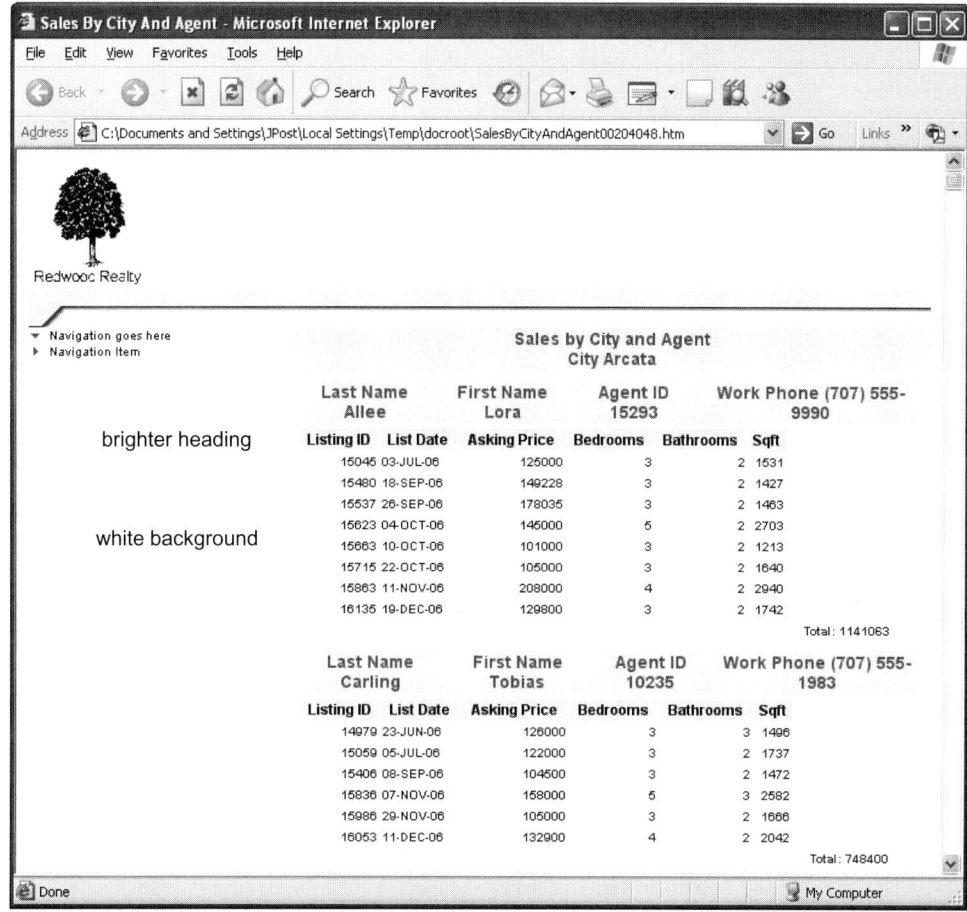

FIGURE 10.37   The new Web report.

In a Web report, the first step is to decide where to put the chart. For this example, you will place it at the end of the report—which means you first have to find the end of the report.

1. Open the **Web Source** for the Sales By City and Agent report. Locate the end of the Web report.
2. Just above the **</BODY>** tag add a new paragraph section with **<P>** and **</P>** tags. Click the space or line between these two tags.
3. Choose **Insert/Graph** on the main menu. Answer the wizard prompts to create the desired chart.
4. Choose the following: **type = Bar**, **X-axis column = City**, and **Y-axis column = sumAskingPricePerCity**. Enter title values, and skip the rest, including the hyperlinks.
5. When the wizard is finished, run the Web layout. To see the chart, scroll to the bottom of the Web page. Figure 10.38 shows the sample chart.
6. It should be similar to the code in Figure 10.38.

The code for the report has been inserted into the Web Source file. Figure 10.39 shows the sample code. It contains only a couple of lines because it relies on the Java

516 Introduction to Oracle

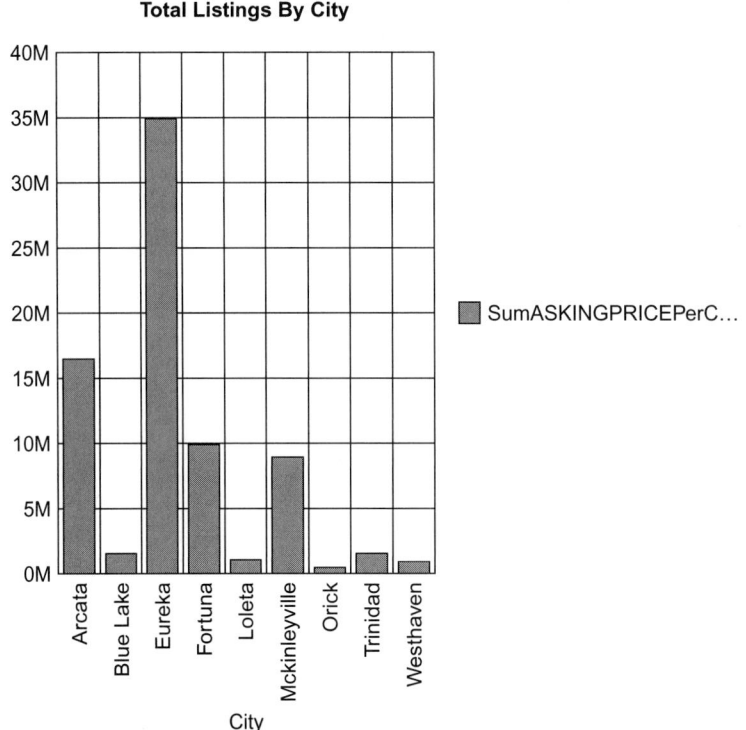

FIGURE 10.38 A chart at the bottom of the Web report.

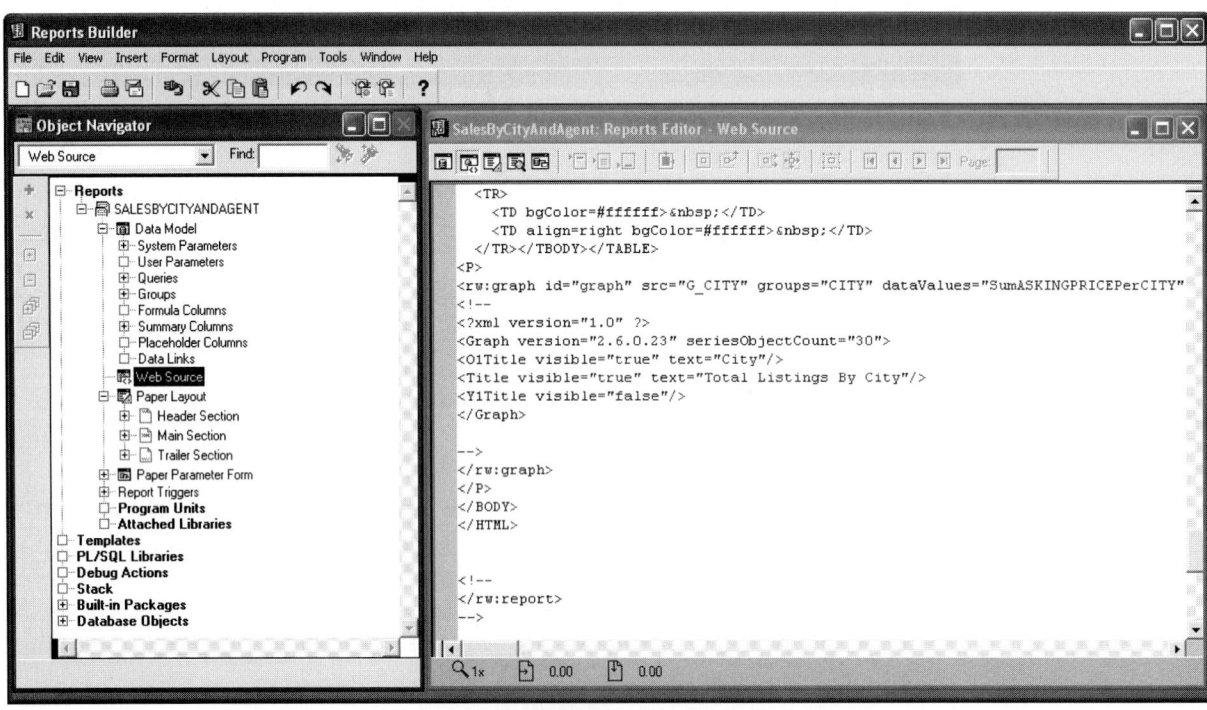

FIGURE 10.39 Inserting a Chart.

graphics code written by Oracle. If you want to change the chart, you could edit the source code. However, altering the tags directly is risky because if you make a mistake the chart might not work at all. In that case, you would reload your backup copy, but there is an easier way. To edit a chart, place the cursor somewhere within the graph tags. That is, between <rw:graph ..> and </rw:graph>. Then choose the menu item **Edit/Settings** to reenter the wizard and make the changes you want.

Adding hyperlinks to charts can provide some interesting options. For example, you can add a link to each bar on a chart so that when a user clicks on a specific bar, it opens a new report with details for that particular data point. The wizard contains details on how to specify a hyperlink. The only catch is that you have to create all of the other reports.

Summary

You will need reports for almost any database project. Even if you want to provide data on the Web instead of paper, the Reports Builder has some useful capabilities that set it apart from the Forms Builder. In particular, reports are commonly designed to display groups of data with subtotals. The report wizard makes it easy to create relatively standard reports, including the grouped and matrix reports.

The Reports Builder gives you considerable control to enhance and customize a report. You begin by creating a data model that uses queries to retrieve the data you need. You can set relationships using groups or master-detail settings. You then use the Paper Layout to configure the report layout and set properties for the various sections. All data is displayed through the use of repeating frames. You use nested repeating frames to display one-to-many relationships. You can also use simple frames to group related items to make it easier to set common properties. For example, you will almost always create a frame for header and footer sections.

Eventually, you should create standardized templates for the reports that establish common properties so groups of reports all have a similar appearance. It is easiest to edit an existing template.

Web reports use the same Data Model and one-to-many relationships as the paper versions. However, the layout control is different because you are limited by Web standards. The cascading style sheet is the best way to set the report's design. You can also create a standard style sheet that you can apply to all related Web reports. Ultimately, dynamic Web reports have to be distributed through the Oracle Application Server.

Key Terms

- break footer
- break header
- cascading style sheet
- custom templates
- data model
- format triggers
- frame
- group filter
- group report
- mailing labels
- master-detail
- matrix report
- overrides
- page footer
- page header
- repeating frame
- report footer
- report header
- report triggers
- system parameters
- tabular report
- user parameter form
- user parameters
- validation triggers

Review

TRUE/FALSE

1. In a master-detail or grouped report with two levels of breaks, the Level 2 footer appears before the Level 1 footer.

2. You cannot easily create a matrix report that includes groups.

3. If a data model contains only one group, you can still create master-detail relationships using frames on the layout editor.
4. You can use a group filter to limit the number of rows displayed in a detail section, and the totals for that section will only include the values displayed.
5. User parameter forms are created once for a report and work the same in both paper-based and Web-based reports.

FILL IN

1. Even on a simple tabular form, you have to use a(n) _____ to hold the data fields.
2. If you have a relationship that has one parent group and two independent repeating groups, you need to create _____ relationships.
3. A custom template at the Default level defines properties for all report types, but _____ define properties for specific report types.
4. Instead of a template, you use a(n) _____ to define properties for a Web report.
5. A(n) _____ allows users to select items that control the data displayed on a report.

MULTIPLE CHOICE

1. Managers want to see a report that displays total commissions earned by quarter from sales in each city. What is the best type of report to use?
   a. Mailing label
   b. Grouped with two levels
   c. Tabular
   d. Matrix
   e. Grouped with one level
2. Managers want a report that shows listings by sale status (sold, for sale, or pending), with an inner level grouping by agent. In which section would you place the heading columns for the detail section consisting of ListingID, Bedrooms, and AskingPrice?
   a. Page header or margin
   b. Break footer for AgentID
   c. Break header for AgentID
   d. Break footer for SaleStatusID
   e. Break header for SaleStatusID
3. In a custom template for a paper-based report, you assign the background color for the overall report in which frame?
   a. Section
   b. Headings
   c. Fields
   d. Summaries
   e. Summary Labels
4. If you reenter the report wizard to change the paper layout, changes to the paper layout will be saved,
   a. but you cannot change the data model.
   b. and the Web layout will be overwritten as well.
   c. but will not overwrite the customized property changes you made.
   d. but you cannot change the template.
   e. but you cannot alter the overall report style.
5. To add a new summary calculation to the report:
   a. You simply place a new field in the appropriate layout frame.
   b. You must first add the field to the data model in the proper group.
   c. You must first create a formula field for calculations.
   d. You must restart the report wizard.
   e. You must alter the query to perform the calculation.

Hands-on Exercises

1. EXTENDING THE CHAPTER CASE

The manager needs a basic report that displays listings by agent. The manager also wants to be able to pick a month and see the listings for sale only in that month. Dates are based on the BeginListDate because that indicates the initial activity by the agents. The report should list basic information about each agent (name and phone), followed by a display of all of the listings signed by that agent, sorted in descending order of AskingPrice. The manager wants to see the total value of the AskingPrice and a count of the number of listings. He intends to print the reports, and each agent should be printed on a separate page.

1. Create a new report using the GroupAbove wizard. In case he changes his mind about printing, create both Web and Paper layouts. Name the report **Agent Listings**.
2. Create the query using the Agent, Listing, SaleStatus, and Properties tables. Be sure to set **SaleStatus = 'For Sale'** and sort by agent name and asking price.

```
SELECT ALL AGENTS.AGENTID, AGENTS.LASTNAME,
AGENTS.FIRSTNAME, AGENTS.WORKPHONE,
LISTINGS.LISTINGID, LISTINGS.BEGINLISTDATE,
LISTINGS.ASKINGPRICE,
SALESTATUS.SALESTATUS,
PROPERTIES.CITY, PROPERTIES.BEDROOMS
FROM AGENTS, LISTINGS, PROPERTIES,
SALESTATUS
WHERE SALESTATUS.SALESTATUS = 'For Sale'
   AND ((LISTINGS.LISTINGAGENTID =
   AGENTS.AGENTID)
   AND (LISTINGS.PROPERTYID =
   PROPERTIES.PROPERTYID)
   AND (LISTINGS.SALESTATUSID =
   SALESTATUS.SALESTATUSID))
ORDER BY AGENTS.LASTNAME ASC,
AGENTS.FIRSTNAME ASC, LISTINGS.ASKINGPRICE
DESC
```

3. There is only one group: Agents, so pick **LastName**, **FirstName**, **AgentID**, and **Workphone**.
4. You need to display **ListingID**, **BeginListDate**, **AskingPrice**, **City**, and **Bedroom** in the detail section.
5. Be sure to compute the Sum of AskingPrice and Count of ListingID.
6. If you have your template available you can use that, or pick the standard beige and add the logo, page number, and date manually.
7. To print one agent per page, open the properties for the agent group (**R_G_Lastname**), and set **Maximum Records per Page = 1**. You should also place the overall total on its own page by setting the **Page Break Before** property of the **M_G_LastName_FTR** frame to **Yes**.
8. Format the AskingPrice column and the total. Be sure the total aligns correctly with the column by using the **Format/Justify/Right** menu option.
9. The user parameter form is relatively interesting because the manager wants the ability to pick a month or to pick all months. In the Data Model, create a user parameter. Set Name = Listing_Month and Datatype = Character. For the List of Values query, hide the first column and use:

```
SELECT 'All' AS MonthID, 'All Months' AS
Month
FROM dual
UNION
SELECT DISTINCT
TO_CHAR(LISTINGS.BEGINLISTDATE,'MM') AS
MonthID,
TO_CHAR(LISTINGS.BEGINLISTDATE, 'Month')
AS Month
FROM LISTINGS
ORDER BY MonthID
```

10. Create another user parameter. Set Name = Listing_Year and Datatype = Character. For the List of Values query, there is only one column:

```
SELECT DISTINCT
TO_CHAR(LISTINGS.BEGINLISTDATE,'YYYY')
AS ListYear
FROM LISTINGS
ORDER BY
TO_CHAR(LISTINGS.BEGINLISTDATE,'YYYY')
```

11. Modify the data model query adding two AND lines immediately before the ORDER BY statement. Note that the test for 'All' months must come first and be sure to include all of the parentheses:

```
AND (('All' = :LISTING_MONTH) OR
(TO_CHAR(LISTINGS.BEGINLISTDATE,'MM') =
:LISTING_MONTH))
  AND (TO_CHAR(LISTINGS.BEGINLISTDATE,
'YYYY') = :LISTING_YEAR)
```

12. Save the report and run it. Print out the first page to hand in.

2. COFFEE MERCHANT

The managers at the Coffee Merchant need to be able to analyze the sales data to see if there are any patterns. In particular, they are interested in looking at quarterly sales and sales by states. They suspect there might be some patterns in each of these two categories, and they are curious to see if there is a pattern across the two categories. Consequently, you need to create a matrix report across those two categories. You will have to create the value of the quarter in the query. The managers also want to separate coffee sales from tea sales, which is defined by the ItemType.

1. Start a new report using the report wizard, and create both Web and paper layouts. Pick the **Matrix with Group** report type and title it **Quarterly Sales By State**.
2. The query is the most challenging part of this report. You need to set up columns for YearQuarter and Value. You will probably have to write the query in SQL and skip the query builder. Use the **Consumers**, **Orders**, **OrderLines**, and **Inventory** tables. Use To_Char to format the OrderDate as 'YYYY-Q' for **YearQuarter**, and compute the Value of an **OrderLine** with **Round(Quantity*Price*(1-Discount),2)**.

```
SELECT ALL CONSUMERS.STATE, INVENTORY.ITEMTYPE,
TO_CHAR(ORDERS.ORDERDATE, 'YYYY-Q') AS
YearQuarter,
Round(ORDERLINES.Quantity*ORDERLINES.Price*
(1-ORDERLINES.Discount),2) AS Value
FROM CONSUMERS, ORDERS, ORDERLINES,
INVENTORY
WHERE ((ORDERS.CONSUMERID =
CONSUMERS.CONSUMERID)
  AND (ORDERLINES.ORDERID = ORDERS.ORDERID)
  AND (ORDERLINES.INVENTORYID =
INVENTORY.INVENTORYID))
```

3. Select **ItemType** as the group variable, **State** for the rows, **YearQuarter** as the matrix column, **Sum(Value)** for the cells, and **Sum(SumValue)** for the total.
4. Save the result. Change the font for the title, and add page numbers and the date. Replace the logo. You can create one of your own, or use the one on the disk.
5. Clean up the formatting, save the report in your folder, and print a copy to hand in.

3. Rowing Ventures

Rowing Ventures needs a report that can be used to distribute the race results via a Web site. The report will use most of the data in the database. You should also create the paper layout version of the form so the company can hand out result sheets at the race. Use the Group Left style and create a query using all of the tables (**Race**, **RaceTimes**, **Boat**, **BoatCrew**, **Person**, and **Organization**. Sort by **StartTime**, **Place**, and **Position**. The report needs two master levels plus the detail. The top level consists of the basic race information. The second level is the data about the boats, organized by the finishing position. The detail level consists of the names of the boat crew. The report does not need totals. Clean up the print layout, then edit the style sheet and make the Web report readable. Add a logo file, and print the first page of the report to hand in to your instructor.

Note that it can be challenging to edit a Group Left layout because the frames are so tightly packed. If you have problems moving fields or frames on the page, try using the frame selection button and use the magnifier to enlarge the screen to help you find the frame handles. Remember that the wizard builds a simple group frame to hold elements for each section, and you might have to move that frame first.

4. Broadcloth Clothing

Broadcloth Clothing needs an important report for the factories: a shipping invoice. The shipping invoice is printed and is sent with each shipment. It is used by everyone from packing to customs to the receiving department and accounting at the customer firm. It is a relatively simple form, but the choice of data is important and the layout has to be readable. Use the **Group Above** report style. You need to display the following data: most of the columns from the Shipment table including the ID values, date, and shipping address. Then supporting data such as **CompanyName**, **ItemID**, **QuantityShipped**, **OrderID**, **ModelID**, **Color**, **ItemSize**, and **ModelDescription**.

Because the invoice needs to be printed separately, be sure to display only one record per page. You should also include page numbers and the printing date. You can create your own logo or use the sample on the disk. It is very important that you create a user parameter for the shipping clerk to choose the ShipmentID—making it easy to find the correct shipping record. Create the invoice and print one page to hand in.

For analysis, the managers want to see a Web report that examines production by model and factory. Create a matrix report that displays production totals by factory and model. Clean up the Web display, print one page and hand it in.

CHAPTER 11

BUILDING AN INTEGRATED APPLICATION

Learning Objectives

In this chapter, you will learn:
- How to use templates to standardize an application.
- How to connect forms and create a startup form.
- How to deploy forms and reports on OAS.
- How to create custom menus.
- How to create help files.

DESIGNING AN INTEGRATED DATABASE APPLICATION

Now that you understand how to create forms and reports, it is time to put everything together and turn them into an application. An *application* consists of a set of forms and reports designed to work together. Most applications are targeted to solve specific problems. The key is that to the user the application appears to be self-contained. You create forms and reports to help the user perform all necessary operations to enter and retrieve data. The user should not have to interact directly with the database, such as writing queries. In fact, the end user probably never knows that the application is running on top of a specific DBMS.

In addition to the standard data-entry forms and the reports, you will also want to create a startup form that guides the user through the application. Users will be able to open new forms and reports and navigate the application by clicking buttons. You can also create custom menus and toolbars both to limit the actions available to the user and to provide standard tools throughout the application. You can also write custom help files and assign topics to individual forms or even sections of forms. With one click, the user can receive customized help. You need all of these elements to create a professional application. Most are not difficult, and several tools exist to help you create the pieces. However, it is time consuming to create all of the elements. Also, the entire application has to be tested and reviewed. Generally, you split large applications into pieces and assign portions to each person. Then you are left with the problem of coordinating everyone and being careful to ensure that all of the pieces fit together.

Several systems analysis and design methodologies have been developed to help groups work together to create large applications. Organizations that specialize in development generally adopt features from several methodologies and have programs to train developers so that everyone follows a similar approach. The common elements in many systems are:

1. Analysis and design, where you identify the user needs, identify common design patterns, and assign schedules.
2. Module development, where individual developers create specific forms and reports. Individual forms and reports are tested and validated at this stage to ensure that each section works correctly.
3. Integration, where you combine all of the pieces into a single application.
4. System testing, which involves testing navigation, usability, and performance to ensure that the application works correctly.
5. Deployment, where you load databases, set up Oracle Application Server, set accounts and security permissions, and make the system available to users.

ORGANIZING REDWOOD REALTY

One of the first steps in designing the application is to identify the basic user tasks and the forms and reports that will be needed to support them. In the case of Redwood Realty, you have already created most of the needed forms and reports in the previous chapters. At this point, you need to collect these forms and reports and put them into a common folder for this chapter. At the same time, you should review the forms so you remember their purpose and their overall layout. Even if you have not completed all of the forms, you should put the pieces together.

Table 11.1 shows the main forms that have been created along with a brief description.

Table 11.2 shows the main reports that have been created for Redwood Realty. You should go through your folders and find these files. It is not critical if you are

TABLE 11.1 List of Redwood Realty forms.

Form	Description	Layout
AgentContacts	Agents and contact list	Main/subform
AgentListings	Listings by agent with search by agent and date	Main/subform
Agents	Simple agents form	Single row
ContactReason	Administration form for ContactReason table	Tabular
Customers2	Basic customers form with logo	Single row
LicenseStatus	Administration form for LicenseStatus table	Tabular
ListingActivity	Listing data with offers in subform	Main/subform
Listings	Main listing form with photo upload	Single row
Properties	Main form for properties	Single row
SaleStatus	Administrative form for SaleStatus table	Tabular
Search	Search for listings	Main/subform
Search2	Variation of search with Properties on second canvas	Main/subform
Search3	Variation of search with Properties on stacked canvas	Main/subform
Search4	Variation of search with Properties and Owners on tab canvas	Main/subform

TABLE 11.2 List of Redwood Realty reports.

Report	Description
AgentSales	Listings by agent with user parameter form to select year and month
CustomerList	Simple list of customers
Listings and Offers	Basic listing data with photo and offers
SalesByCityAndAgent	Grouped sales listing by city and then agent
SalesByMonthAndAgent	Matrix listing comparing sales by agent with user parameter for Sale Status

missing a couple of them, although you might want to take a few minutes and build them. The main thing is to:

1. Create a new folder for this chapter.
2. Find and copy the forms and reports to the new folder.
3. Open some of the forms to familiarize yourself with the layout and style. Take some notes on the styles and elements you like and the things that need to be changed.

A Consistent Look

It is a challenge in a large application project to ensure that all of the forms and reports have a consistent look. Although you could create an application where every form was a different color, it looks unprofessional, and users will quickly complain about the strain of dealing with constantly changing colors. Equally important, common design elements should exist on each form and in approximately the same locations. For example, you might choose to put a "Close" button on every form and place it in the top-right corner. Take a look at the forms you created earlier—it is rare that even two of them will have a similar appearance. Now, imagine what happens when different people create each form.

For every project, you need to establish a style guide. The *style guide* should specify the overall structure of forms and the basic design elements that are to be included on each form. For example, Figure 11.1 shows a sample layout for the forms. It specifies the location of the form title and the logo. It also specifies that every form should have a "Close" button and a standard location for messages. The style guide would also specify the standard background colors and the common font typeface and size. It would probably include properties for column headings and how subforms might be highlighted.

Some developer guidelines might contain specifications for how objects should be named. These items go beyond basic visible properties, but make it easier for developers to communicate and modify forms built by others. For instance, you might specify that all canvases are labeled as Table_Canvas, and that all radio groups begin with the prefix RADIO_.

In most cases, the style guide will be a written document. However, it is wise to put an electronic copy in a convenient location so everyone can refer to it when necessary. You will probably want to create a separate style guide for reports. It would most likely need separate descriptions for printed versus Web layouts. Style guides are often used for multiple projects within a company, so it is a good idea to get assistance from a graphics designer. Also, sample versions of forms and reports should be created and tested with various users to ensure the usability of the design.

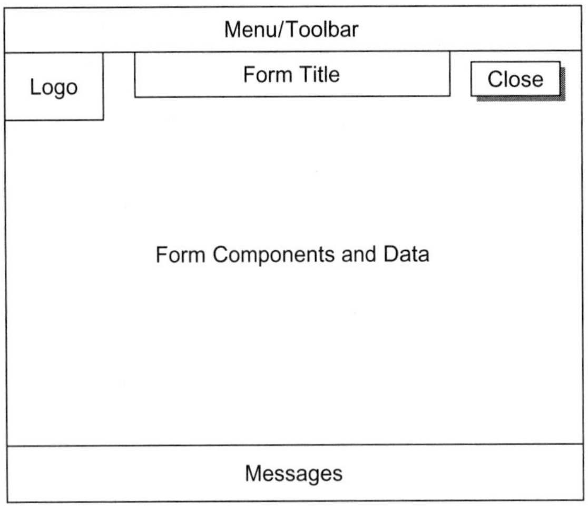

FIGURE 11.1 Sample form layout.

CREATING TEMPLATE FORMS

Once you have a style guide, you can create a template form to set up the layout. A *template form* contains boilerplate objects, graphics, toolbars, program sections, and any other objects that you want to include by default on all forms. It is the ideal way to specify a common layout for your forms. You create a template form using the same tools to create any form, but you generally do not place data items on the form. Then you save the template and make it available to all of the developers. Whenever anyone creates a new form, they begin by using the template form and add their new items to that form. The one drawback to template forms is that there is no easy way to assign a template to an existing form.

Note that the chapter on reports described how to create report templates. In many ways, report templates are more powerful than form templates because you can retrofit a report template to an existing report (although at a cost of losing some customizations).

To understand the process of creating templates, you should build the template to match the style guidelines for Redwood Realty. Feel free to make some adjustments to the layout to suit your individual style. The basic process is to build a form from scratch.

1. Start the Forms Builder but do not open any forms. Rename the Module1 section to **Redwood_Template**.
2. Add a new canvas by selecting the Canvases item and clicking the **Create** button. Rename it **Template_Canvas**.
3. In the Windows section, rename Window1 as **Redwood_Window**. Use the Property Palette to change the title to **Redwood Realty** and set the Primary Canvas to the **Template_Canvas**.
4. Double-click the icon in front of the Template_Canvas to open the canvas design. Use the Property Palette to set its Background Color to **white**.
5. Use **Edit/Import/Image** to import the Redwood logo and place it on the upper-left corner of the form. In the Object Navigator, name the item **img_Logo**.
6. Click the **Text** A button in the toolbar and place a title line at the top of the form. Enter sample text (**Form Title**) and set the font to **Arial** at **14** points. In the Object Navigator, name the item **txt_Title**.
7. Use the **Display Item** tool to add a line of text across the bottom of the form that can be used to display messages. Be sure to keep the box within the marked

area with the white background. Set its properties so that Name = **txt_Message**, Maximum Length = **130**, Database Item = **No**, and Bevel = **None**.

8. By adding the display item, the Forms Builder automatically created a new data block. Use the Object Navigator to rename it to **Template_Block**.

9. To add a Close button to the form, click the **Button** tool, then click near the top-right corner of the form. Use the Property Palette to set Name = **btn_Close** and Label = **Close**. Reduce the size of the button by dragging one of its ends.

10. Add the code for the Close button by right-clicking the button and selecting **Smart Triggers/When-Button-Pressed**. In the PL/SQL editor, enter the code: **EXIT_FORM;** then click the **Compile** button to check it. Close the editor.

11. Save the template form in your forms folder as **Redwood_Template.fmb**.

Any objects or code that you create on the template form will be available to any forms that are built from the template. Both the button and the code in this example are stored with the template.

CREATING AND APPLYING PROPERTY CLASSES AND VISUAL ATTRIBUTES

A template form is designed primarily to set the overall framework of a form. It works well for placing objects that are common to all forms. However, by itself it does not really set enough of the visual elements. For example, developers might still choose their own colors for text boxes, buttons, frames, and other objects added to the form. There is an answer. In fact, there are two answers: property classes and named visual attributes.

A *named visual attribute* is a defined style that affects the visible properties of objects: font, colors, and background patterns. You can create various styles, give them names, and store them on the primary template. Then developers can apply the named collections to objects on the form, and the objects will pick up those styles.

The second approach is to use the object-oriented features of the Forms Builder and create property classes. A *property class* is simply a collection of property values. Unlike named visual attributes, you can assign values to any property. When you apply the property class to an object, it picks up only the properties that can be used for that object. For instance, a text label lacks the Prompt property, so it would ignore any of those settings in the property class.

At this point, you must be wondering how a property class is different from a named visual attribute and which one you should use. The main difference is that named visual attributes can only affect a few properties, while a property class can set any property. The other difference is more subtle: you can change the named visual attribute setting of an object programmatically. This trick makes it easy to change the look of an item dynamically, and is really the only reason you would use a named visual attribute instead of a property class. The other characteristic you should know is that if you assign both a named visual attribute and a property class to the same object, the named visual attribute properties will take precedence.

You follow similar steps to create named visual attributes and property classes, but because the property class is more flexible, that is what you will create now. First, create a property class for text boxes.

1. In the Object Navigator, select the **Property Classes** node and click the **Create** button to add a new class. Name it **cls_Textbox**.

2. It is straightforward to add one or two properties to a property class. For simple character data, you only need to standardize the prompt offset, so open the Property

526 Introduction to Oracle

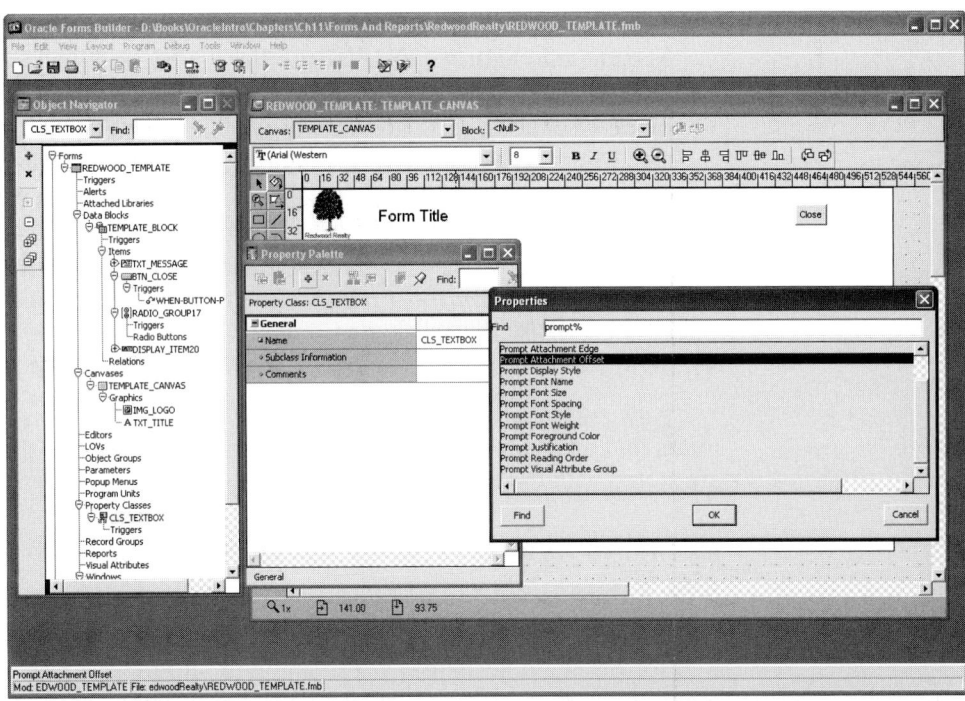

FIGURE 11.2 Adding a property to a property class.

Palette for the new class. Click the **Add Property** button on the toolbar, which opens the property selection window. Find **Property Attachment Offset** and click the **OK** button to accept it. Figure 11.2 shows the main windows in the process.

3. In the Property Palette, assign a value of **7** to the Prompt Attachment Offset and close the Property Palette.

When you need several properties, it is easier to first create a sample item, assign all of the properties the usual way, and then copy those properties to the property class. Currency data requires several properties.

4. Create another Property Class and name it **cls_Currency**.
5. On the form layout, use the toolbox **Text Item** button to add a temporary text box to the form.
6. Open the Property Palette for that item and assign properties for currency data. Justification = **Right**, Data Type = **Money**, and Format Mask = **FML9G999G999G999D00**. You should run the form and test the properties.
7. Now you need to copy the changed properties into the new property class. Hold down the **Ctrl** key and select each of the three changed properties (Justification, Data Type, and Format Mask). Click the **Copy Properties** button in the palette toolbar. Switch to the **cls_Currency** property class by clicking on it in the Object Navigator. The Property Palette should stay open, but you might have to open it. Click the **Paste Properties** button and the three properties will be inserted into the class.
8. Now for the real trick. Open the **Subclass Information** property. Select the **Property Class** option and choose **CLS_TEXTBOX** as the class name. This

approach means that the new currency property class will inherit the attachment offset setting from the cls_Textbox. So, if you want to change the offset, you only need to change it in one place.

9. Delete the temporary text item box and save the form.

To use visual name attributes, the process is similar.

1. In the Object Navigator create an entry for the Visual Attributes node. Name it **vis_att_Blue**.
2. Open the Property Palette to set the basic visual properties. Set Foreground Color = **Blue** and Font Weight = **Demibold**.

Once the visual attribute has been created, it can be assigned to a form object by setting the Visual Attribute Property of the desired item. If you look through the property list of a typical item, you will see that you can assign a different group to the main item, the prompt, the tooltip, and the current record. The current record attribute group is useful for highlighting the currently selected row of data in a tabular list.

APPLYING TEMPLATE FORMS AND PROPERTIES

Once you have created the template along with the visual attribute groups and property classes, developers can use it to create new forms. To see the effect of the template, you will rebuild one of the existing forms: ContactReason. This form is a simple tabular form that is only updated occasionally, but it is easy to create, and you can compare it to the form you built earlier.

1. Clear everything from the Forms Builder, or restart it. Choose the **File/New/Form Using Template** menu option. The Windows Open box prompts you to find the template file. Select the **Redwood_Template.fmb** file and click the **Open** button. Look through the Object Navigator and you will see that your new form has the template items you created.
2. Change the form name to **ContactReasonT**. Fire up the data block wizard to create the new form elements. Choose the **ContactReason** table and add both of its columns. If asked, do not attempt to create a relationship with the existing data block, because that contains the fixed items from the template.
3. In the Layout Wizard, put both columns on the **Template_Canvas**. Be sure to choose the **Tabular** form option with **10** records displayed.
4. When the wizard finishes, you will probably have to move the new frame onto the main body of the form. It likes to place new items below everything else on the form. Restore the canvas size to the bottom of the txt_Message box. Click the title on the form and change it to **Contact Reason**.
5. Find the new **ContactReason** data block in the Object Navigator. If necessary, drag it above the **Template_Block**. Be sure the ContactReason data block is the first one entered when the form opens, so that the query buttons work as expected.
6. Open the Property Palette for the ContactReason data block. Change the **Current Record Visual Attribute Group** property to **vis_att_Blue**.
7. Create a new form trigger for **When-New-Form-Instance**, and enter **EXECUTE_QUERY;** as the code so that the form loads the data automatically. Save the form as **ContactReasonT.fmb**. Compile the code and run the form to test it.

Figure 11.3 shows the new form. Notice that it picks up the structure and colors from the template. In particular, notice on your screen that the currently selected row in the list is highlighted in blue and boldface. You might not need the boldface, but the

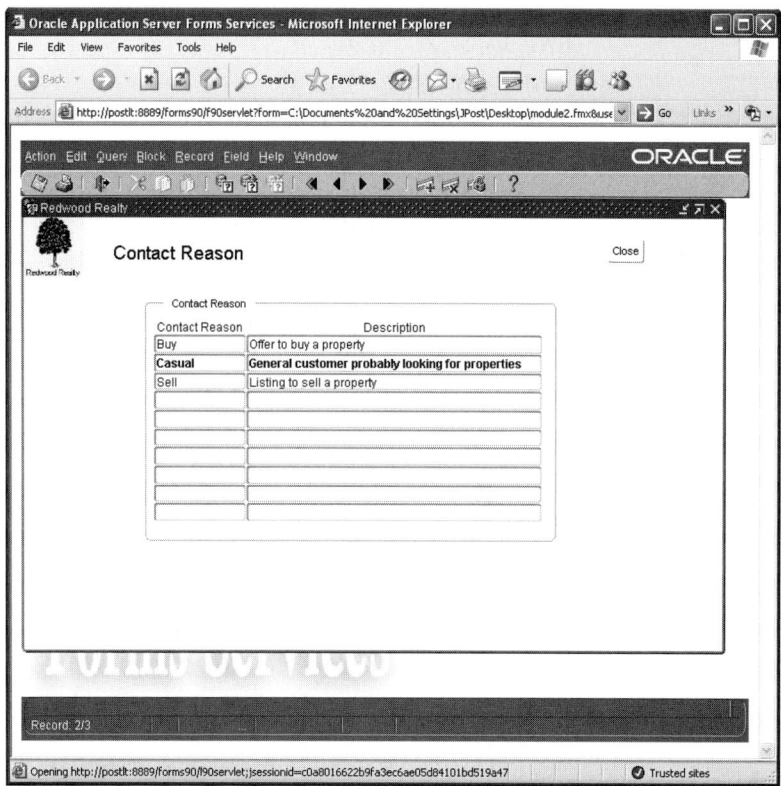

FIGURE 11.3 The new form contains the elements and styles from the template.

contrasting color helps users realize which record will be deleted if they want to delete the record.

There is a way to take an existing form and apply it to the template form, but it is not simple. For smaller forms, it almost always will be easier to start from scratch and rebuild the form. However, someday you might want to rebuild a form using a template, so you should understand the basic steps. For this example, you will rebuild the AgentContact main/sub form. The basic process is to create a blank template-based form and copy all of the items onto it from the AgentContact form.

1. Clear everything out of Forms Builder or restart it. Choose the **File/New/Form Using Template** menu option and pick the **Redwood_Template.fmb** form.

2. Open the existing AgentContact form, placing both it and the new form in the Object Navigator.

3. Using the Object Navigator, expand the **Canvas** and **Graphics** nodes for the **AgentContact** form. Copy the entries (**Frame5** and **Frame8**) by dragging them to the **Canvas/Graphics** node in the new form.

4. Copy the two data blocks (**Agents** and **CustAgentList**) by dragging them from the AgentContacts form to the new module.

5. Use the same process to copy the three **Program Units** to the new form.

6. Copy the form trigger **On-Clear-Details** to the new form. In more complex forms you would also have to copy LOVs and Record Groups.

7. In the new **Template_Canvas**, expand the **Agents** data block and select all of the items. Choose **Tools/Property Palette**, and set the **Canvas** property for all five

CHAPTER 11 Building an Integrated Application **529**

items to the **Template_Canvas**. Do the same thing for the nine items in the **CustAgentList** data block.

8. In both the **Agents** and **CustAgentList** data blocks, set the Scroll Bar Canvas to **Template_Canvas**. You should now be able to display the new canvas.

9. To assign the new styles, select all of the text box items in the Agents frame and use the Property Palette to set the Subclass Information to cls_Textbox.

10. Select the **BidPrice** item in the CustAgentList data block and set its **Subclass Information** to cls_Currency. Also, in its **Data** properties, make sure the **Maximum Length** is at least **15**.

11. Open the properties for the **CustAgentList** data block and set the **Current Record Visual Attribute Group** to **vis_att_Blue**.

12. Delete the old **AgentContact** module from the Object Navigator. Change the title on the form, then run the form to test it. Return to design and adjust the layout as needed. Save the form as **AgentContactT**.

As you can see in Figure 11.4, the template provides the standard look to the new form. As you probably noticed while following the steps, the process is somewhat tedious, and you have to be careful not to make mistakes. The point of the exercise is to show you that it is possible to move a form to a template. However, it is almost always easier to create the template first, then build the form onto the template right from the start.

Also, note that if you change a template later, none of the changes can be pushed to the existing forms. Even if you change a property class or visual attribute group, you

FIGURE 11.4 The template version of the Agent Contact form.

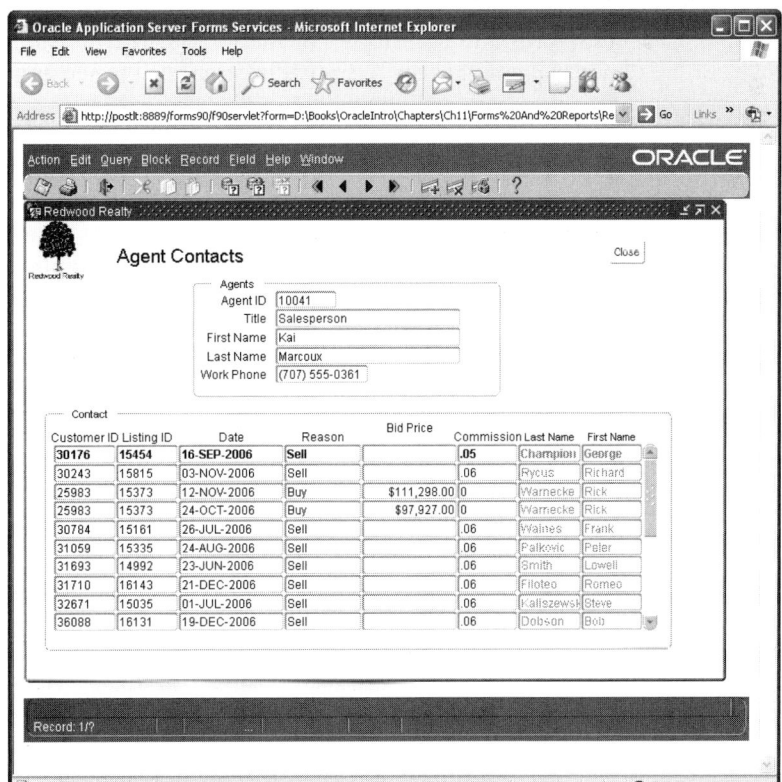

will have to copy all of the changes back into the existing forms. Recall from the reports chapter that report templates are much more flexible. But in both cases, you really want to be absolutely certain about the templates before you begin creating the forms and reports.

CONNECTING FORMS AND REPORTS INTO AN APPLICATION

In almost all cases, users will only see your application. They should never see the underlying database. They will not have Forms Builder or Reports Builder installed on their machines. They will predominantly access your application through a Web browser. That means you need to connect the forms and reports so that all of the data is accessible through your application. In most cases, you will have to create additional forms. These forms are specifically designed to help the user navigate your application. The startup form is the most important. Users must begin with a single form that gives them the entry to your application.

You connect forms together by providing buttons. Users click individual command buttons to open the desired forms or reports. In many cases the process really is simply to open the form and show all of the data. In other cases, you will want to restrict the data displayed on the new form or report. For example, a user might click a button that opens the property form. Do you show them all of the properties, or a single one that matches the property on the existing form? These are navigation issues that you need to identify ahead of time. You need to know exactly what users want to see and how they will use the application.

It is often helpful to sketch a diagram to show how your application will typically be used. You can outline how forms will be connected and when users will want to see or print reports. Go back and look at Tables 11.1 and 11.2 to see a list of the forms and reports available to Redwood Realty employees. Then think about the roles of the employees and their jobs. For the most part, you can split the tasks into two groups: agents and managers. Agents primarily need to see and update data on properties, listings, and contacts. They will also want the search pages, but you should probably pick just one of the search forms. Managers will need access to the same forms and reports because they also work as agents. Additionally, they will want to see the reports that list sales by agent. Finally, a few of the forms, such as the Contact Reason and License Status, are rarely used but need to be accessed by a manager or administrator for when data does change.

In the Redwood application, you might consider creating three separate entry points into the application—one for each of the major tasks. But, it is easier to support users if you use one entry point so that everyone follows the same initial procedures. Sometimes application administration is handled from a completely different startup, but this data is not overly sensitive so it will not be necessary. Figure 11.5 organizes the forms and reports into two groups: the common forms needed for handling listings and customers versus the administrative forms and management reports. You could try to place buttons for all of these forms and reports on the main startup form, but you should try to keep 10 or fewer items on any menu form to avoid overwhelming the users. In this case, you can create a second menu form to hold links to the management-specific items.

STARTUP FORM

Most modern applications use a startup form as the entry point. A **startup form** is the main navigation point for users. It usually contains buttons that direct the user to other forms and reports. Sometimes it is customized for each type of user. It often contains a

CHAPTER 11 Building an Integrated Application

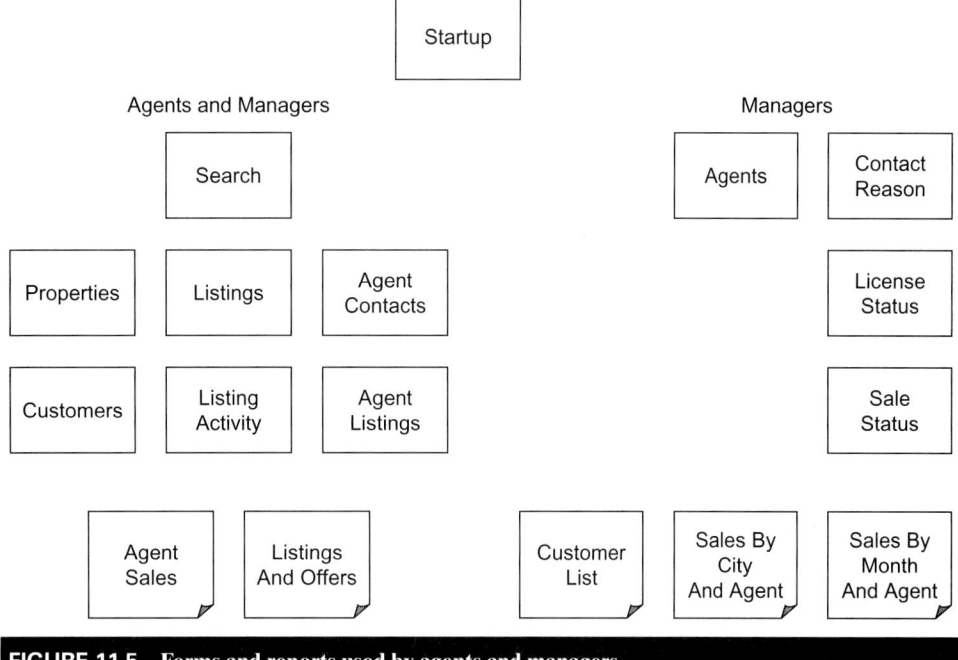

FIGURE 11.5 Forms and reports used by agents and managers.

logo or other graphic to add visual interest. The key to the startup form is to know which items are most important to the users.

It is relatively easy to create a startup form. You just build a blank form and add a logo, title, and buttons to open other forms and reports. The connections to the forms are relatively easy, so you will build those first.

1. Clear the Forms Builder or restart it so you start with a new module. Rename it **Startup**.
2. Add a canvas (**Main_canvas**) and data block (**Main_datablock**) manually. Rename Window1 to **Startup** and set its **Title** property to **Redwood Realty**.
3. Open the canvas in the layout editor, set its background to white, add the Redwood logo (**Edit/Import/Image**), and place a title (**Redwood Realty Information System**) on the top of the screen.
4. Add a push button to the form and set its properties: **Name = btn_Listings**, **Label = Listings**, and **Access Key = L**. Add similar buttons for **Properties**, **Customers**, **Agent Contacts**, **Listing Activity**, and **Agent Listings**. Adjust the sizes so all of the buttons are the same size. Align the buttons in some type of pattern. Be sure to enter a unique access key for each button so users can select an option using the Alt-key key press.
5. Add a **Search** button near the middle of the form and an **Exit** button near the top right. Set the property **Default Button = Yes** for the Search button so that it is automatically selected. Save the form (**Startup.fmb**) and run it to check the button sizes and overall design. Figure 11.6 shows a possible layout for the startup form. Your design can be different, or more colorful, but you should have the same buttons.
6. Now you need to add code to make the buttons function. You already know how to do the Exit button. For the When-Button-Pressed trigger, add the code: **EXIT_FORM;**

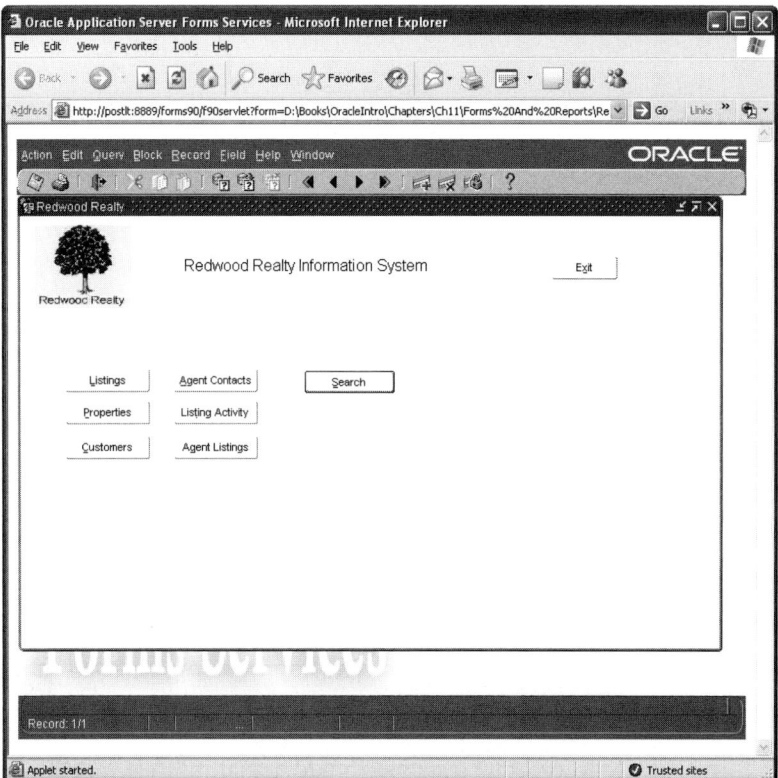

FIGURE 11.6 Initial design of the startup form.

OPENING CONNECTED FORMS

The code to open a form is relatively easy, but you have two choices. You can use CALL_FORM or OPEN_FORM. The two approaches are similar but they have different options. For instance, the OPEN_FORM call has an activate_mode parameter that you can use to prevent the focus from shifting to the new form. On the other hand, CALL_FORM uses its query_mode parameter to force the form to display data directly, without allowing users to enter queries. You can check the Oracle documentation for more details, and if you need one of these features, simply pick the appropriate function call. In most cases, you can use the CALL_FORM. The basic syntax for opening a form is CALL_FORM('form name');

The next problem is that the form name is somewhat tricky. Oracle needs to know where the form is located. You have two main methods of specifying the location of the forms for your application. First, you can edit the server configuration files to tell Oracle the default value of the forms folder. Second, you can specify the complete server pathname of the file to open. When you run a sample form using the Forms Builder, take a look at the URL in the browser address window. You will see that Oracle has been using the complete pathname of each file.

A serious problem exists with using the complete pathname of a file in every form button. What happens when you move the application to another server or need to reorganize the disk drives? Someone would have to find and edit every one of those names. Ultimately, when you deploy an application on the server, the best approach is to configure the server to set the default folders for forms and reports. However, that might not be possible (or easy) for you to do during testing on a local machine.

Programmers use the term *hard-coded* to describe data that is stored inside an application and difficult to change. Instead of writing the folder name into every single trigger, a better answer is to create a global variable to hold the path of the forms folder. Each trigger code call can use that variable. This way, someone only has to change the initial value of the global variable in one location to move the application. You might even consider creating a table in the database to hold this and similar global parameters. Then you simply have to update a couple of data rows to move an application. Because you would normally try to use the server configuration files, this demonstration will not go that far, but it is an idea worth remembering.

1. Because everyone will begin with the startup form, it is a good place to initialize system variables. Create a new trigger in the startup form for the **When-New-Form-Instance** event. Add the code:

   ```
   :GLOBAL.ApplicationPath := 'C:\MyFiles\Ch11\Forms And
   Reports\RedwoodRealty\';
   ```

   Be sure to specify the exact path that identifies where you placed your copies of the forms and reports. Also, be sure to include the last backslash. You are now ready to write the code for the button triggers.

2. For the **Listings** button, open the **Smart Trigger** for the **When-Button-Pressed** event. Enter the code:

   ```
   CALL_FORM(:GLOBAL.ApplicationPath || 'Listings.fmx');
   ```

   Notice the use of the new global variable. The code simply appends the name of the form that you want to open to the path name, to get the complete location of the file. Also, notice the use of the .fmx suffix. The Forms Builder creates this compiled version of the form when you run it. It is a little faster and more secure to use the compiled version instead of the design (.fmb) copy.

3. Create a line of similar code for each of the other buttons on the startup form. Be sure to specify the correct name of the form in each case. Also, compile each module as you go to test for typographical errors.

4. Run the form and test all of the buttons to ensure that each button opens the correct form.

   > **Tip:** If you make a mistake in typing the name of a form to open, the system will not catch the error until you run the form and test the button. Items in quotes are not tested when they are compiled.

As you run through the forms you should notice the dissonance that is created because they were not built on the same template. Even seemingly minor differences in background colors and the lack of the Close button quickly become annoying. You should try to set aside some time to go back and clean up each of the forms by moving them to the form template.

The forms give you a good idea of how the application should run. Ultimately, you will want to add some other buttons within forms to provide some cross-navigation. For instance, you might want to put a button on the Listings form to open the corresponding property.

1. Open the **Listings** form and add a button just to the right of the **PropertyID**. Name it **btn_Property** with a label of **Property**.

This button will be used to open the Property form, but there is a major difference between this button and the one on the startup form. From the Listings form, you want to open the Property form to a specific property—using the PropertyID given on the Listings form. In other words, you have to pass the PropertyID as a parameter to the Properties form. Oracle provides two methods to pass a parameter to a form: (1) using the parameter list of the CALL_FORM function, or (2) assigning the value in a global variable. The global variable approach has a couple of advantages over the parameter method. The global parameter can be used by multiple forms if necessary, and it is easy to adjust the code so that the Properties form can continue to be used without requiring the parameter.

2. Open the **When-Button-Pressed** trigger for the new properties button. Add the code to assign the value to the global variable and open the Properties form:

```
:GLOBAL.PropertyID := :Listings.PropertyID;
CALL_FORM(:GLOBAL.ApplicationPath || 'Properties.fmx');
```

3. Save and close the Listings form and open the **Properties** form. You need to add the code that looks for the new global parameter and adds a Where clause to find that particular property. Create a new trigger for the form's **When-New-Form-Instance** event. Write the code to define the data block's Where clause:

```
DECLARE
    sWHERE VARCHAR2(200);
BEGIN
    If (:GLOBAL.PropertyID IS NOT NULL) Then
        sWhere := 'PropertyID=' || :GLOBAL.PropertyID;
        Set_Block_Property('Properties', DEFAULT_WHERE, sWhere);
    End If;
    Go_Block('Properties');
    Execute_Query;
END;
```

4. To eliminate a warning error message, you should also add one line of code to the startup form. Open the When-New-Form-Instance trigger on the Startup form and add one line to the module:

```
:GLOBAL.PropertyID := Null;
```

If you do not add this line, when you open the Properties form directly, you will see a warning message at the bottom of the screen that the global variable has not been declared. You will most likely find several situations where you can use this trick to open a form to show a specific related record. Notice that it is similar to the multiple canvas approach used in Chapter 9. However, the forms are completely independent and can be used for multiple purposes.

DISPLAYING REPORTS

On most applications, you will also want to add buttons that make it easy for the user to see reports that are associated with a form, or that provide additional information. You might think that you could use a process similar to the buttons that display forms. However, Oracle reports add two challenging elements: (1) the report processor is completely separate from the forms processor, and (2) dynamic reports have to be generated before they can be displayed. The ***Oracle Application Server (OracleAS)*** is the big answer to these two issues. OracleAS runs both the forms and report services, and it has tools to handle dynamic report generation automatically. It runs as a Web-based system, so all forms and reports are delivered directly to the user's browser. Interestingly, it handles Web-based reports differently from paper-based reports. Paper-based reports are generated as Adobe **portable document file (.PDF)** images. Users will need to have the Adobe Acrobat Reader installed, but most computers have that today, and because the users often run on in-house computers, Acrobat Reader can be installed. If Acrobat Reader cannot be made available, you can choose other formats or stick with Web-based reports.

The real key to displaying Oracle reports is to understand that they need to run in a Web browser. Ultimately the application will be moved to an Oracle Application Server, but with OC4J running, you can test everything on your development computer. The OC4J process that you use to test forms actually runs a Web server, and it has the ability to interact with the reports service in addition to the forms. This process provides a relatively easy way to display reports using buttons on forms.

Before showing you the Web-based approach to displaying reports, it is necessary to take a brief detour into the old way that reports were integrated into applications. You are likely to encounter the old approach if you modify existing applications, so you should at least be familiar with the basic method. You do not actually have to follow these steps, but reading through them will also help you understand how the Oracle Reports service works.

1. Create, test, and save a report file using Reports Builder—just as you did in Chapter 10. Close the Reports Builder.
2. Start the Forms Builder and open the form (Startup) where you want to trigger the report. Find the Reports section in the Object Navigator, add a new report object, and give it a name. This is simply an object reference, not the actual report.
3. Add a button to the form giving it an appropriate name and title. The trigger code is the key to running the report:

```
DECLARE
    Report_ID       Report_Object;
    Report_Job_ID   VARCHAR2(100);
BEGIN
    Report_ID := Find_Report_Object('CustomerList');
    Set_Report_Object_Property(Report_ID, REPORT_FILENAME,
    :GLOBAL.ApplicationPath
        || 'CustomerList.jsp');
    Set_Report_Object_Property(Report_ID, REPORT_DESNAME,
    :GLOBAL.ApplicationPath
        || 'CustomerList.html');
    Report_Job_ID := Run_Report_Object(Report_ID);
    Web.Show_Document('file:///' || :GLOBAL.ApplicationPath ||
    'CustomerList.html',
        '_blank');
END;
```

The key to understanding the code is to remember that reports are dynamic, and that the Report Object is just a placeholder. The code finds the specified report, then assigns two critical properties to the object: the source and destination file names. The source filename is just the file that you created with the Reports Builder. The destination is an HTML file that can be sent to the browser, but it has to be stored in some folder. The Run_Report_Object command calls the report server, retrieves the report description, loads the data, and generates the HTML output file. The Web.Show_Document command simply sends the newly generated file to the user in a new browser window. You can actually use the **Web.Show_Document** built-in function to send any HTML file to the user's browser.

The new approach to displaying reports is considerably simpler for you because the reports service does most of the work. It actually still follows the same basic steps of reading the report definition file, loading the data, and generating a temporary file. It just handles those steps automatically. There is one catch to testing this method on your computer: you have to know which TCP port the Web server is listening on. It is probably 8889, but it might be different. The easiest way to find out is to test it with a form.

1. Start the Forms Builder and open the Startup form. Run the form. When the browser window opens and displays the form, look closely at the address line in the browser. You should see "http://name:8889/forms90/f90servlet..." The name will be the name of your computer and the number following the name is the TCP port number that you need. Write down the name and number then close the browser. Leave OC4J running.

2. Test your system to ensure the reports server is working. Find the full pathname of one of your reports, such as CustomerList.jsp. In Windows, start your browser. In the address line enter the following URL, but modify it to match your locations:

   ```
   http://postlt:8889/reports/rwservlet?destype=cache&desformat=PDF&report=c:
   \books\OracleIntro\Chapters\Ch11\Reports\RedwoodRealty\
   CustomerList.jsp&userid=@postdb
   ```

   Be sure to use the name and TCP port for your machine that you obtained in Step 2. The rwservlet is the Oracle program that does all of the work for you. The *destype* parameter simply tells it to write the report to a temporary cache. The *desformat* parameter tells it what type of format to generate. In this case, the setting is PDF for Adobe Acrobat. The report parameter is where you list the full pathname of the report. The *userid* parameter tells the report server how to log into the database. The format for a userid is username/password@servername. However, you really do not want to put the password into plain text in a URL. So, if you leave off the username and password, the report server will first display a form asking the user to log in with their personal username and password. Normally, you want to include the name of the server (probably your computer name) to save the users a step. The main thing at this step is to make sure you get the URL exactly right so that the report is displayed. If you cannot get the report displayed, then make sure OC4J is running. If it still fails, you will probably have to find an Oracle Application Server or a different computer to test everything.

   Tip: If you receive an error message or do not see the report, check the URL carefully. Pay close attention to the full pathname of your report file.

3. Once again, it is best to avoid hard-coding everything into dozens of buttons spread across the forms. You need to create three global variables to make it easier to move the application later. Open the **When-New-Form-Instance** trigger of the **Startup** form. Add these three lines, making sure to modify the first and last lines so they use your machine names and TCP port:

   ```
   :GLOBAL.ReportServerURL := 'http://postlt:8889/reports/rwservlet';
   :GLOBAL.ReportFormat    := 'desformat=PDF';
   :GLOBAL.DatabaseServer  := 'postdb';
   ```

4. Now create a button on the Startup form. Name it **btn_CustomerList** with a label of **Customer List**. For the **When-Button-Pressed** trigger, enter the code to create the URL and display the report. Notice that the code is broken into multiple lines to make it easier to read and to fix errors. Also notice the use of the new global variables so that the only fixed item in the button code is the name of the report:

   ```
   DECLARE
           sURL VARCHAR2(200);
   BEGIN
           sURL := :GLOBAL.ReportServerURL
           || '?destype=cache'
           || '&' || :GLOBAL.ReportFormat
           || '&report=' ||  :GLOBAL.ApplicationPath || 'CustomerList.jsp'
           || '&userid=@' ||  :GLOBAL.DatabaseServer;
           Web.Show_Document(sURL, '_blank');
   END;
   ```

TABLE 11.3 Desformat parameter options for reports.	
Desformat parameter	*Output format*
HTML	Standard HTML with minimal formatting.
HTMLCSS	HTML using a style sheet for some formatting.
PCL	The printer language used by Hewlett Packard.
PDF	Adobe portable document format.
Postscript	The printer language used by many printers.
XML	Extensible markup language often used for transferring data to other systems.

5. Compile everything, save the form and test it. When you click the button, you should get a new browser window that displays the report in PDF format. Add a similar button to open the report for **Listings And Offers**.

The desformat parameter supports several options to provide different types of reports. There are also other parameters that allow you to send reports directly to a printer if desired. You can find all of the options in the Oracle documentation. The choices for the desformat printer are shown in Table 11.3. .PDF is a good default choice, but if necessary, you could create a form and let users pick the format they want to see.

Many of the reports you created in Chapter 10 are designed for managers. Agents will rarely need to use them. Likewise, the three administrative forms would be used by managers instead of agents. Consequently, you should create a secondary menu form for managers.

1. Create a new blank form, name it **Management**, add a blank data block (**Main_Datablock**) and a canvas (**Main_Canvas**). Add the logo and a title (**Management Tasks**).
2. Add buttons for the administrative forms (**ContactReason**, **LicenseStatus**, and **SaleStatus**). Add the simple **Call_Form** trigger code to each button using the correct form name in each case.
3. Add buttons for the three management reports (**AgentSales**, **SalesByCityAndAgent**, **SalesByMonthAndAgent**). Copy the code to open the reports and paste it into each of the three triggers. You should only have to change the name of the report in each button. Be sure to compile everything to check for errors.
4. Save and run the **Management** form to compile it.
5. Close the **Management** form and open the **Startup** form. Add a button that calls the new **Management** form. Compile, save, then run **Startup** and test everything.

Recall that two of the forms (AgentSales and SalesByMonthAndAgent) have user parameter forms. To get the parameter forms to work, you have to tell the report server that these reports use a parameter form.

6. In the **Management** form, open the button trigger for the AgentSales report. Modify the URL to append one additional command at the end:

```
|| '&PARAMFORM=yes';
```

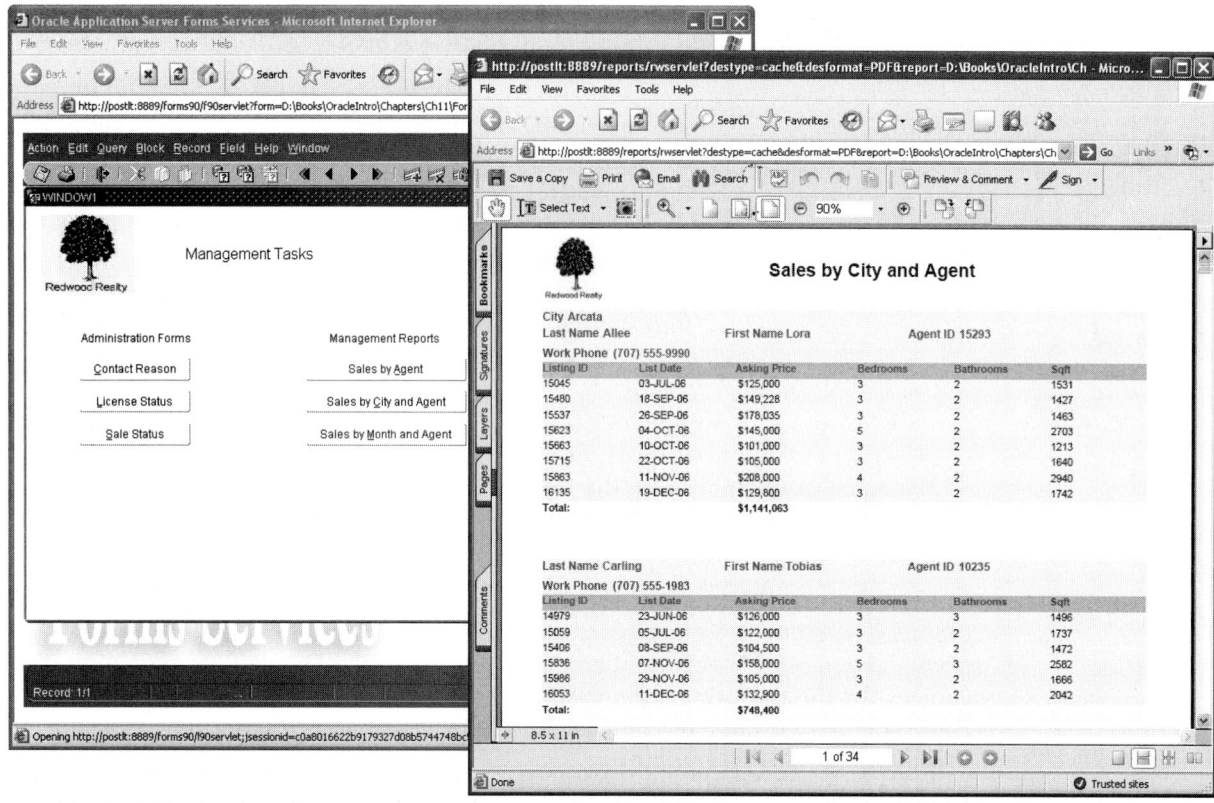

FIGURE 11.7 A management report created by the application.

Be careful with the semicolon, because it signifies the end of the URL string. Be sure to remove it from the previous end of the string. Compile and test the report. Do the same thing for any other reports that use a parameter form. Figure 11.7 shows the Sales report.

DEPLOYING FORMS AND REPORTS IN ORACLEAS

Now that you have an application running, deploy it by moving it to an Oracle Application Server. OracleAS is software that is sold separately from the DBMS and is generally installed on a second server. It is designed to integrate all of the tasks required by an application, including forms and reports. OracleAS provides many additional functions, including a separate security directory called Oracle Internet Directory (OID). But, many of these functions require time to install and manage, so you probably will not have access to all of them. One of the main benefits of OID is *single sign on*, where users log into the directory at the start of the application, and their credentials are available to all of your forms and reports.

The challenge at this point in the text is that you might not have access to an application server. In fact, the full application server is usually installed on a computer that is separate from the database server. This tiered approach provides a robust solution to keeping systems running in large organizations, but makes it difficult to test applications on a limited budget. To experiment with OracleAS, download the partial OracleAS solution: OracleAS Forms and Reports Services. You should be able to install this portion of OracleAS alongside your existing Oracle database—but be sure to create a new database home for it.

OracleAS has several methods to help you set up an application. The first approach is straightforward because it matches the way you have been testing the application.

1. Create a folder on the OracleAS server to hold all of the forms and reports. For example, you might use **E:\OracleAppplications\RedwoodRealty**, but the exact drive and location depends on your server and it might be controlled by a system administrator who will tell you what folder to use. Copy all of the forms (.fmx files) and reports (.jsp files) to that folder. You also need to know the network name of the server.

2. Copy the **Startup.fmb** file to the server folder as well. Using the Forms Builder, open the **Startup.fmb** file on the server. Edit the **When-New-Form-Instance** trigger. Change the global variables to point to the locations on the server. Change **ApplicationPath**, **ReportServerURL**, and the **DatabaseServer**. In most cases, you will not need the port (8889) in the ReportServerURL. OracleAS defaults to the standard port 80 unless it was changed during the installation. Compile the trigger. Save the file. Be sure to run the form at least once to force the system to recompile the Startup.fmx file.

3. You and your users, can now run the application with just a browser. Open a browser window on your computer. In the address line, enter the name of the OracleAS server along with the full path name of the startup form:

    ```
    http://servername/forms90/f90servlet?form=E:\OracleApplications\
    RedwoodRealty\Startup.fmx
    ```

    You will be asked to log in for the first form. You should then be able to click the buttons to open any of the forms or view the reports. You will have to log in again the first time you open a report.

4. Test all of the buttons. If one does not work, you probably forgot to include the **:GLOBAL.ApplicationPath** in the trigger code for that button. You will have to edit the form on your machine, recompile and rerun the form, then copy it to the server.

Of course, the fairly obvious drawback to this approach is that users need to know the full pathname of the startup form. You could make it easier for them by placing a shortcut on their desktops with the correct URL. Or, you could place a small HTML file on the OracleAS server that contains a link to that page. Actually, if you go with the HTML approach, you could replace the entire startup form with a simple HTML page. Or, you could use Oracle Portal to help you customize a dynamic entry page for each person. But you need the full OracleAS with the Internet Directory to run the Portal.

OracleAS provides other methods for specifying the default location of forms and reports. If you place your forms and reports into the default folders, they can all be opened just by specifying the name of the file, without the full pathname. In this case, you would change your GLOBAL.ApplicationPath variable to an empty string (' '). The initial default locations are a little hard to find. The default folder for forms is: **OracleASHome\forms90**, and the default folder for reports is **OracleASHome\j2ee\OC4J_BI_Forms\applications\reports\web**. In both cases, OracleASHome represents the root folder where you installed the OracleAS forms and reports services.

You probably do not want to place all of your forms and reports into the initial default folders. It would be simpler to leave them in the new application folder, and edit the Oracle configuration files to change the default folder locations. Of course, you need administrator rights on the OracleAS system to be able to change configuration files. Also, Oracle now recommends that you use the OracleAS Enterprise Manager to set configuration options instead of trying to edit files directly. If you do have your own version of OracleAS, it is relatively easy to set the configuration for the forms.

1. Start the **OracleAS Enterprise Manager**. Note that this is different from the DBMS Enterprise Manager. Use **http://servername:1810**, with the correct name of the server, and log in with the OracleAS administrator username and password you created when you installed the server.
2. Click the **Forms** entry in the list, then the **Configuration** link.
3. Select the **default** section, click the **Duplicate** button. When prompted, enter **Redwood** as the new configuration name.
4. Select the new **Redwood** section and click the **Edit** button.
5. Find and change three properties. For **Working Directory**, enter the full path name of the folder where you stored the forms on the server. For **Page Title**, enter **Redwood Realty**. For Form, enter **Startup.fmx**. Click the **Apply** button to save the changes.
6. Now, on any computer start a browser. On the address line, enter the URL using the actual name of the server:

```
http://servername/forms90/f90servlet?config=Redwood
```

The Startup form will run. You no longer need the ApplicationPath variable to open the various forms. You can simply use the name of each form. However, you still need the ApplicationPath variable for the reports. It is more complicated to change the default folder for reports. You have to find the engine configuration file and edit or add a SourceDir property. You can find the details in the Oracle documentation. However, since users will rarely need to start reports independently, it is just as easy to use the ApplicationPath variable.

Even the latest version of the starting URL probably is still too hard for users to remember. Ultimately, you really need to add a simple Web page to the server that includes the link. In that case, it probably does not matter if you go through the effort to create the special config file. But, it is useful if you need to deploy an application where no one bothered to use the ApplicationPath global variable and you do not have time to go back to find and edit every single link in the application.

CREATING MENUS

Since you have likely been using Windows for some time, you are familiar with pull-down menus at the top of many applications. When you run an Oracle form, you should notice that there is a default menu that appears on all forms. The standard menu contains tools to help with common tasks, such as the Record tasks to insert or remove rows. In many applications, you will want to limit the actions that users can take. Additionally, you might want to provide some options that are accessible from a standard location on every form. Oracle forms give you the ability to create your own menus that will replace the standard menu.

THE ROLE OF MENUS

In most applications, the purpose of a top menu is to provide easy access to standard tasks. In most cases, you want to keep the menus consistent across all of your forms. However, you do have the ability to provide customized menus for any form. But, since one of the goals of a menu is to make it easy to use the application, you should try to standardize most of the items on the menu. Users will always know where to find the common tasks. They will also know where to look for additional choices.

You will probably want to place a couple of standard items on most database application menus. For example, you generally place a Help link at the far right side of the menu to provide customized help. Likewise, you will need at least some of the standard Record options, such as moving forward and back, or adding and deleting records. Depending on how you create your application, you also might want to leave many of the standard Windows tasks on the menu. Likewise, most people expect to find common Edit items in any application, such as cut and paste.

Beyond these relatively standard tasks, you might think about organizing your menu in terms of application tasks or users. For instance, in the Redwood Realty case, you could have a top-level menu option for agents, and one for managers. Then place common tasks beneath each item. Or, you could set up the menu by using major tasks or entities as the top level: Offers, Listings, and Properties. Once again, you should sketch up a few ideas and show them to users. The users are the ones who should decide how they want to organize their work.

Figure 11.8 shows the standard menu. Open a form and go through the standard items so you know what options you might need to include in your custom menu. In particular, you will most likely need many of the options under the Record and Action items, such as Save, Insert, Remove, and Clear. Users will also probably need the basic Query options of Enter, Execute, and Cancel.

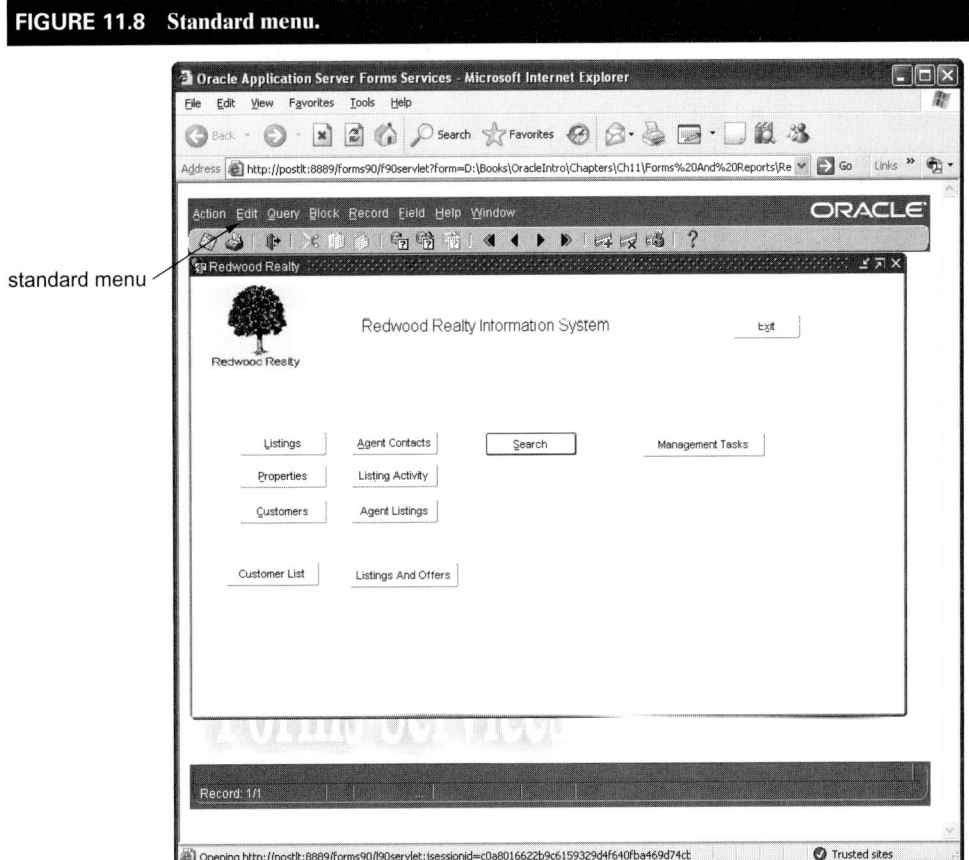

FIGURE 11.8 Standard menu.

BUILDING MENUS

Creating menus is straightforward once you decide what you want to include. You can create pull-down menus using several options. The Forms Builder has an editor to help build menus.

1. Start the Forms Builder and open the startup form. Find the **Menus** section of the Object Navigator and click the **Create** + button to add a new menu. Name the entry **Redwood_Menu**. A *menu module* is a collection that can hold multiple menus for the entire application.
2. Find the **Menus** option under the new Redwood_Menu and click the **Create** + button to add an actual menu. Name it **Main_Menu**.
3. Menus contain items—the entries on the menu itself. You can create *menu items* several ways. Select the **Items** entry under the new Main_Menu and click the **Create** + button to add a new item. Name it **Agents**. Follow a similar process to add items for **Managers**, **Records**, and **Help**.
4. To see the effect of your work, double-click the icon next to the **Main_Menu** entry to open the **Menu Editor**. It contains the four new items displayed horizontally. You can set the labels either by opening the Property Palette for each item, or by clicking on the entry and typing the new label. Figure 11.9 shows the menu editor with the first entry relabeled.

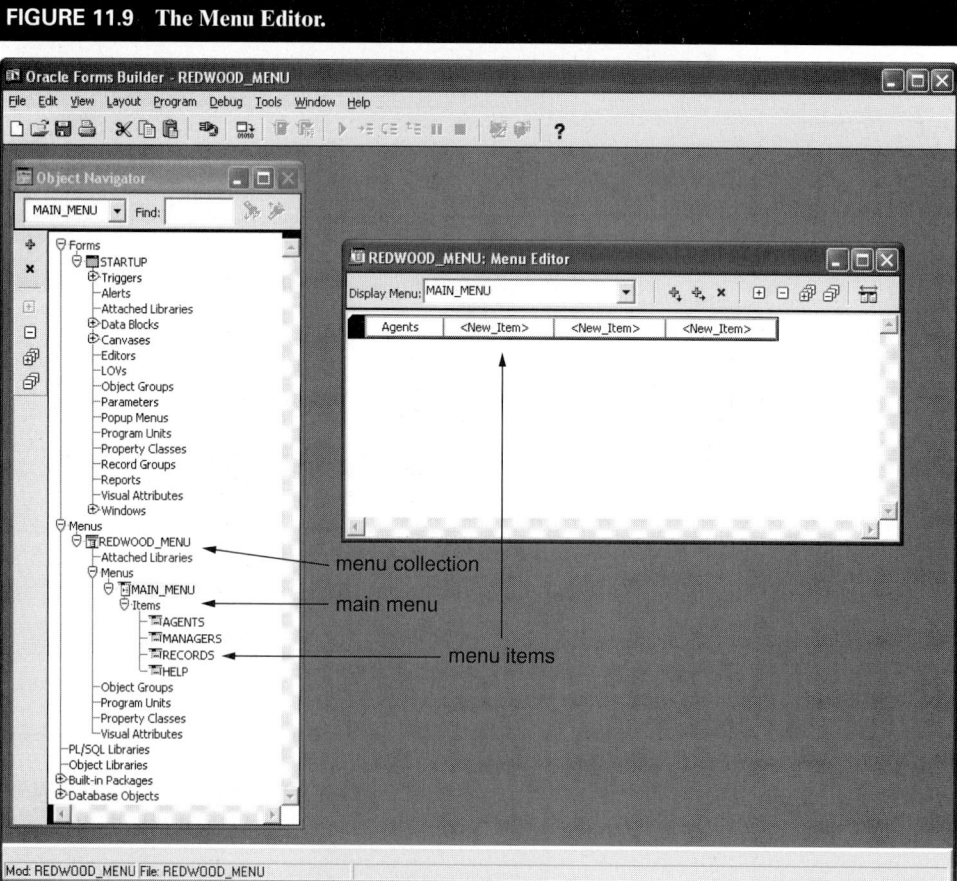

FIGURE 11.9 The Menu Editor.

CHAPTER 11 Building an Integrated Application

The top-level menu items you just added are *parent menu items*. You can now add *child menu items* underneath them to get the pull-down effect. You can even add sub menus to the child menu—these usually expand horizontally.

5. Select the **Agents** item in the **Menu Editor** and click the **Create Down** button to add an entry beneath the Agents. Enter **Offers** as the label. Notice in the Object Navigator that the Agents_Menu has been created with the new Offers item. Repeat the process to add items for **Listings** and **Properties**.
6. Follow a similar process to add child items under **Managers** for **Sales by Agent**, **Sales by City and Agent**, and **Sales by Month and Agent**.
7. Under **Records**, add **Save**, **Insert**, **Remove**, and **Clear**. Figure 11.10 shows the menu layout, but the items can be rearranged if you prefer.

The menu used here is relatively simple. You can add also add separators (lines). By setting the properties of the individual items, you can also create special items. If you check out the properties for the items, you will notice that you can also use icons instead of words. In effect, you can create your own toolbar.

CREATING MENU ACTIONS

Once you identify the menu items, you need to add trigger code so that they actually do something when the user makes a selection. If you include the Edit menu (Cut/Copy/Paste), you can use the Property Palette to set the *Magic* type and choose the corresponding action. The list appears to indicate that you can also use Magic for Help. However, this command probably does not work correctly. Instead, you can use the Built-in Help procedure shown in Table 11.4. Remember that you have not written

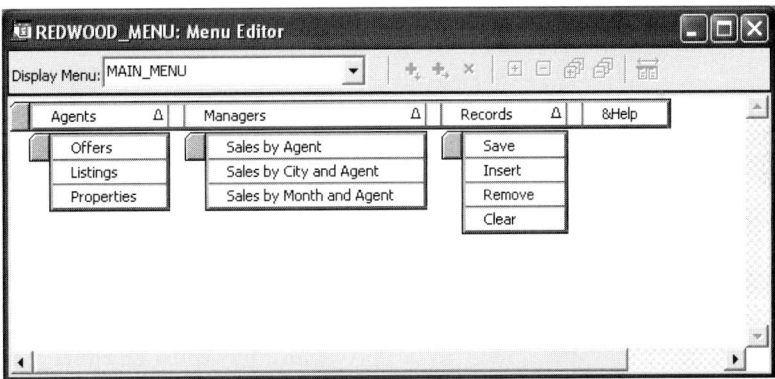

FIGURE 11.10 Menu layout.

TABLE 11.4 Special item formats.

Item type	Description
Plain	Basic text menu entry with trigger code to handle the action.
Check	A property that users can toggle to enable or disable conditions, such as boldface.
Radio	A set of options where users can select only one, similar to a radio group on a form.
Separator	A separator line between entries.
Magic	One of the predefined menu items: Cut, Copy, Paste, Clear, Undo, Help, About, Quit, and Window.

any help files yet, so users will really not get much help. Then why should you enter the command now? The answer is that every menu-item must have an action or the menu will not compile. So, do the easiest one first.

1. Right-click the **Help** item and open the **PL/SQL Editor**. Type **Help;** and compile the module.

There is one more useful trick you can use with menus—setting the access key. An *access key* means that the user can click the Alt-key combination to activate the menu item. You specify the access key in a menu by prefixing the letter with an ampersand (&). By default, the first letter of the top-level menus are automatically set as access keys.

2. Change the label for the Help item to **&Help**.
3. Save the menu and accept the default name (**Redwood_Menu.mmb**).

Of course, you now have to write the trigger code to perform the desired actions for the other menu items.

4. Right-click the **Offers** menu item under **Agents** and select the **PL/SQL Editor** option. In the Editor window, add the code to open the **ListingActivity** form using the global ApplicationPath variable:

```
CALL_FORM(:GLOBAL.ApplicationPath || 'ListingActivity.fmx');
```

5. Repeat Step 5 with the **Listings** and **Properties** menu items to open the corresponding forms.

Opening reports is similar to the forms process, but recall that you use the Web.Show_Document command. You might also recall that the command URL was relatively long because you need to add the ApplicationPath and set the output type. Instead of typing the same long command repeatedly, this is a good place to create a procedure to make life a little easier by handling the repetitive tasks.

1. Select the **Program Units** node in the Object Navigator and click the **Create** button.
2. Choose the **Procedure** option and enter the name: **Display_Report**, then click the **OK** button.
3. The PL/SQL Editor shows the framework of your new procedure. When you call this procedure, you will want to pass it the name of the report to display, so add a parameter to the procedure by typing **(Report_Name IN VARCHAR2)** between the name of the report and the word IS.
4. Enter the Web.Show_Document command as the body of the procedure, but insert the new parameter (Report_Name) as the name of the report. Your procedure should look like this streamlined version:

```
PROCEDURE Display_Report (Report_Name IN VARCHAR2) IS
BEGIN
     Web.Show_Document(:GLOBAL.ReportServerURL
          || '?destype=cache'
          || '&' || :GLOBAL.ReportFormat
          || '&report=' || :GLOBAL.ApplicationPath || Report_Name
          || '&userid@' || :GLOBAL.DatabaseServer
          , '_blank');
END;
```

5. Now you can use this procedure in your menu items. Open the **PL/SQL** trigger for the **Sales by Agent** menu item in the **Managers** menu. Enter the line:

```
Display_Report('AgentSales.jsp');
```

6. Repeat Step 5 for the other two reports in the Managers menu, being careful to enter the exact name of the report for each entry.

Most menu options consist of opening either forms or reports, and you now know how to create menu actions for both. You also know how to add menu options for the basic Magic functions that are built into the menu system. However, if you look at the items under the Records menu, you will see that you need a couple more lines of special code for Save, Insert, and Remove. In fact, you need to know the commands that match the standard menu items so that you can add them to your own menus. You can find the commands in the Object Navigator under the Built-in Packages. The procedures are listed in the STANDARD Extensions. You can use the Help system to get more details about each command. Table 11.5 lists the common menu items and the corresponding commands that you will use.

1. Select the Save item under the Records menu. Open the PL/SQL Editor and enter **Commit_Form;** and compile the module.
2. Look up the item and enter the code needed for the **Insert**, **Remove**, and **Clear** menu entries.
3. At this point, every menu item should have an action. Set the focus to the Menu Editor by clicking any item in the editor window. Then click the **Compile** button on the main toolbar of the Forms Builder to compile the menu.

TABLE 11.5 Common menu items and the PL/SQL replacement commands.

Standard Menu Item	*Command*
Action	
Save	Commit_Form;
Clear All	Clear_Form;
Print	Print;
Exit	Exit_Form;
Edit	
Cut	Magic: Cut
Copy	Magic: Copy
Paste	Magic: Paste
Query	
Enter	Enter_Query;
Execute	Execute_Query;
Cancel	Abort_Query;
Count Hits	Count_Query;
Block	
Previous	Previous_Block;
Next	Next_Block;
Clear	Clear_Block;
Record	
Previous	Previous_Record;
Next	Next_Record;
First	First_Record;
Last	Last_Record;
Insert	Create_Record;
Remove	Delete_Record;
Lock	Lock_Record;
Duplicate	Duplicate_Record;
Clear	Clear_Record;
Scroll Up	Scroll_Up;
Scroll Down	Scroll_Down;

4. If you receive any error messages, find the referenced menu item, fix the problem, and recompile the menu. Eventually you should see only a small message at the bottom of the Forms Builder stating that the module was built successfully. You can also check your folder to see if it contains the compiled (.mmx) file.

DEPLOYING AND USING MENUS

Once the menu has been compiled successfully, you can add it to your forms. When you add it to the startup form, it will become the default menu for all of the forms in the application. The standard way to specify the menu is to change the startup form's menu properties.

1. Open the Startup form. Open the Property Palette for the overall form module (Startup node). The default Menu Module property is set to DEFAULT&SMARTBAR. Change this property to the full pathname of the compiled menu file: **C:\your path\Redwood_Menu**.
2. In the same set of properties, set the **Initial Menu** to **Main_Menu**, which is the top-level menu that you created.
3. You can run the form and test the menu.

However, as you are entering the long full path name of the menu file, alarm bells should be going off in your head. To deploy this application to the server, someone will have to come back and change this value. What do you think the probability is that this change will be made correctly?

A better way to specify a new menu is to use the built-in function Replace_ Menu. This way you can use the global variable to set the full path, and your entire application can be moved simply by having someone change this one variable in one location.

1. If you actually changed the last two properties, go back and delete them and restore DEFAULT&SMARTBAR as the Menu Module.
2. Open the When-New-Form-Instance trigger for the Startup form. Add one line of code at the bottom of the module:

```
Replace_Menu(:GLOBAL.ApplicationPath || 'Redwood_Menu', PULL_DOWN,
'Main_Menu');
```

3. Compile the module, save the form and run it. Test all of the menu options.

As you test the menu shown in Figure 11.11, notice that the new menu remains across all of the forms. What if you want to modify the menu on one of the forms to add some new options? You could write code to add the options dynamically, or to temporarily disable an option. Or, you can create a completely separate menu for a form. The easy solution is to then add a Replace_Menu command to that form's When-New-Form-Instance trigger that specifies the name of the new form. Alternatively, you can embed the complete menu name into the form's properties and specify DO_REPLACE in the Call_Form command that opens the new form. For example:

```
Call_Form(:GLOBAL.ApplicationPath || 'Agents.fmx', HIDE, DO_REPLACE);
```

Of course, remember that specifying the full path name of the menu makes it hard to port the application. If you really need to use this approach, you should not enter any path name—just the file name—and be sure to set up a new configuration on the Oracle Application Server. Then, the configuration file controls the location of all form and menu files.

CHAPTER 11   Building an Integrated Application   **547**

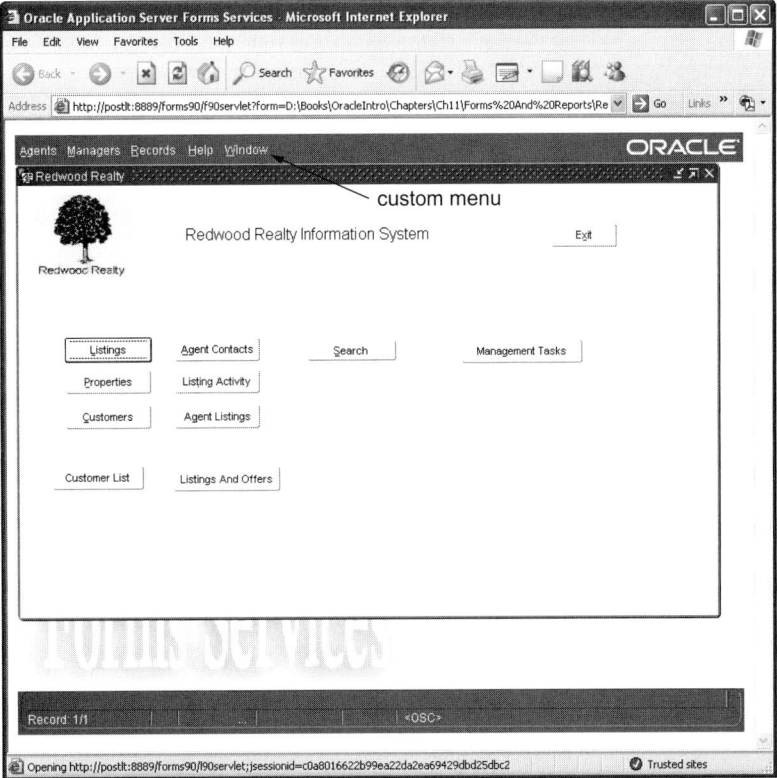

FIGURE 11.11   The new menu in the application.

CREATING HELP FILES

The main functions of the application are looking good. You have the forms and reports, including a startup form that provides easy access to the application. You have a start on the menu that helps users navigate the application and run the forms. But, you have one major piece left to create: a help system. Think of the applications you have used (Word, Excel, Forms Builder, and so on), and think of the times you have relied on the help files. A good help system can make an application significantly easier to use.

Over the years, help systems have started to standardize. People now expect to see certain things when they ask for help: (1) The help should be *context sensitive*, so that the initial help page should be related to the task currently being performed. In a database application, that usually means that if users select the Help menu option or press the Help (F1) key, they will see a help page that explains items on the current form; (2) A help system has a table of contents. A *table of contents* page organizes the help files from the top down. It provides an overview or outline of the primary tasks, and users can expand each section to get more detail on topics in that area; (3) A help system has an index page. An *index page* is a sorted list of key words. Clicking on the word brings up the help pages with matching information about that topic; (4) A help system usually has a *search page* that enables the user to enter words or phrases and search for any topic that contains that phrase.

The nice thing about becoming standardized is that we now have tools that make it relatively easy to provide these features. As a developer, you can concentrate on the actual content of the help page, and the tools will almost automatically create the standard features. But, keep in mind that someone still has to write all of the help pages.

TABLE 11.6 Files needed in a help system.

File Type	Structure and Purpose
Topic Files	HTML files that contain the content displayed to the user. Put only one topic in a file.
Table of Contents	XML files that provide a hierarchical list of topic pages.
Index Files	XML files that list key words and the matching topic page.
Search Index Files	XML files that contain databases used for text searches.
Link Files	XML files that define associative links between topics.
Map Files	XML files that associate topic IDs with the topic files so you can refer to any topic by its ID.
Helpset File	XML file that defines the appearance and operation of the help system.
OHW Configuration File ohwconfig.xml	Server file that tells the system where to find your help files.

As you will see, even a simple application could need dozens or even hundreds of pages for the help system. In large projects, a dedicated team is usually formed just to write, edit, and organize the help files.

THE ORACLE WEB HELP SYSTEM

Oracle has two main help systems: one that runs as Java (.OHJ) and one that runs over the Web as HTML files (.OHW). The process for creating the files is similar for both systems, but since the application is primarily designed to run over the Web, the discussion in this section uses the Web (.OHW) approach.

Ultimately, you need to create several types of files to build your help system. In a large project, you probably would want to purchase a specialized help editor that has generators to create many of the supplemental files, and tracks revisions to the main documents. However, you could create them all by hand using a simple text editor (Wordpad). The types of files that you need to create are listed in Table 11.6.

Before delving into the details of these files and creating a few help pages, you should think about an important question. Since the application runs on the Web, why not use simple HTML pages for the help system? You can use the Web.Show_Document command to open any HTML page, so this approach would work. The main reason for using .OHW is that it already contains procedures for handling indexes and searching. But, with a standard search engine, you could duplicate these facilities fairly easily with standard HTML pages. Ultimately, this question will have to be answered by the MIS organization. Fortunately, the hard part of writing all of the help topics is almost the same in either case, so you do not lose much time if you decide to switch systems later.

CREATING HTML HELP FILES

You need to create a separate HTML page for each topic that you want to display to the user. You will create three pages for this project to demonstrate a couple of features. Ultimately, a project will have dozens or even hundreds of pages. You can use almost any HTML editor, but you might have to add some features by hand, so make sure you can edit the HTML directly.

1. Create a new folder in the RedwoodRealty folder named **HelpFiles**.
2. Create a main help page in HTML and save it as **Redwood.html** in the new folder. If you want to include the logo, make sure you copy the logo file into the same folder. Test the basic HTML by opening the file directly.

CHAPTER 11 Building an Integrated Application 549

```
<HTML><HEAD>
<TITLE>Redwood Realty</TITLE>
</HEAD><BODY>
<H1>Redwood Realty Information System</H1>
<TABLE><TR>
<TD><IMG SRC="RedwoodLogo1.jpg" border="0" height="110"></TD>
<TD>The Redwood Realty information system collects all sales and listings
data for the firm.</TD>
</TR></TABLE>
<H2>Help for Primary Tasks</H2>
<UL>
<LI><A HREF="Agents.html">Agent Tasks</A></LI>
<LI><A HREF="Management.html">Management Tasks</A></LI>
</UL>
</BODY></HTML>
```

3. Create the other two HTML pages (**Agents.html** and **Management.html**). Keep the pages simple with just a couple of lines of text to identify them for now. Be sure to include a link back to the initial file.

```
<HTML><HEAD>
<TITLE>Agents</TITLE>
</HEAD><BODY>
<H1>Help for Agents</H1>
<P>This is the main help file for agents.
Later, we will add more items.</P>
<P><A HREF="Redwood.html">Main help</A></P>
</BODY></HTML>
```

4. Test the files with a standard browser and make sure the links work.

Oracle also lets you define the links using a topic ID instead of the actual file name. However, you can only test these types of links within the Oracle help system. They have the slight benefit of storing all links in one location, which makes it easier to correct broken links. However, many tools exist to check standard HTML help files for links, and these tools will only work if you use standard HTML link tags.

Oracle also supports associative links. An *associative link* uses key words to show a pop-up list of related topics. For example, you can add the following line to both the top-level page and the agents page:

```
<A HREF="alink: agent ">Topics about agents.</A>
```

When the help file is created, the user can click on that resulting link to get a list of all pages that contain the same key word. However, to use associative indexes, you will have to create a link file. Also, the link will be meaningless to a regular browser and can only be used within the Oracle Help system.

The Oracle help system also requires that you create a map file. Internally, the help system refers to pages by an ID. The ID can be numeric or text, but it cannot contain spaces. A common scheme is to use the file name but replace the dot with an underscore.

5. In this example, you would create and save the text file **topics.xml**:

```
<?xml version='1.0' ?>
<map version="1.0">
  <mapID target="Redwood_html" url="Redwood.html" />
  <mapID target="Agents_html" url="Agents.html" />
  <mapID target="Management_html" url="Management.html" />
</map>
```

6. You also need to create a table of contents file similar to what you would see in a book. Create and save the text file **toc.xml** which creates Introduction as the primary heading, with subheadings for Agents and Managers.

```xml
<?xml version='1.0' ?>
<toc version="1.0">
<tocitem text="Introduction to Redwood Realty IS">
  <tocitem target="Redwood_html" text="Introduction to Redwood Realty IS" >
    <tocitem target="Agents_html" text="Tasks for agents." />
    <tocitem target="Management_html" text="Tasks for managers." />
  </tocitem>
</tocitem>
</toc>
```

7. The index is more challenging since you have to decide how to group items together. The following example creates a single entry for Introduction, and another entry for Tasks by users that has two items grouped under it (Agents and Managers). Create and save the text file as **index.html**:

```xml
<?xml version='1.0' ?>
<index version="1.0">

<indexitem target="Introduction" text="Introduction to the system">
  <indexentry target="Redwood_html" text="Introduction" />
</indexitem>

<indexitem target="Tasks by user" text="Tasks by type of user">
  <indexentry target="Agents_html" text="Agent tasks" />
  <indexentry target="Management_html" text="Management tasks" />
</index item>
</index>
```

8. If you want to create associative links, you also need to add a file that groups the links together. If you entered the associative link earlier, you need to add two entries for the agent link. Save the text file as **links.xml**:

```xml
<?xml version='1.0' ?>
<link version="1.0">

<linkitem topic="agent">
  <linkentry target="Redwood_html" text="Introduction" />
  <linkentry target="Agents_html" text="Agent tasks" />
</linkitem>
</link>
```

9. You need a search index file to use the search tools. The catch is that this file is a proprietary binary file. Oracle ships a Text Search Indexer program with the Oracle Java Help system, but not with the Web help system. So, if you download and install the Java help system, you can run the Java help-indexer program to create the search.idx file. Since this step requires that you install Java help and run the Java compiler, the details are beyond the scope of this book, but you can follow the Oracle documentation. If you want to build your help file without creating the index, you can copy an index file from one of the samples that comes with the OHW system. It will not function in your application, but it will enable the rest of the system to work.

10. Now that you have all of the supporting files, you can create the helpset file. The helpset file sets up the help window and tells Oracle what you named all of these other files. It is a little longer, but if you use standard names for your supporting files, you can usually just copy this file and edit a couple of the titles. Save the file as RedwoodHelp.hs:

```xml
<?xml version='1.0'?>
<helpset version="1.1">
```

```xml
<title>Redwood Realty</title>

<maps>
  <mapref location="topics.xml"/>
</maps>

<links>
  <linkref location="links.xml"/>
</links>

<view>
  <label>Table of Contents</label>
  <type>oracle.help.navigator.tocNavigator.TOCNavigator</type>
  <data engine="oracle.help.engine.XMLTOCEngine">toc.xml</data>
</view>

<view>
  <label>Keyword Index</label>
  <type>oracle.help.navigator.keywordNavigator.KeywordNavigator</type>
  <data engine="oracle.help.engine.XMLIndexEngine">index.xml</data>
</view>

<view>
  <label>Search</label>
  <title>Redwood Realty</title>
  <type>oracle.help.navigator.searchNavigator.SearchNavigator</type>
  <data engine="oracle.help.engine.SearchEngine">search.idx</data>
</view>
</helpset>
```

DEPLOYING AND USING HELP FILES

Now that you have all of the topic files and the supporting files that define the help system, you need to integrate them into your application and deploy them. To do that, you need to install the .OWH bundle on your development machine, or move all of the files to an OracleAS system. If necessary, you can download the .OWH files from the OTN Web site. You install the files by unzipping the folder into your Oracle home directory. The ReadMe.txt file contains instructions on configuring and starting the service. Basically, you need to switch to command line and run a Java program to install the system.

The primary step in deploying the actual help files is to find and modify the ohwconfig.xml file. Use the Windows Explorer search option to find where the file is installed on your computer. Then, you have to modify the file slightly so that the system knows where to find your helpset file.

1. Find the **ohwconfig.xml** file and modify it with WordPad. The default location is <Install_folder>\ohw\j2ee\home\applications\auto\ohw\ohw-demo\helpsets. Change the <books > section to add your helpset. Note that you can leave the other helpset definitions in the file, if you want users to have easy access to the additional help. Or you can delete the other entries if they will be too confusing.

```
<books combineBooks="true" useLabelInfo="true">
  <helpSet id="Redwood" location="Redwood/RedwoodHelp.hs" />
  ... leave or delete the other helpset files
</books>
```

2. Create a Redwood subfolder beneath the directory containing the ohwconfig.xml file and copy all of your help files into that folder.

3. Start the OC4J instance that comes with the OWH application—using another Java command listed in the ReadMe.txt file. You should now be able to view

552 Introduction to Oracle

your help files by opening a browser and entering the help URL into the address box:

```
http://localhost:8888/ohw-demo/help/?topic=Redwood_html
```

Now, how do you tie each page to a specific help topic? The answer is that you create a custom help button (or menu entry) for each form and use the Web.Show_Document command. Simply modify the topic ID for each page. When the user clicks the button, the browser will call the help system and display the help topic. Be sure to include the _blank option so the topic is displayed in a new browser window.

4. Open the **Startup** form and edit the **When-New-Form-Instance** trigger. Define a new global variable for the Help server:

```
:GLOBAL.HelpServerURL := 'http://localhost:8888/ohw-demo/help/';
```

5. Now you can use that variable to call the help server. Open the **Redwood_Menu** file, display the **Main_Menu** and change the PL/SQL for the **Help** option to

```
Web.Show_Document(:GLOBAL.HelpServerURL ||'?topic=Redwood_html',
'_blank');
```

6. Save and recompile the menu. Save the Startup form and run it. When you select the Help option, it should bring up the introductory page shown in Figure 11.12.

If this process seems overly painful, note that most organizations that create help files purchase a commercial package to build the help files. These tools automate most

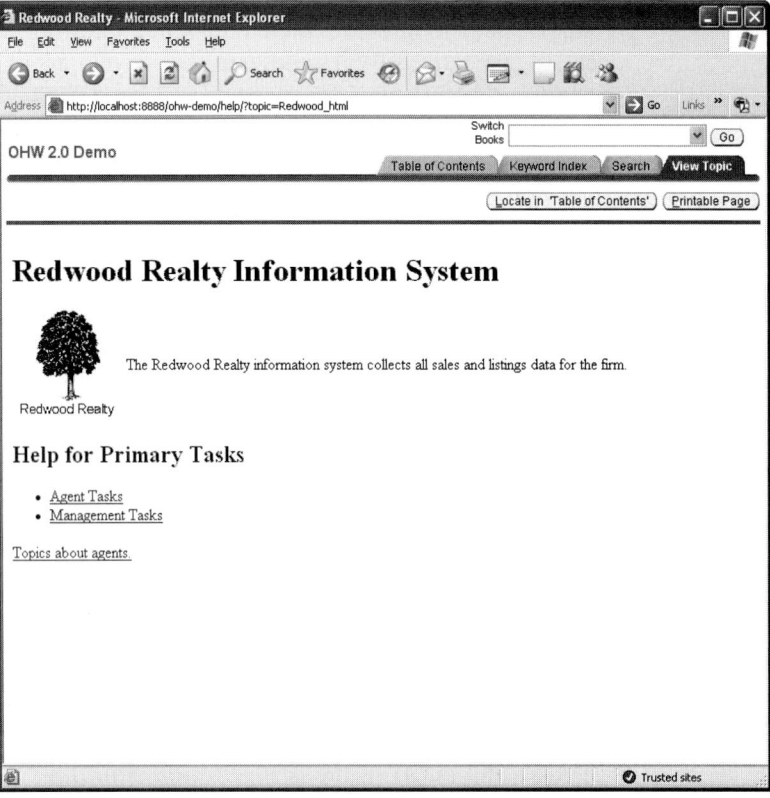

FIGURE 11.12 The help file.

of the process—particularly creating the supplemental files. However, someone still has to write all of the topic files. Also, an OracleAS DBA has to configure the server to run the help files. Finally, as a developer, you still have to write all of the help links into your forms.

In many ways, if you only want Web-based help files, you are probably better off today if you simply write the files in HTML. You can find many editors and tools that make the process easy and test the links for you. You can create your own Table of Contents and index pages with complete control over the design. The only tricky part is the full-text search. For that, you can easily obtain one of the powerful commercial search engines and implement it in a few hours. The search engines are dynamic and do not require you to manually rebuild the indexes.

Summary

You build applications to provide all of the functions needed by users. The forms and reports are the foundation of the application, but you still need to clean them up. It is important that all of the forms and reports have a consistent look and feel, so you first build templates and establish a style guide. Then you have to connect the forms and reports into a single application. All of the forms, reports, and even application management tasks should be accessible through the forms. Most applications have a startup form with buttons to guide users to the needed forms. Deploying the application ultimately means you have to move it to an Oracle Application Server. Through the careful use of global variables to define the services and locations for forms, reports, and help files, you can move your application to another location simply by copying the executable file and modifying the global variables in the startup code. You can also create custom menus to limit user actions and make your application easier to use. Finally, you need to create help files that explain how to use the application and recover from potential problems. You need the OHW (or OHJ) help system to create and run the help files.

It is time-consuming to handle the hundreds of details in creating a consistent, usable application. However, it is time you have to spend. Users need a professional application that is easy to use, performs all of the tasks they need, and contains the customized menus and help files that provide immediate support and guidance.

Key Terms

- access key
- application
- associative link
- child menu items
- context sensitive
- desformat
- destype
- hard-coded
- index page
- Magic
- menu items
- menu module
- named visual attribute
- Oracle Application Server (OracleAS)
- parent menu items
- property class
- search page
- single sign on
- style guide
- table of contents
- template form
- userid

Review

TRUE/FALSE

1. You can modify a form template and reapply the changes to an existing form.
2. Visual attributes created within a form template are automatically applied to data items.
3. Forms and reports are both opened with calls to the Web.Show_Document function.
4. When you create and use a custom menu, it removes the standard menu and toolbar so you need to add items to handle some standard tasks.
5. Any time you modify help files, you will need to rebuild the search index.

FILL IN

1. If you want to set a standard date format to be used whenever a user enters a date, you should create a(n) _____, and assign it to all data items using dates.
2. You have a long list of data items and you want to change the color of the item after the user has entered a value. You should create and programmatically assign a(n) _____ to each item.
3. To specify that a report should be generated in HTML, you would set the _____ parameter when opening the report.
4. To create a menu item that mimics the Edit/Cut command, you need to set the menu item's properties to _____.
5. To provide an overview guide to the entire help file, you need to create the _____ file.

MULTIPLE CHOICE

1. To ensure that all developers on a large project create forms with a consistent look and feel, you need to develop
    a. Report templates
    b. Form templates
    c. A style guide
    d. Property classes
    e. All of the above
2. You created a button on a form to display a report. You will use the _____ PL/SQL function to display the report.
    a. Web.Show_Document
    b. Call_Form
    c. Call_Report
    d. Show_Report
    e. Run_Report
3. To make it easier to move your application to a different location, you need to create _____ that you will use every time you open a form or report.
    a. User parameters
    b. Global variables
    c. Startup forms
    d. Menus
    e. Help files
4. Although you can set a form's menu properties, it is better to use the _____ command because the menu property hard-codes the location of the file.
    a. Show_Menu
    b. DEFAULT&SMARTBAR
    c. Global variable
    d. Replace_Menu
    e. Help
5. Which of the following is NOT a file you need to create when using the Oracle help system?
    a. Topic files
    b. Index file
    c. Title file
    d. Table of contents file
    e. Search index file

Hands-on Exercises

1. EXTENDING THE CHAPTER CASE

You need to clean up the Redwood application so it is ready to use. The steps you have left depend a little on whether you have created all of the forms and reports along the way. If not, you should create them now. However, the most important thing is to create a consistent look and feel, so you need to base all of the forms on the template.

1. Use the template created in this chapter; improve it if necessary. Build new forms and copy all of the existing forms onto template-based forms.
2. Improve the Startup form so that it contains all of the links needed for agents and managers.
3. If you have kept up with all of the changes, the menu probably needs the most work. Most important, you need to add some Query functions. Use the Forms Builder to edit the Redwood_Menu. Insert a new top-level item for

Query. Add menu items for Enter Query and Execute Query.

4. While you are working on the menu, add some of the navigation options to the Records entry. You need at least Previous and Next Record options. Put them at the bottom of the list with a separator between them and the existing editing choices. Save and compile the menu and test it.

5. Print one of the new forms with the menu displayed and hand it in.

2. COFFEE MERCHANT

You probably do not have time to build the complete application for every one of these cases, but you should at least collect the files you do have and build the startup form.

1. Create a new folder for this case in this chapter. Copy the existing forms and reports that you created in earlier chapters into the new folder.

2. Create a startup form manually. Add the data block and canvas—setting the background to white. Add a logo, title, and Exit button with the **Exit_Form;** code.

3. Copy the setup code from the **Redwood Startup** form that defines the global variables. Paste it into the **When-New-Form-Instance** trigger for the **Coffee Merchant Startup** form. Edit the variables to point to the correct locations. For now, comment out the Replace_Menu command.

4. Add buttons to the **Startup** form that open the other forms: **Consumers, Orders, Inventory, InventoryTable, Countries,** and **Employees.** Add a button for the **Quarterly Sales by State** report.

5. Add PL/SQL code to the buttons following the format:

   `Call_Form(:GLOBAL.ApplicationPath || 'FormName.fmx');`

6. For the report button, copy the similar code from the Redwood Startup form and change the name of the report. Compile everything; save the form.

7. Compile all of the existing forms to ensure that you have executable (.fmx) versions in the folder. You might consider adding **Close** buttons to most forms while you are at it. Add **Execute_Query;** code to the **Countries, Inventory, InventoryTable,** and **Employee** forms so they load automatically.

8. Print a copy of the Startup form and hand it in.

3. ROWING VENTURES

You should already have the forms and reports you need for the Rowing Ventures case. Assemble them into a new folder for this chapter and create a Startup form. Be sure to add the initialization code to set the global variables. Add buttons to open the basic forms (Boat, Organization, Person, and Race). Add buttons to open the compound form for Race Day and the Race Results report. Create a new menu for this application. It might be faster to copy the menu you created for the Redwood case and modify it. Be sure to add the Startup form to the menu so people can easily get back to the starting point. Print a copy of the Startup form with the new menu and hand it in.

4. BROADCLOTH CLOTHING

If you have looked through the table list lately for Broadcloth Clothing, you have probably figured out that it is going to be a large application. To this point, you have created only a few of the forms and reports for this company. If you have a spare couple of hours, you could work on creating the other forms and reports. In the meantime, you should build the Startup form. You might need a couple of levels of menu forms, because you really do not want to put 20 buttons on the main form. Instead, work out a hierarchy where the main Startup form directs users to a secondary menu form based on their primary tasks. For instance, you might have secondary forms for Orders, Factory Production, and Shipping. If you want to get creative, you could make the Startup form with tab canvases, where each tab represents one of the primary tasks and its canvas contains buttons specific to that task. Print the menu forms/canvases and hand them in.

CHAPTER 12

MAINTAINING DATABASE SECURITY

Learning Objectives

In this chapter, you will learn:

- How to create user accounts and roles.
- How to control access to objects through roles.
- How to limit access to data through views and application controls.
- How to encrypt data.
- How to establish and monitor security audits.

CREATING AND EDITING USER ACCOUNTS

More people are beginning to understand that computer security is an important topic. In the old days, an organization might hire a security administrator or perhaps a consultant, configure its systems for a certain level of security, and then assume that everything was safe. In a database environment, perhaps the database administrator would be placed in charge of security—along with dozens of other duties. Today, security is more complex and more important than it used to be—particularly as the number of attacks increases and the threats continually evolve. As a result, developers need to consider security aspects earlier in the development stages. Security also needs to be integrated into the overall application, instead of simply tacked on at the end.

To understand computer security tools, you need to have some idea of the basic threats. A complete discussion of computer security is beyond the scope of this book, but you can manage with a few basic principles. One of the most important points is that more money is lost to insider theft than from outside attackers—way more money. It is not even close. Second, in most situations, the greatest threats to loss of data are fairly common things such as fire, flood, failing hardware, accidental deletion, and so on. Yes, you do need to be aware of potential attacks from outsiders—particularly across the Internet. But, it is substantially more difficult to handle the threats from insiders. You have to trust insiders—employees need to be able to do their jobs, and most employees are hardworking, honest people. So, employes and consultants and business partners need access to your systems. They just do not need total access to your systems. So the challenge is to draw that thin line between exactly what data employees do need to access, and what data they should not access. Identifying the needed access rights by various employees is the main reason it is so important for developers to integrate security points early into the application. It is the designers and developers who understand the system best and need to define the roles of the employees.

The three goals of a secure database system are to ensure: (1) confidentiality, (2) integrity, and (3) availability. ***Confidentiality*** means that only authorized people are allowed to see data. For example, health information can only be seen by certain people—which does not include billing clerks. Confidentiality means that you have to secure the database servers, protect the transmission of the data, including reports, and authenticate users so you only allow authorized people to see the data.

Integrity means that the data stored accurately represents the concepts it is recording. It includes recovery from system crashes as much as preventing unauthorized people from changing data. For instance, you do not want to allow employees to change their own salary figures.

Availability is equally important but often ignored. It means that the system must be available when it is needed. That includes backup provisions for systems failures. It also means providing access to authorized users. Some novices in security overreact and tighten security so far that legitimate users have problems using the system.

Availability is also affected by the backup and recovery operations of the database. Backup is critical to the security of any database. However, backup and recovery are covered in Chapter 13 because they require DBA privileges and you need to understand the way that Oracle stores data.

This chapter discusses the major tools that Oracle provides to improve the security of the database. Remember that you will also want to use traditional security tools outside of Oracle such as employee background checks, network firewalls, and physically securing the servers. These techniques are covered in other security books.

USER AUTHENTICATION

Who are you? How does the computer know who you are? These are critical questions in computer security. Unfortunately, they are also difficult problems to solve. Today, the most common method of authenticating users is based on the ***challenge-response*** system: Each person is assigned a unique username and chooses a secret password. Only the user and the computer system know the password, so if the user provides the correct username/password combination when asked, the computer accepts the identity of the user.

In theory, the username/password approach is relatively powerful. Also, it is relatively easy to implement—just remember to encrypt the passwords securely. In practice, the approach suffers from several well-known problems. Most of the problems cannot be avoided. For example, it is hard for people to memorize dozens of passwords, so they pick easy ones or write them down when they are forced to change them. However, one specific problem can be improved. Organizations need to avoid forcing users to log in dozens of times to accomplish their tasks. Instead, many are trying to implement a ***single sign-on*** approach. Users will have one username/password combination within the organization. They will log in one time and be able to use any system where they have access.

Oracle applications support a version of single sign-on, but it requires several components and additional configuration. Remember when you ran the applications created in Chapter 11? You have to log on once to see the forms, and once to see the reports—because the forms and report services use different engines. Now, if the company has several applications, the users will have to log in again for each application.

The single sign-on approach can eliminate or at least reduce the problem. If you install the Enterprise Edition of Oracle, you will have to install and configure the **Oracle Internet Directory (OID)**. OID can handle the user credentials and authentication within all Oracle applications. When you move the application to the OracleAS server, you can configure the server to use OID. If all applications use OID, then the user only has to log in one time. More important, OID supports the **lightweight directory application protocol (LDAP)**, which is a standard method of storing user data. Through this process, OID can pick up user credentials from other platforms, including Microsoft Active Directory or SunONE Directory Server. In other words, users log into their own computers and this authentication is made available to the Oracle servers. So, even across platforms, users only need to sign in one time. It takes a fair amount of work to configure these systems, but it makes life easier for the users and it improves security because authentication is handled at one point and users need to memorize only one set of credentials. Configuration of OIS is beyond the scope of this book, but you should be aware that it exists, and you should plan your applications to take advantage of it.

Without OID or LDAP, you have to create user accounts individually in the Oracle database. It is easier to test your application on a single system database, and then move it to OracleAS and OID later. Consequently, you usually need to create sample user accounts on your own computer for testing purposes. The SQL Command to create a user is:

```
CREATE USER username IDENTIFIED BY password
```

You can also assign quotas on the amount of storage space the user can take, and specify default and temporary tablespaces where their data will be stored. These options are generally used if the user will be creating tables, and in most cases, your application users will not be given those permissions, so the default values are acceptable.

For the Redwood Realty case, you will need a couple of user accounts to test your security settings. The catch is that your own account needs relatively powerful permissions to create those users. You will either need DBA permissions or at least CREATE USER authority.

1. Create a new agent account for Kai Marcoux:

   ```
   CREATE USER MarcouxK IDENTIFIED BY changeme;
   GRANT Create Session To MarcouxK;
   ```

2. Create a new manager account for Tobias Carling:

   ```
   CREATE USER CarlingT IDENTIFIED BY changeme2
   GRANT Create Session To CarlingT;
   ```

You can pick different passwords, but remember what you pick. Also, be careful later with giving permissions to these two accounts because other people reading this book might gain access to your database. As you will see in Chapter 13, if you have DBA permissions, you can use the Enterprise Manager to create accounts and assign permissions. Since you might not have DBA permissions, this chapter will stick with the SQL approach. To help you see the process, Figure 12.1 shows the basic screen to create a user with the Enterprise Manager. You enter the same data (username and password) and it creates the SQL command for you. It is a handy tool if you have permission to use it and if you forget the CREATE USER syntax. But, it is cumbersome to use when you need to create more than one or two accounts at a time. In those situations, you can write a script file that reads the username/password combinations from a file and creates the accounts in a batch.

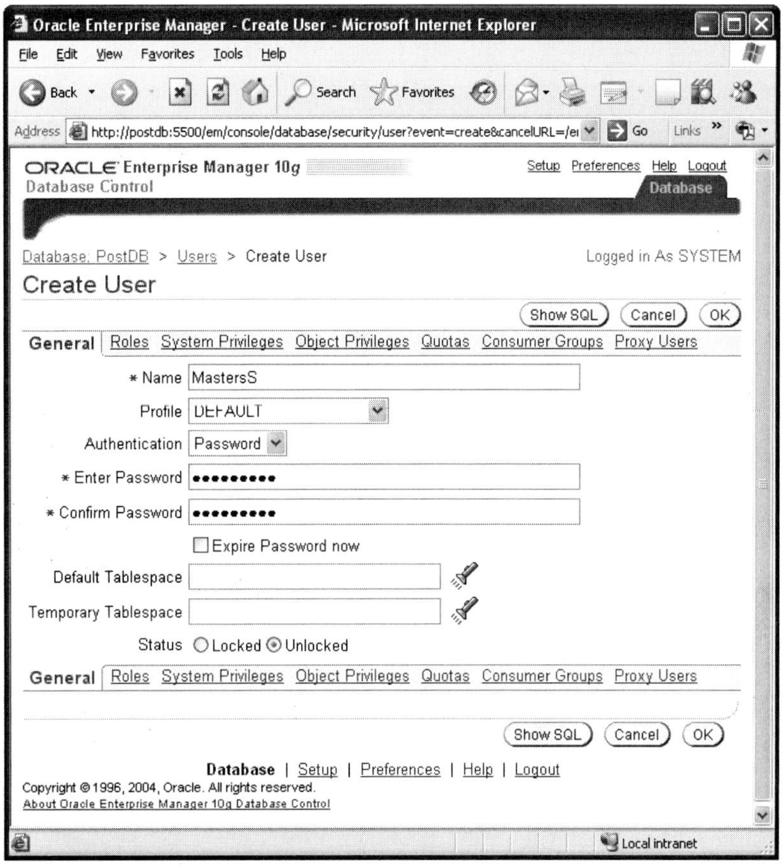

FIGURE 12.1 Creating a user with Enterprise Manager.

Note that the second line (GRANT Create Session) is required to enable the user to log in. Simply creating a user does not give them permission to log in. They must have the permission to create a session.

> **Tip:** If you receive an error message either on the CREATE or GRANT statements, your personal account does not have sufficient privileges to create users. You will have to contact the system administrator and ask for CREATE USER, and CREATE SESSION WITH ADMIN permissions. But the administrator may be reluctant to give you those permissions.

USER ROLES

Chapter 2 briefly listed the two primary SQL security commands GRANT and REVOKE. Recall that GRANT gives permissions to a user to access a table, and REVOKE takes away permissions. The syntax for both commands is straightforward.

```
GRANT privilege [, privilege [, privilege] ...] | ALL PRIVILEGES
ON object
TO user [IDENTIFIED BY password] [, user2 [, user3]...] | PUBLIC
[WITH GRANT OPTION]
```

The one catch with the GRANT and REVOKE statements is that you really do not want to apply them to individual users. Think about the situation for a minute.

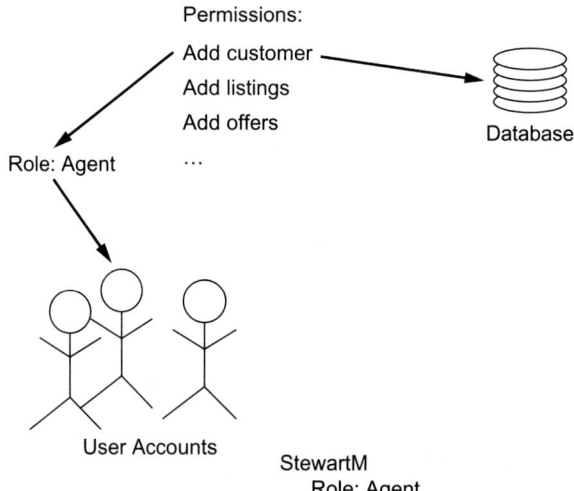

FIGURE 12.2 User roles.

Even in a small firm such as Redwood Realty, you might have 20 or 30 agents and five to 10 managers. What happens when you add a new employee? Someone has to assign all of the needed permissions to the person's account. With dozens of permissions, what is the probability a mistake is made? Even if you keep all of the permission in a script file, the DBA or security manager has to find the correct file and ensure that it is up to date. Also, think about what happens if you need to alter the basic permissions for agents. Not only do you have to define the changes, someone has to identify all of the agents and then correctly apply the changes to each agent account. Now, multiply the complications when a company has thousands or hundreds of thousands of employees.

The answer is to create user roles. A ***user role*** is a set of permissions that are applied to every user in a common group. For example, every employee in a group of payroll clerks would need the same permissions because they perform the job or role. Instead of assigning permissions individually to each user, you create a user role and assign the permissions to that role. Then you assign the role to a user.

Figure 12.2 illustrates the process. As a developer, you identify the various roles needed in your application. Then you determine the permissions needed by each role. Eventually, the security manager assigns the role to individual users who then gain the permissions associated with the role. Note that users can be assigned multiple roles, and they will gain the permissions from each role. It is also possible to create a role that inherits permissions from another role. For example, you might consider assigning the Agent role to the Manager role. That way, managers have all of the permissions of agents, plus the added permissions from the Manager role. But, as your roles and permissions become more complex, make sure you document the entire system someplace. If problems arise, the security manager needs to be able to see how the roles interrelate. Even a simple sketch will help.

SYSTEM AND OBJECT PRIVILEGES

Oracle defines two types of permissions that can be assigned to users and roles: (1) object privileges and (2) system privileges. ***Object privileges*** are specific operations that can be performed on existing database tables, views, procedures and similar objects. For example, an agent needs the SELECT permission to read data in the Customer table. ***System privileges*** are permissions that enable users to modify the database definitions, such as creating a table, user, or view. For instance, you need the CREATE TABLE permission to define new tables in the database, but it is unlikely an agent needs that system privilege, unless the agent needs to run a script that creates a temporary table. Table 12.1 lists some of the common system privileges that you might need sometime. It lists the only the simple privileges that you might consider applying to general users. Oracle has over 150 system privileges, but many of them should only be applied to database administrators or highly trusted and trained managers. The Oracle SQL Reference documentation has a complete list of the system privileges. Most general users will need very few system privileges unless they need to run complex scripts that alter the database. However, you should be familiar with the primary privileges because you will need many of them for your developer accounts.

Object privileges depend on the type of object being referenced. In spirit, they are closest to the GRANT permissions, such as DELETE and INSERT. Table 12.2 is based

TABLE 12.1 Some common system privileges.

ALTER SESSION
ALTER SYSTEM
ALTER USER
AUDIT ANY
BACKUP ANY TABLE
CREATE PROCEDURE
CREATE ROLE
CREATE SEQUENCE
CREATE TABLE
CREATE TRIGGER
CREATE TYPE
CREATE USER
CREATE VIEW
DROP USER
FORCE TRANSACTION

TABLE 12.2 Common object privileges.

Privilege	Table	View	Sequence	Procedure, Function, or Package	User Defined Type
ALTER	X		X		
DELETE	X	X			
EXECUTE				X	X
DEBUG	X	X		X	X
FLASHBACK	X	X			
INDEX	X				
INSERT	X	X			
ON COMMIT REFRESH	X				
QUERY REWRITE	X				
REFERENCES	X	X			
SELECT	X	X	X		
UNDER		X			X
UPDATE	X	X			

on the Oracle SQL Reference documentation. It shows which privileges can be applied to each object type. The table leaves out a few objects and privileges that are not covered in this book. The Table, View, and Procedure privileges are the ones you will use the most.

You will primarily add object privileges to user roles. In fact, the challenge at this point is to identify all of the possible roles needed to use your application. Then you need to define the minimum object permissions needed by each role. Your goal is to provide the smallest set of roles possible to each role so those users can do their jobs effectively.

To identify the permissions you need to assign, you need to be familiar with the concept of *separation of duties*. The situation is emphasized in a classic accounting fraud that has happened many times in organizations with weak controls. A clerk in the purchasing department decides to make some extra money illegally. She sets up a fake supplier company and offers to sell items to your company for low prices. As a purchasing clerk with too much authority, she signs a contract with the firm and places an order. Later, she logs into the system to indicate that the products were received. The accounting department then sends a check to pay for the items—and the check goes to the address controlled by the purchasing clerk. The basic problem is that one person has control over too many steps in the process. As shown in Figure 12.3, you really should use four separate people to handle purchases: (1) a purchasing manager to sign new suppliers as the only person who can add insert rows into the supplier table; (2) a purchasing clerk who can insert rows into the Purchase and PurchaseItem tables but can only select suppliers already existing in the Supplier table; (3) a receiving clerk

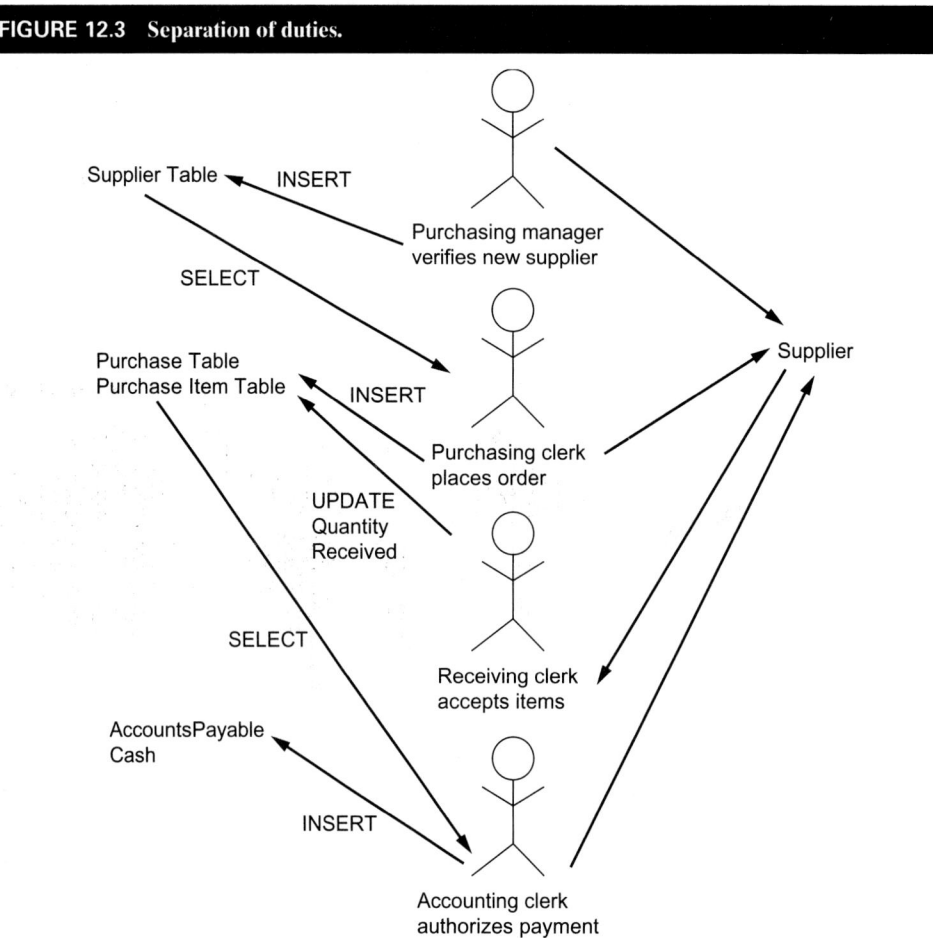

FIGURE 12.3 Separation of duties.

who logs the receipt of items ordered, who can only update the QuantityReceived values; and (4) an accounting clerk who can retrieve data from the three tables and record payments to suppliers in the basic accounting tables. In a tiny company, you might be able to combine a couple of the roles, but you should really keep at least two of them separate. The more people involved in a process, the harder it will be to get all of them to cooperate. That is, a company might accidentally hire one dishonest person, but it is unlikely that it will hire four into the same process. And even if it does, it will be difficult to get all four people to cooperate and remain quiet on a venture that could send them all to jail.

Now that you see the importance of separating jobs, you can start thinking about how to accomplish this process with the database object privileges. Figure 12.3 outlines the major steps. By controlling the permissions on each table, you can force different roles for each job. Of course, if someone assigns all four roles to the same person, it would defeat the purpose. This is yet another reason why it is critical to document your security design. At present, Oracle (or any other DBMS) does not have the ability to automatically control the way roles are assigned. So, you will have to write everything down.

At this point, you need to do three things:

1. Identify the primary objects in your database.
2. Identify the primary roles needed by users of the database, keeping in mind the importance of separation of duties.
3. Determine the permissions that each role needs for each object.

Keep in mind that you can limit object privileges in a table by column. In the purchasing example, you could restrict the receiving clerk to updating only the QuantityReceived column. The Enterprise version of Oracle also has a mechanism to limit access to data by row. For instance, in an employee table, you could restrict an employee to viewing only the single row that matches their EmployeeID. SELECT permissions are relatively easy to implement at the row level. But UPDATE controls require security configuration that requires considerable time and knowledge to set up, so that is not covered here. If you need complex row-level security controls, read the documentation about the *virtual private database (VPD)*.

CONTROLLING USER ACCESS TO OBJECTS

The GRANT and REVOKE statements are the foundation of SQL security. By default, users have almost no permissions, but it depends somewhat on how you create the user account. Using the Enterprise Manager, users are granted the predefined Connect role that contains the CREATE TABLE and a few other permissions you might not need to give to everyone. If you use SQL to create a user, that account initially has no permissions—not even the ability to log in. You should see what default access exists on user accounts before trying to assign new ones. If necessary, you can revoke some of the default privileges.

It can be difficult to assign security permissions properly. In fact, it requires considerable testing. You first go through the application and identify the basic roles and objects. It often helps to create a matrix and fill in the permissions you think each role needs for each object. Then you create the roles and create a sample test user for each major role. After you assign the security permissions, you need to test the entire application from the perspective of each user role. First, make sure that the user can perform all of the tasks required of that role. Second, try to attack the system as that user and make changes or deletions they should not be allowed to perform. Make sure the system stops them.

As you develop and test the permissions, you will almost always have to make modifications. The best approach is to write a PL/SQL script file that assigns all of the permissions. As you make changes, make them to the script file. Revoke all permissions, and then rerun the script file to apply the new versions. As you are testing, keep the older script file versions around in case you make too big of a change and need to go back to an earlier setting. When you are finally satisfied with the results, document the script and store it in a safe place. It provides a good record of the security policies and makes it easier for the security officer to make minor changes in the future.

Note that any GRANT statement can include the **WITH ADMIN** option at the end. This option is powerful and you should rarely use it. It gives the grantee permission to pass on the same privileges to someone else. In other words, you are giving away some of your control over who accesses the object to another person. If you just issue a simple GRANT statement, the recipient or grantee will gain those permissions. If someone else wants the same permissions, they have to come to you (or the DBA) and ask for a similar GRANT command. If you add the WITH ADMIN option, you allow someone to grant others the right to use the object. It can reduce your workload, but you need to really trust that person.

CREATING ROLES

For the Redwood Realty application, the two most important roles are Agent and Manager. You might consider adding application Administrator as a third role, but the company is small enough that it is probably better to let the managers perform those tasks as well. (For example, if the sole administrator is out of town, other managers might not know how to make changes.) But, you could create the Administrator role and simply assign it to all of the managers if you want to plan for future growth. For now, stick with the two basic roles and assume that managers can also be application administrators. The main thing an application administrator would need is the ability to change values in the lookup tables such as SaleStatus.

1. It is straightforward to create both the Agent and Manager roles:

```
CREATE ROLE Agent;
CREATE ROLE Manager;
```

> **Tip:** If you receive an error message, your account does not have permission. You will need the CREATE ROLE system privilege.

Note that these roles are currently empty—they provide no permissions to anything. Nonetheless, you can add them to the two sample users. We will assume for now that Marcoux is an agent and Carling is a manager. Ideally, you would know exactly who are managers and agents when testing, but it will work for now. In a real-world project, you would make a note in your calendar to remove the roles later.

2. Assigning the roles is also straightforward:

```
GRANT Agent to MarcouxK;
GRANT Manager to CarlingT;
```

You would assign the roles to the other users the same way. In fact, it would be a good place to use a substitution variable so you can quickly rerun a GRANT statement and just enter the new username. But you can do that later. The next step is to define the permissions that should be assigned to each role. As you add permissions to the role, the users will automatically acquire those permissions.

CHAPTER 12   Maintaining Database Security   **565**

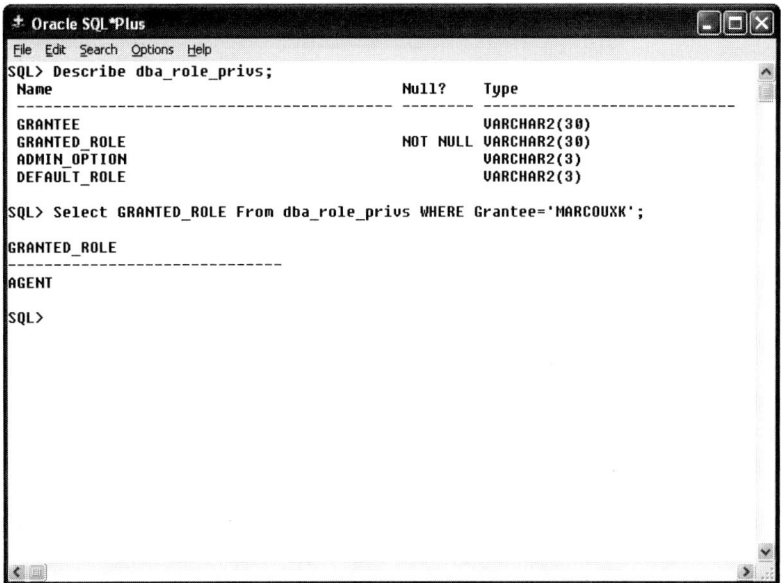

FIGURE 12.4   Using a DBA system table to list roles granted to a user.

You can find the roles assigned to a user, but you either need DBA permissions, or you have to be able to log on as that person. If you have DBA permissions, you can use the dba_role_privs table. The following code shows the table description and then displays the roles granted to MarcouxK:

```
Describe dba_role_privs;
Select GRANTED_ROLE From dba_role_privs WHERE Grantee='MARCOUXK';
```

Note that you must enter the username in upper case characters because that is the way Oracle stores them. Figure 12.4 verifies that MarcouxK has only the Agent role you have granted him.

If you have DBA permissions, you can also use the Enterprise Manager to list or change the roles for any user. If you do not have DBA permissions, you can only identify roles assigned to the current session. You can check your own roles, or you can log in as a user if you know the password. For example, you can log in with one of your test accounts. Use the session_roles view to get a list of the roles assigned:

```
SELECT Role FROM session_roles;
```

GRANTING AND REVOKING PERMISSIONS

The next planning step is to identify the major database objects. Table 12.3 shows the list of tables, forms, and reports along with the desired permissions for the two application roles. Notice that managers are going to be given full access to all of the objects. The one catch is that it is only access to the data not to the underlying table definitions. You do not want managers to have the ability to DROP or ALTER a table. Instead, a value of "All" simply means they have SELECT, INSERT, DELETE, and UPDATE permissions on the table.

Of course, the GRANT and REVOKE statements cannot be used with Oracle forms and reports. However, it is still useful to include them in the permissions table so that you remember to handle them later. In fact, one way to handle report permissions would be to control access to the views used to generate the reports. Even if an agent

TABLE 12.3 Desired permissions by object and role.

Database Object	Agent role	Manager role
Tables		
Agents	Select	All
ContactReason	Select	All
CustAgentList	All	All
Customers	All	All
LicenseStatus	Select?	All
Listings	All	All
Properties	All	All
SaleStatus	Select	All
Forms		
AgentContacts	All	All
AgentListings	All	All
Agents	None	All
ContactReason	None	All
Customers	All	All
LicenseStatus	None	All
ListingActivity	All	All
Listings	All	All
Management	None	All
Properties	All	All
SaleStatus	None	All
Search4	All	All
Startup	All	All
Reports		
AgentSales	Maybe for self	All
CustomerList	All	All
ListingsAndOffers	All	All
SalesByCityAndAgent	Maybe for self	All
SalesByMonthAndAgent	Maybe for self	All

managed to run a report based on its name, the report would simply generate an error message because it would not have access to the view needed to retrieve the data for the report.

For starters, you can add the SELECT permission to the Agent role for the four base tables (Agents, ContactReason, LicenseStatus, and SaleStatus).

1. You could write it as a single statement, but it is easier to read as four separate GRANT statements:

```
GRANT SELECT ON Agents TO Agent;
GRANT SELECT ON ContactReason TO Agent;
GRANT SELECT ON LicenseStatus TO Agent;
GRANT SELECT ON SaleStatus TO Agent;
```

2. Make sure that you create a SQL script file using WordPad or Notepad and add these four statements to the file. Save the file in your folder for this chapter.

3. Now add the broader permissions for the other four tables, and again copy the same list into your script file:

```
GRANT SELECT, UPDATE, INSERT, DELETE ON CustAgentList TO Agent;
GRANT SELECT, UPDATE, INSERT, DELETE ON Customers TO Agent;
GRANT SELECT, UPDATE, INSERT, DELETE ON Listings TO Agent;
GRANT SELECT, UPDATE, INSERT, DELETE ON Properties TO Agent;
```

4. The eight, relatively open permissions for the managers are straightforward. You should be able to use copy and edit functions in WordPad to create this list:

```
GRANT SELECT, UPDATE, INSERT, DELETE ON Agents TO Manager;
GRANT SELECT, UPDATE, INSERT, DELETE ON ContactReason TO Manager;
GRANT SELECT, UPDATE, INSERT, DELETE ON LicenseStatus TO Manager;
GRANT SELECT, UPDATE, INSERT, DELETE ON SaleStatus TO Manager;
GRANT SELECT, UPDATE, INSERT, DELETE ON CustAgentList TO Manager;
GRANT SELECT, UPDATE, INSERT, DELETE ON Customers TO Manager;
GRANT SELECT, UPDATE, INSERT, DELETE ON Listings TO Manager;
GRANT SELECT, UPDATE, INSERT, DELETE ON Properties TO Manager;
```

If you make a mistake or want to remove permissions, you can use the REVOKE command. In fact, you should include a series of REVOKE statements at the top of your permissions script of the form: REVOKE ALL ON Agents FROM Agent, Manager;

To set the permissions for the reports, you need to know what views are used for each report. You can open the Reports Builder and look them up. It turns out that all of the reports use their own internal queries to retrieve data directly from the underlying tables. Because agents and managers all have at least SELECT privileges on the tables, everyone will be able to view the reports. If you had found a view in one of the reports, you would need to assign the SELECT permissions to that view for the appropriate roles.

If you test the forms now, you will quickly find that there is one more significant problem: none of the forms will work. The problem is that every time a form is referenced in a query in a form, it uses the simple name of the table, such as Agents. But, the default schema for the MarcouxK is his own schema, not the Redwood schema. There are two basic ways to configure the system so MarcouxK can access tables in the Redwood schema: (1) Prefix every table and view reference with the schema name, such as Redwood.Agents, or (2) define a public synonym for every table and view. The public synonym approach is the easiest of the two (e.g., CREATE PUBLIC SYNONYM Agents FOR Redwood.Agents), but it requires that you have the system privilege to create a public synonym, or that you convince the database administrator to create them all for you. So, although it takes time, you can edit the forms and change all of the references to the tables and views.

5. Copy all forms and reports for the Redwood Realty application into a new folder for this chapter.

6. Open each of the forms, expand the **Data Blocks** node, edit the property **Query Data Source Name** and add *<your schema name>* as the prefix to any tables. For example, in the **AgentListings** form for the **Listings** data block if the schema is Redwood:

```
(SELECT ListingID, Listings.PropertyID, ListingAgentID, SaleStatusID,
BeginListDate, EndListDate, AskingPrice, HousePhoto, Bedrooms, Bathrooms,
Stories, SQFT, YearBuilt FROM Redwood.Listings INNER JOIN
Redwood.Properties ON
Redwood.Listings.PropertyID=Redwood.Properties.PropertyID)
```

7. Do the same thing for the all of the data block. Remember to change the queries for the **Record Groups** that drive the LOVs. Repeat the process for all of the forms. Is it too late to beg the database administrator for permission to create public synonyms?

Now it is time to test the application.

8. Start **Forms Builder** and open the **Startup** form and edit the initial trigger code so that the global variables point to the new location for your files. Save and compile the form.

568 Introduction to Oracle

9. Use **File/Disconnect** to log yourself out, or close the Forms Builder and restart it. Run Startup and log in as agent MarcouxK/changeme. Work through the forms and reports. Most of them should work. Since Marcoux is an agent, you should be able to see the data in the manager's forms but not change it or add a record.

10. When you test the Search form, it will not work. Why not? Because the form is based on the ListingResults view and you have not yet assigned permissions to that view. Add a line to your permissions script file and run it in SQL*Plus under your login name, and then retest the Search form.

    `GRANT SELECT ON ListingResults TO Agent, Manager;`

    If you have DBA privileges, you can use the dba_tab_privs system table to list all of the privileges that have been granted to either the roles or individual users. The most useful version of the command is:

    `SELECT table_name, privilege FROM dba_tab_privs WHERE Grantee='AGENT';`

    At this point, all of the forms should work. You should also test the forms with the CarlingT login as a manager. Also check the reports.

ENFORCING PRIVILEGES THROUGH VIEWS AND PROCEDURES

By now, you should be aware of some of the problems with using simple privileges on tables. It is difficult to provide the granularity you want. *Granularity* is the ability to specify permissions at detailed levels. For example, you might want to limit access to specific columns or even rows. Technically, the GRANT command allows you to set access to individual columns, but it does not work for rows, so you need other solutions.

You need to know about a couple of useful tricks for limiting access to data in a database. Two of the most powerful tricks are to assign user and role permissions to Views and Procedures instead of giving users access to the base tables. Remember that you can create a view using any tables, columns, and rows that you want. You can name the view almost anything—just not the same as an existing table or reserved word. If users only need to see the data, you simply create the view, restricting the columns or rows that it retrieves, then give the users access to the view but not to the underlying tables.

Views work well for SELECT statements when you need to limit the data that an individual or group can see. They are less useful when you need to allow users to update the data. First, views are not reliably updateable unless they are based on a single table. Second, it is hard to control the update process with a view. When you need to control updates, the best approach is to create a stored procedure that does the update. Then give users access to the procedure and not to the underlying tables. The issues behind these tricks can seem difficult. It is easiest to understand the reasons by looking at a specific case.

Views are useful for restricting access to reports. The Reports Builder generally creates an internal query that pulls data from the underlying tables. You can turn that query into a saved view, base the form on the view, and restrict the permissions to that view. Then even if users guess the name of a report, they will not be able to run it.

1. Start the Reports Builder and open the SalesByMonthAndAgent report. Expand the Queries node under the Data Model node. Open the Property Palette for the Q_1 query, and open the SQL editor by clicking the **SQL Query Statement** property.

2. You need to edit the query slightly, so start Notepad and paste the query into it. Edit the WHERE clause to remove the SaleStatusID line with the bind variable. Add SaleStatusID to the SELECT statement and add the CREATE VIEW line at

the top. Copy the new statement and start SQL*Plus. Paste the command and run it. If you receive an error message, clean up the query and try again.

```
CREATE OR REPLACE VIEW SalesByMonthAndAgent AS
SELECT ALL AGENTS.LASTNAME, AGENTS.FIRSTNAME, SALESTATUS.SALESTATUSID,
LISTINGS.ASKINGPRICE, TO_CHAR(LISTINGS.ENDLISTDATE, 'MM') SALEMONTH
FROM AGENTS, LISTINGS, SALESTATUS
WHERE ((LISTINGS.LISTINGAGENTID = AGENTS.AGENTID)
  AND (LISTINGS.SALESTATUSID = SALESTATUS.SALESTATUSID))
ORDER BY AGENTS.LASTNAME ASC, AGENTS.FIRSTNAME ASC;
```

3. Back in the Reports Builder, replace the Q_1 query with a call to the new view. Make sure you include the correct schema (e.g., Redwood).

```
SELECT ALL LASTNAME, FIRSTNAME, ASKINGPRICE, SALEMONTH
FROM Redwood.SalesByMonthAndAgent
WHERE SaleStatusID = :SALE_STATUS
```

4. Return to SQL*Plus to give managers the right to view the query:

```
GRANT SELECT ON SalesByMonthAndAgent TO Manager;
```

5. In the Reports Builder, you need to add the schema to the LOV for the user parameters. Expand the Data Model and User Parameter nodes. Open the Property Palette for the SALE_STATUS item. Click the **List of Values** property and add the schema name to the tables listed in the SQL query.

```
SELECT ALL  SALESTATUSID, SALESTATUS
FROM Redwood.SALESTATUS
ORDER BY SALESTATUS ASC
```

6. Run the form and use File/Disconnect to test it with both the CarlingT (works) and MarcouxK (should not work) logins.

Controlling access to the views makes it more difficult for unauthorized users to see the reports. However, because the workers have access to the underlying tables, they could still retrieve the data themselves and create their own reports with some other tool. Restricting employees to seeing only data that refers to them is more challenging.

RESTRICTING ACCESS TO SELECTED ROWS AND COLUMNS

The trick of using a view to limit a SELECT statement is the easiest. You already know how to write a SELECT statement to pick individual columns and rows. You know how to turn the SELECT statement into a stored view.

1. Logged in as yourself, create a view for Redwood Realty that displays listings for sales agent Marcoux. To keep it easy, just use his ID number (10041):

```
Create View MarcouxListings AS
SELECT * FROM Listings
WHERE ListingAgentID=10041;
```

2. Now, grant Marcoux access to this view, but do not give permissions to anything else:

```
GRANT SELECT ON Redwood.MarcouxListings TO MarcouxK;
```

Note that you must include the Redwood prefix to indicate the schema. If you leave off the Redwood schema, you would be granting Marcoux access to a MarcouxListings view or table in his own schema—which does not exist.

3. You always have to test your security permission assignments, so log in as Marcoux using his username and password, but plug in the correct name of the server:

   ```
   Connect MarcouxK/changeme@server_name
   ```

4. Test the view permissions:

   ```
   SELECT ListingID, PropertyID, ListingAgentID, BeginListDate
   FROM Redwood.MarcouxListings;
   ```

5. Ensure that Marcoux does not have access to the underlying Listings table:

   ```
   SELECT * FROM Redwood.Listings;
   ```

6. Open a second SQL*Plus window logging in as yourself. You will want to be able to make changes in one window and test them in the other.

Figure 12.5 shows the results of the two queries. The rows from the view correspond to the AgentID for Marcoux, and he can see no other rows. Even if he guesses the name of the underlying Listings table, he cannot retrieve any data from it. In fact, the system will not even acknowledge that the table exists. You can save complex queries as views to control confidentiality—as long as you do not need to use the view to update data.

Of course, it will be a little painful to create different views for every single employee. To make the process easier, you can add a username column to the Agents table. Then you can pick up the username of the current user from the User system variable and restrict the rows based on that value. The detailed steps are not listed here because you will use a similar process in the next section to control updates.

RESTRICTING UPDATES THROUGH PROCEDURES

What happens when you do want users to update the database? Because the MarcouxListings view is based on a single table, you can update it. So, you could

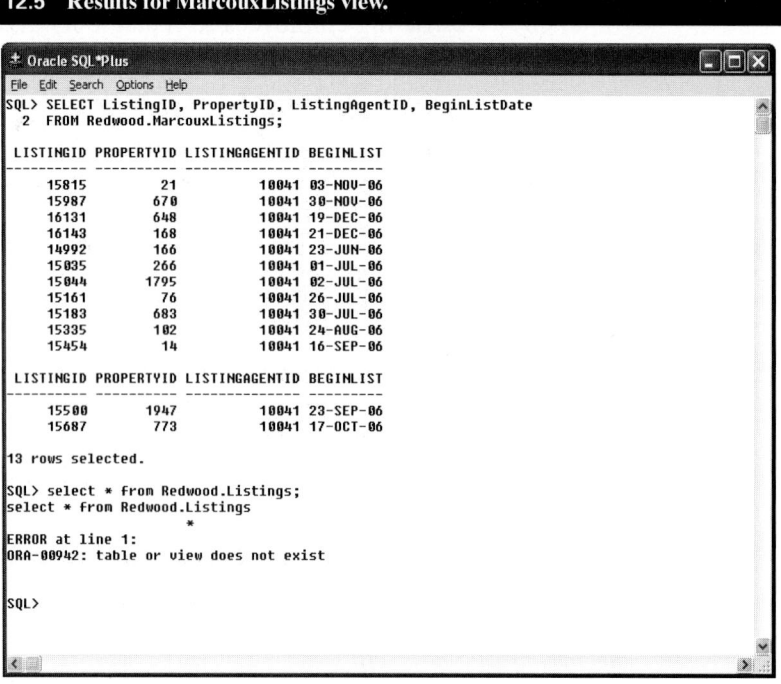

FIGURE 12.5 Results for MarcouxListings view.

CHAPTER 12 Maintaining Database Security **571**

change the permissions so that Marcoux can insert rows into the view, which passes them through to the underlying Listings table using your own login:

```
Grant Insert on Redwood.MarcouxListings to MarcouxK;
```

1. You can now switch to the MarcouxK login and try to insert a row:

```
Insert Into Redwood.MarcouxListings (ListingID, PropertyID,
ListingAgentID, SaleStatusID)
Values (99, 773, 10041, 101);
Commit;
```

2. The INSERT command works. Since this data row is meaningless, you should really switch to your login and delete it:

```
DELETE FROM Listings WHERE ListingID=99;
```

The command seems to have worked fine. What is the security problem?

3. To see some of the problems, switch to the MarcouxK log in and try this insert:

```
Insert Into Redwood.MarcouxListings (ListingID, PropertyID,
ListingAgentID, SaleStatusID)
Values (98, 773, 12963, 101);
Commit;
```

Again, the INSERT command works. Again, you should switch to your login and delete ListingID=98. But, do you see the potential security problem? Marcoux just inserted a false listing for a different agent (Reed). Ultimately, you would want to give additional permissions to the Listings table through the MarcouxListings view. Each additional permission would give Marcoux the ability to make greater changes to the underlying table—even to rows that he does not own.

The answer is to create a procedure that does a tightly controlled update and then give Marcoux permissions only to the procedure.

4. First, revoke his ability to insert data through the view:

```
REVOKE Insert ON Redwood.MarcouxListings FROM MarcouxK;
```

The basic goal at this point is to create a procedure that adds new listings to the database. It should be capable of working for any agent and should automatically insert the ListingID, the agent's ID value, and the For Sale (101) code. Ideally, you would also pick up the PropertyID value from an input form. For example, the agent would go to the Property form to enter the data on the new property and the owner contact information. After entering the listing dates and asking price, the user would click a button and the form would call this procedure and write the data to the Listings table.

5. To have the system automatically generate the ListingID, you will need a sequence for the Listings table, so as the Redwood owner, create the new sequence:

```
CREATE SEQUENCE seq_Listings
INCREMENT BY 1
START WITH 20000;
```

The next step is a little trickier. You want the procedure to identify the agent and find his or her AgentID so it can be inserted correctly. The trick is to create a new column in the Agents table that contains the username for each agent. You could enter each username by hand, but it is easier to use a process and assign usernames as Lastname plus first initial.

6. Add a new Username column to the Agents table and set the default username:

```
ALTER TABLE Agents
ADD (Username   VARCHAR2(100));
UPDATE Agents
SET Username = LastName || SUBSTR(FirstName,1,1);
Commit;
```

Finally, you can create the new procedure that adds new rows to the Listings table:

```
Create or Replace Procedure AddAgentListing(
      PropertyID NUMBER,
      BeginListDate DATE,
      EndListDate DATE,
      AskingPrice NUMBER)
AS
BEGIN
DECLARE
      nAgentID NUMBER;
BEGIN
      SELECT AgentID INTO nAgentID
      FROM Agents WHERE UPPER(Username)=User;

      INSERT INTO Listings (ListingID, PropertyID, ListingAgentID,
            SaleStatusID, BeginListDate, EndListDate, AskingPrice)
      VALUES (
            seq_Listings.NextVal,
            AddAgentListing.PropertyID,
            nAgentID,
            101,
            AddAgentListing.BeginListDate,
            AddAgentListing.EndListDate,
            AddAgentListing.AskingPrice
      );
      COMMIT;
END;
END;
```

The code really has only one trick in it: it uses the User system variable to pick up the username of the agent who is logged in and running the procedure. It uses the Username to look up the matching AgentID. From there, it does a straightforward INSERT on the Listings table. Notice that all of the key values except PropertyID are completely controlled by this procedure. The user does not see those values and cannot change them.

7. Give MarcouxK and other agents the ability to execute this new procedure:

```
GRANT EXECUTE ON AddAgentListing TO Agent;
```

8. Now, switch to the MarcouxK login and test the procedure:

```
EXEC Redwood.AddAgentListing(773, '01-MAR-2006', '01-JUL-2006', 150000);
```

Again, you should switch back to your own login and delete this entry. It will probably have ListingID=20000, but you should check the Listings for AgentID=10041 to be safe, since you might have run the sequence generator a couple of times and changed the value.

If you look closely at the code, you see that the heart is really just a simple INSERT statement. So, the code is not overly difficult to create or implement. However, do you really need to go through this much work? Can you just give agents INSERT, UPDATE, and maybe DELETE access to the underlying Listings table? Well, only you can answer those questions because the answer depends on the specific problem and the company. In the case of a mid-size real estate agency, you can probably argue that the data is not that critical and the owner might trust the agents. But, there is a slight risk that a disgruntled employee could delete or alter important rows of data.

VIRTUAL PRIVATE DATABASE AND LABEL SECURITY

The concept of a virtual private database is relatively new. The goal of a VPD is to restrict the data that users can see to just the data that is somehow related to them. For example, an employee would be able to see and edit only the rows of data about her. A manager would be able to see employee records for all employees in his division. A customer would be able to see its own orders but none of the others. Essentially, the VPD shows the tables and data as if they contain only data about the restricted person or company.

The VPD accomplishes its work by creating views with an additional WHERE clause. It works the same as the methods discussed in the earlier sections. The difference is that once you configure the VPD, it automatically alters all of the queries. That process is good and bad. It is easier to set up by novices, but you have less control over the process. You configure a VPD by establishing fine-grained policies on each table, view, or other object. You can use the Oracle Policy Manager to help you define the policies. Or you can use the SYS_CONTEXT and DBMS_RLS packages to define the restrictions manually. Either way, you need the DBA role to establish these policies.

Oracle has also implemented a *label security* system. Label security is similar to an approach used by many national security and military organizations. It assigns a security level to each piece of data—such as top-secret, secret, or confidential. It also assigns security clearance levels to users and various objects. So, you can only view top-secret data if you have top secret clearance. It is essentially a backup security system. Even if you have top-secret clearance, the access control system limits the data you can see based on your need to know or use that data. Yet, if the access control system is set incorrectly or someone bypasses it, the label system will prevent a low-security clearance person from viewing top-secret data. You have to install the virtual private database toolkit to use the label security system.

LIMITING ACCESS WITHIN AN APPLICATION

The third way to provide detailed controls for viewing or changing data is to write additional security controls directly into the application forms. Look at the Startup and Management forms for the Redwood Realty case again. Moving the management reports to the Management form makes them less obvious to the agents. However, nothing prevents the agents from exploring the application and clicking on the Management button to see the reports. You should consider hiding the Management button so that it can only be seen and used by managers.

The basic approach is to make the Management button invisible by default. You can write trigger code so that when a manager is logged into the system, the Management button is made visible. With the system User variable, you could even control the appearance and access to buttons based on individual users.

1. Start the **Forms Builder** and open the **Startup** form. Open the **Property Palette** for the **Management** button and set **Visible=No**.

The next step is to make the button visible if a manager is logged in. You look at the Session_Roles view to see if the Manager role is assigned. If so, you make the Management button visible. You have to perform the test when the Startup form begins. But, you should create it as a separate function in case you need it later.

2. Select the **Program Units** node in the Object Navigator and click the **Create** button. Choose the option to create a function and name it **IsManager**. Edit the resulting template to return a **Number** and add the code to check the Session_Roles:

```
FUNCTION IsManager RETURN Number IS
BEGIN
    DECLARE
        nRoles NUMBER;
    BEGIN
        SELECT Count(Role) INTO nRoles FROM Session_Roles
        WHERE Role='MANAGER';
        Return nRoles;
    END;
END;
```

3. In the Startup form's **When-New-Form-Instance** trigger, you need to create a global variable to hold the result of the IsManager function so you can use it in other forms. Then test the value to determine if you should make the Management button visible. Add these lines at the end of the existing statements:

```
:GLOBAL.IsManager := IsManager();
IF (:GLOBAL.IsManager > 0) THEN
    SET_ITEM_PROPERTY('BTN_MANAGEMENT', VISIBLE, PROPERTY_TRUE);
    SET_ITEM_PROPERTY('BTN_MANAGEMENT', ENABLED, PROPERTY_TRUE);
END IF;
```

4. Compile and save the function and trigger code changes. Compile the Startup form and run it.

> **Tip:** If you receive an error regarding the Session_Roles table during compilation, use File/Connect to make sure you are logged in to the database.

When you run the form, test run it with the MarcouxK login because he does not have the Manager role. Figure 12.6 shows that Agent users will not see the Management button, so they will not be able to run any of the managerial tools from the Startup form. You should use a similar process to disable any management forms or reports on the main menu.

From a security perspective, this solution is not perfect, because it is mostly cosmetic. A user who knew the name of the Management form could edit the URL in the browser and open the form directly. This approach means the global variables are not available, so the other forms and reports probably will not open until the person finds a way to define them separately. The point is that you should add an additional test to each management form to ensure that only managers can run them.

5. Open the Management form and create a **When-New-Form-Instance** trigger. Add the following code:

```
BEGIN
    DEFAULT_VALUE(0, 'GLOBAL.IsManager');
    IF (:GLOBAL.IsManager < 1) THEN
        EXIT_FORM;
    END IF;
    IF (Not Form_Success) THEN
        EXIT_FORM;
    END IF;
EXCEPTION
    WHEN OTHERS THEN
        EXIT_FORM;
END;
```

CHAPTER 12 Maintaining Database Security

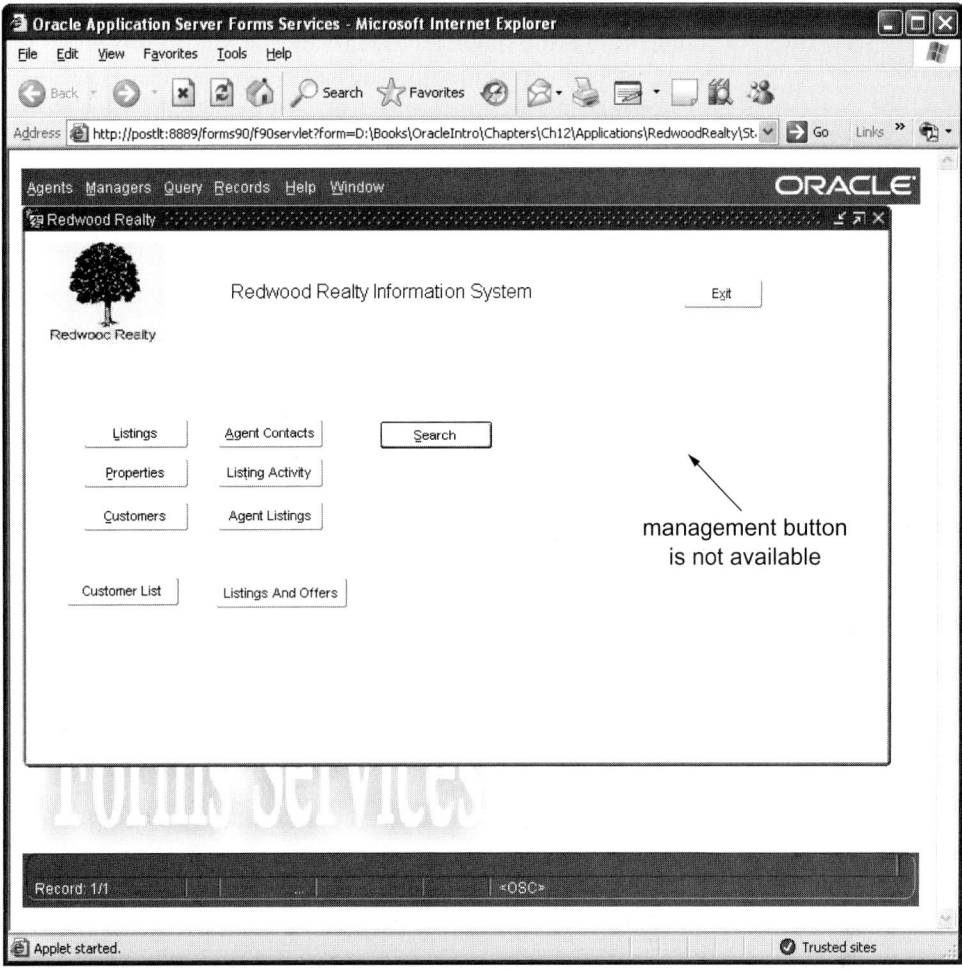

FIGURE 12.6 Startup form run by an agent without the Manager role.

The basic code consists of the initial IF statement which closes the form if the user is not recognized as a manager. However, to prevent the form from crashing when the global variable is not defined, you first have to define a default value for the GLOBAL.IsManager variable. The code also contains two error trapping tests to ensure that you catch all possible errors and still close the form. You can copy this code and put it in the startup triggers for all of the managerial forms.

PROTECTING DATA WITH ENCRYPTION

Encryption is a powerful tool in security, but you need to understand what it can and cannot do. *Encryption* mixes plain-text data with a key value and produces a scrambled encrypted text that hides the original data. Encryption today is commonly discussed in two categories: single key and dual key. With single or symmetric key encryption, the same key is used to encrypt and decrypt the data. With dual or public key encryption, two keys are required. You can encrypt the data with either key, but only the other key will decrypt it. The main advantage of single key encryption is that high-speed algorithms can rapidly encrypt and decrypt data with minimal performance issues. The primary drawback to single key encryption is that it is difficult to protect and distribute the single key. Dual key encryption solves the key-distribution problem but the speed is considerably slower. Most practical systems use dual-key encryption for transmitting messages, and single-key encryption for storing data. Even then, the systems often rely on dual-key simply to distribute a one-time single key that is used for the duration of the session.

Securing Internet Transmissions

Since version 9i, Oracle has concentrated on delivering forms and reports over the Internet. The Web-based approach makes it much easier to distribute applications since users need only a Web browser and an account on the server, and no complex configuration on their individual machines. However, the Internet is an open network where data passes through many different locations on the way from the client to the server. It would be relatively easy for someone to intercept communications and read the data or even make changes to the data. The interception is even easier if the user is on a wireless connection.

Of course, the interception problem exists for any application run over the Internet. The standard solution is to encrypt the transmissions. The requirement for encryption is so common that it is built into the Web browsers. Because the need for encryption is so great, a few companies provide commercial solutions for Web servers. Most use the **secure sockets layer (SSL)** approach originally developed by Netscape. Provisions for SSL are built into most existing Web browsers and servers. However, to configure SSL, you need to obtain a **digital security certificate**. SSL works by creating and exchanging session keys using a **public-key infrastructure (PKI)** approach. The main feature of PKI is that it uses two keys, one private and one public, to encrypt and decrypt data. Several sources explain the usage in more detail, but essentially you encrypt a message with one key and decrypt it with the other. You make one key public and keep the other safe on the server. So, the Web browser can encrypt a message with the public key, and that message is safe because the only way it can be decrypted is by using the super secret private key stored on the server. So, where do you get a super secret private key? That is the point of the digital security certificate. It is used to generate the two keys, and it is used to verify the identity of the company or person that runs the server. The bottom line is that you have to buy a security certificate from a trusted third party (Verisign is currently the largest vendor). Actually, if you are only going to use the security within your own company, you can create your own security certificate.

Once you have a security certificate, install it on your Web server. The process varies depending on the operating system of the server, but you can find instructions on the Web for all common servers. Basically, you set up a new folder and tell the server to encrypt any data being sent to or from that folder and its subfolders. Then you move your application files into the secure folder and configure the ApplicationPath and the OracleAS server configuration files. Users open the Startup form using https on the address line, and all transmissions are encrypted automatically. Figure 12.7 shows the basic process. Even if the user is on a wireless network and someone intercepts the public key or the encrypted data, they will not be able to decrypt the message—because that can only be done with the server's private key.

Encrypting Selected Data in the Database

Generally, you will use access controls to control who can retrieve and change data in your database. However, in some cases you will want to provide additional protection. Think about what can happen if someone steals your main customer order database

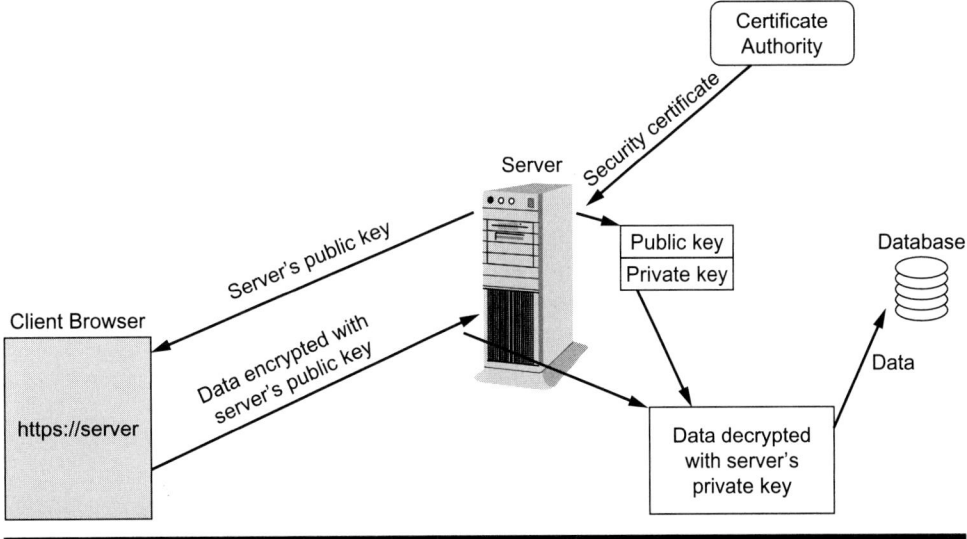

FIGURE 12.7 Public key encryption.

files. With some effort, the attacker might be able to read through the data files and retrieve customer credit card numbers. In California (and other states soon), you would have to notify all of your customers about the breach in security. To protect yourself legally and in terms of public relations, you should encrypt all sensitive data including credit card numbers and national identity or social security numbers.

Oracle provides the dbms_crypto package for PL/SQL that contains industry standard encryption algorithms. You can use this tool to encrypt your data before you store it in the database. However, it is not an automatic process. For one thing, the database administrator has to grant you execute access on the dbms_crypto utilities. This grant must be done while logged in as the sysdba. If you are running your own database server, try logging into SQL*Plus, then:

```
Connect sys/<sys password>@servername as sysdba
Grant Execute on dbms_crypto to <your username>
Disconnect
```

At this point, you can now use the encryption routines in the dbms_crypto package from your account. If you cannot obtain these permissions, you can simply read through the code. These steps are only an introduction. The basic functions are based on examples in the Oracle documentation. Check out the documentation on PL/SQL packages. The following code creates a simple test procedure that encrypts a string and decrypts it:

```
SET SERVEROUTPUT ON
CREATE OR REPLACE PROCEDURE TestEncrypt AS
BEGIN
DECLARE
        input_string VARCHAR2(22) := 'This is plaintext data';
        enc_type Number := dbms_crypto.DES_CBC_PKCS5;
        key_string VARCHAR2(11) := 'my password';
        raw_key RAW(128) := UTL_I18N.STRING_TO_RAW(key_string, 'AL32UTF8');
        encrypted_raw RAW(2048);
        encrypted_string VARCHAR2(2048);
        decrypted_raw RAW(2048);
        decrypted_string VARCHAR2(2048);
```

```
        BEGIN
            dbms_output.put_line('> Input String : ' || input_string);
            dbms_output.put_line('> ========= BEGIN TEST Encrypt =========');
            encrypted_raw := dbms_crypto.Encrypt(
                src => UTL_I18N.STRING_TO_RAW(input_string, 'AL32UTF8'),
                typ => enc_type,
                key => raw_key);
            dbms_output.put_line('> Encrypted hex value : ' ||
                rawtohex(UTL_RAW.CAST_TO_RAW(encrypted_raw)));
            decrypted_raw := dbms_crypto.Decrypt(
                src => encrypted_raw,
                typ => enc_type,
                key => raw_key);
            decrypted_string := CONVERT(UTL_RAW.CAST_TO_VARCHAR2
                (decrypted_raw),'US7ASCII','AL32UTF8');

            dbms_output.put_line(
                '> Decrypted string output : ' || decrypted_string);
            IF input_string = decrypted_string THEN
                dbms_output.put_line(
                    '> String DES Encryption and Decryption successful');
            END if;
    END;
END;
/
```

Test the function by entering **exec TestEncrypt.** Figure 12.8 shows the call and the results. It is straightforward to change the original text or the text used as the key. It takes several more complex steps to use this code to store and retrieve encrypted data in the database. Again, the Oracle security documentation contains more detailed

FIGURE 12.8 Encryption test results.

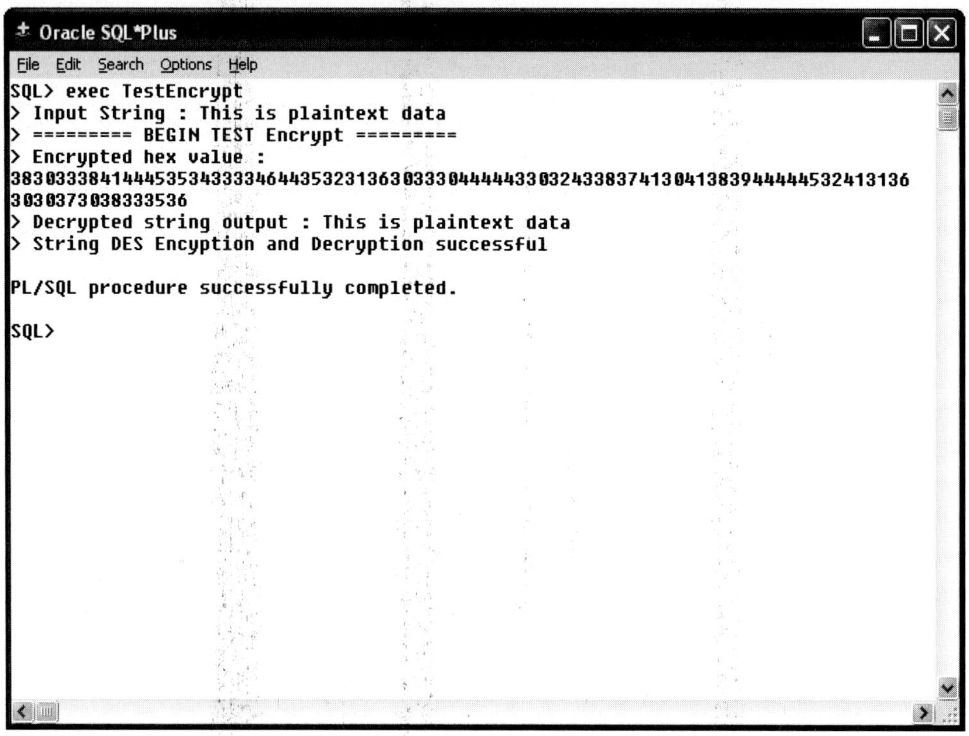

```
SQL> exec TestEncrypt
> Input String : This is plaintext data
> ========= BEGIN TEST Encrypt =========
> Encrypted hex value :
38303338414445353433334644353231363033304444443303243383741304138394444453241 3136
30303730383335 36
> Decrypted string output : This is plaintext data
> String DES Encyption and Decryption successful

PL/SQL procedure successfully completed.

SQL>
```

examples. To store data, the basic process is to replace the standard INSERT code with a trigger that first encrypts each row of data. To retrieve data, you can use a view that calls a stored decryption function.

Recall that the main problem with symmetric keys is that you have to store and distribute it somehow. The problem of storing the encryption key is difficult in the case of encrypting and decrypting data in the database. Where can you put this secret key so that it is secure, yet accessible? The Oracle documentation gives several ideas, but they all have issues. The easiest approach is to embed the key in your procedure code as shown in the example, but if someone breaks into the database they could find the key and use it to decrypt the data. Another possibility is to store it in a file on the server and use operating system controls and a second level of encryption to protect it. But, no approach is going to be perfect. That is a key fact in security: perfection is impossible. You have to find the level that is appropriate for each situation.

PROTECTING SOURCE CODE WITH WRAP

The wrap utility is not exactly an encryption tool, but it does something similar. It renames all variables and mangles your PL/SQL source code to make it difficult for humans to read. The program code still executes correctly on the computer. With this utility, you can distribute your code to customers or install it on your servers. If someone did manage to steal the code, it would be substantially more difficult for them to read it or understand what it does. It would not be impossible, but probably difficult enough to stop most snoopers. You can find more information on the wrap utility in Oracle's security documentation. It runs as a command-line application outside of Oracle with the syntax:

```
wrap iname=input_file [oname=outputfile]
```

Once you wrap PL/SQL script file, you will not be able to edit it. To make changes, you will have to edit the original source file and wrap it again. So, make sure you have secure storage for all of your source files. Also, note that the wrap utility does not obfuscate trigger code. You will have to create separate procedures that are protected and call that procedure from the trigger event.

If you use any of the encryption systems, you need to be sure to use the wrap utility on all of the encryption packages—particularly if you store the key inside the procedure. Even if you store the key in some other manner, you still need to obfuscate the code that retrieves it to make it more difficult for someone to reverse-engineer the process.

AUDITING THE DATABASE

Auditing or monitoring database activity can be a key element in a security plan. Simply setting permissions and encrypting data are not sufficient. At some level, you need to observe the activities in the database so that you can spot problems before they get out of control. Auditing has several benefits:

- It can identify undesirable actions and track which people (accounts) performed those actions.
- By informing everyone of the monitoring, it can deter people who might stray into unacceptable actions.
- It can provide a trail for investigators and legal action.
- It can provide detailed data on how the database is used, helping the DBA tune the database.
- By detecting problems, it can give you better information to help redesign the security permissions.

TABLE 12.4 Oracle auditing types.

Type of Auditing	Description
Statement Auditing	Tracks activity by the type of statement. For example, AUDIT TABLE tracks several DDL statements regardless of the table involved. A broad-based tracking, but it can be applied to individual users or to everyone.
Privilege Auditing	Monitors the use of system privileges such as AUDIT CREATE TABLE. Can be assigned to track individual users or everyone.
Schema Object Auditing	Records the usage of specific statements on individual objects. For instance, AUDIT SELECT ON customers records a note every time someone retrieves data from the customer table. Always applies to all users.
Fine-Grained Auditing	The most detailed specifications, you can create any Boolean condition based on individual columns or specific rows of data. For example, you might track all orders with a value > 100,000.

Auditing tracks user activities and records them to a separate secure location. Of course, that means auditing can quickly generate huge amounts of data. Consequently, you have to decide exactly what types of events and actions you want to monitor. For normal operations, you might choose a small list of critical items to monitor. If you encounter problems or see suspicious activity, you would turn on additional auditing features. Oracle supports many different levels of auditing, divided into the four main categories listed in Table 12.4.

Audits record the name of the operation being performed, the object affected, the user performing the operation, and the date and time of the action. Audit records can be stored in the database itself or written to an operating system file. You store records in the sys.aud$ table using the DBA_AUDIT_TRAIL option. Audit records written to the database contain more information than those written to an operating system audit trail. Note that your database can encounter problems if you run out of space either for the database audit records or in the operating system file. Because detailed audits can record huge amounts of data, someone will have to monitor these files carefully.

You can use the audit statements to trace successfully completed commands (WHENEVER SUCCESSFUL), unsuccessful operations (WHENEVER UNSUCCESSFUL), or both. Sometimes the unsuccessful commands provide the most pertinent information about an attack. If your permissions are set correctly and someone tries to retrieve or delete data, the audit trail will show the attempt.

Oracle also has a separate provision to audit all actions taken using the powerful sysdba and sysoper logins. The AUDIT_SYS_OPERATIONS option records every successful SQL statement to a secure operating system file. A company might use this option to monitor activities by DBAs. A DBA normally has relatively open access to the entire database, and you really have to trust your DBAs. However, if the need arises, you can track the important actions taken by the DBA. Actually, the Oracle system automatically tracks anytime someone connects as sysdba or sysoper. It also always records when a database is started or shut down.

You need access to the fine-grained auditing package (DBMS_FGA) to create detailed audit commands. Using this tool, the security administrator can also create a new event handler. In addition to writing the data to a file, the administrator could write a procedure to send a security alert message or even to shut down certain users or packages.

ENABLING AUDITING

By default, auditing is disabled when an Oracle database is installed. To enable auditing, you have to alter a parameter in one of the configuration files. That means you also have to shut down and restart the database for the change to take effect. You need to be the database owner and the DBA to make this change. If you are running Oracle on your own machine, it is no problem. If you are running on a shared machine, you probably will not be able to get this change made. However, once auditing is enabled, you should be able to write audit statements on objects that you created.

If you are running your own copy of Oracle, you should be able to edit the database initialization file. You can only change the initialization parameters as system DBA. You can try the following steps if you are running Oracle on your own computer, but do not even think about trying them if it is a shared machine.

1. Start SQL*Plus and log in as sys/password@server as sysdba. Set the auditing parameter with the command:

   ```
   ALTER SYSTEM set audit_trail=DB_EXTENDED SCOPE=SPFILE;
   ```

   The DB_EXTENDED parameter stores the SQL statement to make it easier to read the log file. If you just use the DB value, the log file is smaller, but it keeps only the type of statement, not the actual command.

2. The change will not take effect until you restart Oracle. You can try the **SHUTDOWN** command. Wait a couple of minutes and use the Windows Computer Management tool to verify that the Oracle database service is stopped.

3. Restart the database. You can try **STARTUP** in SQL*Plus, but you might have to reboot the server to get all services restarted. When the server restarts, log into SQL*Plus again as sysdba and verify that it picked up the change:

   ```
   Show parameter audit_trail
   ```

If you are working on a shared machine that has been configured for auditing, you can perform these next steps. The simplified format for starting an audit record is:

```
AUDIT <SQL statement> [ON <schema object>]
      [BY <user>]
      [WHENEVER [NOT] SUCCESSFUL]
```

Other options exist, including the ability to write records every time the statement is issued (BY ACCESS) or only write a record once per session to save log space (BY SESSION). Also, notice that you can specify a statement or a statement group without providing an object. This approach records all usages of that statement, regardless of the object. This broad approach tends to generate huge log files, so you should avoid it. However, it is useful for some commands that are rarely issued. For example, AUDIT ROLE or AUDIT ROLE WHENEVER NOT SUCCESSFUL.

1. Start a second version of SQL*Plus and log in with your normal Redwood user account. You are concerned about changes to the employee Agents table, so set audits for any insert or delete commands on that table.

   ```
   AUDIT INSERT on Agents;
   AUDIT DELETE on Agents;
   ```

   Notice that these commands do not have the WHENEVER clause, so they will record all insert and delete commands on the Agents table whether they are successful or not.

2. Create a new agent and delete the row to test the auditing:

```
INSERT INTO Agents(AgentID, Firstname, Lastname)
VALUES (99, 'Barbara', 'Feldon');
commit;
DELETE FROM Agents
WHERE AgentID=99;
commit;
```

You do not want to leave auditing running on a development machine because it will generate too many records, and you will probably forget to clean them up. Plus, the data is not all that useful. So, if you are running your own machine, turn off the auditing.

3. Under your normal user account, you can stop the individual audits you created using the NoAudit command:

```
NOAUDIT INSERT on Agents;
NOAUDIT DELETE on Agents;
```

Viewing Audit Trails

If you are running Oracle on a Windows computer and choose the option to write audit logs to the operating system, all information is written to the standard Event Viewer log. Assuming you have the correct operating system privileges (e.g., a member of the Administrators group), you can use Start/Programs/Administrative Tools/Event Viewer to see or delete the records. You have minimal searching and sorting capabilities in the Event Viewer, but you can save the events to a text file and use other tools to search it.

When you choose the option to store audit data to the database, the records are stored in the sys.aud$ table. You should have SELECT privileges on this table for entries made due to your audit commands. You can write any standard SELECT statement to choose columns, select rows, or sort the listings.

1. To see the events that were logged, format the output and issue a standard SELECT statement:

```
SET linesize 150
COLUMN NTIMESTAMP# FORMAT DATETIME
COLUMN UserID FORMAT A15
COLUMN OBJ$NAME FORMAT A20
COLUMN SQLTEXT FORMAT A40
SELECT TO_CHAR(NTimeStamp#, 'YYYY-MM-DD HH24:MI:SS') AS Time, UserID,
OBJ$NAME,
SQLTEXT FROM sys.aud$;
```

Figure 12.9 shows the sample output. Note that you might not see the second entry for the DELETE command until after you log off the session. In a production system you would eventually have thousands or hundreds of thousands of rows in the audit table—depending on the items you choose to audit.

If you are running your own server, you should also turn off the auditing parameter. As sysdba, you can clear the audit trail table with a standard delete command. The changes will not take effect until you restart your computer, but you can wait until later.

```
ALTER SYSTEM set audit_trail=NONE SCOPE=SPFILE;
DELETE FROM sys.aud$;
Commit;
```

Fine-grained auditing gives you even more control over data that is collected. However, it is not handled through the AUDIT_TRAIL at all. The DBA grants

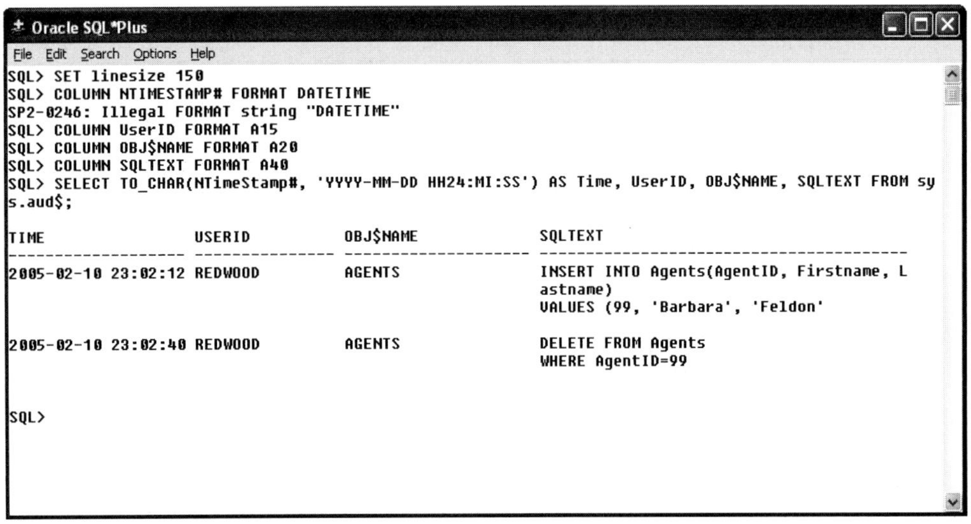

CHAPTER 12   Maintaining Database Security   **583**

```
SQL> SET linesize 150
SQL> COLUMN NTIMESTAMP# FORMAT DATETIME
SP2-0246: Illegal FORMAT string "DATETIME"
SQL> COLUMN UserID FORMAT A15
SQL> COLUMN OBJ$NAME FORMAT A20
SQL> COLUMN SQLTEXT FORMAT A40
SQL> SELECT TO_CHAR(NTimeStamp#, 'YYYY-MM-DD HH24:MI:SS') AS Time, UserID, OBJ$NAME, SQLTEXT FROM sy
s.aud$;

TIME                  USERID          OBJ$NAME             SQLTEXT
-------------------   -------------   ------------------   ----------------------------------------
2005-02-10 23:02:12   REDWOOD         AGENTS               INSERT INTO Agents(AgentID, Firstname, L
                                                           astname)
                                                           VALUES (99, 'Barbara', 'Feldon'

2005-02-10 23:02:40   REDWOOD         AGENTS               DELETE FROM Agents
                                                           WHERE AgentID=99

SQL>
```

FIGURE 12.9   Audit log results.

permissions by adding or removing FGA policies. But these details are beyond the scope of this book.

CREATING TRIGGERS FOR AUDITING

As pointed out in Chapter 4, sometimes you need additional data that is not recorded by the standard audit mechanism. Other times, you want to take additional, immediate actions when some event occurs. To handle these situations, you can write your own audit mechanism using database triggers. The main benefit is that you have complete control as a developer. You do not need the intervention of the DBA, and you can track any data that you want to collect.

A common example is to record changes to employee salaries—particularly large increases. That way, even if someone does circumvent security, the changes will still be flagged and stored in a separate table. You can monitor this table on a regular basis to identify potential problems. Assuming that the database has an Employee table with a column for Salary, the trigger code is straightforward.

1. To test this code, create an Employee table with at least EmployeeID and Salary columns. Add a couple of rows of data.
2. Create a second table to hold audit values. Call it Salary_Audit, with columns for EmployeeID, OldSalary, NewSalary, User, and ChangeDate.

   ```
   CREATE TABLE Salary_Audit
   ( EmployeeID      NUMBER,
     OldSalary       NUMBER(9,2),
     NewSalary       NUMBER(9,2),
     Username        VARCHAR2(50),
     DateChanged     Date,
          constraint pk_Salary_Audit PRIMARY KEY(EmployeeID, DateChanged)
   );
   ```

3. Use SQL*Plus to create a new trigger procedure:

   ```
   CREATE OR REPLACE TRIGGER Audit_Salaries
   AFTER UPDATE ON Redwood.Employee
   ```

```
FOR EACH ROW
BEGIN
   IF (:NEW.Salary > :OLD.Salary*1.20) THEN
      INSERT INTO Redwood.Salary_Audit (EmployeeID, OldSalary,
         NewSalary, Username, DateChanged)
      VALUES (:NEW.EmployeeID, :OLD.Salary,
         :NEW.Salary, User, sysdate);
   END IF;
END;
/
```

4. Now change one of the salaries by more than 20 percent.

```
UPDATE Employee
SET Salary=Salary*2
WHERE EmployeeID=1;
Commit;
```

5. Check the Salary_Audit table to ensure that it recorded the changes.

```
set linesize 150
COLUMN Username FORMAT A20
SELECT * FROM Salary_Audit;
```

Figure 12.10 shows the changes listed in the audit table. If you do not get similar results, go back and check the trigger code carefully. Remember that trigger code cannot be obfuscated with the Wrap utility. And this code really needs to be protected so that no one can see it. The solution is to write the actual code in a separate procedure and protect that procedure with the Wrap utility. Then use a single line in the trigger code to call the new procedure.

Also remember that you will have to set access rights carefully for both the Employee and Salary_Audit tables. In fact, you should simply give users Execute permissions on the new procedure and make sure that they have no access to the underlying table.

FIGURE 12.10 Changes stored from trigger code.

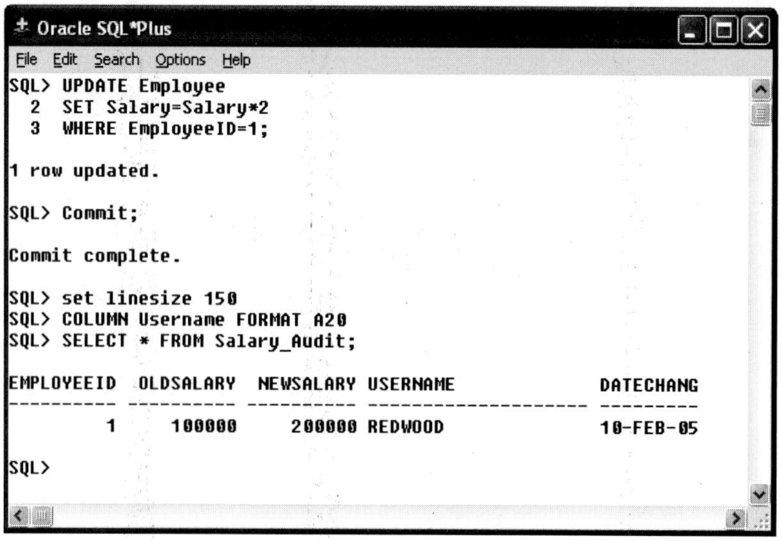

```
SQL> UPDATE Employee
  2  SET Salary=Salary*2
  3  WHERE EmployeeID=1;

1 row updated.

SQL> Commit;

Commit complete.

SQL> set linesize 150
SQL> COLUMN Username FORMAT A20
SQL> SELECT * FROM Salary_Audit;

EMPLOYEEID  OLDSALARY  NEWSALARY  USERNAME              DATECHANG
----------  ---------  ---------  --------------------  ---------
         1     100000     200000  REDWOOD               10-FEB-05

SQL>
```

FINE-GRAINED AUDITING

Fine-Grained Auditing (FGA) is similar to writing trigger code, but it requires less effort and provides additional controls. Audit trail records can be retrieved from the DBA_FGA_AUDIT_TRAIL view. You need DBA permissions to configure FGA policies and to view the audit trail. Most operations are handled through the DBMS_FGA package. For example, you could create a policy to monitor common SQL operations on the Employee table. You can even tell the policy to record notes only for employees who are not in the HRM department:

```
DBMS_FGA.ADD_POLICY(
    Object_schema => 'HRM',
    Object_name => 'Employee'
    Policy_name => 'Monitor_Employee_Table',
    Audit_condition => 'Department <> "HRM",
    Audit_column => 'Salary',
    Statement_types => 'select, insert, update, delete');
```

It is even possible to create a special event handler function that will be called when an audit is triggered. You could use the UTIL_ALERT_PAGER function to send the security administrator a page whenever some critical event is logged.

Summary

Because of the importance and widespread use of database systems, security is critical. Creating secure databases and applications requires the cooperation of the developers, database administrator, security administrator, and ultimately the users. Enterprise databases and applications that span multiple servers and locations are more complex and harder to secure and monitor.

One of the first security challenges is to identify users. Authentication is commonly handled with passwords. But, even if you add more advanced technologies (such as biometrics), you still want to limit the number of times you ask a user to log in. Oracle supports single sign-on, even in an enterprise environment with its ability to authenticate against standard user databases. Once the users are identified, you can grant them various roles. Roles are collections of permissions that apply to a group of users. It is always better to assign permissions to a role and then assign roles to users. Otherwise you will have to wade through and edit permissions for thousands of users individually.

You can assign access rights based on system services or individual data objects. If you need greater control over the rights, you can use stored views and procedures to limit the access and then assign the permissions to the views and procedures instead of giving users direct access to the tables. You can also restrict access to elements on forms by setting the Visible property of items only if a specific role is assigned to the current user.

Encryption is used to protect data in transmission and as backup security for critical data, such as social security numbers and credit card data. Web transmission security is provided outside of Oracle by installing a digital security certificate on the server and activating secure sockets layer for automatic encryption. You can write procedures to call the internal encryption procedures when you need to scramble individual pieces of data. You still need to figure out where to store the value of the encryption key, but encryption protects you if someone steals the entire database.

Auditing user activity is the best way to monitor the system for problems. You can record normal transactions, transactions that exceed some level, or failed transactions. You can create triggers or use fine-grained auditing controls to capture activities on individual columns of data and actions taken by individuals or groups of users. The challenge lies in finding the balance in collecting enough data to spot problems, without overwhelming the system and monitoring everything in the world.

Key Terms

- auditing
- availability
- challenge-response
- confidentiality
- digital security certificate
- encryption
- granularity
- integrity
- label security
- lightweight directory application protocol (LDAP)
- object privileges
- Oracle Internet Directory (OID)
- public-key infrastructure (PKI)
- secure sockets layer (SSL)
- separation of duties
- single sign-on
- system privileges
- user role
- virtual private database (VPD)
- WITH ADMIN

Review

TRUE/FALSE

1. Data encryption is an effective replacement for access controls.
2. The GRANT command can assign UPDATE rights to individual columns in a table.
3. Securing Oracle Web-based applications by encrypting transmissions requires the use of secure sockets layer.
4. Restricting updates by row, or based on the identity of a user, can be handled with the GRANT command.
5. A system is more secure if you assign permissions directly to individual users instead of using roles.

FILL IN

1. You suspect that someone is reading customer order data and selling it to your competitors. You use _____ to check your suspects.
2. When you assign permissions to roles, you need to use them to create _____ so that insider theft would require the complicity of several people.
3. In a form, you can query the _____ view to see if a role is assigned to the current user and make sections of the form visible or invisible.
4. Once the DBA has to give you additional privileges, you can use the _____ package to encrypt data with standard security algorithms.
5. In the enterprise version, Oracle provides support for single sign-on using the _____ tools.

MULTIPLE CHOICE

1. Which of the following is NOT a goal of a security system?
   a. Confidentiality
   b. Integrity
   c. Availability
   d. Query performance
   e. All of these are standard goals.
2. You want to let employees use the Employee table to look up names and phone numbers of other employees but not to see any other data in the table. You also want to keep some names out of the directory listing, the best security approach is to
   a. Create a view and give users SELECT access to the view.
   b. Write an update procedure that inserts the identity of the user.
   c. Create a virtual private database to limit users to see only rows in their department.
   d. Encrypt the salary data.
   e. Keep audit trails on the table access and fire anyone who looks at Salary data.
3. You want to protect a report so that only managers can use it. The best security approach is to:
   a. Create a virtual private database so that users can only see data they created.
   b. Save a view with the necessary data, restrict access to the view, and base the report on that view.
   c. Encrypt all of the data used in the report.

d. Audit the use of the report so every time it is run you receive a page and can check the name of the user.
e. Use the Wrap utility to obfuscate the codes that start the report.

4. To prevent users from altering customer order data created by other employees, the best security mechanism to use is:
    a. Use Oracle Internet Directory and enforce single sign-on.
    b. Use secure sockets layer to protect the transmission of the update data.
    c. Create a procedure to handle the updates and automatically insert the UserID, possibly using VPD to create the procedure.
    d. Encrypt all of the data in the Order table.
    e. Create a user role that only allows certain people to update data in the Order table.

5. You can use the database security system to enforce separation of duties by
    a. Creating different roles to perform each step and not assigning all roles to the same person.
    b. Encrypting all of the data in the database.
    c. Creating a procedure to check that the person who performs the last step in a process can never be the same as the person who performs the first step.
    d. Creating a fine-grained audit trigger that notifies you when one person attempts to do two steps in a process.
    e. Assigning proper system privileges to only one person.

Hands-on Exercises

1. Extending the Chapter Case

You need to work on more of the security configuration for the Redwood Realty case. Most of the work here is applying the examples from the chapter to more of the reports, views, and tables. Most of the work has been done for the tables and forms. At least the agents and managers will be able to use the forms. You might want to think about whether security could be tightened in some areas—but remember that it is a small company, the managers trust the agents, and the database is not holding highly sensitive data.

1. Evaluate the existing security provisions outlined in Table 12.3 and evaluate any changes. Write a short document explaining any proposed changes and the potential benefits and problems that might arise.
2. You need to adjust the reports so that they all pull data from views, and then assign permissions to the views. Even the reports currently open to agents should be based on views if managers want to restrict access in the future. Edit the queries for the **AgentSales**, **CustomerList**, **ListingsAndOffers**, and **SalesByCityAndAgent** reports. Create and save views for each of those queries. Also, if the reports have user parameters, make sure they include the schema name. Assign access rights to the reports based on Table 12.3 and test the reports. Note that you will need to clean up the views to ensure that there are no duplicate column names. You then have to rewrite the report query so that it includes any user parameters. For example, the query for AgentSales becomes:

```
SELECT ALL AGENTID, LASTNAME, FIRSTNAME,
WORKPHONE, LISTINGID, BEGINLISTDATE,
ASKINGPRICE, SALESTATUS, CITY, BEDROOMS
FROM Redwood.AgentSales
WHERE   (('All' = :LISTING_MONTH) OR
(TO_CHAR(BEGINLISTDATE,'MM') =
:LISTING_MONTH))
  AND (TO_CHAR(BEGINLISTDATE,'YYYY') =
:LISTING_YEAR)
```

3. Notice that Table 12.3 says that perhaps agents should be able to get a report listing their own sales. To create this level of security, copy the AgentSales report to AgentSelfSales and the view AgentSales to AgentSelfSales. Edit the report query to point to the correct view. Replace the view with one that only retrieves data for the current user.

```
Create or Replace View AgentSelfSales AS
SELECT ALL Redwood.AGENTS.AGENTID,
Redwood.AGENTS.LASTNAME,
Redwood.AGENTS.FIRSTNAME,
Redwood.AGENTS.WORKPHONE,
```

```
Redwood.LISTINGS.LISTINGID,
Redwood.LISTINGS.BEGINLISTDATE,
Redwood.LISTINGS.ASKINGPRICE,
Redwood.SALESTATUS.SALESTATUS,
Redwood.PROPERTIES.CITY,
Redwood.PROPERTIES.BEDROOMS
FROM Redwood.AGENTS, Redwood.LISTINGS,
Redwood.PROPERTIES, Redwood.SALESTATUS
WHERE Redwood.SALESTATUS.SALESTATUS =
'For Sale'
   AND ((Redwood.LISTINGS.LISTINGAGENTID =
   Redwood.AGENTS.AGENTID)
   AND (Redwood.LISTINGS.PROPERTYID =
   Redwood.PROPERTIES.PROPERTYID)
   AND (Redwood.LISTINGS.SALESTATUSID =
   Redwood.SALESTATUS.SALESTATUSID))
   AND (UPPER(Redwood.Agents.Username) =
   User)
ORDER BY Redwood.LISTINGS.ASKINGPRICE DESC ;
```

4. Create a view for the **CustomerList** report and change the report to use the view. Both agents and managers should be able to print this report. Do the same for the two queries in the **ListingsAndOffers** report. If you have time, do the same for the **SalesByCityAndAgent** report, but note that you will have to clean up the view to remove duplicate columns. Fix it so that it only retrieves the data needed for the report.

5. Find the list of sequences in the Redwood case and assign SELECT permissions to them for both Agent and Manager roles. To get a list, use

```
SELECT sequence_name FROM user_sequences;
```

6. Add a button to the startup form so agents can open the AgentSelfSales report. Use the startup form and log in with the MarcouxK account. Test the AgentSelfSales report. Print the screen and hand it in.

2. Coffee Merchant

To configure security for the Coffee Merchant case, you first have to identify the primary objects and the main user roles. As a small company running the basic order application, the company probably just uses a single role for employees. However, it makes sense to use an administrator role to handle updates to some base tables that seldom change: Countries, Employees, and Inventory.

1. Create a new folder for this case in this chapter. Copy the existing forms and reports that you created in earlier chapters into the new folder. Open the Startup form and change the ApplicationPath in the starting trigger.

2. Create two roles: Clerk and CoffeeAdmin. You can reuse the users created for the Redwood case (maybe they moonlight at the coffee shop). So grant the Clerk role to MarcouxK and CoffeeAdmin to CarlingT.

3. Grant permissions to the roles to access the tables. The CoffeeAdmin role has standard access (SELECT, INSERT, UPDATE, DELETE) to all tables. The Clerk has SELECT access to all tables except the Employee table. They have INSERT, UPDATE, and DELETE permissions on the Orders and OrderLines tables.

4. Clerks need to retrieve EmployeeID, FirstName, and LastName from the Employees table for the Orders form. Create a view and grant Clerk the ability to see just those three columns. Rewrite the LOV in the Orders form to use that view.

5. Remember that you will have to set the Schema name into all of the form queries, or create public synonyms for all of the forms, views, and sequences. You will also have to grant both clerks and administrators Select access to the seq_Orders sequence.

6. For the QuarterlySalesByState report, convert the report's query to a view. For now, give both the Clerk and Administrator roles select permission on the view.

7. Run the Startup form. Test the buttons and other forms. Test the report. Print the screen and hand it in.

3. Rowing Ventures

Security in Rowing Ventures can be relatively weak because the data is not that critical, and there is no money involved. You might worry about someone altering race results, but on race day there are enough checks and balances that it is not an issue. For example, race results are written on paper by the judges first, so you always have those as backup. It might be possible for someone to come back a month later and try to alter your electronic copy of the results, but there would be little to gain. You do still need to create at least one role, and you need to configure the tables and views so they can be used by members of that role. Since this case has a relatively small number of tables and views, you should try to create public synonyms for them. If you can get permission to create public synonyms, you can create them with

```
Create public synonym RaceTimes for
<schema>.RaceTimes;
```

If you cannot get the necessary privilege for your account, you will have to modify the queries in the forms and reports. You can assign the new RaceClerk role to the MarcouxK user and log in with that account to test everything. Remember to check the ApplicationPath. Also remember to check for sequences and assign permissions to them.

Since you are somewhat concerned about the possibility of people altering the race results after the fact, you should consider adding auditing to the RaceTimes table. If auditing is turned off, you can write a short trigger program to capture the changes to a new table.

4. BROADCLOTH CLOTHING

The Broadcloth case has several tables, views, and sequences. Again, you can either assign public synonyms or alter the forms and reports to use the schema name. Because of the complexity of the case, it will take time to create all of the roles and permissions needed. Instead of trying to create all of the roles for this assignment, it is best to just develop a plan. Create a table that lists all of the suggested roles and the access rights you plan to grant to each object for the various roles. Print the access plan and hand it in. Include explanations on a separate page if necessary.

CHAPTER 13

DATABASE ADMINISTRATION

Learning Objectives

In this chapter, you will learn the basics of:

- Why companies need a DBA.
- How to use the Enterprise Manager to perform basic DBA tasks.
- How to configure storage files and space utilization.
- How to export and import data.
- How to maintain and update the database.
- How to back up the database and recover from crashes.
- How to monitor and improve database performance.

OVERVIEW OF A DBA'S DUTIES

At the most basic level, a *database administrator (DBA)* is in charge of keeping the database running and monitoring its performance. With Oracle databases, this is often a full-time job. Large companies often hire multiple DBAs if they run several applications. Oracle provides dozens of tools and literally hundreds of predefined views that provide information to help you monitor, configure, and fine-tune the databases. It takes time to learn the alternatives, and experience to spot problems and find the best solutions. If you want to become a DBA, you will ultimately need to read dozens of specialty books on the subject and work with large databases to gain experience. This chapter merely provides an introduction to the fundamental tasks and points out some of the common tools available.

DBAs are responsible for several day-to-day tasks to keep the database running at peak performance. Often, one of the first steps is installing the database. While that might sound easy, it can be one of the most difficult steps. You need to select the proper options, configure the storage, and help define the database structure. You also have to allocate the storage. You have to estimate the amount of space needed, analyze the performance issues of various tables, and keep an eye on growth. As the database runs, you have to monitor the performance of several items. Oracle provides several monitoring tools, and you can automate many of the processes, but if you see problems arising, you have to catch them early, and find solutions.

DBAs are also responsible for patches and updates to the DBMS. Patches are released on a regular schedule to fix bugs and to fix security problems. Some, such as the critical security patches, are more important than others. The DBA is generally the primary contact with Oracle and receives notices of patches, updates, and new features. The DBA also needs to help developers plan for these new features and test the updates before they are installed on the production system.

DBAs play important roles in ensuring the security of the database. They are responsible for ensuring that backups are made on a regular basis and that the physical backups are stored in a secure location. When things go wrong, they are responsible for reinstalling everything and recovering the data. Sometimes, the DBA is also responsible for developing a security plan for the database systems and for monitoring the system and audit logs. For example, a sudden performance slowdown could be the result of an attack on the system, so the DBA needs to watch for these problems and know how to track potential intruders.

All of the examples and exercises in this chapter require that you have an account that has at least a DBA role. For some tasks, you might need even more privileges, such as the SYSDBA account. If you are running your own copy of Oracle, you will have these privileges, although you might want to create a new user account and grant it the DBA role. When you install Oracle, it automatically creates the system and sysdba accounts. You entered passwords for those accounts when you installed the system. Go back to your notes and look up the passwords you entered. On the other hand, if you are running Oracle on a shared system at school, you might have problems obtaining the DBA permissions, and it is highly unlikely that the administrator would give you the system or sysdba account access. In that case, you can read through the examples in this chapter. If you really want to understand the DBA tools, you will ultimately have to install your own copy of Oracle and experiment with it. When you are learning, it is best to work on a copy that no one else is using.

There is one more major piece of advice: As you work with DBA tasks, it is critical that you keep a notebook. The notes can be electronic. In fact, you often should copy and paste fragments of SQL scripts. Just be sure to keep the notes organized and annotated so that you remember why you need the scripts. Think of the process as a science lab. Every experiment you perform in a science lab gets documented in your lab notebook. You have to do the same thing when you experiment with Oracle commands and options. Many times, you will fail to get the commands right on the first try. You will experiment and change lines, fix syntax errors, and test other options. Eventually, when the commands finally work, you need to know why, and what to do next time. Write everything down. One approach is to use a paper notebook. Another is to keep a WordPad window open and write all of your steps, scripts, and reasons into the notebook. Just be sure to save it repeatedly in a safe location so you can recover it when you crash the entire system.

USING THE ENTERPRISE MANAGER

The *Enterprise Manager (EM)* is Oracle's Web-based approach to helping DBAs monitor and control the databases on their systems. By providing a single entry point for most tasks, it makes it easier to find the various options. However, the EM has been revised several times through the latest versions of the Oracle DBMS. Most professional DBAs find that it is eventually easier to monitor and control Oracle using SQL statements. In fact, many of the tools in the EM are simply front-end forms that generate and run SQL statements. One of the best things about these tools is that they will show you the SQL statements. As you learn the DBA tools and commands, you can use the EM to help create the basic SQL statements. Then you can write the statements into your DBA notebook and even create your own SQL scripts for the next time.

At this point, you should look at the overall structure of the Enterprise Manager so you know where to find some of the basic tasks. Starting the EM is one of the first challenges. It runs as another Web-based service on the Oracle database server. If you installed it to the standard location, it listens on TCP/IP port 5500. If you installed it somewhere else for some reason, you need to consult your notes for its location. The Oracle installation tool writes a short text file when the installation is complete and records all of the port information for you. The second challenge is that you should probably log in using the standard Oracle system account, with the password you created during the installation. You might be able to use your regular username and password, but it might not have sufficient privileges.

1. This is a good time to review the notes you took when you installed Oracle.
2. Start the Enterprise Manager by opening your Web browser and entering the address using the name of the server that is running the database. Log in when asked.

```
http://<servername>:5500/em
```

If you receive an error message and the EM does not start, it might be because the server name or port number is wrong. The other possibility is that the listener did not start correctly. If so, you can try shutting down the entire server and restarting it. Figure 13.1 shows a portion of the main page of the EM. The specific items, such as the Instance Name and charts, will be different on your screen. Notice that most of the screen is devoted to monitoring activities and problems. As a DBA, the monitoring features are the ones you most need on a daily basis.

For now, focus on the four link options at the top left of the screen: Home, Performance, Administration, and Maintenance. You are currently on the Home page, so it is not shown as a link.

3. Click on the Administration link.

Figure 13.2 shows the organization of options by primary database objects. Note that you might not have the Enterprise options available if you did not install the Enterprise edition. Now you can start to see some of the control options available to the DBA.

4. To review a task that you performed in the last chapter, find the Security section and click on the Users link.

Figure 13.3 shows a partial list of the users. Again, your list will probably be a little bit different. But, it should contain the user you created in Chapter 13. Also, notice that you could use the Create button to create a new user. The Edit button lets you change basic information about the user account, including the password and the roles assigned to the user. The Delete button will completely remove a user account from the database. Be careful with deleting users. You might want to edit the account first and lock it for a while to make sure no one needs it. It is much easier to reactivate an account by unlocking it than it is to create it from scratch and assign all of the correct roles and system privileges. You should click through a few of the user account screens to become familiar with them. However, be aware that many DBAs do not like this approach to creating users. If you try to create a user and look carefully at the SQL,

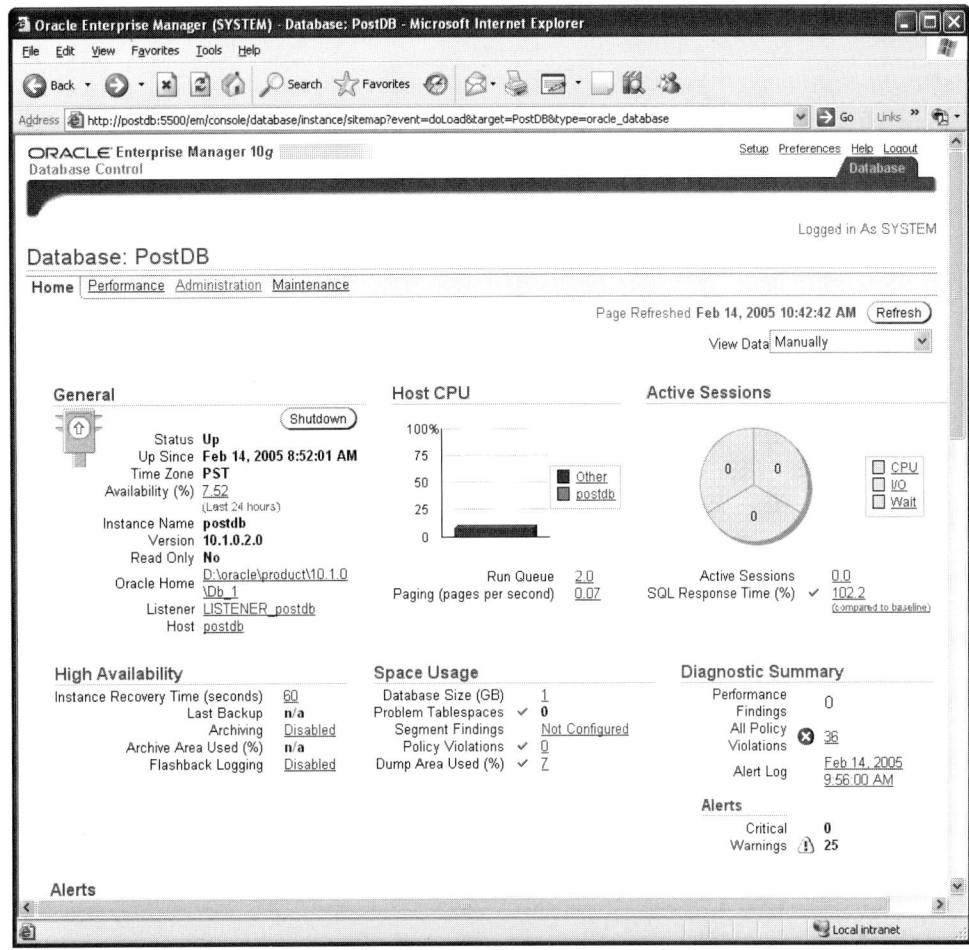

FIGURE 13.1 The Enterprise Manager main page.

you will see why. This approach automatically assigns the Connect role to users, and the Connect role grants relatively powerful privileges to users—especially the CREATE TABLE role. That is your first important DBA lesson: The tools might be easy to use, but you need to be careful and fully understand exactly what they are doing behind the scenes.

5. Click the Database link near the top-left of the page to return to the Administration page.

Take a minute to look at the sections and options. The Security section, which we discussed in Chapter 12, is straightforward. The Schema section should make sense because it lists the tables, indexes, views, sequences, procedures, and other items created for a specific database. You could use it to create new tables, but again, most DBAs recommend using SQL instead. With SQL you can keep a script file and use it any time you need to recreate a table or rebuild the database. The Enterprise and Warehouse options are beyond the scope of this book. However, one of the major topics you need to explore is data storage.

594 Introduction to Oracle

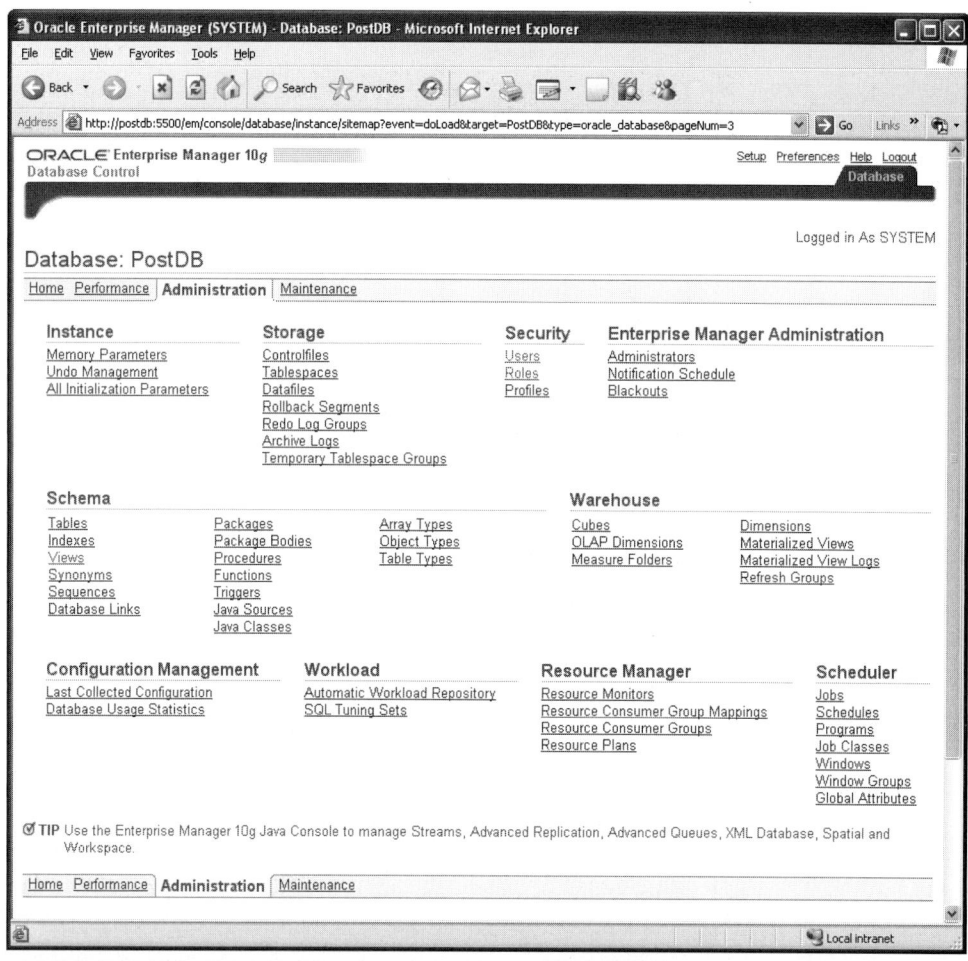

FIGURE 13.2 Enterprise Manager Administration page.

UNDERSTANDING ORACLE STORAGE FILES

Whether you are installing a database, making backups, or monitoring performance, you need to understand the overall storage system used by Oracle. Look again at the options in Figure 13.2 and you will see several entries under the Storage management section:

- Control files
- Tablespaces
- Datafiles
- Redo log groups
- Archive logs

You might also see rollback and temporary group tablespaces, but rollback segments are not used anymore, and you cannot really alter the temporary group tablespaces.

As a DBA, you need to understand a few things about each of the data file types. Ultimately, the DBMS has to put the table rows and data someplace. In actuality, the DBMS has to work with the operating system to store data in files. Oracle has defined a set of file types that it uses to work with diverse operating systems. Each

CHAPTER 13 Database Administration **595**

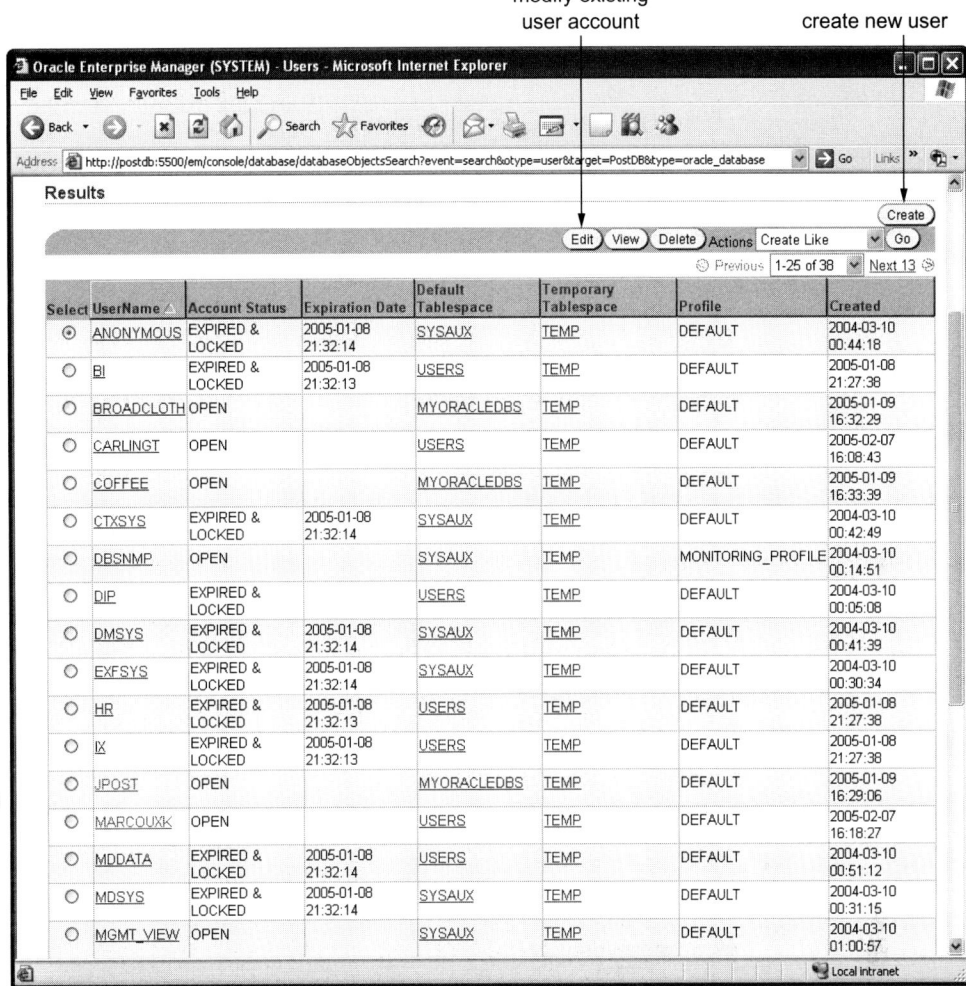

FIGURE 13.3 Enterprise Manager Administration/Security/Users page.

file type has a specific purpose and can be controlled by the DBA to improve reliability and performance.

Before looking at specific file types, you might want to review some hardware issues dealing with physical disk drives. Remember that disk drives are one of the slowest elements of a computer—because they are mechanical. Speed depends on the physical rotation of the platters. Because of the mechanical aspect, they are also the most likely element to crash. And when drives crash, it is expensive and often impossible to retrieve data. If you are going to optimize drive storage, you will have to learn about current issues in storage; but most of them are outside the control of Oracle and are not covered in this book. For example, you can dramatically improve performance by using a ***redundant array of independent drives (RAID)*** as the primary data storage. This technique uses the operating system and the drive controller to automatically write data for a single file across multiple drives. Since each disk spins independently of the others, you are creating a parallel process that can operate many times faster than a single drive. You can also have the storage system write copies of each record to multiple drives, automatically creating its own backup. Even if one drive in the array fails, the system can instantly pick up the backup data from the others. Using the same features, you can shut down one drive and replace it while the others continue to operate, making it possible to repair and upgrade the storage system while the database remains online continuously.

PROTECTING CONTROL FILES

A control file is a special binary file that tells Oracle how the data is stored on your system. By default, Oracle creates three exact copies of the control file. On startup, Oracle tries to read the configuration data in one of the files. If it eventually fails on each copy, the database will not open, and you have serious problems to solve. To be safe, it is highly recommended that at least one of the copies be stored on a different computer on the network. At a minimum, it should be stored on a different disk drive. Then if one drive or server crashes, Oracle can quickly recover by using the control file stored on the secondary computer. This approach is particularly important when you want to maintain high availability of the database. The flip side is that if you are running a single server and lose the control file, you have probably already lost big chunks of your database. So, you will probably have to reload the backup files anyway, which should also restore the control files. But, it will take some time.

1. Assuming you still have the Enterprise Manager running, return to the Administration page and click on the **Controlfiles** link under the **Storage** heading.

   As shown in Figure 13.4, you should see a list of the three control files and their locations. If you installed your own copy of Oracle, the three files are probably in the same directory. You can click on the Record Section to see some basic information about the size of the control file, but you cannot edit any of the data. You cannot change the locations at this point. You would need to change a database initialization parameter. You would need to log into SQL*Plus with the sysdba role and issue an ALTER SYSTEM command to do that. Do not attempt it now, but you might need to know the syntax in the future:

```
ALTER SYSTEM SET control_files=<filename1>, <filename2>, … <filename8>
SCOPE=SPFILE;
```

Because the control file is so important, you would also have to stop and restart the database before the changes could take effect. This static nature of the parameter is why you cannot use the EM to alter its value. Once you have the control files configured properly, you will almost never change it. Note that you can also use the operating system to maintain a mirror backup of the control files if you do not want to alter the Oracle configuration.

CREATING TABLESPACES AND DATAFILES

A *tablespace* is a special Oracle invention. It is a logical collection of items from the database. As DBA, you assign various objects (and effectively, users) to a tablespace. You can create as many tablespaces as you want, and you can choose what to store in each tablespace. For example, you might decide to store all of the tables and other objects for the Redwood Realty case in one tablespace, and data for each of the other cases in different tablespaces. You might go even further and store just the table data for Redwood in one tablespace and all of the indexes for it in a second tablespace. Or, you could go the other way, and store everything into one giant tablespace. What difference does it make, and how should you make that decision?

Figure 13.5 illustrates the main Oracle data storage terminology. A tablespace is a logical collection of data. User schema objects are assigned to a tablespace. Data written to a tablespace is stored in one or more datafiles. A **datafile** is a physical file in the

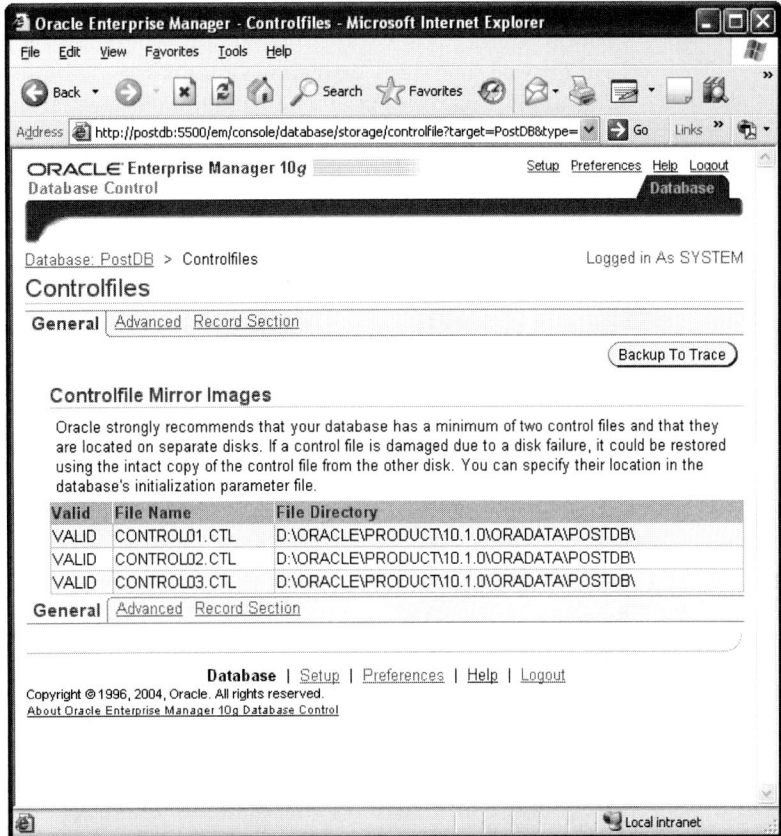

FIGURE 13.4 Location of current control files.

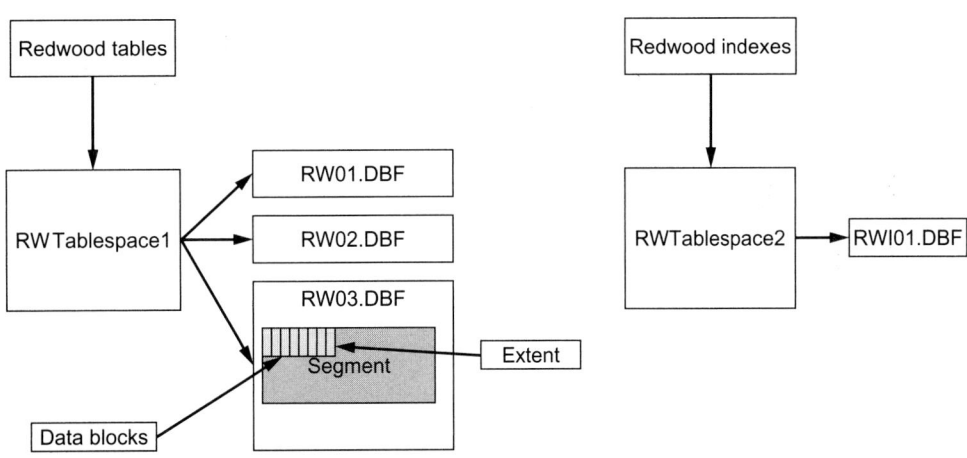

FIGURE 13.5 Oracle tablespaces and datafiles.

operating system. If you define a datafile named RW01.DBF, you can find that file in your operating system. Data is stored in a proprietary data format that other programs cannot read. When you create a datafile, you specify an initial size and an increment. When the datafile is full, Oracle extends the file by the size of the increment. You could choose to create a few huge datafiles for your database, or break them down into several smaller datafiles. The choice will affect the performance of the database. In general, multiple files will be faster, but it depends on the size of the data items. Also, bear in mind that many operating systems impose limits on the number of files that one program (Oracle) can keep open at a time. The other limitation is that a datafile can be assigned to only one tablespace.

Data is stored in the datafile as segments. **Segments** are specialized collections, so that a table segment holds table data and an index segment holds index data. A segment contains multiple **extents**, which are collections of contiguous data blocks. A **data block** is the smallest piece of data that is read from or written to a datafile. The DBA can specify the size of the data block when the database is defined. For example, if you are creating a database that holds pictures or other large binary objects, you would set a larger data block size than if you are storing a few small numbers. In practice, an extent is the smallest set of data read or written at one time. All of the data blocks within an extent would be read at the same time. Remember that disk drives are relatively slow, so the purpose of the extent is to retrieve data blocks in groups and hold them in a local memory cache to speed up the process.

Before your eyes completely glaze over, how much of this detail do you really need to know? The good news is that you usually pick the option to create locally managed extents, and the DBMS handles the details for you. This process is efficient for most business data. However, if you encounter more extreme situations—such as huge databases, or large binary objects—you can improve performance by altering these parameters. The bad news is that you will probably have to experiment to find the values that work the best.

Before trying to create a tablespace, you should also know that there are three types of tablespaces: (1) permanent, (2) temporary, and (3) undo. Permanent tablespaces are used to hold data from tables and indexes. Temporary tablespaces are only used to hold data for short-term activities within the system, such as sorting. Undo tablespaces are used to help rollback transactions that are not committed. You almost never need to create new temporary or undo tablespaces. You might create new ones if you have a complex data storage disk array and want to move them to faster hardware to improve performance.

1. From the main **Administration** page, click on the **Tablespaces** link under the **Storage** heading.

Figure 13.6 shows a sample tablespace listing. Your listing and the percent utilization is likely to be different. Notice the standard temporary and undo tablespaces. The System, SysAux, and Users tablespaces are always installed by default. Most installations also include the Example tablespace. When you create a new user, you can specify which tablespaces should be used for permanent and temporary data. The Users and Temp tablespaces are the defaults.

Think about what can go wrong if you assign all users to the same tablespace. In particular, they will all share the same underlying datafiles. If something goes wrong with one application, it could knock out all of them. It makes more sense to put different applications (users or schemas) into different tablespaces.

2. Click the **Create** (Create) button to add a new tablespace. Enter **Redwood** as the name of the new tablespace. Make sure the default **Permanent** and **Read Write** options are selected.

3. Near the bottom-right corner of the screen, click the **Add** (Add) button to add a new datafile.

4. Enter **Redwood01** as the new file name. Note the location of the file directory. You can use this option to place the datafile on a high-speed storage area

CHAPTER 13 Database Administration 599

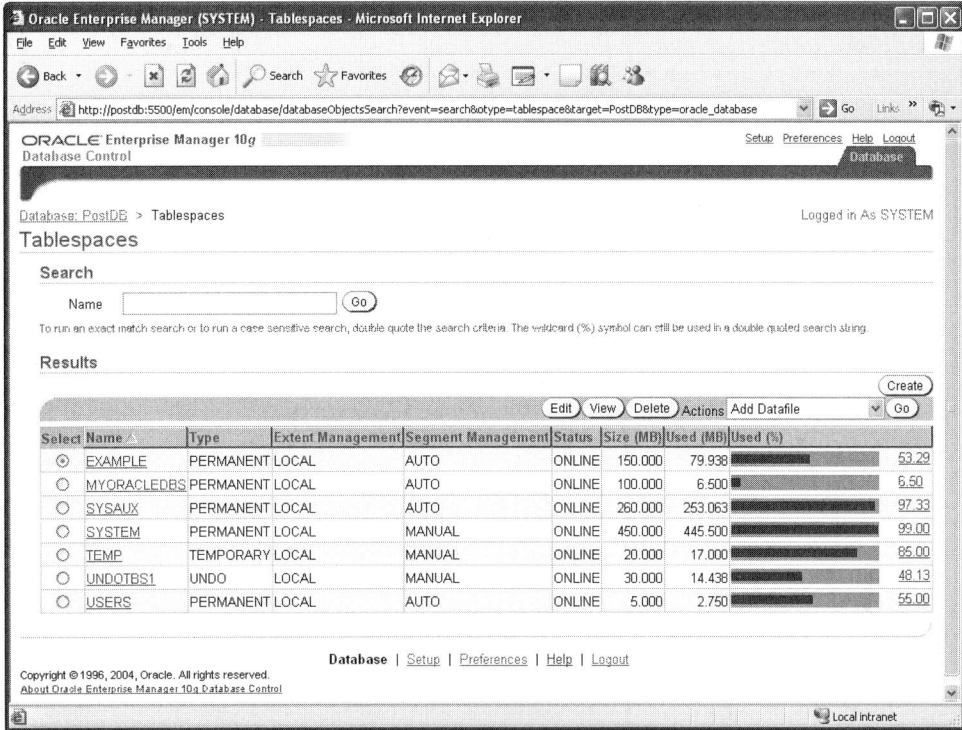

FIGURE 13.6 Sample tablespaces.

network or other fast drive. Leave the default value. Set the file size to **100 MB**. Select the options to **automatically extend** the file by **20 MB**. Click the **Continue** (Continue) button.

Figure 13.7 shows the input screen for creating the new datafile. Your file location will be different, but the other options should be similar. When finished with this page, the data file will be created and you will see the tablespace creation screen again as shown in Figure 13.8.

5. Click the **OK** (OK) button near the top-right corner of the screen to create the tablespace.

As you can see, the new tablespace has been added to the list of tablespaces. You can now assign schema objects to this tablespace. Of course, existing objects will remain at their current location. To move the data, you would create a new Redwood schema and assign it to this new tablespace. Then rebuild the tables for the case and use SQL to transfer the data into the new tables. Then you can delete the old tables. In most cases, you want to plan ahead and build the tablespaces and datafiles before you create the tables and begin storing data. Actually, the developers will probably build the sample application on a development machine first. Then you can use the knowledge of the tables and data types to determine the best tablespace and datafile structures needed for the production machine.

Over time, tablespaces can become cluttered. Deleting rows or other items in tables can cause the tablespace to become fragmented. Segments that were once contiguous begin to get pieces of empty space among them. By itself, an individual piece is

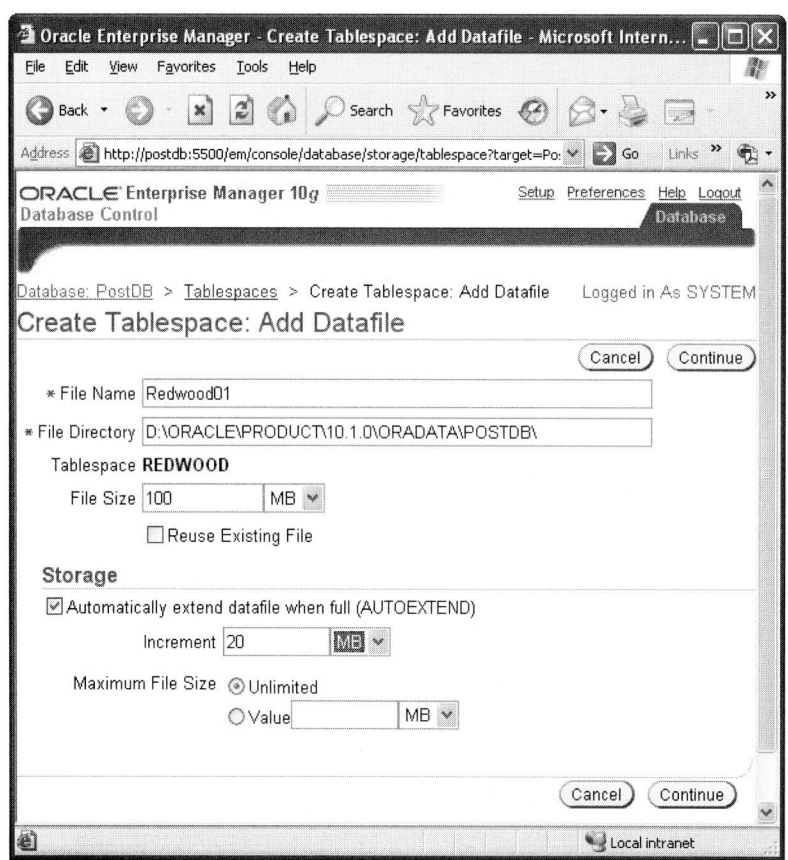

FIGURE 13.7 Creating a new datafile.

too small to be reused, but taken together, they can add up to a lot of wasted space. Periodically, you need to analyze the tablespaces and reclaim this fragmented space. You should be able to do this through the Run Segment Advisor in the drop-down list of the tablespace screen. But only attempt it when the system load is light and you have plenty of time. Eventually, you should be able to choose the shrink options to compact the tablespace.

CONFIGURING UNDO AND REDO OPERATIONS

To provide consistency in transactions, Oracle maintains an ***undo tablespace***. All changes to the data are written to this log. If a transaction fails to complete, either because of a recovery operation or because your code issued a Rollback command, Oracle uses the log to return the database to a consistent point. The DBMS also uses the log to provide read consistency to user queries. For example, if a query starts at 9:00 and runs for 10 minutes, some of the data might be changed or deleted by other users before the query completes. The undo log enables the DBMS to report a consistent set of data at the time the query started. When data is altered, the original values are written to the undo tablespace until the changes are committed. If the undo tablespace fills up, some transactions might fail. As DBA, you never want transactions to fail. So, you have to ensure that the undo tablespace is big enough to hold all of the active transactions. You can control the size of the tablespace. You can also control the retention

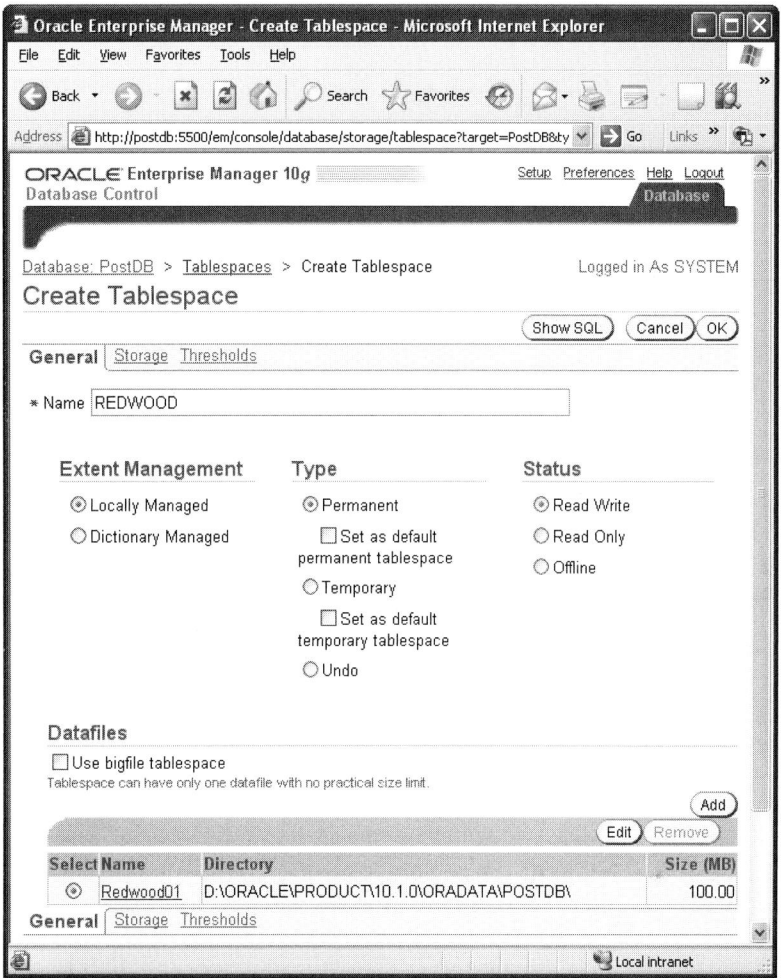

FIGURE 13.8 Creating a new tablespace.

time. To provide consistent data for queries, the retention time should exceed your longest running query. Of course, it costs money to buy drive space, so you want to make the undo tablespace large enough not to fail, but you cannot afford to overkill it either. Although, if it comes down to a choice between another $1,000 of disk space or your job, pick the drive space, and set the undo tablespace to auto extend. For complex situations, Oracle provides an Undo Advisor to help you adjust the parameters.

Redo log files are similar to undo tablespace, but they have a slightly different purpose. They are used for recovering transactions if the database fails. All changes are written to the active redo log. The redo log is circular—when the log writer reaches the end of the file, it goes back to the beginning and overwrites the data. Obviously, the redo log file has to be large enough to handle your largest transaction, but that is rarely a problem. It is more important to create multiple redo log files and protect them from crashing. By default, Oracle creates two files and switches to the second if something happens to the first one. By placing the files on multiple disk drives, you can avoid losing transaction data if one drive crashes. You use the ALTER DATABASE ADD LOGFILE GROUP command to add new log files.

CONFIGURING SPACE FOR SCHEMA OBJECTS

Oracle provides several parameters and options for defining the way tables, indexes, and other schema items are stored. For relatively small databases, you can almost always use the default values and let Oracle manage the storage. You can also rely on the external capabilities of the storage systems, such as RAID devices, to improve performance and handle automatic backups. However, eventually you will encounter tables that need additional tweaking. You can use these parameters and options to optimize the storage for those tables that fall beyond the average.

First, you can define the tablespace for any table. By defining tablespaces on specific drives, you can move heavily used data to the fastest drive systems. Second, when you create a table, you can use your knowledge of the type of data it will hold to fine-tune the data block storage mechanism by setting a couple of useful parameters. Third, you can use partitioning and clustering to split a table so that portions are stored in different locations.

SETTING TABLE STORAGE PARAMETERS

A data block is the smallest unit of disk storage spaced used by Oracle. You can control the size of the data block when you create a datafile. However, you can also control how the data blocks are used with the PCTUSED and PCTFREE parameters. These two values can usually be specified when you create a table or an index. For example,

```
CREATE TABLE <tablename> (row definitions …) PCTFREE=10 PCTUSED=40;
```

The **PCTFREE** parameter is the easiest to understand. Figure 13.9 shows the basic structure of a single data block. The data block is filled with data as INSERT commands are issued. Some space is also taken by overhead that Oracle uses to track data within the data block. If you specify a PCTFREE parameter of 20, Oracle will allow the data block to fill until 20 percent of free space remains. At that point, Oracle will no longer insert new data into this data block. Instead, a new data block will be created, and new rows will go to that data block. A link point will be placed in the first data block, pointing to the continued data in the second block. But, what is the purpose of reserving the free space? This space is used to hold updates to the rows that are already

FIGURE 13.9 Effect of the PCTFREE parameter.

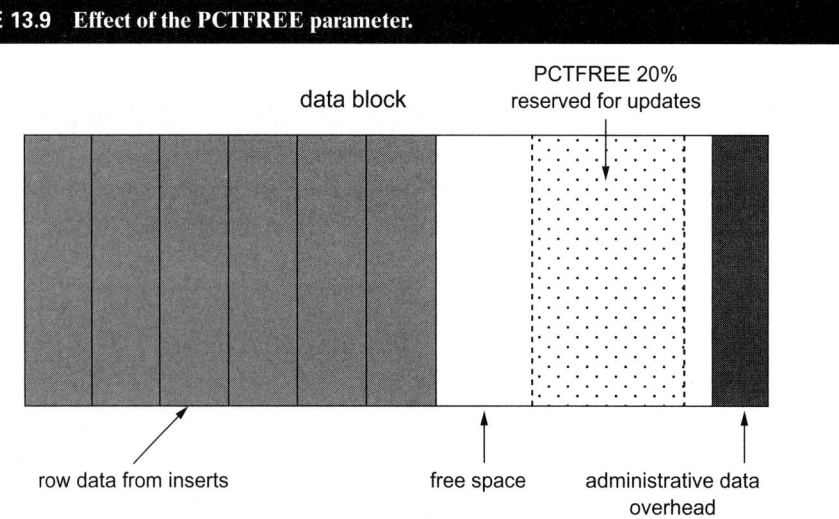

stored in the data block. With some tables, when you update a row, the new data is larger than the old. The data block needs space in which to put this expanded row. If you know that a certain table will experience growing data rows on updates, you can reserve larger amounts of free space. As much as possible, you want the system to keep related data together so that it can all be retrieved from the datafile at the same time. The default value of PCTFREE is 10 percent.

Table 13.1 lists the primary effects of choosing smaller or larger values of PCTFREE. Essentially, if you know that most table rows will be the same size, you should use a smaller value for PCTFREE. If rows tend to grow in size, you will need a larger value. You would like to avoid running out of space in the data block. When Oracle tries to update a table row and does not find enough space in the data block, it migrates the row to a new data block. This process slows down the data write, and slows down future retrievals because Oracle has to read multiple blocks to find related data.

Now that you understand how data is stored in a data block, you will be able to see the role of the PCTUSED parameter. It comes into play only after a data block has been filled by reaching its PCTFREE level. The next question Oracle faces is what to do when table rows are deleted. If one row of data is deleted, and the total free space now exceeds the PCTFREE parameter, should Oracle start using the data block for inserts again? The answer is no. Oracle waits until the percentage of space used drops below the **PCTUSED** level. The default value is 40 percent. So, Oracle will not begin adding rows to a block again until the block is at less than 40 percent capacity. If you specify both PCTFREE and PCTUSED, note that they must add to 100 or less. Larger values of PCTUSED improve space utilization, but increase processing costs for INSERT and UPDATE commands. Remember also that the PCTUSED parameter is ignored when the tablespace is locally managed and segment space management is set to AUTO.

Table 13.2 describes Oracle's primary recommendations for setting the PCTFREE and PCTUSED parameters. Using your knowledge of the data, you can fine-tune the

TABLE 13.1 Effects of choosing PCTFREE values.

Smaller PCTFREE	Less room for updates to existing table rows. Inserts fill the block with less wasted space. May require fewer total data blocks, saving space with faster retrieval.
Larger PCTFREE	More room for updates to existing table rows. May require more blocks. May improve Update performance because the database does not have to migrate rows.

TABLE 13.2 Oracle recommendations for PCTFREE and PCTUSED.

Table Characteristics	Settings	Reasoning
Default	PCTFREE=10 PCTUSED=40	Default values for general purpose tables.
Many UPDATE statements increase the size of rows.	PCTFREE=20 PCTUSED=40	More free space to allow rows to grow. PCTUSED reduces processing during high update activity.
Row sizes rarely change.	PCTFREE=5 PCTUSED=60	Need less free space since row space can be reused. PCTUSED reduces wasted space, allowing space to be reused faster.
Large table and most activity is read only.	PCTFREE=5 PCTUSED=40	With a large table, you want to minimize the empty space.

storage to reduce the storage space required and improve the performance. In small databases, you can usually just let Oracle manage the storage space. However, you should know that you can use these various options to improve the performance of large tables.

DEFINING CLUSTERS

A *cluster* consists of a group of tables that share the same data blocks. Remember that Oracle reads an entire data block from the drive at one time. Data stored in the same data blocks can be accessed quickly. You want to cluster data together when it will often be retrieved at the same time. For example, In the Redwood case, it is common to retrieve columns from the Properties table whenever you pull something from the Listings table. Looking at the table definitions, you can see that they are linked by the PropertyID column. In fact, to create a cluster, you create an index that links the two tables on this clustered key (PropertyID).

Generally, you want to create clusters on tables that are often queried together, but that have few updates. You can improve the performance of the cluster by specifying several storage parameters, including the PCTFREE and PCTUSED values. The SIZE parameter specifies the estimated number of bytes required by an average cluster key and its associated rows of data. It is used by the storage system as a hint to help it store data efficiently. Assuming your account has adequate privileges, you use the CREATE CLUSTER command to set up the cluster:

```
CREATE CLUSTER Listing_Properties (PropertyID NUMBER)
PCTUSED 80
PCTFREE 5
SIZE 200
TABLESPACE users;
```

Once the cluster has been defined, you can create the tables in that cluster using the standard CREATE TABLE command by adding the CLUSTER statement at the end. For example,

```
CREATE TABLE Listings (
   ListingID NUMBER      NOT NULL,
   <other columns>,
     Constraint pk_Listings PRIMARY KEY (ListingID),
     Constraint fk_Listings_Properties FOREIGN KEY (PropertyID)
     REFERENCES Properties(PropertyID)
)  CLUSTER Listing_Properties (PropertyID);
```

You will need to create both tables in the same cluster. Once the cluster and tables have been defined, you need to create a cluster index before you try to insert any rows into the tables. Again, you can control several storage options. For example, you can improve performance by putting the index on a disk drive that is independent from the data cluster drive by specifying a different tablespace. The basic command is straightforward:

```
CREATE INDEX Listing_Properties_Index
ON CLUSTER Listing_Properties
TABLESPACE users
PCTFREE 5;
```

Once the cluster, new tables, and the index have been defined, you can copy data into the tables. Notice that the order of these steps is critical. But, it also means that you must know ahead of time that you want to use clustering. It is possible to set up a cluster after the application has already been running, but it takes more effort. You would have to rename the original tables, create the cluster with the new tables, then transfer the data using SELECT INTO statements. When you have retested the entire application, you can then drop the renamed original tables.

If you are testing these commands on your database, you will want to drop the cluster before continuing. Remember that when dropping a cluster you have to drop the tables at the same time:

```
DROP CLUSTER Listing_Properties INCLUDING TABLES;
```

CREATING PARTITIONS

In many respects, partitions are the opposite of clusters. Your goal is to separate the data in a table so that portions are physically stored in different locations. Partitions have several advantages in a ***very large-scale database (VLSD)***. Organizations today have VLSDs consisting of hundreds of gigabytes or even terabytes of data. The main advantages of partitioning tables and indexes are:

- Reduce the risk of loss due to data corruption, since failures would generally be limited to a single partition.
- Simplify backup and recovery because individual partitions can be handled separately with smaller amounts of data.
- Improve disk performance by allocating partitions to different disk drives. More active data can be stored on faster drives.
- Improve manageability, performance, and reliability. Performance is improved in part because indexes are partitioned, speeding lookups and joins.

Partitioning is transparent to the SQL commands and applications, so it can be done without altering the existing operations. However, the DBA can take advantage of special commands to work with just selected partitions if needed.

Oracle provides several ways to partition tables. At heart, they all allow separating a table by rows and columns. The three primary methods are range, hash, and list partitioning. ***Range partitioning*** splits the rows of a table into different partitions based on ranges of column values. For example, eventually you might split the Listings table based on the BeginListDate. Anything with an older date will be stored on a cheaper but slower disk system because the data is not accessed very often. Effectively, properties for each agent would be stored separately. You define partitions when you create the table. So, you either have to know ahead of time that you will use partitions, or you have to create a new table and copy in the old data. The syntax for ranges is straightforward, but you need to know the range values for each partition. Assuming that you have older data for Redwood Realty, you might use:

```
CREATE TABLE Listings2(
   ListingID      NUMBER     NOT NULL,
   PropertyID     NUMBER     NOT NULL,
   BeginListDate  DATE,
   <other columns>,
   <constraints>
)
PARTITION BY RANGE (BeginListDate)
(  PARTITION List2004 VALUES LESS THAN ('01-JAN-2005') TABLESPACE List04,
   PARTITION List2005 VALUES LESS THAN ('01-JAN-2006') TABLESPACE List05,
   PARTITION List2006 VALUES LESS THAN ('01-JAN-2007') TABLESPACE List06,
   PARTITION List2007 VALUES LESS THAN ('01-JAN-2008') TABLESPACE List07,
   PARTITION Future   VALUES LESS THAN ('01-JAN-2100') TABLESPACE List00
);
```

Notice that the ranges are arranged in order. Items that do not meet the first condition are tested against the second, and so on, until the appropriate partition is found.

Also notice that each partition is stored on a separate tablespace in this example. Of course, it would be necessary to create those tablespaces before running this command.

Hash partitioning is split rows based on a single key value, and you use it when you are unable to identify specific ranges for the values. In the Redwood case, you might want to split the Listings table based on the ListingAgentID. Effectively, listings for agents would be stored in different partitions. This approach has the benefit of isolating the data for each agent. If a disk drive crashes, only the listings for a few agents would be affected; the rest of the agency could continue as usual. You can specify the number of partitions, so in this case you would probably not completely separate listings by agent, but would create four or five groups. Again, you define a hash listing when you create the table:

```
CREATE TABLE Listings3 (
    ListingID        NUMBER      NOT NULL,
    PropertyID       NUMBER      NOT NULL,
    ListingAgentID   NUMBER      NOT NULL,
    <other columns>,
    <constraints>
)
PARTITION BY HASH (ListingAgentID)
Partitions 4
STORE IN (List1, List2, List3, List4);
```

List partitioning is more flexible than range or hash partitioning. The list enables you to identify exactly which items will be stored together based on specific values. A common example is to partition rows of data based on the state. For example, you might partition the Properties table based on the state code:

```
CREATE TABLE Properties2 (
    PropertyID       NUMBER      NOT NULL,
    OwnerID    NUMBER      NOT NULL,
    State      NVARCHAR2(20),
    <other columns>,
    <constraints>
)
PARTITION BY LIST (State)
    (PARTITION Pacific VALUES ('CA', 'OR', 'WA'),
     PARTITION SouthWest VALUES ('AZ', 'NM', 'TX'),
     PARTITION NorthWest VALUES ('ID', 'MT', 'UT', 'WY')
);
```

Oracle also provides options to create subpartitions that enable you to break a partition into even smaller groups. If you find you no longer need partitions, you can use the COALESCE option of the ALTER TABLE command to combine data from multiple partitions. Or, if the table is small enough, you could just create a new table and copy the data into it with SQL.

EXPORTING AND IMPORTING DATA

Transferring data from one database to another can be challenging. Often, you will want to transfer all of the data for a table at one time. You will find you need this approach when creating a new database, transferring data from non-Oracle data sources, or copying a database to a new location. You have three basic choices in Oracle, each with different ideal uses. The simplest, but slowest is to create SQL script files with multiple INSERT statements. By far, the fastest is to use the new Data Pump utility. However, it transfers files using a proprietary Oracle format. The third approach uses the SQL*Loader and is more flexible but requires more configuration.

USING SQL SCRIPTS

One approach to transferring data is to create a text script file consisting of multiple INSERT statements. The strength of this approach is that it works almost all of the time and files can be loaded running a script in SQL*Plus. Recall that we have used this approach to build and load the tables used in this book. We chose the approach primarily because it is most likely to work on everyone's configuration. The drawbacks are that: (1) the files are relatively large, (2) it is relatively slow, and (3) the files are difficult to create. The first two drawbacks mean that it will work for small databases, but will be difficult to use for large tables of data. You can reduce the file size slightly by simplifying the INSERT statements, but it will remain slow because every single row is handled separately. We actually got around the third problem by writing a custom program to create the insert statements.

USING THE DATA PUMP

A second approach to transferring data is to use the Oracle bulk export and import commands. These can only be run by a DBA, with the password for the System user. More important, they export data in a proprietary Oracle format so you cannot use them to transfer data to or from other applications. On the other hand, they are the only recommended method for transferring an Oracle database across hardware platforms, such as from Windows to Linux. You can use the export and import commands to deal with a single table or tablespace, and with the entire database. Older versions of Oracle used the exp and imp commands, but these have been replaced with newer **data pump** commands that are substantially faster. You can find details in the Oracle Utilities documentation.

To export and then import an entire database, you need the EXP_FULL_DATABASE and IMP_FULL_DATABASE roles. These are often reserved for the built-in System user. You really do not want to do them now because they take time and disk space, but a DBA needs to be familiar with the commands.

1. As DBA or sysdba, create an Oracle directory that points to the location where you want to store the files:

    `CREATE DIRECTORY dpump_dir1 AS 'c:\temp\datafiles';`

2. Switch to the command line mode. These commands are operating system commands and are not run as SQL commands.

3. Make sure the Oracle_Home\bin folder is in the path, or switch to that folder. Run the command:

    `expdp system/<password> FULL=y DIRECTORY=dpump_dir1 FILE=exportdata.dmp`

4. Copy the **expportdata.dmp** binary file to the new system. It will be huge, so be sure to use a binary copy method.

5. Create a database on the new server and create the directory on this copy.

6. Run the import command:

    `impdp system/<password> FULL=y DIRECTORY=dpump_dir1 FILE=exportdata.dmp`

> **Tip:** The expdp and impdp commands need to be run on the server. The directories are server-based folders and you will need server permissions to access the specified folder.

If you are moving data to an entirely different system, you might want to reassign the datafiles and tablespaces. You can even change the schema if necessary. You first have to create the new datafiles, tablespaces, or schemas on the new database. Then on the impdp command line, use the remap_datafile, remap_tablespace, or remap_schema parameter and specify the old value and the new value.

USING SQL*LOADER AND EXTERNAL TABLES

SQL*Loader is designed to import data from external files. For years, a common way to exchange data across diverse systems has been to create a ***comma-separated values (.CSV)*** text file. One row in the file represents one row of data. In other words, the rows are delimited by the return character stored in the text file. The columns are usually delimited by commas. Text data—particularly text that contains special characters such as commas—is enclosed in quotes. For example, a portion of the Agents data for the Redwood case with four rows and only some of the columns could be stored as:

```
10041,'Kai','Marcoux',03-Oct-1996,12-Dec-1970,'M','(707) 555-0361'
10235,'Tobias','Carling',19-Dec-2000,19-Oct-1975,'M','(707) 555-1983'
10429,'Elizabeth','Dahlen',23-May-2005,03-Oct-1969,'F','(707) 555-7218'
10497,'Ramanathan','Rowe',05-Sep-1997,23-Oct-1953,'M','(707) 555-9839'
```

Spreadsheets and most data-intensive programs usually have a simple option to save data in this format. Oracle's SQL*Loader routine can be used two ways: (1) as a standalone command-line utility, or (2) to create an external table connection. The first approach can be used to bulk-transfer data from one system to another. Note that the first approach can only insert records into an empty table. To add rows to a table, first load them into a temporary table, then use SQL to copy them to the desired location. The second approach could also be used that way, but it can also be used when the text file needs to be changed and reread.

Generally, when you use the batch method of running SQL*Loader, you create a control file that defines the data file. Note that you usually need to run the commands on the database server, so you will need an account on that machine. You can run the load across a network connection if the sqlldr.exe file has been installed on your computer.

1. Using SQL*Plus, create a new version of the Agents file for the Redwood case. The **CreateAgent2.sql** file on the data disk will create the table for you.
2. Copy the **Agents.csv** file from the data disk to a folder on the server.
3. Create a text file to describe the columns of the .CSV file and its location. Name the file **Agents2.ctl**, and put it in the same folder as the .CSV file:

```
load data
  infile 'Agents.csv'
    into table Agents2
  fields terminated by "," optionally enclosed by "'"
     (AgentID, FirstName, LastName, HireDate, BirthDate, Gender,
       WorkPhone, CellPhone, HomePhone, Title, TaxID, LicenseID,
       LicenseDate, LicenseExpire, LicenseStatusID)
```

4. Switch to command mode on the computer that has the sqlldr.exe file installed—usually the server. Change to the folder that holds the control file and type the command to run the loader, using your username, password, and server names.

```
sqlldr username/password@server control=Agents2.ctl
```

5. Start SQL*Plus and check to ensure that the rows have been added. If you are going to continue with the next version of the load command, delete the rows.

```
SELECT Count(*) FROM Agents2;
DELETE   FROM Agents2;
Commit;
```

CHAPTER 13   Database Administration   **609**

The batch approach works well for DBAs when you occasionally need to transfer files. But, what if users routinely generate new versions of the data file and want to import the data regularly? The process can be automated only by using script files on the operating system.

Oracle provides the ability to create ***external tables*** to handle cases where you need more flexibility in importing data. The external table uses the same approach as SQL*Loader, except that you create the definition within Oracle. Once you have defined the external table, you can run SQL commands to retrieve data. In most cases, you will just retrieve the values you need and transfer them to a regular internal table. Once you have defined the external table, you can use the SQL commands whenever you want. If necessary, you could create Oracle procedures to examine the data on import or perform computations or corrections as the data is retrieved.

1. If you have not already done so, create the Agents2 table using the **Agents2.sql** script with the student files. Make sure any existing data is deleted. Also, copy the **Agents.csv** file to a folder on the database server machine.

2. You need to create a directory to tell Oracle where the .CSV file is located. Be sure t enter the correct folder name on your server:

   ```
   create or replace directory csv_dir as 'c:\temp';
   ```

3. In SQL*Plus, run the command to define the external table. You can use the AgentsExternal.sql script file stored on the data disk:

   ```
   CREATE TABLE Agents_ext
       (AgentID          INTEGER,
        FirstName        NVARCHAR2(30),
        LastName         NVARCHAR2(30),
        HireDate         DATE,
        BirthDate        DATE,
        Gender           NVARCHAR2(10),
        WorkPhone        NVARCHAR2(20),
        CellPhone        NVARCHAR2(20),
        HomePhone        NVARCHAR2(20),
        Title            NVARCHAR2(30),
        TaxID            NVARCHAR2(30),
        LicenseID        NVARCHAR2(30),
        LicenseDate      DATE,
        LicenseExpire    DATE,
        LicenseStatusID  INTEGER
       )
       organization external (
       type oracle_loader
       default directory csv_dir
       access parameters (
          records delimited by newline
          fields terminated by ','
          optionally enclosed by '"' lrtrim
          missing field values are null
       )
       location ('Agents.csv')
   )
       reject limit unlimited;
   ```

4. Test the connection by counting the number of rows in the external table:

   ```
   SELECT Count(*) FROM Agents_ext;
   ```

> **Tip:** If there are errors in the file definition, you will see several error files in the folder holding the .CSV file after you try the SELECT command.

5. You can now copy the rows into the internal table with a standard INSERT INTO command:

```
INSERT INTO Agents2
SELECT * FROM Agents_ext;
```

Of course, the SELECT statement could have contained function calls to round off numbers, convert dates, or perform complex lookups or calculations on the data. This process is often used when you need to clean up the data while importing it.

6. Since you do not need this new data, drop both the Agents2 and the Agents_ext tables. Be careful to delete the Agents2 table and not the Agents table.

```
DROP Table Agents2 PURGE;
DROP Table Agents_ext;
```

SQL*Loader, both in batch mode and using external tables, has additional parameters to deal with other file types. For example, you can specify a fixed format, where each column of data begins in a specific column and has a predefined width. You can use the trim statements to remove leading and trailing spaces in those cases.

On the other hand, SQL*Loader does not export .CSV files. If you want to create those, you need to write your own SELECT statement in SQL*Plus. Basically, use the concatenation operator to build one long string for each row. For example:

```
SELECT AgentID || ',' || '"' || LastName || '"' || ',' || '"' …
```

Add the rest of the columns to the query and test it. Once it works, redirect the output to a file and run the query. Another trick is to use different software. For instance, you can import the data into an Excel spreadsheet and then use Excel to save the CSV file. Although Excel will not work for large tables, you could find other packages and use the same trick.

MAINTAINING THE DBMS

One of the roles of the DBA is to maintain the DBMS. That includes monitoring for problems—particularly the space issues. But, it also means planning for changes to the DBMS software. Commercial software continually evolves—both through patches and upgrades. **Patches** are generally released to solve specific, immediate problems. For example, you might receive a notice that Oracle has been patched to solve some security issue. **Upgrades** are major changes or additions to the DBMS software. Sometimes upgrades are simply accumulated patches released as a complete package so you can make all of the changes at once. Other times, major sections of the DBMS software are rewritten. These larger changes are usually released as a new major version with a big number change, such as from Oracle 9i to 10g.

PATCHES AND UPDATES

Patches and minor version upgrades are usually relatively safe to install. They rarely change the way the underlying database is organized, and you might even be able to leave the database operational while you make the change. Major upgrades are usually more challenging. They often require existing databases to be converted to a new storage format.

It can be a challenge to keep up with patches. Oracle has adopted a regular schedule for releasing critical security patches. You can get on the mailing list so that you will receive an e-mail notice whenever the patches are released. Other patches are released almost randomly, and you have to check the Oracle Web site periodically to see if you need the changes. For the most part, if your applications are running correctly, you should only install critical patches. Any time you change your system, you will have to test your databases and applications to make sure they continue to work correctly.

Oracle only provides patches to customers that hold maintenance contracts. Most educational accounts are granted maintenance contracts, but there might be only one authorized contact user. With the maintenance contract, you want to set up an account on the Oracle *MetaLink* Web site (http://metalink.oracle.com). In most companies, one DBA will be responsible for this account. This DBA also can grant other users from the company permission to register. The MetaLink site provides news and information on patches and updates. MetaLink is different from OTN and requires a separate account registration. MetaLink provides detailed information on database administration, so it is a good starting point to learn more about the tools available. You can also use the Bug and Patch search systems to look for bug fixes and patches. Figure 13.10 shows a version of the MetaLink path search screen. This version shows the latest patch versions organized by products and components. You can also search by keywords or patch number. From here, you can download specific patches and run the installation program.

FIGURE 13.10 MetaLink patch search.

You can also configure Enterprise Manager to run a RefreshFromMetalink job every day. Actually, the job is already configured; all you have to do is choose **Setup/Patching Setup** and enter your MetaLink username and password. The EM will check for updates and download the data for display in the **Critical Patch Advisories** section of the EM. When you see a critical patch in the list, you can click the **Patch Advisories** link to get more information. By following the links, you can start a patch job that will automatically install the patch for you. This process is usually easier than manually downloading the patch from MetaLink, configuring the patch engine, and installing the patch.

Upgrades, particularly major version upgrades require considerably more planning. Most major releases come with detailed instructions on how to convert the data from the old format to the new format. Nonetheless, it takes time to upgrade all of the data. You might choose to shut down the database application during the conversion, in which case you have to find a time when the business operations will not need the system. The other alternative is to convert the database at one point in time, then transfer the changes into the new system once it is running. Major upgrades might also require updates to forms and reports. In any case, you will definitely have to set up a temporary server and test everything before attempting the conversion.

STARTING AND SHUTTING DOWN THE DATABASE

You should rarely need to actually shut down an Oracle database. However, some situations require it, such as changing database parameters, performing a full data backup, or for some upgrades.

If it works, the easiest way to shut down a database is to log into the Enterprise Manager using the sys account as sysdba and click the Shutdown button. However, early versions of the software appear to have problems handling passwords and this approach might not work. You can also try using SQL*Plus and issue the *shutdown* command.

As shown in Table 13.3, the shutdown command has some options that give you control over the process. The options are listed in order of most polite to emergency (top to bottom). Generally, you will use either the transactional or immediate options. The default normal option is too slow, since you have to go around and tell all of the users to disconnect. The abort option is for emergencies only because it potentially leaves the database in an inconsistent state and requires that you run recovery when you restart.

TABLE 13.3 Shutdown options.

Shutdown Command Option	*Description*
Shutdown normal (default)	No new connections are allowed, but the system waits for all users to disconnect before shutting down.
Shutdown transactional	No new connections are allowed. No new transactions can be started. After all transactions are completed, the database shuts down.
Shutdown immediate	No new connections are allowed. No new transactions can be started. Uncommitted transactions are rolled back.
Shutdown abort	All transactions are terminated. Current SQL statements are terminated. The database will have to go through recovery when it restarts. Avoid this option except in emergencies.

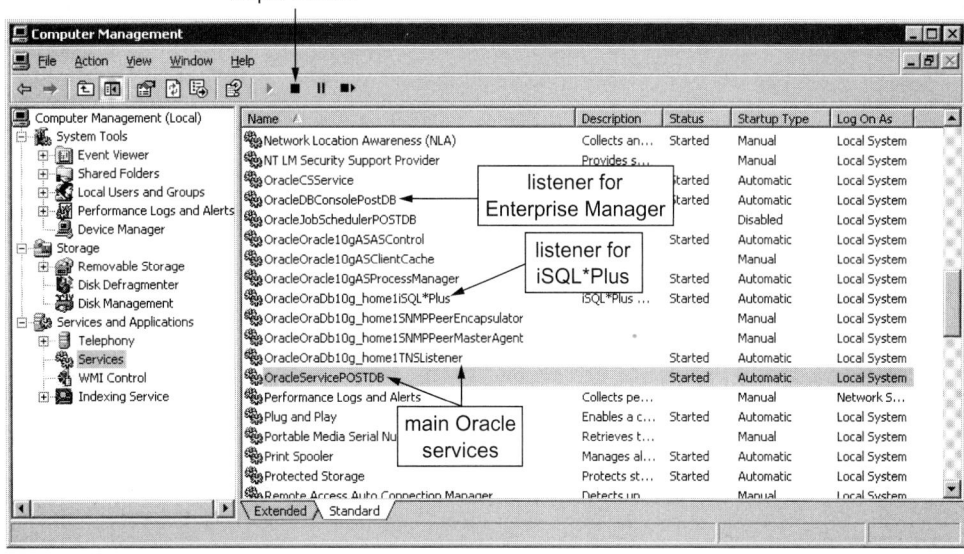

FIGURE 13.11 Shutting down Oracle with the Windows service manager.

If you cannot get the database to shut down with one of these commands, you can also force it to shut down by stopping the underlying database services. Also, an Oracle shutdown command does not stop the underlying services. Sometimes you need to force a complete shutdown so the service can reinitialize. As shown in Figure 13.11, stopping a service is straightforward. However, you will probably need to be a member of the Windows Administrators group on the server.

1. Log into the Windows server as an administrator.
2. Start the **Administrative Tools/Computer Management** program. Expand the **Services** node and scroll down to the section of **Oracle...** entries.
3. Select the **OracleService<name>** entry. Yours will be different because the name of the service is based on the name of the database.
4. Click the **Stop** button. You can repeat the process with the **TNSListener** and the **iSQL*Plus** services, but they rarely need to be restarted.

There is one tiny catch: when you shut down the main Oracle database service, it will also shut down the Enterprise Manager listener (DBConsole). That means you cannot use the Enterprise Manager to restart the database. Sometimes, the DBConsole service will not restart unless you reboot the entire server. That drawback simply means that you might not be able to use the Enterprise Manager. Yet another reason why DBAs learn to use the SQL commands.

Most of the time when you restart a database, you simply reverse the procedures used to shut it down. If you stopped the Windows database service, you have to restart it. If you issued a shutdown command, you will send a startup command. However, the *startup* command has an option that can be useful in some circumstances.

Table 13.4 shows the startup options. Generally, you will simply start the database and let everyone use it. The other choices are used for specific administrative situations. In particular, the *startup restrict* command is useful because it gives you full access to the database and you do not have to worry about concurrency issues with other users. Of course, the business cannot run while you are running in this mode, so

TABLE 13.4 Startup options.

Startup command option	Description
Startup	Starts the instance, mounts the database, and allows everyone to log in.
Startup nomount	Starts the instance, but does not mount the database. Used when you want to create a new database.
Startup mount	Starts the instance, sets up the database, but does not open it. Used for configuring red logs files and performing full database recovery.
Startup restrict	Starts and mounts the database, but only certain users (DBAs) can log in. Useful when you need to export data, load large tables, or during upgrade migrations.

use it sparingly. When you have finished with your work, you can open the system up again with the command:

```
ALTER SYSTEM disable restricted session;
```

BACKING UP THE DATABASE

Now that you have seen how Oracle stores data, and you know how to shut down and restart the database, you can learn the truly critical task of backing up the database. Databases form the foundation of many business processes. Without the data stored in them, a company would be lost. Managers rely on the stability of the information system, and databases are one of the most important components. It is essential that every database have a backup plan that is followed. Remember that data is stored on mechanical disk drives. No matter how well you protect the drives, there is a probability that they will fail, simply because they are mechanical devices. More serious recovery issues arise in the event of a natural disaster such as a fire or flood. Then you have to be able to recover the data and load it on a different machine in a safe location.

COMPLICATIONS IN BACKING UP DATABASES

Remember that a major strength of a DBMS is its ability to handle multiple users. But supporting multiple users makes it much harder to handle backups. For starters, it is difficult to kick everyone off the database, stop the database, and make a copy. In other words, changes are constantly being made to the database.

Figure 13.12 illustrates the complications and how they are handled by Oracle. A full backup is made of the database when it is in a consistent state. To support recovery, Oracle writes all data changes to a redo log. Actually, there are always at least two redo log files at any time. However, the catch is that when you first install a database, the redo log files are not archived. That means when a file fills up, the system starts back at the beginning of the file and overwrites the oldest data. When you overwrite data, you might not be able to recover after a crash. So, the first step is to turn on the archive feature:

1. Start the **Enterprise Manager** and log in with the sys account as sysdba.
2. Select the **Maintenance** link. Under the **Backup/Recovery** list, select the link to **Configure Recovery Settings**.
3. Figure 13.13 shows some of the options on the Recovery Settings page. Check the option to set the ArchiveLog mode. You can also enter a disk drive folder where the archives will be stored.

CHAPTER 13 Database Administration

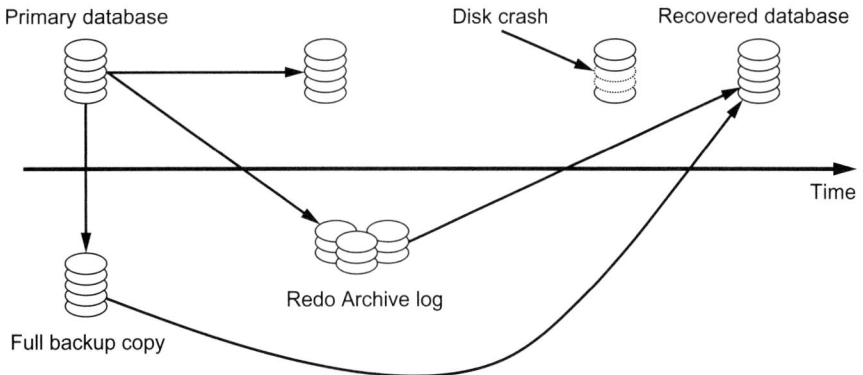

FIGURE 13.12 Recovering an active database.

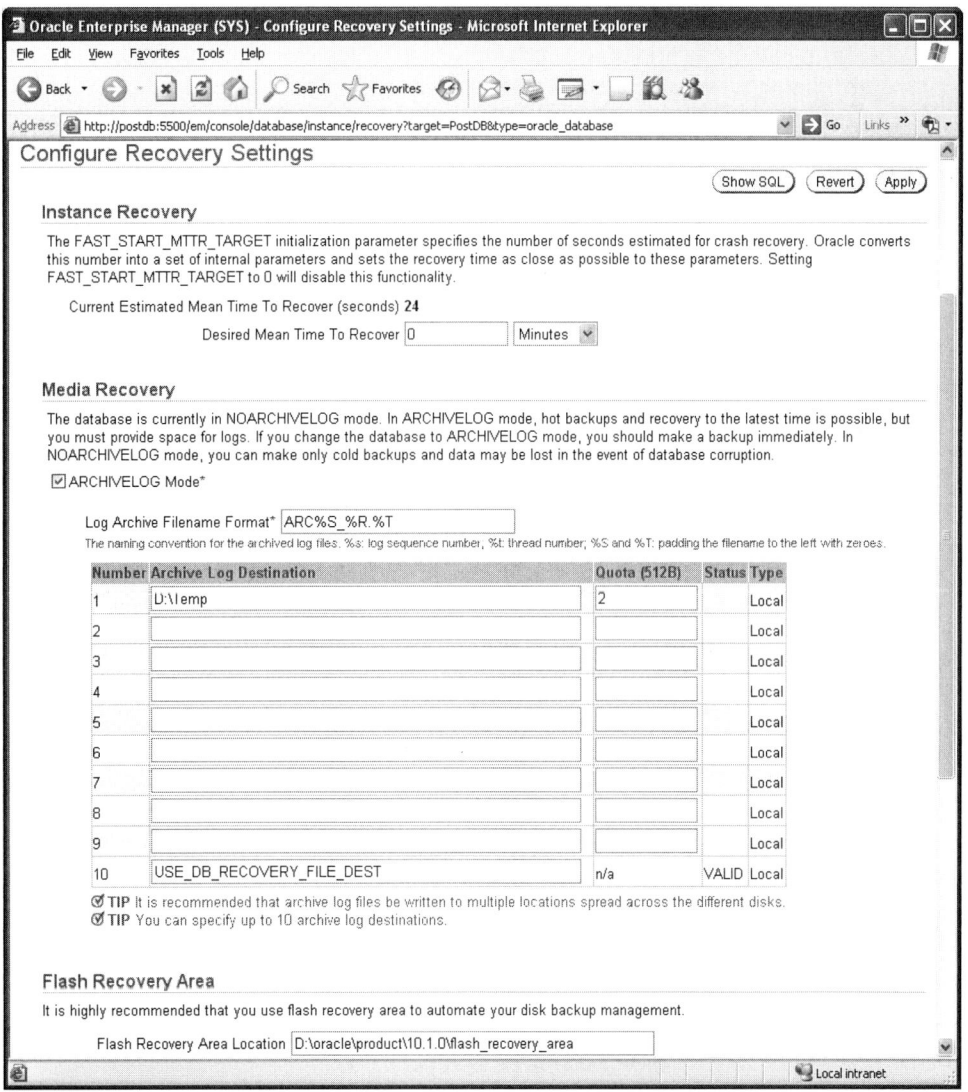

FIGURE 13.13 Configuring the ArchiveLog property.

4. Scroll to the bottom of the form and choose the option to write the changes only to the startup file. The changes will take effect when you stop and restart the database.
5. Scrolling down the form, you can also check the option to establish a **flash recovery area**. When you have made all of your changes, click the **Apply** button. Ultimately, you will have to reboot the server for the changes to take effect.

Setting up a flash recovery area causes all ongoing changes to be written to a special folder. Data is only held for a limited time, but it is particularly useful when users make mistakes. With the flash recovery area, users can basically undo their operations, even after they have been committed. So, if a user somehow drops the Customers table, you can quickly restore it from the flash recovery area—without having to go through a formal database recovery operation.

> **Tip:** Interactions between the EM and the Windows security system might prevent you from setting the ArchiveLog mode on some machines.

SHUTDOWN AND SYSTEM BACKUPS (COLD)

You have limited choices if you do not set the ArchiveLog mode. Without it, you are generally restricted to cold backups. Essentially, you shut down the database and use operating system utilities to copy the files. This approach actually works well if your business does not need to operate 24 hours a day. You can pick a time slot, automatically shut down the database, and let the operating system make backups of the files. The backup files should always be in a consistent state, so recovery is easy. Just shut down the database, restore the files, and restart the database. Of course, you will lose any changes that took place since the most recent backup. So, be sure to make backup copies fairly often.

Although this approach might seem limiting, it means you can choose to rely on the hardware and operating system features to provide continuous backup for you. In particular, you can put the database files on a RAID system. These systems can automatically back up every piece of data that is written to the drives. You can also get software that will create mirror copies of the drives in a distant location—if they are connected by a high-speed network. With this process, the hardware effectively maintains a continuous backup, so you might not need the Oracle log file approach.

To back up your files manually, you need to make sure you get all of them. Also, remember that you will want to back up the system software and registry database so that you can restore the current version of the DBMS if necessary. You can find the location of the database files using the Enterprise Manager.

1. Start the **Enterprise Manage**r and log in as system or sysman.
2. Click the **Administration** link from the main page. The list of file types is under the **Storage** heading. Select **Controlfiles** and **Datafiles** links.
3. Click the **Maintenance** link, then the **Configure Recovery Settings** under the **Backup/Recovery** heading to get the archive files.
4. Start SQL*Plus and examine the DB_RECOVERY_FILE_DEST parameter to get the location of all flashback files, and the SPFILE parameter to get the location of the startup file:

```
SHOW PARAMETER db_recovery_file_dest;
SHOW PARAMETER spfile;
```

Table 13.5 shows the default locations and typical names for the files. You can also use the Windows search utility to look for similar files that someone might have

CHAPTER 13 Database Administration   617

TABLE 13.5 Oracle file names and common locations.

File type	Typical Name	Typical Location
Control File	CONTROL01.CTL	ORACLE_HOME\Oradata*DBName*\
SPFile	SPFILE<*DBName*>.ORA	ORACLE_HOME\<*instance*>\Database
Password file	PWD<*DBName*>.ORA	ORACLE_HOME\Database\
Data Files	SYSTEM01.DBF	ORACLE_HOME\Oradata*DBName*\ Plus other locations if you create your own tablespaces and datafiles.
Archive Logs		Depends on what you entered.
Flash Recovery Area		ORACLE_HOME\flash_recovery_area
Redo Logs	REDO01.LOG	ORACLE_HOME\Oradata*DBName*\

configured. Note that you really want to back up all of the files in the Oracle_Home\Oradata*DBName*\ folder, along with all of the files in the flash_recovery_area.

Even on your development machine, you should consider making backup copies of these files. In particular, you should always have a backup copy of the startup SPFILE. If anything goes wrong while you are working with the administration tools, you can shut down the database and copy the saved version of this critical configuration file.

CONTINUOUS BACKUPS AND ARCHIVES (HOT)

When you do have the ArchiveLog mode set, Oracle can automatically make backup copies on the live database. It simply writes the backup as of a point in time. If anything goes wrong, you can restore the main backup database, and Oracle will add the changes from the archive logs.

The Enterprise Manager provides options to help you create backup files. You can also run the ***recovery manager (RMAN)*** and issue command-line statements to generate backup copies. With RMAN, it is easy to backup anything from the entire database, to tablespaces, or individual datafiles. Run RMAN using the command line mode on the server. The basic steps are:

1. Start a command-line session, and log into the recovery manager using the sys account with the correct password and database name:

   ```
   rman target sys/password@database
   ```

2. Set the national language character set and date format:

   ```
   NLS_LANG=American
   NLS_DATE_FORMAT='Mon D YYYY HH24:MI:SS'
   ```

3. You can view the current configuration:

   ```
   show all;
   ```

4. You probably should configure the backup device. The default is set to disk, which is easier in most cases. Once the file has been written, you can use operating system utilities to copy the file to tape and move it offsite. However, you need to tell RMAN which folder to use for the backup files:

   ```
   configure channel device type disk format 'd:\temp\ora_df%t_s%s_s%p';
   ```

   The file name is expanded by RMAN to include the date and backup sequence information.

5. You only have to configure the devices once. From there you simply issue a backup command. The easiest command is to back up the entire database, but unless you have plenty of time and spare disk space, you probably do not want to run this command on your development machine now:

```
backup database;
exit;
```

You can use the exit command at any point to exit the recovery manager. Remember that you need to set the ArchiveLog property for RMAN to function correctly. Of course, archiving all of the changes to your database will eat up a fair amount of disk space. For that reason, most developers do not bother with backup on their desktop databases.

In a production database, you need to decide early in the process how you want to handle backups. Given the relatively low price of data storage products, it makes sense to let the RAID hardware do the job for you. It can simplify the management of the database, and it provides continuous backups. However, you should seriously consider configuring the flashback recovery area. This approach serves a different purpose—it is designed to help users recover from mistakes without having to call on the DBA to restore the database. It is easy to control the amount of storage allocated for the flash area, and you can quickly undo drastic changes made by the users.

MONITORING AND IMPROVING DATABASE PERFORMANCE

Large databases can be challenging to run. As the amount of data and number of users increases, the system can begin to slow down—sometimes dramatically. Queries that worked well during development suddenly take several minutes to run. Users click options on forms and have to wait. As a DBA, you are often called upon to find ways to improve the database performance. In fact, a great deal of a DBA's time is spent monitoring the database performance and proactively searching for causes and solutions before they become noticeable to users.

Unfortunately, there are rarely simple answers to improving database performance. Each database seems to have its own bottlenecks and problems. In some cases, you can improve results by adding new hardware—particularly system RAM, faster disk drives (RAID), or moving to a cluster-based system with multiple processors. But, before you spend the extra money, you still need to find the source of the problems to determine which approach you should take. Also, as you have seen in the discussion on data storage, Oracle has several options for improving performance by changing the way data is stored and retrieved. In some cases, you can get dramatic improvements simply by changing the storage methods. Finally, queries can be a major cause of performance degradation. Most queries can be written in several different ways, and it is not always obvious which method is the best. To evaluate queries, turn to the Query Optimizer.

MONITORING TOOLS

Oracle provides several monitoring tools to notify DBAs of impending problems. In particular, you should jump if you see any of the default alerts appear in the Enterprise Manager: Table Space Usage, Snapshot Too Old, Recovery Area Low on Free Space, and Resumable Session Suspended. All of them indicate that the database is running out of disk space in a particular area. The Table Space Usage alert fires a warning message at 85 percent of capacity and a critical alert when it is 97 percent full. You can also configure the alerts to send you e-mail messages—which means you could have them sent to your pager or cell phone in case of a major emergency. If you imposed absolute space constraints on your tablespaces, you can solve the problem by adding new datafiles. If you used the auto-extend feature of the tablespace, you will probably have to find new disk drives. You can also create your own alerts based on almost any condition you need. Alerts are created based on *metrics*.

1. Log into the **Enterprise Manager** and click the **Performance** link.
2. Scroll to the bottom and select the **All Metrics** link under the **Related Links** section.
3. Clicking the **Manage Metrics** link enables you to change the threshold values for the various items to trigger the alert. Clicking the **User-Defined Metrics** link enables you to create your own metrics.

Figure 13.14 shows the list of standard metrics defined in Oracle. Clicking on any of the items generates a page that shows the detailed statistics evaluated for that particular item. For example, if you click the **Tablespaces Full** metric, you will be given a page listing each tablespace and its percentage utilization. Of course, the statistics generated on your development machine are usually not very exciting—particularly if you have not been running any big jobs. But remember this section of the Enterprise Manager, because it provides a quick way for the DBA to spot potential problems and drill down to see the cause.

FIGURE 13.14 Metrics used for standard alerts.

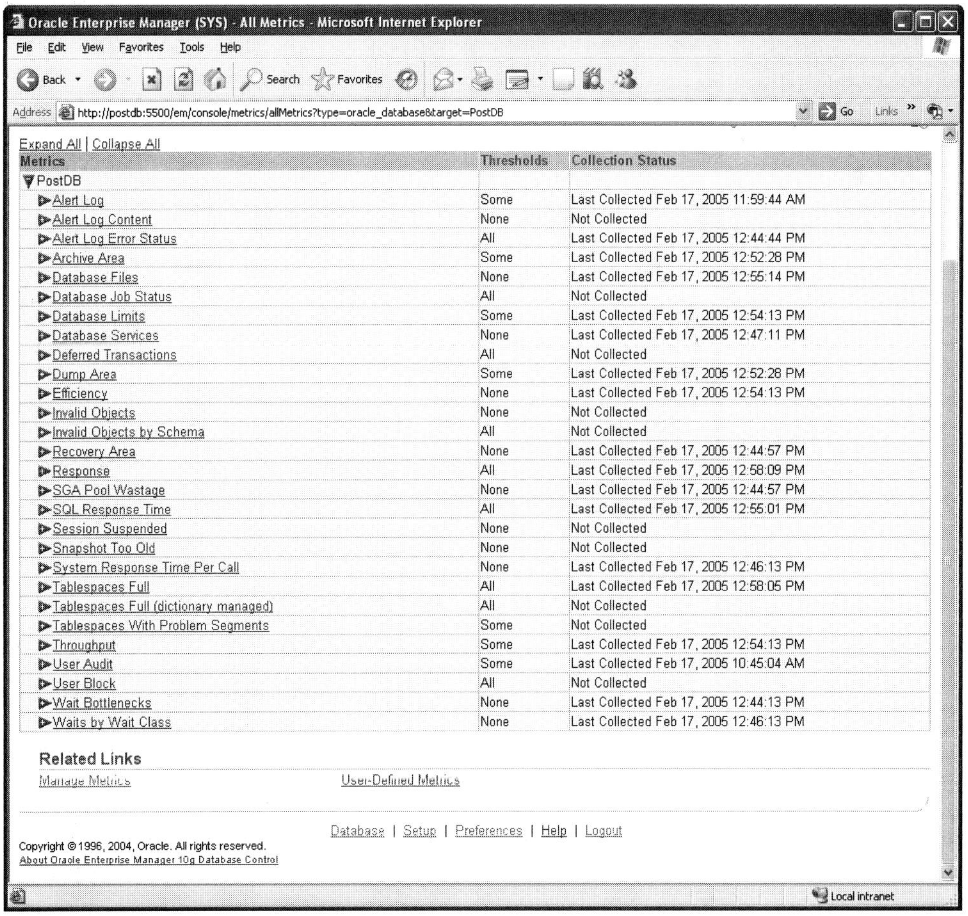

620 Introduction to Oracle

If you want to receive more immediate notification of problems, you can configure the system to send e-mail messages.

1. First, configure the server so that it knows how to connect to a mail server. From any **Enterprise Manager** page, click the **Setup** link, then the **Notification Methods** link.
2. Enter the full name of the outgoing **SMTP mail server**. You need to get this name from your network administrator, and you might need to get network security configured to allow your database server access to the mail server. Fill in the e-mail address that will appear as the sender's address. (This is probably not your address.)
3. Enter your e-mail address. Click the **Preferences** link, and then the **General** link. Add your e-mail address to the list.
4. Select the rules that will trigger messages. Click the **Rules** link in the **Notification** section. Select the option button in front of the desired alert, then click the **Assign Methods** button and check the option to send an e-mail.

Figure 13.15 shows the Preferences screen where you select an event. It also shows the location of the Setup and Preferences links needed to establish the e-mail server data. You probably want to be cautious and limit the number of events that will send you e-mail. If you receive constant messages, you will learn to ignore all of them.

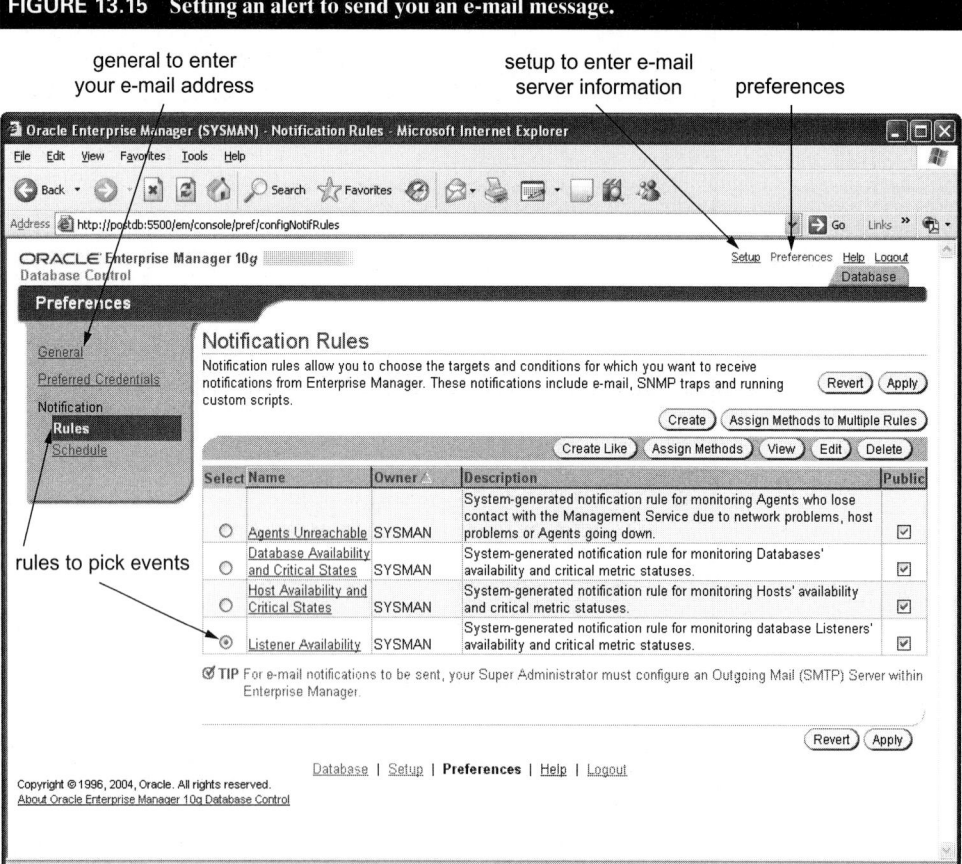

FIGURE 13.15 Setting an alert to send you an e-mail message.

Beyond simple alerts, Oracle includes the self-diagnostic engine: *Automatic Database Diagnostic Monitor (ADDM)*. The ADDM periodically collects usage statistics and analyzes the data to look for problems. It also makes recommendations on how to tune the database and improve performance. Generally, it focuses on three major types of problems:

- Resource bottlenecks, such as insufficient CPU cycles.
- Poor connection management, where an application makes too many connections to the database, instead of reusing a single connection.
- Lock contention, where multiple users are holding on to data too long, causing others to wait for the concurrency lock to be released.

The Enterprise Manager provides charts of the more important statistics monitored by ADDM. You can see these charts from the Performance link of the Enterprise Manager.

5. Click the **Performance** link in the **Enterprise Manager** to see the default statistics.

Figure 13.16 shows some of the statistics, but the chart is unexciting because it is a development machine with almost no queries being run. You are looking for peaks—particularly at certain times of the day. You can click on any of the charts to see more

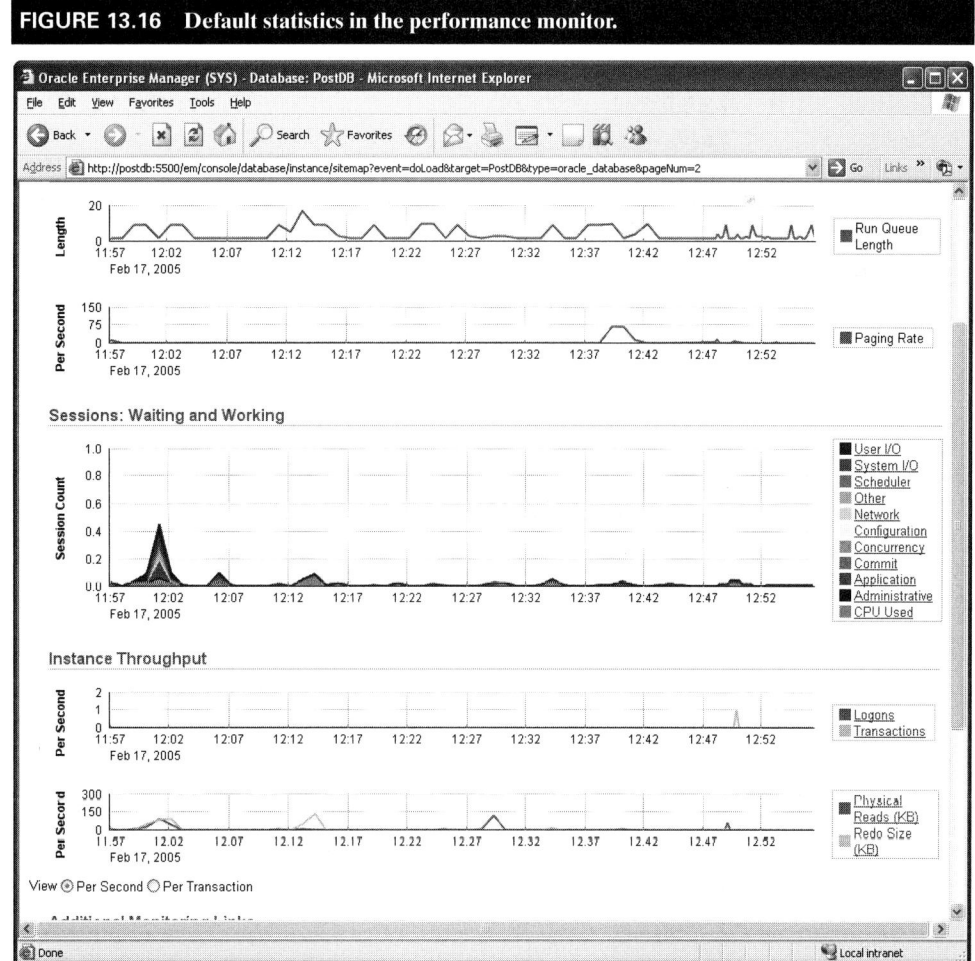

FIGURE 13.16 Default statistics in the performance monitor.

detailed information. For example, the Per Second chart provides detail on the CPU, Memory, and Disk I/O utilization rates over time.

6. Scroll the page down and click the **Top SQL** link under the Additional **Monitoring Links** section.

Figure 13.17 shows an example of the performance monitor for the top SQL commands. Again, only a few commands were run during the monitoring time period. In a production environment, you would see the queries that are eating up the most resources. Those are queries that you need to be concerned about. Even small gains in performance for the top queries will provide decent gains across the system. The EM makes it easy to click on each query to learn the details, and to run the SQL Tuning Advisor. That tool is explained in the next section, so hold off running it for now.

When you do spot problems—particularly when you receive a critical alert message—you can often click on items to gain more detailed information. Additionally, the alert usually provides some suggestions for how to resolve the problem. Oracle also provides several **tuning advisors**—automated tools that analyze the problem and suggest corrections. Table 13.6 lists the major advisors and describes their primary purposes.

FIGURE 13.17 Performance monitor showing the top SQL commands.

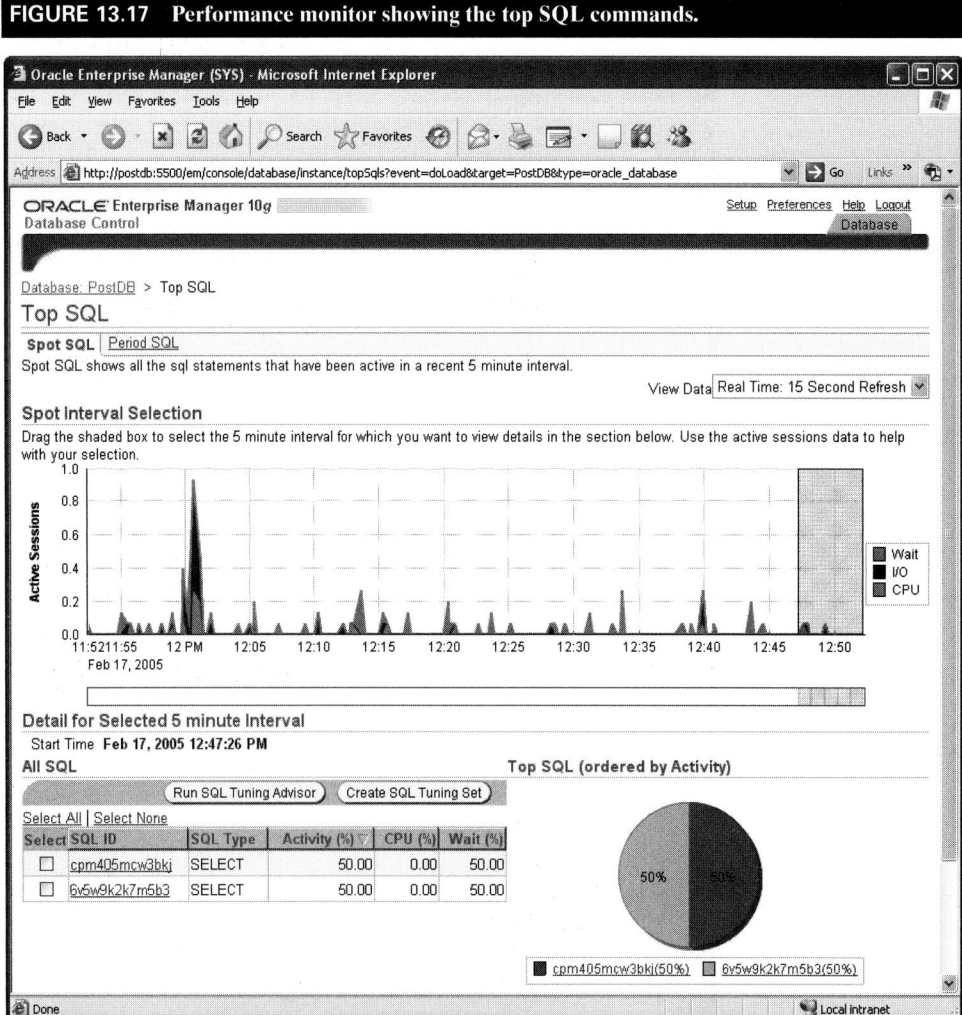

TABLE 13.6 Tuning advisors.

Advisor	Description
ADDM Advisor	The automatic analyzer examines usage, self-diagnoses problems, and recommends overall improvements.
SQL Tuning Advisor	Analyzes SQL statements and recommends rewrites to improve performance on individual queries.
SQL Access Advisor	Analyzes SQL statements and recommends indexes and materialized views.

Memory Advisor
  Shared Pool Advisor
  Buffer Cache Advisor
  PGA Advisor
	Analyzes the use of system memory and can automatically reconfigure it for optimal performance. You can also run SGA and PGA advisors manually.

Segment Advisor	Analyzes segments to decide if you should run the shrink option to compact the space. It also maintains usage reports that are useful for capacity planning.
Undo Advisor	Identifies problems in the undo tablespace and helps set the optimal size, threshold values, and retention period for the undo and flashback segments.

You can run any of the advisors from the **Enterprise Manager**. Return to the **Home** (Database) page and click the **Advisor Central** link under the **Related Links** section. The ADDM advisor works best after it has collected usage statistics for several days—especially over peak time periods. Memory and disk I/O tuning is relatively technical, so unless you want to become an expert in these areas, the best advice is to implement the suggestions offered by the advisors.

The primary system advisor, the ADDM, looks at the snapshots of data taken every hour and makes recommendations on how to improve the system performance. To see the report:

1. Select the **Performance** link and click the **Advisor Central** option under the **Related Links** list.
2. Pick the **ADDM** advisor. If necessary, **refresh** the chart. Choose a time period by clicking on a snapshot icon under a relatively busy time slot. Click the **OK** button.

Figure 13.18 shows that if the ADDM advisor finds problems, they will be displayed in a list at the bottom of the screen. You can go through each option and decide whether the problem is serious enough to require changes.

3. Click on one of the links to get a more detailed description and suggested improvements.

Figure 13.19 shows a problem with the memory configuration and suggests how performance can be improved. In most cases, you can click the **Implement** button and the EM will help you make the changes. You generally need to be running with the sysdba account to actually make changes to the database.

OPTIMIZING QUERIES

Queries can become a problem within an application—particularly as the size of the database increases. Because queries are so important to performance, Oracle has continually improved its query optimizer. Now, all queries are automatically scanned and the optimizer chooses the best approach for each query. It accomplishes this task by

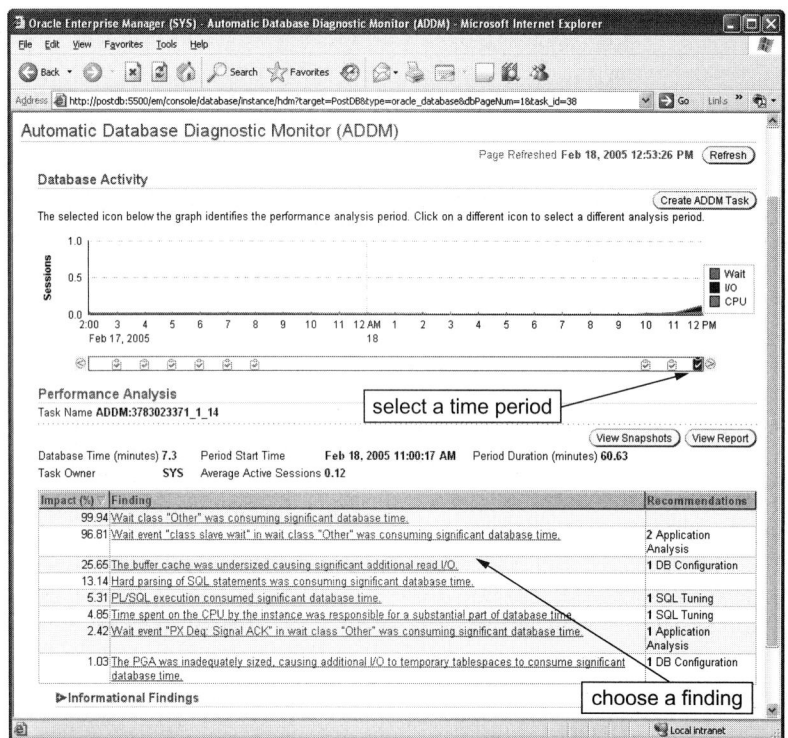

FIGURE 13.18 Automated performance analysis problems found.

looking at basic statistics about the tables, such as the number of rows, and the degree of repetition within a column. However, this automated query optimizer has only fractions of a second to make a decision and choose the best approach. Also, it is limited by the current structure of the database. Consequently, Oracle also provides the ability for you to run a more intensive analysis of the query. In fact, you have two major tools: the SQL Tuning and Query Access advisors.

The *SQL Tuning* advisor performs a more intensive analysis of a specific query and makes suggestions on how to improve it. In the process, it creates a *SQL Profile* to hold its main decisions. Later, when the query is run again, it uses the optimizer hints in the Profile along with current statistics to improve its approach to the query. Usually, you want to run the SQL Tuning advisor on the queries that take the most time to process. The easiest approach is to use the Enterprise Manager and let it identify the most important queries. Recall from Figure 13.17 that the performance monitor tracks these queries for various time intervals. You can tune any of these queries simply by selecting it from the list.

1. In the EM, switch to the **Performance** monitor. Click the **Top SQL** link under the **Additional Monitoring Links** heading.
2. Click on the bar below the chart to select a time period with relatively heavy database activity. Click one of the **SELECT** queries.

Figure 13.20 shows that the tuning advisor displays the *execution plan* for the query. This plan shows the overall approach that Oracle will use. With practice, you can read through the plan to look for potential problems. For example, you might see tables being used that are unnecessary. You might see a step that carries a high processing cost—which is a good place to start looking for improvements. The Oracle

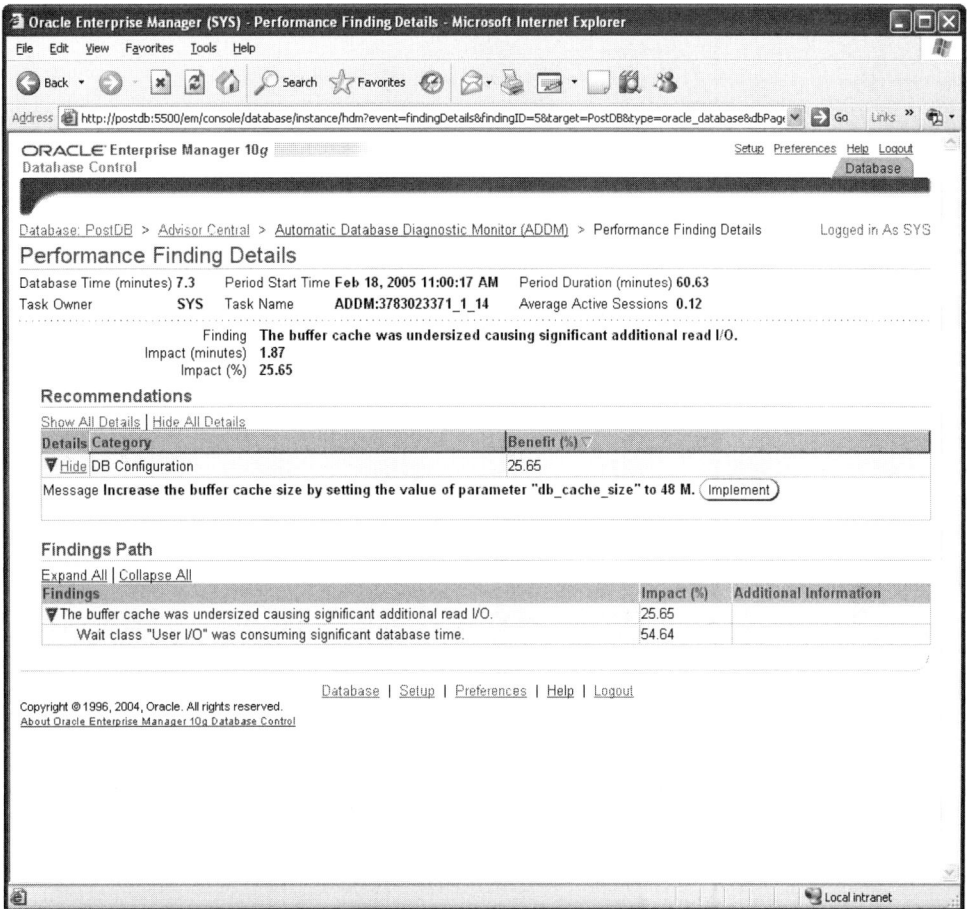

FIGURE 13.19 Suggestions to fix database problems.

documentation also points out that you should avoid calling a view from within a query. It is better to rewrite the view's SQL statements inside the main query to allow the optimizer to work across the entire query. In fact, in most cases, it is best to let the tuning advisor make most of the decisions:

3. Click the **Run SQL Tuning Advisor** button.

After a few seconds, or longer if it is a big query, Figure 13.21 shows the recommendations of the Tuning advisor. In this case, the underlying statistics had not been gathered for the tables yet. Click the **Implement** button and the system will run the job to gather the statistics for the desired tables. Remember that the query optimizer uses that data to find the fastest query approach. The recommendations you receive will depend on the query and the problems encountered. As long as your query is well-formed, most recommendations will be straightforward.

One of the most important ways to optimize a query is to add indexes to a table. An index stores values that are commonly searched in a sorted order (B Tree), or directly associated with the key (hashed). Either way, an index can speed up data searches and retrieval by hundreds of times. For example, a B-Tree index can search over 1 million rows of indexed data with less than 20 lookups. A hashed index, with relatively simple key values, can find an index entry with only one lookup. In relational databases, indexes are critical on joined columns. Consequently, the DBMS will usually automatically create

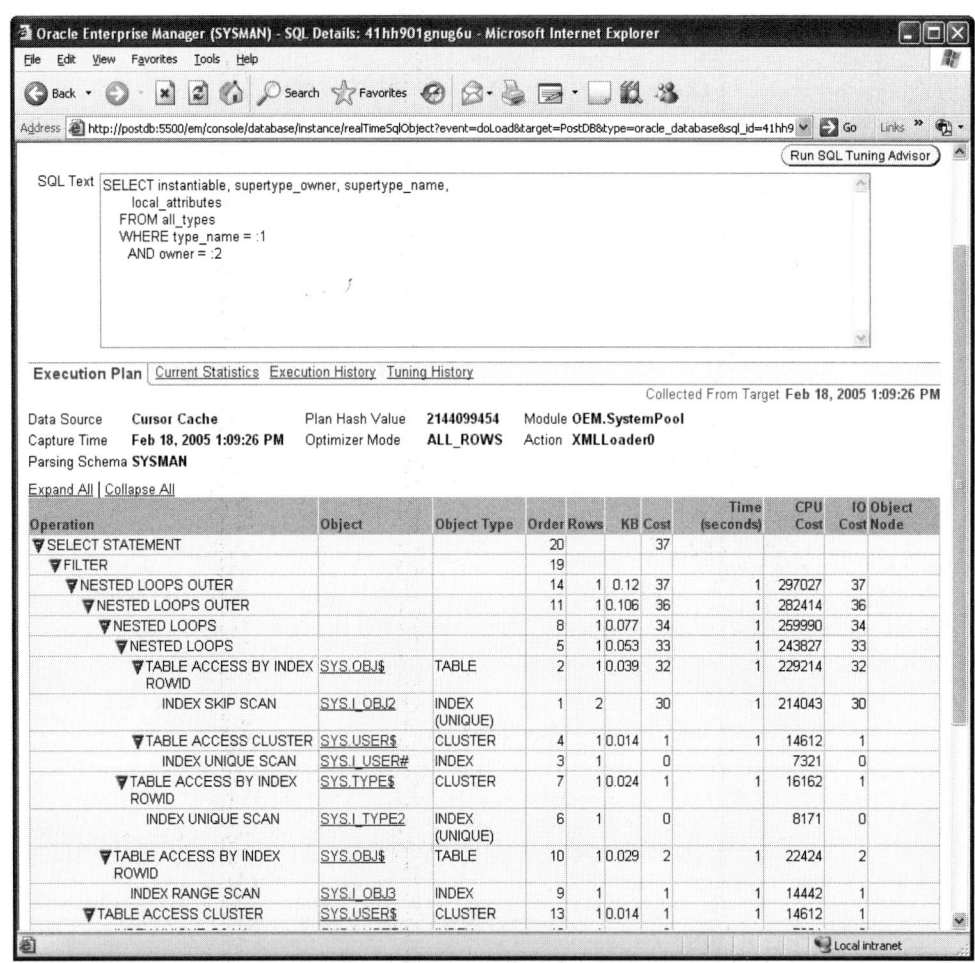

FIGURE 13.20 Query execution plan.

indexes for key columns. However, indexes carry a cost—whenever a row is inserted into a table, the DBMS has to update the row and change all of the indexes. According to the Oracle performance tuning documentation, each index requires about three times the resources as the original DML. So adding three indexes to a table will slow down an INSERT command by about ten times. You need to carefully balance the need to retrieve data with the speed required for updates. In fact, this dichotomy is the main reason for the importance of data warehouse systems. A data warehouse can use *materialized views* where data is denormalized and stored together, along with indexes on most columns. The data warehouse is not used for transactions—only for analysis. So the system can build many indexes and not worry about performance problems during updates.

Even in a transaction environment, you might want to add more indexes. But how do you know what indexes to add? The answer is to run the *SQL Access advisor*.

1. From the home EM page, click the **Performance** link, then the **Advisor Central** option under the **Related Links** section.
2. Select the **SQL Access Advisor**.

Figure 13.22 shows that the SQL Access advisor can examine queries from several sources. The simplest is to analyze the recent SQL activity. However, you can also create a Workload, which consists of a set of SQL queries. An easy way to create a SQL

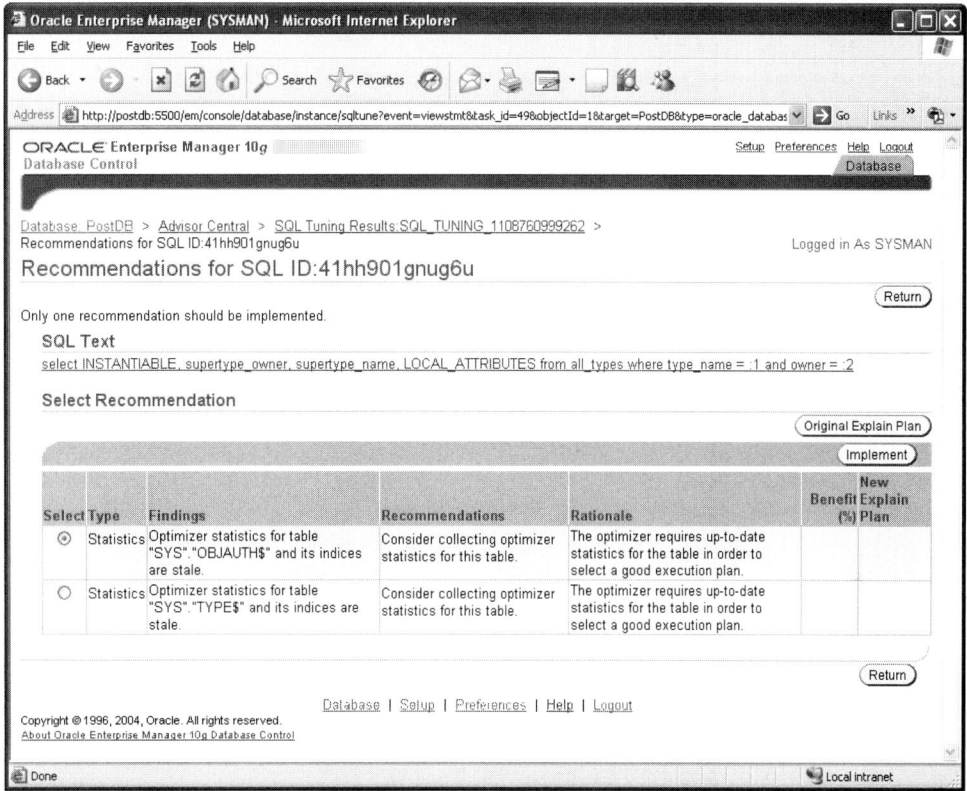

FIGURE 13.21 Tuning advisor recommendations.

repository is to add individual statements to the group using the Top SQL option. You can also create a Workload table manually and add your own group of SQL statements. This approach is useful for testing multiple queries on a form or a report. The Oracle documentation explains how to create the table and store the SQL statements as strings. Finally, you can have the advisor analyze all of the tables in a schema. Chose the option to create a hypothetical workload and pick the tables from your schema.

3. Work through the Advisor screens. For a transactions database, stick with **Indexes**, but you can select the **Comprehensive Mode**. For scheduling, change the **Schedule Type** to **Standard** and run the job **Immediately**.
4. Submit the job, then wait a short time and click the **Refresh** button. Once the job has completed, you can click its name in the **Results** list to see any recommendations.

> **Tip:** The Advisor might not work on your development machine. There is a reason real DBAs use SQL instead of the Enterprise Manager.

Even if the advisor suggests creating several new indexes, you should be cautious. Look carefully at the table and determine if it will have to handle a substantial number of updates or insertions every day. If so, you should try to hold down the number of indexes.

You should probably test the SQL functions used in the forms and reports of the Redwood Realty case. Since the application is not running in production mode, you will have to add the SQL statements manually and then run the advisor. This process is easiest to do using SQL*Plus. The nice aspect of SQL*Plus is that you do not need the DBA

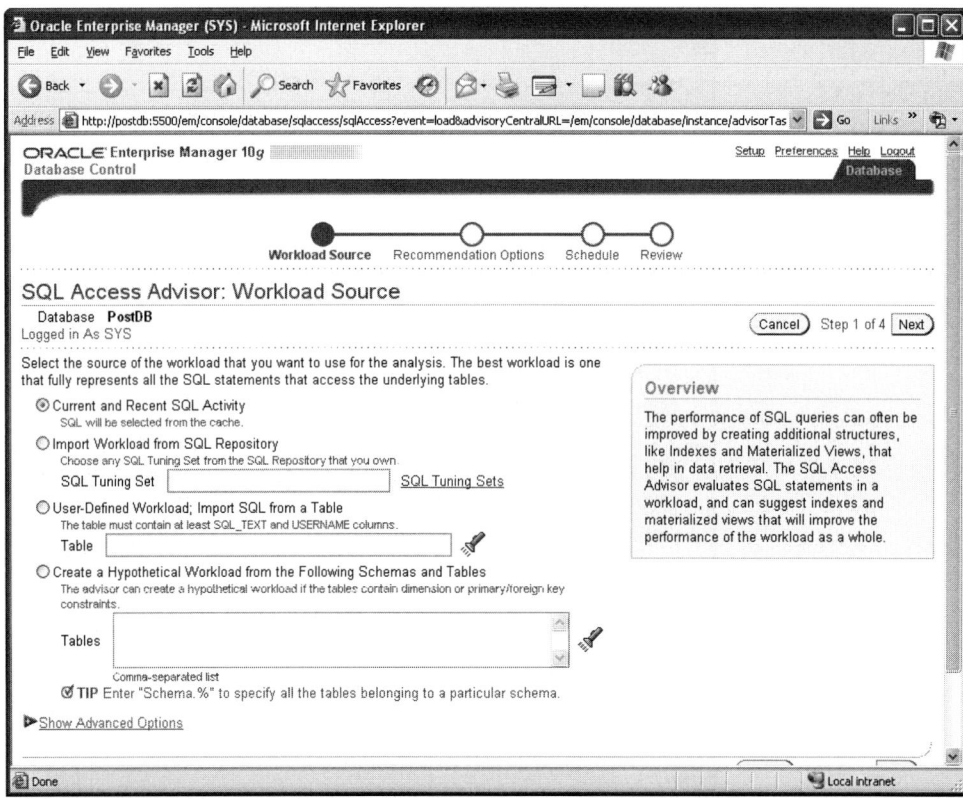

FIGURE 13.22 Configuring the SQL Access advisor.

role. You only need to be granted the Advisor role and have Execute permission on the DBMS_Advisor package. You will need to get the DBA to grant you these privileges:

```
GRANT Advisor to <username>;
GRANT EXECUTE on DBMS_Advisor to <username>;
```

It takes several steps to set up and run the advisor. The easiest way to do the setup is to modify a standard SQL script. You simply have to enter your own SQL statements. The procedure is shown here, but you should copy it from the student disk to save typing it:

```
Create or Replace Procedure SetupAccessAdvisor AS
BEGIN
DECLARE
  task_id NUMBER;
  task_name VARCHAR2(30);
  workload_name VARCHAR2(30);
  username VARCHAR2(30) := 'REDWOOD';
  sql_text CLOB;
BEGIN
  workload_name := 'Main_Workload';
  task_name := 'First_Task';

  DBMS_ADVISOR.CREATE_TASK(DBMS_ADVISOR.SQLACCESS_ADVISOR,
  task_id, task_name);
  DBMS_ADVISOR.CREATE_SQLWKLD(workload_name, 'Main Workload');
  DBMS_ADVISOR.ADD_SQLWKLD_REF(task_name, workload_name);

  sql_text := 'SELECT ALL Redwood.LISTINGS.LISTINGID,
  Redwood.LISTINGS.PROPERTYID,
```

```
        Redwood.LISTINGS.BEGINLISTDATE, Redwood.LISTINGS.ENDLISTDATE,
        Redwood.LISTINGS.ASKINGPRICE, Redwood.LISTINGS.HOUSEPHOTO,
        Redwood.PROPERTIES.CITY
        FROM Redwood.LISTINGS, Redwood.PROPERTIES, Redwood.SALESTATUS
        WHERE Redwood.SALESTATUS.SALESTATUS = ''For Sale''
        AND ((Redwood.LISTINGS.PROPERTYID = Redwood.PROPERTIES.PROPERTYID)
        AND (Redwood.LISTINGS.SALESTATUSID =
        Redwood.SALESTATUS.SALESTATUSID))
        ORDER BY Redwood.LISTINGS.BEGINLISTDATE ASC';

    DBMS_ADVISOR.ADD_SQLWKLD_STATEMENT (
            workload_name => workload_name,
            priority => 1,
            executions => 20,
            username => username,
            sql_text => sql_text
);
    sql_text := 'SELECT ALL Redwood.CUSTAGENTLIST.LISTINGID,
    Redwood.CUSTAGENTLIST.CONTACTDATE, Redwood.CUSTOMERS.FIRSTNAME,
    Redwood.CUSTOMERS.LASTNAME, Redwood.CUSTAGENTLIST.BIDPRICE,
    Redwood.CUSTAGENTLIST.COMMISSIONRATE
    FROM Redwood.CUSTAGENTLIST, Redwood.CUSTOMERS
    WHERE (Redwood.CUSTAGENTLIST.CUSTOMERID =
    Redwood.CUSTOMERS.CUSTOMERID)
    ORDER BY Redwood.CUSTAGENTLIST.CONTACTDATE ASC';

    DBMS_ADVISOR.ADD_SQLWKLD_STATEMENT (
            workload_name => workload_name,
            priority => 1,
            executions => 20,
            username => username,
            sql_text => sql_text
);
    DBMS_ADVISOR.EXECUTE_TASK(task_name);
END;
END;
/
```

1. Copy and edit the SQL script (**SQLAdvisor.sql**). Change the **username** and edit the queries so they work with your username/schema. Hint: Use global search and replace on **Redwood**.

The script seems long, but basically, it sets up a single task and a workload. It then assigns the task to the workload. Then it creates two SQL statements and adds them to the workload. The last step is to run the advisor. You can enter any SQL statements you want, and you can add an unlimited number of them. Realistically, you want to keep the statements manageable or you will have trouble dealing with the recommendations. It makes sense to add all of the statements needed for a form or a report. Notice that when a SQL statement includes a quoted string, you have to repeat the quotation mark because you are actually creating the entire statement as a string. Check the "For Sale" entry for details.

2. Fix any errors that arise. Run the script:

```
Execute SetupAccessAdvisor
```

3. At this point, the system has evaluated the queries. Now you need to see the results and recommendations. The advisor creates a recommended SQL script that you can run. To see the script, you need to create a temporary variable, retrieve the results into it, and print the variable:

```
VARIABLE buf CLOB;
Set long 50000;  --maybe longer?
Execute :buf := DBMS_ADVISOR.GET_TASK_SCRIPT('First_Task');
Print :buf;
```

In this example, the system created two major recommendations: (1) create three materialized views and collect statistics on one of those views, and (2) create an index on the SaleStatus table. The primary script is:

```
whenever sqlerror CONTINUE

CREATE MATERIALIZED VIEW LOG ON "REDWOOD"."CUSTAGENTLIST" WITH ROWID;
CREATE MATERIALIZED VIEW LOG ON "REDWOOD"."CUSTOMERS" WITH ROWID;
CREATE MATERIALIZED VIEW "REDWOOD"."MV$$_00690001"
    REFRESH FAST WITH ROWID
    ENABLE QUERY REWRITE
    AS SELECT REDWOOD.CUSTOMERS.ROWID C1,
       REDWOOD.CUSTAGENTLIST.ROWID C2,
       "REDWOOD"."CUSTAGENTLIST"."BIDPRICE" M1,
       "REDWOOD"."CUSTAGENTLIST"."COMMISSIONRATE" M2,
       "REDWOOD"."CUSTAGENTLIST"."CONTACTDATE" M3,
       "REDWOOD"."CUSTAGENTLIST"."LISTINGID" M4,
       "REDWOOD"."CUSTOMERS"."FIRSTNAME"   M5,
       "REDWOOD"."CUSTOMERS"."LASTNAME" M6
    FROM REDWOOD.CUSTAGENTLIST, REDWOOD.CUSTOMERS
    WHERE REDWOOD.CUSTAGENTLIST.CUSTOMERID =
    REDWOOD.CUSTOMERS.CUSTOMERID;
begin
dbms_stats.gather_table_stats('"REDWOOD"','"MV$$_00690001"',NULL,
    dbms_stats.auto_sample_size);
end;
/

CREATE INDEX "REDWOOD"."_IDX$$_00690007"
    ON "REDWOOD"."SALESTATUS" ("SALESTATUS")
    COMPUTE STATISTICS;
whenever sqlerror EXIT SQL.SQLCODE
begin
  dbms_advisor.mark_recommendation('First_Task',1,'IMPLEMENTED');
  dbms_advisor.mark_recommendation('First_Task',2,'IMPLEMENTED');
end;
/
```

In general, materialized views are used for data warehouse and decision support applications. Essentially, they denormalize the tables and take periodic snapshots of the database. They can make a huge difference in some applications. However, they might not be as useful in a transaction database, so you should not attempt to implement them in this situation. In fact, the ADD_SQLWKLD_STATEMENT procedure has several options, so you could have told it to look only at indexes for improvements and ignore materialized views. The suggested index for the SaleStatus table is an excellent idea. The table is often used in queries and its data rarely changes.

You can gain a little more information about the proposed changes by looking at the User_Advisor_Recommendations view. It lists the two proposed changes and the potential benefit. The view has several additional columns, but the main values can be obtained with:

```
SELECT Finding_ID, Type, Rank, Benefit_Type, Benefit
FROM User_Advisor_Recommendations
ORDER BY Rank ASC;
```

Finally, note that if you want to change the SQL and rerun the set up procedure, you will have to either rename the task and workload or delete the existing values:

```
execute DBMS_ADVISOR.DELETE_TASK('First_Task');
execute DBMS_ADVISOR.DELETE_SQLWKLD('Main_Workload');
```

You might be interested to know that if you want to manually investigate a single query, you can run the EXPLAIN PLAN command directly from SQL as well. However, it takes time to learn to read the plan and figure out how to improve a query. For most cases, the automated analyzers do a good enough job.

OBTAINING USEFUL INFORMATION FROM SYSTEM VIEWS

Virtually everything handled by Oracle is stored in a table. For example, the table names, columns, relationships, and view definitions are stored in system tables. Similarly, performance and monitoring data are stored in system tables. As DBA, you could retrieve data from many of these tables directly. However, Oracle has created several standard views that make it easier to get the data you want—using slightly more understandable names. This section presents some of the views that you might find useful. Many of the DBA views begin with the dba_ prefix. Many of the newer system monitoring views use the V$ prefix. Literally thousands of views have been defined, so this section presents only a small portion of them. One of the first tricks you should know is that you can get a list of all of the current views from the view dba_views, and you can use the Describe command to see what columns are included in a specific view. First, log in with an account that has the DBA role, then issue a few basic commands:

```
Describe dba_views;
SELECT view_name FROM dba_views WHERE view_name LIKE 'DBA_ROLE%';
SELECT Comments FROM dba_tab_comments WHERE table_name = 'DBA_ROLES';
```

The dba_tab_comments view holds comments on tables or views that have been added to the data dictionary. Sometimes you can also see comments on specific columns using the dba_col_comments view. These three views and the describe command enable you to find at least some information on any of the views available to you. From there, you can search the Oracle documentation for more details and usage notes. Note that most of the views contain detailed usage and control information in addition to the owner and name. Table 13.7 shows only some of the more common views with a brief description of its purpose.

TABLE 13.7 Common DBA views.

DBA View	Description
dba_views	List of all views available to the DBA. Individual users can use user_views instead.
dba_tab_comments	List of comments for tables and views.
dba_col_comments	List of comments for specific columns.
dba_tablespaces	Data on tablespaces. Also look at dba_segments and dba_data_files.
dba_tables	List of table names and storage data. Also look at dba_indexes.
dba_tab_cols	List of columns in tables.
dba_procedures	List of procedures and functions in the database. Also look at dba_triggers.
dba_sequences	List of sequences in the database.
dba_synonyms	List of synonyms. Also look at dba_directories.
dba_users	List of all users.
dba_roles	List of all roles.
dba_role_privs	List of roles assigned to users (or other roles).
dba_sys_privs	List of system privileges assigned to users.
dba_tab_privs	List of all granted privileges in the database.

TABLE 13.8 A few V$ performance views.

V$ View	Description
v$fixed_table v$fixed_view_definition	A list of all V$, X$, and GV$ views. The SQL query used for each view.
v$database v$instance v$tablespace v$datafile v$controlfile v$option v$version	Configuration data about the database.
v$open_cursor v$sql v$sqlarea v$sql_plan	Cursors and SQL statements.
v$sort_usage v$sysstat v$transaction v$osstat v$session v$session_wait_history v$lock v$locked_object	Overall system and session performance.
v$archive v$backup_datafile v$recovery_status v$recovery_file_dest v$rollstat v$undostat	Archives, backup, and recovery, and rollback performance.

Oracle also has several hundred dynamic views that are largely used to monitor performance of the database. The majority of these are prefixed with a V$, and referred to as the V$ views. However, there are also a few X$ and GV$ views. You can find a list of all of these views in the v$fixed_table view. However, you will have to turn to the Oracle documentation for details on how to use each view. Table 13.8 lists some of the V$ views to give you an idea of the purpose and scope of these views. Remember that these views contain lists of performance statistics, such as the number of current users and space utilization.

Summary

This chapter explains some of the roles of the DBA and some of the Oracle DBA tools. Remember that it takes several books and a couple of years of experience to become a DBA. However, even application developers need to know a few things about how an Oracle database is configured, managed, and monitored. Oracle gives you considerable control over storage locations and space utilization through the logical tablespaces and physical datafiles. You also need to know the locations of control files, and redo and undo archive files when it comes time to back up the database. You can use table storage parameters to assign data to specific files through the choice of the tablespace. You can also cluster related data together or split large tables into partitions so that more active data can be placed on faster drives.

Oracle can easily export and import the entire database or selected tables. But it uses proprietary binary data files for this purpose so these options cannot be used with other software packages. You can use SQL*Loader and external tables to import data files created by other applications, including free-format .CSV files or fixed-format print files.

DBAs are responsible for backing up the database and keeping the software patched and up to date. Backups are tricky because the business might need to run 24 hours a day, seven days a week and that data is constantly changing. With archive log files, Oracle can make a backup even while changes are being written to the database. Otherwise, you can rely on hardware solutions to continuously back up data, such as RAID devices.

DBAs and application developers have to work together to improve the performance of the database and the applications. Major performance gains are usually found by redesigning an application and a query instead of waiting until a problem arises and trying to tweak the database settings. The SQL Tuning and SQL Access advisors can help you spot problems and suggest improvements if you need help with query performance. Oracle also collects several dynamic statistics that the DBA can monitor either through a visual tool such as the Enterprise Manager, or through the dynamic V$ views.

Key Terms

- Automatic Database Diagnostic Monitor (ADDM)
- cluster
- comma-separated values (.CSV)
- data pump
- database administrator (DBA)
- Enterprise Manager (EM)
- execution plan
- external tables
- hash partitioning
- list partitioning
- materialized views
- MetaLink
- metrics
- patches
- PCTFREE
- PCTUSED
- range partitioning
- recovery manager (RMAN)
- redo log files
- redundant array of independent drives (RAID)
- shutdown
- SQL Access advisor
- SQL Profile
- SQL Tuning
- SQL*Loader
- startup
- startup restrict
- tablespace
- undo tablespace
- upgrades
- very large-scale database (VLSD)

Review

TRUE/FALSE

1. A tablespace is the same thing as a datafile and each tablespace represents one datafile.
2. Hash partitions are particularly useful when you need to store related items together, such as tables joined on a common key.
3. The Oracle data pump exports data efficiently, but always stores it in a proprietary format.
4. Oracle upgrades for a major version number (such as 9i to 10g) usually require a conversion of the datafiles that require shutting down the database.
5. The Enterprise Manager is the only place where you can see the statistics needed to monitor the status of the database.

FILL IN

1. In the Enterprise Manager, the _____ section provides access to several tools to help you improve the performance of the database.
2. If you want to create a table that stores older data on slower, but cheaper, disk drives, and recent data on high-speed drives, you would group the data by years by using _____.
3. If you choose not to use RAID drives to continuously back up your database files in hardware, you need to turn on the _____ property so Oracle can make continuous backups itself.
4. You have been asked to load data into Oracle that is currently stored in a spreadsheet file. You will probably use the _____ tool.
5. A list of the system views that provide information about the database can be found in the _____ view.

Multiple Choice

1. Users are reporting that two forms in an application are painfully slow. You think it might be some poorly written queries, but you are not certain. You should use the _____ tool to help determine the problem and identify possible solutions.
   a. SQL*Loader
   b. SQL Access Advisor
   c. Hash partitioning
   d. ARCHIVELOG
   e. PCTFREE

2. If you are creating a table that is large, but contains data that does not change very often, you should change the space utilization parameter closer to:
   a. PCTFREE=5
   b. PCTUSED=5
   c. PCTFREE=40
   d. PCTUSED=40
   e. List partitioning

3. If you choose to back up your database manually using system utilities, which of the following files is the LEAST important:
   a. CONTROL01.CTL
   b. SYSTEM01.DBF
   c. SPFILEmydb.ORA
   d. REDO01.LOG
   e. IFBLD90.EXE

4. You can download patches manually or configure Enterprise Manager to do it automatically, but in both cases, you need a customer account on the _____ site.
   a. OTN (Oracle Technology Network)
   b. MetaLink
   c. Java
   d. RMAN
   e. Patch.Oracle

5. As DBA you can configure Oracle Enterprise Manager to e-mail you customized notices of events by configuring the
   a. patches
   b. SQL Profile
   c. data pump
   d. metrics
   e. SQL Tuning

Hands-on Exercises

1. Extending the Chapter Case

Similar to the example in the text, you need to improve the performance of the report Sales by Month and Agent. Build the test query using SaleStatusID=101 because that condition returns the most data. From the report created in Chapter 10, the modified query is:

```
SELECT ALL AGENTS.LASTNAME,
AGENTS.FIRSTNAME,
LISTINGS.ASKINGPRICE,
TO_CHAR(LISTINGS.ENDLISTDATE, 'MM')
SALEMONTH
FROM AGENTS, LISTINGS, SALESTATUS
WHERE SALESTATUS.SALESTATUSID = 101
  AND ((LISTINGS.LISTINGAGENTID =
  AGENTS.AGENTID)
  AND (LISTINGS.SALESTATUSID =
  SALESTATUS.SALESTATUSID))
ORDER BY AGENTS.LASTNAME ASC,
AGENTS.FIRSTNAME ASC
```

1. Copy and edit the SQLAdvisor.sql file on the student data disk. Replace the first SQL query with the new one. Be sure you add second quote marks to the 'MM' format. Also make sure you replace REDWOOD with your username.
2. Delete the second query and the ADD_SQLWKLD_STATEMENT text for it.
3. Run the new statement to create the procedure. Clean up any problems.
4. If necessary, delete any prior tasks and workloads.

```
Execute
DBMS_ADVISOR.DELETE_TASK('First_Task');
Execute DBMS_ADVISOR.DELETE_SQLWKLD
('Main_Workload');
```

5. Execute the new procedure, then retrieve the suggested changes:

```
VARIABLE buf CLOB;
set long 50000;
Execute :buf := DBMS_ADVISOR.GET_TASK_SCRIPT
('First_Task');
Print :buf;
```

6. Examine the suggestions and briefly explain why or why not you would implement them. Hand in your conclusions.

2. COFFEE MERCHANT

The Coffee Merchant reports and forms are straightforward. You could run performance tests on them if you have DBA privileges. However, if you look at the tables and think about how they are used, you already know a few methods that could improve performance.

1. Log into SQL*Plus for the Coffee Merchant case. This step is easier if you have a separate schema for this case. Get a list of the tables available to you:

   `SELECT table_name FROM user_tables;`

2. Of the seven tables, identify the ones that change infrequently. Make a recommendation of how the table storage could be changed to reduce space and improve performance.

3. Over time, you notice that the managers frequently search the orders based on the names of the customers. To facilitate these searches, you decide to add an index to the Consumers table based on LastName. First, retrieve data for a couple of names to get a feel for the performance:

   ```
   SELECT ConsumerID, City, LastName
   FROM Consumers
   WHERE LastName IN ('Samuel', 'Bloom', 'Mauch');
   ```

4. Also test an insert command and note the performance:

   ```
   INSERT INTO Consumers (ConsumerID,
   FirstName, LastName, Street, City, State,
   ZipCode) VALUES (99, 'Barbara', 'Feldon',
   '123 Michigan', 'Chicago', 'IL', '60601');
   ```

5. Now create an index on the LastName column:

   ```
   CREATE INDEX ConsumerLastName on
   Consumers("LASTNAME")
         Compute Statistics;
   ```

6. Retest the select statement from Step 3. Retest the insert statement, but change the data slightly:

   ```
   INSERT INTO Consumers (ConsumerID,
   FirstName, LastName, Street, City,
   State, ZipCode)
   VALUES (86, 'Max', 'Smart', '123 State',
   'Chicago', 'IL', '60601');
   ```

7. Did you notice a difference in performance? Write a short paragraph and explain why you did or did not notice a difference. What conditions would emphasize the difference in performance? Hand in your comments.

3. ROWING VENTURES

The Organizations.csv file on the student data disk contains data entered into a spreadsheet that you need to import into the Organization table. It was exported from Excel as a standard .CSV file, with the columns:

```
OrganizationID, Phone, Address, City,
State, PostalCode, Nation,
OrganizationName, NewsOutlet
```

Open the file in WordPad and you will see some potential issues. For instance, some columns are missing data and most of the text columns are not delimited with quotation marks. These two issues should not be serious, but you will have to double-check the data to ensure that it is correct. More important, notice that the last organization was given the same ID number as the one before it. This entry is not an accident, so do not try to fix it. The goal is to see what happens when you try to import the file. Your task is to import the file using either SQL*Loader from the command line, or by creating an external table. When you have succeeded, use a SELECT statement to show some of the columns from the new rows and print the list. Also, write a short paragraph to explain how the database responded to the duplicate ID value and how you would search for that problem if you had a huge list to import.

4. BROADCLOTH CLOTHING

Assuming you have DBA permissions, identify the tablespaces, datafiles, and all system files used by your database to handle the Broadcloth Clothing database. If possible, perform a shutdown of the database and make a cold backup copy of all of the files. If you have a tremendous amount of courage, try deleting one of the existing files and restart the database. When it fails, shut down the database and restore your backup copy. Note: do not even think about attempting this last step if anyone else uses the database.

GLOSSARY

Access key A key used in combination with the Alt key to select a menu item.

Action query Commands INSERT, UPDATE, or DELETE, causing changes to data.

Active row The only row available to the PL/SQL program via the cursor.

Administration tools They help the DBA configure and monitor the DBMS status and performance.

Aggregate function A function that operates on multiple table rows simultaneously and returns one row of output.

Alert A special popup window used to display critical messages to the user. Avoid using it as much as possible.

Alias An alternative name for a table or column.

Anonymous block An unnamed block containing SQL and PL/SQL statements that are compiled and executed.

Application A complete system that performs a specific collection of tasks. It typically consists of integrated forms and reports and generally contains menus and a help system.

Application A set of forms and reports that work together to accomplish a specified set of tasks.

ASC/DESC Optional phrase indicating sorting in ascending/descending order.

Associations Connections between classes or entities that usually represent business rules. For example, the relationship between orders and customers.

Associative link A key word within a help topic that has a link to a list of related topics.

Asterisk (*) SELECT list entry indicating that Oracle is to retrieve *all* of the table's columns.

Atomic Values cannot be broken down any further.

Attributes The features or characteristics of entities.

Auditing Collecting logs on computer operations and monitoring database activity to check for problems or undesirable activity.

Automatic database diagnostic monitor (ADDM) A DBA tool that runs in the background to monitor performance. From the Enterprise Manager, you can request an analysis of the performance and ADDM will make suggestions on parameters that can be changed to improve the overall performance.

Availability A security condition that ensures that authorized people can access data they need when they want it.

Base table A table that contains data about a single, basic entity. Usually, it does not contain any foreign keys.

BETWEEN operator A convenient way to search for rows whose column values lie within a particular range of values.

Block Contains SQL and PL/SQL statements.

Break footer The section of a report that is printed at the bottom of a control section, usually used to display subtotals.

Break header The section of a report that is printed at the start of a control section, usually used to display column headings.

Calling The action of executing a function or procedure from another procedure or SQL*Plus.

Canvas The main display area of a form. You can have multiple canvases or drawing pages on one form.

Cascading style sheet (CSS) A set of layout and visual properties used to provide a common look for Web pages.

Challenge-response A security method commonly implemented with a username/password combination in computer systems.

Character function A function that manipulates character strings and returns a character string result.

Check box A form element used for multiple selection of related items. By convention, it is displayed as a square box and users can select several items from the list.

Check constraint Enforces a logical expression on a column that must evaluate to true for all values in the column.

Child menu items Second level or entries that pop up in a menu when a first-level item is selected.

Class A descriptor for a set of objects with similar structure, behavior, and relationships. A class represents an entity and its properties.

Cluster A group of tables that share the same data blocks. Used to associate related data tables to reduce the drive's read and write time.

Column alias An alternative name for a SELECT list column.

Column subset view A view that hides selected columns from some users.

Comma-separated values (CSV) A text file used to transfer data to diverse systems where data in columns is separated by commas, strings are usually delimited by quotes, and each row in the file represents one row in the database table.

Commit The command that makes permanent any changes made since the last commit statement was executed.

Communications network Connects users to other computers.

Compile When Oracle converts the higher level PL/SQL instructions into a lower-level format that a computer can execute more quickly.

Complex view A view containing a subquery that retrieves data from multiple tables, or groups rows using a GROUP BY or DISTINCT clause, or contains a function call.

Component query Each SELECT statement in a compound query.

Composite primary key A multicolumn primary key is also called a *compound primary key* or a *composite primary key.*

Compound query SELECT statements that contain set operators.

Concatenation The act of combining together, end-to-end, a consecutive series of symbols.

Confidentiality A security restriction where only authorized people are allowed to see data. It prevents even read or SELECT access to unauthorized people.

Constant A value that occupies storage space, exists as long as the PL/SQL block is available, and holds a value that does not change during the PL/SQL code's execution.

Constraint A restriction on the value a column can take on.

Constraint naming convention Any convention established to name a constraint is called a *constraint naming convention.*

Context sensitive (help) A help topic that is tied to a specific task or location within an application.

Conversion function A function that converts data from one data type to another.

Correlated subquery A subquery that references one or more columns in the outer query.

Correlation names During trigger execution, they contain the old and new column values for the affected row.

Cursor The memory locations allocated by the PL/SQL engine to hold the rows returned by a SELECT statement.

Cursor FOR loop A cursor controlled automatically by a FOR loop. You do not have to open or close the cursor, and you do not have to issue a FETCH instruction.

Custom template A set of layout and visual attributes that you store so that reports all have the same style.

Data block An internal form element used to support the transfer of data from the database to the form.

Data Block Wizard The main wizard you start when you want assistance in creating a form. When finished, it usually calls the Layout Wizard.

Data dictionary Data tables that hold the definitions of all of the data tables and that describe the type of data that is being stored.

Data engine The part of the database system that handles most of the actual exchanges with the computer system.

Data model (report) The internal definition of data required for a report that is used to transfer data from the database.

Data pump An Oracle utility for exporting and importing bulk data.

Data type The *data type* specifies, or limits, the type of data that the field holds.

Database A collection of data stored in a standardized format, designed to be shared by multiple users. A collection of tables for a particular business situation.

Database administrator (DBA) A person in charge of keeping the DBMS running and monitoring its performance.

Database management system (DBMS) Software that defines a database, stores the data, supports a query language, produces reports, and creates data entry screens.

Date function A function that returns a date or time result.

Declaration section An optional section of a PL/SQL block that begins with DECLARE and defines any variables or constants required in the program block.

Delimited names *Delimited names* refers to object names—tables, columns, etc.—that are enclosed in a set of double quotation marks such as the "CreditLimit" identifier.

Derived table The results returned by the database system when you query (SELECT) the database.

Desformat (parameter) A reports services parameter that specifies what format to generate.

Destype (parameter) A reports services generation parameter used to set the destination.

Developer A person who designs the databases, writes queries, and builds the forms and reports.

Developer suite An integrated development environment that combines the power of application development and business intelligence tools in a single interface.

Digital security certificate An electronic file that uses public key encryption to authenticate a Web server and generates keys to encrypt data transmissions between a Web browser and the server.

Disabled constraint A *disabled constraint* is a constraint that is named but not enforced.

Discretionary access control Allowing different users to see subsets of rows and columns from the same base tables.

Display columns The columns that appear following SELECT and preceding FROM in a query.

Distribution A frequency count of values in each category.

Domain constraints *Domain constraints* define specific data values or value ranges that are permitted in columns in which they appear.

DUAL A table that Oracle defines and which contains one row and one column. It is used to display a value such as a calculation that is not a column of any particular table.

Encryption A procedure that mixes plain-text data with a key value to produce a scrambled text that hides the original data.

END A keyword that closes the PL/SQL block.

Enterprise Manager (EM) Oracle's Web-based system tool to help beginning DBAs monitor and control databases.

Entity an *entity* or *object* is a person, place or thing (a noun) that the business wants to record and track.

Entity-relationship diagram (ERD) A graph that shows the associations (relationships) between business entities.

Environment variable A SQL*Plus system variable that determines how various elements appear when they are displayed.

Equijoin The most common type of join condition looks for matching values in two tables.

Exception An error condition or unexpected result that occurs when executing a PL/SQL block.

EXCEPTION statement A structure command used within trigger code to catch runtime errors. If an error arises, the forms processor jumps to the exception section code.

Exception-handling section An optional section of a PL/SQL block that begins with the keyword EXCEPTION and gets program control whenever any of a number of errors occurs.

Executable section The code that is enclosed between BEGIN and END statements and that contains the PL/SQL code and SQL statements to be executed.

Execution plan An explanation of how Oracle is going to evaluate a query. Sometimes useful when you want to see why a query is taking so long to run.

Exists A relational operator that determines whether a condition is true in a subquery.

Explicit cursor A cursor that you must explicitly manage (define, open, fetch, and close) in conjunction with a PL/SQL block that returns more than one row from a database table.

External tables A file outside of Oracle that has been defined via SQL*Loader to represent a pseudo table. Often used with comma-separated values files. Once defined, you can use SQL commands to transfer data from external tables.

Fire The term used for executing a trigger.

First normal form A table is in first normal form (1NF) when there are no repeating groups within it.

Fixed-length character *Fixed-length character* data means character data in which the fields for different records are identical in length.

Fixed-precision number A *fixed-precision number* contains a specific number of decimal places.

Flashback drop Beginning with Oracle 10g, a dropped table is moved to a recycle bin. This is called a *flashback drop*, because you can recover the table later.

Floating-point number A *floating-point number* contains a variable number of decimal places.

FOR loop A program loop that executes a predetermined number of times.

Foreign key A column in one table that is a primary key in another table.

Foreign key constraint While primary key constraints ensure the integrity of the data in a table and uniquely identify each row, a *foreign key constraint* specifies that a field must exist as a primary key in another, referenced table.

Format model A set of characters that describe how an item of data should be displayed, and how the data can be entered by the user. See Table 8.3 for examples, but the list of allowable characters is long, so check the documentation for the complete list.

Format triggers Code that is executed every time a targeted object is displayed on a report.

Forms Interactive applications that are used to enter and edit related data stored in tables.

Forms and reports services A separate part of the Oracle system that supports creation, debugging, and deployment of database forms and reports.

Forms debugger A forms tool that enables you to step through your trigger functions line by line to see exactly how the code is being processed. You can also examine the values of variables and form data.

Frame (form) A tool used on a form to group items together. It could be an aesthetic grouping or a functional grouping such as those used for radio buttons.

Frame (report) A tool used to group items together. Useful for setting common properties for all items within the frame.

Full outer join A join condition that returns rows from either joined table that do not have matching rows in the other table along with those that do have matches in both.

Function A predefined series of calculations that accepts zero or more input values, or parameters, and returns an output parameter.

GLOBAL prefix The syntax for declaring a global variable. See scope and lifetime.

Global variable A variable that can be referenced by the host environment from outside the PL/SQL block.

Granularity The ability to break a security permission problem down to detailed levels. For example, instead of granting access to an entire table, a more granular system enables you to grant permissions to specific rows.

Grid form (See *tabular form*.)

GROUP BY clause Optional SELECT statement clause that partitions the rows returned by the SELECT statement into groups.

Group filter (property) A tool for restricting the records displayed on a report.

Group function (See *Aggregate function*.)

Group report Sometimes called a control break report, it breaks a listing into groups and usually displays headings and subtotals for each section.

Hard coded Writing data and magic numbers directly into a form. It makes them difficult to change later. Better to define global variables so data is defined in only one location.

Hash partitioning A table storage method that stores and retrieves data based on a single key value. It isolates data based on individual values, but also provides rapid retrieval when the hash key is unique.

HAVING clause Optional SELECT statement clause that filters groups.

Header section The section of a named block that contains the name of the block and whether the block is a function or a procedure.

Implicit cursor A cursor that the PL/SQL engine automatically manages (defines, opens, processes, and closes) whenever a PL/SQL block SELECT statement returns zero or one row.

IN A parameter designator that allows a value to be passed into the function or procedure but that cannot be changed within the function or procedure during its execution.

IN operator Specifies a condition that is true if table column values match one of the values in a list of acceptable values.

IN OUT A parameter designator that allows a value to be passed into a function or procedure, changed within the function or procedure, and passed back to the calling procedure.

Index page A sort list of key words used in a help system.

Infinite loop A loop that does not stop.

Information overload A state reached by users when a form tries to display too many things at one time.

Inheritance The ability to define new classes that are derived from higher level classes. A new class inherits all prior properties and methods of the higher class.

Inline view The subquery following the FROM statement and enclosed in parentheses.

Inner join A join of two or more tables that returns only rows that satisfy the join condition.

Integer An *Integer* is a whole number with no fractional part—you omit the scale part of the declaration.

Integrity A security restriction that indicates data is stored accurately and represents the concept it is recording. It includes database recovery activities in addition to preventing unauthorized people from modifying data.

Integrity constraint *Integrity constraints* are rules that are applied to tables, and table columns in which they appear, that constrain the values that are inserted into the tables.

Items Various objects placed on forms including labels and text boxes.

JInitiator A Java application provided by Oracle that runs within a Web browser to process forms. It must be installed on user computers.

Join A temporary relationship you create between two tables. Often this relationship is formed by associating rows from one table with rows from another table based on columns in each that have the same value.

Join column The primary and foreign key columns which Oracle uses to join two tables together.

Join condition The condition that Oracle evaluates to determine if the two values meet the criteria for joining two tables.

Join, natural An equijoin in which the column *names* match in both tables.

Join, non-equality A join condition that uses a relational operator other than the equality operator between two column names in the ON or WHERE clauses.

Join, outer A join condition that returns rows when join conditions are met and even when one of the join column conditions contains a null value.

Label security A complex security system in which you can assign security levels to users and to data. It is applied in addition to traditional access rights systems. For example, data could be labeled top secret and only users with top secret clearance could see the data.

Layout Wizard The main tool to initially place items from a data block onto a canvas. It reduces the typing required. Even after the form has been created, you can call the wizard again to make major changes.

Left outer join A join that returns rows from the left table even when it returns a null value.

Lifetime (variable) The time between when a variable is created and when it is destroyed. Somewhat related to scope, a variable exists only within the frame in which is was created. Values assigned during a form event will disappear when the trigger code finishes. Even if the same trigger is fired again, the earlier values are gone.

Lightweight directory application protocol (LDAP) A standard that defines how data about people should be stored and retrieved in a centralized directory. It is supported within OID to make it possible to share security identifiers across systems.

LIKE operator Uses wildcard characters to search for patterns of characters in a character string.

List of Values (LOV) A list of all possible entries that could be selected for a specific text box. The list can be filtered and searched by the users. It efficiently downloads only portions of the list at a time.

List partitioning A table storage method that splits the rows of a table into different physical partitions based on groups of data in a specified column. Commonly used to split data by state code.

Magic (menu item) Menu items with prewritten tasks, such as copy and paste.

Mailing labels An *n*-up report that displays data in groups across a page. Commonly used for mailing labels because of available paper forms, it can also be used whenever you want multiple, separate columns of data.

Many-to-many A relationship in which one row of a table is related to possibly many rows of another table. Correspondingly, one row of the second table is related to possibly several rows of the first table.

Master-detail (report) A report with two sections where there is a one-to-many relationship between the master and detail sections.

Materialized view A snapshot of a table at a particular point in time. Used for speeding up queries with time-consuming joins. Copies of the data are stored in a temporary location, so the system only needs to perform a join once in a while to refresh the data.

Matrix report A cross tab report that shows aggregate values for two control variables. One control variable defines the rows, the other the columns.

Menu item A specific menu choice.

Menu module A tool for holding submenus when building a menu tree.

MetaLink The primary support group within Oracle, generally the best location for patches and upgrades. The account can be integrated into Enterprise Manager to automate some software maintenance tasks.

Metrics Literally, measures of database activity and performance.

Multiple column subquery A subquery that returns more than one column to the outer SQL statement.

Multiple row subquery A subquery that returns two or more rows to the outer SQL statement.

Mutating table A table that is being modified by a DML statement that has triggered the event.

Named block A PL/SQL block that has a name and that is stored in the database and referenced by its name.

Named visual attribute A defined style that affects the visible properties (font, colors, patterns, and so on) of objects.

National character set A character set that permits storage of information from languages whose individual characters cannot be represented by an eight-bit coding scheme.

Native code Machine code that executes on a particular computer directly without separate, line-by-line interpretation.

Normalization The process of creating a well-behaved set of tables to efficiently store data, minimize redundancy, and ensure data integrity.

NOT NULL The *NOT NULL* constraint prevents a column's values from being empty, or NULL.

NULL A reserved word meaning that a value is unknown.

Numeric function A function that performs calculations and returns a numeric result.

Object Navigator A hierarchical listing of all the elements on a form. It can show multiple forms within a tree structure.

Object privileges Specific operations that can be performed on existing database tables, views, procedures, and similar objects. You can grant or revoke object privileges to roles.

One-to-many A relationship in which one and only one row of one table is related to possibly many rows of another table. However, every row in the second table is related to exactly one row in the first table.

Operator precedence Refers to the order in which Oracle evaluates subexpressions.

Oracle Application Server (OracleAS) The software system that processes forms and reports on the server. It also has tools to handle authentication and security.

Oracle Containers for Java (OC4J) A self-contained Web server application that processes the server-side elements of forms and reports. You need to run an OC4J instance to test forms, otherwise they have to be run on an Application Server.

Oracle data dictionary The *Oracle data dictionary* contains tables of information about its own tables and all objects in the database.

Oracle Internet Directory (OID) A centralized application used to support single sign-on within Oracle applications.

ORDER BY clause Optional SELECT statement clause that sorts returned rows into order specified by listed column names.

OUT A parameter designator that allows a value to be changed within the procedure or function and passed back to the statement through the parameter.

Overrides A secondary style that you can specify for an item on a report that overrides or takes precedence over definitions from the template.

Page footer The section of a report that is printed at the bottom of every page.

Page header The section of a report that is printed at the top of every page.

Parameter The list of values, separated by commas and enclosed in parentheses, that follow the function or procedure name and through which information passes to or from the function or procedure.

Parent menu items The first level of entries in a menu.

Patches Updates to the underlying DBMS software. They can be managed and applied through the Enterprise Manager tool.

P-code A portable form of code for a function or procedure that executes on any computer platform by the PL/SQL engine.

PCTFREE (parameter) A storage parameter used with CREATE TABLE that specifies the point at which a new storage data block is added to a tablespace.

PCTUSED (parameter) A storage parameter used with CREATE TABLE that specifies the release point at which Oracle will again begin using a storage data block.

Point (typography) A measure of font size. In a 72-point font, upper-case characters are about one inch tall. Sometimes used as a measure of 1/72 of an inch.

Precision *Precision* refers to the total number of digits that are stored in a number, and scale specifies the number of digits to the right of the decimal space.

Primary key A column or set of columns that contain values to uniquely identify each row within a table.

Primary key constraint A *primary key constraint* ensures that all values in the column in which it is declared are not null and are unique.

Private variable A variable that is not available outside the PL/SQL block in which it is declared.

Procedure A named PL/SQL block that is stored on the Oracle server and that performs some action or series of actions.

Property class A collection of property values used to apply standard styles to multiple objects.

Property Palette A small window used to see and modify properties or attributes of items on a form, including the form itself.

Pseudocolumn It appears to be a field from a database table, but it is a command that returns a value.

Public-key infrastructure (PKI) Encryption using public keys requires generation and storage of public keys. When encryption is used to authenticate servers, a central organization needs to validate the real-world identity of a company when issuing a digital security certificate.

Qualified name A two-part name that designates both the table name and the column name it contains.

Query The ability to ask questions of the database and receive answers from it.

Query processor Part of the DBMS that uses the PL/SQL language to determine how to store and retrieve data in response to user and application requests.

Radio button A form element used for multiple selection of related items. By convention, it is displayed as a round button, and the choices are mutually exclusive.

Range partitioning A table storage method that splits the rows of a table into different physical partitions based on ranges of data values. For example, you might partition a table based on date values so that older data is stored on slower, less costly drives.

Record A composite structure that has the same structure as the row Oracle retrieved with the explicit cursor.

Record Group An internal form structure that holds the SQL SELECT statement to retrieve data. Often used to fill a list of values.

Recovery manager (RMAN) An Oracle tool that runs from the command line to configure backup operations and recover the system in the event of a crash.

Redo log files Files that hold transaction records for recovering the database in case of a crash. Best stored on separate disk drives.

Redundant array of independent drives (RAID) A storage system consisting of several inexpensive drives that spin independently of each other. Data is written in stripes across the multiple drives to improve performance and provide redundancy.

Referential constraint This is known as a *referential constraint.*

Referential integrity A data integrity constraint in which data can be entered into a foreign key column only if the data value already exists in the related primary key of a base table.

Regular expression functions A function that manipulates regular expressions to search character string data.

Relational database A collection of related tables logically connected by the data that each holds.

Relationship The association between two entities. (See association.)

Repeating frame (report) Used to display multiple rows of data. All data on a report must ultimately be in a repeating frame.

Report footer The section of a report that is printed one time at the end of the report.

Report formatting command Commands to create report headers and footers, suppress the display of duplicate information, format columns of character strings and numbers, and perform calculations.

Report header The section of a report that is printed one time at the start of the report.

Report triggers Event triggers to run code that is related to stages of the form processing but unrelated to your data.

Right outer join A join that returns rows from the right table even when it returns a null value.

Rollback The SQL statement that reverses the result of one or more SQL statements that make up a transaction.

ROLLBACK Undo any pending changes to a database.

Row It holds data for a single instance of an object.

Row subset view A view that hides selected rows from some users.

Row-level trigger A trigger that fires for each row affected.

Runtime error An application problem that arises while the form is being processed, such as a divide-by-zero error. The error can be observed only while the form is running. It can be trapped with the EXCEPTION statement.

Scalar subquery A subquery that returns one row and one column.

Schema object *Schema objects* or *database objects* are the names given to all the objects stored in the user schema.

Scope (variable) A description of when a variable is accessible. A global variable is accessible across the entire application. A variable declared within a procedure can be accessed only within that procedure.

Script Any SQL commands you save in a file.

Search columns Column names that appear in the WHERE clause.

Search condition Follows the WHERE clause and identifies specific rows in a table or tables that Oracle is to retrieve by specifying expressions and values that must match or be true for the rows to be retrieved.

Search page A tool inside a help system that enables users to search based on key words and phrases.

Second normal form A table is in second normal form (2NF) if it is in 1NF and every non-key column depends on the entire key and not just part of it.

Secure sockets layer (SSL) An Internet protocol that uses public keys to encrypt data transmissions between a Web browser and the server.

Security subsystem The portion of the database system responsible for identifying users and enforcing access rights to control the actions of all users.

SELECT list A list consisting of comma-separated lists of table columns and expressions.

Self join A join condition that returns rows from the same table, joining a table to itself and then evaluating the join condition.

Separation of duties A security concept that dictates that multiple people within an organization should be involved in financial transactions to make it more difficult for one person to steal money.

Sequence A database object that generates a series of unique integers.

Sequence of primary events The order in which events are fired on a form. One of the challenges of an event model is placing code under an event that fires at exactly the proper time.

Session An individual connection to an Oracle database server.

Set operator Operators that combine the results from multiple SELECT statements into one query.

Shutdown (command) The process of telling the Oracle software to clean up and stop the database.

Simple loop A program loop that executes repeatedly until you explicitly end it.

Simple view A view that is defined on *one* base table.

Single row function A function that operates on one table row at a time and returns one row for each input row.

Single row subquery A subquery that returns zero or one row to the outer SQL statement.

Single sign-on The ability for users to log into a network one time and have their credentials automatically applied for all services and applications.

Smart trigger A method for creating the most commonly used events for an object on a form. Right-click an item to choose a smart trigger event.

SQL Access advisor A tool that analyzes groups of SQL statements and makes suggestions on how best to store the data. It identifies when you should add indexes and materialized views.

SQL Profile A set of queries and suggestions to improve the queries. The query analyzer users the profile statistics to improve query performance.

SQL Tuning (advisor) A tool that analyzes a SQL query and offers suggestions to improve the performance.

SQL*Loader An Oracle utility for importing data from external files, particularly comma-separated value files.

SQL*Plus commands Oracle's own extension to SQL commands that provides a wide variety of commands to format results, display table definitions, and edit and save files.

Stacked canvas A canvas with two major sections—one of which overlays the other. A viewport displays the visible portion of the top canvas.

STANDARD Extensions A section of the object navigator under Built-in Packages that lists commonly used form functions and provides explanations and examples.

Startup (command) The command to restart an Oracle DBMS after it has been shut down.

Statement-level trigger A trigger that fires once for a DML event, regardless of the number of rows affected.

Startup restrict (command) A variation of the startup command that allows administrators to log in and perform tasks while blocking other users.

Style guide A description of the overall layout and style of an application.

Subprogram A computer program contained within another program that operates semi-independently of the enclosing program and that can be invoked from the enclosing program.

Subquery A query that is contained within another SQL statement—often a query itself.

Substitution variable It is used in a SQL statement as a substitute for a value at the time the SQL statement is executed.

Super class The parent class of a derived class.

System parameters Predefined variables used to control environmental issues for a report, such as the number of copies or destination printer name.

System privilege A privilege that allows a user to perform selected actions in Oracle such as creating tables, creating views, and so on.

System privileges Permissions that enable users to modify database definitions, such as creating a table, user, or view.

Tab canvas A canvas with multiple sections, where each section is selected by clicking on a tab. Generally, the sections contain related forms, such as a Customer form for a related Order form.

Table A structure that consists of rows and columns and holds data that represents a single entity in the business model.

Table alias A short name used in place of the actual table name in a query.

Table list A list following the FROM clause containing one or more tables from which the result data is retrieved.

Table of contents An introductory page to a help system that provides a broad-level perspective of the help topics.

Tablespace Oracle's term for a logical collection of items from the database. A tablespace maps to physical data files.

Tabular form A form where data is displayed in a table with rows and columns. Useful when there is a limited number of columns, and users need to see and compare multiple rows.

Tabular report A simple report listing rows and columns.

Template form A standard set of styles used as the foundation for all forms in an application.

Third normal form A table is in third normal form (3NF) if it is in 2NF and each non-key column depends on the whole key and nothing but the whole key.

Tools Various objects predefined by Oracle to perform specific tasks on a form, such as text boxes and lines.

Transaction A group of SQL statements that are a logical unit of work. Statements in a transaction are a cohesive, inseparable group whose individual statements must succeed or fail together.

Trigger A database procedure that runs when an INSERT, UPDATE, or DELETE statement is run against a specified database table.

Truncate When referring to a table, it is the action that removes all the table data without saving any rollback (undo) information.

Undo tablespace A special tablespace area to temporarily hold database changes. Users can use the Rollback command to release the changes and revert to the prior versions of data and tables.

Unified Modeling Language (UML) A standardized modeling language for designing and documenting computer and business systems.

UNIQUE constraint A *UNIQUE constraint* specifies that each of the values in the column in which it occurs must be the only one of its kind—no value may be repeated.

Upgrades Major version changes to the underlying DBMS software. They generally require new licensing and often require restructuring the existing database files.

User parameter form A predefined form to make it easier for users to enter values for user parameters on reports.

User parameters Variables defined and used in report queries. When the report runs, the user enters a value for each parameter and the report query is modified based on the value.

User role A set of permissions that are applied to every user in a common group. You should always apply permissions to roles instead of to individual users.

User schema The Oracle database allows a large number of concurrent users to share the same database system, which is usually stored on a separate server. Database files stored and maintained by Oracle provide security by keeping a user's database tables and other objects in a separate, protected area. This area is called a *user schema*.

User-defined exception An exception or error that the user defines.

UserID (parameter) The standard username/password@servername identifier used to tell the reports services how to connect to the database.

Validation triggers Triggers used to check the data returned from the user parameter form.

Variable A PL/SQL reserves temporary storage to hold values contained wholly within the PL/SQL block.

Variable-length character *Variable-length character* data is data whose length can vary from one record to another.

Variable, local (See *Private variable*.)

Vertical join compound queries are called *vertical joins* because the retrieved rows are formed based on columns instead of rows.

Very large-scale database (VLSD) Huge databases consisting of terabytes of data that generally require detailed storage configuration to optimize storage and retrieval times.

View An object that displays a subset of the rows and columns of a base table.

Viewed table A named, derived table.

Viewport A window used to display the portion of a canvas that is stacked on top of a second canvas.

Virtual private database (VPD) An Oracle tool that uses views to define subsets of data for any particular role. In essence, each person sees only the specific data rows related to his or her job.

WHERE clause Optional SELECT statement clause that defines the filter or search conditions that each row in the table(s) must meet to be returned.

WHERE clause An entry in the Database section properties for a query to filter or limit the rows to display. You can use bind parameters to dynamically alter the data retrieved for list queries.

WHILE loop A program loop that executes until a specified condition occurs.

Wildcard character Special symbols that stand for one or more characters in a search string.

WITH ADMIN OPTION A clause used with SQL GRANT commands that give the recipient the ability to pass on the specified permission to other users.

INDEX

Symbols

& (ampersand), 81
* (asterisk)
   in error message, 51, 52
   one-to-many relationship and, 5
   SELECT statement and, 200, 203
@ (at sign) command
   locate, load, and run script file with, 80
   .sql suffix and, 149
/* (begin comment), 83
{} (braces), 63
[] (brackets), 63
:= (colon-equals) statement, 426
$ (dollar sign) command, 82
*/ (end comment), 83
- (hyphen)
   comments, 83
   SQL*Plus and, 253
% (percent wildcard character), 209
|| (pipe symbols), 219
(pound sign), 232
/ (slash), 348
_ (underscore wildcard character), 209

A

abort option of shutdown command, 612
aborting long SQL*Plus display, 205
ACCEPT command, 168
access, restricting. *See* restricting access
access key, 544
accessing multiple tables in another schema, 309–310
account
   creating, 19
   DBA, 32
   locking, 592
   SYSDBA, 591
   system, 95, 591, 592
   See also user accounts
Acrobat Reader (Adobe), 534–535
action query, 142–143. *See also* UPDATE command
ADD_LIST_ELEMENT command, 427
ADDM (Automatic Database Diagnostic Monitor), 621–622, 623, 624
Administration page of Enterprise Manager, 32, 592, 593, 594
administration tools, 16
Adobe Acrobat Reader, 534–535
AFTER trigger
   audit table, creating, 184
   creating, 183–185
   testing, 185–186
Agent Contact form, template version of, 529
Agents table (Redwood Realty)
   constraints of, 144
   creating, 117–118
   description of, 34, 143

inserting row into, 145–146
structure of, 116, 117, 144
aggregate function
   AVG, MAX, and MIN, 241–242
   description of, 221, 239–241
   SUM and COUNT, 242–246
alert forms, adding, 424
Alert message, 423
alerts
   e-mail, 620
   standard, 618–619
alias
   column, 219
   definition of, 172
Align Left button, 386
aligning columns, 485–486
alignment options, 387, 388
ALL operator
   description of, 288
   in subquery, 292–293
   using, 290–291
ALL view, 126
all_dependencies view, 134
all_views view, 310
ALTER command, 49
ALTER DATABASE ADD LOGFILE GROUP command, 601
ALTER SEQUENCE statement, 156
ALTER SYSTEM command, 596
ALTER TABLE statement
   COALESCE option, 606
   columns
      adding, dropping, or renaming, 122–124
      default value or data type, changing, 121–122
   constraints
      adding, enabling, or disabling, 119–120
      dropping or renaming, 120–121
   description of, 66, 119
   dropping unused column, 124
   marking column as unused, 124, 125
ALTER TRIGGER statement, 190–191
ALTER USER statement, 97
American National Standards Institute (ANSI)
   SQL and, 48, 49
   SQL99 compliant form of join, 266, 267
ampersand (&), 81
anonymous block
   creating, 325
   declarative section of, 321–323
   description of, 320–321
   exception handling section of, 324–325
   executable section of, 323–324
   with explicit cursor, testing, 339
   handling exceptions, 330–333
   modifying, 329–330
   running, 328–329

SQL*Plus environment, setting up, 328
   writing, 325–328
ANSI (American National Standards Institute)
   SQL and, 48, 94
   SQL99 compliant form of join, 266, 267
ANY operator
   description of, 288
   in subquery, 292–293
   using, 290–291
Apache Jakarta framework, 454
apostrophe, 145, 146, 200
application
   connecting forms and reports to
      deploying in OracleAS, 538–540
      displaying reports, 534–538
      opening forms, 532–534
      overview of, 530
      startup form, 530–532
   deploying on server, 532
   description of, 2, 521
   designing
      applying template forms and properties, 527–530
      overview of, 521–522
      property classes and visual attributes for, 525–527
      style guide and, 523–524
      template form for, 524–525
      user tasks, forms, and reports, identifying, 522–523
   Help files
      deploying and using, 551–553
      HTML, creating, 548–551
      .OHJ and .OHW, 548
      overview of, 547–548
   identifying forms for, 522–523
   limiting access within, 573–575
   menus
      actions, creating, 543–546
      building, 542–543
      deploying and using, 546–547
      role of, 540–541
   naming conventions for, 523
   restricting access within, 573–575
   See also specific applications
Application Server. *See* Oracle Application Server
applying
   custom templates to reports, 507
   template forms and properties, 527–530
ArchiveLog mode, 614–616
arrow keys, 485
assigning
   default value to column, 118
   security permissions, 563–564
association, 5. *See also* relationship
associative link, 549, 550

■ 645 ■

asterisk (*)
  in error message, 51, 52
  one-to-many relationship and, 5
  SELECT statement and, 200, 203
at sign (@) command
  locate, load, and run script file with, 80
  .sql suffix and, 149
atomic element, 9
attributes
  description of, 4
  table and, 6
  visual, 525–527
audit table
  creating, 184
  displaying, 186, 187
auditing
  database
    creating triggers for, 583–584
    overview of, 579–580
    viewing audit trails, 582–583
  enabling, 581–582
  fine-grained, 582–583, 585
  table operations, 183–184
  See also AFTER trigger
AUDIT_SYS_OPERATIONS option, 580
authenticating users, 557–559
Automatic Database Diagnostic Monitor (ADDM), 621–622, 623, 624
automating Execute Query step on forms, 398
availability of system, 557
AVG function, 221, 241

B

back-end database server, 2
backing up database
  cold backups, 616–617
  complications in, 614–616
  hot backups, 617–618
  overview of, 614
base table
  description of, 14, 65
  view and, 299
BEFORE trigger
  creating, 181–182
  testing, 182–183
BEGIN key word, 323
BETWEEN . . . AND operator, 208–209
Binary data type, 4
binding styles, 52–53
block
  anonymous
    creating, 325–333
    declarative section of, 321–323
    description of, 320–321
    exception handling section of, 324–325
    executable section of, 323–324
    handling exceptions, 330–333
    modifying, 329–330
    running, 328–329
    SQL*Plus environment, setting up, 328
    syntax, 321
    writing, 325–328
  data
    creating, 415–417
    creating query for, 394–395

description of, 376, 415
PCTUSED and PCTFREE parameters and, 602–604
for query, creating, 417–420
search, performing, 420–421, 422
tables and, 415
description of (See PL/SQL)
executing DML statement in, 342–346
named, 347
Boat table (Rowing Ventures), 38
BoatCrew table (Rowing Ventures), 38
borders, adding to report, 486–487
braces ({}), 63
brackets ([]), 63
BREAK command, 254
break footer, 474
break header, 474
breaking runaway query, 204–205
Broadcloth Clothing database example, 41–44
BTITLE command, 253–255, 256
building
  forms, 373
  menus, 542–543
built-in functions, 428
business components data model, creating, 454–456
business rules, designing database and, 91–92
Button tool, 525
buttons, connecting forms and reports to application with, 530

C

C language, 320
calculations
  column alias and, 219
  dates and, 217–218
  mathematical operators, 216–217, 218
  numeric functions and, 225
  SELECT statement and, 216
CALL statement, 360
CALL_FORM call, 532
calling
  function, 347, 350–352
  procedure, 347
  stored procedure, 360–361
call-level interface, 53
Cancel Query button, 386
canvas
  creating, 415–417
  description of, 376, 379
  multiple, working with
    adding canvas, 443–444
    evaluating methods of creating, 450–451
    limitations of, 451
    stacked canvas, 444–447
    tab canvas, 447–450
  role of, 414–415
capitalization, 107, 159
capturing files for printing, 76
cascading style sheet, 510–511
CASE structure
  COUNT function and, 245–246
  description of, 161–162
  updating data using, 162–163, 164

challenge-response system of authenticating user, 557
character data types, 101–102
character function, 222–223, 224
characters
  fixed-length, 101
  number format, 231, 233
  in search condition, WHERE clause and, 207–208
  variable-length, 101
  white space, 50
  wildcard, 209
chart, adding to Web report, 514–517
check boxes, 398
CHECK constraint, defining, 115
child menu item, 543
Choose Destination Location dialog box, 384
class
  attributes and, 4
  definition of, 92
CLEAR SCREEN command, 74
client computer, 2
Close button, 384
closing explicit cursor, 338
clusters, defining, 604–605
COALESCE option of ALTER TABLE statement, 606
Codd, E. F., 6, 48
code
  protecting with wrap utility, 579
  for trigger, 427–428
  writing good error-handling, 434
Coffee Merchant database example, 35–38
cold backups, 616–617
collecting user choices for search form, 460–461
colon-equals (:=) statement, 426
column alias, 219
COLUMN command, 76–77, 251–253
column constraint
  creating, 115–118
  description of, 110
  reviewing, 129–132
column list
  omitting, 147–149
  specifying, 145–146
column names, listing, 75–76
column subset view, 300
columns
  adding or dropping, 66, 122–124
  adjusting prompts and widths of in forms, 380, 381
  aligning and justifying, 485–486
  assigning default values to, 118
  comments, adding, 107–109
  concatenating, 219–221
  correlation name for, 180–181
  data type, changing, 121–122
  default value, changing, 121–122
  display, adding to forms, 406–407
  dropping unused, 124
  formatting
    as numeric, 478
    in SQL*Plus, 76–77, 251–253
  marking as unused, 124, 125
  modifying in all rows, 160–161
  moving items to single, 381

Index 647

columns (*continued*)
  renaming, 122–124
  restricting access to selected, 569–570
  reviewing information on, 128–129
  setting formats with Property
    Inspector, 481
  updating
    CASE structure, using, 162–163, 164
    value of in multiple rows, 160
comma in SQL statement, 50
command button, adding to form, 393
commands for standard menu items, 545
comma-separated value, 608
COMMENT command, 107–109
comments
  adding to tables and columns, 107–109
  in anonymous block, 321–322
  reviewing, 132–133
  in script file, 83
COMMIT command
  description of, 49, 71–72, 174–175
  DML statements and, 142
  ending transaction with, 179
committing transaction, 72
communications network, 17
comparison operators
  ANY and ALL operators and, 290–291
  correlated subquery and, 294–296
  search conditions and, 206–207
Compile button, 525
Compile PL/SQL code button, 393
compiling
  function, 348
  PL/SQL block (*See* PL/SQL)
  See also recompiling
complex view
  creating, 305–306
  description of, 300
  multiple table, examining, 307–309
  one-table, examining, 306–307
component query, 282
composite data type, creating, 15
composite/compound primary key
  declaring, 111–112
  description of, 8, 94
compound query, 282–283
computing subtotals for grid
  data, 441–443
concatenating columns, 219–221
confidentiality, 557
configuring
  Oracle network on developer
    machine, 23–24
  space for schema objects, 602–606
  undo and redo operations, 600–601
Connect role, 563, 593
connecting
  forms and reports to application
    deploying in OracleAS, 538–540
    displaying reports, 534–538
    opening forms, 532–534
    overview of, 530
    startup form, 530–532
    query form values to data action
      procedure, 462–463
constant (PL/SQL), 321, 322–323
constraint
  adding, enabling, or disabling,
    119–120, 121

column and table
  creating, 115–118
  description of, 110
  reviewing, 129–132
defining
  CHECK, 115
  foreign key, 112–113
  Not Null, 113–114
  primary key, 111–112
  UNIQUE, 114–115
definition of, 65, 99
disabled, 119
domain, 110
dropping or renaming, 120–121
foreign key, 112–113, 120
integrity
  description of, 110
  enforcing, 179
  inserting row and, 146–147
naming, 110–111
NULL value and, 99
primary key, 111–112, 120
range, 110
referential, 112
table
  creating, 115–118
  description of, 110
  reviewing, 129–132
  types of, 110
  UNIQUE, defining, 114–115
constraint name, 130
Consumers table (Coffee Merchants), 36
context sensitive help, 547
ContractReason table (Redwood
  Realty), 34
control files, protecting, 596, 597
controlling
  data in reports
    filters and, 503–504
    overview of, 500
    triggers, creating, 504
    user parameters and, 500–503
  user access to objects, 563–564
conversion function, 226–227, 230–236
Copy Properties button, 526
copying
  output to spool file, 77
  template, 505
correlated subquery
  comparison operators and, 294–296
  description of, 287
  EXISTS operator and, 296–298
  writing, 294
correlation name, 180–181
COUNT function
  syntax, 243
  uses of, 243–246
  variations of, 242
counting loop, 335
Countries table (Coffee
  Merchants), 36–37
coxswain, 40
CREATE CLUSTER command, 604
CREATE command, 49
CREATE ROLE system privilege, 564
CREATE SEQUENCE
  statement, 153–154
CREATE SESSION privilege, 96–97
CREATE SYNONYM statement, 310

CREATE TABLE AS statement, 136
CREATE TABLE statement, 65, 100
CREATE TRIGGER statement, 180
CREATE TYPE command, 15
CREATE USER statement,
  95–96, 558–559
CREATE VIEW statement, 300–301
Cross Product tool, 494
.CSV text file, 608
Ctrl+A (select), 58
Ctrl+C
  copy, 58
  interrupt current instruction, 205
Ctrl+click (select item), 376
Ctrl-H (Help system), 428, 429
Ctrl+L (list of values), 397
Ctrl+V (paste), 58
Ctrl+Z (Undo), 480
cursor
  ADD_LIST_ELEMENT
    command and, 427
  implicit, 329, 333
  types of, 323
  See also explicit cursor
cursor FOR loop, 339–341
CustAgentList table (Redwood
  Realty), 35
custom templates
  applying to reports, 507
  designing, 505–507
  overview of, 504–505
  registering, 507–509
Customers table (Redwood Realty)
  adding primary key constraint to, 120
  description of, 34
customizing
  reports
    data group structure and
      frames, 493–495
    data model and, 489–492
    fields, adding, 492–493, 494
    overview of, 489
  SQL*Plus environment, 78–80
  Web report
    cascading style sheet and, 510–511
    chart, adding, 514–517
    dynamic report environment, 510, 511
    modifying, 511–514
    overview of, 509
    style sheet, 512–514

D

data
  displaying with form queries, 384–385
  encrypting selected, 576–579
  format masks, setting, 407–408
  integrity of, 557
  modifying using one-table
    view, 304–305
data block
  creating, 415–417
  creating query for, 394–395
  description of, 376, 415, 598
  PCTUSED and PCTFREE
    parameters and, 602–604
  for query, creating, 417–420
  search, performing, 420–421, 422
  tables and, 415

data block wizard, 378–379, 380, 403–404, 405
data connection, creating, 453–454
Data Control Language statements, 49, 72–73
Data Definition Language (DDL) statements
 CREATE TABLE, 65, 100
 description of, 49, 64
 ROLLBACK statement and, 49, 69, 71–72, 175–176
 See also ALTER TABLE statement
data dictionary
 description of, 16, 126
 views, 126–128
data engine, 16
data function, 226–229
Data Link tool, 495
Data Manipulation Language (DML) statements
 DELETE, 49, 69–71, 168–170, 299
 description of, 49, 66
 executing in PL/SQL blocks, 342–346
 INSERT, 49, 67–68, 144–145, 152–153, 607
 performing on view, 304–305
 ROLLBACK, 69, 175
 subquery and, 299
 transactions and, 174
 TRUNCATE, 49, 69
 See also UPDATE command
data model of report, 489–492
Data Model toolbox, 494
data pump, 607–608
data trigger, form trigger compared to, 424–425
data types
 character, 101–102
 of column, changing, 121–122
 conversion functions and, 226–227, 230–236
 date and time, 103–105
 examples of, 4
 image, 105–106
 listing, 75–76
 numeric, 102–103
 overview of, 100–101
 storing complex, 14–15
database
 description of, 1
 images, adding to, 391–394
 initializing, 143, 325, 326
database administrator (DBA)
 description of, 2, 16, 590
 Enterprise Manager and, 31, 591–594
 privileges of, 73
 query tools and, 31
 responsibilities of, 590–591
 system views and, 631–632
 tracking actions taken by, 580
 See also maintaining DBMS; storage files
database management system. *See* DBMS
database object, 95
database system, modeling, 4–5
database transaction. *See* transaction

datafile
 creating, 597–600
 description of, 596–597
date
 calculating with, 217–218
 converting string to, 232–235, 236
 converting to character string, 230–232
 formatting, 514
 inserting
  in report, 487–488
  in table, 149–151
 in search condition, WHERE clause and, 207–208
DATE data type, 4, 5, 103–105
date format model symbols, 150
date-related format model elements, 234
DBA. *See* database administrator
DBA view, 126
dba_col_comments view, 631
dba_role_privs table, 565
dba_tab_comments view, 631
dba_tab_privs table, 568
DBConsole service, shutting down, 613
DBMS (database management system)
 components of, 1–2
 description of, 1
 installing, 17–19
 integration into operating system, 16
 maintaining
  overview of, 610
  patches and updates, 610–612
  shutting down, 612–614
 personal, 2
 removing, 19–21
 server-based, 2–4
DBMS_CRYPTO package for PL/SQL, 577–579
DBMS_ERROR_CODE statement, 434
DBMS_FGA package, 580, 585
DDL statements. *See* Data Definition Language (DDL) statements
debug mode, tools available in, 430
debugging
 handling errors and, 431–434
 trigger, 428–431
declarative section of anonymous block, 321–323
declaring variables to hold column values and explicit cursor, 336
DECODE function, 236–237
Default template, 505
default value
 assigning to column, 118
 of column, changing, 121–122
Define Column button, 484
defining
 clusters, 604–605
 constraint
  CHECK, 115
  foreign key, 112–113
  Not Null, 113–114
  primary key, 111–112
  UNIQUE, 114–115
 form events, 422–424
 one-table view, 300–304
 tablespace, 602
 trigger, 180
definition of view, reviewing, 310–311

DELETE command
 description of, 49, 69–71, 168
 subquery and, 299
 WHERE clause and, 169–170
deleting
 column, 122–123
 records, 72
 rows
  all rows, 169–171
  selected rows, 168–169, 170
 users, 592
 See also dropping; removing
delimited name, 100
deploying
 forms and reports in Oracle Application Server, 538–540
 Help system, 551–553
 menus, 546–547
derived table, 65
DESCRIBE command
 description of, 75–76
 listing names, structures and comments in table using, 124–126
desformat parameter options for reports, 536, 537
designing
 application
  applying template forms and properties, 527–530
  overview of, 521–522
  property classes and visual attributes for, 525–527
  style guide and, 523–524
  template form for, 524–525
  user tasks, forms, and reports, identifying, 522–523
 custom template, 505–507
 form, 413
 form trigger, 421–422
 relational database
  business rules and, 91–92
  identifying user requirements, 92
  normalizing design, 93–95
  recognizing business objects, 92–93
destination filename, 535
detail section of report, 474
developer, 2
developer machine
 auditing and, 582
 configuring Oracle network on, 23–24
Developer Suite tools, 2, 17, 21–24. *See also* Forms Builder; Reports Builder
digital security certificate, 576
direct execution, 52–53
disabled constraint, 119
disabling trigger, 190–191
discretionary access control, 300
disk drive, 595–596
display columns
 adding to forms, 406–407
 description of, 267
Display Item tool, 524–525
displaying
 audit table, 186, 187
 data from single table
  breaking runaway query, 204–205
  DISTINCT phrase and, 204
  filtering results with search conditions, 205–211

displaying data from single
    table (*continued*)
        overview of, 199
        SELECT statement and, 201–202
        selecting all columns, 203
    data with form queries, 384–385
    images on reports, 499–500
    names
        of sequences, 154–155
        of tables, 127
    reports, 534–538
    stacked canvas, 446
    trigger information, 190, 191
    view information, 310–311
    See also listing; reviewing
DISTINCT keyword and COUNT
    function, 243
DISTINCT phrase of SELECT
    statement, 204, 212
distribution, 280, 281
DML statements. *See* Data Manipulation
    Language (DML) statements
dollar sign ($) command, 82
domain constraint, 110
DOS command-line
    editing SQL commands, 55
    entering and running SQL
        commands, 54–55
    logging into Oracle using, 53–54
    downloading .OWH files, 551
drawing line, 487
DROP command, 49
DROP SEQUENCE statement, 156–157
DROP TABLE statement, 66, 133–134
DROP USER statement, 99
dropping
    column, 122–123
    constraint, 120–121
    function, 355–356
    procedure, 364
    sequence, 156–157
    table, 133–134
    trigger, 191–192
    unused column, 124
    view, 311–312
    See also deleting; removing
dual key encryption, 575–576
DUAL table
    description of, 156
    error message about, 437
    querying, 216
    uses of, 235

E

editing
    chart, 517
    function, 349–350
    SQL command
        in DOS window, 55
        in *i*SQL*Plus, 61–62
        in SQL*Plus for Windows, 57–59
    trigger, 424–428
    See also modifying
"eight", 40
ELSIF clause, 342
EM. *See* Enterprise Manager
e-mail alerts, 620
embedding SQL statement, 53

Employees table (Coffee Merchants), 36
enabling
    auditing, 581–582
    constraint, 119
    trigger, 190–191
encryption
    overview of, 575–576
    public key, 577
    of selected data, 576–579
ending loop, 334
enforcing privileges through views and
    procedures, 568–575
Enter key
    SQL statements and, 50
    SQL*Plus and, 74
Enter Query button, 29, 384, 386
entering
    data directly into text boxes, 462
    SQL command
        in DOS window, 54–55
        in *i*SQL*Plus, 60–61
        in SQL*Plus for Windows, 56–57
Enterprise Manager (EM)
    Administration page, 32, 592, 593, 594
    control files and, 596, 597
    creating user with, 558–559
    DBAs and, 591–594
    default alerts, 618–620
    description of, 16–17, 31
    listing or changing user roles, 565
    location of database file, finding, 616–617
    logging into, 18
    main page, 593
    Recovery Settings page, 614–616
    RefreshFromMetalink job, running, 612
    Schema section, 593
    Security section, 593, 595
    starting, 31–32
    tablespaces and datafiles, creating,
        598–600, 601
    tuning advisors, running, 623
Enterprise Manager listener, shutting
    down, 613
entity, recognizing when designing
    database, 92–93
entity-relationship diagram (ERD), 4
environment variables
    Forms Builder and, 375
    PAGESIZE, 77–79, 83
    setting, 78–80, 250–251
    TERMOUT, 83
equijoin, 264–265, 266
error handling, 431–434
error message
    about dual table, 437
    calling function, 351–352
    compiling and, 349
    CREATE USER or GRANT
        statements and, 559
    deleting rows and, 168
    dropped table and, 134
    online help, obtaining, 51–52
    Session_Roles table and, 574
    trigger
        creating, and, 182
        testing and, 188–189
exception, 324
exception handling section of anonymous
    block, 321, 324–325, 330–333

EXCEPTION statement, 431–433
executable section of anonymous block,
    321, 323–324
Execute Query button, 29, 382, 386
executing
    SQL statement in buffer with
        substitution variables, 166–168
    stored script file, 80
execution of SQL statements, 52–53
execution plan for query, 624, 626
exercises
    Broadcloth Clothing database, 41–44
    Coffee Merchant database, 35–38
    end-of-chapter, 33
    Redwood Realty database, 33–35
    Rowing Ventures database, 38–41
EXISTS operator and correlated
    subquery, 296–298
EXIT statement, 334
EXIT WHEN statement, 334
exiting
    *i*SQL*Plus, 62
    SQL*Plus for Windows, 59
expdp command, 607
EXPLAIN PLAN command, 631
explicit cursor
    closing, 338
    description of, 323, 333
    loop constructs and, 335
    looping and fetching rows from, 337
    opening, 337
    processing rows using, 335–339
    processing using FOR loop, 339–341
    testing, 339
exporting data
    with data pump, 607–608
    with SQL script, 607
    with SQL*Loader, 608–610
extensions to SQL. *See* SQL*Plus
    commands
extents, 598
external tables, creating, 609–610

F

FETCH command, 337
Field button, 492
fields, adding to reports, 492–493, 494
File menu, Save As command, 361
filenames, case sensitivity of, 512
Fill Color button, 483
filtering
    groups, 247–249
    table rows with WHERE clause
        comparison operators, 206–207
        logical operators and, 210–211
        overview of, 205–206
        rules for characters and dates,
            207–208
        SQL operators and, 208–210
filters, using to limit reports, 503–504
Find box
    List of Values window, 397
    Property Palette, 389
Fine-Grained Auditing, 580, 582–583, 585
first normal form
    description of, 9–11
    designing database and, 94
fixed-length character, 101

fixed-precision number, 102–103
flash recovery area, 616
flashback drop, 134
FLASHBACK TABLE command, 135
Flex Off button, 480
Flex On button, 480
floating-point number, 103
.fmx suffix, 533
folders, saving forms in, 417
F1 (format mask options), 407
footer section of report, 474
FOR loop
    description of, 333, 335
    processing explicit cursor with, 339–341
FOR UPDATE phrase and SELECT statement, 200
foreign key
    description of, 13–14, 94
    in Redwood Realty database, 33–34
foreign key constraint
    adding, 120
    defining, 112–113
form events, defining, 422–424
Format Mask property, 439, 486
format masks, setting, 407–408
format model, 77, 150, 230
format trigger, 504
formatting
    column
        as numeric, 478
        in SQL*Plus, 76–77, 251–253
    numbers or dates on Web report, 514
    template, 505
forms
    automating Execute Query step, 398
    Broadcloth Clothing examples, 42–43
    building from scratch, 524–525
    Coffee Merchants example, 37, 38
    command button, adding to, 393
    computing subtotals for grid data, 441–443
    creating, 376
    deploying in OracleAS, 538–540
    description of, 372
    display columns, adding, 406–407
    format masks, setting, 407–408
    identifying for application, 522–523
    image, adding to, 390–391
    input, validating, 438–441
    list of values, creating, 395–398
    lookup columns, adding, 394–395
    main
        creating, 402–406
        description of, 373
        simple, creating, 377–385
    modifying
        layout editor and, 385–387
        object navigator and, 387–388, 389
        Property Palette and, 388–390
    opening, 532–534
    passing parameters to, 534
    permissions for, 565, 567–568
    radio buttons and check boxes for, 398–401
    Redwood Realty example, 35, 36
    reports compared to, 473
    Rowing Ventures example, 40–41
    security Internet transmission of, 576
    simple example of, 29–30
    specifying location of, 532, 539
    structure of, 376–377, 413–415
    sub, creating, 402–406
    tabular, creating, 402, 403
    testing with Run Form button, 382–384
    tools for, 435–438
    types of, 373–374
    See also canvas; data block; Forms Builder; menus; trigger; Web forms
Forms and Reports services, installing, 17, 25–26, 472
Forms Builder
    debug buttons, 430
    main form, simple, creating, 377–385
    menus, building with, 542–543
    overview of, 28–29
    Windows environment variable and, 375
    wizards, 378–382, 395, 403–404, 405
forms debugger, testing, 429–431
Forms Designer, JDeveloper compared to, 451
forms services architecture, 374–376
formula column, 493
"four", 40
frame title for form, 380–381
frames
    adding, 416
    description of, 415
    repeating frame, 497
    reports and, 483
    text items, adding inside, 419
frequency distribution, creating, 245–246
FROM clause of SELECT statement and join condition, 264, 265–266
front-end tier of three-tier system, 3
F2 (layout editor), 385
full outer join
    description of, 274
    using, 279
function
    built-in, 428
    calling, 347
    character, 222–223, 224
    conversion, 226–227, 230–236
    creating and storing, 348–350
    data, 226–229
    description of, 221
    dropping, 355–356
    group, 240
    invoking, 350–352
    listing, 353–355
    modifying, 352–353
    numeric, 223, 225–226
    overview of, 347–348
    in PL/SQL, 321
    recompiling modified, 353
    special, 236–239, 240
    See also aggregate function; single row function; specific functions

G

global variable
    description of, 322, 533
    lifetime of, 435
Google search engine, 95

GRANT command
    as Data Control Language statement, 49
    syntax for, 73
    user roles and, 559–560
    WITH ADMIN option, 564
granting
    permissions to users, 565–568
    privileges to user name, 96–97
granularity, 568
grid data, computing subtotals for, 441–443
grid form, creating, 402, 403. See also tabular form
group breaks in report, 474–475
GROUP BY clause of SELECT statement, 240, 246–247
group filter property, 503–504
group function, 240. See also aggregate function
group report, 470–471
grouping
    aggregate information, 247–249
    results, 246–247

H

handling
    errors, 431–434
    exceptions, 330–333
hard coding, 426, 533
hash partitioning, 606
HAVING clause of SELECT statement, 200, 240, 247–249
header section
    of named block, 347
    of report, 474
Help system
    deploying and using, 551–553
    functions and, 428, 429
    HTML files, creating, 548–551
    .OHJ and .OHW, 548
    overview of, 547–548
helpset file, 550–551
hiding stacked canvas, 446
hierarchy of object inheritance model, 15–16
HOST command, 82–83
hot backups, 617–618
HTML Help files, creating, 548–551
HTML reports, creating, 255–258
hyperlinks, adding to charts, 517
hyphen (-)
    comments and, 83
    SQL*Plus and, 253

I

icons
    traffic light, 382
    Web Source, 511
identifying user requirements for database, 92
IF statement
    executing DML statement in blocks and, 342–346
    making alternative choices using, 342, 343
    overview of, 341–342

IF/THEN statement, 342
image data types, 105–106
images, adding
    to database, 391–394
    to forms, 390–391
    to reports, 499–500
impdp command, 607
implicit cursor, 323, 329, 333
importing data
    with data pump, 607–608
    with SQL script, 607
    with SQL*Loader, 608–610
IN operator
    description of, 209, 288
    multiple row subquery and, 289–290
IN OUT parameter, 347
IN parameter, 347
INCREMENT BY clause of CREATE
        SEQUENCE statement, 154
index, adding to table, 625–626
index page for help files, 547, 550
infinite loop, 334
inheritance, 15
INITCAP() function, 222
initializing
    database, 143, 325, 326
    system variables, 533
inline view, 213
inner join
    description of, 265–266
    syntax for, 477
    using, 266–269
input on form, validating, 438–441
INSERT command
    description of, 49, 67–68, 144–145
    importing and exporting data and, 607
    SELECT subquery and, 152–153
Insert Date and Time button, 506
INSERT INTO command
    description of, 145
    omitting column list, 147–149
Insert Page Number button, 506
inserting
    data from other tables, 152–153
    dates and times, 149–151
    row
        integrity constraints and, 146–147
        overview of, 145–146
        without specifying column names,
            147–149
installing
    Application Server, 24–25
    DBMS, 17–19
    Developer Suite tools, 17, 21–24
    Enterprise Manager, 592
    forms and reports services, 17,
        25–26, 472
    JDeveloper, 451–452
    JInitiator Java application, 376,
        382–383
    security certificate on Web server, 576
    updates, 610–612
integer, 102
integrity constraint
    description of, 110
    enforcing, 179
    inserting row and, 146–147
integrity of data, 557
interface tools. *See* *i*SQL*Plus; SQL*Plus

International Standards Organization
    (ISO), 48
Internet
    connecting through, 2
    protocols, Oracle 10g and, 17
    security transmissions with
        encryption, 576
INTERSECT set operator, 283, 286
INTERVAL data type, 103–105
Inventory table (Coffee Merchants),
    36–37
invoking
    function, 350–352
    procedure, 347
    stored procedure, 360–361
IS NULL operator, 209–210
ISO (International Standards
    Organization), 48
*i*SQL*Plus browser window
    description of, 27, 59
    displaying table columns in, 148
    drawbacks to, 28
    editing SQL commands and, 61–62
    entering and running SQL commands
        and, 60–61
    exiting, 62
    idle time value and, 204
    logging into Oracle using, 59–60
    running simple query with, 29
    SELECT statement and, 64
    SQL*Plus commands and, 74
    starting, 28
items
    canvas and, 414–415
    child menu, 543
    description of, 376
    frames and, 415
    parent menu, 543
    in quotation marks, testing of, 533
    selecting, 376
    text, adding inside frames, 419

J

Java engine, as requirement, 3, 4
Java help-indexer program, 550
Java Server Page, creating, 456–457
Java 2 Enterprise Edition (J2EE), 451
Java-based Web applications, 374
JDeveloper
    Attribute screen, 456
    business components data model,
        creating, 454–456
    data connection and workspace,
        creating, 453–454
    Forms Designer compared to, 451
    installing, 451–452
    Java Server Page, creating, 456–457
    modifying listings table and setting up
        server files, 452–453
    search form, adding, 457–463
    Struts controller, 459–460
JInitiator Java application, 376, 382–383
join
    description of, 264
    full outer, 279
    inner
        description of, 265–266
        using, 266–269

    natural
        description of, 266
        using, 269–270, 271
    non-equality, 280–282, 283
    outer
        description of, 273
        using, 273–276, 279, 280
    self
        description of, 273
        using, 276–279
    syntax for, 476–477
    three-table, 270–272
join column, 267
join condition, 264
join operation, 94
joining three or more tables, 270–272
J2EE (Java 2 Enterprise Edition), 451
justifying columns, 485–486

K

keyboard shortcuts
    Ctrl+A (select), 58
    Ctrl+C
        copy, 58
        interrupt current instruction, 205
    Ctrl+click (select item), 376
    Ctrl-H (Help system), 428, 429
    Ctrl+L (list of values), 397
    Ctrl+V (paste), 58
    Ctrl+Z (Undo), 480
    F1 (format mask options), 407
    F2 (layout editor), 385

L

label security, 573
layout editor, 385–387
layout wizard, 378, 379–381, 382, 403
LDAP (lightweight directory application
    protocol), 558
left outer join, 274–276
LicenseStatus table (Redwood Realty)
    description of, 35, 143
    structure of, 144
lifetime of variable, 434–435
lightweight directory application
    protocol (LDAP), 558
LIKE operator, 209
limiting access. *See* restricting access
line, drawing, 487
link file, 549
list box, creating, 416–417
List of Values wizard, 395
list of values (LOV), creating, 395–398
list partitioning, 606
listing
    function, 353–355
    names, structures and comments in
        table, 124–126
    procedure, 362–364
    tables, 126–128
    See also displaying; reviewing
Listings table (Redwood Realty)
    adding foreign key constraint to, 120
    creating, 118
    describing, 124–126
    description of, 34
local variable, 327

location
  of database file, finding, 616–617
  of forms, specifying, 532, 539
locking account, 592
logging in
  to database, 26, 27
  to Personal Oracle with another username and password, 96, 97
  steps for, 28
  using DOS command-line, 53–54
  using iSQL*Plus, 59–60
  using SQL*Plus for Windows, 56
logical operators
  description of, 158
  WHERE clause of SELECT statement and, 210–211
logos, adding to forms, 390–391
looping structures
  cursor FOR loop, 339–341
  in PL/SQL
    explicit cursor and, 335
    overview of, 333–335
LOWER() function, 222
LPAD function, 223, 224

M

Magic functions, 543, 545
Magnify tool, 493
mailing labels, 470, 471–472
main form
  creating, 402–406
  description of, 373
  simple, creating, 377–385
main/sub form approach, 374, 375
maintaining DBMS
  backing up
    cold backups, 616–617
    complications in, 614–616
    hot backups, 617–618
    overview of, 614
  overview of, 610
  patches and updates, 610–612
  performance issues
    monitoring tools, 618–623, 624, 625
    optimizing queries, 623–631
    overview of, 618
  shutting down, 612–614
  system views, 631–632
maintenance contracts, 611
many-to-many relationship, 7, 93
map file, 549
Margin button, 506
marking column as unused, 124, 125
MARKUP command, 255–256
master-detail report, 495
materialized views, 626–630
mathematical operators, 216–217, 218
matrix report
  description of, 470, 471, 472
  enhancing, 483–485
MAX function, 241–242
Menu Editor, 542
menu module, 542
menus
  actions, creating, 543–546
  building, 542–543
  deploying and using, 546–547

role of, 540–541
standard, 541
MERGE statement
  description of, 171–172
  executing, 173–174
  source table, creating, 172–173
  syntax, 171
merging rows, 171–174
MetaLink Web site, 611
metrics, 619
middle tier computer, 472
MIN function, 241–242
MINUS set operator, 283, 285–286
modeling database system, 4–5
model-view-controller approach, 454
modifying
  anonymous block, 329–330
  base template, 505
  data using one-table view, 304–305
  forms
    layout editor and, 385–387
    object navigator and, 387–388, 389
    Property Palette and, 388–390
  function, 352–353
  procedure, 361–362
  Web report, 511–514
  WHERE clause, 458–459
  See also editing
module binding, 53
monitoring tools
  ADDM (Automatic Database Diagnostic Monitor), 621–622, 623, 624
  Enterprise Manager default alerts, 618–620
  query optimizer, 623–631
MONTHS_BETWEEN function, 165, 229
multiline comments in script file, 83
multiple column subquery, 287
multiple row subquery
  ANY and ALL operators and, 292–293
  description of, 287
  IN operator and, 289–290
  writing, 288–289
multiple table view, creating and examining, 307–309
multiple-row function. See aggregate function
multitable queries, 264–265
mutating table, 189

N

named block, 347
named visual attributes, 525–527
naming
  constraint, 110–111
  sequence, 154–155
  table, 100
  trigger, 180
  variable, 322
  See also renaming
naming conventions for application, 523
national character set, 65
native code, 354
natural join
  description of, 266
  using, 269–270, 271

network, configuring on developer machine, 23–24
Next Record button, 29, 383
non-equijoin condition, 273
non-equijoin query, 280–282, 283
normal forms
  first normal form, 9–11
  overview of, 8–9
  second normal form, 11–12
  third normal form, 12–13
normalization and designing database, 93–95
NOT EXISTS operator, 297
NOT NULL constraint, defining, 113–114
notation, 93–94
notebook, keeping, 591
Notepad, creating SQL and SQL*Plus commands using, 58–59
NULL value
  aggregate functions and, 240
  constraint and, 99
  ORDER BY clause and, 212–213
Number data type, 4, 5
number format characters, 231, 233
numbers
  fixed-precision, 102–103
  floating-point, 103
  formatting, 514
numeric, formatting column as, 478
numeric data types, 102–103
numeric function, 223, 225–226
NVL and NVL2 functions, 237

O

Object Navigator
  Built-in Packages section, 428
  description of, 376
  forms and, 387–388, 389
  template in, 505–506
Object Navigator window (Reports Builder), 481–483
object privilege, 73, 560–563
object-oriented programming (OOP), 14–16. See also PL/SQL
objects
  recognizing when designing database, 92–93
  user access to, controlling, 563–564
  user schema and, 95
OC4J (Oracle Containers for Java) application, 376, 535
ohwconfig.xml file, 551
OID (Oracle Internet Directory), 538, 558
ON DELETE CASCADE clause, 168
ON statement, 271
ON_ERROR trigger, 433–434
one-table view
  defining and querying, 300–304
  modifying data using, 304–305
one-to-many relationship, 5, 93
one-to-one relationship, 93
On-Insert trigger, 436
online help, obtaining, 51–52
OPEN_FORM command, 450–451, 532
opening
  explicit cursor, 337
  forms, 532–534

Index **653**

opening (*continued*)
  reports, 544
  See also starting
operating system, DBMS integration
    into, 16
operator precedence
  description of, 210
  mathematical, 216
operators
  ALL
    description of, 288
    in subquery, 292–293
    using, 290–291
  ANY
    description of, 288
    in subquery, 292–293
    using, 290–291
  BETWEEN . . . AND, 208–209
  comparison, 206–207, 290–291, 294–296
  EXISTS, and correlated subquery,
    296–298
  IN
    description of, 209, 288
    multiple row subquery and, 289–290
  INTERSECT set, 283, 286
  IS NULL, 209–210
  LIKE, 209
  logical
    description of, 158
    WHERE clause of SELECT
      statement and, 210–211
  mathematical, 216–217, 218
  MINUS set, 283, 285–286
  in non-equijoin query, 280
  NOT EXISTS, 297
  relational, 158
  UNION ALL set, 283, 285, 286
  UNION set, 283, 284–285
optimizing queries
  index, adding to table, 625–626
  overview of, 623–624
  SQL Access advisor, 626–630
  SQL Tuning advisor, 624–625
  User_Advisor_Recommendations
    view, 630–631
option button, 398
ORA error codes, 51–52
Oracle Application Server (OracleAS)
  deploying forms and reports in,
    538–540
  description of, 534
  forms and reports services and, 26
  installing, 24–25
  as middle tier in three-tier system, 2–3
Oracle Containers for Java (*OC4J*)
  application, 376, 535
Oracle Developer Suite, 2, 17, 21–24.
  See also Forms Builder;
    Reports Builder
Oracle Internet Directory (OID),
    538, 558
Oracle Technology Network, 17
OracleAS. *See* Oracle Application Server
OracleAS Enterprise Manager, 540
ORDER BY clause
  alias and, 219
  concatenating columns, 219–221
  NULL values and, 212–213
  overview of, 211–212

SELECT statement and, 200
  Top-N queries, 213–215
order form, 374
OrderLines table (Coffee Merchants), 36
Orders table (Coffee Merchants), 36
Organization table (Rowing
    Ventures), 38
OUT parameter, 347
outer join
  description of, 273
  using, 273–276, 279, 280
output from trigger, viewing, 187–188
override, 505

P

page footer, 474
page header, 474
Page Layout view (Reports Builder),
    479–481
page numbers, inserting in report,
    487–488
PAGESIZE environment variable,
    77–79, 83
Paper Design window (Reports Builder),
    478–480
Paper Layout button, 480
Paper Layout window, template in, 505–506
parameter
  description of, 347
  passing to forms, 534
parameter forms, 537–538
parent menu item, 543
parentheses in SQL statement, 50
partitions, creating, 605–606
passing parameters to forms, 534
password
  case-insensitivity of, 96
  case-sensitivity of, 98
  changing
    other user's, 97–98
    own, 98–99
PASSWORD command, 98–99
Paste Properties button, 526
patches, 591, 610–612
p-code (pseudocode), 353
PCTFREE parameter, 602–603
PCTUSED parameter, 603–604
.PDF (portable document file) image,
    534–535
percent wildcard character (%), 209
performance
  of computer and running code,
    422–423
  of database
    monitoring tools, 618–623, 624, 625
    optimizing queries, 623–631
    overview of, 618
  period in SQL statement, 50
  permanent tablespaces, 598
  permissions
    granting and revoking, 565–568
    security, assigning, 563–564
    user roles and, 559–560
    See also privileges
Person table (Rowing Ventures), 38–39
personal database system, 2
Personal Oracle
  changing

other user's password, 97–98
  own password, 98–99
  system privileges for user, 96–97
  logging in with another username and
    password, 96, 97
  removing user, 99
  SYSTEM account, 95
  user, creating, 95–96
pipe symbols (||), 219
PKI (public-key infrastructure), 576
placeholder column, 493
planning
  form, 413, 434
  report, 474–475
  See also designing
PL/SQL (Programming
    Language/Structured Query
    Language)
  anonymous block
    creating, 325–333
    declarative section of, 321–323
    exception handling section of,
      324–325
    executable section of, 323–324
    overview of, 320–321
  benefits of, 320
  block
    executing DML statement in,
      342–346
    named, 347
    types of, 320–321
  common commands, 426
  DBMS_CRYPTO package for,
    577–579
  explicit cursor, 333
  function
    creating and storing, 348–350
    dropping, 355–356
    invoking, 350–352
    listing, 353–355
    modifying, 352–353
    overview of, 347–348
  IF statement and, 341–346
  implicit cursor, 333
  loops in, 333–335
  overview of, 319
  procedure
    advantages of, 356–357
    creating and storing, 357–360
    description of, 321, 356
    dropping, 364
    invoking, 360–361
    listing, 362–364
    modifying, recompiling, and saving,
      361–362
  replacement commands for common
    menu items, 545
point, 380
POPULATE_GROUP_WITH_QUERY
    function, 427
POPULATE_LIST function, 427
portable document file (.PDF) image,
    534–535
Post-Item event, 424
Post-Text-Item trigger, 435
pound sign (#), 232
precision, 102
predefined exception, 324–325
Pre-Form trigger, 427

654   Index

Pre-Text-Item trigger, 435
Previous Record button, 29, 383
primary key
   description of, 7–8, 93–94
   generating, 435–438
   in Redwood Realty database, 33–34
   sequence values, using for, 155–156
primary key constraint
   adding, 120
   defining, 111–112
printing, capturing files for, 76
private variable, 321
Privilege Auditing, 580
privileges
   checking, 73–74
   creating users and, 559
   DBA account and, 32
   enforcing through views and procedures, 568–575
   granting and revoking, 73
   granting to user name, 96–97
   object, 73, 560–563
   system, 73–74, 96–97, 560–561, 564
   types of, 73
   See also permissions
problem, identifying, 4
procedure
   advantages of, 356–357
   calling or invoking, 347, 360–361
   creating and storing, 357–360
   description of, 321, 356
   dropping, 364
   listing, 362–364
   modifying, recompiling, and saving, 361–362
   restricting updates through, 570–573
processing
   explicit cursor using FOR loop, 339–341
   rows using explicit cursors, 335–339
Programming Language/Structured Query Language. *See* PL/SQL
Program/Run Paper Layout menu option, 472
Program/Run Web Layout menu option, 472
PROMPT command, 83
properties, applying, 527–530
Properties table (Redwood Realty), 34–35
property classes, 525–527
Property Inspector, 481
property palette
   canvas and, 415
   description of, 376
   forms and, 388–390
protecting
   control files, 596, 597
   source code with wrap utility, 579
pseudocode (p-code), 353
pseudocolumn, 155
public key encryption, 575–576, 577
public synonym approach, 567
public-key infrastructure (PKI), 576
punctuation for SQL, 50–51
PURGE command, 135–136
purging recycle bin, 135–136

Q

"quad", 40
qualified name, 267
query
   action, 142–143
   basing form on, 394–395
   breaking runaway, 204–205
   component, 282
   compound, 282–283
   data block and, 394–395, 417–420
   data displaying with form queries, 384–385
   display column, adding from, 406–407
   execution plan for, 624, 626
   EXISTS, 297
   multitable, 264–265
   non-equijoin, 280–282, 283
   running simple with *i*SQL*Plus browser window, 29
   testing, 394
   Top-N queries, 213–215
   See also subquery
query optimizer
   order of join and, 270
   performance and, 623–631
query processor, 16
query statements, 49, 142
query system, testing, 384–385
query tools and users, 30–31
querying
   database, 63
   one-table view, 300–304
   See also SELECT statement
quotation marks
   double
      delimited names and, 100
      in SQL statement, 50
      use of, 220
   items in, testing of, 533
   single, use of, 145, 146, 220

R

Race table (Rowing Ventures), 38
RaceTimes table (Rowing Ventures), 38
radio buttons
   forms, adding to, 398–401
   groupings, adding, 416
RAID (redundant array of independent drives), 595–596
range constraint, 110
range partitioning, 605–606
real estate profession, 33
recognizing business objects, 92–93
recompiling
   modified function, 353
   modified procedure, 362
   See also compiling
record group, 395
records
   definition of, 339
   deleting, 72
recovering active database, 614, 615
recovery manager (RMAN), 617–618
Recovery Settings page of Enterprise Manager, 614–616
recycle bin
   description of, 134
   purging, 135–136
   viewing, 135
redo log file, 601, 614
redundancy, building in, 3
redundant array of independent drives (RAID), 595–596
Redwood Realty case examples
   Agent Contact form, template version of, 529
   connecting forms and reports to application, 530
   database
      building, 201
      overview, 33–35
   forms for, 522
   initializing, 267
   LicenseStatus table
      description of, 35, 143
      structure of, 144
   Listings table
      adding foreign key constraint to, 120
      creating, 118
      describing, 124–126
      description of, 34
   menus for, 541
   overview of, 33
   OwnerID information, adding to tab canvas, 448–450
   reports for, 523
   user roles, creating, 564–565
   See also Agents table
referential constraint, 112
referential integrity, 14, 134
RefreshFromMetalink job, running, 612
registering custom templates, 507–509
regular expression, 209
relational database, designing
   business rules and, 91–92
   identifying user requirements, 92
   normalizing design, 93–95
   recognizing business objects, 92–93
relational database model
   description of, 1
   normal forms
      first normal form, 9–11
      overview of, 8–9
      second normal form, 11–12
      third normal form, 12–13
   object relational model and, 14–16
   overview of, 6
   primary keys and, 7–8
   relationships and foreign keys, 13–14
relational operators, 158
relationship
   description of, 5
   foreign key and, 13–14
   identifying among entities, 93
removing
   DBMS from computer, 19–21
   scroll bar from form, 389
   table with SQL statement, 28, 66
   user, 99
   See also deleting; dropping
RENAME command, 49, 136
renaming
   column, 123–124
   constraint, 120–121
   table, 136
   See also naming

repeating frame, 497
Replace_Menu built-in function, 546
report trigger, 504
report wizard. *See* Reports Builder
reports
  borders, adding, 486–487
  Broadcloth Clothing examples, 43–44
  Coffee Merchants example, 37, 39
  columns, aligning and justifying, 485–486
  controlling data in
    filters and, 503–504
    overview of, 500
    triggers, creating, 504
    user parameters and, 500–503
  creating and testing, 472–473
  creating manually, 495–499
  customizing
    data group structure and frames, 493–495
    data model and, 489–492
    fields, adding, 492–493, 494
    overview of, 489
  date, inserting, 487–488
  deploying in Oracle Application Server, 538–540
  displaying, 534–538
  displaying images on, 499–500
  as dynamic, 535
  enhancing, 483–485
  Format Mask, setting, 486
  formatting with SQL*Plus commands, 250
  forms compared to, 473
  grouping levels for, 477, 478
  headers, footers, and dimensions, setting, 253–255, 256
  HTML, creating, 255–258
  identifying for application, 522–523
  master-detail, 495
  matrix
    description of, 470, 471, 472
    enhancing, 483–485
  opening, 544
  page numbers, inserting, 487–488
  paper, and Web publishing, 469–470
  permissions for, 565–567
  Redwood Realty example, 35, 37
  restricting access to with view, 568–569
  Rowing Ventures example, 41
  security Internet transmission of, 576
  shading, adding, 486–487
  simple example of, 29, 30, 31
  sorting detail listing, 481–483
  structure of, 473–475
  text box, adding, 488
  types of, 470–472
  See also custom templates; Reports Builder; Web report, customizing
Reports Builder
  limitations of, 473
  Object Navigator window, 481–483
  overview of, 28–29, 469, 472–473
  Page Layout view, 479–481
  Paper Design window, 478–480
  working with, 475–478
resizing static image with mouse, 390
restarting database, 613–614

restoring dropped table, 135
restricting access
  within application, 573–575
  to report with view, 568–569
  to selected rows and columns, 569–570
  to updates through procedures, 570–573
  with virtual private database, 573
results, grouping, 246–247
reversing operations since last COMMIT, 72
reviewing
  column information, 128–129
  table and column comments, 132–133
  table and column constraints, 129–132
  See also displaying; listing
REVOKE command, 49, 73, 559–560
revoking permissions from users, 565–568
right outer join, 274–276
RMAN (recovery manager), 617–618
ROLLBACK command
  deleting table rows and, 69
  syntax for and uses of, 175–176
  as Transaction Control statement, 49, 71–72
row subset view, 300
rowing, 40
Rowing Ventures database example, 38–41
row-level trigger
  description of, 179
  statement-level trigger compared to, 186–187
rows
  adding using MERGE statement, 173–174
  deleting
    all rows, 169–171
    overview of, 70–71
    selected rows, 168–169, 170
  description of, 7
  duplicate, 204
  filtering with WHERE clause
    comparison operators, 206–207
    logical operators and, 210–211
    overview of, 205–206
    rules for characters and dates, 207–208
    SQL operators and, 208–210
  inserting
    integrity constraints and, 146–147
    from other tables, 152–153
    overview of, 67–68, 145–146
    without specifying column names, 147–149
  merging, 171–174
  processing using explicit cursors, 335–339
  restricting access to selected, 569–570
  sorting using ORDER BY clause, 213–215
  updating
    MERGE statement, using, 173–174
    overview of, 68–69, 159–161
    See also multiple row subquery; single row function
RPAD function, 223, 224, 340
Run Form button, 382–384
Run Paper Layout button, 478
Run Segment Advisor, 600

Run Web Layout button, 509
runaway query, breaking, 204–205
running
  anonymous block, 328–329
  code, frequency of, 422–423
  SQL command
    in DOS window, 54–55
    in *i*SQL*Plus, 60–61
    in SQL*Plus for Windows, 56–57
Run_Report_Object command, 535
runtime error, 431

S

sales form, computing subtotals for grid data, 441–443
SaleStatus table (Redwood Realty), 35
Save button, 29, 384
savepoint, rolling back database to, 175
SAVEPOINT command, 49, 72, 176–178
saving
  data, three-tier system and, 3
  form while building, 417
  SQL and SQL*Plus commands for reuse, 58–59
  template file, 506
scalar data type, 323
scalar subquery, 287–288
schema, creating triggers and sequences in, 284
schema object
  configuring space for, 602–606
  description of, 95
Schema Object Auditing, 580
Schema section of Enterprise Manager, 593
scope of variable, 434–435
script
  description of, 58
  running with SQL*Plus, 26–27
script file
  building and running, 83–85
  commenting in, 83
  creating two tables and inserting data, 62–63
  executing, 80
  HTML report and, 255–258
  modifying, 78
  running in SQL*Plus and reviewing in browser, 257–258
  .sql suffix for, 149
  substitution variable, using in, 81–82
scroll bar for form
  adding, 380–381
  removing, 389
  tabular form and, 402
scrolling
  table, 29
  tabular form, 402
sculling, 40
search, performing, 420–421, 422
Search button, trigger code for, 421
search column, 267
search condition
  characters and dates in, 207–208
  comparison operators and, 206–207
  logical operators and, 210–211
  overview of, 205–206
  SQL operators and, 208–210

656 Index

search form, adding to Web page, 457–463
search page for help files, 547, 550
second normal form, 11–12
Secure Sockets Layer (SSL), 576
security certificate, digital, 576
security features
    auditing database, 579–585
    discretionary access control, 300
    installing Oracle tools and, 17
    See also encryption; restricting access
security issues
    DBA and, 591
    user accounts and, 556–557
    See also password
security patches, 610–611
security permissions, assigning, 563–564
Security section of Enterprise Manager, 593, 595
security subsystem, 16
segments, 598
select list, 200
Select Parent Frame button, 483
SELECT permission, adding, 566
SELECT statement
    description of, 49
    to display data from single table
        breaking runaway query, 204–205
        DISTINCT phrase, 204
        filtering results with search conditions, 205–211
        overview of, 199
        selecting all columns, 203
        writing, 200–202
    DISTINCT phrase, 204, 212
    FROM clause and join condition, 264, 265–266
    GROUP BY clause, 240, 246–247
    HAVING clause, 240, 247–249
    including computations in
        column alias and, 219
        dates, 217–218
        mathematical operators, 216–217, 218
        overview of, 216
    iSQL*Plus interpreter, using, 64
    listing tables, 126–128
    ORDER BY clause
        alias and, 219
        concatenating columns, 219–221
        NULL values and, 212–213
        overview of, 211–212
        Top-N queries, 213–215
    syntax, 63
    view and, 126
    WHERE clause
        comparison operators, 206–207
        filtering rows and, 68
        logical operators, 210–211
        rules for characters and dates, 207–208
        search condition and, 205–206
        SQL operators, 208–210
Select tool, 493
selecting
    items, 376
    text boxes, 386

selection construct. See IF statement
self join
    description of, 273
    using, 276–279
semicolon in SQL statement, 50–51, 538
separation of duties, 562–563
sequence
    altering or dropping, 156–157
    creating, 153–155, 284, 435–438
    description of, 153
    of primary events, 423
    primary keys and, 155–156
    trigger compared to, 181
server
    attaching to forms running on, 430–431
    deploying application on, 532
    installing security certificate on, 576
    Web, TCP port for, 535
server-based database system, 2–4
service, stopping, 613
session, description of, 174
Session_Roles table, 574
set operators
    INTERSECT, 286
    MINUS, 285–286
    overview of, 282–283
    UNION and UNION ALL, 284–285
SET VERIFY OFF command, 166
SET_ITEM_PROPERTY function, 427
shading, adding to report, 486–487
Shift key
    drawing line and, 487
    resizing static image with mouse and, 390
shortcut for SQL*Plus for Windows, creating, 56
shortcuts. See keyboard shortcuts
SHOW ERRORS command, 349
Show_Alert function, 424
shutdown command, 612–613
shutting down database, 612–614
SIGN( ) function, 225
simple loop, 333, 334
simple view
    defining and querying, 300–304
    description of, 300
    modifying data using, 304–305
single key encryption, 575–576, 579
single row function
    categories of, 222
    character, 222–223, 224
    conversion, 226–227, 230–236
    date, 226–229
    description of, 221
    numeric, 223, 225–226
    special, 236–239, 240
single row subquery, 287–288
single sign on, 538, 557–558
slash (/), 348
smart trigger, 377
sorting and SELECT statement, 211–215
source code, protecting with wrap utility, 579
source filename, 535
special function, 236–239, 240
specifying location of forms, 532, 539
SPOOL command, 76
spool file, copying output to, 77
SQL Access advisor, 626–630

SQL operators
    IN, 209
    BETWEEN . . . AND, 208–209
    IS NULL, 209–210
    LIKE, 209
SQL Query tool, 495
SQL Reference manual, 100
SQL script, importing and exporting data using, 607
SQL statements and DBA, 591–592
SQL (Structured Query Language)
    binding styles, 52–53
    call-level interface, 53
    description of, 1–2, 48–49
    direct execution, 52–53
    embedding statement, 53
    module binding, 53
    online help, obtaining, 51–52
    SQL*Plus compared to, 53
    statement, anatomy of, 50–51
    table types and, 65
    view, creating in, 417–418
SQL (Structured Query Language) statements
    case-insensitivity of, 52
    editing
        in iSQL*Plus, 61–62
        in SQL*Plus for Windows, 57–59
        in SQL*Plus in DOS window, 55
    overview of, 62
    running
        in iSQL*Plus, 60–61
        in SQL*Plus for Windows, 56–57
        in SQL*Plus in DOS window, 54–55
    text editor, creating using, 58
    types of, 49
    See also specific statements
.sql suffix, 149
SQL Tuning advisor, 624–625
SQL*Loader, 608–610
SQL*Plus commands
    ACCEPT, 168
    BREAK, 254
    capturing files for printing, 76
    COLUMN, 251–253
    DESCRIBE, 75–76
    description of, 49, 53, 74–75
    displaying list of, 75
    executing script files, 80
    formatting, 76–78
    HOST, 82–83
    MARKUP, 255–256
    PROMPT, 83
    report formatting, 250
    SET VERIFY OFF, 166
    TERMOUT and PAGESIZE environment variables, 83
    TTITLE and BTITLE, 253–255, 256
SQL*Plus for Windows
    description of, 55–56
    editing SQL commands, 57–59
    entering and running SQL commands, 56–57
    exiting, 59
    logging into Oracle with, 56
SQL*Plus interface
    aborting long display, 205
    columns, formatting, 251–253
    drawbacks to, 28

Index

SQL*Plus interface (continued)
　Enter key and, 74
　entering statements in, 50
　environment variables, setting, 78–80, 250–251
　error message in, 51–52
　HELP command, 82
　HTML reports, creating, 255–258
　page and report headers, footers, and dimensions, setting, 253–255, 256
　report formatting features, 249–250
　running script with, 26–27
　setting up for PL/SQL block, 328
　SQL compared to, 53
　substitution variables, 81–82
　table, creating, 106–107, 108
　using in DOS window, 54
　See also SQL*Plus commands
SSL (Secure Sockets Layer), 576
stacked canvas, 444–447
standards for SQL, 48–49
START command
　description of, 74, 80
　.sql suffix and, 149
START WITH clause of CREATE SEQUENCE statement, 154
starting
　database, 612, 613–614
　Enterprise Manager, 31–32, 592
　*i*SQL*Plus, 28
　SQL*Plus, 26
　See also opening
startup command, 613–614
startup form, 530–532
Statement Auditing, 580
statement-level trigger
　creating, 186–188
　description of, 179
　modifying and recompiling, 189–190
　testing, 188–189
States table (Coffee Merchants), 35–36
stopping
　OC4J service, 383
　service, 613
storage files
　control files, protecting, 596, 597
　overview of, 594–596
　schema objects
　　clusters, 604–605
　　configuring space for, 602–606
　　data block, 602–604
　　partitions, 605–606
　tablespaces and datafiles, creating, 596–600, 601
　undo and redo operations, configuring, 600–601
stored procedure
　advantages of, 356–357
　creating, 358–359
　invoking, 360–361
structure
　of form, 376–377, 413–415
　of report, 473–475
Structured Query Language. *See* SQL
Struts controller (JDeveloper), 459–460
style guide, 523–524
style sheet
　cascading, 510–511
　modifying for Web pages, 512–514

sub form, creating, 402–406
sub-class and object-oriented programming, 15
subprogram, 321
subquery
　correlated
　　comparison operators and, 294–296
　　description of, 287
　　EXISTS operator and, 296–298
　　writing, 294
　in DML statement, 299
　multiple column, 287
　multiple row
　　ANY and ALL operators and, 292–293
　　description of, 287
　　IN operator and, 289–290
　　writing, 288–289
　overview of, 286–287
　SELECT, 152–153
　single row, 287–288
　WHERE clause and, 287, 288
substitution variables
　executing SQL statement in buffer with, 166–168
　script files and, 81–82
　UPDATE statement and column, adding and updating contents of, 165–166
　overview of, 163–165
subtotals for grid data, computing, 441–443
SUM function, 221, 242
summary column, 493
super class, 15
sweep rowing, 40
symmetric key encryption, 575–576, 579
synonyms to simplify table references, creating, 309–310
syntax
　aggregate function, 240
　ALTER TRIGGER statement, 190
　anonymous block, 321
　CASE structure, 161
　COUNT function, 243
　CREATE SEQUENCE statement, 153
　CREATE TABLE AS statement, 136
　CREATE TABLE statement, 65, 100
　CREATE TRIGGER statement, 180
　CREATE USER statement, 95
　definition of, 63
　DELETE statement, 69, 168
　DROP TABLE command, 134
　EXISTS query, 297
　forms trigger, 425
　GRANT statement, 73, 559
　IF statement, 341
　inner join, 266
　INSERT command, 67, 144
　MERGE statement, 171
　outer join, 274
　REVOKE statement, 73
　ROLLBACK statement, 175
　SELECT statement, 63, 200
　set operation, 283
　SPOOL command, 76
　UPDATE statement, 68, 157–158
sys.aud$ table, 580, 582
SYSDATE function, 118, 165

SYSDBA account, 591
SYSDBA and SYSOPER logins, 580
system account, 95, 591, 592
system parameters
　description of, 500
　list of, 501
system privilege
　changing for user, 96–97
　CREATE ROLE, 564
　description of, 73–74
　user accounts and, 560–561
system views, 631–632

T

tab canvas, 447–450
tab order on form, 387–388
table alias, 271
table browser list of data block wizard, 378, 379
table constraint
　creating, 115–118
　description of, 110
　reviewing, 129–132
table list, 200
table of contents for help files, 547, 550
Table Space Usage alert, 618
table trigger. *See* trigger
tables
　altering, 119
　audit, 184, 186, 187
　base, 14, 65, 299
　clusters, defining, 604–605
　comments, adding, 107–109
　creating
　　from other table, 136–137
　　overview of, 65, 99–100
　　SQL*Plus, using, 106–107, 108
　data block and, 415
　data types
　　character, 101–102
　　date and time, 103–105
　　image, 105–106
　　numeric, 102–103
　　overview of, 100–101
　derived, 65
　description of, 6
　displaying list of names of, 83–85
　dropping, 133–134
　DUAL
　　description of, 156
　　error message about, 437
　　querying, 216
　　uses of, 235
　ensuring identicalness of, 286
　entities and, 93
　external, creating, 609–610
　index, adding to, 625–626
　joining
　　with natural join, 270, 271
　　overview of, 264
　　and retrieving columns from both, 267–268
　　three or more tables, 270–272
　　when join columns have same name, 268–269
　listing, 126–128
　mutating, 189
　naming, 100

658 Index

tables (*continued*)
  partitions, creating, 605–606
  removing, 66
  renaming, 136
  restoring dropped, 135
  scrolling, 29
  splitting, 13
  storage parameters, setting, 602–604
  tracking modifications to, 179
  types of, 65
  viewed, 65
  See also columns; constraint; rows
tablespace
  creating, 598–600, 601
  defining, 602
  description of, 596–597
  types of, 598
tabular form
  creating, 402, 403
  description of, 373, 374
tabular report, 470
TCP port for Web server, 535
telephone book sort, 212
template forms, 524–525, 527–530
templates, custom
  applying to reports, 507
  designing, 505–507
  overview of, 504–505
  registering, 507–509
temporary tablespace, 598
TERMOUT environment variable, 83
testing
  AFTER trigger, 185–186
  anonymous block with explicit cursor, 339
  BEFORE trigger, 182–183
  form with Run Form button, 382–384
  forms debugger, 429–431
  query, 394
  query system, 384–385
  reports server, 535–536
  statement-level trigger, 188–190
text boxes
  adding to report, 488
  entering data directly into, 462
  selecting, 386
Text Color button, 506
Text data type, 4
text editor, creating SQL and SQL*Plus commands using, 58–59
Text Item button, 526
text items, adding inside frames, 419
third normal form, 12–13
three-table join, 270–272
three-tier system, 2–3
time
  converting string to, 232–235, 236
  converting to character string, 230–232
  inserting, 151
time-related format model elements, 234
TIMESTAMP data type, 103–105
TO_CHAR function, 226, 230–232
TO_DATE function, 150, 226, 230, 232–235, 236
TO_NUMBER function, 230, 235–236
tools
  administration, 16
  Button, 525
  Cross Product, 494

Data Link, 495
in debug mode, 430
Developer Suite, 2, 17, 21–24
Display Item, 524–525
for forms, 376, 435–438
Magnify, 493
monitoring
  ADDM (Automatic Database Diagnostic Monitor), 621–622, 623, 624
  Enterprise Manager default alerts, 618–620
  query optimizer, 623–631
query, 30–31
Select, 493
SQL Query, 495
Top-N query, 213–215
tracking modifications to table, 179
transaction
  beginning and ending of, 176, 179
  description of, 71, 174
Transaction Control statements
  COMMIT, 49, 71–72, 142, 174–175, 179
  description of, 49, 71
  ROLLBACK, 49, 69, 71–72, 175–176
  SAVEPOINT, 49, 72, 176–178
TRANSLATE function, 237–239, 240
trapping errors, 431–434
trigger
  AFTER
    audit table, creating, 184
    creating, 183–185
    testing, 185–186
  for auditing, creating, 583–584
  BEFORE
    creating, 181–182
    testing, 182–183
  code for, 427–428, 579
  creating, 180–181, 284, 424–428
  debugging, 428–431
  defining, 180
  description of, 143, 178–179
  designing, 421–422
  disabling or enabling, 190–191
  displaying information about, 190, 191
  dropping, 191–192
  editing, 424–428
  enabling, 190–191
  form events, defining, 422–424
  format, 504
  forms and, 377
  naming, 180
  ON_ERROR, 433–434
  On-Insert, 436
  output from, viewing, 187–188
  Post-Text-Item, 435
  Pre-Form, 427
  Pre-Text-Item, 435
  for reports, creating, 504
  row-level
    description of, 179
    statement-level trigger compared to, 186–187
  sequence, compared to, 181
  smart, 377
  statement-level
    creating, 186–188
    description of, 179
    modifying and recompiling, 189–190

  testing, 188–189
  uses of, 179
  validating form input and, 438–441
  validation, 504
  variable and, 434–435
  When-Button-Pressed event, 421
  When-New-Form-Instance, 438, 534
  When-Validate-Item, 424, 439–440
  wrap utility and, 579
trigger event, 180
TRUNC function, 229
TRUNCATE command, 49, 69
TRUNCATE TABLE statement, 170–171
TTITLE command, 253–255, 256
tuning advisors, 622–623
typeface, changing, 486

U

UML (uniform modeling language), 4
underscore wildcard character (_), 209
Undo (Ctrl+Z), 480
undo log file, 600–601
undo tablespace, 598
uniform modeling language (UML), 4
uninstalling DBMS from computer, 19–21
UNION ALL set operator, 283, 285, 286
UNION set operator, 283, 284–285
UNIQUE constraint, defining, 114–115
unused column, marking or dropping, 124
UPDATE command
  CASE structure and, 161–163, 164
  description of, 49, 157–158
  rows and, 68–69
  substitution variables and column, adding and updating contents of, 165–166
  overview of, 163–165
  WHERE clause of, 158, 159–160
Update Layout property of frame, 381
updates
  installing, 610–612
  restricting through procedures, 570–573
updating rows using MERGE statement, 173–174
uploading image to database, 392–393
UPPER function, 221, 224
user access to objects, controlling, 563–564
user accounts
  creating, 558–559
  overview of, 556–557
user authentication, 557–559
user input, validating, 438–441
user parameter form, 502
user parameters, 500–503
user roles
  creating, 564–565
  description of, 559–560
user schema, 95
user tasks, identifying, 522–523
USER view, 126
User_Advisor_Recommendations view, 630–631
user_cons_columns view, 130–131
user_constraints view, 129–132

user-defined exception, 324
user_errors view, 354
userid parameter, format for, 536
username, case-insensitivity of, 96
user_objects view, 354, 362
users
　authenticating, 557–559
　changing password for, 97–98
　creating, 592–593
　deleting, 592
　errors and, 434
　granting privileges to, 96–97
　informing of mistakes, 438
　query tools and, 30–31
　removing, 99
　sessions and, 435
　steps important to, 438
user_sequences view, 154–155
user_source view, 354, 355, 362
user_tab_columns view, 128–129
user_tab_comments view, 132–133
user_tables view, 127, 128, 299
user_triggers view, 190, 299
user_views view, 310
UTIL_ALERT_PAGER function, 585

V

validating form input, 438–441
validation trigger, 504
VALUES clause of INSERT INTO
　　command, 145
variable
　declaring, to hold column values and
　　explicit cursor, 336
　environment, 78–80, 83, 250–251, 375
　global, 322, 435, 533
　initializing system, 533
　lifetime of, 434–435
　local, 327
　naming, 322
　PL/SQL, 321, 322
　private, 321
　scope of, 434–435
　substitution
　　executing SQL statement in buffer
　　　with, 166–168
　　script files and, 81–82
　　UPDATE statement and, 163–166
　system, 533
variable-length character, 101
V$ performance views, 632
Verisign, 576
vertical join, 283

very large-scale database (VLSD), 605
viewed table, 65
viewing audit trails, 582–583
viewport, 444
views
　benefits of, 300
　complex
　　creating, 305–306
　　description of, 300
　　multiple table, examining, 307–309
　　one-table, examining, 306–307
　creating in SQL, 417–418
　data dictionary, 126–128
　description of, 126, 299–300
　dropping, 311–312
　enforcing privileges through, 568–569
　listing definitions, 310–311
　materialized, 626–630
　one-table
　　defining and querying, 300–304
　　modifying data using, 304–305
　restricting access to selected rows and
　　columns using, 569–570
　synonyms to simplify table references,
　　creating, 309–310
　system, 631–632
　User_Advisor_Recommendations,
　　630–631
　See also specific views
virtual private database (VPD), 563, 573
visual attributes, 525–527
VLSD (very large-scale database), 605
VPD (virtual private database), 563, 573

W

Web browser, displaying reports in, 535
Web forms
　Attribute screen, 456
　business components data model, cre-
　　ating, 454–456
　data connection and workspace, creat-
　　ing, 453–454
　Java Server Page, creating, 456–457
　JDeveloper and, 451–452
　modifying listings table and setting up
　　server files, 452–453
　search form, adding, 457–463
Web publishing and paper reports,
　469–470
Web report, customizing
　cascading style sheet and, 510–511
　chart, adding, 514–517
　dynamic report environment, 510, 511

　modifying, 511–514
　overview of, 509
　style sheet, 512–514
Web sites
　Google search engine, 95
　Java, 4
　MetaLink, 611
　ORA error codes, 51–52
　Oracle Technology Network, 17
Web-based approach to forms services
　architecture, 374–376
Web.Show_Document command,
　535, 544
WHEN OTHERS statement, 432
When-Button-Pressed event, 421, 534
When-Create-Record event, 436–438
When-New-Form-Instance trigger,
　438, 534
When-Validate-Item trigger, 424, 439–440
WHERE clause
　DELETE statement and, 70, 169–170
　join condition and, 264, 267
　modifying, 458–459
　SELECT statement and
　　comparison operators, 206–207
　　filtering rows and, 68
　　logical operators, 210–211
　　overview of, 200
　　rules for characters and dates,
　　　207–208
　　search condition and, 205–206
　　SQL operators, 208–210
　subquery, using in, 287, 288
　testing columns and, 420
　UPDATE command and, 158, 159–160
WHILE loop, 333, 334
white space character, 50
wildcard character, 209
Windows service manager, shutting down
　database with, 613
Windows XP and debug console, 430
wizards
　in Forms Builder, 378–382, 395,
　　403–404, 405
　in JDeveloper, 452
workspace, creating, 454
wrap utility, 579, 584
writing
　anonymous block, 325–328
　correlated subquery, 294
　good error-handling code, 434
　SELECT statement to display data
　　from single table, 200–202
　single row subquery, 287–288